An American History

FREEDOM AND CRISIS

An American History

FREEDOM AND CRISIS

ALLEN WEINSTEIN, Smith College

R. JACKSON WILSON, Smith College

First Edition
987654321
Copyright © 1974 by Random House, Inc.

E
178
W43
1974b

Library of Congress Cataloging in Publication Data
Weinstein, Allen.
Freedom and crisis. [New York] Random, 1974
813 P
1. United States—History. I. Wilson, Raymond Jackson, joint author. II. Title.
E178.W43   1974b   973   73-18072
ISBN 0-394-31626-6

Manufactured in the United States of America

Grateful acknowledgment is extended to the following for permission to reprint previously published material:

Joan Daves:—From "I Have a Dream" by Martin Luther King, Jr. Copyright © 1963 by Martin Luther King, Jr.
Doubleday & Co., Inc.:—From *Six Crises* by Richard Nixon. Copyright © 1962 by Richard M. Nixon.
Alfred A. Knopf, Inc.:—From *In the Court of Public Opinion* by Alger Hiss. Copyright © 1957 by Alger Hiss.
Random House, Inc.:—From *Witness* by Whittaker Chambers. Copyright 1952 by Whittaker Chambers.
Charles Scribner's Sons:—From *The Spirit of St. Louis* by Charles A. Lindbergh. Copyright 1953 by Charles Scribner's Sons.

CONTENTS

SPECIAL FEATURES *(continued)*

MAPS AND CHARTS

MAPS AND CHARTS *(continued)*

Freedom and Crisis is a book of discovery about the American past. The reader will quickly recognize, by glancing at the table of contents or by flipping through the pages, that this book is different from the ordinary "text." The difference is embodied in the way that *Freedom and Crisis* organizes the American experience.

Units are arranged in pairs of chapters. Every pair opens with a dramatic narrative of a significant episode in the American past. Each episode was chosen not only because it conveys an exciting story but also because it introduces many aspects of American life during the period under investigation. The chapter that follows then locates the episode within its appropriate historical context, interpreting the major forces that shaped the actions described in the episode.

This remains the book's basic format: a narrative chapter on a single episode, based on fresh documentary research, followed by an explanatory chapter linking historical fact and interpretation to the episode itself. The account of Bacon's Rebellion in Chapter 1, for example, is followed by a chapter on seventeenth-century plantation colonies. Similarly, Charles Lindbergh's exciting trans-Atlantic flight serves as the basis for a chapter on technological changes in twentieth-century America.

The only exceptions to this pattern are the book's first and last chapters. The Prologue on the period of discovery and exploration and the Epilogue on the United States since 1960 cover a variety of themes. Such variety could best be presented, we felt, by means of a series of smaller dramas. Each of these "mini-episodes" then leads to a discussion of the historical setting of the event portrayed.

We have employed this novel approach to an introductory book on American history for one very good reason. Our primary concern from the start has been to write a book that would hold the interest of today's students, perhaps the most inquisitive but skeptical generation of students ever. To do this, we felt that a book had to be readable and realistic. *Freedom and Crisis* is both. The book dramatizes critical moments in the

American democratic experience and deals candidly with both the extension and the denial of liberty at those times.

Freedom and Crisis is not a traditional book on United States history, then. Often such traditional books are written in the belief that there exists a certain body of data (election results, dates and outcomes of wars, treaties, major laws, and so forth) that comprises American history. We accept this idea only to the extent that most of the data of conventional texts can be found somewhere in this book. Sometimes, however, the information is located in maps, charts, and special features rather than in the text itself.

Frequently overlooked by students (and even by some teachers) is the point that this central body of data, the "facts," emerges only after a certain selection on the part of historians. There exists, after all, an almost infinite number of facts that could be chosen to represent the history of the human experience. In writing this book, we simply carried the usual selection process a step farther. Half the book is devoted to selected dramatic episodes. When linked to the accompanying chapters, the episodes form our bedrock of factual material. Using this foundation, students can then inquire into the fundamental questions of American history.

Most episodes can be read simply as absorbing stories. Thus readers will discover much about the country's past merely by studying such vivid incidents as the Boston Massacre, the Aaron Burr conspiracy, a New York City election riot, the Wounded Knee massacre, the Triangle fire, the Philippines revolt, the Bonus March, and the attack on Pearl Harbor. But by using the interpretative chapter accompanying each episode, students will develop the ability to extract greater meaning from the facts in these dramas and, at the same time, acquire an understanding of related historical events.

Freedom and Crisis moves chronologically through the American experience, but certain themes recur and receive particular attention. The book devotes several episodes, for example, to patterns of race and ethnic relations, especially the treatment of blacks, Indians, immigrants, and other oppressed minorities. The struggle for political liberties and economic betterment, class conflicts, territorial expansion, technological change, and basic ideological and cultural disputes are also treated.

The constant interplay of factual drama and careful interpretation is the book's distinctive feature. Facts and concepts cross paths on each page, thereby avoiding the usual unhappy classroom extremes of concentrating either on what happened or on why it happened. *Freedom and Crisis* has no room for empty historical abstractions that leave students without a factual anchor. Nor does an uncontrolled flood of rampaging facts lacking solid conceptual boundaries spill endlessly off the printed pages. The paired chapter format, we believe, avoids both these extremes.

The episodic-explanatory chapter pairs present a concise but comprehensive introduction to the history of the United States. Yet although the book covers the American experience, we wrote with less direct concern for coverage than for concreteness, drama, and interpretive depth. Almost every detail included in the narrative episodes has a larger meaning, so that students and instructors must work outward in this text from concrete detail to generalized understanding.

We make no apologies for this approach to studying and learning history, since professional historians use it daily. History as an act of inquiry involves putting great questions to small data, discovering general significance in particular events. *Freedom and Crisis* evolved from our belief that students are both willing and able to engage in the same process of inquiry as professional historians. In this manner each incident in the American odyssey, from the earliest European discoveries to our generation's exploration of the moon, can become a personal act of discovery for the reader, risky but rewarding.

The chapters that follow chart our personal roadmap through the American experience. The book will achieve its purpose only if it stirs the reader into beginning his or her own private journey through the past.

An
American
History

FREEDOM AND CRISIS

PROLOGUE

The Exploration and Conquest of America

Christopher Columbus, by the Italian artist Sebastiano del Piombo. This portrait was not painted from life; no one is sure what the great explorer looked like.

The Voyages of Columbus

THE SAILORS muttered, schemed mutiny, and talked of throwing the admiral overboard. He must be a madman, they said, to think that he would find land by sailing westward from Spain. The men had left Palos in three ships in August 1492. They grumbled almost from the beginning. Their complaints grew even louder after their departure from the Canary Islands in September. Finally, on October 10, they complained to the admiral himself, Christopher Columbus. He tried to pacify them with talk about the riches they would earn from their successful voyage to the East Indies and China. No one, after all, had ever sailed to China from the west. He added that it was useless to complain. He had set out for the Indies and would keep on until he found them, "with the aid of Our Lord."

The sailors' grumbling ended when land was sighted the following evening. The island where the Spaniards landed on October 12 was a small one in the Bahamas. Columbus named it San Salvador (Spanish for "Holy Saviour"). The natives of the island he called "Indians;" he was convinced that he had arrived in the East Indies.

Columbus searched everywhere for signs that would confirm his arrival at his original goal, the East Indies. Every island encountered was assigned the name of a place described by Marco Polo in his chronicle.[1] Thus he called the island of Cuba "Cathay." The admiral even carried letters from the king of Spain to the Great Khan, the Mongol ruler. On October 19 Columbus set sail from San Salvador for the mainland. After reaching Cuba, he sailed to Hispaniola, which he believed was the shore of "Cipango" (Japan). Thinking that the ruler's capital city lay just over the horizon, he sent one of his men, an interpreter, with greetings to him. The messenger found no magnificent walled city in the distance, only a scraggly village of naked Indians. Columbus left a small settlement of sailors on Hispaniola and returned to Spain.

---

[1] Marco Polo, a famous Italian traveler, spent many years in the Far East during the late thirteenth century. His account of his travels and particularly of the realm of the Mongol ruler of China, Kublai Khan, strongly influenced later explorers.

Columbus intended to set up trading colonies in the regions he had discovered, and it mattered little to him that these regions were already inhabited. Most of the Indians he had met were as friendly as the Lucayans, the tribe on San Salvador. He wrote:

> The people of this island are artless and generous with what they have, to such a degree as no one would believe. If it be asked for, they never say no, but rather invite the person to accept it, and show as much lovingness as though they would give their hearts.

Columbus responded to this display of friendliness with calculated aggression. "These people are very unskilled in arms," he remarked elsewhere, "and with fifty men they could all be subjected and made to do all that one wished."

Columbus returned from Spain not with 50 but with 1,500 men in 17 ships. This second voyage took place in 1493. The Spanish monarchs, Ferdinand and Isabella, confidently expected to reap quick profits in gold, jewels, and other forms of treasure. The people who came in this convoy represented the full range of Spanish ambition in the new lands. Among them were

missionaries who wished to convert the Indians to Christianity. There were artisans who planned to fashion the Indians' reported treasure in gold and jewels into exquisite forms suitable for the Spanish monarchs. There were also knights and young courtiers who would direct the military and political affairs of the settlements, and ordinary soldiers who would handle the actual fighting. Field laborers came to tend crops. The ships also transported domestic animals, foodstuffs, and seeds for planting. No women accompanied the expedition.

The entire expedition landed on the north coast of Hispaniola after searching fruitlessly for traces of the garrison that Columbus had left from his first voyage. Within days the Spaniards began developing on this tropical island the entire physical and social framework of a Spanish town, which they named Isabela. They laid out streets and a central plaza. They constructed the public buildings that they considered vital to a Spanish colony: a fort, a church, an arsenal, a storehouse, and a hospital.

Columbus' more ambitious plans never materialized, however. His men found neither precious metals (except in small supply) nor the

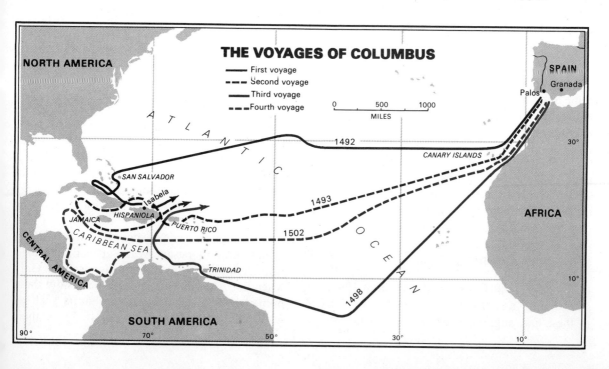

THE VOYAGES OF COLUMBUS

— First voyage
--- Second voyage
— Third voyage
--- Fourth voyage

0   500   1000
MILES

NORTH AMERICA

SPAIN
Granada
Palos

ATLANTIC

1492

CANARY ISLANDS

30°

SAN SALVADOR

Isabela

1493

JAMAICA

HISPANIOLA

PUERTO RICO

1502

CARIBBEAN SEA

AFRICA

CENTRAL AMERICA

OCEAN

TRINIDAD

1498

10°

SOUTH AMERICA

90°   70°   50°   30°   10°

fabled Asian cities that the admiral still believed were just over the horizon. Instead, cruel treatment of the Indian tribes by the Spanish led to a rebellion during which Columbus' cannons and crossbows proved most effective. After three years of sporadic warfare with the Indians of Hispaniola, the Spanish had wiped out two-thirds of the native population and enslaved most of those remaining.

When Columbus returned to Spain a second time in 1496, he brought no substantial treasure with him. Still he persuaded Ferdinand and Isabella to finance a third voyage in 1498. This time, however, enemies of Columbus tried to convince the Spanish rulers that the admiral had abused his power. They dispatched an investigator to Hispaniola, who sent Columbus back to Spain in chains. But Columbus convinced the king and queen of his innocence, and they released him. He then made a fourth and last voyage in 1502. He sailed along the eastern coast of Central America before returning home.

The "Admiral of the Ocean Seas" found little tangible wealth for Spain on his voyages. His only consistent source of revenue during the decade he ruled Hispaniola was the slave trade; Columbus shipped hundreds of Indians to Spain as a form of wealth in order to placate the royal court. Few Spaniards at the time seemed grateful for his labors. When his two children walked through the streets of Granada, mobs of townspeople reportedly pursued them shouting, "There go the sons of the Admiral of the Mosquitoes, who has found lands of vanity and delusion, the grave and misery of Castilian gentlemen!"

The Many "Discoveries" of America

CHRISTOPHER COLUMBUS came to America for the same reason that many other Europeans would come to the New World: to discover new sources of wealth. Finding such riches, Columbus believed, would bring glory to his own name, to his sponsors—the monarchs of Spain—and to his Christian faith. Columbus did indeed win glory, not through riches but as the man who discovered America. In truth, of course, Columbus did not discover America. He rediscovered it.

THE FIRST AMERICANS

Human beings first came to the Western Hemisphere some 20,000 years before Columbus. Until these first migrants came, America had been an uninhabited land mass, distant and separated from civilization's main centers in the Old World.

Almost nothing is known about why these prehistoric pioneers came. They were probably roving Mongolian hunters who first wandered across Siberia and, from there, across the Bering Strait (then dry land) into what is now Alaska. They knew nothing about pottery making or weaving. They were unfamiliar with the plow or the wheel. Their descendants continued to trek slowly southward and eastward for a long time. It took several thousand years for them to spread throughout the entire Western Hemisphere. Only when they had settled at various points did these nomads begin acquiring fixed habits such as growing food and raising animals. From their

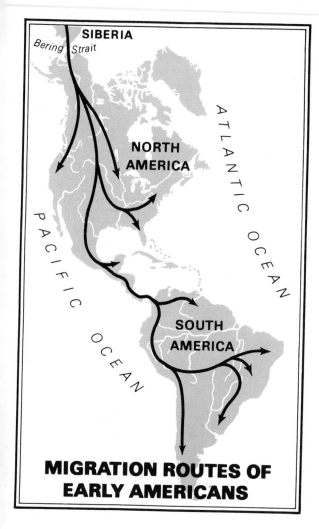

MIGRATION ROUTES OF EARLY AMERICANS

tinents of Mu and Atlantis. A few even argued that they were the defeated Trojans of Homeric legend.

It seems clear, though, that while the Indians were the first, they were not the only people to "discover" America before Columbus. Over most of these pre-Columbian explorers hangs a heavy cloud of myth, pierced by a few rays of historical fact. Several archaeologists argue that Polynesian sloops or Japanese fishing boats or Chinese junks first brought people to the American continent. Other scholars believe that if a recently translated inscription found in Brazil is genuine, it proves that a boatload of Jews or Phoenicians sailed here from the Red Sea as early as the sixth century B.C.

Irish folklore insists that Saint Brendan steered westward in the sixth century A.D. and found the New World, but, homesick for the Emerald Isle, sailed right back into martyrdom. Not to be outdone, the Welsh assert that certain archaeological remains in the American South indicate that the legendary Prince Madoc not only sailed from Wales to the New World in 1170 but even founded colonies here. One Italian professor insists that the Etruscans took time out from governing the Po Valley to discover America in 1100 B.C.

ranks evolved all the Indian tribes and cultures of the Western Hemisphere.

OTHER PRE-COLUMBIAN DISCOVERERS

Not long ago, many people preferred to believe that the first settlers in America belonged to advanced civilizations. Many wonderful tales claimed that our first families were something other than simple Asian hunters. Some people believed that the earliest Americans were remnants of the lost tribes of Israel. Others claimed that early settlers had fled the mythical lost con-

THE VIKINGS

The most believable claim for European penetration of the Western Hemisphere before Columbus involves the Vikings. These Scandinavian adventurers (also called Norsemen) were courageous seamen. In the ninth century they established a settlement in Iceland. From this base of operations they conducted daring voyages of exploration farther westward.

Vikings led by Eric the Red discovered and settled Greenland during the tenth century. Around the year 1000 Eric's son Leif anchored his ship off the coast of what is now Newfoundland. He called the place Vineland the Good, and he and his men spent the winter there before returning to Greenland. A decade later, other

In this fanciful engraving, Ferdinand and Isabella watch Columbus' departure. This type of ship, the caravel, was an improvement over heavier vessels used earlier.

Vikings sailed from Iceland to found a colony of farmers and tradesmen in Vineland. After spending two or three years fighting hostile Indians, however, they abandoned their settlement and returned to the Greenland base.

SPANISH AND PORTUGUESE EXPLORATION

Nothing permanent came from the Viking explorations or any other pre-Columbian voyages to the New World (if they occurred). Europe in the eleventh century had little interest in westward exploration. Furthermore, the Viking settlers had neither adequate weapons nor the manpower to protect themselves against the native inhabitants over a long period.

Five hundred years later, Europeans were better prepared to accept the costs and consequences of large-scale overseas expansion. By 1492 some countries already had decades of experience exploring beyond the borders of Europe. Columbus' first voyage would have remained as unimportant an incident as the earlier European discoveries of America if others had not been ready and willing to follow him.

Greatest among the exploring nations of Europe in the fifteenth century were Portugal and Spain. Their motives were chiefly economic. For centuries, luxury products such as spices, jewels, and silk had come from Asia overland or across the Indian Ocean. In either case, the Italian middlemen transported the goods from the eastern end of the Mediterranean Sea into western Europe. They had a monopoly on the trade and charged high prices. Nations on the Atlantic—Portugal and Spain, for example—decided to bypass the Mediterranean (and the Italians) and do their own trading with the East.

The Portuguese concentrated mainly on finding a route around Africa and then eastward to India and China. In the early fifteenth century Prince Henry the Navigator sponsored a school of navigation on his country's southwestern coast. He devoted his life to sending out fleets of ships to explore the west coast of Africa. The Portuguese sailed farther south along the African coast year by year. In 1488 Bartholomeu Dias voyaged as far as the Cape of Good Hope, at the tip of Africa. Vasco da Gama sailed around the cape and reached India in 1498, returning to Portugal with a rich cargo the following year. In 1500 Pedro Cabral, headed for India, was blown off course by trade winds and landed in what is now Brazil. This region of South America, claimed by Portugal, was the only area in the Western Hemisphere that the Portuguese exploited. They were more interested in developing a trading empire in the lands around the Persian Gulf and the Indian Ocean.

Meanwhile, the Spanish were sailing westward to reach Asia. This, of course, was Columbus' goal. He never surrendered his belief that the lands he had found were simply the fringes of Asia and, therefore, that he had all but discovered the legendary westward passage to the East. "It is no farther from Panama to the Ganges," he once wrote, "than from Pisa to Genoa."

The honor of having two continents named after him went not to Columbus but to a Florentine bank manager, Amerigo Vespucci. He claimed to have sailed to America several times. In widely read letters he described his experiences in what he called the New World. In 1507 a geographer named Martin Waldseemüller suggested calling the new land "America, because Americus discovered it." (*Americus* is the Latin form of Vespucci's first name.)

In 1519 the Portuguese explorer Fernando Magellan, with Spanish backing, sailed around the southern tip of South America. He crossed the Pacific and thus found the route to the East. Magellan was killed by natives in the Philippine Islands. But his navigator, Sebastian del Cano, continued westward in the only ship that remained of the original five. He returned to Lisbon in 1522, having completed the first voyage around the world. The people of Europe then realized what scholars had long known—namely, that the world is round. And they realized, too, that a whole New World lay to the west between Europe and Asia.

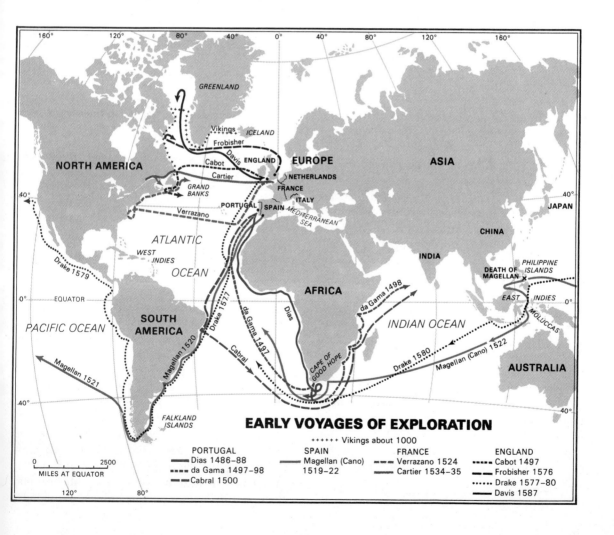

EARLY VOYAGES OF EXPLORATION

+++++ Vikings about 1000

PORTUGAL	SPAIN	FRANCE	ENGLAND
Dias 1486–88	Magellan (Cano)	Verrazano 1524	Cabot 1497
da Gama 1497–98	1519–22	Cartier 1534–35	Frobisher 1576
Cabral 1500			Drake 1577–80
			Davis 1587

MILES AT EQUATOR 0 — 2500

Moctezuma's Defeat

An Indian view of Cortés on his march to Mexico City. The eagle perched on the cactus, at right, was the Aztec national symbol and today forms the Mexican coat of arms.

FOR DAYS the Emperor Moctezuma[2] slept badly and ate little. He feared for the safety of his Aztec kingdom. Ships had been sighted on the Atlantic coast, and Moctezuma anxiously awaited the return of messengers sent to greet the strangers. These envoys carried gifts of gold and precious jewels, which the emperor hoped would induce the strangers to leave Mexico at once. Moctezuma believed that the strangers might be ancient Aztec gods, returned to claim their kingdom. He was a deeply religious man and a cautious ruler. Wishing neither to offend his gods nor lose his throne, he fretted impatiently as he awaited his envoys' return. He hoped that events would not force him to choose between resisting the gods and surrendering his power.

When the messengers finally returned, Moctezuma prayed to the supreme Aztec god. Aztec religious practice at times of crisis decreed that human captives taken in battle be sacrificed to the gods. The emperor ordered two Indian captives brought to the largest temple in his capital. There his priests performed the Aztec ritual of thanksgiving, described thusly in a later Aztec account:

> Their breasts were torn open, and the messengers were sprinkled with their blood. This was done because they had completed a difficult mission: they had seen the gods, their eyes had looked on their faces. They had even conversed with the gods!

After the ceremony, the messengers reported to the emperor. They told of walking many miles to the coast and then sailing canoes on the coastal waters until they reached the strangers' gigantic white-sailed ships. On board one of these, the messengers were led before a light-skinned but sunburned man, stocky and heavily bearded, who wore a warrior's armor. This was obviously the leader, the "god" himself. The messengers paid homage to him in the usual Aztec fashion by kissing the ground at his feet.

Moctezuma believed that this leader was the returning Aztec deity, Quetzalcoatl. The messengers spoke the emperor's words to him: "If the god will hear us, your vassal Moctezuma, who guards Mexico for you, has sent us to render

---

[2] The form "Montezuma" has been commonly used in English but is not in accord with Mexican usage.

homage." The messengers then dressed the stranger in Quetzalcoatl's traditional clothing: a serpent's mask, armor, and other adornments heavily jeweled and encrusted with solid gold. All these were gifts of welcome from Moctezuma. The other strangers—also light-skinned, bearded, and armed—crowded around their leader. Finally the "god" said: "And is this all? Is this your gift of welcome? Is this how you greet people?"

The "god" then ordered the Aztec messengers chained by the neck and feet, after which his men fired a ship's cannon. This unfamiliar weapon frightened the Aztecs so much that they fainted. When they awoke, their chains were removed and the "god" ordered them to fight his own men hand to hand. Fearing Moctezuma's anger, they refused. The leader of the strangers laughed and sent the messengers on their way.

Racing to report these fearful events to the emperor, the messengers retraced their original journey toward the Aztec capital, Tenochtitlán. This city had at least a quarter of a million people. Its palaces and temples rose along the canals and causeways of an island in a lake. Here Moctezuma received his messengers' report. He was frightened, particularly by their description of the strangers' cannon that "shatters a tree into splinters," the iron armor they wore, and the "deer that carry them on their backs wherever they wish to go." (These "deer" were actually horses, which the Indians had never seen before.) The emperor hung on the messengers' every word and afterward "was filled with terror as if he were conquered by despair." The messengers had confirmed all the earlier Aztec omens and signs, the predictions of priests and magicians that announced either the return of Quetzalcoatl himself or the arrival of strangers as powerful as gods. From this time on, Moctezuma brooded over a single question: What did the "god" expect of him? He was soon to learn.

The strangers were first sighted on the coast in the Aztec calendar year "13-Rabbit" (1519). Their leader was a Spanish soldier and adventurer named Hernando Cortés. Not long after his men debarked, some of them wanted to leave, so

Cortés scuttled all but one of the ships. After the return of his first messengers, Moctezuma sent wizards and magicians to greet the "gods" as they marched inland toward Tenochtitlán. But the strangers seemed repelled by the Aztec religious practice of human sacrifice, and sent the wizards away. Thousands of once-loyal Indians from Aztec subject tribes joined Cortés on his march; the procession stretched out for miles along the royal road. Everywhere the Spanish soldiers asked local villagers about Moctezuma and his wealth. They destroyed one entire tribe that attacked them. Their ranks continued to grow.

Moctezuma tried one final time to appease the oncoming "god" and his followers by sending presents of golden feathers and necklaces. "They picked up the gold and seemed to be transported with joy," noted one Aztec at the scene. "They hungered like pigs for that gold." An Aztec envoy claimed to be Moctezuma. The Indian allies of Cortés, knowing that he was not, taunted him: "You cannot deceive us. You cannot make fools of us. You are not Moctezuma. He is there in his city. He cannot hide from us. We are coming to see him, to meet him face to face." By the time the strangers reached the outskirts of Tenochtitlán, even the Aztecs' two strongest subject tribes had joined the Spaniards' triumphal procession.

To his advisers Moctezuma seemed "weak and listless and too uncertain to make a decision. He did nothing but resign himself and wait for them to come and for whatever was to happen." Many of the emperor's nobles and war chiefs urged him to keep the strangers out of the city. After all, there were hundreds of thousands of Aztec warriors and only a few hundred Spaniards. Even with their Indian supporters, the Spaniards were smaller in number than the Aztecs.

In the end, however, Moctezuma decided to welcome the "god" in friendship and allow him and his men to march peacefully across a causeway that led into the city. On an ordinary day thousands of Aztecs would be crossing this route. On this August morning, according to a

A sixteenth-century map presents a stylized view of Tenochtitlán. At the center stands the plaza with a great pyramid temple where important sacrifices took place. Causeways lead across Lake Texcoco to "suburbs"–here depicted as European fortresses. One Spaniard wrote on entering the city: "Gazing on such wonderful sights, we did not know what to say. Some of our soldiers even asked whether the things we saw were not a dream."

later chronicle, "all lay quiet: the people did not go out. The roads were empty and clear and the common folk said, 'Now we shall die; we shall perish.'"

Moctezuma waited for Cortés just inside the city's boundaries, dressed in his imperial finery and attended by Aztec princes, knights, and priests. The emperor himself draped "Quetzalcoatl" and his men with flowers, gold garlands, and other presents in an elaborate ceremony of welcome. He bowed his head low before the "god" and said: "Our lord, you are weary. The journey has tired you, but now you have come to your city." Cortés in turn ordered his Indian translator to "tell Moctezuma that we are his friends. There is nothing to fear. We love him well." The strangers then took Moctezuma by the hand and patted him on the back to show their affection. Dismounting from their horses, they accompanied Moctezuma and his chiefs into the royal palace.

Within a week the emperor was a prisoner of the Spanish, held under guard in his own quarters. His chief nobles had fled into hiding. From the moment of his captivity the emperor's hold over his subjects grew weak. Even when he finally recognized that the strangers were not gods but mortals like himself, Moctezuma was reluctant to oppose them. He offered to share Aztec wealth in gold, silver, and jewels with the strangers, an offer greedily accepted by Cortés.

Despite Moctezuma's pledge of fidelity, the Spaniards kept him in a state of virtual imprisonment. Finally, the emperor briefly recovered his self-assurance as his people prepared for war against the small band of intruders. Moctezuma ordered Cortés and his men to leave. Early in 1520 Cortés did withdraw most of his soldiers and Indian allies for a campaign against a competing Spanish expedition that had just landed on the coast.

In Tenochtitlan, meanwhile, one of Cortés' lieutenants led a foolish attack on Aztec warriors conducting a religious ceremony. In the struggle that followed, the Spaniards found themselves under siege in the royal palace, with all of Aztec Mexico in arms against them. Moctezuma re-

mained a prisoner. By now his nobles and people had turned against him. They denounced him for having cooperated with their enemies, put his servants to death, and finally deposed him in favor of his brother, Cuitlahuac, a man committed to total destruction of the Spaniards.

Cortés had returned by this time. In the midst of an Aztec attack on the palace that raged for four days, Moctezuma was killed. Aztec accounts insist that this tragic figure was killed by the Spaniards. The Spaniards claimed that Moctezuma was fatally wounded by rocks hurled by his own people while he pleaded with them to throw down their arms. Either account could be true. In any case, Moctezuma's death made little difference to the outcome of the battle itself, which went badly for the Spaniards.

After four days, Cortés decided to abandon the capital. Thousands were killed in his retreat. But the Spaniards and 75,000 Indian allies returned to besiege Tenochtitlán. In 1521, after months of grisly warfare, Aztec power finally collapsed. Moctezuma's beautiful capital city lay in ruins, burned to the ground during the fighting. (Later, Mexico City would be built over it.) The Aztec population, reduced to starvation, was enslaved by the Spaniards and their Indian allies.

Moctezuma's worst fears had come true. His empire had been reduced to ashes, its people destroyed or driven from their homes, their culture abandoned. As one Aztec poet wrote:

> Broken spears lie in the roads;
> we have torn our hair in our grief,
> The houses are roofless now, and their
> walls
> are red with blood.

And the emperor himself might have written these lines from another lament chanted by the Aztecs in their anguish:

> Weep, my people:
> know that with these disasters
> we have lost the Mexican nation.
> The water has turned bitter,
> our food is bitter!
> These are the acts of the Giver of Life.

The Indian Cultures of America

THE AZTEC EMPIRE ruled by Moctezuma was built upon the achievements of earlier Indian cultures. The Indians of America, like peoples all over the world, progressed from simple to more complex ways of living. In Latin America (America south of the Rio Grande) Indian cultures reached a high point under the Aztecs, the Mayas, and the Incas. In North America north of the Rio Grande, Indian life was simpler, though no less varied.

THE AZTECS

The heart of the Aztec Empire was the Valley of Mexico, the region around what today is Mexico City. It had been inhabited long before the Aztecs ruled it. First came the people of Teotihuacán, who constructed a great city near the later site of Tenochtitlán. Teotihuacán flourished during the fourth and fifth centuries A.D. Here the Indians built pyramids, palaces, and religious temples.

A later people in the Valley of Mexico, the Toltecs, built another great city, Tula, somewhat to the north of Teotihuacán. Under the leadership of a strong king named Quetzalcoatl, the Toltecs conquered a sizable territory, built beautiful palaces, and erected huge stone sculptures. Although Toltec rule collapsed, Indians in the Valley of Mexico retained Toltec cultural patterns. For example, they began worshiping Quetzalcoatl as a god. They believed that he had departed to the east, abandoning his people. One day he would return by ship from the other end of the world. This legend was the basis for Moctezuma's initial fear that Cortés and his men were returning deities.

The Aztecs came into the Valley of Mexico from the north about 1215. They were simple warriors. Neighboring peoples helped to educate them in the fine arts and skills that had been handed down from the Toltecs. The Aztecs needed little training in the art of warfare, however. Within decades of their arrival in the valley, they had conquered every major city-state in the area. They then began extending their rule outward in all directions.

The Aztecs, like the Spanish, had a passion for military conquest. But the two peoples held opposing views on warfare. Wholesale, indiscriminate slaughter of "pagan" peoples (such as Moctezuma's Aztecs) in warfare seemed quite acceptable to the Christian troops of Cortés. But these same troops were revolted by the individual ritual slaughter that the Aztecs engaged in.

Most tribes in the Valley of Mexico (including Cortés' Indian allies) practiced human sacrifice to some extent. None, however, performed it with as much frequency and gusto as the Aztecs. They considered it necessary for life itself. Calling themselves "people of the sun," the Aztecs believed that their major deity required a constant supply of fresh human blood lest he, as the source of all life, dry up. In order to secure this supply, they had constantly to capture enemy warriors for sacrifice. For the Aztecs, then, the purpose of war was not merely to conquer territory but to capture enemy warriors.

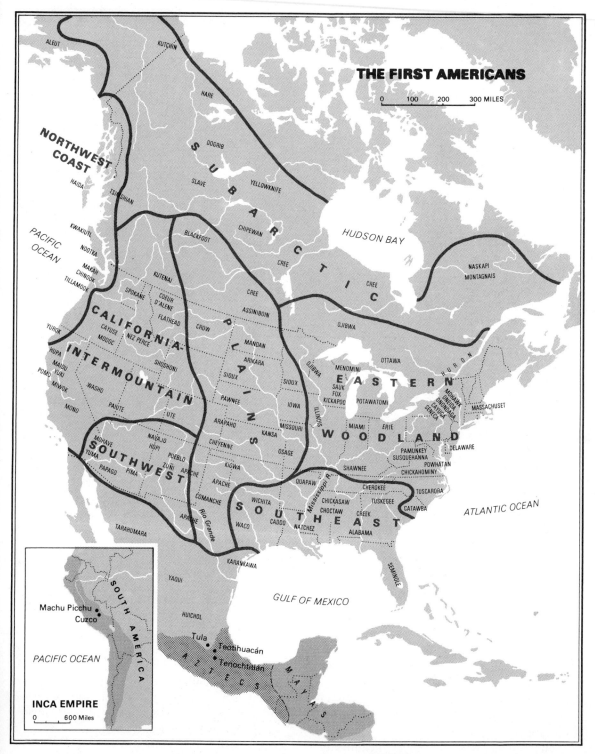

THE FIRST AMERICANS

0   100   200   300 MILES

NORTHWEST COAST

ALEUT

KUTCHIN

HARE

DOGRIB

S U B A R C T I C

HAIDA

TSIMSHIAN

SLAVE   YELLOWKNIFE

KWAKIUTL

NOOTKA

MAKAH

CHINOOK

TILLAMOOK

CHIPEWAN

BLACKFOOT

CREE

HUDSON BAY

PACIFIC OCEAN

KUTENAI

SPOKANE

COEUR D'ALENE

FLATHEAD

CREE

CREE

NASKAPI

MONTAGNAIS

YUROK

CALIFORNIA

CAYUSE

NEZ PERCE

CROW

ASSINIBOIN

OJIBWA

HUPA

MODOC

INTERMOUNTAIN

SHOSHONI

MANDAN

ARIKARA

P L A I N S

OJIBWA

OTTAWA

E A S T E R N

HURON

MAIDU

YUKI

WASHO

SIOUX

SIOUX

IOWA

MENOMINI

MOHAWK

ONEIDA

ONONDAGA

CAYUGA

SENECA

POMO

MIWOK

PAWNEE

SAUK

FOX

KICKAPOO

POTAWATOMI

MASSACHUSET

MONO

PAIUTE

UTE

ARAPAHO

MISSOURI

ILLINOIS

MIAMI

ERIE

W O O D L A N D

MOHAVE

NAVAJO

HOPI

CHEYENNE

KANSAS

OSAGE

SHAWNEE

PAMUNKEY

SUSQUEHANNA

POWHATAN

DELAWARE

YUMA

PUEBLO

ZUNI

APACHE

SOUTHWEST

KIOWA

CHICKAHOMINY

PAPAGO

PIMA

APACHE

QUAPAW

CHEROKEE

TUSCARORA

COMANCHE

Rio Grande

WICHITA

S O U T H E A S T

CHICKASAW

CHOCTAW

TUSKEGEE

CATAWBA

TARAHUMARA

APACHE

WACO

CADDO

CREEK

ALABAMA

ATLANTIC OCEAN

NATCHEZ

KARANKAWA

YAQUI

SEMINOLE

GULF OF MEXICO

HUICHOL

Tula

Teotihuacán

Tenochtitlán

A Z T E C S

M A Y A S

S O U T H   A M E R I C A

Machu Picchu

Cuzco

PACIFIC OCEAN

INCA EMPIRE

0   600 Miles

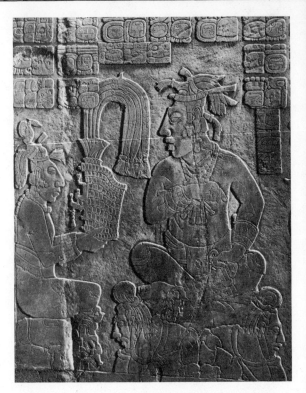

Latin American artists and craftsmen produced works of outstanding quality. The great stone head at left, which stands eight feet high and weighs twenty tons, was carved by the Olmec people of Mexico, forerunners of the Toltecs. Another early culture—the Chavin of Peru—specialized in fine metalwork. The hammered silver object at top left represents the head of a puma. The Mayan stone relief above depicts a god receiving offerings from a priest, with writing overhead. This sculpture is known as the Panel of the Slaves because of the figures upon which the god sits.

The Aztecs ruled a large territory. Their empire can best be understood as a feudal realm. Within it a number of semi-independent city-states competed with one another for influence. While paying formal tribute to the emperor, city-states often ignored orders that came from the far-off capital.

Tenochtitlán was the most beautifully planned and elaborately defended city in the Western Hemisphere at the time that Cortés and his men entered it. About 250,000 people lived within its boundaries or in the surrounding Aztec city-states. When the first Europeans viewed the dazzling palaces, temples, and marketplaces along the city's canals and causeways, they could hardly believe their eyes.

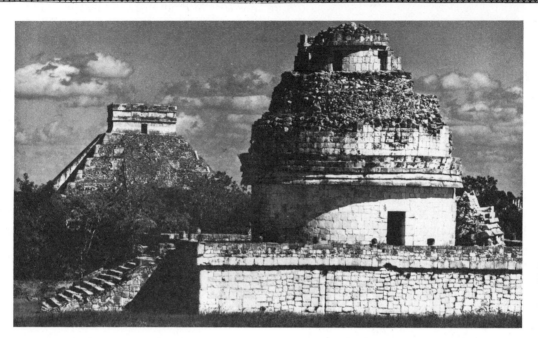

The Mayan buildings above are among several at Chichen Itzá. *At left is a temple to Kulkulcan, the Mayan counterpart of Quetzalcoatl. The round structure at right is an astronomical observatory.*

High in the Andes lies the Inca town of Macchu Picchu, below. Undiscovered by Spanish conquerors, it remained hidden in the mountains until an American explorer stumbled across it in 1911.

The Aztecs built upon the achievements not only of the peoples of the Valley of Mexico but also of those in nearby regions, notably the Mayas. Mayan culture surpassed that of both the Aztecs and the Toltecs.

Mayan civilization reached its height between 200 and 900 A.D. in what is now southeast Mexico and Guatemala. The people were not united under one government, but they lived clustered about such ceremonial cities as Tikal and Palenque. Later cities, influenced by the Toltecs, include the famous Chichen Itzá. It is built on a grand scale, with large open plazas and high stepped pyramids.

The most striking Mayan remains are intricately carved limestone sculptures. Many of these depict gods and priests. Most are also covered with symbols, for the Mayas were the only Indians to develop a true system of writing. This system is not yet completely understood, but much of it seems to be related to time keeping, which was important in Mayan religion. To the Mayas each day had a sacred meaning, and their priests worked out a series of intricate calendars. One calendar—of 365 days, like our own—was more exact than any other calendar used in Europe at the time of Columbus. Because keeping time was so important, Mayan priests were excellent astronomers and mathematicians; they developed a number system based on twenty and including the useful concept of zero.

Mayan culture declined after the Toltecs invaded in the twelfth century. By the time Europeans arrived in the sixteenth century, Mayan glory had long since faded.

THE INCAS

The Mayas have sometimes been thought of as the Greeks of pre-Columbian America because of their cultural achievements. Similarly, the Incas have been compared to the Romans because of their imperial political and administrative organization. The Inca Empire sprawled over the western part of South America. It covered large portions of modern Ecuador, Chile, Peru, and Bolivia—in other words, most of the land available for cultivation in the Andean Plateau. In the eleventh century, at roughly the same time the Toltecs were invading the Mayan region, the Incas began extending their control over the Andean Plateau. At its peak in the sixteenth century, the Inca Empire stretched along a land mass 1,500 miles long and 300 miles wide. It was bound together in a much more systematic way than the Aztec Empire.

The Inca emperor, known himself as "the Inca," was considered a divine figure. He ruled from the capital city of Cuzco, high in the Andes Mountains. Cuzco was connected to all parts of the empire by an excellent system of roads and runners. Along the roads and in other central locations were state-owned granaries, where food was stored in case of shortages.

Inca roads were supremely useful for moving troops. "Not an insurrectionary movement could occur, not an invasion on the remotest frontier," wrote an American historian, "before the tidings were conveyed to the capital, and the imperial armies were on their march across the magnificent roads to the country to suppress it."

The Incas had a more efficient war machine than the Aztecs. But it too was no match for the Europeans. An adventurer named Francisco Pizarro had heard of a rich inland kingdom while voyaging along the Pacific coast in the 1520s. He led a group of Spaniards into the Inca domains in 1531. They found the empire in the throes of a civil war between two sons of the previous emperor. The more successful imperial contender, Atahualpa, had recently won control.

Because of this civil war, Inca forces were weakened and divided. They could not muster effective resistance when Pizarro attacked. The climax of Pizarro's campaign came in a scene resembling the episode in Tenochtitlán when the Spaniards slaughtered peaceful Aztecs at worship. Pizarro lured Atahualpa to a meeting, where he ordered Spanish troops to cut down thousands of poorly armed, unsuspecting Inca soldiers. Pizarro promised to release the Inca emperor after payment of a fantastic ransom in gold and silver, worth an estimated $10 million. Once the ransom had been delivered, the unscrupulous Spaniard had Atahualpa executed.

NORTH AMERICAN CULTURES

The complex societies developed by the Aztecs, Mayas, and Incas contrasted with the simpler cultures of most North American Indians at the time of the European influx. In Latin America the Indian population was large; there were probably over 15 million Indians in the region when the whites came. Societies were stable. People built cities and made a living by farming settled areas. (Corn, the staple crop for almost all American Indians, was probably first brought under cultivation in Mexico.) In America north of the Rio Grande, on the other hand, the Indian population was much smaller; it probably totaled no more than a million when Europeans arrived. Tribal groupings were smaller, and many were nomadic at least part of the year. Although many groups were semisettled and did some farming, several lived almost entirely by hunting and gathering.

Remnants of some relatively advanced Indian cultures still exist in several regions of North America. One such culture flourished in southern Arizona, where an Indian-built complex of irrigation canals dating to the eighth century suggests highly sophisticated farming techniques. In the Mississippi Valley early Indians known as Mound Builders heaped earth and rubble into pyramids and other structures. These were used as temples or burial mounds and have yielded many beautiful works of art.

A striking feature of North American Indian life at the time of European penetration was the remarkable variety of tribal cultures. In order to simplify matters, scholars have tended to group tribes into a few so-called culture areas—regions where most Indians followed the same pattern of living.

In the Southwest the oldest inhabitants were the Pueblos, peaceful farmers who lived in adobe

Indians of a vanished era scratched these mysterious figures on a cliff wall in Wyoming. They may represent priests or perhaps gods held sacred by the tribe.

villages built on high mesas. Latecomers to the region included the more nomadic and warlike Apaches and Navajos. Indians of the Southwest excelled in weaving and making pottery and jewelry.

In the large area to the north between the Rockies and the Mississippi River lived the Plains Indians. Though they did some farming, hunting was also important to them. After the coming of the whites—and with them the horse—tribes such as the Cheyenne, the Pawnee, and the Sioux gave up farming altogether and lived entirely by hunting buffalo, which roamed the plains in vast numbers. They killed the animals not only for food but also for clothing and for making the skin-covered tepees in which they lived.

Between the Rockies and the Pacific Ocean, in the California-Intermountain culture area, roamed many small groups of Indians. In the mountain regions life was hard; tribes such as the Shoshoni and Ute made a poor living gathering wild plants and eating small animals such as rabbits and snakes. In California—home of the

In America north of the Rio Grande, Indians created a number of distinctive styles. Typical of the Mound Builder culture is the kneeling stone figure at left, found in Tennessee. From New York State is the Cayuga Iroquois mask above, braided from corn husks. Masks like this were worn by members of the so-called False Face Societies—secret organizations whose members performed dances and other rituals to heal the sick. Below is a slate canoe sculpted by a Haida Indian of the Northwest. The figure in front is a shaman, or medicine man. He wears a crown of bear claws set in a rope of twisted cedar bark. The reclining figure at the back, with closed eyes, probably represents a dead person.

Navajo Indians of the Southwest are noted for their sand paintings, like the one above. Each one, combining sacred symbols and used as part of a healing ceremony, is formed by a priest in the morning and destroyed before nightfall. At right above are blanket bands woven by the Sioux Indians of the Great Plains. These were made after the white man came with beads for trade; in the early days, women fashioned similar designs using dyed porcupine quills or wampum (beads drilled from clam shells). The whale statuette at right was carved by a Chumash Indian of California.

Pomos, Hupas, and others—acorns were a staple food. Life was easier there, and people had time to make some of the finest basketry in the world.

The Northwest Coast region stretched along the Pacific shore of what is now Oregon, Washington, and British Columbia. Tribes such as the Kwakiutl, Nootka, and Tlingit thrived on salmon and other fish that teemed in local waters. From the cedars of the Northwest forests expert crafts-men carved handsome canoes, household objects, and totem poles.

The plains of Canada were the home of small bands of Subarctic hunters such as the Crees. They led a hand-to-mouth existence, dependent on caribou, moose, and fish. To them we owe the birchbark canoe, snowshoes, and the toboggan.

The first Indians to greet many explorers of

North America were those of the Eastern Woodlands, the culture area east of the Mississippi River. These tribes lived by a combination of farming and hunting. Most of them dressed in deerskins and lived in bark-covered wigwams. In what is now the New York State region lived the famous Iroquois confederacy. This league of five tribes consisted of the Mohawks, Oneidas, Onondagas, Cayugas, and Senecas. The American Southeast was the home of such tribes as the Cherokees, Creeks, and Seminoles.

THE INDIAN WAY

Clearly, Indian life differed a great deal from group to group and place to place. But certain characteristics were common to almost all Indians and set them apart from other peoples—especially the Europeans who settled in America. One of these characteristics was the Indian attitude toward land. A tribe might have hunting rights to a certain territory, but its members no more owned this territory than the sky above it. Even among the complex farming societies of Latin America, land belonged to the community or perhaps to a god or spirit. Indians had no idea of individual ownership.

Indians also had different attitudes about warfare. For them it was as much a ceremony as a conflict. Even in the Aztec Empire, where territory and tribute were important, the basic goal of war was to capture prisoners for a religious purpose. To many North American tribes, war was almost a game. Plains fighters, for example, achieved as much glory for touching an enemy in battle as for killing him. European techniques of warfare, such as long sieges, were strange to the Indians.

The first Europeans who came to America were accustomed to monarchs, and to strong monarchs at that. But even a ruler of Moctezuma's importance did not possess absolute power. He was, in fact, elected to his post, and many of his duties were merely ceremonial. Few chiefs of North American tribes had the authority to rule by themselves. When there was an issue to be decided, all the respected elders of a band would gather together and, after lengthy deliberations, reach a unanimous decision.

Indian religious concepts were, of course, unlike those of Christianity. The idea of an afterlife was, at most, vague. There was no one God but often a multitude of gods or spirits. (The Aztecs worshiped some 300 deities.) An Indian was believed to have his own guardian spirit that helped him through life. Such spirits were also thought to inhabit trees, animals, rivers, and mountains. From Moctezuma down to the poorest Cree hunter, every Indian was guided by omens and signs and trusted in what we would call magic.

THE EUROPEAN IMPACT

Europeans of the fifteenth and sixteenth centuries were not noted for their tolerance toward those having different beliefs. When they encountered customs and values unlike their own—whether in America or Asia or Africa—they concluded that the strangers' ways were "barbaric" or "uncivilized." This helps to explain the ferocity with which whole societies in the New World were destroyed.

Technology played a large role, too. The Aztecs' amazement at the horses and the cannon of the Spaniards was echoed a thousand times over when Indians saw their first sailing ships, their first firearms, even their first iron pots. They had no beasts of burden (other than the llama of the Andes). Thus, though they knew the principle of the wheel, the Indians never developed it to make carts or wagons.

Finally, there was the impact of population. The first Europeans who landed in America came in small groups: Columbus' first voyage brought 90 men. Cortés landed in Mexico with 650. Pizarro marched into the Inca capital with fewer than 200. But thousands followed these early adventurers. In North America, especially, the Indians soon found themselves vastly outnumbered by peoples for whom their own organization and technology were no match.

Hernando de Soto tried to persuade Cabeza de Vaca to accompany him to Florida. But the latter, a proud man, refused to serve under another commander.

De Soto at the Mississippi

IN TIME American Indians adopted at least some European ways. These included language, religion, guns, horses, and—unfortunately—alcohol. Europeans, too, learned new customs. They not only grew Indian crops but also adopted Indian words, made roads out of Indian trails, and used Indian wampum as a medium of exchange. One Spanish explorer even became an Indian medicine man!

In 1528, seven years after Cortés had conquered the Aztecs, a Spanish expedition under Pánfilo de Narváez sailed to North America to explore Florida.[3] Soon after landing on the mainland, the expedition sailed west and was shipwrecked off the coast of Texas. One of the few survivors was an official named Álvar Núñez Cabeza de Vaca. Captured by Indians, he es-

caped certain death at their hands by practicing the healing arts. The Indians allowed him a small measure of free movement in return for the prayers and crude treatments they thought were responsible for the miraculous cures of their sick.

In 1534, after six years of close confinement, Cabeza de Vaca found three other survivors of the shipwreck. These men, who had been enslaved by other tribes, included a black explorer named Estevanico. The four men escaped from their captors and struck out across the interior of Texas and New Mexico toward Spanish territory. They were thus the first non-Indians to cross the American Southwest. They moved from Indian village to village, and everywhere they were treated with enormous respect and friendship because of their reputations as medicine men. "Frequently," Cabeza de Vaca later wrote, "we were accompanied by three or four thousand persons, and had to breathe upon and sanctify

---

[3] To the Spanish and other Europeans of this period, the term "Florida" referred not just to the peninsula but also to what is now the entire southeastern United States.

the food and drink for each, and give them permission to do many things they would come to ask.''

Finally, in July 1536 the four men reached Mexico City. There they reported their incredible adventures to the Spanish viceroy, recounting tales of all the gold they had seen in their travels. Cabeza de Vaca returned to Spain the following year. He hoped to lead an expedition to Florida, then only barely explored, in order to continue his quest for wealth. But in 1538 this responsibility was given to another leader, Hernando de Soto. He himself had recently returned from America, where he had been one of Pizarro's chief lieutenants in the conquest of the Inca Empire.

In May 1539 De Soto left Cuba with the largest Spanish expedition yet dispatched to North America—nine ships with over 550 soldiers, 200 horses, and dozens of glory-seeking noblemen. It landed near Tampa Bay and soon met another survivor of Cabeza de Vaca's earlier expedition, Juan Ortiz. He had married an Indian chief's daughter and lived among the local tribes for the past twelve years. Ortiz joined the party as a translator. On the basis of his knowledge of tribal life, he cautioned the Spaniards against hoping to find precious metals or Indian empires nearby. Discouraged, many of the noblemen urged their leader to return to Cuba. De Soto refused "till I have seen the poverty of the country with my own eye." Instead, he ordered his ships to return to Cuba, and his men proceeded to march up the west coast of Florida, using Indians as porters.

For the next three years the Spaniards wandered north through what is now Florida, across Georgia into South and North Carolina and Tennessee. Next they continued through Alabama and Mississippi and westward into Arkansas, Oklahoma, Louisiana, and Texas. During their travels they stopped mainly to rest horses and men. They discovered no great stores of gold and silver, however, although De Soto did seize whatever valuables he could find. After professing friendship for one Indian queen who had greeted him warmly with a gift of pearls, De Soto took her prisoner and ordered his men to dig up Indian graves in order to steal the pearls buried with dead tribal chieftains. Through its bitter wanderings his expedition learned the truth of Ortiz' cautions. These new lands did not hide wealthy Indian kingdoms like those in Mexico and Peru.

Furthermore, the Indians became increasingly hostile as word of De Soto's thievery spread. Reaching the Indian village of Mabila (near what is now Mobile) in October 1540, De Soto's party fought a savage battle for survival against a large band of Indians. Eighteen Spaniards were killed and 150 wounded. By burning down Mabila, the Spaniards won the battle and killed many Indians; but they also lost many of their horses and most of their baggage. The exhausted survivors pleaded once more with De Soto to turn back. Although he had secret information that his ships waited along the Florida coast, only six days' march from Mabila, De Soto "determined to send no news of himself until he had found some rich country." The remainder of his expedition continued to press farther into the interior, heading northwest from Mabila and finally quartering for the winter in another Indian village.

Before setting out again in the spring of 1541, De Soto ordered the local chiefs to provide him with porters to replace those who had deserted or been killed. The Indians responded by attacking De Soto's party at midnight, setting the village on fire. A dozen Spaniards perished in the flames. The majority escaped—but without their clothes, most of which were burned. Wearing garments made of animal skins and matted leaves, De Soto and his men continued their wanderings. In June 1541 they "saw the great river." Earlier Spanish explorers had seen the Mississippi River only where it emptied into the Gulf of Mexico, but De Soto and his men viewed a more spectacular sight:

The river was over a mile wide. If a man stood still on the other side, it could not be discerned whether he was a man or no. The river was of great depth, and of a strong current. The water was always muddy. There came down the river continually many trees and timber.

The Spaniards set up quarters along the river bank and built barges to make a crossing. Then they floated across the Mississippi into Arkansas and resumed their journey.

De Soto's men had heard tales of the buffalo and of "the other sea" to the west. They marched through Arkansas and into Oklahoma, where they began encountering bands of Plains Indians. After a long western trek they turned back toward the southeast and camped in Arkansas. De Soto had already lost over 250 men. He began to despair of finding any new source of great riches.

The Spaniards continued to spread terror in Indian villages along their way, slaughtering thousands. But they found no wealth. Sensing the growing frustrations of the Spaniards, the Indians stiffened their resistance. De Soto's anguish sharpened. "His men and horses every day diminished, being without succor to sustain themselves in the country, and with that thought he

fell sick." The expedition by then had retraced its steps back into Louisiana. De Soto, realizing that he would die soon, called his men together one final time on May 20, 1542. Before designating his successor, Luis de Moscoso, De Soto thanked his men for their loyalty through great hardships. He pleaded that they "forgive him any wrongs they might have received at his hands." The next day De Soto was dead. One chronicler of his journey wrote that he had been "advanced by fortune, that he might fall the greater depth."

Moscoso, who later led the survivors back to safety in Mexico, wanted to conceal De Soto's death from the Indians. De Soto had tried to convince them that Christians were immortal and therefore to be feared rather than fought. Moscoso arranged for De Soto's body to be buried secretly. Later "he ordered the corpse to be taken up at night," wrapped in blankets, and weighted with sand. Then the European who discovered the Mississippi "was carried in a canoe, and thrown into the midst of the river."

Spain and America — "Glory, God, and Gold"

IN THE FIFTY YEARS after Columbus' first voyage a host of Spanish explorers and conquerors performed incredibly daring and ruthless feats all over America. Like Columbus, they dreamed of fame, of winning converts to the Christian faith, and of wealth. Spanish goals have been summed up as "glory, God, and gold."

A few Spaniards, like Cortés and Pizarro, stumbled upon fortunes. More typical were the experiences of Cabeza de Vaca and De Soto. Juan Ponce de León (who had sailed to America on Columbus' second voyage) failed to find either gold or a legendary fountain of youth when he explored Florida in 1513. After trying unsuccessfully to found a settlement on the peninsula in 1521, he was wounded by Indians and died on his return voyage to Cuba. Francisco Vásquez de Coronado—encouraged by the tales of Cabeza de Vaca and Estevanico—explored much of the Southwest in 1540-42, searching for the "Seven Cities of Cibola," said to be full of riches. When found, they turned out to be nothing more fabulous than the simple adobe villages of the Pueblo Indians.

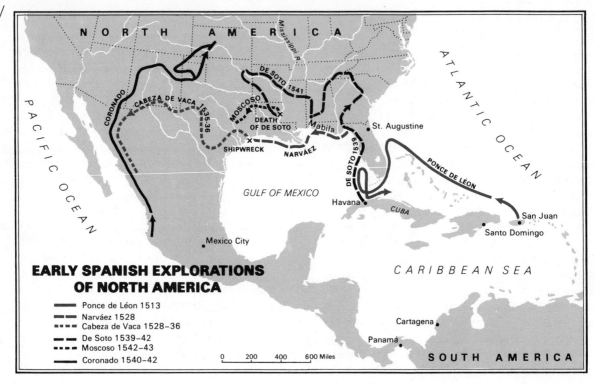

**EARLY SPANISH EXPLORATIONS
OF NORTH AMERICA**

— Ponce de Léon 1513
– – Narváez 1528
■■■■ Cabeza de Vaca 1528–36
— ■ — De Soto 1539–42
■■■■ Moscoso 1542–43
— Coronado 1540–42

0   200   400   600 Miles

CREATING AN EMPIRE

In spite of all these setbacks, the Spanish continued to come to the New World in tremendous numbers. They formed political units and appointed Spanish rulers. (After his expedition, Cabeza de Vaca served as governor of Paraguay. De Soto was governor of Cuba at the time of his expedition.) They built missions, military outposts, and towns. In short, they created an overseas empire. Eventually, there were four large provinces: New Spain, which stretched from Mexico through the western United States and included Spain's Caribbean possessions, and the three South American provinces of New Granada, Peru, and La Plata. The Spanish colony established at St. Augustine, Florida, in 1565 is the oldest existing permanent European settlement in what is now the United States.

By 1600 a quarter of a million Spaniards had settled in the Western Hemisphere. Into their lands they introduced crops previously unknown in America—among them wheat, rye, oats, and barley. They found that bananas, peaches, and citrus fruits would grow well in America, too. Sugar cane became an especially important crop in tropical regions. The Spanish also brought draft animals—horses, mules, and oxen—and livestock, including cattle, hogs, and sheep. And the newcomers quickly learned to grow native American crops: corn, tomatoes, potatoes, beans, cacao, and tobacco.

Spanish America soon boasted flourishing cities with great cathedrals. The first universities in America were founded at Mexico City and Lima in 1551. These two university locations were not accidental, for Spanish civilization in the Americas prospered on gold and silver acquired from the Aztec and Inca empires. Fabulously rich silver mines were discovered in Mexico and Peru in 1545. Silver and, to a lesser extent, gold were for many decades Spain's chief exports from the New World. Each year royal treasure fleets sailed from Havana and other Atlantic ports carrying this precious cargo collected in America.

THE INDIANS

After the Spanish conquests of America most Indians were virtually enslaved by their conquerors. Thousands of them labored in the mines to dig and smelt silver and gold. Others farmed and tended livestock.

Spanish friars and priests protested against mistreatment of the Indians. In time, the Spanish crown passed laws designed to limit the abuse of native labor. These efforts, however, were not notably successful in preventing cruelty and exploitation. Cortés, Pizarro, De Soto, and other Europeans of that time regarded Indians as

barely human. After a century of Spanish rule the Indian population of Mexico had declined through disease and maltreatment from over 5 million to only 1 million. Elsewhere in the New World—in Peru and the Caribbean islands, for example—the Indian population decreased at comparable rates and for similar reasons.

As a result, Indian culture was greatly weakened. Spanish missionaries worked to destroy "pagan" religions and convert New World peoples to Christianity. Through intermarriage with the Spanish a new mixed class—the *mestizos*—was created. Accepted by neither the Indians nor the Spaniards, its members were often homeless and rootless outcasts.

AFRICAN SLAVES

As many Indians died or fled beyond the range of Spanish settlements, another steady source of

One of the richest sources of silver in the world was a mountain known as Cerro Rico, at Potosí, Bolivia. In this 1584 painting, Indian laborers using llamas struggle up and down the hillside while other workers sort and stack the ore for shipment to Spain.

cheap labor seemed necessary. Most Spaniards regarded manual labor as undignified, and raising crops like sugar cane required a large labor force. So the Spanish began importing black slaves from Africa. The first slaves came as early as 1510. Many thousands were shipped in later years.

In spite of the horrors of the Atlantic crossing, many African slaves survived the hard life, and their numbers increased. They were more resistant to diseases of the whites than the Indians, as they had already been exposed to them in Africa. They also proved to be better at agriculture because of previous experience. Many Indians—especially those in the Caribbean and in North America—had done relatively little farming.

THE EFFECTS OF EMPIRE BUILDING ON SPAIN

Spain dominated sixteenth-century European politics, diplomacy, warfare, and economic life. The country's two rulers for most of the century were Charles V, king of Spain from 1516 to 1556, and his son Philip II, who ruled from 1556 to 1598. Gold and silver from its American possessions flowed into Spain throughout the sixteenth century. The crown's share (usually a quarter of the total) often went to sponsor military expeditions against foreign enemies in Europe.

The vast influx of precious metals had serious consequences for the Spanish economy. It caused an enormous rise in prices—that is, inflation. Prices rose about 400 percent in Spain during the sixteenth century. The Spanish government often found it impossible to collect enough tax revenue to pay its debts.

Furthermore, inflation made it difficult for Spanish farm or manufactured goods to compete with cheaper foreign imports. Thus the same influx of precious metals that gave Spain temporary dominance in Europe also helped cripple her long-range chances as a food-producing, manufacturing nation.

MERCANTILISM

Spain's overwhelming desire for precious metals grew out of a certain view of economic life held by most European governments. A Catholic missionary might have viewed Cortés' looting and De Soto's grave robbing as shameful. But any European monarch would have considered these exploits the fulfillments of his nation's economic prosperity and power. The true measure of such prosperity, according to this view, was the amount of gold and silver a country controlled. Later economic writers gave the name *mercantilism* to this set of ideas, which governed the economic behavior of European nations since the fifteenth century.

Spain alone had the mines from which to acquire gold and silver directly. Every other European power turned to foreign commerce to increase its stock of precious metals. The goal was to maximize exports of a nation's manufactured goods and minimize imports from other countries. This is known as a favorable balance of trade.

Mercantilists believed that gold and silver could best be kept within a country by achieving such a favorable balance of trade. To this end, the ships of Portugal, the Netherlands, England, France, and other European nations crossed and recrossed the oceans in search of new opportunities for trade. Spain, by contrast, never developed a strong commerce, partly because of her smug certainty that New World mines would provide all the gold and silver she needed.

Unfortunately for Spain, those sources ran dry in the seventeenth century. Her great period of national prosperity waned. So did her political and military influence in Europe. What endured from decades of Spanish conquest and plunder was not the treasure itself. Instead, there remained a vast imperial domain, studded with great plantations, ranches, and orchards. Through it ran an equally impressive network of Catholic missions and churches, strung like rosary beads along the length of Spanish America. And over all lay the veneer of Spanish language and culture.

Sir Francis Drake was described by a Spaniard as "of medium stature, blonde, rather heavy than slender, merry, careful." The vignette shows him receiving homage from a group of Indians.

The Return of the *Golden Hind*

THE HUNDRED-TON SHIP glided smoothly across the harbor toward the English town of Plymouth. The few small fishing boats it passed seemed dwarfed by the huge vessel, which had the words "Golden Hind" painted on her bow. From the *Golden Hind*'s top deck came a shout, evidently directed by its captain at one of the fishing boats: "Is the queen alive and well?" The puzzled fisherman shouted back the answer—and a warning: "Her majesty is in good health, but there is pestilence in Plymouth."

The captain of the *Golden Hind* listened

without comment to the news of Queen Elizabeth and the plague warning. Then he went to his cabin, where he wrote these words in the ship's log:

> We safely, with joyful minds and thankful hearts to God, arrived at Plymouth, the place of our first setting forth, after we had spent two years, ten months, and some odd days besides, in seeing the wonders of the Lord in the deep, in discerning so many admirable things, in going through with so many strange adventures, in escaping out of so many dangers, and overcoming so many difficulties.

Thus, on September 26, 1580, Francis Drake completed the record of his voyage around the world. It was the first such trip after Magellan's voyage, and it was the first trip ever made by a captain sailing his own ship for the entire distance.

Drake fretted anxiously after the *Golden Hind* docked in Plymouth. He awaited news from the queen. Would she welcome back in triumph the daring "sea dog" who had established English naval power over the entire globe while sacking Spanish treasure ships for the royal treasury? Or would she condemn him as a pirate? Earlier she had seemed to approve of his adventures, but now Spain was protesting. And Spain was still Europe's leading power.

The first messages from London were ominous. The Spanish ambassador had demanded the return of Drake's booty—the gold, silver, and precious jewels that had been seized from Spain's American treasure houses. London merchants feared retaliation, and some of the queen's advisers preferred to sacrifice Drake rather than risk war with King Philip of Spain. "Lie close," came one message to Drake, advising him to remain in Plymouth "until she changes her mind."

Meanwhile, Drake deposited the spoils of his voyage in Plymouth Castle for safekeeping: twenty tons of silver bullion, five blocks of gold (each eighteen inches long), and a quantity of pearls, other precious jewels, and jeweled objects. No one knows the precise value of Drake's entire treasure. According to estimates, the total came to at least $25 million (in modern American currency), perhaps much more. This was a huge sum for a small and not very wealthy country like sixteenth-century England.

Drake and his crew remained on board the *Golden Hind*, partly because of the pestilence in Plymouth and partly because of Drake's fear that Elizabeth might order his arrest on shore. Finally, word came from London summoning Drake before the queen. He was not to fear, ran the message, because Elizabeth would protect him. Her Majesty wanted to see some of the "curiosities" he had collected on his voyage and, of course, wished a full account of the trip. Drake ordered five packhorses loaded with gold, jewels, and other booty for the queen's inspection. In London he spent six hours in private audience with Elizabeth, displaying samples of the treasure he had captured and regaling her with tales of his voyage.

This was not the first of Drake's maritime adventures. He had learned his trade working with his cousin John Hawkins. In 1567 he commanded his own ship on a voyage with Hawkins carrying cargoes of slaves from Africa to the New World. Drake and Hawkins transacted business in the slave trade without apparent concern for the people being sold. They combined a passionate zeal for financial gain with an equally earnest belief in two pillars of faith: England and Protestantism.

Queen Elizabeth supported and encouraged Drake's slave trading and semiofficial piracy. She hoped to add funds to her royal coffers while reducing Spanish power. She commissioned Drake as a privateer in 1570. The following year, he led a group of seventy sailors in an ambush of a Spanish mule train lumbering across the Isthmus of Panama with a cargo of silver from Peru. After pillaging a Spanish town on the Panama coast, Drake returned safely to England with his booty in mid-1573.

Drake's round-the-world trip began in 1577. Starting with 5 ships and 164 officers and men, Drake set out to circle the globe in order to break Spain's monopoly in the Pacific. His squadron sailed past the Cape Verde Islands, where he captured Spanish and Portuguese ships. Proceeding southward along the east coast of South America, Drake beat back an attempted mutiny, losing ships and men along the way. He rounded Cape Horn and reached the Pacific in September 1578 with only one remaining vessel, the *Pelican* (later renamed the *Golden Hind*).

Then Drake turned north, seizing treasure and provisions from Spanish ships and towns along the way. To escape enemy attack, he kept heading north, sailing, he wrote, "on the backside of America to 43 degrees Northerly latitude." Along the coast of California he stopped

Drake's campaign of the 1580s was his first act of open warfare against the Spanish. He commanded a fleet of twenty-nine ships. One successful episode was the sack of Santo Domingo, above. While the fleet lies at anchor, foot soldiers—their ranks bristling with spears—attack the walled city from the left. Drake was a daring man who much enjoyed what the English of his day called "singeing the king of Spain's beard."

at a "fair and good bay"—what may be the San Francisco of today. He claimed the lovely harbor and its surrounding territory for England, "calling this country Nova Albion[4] and setting up a monument of our being there, as also of her Majesty's right and title to the same."

Drake then searched, as had Columbus and other European explorers before him, for some

[4] *Nova* is Latin for "new"; "Albion" is an ancient name for England.

body of water connecting the Atlantic and Pacific. This would have allowed him to return to England by sailing eastward. Finding none, though, he voyaged westward to the Spice Islands (the Moluccas—now part of Indonesia). There he loaded a cargo of valuable pepper. He continued west, rounded the Cape of Good Hope, and sailed up the west coast of Africa to reach Plymouth in September 1580.

Drake's account of his voyage clearly excited Elizabeth's imagination. Despite protests by the Spanish ambassador, Bernardino de Mendoza, she refused to disguise her admiration for the returning privateer. "Drake has returned to court," Mendoza wrote to Philip II, "where he passes much time with the queen, by whom he is highly favored and told how great is the service he has rendered her." Elizabeth ordered the treasure cargo of the *Golden Hind* brought from Plymouth to London. She went through the motions of signing a royal decree formally directing that the treasure be registered and returned to its rightful Spanish owners. But not a penny of it ever left England. Drake made a handsome profit. So did the noblemen who had sponsored his voyage as shareholders. Despite Mendoza's continuing protests and threats, the bulk of the precious cargo remained in the Tower of London as part of Elizabeth's royal treasury.

Drake, meanwhile, became a popular hero, particularly after the queen made a journey to visit the *Golden Hind*. Elizabeth's leading sea dog had sailed the ship around the coast and up the Thames River to Deptford. Leading a procession of royal barges, the queen sailed down the Thames from London to Deptford on April 4, 1581. She boarded the *Golden Hind*, where a great banquet was served on deck. Afterward, Elizabeth ordered Drake to kneel.

The monarch then informed Drake that the king of Spain had asked her to chop off his head and that she held a gilded sword in her hand that could do the job. At this time, she handed the sword to the French ambassador, doubtless much to his surprise, and asked him to lay the blade across Drake's shoulder while she knighted him "Sir Francis."

Knighting Drake was not a step Elizabeth took lightly. She realized that Spain would be insulted by her honoring the very man whom Spain considered to be a foul pirate. Yet she also realized—and this perhaps explains her action—the degree to which English pride had become identified with Drake and his exploits. Few actions taken during her long reign were as popular as her knighting of Drake. His fame, wrote one contemporary, now "became admirable in all places, the people swarming daily in the streets to behold him, vowing hatred to all that dared mislike him. Books, pictures, and ballads were published in his praise. His opinion and judgment concerning marine affairs stood current." Whatever the wealthy and well-born might have thought of Drake—for he did have powerful enemies in Elizabeth's court—ordinary Englishmen idolized him.

Drake returned to raid Spanish America during the 1580s. In 1586 he led ships that attacked the coastal cities of Santo Domingo, Cartagena, and St. Augustine. He then played a major role in defending his country against the Spanish Armada. This great fleet was sent by Philip II in 1588 to invade England. Drake commanded the English ships that sailed out to meet the Spanish fleet. Among his captains was his cousin John Hawkins. Hammering at the Spanish galleons and aided by a severe storm, the English inflicted a crippling defeat upon the enemy. The English victory marked the end of Spanish naval power.

Drake continued his privateering until the time of his death in 1596. He died on board ship, off the coast of Panama, while engaged in one last campaign against the Spanish.

England as a Colonizing Power

As Early As 1497, the English crown—in the person of Elizabeth's grandfather Henry VII—had sent an exploratory expedition to the New World. It was captained by John Cabot, a Genoese born Giovanni Caboto. Cabot sailed along the Grand Banks area off Newfoundland looking unsuccessfully for a northwest passage—a short northern water route from the Atlantic to the Pacific and thus to the Far East. A second voyage by Cabot in 1498 confirmed both the presence of fish and the absence of Chinese. For the next sixty years, England showed little interest in overseas ventures. Her monarchs were too involved on the Continent to challenge Spanish power on the seas.

OTHER EUROPEAN VENTURES

In 1524 the French king, Francis I, employed a Florentine navigator named Giovanni da Verrazano. His aim was also to seek a northwest passage. Verrazano charted much of the North American coastline from North Carolina to Maine, but his assigned mission, like Cabot's, was clearly impossible.

A decade later, Jacques Cartier sailed from France with the same goal and with similar results. He made three trips up the St. Lawrence River between 1534 and 1541, but he, of course, did not find the East. (He did, however, name the rapids above Montreal "La Chine"—French for "China.") Nor did Cartier find any precious metals.

Throughout most of the sixteenth century, the great majority of Europeans who sailed north of Spanish settlements in the New World were neither explorers nor adventurers. They were summertime fishermen. Each spring they left their home ports along Europe's Atlantic coast to catch, dry, salt, and pack codfish along the Grand Banks. Living in closely knit, temporary international communities, these fishermen devised their own "Common Market" in codfish. They divided the fishing grounds among themselves during the day, visiting and exchanging goods in the evening.

ELIZABETHAN ATTITUDES

Queen Elizabeth came to the throne of England in 1558. Under her strong leadership the English

Queen Elizabeth ruled England, in her words, with the body of a woman "but the heart and stomach of a king."

began to assert themselves both in Europe and abroad. The time had come to challenge Spanish power and obtain a share of New World wealth. Drake and Hawkins were the most famous of England's sea dogs, but there were many others. Martin Frobisher sailed to Labrador in 1576 searching for a northwest passage, and he made additional voyages the following two years for the same purpose. (Frobisher later commanded a ship against the Spanish Armada.) John Davis—also an Armada captain—was equally noted for his explorations in Arctic waters. He later discovered the Falkland Islands off the coast of South America.

The voyages of her sea dogs made the New World appear so attractive to Elizabeth that she took yet another step. In the 1580s she began to authorize other English adventurers—not pirates this time but enterprising businessmen among the nobility—to explore and to found settlements. Their objectives were described as those "remote heathen and barbarous lands, countries and territories not actually possessed by any Christian prince or people." This language meant that Elizabeth's adventurers were to establish colonies in those portions of the New World north of Spanish settlements.

Elizabeth and her advisers had various reasons for wanting to colonize the New World. Economically, colonies were important to England as a mercantilist nation. It was hoped that, once established, they would yield precious metals while serving as an outlet for English manufactures.

The desire for gold and silver was whetted by England's fierce rivalry with Spain. Drake and others had proved that the Spanish were by no means invincible, that English daring was a match for Spanish experience. This rivalry in turn was heightened by religious differences. Under Elizabeth's father, Henry VIII, England had broken away from the Roman Catholic Church. Elizabeth had established the Church of England—the Anglican Church, a kind of middle ground between extreme Protestants on the one hand and Roman Catholics on the other. Throughout her reign—and later as well—Catholic countries like Spain tried to restore England to Catholicism. This was one goal of the planned invasion by the Spanish Armada.

Another factor in early colonization schemes was the belief that England was overpopulated. The countryside seemed to be filled with vagabonds. Actually, the problem was unemployment rather than overpopulation. For several decades landowners had been involved in the process of *enclosure*—fencing in what had been common farmland—in order to raise sheep. (Wool growing was more profitable than raising crops.) As a result, many farm laborers were forced off the land. Colonies were seen as a means of ridding England of these "sturdy beggars."

TRADING COMPANIES

Though the English crown looked favorably on the idea of colonies, it did not officially sponsor them. Instead, they were established by private trading companies.

A trading company was a joint-stock company in which individual members invested by buying shares. Drake's round-the-world voyage in 1577–80 was a joint-stock effort—one that proved extremely profitable for its shareholders. A joint-stock company received a charter from the English government that granted it certain monopoly privileges. No one else could trade or settle in the region over which a particular company had control.

One of the first trading companies founded by the English was the Muscovy Company, organized in 1553 for trade with Russia. The most successful was the East India Company, founded in 1600 to exploit the riches of the East.

SIR HUMPHREY GILBERT

Perhaps the first man to recognize clearly the potential benefits to England of New World colonies was Sir Humphrey Gilbert. Like many

(continued on page 34)

THE LAND
THE EXPLORERS
FOUND

The first Europeans who came to America were not literary men, but adventurers with a purpose—to discover routes to the East, or gold, or land for settlement. Still, they were curious and observant, and kept good records of what they saw. Coming from a populated land of cities and farms, they were struck by America's seeming emptiness, its great forests, its plentiful wild game and fruits.

One of the oldest accounts of America was written by an anonymous Viking chronicler about land not unlike this shoreline at Mt. Desert, Maine: ''They found it a fair, well-wooded country. It was but a short distance from the woods to the sea, and there were white sands, as well as great numbers of islands. They found neither dwelling of man nor lair of beast.''

[For further information on the foreign observers quoted in this essay, see ''Notes on Sources.'']

PICTORIAL ESSAY 1

Whoso maketh navigations to those countries hath not only extreme winds and furious seas to encounter, but also many monstrous and great islands of ice—a thing both rare, wonderful, and greatly to be regarded.

We were forced sundry times, while the ship did ride here at anchor, to have continual watch, with boats and men ready with hawsers to fasten onto ice that was tossed to and fro in the harbor with the ebb and flood. The men would haul the ice away with force of oars so that it would not endanger our ship.

[DIONISE SETTLE, WITH MARTIN FROBISHER, 1577]

Ice floes near Baffin Island

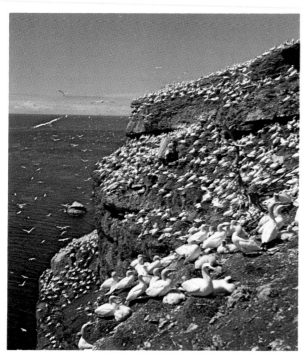

Gannets near the coast of Canada

Along the shore, Cape Cod

Newfoundland we found very subject to fogs and mists. The ground of it is very rocky, and upon it there is great store of fir trees, and in some places red. About the shore it hath great abundance of codfish.

The three Islands of Birds are sandy red, but with the multitude of birds upon them they look white. The birds sit there as thick as stones lie in a paved street. The greatest of the islands is about a mile in compass. The second is a little less. The third is a very little one, like a small rock. At the second of these three lay on the shore in the sunshine about thirty or forty walruses which, when our boat came near them, presently made into the sea, and swam after the boat.

[CHARLES LEIGH, 1597]

Near this cape we came to anchor in fifteen fathoms, where we took great store of codfish, for which we called it Cape Cod. Here we saw schools of herrings, mackerels, and other small fish in great abundance. This is a low sandy shore, but without danger. We came to anchor again in sixteen fathoms. This cape is well near a mild broad, and lieth north-east east. The captain went here ashore and found the ground to be full of peas, strawberries, huckleberries, etc., then unripe.

[BARTHOLOMEW GOSNOLD AND BARTHOLOMEW GILBERT, 1602]

Adirondack Mountains, New York State

This region is almost an island, surrounded by the great river Saint Lawrence, which passes through several lakes of great extent. On the shore of this great river there are very high mountains, and the air is temperate. All these places abound in game. Fishing is abundant, there being many varieties, both those which we have in France, as also others which we have not. There are likewise many birds in their time and season. The country is traversed by numerous rivers, brooks, and ponds, connecting with each other and finally emptying into the river St. Lawrence and the lakes through which it passes. The country is very pleasant in spring, is covered with extensive and lofty forests, and filled with wood similar to that which we have in France.

[SAMUEL DE CHAMPLAIN, 1615]

Wild grapes

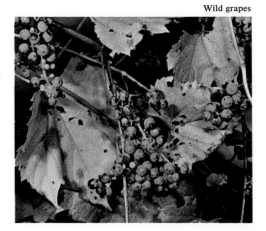

We saw in this country many vines growing naturally, which growing up, took hold of the trees as they do in Lombardy. If they were tended in good order by husbandmen, without all doubt they would yield excellent wines. Having oftentimes seen the fruit thereof dried, which was sweet and pleasant and not differing from ours, we think those here do esteem the same, because in every place where they grow, they take away the under branches growing round about, that the fruit thereof may ripen better.

[GIOVANNI DA VERRAZANO, 1524]

Southern forest and underbrush

The Indians led us into a country difficult to traverse and strange to look at, for it had very great forests, the trees being wonderfully tall and so many of them fallen that they obstructed our way so that we had to make long detours and with great trouble. Of the trees standing many were rent from top to bottom by thunderbolts, which strike very often in that country, where storms and tempests are always frequent.

[ÁLVAR NÚÑEZ CABEZA DE VACA, 1528]

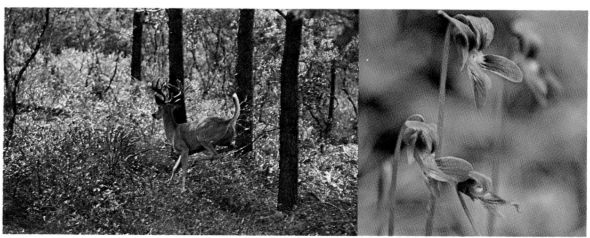

White-tailed deer

Wild violets

Deer in some places there are in great store. Near unto the seacoast they are of the ordinary bigness of ours in England, and some less, but further up into the country, where there is better food, they are greater. They differ from ours only in this: their tails are longer, and the snags of their horns look backward.

[THOMAS HERIOT, 1585]

Mother opossum with young

Trees and swampland, Florida

The animals we saw included one that carries its young in a pouch on its belly as long as the young are small, until they are able to look for their sustenance. Even then, when they are out after food and people come, the mother does not move until her little ones are in the pouch again.

[ÁLVAR NÚÑEZ CABEZA DE VACA, 1528]

An Indian guided them through an immense pathless thicket of wilderness for seven days, where they slept continually in ponds and shallow puddles. Fish were so plentiful in them that they were killed with blows of cudgels.

["A FIDALGO OF ELVAS," WITH HERNANDO DE SOTO, 1541]

Countryside around Jamestown

Island in the Caribbean

All this coast, and the part of the island which I saw, is mainly a beach. The island is the loveliest thing that I have seen, for, if the others are very lovely, this is more so. It has many trees, very green and tall. The singing of little birds is such that it seems that a man could never wish to leave this place. The flocks of parrots darken the sun, and there are large and small birds of so many different kinds and so unlike ours, that it is a marvel. There are, moreover, trees of a thousand types, all with their various fruits and all scented, so that it is a wonder. I am the saddest man in the world because I do not recognize them.

[CHRISTOPHER COLUMBUS, 1492]

Parrot fish from the Bahamas

Cuban parrot

←*The territory for pleasantness of seat, for temperature of climate, for fertility of soil, and for the commodity of the sea, besides multitude of bears (being an excellent good victual), was not to be excelled by any other whatsoever. To the northwest the farthest place of our discovery was distant from Roanoke about 130 miles. Our passage thither lay through a broad sound, but all fresh water. The channel was of a great depth, navigable for good shipping, but outside the channel the sound was full of shoals.*

[RALPH LANE, 1585]

In this river we saw many crocodiles of sundry bignesses, but some as big as a boat, with four feet, a long broad mouth, and a long tail, whose skin is so hard that a sword will not pierce it. His nature is to live out of the water as a frog doth, but he is a great devourer, and spareth neither fish, which is his common food, nor beasts, nor man.

[JOHN HAWKINS, 1564]

A crocodile, from an early engraving

Grasslands on the Great Plains

Now we will speak of the plains. The country is spacious and level. No settlements were seen anywhere. In traversing 250 leagues, the other mountain range was not seen, nor a hill nor a hillock which was three times as high as a man. The country is like a bowl, so that when a man sits down, the horizon surrounds him all around at the distance of a musket shot. There are no groves of trees except at the rivers.

[PEDRO DE CASTAÑEDA, WITH FRANCISCO VÁSQUEZ DE CORONADO, 1541-42]

One of the earliest depictions of the buffalo, 1558

The buffalo's shape and form are so marvelous and laughable, or frightful, that the more one sees it the more one desires to see it, and no one could be so melancholy that if he were to see it a hundred times a day he could keep from laughing heartily as many times, or could fail to marvel at the sight of so ferocious an animal. They are so thickly covered with wool that it covers their eyes and face, and the forelock nearly envelops their horns. This wool, which is long and very soft, extends almost to the middle of the body, but from there on the hair is shorter.

[JUAN DE OÑATE, 1598]

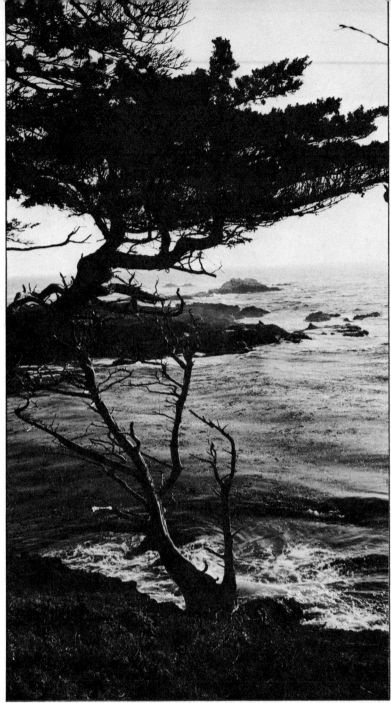

California coastline near Monterey

We arrived at Monterey in the evening. The next day the men landed. Mass having been said and the day having cleared, there having been much fog, we found ourselves to be in the best port that could be desired. Besides being sheltered from all the winds, it has many pines for masts and yards, and live oaks and white oaks, and water in great quantity, all near the shore.

[SEBASTIÁN VIZCAÍNO, 1602]

Roanoke—the island at center—was protected from the sea by the Outer Banks, including Hatteras (here called "Hatorasck"). Sunken ships lie in the foreground.

other Englishmen of Elizabeth's day, Gilbert was attracted to the profits and glory that came from combining New World trade with a bit of officially sanctioned piracy. Gilbert moved past these concerns, however, and persuaded Queen Elizabeth to grant him a charter to discover and claim any North American lands not already claimed by any other European countries.

Gilbert promised the crown a fifth of all the precious metals he found, a far smaller percentage than Drake had given Elizabeth from the cargo of the *Golden Hind*. He also vowed to foster the official Anglican religion in the New World. In turn he received royal authority to found and govern a colony in North America.

Gilbert made two attempts at colonization. In 1578 he was forced back by bad weather or perhaps diverted by the more attractive possibilities of piracy. (Historical accounts differ on this point.) He tried again in 1583 with a larger expedition. This time he reached Newfoundland and took possession of a surprised international colony of summer fishermen. Soon afterward, however, he perished in a storm.

RALEIGH AND ROANOKE

The dream of an English colony in America was carried further by Gilbert's half brother, Sir Walter Raleigh. He took over Gilbert's charter in 1584 on even more favorable terms than those granted his relative. Raleigh sent out an advance party that year to search for a suitable site. The party found one, which it called Roanoke Island, along the Atlantic coast south of Chesapeake Bay. Raleigh named the entire coastal region Virginia in honor of England's "Virgin Queen."

In 1585 Raleigh dispatched an expedition of settlers to Roanoke Island. They spent most of their time roaming through the countryside searching for gold. They also explored nearby rivers looking for the Pacific Ocean. In other words, they did everything but colonize. The entire settlement returned the following year with Drake after his sacking of St. Augustine.

In 1587 Raleigh sponsored a third expedition, this time commanded by an artist, John White. He helped the 118 settlers establish a colony at Roanoke Island before he went back to England for additional supplies. Unfortunately for the new settlement, White could not return promptly with the supplies. England was in the grip of a Spanish invasion scare, and several years passed before the defeat of the Armada and the return of tranquility to Elizabeth's realm.

White sailed back to America in 1591. When he reached Roanoke, he found the settlement in ruins. The entire colony had vanished without a trace except for the single word *CROATOAN* (the name of a nearby island) carved on a doorpost. White's own daughter and granddaughter were among the missing. Despite a thorough search of the entire neighboring area, including Croatoan Island, none of the Roanoke colonists was ever found. They may have starved or been killed or captured by Indians. Their fate remains a mystery. Future English settlements in North America proved more fortunate, more lasting, and less mysterious.

1. Is it accurate to say that Columbus did not discover America, but rediscovered it? Why have so many different peoples made claims about the discovery of America?
2. Why did Portugal and Spain take the lead in trying to find new routes to India and China?
3. In what ways were the Aztec, Mayan, and Inca cultures more complex than those of other American Indians? How would you refute the charges of European explorers that the Indians were primitive?
4. Do you think that the European attitude toward land was preferable to that held by the Indians? What about attitudes toward warfare? Toward government? Toward religion?
5. Of the three Spanish goals in the New World—"glory, God, and gold"—which was the most important? Why? With which of these goals did the Spanish have the most success? The least success?
6. Why did the Spanish import blacks from Africa? Why did they prefer black slaves to Indian slaves? Some historians have held that the Spanish came to the New World as conquerors and not as colonizers; do you think this view is correct?
7. What effects did the influx of large amounts of gold and silver have on Spain?
8. How would you summarize the theory of mercantilism? Do nations today believe in the same doctrine? Why or why not?
9. Why was England so late in becoming a colonizing power? Were Queen Elizabeth's reasons for undertaking colonization the same as Spain's?

Beyond the Text

1. Improvements in sailing techniques and instruments aided explorers in the Age of Discovery. Investigate the significance of the following: Martin Behaim; astrolabe; tables of ephemerides; caravel; square rigging; cross-staff.
2. The Aztec Empire is sometimes called a feudal realm. Analyze the correctness of this view by determining (a) the various parts of the empire; (b) the duties of the parts of the whole; and (c) the duties of the whole to the parts.
3. The text refers to the Mayas as the Greeks of pre-Columbian America and the Incas as the Romans. What are the bases for these comparisons? Explain why you think they are accurate or inaccurate.

Bibliography

Nonfiction

Gibson, Charles, *Spain in America.**
Haring, Clarence H., *The Spanish Empire in America.**
Innes, Hammond, *The Conquistadors.*
Josephy, Alvin M., Jr., *The Indian Heritage of America.**
Leon-Portilla, Miguel, *Broken Spears: The Aztec Account of the Conquest of Mexico.**
Morison, Samuel E., *Admiral of the Ocean Sea.*
———, *The European Discovery of America: The Northern Voyages, 500–1600.*
Notestein, Wallace, *The English People on the Eve of Colonization, 1603–1630.**
Parry, John H., *The Age of Reconnaissance.**
Sauer, Carl O., *Sixteenth-Century North America.*
Vaillant, George C., *Aztecs of Mexico.**

Fiction

Bandelier, Adolf G., *The Delight Makers.**
De Madariaga, Salvador, *Heart of Jade.*
Stacton, David, *A Signal Victory.*

*a paperback book

UNIT ONE

COLONIAL

During the seventeenth century, Englishmen managed to establish their first successful settlements in North America. Their ''plantations'' (as they called their new colonies) were carved out of the wilderness. The English did not encounter Indian civilizations as advanced as those the Spanish found in Latin America. Nor did they find gold or silver. What they found was land, land that sometimes seemed impossible to conquer.

The early English settlements held on by a thin thread. They were paid for in blood and suffering. Thousands of English people came to America, and at first almost as many died as made the long, difficult voyage. But two successful centers gradually developed, one in Virginia and the other in Massachusetts. From these beginnings, English colonists spread out into Maryland and the Carolinas, into Connecticut and Rhode Island, and into New York and Pennsylvania.

The two centers of settlement, Virginia and Massachusetts, were similar in many ways. Their colonists had the same basic problems of

AMERICA

getting food, building shelters, and dealing with the Indians. And, at first, colonists in both regions tried to fulfill common ideas about how a colony should work and be governed. Both colonies were distinctly English in language, government, and social life.

For all the similarities, there were deep and important differences between the plantation colonies and New England. Types of soil and climate made one kind of agriculture possible in the South but not in the North. This difference led to a second. Southern agriculture could use black slave labor from Africa. New England settlers had nothing particular against slavery, but their economy had little use for it. A third difference was that most of the settlers in New England were deeply religious men and women, known as Puritans, who wanted to remake both church and society.

This unit of *Freedom and Crisis* tells stories of fear, confusion, and violence in the two colonies of Virginia and Massachusetts in the seventeenth century. The unit also provides chapters that give background information about

the larger forces that shaped the dramatic events.

Chapter 1 deals with a political uprising in Virginia known as Bacon's Rebellion. Its accompanying chapter is a general study of the plantation colonies in the South. In Chapter 3 the focus is on a witchcraft scare in the village of Salem, Massachusetts. It is followed by a broad treatment of society in Puritan New England.

Both Bacon's Rebellion and the Salem witchcraft episode tore deeply at the two small colonies in which they occurred. Virginia and Massachusetts were still unsteady outposts, and they were deeply threatened by these moments of crisis. But they survived their difficult times and achieved stability.

Both stories are full of foolishness and cruelty. In each story, too, there is some courage and good sense. When men and women experience crises, they often disclose essential facts about themselves. Thus these episodes, and the chapters that accompany them, reveal much about the nature of seventeenth-century English colonial society in North America.

Bacon's Rebellion

THE YEAR WAS 1675. Thomas Mathew, a Virginia tobacco planter with a large plantation on the south bank of the Potomac River, observed with his neighbors three strange and ominous signs. First there was a large comet, "streaming like a horse tail, until it reached almost the horizon." The other two signs were even more unusual. Flights of pigeons that filled a quarter of the sky came into Virginia from the interior. When they roosted at night, their weight broke even large tree limbs. According to Mathew: "This sight put the old planters under portentous apprehensions, because the like was seen when the Indians committed the last massacre." The third "strange appearance" that Mathew observed was "swarms of flies about an inch long and big as the top of a man's little finger, rising out of spigot holes in the earth, which ate the new-sprouted leaves from the tops of the trees, and in a month left us."

As Thomas Mathew tried to interpret the meaning of the three omens, he might have thought of the hurricane that had recently devastated the colony. Or he might have remembered a drought that had spoiled almost an entire year's tobacco crop—the English planters' most important economic asset. More than likely, however, Mathew and his neighbors thought of Indians. There had been problems recently with a tribe of friendly Doeg Indians, who lived just across the Potomac River in Maryland. Mathew himself had neglected to pay for

At the head of his "army," Nathaniel Bacon strides through the streets after setting fire to Jamestown. This re-creation of the event was painted by illustrator Howard Pyle.

some goods that he had bought from the Doegs. In retaliation, the Doegs had tried to steal some of Mathew's hogs, but a band of Englishmen had tracked the Indians down and killed one or two of them. Mathew also knew that a band of Susquehannah Indians, much more warlike than the Doegs, had moved down from farther north to the Maryland side of the Potomac. Technically, both the Doegs and the Susquehannahs were friendly and lived under Maryland's protection. But the Potomac region was crowded—with Virginians, Marylanders, Doegs, and Susquehannahs. Any Englishman who had lived through or even heard about earlier Indian wars expected trouble.

Trouble came to Mathew's door. He owned another plantation several miles up the Potomac, run by an overseer and a herdsman named Robert Hen. On a Sunday morning in July 1675 some people on their way to church passed near Hen's house and saw him lying in his doorway, hurt. An Indian lay nearby. Both men had been "chopped on their heads, arms and other parts, as if done with Indian hatchets." The Indian was already dead, and Hen was dying. But he had time to gasp, "Doegs! Doegs!" before he died. Then a boy who had been hiding under a bed in the house came out and told the people that "Indians had come at the break of day and done these murders."

Stealing hogs was one thing, but the death of an Englishman was much more serious. The Virginians had a militia[1] to deal with such matters, and the local leaders called the farmers to arms. Years later, Mathew recalled what happened:

> Of this horrid action, Colonel Mason, who commanded the militia regiment of foot, and Captain Brent, the troop of horses in that county, having speedy notice, raised thirty or more men. They pursued the Indians twenty miles up and four miles over the river into Maryland. Landing at the dawn of day, they found two small paths. Each leader took a separate path, and either found a cabin, which they silently surrounded.

The English were not nearly so skilled at forest warfare as the Indians. But this time they were able to catch their enemy by surprise—probably because the Indians knew that it was against English law for Virginia militia to cross into Maryland.

> Captain Brent went to the Doegs' cabin. Speaking the Indian tongue, he called to have a *Matchacomicha Weewhip,* a Council, such being the usual manner with Indians. The king came trembling forth, and would have fled, when Captain Brent, catching hold of his twisted lock (which was all the hair he wore), told him he was come for the murderer of Robert Hen. The king pleaded ignorance, and slipped loose. Brent shot him dead with his pistol. The Indians shot two or three guns out of the cabin; the English shot into it. The Indians thronged out at the

---

[1] A colonial militia consisted of citizens who could be called upon to form an army in case of need.

door and fled. The English shot as many as they could, so that they killed ten, and brought away the king's son of about eight years old.

So far, the Virginians' mission of revenge had been successful, at least by their own standards. They had taken ten Indian lives for one English life. And at this point they were not troubled by the fact that they had illegally invaded a sister colony. They did not even mind the fact that they had no way of knowing whether or not these particular Indians had actually been involved in the murder of Hen. But the other half of the company of militia was about to make a very costly mistake.

The noise of the shooting awakened the Indians in the cabin which Colonel Mason had encompassed. They likewise rushed out and fled. The company shot fourteen before an Indian came and with both hands shook Colonel Mason (in a friendly way) by one arm, saying "*Susquehanougs Netoughs*! Susquehannah friends!" and fled. Whereupon Colonel Mason ran among his men, crying out, "For the Lord's sake, shoot no more! These are our friends, the Susquehannahs!"

Mason and Brent took their militia back to the Virginia side of the Potomac. They had won a military victory, in which thirty Virginians had killed almost as many Indians. They had punished the Doegs. But in doing so they had caused more problems than they had solved, for the Susquehannahs would want revenge.

BACON'S REBELLION

A fort of the Susquehanna Indians, as depicted in an early European print. The shelters, typical of this region, were probably made of bark; each was inhabited by several families.

The Susquehannahs who had escaped Colonel Mason's troops went upriver to a fort that their tribe had built on the Maryland side. The main body of the tribe had about a hundred warriors, plus their wives and children. They had built an English-style fortress with walls made of tree trunks sunk into the ground. At the corners were firing platforms, and the square was surrounded by a ditch.

With the Susquehannahs safely inside their fort, the English had time to stop and think. The governor of Maryland sent a protest to the Virginia capital at Jamestown concerning the Virginians' illegal invasion of Maryland territory. A month passed without any serious trouble, and the governor of Virginia, Sir William Berkeley, ordered an investigation. He told two militia leaders to call together all the officers in the northern area of Virginia to conduct an inquiry. Berkeley wanted to move cautiously. He had kept peace with the Indians for over thirty years, and he did not want an Indian war now. But the militia leaders violated their orders. Instead of calling out the officers of the militia to make an investigation, they called out the troops. And, without authority, they asked for help from Maryland. Altogether, about a thousand men were quickly assembled from the two colonies. Before Governor Berkeley knew what was happening, they set out up the Potomac to attack the Susquehannah fort.

The English arrived at the Indian fort in late September 1675, about two months after the murder of Robert Hen. The commanders asked the Indians for a council, just as they had done at the Doeg cabin. The Indians sent out four of their "great men." The English betrayed the truce by axing the Susquehannah chiefs to death. Then they attacked the fort.

The Susquehannahs were ready, however. They resisted the English successfully for several weeks, "shooting many of our men, and making frequent, fierce and bloody sallies. And when they were called to, or offered parley, they gave no other answer than 'Where are our four *Cockarouses* (Great Men)?' "

The Indians kept themselves from starving by stealing English horses for food. But finally they had to escape. Seventy-five braves crept out of the fort at night, with their families, and killed ten sleeping English sentries in the process. In the morning the English militia awoke to find only three or four old people left in the fort. The Susquehannahs, bitter at the murders of their chiefs, broke up into small bands of roving warriors, determined to take revenge. In a body, contained within their fort, they could have been controlled by the English. Now there was no way to keep track of them.

So far, every move the English had made was wrong. Governor Berkeley was outraged by the open murder of the Susquehannah chiefs. At the next meeting of the House of Burgesses (the lower house of the Virginia legislature) he declared: "If they had killed my grandfather and grandmother, my father and mother and all my friends, yet if they had come to treat of peace, they ought to have gone in peace!"

But more than the governor's sense of honor had been damaged. The militia had lost fifty men in its siege of the Susquehannah fort. (This loss in a colony of 30,000 inhabitants is comparable to the loss of more than 20,000 soldiers in twentieth-century America.) Moreover, the roaming Susquehannahs soon began to make themselves felt. In January 1676 they raided some settlements on the upper Rappahannock and Potomac rivers and killed or captured thirty-six people.

Then the Indians surprised Berkeley by sending him a proposal of peace. The Susquehannahs, too, had their idea of justice. The Susquehannah chief told the governor that since the Indians had now killed ten English settlers for every one of the murdered Great Men, they were satisfied. There need be no more war. But if the English wanted war, the chief concluded, his people were ready to fight to the last man.

The "Indian troubles" had reached a critical point, and a policy decision had to be made. The murder of Hen, the attacks on the Doeg and Susquehannah cabins, the disastrous campaign against the Susquehannah fort, and the Susquehannah attacks of January could all be regarded as a series of small incidents. They grew out of a misunderstanding between Thomas Mathew and the Doegs. All in all, about an equal number of Indians and whites had been killed. And the Susquehannahs seemed ready to call off the fighting. Thus Governor Berkeley replied to them in a peaceful way, and during April and May the Susquehannahs killed no whites, though they did steal some livestock.

There were really two conflicts in Virginia. The first, obviously, was between whites and Indians. The second was between small, frontier planters and the royal government. The small planters, like other frontiersmen throughout American history, believed that the solution to the first conflict was simply to wipe out all the Indians. Good land was already becoming scarce in the settled areas of Virginia, and whites were crowding north and west. The tobacco planters on the frontier had a very simple program. Every Virginian was armed, and most had horses. So volunteers would gather wherever there was the slightest hint of Indian trouble.

The difficulty with this policy was that it offered no real way of dealing with the many small tribes of friendly Indians that lived in permanent "plantations" (reservations) among the whites. These friendly tribes, such as the Doegs of Maryland, had technically become subjects of the English ruler many years earlier. They had a legal right to their lands under English law, and they were a valuable source of beaver skins—a commodity second only to tobacco in economic importance in Virginia.

Governor Berkeley, as head of the royal establishment, wanted a policy of peace and order that would protect the friendly tribes and the beaver trade. He also wanted Indian policy to rest in the hands of the government at Jamestown, not in the hands of hundreds of small planters scattered along the edges of the wilderness. Berkeley's Indian policy, in other words, was generally defensive, while that of the small planters was offensive. The government's policy, which was slow, cautious, and centralized, conflicted with the farmers' wish for drastic and immediate action.

The governor made the next move. He called the Virginia legislature into session in early March and had an act passed that declared war on the Indians and provided for defense against them. The colony would build a fort at the falls of each river and create a permanent army of approximately 500 men. Parties of horsemen would conduct regular patrols between the forts. To prevent a repetition of the murders of Indians that had occurred the preceding winter, the act provided that the governor's personal permission would be necessary for any attack on an Indian fort or village—a permission that might take days to obtain.

To the planters on the frontier, Governor Berkeley's plans made about as much sense as, to us, trench warfare would against helicopters and paratroops. The English forts would be separated by miles of forest, through which the Indians could move at will. The forts, with their permanent garrisons, would be expensive. Tobacco prices were very low, and many planters could hardly make ends meet. Paying taxes to support a useless military policy would only add to their economic troubles. Furthermore, it would not provide them with any real security from the Indians.

According to the report of a royal commission that later investigated the episode, the "vulgar sort" began to protest the governor's policy. Berkeley himself summed up the situation with classic simplicity and accuracy: "How miserable the man is," he wrote home to England, "that governs a people where six parts of seven at least are poor, indebted, discontended, and armed."

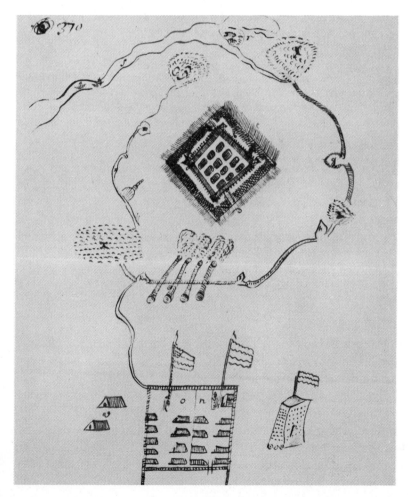

The royal commissioners sent to investigate Bacon's Rebellion included this plan of the Susquehanna fort in their report to the king. The square fort, top, is surrounded by swamps (marked "x"). Below are the tents of the English. At left ("o") is "the Virginians main Garde." At right ("n") is "the Merrylanders main Garde."

According to the report of the royal commission, the plain people of Virginia were near rebellion:

> The unsatisfied people finding themselves still liable to the Indian cruelties, and the cries of their wives and children growing grievous and intolerable to them, gave out in speeches that they were resolved to plant tobacco rather than pay the tax for maintaining the forts; that the erecting of the forts was a great grievance and cheat, and of no more use than another plantation with men at it; and that it was merely a design of the grandees [wealthy planters] to take all the tobacco into their own hands.

One group of angry planters from Charles City County went so far as to send out a call to arms against the Indians. When they brought a petition to the governor asking him to support an attack on the Indians, Berkeley angrily sent the petititoners away and "bid a pox take" them. The Charles City County men decided to gather in arms anyway, and they set up a camp on the James River, where they were joined by men from Henrico County. They were now in open rebellion against the royal government. According to the report of the royal commission sent to investigate:

> The rout [the "giddy-headed multitude"] being got together now, wanted nor waited for nothing but one to head and lead them out on their design. It so happened that one Nathaniel Bacon, Jr., a person whose lost and desperate fortunes had thrown him into that remote part of the world about fourteen months before, was fit for such a purpose.

After months of trying to restore peace and maintain a cautious Indian policy, Governor Berkeley was faced with a collective force of about 300 rebellious men, ready to defy his orders and follow a young and vigorous leader. In the weeks that followed, concern about the Indians became almost irrelevant, or at least secondary. Nathaniel Bacon and Governor Berkeley conducted a bitter and violent personal contest for control of Virginia. This contest is known as Bacon's Rebellion.

Sir William Berkeley, the governor, and Nathaniel Bacon, Jr., the rebel, were in many ways very much alike. In fact they were even cousins by marriage. Both came from wealthy English families. Each held a degree of Master of Arts from great English universities—Berkeley from Oxford and Bacon from Cambridge—in a day when most people could not even read. In addition, Bacon had traveled across Europe in the company of a tutor, and he had studied law in London for two years. Governor Berkeley, who had even written a play while still in England, was something of an amateur scholar and scientist. Most important, both men were enormously proud and quick to anger.

The two crucial differences between Berkeley and Bacon were age and position. Sir William Berkeley was almost seventy years old when the Indian troubles erupted. He had been governor of Virginia off and on since the early 1640s. In his youth, he had gained fame as a vigorous leader in the English wars against the Indians. Now he was tired. He wrote home to his king saying that his bones could not bear another six months in office. His age had also made him extremely irritable.

Sir William Berkeley—shown here before the time of Bacon's Rebellion—was not always a harsh ruler. But after his bloody revenge on the insurgents, King Charles II remarked, "The old fool has killed more people in that naked country than I have done for the murder of my father."

Nathaniel Bacon, on the other hand, was only in his twenties. He was extremely vain and ambitious, according to contemporary accounts. And he had a fortune and a career to make. The governor had an office: he was the king's principal servant in the largest and most profitable English colony in America. Bacon was a young planter with two plantations near the frontier, a born leader without an official position and without a following.

When the men of Charles City and Henrico counties gathered on the James River, Bacon had been in Virginia only a little over a year. But he had a great deal of money, and he was quite dashing. As soon as Bacon had come to Virginia, Berkeley had appointed him to the Governor's Council, the upper house of the Virginia legislature. His fortune, his dash, and his position—together with the fact that he lived near the western frontier—made him a ripe candidate for the leadership of the rebellious planters camped near his home. As the royal commission of investigation described him:

> He was said to be indifferent tall but slender, blackhaired and of an ominous, pensive, melancholy aspect, not given to much talk, or to make sudden replies, of a most imperious and dangerous hidden pride of heart, despising the wisest of his neighbors for their ignorance, and very ambitious and arrogant. But all these things lay hidden in him until he became powerful and popular.

This description, recorded after Bacon was dead, was written by the commissioners of a king whose authority Bacon had defied. The people whom Bacon led had kinder words for him, but both his friends and enemies agreed that Nathaniel Bacon was a man of hot temper and quick to violence.

According to the report of the royal commission, Bacon was mildly tricked into taking command of the rebel army. He was

> in company of one Crews, Isham, and Bird, growing to a height of drinking, and making the sadness of the times their discourse. Crews and the rest persuaded Mr. Bacon to go over and see the soldiers on the other side of the James River, and to take a quantity of rum with them to give the men to drink. And (as Crews and others had before laid the plot with the soldiers) they all one once in the field shouted and cried out "Bacon! Bacon! Bacon!"—which, taking fire with his ambition, easily prevailed on him to head them.

After this staged and somewhat alcoholic demonstration, Bacon and his "soldiers" made a decision. They would ask the governor once more for a commission to go to war with the Indians. If Berkeley refused again, they would fight anyway.

> Bacon's friends told him they would go along with him to take revenge on the Indians, and drink damnation to their souls to be true to him. And, if he could not obtain a commission, they would assist him as well and as much as if he had one. He boasted what great service he would do for the country, and subtly and secretly seduced the vulgar and most ignorant people (two-thirds of each county being of that sort) so that their whole hearts and hopes were set now upon Bacon. Thus Bacon encouraged the tumult. And as the unquiet crowd followed him, he listed them upon a large paper, writing their names circular-wise, so that the ringleaders might not be found out.

During the next few days Bacon recruited about 300 men to his cause. When Governor Berkeley angrily refused him the commission, Bacon led his troops into the forest. Berkeley rode out from Jamestown with a troop of "gentlemen" to try to stop Bacon, but he was too late. All he could do was to proclaim Bacon and his followers "rebels and mutineers."

In the meantime, Bacon and his men had marched off to the southwest. They found no Susquehannahs. Gradually, as provisions ran low, the force dwindled away to about fifty men, tired, restless, and hungry. Finally, they came upon a well-built fort belonging to a tribe of Indians called Occaneechees. The Occaneechees were friendly. In fact, they made their living partly by serving as middlemen in the beaver trade between the English and Indians who lived farther south and west. Their fort was many miles from the nearest English plantation, on an island in the Roanoke River. There was no evidence that they had been involved in the recent troubles.

The Occaneechees greeted Bacon and his followers warmly, sending out canoes to bring them to the island fort. Bacon explained that he was hunting Susquehannahs. The Occaneechee chief informed him that there was a band of Susquehannahs nearby and that, as a gesture of good will, the Occaneechees would wipe them out. Bacon agreed, and remained safe at the Occaneechee fort with his men while the small Susquehannah party was destroyed. A few prisoners were brought back to the Occaneechee fort and tortured to "entertain" the English.

Eyewitness accounts of what happened next are confused. For some reason Bacon ordered his men to surround the Occaneechee fort and keep as many Indian women and children outside as possible. This tense situation was broken by a shot that killed one of Bacon's men.

But the English were already at the fort walls, ready to fire in through the portholes. For a day and a half they poured shot in on the Indians. They also "fell upon the women and children without, disarmed and destroyed them all," according to a version of the event written by one of Bacon's own followers. When the battle was over, the Occaneechees had been destroyed. Bacon felt no need to justify the attack or make any distinctions between Indian friends and enemies. He said simply: "We fell upon a town of Indians, beginning our fight after midnight close at their portholes."

Bacon had not fired a shot at the Susquehannahs. Instead, he had destroyed a friendly tribe—men, women, and children. But, like most of his followers, his aim was to kill Indians, not to conduct careful negotiations or make fine distinctions between friends and foes. He rode with his band of Indian fighters back to Henrico County, boasting of a great victory.

While Bacon was killing Occaneechees on the far-off Roanoke, Governor Berkeley was busily trying to repair his collapsing political popularity. He had not called for the election of a new House of Burgesses in more than fifteen years. So he called for a new election, and he even provided that all freemen could vote (the vote was normally restricted to property owners). This move was designed to appeal to the "rabble" who supported Bacon.

The governor also offered to pardon Bacon, if Bacon would apologize. But Bacon refused, saying that "Indians in general were all enemies," and that he would not stop warring against them. The governor's policy backfired. In the new election the House of Burgesses was packed with Bacon men. The two commanders who had attacked the Susquehannah fort in the fall of 1675 were elected. Bacon himself was voted a burgess from Henrico County.

The new assembly opened on June 5, 1676. Bacon came cautiously down the river to Jamestown in a sloop with thirty armed men. He anchored out of gunshot range of Jamestown and waited to see what the governor would do. Berkeley, now angry and bitter, reacted in a way that Bacon might easily have anticipated. He sent a visiting ship, the *Adam and Eve,* to capture Bacon's little sloop. Bacon, the rebel, the wealthy young planter and recently elected member of the House of Burgesses, was taken into Jamestown as a military prisoner.

The governor now had Bacon in his power, but he also had to face the people of Virginia and their elected legislators. Actually, Berkeley's concern for order and calm had won out. He decided to liberate Bacon and return him to his place on the Governor's Council.

A contemporary mural depicts Jamestown in the early years. In the foreground is the James River. Farmers beyond the town would take refuge inside the palisade in case of attack.

He also promised him a commission to fight the Indians. Bacon, in return, agreed at last to humble himself.

In a dramatic gesture Berkeley stood stiffly before the House of Burgesses and said, "If there be joy in the presence of the angels over one sinner that repenteth, there is now. For we have a repentant sinner before us. Call Mr. Bacon!" Bacon entered the chamber and knelt before Berkeley, begging the pardon of God, the king, and the governor. Berkeley paused for a moment and then said three times, "God forgive you; I forgive you!"

Both Berkeley and Bacon were probably just acting. Berkeley was not really interested in angelic rejoicing over a repentant sinner. He was trying chiefly to maintain peace and order until he became powerful enough to subdue Bacon for good. Bacon, on his part, was interested only in the commission that would officially make him "General of Virginia."

Neither man got what he wanted. Berkeley delayed the commission, and after a few days Bacon suddenly disappeared from Jamestown. For ten days rumors about his activities filled the air. Then, on June 23, Bacon reappeared, this time at the head of an army of about 400 men, all armed, with more than a hundred on horseback. He had not come to beg the governor's pardon this time. He had come instead to demand his commission, and to take it by force if necessary.

The scene that followed was partly drama, partly farce. Bacon approached the little statehouse between two files of his own foot soldiers. The governor, with his council, came out to meet him. Berkeley opened his coat and shirt and pointed to his chest, offering Bacon a coward's chance: "Here! Shoot me! Before God, a fair mark! Shoot!" The governor repeated this insulting invitation several times. Bacon, with equal sarcasm, made a gentle reply: "No, may it please your honor, we will not hurt a hair of your head—nor of any other man's. We are come for a commission to save our lives from the Indians. You have so often promised it, and now we will have it before we go."

Berkeley once more refused the commission, and he turned his back on Bacon to walk toward his office at the other end of the statehouse. The members of the House of Burgesses, meeting inside, had all crowded to the windows to watch. Bacon followed the governor, shouting and waving his arms, and then suddenly commanded his men to air their cocked flintlocks at the burgesses in the windows.

Bacon swore and shouted, "I'll kill governor, council, assembly and all, and then I'll sheath my sword in my own heart's blood."

The burgesses were terrified. Bacon gave an order for his men to fire if he drew his sword. Bacon's men were shouting, "We will have it! We will have it!"

Then one of the frightened burgesses waved a handkerchief from the window, shouting back, "You shall have it! You shall have it!"

Bacon had won in this showdown, simply by commanding a superior armed force. The governor had no alternative but to give in or lose his office, perhaps even his life, to the rebels. The assembly made Bacon "General of the Virginia War." A day or two later, the burgesses adjourned to go to their plantations. Berkeley went home to sulk. Bacon led his troops back west, this time with an official commission in his hands. He quickly set about appointing junior officers, to whom he gave the power to take horses, ammunition, and other goods from the plantations of Virginia for the Indian war he planned to wage. It was rumored that he was preparing to fight any royal troops that might be sent over from England to put down his rebellion. For the time being, Bacon was in control of Virginia.

For the next few weeks Berkeley did nothing. Nor did Bacon seem to do much besides getting his army organized. Probably a few scouting parties searched for Indians, but there was no action. Bacon had

After signing a treaty with the Potomac Indians in 1677, the English presented their chief with this silver medal, inscribed—somewhat carelessly—"Patomeck."

become more interested in his rebellion than in fighting Indians. At the end of July he assembled all his forces at Middle Plantation, the future site of Williamsburg, a few miles from Jamestown. Berkeley, in despair, fled across the Chesapeake to a plantation on the Eastern shore, abandoning the government.

At Middle Plantation, Bacon held what amounted to a political convention. He sent out an oath for all Virginians to swear, promising they would be loyal to him and even fight royal soldiers in his defense. On August 3 he also issued a "Manifesto and Declaration of the People." It stated the rebels' case against the Indians very clearly. All Indians were enemies and outlaws and ought to be wiped out. The governor had treated them as "darling and protected" subjects, as "quiet and honest neighbors." And, according to the manifesto, the governor had used the beaver trade solely to enrich himself and a small group of friends. This trade had enabled the Indians to arm and murder English settlers. Bacon's solution was simply to put an end to the trade by putting an end to both groups of traders. He ordered the arrest of Berkeley and his associates and promised death to all the Indians.

Bacon's manifesto also introduced a new element into the rebellion. At Middle Plantation, for the first time, Bacon's movement took on a tone of a political revolution. Everyone who wrote about the rebellion at the time agreed on one fact—that Bacon's followers were of the "poorer sort," whereas Berkeley's were "gentlemen" or "grandees." The manifesto recognized this apparent class division for the first time.

The manifesto was full of brilliant political rhetoric, the product of Bacon's excellent education. "If virtue be a sin," Bacon began, then he and his followers were guilty. But, he continued, "we cannot in our hearts find one single spot of rebellion or treason." Instead, Bacon appealed "to the country" to examine its rulers, not its rebels. Over the years Governor Berkeley had gathered around him the wealthiest planters of the colony. These Virginians were a ruling elite—or so Bacon's rebels thought. This elite were men of "vile" education and background, Bacon charged. But they had been suddenly made into "grandees" by "mysterious wiles." Altogether, they were nothing but "sponges who have soaked up the public treasure, unworthy favorites and juggling parasites, whose tottering fortunes have been supported at the public charge."

Bacon marshaled the "people" against these so-called grandees. He insisted that the king would finally side with the people, once the political corruption of the ruling planters was exposed. Bacon demanded the surrender of Berkeley and nineteen of his "wicked counselors" within four days. After that time, he declared, anyone who hid or protected any of the "oppressors" would be considered "traitors to the people." Bacon signed the manifesto: "Nath. Bacon, Gen'l. by the Consent of the People."

Up to now, Bacon had been declared a "rebel and mutineer" by proclamation of the governor. But by marching back to Middle Plantation, sending out "Bacon's oaths" to all the counties of the colony, and issuing the manifesto and declaration, Bacon had become a rebel by even his own definition. In a conversation with John Goode, a Henrico County neighbor, Bacon tried to work out a strategy for resisting England and liberating the colony:

> BACON: There is a report that Berkeley has sent to the king for two thousand redcoats.[2] Tell me your opinion. May not five hundred Virginians beat them, we having the same advantages against them the Indians have against us?
> GOODE: On the contrary, I think five hundred redcoats may either subject or ruin Virginia.
> BACON: You talk strangely. Are we not acquainted with the country, so that we can lay ambushes? Can we not hide behind trees? Are we not as good or better shots than they?

But Goode pointed out to Bacon that with their fleet the English could easily win.

> GOODE: They can accomplish what I have said without hazard by landing where there is no opposition, firing our houses and fences, destroying our cattle, preventing trade and cutting off imports.
> BACON: I am confident that it is the mind of this colony, and of Maryland as well as Carolina, to cast off their governors. And if we cannot prevail by arms, we may retire to the Roanoke [River] and establish our own government there.

By this time, both Bacon and Goode were becoming angry.

> GOODE: Sir, this design will produce utter ruin. I hope you will excuse me from having any part in it.
> BACON: I am glad to know your mind, but I think this proceeds from mere cowardice.

At any rate, if a revolution was part of Bacon's plan, he seemed to have won easily. Berkeley had abandoned most of Virginia, and many of the planters appeared ready to follow Bacon. Without any real authority Bacon ordered the election of a new House of Burgesses to meet in Jamestown on September 4.

In this early English drawing, Virginia Indians feast on fish and corn. When the colonists were hungry, the Indians gave them grain. Later, when the Indians were starving, the whites traded them 400 bushels for "a mortgage on their whole countries."

[2] English troops were given this name because of their scarlet uniforms.

When he had completed all these successful but dangerous political actions, Bacon gathered his troops and set out west in search of the Indians. They were still supposed to be his principal concern. Once again, he did not pursue the Susquehannahs, the real "enemy." Instead, he plunged his army into the Great Dragon Swamp to search for the village of a small, friendly tribe, the Pamunkeys. (Some suspected them, wrongly, of planning opposition to the English.) The swamp was a difficult place for Indians to maneuver in; it was nearly impossible for armed Englishmen. Bacon's army, which at first probably numbered a thousand, gradually dwindled down to about 150 wet, tired men who were running low on food. Several times, Bacon had to make fiery speeches to whip up the falling spirits of his men:

> I would rather my carcass should lie rotting in the woods, than miss doing the service the country expects from me. All you gentlemen that intend to abide with me must resolve to undergo all the hardship this wild can afford, and if need be to eat chestnuts and horseflesh before you return.

Finally, after days of marching back and forth across the swamp, Bacon stumbled on the Pamunkey village. His men immediately charged and opened fire. The Indians did not resist but simply ran. The English killed eight Pamunkeys, and captured forty-five more. This was Bacon's second "victory" over the Indians. He stumbled out of the swamp toward Jamestown (expecting to find the new House of Burgesses ready to meet). He had the captured Pamunkeys tied in a row as evidence of his success as an Indian fighter.

When Bacon emerged from the swamp, instead of finding a victory celebration, he was confronted with the shocking news that Berkeley had somehow managed to occupy Jamestown again. The governor had a thousand troops. He also had several large English ships on the James, with heavy guns, ready to defend the capital.

The shrewd old governor had played a sly trick. He had won control of Virginia's waterways. The colony in 1676 was as much water as land. The Chesapeake Bay and rivers like the James, the York, and the Potomac led everywhere into the settled areas of the colony. Bacon too had realized this early in the rebellion, and he had taken over two or three large merchant ships and armed them with cannon from Jamestown's fort. It was hoped that these ships could capture any other vessels that might sail from England, including warships of the royal navy.

Early in September, while Bacon was hunting Indians in the Great Dragon Swamp, his little fleet sailed the thirty miles across the Chesa-

Dancing in a circle, Indians brandish bunches of leaves and other religious symbols. When left alone, the tribes of Virginia were usually industrious and peaceable.

peake to attack Berkeley on the Eastern shore. The rebel "navy" had 300 men, more than enough to capture Berkeley. But the governor shrewdly sent word to the captain of the fleet that he wanted to negotiate. The captain went ashore and, unfortunately, accepted too much of Berkeley's wine. While Bacon's captain drank, a small boatload of men loyal to Berkeley rowed out to the largest ship. With the help of the English sailors on board—who had been forced to join Bacon's forces against their will—Berkeley's men quickly captured the ship and disarmed Bacon's troops. By threats and promises Berkeley quickly raised an army and sailed back to Jamestown. The detachment of men Bacon had left there abandoned the town, and Berkeley went ashore and fell to his knees to praise God for his mercy and help.

An Indian watchman crouches in a small hut in the midst of a corn field. As a sort of living scarecrow, he frightens away birds and other animals that might destroy the Indians' crop.

This was the situation Bacon confronted when he marched out of the Great Dragon Swamp. In bitter anger he led his troops on a forced march toward Jamestown, picking up recruits along the way. Finally, after a march of forty miles in one day, the men reached the outskirts of Jamestown. Bacon kept his tired men up all night, cutting down trees and digging a trench by moonlight, ready for the charge he was certain would come from the town and the cannon that would be trained on him from the ships in the river.

The next day, however, when no attack came, Bacon decided to move up heavy cannon of his own to fire at Jamestown's fortifications. To cover his men while they put the guns in place, Bacon sent scouts out to bring in the wives of some of Berkeley's leading supporters. He forced the women to stand between his men and Berkeley's guns while places were dug for the guns. Then they were released.

Finally, Berkeley decided to attack. Bacon described the battle this way:

> Yesterday, they made a sally, with horse and foot in the van [the front]. The forlorn [the lead] was made up of such men as they had compelled to serve. They came up with a narrow front, pressing very close upon one another's shoulders, so that the forlorn might be their shelter. Our men received them so warmly that they retired in great disorder, throwing down their arms, as also their drums and dead men. They show themselves such pitiful cowards.

Bacon was right. Even the governor's supporters agreed that their men went out "like scholars going to school, with heavy hearts; but they returned home with light heels."

Once Berkeley's heavy-hearted "scholars" were safely back inside Jamestown, they began to mutter of mutiny. Even the governor's officers encouraged the talk of desertion. Finally, Berkeley had no more than twenty men on whom he could rely. Under the safety of nightfall, he loaded his ineffective troops once more into the ships and slipped off down the James.

Bacon had won again, or so it seemed. But every one of his victories added together meant nothing. He was finally forced to realize that, in the long run, his situation was hopeless. In the first place, the governor still had the only useful ships in the colony, and he could take control of every other ship that sailed into Virginia from the Atlantic. This meant that Berkeley could land forces anywhere in the colony. Bacon had taught Berkeley a difficult lesson: controlling the statehouse was not the same thing as controlling the colony.

Now Bacon had to learn the same lesson. For him, occupying Jamestown was worthless as long as Berkeley was armed with ships and the title of royal governor. More important, Bacon realized that Berkeley would certainly have already sent home to England for help. Any morning tide might bring in royal warships and the king's redcoats to occupy the colony. Bacon might kill Pamunkeys. He might even drive the governor again and again to the Eastern shore. But the entire colony of Virginia had fewer people than the city of London alone. And the English king had the world's greatest navy to pit against Bacon's army, which was tiny by European standards.

So, despite his dramatic capture of Jamestown, Bacon was doomed. There would be no time to unite the people against Berkeley's supporters. The new House of Burgesses Bacon had ordered would never meet. Sooner or later, Bacon and his officers would either have to die in battle or be hanged as traitors. There was no way out. After occupying Jamestown, Bacon waited until night and then burned down every building in the town, even the church. From their ships down river Berkeley and his troops could see the fires light the harvest sky.

Over the next few weeks Bacon tried to strengthen his position by issuing new oaths of loyalty and enlisting new recruits. But because Berkeley did not venture off the Eastern shore, Bacon's men could do nothing. They must have realized as well as Bacon that the rebellion had failed. They grew disorderly and began to loot plantations, much to their general's dismay.

But Bacon faced an even more serious problem. In either the Great Dragon Swamp or the trenches outside Jamestown he had become ill with dysentery—the "bloody flux," as it was called then. He had also become so infested with lice that his clothes had to be frequently burned. On October 26 he died. If he was buried, no one knows where, for his grave has never been found.

Bacon's death brought about the quick collapse of his rebellion. In a sense, Bacon *was* the rebellion. While he was alive, it had no real chance of success. With him dead, though, it simply did not exist.

When Berkeley received the welcome news that his enemy had died, he began to attack the remainder of Bacon's followers with his ships. Here and there, small groups of rebels fought back. In one battle a dozen or so rebels were killed. But, on the whole, the rebels did not resist. Most of them drifted quietly back to their homes without reprisal. But the governor was bitter. Between the time of Bacon's death and March of 1677 he had twenty-three rebels hanged.

Finally, when it was no longer needed, help came from England. News of Bacon's Rebellion had caused great concern in London, and the king had sent over several warships, a thousand redcoats, and a royal commission of investigation. The English expected to find Bacon in command and Berkeley either dead or imprisoned. What they found instead was the governor securely in control and Bacon dead. Still, their instructions provided that if Berkeley were still alive, he should return to England as soon as possible. The governor delayed returning in order to hang rebels, but he finally set sail for London in March. He never returned. He reached London in June and died in July, without ever seeing the king to explain what had happened.

With Bacon and Berkeley dead and British troops stationed for the first time in Virginia, there was peace. For the next ninety-nine years Virginia remained loyal to England.

The Plantation Colonies

WILLIAM BERKELEY never stopped complaining that Nathaniel Bacon was a recent immigrant, a man who had been in Virginia for less than two years when he became a rebel and mutineer. But the governor himself was an immigrant, as were most of the planters. Virginia was an immigrant society. The colony had existed for only about seventy years when Bacon's Rebellion occurred. Probably a majority of the people in the colony had been born not in Virginia but in England, not in the New World but in the Old. This fact, though obvious, is sometimes too easily forgotten, and it helps explain not only Bacon's Rebellion but much of the history of early America.

Like the first immigrants, the Indians, and like earlier Europeans before them, the English came to Virginia and the other colonies for one basic reason: to improve their lives. And, like the earlier immigrants, the English came without any real plans or much information. They had hopes instead: hopes of finding gold and silver as the Spanish had done in Mexico and Peru; and, like many explorers, hopes of finding a northwest passage to the wealth of the East.

Some Englishmen hoped to convert the Indians to Christianity. Then, too, the desire to make England a great and powerful nation moved many Englishmen either to become immigrants or to give money and support to colonization. A straightforward itch to travel, to see new sights, was sometimes as important as any other motive for colonization.

All these motives—the desire for wealth, the missionary spirit, patriotism, adventure—were mixed together, sometimes in the same person. But underlying them all, from the beginning of English colonization to the American Revolution—and probably to the present—was the idea that the New World meant wealth. To most Europeans, America meant gold, land, or profitable trade. Almost all the immigrants who came here voluntarily thought of the New World as a place where they could improve their way of life. (Though their immediate goals were different, the ancestors of the Indians had had this basic purpose thousands of years earlier.)

The problem that brought on Bacon's Rebellion was no different from the problem that existed in every part of America: Whose fortune was going to be improved first and most? And who was going to pay the price? There was an almost comic character to Bacon's marches to the west and back to the east, his inability to decide whether to fight Indians or his own government.

This many-chimneyed house in Surrey County, Virginia, was supposedly fortified as a stronghold by Nathaniel Bacon. It comes complete with ghosts.

**VIRGINIA LAND GRANTS,
1606–20**

— 1606 grant to Virginia Company of London
— 1606 grant to Virginia Company of Plymouth
▓ 1606 grant to the Council for New England

on the other. The curious fact that Bacon destroyed both Indian forts and his own capital city is a pointed illustration of the colonists' dilemma.

In 1676 the 30,000 Englishmen of Virginia thought of themselves as a small, weak group, virtually at the mercy of both the Indians and the English crown. The people who followed Bacon into his rebellion were lashing out blindly at both opponents, without much hope of real success on either front. To understand what made Bacon's followers act the way they did, their rebellion must be seen as one chapter in the story of the English conquest of North America.

THE FOUNDING OF VIRGINIA

The history of Virginia began with a document issued by the English king, James I, on April 10, 1606. Since the 1580s Englishmen had been making unsuccessful stabs at colonization. Now a new group of "knights, gentlemen, merchants, and other adventurers" was ready for another try. They petitioned the crown for the right to create a colony. The king granted the petition by issuing the charter of 1606, which marks a kind of official beginning of the history of not only Virginia but the entire United States.

The charter first asserted the king's claim to most of North America—"that part of America, commonly called Virginia," between 34 and 45 degrees north latitude. This included everything from Cape Fear in North Carolina to what is now Bangor, Maine—a total of about 2 million square miles of land. Then, the charter granted the right to plant colonies to two groups of "loving subjects." There would be two trading companies, one based in London and the other in the town of Plymouth. Each company could begin by creating one colony. The London Company could settle anywhere between 34 and 41 degrees north latitude, an area extending from Cape Fear to what is now New York City. The Plymouth Company could establish its colony anywhere between 38 and 45 degrees, which included the coast between approximately Wash-

But all the marching and countermarching grew out of one crucial fact. In Virginia, and all the other English colonies, there were three principal factors: Indians, English colonists, and England herself. Obviously, each had different ideas about how to divide the natural wealth of the New World. Bacon and the colonists stood literally between the Indians on the one side and England ington, D.C., and Bangor. If both companies decided to found their colonies in the overlapping area, they had to settle at least a hundred miles apart.

The king did not grant all of his 2 million square miles in America to the two Virginia companies. Far from it. Each company got control of only 10,000 square miles of land. From their first seats the Virginia and Plymouth companies were given control of the coastlines for fifty miles north and south and of the land a hundred miles inland. They could also control the ocean for a hundred miles out to sea.

The rest of America, however, remained firmly in the king's hands. More important, the government of the companies would be in the hands of a Royal Council of thirteen men appointed by the king. These appointees were responsible directly to the king. If the colonists discovered any gold or silver, furthermore, they would have to pay a fifth of it to the crown.

Within these limits the merchants of the London and Plymouth companies had the right to send over colonists (called planters) and to develop trade, agriculture, and industry. The charter of 1606 said nothing about self-government or freedom of religion. The merchants who financed the colonies were interested primarily in making money. It cost a great deal to outfit ships and buy tools, seed, and livestock for the first settlers. The shareholders who put up the money to back these ventures expected to have it returned with a reasonable margin of profit.

The first settlers might find gold. They could trade with the Indians. They could cut lumber for shipment back to England. Most important, they could try raising a cash crop[1] that was not grown in England—rice, for example, or sugar or citrus fruit. The merchants at home in England could then import the crop at a profit. The colonists (and the Indians) would, in turn, buy from the merchants such necessities as cloth, tools, nails, and furniture. If their colony worked out as the merchants of the London Company hoped, it would be the perfect mercantilist dream: a source of imports and a market for manufactured goods that would free England from dependence on Spanish, French, or Dutch markets. England could take a giant step toward becoming a self-sufficient kingdom, to the profit of her merchants and her government.

Settling Jamestown Such were the ideas and expectations of the merchants. The 120 Englishmen who sailed in three ships for Virginia in December 1606 probably had the same kinds of ideas in mind. After a long voyage, 104 of them reached the entrance to Chesapeake Bay on April 29, 1607. For two weeks they explored the bay and some of its rivers. Finally, they chose a point of land about thirty miles up the river that they had already named after King James. They landed and unloaded their supplies. Their settlement, too, they named after the king: James Fort, or Jamestown.

Things went smoothly at first, and after about seven weeks the leaders of the colony sent back their first report to the Royal Council for Virginia. The report complained a little but presented a generally optimistic picture—the kind that was to lure thousands of other Englishmen over the Atlantic in the coming years.

In this pleasant land, the colonists reported, they had already accomplished the first tasks of planting: "Within less than seven weeks, we are fortified well against the Indians. We have sown good store of wheat. We have sent you a taste of clapboard.[2] We have built some houses." The only note of caution in the first report was a request that new supplies and people be sent as quickly as possible, lest the "devouring Spaniard lay his ravenous hands upon these gold-showing mountains."

This was the Englishmen's "Virginia." For the king it was a vast region with enormous possibilities for the crown and the nation. For the merchants it was an investment that could

---

[1] A cash crop is one raised in quantities to sell for income. Cash-crop farming contrasts with subsistence farming, where crops are raised primarily to feed the farmer's own family.

[2] By "a taste of clapboard," the writer meant a small amount of split oak (used for making barrels).

pay off handsomely. For the colonists it was a fair land with great rivers, rich soil, and "gold-showing mountains." No one, neither the king nor the merchants nor the settlers, could see Jamestown for what it really was—a death trap.

Hardship and Disease The land called Virginia had already claimed the lives of the entire Roanoke settlement. It also killed hundreds of the people who came to Jamestown. In 1607 the 104 "first planters" came. In the next year and a half two groups of reinforcements totaled almost 200. Out of this group of 300, only 80 men were left alive in the summer of 1609—about one out of four.

The first really large "supply," as it was called, arrived in 1609. This group of 600 included women and children for the first time. But, by the next summer, only 60 people were left alive. This meant that, in the first three years, the odds of staying alive in the new settlement were only about one out of twelve. Nor did things get much better as time passed. In the first seventeen years of settlement, about 10,000 Englishmen sailed to Jamestown. But the surviving population in 1624 was only 1,275.

At the beginning, Virginia colonists spent too much time looking for gold and not enough growing crops. This was partly the fault of the English shareholders, who wanted a quick return on their investment. Even after the settlers began farming more extensively, they underwent some lean years because they had to rely for many of their supplies on imports from England.

In the next fifty years, up to the time of Bacon's Rebellion, survival became easier, and the population of Virginia[3] grew to about 30,-000. But it grew slowly, and Bacon's followers could remember how difficult and dangerous settling the colony had been. Nearly everyone had a friend or a relative who had died as a result of one of the dangers of the place: Indians, starvation, or disease. Despite their success, Virginians in 1676 still regarded their hold on the New World as weak and uncertain. The possibility of death and failure still seemed to lurk around every corner. Life was full of risks—a fact that helps explain the willingness of Bacon's followers to take up arms against both the Indians and the government for reasons that seem so petty today. The experience of colonization in the seventeenth century was one that combined hope and optimism with danger and death.

What turned Virginia into such a slaughterhouse was disease. The town was located on marshy ground where mosquitoes flourished during the summer, and a hundred of the first settlers died from malaria. (At that time, of course, no one knew of the connection between mosquitoes and malaria.) Probably even more settlers died from diseases brought over from England—mainly the plagues that were simultaneously killing Europeans by the hundreds of thousands. The ships that came to Virginia in the early years were terribly overcrowded, like immigrant ships throughout most of American history. Disease spread quickly and easily among the passengers. One ship, one of the unluckiest on record, lost about 130 out of 180 passengers before even sighting Virginia. Then there was dysentery (the "bloody flux" that had killed Bacon).

It took an English immigrant about two years to develop immunities to the unfamiliar bacteria in his new homeland—to become "seasoned," as the Virginians put it. Many died before they could obtain immunity. Even in Bacon's day the chances of surviving the first two years were probably not much better than two out of three.

One of the early records of Jamestown summed up the horrors of the sickness this way:

> There were never Englishmen left in a foreign country in such misery as we were in this new-discovered Virginia. If there were any conscience in men, it would make their hearts bleed to hear the pitiful murmurings and outcries of our sick men, every night and day. In the mornings, their bodies were trailed out of their cabins like dogs to be buried.

[3] As other colonies were established along the Atlantic coast in what had originally been known as Virginia, the term became restricted in meaning. By the time of Bacon's Rebellion, "Virginia" referred to the colony only.

Almost everyone who has ever heard of Virginia has heard of John Smith. But few people know that Smith's life was a lonely one, and that what he achieved he achieved alone—as explorer, expansionist, writer, and mapmaker. For the close bonds of family life Smith substituted his love for the New World. He called Virginia and New England his "children who never had a mother."

Born in Elizabethan England on January 9, 1580, Smith was never content to sit still. He sought adventure, wandering all over Europe. When he returned to England in 1604, he was ready for another challenge—exploration of the New World. He joined the Jamestown expedition of 1607 as one of its leaders.

Life was hard for the early Virginia settlers. Smith continually negotiated with the Indians for needed provisions, and he led many trade expeditions. On one such venture he was captured by the Indians. Smith was exhibited as a prisoner before the Indians and then taken before their chief, Powhatan. A group of braves forced Smith's head against some stones and were about to club him to death. Then came the dramatic event that has preserved the legend of John Smith. He described it, speaking of himself in the third person: "Pocahontas, the king's [chief's] dearest daughter, when no entreaty would prevail, got his head in her arms and laid her own upon his to save him from death."

Did this really occur? Smith was known to be a braggart. There were no witnesses. He said nothing about the incident in his *True Relation* in 1608, an account of the early days of Virginia. He did not tell the story until 1624, in his *Generall Historie of Virginia.* In any case, American folklore and history have preserved the tale.

Whether or not Smith's Pocahontas story is true, he did become an expert on Indian customs and strategy. With Indian advice and assistance, he saw to it that corn was grown in Jamestown.

Much of Smith's time was also devoted to exploring. His maps and descriptions were so accurate that they were the sole authority on which Lord Baltimore's Maryland charter was based.

Meanwhile, the London Company was beginning to view Smith as a young upstart and soldier of fortune. So when he was severely burned by a gunpowder explosion and forced to return to England for medical help, the company employed someone else to take his place.

In 1614 Smith made a fishing and exploring voyage to the northern part of the Virginia grant. Again he made a surprisingly accurate map. He called the region New England and assigned the name "Plimouth" to the mainland opposite Cape Cod. Smith made several other attempts to return to America, but they all failed. Still he continued to work for colonization.

"How I have lived, spent my time and been employed, I am not ashamed who will examine," Smith once said. These words could have been his epitaph.

Relations with the Indians For those who managed to stay on their feet, there was the problem of the Indians, who wasted little time in making their first attack. On May 20, 1607, just six days after the landing at Jamestown, several hundred Indians rushed out of the woods at the men planting their first crop of wheat. The English, having an enormous advantage in weapons, defeated their attackers. The Indians very quickly learned that they could not win large battles, and they began ambushing individuals and small groups that wandered too far from the protective walls of Jamestown's crude fort.

The English found their Indian neighbors utterly unpredictable. The Indians were usually willing to trade. They sold beaver hides cheaply enough. They also helped the English plant their first crops of corn. But it was difficult to work out long-range, overall policies. The Indians of the area were broken up into many small tribes and clans, each of which had its own ideas of how to deal with the strangers.

Fortunately, there was a loose confederation among the tribes in the area under a ruler named Powhatan. The English decided to "crown" Powhatan with a copper crown sent from England. In English theory the ceremony made Powhatan and all his people subjects of James I. This move, combined with the Indians' real desire to trade what they thought were worthless beaver skins to the foolish whites, kept an unsteady peace, as long as the English stayed close to their fort and muskets. Even this uneasy truce kept the English hemmed inside the unhealthy Jamestown settlement. They were so crowded that at one point they were even planting in the streets of their little town.

Finally, in 1613, the English won a long peace with Powhatan by the simple tactic of kidnapping his daughter Pocahontas and holding her as a hostage. They converted her to Christianity, and one Englishman, John Rolfe, married her and took her to England. There she became the central attraction of an otherwise dull London social season. The English colonists had first seen Pocahontas as a naked girl doing cartwheels in front of her father's lodge. Seven years later, she was being introduced at the court of King James. (And a year after that, she was dead of smallpox.)

Thus by trickery and trade the English managed to live among the Indians for the first fifteen years of Virginia history. However, Indian resentment was growing because of white inroads on their lands. In 1622, with Powhatan dead and Pocahontas all but forgotten, the Indians massacred some 400 whites—almost a fourth of the total population. The English had spread up and down the James in the ten years of peace that followed the marriage of Rolfe and Pocahontas. On their isolated plantations they were easy targets for the Indians. But when they recovered from the Indian attack, the colonists were just as angry as Bacon's followers would be fifty years later. They attacked the Indians' villages and adopted a new policy of destroying their enemy's corn crops in order to starve them out. In a few years the Indians were beaten and stopped fighting.

Once more there was an uneasy truce, this time for almost twenty years. Then, in 1644, there was another massacre, in which the Indians took about 500 lives. The whites' new counterattack was led by Sir William Berkeley, who personally captured the Indians' chief. The peace that Berkeley made lasted a generation—until Bacon's Rebellion. Berkeley's success made him proud of his record in dealing with the "Indian problem." This pride helps account for his bitterly angry response to the young upstart Bacon in 1676.

Ironically, Berkeley had little reason to be proud, and Bacon had just as little reason for attempting to wipe out the Indians by force. They were just two men in a massive flow of white Europeans into North America, a flow that would soon reach into the millions. In the long run, the Indians were certain to lose their continent, and nothing that people like Berkeley or Bacon did was likely to change the result. No matter how many thousands died of malaria and dysentery at Jamestown, thousands of others kept coming to the New World.

In 1607 there were about 10,000 Indians in

The 1622 Indian attack on Virginians, as imagined by an artist. Gory pictures of Indian atrocities appealed to Europeans, who held contradictory views of native Americans as either violent brutes or noble savages untouched by the vices of civilization.

Virginia ready to oppose the 104 white men who sailed up the James. By 1670 there were about 30,000 whites and only 4,000 Indians. Few of the "missing" 6,000 Indians were combat casualties. They had died of European diseases to which they had no inherited immunities. Some had been starved out by the collapse of their economy and their way of life. Others had moved west to escape the whites.

There was a profound difference in the relationship to the environment of the Indians and the Europeans. The Indians lived in nature. They farmed in small areas and hunted for food only. Left to themselves, they would probably have kept a stable population for centuries. The whites, in contrast, used up the environment. They took unlimited quantities of beaver, for example, not for food but for skins to make into hats. And they needed ever more and larger fields for their tobacco. The landscape of Virginia, which could have supported 10,000 Indians forever, was literally transformed into hats and tobacco smoke for Europeans thousands of miles away.

At first, the Indians cooperated. They loved the white man's cheap jewelry, his cloth, and his tools. For these things they could trade beaver skins. The white man's demand for beaver was practically unlimited, and the Indians were skillful hunters and trappers. The only difficulty was that the slow, exposed beaver was a very vulnerable animal. In the space of one man's lifetime, beaver would become scarce in areas near white settlements. This meant that the Indians had lost their cash crop for trade with the whites.

The Indians were then doomed. They might lash out blindly as in the attacks of 1622 and 1644 in Virginia. But one by one the tribes of Powhatan became dependent on the whites. Tribes like the Doegs and the Pamunkeys were put on their own reservations under the so-called protection of colonial governments in Virginia and Maryland. Ironically, it was against these already beaten and ruined tribes that Bacon and his followers aimed their cruel and useless attacks.

PROBLEMS OF GOVERNMENT

In some ways Bacon's Rebellion was only one episode in a long conflict between the Indians and the English. But the rebellion involved more than the "Indian problem"—or, from the Indians' viewpoint, the "white problem." Bacon and the planters who sided with him also were interested in the way Virginia ought to be governed. The problem of the colony's government was as old as Jamestown. During the seventy years before Bacon's Rebellion, Virginia had never really developed a stable system of government, and Bacon's mutiny occurred within a tradition of political instability and unrest.

The trouble had begun even before the first ships entered Chesapeake Bay. The charter of 1606 provided that the Royal Council in England would appoint a local council to govern the colony. There were six councillors aboard the first fleet. During the first two years, while the planters died by the dozen, the councillors argued among themselves, chiefly over matters of rank. Of the first ten men appointed to the Jamestown council, one was tried for mutiny and executed in Virginia. Two died. Two others went back to England voluntarily, and four were sent back to London under arrest. The tenth and probably the luckiest man was a sea captain who spent almost no time in Jamestown. By 1609 it was clear that the system of council government would not work. The colony obviously needed a single governor with broad powers.

In the meantime, the London Company was having its problems. The Jamestown colony was not making a profit, and the first two years of settlement had cost a great deal of money. So the company petitioned King James for a new charter granting more generous terms. The new charter of 1609 eliminated the Plymouth Company entirely. It vastly increased the size of the land grant to the other company, now known as the Virginia Company. This company now owned a strip of land 400 miles wide and extending "up into the land from sea to sea." The new charter also gave control of the company to its investors, the stockholders. Any person could become a stockholder by buying a share for about £12[4] or by becoming a settler in the colony. At the end of seven years the company would divide whatever profits there were. At the same time each stockholder would receive land—100 acres for each share he owned.

This new charter greatly strengthened the Virginia Company. It could now raise money by selling stock. And it now owned an enormous area of land. For the colonists, however, the new charter had other effects. It replaced the old governing council with a single governor. Appointed by the company for a life term, he had almost absolute power over the colony. For nine years Jamestown was ruled by a set of very harsh laws. They may have saved the colony, because its death-trap atmosphere made strong discipline necessary. But these laws were made in the interests not of the colonists but of the company in England. In early Jamestown, as in Bacon's time, there was an inevitable conflict of interest between those who actually went to Virginia and those who stayed behind in England.

The charter was revised again slightly in

---

[4] It is difficult to work out present-day equivalents for seventeenth-century money. This figure might be roughly estimated as equal to $1,000 today.

This plain but stately building, the so-called Capitol, housed the Virginia legislature after the capital was moved to Williamsburg in 1699. The Governor's Council met in one wing, while the House of Burgesses met in the other.

1612, mainly because the Virginia Company was going bankrupt and needed a new source of money. This time, the king gave the company the right to conduct a lottery. From then on gambling was the main source of the English capital invested in Virginia. Over the long run, the company spent about £200,000—an enormous sum of money in that day—on settlement. It made no profit at all. As a business venture, Virginia was a total failure.

Land Allocation   In 1618 it was time to divide lands and profits under the charters of 1609 and 1612. There were no profits, but the Virginia Company did grant 100 acres to every colonist who had paid his way to Virginia since 1607. At the same time, the company made a very important change in the land system. Before 1618 all the land had belonged to the company and had been farmed for it by the colonists. A new company charter ruled that every new Virginia settler would get 50 acres of land for himself and 50 acres for every member of his family over fifteen. The colonist would also receive 50 acres for each servant brought or sent over. This meant that an Englishman with a wife, two grown children, and three servants would own 400 acres of land as soon as he reached Virginia.

Prospective settlers who could not afford to pay for their passage to Virginia could come over as servants. A man or woman signed a paper called an indenture, promising to work for a specified master for a period of years, usually seven. At the end of the period the indentured servant gained his or her freedom. At the same time, the former servant received farmland in the usual way—100 acres for himself or herself and 50 acres each for a spouse or a grown child.

Much of Virginia was settled under the rules of 1618. Together they became known as the headright system, since a colonist was entitled to a certain amount of land for each "head" he brought to Virginia. At the same time, the company also made huge grants of free

The Founding of Maryland

From the beginning of the colonial period, the major and possibly the most consistent inspiration of New World ventures was the hope of acquiring title to land. This good fortune befell one Englishman beyond most people's wildest dreams. He was George Calvert, the first Lord Baltimore. In 1632 King Charles I of England granted him a charter to a 10-million-acre tract of land in the New World. Lord Baltimore died before the grant was made official, bequeathing the charter to his son Cecil.

Cecil Calvert was now the proprietor of a colony to be carved out of territory originally granted to the Virginia Company. Furthermore, it was to be ruled exclusively by him. The Virginia Company objected, claiming title to the land. The second Lord Baltimore was forced to remain in England the rest of his life, continually defending his interests. He

Cecil Calvert, second Lord Baltimore

chose his younger brother Leonard to act as his lieutenant-governor and foster his ideals.

Baltimore was committed to the idea of religious toleration. As a Roman Catholic in Anglican England, he wanted to establish a colony where freedom of worship would be a cornerstone. He also felt strongly that everyone should have the opportunity to own land. In his advertisements he promised generous allotments to everyone who would transport settlers to his colony.

On March 27, 1634, the first arrivals—some 200 people—established a settlement, St. Mary's City, between the Potomac River and Chesapeake Bay. A chronicler of the expedition described it as "a spot so charming in its situation that Europe can scarcely show one to surpass." The colony was called Maryland in honor of the king's wife, Henrietta Maria.

The Maryland charter gave the land unconditionally to the Calvert family as proprietors. Leonard Calvert, though, "in order to avoid any appearance of injustice and afford no opportunity for hostility, bought from the [Indian] king thirty miles of that land, delivering in exchange axes, hoes, cloth, and hatchets."

From the outset Lord Baltimore had no intention of duplicating the mistakes made at Jamestown. He legalized landowning because he wanted the freemen to reap the products of their own labor. He emphasized the necessity of growing food crops as well as tobacco. This foresight enabled Maryland to escape the famine that had beset earlier colonial undertakings.

In 1649 a group of Puritans in Virginia were having difficulties with the Anglican governor, Sir William Berkeley. They were invited to settle in Maryland. That same year the Maryland assembly passed the Toleration Act, which granted religious freedom to anyone who professed belief in Jesus Christ. Maryland was thus the first colony to make official provision for liberty of conscience.

land to various people—some as large as 200,000 acres.

From 1618 on, Virginia was really not much more than a focus of speculation in real estate. In fact, much of American history has been a story of land sales, grants, and speculation. In 1676 the people who followed Bacon into rebellion were interested in opening up new land. They were ready to wipe out any Indians who stood in their way. The English had moved into the Indians' neighborhood, just as later groups of immigrants would move into English neighborhoods. The result, both in 1676 and later, was conflict between old settlers and new ones that often led to violence.

Governors and Assemblies The new land policy of 1618 changed the character of Virginia. It made the colonists much more independent of the Virginia Company, since they now owned their land directly. But they were still ruled by a governor who was appointed in England and who served for life. The company tried to soften this contradiction by allowing the settlers to elect representatives to pass some of their own laws.

In 1619 the first elected legislature in America met in Jamestown. The governor was present. So were the appointed members of his council, which still existed as an upper house of the legislature to give advice to the governor. There were also twenty-two elected burgesses, two from each of the eleven regions into which the colony was divided. This House of Burgesses formed the lower house of the Virginia legislature. Their first meeting lasted only six days. But the burgesses passed a number of laws and helped to establish a principle that the colonists would be governed partly by their own elected representatives, not just by men appointed in England.

Gradually, during the next hundred years, Virginia's political system became a model for many of the other colonies being settled by the English: a governor appointed in England; an upper house or council, also appointed; and an elected lower house. A regular pattern developed in colonial politics. Any conflict of interest between the Americans and the English became

contests between the governors and the assemblies. Only when this system broke down, as it did under Governor Berkeley, did the colonists resort to force.

The changes of 1618 might have brought stability to Virginia. The colony seemed to be a safer place (at least until the Indian attack of 1622). The land system was fair. The House of Burgesses was functioning. But, back in London, the Virginia Company was in trouble. The king took away its privilege of holding a lottery, and it went bankrupt. In 1624 the government abolished the company, and the king took over control of Virginia, making it a royal colony. From then on the monarch appointed the governors—as he did Berkeley in 1642, for example. The royal governor, in turn, appointed members of the Governor's Council—as when Berkeley appointed Bacon in 1674. But the king did allow the settlers to continue to elect their own burgesses—as they did when Bacon was elected in 1676.

A GROWING ECONOMY

Thus the settlers coped in various ways with the problems of disease, Indians, and government. Another crucial problem was that of earning a living. The colonists could grow enough to feed themselves during most years. What they needed was a crop that they could sell in England to obtain the money to buy tools, clothing, furniture, and other manufactured articles. Without a cash crop their lives would remain primitive and their progress slow.

The Virginians experimented with grapes and olives, oranges and lemons, silkworms, and a dozen other possibilities. They finally settled on tobacco. John Rolfe made one great contribution to Virginia by marrying Powhatan's daughter. But an even greater contribution was his successful cultivation of the first smokable tobacco in 1612.[5]

[5] The tobacco grown by Indians in North America was too harsh for European tastes. Rolfe introduced a different species, that grown by Indians in Latin America.

70 / Tobacco   From 1612 on, tobacco growing was like a fever in Virginia. It was even planted in the streets of Jamestown. The Virginians used it instead of money. They paid taxes with it, and used it to pay their public servants, soldiers, and preachers. Most important of all, they loaded it on ships to sell in England and the Netherlands. In 1617 they managed to load about 20,000 pounds of tobacco. Two years later, the quantity had already tripled. By 1700 production had gone up to 20 million pounds a year. This total had increased to 50 million pounds by the time of the American Revolution. Tobacco was the staff of life in Virginia and also in the neighboring colony of Maryland. Maryland was a successful tobacco colony from the beginning, and avoided early years of starvation and death.

Tobacco was, in some ways, the perfect colonial crop. It was not grown in England, so Virginia was not competing at home with any English product. Tobacco was also profitable. One man's labor in a tobacco field earned as

Tobacco—here shown in an English book of 1596—had its enemies. King James called smoking "loathesome to the eye, hateful to the nose, harmful to the brain."

much as the work of six men in a wheat field. Also, a tobacco planter did not have to clear much land; one man could farm only about 1 1/2 acres of tobacco, but his yield would be about 1,500 pounds of tobacco a year.

Furthermore, there was a ready market for tobacco all over Europe, and, per pound, it brought more income than wheat or timber. When prices were good, the Virginia or Maryland planter would get enough to buy all the tools or furniture or clothing his family needed for the year. He might also clear enough money to pay the passage of an indentured servant, who was worth another 50 acres of land under the headright system and who would produce another 1,500 pounds of tobacco each year for the next seven years.

But there were problems, of course. Tobacco wore out land very rapidly. Newly cleared woodlands were good for only four or five years. After this period the crop yield thinned, and the planter had to clear more land. Soon good land was scarce. Virginia became, in an odd way, crowded. Finding more good new land meant moving farther and farther up the rivers—the James and the York first, then the Rappahannock, the Potomac, and others. This migration brought the planters into continuous conflict with the Indians, and helped cause the attacks of 1644 and 1676. Most of Bacon's rebels were actually planters who had moved out into the new areas and wanted even more land for their tobacco.

A second problem with tobacco was that it made the planters dependent on prices in the London market, a market over which they had no control. No one knew, when he planted tobacco in the spring, whether the price in the fall would be enough to meet his expenses. During a bad year the planter still had to have tools and clothing. Then he had to buy on credit. Tobacco planters all over Virginia gradually accumulated debts to the English merchants who supplied them with manufactured goods. These debts were passed on from father to son, from generation to generation, as part of the plantation estate. The annual crop and prices were

Slaves gather for festivities on a Carolina plantation. According to one expert,
both the drum and the dance depicted are of Yoruba origin. (Many American slaves were
descended from the Yoruba people, whose home is near the coast of West Africa.)

the most important facts in the life of any Virginian or Marylander.

After 1619 the English government required that all Virginia tobacco had to be shipped to England for the benefit of the mother country. If the English price happened to be low, the planters could not sell to the Dutch or anyone else in order to get higher prices. They were at the mercy of the English traders. This restriction of trade angered many planters, especially during bad years.

All these problems came to a head in the years just before Bacon's Rebellion. Tobacco prices were very low, and Bacon's indebted followers were in deep trouble. When Bacon thought of the possibility of independence for Virginia and Maryland, he was also aware that the Dutch would gladly protect Virginia from England in return for controlling the colony's tobacco crop. Exactly these same kinds of ideas

and problems involving market restrictions occupied the minds of the leaders of the American Revolution a century later.

Slavery Another difficulty with the tobacco economy was that it required a good deal of labor. Crops like wheat or corn needed more land, but they did not demand much handwork. Tobacco was (and still is) a crop requiring careful tending, from the first planting to the packing of the cured leaves almost a year later.

Virginia and Maryland were in a mixed situation. In one sense they were crowded, because fresh new land was becoming more and more scarce. But in another sense they were underpopulated, because there was a shortage of labor needed to cultivate the expanding tobacco crops. During most of the years before Bacon's Rebellion this problem was met by importing white indentured servants from England, at the rate of about a hundred a month up to 1690. The

FOUNDING OF THE THIRTEEN ENGLISH COLONIES

COLONY	EARLY SETTLEMENTS	YEAR FOUNDED	TYPE OF COLONIAL GOVERNMENT
CONNECTICUT	Windsor	1633	Self-governing corporate
	Wethersfield	1634	
	Hartford	1636	
	New Haven	1638	
DELAWARE	Zwaanedael (Lewes) (settled by Dutch)	1631	Proprietary to 1682/Part of Pennsylvania, 1682-1703/ Self-governing corporate after 1703
	Fort Christina (Wilmington) (settled by Swedes)	1638	
GEORGIA	Darien	1721	Proprietary 1732-54/Royal after 1754
	Savannah	1733	
	Augusta	1735	
MARYLAND	St. Mary's	1634	Proprietary 1632-91/Royal 1691-1715/ Proprietary after 1715
	Annapolis	1648	
MASSACHUSETTS	Plymouth	1620	Self-governing corporate 1620-91/Royal after 1691
	Gloucester	1623	
	Salem	1626	
	Boston	1630	
NEW HAMPSHIRE	Rye	1623	Proprietary 1622-41/Part of Massachusetts, 1641-80/Royal after 1680
	Portsmouth	1624	
NEW JERSEY	Gloucester	1623	Proprietary 1664-1702 (divided into East Jersey and West Jersey 1676)/Royal after 1702
	Hoboken	1630	
	Hackensack	1639	
	Swedesboro	1641	
	Elizabeth	1664	
NEW YORK	New Amsterdam (New York) (settled by Dutch)	1609	Colony of Dutch West India Company, 1624-64/ Proprietary 1664-85/Royal after 1685
	Kingston (settled by Dutch)	1615	
	Fort Orange (Albany) (settled by Dutch)	1623	
NORTH CAROLINA	Edenton	1658	Part of Carolina proprietary colony 1670-1712/ Separate proprietary colony 1712-29/Royal after 1729
	Currituck	1672	
	Bath	1705	
	New Bern	1710	
PENNSYLVANIA	Marcus Hook (settled by Swedes)	1640	Proprietary
	Bristol	1681	
	Philadelphia	1682	
	Germantown	1683	
RHODE ISLAND	Providence	1636	Self-governing 1636-44/ Self-governing corporate 1644-63/Royal after 1663
	Portsmouth	1638	
	Newport	1639	
	Warwick	1643	
SOUTH CAROLINA	Charleston	1670	Part of Carolina proprietary colony 1670-1712/ Separate proprietary colony 1712-29/Royal after 1729
	Beaufort	1711	
VIRGINIA	Jamestown	1607	Self-governing corporate 1607-24/Royal after 1624
	Hampton	1610	
	Newport News	1611	

Each colonial government had a governor and a legislature. All the legislatures except that of Pennsylvania had two houses. The upper house was usually called the council. The lower house was generally known as the assembly.

There were three main types of colonial governments—royal, proprietary, and self-governing. In a royal colony, the governor and council were appointed by the crown; the assembly was elected by freemen. In a proprietary colony, the proprietor (or his appointee) was appointed by the crown. He in turn named the council, while freemen elected the assembly. In a self-governing colony, freemen elected the governor, the council, and the assembly. In a self-governing corporate colony, directors of the corporation appointed the governor and council; freemen elected the assembly.

For additional information on the original thirteen colonies, see maps on pages 74, 103, and 109.

servants did not get their own land for seven years, and in the meantime they worked in existing tobacco fields.

There was, however, another source of cheap labor that did not use up land, a source that eventually made Virginia and the other Southern colonies very different from the rest of the country: black people from Africa. The first "Negars," as they were called, came into Virginia in 1619. They came not as slaves but as indentured servants. They did not come in large numbers until about the time of Bacon's Rebellion. In 1650 there were still only 300 blacks in Virginia. In 1671 the number had risen to 2,000. Ten years later, in 1681, there were 3,000.

At about the same time, the legal status of the blacks as slaves for life was spelled out. In 1670 the House of Burgesses passed a law that sealed the fate of black people, though it did not refer to them by race directly: "All servants not being Christians [that is, not being white Europeans] imported into this colony by shipping shall be slaves for their lives."

PLANTATION SOCIETY

Slavery did not become basic to Virginia until the eighteenth century. But already the way was being prepared for the kind of society Americans associate with the word "plantation": a society of vast estates, in which the planter lived like a great lord (a "grandee," Bacon's men would have said), supported by the labor of blacks whom he owned and bred as he did his horses or cattle. Virginia eventually became such a plantation society, as did Maryland, the Carolinas, and Georgia. By the middle of the eighteenth century all the Southern colonies were basically alike, with large plantations involved in staple farming that used slave labor.

Bacon's Rebellion took place during the early stages of the change. Before 1670 or so Virginia was still a region of small farms. Settlers usually owned a few hundred acres and still worked the land themselves with the help of their sons and perhaps one or two servants. The

servants themselves would soon be free, and they would, in turn, become small planters. After approximately 1700, Virginia was controlled by a growing class of great planters, whose estates consisted of thousands of acres and whose great fortunes (and debts) rested squarely on the shoulders of black men and women.

Bacon's Rebellion can be explained, in part, as a personality conflict between the governor and the young revolutionary. It can also be understood as the outcome of troubles between the Indians and the white settlers. But it did have a political content, too. Whenever the rebels and the government talked about this political content, both always referred to the battle between the "poorer sort" and the "grandees." The rebellion took place during the first years of the expansion of slavery. Bacon's followers—some of them, at least—probably sensed the new kind of society growing up around them. They feared the growth of an aristocracy, which would control local governments and also enlist the power of the royal governor most of the time. Those who supported Berkeley probably looked forward to the creation of just such a planter aristocracy.

In 1676 the two groups—the rebels and the government—were in fact roughly equal economically. How they differed was essentially in their way of looking into the political future, of interpreting the kinds of changes that were occurring in Virginia. Virginia, Maryland, the Carolinas, and Georgia grew into the kind of society that Berkeley would have favored. The colonies were loyal to the king and his governors most of the time—at least until the 1770s, when planter-aristocrats like Thomas Jefferson and George Washington finally felt able to throw off English support, protection, and control.

Washington and Jefferson were great patriots, political leaders, and statesmen. But whatever else they were, Bacon's men would have recognized them as slaveholding "grandees." It is odd in some ways that Jefferson—a wealthy Virginian with slaves—should have written "All men are created equal." But the contradiction was not new; it lay at the heart of Virginia's history. An immigrant in Virginia could easily

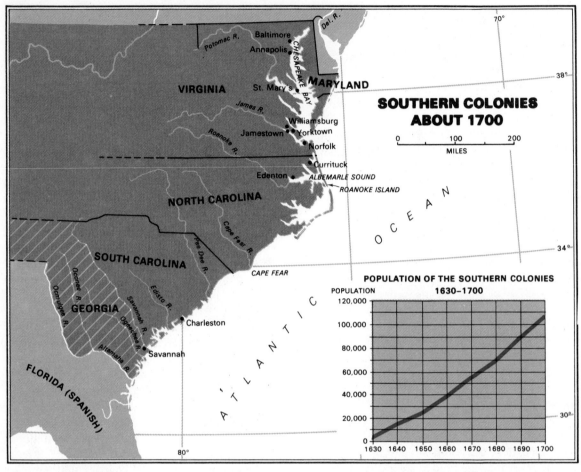

SOUTHERN COLONIES ABOUT 1700

POPULATION OF THE SOUTHERN COLONIES 1630–1700

Permanent English settlement in the Southern colonies began after the Virginia grant of 1606. From then on, English kings carved big chunks of land out of Virginia to form the four other Southern colonies.

Land north of the Potomac River was given in proprietorship to Lord Baltimore in 1634. Land south was given to eight noblemen as proprietors by King Charles II in two separate grants in 1663 and 1665. The king hoped that this new colony, Carolina, would serve as a buffer state, protecting Virginia from Indian and Spanish attack. The first settlers to Carolina came in 1653 from Virginia. They settled in the northeast, along Albemarle Sound. Carolina was treated as one colony until 1712, when it became known as North Carolina and South Carolina.

The last mainland colony to be claimed was the land southwest of Carolina, between the Savannah and Altamaha rivers. Georgia was founded not as a proprietory nor as a corporate colony, but rather under the trusteeship of a group of Englishmen. The most famous of these trustees was James Oglethorpe. Oglethorpe's goal was to create a refuge for worthy Englishmen imprisoned for debt. The founding of this new colony was greeted with delight by South Carolinians, who saw Georgia as a bulwark against the Spanish in Florida. By 1700 the population of the Southern colonies (excluding Georgia) was 104,588. Virginia was the most populous.

obtain a plantation of 150 acres of tobacco land. He could elect his own representatives—even a rebel like Bacon—to the House of Burgesses. These conditions might make it seem that all men (at least all *white men*) were in fact equal.

But these democratic realities existed in an economy of tobacco and of slavery, an economy that tended to produce, inevitably, an aristocratic social structure. The contradiction was present in Bacon. He was a wealthy man, a member of the Governor's Council, and the son of an aristocrat—but still the enemy of the "grandees." The same kind of contradiction existed in Thomas Jefferson a century later.

1. Why did Bacon turn his attention to liberating Virginia from England? Why did his control of the statehouse not give him control of the colony? For what reasons did his rebellion fail?
2. Can it be said that Bacon's Rebellion was as much a class conflict as a sectional one? Would it be accurate to call it a democratic movement?
3. For what reasons did people migrate to Virginia? Which reason do you think was most important? Why?
4. Why was the Virginia colony a failure as a business venture? Why did the London Company provide that each new settler receive 50 acres of land for himself and for each member of his family, including servants?
5. Who benefited more from the establishment of the House of Burgesses—the London Company or the settlers? In what ways did the conflicts of interest between the colonists and the English become contests between the governors and their assemblies?
6. Why did planters prefer cultivating tobacco to wheat? What were its disadvantages as a staple of the plantation economy?
7. What was the connection between Bacon's Rebellion and the price of tobacco?

Beyond the Text

1. Not everyone who wanted to come to the English colonies could pay the costs of transportation and settlement. Prepare a report on indentured servants, focusing on the kinds of problems they faced and the objections some settlers had to them.
2. Although slavery was well-rooted in the English colonies by 1700, the first blacks who came were indentured servants. Research one of the following topics: (a) Why were black indentured servants enslaved but not white ones? (b) How valid is the argument that prejudice against black people preceded their enslavement and may have caused it? (c) Does it matter today whether color prejudice caused or resulted from the institution of slavery?
3. Debate the topic: Nathaniel Bacon—Rabble Rouser or Reformer?

Bibliography

Nonfiction

Barbour, Philip L., *The Three Worlds of Captain John Smith.*
Craven, Wesley F., *The Colonies in Transition.**
Degler, Carl N., *Out of Our Past.**
Jordan, Winthrop D., *White Over Black.**
Middleton, Arthur P., *The Tobacco Coast.*
Morton, Richard L., *Colonial Virginia.* 2 vols.
Pomfret, John E. and Floyd M. Shumway, *Founding the American Colonies.**
Washburn, Wilcomb, *The Governor and the Rebel.**
Wertenbaker, Thomas J., *Torchbearer of the Revolution.*
Wright, Louis B., *The Atlantic Frontier.**

Fiction

Fletcher, Inglis, *The Wind in the Forest.*
Gerson, Noel B., *Daughter of Eve.*
Schachner, Nathan, *The King's Passenger.*

*a paperback book

3

Witchcraft at Salem Village

THE TWO GIRLS were strangely sick. Betty Parris, who was nine years old, and her cousin, eleven-year-old Abigail Williams, often stared dully into space. Sometimes they went down on their hands and knees and made hoarse, choking sounds. At other times they simply fell to the floor and screamed. The girls lived in the house of Betty Parris' father, Samuel, a minister. The house stood in the center of a small settlement called Salem Village, Massachusetts. It was January 1692.

At first Samuel Parris kept quiet about the girls' behavior. But, as the minister of the town, he was more carefully watched by his neighbors than any other man. His house stood at the center of the village. It was just down a dirt road from the tavern and not far from the only meeting house, or church. Something had to be done, so Samuel Parris sent for the village doctor. Since the minister's family was considered the most important family in the village, the doctor proceeded seriously and carefully. He examined the girls, consulted his medical books, and tried various medicines. Nothing worked, and his books gave him no clue. Finally, he gave up. The girls, he told the Reverend Parris, were not physically sick at all, but they had been touched by "the evil hand."

No one in Massachusetts in 1692 needed to be reminded that the doctor was talking about witchcraft. Four years earlier, in Boston, an Irish woman called Witch Glover had been hanged for bewitching four

A crude English drawing of 1655 shows the hanging of witches. A hangman climbs up to check the bodies. Below stand three condemned women and various officers of the law.

Matthew Hopkins was a witch finder, known for his expertise in discovering witches. Such informers were paid for their work. The two witches are shown with their "imps," or "familiars"—animals housing evil spirits that performed various services for their owners.

children. One of Boston's most famous ministers, Cotton Mather, had taken one of the bewitched children into his own house to try to cure her. Mather had then published a book on witchcraft, a book read in every town of the Massachusetts Bay Colony. (Samuel Parris had a copy.)

Practically every citizen of the colony believed that the devil actually did visit the earth, persuading men and women to join him, and giving them a witch's power to torment innocent people. All over

Europe at this time witches were being accused, convicted, and hanged or burned at the stake. The people of Salem Village were just as superstitious as Europeans and other Americans. Cotton Mather was one of the best-educated men in the colony. Samuel Parris had attended Harvard College. The doctor who first examined Betty Parris and Abigail Williams was an educated scientist. All of these men believed in witchcraft. If such educated community leaders accepted the idea that an evil hand was at work, what could be expected of the plain farmers of Salem Village?

As soon as gossip leaked out about Betty Parris and Abigail Williams, their young friends began to have similar fits. Between January and September of 1692 a group of about a dozen girls steadily acted bewitched. They accused one adult after another of being the tormenting witch. Betty Parris was the youngest of the afflicted children; the oldest of the group were two young women of twenty. Today they would probably all be called teen-agers. This group of teen-aged girls was joined from time to time by other afflicted persons, some of them adults, but most of them young people. A few adults argued that the girls were only pretending and that a good spanking would cure them. But most of the people of Salem Village, of nearby Salem Town, and of the whole Massachusetts Bay Colony took the girls' fits seriously.

At first the girls did not name anyone as their tormentors. All over Salem Village parents and other relatives prayed and fasted. Samuel Parris called in the ministers of several neighboring towns, and they too prayed and fasted. The questions in their minds were: Who was bewitching the girls? Whom had the devil persuaded to join him in witchcraft? Finally, on February 25, some of the girls called out three names. Whether the afflicted children had a plan or not, they were very shrewd. They named three women who were, for different reasons, not respected in the community.

The first was Tituba, a slave in the house of Samuel Parris. Tituba was from one of the islands of the West Indies, where Samuel Parris had worked as a merchant before coming to Salem to preach in 1689. She probably was part black and part Indian. Tituba was married to another slave, John Indian, who also belonged to Parris. During dark winter afternoons in the Parris kitchen, Tituba had no doubt told weird stories of the islands to Betty and Abigail. She had also shown magic tricks to the village girls who were now afflicted.

The second person identified by the afflicted girls was Sarah Good. In her own way Sarah Good was even more vulnerable than Tituba. Her husband was a laborer who had never held a job for long. Sarah herself was something of a hag. She smoked a pipe, muttered to herself, and often went begging from door to door in the village.

Cotton Mather did not speak out against the witch trials at the time, but later stated that he thought they had been unfair. He himself believed in "curing" witches through fasting and prayer.

The third supposed witch was a prosperous old woman named Sarah Osburne. After her husband had died, she had offended the town by living with an overseer on her farm. Although she had eventually married the man, she had stopped going to church. Thus she had developed a bad reputation generally.

In 1692 there were no regular judges in Massachusetts. Court cases were presided over by members of the colonial legislature known as assistants. So the parents and relatives of some of the afflicted children went to the two assistants of Salem Town and asked for the arrest of Tituba, Sarah Good, and Sarah Osburne.

March 1 was an exciting day for the village. The constables and uniformed military guard went out with drums to meet the two assistants coming from Salem Town. With this military escort the assistants marched into the meeting house, which had been converted into a courtroom. The assistants took their seats on a platform at the front of the church, with the afflicted girls facing them in the front pew. Almost everyone else in the village crowded in. Sarah Good was then brought forward for preliminary questioning.

One of the assistants, John Hathorne, was a stern, dark man who took his work very seriously. He leaned forward toward cranky old Sarah Good and began to question her:

HATHORNE: Sarah Good, what evil spirit have you familiarity with?
SARAH GOOD: None.
HATHORNE: Have you made no contract with the devil?
SARAH GOOD: No.
HATHORNE: Why do you hurt these children?
SARAH GOOD: I do not hurt them. I scorn it.
HATHORNE: Who do you employ, then, to do it?
SARAH GOOD: I employ nobody.
HATHORNE: What *creature* do you employ, then?
SARAH GOOD: No creature. But I am falsely accused.
HATHORNE: Have you made no contract with the devil?
SARAH GOOD: No.

Up to this point, Hathorne had not shaken this stubborn woman. She simply denied everything, saying in a tough old voice, "I scorn it!"

But Hathorne and the other assistant, Jonathan Corwin, had made a decision before opening the court. They would accept the testimony of the afflicted children about who it was that tormented them. According to this decision, even if Sarah Good were standing innocently before the judges, her "shape," or spirit, might attack the girls. If the

Known as the Witch House, /81
this gabled building in Salem
dates back to 1675. It
received its name because it
was once the home of
Jonathan Corwin. Some
preliminary hearings in the
witchcraft trials took
place here.

afflicted girls said that Sarah Good's shape was pinching or hurting them, then she would be put in jail for a full-scale witch trial and possible hanging.

According to the legal procedures of the day, Sarah Good was not told of this decision in advance. Nor was she represented by a lawyer. Hathorne's next move was very important. It established the pattern for all the hearings that would follow. The clerk's record of the testimony continued:

> Hathorne desired the children all of them to look upon her and see if this were the person that had hurt them. And so they all did look upon her, and said this was one of the persons that did torment them. Presently they were all tormented.

Here was the key to Hathorne's prosecution of the witches: "Presently they were all tormented." Here, for the first time, the afflicted girls learned that their moaning and screaming could attract attention. After a short time the girls quieted down. They said that they were being tormented by the shape of Sarah Good, the cranky old woman who, at that moment, was standing so still in the meeting house. Hathorne returned to the attack. Sarah Good held her ground for a moment, but then she began to break down:

> HATHORNE: Sarah Good, do you not see now what you have done? Why do you not tell us the truth? Why do you thus torment these poor children?
> SARAH GOOD: I do not torment them.
> HATHORNE: Who was it, then, that tormented the children?
> SARAH GOOD: It was Osburne.

In her panic Sarah Good tried to save herself by pointing an accusing finger at Sarah Osburne. But in doing so she sealed her own fate. Hathorne and Corwin reasoned this way: Sarah Good was not afflicted. Therefore, unless she were a witch, how could she know that Sarah Osburne attacked the children? Hathorne could see that the hag was going to pieces, and he hurried the process:

> HATHORNE: What is it you say when you go muttering away from persons' houses?
> SARAH GOOD: If I must tell, I will tell.
> HATHORNE: Do tell us then.
> SARAH GOOD: If I must tell, I will tell. It is the commandments.

Hathorne sensed that she was lying. Sarah Good might still have saved herself if she could have repeated even some of the Old Testament commandments. But when Hathorne asked her to name one, she hedged:

> HATHORNE: What commandment is it?
> SARAH GOOD: If I must tell, I will tell. It is a psalm.
> HATHORNE: What psalm?

As the clerk of the court recorded, "After a long time, she muttered over some part of a psalm." He also recorded: "Her answers were given in a very wicked, spiteful manner, with base and abusive words and many lies." Sarah Good was taken away, and her husband was questioned briefly. The clerk recorded this curious testimony:

> It was here said that her husband had said that he was afraid that she either was a witch or would be one very quickly. The worthy Mr. Hathorne asked him his reason why he said so of her. He answered that it was her bad carriage [attitude] to him, and indeed, said he, I may say with tears that she is an enemy to all good.

Once finished with questioning Sarah Good, Hathorne and Corwin then called Sarah Osburne, who quickly panicked. She tried to claim that she herself had been bewitched. To save herself, she tried to throw suspicion on Tituba's husband, John Indian, by claiming that she had been attacked by a "thing like an Indian, all black." But the afflicted girls would not let her join their circle. They accused her just as they had Sarah Good, and she was taken away. The assistants then sent for Tituba, who was to be the star of the day.

Tituba's situation was frightening. Samuel Parris owned her as a slave. As the village minister, he claimed to own her soul. Between the time little Betty Parris first accused Tituba until she testified, Parris had sometimes beaten her and sometimes prayed for her. By March 1 she

SALEM IN 1692

Boundaries of Salem Village   □ House

LOCATIONS IN SALEM TOWN

1 Courthouse
2 Prison
3 Meeting house
4 Place of execution
5 English
6 Bishop
7 Corwin
8 Hathorne
9 Gedney

had worked out a shrewd plan. She would confess. But she would also save herself by throwing greater suspicion on others and by claiming that she was no longer working with the devil. Once more Hathorne took the lead in the questioning. At first, Tituba's answers sounded like Sarah Good's, and the afflicted girls behaved the same way:

HATHORNE: Tituba, what evil spirit have you familiarity with?
TITUBA: None.
HATHORNE: Why do you hurt these children?
TITUBA: I do not hurt them.
HATHORNE: Who is it then?
TITUBA: The devil for aught I know.

But then Tituba began to execute her plan. As soon as she began to confess, the afflicted girls calmed down. It was as though Tituba's confession released them from their spells for the time being.

HATHORNE: Did you ever see the devil?
TITUBA: The devil came to me and bid me serve him.
HATHORNE: Who have you seen?
TITUBA: Four women sometimes hurt the children.
HATHORNE: Who were they?

At this point Tituba had to be careful. The children were cooperating by not acting tormented. But she had to name names that the assistants and the village farmers would accept. She also had to try to protect her husband, John Indian. Sarah Osburne had testified that she was bewitched by "a thing like an Indian, all black." Tituba invented a "tall man from Boston," dressed in black, to throw suspicion off John Indian. When she named Sarah Osburne and Sarah Good as witches, Tituba called them Goody. (This was an abbreviation of "Goodwife," a way of addressing married women of the lower class.) But she claimed that she did not know who the other witches were.

Then Tituba began to weave a tale of witches, devils, and strange animals. The citizens of the village listened in fascinated horror.

TITUBA: There is four women and one man. They hurt the children. And they lay all upon me and they tell me if I will not hurt the children, they will hurt me.
HATHORNE: What also have you seen?
TITUBA: Two rats, a red rat and a black rat.
HATHORNE: What did they say to you?
TITUBA: They said serve me.
HATHORNE: Why did you not tell your master?
TITUBA: I was afraid they would cut off my head if I told.
HATHORNE: What attendants hath Sarah Good?
TITUBA: A yellow bird. And she would have given me one.
HATHORNE: What meat did she give it?
TITUBA: It did suck her between her fingers.
HATHORNE: What hath Sarah Osburne?
TITUBA: A yellow dog. She had a thing with a head like a woman, with two legs and wings.
HATHORNE: What else have you seen with Osburne?
TITUBA: Another thing. Hairy. It goes upright like a man. It hath only two legs.
HATHORNE: What clothes doth the man [the "tall man from Boston"] go in?
TITUBA: He goes in black clothes. A tall man with white hair, I think.

At the mention of these creatures, the afflicted girls began to behave strangely again. The timing was perfect. Hathorne had to ask Tituba who was bewitching the girls. His question gave Tituba a chance to end her testimony in a helpful way. She could again throw suspicion on someone else. Doing so would prove that she wanted to help hunt down the witches. But then she could claim that she could no longer "see." This would prove that she was free from the devil's spell herself. Things worked out perfectly:

> HATHORNE: Do you see who it is that torments these children now?
> TITUBA: Yes, it is Goody Good. She hurts them in her own shape.
> HATHORNE: And who is it that hurts them *now*?
> TITUBA: I am blind. I cannot see.

Tituba, Sarah Good, and Sarah Osburne were questioned several more times during the next few days. On March 7 they were sent to jail in Boston to await a full trial. Sarah Osburne fell ill and died on May 10 without a trial. Sarah Good had a baby in jail, who died—confirming everyone's suspicions that she was an evil woman.

With the three witches in jail, Salem Village might have calmed down. But Tituba had said that four women, plus the tall man from Boston, were tormenting the afflicted girls. And the girls continued to be afflicted. This meant that more witches were on the loose.

Shortly after Tituba, Sarah Good, and Sarah Osburne had been taken away, Salem Village had a day of fasting and prayer. Once more the ministers of the neighboring towns came to meet with Parris. Once more the girls were watched, prayed over, and questioned. Finally, they called out a name, a name that shocked everyone and started the trials off in a new direction. The girls named Martha Cory, who was not a slave like Tituba, not a hag like Goody Good, and not a sinner like Goody Osburne. Martha Cory was an upstanding member of the village congregation. For the first time the girls had accused an adult with a solid reputation. If Martha Cory could be successfully attacked, then no woman in Salem Village would be safe.

The warrant for Martha Cory's arrest was dated March 19. But because that day was a Saturday, she was not to be arrested until the following Monday, March 21. On the Sunday between she bravely showed up at church, where a visiting minister, Deodat Lawson, was to conduct the church service. Lawson had once been the minister of Salem Village and was now living in Boston. He came to Salem to witness the witchcraft proceedings, and he had spent the night in Parris' house, where he watched Abigail Williams go through a violent fit of hysteria. The next morning, Lawson went to the meeting house to preach.

It was no ordinary Sunday service. Goodwife Cory herself came bravely to church, and there, during prayers and the sermon, the afflicted girls had fits. Ordinarily, it was a serious offense to whisper, doze off, or even look out the window during church services. In the meeting houses men were assigned the job of patrolling the aisles during the sermon—which might last several hours—to prod or even hit people who misbehaved or did not pay attention. But the afflicted girls broke all the usual rules. Abigail Williams yelled out at the minister, and she was imitated by several of the other girls. Finally, Abigail pointed to an exposed beam above the head of Martha Cory and called out, "Look where Goody Cory sits on the beam, suckling her yellow bird betwixt her fingers."

The girls had learned Tituba's lessons well. From the time of her confession to the end of the trials, they often mentioned strange animals, especially the yellow bird. Martha Cory, of course, was simply sitting in her pew. But when the girls cried out, all eyes looked overhead to the beam where her shape was supposed to be sitting with its sinister yellow bird. When Martha Cory came before the assistants the next day, most of the villagers had already made up their minds that she was guilty.

The visiting minister, Deodat Lawson, wrote an account of Martha Cory's examination by Hathorne and Corwin:

> On Monday the 21st of March, the magistrates of Salem were appointed to come to the examination of Goodwife Cory. And about twelve of the clock, they went into the meeting house, which was thronged with spectators. Mr. Noyes [a minister from Salem Town] began with a very pathetic prayer. Goodwife Cory, being called to answer what was alleged against her, desired to go to prayer. This was much wondered at, in the presence of so many people.

Martha Cory was a very proud and rugged woman. When two officers of the town had first come to her farm to ask her about the charges of witchcraft, she had laughed at them. Now, in her examination, she was trying to beat the village at its own game. If they could pray, then she would pray herself. But Hathorne refused:

> The magistrates told her they would not admit it. They came not there to hear her pray, but to examine her in what was alleged against her. The worshipful Mr. Hathorne asked her why she afflicted these children. She said she did not afflict them. He asked her who did, then? She said, "I do not know. How should I know?"

Hathorne began with the same questions he had put to Sarah Good and Sarah Osburne. Once more, the suspected witch denied everything. Once more, the afflicted girls involved the suspect more deeply by having fits. This time, however, they refined their techniques. Every time Matha Cory moved an arm or bit her lip, the girls acted afflicted in exactly the same parts of their bodies:

The number of afflicted persons were about that time ten. Those were most of them at Goodwife Cory's examination, and did vehemently accuse her in the assembly of afflicting them, by biting, pinching, strangling, etc. And that they did in their fit see her likeness coming to them, and bringing a book to them. She said she had no book. They affirmed that she had a yellow bird that used to suck betwixt her fingers. Being asked about it, she said she had no familiarity with any such thing. She was a Gospel woman, which title she called herself by. And the afflicted persons told her, Ah! She was a Gospel witch.

It was observed several times that if she did but bite her under lip in time of examination, the persons afflicted were bitten on their arms and wrists and produced the marks before the magistrates, ministers, and others. If she did but pinch her finger, or grasp one hand hard in the other, they were pinched and produced the marks before the magistrates and spectators.

Then the afflicted girls threw terror into the entire audience by saying that there was a gathering of witches that very moment in front of the meeting house!

The afflicted persons asked her [Martha Cory] why she did not go to the company of witches which were before the meeting house mustering? Did she not hear the drumbeat? They accused her of familiarity with the devil, in the shape of a black man whispering in her ear. They affirmed that her yellow bird sucked betwixt her fingers in the assembly.

She denied all that was charged upon her, and said they could not prove a witch. She was that afternoon committed to Salem prison.

Martha Cory was the first respectable woman to be accused of being a witch. Once the afflicted girls had succeeded in their attack on her, they were able to accuse anyone in the village. During the last week of March and the first days of April, several women with sound reputations were arrested and brought before the assistants. The village was in a deepening panic. Neighbors began to suspect each other, and people quickly forgot the difference between evidence and common gossip.

The panic spread from Salem Village to Salem Town, and then to the rest of the Massachusetts Bay Colony. By April 11 the examinations had to be moved to the larger meeting house in Salem Town. The deputy governor and several other leading citizens of the colony came up from Boston to observe the proceedings. The afflicted girls were no longer a local phenomenon. Now they were watched and wondered at by people all over Massachusetts.

In the middle of April, with spring well on its way, the first break showed in the ranks of the afflicted girls. One of the women identified as a witch in early April was Elizabeth Proctor, whose husband owned a large farm in the southern part of the village. The Proctors' maid, Mary Warren, was one of the afflicted girls. But the Proctors did not believe in witchcraft at all, and, furthermore, they had the courage to say so in public. At Elizabeth Proctor's examination some of the girls had screamed out that her husband, John, was also a witch—or a wizard, as male witches were called. This accusation alarmed Mary Warren. She did not like Mrs. Proctor at all, but she seems to have had a twenty-year-old's crush on John Proctor, who was a middle-aged man. Outside the meeting house, she began to admit that the afflictions were all a sport, that John Proctor was not a wizard at all.

When the other afflicted girls found out about Mary Warren's betrayal, they accused *her* of being a witch. So, on April 18, she was arrested and brought before the assistants. Suddenly, she had moved from the favored pew of the afflicted girls into the seat of fear where she had watched grown men and women collapse in panic. This was a crucial point in the trials. If Mary Warren could hold her ground against the screams of the afflicted girls, the stares of the audience, and the sternness of Hathorne, then the trials might come to a halt.

Samuel Parris himself kept the official record of the scene:

[As soon as she was coming toward the bar, the afflicted fell into fits.]

HATHORNE: Mary Warren, you stand here charged with sundry acts of witchcraft. What do you say for yourself? Are you guilty or not?
MARY WARREN: I am innocent.
HATHORNE: Hath she hurt you (speaking to the sufferers)?

Some were dumb. Betty Hubbard [one of the afflicted girls] testified against her, and then said Hubbard fell into a violent fit.

HATHORNE: You were a little while ago an afflicted person. Now you are an afflictor. How comes this to pass?
MARY WARREN: I look up to God and take it to be a great mercy of God.
HATHORNE: What? Do you take it to be a great mercy to afflict others?

This trick question of Hathorne's took Mary Warren by surprise. At the same time, all the afflicted girls began to howl. It was too much for the young woman to bear. She broke down and became incoherent. She struggled from time to time to regain control of herself, but it was no use. By now the fits may have become real hysteria, which Mary Warren and some of the other girls could no longer start or stop at will.

Now Mary Warren fell into a fit, and some of the afflicted cried out that Goody Cory and Proctor and his wife came in their apparition [shape] and struck her down.

Mary Warren continued a good space in a fit, and she did neither see, nor hear, nor speak.

Afterwards, she started up, and said, "I will speak," and cried out, "Oh I am sorry for it. I am sorry for it," and wringed her hands, and fell a little while into a fit again. And then she came to speak, but immediately her teeth were set, and then she fell into a violent fit, and cried out, "Oh, Lord, help me! Oh, Good Lord, save me!"

And then afterwards she cried again, "I will tell! I will tell!" And then she fell into a dead fit again.

The afflicted girls had won. Mary Warren was taken to Salem to jail, where she was questioned again and again by the assistants and ministers. Finally, on May 12, she admitted that both the Proctors were witches. By then, she was probably completely out of touch with reality. She confessed that she herself had "signed the devil's book," and she wildly accused several other people of witchcraft.

What happened in Massachusetts in 1692 was really quite simple. A group of teen-aged girls caused a brief revolution. In January they were ordinary girls, taking orders from adults, working very hard in their homes, listening to long sermons in church on Sundays and other days. By the spring of 1692 they held an enormous amount of power—even the power of life and death—over a large number of the adult citizens of Massachusetts. They had begun by accusing poor old women and slaves. But within a few weeks they were charging ministers, merchants, and other solid citizens. The girls probably had no plan, at least not at the beginning. Still, they were able to terrify tough old pioneer farmers. They were also able to use the power of the Massachusetts government to send innocent men and women to the gallows.

As panic gripped Salem and the rest of the colony during the summer of 1692, displays of both courage and cowardice could be seen, sometimes in the same family or individual. One such mixture of responses occurred in the case of George Jacobs, a toothless village elder who shuffled about with the aid of two canes. Jacobs' household included his son and daughter-in-law—"a woman crazy in her senses who had been so several years," according to local gossips. There were four grandchildren, the eldest a teen-ager named Margaret. Jacobs' servant, Sarah Churchill, was one of the afflicted girls.

Old Jacobs, like John Proctor, had scoffed openly at the girls' claims that they were possessed by witches. He even went so far as to mock his own servant, Sarah, as a "witch bitch." Unfortunately for Jacobs, no one in Salem in 1692 could make such remarks and escape reprisal. On May 10 Jacobs was summoned to answer to charges of being a wizard. Jacobs, like John Proctor and Martha Cory, was crisp and caustic in his examination, because he considered the accusation completely ridiculous:

HATHORNE: Here are them that accuse you of acts of witchcraft.

JACOBS: Well, let us hear who they are and what they are.

HATHORNE: Abigail Williams.

JACOBS: (Laughing) I am falsely accused. Your worships, all of you, do you think this is true?

HATHORNE: Nay, what do you think?

JACOBS: I never did it.

HATHORNE: Who did it?

JACOBS: Don't ask me. I am as innocent as the child born tonight. You tax me for a wizard. You may as well tax me for a buzzard.

But it was no use. Old Jacobs was sent away to the Boston jail. His son and namesake, George, Jr., did not wait to undergo a similar examination. Instead, he fled the colony, leaving not only his crazed wife but also their four children to face alone the consequences of having had a close relative declared a wizard. The consequences were not long in coming. The town officers soon dragged Mrs. Jacobs before the afflicted ones. At first the girls did not recognize her. Then one of them, probably her former servant, Sarah Churchill, cried: "Don't you know the old witch? And then they cried out at her, and fell down in their fits." Mrs. Jacobs spent the next ten months in prison as a suspected witch, with her three youngest children left to the care of sympathetic neighbors.

Margaret, the oldest child, had even worse luck. She was brought in to give testimony against her grandfather. Afraid that she herself would be denounced as a witch, Margaret confessed in order to save her life, accusing both her grandfather and the Reverend George Burroughs[1] of being wizards.

By the time of George Jacobs' examination, almost two dozen more people had been arrested, and many more were being accused every day. By the last week of May nearly fifty people had been sent to the dark, crowded Boston jail, waiting for their final trials. The accused were no longer outcasts or simple local farmers. One of those arrested in May, for example, was Philip English, the foremost shipowner of Salem. (He later escaped from jail and fled to New York.)

Samuel Sewall, of the Court of Oyer and Terminer, was the only witch-trial judge to admit error. In 1697 he made a public confession at the Old South Church in Boston.

At last, on May 28, the afflicted girls named the Master Wizard. They had been questioned for weeks by the assistants and ministers

---

[1] Burroughs, at this time living in Maine (still part of Massachusetts), was formerly the minister of Salem Village.

about the "tall man from Boston" whom Tituba had first mentioned on March 1. Everyone presumed that he was the guiding hand behind the entire witches' plot. The magistrates summoned him to court, and on May 31 a tall man from Boston walked into the Salem meeting house. His name was John Alden. He was the son of the Plymouth Colony's famous lovers, John and Priscilla Alden. This John Alden was more famous as a soldier than a lover, for he was a sea captain who had fought bravely in recent battles with the Indians.

Alden would never have come to Salem by his own choice, since he thought that the accusation of witchcraft was insanely foolish. But the deputy governor of the colony, William Stoughton, ordered him to appear for questioning. So Alden marched into court to face his accusers. Later, writing in the third person, he gave an angry description of what took place:

> John Alden was sent for by the Magistrates of Salem upon the accusation of a company of poor, distracted, or possessed creatures or witches. And being sent by Mr. Stoughton, arrived there the 31st of May, and appeared at Salem Village before Mr. Gedney [a third assistant], Mr. Hathorne, and Mr. Corwin.
>
> Those wenches being present, who played their juggling tricks, falling down, crying out, and staring in people's faces, the Magistrates demanded of them several times who it was of all the people in the room that hurt them?

Could the girls identify a man they had never seen before—except for his shape? For a moment the girls were helpless.

> One of these accusers pointed several times at one Captain Hill, there present, but spoke nothing. The same accuser had a man standing at her back to hold her up. He stooped down to her ear. Then she cried out Alden, Alden, afflicted her. One of the Magistrates asked her if she ever had seen Alden. She answered, "No." He asked her how she knew it was Alden. She said the man had told her so.

The assistants had to be careful, for Alden was an important man and a war hero. They ordered a ring of men to stand in the street; then they took the girls outside to see whether they could pick Alden out of the ring. Somehow, the girls immediately selected him, and the assistants ordered him arrested. His sword was taken from him, and he was brought back inside. But Alden was no poor slave or hag of Salem Village. He stood his ground to the end:

> Mr. Gedney bid Alden confess, and give glory to God. Alden said he hoped he would give glory to God, but appealed to all that ever knew him, and challenged any one that could bring in anything that might give suspicion of his being such a one [a wizard]. They bid Alden look upon the accusers, which he did, and then they fell down. Alden asked Mr. Gedney, what reason could be given why Alden looking upon *him* did not strike *him* down as well? But no reason was given that I heard.

Judge William Stoughton was a stubborn and overbearing magistrate. But he donated generously to Harvard College, which named Stoughton Hall in his honor.

> Alden told Mr. Gedney that there was a lying spirit in them [the afflicted girls], for I can assure you that there is not a word of truth in all these say of me. But Alden was again committed to the marshal.

Alden spent the next fifteen weeks awaiting trial, not in prison but under guard at his Boston home. This special treatment was due to his friendship with the colony's leading ministers—men like Cotton Mather of Boston—and with crown officials like the governor himself. These ministers met with Alden from time to time in order to pray and fast for his deliverance, but whether they meant "deliverance" from the charge itself or from being a wizard was uncertain.

Although Alden was a strong and self-assured man, he began to doubt his chances of escaping trial. Finally, in September 1692, after several witches had been hanged, he fled to friends in neighboring Duxbury and pounded on their door at midnight, shouting: "The devil is after me!" His friends smuggled Alden to safety in New York. There he joined other well-to-do or prominent individuals who had left Massachusetts rather than face the Salem court. There was no democracy among witches in the Bay Colony. With wealth or influence one had a far better chance of reaching safety in colonies like New York than did the ordinary citizen accused of witchcraft. The following year, Alden was declared innocent by special proclamation, and the tall man from Boston returned to Massachusetts, his person and property untouched.

Meanwhile, during the storm of arrests and imprisonments, a ship from England was bringing the man who would eventually control the outcome of events—Sir William Phips. He had recently been appointed the first royal governor of the Massachusetts Bay Colony.

Sir William Phips was born in New England, the son of a poor farmer in Maine. He had made a fortune in Boston. He had added to it in the Caribbean Islands, not far from where Samuel Parris had worked as a merchant and had bought Tituba and John Indian. Phips found a sunken Spanish ship near Haiti and raised a treasure in gold worth well over a million dollars. England's king at the time, James II, had knighted Phips as a reward. Sir William was also the hero of several battles against the Indians and the French in America. After a trip to England he was returning home as a wealthy hero and the governor of Massachusetts.

When Sir William's ship sailed into Boston harbor in May 1692, he knew nothing of the witchcraft trials because he had been at sea for weeks. He was horrified at the news. Like almost everyone else at the time, Phips believed in witchcraft. But he was determined to get to the bottom of things. Dozens of suspected witches were in Boston jail awaiting trial. At the end of May Phips appointed a special court to try the prisoners. He named seven judges, with his deputy governor, William Stoughton, as the chief justice. The court was called a Court of Oyer and Terminer.[2] Verdicts of innocent or guilty were to be handed down by a jury picked from the men of Salem Town, where the trials were to take place.

The prisoners had to put their faith in the court. The judges were men of high standing in the colony. They would probably be very careful about hanging men and women who had been accused by a group of hysterical young girls. What the prisoners did not know, at first, was that most of the judges were just as severe as Hathorne.

Before they opened the Court of Oyer and Terminer, the judges made several decisions that were harmful to the suspected witches. First, they decided that the records of the earliest examinations before Hathorne and Corwin would be admitted as evidence. The new court would, therefore, hear only testimony gathered since the first examinations. Second, the judges decided to accept the testimony of the afflicted girls about the shape of the witches. Third, the court would not punish any witch who confessed. This meant that confessions were rewarded, and it encouraged some, like Tituba, to name innocent suspects in their confessions. All these rules meant that the accused witches hardly had a chance for a fair trial.

On June 2 the judges first tried a woman named Bridget Bishop. Stoughton probably chose her because the case against her was strong. She was the wife of a tavern keeper, and she had a very bad reputation. Also, several confessing witches had said that she was one of their leaders. The jury quickly found her guilty, and the judges sentenced her to death. She was given a few extra days of life by an embarrassing discovery. There was no Massachusetts law providing the death penalty for witches. The colonial legislature, known as the General Court, quickly passed such a law. On June 10 the sheriff took Bridget in a cart to the top of Gallows Hill, where she was hanged. The first witch was gone.

But many more suspects were waiting, and Hathorne and Corwin were still conducting examinations in the village. Sometimes as many as fifty new witches were accused in a single day, no longer just in Salem Village but all over eastern Massachusetts. One week, then two weeks passed after the hanging of Bridget Bishop. But still the judges did not meet again. They were quarreling among themselves about the meaning of the afflicted girls' testimony concerning shapes. This kind

---

[2] This old English term was derived from French words meaning "to hear" and "to determine."

Margaret Sewall, a sister-in-law of the judge, lived in Salem at the time of the trials. Her dignified appearance was the ideal of New England Puritans.

of evidence, which was called spectral evidence (from "specter," meaning "ghost"), was considered all-important. Without it there would not be a case against a single suspected witch. The quarreling judges turned to the ministers of Boston and nearby towns to decide the question. The ministers finally decided that spectral evidence should be used, as long as the judges and jury were careful with it.

On June 28 the court met again to try Rebecca Nurse. Goodwife Nurse was from a large and prosperous farm family of Salem Village. She was an old woman and nearly deaf. But she was a member of the church, and before the witchcraft panic she had been a respected old grandmother. The jury took the ministers' advice about being careful in admitting spectral evidence. This time, they ignored the shrieking, afflicted girls and brought back a verdict of not guilty. Chief Justice Stoughton quickly bullied the jury into reversing its verdict, however. Then Rebecca Nurse's relatives went to Governor Phips and persuaded him to stop the hanging. But it was no use. When Stoughton and others heard about Phips' action, they insisted that he change his mind.

Neither the jury nor the governor could save Rebecca Nurse, and on Tuesday, July 19, she was hanged. Four other women were hanged on the same day. One was the old hag of Salem Village, Sarah Good. When she was about to die, one of the ministers tried to persuade her to confess. Goody Good might well have done so. She had spent months in prison. One child had died there with her. A second child had been arrested as a witch, though she was only five years old. But these things had only toughened the old hag's will. "You are a liar," she spat back at the preacher. "I am no more a witch than you are a wizard. If you take my life away, God will give you blood to drink." With that, she went up the ladder to the waiting rope.

Meanwhile George Jacobs' granddaughter Margaret, in prison, summoned up the courage to recant her confession. She wrote denying her previous accusations against Old Jacobs and Burroughs, who had both been sentenced to die.

The humble declaration of Margaret Jacobs unto the Honored Court now sitting at Salem:

I was cried out upon by some of the possessed persons. The Lord above knows I knew nothing. They told me if I would not confess, I should be put down into the dungeon and would be hanged. But if I would confess, I should have my life. This did so affright me, with my own vile, wicked heart, to save my life made me make the confession I did, which confession is altogether false and untrue. What I said was altogether false, against my grandfather, and Mr. Burroughs, which I did to save my life and to have my liberty. But the Lord, charging it to my conscience, made me in so much horror that I could not contain myself before I had denied my confession, which I did, though I saw nothing but death before me, choosing rather death with a quiet conscience than to live in such horror.

Margaret's statement had no effect on the judges, and they did not alter their decision. Old Jacobs was hanged on August 19, together with John Proctor and three other witches. Proctor's wife, Elizabeth, was spared because she was pregnant.

Old Jacobs was told of Margaret's recantation before his execution. Although his property had already been confiscated, he showed his pleasure at Margaret's brave act of conscience by including her in his will. The girl managed to visit Burroughs before his own execution later in August, and she received his forgiveness.

After her grandfather's death, Margaret wrote from prison to her vanished father describing her experiences. She ended her letter by stating simply: "My mother, poor woman, is very crazy, and remembers her kind love to you." Since Margaret's letter was placed later in the Salem court records, it probably never reached her father.

At the September meeting of the Court of Oyer and Terminer, one man refused to plead either innocent or guilty. He was Giles Cory, the husband of Martha Cory, who had already been condemned. Under an old English law Cory was taken into a vacant field beside the prison in Salem Town and tortured. Heavy stones were piled on his chest, but he would not surrender and say either "innocent" or "guilty." Instead (according to legend), he said only "More weight!" By afternoon he had been crushed to death. Three days later, on September 22, the sheriff hauled eight more convicted witches to the top of Gallows Hill to die, bringing the total dead to twenty—not counting the several who had already died in prison.

After the hangings of September 22, as suddenly as it had begun, the panic was over. The afflicted girls had gone too far. In the early fall of 1692 they began to accuse almost everyone, including the pious wives of well-known ministers. One girl even claimed that Cotton Mather, the colony's leading minister, was a wizard. Several of the girls began to see the shape of Lady Mary Phips, the governor's wife! These charges simply could not be accepted.

The trials that began in Salem Village were stopped by some of the leading citizens of the colony. They had finally become convinced that the entire affair had been a terrible mistake. On October 26, before the Court of Oyer and Terminer opened again, the General Court ordered a new meeting of ministers to consider the problem. Three days later, the General Court dismissed the trial court, and Governor Phips began releasing prisoners on bond. In November, following the advice of the ministers, the governor established a new court, with new rules. In the new trials spectral evidence would not be accepted. And, just as important, confessing witches would be hanged. Under these new rules there could be almost no convictions. One by one, the prisoners were tried and found innocent. Five still insisted on confessing, and they were sentenced to hang; but Phips overruled the court and allowed even these five to live. It was too late for Sarah Good, Martha Cory, John Proctor, Old Jacobs, and the rest who had died. But the Salem witch trials were over at last.

Salem and the rest of the colony then started the impossible task of settling accounts. The released prisoners were required to pay for food and time in prison. Some remained in jail for several months until these charges were paid. Samuel Parris' congregation voted to dismiss him, and he left Salem Village in disgrace. No one knows what happened to little Betty Parris, but her younger brother went insane and died a young man.

In January 1697, five years after Betty Parris and Abigail Williams had first been afflicted, the General Court voted a fund of £598 (worth about $30,000) to be distributed among the relatives of the dead and the surviving witches. The money proved small compensation for the terrible anguish endured. When it was divided up, the lives of Martha Cory and Giles Cory turned out to have been worth about fifty dollars.

After any tragedy people's minds eventually turn to other matters. In Salem Village the families of the dead gradually and painfully made peace with the families of the afflicted girls. By 1706 the little town was calm. But on August 25 of that year, the meeting house was once more filled to overflowing. A young women named Anne Putnam had come to ask for admission to membership in the church. According to New England church custom, she had to make a public confession, after which the members of the church would vote on whether to accept her.

As a young girl of twelve, Anne Putnam had been one of the most active of the afflicted girls. She probably had accused more "witches" than anyone. Now, at the age of twenty-six, she was asking for full admission into the adult community. She stood at her place in the meeting house. The rest of the congregation was seated while the new minister read her confession:

I desire to be humbled before God for that sad providence in the year about '92. I, then being in my childhood, was made an instrument for the accusing of several persons of a grievous crime, whereby their lives were taken away from them. I now have good reason to believe they were innocent persons. What was said or done by me against any person, I can truly say I did not out of any anger,

(continued on page 97)

GAINING A FOOTHOLD IN THE NEW WORLD

After some shaky beginnings, the English colonies in North America took root and flourished. The land soon boasted farms, towns, and busy harbors. (The South Carolina plantation shown here, built in the early eighteenth century, exported rice and indigo.) Foreigners who traveled to the country during its early days were interested in the economic reasons for its success. How did people make a living? Were Americans better off than their counterparts in other countries? What were a newcomer's chances of prospering?

Henry Wansey, an English visitor, thought that the keys were freedom and hard work. He wrote: "Everyone is at full liberty to follow the bent of his genius. Three fourths of the people are actively employed in either agriculture, trade, or commerce. There are but few idle drones in the hive, and, with all these advantages, their rapid progress to wealth and improvement is certain, and must be great beyond conception."

[For further information on the foreign observers quoted in this essay, see "Notes on Sources."]

PICTORIAL ESSAY 2

A view of early Baltimore, with tobacco growing on the hill at right

All of Maryland that we have seen is high land, with few or no meadows, but possessing such a rich and fertile soil, as persons living there assured me, that they had raised tobacco off the same piece of land for thirty consecutive years. The inhabitants, who are generally English, are mostly engaged in this production. It is their chief staple, and the means with which they must purchase everything they require.

[JASPAR DANCKAERTS, 1679]

The Blue Mountains, [the Catskills] which reared their towering summits above all the other mountains, were now seen before us towards the north, but at a great distance. The farms became very numerous, and we had a view of many grain fields between the hills.

[PETER KALM, 1748]

A New York farm, with the Catskills in the background

Swedes trading with the Indians

In dealing with the Indians, you must be positive and keep to your word, for if they persuade you to lower your price, they will spend time in higgling for further reductions, and seldom conclude any bargain. Sometimes you may with brandy or strong liquor dispose them to give you ten times the value of your commodity. At other times they are so stubborn that they will not offer half the market price, especially if they are aware that you plan to influence them with drink, or that they think you have a desire for their goods, which you must appear to slight and disparage.

[JOHN LEDERER, 1669]

Sawmill operated by water power

New England produces very good timber. The firs are of an extraordinary growth, for masts, yards, and planks. The sumac is much used by the tanners and dyers. The cedar produces sweet gums, besides being extremely useful in making shingles for coverings for their dwellings, as being the most durable and least injured by the weather. But the treasure and glory of the woods are the monarch oak, the spruce, and fir trees, which are in such abundance that the navy of England might be supplied with all sorts of naval stores at a cheaper rate than from the Baltic.

[THOMAS ANBUREY, 1778]

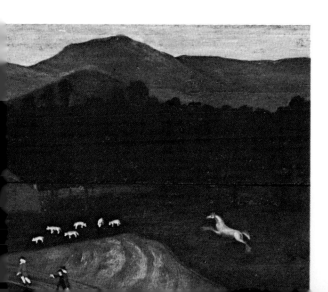

The fishermen take yearly upon the coasts many tons of cod, hake, haddock, and pollack, which they split, salt, and dry at their stages, making three voyages in a year. When they share their fish at the end of every voyage, they separate the best from the worst. The first they call merchantable fish. These they sell to the Massachusetts merchants, who send them to Lisbon, Bilbao, Bordeaux, Marseilles, and other cities of France. The refuse fish they sell to the Caribbean islanders of Barbados, Jamaica, and so on, who feed their Negroes with it.

To every shallop belong four fishermen—a master or steersman, a midshipman, a foremastman, and a shore man who washes the fish, dries it, and tends their cookery. These often get in one voyage £8 or £9 a man for their shares, but it does some of them little good. For the merchant at the end comes in with a traveling tavern—a boat laden with the legitimate blood of the rich grape, and with brandy, rum, and tobacco. Coming ashore, he gives them a taste or two, which so charms them that for no persuasions that their employers can use will they go out to sea for two or three days, nay sometimes a whole week, till they are wearied with drinking. If a man of quality chance to come where they are roistering, he must be sociable and rolypoly with them or else be gone. For when wine in their guts is at full tide, they quarrel, fight, and do one another mischief.

[JOHN JOSSELYN, 1674]

Unloading and drying fish at Newfoundland

Launching the ship *Fame* at Salem, Massachusetts, 1802

*The principal branch of American
manufacture is the building of vessels. The
Americans excel in naval architecture,
and in this particular point certainly rival
the most industrious people of Europe.
The annual tonnage of vessels built in the
different yards is estimated at about
100,000 tons.*

[FELIX DE BEAUJOUR, 1810]

Trade card of a manufacturer of spermaceti (whale oil) candles

*In Rhode Island and particularly in the small town of
Nantucket, famed for its fisheries, spermaceti candles are
made, which in whiteness rival those of wax, but they
do not give so pure and equal a light.*

[FELIX DE BEAUJOUR, 1810]

Wasteland, unhealthy climate, poor people, ragged clothing—such is approximately the general idea of this continent in Europe. But oh how far from the truth is this! The land requires too little work to remain uncultivated. The robustness of the men and the fine color of the women attest to the healthiness of the climate. Not only the abundance, but also the luxury in which people live belies their reputed poverty. And the pleasure which everyone who is introduced to their society experiences is incontestable evidence of their gracious manner of living. The [American] peasant does not know what misery is; he eats meat four times a day and drinks tea twice a day. If money is scarce, everything is cheap. At present such is the compeition here among ships from Europe (where perhaps they imagined that the Americans were all naked) that they are obliged to sell their merchandise at a loss. The quantity of all kinds of lumber, fish, oil, blubber, material for soap, flour, and salt meat will, before long, bring to this continent enough money to enable it to be recognized as a wealthy country.

[FRANCESCO DAL VERME, 1783]

Elijah Boardman, a wealthy Connecticut merchant

In the heart of New York City's commercial district, 1797

Merchants' counting house in Philadelphia

Table for converting currency

Philadelphia, if we consider that not eighty years ago the place where it now stands was a wild and uncultivated desert, inhabited by nothing but ravenous beasts and a savage people, must certainly be the object of everyone's wonder and admiration. It contains about 3,000 houses, and 18 or 20,000 inhabitants.

The Pennsylvanians, as to character, are a frugal and industrious people: not remarkably courteous and hospitable to strangers, unless particularly recommended to them; but rather, like the inhabitants of most commercial cities, the reverse. They are by far the most enterprising people upon the continent. As they consist of several nations, and talk several languages, they are aliens in some respect to Great Britain: nor can it be expected that they should have the same filial attachment to her which her own immediate offspring have. However, they are quiet, and concern themselves but little, except about getting money.

[ANDREW BURNABY, 1760]

Forges are established in New Jersey, Pennsylvania, Maryland, and Virginia. In several states, particularly the northern ones, utensils of iron the most necessary for agriculture and building are manufactured.

[FELIX DE BEAUJOUR, 1810]

Air furnace for casting iron, from an early advertisement

Went with a party to see Dickson's cotton manufactory. There are two large buildings four stories high and eighty feet long. Twelve or fourteen workmen from Manchester. All the machinery in wood, steel, and brass was made on the spot from models brought from England and Scotland. They are training up women and children to the business, of whom I saw twenty or thirty at work. They give the women two dollars a week, as well as board and lodging. The children are bound apprentice till twenty-one years of age, with an engagement to board, clothe, and educate them.

[HENRY WANSEY, 1794]

Early American flask, decorated with an eagle

Carding machine constructed by English immigrant Samuel Slater in 1790

malice, or ill-will. What I did was done ignorantly, being deluded by Satan. I desire to lie in the dust, and to be humbled for it, and earnestly beg forgiveness of God, and from all those unto whom I have given just cause of sorrow and offence.

The minister finished reading, and he then asked the congregation to vote. Sitting in the meeting house were many relatives of the innocent men and women whom Anne Putnam had helped to imprison and hang. They must have frowned and clenched their hard farmers' fists. But they voted along with the rest of the congregation, unanimously, to accept Anne Putnam's plea for forgiveness. Shakily, she sat down. The story of the Salem witches had finally ended.

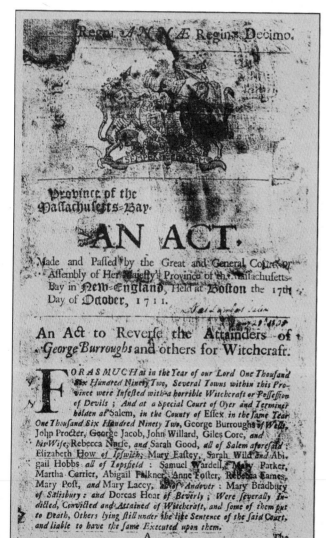

In 1711 the legislature of Massachusetts Bay passed an act to reverse the attainders of those executed for "a horrible witchcraft" in 1692. This meant mainly that lands and other property they had forfeited could be restored to their heirs.

Puritan New England

THE GOVERNOR kept a careful journal, beginning in late March when the ship still rode at anchor in England. Now, more than two months later, he was nearing the part of America that John Smith had named New England. On June 5, 1630, the ship's crew took a sounding and touched the bottom at about eighty fathoms (less than 500 feet). Even though it was early summer, the weather was still cold and foggy on the North Atlantic. In the afternoon the mists cleared enough for the governor to catch his first sight of the coast of what is now Maine. The next day, the ship slowed, and the men fished. The governor noted carefully that in less than two hours, they had taken in sixty-seven cod, some as large as three feet around. Such details might prove helpful to other Englishmen who came later.

On June 11 the governor's ship, the *Arbella,* was near enough to shore to turn south and begin the easy search for its destination, Massachusetts Bay. The entry in the journal was more relaxed than usual:

was later renamed Salem.) The governor was John Winthrop, and he was the head of the Massachusetts Bay Company. He and several hundred other Englishmen had come to Massachusetts Bay to establish the second important English colony in North America.

Winthrop and the colonists he governed were known as Puritans. They created in New England a distinctive set of communities. It was a strict, intensely religious society that finally became the setting for the witchcraft episode of 1692.

BACKGROUND OF THE PURITAN MIGRATION

Some weeks before he caught sight of the Maine coast, Winthrop had assembled his fellow passengers on the *Arbella*. He then delivered a lecture on why they had left their homes and were coming to New England. He did not mention the kinds of reasons a Virginian might have given, such as gold or trade with the Indies. Instead, he claimed, he and his followers were embarked on a religious mission—"To serve the Lord and work out our salvation under the power and purity of his holy ordinances." If they succeeded, Winthrop promised them:

> We shall find that the God of Israel is among us. When ten of us shall be able to resist a thousand of our enemies, when he shall make us a praise and glory, men shall say of succeeding plantations: "May the Lord make it like that of New England." We must consider that we shall be as a City upon a Hill; the eyes of all people are upon us.

The *Arbella* was the lead ship of a fleet of seventeen that brought over 1,000 settlers. In the next ten years 20,000 more came. By 1640 a string of Puritan towns stretched up and down the coast from Boston. No doubt many of the settlers and even more of their servants came for land or adventure. But basically, this great migration was a religious movement, a crusade. The migrants were escaping from an England they believed was powerfully corrupt. They

John Winthrop was a man of refinement and sensitivity. Though some questioned his arbitrary rulings (he had no faith in democracy), none doubted his integrity.

Then we tacked and stood west-southwest. We had now fair, sunshine weather, and so pleasant a sweet air as did much refresh us. And there came a smell off the shore like the smell of a garden. There came a wild pigeon into the ship, and another small land bird.

It took four more days to reach port, a small English settlement called Nahumkeck. (The town

The Pilgrims

Ten years before Governor Winthrop arrived to found the Massachusetts Bay Colony, a small ship called the *Mayflower* made its way toward the shore of eastern Cape Cod. The 102 passengers aboard were the Pilgrims. They had come to the New World with the hope of establishing a colony where they could worship as they wished.

Because of errors in navigation the *Mayflower* was off course. It was about to drop anchor near land that was not legally within the Pilgrims' charter. Several passengers, while still at sea, had said "that when they come ashore they would use their own liberties; for none had power to command them."

Responding to this unrest and need for a sure legal footing, the Pilgrim leaders drew up, on November 11, 1620, what became known as the Mayflower Compact. Forty-one men promised to "covenant and combine ourselves together into a civil body politic . . . and by virtue hearof to enact, constitute, and frame such just and equal laws . . . for the general good of the colony, unto which we promise all due submission and obedience." This short document was the first agreement for self-government ever enacted in the New World. It was to become the precedent for other covenants in New England, forming the basis of town and church government there.

Meeting hardships was not new to these men and women. While they were in England, the government had arrested and tried many of them because of their failure to conform. They belonged to a group that originated as part of the general movement known as Puritanism, but they were more radical. They did not want to reform the Church of England from within. Instead, they wanted to sever all connections with it. Thus they were called Separatists.

Since the crown required all Englishmen to support the established church, the Separatists made their way to the Netherlands in 1607, where there was greater religious toleration. There, however, the Separatists felt that they were exiles. By 1620 they were able to secure a charter from a London trading company and set sail for the New World. Once the Pilgrims had arrived in America, they explored Cape Cod. Shortly before Christmas in 1620, they chose the site of their new home—the rocky western shore of the cape—called "Plimouth" on John Smith's map of New England.

The first winter in Plymouth was severe. By autumn, after the first successful harvest, they celebrated. "Our harvest being gotten in, our governor sent four men on fowling [shooting birds] that we might after a special manner rejoice together after we gathered the fruit of our labors." So wrote Pilgrim Edward Winslow in 1621 to a friend in England, describing the first thanksgiving, a harvest celebration that grew out of an old English tradition. It was a time of joy and good spirits, not as solemnly religious as sometimes pictured.

Plymouth Colony merged with the larger Massachusetts Bay Colony in 1691. But it did not lose its identity as the first permanent English settlement in America north of Jamestown.

Landing of the Pilgrims

hoped to build a more perfect, more Christian, and more Protestant society in the New World.

The Puritans had been battling the devil for decades in England before some of them migrated to America. Although thousands of them followed the Winthrop party, even larger numbers remained in England to defend their religious beliefs against the monarchy and England's established church.

The Church of England, or Anglican Church, had become the established church of England during the sixteenth century. It closely resembled the Roman Catholic Church in many aspects. Its clerical organization remained largely the same. Archbishops were the chief religious officers; bishops ranked below them; and priests served as the foot soldiers in God's army. Many beliefs and ceremonies of the Church of England were essentially Catholic, too. However, traditional Roman Catholics were dissatisfied with the compromise. And so were radical Protestant critics of the Anglican Church. The most important of these were known as Puritans.

Puritan Beliefs   English Puritans believed that most Anglican priests were unfit preachers and ungodly men. Most of the ministers, by their own admission, had not undergone a personal religious conversion. How could a minister preach properly, Puritans asked, if he was a sinful man who would spend his eternity in hell?

The Puritans also believed, along with other radical Protestants, that life presents man with two basic facts. First, God is absolutely good and powerful. Second, man is born in sin and is helpless before God's judgment. God, being generous and merciful, selects some people before their birth to be saved and live for eternity with him in heaven. Others he damns. This doctrine became known as predestination, the belief that people are destined before birth—*pre*destined— for heaven or hell.

Puritans considered those who were predestined for salvation a separate company of God's chosen people, a community of the elect on earth. Puritans distinguished these people, the invisible

church of the saved, from the existing, visible churches on earth. The Puritans worked to make their visible churches into the closest possible imitation of God's invisible congregation.

Each Puritan congregation was to be a close-knit religious and civil community. Members would not only pray but live together in complete devotion to God. Puritans would not tolerate ungodly moral behavior. What they considered disturbing about both the Roman Catholic and Anglican churches was that they allowed their members to live too much of their lives uncontrolled by religious teachings. The Puritans saw their congregations as communities of believers set apart from the rest of the world.

Harassment and Danger   The Puritans pursued their efforts to reform the Anglican Church throughout the reigns of Queen Elizabeth (1558–1603) and her successor, King James I (1603–25). Both Elizabeth and James regarded the Puritans as annoying and subversive religious fanatics, whose constant demands for changes in church doctrines and practices undermined the country's stability. Both rulers harassed the Puritans by imprisoning them and persecuting them in other ways. Open conflict broke out when James' son, Charles I, became king in 1625.

Charles quarreled with Parliament and its Puritan leaders over the power each should possess. At the same time, Charles' leading Anglican bishop, William Laud, harassed the Puritans for their religious beliefs. Laud dismissed Anglican ministers whom he felt had been influenced by Puritan ideas. In one famous case, for example, a Puritan who published a book attacking Laud was fined and imprisoned and had his ears cut off.

In 1629 Charles I dissolved Parliament and announced that he would begin ruling England alone. This stripped the English Puritans of their political protectors in Parliament. Many decided to fight the king and Laud openly, to go to war if necessary.

It was a time of disorder and confusion. The king was battling Parliament for political control of the nation. The various religious groups—Puritans, Anglicans, and Roman Catholics—struggled for supremacy. While new merchant classes grew wealthy in the cities, thousands of unemployed farmers and laborers went ragged and hungry in the countryside.

The atmosphere in England was especially dangerous and unsettled for Puritans. A minister might go to bed at night not knowing whether he would wake up in his own home or in a royal prison. It was partly because of this tense atmosphere that a number of leading Puritans decided to migrate to the New World. This was the group, led by Winthrop, that established settlements at Massachusetts Bay in 1630.

The Puritan Mission Winthrop and his associates did not think that, by settling in America, they were abandoning their friends and fellow Puritans in England. Rather, they felt they might serve their religion best by establishing a model community in the New World. The Puritans saw their basic task as the complete reformation of religion in England and the rest of Europe. Believing themselves to be inspired by God, they had little fear of acting boldly to achieve their ends. They kept stern discipline among themselves and sought, as much as possible, to make each man responsible for controlling his own actions. Along with this belief in self-control, which was preached daily by Puritan ministers, went an elaborate set of regulations imposed *by* Puritans *on* Puritans.

Because they were trying to create a new and holier religious society, the Puritans were determined above all to govern themselves properly. Each Puritan congregation became a little political community, and controlled its own affairs. Each congregation elected its own minister and officers, as Salem Village had elected Reverend Parris. Since all congregations were thought to be equal in relation to God, none was subordinate to any other. Instead, all of them cooperated voluntarily in matters of common concern.

Each Puritan family also became a miniature community. The father, like a magistrate, directed the spiritual and moral lives of other members in the family. Even the Puritan's own soul was seen as a tiny community. Here God battled the devil daily, trying to govern a person's actions and impulses. Whether in his church, his family, or his own soul, a Puritan had to keep constant vigilance to ensure that God's purposes were being followed and the devil's rejected. The Salem community's vigilance in 1692 concerning the witches was, from the Puritans' point of view, only the response of godly and watchful people.

POLITICAL AND RELIGIOUS ORGANIZATION

The northern region of the first Virginia grant had interested the English since the original charter of 1606. After a few unsuccessful attempts at colonization in New England, the Plymouth Company was dissolved. However, other groups obtained their own charters and had greater success. One such group—with a charter from the Virginia Company—was the Pilgrims (see page 100). Other Englishmen, forming the Council for New England, obtained a grant to all the land from 40 to 48 degrees north latitude and from sea to sea. Some early settlements in Maine were made under this charter.

In March 1629 another liberal grant was obtained by a group of John Winthrop's friends and associates. Some element of trickery, perhaps even bribery, may have been involved. In any case, Charles I overcame his fear and suspicion of the Puritans long enough to give some Puritan gentlemen rights to settle in an area roughly the depth of the present state of Massachusetts, but extending from the Atlantic all the way to the South Sea (the Pacific). The land, according to the language of the charter, was "in the bottom of a certain bay there, commonly called Massachusetts, alias Mattachusetts, alias Massatusetts Bay."

The Puritan gentlemen and the king's advisers must have winked a bit when they agreed that the principal end of the colony would be to

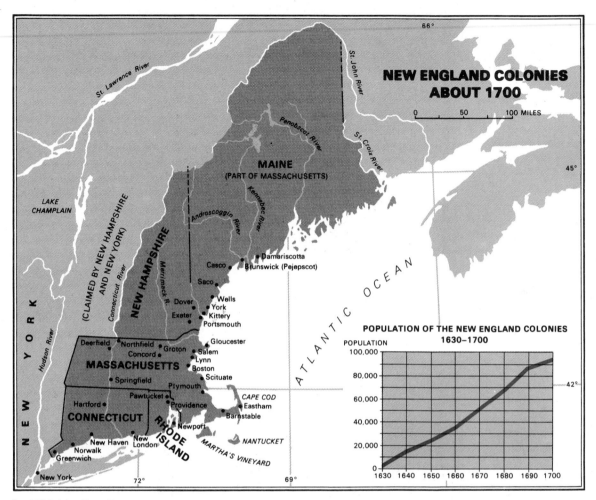

NEW ENGLAND COLONIES ABOUT 1700

0   50   100 MILES

MAINE
(PART OF MASSACHUSETTS)

St. Lawrence River

St. John River

Penobscot River

St. Croix River

Kennebec River

Androscoggin River

LAKE CHAMPLAIN

NEW HAMPSHIRE
(CLAIMED BY NEW HAMPSHIRE AND NEW YORK)

Connecticut River

Merrimack R.

Hudson River

N E W   Y O R K

Damariscotta
Casco
Brunswick (Pejepscot)
Saco
Dover • Wells
York
Exeter • Kittery
Portsmouth
Gloucester
Deerfield • Northfield • Groton
Concord • Salem
Lynn
Boston
MASSACHUSETTS
• Springfield
Scituate
Plymouth
Pawtucket •
Hartford • Providence
CONNECTICUT
RHODE ISLAND
New Haven New London
Norwalk
Greenwich
New York

CAPE COD
• Eastham
Barnstable
Newport
NANTUCKET
MARTHA'S VINEYARD

A T L A N T I C   O C E A N

66°

45°

42°

72°   69°

POPULATION OF THE NEW ENGLAND COLONIES 1630–1700

POPULATION
100,000
80,000
60,000
40,000
20,000
0
1630 1640 1650 1660 1670 1680 1690 1700

By 1700, the New England colonies had a population of 92,763. Over three fourths of this total lived in Massachusetts and Connecticut. Northern New England, as can be seen, had not yet taken on the form familiar to us today.

Maine's English beginnings went back to a grant to proprietors Sir Ferdinando Gorges and John Mason. In 1622 they received the land between the Merrimac and Kennebec rivers. They did little to build up a colony. Most early settlers came from Massachusetts, and the region remained part of that state until 1820.

In 1629 Gorges and Mason divided their lands. Mason received the region between the Piscataqua and Merrimack rivers, which he named New Hampshire. Like Maine, it had many ties to Massachusetts. The colony became a separate royal province in 1679. Both New Hampshire and New York claimed it, but there were no English settlements in the region until the eighteenth century.

"incite the natives of the country to the knowledge and obedience of the only true God and Saviour of mankind, and the Christian faith." (The Puritans of New England usually worried a little more about the Indians' rights than did the Virginians—but only a little. And the Puritans usually tried a little harder than the Virginians to convert the natives to Christianity—but only a little.)

In order to control the new colony, the charter of 1629 established a corporation known as the Governor and Company of Massachusetts Bay in New England. The king appointed the first governor. Thereafter, according to the char-

An old sketch depicts the Plymouth meeting house, built in 1683. In the early days, the Pilgrims met for services in the lower story of the fort that stood at one end of their settlement.

ter, the freemen, or stockholders, would elect a new governor each year. Also, the stockholders were to meet four times a year in a Great and General Court to pass regulations for the company. In form the company was an ordinary trading company, created to do business in much the same way as the Virginia Company or any other English joint-stock corporation.

By a stroke of luck, oversight, or genius—or some combination of the three—the charter did not specify that the governor had to live in England or that the meetings of the General Court had to take place there. (Most trading company charters made specific provisions for matters of this sort.) This made it possible for Winthrop and his colleagues to take the charter itself to America and change it from a trading-company charter to a political constitution.

Fewer than ten of the original migrants were stockholders of the Massachusetts Bay Company. Technically, only they had the power to vote in and govern the colony. Thus most of the colonists should have been politically powerless, as were their counterparts in Virginia. But Winthrop and the other leaders quickly made a decision. They admitted all adult male church members to full membership in the company,

with the right to vote in elections. Through this device the Puritans turned the original Massachusetts Bay Company, chartered as a trading company, into a political unit known as the Massachusetts Bay Commonwealth. This decision allowed the Puritans to maintain a government fitted to their religious purposes. The colony's chief magistrate was the governor. He, in turn, was advised by a council of assistants elected by the colony's freemen—that is, its adult male church members.

The Church   The political institutions of the Bay Colony were supported and reinforced by its churches. Organizing a church—gathering, as the Puritans called it—was usually the first task of any group of Puritan migrants who came to Massachusetts Bay. Usually, in fact, settlers formed their church even before they organized a town government.

The Puritan church generally had a pastor in charge. He was assisted by another minister known as a teacher. Neither one could become a civil official of the town, and ministers did not have the right to judge and punish offenders in ordinary, nonreligious matters. Instead, town or colony officials handled such cases. At Salem in 1692, for example, the accused witches were tried by a special colony court, even though their offenses had a basically religious origin and meaning.

The Puritans tried to keep religious and civil powers separate, primarily to purify and strengthen the church. Thus, New England congregations—unlike the Anglican and Roman Catholic churches—generally owned no property, not even their own church buildings. Congregations worshiped at a meeting house owned by the town and used often for town meetings and other civil occasions.

The first Puritan church founded in New England by Winthrop's group was established at Salem in 1629. The Salem church served as a model for later congregations. The following account of its organization, written by a Puritan, illustrates how seventeenth-century New Englanders thought about their religious institutions:

> The Salem residents picked the 6th of August for entering into a solemn covenant with God, and one another, and also for the ordaining of their ministers; of which they gave notice to the church of Plymouth (that being the only church that was in the country before them). The people of Salem made choice of Mr. Skelton for their pastor, and Mr. Higginson for their teacher. And accordingly it was desired of Mr. Higginson to draw up a Confession of Faith and Covenant in Scripture-language; which being done, was agreed upon. Thirty copies of the Confession of Faith and Covenant were written out for the use of thirty persons who were to begin the work. When the 6th of August came, it was kept as a day of fasting and prayer, in which after the sermons and prayers of the two ministers at the end of the day, the foresaid Confession of Faith and Covenant being solemnly read, the forenamed persons did solemnly profess their consent thereunto.

A church came into being, then, by the direct action of the members of the community. They looked to no outside power, no bishop or king. They created their own institution for their own purposes, and they chose their own leaders. Making such covenants, or compacts, soon became a deeply ingrained habit in New England.

Similar Puritan churches were organized throughout northeastern America within a decade of the *Arbella*'s arrival in 1630. They extended northward into what is presently New Hampshire and Maine and as far south as Connecticut. A small minority of dissenters from Puritan control established settlements in Rhode Island in 1636. That same year the Reverend Thomas Hooker, a restless Puritan minister, led another group of Puritans that set up the first towns in Connecticut. Other Puritans migrated to New Haven, which organized as a separate colony in 1638 but joined Connecticut in 1662.

Thus the expansion of New England took place as a direct result of the migration of whole congregations. They maintained close contact

The town of Boston (shown here in the 1640s) was founded in 1630, when Winthrop and others moved there from Charlestown, across the harbor. They named their settlement after Boston, England. The name is a shortened version of St. Botolph's Town.

with one another on matters affecting their common religious beliefs. New England's expansion, like its original settlement, had a basically religious character, and often (as at Salem in 1692) ministers from one congregation were called to consult with other ministers during periods of crisis.

The Town   Clearly, individual men and women did not simply decide to migrate to New England and then purchase land, as was the practice in Virginia. In most Puritan towns a congregation asked for a land grant from the colony's legislature in Boston, the General Court.

Once the grant was made, the General Court usually created a unit called a township. Within the township the congregation established a village or town. Almost every Puritan town, at the start, set aside a portion of its land for a meeting house that would serve as a church, town hall, and sometimes as a school. Some lands outside the town were set aside for common use as pasture or woodland. The rest of the lands were then divided among the residents for farming and grazing livestock. The purpose of this careful, step-by-step planning was to ensure that the Puritans achieved their major purpose—the development of a united community to practice true religion.

Once it was founded, the town became the center of life. Its citizens exercised close watch not only on their own actions but on the behavior of their neighbors as well. There were no hermits or solitary spinsters in Puritan towns, since the community was too close-knit to allow this.

All town residents gathered in the meeting house on Sundays, when it was used as the church. They also met there during the week, either to hear the ministers or attend to town business. Children attended the grammar school located near the center of the community, and they played on the common land. Most people lived within the village itself, both as a protection against Indian attack and in order to cement community ties.

Puritans considered themselves a people joined by covenant with God. The town was the political pillar of this covenant just as the church was its religious pillar.

The Family   There was yet a third pillar, as important in daily life as either the church or the town: the family. The Puritans migrated from England in families, not as individuals. Men who migrated to New England without their families were either sent back to England or ordered to bring their wives and children as quickly as possible. Those settlers who came as bachelors or spinsters—whether free settlers, servants like Mary Warren, or slaves like Tituba—were placed immediately under the supervision of a family. The male head of every family was responsible for the conduct of all its members. Each person in a Puritan community was under strict moral supervision within some family.

Puritans considered the family unit to have been created by God as a means to fulfill divine aims. The responsibilities of a Puritan parent, other than feeding, clothing, and sheltering those within his or her care, were basically religious ones. Parents were expected to train and educate their children to become adult members of the community. Parents were expected especially to prepare a child by proper religious teaching to wait in readiness for God's saving grace, should it come.

Puritan men and women were not unfeeling. Often they fell deeply in love with one another. But they believed that the primary purpose of marriage was not merely to satisfy these personal emotions. Marriage allowed a husband and wife to devote their love to the glory of God by using their family as what one writer called a spiritual center for the training of God's elect.

Thus at each level in Puritan society—as members of a church, a town, and a family—men and women worked to fulfill the ideal of a holy community.

Compared with modern Americans, the Puritans of New England had little sense of privacy. They always thought of themselves as members of some group—a household, a town, a congregation, a commonwealth, and, hopefully,

(continued on page 110)

Anne Hutchinson

The population of Massachusetts Bay Colony was strikingly uniform. There were no racial distinctions. Nearly everyone was of English stock. Community behavior was rooted in English tradition, refined and narrowed according to Puritan standards. But one woman refused to conform. Anne Hutchinson, almost from the moment she arrived in the colony in 1634, protested against the authority of the clergy. She thus became a center of controversy.

According to Governor Winthrop, Anne Hutchinson was ''a woman of haughty and fierce carriage, of a nimble wit and active spirit, and a very voluble tongue.'' She settled in Massachusetts Bay Colony when she was forty-three, with her husband and family. (She was eventually to have fifteen children.) This strong-minded woman took it upon herself to interpret the Bible, preaching what was called the Covenant of Grace.

A person who was said to live under a Covenant of Grace possessed a strong sense of oneness with God, no matter what his or her conduct in everyday affairs. Such a person felt sure of being God's elect and therefore certain of salvation. A person who was said to live under a Covenant of Works was one who had no such sense of God's approval. Instead, he or she hoped to win salvation by good deeds.

Mrs. Hutchinson might have been allowed to believe as she chose if she had kept her views to herself. But she insisted on relating them in public meetings. And her disciples spread her ideas, couched in sweet slogans—''free grace,'' ''gospel truth,'' and ''glorious light.''

As the movement grew, orthodox Puritans became alarmed. The issue finally came into the open in November 1637, when Anne Hutchinson was summoned before the General Court. There she confronted her archenemy, Governor Winthrop, who presided over the trial. She defended herself

well until she started talking about her revelations. This sealed her doom. It was a cardinal principle of the Puritan faith that no one was thus inspired, not even the ministers. So it surprised very few when Winthrop said, ''Mrs. Hutchinson, the sentence of the court you hear is that you are banished from out of our jurisdiction as being a woman not fit for our society.''

Fortunately, Roger Williams offered Anne Hutchinson refuge in his colony of Rhode Island. She and her followers went there in 1638 to found what became the town of Portsmouth. Four years later, after the death of her husband, Mrs. Hutchinson settled in New York, near Pelham Bay. In August 1643 she and five of her children were killed by Indians—an event regarded by some in Massachusetts as a sign of divine providence.

Massachusetts Bay was not a place of toleration, as is obvious from what happened to Anne Hutchinson. After she left the colony, the atmosphere of intolerance prevailed, to reach a climax at Salem in 1692.

William Penn, the Quaker who founded Pennsylvania, maintained excellent relations with the Indians. This romanticized painting by Benjamin West portrays Penn (center) signing a treaty with the Delawares in 1682.

The land between the Southern colonies and the New England colonies was known as the Middle Colonies. This region early attracted settlers from many different countries in Europe, and from other colonies.

The Dutch staked one of the first claims in the Middle Colonies on the basis of explorations by Henry Hudson in 1609. Dutch merchants established fur trading posts at Fort Orange (Albany), on the Connecticut River, and on the Delaware River. They called the land they claimed New Netherland. Dutch merchants negotiated a famous real estate deal with the Indians. They purchased Manhattan Island for twenty-four dollars' worth of goods, and changed its name to New Amsterdam.

The Dutch were also responsible for the settlement of Delaware. A Dutchman obtained a charter that organized a company headed by Swedes and Dutchmen. Fifty Swedes sailed up the Delaware River in 1638 and established Fort Christina, on the site of present-day Wilmington. Several Finnish families joined them later. The colony was called New Sweden.

In 1655 the Dutch strengthened their hold on this region by seizing Fort Christina. But New Sweden did not remain in Dutch hands long. King Charles II of England did not like having Dutch settlements wedged in between the English colonies. In 1664 he declared that all the territory between the Connecticut and Delaware rivers belonged to this brother

James, the Duke of York. The Dutch, realizing they were in no position to fight, surrendered when an English fleet sailed into New Amsterdam. Thus ended Dutch colonial power in mainland America. The new proprietor, the Duke of York, promptly renamed the colony New York.

Included in James' grant was the region of New Jersey, which had been settled by Swedish and Dutch pioneers. James gave the land to two of his friends, Lord John Berkeley and Sir George Carteret. The province was soon divided into East Jersey and West Jersey. In 1702 England claimed all New Jersey as a royal colony. There is still a Board of Proprietors for East Jersey and one for West Jersey.

The most successful of the Middle Colonies was Pennsylvania. William Penn, a Quaker, received the land from Charles II in 1681. He envisioned his colony as a refuge for fellow Quakers. Arriving in Pennsylvania in 1682, he carefully studied his property before selecting the site of Philadelphia. Attracted by the prospect of good land, political liberty, and religious toleration, people flocked to Pennsylvania. By 1700 Philadelphia had 10,000 people. It would eventually outstrip Boston as the largest city in colonial America.

In 1682 Penn convinced the Duke of York to grant him control of the southern portion of the Delaware River. This area already inhabited by Swedes and Dutch, was known as "the lower counties." It became the colony of Delaware in 1704.

This engraving of 1651 is the earliest known view of Manhattan when, as New Amsterdam, it still belonged to the Dutch. In 1664 the English sailed into this harbor, took the fort, and seized the colony, renaming it New York.

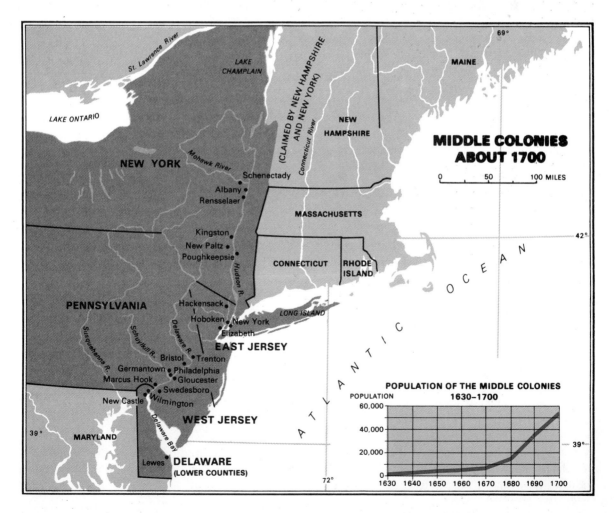

MIDDLE COLONIES ABOUT 1700

0   50   100 MILES

LAKE ONTARIO

St. Lawrence River

LAKE CHAMPLAIN

69°

MAINE

NEW YORK

Mohawk River

Schenectady

Albany
Rensselaer

Kingston

New Paltz

Poughkeepsie

Hudson R.

(CLAIMED BY NEW HAMPSHIRE AND NEW YORK)

Connecticut River

NEW HAMPSHIRE

MASSACHUSETTS

42°

CONNECTICUT

RHODE ISLAND

PENNSYLVANIA

Susquehanna R.

Schuylkill R.

Delaware R.

Hackensack

Hoboken   New York

Elizabeth

EAST JERSEY

Bristol   Trenton

Germantown   Philadelphia

Marcus Hook   Gloucester

Swedesboro

New Castle   Wilmington

WEST JERSEY

MARYLAND

Delaware Bay

Lewes   DELAWARE
(LOWER COUNTIES)

LONG ISLAND

ATLANTIC OCEAN

39°

39°

72°

POPULATION OF THE MIDDLE COLONIES 1630–1700

POPULATION

60,000							
40,000							
20,000							
0							

1630 1640 1650 1660 1670 1680 1690 1700

God's elect. Their lives were remarkably public. If they sinned, they made public confessions before the whole congregation (as Anne Putnam did in 1706). They believed, furthermore, that it was their duty to prevent their neighbors from sinning. In a way, the afflicted girls of Salem Village who called their neighbors witches were acting in the oldest of New England traditions. Much of the testimony in the witchcraft trials was nothing but neighborhood gossip. But in New England gossip had often been a public virtue. Not one of the accused witches of Salem Village ever reacted by saying, "It's none of your business!"

DISSENTERS—AND THE DEVIL

In every age certain people aim in different ways at perfection. Some try to make their homes and families run as perfectly as possible. Others work to perfect their own talents. Still others try to make their society perfect through political groups or governments. Some even try to perfect the entire world. These are the most ambitious of all perfectionists. They usually believe completely in the moral rightness of their own cause. They are, most often, the world's radicals, who try to make extreme changes in the way people live and what people believe.

The Puritans were religious radicals. Few of them believed that human beings could become perfect by themselves. Even those who considered themselves saved by experiencing conversion still spent their lives fighting the influence of the devil within them.

Almost from the founding of the New England colonies, Puritan magistrates and ministers—the spokesmen for the community—came under attack from a few settlers who were religious perfectionists of a different kind. Some of these critics of New England Puritanism are familiar to Americans today. Anne Hutchinson was one such critic (see page 107). Others were Roger Williams, the Baptists, and the Quakers.

These individuals and groups were not fighting to make all people free. Rather, they quarreled with the Puritans over differences in religious ideals. People like Mrs. Hutchinson, Williams, and the Quakers believed that an individual should perfect his own direct relation with God. The Puritans, on the other hand, believed in perfecting the community. God did not ordinarily deal with each individual directly, the Puritans argued, but only with groups of worshipers—that is, churches—with whom he entered into his agreements and covenants.

Roger Williams Roger Williams arrived in Massachusetts from England in 1631. Not long afterward, he began complaining about the way leaders like Winthrop ran the colony. Roger Williams was a Separatist, with beliefs similar to those of the Plymouth Pilgrims. He was outraged, for one thing, that the Puritans of Massachusetts Bay had not formally broken with the Church of England. He felt also that it was unholy of the Puritans to compel both the "saints" and other persons to attend church together. The elect should worship only with one another.

Williams also attacked the government. He believed that civil magistrates should not help enforce religious discipline in the churches by punishing those who violated church rules. The Puritans, on the other hand, believed that the main purpose of government was to punish violators of religious discipline. If Williams' views had been accepted by the magistrates, an episode such as the Salem trials would probably never have occurred. However, if Williams' views had been accepted, there would probably have been no Puritan commonwealth at all.

Williams even challenged the legality of the royal charter under which the Puritans had founded their colony. He claimed that the new residents of Massachusetts Bay had no right to settle there without having first purchased the land from the Indians. This the Puritans—along with most other English settlers on the American mainland—often failed to do.

Williams was a most likable and charming individual; Governor William Bradford of Plymouth called him "a man godly and zealous, but very unsettled in judgment." Many Puritans listened with interest to his complaints. Some were sympathetic, but others were outraged.

Williams settled finally in Salem, where he became assistant minister and then minister of the Salem church. For the next five years he kept the entire colony on edge with constant attacks on its doctrines and practices. Because they respected Williams as a godly and talented man, Winthrop and his fellow magistrates tolerated his attacks for several years before deciding to banish him. In 1636 Williams fled. With other dissenters from Puritan rule he helped found the new colony of Rhode Island. In his few years at Massachusetts Bay, Williams had brought into question every major principle of Puritan society. It is more surprising that the Puritans tolerated him for years than that they finally banished him.

Other Sects   Within a decade of founding Massachusetts Bay, the Puritans had dealt with two major critics of their holy community, Roger Williams and Anne Hutchinson. During the rest of the seventeenth century such attacks continued, sometimes from within the community itself, sometimes from outside.

The Puritans have been regarded as intolerant because they excluded other religious groups from Massachusetts. Few Puritans would have been disturbed by this charge. After all, they would have argued, they came from England to found a model religious commonwealth in this unsettled and isolated region. Why should they offer a haven to any of their religious enemies?

One group frowned upon in Puritan New England were the Baptists. They too had split away from the Church of England. But their Protestant beliefs differed from those of the Puritans. Three Baptist ministers traveled from Rhode Island to Massachusetts in 1651 to preach Baptist views. They attacked the close cooperation between clergy and magistrates that existed in Massachusetts. They denounced the Puritan practice of baptizing infants instead of delaying the ceremony until a person had experienced an adult conversion. This was a direct challenge to Puritan church practices. The three Baptists were

fined and banished. One of them refused to pay his fine, and he was publicly whipped.

A number of Quakers who came into the colony during the 1650s and 1660s received even harsher treatment. Quakers denied the need for any church discipline of the kind practiced in Massachusetts Bay. They preached that God infused his spirit into individuals directly. Because they believed that each person was inspired by an individual divine "inner light," Quakers could see little use in the controls exercised by the Puritan community over all its inhabitants.

The Puritan magistrates and ministers, for their part, could see only danger in allowing Quakers to preach freely in New England. They dealt with the Quaker intruders first by threats and then by punishments that ranged from imprisonment to public whippings. Eventually, the Puritans resorted to mutilation (cutting off a Quaker's ears was the favorite device) and finally to hangings. Nothing, however, seemed to deter the Quakers, who kept entering the colony despite the certainty of punishment or even death. One Quaker woman named Mary Dyer suffered through two executions before dying. Freed at the last moment while on the gallows waiting to be hung in 1659, Mrs. Dyer was banished from the colony. She returned the following year, when she finally executed, suffering what Quakers have called her double death.

The Devil as Reality   Although the Puritans could not prevent the worship of God by other Protestant groups in New England after the 1660s, they still made every effort to banish the devil. Along with all of Christian Europe during the seventeenth century, New England Puritans responded to what they believed were supernatural events. Sometimes these might be signs from God; other times they originated with the devil. Famines, fires, floods, Indian wars, good harvests and bad—in fact most crises in the life of New England society—were usually explained in religious terms, as such events had been explained in biblical times. God was forever warning, punishing, or rewarding his people through these signs.

Even in the early days, New England was noted for commerce and manufacturing. Here workers—including a smith, a tailor, and a shoemaker—ply their trades.

The devil made many appearances in Puritan New England, according to its residents, in order to destroy God's holy experiment there. The devil might show himself through a natural event like a famine. He might inspire the appearance of religious heretics like the Quakers. Or he might appear supernaturally, through witches and wizards. The Puritans uncovered many such agents of the devil in their midst during the seventeenth century. Even before the events at Salem in 1692, a number of witches and wizards had been tried in New England. Several had been hanged.

Two things set the Salem witch trials apart from earlier ones. First, in the earlier witch trials those who confessed were punished while those who denied the charges often managed to go free. In the Salem trials the reverse was true. Second, all the earlier witchcraft trials had concerned isolated individuals. Salem was the only case in which large numbers of witches were discovered, and the community divided into the accused and their accusers.

PURITAN SOCIETY IN CRISIS

The Salem trials came at the end of several decades of Puritan decline and at a time of great social change in New England. The trials could

have taken place only because of these changes. Understanding what motivated these changes, then, can help explain the events at Salem.

The Merchant Class In the beginning the Puritans, like other Englishmen who settled in the New World, needed something to sell in order to keep their community operating. The settlers of Virginia had found a single product, tobacco, to export to England. The Puritans had no such export, and the success of their colony depended in large measure upon trade.

New England merchants, almost all of them Puritans, began to take over from merchants in the mother country by filling English demands that could not be met during the Civil War.[1] New England's first important export was fish, and its fishermen prospered during the seventeenth century. Soon merchants in seaports along the New England coast towns, like Salem and Boston, began exporting not only large quantities of fish but also lumber and other products, often in ships built in New England. Merchants also began developing trade with the English West Indian islands (where many Puritans had also settled), picking up cargoes of sugar to sell in England. Sometimes the ships also shuttled Puritan passengers back and forth. John Winthrop's son, for example, settled in the West Indies. The Reverend Samuel Parris and his family—along with their slaves Tituba and John Indian—came to Salem aboard a New England merchant ship.

As New England's merchants prospered, they developed close ties with each other and became an upper class of wealth and power in the various Puritan communities. By the 1690s merchants were the most powerful economic group in New England life. They became not only wealthy but also politically powerful. The Puritan tradition of Massachusetts Bay held that

---

[1] Religious and political differences in England led in 1642 to war between the forces of King Charles I and those of Parliament under Oliver Cromwell. As a result of the Civil War, Charles was executed in 1649, and a Puritan Commonwealth was established. After Cromwell's death the monarchy was restored. The son of Charles I came to the throne as Charles II in 1660.

power ought to be exercised largely by magistrates and priests to regulate the community's religious life. Thus its people were concerned by the rise of a merchant class powerful enough to resist earlier authorities.

Changing Church Practices The rise of a merchant class was not the only problem faced by Puritan leaders. By the 1660s Puritans had to ease the severe tests for church membership that they had established in the early years of the Massachusetts Bay Colony. The early Puritan settlers believed that only those who had received God's grace through conversion should be allowed into church membership. But by the 1650s Puritans were faced with a serious problem. If the baptized children of church members were not themselves saved by conversion as adults, could their children be baptized?

In 1662 the Puritans settled on a compromise solution known as the Halfway Covenant. According to this important compromise, children of those baptized church members who had not experienced conversion would still be baptized, but they would be only halfway church members. That is, they could help govern the affairs of the church and community. But they could not receive all the religious privileges of full membership until they had experienced conversion and were saved. In the decades that followed, church membership became easier and easier to acquire. Finally, many congregations began admitting to full membership anyone who claimed simply to be leading a decent life, even though he or she might make no claim to conversion or salvation.

Few Puritan ministers were happy with this turn of events. They complained about the loss of zeal among the second and third generations. Ministers after the 1660s preached many sermons about this decline. They felt the Puritans had abandoned their original mission of building a lasting community of God's elect in America. Times had changed in New England, the ministers believed, and for the worse. Even all the good things that had happened—the arrival of thousands of new immigrants from England,

the expansion of trade, the prosperity of Puritan farmers, the rise of new people of wealth in land and trade, expansion into frontier areas—all these had only made it more difficult to fulfill the original religious purpose of Puritan settlement. As far as the ministers of the 1660s and their successors could see, New England had indeed departed from the aims of its Puritan founders. For this reason, no matter how wealthy New England became, God would still find means of punishing his people for turning their thoughts away from him and toward themselves.

Loss of Self-Government One part of God's punishment, the ministers believed, was political: the loss of some of the Puritan magistrates' governing power. This occurred in the decades that followed 1660, with restoration of the monarchy in England. Charles II determined to increase royal influence over New England. Until his reign it had run its own affairs with hardly any interference.

Charles did little more than meddle in the affairs of Massachusetts Bay. In 1684, however, he revoked the Massachusetts Bay charter, that same document that the Puritans had brought with them on the *Arbella*.

When Charles' brother James II became king in 1685, he sent a royal governor to rule all the New England colonies, except Connecticut and Rhode Island. James' choice as governor was a tough Anglican nobleman named Sir Edmund Andros. He had little use for the Puritan leaders of New England. Andros organized the colonies into a single government called the Dominion of New England, which he placed for the first time under direct royal supervision.

After fifty years of having ruled themselves, the New England Puritans were subjected to the very kind of control they had left England to escape. Little wonder that many devout Puritans began to see this loss of colonial self-government as God's punishment for having departed from the colony's original mission. The ministers preached this viewpoint, and many in their congregations believed it.

James II was overthrown in 1688 in a

bloodless revolution. New monarchs from the Netherlands, William and Mary, were placed on the English throne. New England now looked for deliverance from Governor Andros' rule. God seemed to be favoring his chosen people in New England once again, or so it appeared for a brief moment. The citizens of Boston threw Andros into prison, restored the old magistrates, and waited for word from England on whether the old charter would be restored.

They were disappointed. King William recalled Andros and accepted the temporary restoration of Puritan rule. But he too was determined to establish royal control once and for all in New England. The Massachusetts Bay magistrates sent their most important minister, Increase Mather (Cotton Mather's father), to England to appeal for restoration of the old charter. Mather failed.

According to the terms of a new charter of 1691, some of the political power of the Puritan magistrates was destroyed. Puritan rule in New England was ended. Until 1691 only church members could vote for the legislative officials of the colony, who, in turn, elected the governor. The new charter provided instead for a governor appointed by the king, a royal official who would be responsible not to the citizens of Massachusetts Bay but to the crown. Furthermore, the new charter established a property requirement for colony-wide voting. It also ended the previous religious requirement, that only Puritan church members could vote.

As a final check on Puritan domination of Massachusetts life, the new charter decreed religious toleration in New England. By this time Puritans, Quakers, Baptists, Anglicans, and other Protestant groups were free to worship in England. Now these groups, and others, were also free to worship in Massachusetts Bay. The government of Massachusetts, after these changes, was almost exactly like the royal government of Virginia.

A Time of Anxiety   This was the setting for the Salem witch trials. It seemed fitting that the same ship that brought the Reverend Increase Mather from England in 1692 also brought the colony's new charter and the newly appointed royal governor, Sir William Phips. Things that other men might view simply as signs of change were regarded by orthodox Puritans as signs of decline. For many citizens of Massachusetts Bay the rapid pace of change in their colony's economic, religious, and political life had become very unsettling by the 1690s. The present seemed uncertain; the future, unpredictable.

New people of wealth, merchants and landowners, had become numerous in the previous decades. They still lacked, however, the means to protect their wealth through an equal degree of political power. This concern surfaced, for example, during the Salem trials. Great merchants like Philip English, colonial notables like John Alden, and even devout ministers like George Burroughs all found it difficult, if not impossible, to defend themselves against the charges of hysterical teen-agers. Long-established Puritan magistrates felt as insecure as the accused witches. No one in New England during the 1680s and early 1690s could really tell what the new royal government had in store for him or her.

The Salem witch trials took place against a backdrop of fear that ran through the entire colony. An uneasy sense of great and disorderly change seemed to mark most aspects of life in Massachusetts Bay Colony when the first afflicted girls made their appearance in Salem. The events at Salem were partly a symptom of this general disorder. By the time they had ended, even more chaos had been created in Massachusetts because of them.

John Winthrop's orderly, stable, and godly "City upon a Hill" had become, sixty years later, a quarrelsome, unstable, and divided community. No wonder that the Reverend Samuel Willard (a leading minister), in searching for the wisdom to understand the Salem witch trials, prayed: "Lord, lead me through this labyrinth." Although he spoke only for himself and only about Salem, Willard's prayer had a special meaning for confused, anxious New Englanders.

1. Give as many reasons as you can to explain why the witch trials took place when they did and why people believed the girls' charges.
2. Compare the Puritan migration with that of the settlers who went to the plantation colonies.
3. Was the Puritan doctrine of predestination a hopeful one? What did the Puritans mean when they distinguished the "invisible" from the "visible" church?
4. Why did the Puritans try to keep civil and religious powers separate? In what way was this shown in the witch trials?
5. Do the Puritans deserve to be called religious radicals? In what way did their religious views create a climate favorable to witch hunts?
6. Why might there have been no Salem witch trials if the views of Roger Williams had prevailed in Massachusetts Bay Colony? Why might there have been no Puritan colony at all if his views had prevailed?
7. In what ways were the Salem witch trials different from those that had gone before?
8. Explain why many Puritans were able to become successful merchants. What effects did this have on the colony?
9. How did changes in religious and political organization create a climate of anxiety in Puritan New England?

Beyond the Text

1. The authors write of the stern discipline that prevailed among the Puritans and of "an elaborate set of regulations imposed *by* Puritans *on* Puritans." Investigate and report on the kinds of behavior the Puritans frowned upon. Give examples of the persistence of their kind of regulation.
2. Dramatize the heresy trial of Anne Hutchinson. In order to make this as authentic as possible, research what people wore at the time and what their homes looked like, as well as the background of the trial itself. For everyday life, see Edwin Tunis, *Colonial Living*.
3. Many Puritan merchants prospered by engaging in a lucrative "triangular trade." Examine the significance of this trade.
4. The McCarthy investigations of the 1950s were often called "witch hunts." How would you compare them with the Salem trials?

Bibliography

Nonfiction

Bailyn, Bernard, ed., *The New England Merchants in the Seventeenth Century.**
Demos, John, *The Little Commonwealth.**
Hall, Michael G., et al., eds., *The Glorious Revolution in America.**
Miller, Perry, *The New England Mind: From Colony to Province.**
———, *The New England Mind: The Seventeenth Century.**
Morgan, Edmund S., *The Puritan Dilemma.**
———, ed., *The Puritan Family.*
Nissenbaum, Stephen and Paul Boyer, *Salem-Village Witchcraft.**
Powell, Sumner C., *Puritan Village.**
Rutman, Darrett B., *Winthrop's Boston.**
Starkey, Marion L., *The Devil in Massachusetts.**

Fiction

Cannon, Legrand, *Come Home at Even.*
Forbes, Esther, *A Mirror for Witches.**
Hawthorne, Nathaniel, *The Scarlet Letter.**
Miller, Arthur, *The Crucible.**
Rees, Gilbert, *I Seek a City.*

*a paperback book

UNIT TWO

REVOLUTIONARY

The America of Bacon's Rebellion and the Salem trials was little more than a series of isolated settlements scattered along eastern North America. The planters of Virginia and the Puritans of Massachusetts, like other early colonists, were still basically Europeans. They still identified with their European homes, languages, and governments. Their idea of ultimate authority still centered in Europe. In fact, both Bacon's Rebellion and the Salem hysteria were settled by the exercise of British power—by Governor Berkeley (backed by English soldiers) in Virginia and through Governor Phips in Massachusetts.

By the mid-eighteenth century—just two generations after Anne Putnam's final confession—all this had changed. With remarkable speed, the colonists, overcoming many problems, had created a new society. From Georgia to Maine, the line of settlement was almost solid. The population was expanding. Cities like Boston, Philadelphia, and New York were as large and as rich as many in Europe.

This new society was, on the whole, British. It

AMERICA

absorbed the Germans, the Dutch, and the Swedes who had settled along the seaboard. As it grew, however, this new society was becoming more conscious of its identity as American rather than British. Finally, in the 1770s, the Americans reached a frightening and fateful conclusion: that they should break away from Britain and found a new, independent nation. In this unit of *Freedom and Crisis*, you will read about the experience of those Americans who demanded their independence, won it, and created a new government for what they decided to call the United States of America.

On March 5, 1770, a squad of British soldiers fired their weapons into a noisy crowd of Boston citizens. When the shooting stopped, five Americans were fatally wounded and six others had been hurt. Boston's political leaders quickly labeled the event a "massacre." It was one event in a growing conflict between the thirteen American colonies and the British crown, a conflict that finally led to war. The Boston Massacre is the subject of Chapter 5. Chapter 6 is about the chain of events that led up to it and beyond it to independence.

To everyone's surprise (even their own), the Americans somehow managed to win the Revolutionary War. The American hero of the Revolution, George Washington, retired to his Virginia plantation. Soon, however, he began to realize that something was wrong. Like thousands of other Americans, he came to feel that the government he had helped create was not working and had to be replaced. For Washington, and for most of his fellow citizens, this decision was not sudden nor lightly made. Washington reached his conclusion slowly, sometimes painfully, and as a result of very concrete experiences. Chapter 7 is about those experiences, and Chapter 8 is about their outcome, the new Constitution of the United States.

The people that had entered the eighteenth century as small, weak, and European, prepared to enter the nineteenth as proud Americans. They were certain that they would conquer not only their continental wilderness but a host of other difficulties as well.

The Boston Massacre

SOME CALLED the eleven-year-old boy Christopher Seider, others, Christian Snider. Whatever his real name, Christopher Seider (let us call him that) stood in a crowd outside Ebenezer Richardson's home in Boston's North End on the windy morning of February 22, 1770. Seider was one of several hundred Bostonians gathered there, many of them youngsters like himself. They had penned Richardson and his family inside as they pelted the house with eggs, fruit peelings, sticks, and stones. The crowd broke most of the house's glass windowpanes. One rock struck Richardson's wife. Others barely missed his two daughters. Richardson took an unloaded musket to the window and aimed it at the mob outside. The crowd broke down his front door, but continued to stand outside—probably because of its healthy respect for the gun—and bombard the house with stones.

Richardson then loaded his musket with small birdshot pellets. He fired and hit several members of the crowd, some of whom were injured slightly. Christopher Seider, less fortunate than others, fell to the ground with eleven pellets in his chest and abdomen. He died that evening.

The angry crowd surged into the house after the boy fell. It cornered Richardson, who surrendered without further resistance. The mob would probably have lynched Richardson except for the timely appearance of William Molineux, one of Boston's leading opponents of

Effective propaganda but inaccurate history is Paul Revere's engraving of the Boston Massacre. The British soldiers did not fire a coordinated volley point-blank at the Americans. Nor did Captain Preston order the shooting, as he appears to be doing here. Revere also added other special touches of his own, such as labeling the Custom House (at right) Butcher's Hall. Revere's drawing appeared in the Boston Gazette *on March 12, a week after the event. The accompanying full-page account, equally inaccurate, played upon readers' emotions in describing what the journal called "the consequences of quartering troops in a populous, well-regulated town."*

British authority. Molineux persuaded the angry crowd to turn Richardson over to the law officials. Within the hour Richardson appeared before four justices of the peace and a thousand onlookers in Faneuil Hall. Witnesses were heard at the open hearing, and Richardson was held in jail until the next session of the Massachusetts Superior Court. The charge against him was that of "giving Christopher Seider a very dangerous wound." After Seider died, the charge became murder.

Before his death Seider had been unknown to most of Boston's 16,000 residents. On February 26, however, he received the "largest funeral perhaps ever known in America" up to that time. Several thousand Bostonians braved snow-clogged streets to pay tribute to his memory. The funeral was organized by one of Boston's leading citizens, Samuel Adams, a lawyer and former town official with a reputation as an effective political agitator.

Seider's death provided Adams, and the cause of colonial resistance, with a ready-made juvenile martyr to British "tyranny." It was disclosed that Richardson had served in previous years as an informer for the British customs commissioners. These commissioners had been sent to Boston in 1767 to collect duties on colonial imports set by Parliament in the Townshend Acts.

Merchants in Boston, along with many other inhabitants of the North American colonies of Great Britain,[1] disliked these duties. They felt that the British Parliament had no right to tax Americans. So they organized a boycott of British goods, the nonimportation agreement. Protesters against British authority were known as Patriots. The most militant were organized into a group called the Sons of Liberty. Colonists who backed the British government were known as Loyalists or Tories.

In port cities like Boston, mob demonstrations against the British were frequent after 1767. Some were spontaneous. Others were organized by Patriot leaders like Samuel Adams and William Molineux. Such mobs often included some of the city's most respectable merchants and politicians.

The mob that stormed Ebenezer Richardson's house had gathered spontaneously. Richardson had just tried single-handedly to break up another, more purposeful, mob from interfering with a merchant who was reportedly violating the nonimportation agreement.

A few days later, after Christopher Seider's death, Boston's townspeople poured into the streets again, this time not as a mob but as a funeral procession. The following opinion appeared in the *Gazette*, the

---

[1] In 1707 England was united with Scotland. After this date the governmental unit as a whole is usually referred to as Great Britain. Its overseas possessions together became known as the British Empire.

unofficial newspaper of the Sons of Liberty: "Young as he was, Seider died in his country's cause, by the hand of an execrable villain, directed by others, who could not bear to see the enemies of America made the ridicule of boys."

During the two years before this incident, a bitter struggle had taken place between Patriots and the royal government of the Massachusetts colony. Both sides aimed to control Boston's economic and political life. The royal governor of Massachusetts, Francis Bernard, wanted British troops sent from Canada to discourage mob violence. But he could not request them without the consent of the Governor's Council, the upper house of the Massachusetts legislature. Its members generally opposed British control. London authorities, however, could order troops—and did.

In October 1768 Boston witnessed the arrival of the first redcoats from the two regiments to be stationed there—the 14th and the 29th. In time their numbers in Boston ranged from 600 to 1,000 men. Their presence angered Bostonians intensely, and patriotic sentiment increased tenfold. In the months between their arrival and the death of Christopher Seider, tempers flared frequently on both sides.

British soldiers disembark at Boston's Long Wharf in October 1768. According to engraver Revere's caption, the troops then marched up King Street "with insolent parade."

Thomas Hutchinson, a loyal servant of the crown, moved to England in 1774 and never returned to America. But he loved Boston and was homesick for it until he died in 1780.

During these months the troops controlled their sentry posts. The Patriots controlled the merchants and the town meeting.[2] Crown officials controlled Boston by day. The mobs, when they appeared, controlled the streets at night. The royal governor controlled only his temper. He resigned in 1770 in favor of Thomas Hutchinson, who became lieutenant governor. As far as anyone could judge, none of these authorities controlled Boston itself with any certainty. Both royal officials and Patriot leaders freely predicted that any major incident could trigger an open rebellion against British authority in that edgy community.

Relations between Bostonians and the British troops were sometimes friendly, sometimes hostile. Two groups among the unwanted soldiers made them even less welcome than they would otherwise have been. There were many Irish Catholics, whose presence offended the town's Protestant citizens. There were also a number of black troops, a fact that did not please those Bostonians who kept either slaves or black servants.

Any occupying army, of course, must expect hostility from those whose territory it controls. The British army was no exception. What proved particularly galling to the troops and their officers, however, was not the understandable bitterness of private citizens. It was the crippling hostility of public officials, especially the magistrates of Boston's court system. Ordinary soldiers complained about unfair treatment at the hands of American justices of the peace with the same kind of outrage felt by colonial merchants at their treatment by British customs commissioners. On both sides almost no one believed that justice could be secured from the other's courts, and there was much truth to these complaints.

By late 1769 it had become clear that both the Townshend Acts and the dispatch of troops to Boston had failed as British policies. Officials in London received pessimistic letters on the situation from General Thomas Gage, the British commander in North America.

British officials in the colonies such as Gage, Bernard, and Hutchinson, along with most American Tories, believed that the Patriots wanted not only to abolish the customs duties but to end British rule entirely. They viewed the Patriots, in Gage's words, as "an illegal combination of people" conspiring to stir popular feeling against Britain as a first step along the road to revolution. The Patriots, for their part, did not consider themselves conspirators. But they did view the British authorities and Tories in this light, as schemers trying to deprive provincial America both of its traditional liberties and its hard-

---

[2] Boston was governed by a town meeting consisting mostly of voters. It met at Faneuil Hall whenever the need arose. It could bring as many as 3,000 people together for several days running.

earned income. "There was a cursed cabal [group of plotters], principally residing in this town," Samuel Adams wrote in 1769 of Boston's Loyalists, "who were perpetually intriguing to bring about another parliamentary tax act; for no other purpose than that they might feast and fatten themselves upon the spoils and plunder of the people." Adams wrote that he thought it possible that the British "in calling for a military force under pretence of supporting civil authority, secretly intended to introduce a general massacre."

That the 600 harassed British soldiers who occupied Boston in early 1770 "secretly intended to introduce a general massacre" against Boston's 16,000 residents may seem improbable today. But at the time many Bostonians believed it, and they acted accordingly. Tensions ran high in the early months of 1770. Each group feared an attack that it believed its opponents had plotted well in advance. More often than not, however, the violence that actually flared up was unplanned and disorganized.

One such incident took place on March 2, 1770, only four days after Christopher Seider's funeral. It began at John Gray's "ropewalk,"[3] a large plant where a number of workers produced rope and cable. Temporary laborers' jobs were often available there. These attracted unemployed townspeople and British troops, who frequently needed extra money. On this particular day a British soldier named Thomas Walker of the 29th Regiment entered the plant and asked for work. Ropemaker William Green, a Bostonian, asked him: "Soldier, do you want work?" "Yes, I do," replied Walker. Green responded with an amused smirk, "Well, then go and clean my outhouse." The other ropemakers roared with laughter, but Walker's face turned red with fury. "Empty it yourself!" he shouted at Green. After the pair exchanged hard words for a moment longer, the fight began.

The ropemakers pounced on Walker and pummeled the unfortunate soldier badly before he managed to get away. He returned shortly with other redcoats, and the slugfest resumed. Both sides fought mainly with wooden clubs, although the soldiers also slashed away at times with their swords. Soon Gray's ropewalk was jammed with troops and ropeworkers, cracking their clubs against all comers. Both sides suffered casualties, some quite severe, until the soldiers were driven from the factory.

The following day, Saturday, March 3, a trio of redcoats returned to the ropewalk, where they renewed the battle against workers on the

---

[3] At this time rope was made in a long, low building. A ropemaker walked backward from one end to the other, paying out fiber from a bundle at his waist and braiding it as he walked.

scene. This time, one of the soldiers suffered a fractured skull and arm before he and his friends withdrew. Sunday, March 4, seemed more peaceful, although a group of British officers visited the ropewalk searching for a missing British sergeant, whose comrades had reported him killed by the townspeople.

Although the sergeant's body was never found, rumors spread among the troops that the Bostonians planned some larger dramatic gesture of revenge against the British soldiers. One private "remembered some ropemakers asking where the 29th [Regiment] planned to bury its dead." A Bostonian later swore that he heard four soldiers from the 29th say that "there were a great many townspeople who would eat their dinners on Monday next [March 5], who would not eat any on Tuesday."

The day of Monday, March 5, passed without incident. A foot of snow covered the ground. Bostonians who braved the cold, windswept city walked cautiously over the ice sheets that covered most of the streets. Boston had no street lamps then. As darkness fell, people had only a first-quarter moon to light their way. Snow covered King Street, where stood both the Custom House and the Main Guard, British army headquarters.

No one in Boston knew that in London, earlier in the day, the British Parliament had repealed most of the controversial Townshend Acts (all but the one on tea). This was a stunning victory for colonial protesters. The news of the repeal, though, reached Boston only in late April. And by that time Bostonians were preoccupied with the events that took place on King Street on the bitter cold evening of March 5. It was then that the fragile structure of civic peace in Boston finally collapsed.

The incident began as had similar ones in the past—with a soldier, a sharp-tongued young Bostonian, and a fight. The soldier, Private Hugh White of the 29th Regiment, was on guard duty at a sentry box on the corner of King Street and Shrimton's Lane, down the street from both the Main Guard and the Custom House. Along came a young wigmaker's apprentice named Edward Garrick. Garrick spotted a British officer named Goldfinch, and shouted within earshot of Private White: "There goes the fellow that won't pay my master for dressing his hair." Joined by another apprentice, Garrick strolled through the King Street area, later returning to White's sentry post, where he resumed his criticism of Captain Goldfinch. At this point, Private White defended the officer as a gentleman who would pay all his debts. "There are no gentlemen in the 29th Regiment," shouted Garrick, whereupon White left his post and joined Garrick in the street.

"Let me see your face," ordered White. Garrick obliged, and White immediately smashed his musket into the young wigmaker's head. Garrick cried out in pain, and his companion began exchanging curses with the angry sentry. Within minutes a crowd of some fifty townspeople had gathered in the street, surrounding the lone sentry, shouting at him to stand and fight them. White loaded his musket, retreated down the block to the steps of the Custom House, fixed his bayonet, and faced the angry crowd.

The mob began throwing large chunks of ice at White, screaming as they flung the missiles: "Kill him, kill him, knock him down. Fire, damn you, fire, you dare not fire." The town watchman suddenly appeared on the scene and urged the sentry to restrain himself, pleading that most people in the mob were youths who would not hurt him. As the crowd continued nevertheless to pelt him with ice, White responded: "Damn them; if they molest me I will fire." Finally, he shouted for assistance from the nearby regimental headquarters: "Turn out, Main Guard!"

Meanwhile, similar mobs had gathered elsewhere in Boston. Just a few blocks from King Street, soldiers strolled along Brattle Street carrying clubs, bayonets, and other weapons while a solitary Bostonian ran up and down the immediate area shouting the usual call for a mob to gather: "Town born, turn out! Town born, turn out!" A crowd collected quickly at a regimental encampment called Murray's Barracks near Brattle Street. Soon volleys of snowballs hurled at the soldiers accompanied the shouts of bystanders. Several British officers, including Captain Goldfinch, ordered the soldiers back into the barracks to forestall bloodshed. More than once, officers knocked their own troops to the ground to prevent them from shooting into the onrushing crowd.

Another throng gathered in Dock Square, only two blocks from Private White's sentry post on King Street. Several hundred townspeople poured into the empty stalls of Boston's town market. They ripped the legs off produce and butcher tables and shouted "Fire!" to attract additional recruits from the neighborhood.

The cry of "Fire!" repeated endlessly through the dark Boston streets attracted a number of sleepy townspeople. Boston depended on volunteer firefighting companies composed of residents. So groups of such firefighters carrying buckets joined the three separate crowds of agitated Bostonians spoiling for a fight with the soldiers. At one point, church bells began tolling the additional call for firefighters.

Bostonians of all ages converged on King Street—some with buckets, others with sticks. Many ran from the Dock Square and Murray's Barracks fracases once those incidents had quieted down. The crowd in King Street varied in size from several dozen to several hundred over the next hour, as men and boys moved along the town's cramped lanes and alleys. "There is no fire," shouted one youth to a bystander. "It is the soldiers fighting." "Damn it, I am glad of it," came the response. "I will knock some of them on the head." A number of Bostonians left the sidewalks to join the unruly scene in the streets.

The mob that gathered in King Street surrounded White's sentry post but made no immediate attempt to overwhelm him. Meanwhile, the British officer of the guard that evening, Captain Thomas Preston, had been summoned from his dinner table by White's urgent request for reinforcements. He went to the Main Guard on King Street, and he surveyed the crowd. By now it had grown to at least 300 or 400 (accurate estimates were difficult). After deciding to help the beleaguered White, Preston ordered up a relief party of sentries—six privates and a corporal. He then marched with them toward the menacing crowd, their muskets empty and shouldered but their bayonets fixed.

Preston's few soldiers managed to push through the crowd, loading their muskets after reaching White's empty sentry box. White still confronted the large throng from a position on the Custom House steps. At Preston's orders and without interference from the bystanders, he joined the other soldiers.

Preston had ordered the sentries out primarily to relieve White. Having done so, the captain tried to march his soldiers back toward the Main Guard. The surrounding mob either would not or could not allow the troops through, so great was the press of bodies. Some people in the throng began shouting at the redcoats: "Damn you, fire. You can't kill us all." Within moments Preston found himself and his men cut off from assistance. He ordered his soldiers to deploy at one side of the Custom House. The men formed a curved line with their backs to the Custom House. Although they tried to keep the crowd from encircling them, some Bostonians managed to slip behind the soldiers' tightly formed ranks.

The crowd, obviously leaderless, shuffled angrily yet uneasily around the nervous redcoats, uncertain whether to attack or withdraw. To add to the confusion, the church bells kept tolling. Every few moments, more bucket-carrying Bostonians arrived at the scene. Many exchanged their buckets quickly for clubs or ice chunks when they

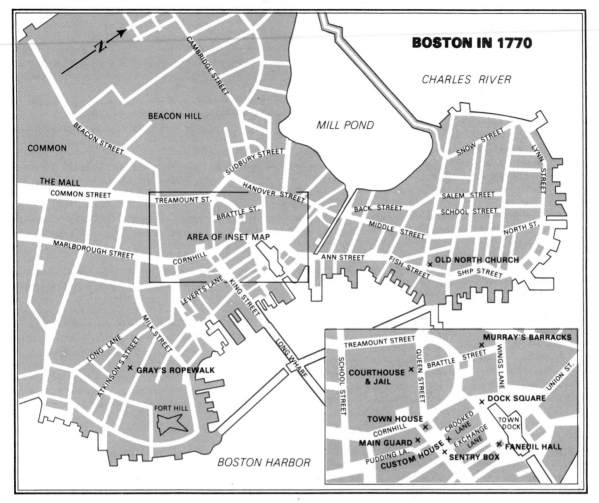

learned the circumstances. Preston shouted for the crowd to disperse but received in return only laughter, hooting, and a pelting with snowballs. The crowd taunted the soldiers to shoot, and the small company of British troops clenched tightly at their weapons.

The only town official to brave the mob scene was one James Murray, a Tory justice of the peace, who arrived at King Street to read the Riot Act. By law, the statute forbidding riotous gatherings had to be read to a mob before it took effect. The crowd knew this. They knew, therefore, that Preston and his men would be on questionable legal ground if they fired without having first ordered the mob to disperse by a reading of the Riot Act.

The mob wanted to prevent the reading. A volley of snowballs and ice chunks soon sent Murray scurrying toward safety. The mob's anger increased when some of its members recognized at least two of the sentries, Privates Matthew Kilroy and William Warren, as participants in the battle at the ropewalk four days earlier. At the same time, Private White himself spotted a familiar face in the crowd. It belonged to a young woman named Jane Whitehouse who lived near his own Boston living quarters. "Go home," he cried, taking her arm and pushing her toward the corner. "Go home, or you'll be killed."

The mob soon abandoned all restraint short of directly assaulting the soldiers. Individuals began pushing forcefully against Preston's troops, daring them to fire, denouncing them as cowards and scoundrels, challenging them to fistfights. "Why do you not fire? Damn you, you dare not fire. Fire and be damned." There were small duels, as townsmen carrying clubs beat them against the guardsmen's musket barrels and bayonets. Preston continued to shout demands that the crowd disperse, at the same time restraining his frightened band of soldiers from opening fire. Several times the captain was approached by Patriot leaders in the mob who asked whether he intended to fire. Each time he responded, "By no means, by no means."

A Tory dignitary in the crowd urged the captain to disperse the unruly rioters with a warning volley of musket shot. At this, stressing his desire to prevent bloodshed, Preston placed himself directly in front of the muskets so that he would be the first victim of any shooting. The crowd cheered at Preston's embarrassment, which at the moment seemed an almost perfect reflection of the overall British situation in Boston—the incapability of either maintaining public order or withdrawing gracefully.

No more than a foot or two separated the line of soldiers from the nearest rioters. Suddenly a club went sailing from the midst of the crowd into the dimly lit street, hitting Private Hugh Montgomery. The private fell to the ground and dropped his musket on the ice. No one knows why that particular individual threw that particular club, any more than we know what emotions Private Montgomery felt as he staggered to his feet and recovered his musket. One can guess easily at both. We do know that Montgomery immediately shouted, "Damn you, fire," and proceeded to pull his trigger. Within seconds members of the crowd lunged at Preston and his troops, swinging their clubs wildly. The soldiers managed to fight off these blows. In an interval of from fifteen seconds to two minutes (the exact time remains unclear), the other troops also fired their weapons.

Preston neither ordered the shooting, nor did he—stunned at Montgomery's impulsive action—order it to stop. When the shooting stopped, the crowd continued to advance on the small group of soldiers, although few people got close enough to swing their clubs. The soldiers parried blows by members of the mob while reloading their muskets. They fired another round. Again the firing took place sporadically, with single shots being fired over a period of minutes. This time, several people in the crowd were wounded, and some fell to the ground. Finally, the crowd began to disperse, although it regrouped quickly when the firing had stopped, this time to recover the bodies of

A plan of the scene of the Boston Massacre was drawn by Paul Revere for use at the trial of Preston's men. More accurate than his engraving of the event, it shows the location of the chief buildings nearby and the places where four of the dead fell.

Although only a mediocre artist, Paul Revere was a fine silversmith in addition to being an ardent Patriot. As a skilled craftsman, he cast cannon for the army, printed the first Continental money, and designed the state seal still used by Massachusetts.

those who lay dead or wounded. The soldiers, fearing another attack, raised their muskets to fire a third round. By now, Preston had regained his composure and personally shoved down his soldiers' gun barrels before they could shoot, shouting, "Stop firing! Do not fire!"

The mob drew back for the moment, carrying the bodies of those hit by the troops. Preston's soldiers began to explain to their agitated captain that they had fired after hearing what they believed to be *his* command. While emergency hospitals for the wounded sprang up in nearby homes, Preston marched his company back to the Main Guard. He then turned out the entire guard and placed it in formation on King Street between the Main Guard and Boston's Town House (the Old State House). The troops were drawn up in street-firing position, an eighteenth-century tactic for controlling urban riots in narrow streets. Rows of soldiers stood in single-file formation. The man at the head of the line would shoot, then move to the back of the line. There he reloaded and waited his turn at the front to shoot once more.

In front of the Custom House, small groups of Bostonians passed grimly along King Street and stared at the bloodstains splattered on the icy thoroughfare. Word had spread quickly through town that, as a result of the shooting, five men lay dead or dying. Among the dead was one who would soon become the most famous martyr of the evening's bloodshed, Crispus Attucks. (Accounts differ as to whether he was a free black, a runaway slave, or an Indian of the Natick tribe.) Four others were also killed—an Irish Catholic immigrant named Patrick Carr; Samuel Gray, the son of the ropewalk owner; seventeen-year-old Samuel Maverick; and a young apprentice sailor named James Caldwell. Almost from the moment of these deaths, Bostonians began referring to the episode as a massacre. (Over 10,000 people attended the funeral held for the five men on March 8.)

The withdrawal of Preston's men did not dispel the threat of an even greater massacre that very night, as angry Bostonians filled the streets, hurling curses at the British troops and crying "To arms!" Every church bell in Boston began pealing. Even the town's official drums—which generally summoned the militia to combat—beat solemnly to announce the tragedy. Within an hour after the so-called massacre itself, more than a thousand citizens crowded King Street. Rumors spread quickly among the townspeople that the soldiers planned a wholesale slaughter of the inhabitants. Local Tories were attacked and beaten in the streets. British officers and soldiers also found it dangerous to walk through Boston without armed escorts that night.

Moderate Patriot leaders pleaded with Lieutenant Governor Hutchinson, the leading civil official in town, to remove Preston's troops from King Street before their presence provoked further retaliation from the crowd. Hutchinson approached the troops and exchanged some harsh words with Preston. But he declined to order the soldiers back to quarters. Instead, he addressed the people from a balcony of the Town House. He urged them to retire peacefully, promising that he would do everything possible to ensure a full inquiry into the shooting. "The law shall have its course," he shouted. "I will live and die by the law." Apparently, this was the view of the many Bostonians in the crowd who left quietly. Hundreds remained, however. They demanded both immediate action against the British soldiers and removal of the troops from Boston's streets. Preston's superior officer, Lieutenant Colonel Maurice Carr, feared a renewed confrontation between the crowd and the troops. He ordered the soldiers on King Street to abandon street-firing formation and return to their barracks. As the troops marched off, the crowd—now silent and somber—dispersed.

At 2 A.M. on March 6 the town sheriff served a warrant on Captain Preston for his role in the episode. Preston surrendered an hour later. A few hours afterward, the eight redcoats in Preston's sentry party were also imprisoned. All nine were charged with murder. Scattered incidents between individual soldiers and townsmen punctured the morning calm on March 6, but Boston remained generally quiet.

After the arrest of Preston and his men, Boston drew back from the brink of civil disorder. Hutchinson and Carr were not the only ones who feared a bloodbath. Most responsible Patriot leaders shared their anxieties. They believed that the continued presence of troops among angry townspeople would only provoke violence on an uncontrollable scale. So they urged the removal of British troops from the town itself to Castle William, an island fort in Boston harbor.

Bostonians were still outraged over the massacre. At a town meeting on March 6, which was dominated by Samuel Adams and other Patriots, people demanded removal of the British troops. Hutchinson tried to compromise between his loyalty to the crown and his recognition of the town's anger. He ordered only Preston's regiment, the 29th, to Castle William.

The town meeting remained dissatisfied. On March 10 it sent a committee led by Samuel Adams to see Hutchinson. The group demanded that the remaining British regiment be ordered out of town. Hutchinson and his advisers had no choice but to submit. They ordered the 14th Regiment, the last British troops in Boston, to depart the following day for Castle William. Boston now returned to the control of its own, Patriot-dominated town meeting. The remaining royal dig-

Samuel Adams, who did much to bring about American independence, cared more for causes than his own comfort. Friends helped support him and his family and he lived his last years in what he called "honorable poverty."

nitaries—Hutchinson, the customs commissioners, and lesser officials—could not direct the course of events without assistance from troops. The Patriots had no further need for nightly mobs to confront crown authority. Thus the immediate threat of civil disorder ended.

With the troops gone from Boston, the Patriots turned their attention to settling accounts with the imprisoned soldiers. On March 12 the *Gazette* employed the term "massacre" in connection with the events of March 5. This was the first public use of the term. A week later, on March 19, Boston's town meeting approved printing a version of the events that justified the behavior of the rioters and condemned the British soldiers. Entitled *A Short History of the Horrid Massacre at Boston,* the pamphlet was dispatched on fast ships to England to soften British anger at the Bostonians' conduct toward the troops. The Patriots decided not to distribute the pamphlet in Boston itself, lest it prejudice the soldiers' trials.

Also on March 19, the town meeting petitioned Hutchinson for an early trial of the prisoners. The lieutenant governor and other Loyalists resisted, considering the aroused state of emotions in Boston regarding Preston and his men. "I have assurances from the court," Preston wrote General Gage on April 1, "that they will continue [postpone] the trial until the last week in May although great pains are being taken to intimidate the judges and compel them to bring it on sooner." Hutchinson's concern for a fair trial seemed even more understandable after the end of Ebenezer Richardson's trial. On April 21 a Boston jury found Richardson guilty of killing Christopher Seider. They did so despite the judge's instruction from the bench that Richardson had clearly committed justifiable homicide in self-defense.

Soon after the massacre, both Tories and Patriots began arguing that the incident had been part of a prearranged scheme of wholesale murder on the part of their opponents. Such assertions appeared in versions of the incident prepared by the British military authorities and in the town meeting's *Short History*. A later town meeting on May 15 issued statements that referred to "a deep-laid and desperate plan of imperial despotism for the extinction of all civil liberty" in the American colonies. Hutchinson viewed the behavior of Adams and the Patriots as simply the "designs of particular persons to bring about a revolution, and to attain to independency." In the aftermath of the massacre, belief in conspiratorial plots hardened into obsessions on both sides. Loyalists and Patriots seemed worlds apart, and Boston was split into two camps. "They call me a brainless Tory," said one local gentleman. "But tell me which is better—to be ruled by one tyrant three thousand miles away, or by three thousand tyrants not one mile away?" Aware of this tension, Hutchinson and other crown dignitaries employed various legal devices to delay proceedings against Preston and his soldiers. They were finally indicted in September.

John Adams was forty-one when this drawing was made, in 1776. His grandson later described him as "grave and imposing, but not unbending" and as one who "delighted in social conversation."

Preston's trial began on October 24. Ironically, one of his prosecutors was a well-known Tory, Samuel Quincy. And his defense was undertaken by two of the colony's leading Patriot lawyers, John Adams (Samuel Adams' cousin) and Josiah Quincy (Samuel Quincy's brother). There is some evidence that Samuel Adams and other Patriot leaders encouraged John Adams and Josiah Quincy to act as defense counsel, not wishing the British government or public to feel that Boston had failed to provide a fair trial.

Whatever the motives, Adams and Quincy performed brilliantly. Actually, Preston's chances for acquittal seemed good from the start, especially since five acknowledged Tories were among the jury. The failure or inability of Patriot leaders to pack the jury with hostile Bostonians suggests that the Patriots were less concerned with convicting Preston and his men than with exploiting the trial as propaganda.

A parade of prosecution and defense witnesses testified to the different British and Bostonian versions of the events on King Street. James Brewer's testimony for the prosecution summarized the claim that the soldiers had lacked sufficient provocation to fire into the crowd.

Q. Did you see anything thrown at the soldiers?
A. No.
Q. Did you hear anybody call them names?
A. No.
Q. Did you hear any threatening speeches?
A. No, except that the people cried "Fire! Fire!" The word "fire" was on everybody's mouth.
Q. Did you take that to be the cry of fire, or bidding the soldiers fire?
A. I cannot tell now what I thought then.
Q. Did you see anything extraordinary, to induce them to fire that gun?
A. Nothing, but a short stick was thrown, which seemed to go clear over all the soldiers' heads.

A typical statement for the defense came in the testimony of Newton Prince:

I ran to the door of my house and heard the cry of fire. I went out and asked where the fire was; somebody said it was something better than fire. I met some with clubs, some with buckets and bags, and some running before me with sticks in their hands. There were a number of people by the west door of the Town House. They said, "Let's go and attack the Main Guard." After a while they huzzahed and went down King Street; they went down to the Custom House, and

> I went down. There were people all round the soldiers. I saw people with sticks striking on the guns.

> Q. Did you hear at that time they were striking, the cry of "fire, fire!"?
> A. Yes, the crowd said "Fire, fire, damn you! Fire, fire, you lobsters![4] Fire, you dare not fire!"

At several points during Captain Preston's trial—and later during the other soldiers' trial—John Adams threatened to resign as defense attorney because his co-counsel, Josiah Quincy, wished to introduce evidence that Bostonians had triggered the violence. Adams felt that the British soldiers could be acquitted without putting Boston and the Patriot cause itself on trial.

From the manner in which they dealt with Boston itself, the closing arguments by prosecution and defense lawyers used at the soldiers' trial illustrated the basic issues of Preston's case as well. The chief prosecutor, Robert Treat Paine, tried to absolve the mob itself of blame for the shooting. He answered yes to his own question: "Was it lawful for the inhabitants of Boston to walk the streets that evening and with sticks? Was it lawful for them to run about crying 'fire!'?" And he responded no to this critical question: "Must they be answerable for the rude speech of every person that happens to be near them, when it does not appear they assented to them and joined in putting them in execution?" In other words, Paine thundered, Preston's company of sentries had no lawful right to fire into the crowd. They were, therefore, guilty of murder.

While Paine defended the radical mob's behavior, lawyer Josiah Quincy (defense lawyer for the sentries as well as for Preston) denied the importance, perhaps even the existence, of such a mob. He insisted that

> Boston and its inhabitants have no more to do with this cause than you or any other two members of the community. The inhabitants of Boston, by no rules of law, justice, or common sense, can be supposed answerable for the unjustifiable conduct of a few individuals hastily assembled in the streets.

In other words, Quincy argued that the crowd's responsibility for provoking the incident was essentially different from the soldiers' guilt or innocence of the murder charge itself. Yet Quincy went on to defend the soldiers' innocence of murder, at the same time defending Boston against those who would criticize it.

Who, then, was to blame for the massacre? The prosecutor pointed to outside agitators who had provoked the violence, and he mentioned

---

[4] "Lobsters" was a slang term for British soldiers because of the red coats they wore.

two such groups in his summation. One was "sailors and foreigners of the lower class who are fond of mingling with such commotions and pushing on a disorder of which they feel not the consequences." The other was the British army. The crowd's threatening words and hostile stirrings were only natural "among a free people oppressed and galled with the ravagings of an ungoverned soldiery, and were not to be construed as evidence of an insurrection or a design to put in execution the supposed threats." John Adams picked up the outsider theme and made it the pivotal argument of his defense summation. Although the British did not come out unscathed, the soldiers' defender obviously directed his eloquence against the mob itself. But *what* mob? Composed of *whom*?

> The plain English is, gentlemen, that most of the mob was probably a motley rabble of saucy boys, Negroes and mulattoes, Irish teagues,[5] and outlandish jack tarrs [sailors]. There was a mob in Boston on the 5th of March that attacked a party of soldiers. And indeed, from the nature of things, soldiers quartered in a populous town will always occasion two mobs where they prevent one. They are wretched conservators of the peace!

Judge Edmund Trowbridge, shrewdest of the three-judge panel that presided at both trials, told the jury that if they were satisfied "that the sentinel was insulted and that Captain Preston and his party went to assist him, it was doubtless excusable homicide, if not justifiable." Trowbridge went on to deny the conspiracy theories of the massacre. He stated that there had been "no concerted plan on either side," only the provocative actions of an angry crowd and the nervous reaction of frightened soldiers. In that situation "any little spark would kindle a great fire—and five lives were sacrificed to a squabble between the sentry [Private White] and Piemont's barber's boy [Edward Garrick]." The jury at Preston's trial appeared to agree with the judge. On October 30 it found the officer not guilty.

The second trial began on November 27 and ended on December 5. Six of the eight soldiers were also found not guilty. The two others, Matthew Kilroy and Hugh Montgomery, were found guilty of manslaughter. Both soldiers later used a legal technicality to avoid imprisonment. Nine months from the day of the massacre itself, the eight men who had fired their weapons into the King Street crowd had all returned to their military posts. As for the massacre, its fame was only beginning.

[5] "Teague," from the Irish name "Tadhg," was a nickname for an Irishman.

Boston was peaceful for a brief period after repeal of the Townshend Acts. In colony after colony during 1770 merchants repudiated their nonimportation agreements. They swiftly resumed trade with Great Britain so that competitors from other areas would not take over their business. Only Boston held firm, demanding that England repeal the remaining duty on tea and renounce similar taxes in the future. Finally, Boston too had to accept the inevitable and abandon nonimportation.

By the end of 1770 the Patriot movement had lost momentum throughout British North America. The spark of rebellion that had flared momentarily at the time of the massacre now flickered low. Samuel Adams confessed in a letter of April 1771:

> The generality are necessarily engaged in application to private business for the support of their own families. When at a lucky season the public are awakened to a sense of danger, and a manly resentment is enkindled, it is difficult, for so many separate communities as there are in all the colonies, to agree in one consistent plan of opposition.

Boston, as Samuel Adams recognized, was the symbol and center of colonial resistance. The game of rebellion would continue to be played first in that throbbing seaport town, where so many prominent and provincial political, economic, and intellectual leaders resided. As part of their campaign to rekindle colonial resistance to Great Britain, Boston's Patriots produced a number of posters, pamphlets, engravings, and poems. Many of them dealt with the massacre. The events of March 5 began filtering into the daily language of patriotic protest as

The Green Dragon Tavern, on Water Street in Boston, was a favorite gathering place for the Sons of Liberty. It was here that they planned the Boston tea party.

American Patriots reviewed for their audiences the major lessons of the
massacre—namely, that the proper response to tyranny was resistance, and that true resistance usually meant the sacrifice of life as well as property. The following appeared in the Boston *Gazette*:

Let THESE Things be told to Posterity!

And handed down
From Generation to Generation
'Till time shall be no more!
Forever may AMERICA be preserved,
From weak and wicked monarchs,
Tyrannical Ministers,
Abandoned Governors,
Their Underlings and Hirelings!
And may the
Machinations of artful, designing wretches,
Who would ENSLAVE THIS People
Come to an end.

Every March 5, in the years that followed the King Street killings, Boston remembered. On that anniversary day a major speech was given to commemorate the five martyrs. The speeches were highly emotional in tone. They were concerned more with evoking the images of bloodstained streets and dying victims than with asserting political and constitutional arguments for freedom. Leading Patriots delivered the orations. For example, John Hancock spoke in 1774. The 1775 oration was given by Joseph Warren, whose heated remarks stirred a large audience in Faneuil Hall. When Warren cried out the words "bloody massacre" for the first time, an irreverent listener, presumably a Tory, is said to have shouted back, "Oh fie!" Many of those in the gallery, believing that the speaker had shouted "Fire!" began jumping out of windows. They collided on the ground with a passing regiment of parading British soldiers, whose fife and drum contingent blared so noisily that some of those inside the hall began to suspect another massacre. The incident amused bystanders and participants alike. But New England had no further humorous moments in connection with the annual observances of the massacre. On March 5 of the following year, Peter Thatcher addressed the gathering with a passionate plea for American independence. It concluded simply: "O God, let America be free!"

6

The Coming of Independence

In Many Ways, there was nothing new about the crisis of 1770 in Massachusetts. The troubles of Governors Bernard and Hutchinson had been experienced earlier by many other royal officials in other colonies. At least as far back as the days of Sir William Berkeley in Virginia, the relationship between American colonists and royal officials had been a troubled one. Powerful stresses and strains were built into the very structure of the British Empire. Many royal governors had complained about how the colonists tried to escape, bypass, or limit British control of colonial life and trade.

What had changed in the years since Berkeley had less to do with the type of quarrel between governors and colonists than with the context of their argument. Conflicts in Boston and elsewhere grew heated in the 1760s. They stemmed from rapidly changing views on both sides of the Atlantic. These views involved colonial rights and obligations as British subjects.

The situation of the colonists before the 1760s had seemed obvious. They swore, and felt, loyalty to the British crown. But they gave their own colony first allegiance. Public life centered in colonial counties, towns, and cities. Within each province colonists had always taken certain rights and privileges for granted. Among these were the common law, the protection of private property, the right to representative legislatures, and the privilege of trial by jury.

Colonial obligations to the mother country seemed equally clear. Many of these involved trade and its regulation.

A CENTURY OF "SALUTARY NEGLECT"

In general, the British government followed a mercantilist policy in relation to its American colonies. The British believed that all their colonies existed mainly to bring benefits to the mother country. Mercantilism, in theory, represented a reasonable division of economic labor between colonies and mother country. The mother country would produce most of the manufactured goods needed by the empire. The col-

British restrictions on colonial commerce were a basic cause of the American revolution. In this dockside scene, Virginia tobacco is being loaded for export.

onies would produce raw materials. In some cases Britain even paid bounties (as on naval stores[1] and indigo) to encourage colonial production. With other products, such as tobacco, Englishmen living at home were forbidden to compete with colonial producers.

In carrying out its mercantilist policies, England passed a number of trade regulations known as the Navigation Acts. Their purpose was to ensure that American commerce would "terminate in the advantage of the Mother State, unto whom it owes its being and protection." Another purpose was to limit the amount of colonial produce carried to Europe in foreign ships, especially those of the Dutch.

The Navigation Act of 1660 was a major trade law affecting the American colonies. It declared that goods from the American colonies could be transported in English ships only. The English crown also wanted to limit profits made by colonial shippers from the sale of American produce. So the 1660 Navigation Act enumerated certain commodities such as tobacco, sugar, indigo, and cotton (most of English America's leading exports). These commodities could be shipped to points outside the empire only from England. Later acts added to the enumerated list new sources of trade almost as fast as Americans developed them—molasses, naval stores, rice, and furs.

It was easier to pass such laws than to enforce them. Smuggling was common. It was not difficult for a colonial merchant to ship enumerated goods to French colonies in America or even to mainland Europe. Breaking the law was all the easier because British colonial administration during the seventeenth and eighteenth centuries was very disorganized. Several different royal agencies in the British government helped to set early policies for the mainland colonies.[2] In 1696 an agency known as the Board of Trade was created to bring some degree of order to

[1] Naval stores were certain products needed to operate British navy and merchant ships; they included hemp, tar, and resin.

[2] That is, British North American colonies other than those in the West Indies.

colonial administration. Throughout the eighteenth century the Board of Trade had primary responsibility for shaping royal policy in America. (It was the Board of Trade, for example, that approved the dispatch of troops to Boston in 1768.)

Administrative reorganization did not solve all of Britain's colonial problems. For one thing, political conflicts, both internal and external, often preoccupied the mother country. Those responsible for colonial regulation were generally too busy with other concerns to worry about widespread smuggling in America. Even if British officials had wished to enforce the laws more rigorously, they had few customs officers and few ships for coastal patrol. Thus, from the viewpoint of British imperial control, the century after 1660 was accurately called a period of "salutary neglect."

As far as the colonists were concerned, they had relatively few complaints about the imperial system during this period. It seemed to meet the needs of a largely undeveloped, labor-starved group of provinces that specialized in producing raw materials. Colonial commerce and agriculture matured under mild royal supervision. Successive Board of Trade members rarely interfered when American merchants violated the Navigation Acts with regularity.

Colonial Government From his distant London office, a British administrator may easily have winked at American violations of the law. It was much more difficult, however, for a royal governor stationed in one of the colonies to keep his good humor.

By 1760 eight of the thirteen colonies were under direct royal control (see chart, p. 72). In these colonies, governors like Francis Bernard or Thomas Hutchinson received their appointments directly from the king. In every royal colony except Massachusetts (where the council was elective), the governor appointed a council, which usually included the wealthiest and most distinguished citizens in the colony.

On paper a royal governor looked unbeatable. His duties were numerous. He enforced royal legislation. He summoned and adjourned colonial assemblies—or dissolved them whenever their actions threatened royal authority. He vetoed colonial statutes if they conflicted with British law. He also commanded the provincial militia and appointed local judges. Despite these impressive powers, governors, like Bernard in Massachusetts, often found themselves isolated among unfriendly colonists and lacking the means to enforce royal authority against colonial assemblies.

In a way, the colonial assemblies were the key. For although the king appointed the colonial governors, the assemblies paid their salaries. And they did so irritably, ungenerously, and on a year-to-year basis. Each mainland British colony had an assembly that controlled the colony's purse strings. In each colony the assemblies had established their right long before the 1770s to initiate legislation, levy taxes, and appropriate money—including the governor's salary—on a yearly basis. Except for Pennsylvania, all the colonies had two-house (bicameral) assemblies. The elected lower house passed laws, assessed taxes, and dispensed funds. The upper house, appointed by the king in royal colonies, advised the governor.

By passing tax measures that had only limited duration, an assembly ensured that it would be called into session regularly by any royal governor who needed more revenue quickly. Moreover, by stating how money raised by specific taxes should be spent, an assembly further limited the governor's freedom of action. In extreme cases of conflict with crown officials, a colonial assembly might resort to the effective practice of withholding salaries. The source of an assembly's power came not only from the fact that it was elected by the people. There was also widespread awareness of its actions among voters and nonvoters alike, through such means as newspapers, political meetings, and even sermons.

Estimates differ concerning the number of colonists who met the requirements for voting in the mid-eighteenth century. Voters had to be Christians, though not of any particular religious

Benjamin Franklin

"Americans do not inquire concerning a stranger, *What is he?* but, *What can he do?*" Benjamin Franklin commented thus on the opportunities available to anyone in colonial America. In America, he observed, any industrious young man could become "self-made," rising from poverty and obscurity to fame and wealth. One such individual was Franklin himself. On his deathbed in 1790, he could claim to have been a printer, author, scientist, inventor, philanthropist, and diplomat.

Franklin was born in Boston in 1706, the fifteenth child and youngest son of a family of seventeen children. He left school at the age of ten. First he was an apprentice to his father, a candle- and soap-maker, and then to his brother, a printer. At the age of seventeen he ran away to Philadelphia.

Within seven years Franklin had bought the weekly newspaper, the *Pennsylvania Gazette.* He rescued it from near-bankruptcy, so that it ran profitably for the next thirty-six years. Its success was due largely to Franklin's boldness in politics and his sense of humor.

During these same years Franklin created the overwhelmingly popular *Poor Richard's Almanack,* published yearly from 1732 to 1757. It contained local information for all the colonies and sayings on the virtues of thrift and hard work. It was "Poor Richard" who said that "A penny saved is a penny earned" and "Time is money."

Franklin grew wealthy. He devoted much of his energy to making Philadelphia a better city. (This combination of wealth and public service had become typically American.) He initiated streetlighting, police and fire protection, and a colony-wide militia. He helped establish a circulating library—the first in the United States—the American Philosophical Society, and the University of Pennsylvania. His scientific and inventive genius, typically American in its practical outlook, extended from experiments in electricity to the invention of bifocal

Yale University
Art Gallery

glasses and the Franklin stove. By the age of forty Franklin was a distinctly successful man. But, he wrote his mother, he would rather have it said that "he lived usefully," than "he died rich."

Unquestionably Philadelphia's most prominent citizen, Franklin was sent to London in 1757 to act as agent for Pennsylvania. He emerged as a spokesman for American independence. When he returned home, the Revolution had already broken out. He served in the Second Continental Congress and in 1776 went to France to negotiate for financial and military aid. Franklin charmed the French with his wit, wisdom, and kindness. His personal popularity added much to the success of his diplomatic mission.

When Franklin returned to his beloved Philadelphia, he received a hero's welcome. He was elected president (mayor) of the city. And at the age of eighty-one he became a delegate to the Constitutional Convention. His interest in the welfare of mankind prompted him to sign a petition to Congress calling for the abolition of slavery. Death claimed him three months later. Philadelphia lost its most famous citizen, and the young nation lost a man who embodied its very spirit.

denomination. They were required to own a certain amount of property. The property requirement usually involved owning an amount of land or its monetary equivalent that was not unreasonably high. In almost every colony property qualifications for voting were met by a large majority of the *white, free, male* population. (These were, of course, important restrictions, since they excluded free blacks, slaves, and women.) The exact proportion of voters probably ranged from 50 to 75 percent in most colonies. In Massachusetts, for example—a colony composed mainly of small family-owned farms—more than 80 percent of the male population could have voted at the time of the Revolution.

Whatever royal governors or imperial legislation might have said on the matter, every colonial assembly already exercised the functions of local self-government by 1750. The assemblies had a long tradition of victory in asserting their claims for colonial autonomy. Supporting the assemblies' actions were majorities of each colony's qualified voters. Even most leading Tories—men such as Thomas Hutchinson, for example—argued for a greater measure of internal self-government in the American provinces.

CONFLICT WITH FRANCE

From their earliest days the mainland English settlements had waged almost continuous warfare against Indian tribes and European settlements along their borders. As the seventeenth century drew to a close, the chief European rival for control of North America was France. Her trading posts and fortified settlements ringed the British colonies like a vise from the eastern tip of Canada to the mouth of the Mississippi River. Aiding the French were thousands of Indians—great tribes like the Hurons—with whom they traded furs. The powerful tribes of the Iroquois Confederation, however, were allies of the British.

France and Britain fought a series of four wars between 1689 and 1763. At stake were territories in Europe and possessions throughout the overseas empires of the two nations. In America, British troops were aided by American militia and their Indian allies in their fight against combined French and Indian forces.

The first of these wars, known in America as King William's War (1689–97), ended inconclusively. In the next war, Queen Anne's War (1702–13), the British won most of the battles, both in Europe and America. As a result, Britain acquired Nova Scotia, Newfoundland, and the Hudson Bay region of Canada. The third conflict, called King George's War (1740–48) in America, ended as indecisively as King William's War. But the French and Indian War, the fourth and last round of fighting, was much more decisive. It began in the spring of 1754.

The Albany Congress   As war began, the American colonies displayed in dramatic fashion their divided condition and mutual suspiciousness. What made the display even more striking was the fact that the first attempt to achieve intercolonial unity was organized by none other than the British Board of Trade.

The Board of Trade wanted the colonists to meet with Britain's Iroquois allies. The purpose of the meeting was to discuss defense measures to be taken against the French and their Indian allies. The British also wanted to encourage cooperation among the various colonial militias, which had been sadly lacking up to this time. The result was the Albany Congress, which met in June and July of 1754. Seven colonies sent delegates. Among them were Thomas Hutchinson of Massachusetts and Benjamin Franklin of Pennsylvania (see page 141).

Once the meeting began, Franklin went beyond the British agenda and proposed instead a general plan of intercolonial union. According to Franklin's plan of union, the king would appoint a president-general, a kind of supergovernor, presumably with the usual lack of enforcement authority. The provincial assemblies would be represented in proportion to their tax payments in a grand council, a kind of superassembly somewhat like our present-day Congress. Taxes on each colony would support the grand

British General Braddock was ambushed by French and Indians near Fort Duquesne (the site of Pittsburgh). After having five horses shot from under him, he was mortally wounded.

council's control of intercolonial defense, Indian relations, and westward expansion. The central body would be allowed to raise an army and navy and build forts and settlements. The president-general, however (like the royal governors), could veto any laws in the king's name.

The Albany Congress approved the essential outlines of Franklin's plan and submitted it to the colonial assemblies. Four of these simply ignored the proposal. The other three rejected it, agreeing with the Boston town meeting that the Albany Plan endangered popular liberties.

The French and Indian War In the beginning this conflict (also known as the Seven Years' War) went badly for the British. Colonial assemblies were reluctant to contribute men and money to the fight. The result was a series of British defeats along the frontier line with

French Canada.[3] Not until William Pitt became prime minister in 1757 did the British war effort begin to take shape. For one thing, Pitt shifted the war's main emphasis from Europe (on which it had centered during the earlier three Anglo-French conflicts) to the empire. Here Pitt assigned most of Britain's military strength. Pitt bankrupted the national treasury to pay for additional regiments of British troops to send to America.

In order to win over the colonial assemblies, Pitt directed British military officials to assume the costs of feeding and arming colonial militia. The British also promised to repay the assemblies for money they spent to supply and pay

[3] One American who got his first taste of battle in this conflict was George Washington. As a young officer with British General Edward Braddock, he took part in an unsuccessful campaign against the French near what is now Pittsburgh.

George III, long thought to have become insane in later life, probably suffered from a rare inherited disease.

additional volunteers. Such generosity swelled the ranks of colonial regiments that fought alongside British redcoats in subduing the French.

The British won a series of military victories under aggressive new commanders such as James Wolfe and Jeffrey Amherst. In 1759 they captured Quebec from the French, who were led by the Marquis de Montcalm. Within a year all of French Canada lay in British hands. In the Treaty of Paris in 1763, France surrendered all of her North American possessions east of the Mississippi from Canada to Florida. The exception was Louisiana, which France had earlier ceded to its ally Spain.

During the war all did not go smoothly between Britain and her colonies. For one thing, Pitt insisted on rigorously enforcing the Navigation Acts in America. British warships pa-

trolled in force to choke off trade with the enemy.

Northern colonial merchants were also outraged by Britain's intensified hunt for smuggled goods through the use of so-called general writs of assistance. These were unlimited search warrants good for the entire period of a king's reign. They allowed customs officers to enter any building in daytime to hunt, without having prior evidence, for illegally imported goods.

After the death of King George II in 1760, Boston merchants (many of whom later led the nonimportation campaign) retained James Otis, one of the colony's best lawyers, to argue the illegality of the writs in order to prevent their renewal under the new king, George III. Otis lost his case, and the writs were upheld. Often during the following decade, royal customs officials barged unannounced into Boston warehouses and homes searching for smuggled goods.

INCREASED BRITISH CONTROL

After the French and Indian War it became clear that the British intended to regulate their American provinces much more closely and thoroughly in the future than they had in the past. One important decision involved the new trans-Appalachian territories recently acquired from the French. Even before 1754, settlers had begun moving into the rich Ohio Valley. Land companies were organized to take control of the region's fur trade and to explore other opportunities. Then the British government issued the Proclamation of 1763 banning, for an indefinite time, settlement and land grants beyond the crest of the Appalachian Mountains. Land speculators (among them George Washington) denounced British efforts to close off the West. American settlement and land speculation continued.

Another problem was financial. Who would pick up the tab for Britain's costly victory over France? Pitt's war strategy had succeeded, but in the process England had spent £82 million. Despite heavy wartime taxation, the British national debt had run up to £130 million by 1764. Every leading British minister during the

1760s and 1770s agreed that it was only fair for the American colonies to share in paying off the war debts. After all, they reasoned, the mainland provinces had achieved virtually complete security on their borders at almost no cost to themselves.

Americans disagreed with the British argument that Parliament had the right to tax colonists along with other British subjects. Throughout the eighteenth century most Americans had accepted Parliament's right to legislate for the colonies while denying its right to tax them. Colonial assemblies believed that they had won the exclusive right to initiate taxes within their own provinces.

The Sugar Act When George Grenville became British finance minister in 1763, he made an embarrassing discovery: the customs service in America cost the British government four times as much in salaries as it collected in revenues! Grenville's solution was a revenue-raising bill that came to be known as the Sugar Act.

Earlier in the century the British had taxed foreign molasses at the rate of sixpence a gallon in order to encourage colonials to purchase this product from the British West Indies. The regulation was largely ignored. American rum distillers found it much cheaper to bribe customs officials (at a penny a gallon) so they could smuggle in cheaper molasses from the French West Indies. Grenville's Sugar Act of 1764 was designed to eliminate such colonial trading freedom.

The new statute lowered the molasses duty from six to three pence. The new duty applied to both British and foreign molasses entering the colonies. This provision transformed a trade-regulating device into a revenue-producing tax. The Sugar Act also placed new tax duties on such commodities as sugar, indigo, wine, and textiles.

More upsetting to the colonists than the taxes themselves was Parliament's obvious determination to enforce their collection. Colonial shipowners now had to file official papers for every vessel leaving or entering American har-

NORTH AMERICA IN 1754

NORTH AMERICA IN 1763

PROCLAMATION LINE

British
French
Spanish
Russian
Unexplored or disputed

bors. Moreover, accused violators of the Sugar Act would be tried in admiralty (naval) courts distant from their hometowns or cities. Such courts operated without juries and under rules according to which a defendant was considered guilty until proved innocent. Provincial merchant smugglers had come to depend on sympathetic local juries or judges (men like Boston's justice of the peace William Molineux, who had persuaded a mob to surrender Ebenezer Richardson). Local jurors and judges generally gave violators of British trade regulations what the defendants wished—freedom, not justice.

A storm of protest over the Sugar Act spread quickly through the colonies. It was sparked by commercial cities like Boston, which reminded their rural countrymen of the stake all Americans had in the new British policies. "If our trade may be taxed, why not our lands?"

asked the Boston town meeting in a thumping denunciation of the Sugar Act. "Why not the produce of our lands and everything we possess or make use of?" Widespread smuggling continued. Yearly collections of revenue from the Sugar Act averaged a ridiculously small £20,000.

Grenville (and many other British officials) failed to realize that, to provincial Americans, their freedom as British subjects involved the right of their assemblies alone to levy taxes over them. Americans were as much concerned with the precedent set by the Sugar Act as with its actual enforcement. The rights of Englishmen, colonists argued, depended upon a person's right—as James Otis put it—to be "free from all taxes but what he consents to in person, or by his representative." Actually, the colonists did lack representation in Parliament; by and large, however, they did not want it. They recognized

American colonists sometimes used violent methods to intimidate those who were supposed to collect Stamp Act taxes. With the tax collector looking on in dismay, a New Hampshire mob stones his effigy and carries a coffin through the streets.

shrewdly that this would lead to tighter English control of provincial affairs.

Additional Regulations Colonial protests over the Sugar Act did not lessen Grenville's interest in squeezing additional revenue out of North America. In March 1765 Parliament passed the Stamp Act. It required Americans to buy tax stamps for newspapers, legal documents, and other types of printed matter. Englishmen had paid such a tax for decades. Grenville made certain to mention that revenues raised from the new tax, which was to take effect in November 1765, would be applied entirely to "the defense of the colonies."

A related measure sponsored by Grenville was the Quartering Act, passed in May 1765. It obliged colonial assemblies to furnish British troops stationed in their colonies with adequate living quarters and provisions. Many colonists considered the timing strange. Britain had kept almost no royal troops garrisoned in America when the French, the Spanish, and the Indians menaced the western borders of almost every colony. Now she planned to station soldiers in America after this threat had been removed. Americans realized that the troops were actually being sent to enforce royal authority—which they did with mixed results in Boston three years later.

The Stamp Act and Quartering Act fed the growing suspicion of Britain among knowledgeable Americans. Had the British government deliberately set out to deny them freedoms they had previously exercised? Some of these might be called negative freedoms—the absence of British taxation, the lack of a British army in their midst, lax enforcement of the Navigation Acts. Others were positive—trial by local juries, the liberty to expand westward.

None of the king's ministers would have denied that Britain meant to change its permissive ways in North America. They would have argued that Parliament did not wish to deny legitimate colonial rights. It wanted only to remind the mainland colonies of their equally legitimate responsibilities toward the mother country. In practice, however, Britain's effort to tighten the parental screws triggered an immediate protest from her fully grown New World children.

American Opposition The Stamp Act generated the first successfully organized intercolonial opposition to British policy. It took the form of almost complete resistance to buying the required stamps. For a lawyer, merchant, newspaper editor, small businessman, or even a planter, the stamps represented both a costly expense and an illegal parliamentary attack on colonial liberties. As usual, resistance centered in the commercial cities and towns, to which Britain had sent most of the stamps and tax collectors. For the first (but hardly the last) time in the struggle, Boston became the center of both legal and violent protest.

The Massachusetts assembly took the lead in June 1765, when it proposed an intercolonial meeting to unify opposition to parliamentary taxation. Boston mobs—often organized by the same Sons of Liberty who would prove so effective later in the decade—ransacked the homes of several British officials, including the chief royal stamp collector. The mobs also burned Lieutenant Governor Thomas Hutchinson's elegant mansion to the ground, destroyed important government records, and forced several stamp distributors to resign their offices. Riotous Sons of Liberty played a similar role in New York City and elsewhere.

Meanwhile, peaceful forms of protest were having an even more unsettling effect on British policy. As early as May 1765, a young lawyer named Patrick Henry introduced a series of resolutions in the Virginia House of Burgesses. They asserted that this body alone had the right to tax Virginians. The House of Burgesses adopted the more moderate of Henry's resolutions, but it rejected his call for outright resistance to collection of stamp taxes. Most other colonial assemblies followed Virginia's lead and passed similar resolutions, all of which Parliament ignored.

But the British government could hardly

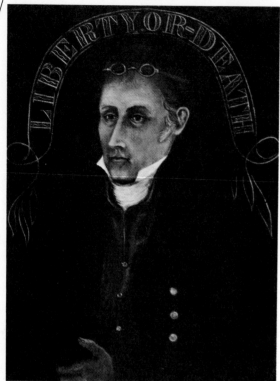

Patrick Henry's famous phrase was part of a 1775 speech urging Virginia to prepare for her own defense.

overlook the resolutions passed by an intercolonial Stamp Act Congress, first proposed by Massachusetts. The assemblies of nine colonies were represented when this congress convened in October 1765 in New York City. Although the congress assured Parliament of "all due subordination," it denied that Britain had the right either to tax the colonists or to try Americans in admiralty courts. Furthermore, the delegates demanded immediate repeal of both the Sugar Act and the Stamp Act.

In order to put teeth into these demands, more than a thousand colonial merchants from all the major trading cities quickly organized an effective boycott of British manufactured goods. This was the first of several times that colonial economic pressures through such nonimportation agreements forced changes in British policy. The merchants played a crucial role in the struggle with Britain—so crucial that the strength

of colonial resistance at any given moment depended to a large degree on the extent of merchant support.

Some Americans—including militants like Samuel Adams—began to advocate independence and revolution. They argued that a people had the right to change or overthrow a government that systematically violated people's rights. Such opinions frightened members of Parliament. William Pitt urged repeal of the Stamp Act on the grounds that doing so would restore the loyalty of most moderate Americans and isolate the minority of radicals: "If we repeal the Act, we shall have all the sober part of America on our side, and we shall easily be able to chastize the few hot-headed republicans among them." Pitt might also have reminded his colleagues that the Stamp Act had proved a total failure. It earned no revenue, since no Americans could be found who were brave enough to collect the tax. American business continued as usual—unstamped—while British manufacturers suffered from an almost total boycott of their goods in America.

Responding finally to this mixture of economic and political factors, Parliament repealed the Stamp Act in March 1766. The most important long-term effect of the Stamp Act protests was that Americans of all classes and backgrounds had begun learning the habit of resistance.

A DEEPENING CRISIS

Americans might have celebrated the repeal of the Stamp Act a bit more heartily had not Parliament coupled its repeal with passage of another measure. This was the Declaratory Act, which reaffirmed colonial subordination. It also asserted Parliament's right to pass any law it wished (presumably, therefore, any *tax* law), "to bind the colonies and people of America."

In 1767 a new British finance minister, Charles Townshend, exercised this option. He secured a new program of colonial duties, to be placed on imports of items such as paper, tea, lead, paint, and glass. Townshend believed somewhat naïvely, that his move would produce much-needed revenue. Instead, he succeeded only in raising again the unsettled issues of the Stamp Act crisis.

Once more, Massachusetts led intercolonial resistance. Its assembly sent a Circular Letter to the other colonial legislatures urging some form of united opposition similar to the Stamp Act Congress. The Circular Letter denied that Massachusetts advocated independence. Still, the British government considered the letter dangerous enough to demand that the assembly rescind it. When the assembly refused, Governor Bernard, on orders from London, prevented the legislators from meeting in 1768. Special town meetings summoned delegates to an extralegal convention to discuss the matter. It was at this point that two regiments of British troops were sent to occupy Boston and protect the unpopular customs commissioners.

The civic turmoil during the next two years was to lead directly to the Boston Massacre. New York City was also the scene of protests and mob violence after Parliament had dissolved the New York assembly for refusing to obey the Quartering Act.

As with the Stamp Act, however, the peaceful boycott of British goods by colonial merchants proved more effective with Parliament than threats or violence. Boston's nonimportation agreement was followed in other cities, among them Providence, Newport, and New York. In the Virginia assembly a set of resolutions sponsored by George Washington supported Massachusetts' Circular Letter. When the royal governor dissolved the assembly, its leaders regrouped informally and endorsed a nonimportation campaign. Throughout the colonies unrest died down only after Parliament had repealed all of the Townshend duties except the tax on tea. The king's new prime minister, Lord North, insisted that this tax remain in order to uphold the supremacy of Parliament in America.

Lacking a dramatic rallying point against Britain, many American Patriots lapsed back easily into provincial loyalties. Even dogged fighters like Samuel Adams were hard-pressed to keep alive much bitterness toward royal authority during the few relatively quiet years that followed repeal of the Townshend Acts. Customs commissioners went about their business. British troops remained quartered in the colonies. And royal governors began to act more confidently.

To counteract this apathy, Samuel Adams and other Sons of Liberty in Boston created a Committee of Correspondence to publicize complaints against the British. The idea spread throughout the colonies and revived intercolonial cooperation. The committees found something juicy to write about when Rhode Islanders burned a British customs patrol boat, the *Gaspée*, after it ran aground in Narragansett Bay. The incident, which occurred in June 1772, led to a royal investigation. To the Patriots' delight, the investigators could find no sign of the culprits. The incident also probably served as a model for another one, involving a shipload of tea, which took place in Boston harbor in December 1773.

The Boston Tea Party   Tea was the colonists' most popular beverage. Few Americans liked Lord North's decision in May 1773 to aid the financially ailing British East India Company by granting it a monopoly in America. Previously, the company had sold its tea to British wholesalers. They in turn sold to American wholesalers, who distributed the tea to local merchants. The British government now proposed to allow the East India Company to sell tea directly through its own agents in America. This step would eliminate both British and colonial middlemen.

The immediate effect was to reduce the retail price of tea considerably. But Americans grasped almost immediately the long-term effect of this action. In return for cheaper tea, they were being asked to accept a new royal interference in normal patterns of colonial commerce. If Parliament could so easily dispose of a profitable longstanding colonial tea trade, then no portion of America's commerce would be safe from British interference.

Public protests against the Tea Act spread

quickly throughout the colonies. They were fueled by passionate letters exchanged by the Committees of Correspondence and by the almost unanimous opposition of colonial newspapers. Once again the British government had unintentionally revived the colonial resistance movement. In New York and Philadelphia royal authorities, fearing violence, ordered the first East India Company tea ships back to Britain without attempting to unload them. In Charleston the tea was simply locked in a warehouse and not offered for sale.

Bostonians, as usual, thought of a more effective way to rally patriotic sentiment and provoke royal anger. On December 16, 1773, a ship called the *Dartmouth* was docked while its captain decided whether to try to unload her cargo of tea. That night, led by the Sons of Liberty, a band of townspeople disguised as Indians boarded the *Dartmouth*. A huge crowd of Bostonians gathered at dockside and cheered as the "Indians" dumped the cargo overboard.

Aftermath: The Intolerable Acts Parliament responded to this "tea party" by passing a series of laws designed to punish Boston. These so-called Coercive Acts took away the city's liberties. One of them closed the port to all commerce until its residents had paid for the spoiled tea. Another authorized the transfer of cases involving British officials from Massachusetts to England in order to escape the hostility of local judges and juries. A third act revised the fundamental structure of Massachusetts' government to strengthen royal authority in the colony. The upper house (Governor's Council) would now be appointed by the king and no longer elected. Town meetings, in which the Sons of Liberty engaged in their most effective organizing, could be held only once a year. Once more British troops appeared in Boston. General Gage, commander-in-chief of all British troops in America, became military governor of Massachusetts. For Bostonians, British occupation and interference with normal political and economic life was far more sweeping than it had been during the controversy over the Townshend duties.

Another statute passed by Parliament at this time was the Quebec Act, which applied to the recently conquered French territory that Americans had already begun settling. The law recognized Roman Catholicism and French civil law—both unpopular with the largely Protestant and largely English colonists of the thirteen colonies. They dubbed the Coercive Acts and the Quebec Act the Intolerable Acts.

Supplies and pledges of support from all over the provinces flowed into Boston. The Intolerable Acts achieved something that had previously eluded Samuel Adams and the Sons of Liberty—the unification of colonial resistance to Britain.

OUTBREAK OF THE REVOLUTION

In June 1774 the Massachusetts assembly asked other colonies to send delegates to a congress where they could agree on common action against the Intolerable Acts. Fifty-five delegates from twelve colonies attended the First Continental Congress, which met at Philadelphia in September. (Georgia was unrepresented at this time but later sent delegates.) The Congress rejected by one vote a compromise proposal for a new scheme of colonial government similar to Franklin's 1754 Albany Plan. The Congress then endorsed a set of resolutions proposed originally by a convention in Suffolk County, Massachusetts. These Suffolk Resolves demanded direct resistance to the Intolerable Acts. The Congress also adopted John Adams' Declaration of Rights and Resolves, a statement of the colonists' constitutional arguments.

The most practical step taken by the Continental Congress involved creating an association to enforce a complete boycott against Britain. Delegates vowed not to import, export, or consume British goods until the crisis had been settled. Before adjourning in October 1774, the delegates also decided to meet again in May 1775.

King George and his ministers had earlier believed that colonial resistance was confined to

In a contemporary British cartoon, Father Time displays a lantern slide to Britannia (the personification of Britain). At center is an exploding teapot—symbolizing the Boston tea party—with victorious American troops at right and defeated redcoats at left.

Massachusetts. Now they convinced themselves that stern measures in that colony would dampen unrest elsewhere. "The New England governments are in a state of rebellion," George III remarked in November 1774. "Blows must decide whether they are to be subject to this country or independent."

General Gage, ordinarily as stubborn as George III himself about punishing colonial resistance, had been sobered by his new role as governor of Massachusetts. He tried to warn London what lay ahead. The provincial militia was then gathering on the outskirts of Boston. To subdue it and reassert parliamentary authority in Massachusetts, Gage wrote Lord North, would require 20,000 additional troops. Until their arrival, Gage recommended that Britain suspend the Coercive Acts in order to reduce tensions in

America. But his superiors responded by declaring Massachusetts in a state of rebellion. They sent Gage an additional 3,500 men. And they directed the general to suppress the rebellion and arrest "the principal actors in the provincial Congress." Gage attempted to obey this order on April 19, 1775, and, in the process, began the American Revolution.

Open Hostilities in Massachusetts Not surprisingly, the conflict began in Boston. Massachusetts Patriots had been drilling for months, organized into extralegal militia companies sometimes called Minutemen. Gage had been informed that the Patriots were storing arms at Concord, west of Boston, and that Samuel Adams and John Hancock were also in the vicinity. The British general sent a force of some 700

Canada and Its Neighbors

The original European settlers in Canada were the French, who first came in the early seventeenth century. Like the English in Virginia, these colonists were sent by a trading company operating under royal charter. The stockholders were allowed to set up a fur trade, but they were also committed to establish colonies in Canada.

Once in Canada, however, men were lured from the stern task of hacking out pioneer farms by the free life of the forest and by dreams of a quick fortune made in the fur trade. They became hunters and trappers—often living with the Indians—rather than settling down to raise large broods of children. By 1660 there were only 2,000 inhabitants in New France, compared with 75,000 in the thirteen English colonies. This scant population did not produce enough food to support itself, nor was it a match for hostile Indians. The French government took over the colony in 1663.

Quebec in 1758

During the next hundred years the government made a systematic effort to people New France. Population did increase, but in 1760 the colony fell to the British in the French and Indian War. By 1763, the British controlled the four chief regions of Canada—Quebec, Nova Scotia, Newfoundland, and Rupert's Land. These provinces, along with the thirteen colonies and British possessions in the Caribbean, formed Britain's American empire.

Renewed imperial controls, which followed the British victory of 1763, ran counter to a rising desire for independence in the thirteen colonies. Americans hoped that Nova Scotia and Quebec would sympathize with their grievances against Britain. (They did not consider Newfoundland or Rupert's Land, as they were too far away.)

Although part of the same empire, Nova Scotia and Quebec did not cast their lot with the thirteen colonies. Few of the American protests applied to Nova Scotia. The closing of the western lands did not affect the colony, which had many empty acres of its own. Nor was Nova Scotia a Massachusetts, ready to stand on its own feet in world trade.

In Quebec support for the colonies to the south was not forthcoming either. The Catholic Canadians had little love for the Protestant Americans, nor much interest in English traditions of government. In Quebec the French were a majority. But if Quebec combined with the other colonies, the French would be a minority. In addition, because of decades of warfare, the colonists of France and those of Britain still regarded each other more as enemies than as friends.

Despite Canadian neutrality, the American Revolution had a profound influence on Canada. She became a refuge for supporters of the crown—Tories to the Americans, United Empire Loyalists to the British. Over 40,000 moved north to Canada. Their descendants live there still.

regulars to confiscate the arms and arrest the Patriot leaders.

On April 19, arriving at Lexington on their way to Concord, the British found about 70 Minutemen assembled on the town common. The British commander ordered the Americans to disperse. Then someone—whether British or American remains unclear—fired a shot. Just as had happened six years earlier during the Boston Massacre, a single shot led to additional firing and a state of general confusion. When the smoke cleared, the Minutemen had fled, leaving eight dead and ten wounded. The British continued to Concord, arriving about 8 at night. Most of the colonial arms stored there had already been removed. The British destroyed what supplies they could find and fought several skirmishes with small groups of Minutemen.

Meanwhile, colonial militia had converged on Lexington and Concord throughout the day, the alarm having been spread the previous night by a few Boston Sons of Liberty, including Paul Revere. Some 900 British reinforcements joined the first detachment at Lexington for the march back to Boston. But they found themselves outnumbered and outvolleyed by more than 4,000 colonial marksmen, who fired from behind stone walls and other cover. The colonists peppered the British troops with musket fire along their twenty-mile retreat. Even the additional redcoats sent by Gage to protect the retreat failed to prevent it from turning into a chaotic stampede.

By the time the British troops straggled back to safety in Boston, they had lost 73 men and suffered 149 wounded, compared to American casualties of 49 killed and 39 wounded. More ominously still, the Minutemen did not return to their homes. They began instead to surround Boston, and their ranks grew. First they came from other Massachusetts towns. Within days volunteers began arriving from other colonies as well. Gage and his undermanned British garrison now found themselves under siege from all sides.

Two months later, reinforced by only 1,100 troops, Gage attempted to break the colonial lines ringing Boston. He fought colonial militia

entrenched on two strategic high points, Breed's Hill and Bunker Hill. After a furious day's fighting, on June 17, the British cleared both hills of American soldiers. The cost was high. The British suffered more than 1,000 killed or wounded out of an attacking force of 2,000 men. The Americans counted fewer than 450 men killed, wounded, or captured. As one of Gage's officers aptly remarked, "another such victory would have ruined us."

The Second Continental Congress In May 1775, while 16,000 colonial militia penned the British garrison in its uncomfortable quarters among Boston's hostile townspeople, the Second Continental Congress met at Philadelphia. Its members now confronted not merely colonial protests but also the newer reality of armed revolt. One of the first acts of the Congress was to appoint one of the delegates, George Washington of Virginia, as commander-in-chief of Continental forces. Delegates also prepared to requisition men and supplies for the new army.

Some of the men at Philadelphia still considered the revolt a temporary break with Britain. They believed that the grievances that had inspired it could be resolved by compromise. In deference to these moderates, the Continental Congress, in July 1775, adopted a conciliatory document that came to be known as the Olive Branch Petition. The delegates, "as faithful subjects," requested the repeal of all oppressive legislation and an end to tyranny.

The Second Continental Congress also passed a Declaration of the Causes and Necessities of Taking up Arms. This document was drafted by John Dickinson of Pennsylvania and a new delegate from Virginia, Thomas Jefferson. It defended colonial resistance as the only alternative to "unconditional submission to the tyranny of irritated ministers." It also denied that the American aim was complete independence and promised to lay down arms once Britain ceased its abusive behavior.

The declaration was a response to the so-called Conciliatory Act, passed by Parliament the previous February. The act had promised to exempt from British taxes those colonies that paid for royal expenses voluntarily. The declaration rejected this idea and signaled the colonists' continued opposition to British policies.

SEVERING TIES WITH BRITAIN

All of the actions taken to strengthen intercolonial resistance reinforced Lord North's belief, shared by George III, that the Americans wanted complete independence. Various proposals for compromise were defeated by Parliament. The British government's answer to the Olive Branch Petition was to send 25,000 additional troops to America. Britain also began to hire foreign mercenary soldiers. In August 1775 the king formally declared the colonies to be "in open rebellion." In December Parliament outlawed trade with the colonies and declared American ships and cargoes subject to confiscation.

As far as Britain was concerned, she was at war with rebellious subjects in a conflict that permitted only one solution: the colonists' submission as dutiful children to the mother country and the king. As far as a growing number of Americans were concerned, the colonies had no choice left but to fight. This involved taking a more serious step toward independence: repudiating the basic symbol of British power and colonial allegiance to it—the British monarchy.

People do not usually surrender their customary loyalties easily or without overwhelming reasons. Many of the delegates at Philadelphia shrank from defying the king himself. To strike such a blow at the symbol of monarchy required someone who hated both the British crown and the ruler on whose head it now rested. The man who struck the blow was a recently arrived immigrant from England named Thomas Paine.

Thomas Paine left England in 1774 for the colonies. He was a failure in marriage and a failure in business. More important, however, he was an ardent republican who believed in rule by the people rather than by a monarch. He made an enormous impact in America with his anonymously printed pamphlet, *Common Sense*, which first appeared in January 1776. Paine's pamphlet

An American cartoon satirizes the British retreat from Concord. British troops, portrayed with jackass heads, stop to burn and plunder in this distorted but lively drawing.

sold 150,000 copies in the critical months from January to July 1776.

Common Sense contained outspoken attacks on George III as "the royal brute of Britain." Paine also assailed the idea of monarchy itself. He wrote: "Of more worth is one honest man to society and in the sight of God, than all the crowned ruffians that ever lived." Under Paine's influence enthusiasm for republican government spread quickly throughout the colonies.

In May 1776 the Continental Congress adopted John Adams' proposal urging all provincial assemblies to suppress any remaining vestiges of royal government, to establish constitutions, and to create new state governments based upon popular consent. Royal authority had already collapsed throughout the colonies by this time, as British officials fled to safety and American Tories retreated into silence. Colonial assemblies began functioning as independent, provisional state legislatures.

The Second Continental Congress had already begun acting like a provisional national government. It sought diplomatic and military assistance abroad. It authorized Americans to attack English shipping in retaliation for the British embargo on American trade. In addition, it opened American ports to foreign shipping, thus formally ending any further pretense at recognizing England's right to regulate American trade.

The decisive step in the move toward independence came on May 15. Virginia's new revolutionary legislature instructed its delegates to the Congress to introduce a resolution proposing both independence and an intercolonial confederation. Many Virginians were already convinced that Britain was indifferent to colonial interests. This belief grew stronger after the efforts made by Virginia's last royal governor, Lord Dunsmore, to recruit slaves into the British army by promising them freedom. Rumors of a British scheme to stir up a slave rebellion swept the South in 1776. Such rumors probably helped some fearful Southerners overcome their reluctance and endorse a complete break with the mother country.

Richard Henry Lee introduced Virginia's independence resolution into the Congress. A five-man committee was assigned the task of preparing an appropriate document defending colonial actions. The committee consisted of John Adams, Benjamin Franklin, Thomas Jefferson, Roger Sherman of Connecticut, and Robert Livingston of New York. The thirty-three-year-old Jefferson, the youngest man in the Congress, became chairman of the committee. Adams and Franklin made suggestions, but the essential draft was largely Jefferson's.

By late June more moderates had accepted the idea of a complete break. On July 2 Congress finally voted to approve Richard Henry Lee's earlier motion "that these united colonies are, and of right ought to be, free and independent states." Jefferson's Declaration of Independence was then submitted to the full membership of the Congress. Delegates altered some of the wording, but they made few substantial changes except to strike out a rather questionable passage blaming George III for the existence of slavery in America.

Most of Jefferson's draft had a familiar ring to the delegates. Perhaps most original was its attempt to attribute colonial oppression to royal rather than parliamentary tyranny. Much of the Declaration consisted of a list of the alleged "injuries and usurpations" by George III that had forced America to resort to rebellion. Some of the complaints were reasonable: the king's interference with representative assemblies, his abuses of civil rights, his use of an army of occupation without colonial consent, and his allowing Parliament to tax the colonies and restrain their trade. Other grievances had plainly been designed to arouse American fears, not to gain foreign support. Of such nature were charges that the king had incited slave and Indian insurrections, "plundered our seas, ravaged our coasts, burnt our towns, and destroyed the lives of our people."

Jefferson's preamble to the Declaration attempted to justify a people's right to rebellion and to alter their form of government. He employed concepts that were thoroughly familiar to his associates in Congress and to his American readers. These included (1) the duty of a government to protect a people's unalienable "natural rights"—among which are "Life, Liberty, and the Pursuit of Happiness"; and (2) government's origin in the consent of those governed. The preamble also spoke of the obligation of a people to alter or abolish their government whenever their rights were persistently violated—in other words, it defended their right to revolution. (For the complete text of the Declaration see the back of this volume.)

John Adams later said that there was "nothing new" in Jefferson's Declaration. Its author would have agreed. Most of these ideas had been included in earlier statements of independence. What was new about the Declaration, which Congress adopted on July 4, 1776, was its suggestion that Americans had become a single, separate people, and the "united colonies" a single, separate nation. The president of the Continental Congress, John Hancock, reportedly said as he signed the Declaration (the first to do so): "We must be unanimous; there must be no pulling different ways; we must all hang together." To which Benjamin Franklin supposedly replied: "Yes, we must indeed all hang together, or most assuredly we shall all hang separately." The exchange probably never occurred. But it suggests an important symbolic truth. During the previous decade, colonists had come to think of their loyalties as national. They had begun to see themselves as Americans, not just as Massachusetts people, New Yorkers, or Virginians.

From a sense of shared grievances and efforts at common action, a broader definition of national loyalty had begun to evolve. This pattern of allegiance would be strengthened immeasurably in the revolutionary struggle that loomed ahead. Even for many of those who had hoped for a compromise settlement, there seemed to be no choice but to acknowledge their mutual peril as *Americans* in revolt.

The Declaration of Independence, as seen by a Chinese craftsman. Porcelain platters like this were made for the export trade in the nineteenth century. It is difficult to identify any particular signer since they look so much alike—and so remarkably Chinese!

1. How did the Navigation Acts implement mercantilism? Why was it necessary for colonial products to be carried only in British ships? Why were certain articles "enumerated"?

2. To what period does the phrase "salutary neglect" refer? Why did it end when it did?

3. Although appointed by the king, colonial governors were generally controlled by the colonial assemblies; why?

4. Were the results of the French and Indian War favorable to Britain? To her American colonies? Why did Britain decide that the colonies should share in the cost of the war?

5. What is the difference between a trade-regulating device and a revenue-producing tax? Why did the colonists regard the former as legitimate, but not the latter?

6. Which groups of colonists were most offended by the Stamp Act? What steps did they take to oppose it? Were their efforts successful?

7. Do you think Parliament's response to the Boston Tea Party was too harsh?

8. Why was the Declaration of Independence directed against the king and not against Parliament? Which of the grievances that it lists would you consider accurate? Which do you regard as propaganda?

9. List what you would consider to be the main causes of the American decision to become independent.

Beyond the Text

1. A major cause of rivalry between the French and the British in North America was the fur trade. On an outline map, designate the centers of the French and British fur trade, with special reference to the importance of the Mississippi Valley.

2. Pontiac's Rebellion played a crucial role in Indian-white relations. Give an oral or written report on this episode, focusing on its causes and effects.

3. Write broadsides or articles for imaginary colonial newspapers, both Patriot and Loyalist, on (a) the Boston Massacre; (b) the Boston Tea Party; or (c) the Declaration of Independence.

4. Assume that Sam Adams has fallen into the hands of the British; put him on trial for treason. Divide the class into prosecution, defense, and jury, with the teacher acting as judge.

Bibliography

Nonfiction

Alden, John R., *American Revolution, 1775–1783.**

Andrews, Charles M., *Colonial Background of the American Revolution.**

Bowen, Catherine D., *John Adams and the Revolution.*

Douglass, Elisha P., *Rebels and Democrats.**

Gipson, Lawrence H., *The British Empire Before the American Revolution.* 15 vols.

———, *The Coming of the Revolution.**

Jensen, Merrill, *Founding of a Nation.*

Maier, Pauline, *From Resistance to Revolution.**

Miller, John C., *Sam Adams: Pioneer in Propaganda.**

Morgan, Edmund S., *The Birth of the Republic, 1763–1789.**

Wright, Esmond, ed., *Causes and Consequences of the American Revolution.**

Zobel, Hiller B., *Boston Massacre.**

Fiction

Allen, Hervey, *The Forest and the Fort.**
Colver, Alice, *The Measure of the Years.*
Roberts, Kenneth, *Oliver Wiswell.*
Swanson, Neil, *The Unconquered.*

*a paperback book

7

George Washington and the Transition to Nationhood

FRIDAY, OCTOBER 19, 1781. A bright sun makes the weather warm for midautumn. A sense of expectancy hangs over the small Virginia hamlet of Yorktown, which stands on a low cliff above the York River, just a few miles from Jamestown. Inside Yorktown are about 7,000 British troops, commanded by Charles, Lord Cornwallis, the best of King George's generals in America. Facing Yorktown on the south and east are American and French armies under the command of George Washington. They have been digging trenches, mostly at night, edging closer and closer to the British lines. The Americans have some brass cannon advanced to within a few hundred feet of Cornwallis' defenses. The cannon will not be fired. Beyond the town, down the York River toward Chesapeake Bay, lies a fleet of French warships, preventing a British retreat by sea. The password of the day for Washington's troops: "Independence." The order of the day for Cornwallis' army: "Surrender."

At about two o'clock in the afternoon, along a road leading south out of Yorktown, the American and French armies lined up in formation, the Americans on one side of the road, the French on the other. Finally, the British came marching down the road. Their fife and drum corps played a melancholy tune entitled "The World Turned Upside Down." Cornwallis was "indisposed," so at the head of the British troops came an Irish brigadier, Charles O'Hara, Cornwallis' second in

The British surrender at Yorktown effectively ended the Revolution. American artist Charles Willson Peale (who himself fought in the war) depicted Washington at this time with the Marquis de Lafayette, center, and Washington's aide, General Tench Tilghman, at right.

> York, Virginia 17th Octr. 1781
>
> Sir
>
> I propose a Cessation of Hostilities for Twenty four hours, and that two Officers may be appointed by each side to meet at Mr. Moore's house to settle terms for the surrender of the posts of York & Gloucester. I have the honour to be
>
> Sir
>
> Your most obedient & most humble Servant
>
> Cornwallis
>
> His Excellency
> General Washington
> &c. &c. &c.

command. He rode up to the French commander, the Comte de Rochambeau, who sat on horseback among a group of American and French officers. O'Hara offered to surrender his sword. Rochambeau refused it, and pointed silently toward Washington, the commander of the joint French-American force.

There was a moment of painful formality. Since Cornwallis himself had not approached the American commander, Washington refused to accept the sword from a second in command. The honor, he said, belonged to his second in command, Major General Benjamin Lincoln of Massachusetts.

Down the road from Yorktown came the tough, veteran British regiments. These were troops that had fought the Americans from New York to Charleston, year in and year out since 1776. General Lincoln

(continued on page 161)

Life and Leisure in the Young Republic

"The eighteenth century's greatest epoch was undeniably the time when long-oppressed and devastated America appeared on the world theater and presented herself before amazed Europe in full youthful power as a separate self-governing state." So wrote Axel Klinkowström, who visited the new nation shortly after its birth, and commented favorably on the American people. (Those shown here are strolling past a town house in Philadelphia.) Indeed, the Revolutionary period was an exciting time for the United States. But Americans continued to savor the pleasures of home and the world around them. Having ensured their economic survival and political independence, they were now creating a distinctive life of their own.

[For further information on the foreign observers quoted in this essay, see "Notes on Sources."]

PICTORIAL ESSAY 3

Mary Lightfoot of Virginia, age seven

The European instructors brought to teach in America have always admired the docility and modesty with which girls behave whenever they find themselves in a school with a regular discipline, at least if they are not spoiled to begin with. These qualities are united to a certain freeness and maturity of judgment rarely found elsewhere.

[GIOVANNI GRASSI, 1810-17]

Pennsylvania Germans singing a birthday song

At Bethlehem, I went to the house of the "single men." I entered the manager's apartment, and found him busy copying music. He had in his room a piano, made in Germany. I talked music with him, and discovered that he was not only a performer but a composer as well. When we went into the chapel together, I asked him to play the organ. He played some improvisations, into which he introduced a great deal of harmony and chords in the bass.

[MARQUIS DE CHASTELLUX, 1782]

In the United States on the seventh day of every week, the trading and working life of the nation seems suspended. All noises cease. A deep tranquillity, say rather the solemn calm of meditation, succeeds the turmoil of the week, and the soul resumes possession and contemplation of itself. Laying aside for a while the petty passions which agitate life and the fleeting interests which engross it, the American strays into an ideal world, where all is great, eternal, and pure.

[ALEXIS DE TOCQUEVILLE, 1835]

"The First, Second, and Last Scene of Mortality," needlework by Prudence Punderson of Connecticut

At about seven or eight o'clock of the evenings when there are no formal dinners they have tea. At tea the whole family is reunited and friends, acquaintances, and even strangers are invited. Tea in the evening is accompanied by a boring and dull etiquette. The mistress of the house serves, and passes the cups around. Until you turn over the cup and put the spoon on top they will keep bringing you fresh cups. There are a thousand stories, true or false, of Frenchmen, ignorant of this customary signal, who were drowned with that beverage.

[M.-L.-E. MOREAU DE SAINT-MÉRY, 1794-98]

A Rhode Island family at tea

The theater is on the southeast side of the park, and is a large, commodious building. The interior is handsomely decorated and fitted up in as good style as the London theaters, upon a scale suitable to the population of the city. The scenes are well painted and numerous. The machinery, dresses, and decorations are elegant and appropriate to the performances, which consist of all the new pieces that appear in London, and several of Shakespeare's best plays.

[JOHN LAMBERT, 1806]

MUSIC,
Taught by GEORGE FOOSE.

MR: FOOSE having taken a Room in Crown-Street, (No. 15,) purposes to teach young Gentlemen the HARPSICHORD, VIOLIN, and GERMAN FLUTE, three times a Week.— He will also attend Ladies and Gentlemen who may be desirous of acquiring that graceful and favourite accomplishment at their own apartments, and from his knowledge as a Teacher, flatters himself of giving universal satisfaction.

☞ He likewise Tunes Harpsichords and Forte Pianos.
58

Newspaper announcement of a music teacher, 1785

Playgoers watching an English farce at the Park Theater, New York City

Shopping at the furniture store of Duncan Phyfe, New York City

Blindfold an Englishman and convey him to New York, unbind his eyes, and he will think himself in an English city. The same sort of streets; shops precisely the same; the same beautiful and modest women crowding in and out of them; the same play-houses; the same men, same dress, same language. He will miss by day only the nobility and the beggars, and by night only the streetwalkers and pickpockets.

[WILLIAM COBBETT, 1817-19]

An English fashion plate of the late eighteenth century

The taste in dress is chiefly English, extremely simple, neat, and elegant. The finest cloth and the finest linen are the greatest adornment. The women (as everywhere), seeking to please, allow themselves more variety of ornament than the men. Every year dressed dolls are brought from Europe, which, silent, give the law of the mode. However, distinction of rank among the feminine half is not striking as a result of any distinct costume. In the item of dress, each selects according to her taste, means, and circumstances.

[JOHANN DAVID SCHOEPF, 1783]

The dinner was served in the American, or, if you will, in the English, fashion. It consisted of two courses. One included the entrées, roast, and warm side dishes, the other, the sweet pastries and preserves. When the second course is removed, the cloth is taken off, and apples, walnuts, and chestnuts are served. It is then that healths are drunk; the coffee which comes afterwards serves as a signal to rise from table.

[MARQUIS DE CHASTELLUX, 1780]

A dinner party in Boston

The crafts are greatly respected in this country. They have taken on a different character than in Europe. The rich merchant continues, in spite of his success and the public offices he may have held, to put his hands to his own work.

[AXEL KLINKOWSTRÖM, 1820]

A quilting bee in the South

Dancing, for the inhabitants of the United States, is less a matter of self-display than it is of true enjoyment. At the same dance you will see a grandfather, his son and his grandson, but more often still the grandmother, her daughter, and her granddaughter. If a Frenchman comments upon this with surprise, he is told that each one dances for his own amusement, and not because it's the thing to do.

[M.-L.-E. MOREAU DE SAINT-MÉRY, 1794-98]

Merrymaking at a Wayside Inn, by Paul Svinin

The End of the Hunt, artist unknown

Hunting in Virginia was a far different thing from its English original. The meaning of the latter is simple and explicit. A party of horsemen meet at an appointed spot and hour, to turn up or turn out a deer or a fox, and pursue him to a standstill. Here a local peculiarity—the abundance of game—upsets all system. The practice seemed to be for the company to enter the wood, beat up the quarters of anything from a stag to a snake, and take their chance for a chase. If the game went off well and it was possible to follow it through the thickets and morasses, ten to one that at every hundred yards up sprung so many rivals that horses and hunters were puzzled which to select. Every man, if he chose, could have a deer to himself—an arrangement, I was told, that proved generally satisfactory, since it enabled the worst rider, when all was over, to talk about as many difficulties surmounted as the best.

[JOHN BERNARD, 1799]

Tombstone of a minister, from a New England graveyard

The inhabitants of Marlborough [Massachusetts] are nearly all Congregationalists. The prayers of those Congregational ministers whom I have heard have been of a general and tolerant nature which embraces all sects and denominations of Christians, beseeching the safety and welfare of all men with-out respect of persons. Their sermons were generally zealous, but devoid of all absurd tenets, dogmas, and denunciations. Faith *was earnestly recommended, but the necessity of* good works *was strenuously enforced.*

[JOHN LAMBERT, 1808]

Princeton is a college built by the state of Jersey some years before the war. I dismounted to visit this vast edifice for a moment. I was almost immediately joined by Mr. Witherspoon, the president. From him I learned that this college is a complete university and that it can contain two hundred students and more. There is only one class of the humanities. Two others are devoted to perfecting the young men in the study of Latin and Greek, a fourth to natural philosophy, mathematics, astronomy, etc., and a fifth to moral philosophy.

[MARQUIS DE CHASTELLUX, 1782]

Nassau Hall at the time of the Revolution

directed them into a field encircled by French soldiers. One regiment after another formed in the surrender field, saluted and laid down its weapons, and then marched out again. Some of the British troops were drunk, some cried, others cursed. Some marched quietly, probably glad that they no longer had to endure the American and French artillery bombardment of the past several days. But drunk or sober, cursing or quiet, they were prisoners, all 7,000 of them. No one knew it then—and a peace treaty would not come for two more years—but the War for American Independence was over.

For Washington it had been a difficult, sometimes bitter, six years since he had taken command of the militia that surrounded Gage's force in Boston. There had been times when he had rubbed his neck nervously and wondered whether it had been made for a noose. At one time or another the British had managed to occupy Boston, New York, Philadelphia, and Charleston—all the important coastal cities. In the summer and fall of 1776 the British had landed a huge army of 20,000 men on Staten Island, in New York harbor. This force had methodically driven Washington out of Long Island, then off Manhattan and down into New Jersey. Washington's troops did not fight well, and their weapons were poor. The Americans ran away so fast that at one point the British buglers ridiculed them by blowing a fox-hunting call to signal a charge.

Gradually, Washington had to learn a hard lesson. He was involved in a type of guerrilla warfare. The enemy used larger and better-trained armies in the field. Thus the Americans, without a well-organized force, could pursue only a hit-and-run strategy. Washington had to learn, too, that the British could afford to lose major battles, but that he could not. One smashing defeat and the movement for independence would be lost. The men whom Americans now celebrate as the Founding Fathers—the Adamses, Jefferson, Franklin, Washington, and the others—would simply be hanged as traitors. The British, on the other hand, could afford to lose one army after another until their people and politicians back home grew tired of the war.

Washington learned these lessons. He kept his army on the move. Sometimes he surprised the enemy. This happened with a force of German mercenaries at Trenton on the morning after Christmas in 1776, when he crossed the half-frozen Delaware River to wake the enemy to the sound of his guns. But every time large numbers of British made an important move near the coast, Washington was practically helpless. In the summer of 1777, the year after he had chased Washington out of New York, the British General Sir William Howe decided to take Philadelphia. Washington resisted at Brandywine, just south of the city. But the British overcame his force and ran the Continental Congress out of Philadelphia. Washington tried to make another stand at Germantown but was unsuccessful. He then retired to Valley Forge, between Philadelphia and Trenton, to spend a cold and hungry winter. Washington's steadiness of purpose encouraged the small band of soldiers whose sufferings he shared.

The Americans had a real chance only when the British marched inland from the coast. Then their huge fleet gave them no protection, and their lines of supply and reinforcement were stretched too far. In the summer of 1777, while Howe was capturing Philadelphia, British General John Burgoyne pushed down from Canada toward Albany, a long and difficult overland march. Burgoyne was met at Saratoga in September by several American forces. There he was beaten into surrender. This defeat saved the Revolution by encouraging the French to enter the war on the side of the Americans. Similarly, in the South the British could take Charleston easily enough. But when they went inland, during 1780 and 1781, the Americans turned them back time after time.

Finally, at Yorktown, Cornwallis' army was cornered. The British force had fought its way in a twisting path up from Charleston, across South Carolina, North Carolina, and half of Virginia. During this campaign Cornwallis had been able to move through the country almost at will. But he had not been able to control the countryside or defeat the Americans. At last, in October 1781, Washington put together a superior force outside Yorktown. It consisted of his own Continental army, some militia units, and some French troops. In the Chesapeake, giving decisive help, was the French fleet.

War broke out in April **1775**, with clashes at Lexington and Concord. In May, Ethan Allan and his "Green Mountain Boys," a small colonial force from what is now Vermont, captured Fort Ticonderoga and Crown Point. In the fall, Americans led by Richard Montgomery and Benedict Arnold launched an unsuccessful assault against Canada in an effort to get Quebec to join the rebellion.

The next year, **1776**, saw action in both South and North. At Moore's Creek Bridge, Patriots were victorious against a group of Loyalists. Americans also repulsed a British naval attack on Charleston. The British were forced to evacuate Boston in March. However, they defeated the Americans decisively at the Battle of Long Island (August 27) and the Battle of White Plains (October 28). Washington retreated southward, but on December 26 routed German mercenaries at Trenton. Eight days later he defeated Cornwallis at Princeton.

The two chief campaigns of **1777** took place in the North. In June Burgoyne invaded the United States from Quebec. He took Fort Ticonderoga, but was stopped at Bennington on August 16 by New Hampshire militiamen. After defeats at Saratoga in September and October, he surrendered on October 19—a loss that led to the alliance between the United States and France. Meanwhile, Howe left New York for Philadelphia. Washington failed to stop him at Brandywine (September 11) and Germantown (October 5), and went into winter quarters at nearby Valley Forge.

In **1778**, the British, now led by Sir Henry Clinton, evacuated Philadelphia. That summer, George Rogers Clark, a Kentucky militiaman under orders from Virginia, led 175 men into the west and succeeded in seizing the British forts at Kaskaskia, Cahokia, and Vincennes. A setback to the American cause was Clinton's capture of Savannah in December.

After an indecisive period throughout **1779**, the year **1780** brought increased conflict. Clinton took Charleston in the spring and Cornwallis defeated an American force at Camden on August 16. But an American victory at King's Mountain (October 7) kept Cornwallis from progressing farther.

In **1781**, Cornwallis was victorious at Guilford Courthouse (March 15). Heavy losses followed, however, and he was forced to retreat to Wilmington. Late in the summer he made his way to Yorktown. There he was trapped by land forces under Washington and Rochambeau and a fleet under the Comte de Grasse. Cornwallis' surrender on October 19 ended the war.

fter Cornwallis surrendered, the British could have continued the war. They might have sent another army, and yet another, and then a new fleet. But the French were tying the British down in the

THE REVOLUTIONARY WAR

← U.S. moves
← British moves
✴ Battle

0   MILES   200

LAKE HURON

QUEBEC

Detroit

LAKE ONTARIO

LAKE ERIE

Montreal

St. Lawrence R.

LAKE CHAMPLAIN
Crown Point
Fort Ticonderoga

Quebec

MONTGOMERY 1775

ARNOLD 1775

MAINE
(part of Mass.)

N.H.

BURGOYNE 1777

N.Y.   Saratoga
Bennington
Albany   Lexington
Concord   Boston
MASS.

CONN.   R.I.

Hudson R.

Q

Cahokia
Kaskaskia   Vincennes

CLARK 1778

Fort Pitt

Mississippi River

Ohio River

INDIAN LANDS

PROCLAMATION LINE OF 1763

ALLEGHENY MTS.

PA.
Trenton
Philadelphia
Brandywine

New York

AREA OF INSET MAP

N.J.

HOWE 1777

Mount Vernon
Annapolis
DEL.
VA.   MD.

Potomac R.

Chesapeake Bay

WASHINGTON-
ROCHAMBEAU 1781
Yorktown

HOWE 1777
(UP CHESAPEAKE BAY TO DEL.)

CLINTON 1780

DE GRASSE 1781
(FROM THE WEST INDIES)

ATLANTIC OCEAN

CORNWALLIS 1781
Guilford Courthouse

N.C.

King's Mountain

Moore's Creek Bridge

CORNWALLIS 1780
Camden
S.C.
Wilmington

GEORGIA
Charleston
Savannah

WEST FLORIDA

EAST FLORIDA

GULF OF MEXICO

Washington's campaigns
←--- 1776–77
←— 1777–79

NEW YORK

PENNSYLVANIA

Delaware River

Morristown

Princeton

Valley Forge
Germantown
Brandy-
wine
Philadelphia
Wilmington

Trenton

Monmouth

NEW JERSEY

White Plains

Hudson R.

Long Island
New York

0   MILES   30

West Indies and in Europe, and the British were tired of the American war. When Lord North, the prime minister, received the news of Yorktown on a Sunday in November, he exclaimed wildly, "It's all over!" He soon resigned, and the British evacuated Charleston. Peace negotiations opened in Paris in April 1782 among British, French, and American commissioners. Their dealings were lengthy, but it gradually became clear that the fighting was over.

After Yorktown General Washington rested for a week at Mount Vernon—his first time there in six years. Then he moved his army to Newburgh, New York, to await the outcome of peace negotiations. The American Congress ratified the peace treaty, the Treaty of Paris, in April 1783. But the British did not evacuate New York until November. At last, early in December of 1783, Washington decided that his war was over. He asked his officers to meet him at an inn to say goodby. One of them, a member of Washington's staff, wrote a moving account of the scene:

> The time now drew near when the Commander-in-Chief intended to leave for his beloved retreat at Mount Vernon. On Tuesday, the fourth of December, it was made known to the officers then in New York that General Washington intended to commence his journey on that day.

At twelve o'clock the officers repaired to Fraunces' Tavern in Pearl Street, where General Washington had appointed to meet them and to take his final leave of them. We had been assembled but a few moments when His Excellency entered the room. His emotion, too strong to be concealed, seemed to be reciprocated by every officer present.

After partaking of a slight refreshment, in almost breathless silence, the General filled his glass with wine, and turning to his officers, he said, "With a heart full of love and gratitude, I now take leave of you. I most devoutly wish that your latter days may be as prosperous and happy as your former ones have been glorious and honorable."

After the officers had taken a glass of wine, General Washington said, "I cannot come to each of you, but shall feel obliged if each of you will come and take me by the hand."

General Knox, being nearest to him, turned to the Commander-in-Chief, who, suffused in tears, was incapable of utterance, but grasped his hand, when they embraced each other in silence. In the same affectionate manner, every officer in the room marched up to, kissed, and parted with his General-in-Chief.

Such a scene of sorrow and weeping I had never before witnessed, and hope I may never be called upon to witness again.

But the time of separation had come, and waving his hand to his grieving children around him, he left the room, and passing through a corps of Light Infantry that had been paraded to receive him, he walked silently on to Whitehall, where a barge was waiting. We all followed in mournful silence to the wharf, where a prodigious crowd had assembled to witness the departure of the man who, under God, had been the great agent in establishing the glory and independence of these United States. As soon as he was seated, the barge put off into the river, and the great and beloved General waved his hat and bid us a silent adieu.

From the New Jersey shore Washington rode south to Philadelphia, then on to Annapolis, Maryland, where Congress was in session.[1] The "General-in-Chief" was by far the most popular and respected man in America. The new nation had a weak government, few traditions, and almost no leaders of national stature. Washington could easily and quickly have claimed political powers equal to his military powers. But he chose to resign. He went to Annapolis to turn in his commission as general of all Continental forces. In a draft of a speech to Congress, he spoke of an "affectionate and final farewell" and of taking "ultimate leave" of public office.

For some reason, though, when Washington actually delivered the speech to Congress on December 23, he struck out the words "final" and "ultimate." At the end of his address Washington said only that he was taking "leave of all public employments." His farewell was only "affectionate," not "final."

[1] After the Continental Congress was forced to leave Philadelphia, it met in several towns for varying lengths of time. It held sessions in Annapolis for a year, beginning in November 1783.

The General Washington who resigned his commission was in many ways the simplest and most straightforward of men. Even his very few enemies recognized his almost perfect honesty and forthrightness. But Washington also embodied some important paradoxes of the American Revolution and the American situation in general. He was, to begin with, an aristrocrat who (along with other aristocrats) had somehow led the first modern revolution, a revolution with many democratic overtones. Furthermore, history had placed Washington at the absolute center of the revolutionary stage. It is probably true that if he had been killed or captured or become ill, the Revolution would have collapsed very quickly. But Washington himself was not a true revolutionary. The words and ideas of other men—Samuel Adams, Thomas Jefferson, and Thomas Paine—had made the Revolution. Washington had simply followed along in the movement toward revolution. He never seemed to want his power or his place at center stage very much. More than any other revolutionary leader in history, he seemed at the end to want out, to return to Mount Vernon by Christmas Day 1783, and to stay there.

These paradoxes in Washington point to some larger problems of his country. In the last analysis, his power and influence had been military. He was not a great general in the tactical sense. But he was the only general, over the long haul from 1775 to 1783, whom everyone could trust. And, as a general, he had maintained the only real unity and sense of nationality the Americans had. Now the fighting was over, the army broken up, and Washington back at Mount Vernon. Could Americans create a political unity to replace the military one that had won the Revolution? Would political leaders come forward who could unify the former colonies the way Washington had managed to hold the Continental army together at Valley Forge? And would political institutions be developed to replace the war as a means of making Virginians and New Yorkers into one people? These were the questions that were raised, indirectly, by Washington's retirement to Mount Vernon. And the indirect questions soon became more tangible.

When Washington rode home at the end of 1783, he had no wish to raise any such questions. Indirect or direct, they simply were not much on his mind. He was a public figure, and he knew it. From the time of the Revolution on, his life would always be full of public affairs. His days would be taken up with receiving distinguished visitors in his Virginia home. And an incredible amount of his time would always be absorbed with writing to important political figures, in both Europe and America. (His letters fill thirty-nine thick volumes.) But thinking about public affairs, entertaining important visitors, and keeping up a

Mount Vernon in 1790. On the lawn stroll Washington and his wife, arm in arm. With them are her two children—Nelly Custis at left and George Custis (with his tutor) at right.

steady correspondence on the issues of the day—all these did not necessarily involve a direct participation in politics and government. What Washington wanted in 1783 was time, time to rest, time to build his plantation and attend to the thousands of acres of land he owned in the west. He wanted time for his wife, Martha, and the rest of his family, time for horses, dogs, and foxes.

At first it seemed to work. Washington enjoyed his self-imposed retirement. Since it was winter, there was little farm work to supervise. The roads were bad, and not very many visitors came. The general seemed to believe he could turn himself into a gentleman planter again. To old military comrades he wrote: "The tranquil walks of domestic life are now beginning to unfold themselves. I am retiring within myself." He described himself as a "wearied traveller," home at last "after treading many a painful step with a heavy burden on his shoulders."

Turning inward for Washington had always meant Mount Vernon. This great estate was the center of Washington's conception of himself as a private man. Mount Vernon always represented the opposite of his public life. It was his refuge and sanctuary.

Mount Vernon was indeed a comfortable sanctuary. The great

mansion that is now an American landmark was not yet finished, but it was rich, large, and beautiful. It stood on the Potomac River, about fifteen miles south of present-day Washington, D.C. Around the house lay the plantation, some 8,000 acres of land, covering four full miles along one bank of the river. The plantation was built and sustained by about 200 slaves. Everything about it was on a grand scale. The working land was divided into several different farms, with names like "River Farm" and "Muddy Hole Farm." From these farms came huge quantities of food. The plantation as a whole produced eight tons of pork every year for the slaves and the rest of Washington's "family." Other items of food—including enormous quantities of fish from the Potomac—were produced by the wagonload or barrelful.

And so, in Washington's heart, Mount Vernon was the visible, touchable focus of his private life. Another focus—that of politics, revolution, war—always pulled him away from Mount Vernon, out into the world of Virginia and American politics. When Washington resigned his commission in 1783, not only had he just left the army, but he had also returned home in a very special sense. He was fifty-one years old. He was healthy (except for the bad teeth that bothered him all his life). Yet he was a healthy man on the downhill side of middle age. For all he or anyone else could tell, he had already reached his peak of fame, public service, and involvement in politics. If he had never again left Mount Vernon, he probably would still have been known as the "Father of His Country."

There were two flaws, however, in the picture Washington had of himself. More than any other man in the country, he *was* the American cause. In an almost unique way, vanity and patriotism were the same emotion in him. He was so closely identified with his new country that any ambition for it almost amounted to an ambition for himself—and vice versa. In an odd sense, Washington could actually have no private life. The second flaw was that he was in some ways a poor man. He would have to build his fortune rather than retire on a fortune ready-made. The war had been expensive for him and his plantation. Slaves had been sold, and crops had spoiled. Washington had accepted no salary as commander-in-chief.

As Washington added up his accounts in 1784, he found himself short of money. At the end of the year he could not have put his hands on more than £86 in cash (about $500). In land he was rich—at least on paper. Besides Mount Vernon, he owned well over 30,000 acres in the west, which he had bought before the war. Some of this land was just west of Pittsburgh. More was farther down the Ohio River near the present city of Cincinnati. The land was a speculation, however, only a potential source of wealth. It was worth very little at this time. Mount Vernon with its slaves was a great plantation, but the land was poor. (From Berkeley's time on, tobacco had been a great depleter of soil.) The plantation was simply not a paying proposition in any substantial way.

Washington's wealth made him one of the richest men in America. But it was an odd form of wealth. Either it was impossible to turn into ready cash, like Mount Vernon itself, or it was potential wealth, like the western lands. Washington's other assets—fine horses, clothes, furniture, and dogs—were all luxuries, not real wealth.

In many respects, Washington's financial future rested on the lands in the west. The value of those lands, in turn, depended on getting settlers to the west, improving road and water transportation, and extending orderly government into the Ohio Valley. In a very concrete way, then, Washington's future was tied to the nation's. He was not a narrow man, and he was certainly not selfish. But it was clear to him that he had a great stake in the new Republic. If it prospered, so would he. And if it became a respectable nation among nations, his work in shaping it would have been worthwhile and his reputation and honor secure.

These kinds of concerns and reflections drew the retired general back toward public life. Mount Vernon could not be walled off from the world, nor could Washington daydream for long on "the tranquil walks of domestic life." He had too much energy and too much of the habit of participation and power. These traits were reinforced by his great pride in himself and his country. When Washington's economic circumstances were added to such a picture, almost anyone could easily have predicted that his retirement would be either very short or very incomplete.

The most direct temptation to involvement beyond Mount Vernon led west, to the Ohio Valley lands. Several issues were on Washington's mind. He was angry that land speculators were illegally offering his Ohio land for sale in Philadelphia and New York markets. Trespassers, or "squatters," were living on his land near Pittsburgh, without paying rent or recognizing Washington's title. Also, several Virginians, including Thomas Jefferson, were talking about opening up a trade route from the Chesapeake Bay area to the west. They planned to use the Potomac River and some of the branches of the Ohio for water transportation, possibly building canals or new roads across the short stretches between the eastern and western rivers. Washington was very interested in such schemes. They would help his state and the nation. And, obviously, opening the west for settlement and trade would also be to his own economic advantage.

All these concerns put Washington on horseback in early September 1784 for a trip west. He was accompanied by his nephew, an old friend and his son, and three servants. The group started northwest along the Potomac toward the Allegheny Mountains and Pittsburgh. From there they planned to go by boat to the lands down the Ohio. On the way Washington traveled over what was known as Braddock's Road, through territory he had scouted, surveyed, and fought in as a young soldier thirty years earlier in the French and Indian War. Now the French were gone, the country was filling with farmers, and the British were surrendering the entire Ohio Valley to the Americans.

Washington traveled as the first citizen of the United States. But he traveled to argue with plain farmers who were living on his land and who were not ready to surrender what they thought of as their rights, even to the Revolutionary General-in-Chief. Trying to maintain a pace of five miles an hour, Washington finally reached his land on September 18. In his diary he kept a running account of his encounter with the squatter farmers:

> September 19th: Being Sunday, and the people living on my land *apparently* very religious, it was thought best to postpone going among them till tomorrow.
>
> 20th: Went early this morning to view my land, and to receive the final determination of those who live upon it. Dined at David Reed's, after which Mr. James Scot and Reed began to inquire whether I would part with the land, and upon what terms. They did not conceive they could be dispossessed, but to avoid contention they would buy if my terms were moderate. I told them I had no inclination to sell. However, after hearing a great deal of their hardships, their religious principles, and unwillingness to separate or remove, I told them I would make a last offer: the whole tract at 25 shillings per acre. Or they could become tenants upon leases of 999 years.

The "tenants" discussed the question among themselves for a long time, while Washington sat gravely to one side. Then they turned back to him and said that they would not buy, move off, or pay rent. Washington would have to sue them:

> They had a long consultation. They then determined to stand suit for the land. I told them I would receive their answers individually, and accordingly I called them by name as they stood. They severally answered that they meant to stand suit, and abide the issue of the law.

Washington probably saw cabins like this one on his trip west. The chimney was a refinement; many such buildings had only a hole in the roof for escaping smoke.

Washington had come face to face, on a very practical level, with a problem that was worrying many wealthy Americans who lived in the East: Would the settlers in the new lands beyond the mountains be subject to rules and laws made in the East? Could the frontier be governed? Or would the new areas be lawless and separate from the

United States? Theoretically, as educated Americans looked toward the Mississippi River, the wilderness seemed to be both a tremendous opportunity and a tremendous problem. But Washington did not have to think on a theoretical level. (He was not much of a philosopher by nature, anyway.) He had already encountered the problem, and it had the most direct and worrisome kinds of consequences for him. If the time came for using governmental power to deal with such problems, he would be ready to see that power put to use.

The question of power and the western lands presented itself in yet another way on Washington's trip. The general had planned to go down the Ohio to his other lands, but every traveler he met coming east advised him to stay away. The Indians, they said, were on the warpath. He was told over and over that it would be dangerous to travel much farther into the Ohio country. He decided to head for home, having accomplished almost nothing. Some day, he thought to himself and later wrote to his friends, the United States would have to deal aggressively with the Indians. The government would have to buy land, make treaties, and, if necessary, use force. The problems and opportunities of westward expansion seemed always to demand more power and stronger government.

After Washington returned from his trip west, he had this map printed on the basis of his sketches. Cumberland, lower right, is on the Potomac River in Maryland. The land to the north ("Glades of Great Yough") is part of Pennsylvania.

So far, Washington had met only disappointment. But his return trip had its rewards. He decided to head for home by a southern route up the Cheat River, a tributary of the Monongahela that cuts south into what is now West Virginia (see page 215). From there he would cross the mountains to the upper reaches of the Potomac, looking for places to build connecting roads between the two rivers. If such roads were possible, all the future produce of the Ohio Valley could come down the Potomac to Virginia instead of going north and east to New York or down the Mississippi to New Orleans. Virginia could become the commercial center of the new nation.

Washington headed up the Cheat on September 23. His trip took eleven days. Along the way he carefully noted every twist and turn of the rivers, every rapids, every stretch along which roads might be built. The going was rough. The discomfort, however, had been worth it. For Washington believed that this part of the trip was a success. He felt that he had found the key to the future of the west, of his own lands, of Virginia, and of the struggling economy of his young nation.

When Washington reached Mount Vernon on October 4, he went to work on a series of detailed reflections about his trip:

> 4th: Reached home before sundown, having travelled on the same horses since the first day of September, by the computed distances, 680 miles.
> And, 'tho I was disappointed in one of the objects, namely to examine the land I hold on the Ohio and Kanawha, and rescuing them from the hands of land jobbers and speculators, I say notwithstanding this disappointment, I am well pleased with my journey.

Page after page in his diary he filled with his thoughts and calculations—detailed estimates of distance, of what rivers were navigable and how far, and where the lines of trade might eventually run. He began with an analysis of river transportation in northern Virginia. All the rivers, taken as a network, "could afford water transportation for all that fertile country between the Blue Ridge and the Allegheny Mountains." This filled Washington with proud confidence about the economic future of Virginia. But his thoughts ran well beyond the boundaries of his state, far to the west. The trade of western Virginia, great as it might become, was still "trifling, when viewed upon that immeasurable scale which is inviting our attention!"

Here was the key to Washington and to many others like him in the new nation. They had won independence. Now their minds were free to concentrate on the richest kinds of visions about the future of their country—especially, a new empire to the west! Part of Washington's mind may have been tied to Mount Vernon and visions of retirement. But now he was thinking of expansion.

Nor were his reflections vague and abstract. Washington rummaged among all the maps and papers in his possession and worked out in surprising detail a scheme for connecting the Ohio Valley to the Atlantic, preferably through Virginia—past his own great mansion, in fact, down the Potomac to Chesapeake Bay. Detroit, he calculated, would be the critical point in the Ohio Valley. It would control all the commerce of the Great Lakes region—as far west, Washington figured, as the Lake of the Woods in northern Minnesota! According to Washington's estimates, the total distance from Detroit to Alexandria, Virginia, was only a little over 600 miles. The distances from Detroit to Philadelphia and New York were over 700 and 900 miles respectively. So Virginia had the advantage. It would not be Philadelphia, New York, or Boston that would become the economic and commercial capitals of the Republic. It would be Alexandria. (This city is just across the river from Washington, D.C., today—though Washington had no idea in 1784 that the federal capital would ever be created.)

All these calculations were of great importance for Washington. His mind ran in large strategic channels:

> Hitherto, the people of the western country have had no excitements to industry; they labor very little. But let us open a good communication with the settlements west of us, and see how astonishingly our exports will be increased.
>
> No well-informed mind need be told that the flanks and rear of the united territory are possessed by other powers, and formidable ones too. It is necessary to apply the cement of interest to bind all the parts of the country together by one indissoluble band, particularly the Middle States and country back of them.

Washington had focused on a problem that would occupy him for a long time to come: how to apply the "cement" of economic interest—trade—to hold the nation together and make it powerful. If the United States failed to achieve this unity and power, the west might very soon form a new nation and separate from the United States, or it might even join with Spain or Great Britain.

As a result of his trip, Washington could see more clearly than before just how closely his own life was related to such large questions. His patriotism, which was intense and powerful, was not merely a notion or an ideal. It was also directly tied to his own stake in the future of the Republic that he had done so much to bring into existence.

All these reflections led to a simple set of questions: Would Americans have the good sense to see how much was at stake and what had to be done? Would the governments of Virginia and the other states support projects to make the new commerce come to life? Would the central government be stable and powerful enough to maintain the unity of the nation and hold the west in line? The symbolic questions that had ridden with Washington from New York to Virginia in 1783 were gradually becoming more and more real.

For Washington himself, a chain of events had begun that was to lead him eventually to join in overthrowing the existing government of the United States, creating a new constitution and government, and becoming the nation's first President. The chain ran clearly from his farmhouse confrontation with his Pennsylvania squatters in 1784 to the presidency four years later. One link in the chain was the observations he had made on the trip home. Another was his careful reflection on western trade. Now came the next link: an attempt to get Maryland and Virginia to cooperate in opening up the Potomac to trade.

When Washington reached home in October 1784, he moved quickly from reflections on the west to practical politics. He traveled to the new capital of Virginia at Richmond to lobby for his Potomac project. It was clear that Maryland would have to cooperate, since the Potomac formed the border between the two states. So Washington was appointed commissioner to arrange for similar legislation in the two states. It took him only three days to hurry to Maryland's capital, Annapolis, even though it meant missing his second Christmas at home since the war. Mount Vernon suddenly became a political clearing house. Washington was acting the politician in ways he had not practiced since he was a young man. He drafted laws, and copies passed through his home on their way to and from Richmond and Annapolis.

By the end of December everything was falling into place. Washington worked far past his usual nine o'clock bedtime on the project. As he wrote to his young friend James Madison on December 28, 1784: "It is now near 12 at night, and I am writing with an aching head, having been constantly employed in this business since the 22nd without assistance." His eyes and hand were tired, and the letter was messy: "I am ashamed to send such a letter, but cannot give you a fairer one." But the work was worth it.

Everything was complete by the first week in January. The legislatures of both Maryland and Virginia had appropriated money and joined in creating a joint-stock company to open up river transportation to the west. Washington was soon named president of the Potomac River Company, as it was called. Throughout the next two years he paid very close attention to its affairs. He fussed over the details of planning and surveying and suffered through all the delays. He went about the project with such energy that Madison made a very shrewd observation about him: "The earnestness shows that a mind like his, capable of grand views, and which has long been occupied with them, cannot bear a vacancy."

Commissioners from Maryland and Virginia met several times, at least once at Mount Vernon itself. Then, in January 1786, just a year after the Potomac Company was formed, the Virginia legislature took a surprising step that would soon have even more surprising consequences. The legislature suggested that delegates from all the states meet at Annapolis to discuss trade, taxes, and other matters of common concern. Such a meeting seemed innocent enough, but in fact it bypassed the existing central government completely. Washington thought carefully about the proposal. In many ways, it had grown directly out of his own work on the Potomac Company. But it raised large questions about the political future.

Washington was optimistic. He wrote a French friend:

> The country is recovering rapidly from the ravages of war. The seeds of population are scattered far in the wilderness. Agriculture is prosecuted with industry. The works of peace, such as opening rivers, building bridges, etc., are carried on with spirit.

Despite the apparent prosperity, there was a problem of government, a problem that made Washington and many of his friends increasingly uneasy. During the Revolution the states had written a constitution, the Articles of Confederation, to bring a central government into being. This government was weak, Washington thought, too weak to fulfill the vision of empire he believed in. If the central government was weak, the states would constantly quarrel with one another. All during 1785 Washington's letters were filled with complaints:

> Contracted ideas and absurd jealousy are leading us from those great principles which are characteristic of wise and powerful nations, and without which we are no more than a rope of sand. The Confederation appears to me to be little more than a shadow without the substance. If we are afraid to trust one another, there is an end of the Union. We are either a united people, or we are not. If we are not, let us no longer act a farce by pretending to it.

Because of these fears and doubts, Washington was concerned about the meeting at Annapolis, which was finally scheduled for September 1786. But the result of the meeting was only more anxiety. Only five states sent delegates. None at all came from New England. Here lay one source of Washington's frustrations. Out in the country, there was activity and opportunity. A great nation was waiting to be built as it had waited in 1775 to be born. But the state governments, Washington felt, seemed to care nothing for the opportunity. Still, the few delegates who did come to Annapolis accomplished one thing. They recommended another meeting—a convention to begin in Philadelphia in May 1787—to consider what ought to be done to strengthen the Articles of Confederation.

Washington's reaction to the Annapolis Convention was a mixture of frustration and hope—frustration because more had not been accomplished and hope for a more promising meeting to be held in Philadelphia the following year. Other news soon burst in to trouble him further. An armed rebellion of some kind was under way in Massachusetts. Most of the rebels were farmers. They seemed to come mainly from the western part of the state. (They probably were men much like the tenants on Washington's Pennsylvania lands.) In September bands of these men had kept courts from sitting in many sections of Massachusetts. Memories of 1776 crowded in on Washington. This time, however, it was an *American* government that was being threatened by mobs.

Friends sent Washington warped reports of the rebellion. It had a leader, a Revolutionary War captain named Daniel Shays. It was well organized and might even have foreign support (from old Tories, probably). Shays and his followers believed in some kind of radical division of all private property. They wanted all debts canceled, all taxes abolished. They were threatening to raid the federal arsenal at Springfield. Then they planned to march on Boston and bring down the established government.

These reports were wildly exaggerated, though Washington had no way of knowing it. Daniel Shays was not so much a leader of an organized movement as a surprised farmer who somehow found himself signing statements drawn up by the rebels. The rebels did not believe in abolishing private property, debts, or taxes. They were protesting more personal economic difficulties—namely, the seizure of their farms to pay their debts. The only time they threatened the Springfield arsenal, in January 1787, they were fired on by government cannon and ran away without returning a single shot. Once it reached the Springfield area, the Massachusetts militia (led by Benjamin Lincoln of Yorktown fame) easily put the rebellion down without a real battle.

To Washington, however, and to most men of wealth all along the eastern coast, Shays' Rebellion was like a sudden thunderclap. Washington's informants were in near panic, and he shared their fears. The leaders of the Revolutionary movement in the 1770s had always wildly exaggerated the dangers of British actions, as though every new tax meant tyranny or slavery. Now Washington and many of his friends exaggerated the significance of Shays' Rebellion. A few hundred farmers turning out to close some county courts seemed to spell the eventual downfall of the whole federal Republic.

On the last day of October Washington sat at his writing table working on two long and important letters. The first was addressed to an organization of former Continental officers, the Society of the Cincinnati. Washington had been president of the Cincinnati for three years. They were scheduled to hold a general meeting and elect a president in May 1787 at Philadelphia. The time and place were exactly those chosen for the new convention to revise the Articles of Confederation. Washington's letter was a careful defense of his decision not to attend the meeting and not to serve again as president. He cited his heavy correspondence, his work on the Potomac Company, and problems with his health. All these increased his determination to pass the rest of his days "in a state of retirement." More than anything else, the general said, he wanted "tranquility and relaxation."

Washington's second letter was about Shays' Rebellion. It seemed to say that no matter how much he wanted retirement, Washington would not be able to stay away from politics:

> I am mortified beyond expression when I view the clouds that have spread over the brightest morn that ever dawned upon any country. You talk of employing influence to appease the present tumults in Massachusetts. Influence is no government. Let us have a government by which our lives, liberties and properties will be secured; or let us know the worst at once.
>
> These are my sentiments. Let the reins of government be braced and held with a steady hand. If the Constitution is defective, let it be amended, but not trampled upon whilst it has an existence.

It seemed obvious to Washington that the Articles of Confederation were not working. The central government was simply too weak. It was also bankrupt. It could not, according to its constitution, raise taxes without the consent of all the states. Nor could it be changed without the agreement of every state.

Some people were content with this kind of government. The nation's troubles would work out in time, they thought. After all, Massachusetts had proved perfectly able to handle Shays' Rebellion. A people's first loyalties ought to be to its local and state governments, not to any central government. Washington disagreed, however. For him the questions were: How soon could reforms be made? Would they cause new turmoil, like Shays' Rebellion? Who should lead the movement for a stronger government?

During the winter and early spring of 1786–87, questions about the nation's future began to focus on Washington himself. He had more prestige than any man in America. No one else had a reputation approaching his as a man of honor, good sense, and character. If he wanted a stronger national government, how could he hold back from participating in the movement to abandon the old constitution and write a new one?

The Virginia legislature nominated Washington as a delegate to the Philadelphia Convention. Some of his most faithful young followers, among them James Madison and Alexander Hamilton, kept urging him to join the movement. Others advised him to hold back, not to risk his flawless reputation on a venture that might prove to be an embarrassing failure. Month after month, Washington made excuses. Some were valid. He did have an aching rheumatism that forced him to go around the Mount Vernon farms with one arm in a sling. There were deaths in the family, financial troubles, and even a brief quarrel by letter with his mother. All these things reminded him that his life was full enough without involving himself in the creation of a new constitution.

In the end, though, Washington had no choice. The pressure from his friends was too powerful. His fears for his country were too strong. And, in the last analysis, he wanted to be part of a great event, to stand somewhere near the center of activity. In his letters of the spring Washington referred often to his reputation. He was as close to being vain as he had been in twenty years. It may have been this vanity that provided the final tiny weight needed to tip the balance toward Philadelphia and away from Mount Vernon—though his rheumatism was better, too.

Philadelphia was miserable in May. It rained day after day. Most of the delegates were late in arriving. On the day the Convention was set to open, only Virginia and Pennsylvania were represented. Gradually, enough delegates drifted into town to conduct business. To no one's surprise, Washington was unanimously elected president of the Convention. Week after week he sat in the chair, listening and wondering whether or not a new government could be created. Would the people accept this new Constitution? Would it work?

When the sections of the Constitution outlining the powers of the new office of President of the United States were being discussed, Washington must have listened with special care. Not a man in the room doubted that the office would belong to him if he would have it.

During the whole Convention Washington made only one speech on an unimportant subject. He had a talent for knowing when to be quiet and follow the lead of others who were quicker with words and ideas than he could ever be. Washington was always alert. He could

On Washington's journey to New York City for his inauguration, Americans welcomed him everywhere. The citizens of Trenton, New Jersey, erected a triumphal arch on the bridge over the Delaware River. The President-elect approaches on horseback, right.

follow a point in political theory or philosophy very well. But he made few. If he was a leader in Philadelphia, it was because other people trusted in his character, not because he led the way toward the new frame of government.

After the new Constitution had been created, Washington hoped for its ratification. Once more he did not actually lead. Younger men with more interesting minds—especially men like Madison and Hamilton—carried the burden of trying to explain the Constitution to an extremely suspicious public.

After a precarious struggle the Constitution was ratified by the required number of states. The Articles of Confederation were set aside. A presidential election was held, and Washington was, almost inevitably, given all the electoral votes.

The new President left Mount Vernon for New York[2] in mid-April 1789. From town to town—Alexandria, Wilmington, Philadelphia, Princeton—the citizens and the militia turned out for ceremonies. The trip took seven days. Finally, on April 23 Washington took a barge across the Hudson to Manhattan. There were more salutes, bells, and cheers as he reentered the city he had left from Fraunces Tavern. A week later, Washington was inaugurated on an open porch that looked down on a crowd in Wall Street. The judge who administered the oath turned to the cheering crowd and shouted, "Long live George Washington, President of the United States!"

---

[2] New York City was the capital of the United States until June 1790.

8

Creating a New Government

LATE IN THE YEAR 1799 George Washington died. It was the middle of December, cold and wet, but he was back home, at Mount Vernon. For eight years he had served as first President of the new Republic, and then had come a brief and final period of retirement. Washington's health had been good almost to the end, and he died gently. "I am just going," he said to a friend. "Have me decently buried and do not let my body be put into a vault in less than two days after I am dead. Do you understand me?" "Yes, sir," answered the friend. "'Tis well," said Washington, and soon he was dead. His body had to be measured for the coffin, and the doctor recorded that he was "in length, six feet, three-and-one-half inches, exact."

The measurement of Washington's "length" and his last words are interesting. His height, which was extraordinary in a day when most men were much shorter than they are today, was in keeping with the almost gigantic reputation he had acquired. There have been times, during his lifetime and the centuries since, when he seemed more than human, when he seemed to rise above his surroundings just as his enormous monument does today. Washington's last statement, "'Tis well," says a good deal about the kind of philosophical calm he seems to have won for himself during the long, difficult period between the Revolution and his death. About a month before he died, Washington heard from a friend about recent political troubles in the nation's capital. He would say nothing, Washington replied, because "the vessel is afloat, or very nearly so, and considering myself as a passenger only, I shall trust to the mariners whose duty it is to watch, to steer it into a safe port."

Washington had come a long way since he took command of the straggling little army outside Boston in 1775. Now, at the end of the century, the "vessel was afloat." The Revolution had been won, difficult times had been endured, and the country had a government that looked promising. Washington had survived two presidential terms. John Adams, the second President, was now completing his term. The next year, the first year of the new century, a third President

In 1787 the first covered wagon left Ipswich, Massachusetts, for new land near Marietta, Ohio. Settlement of the west was a continuing problem for the Confederation.

The Northwest Ordinance

The "ordinance for the government of the territory of the United States northwest of the River Ohio" was approved by Congress in July 1787. This far-reaching legislation is considered the most significant act passed under the Articles of Confederation. The ordinance was a plan for the democratic and orderly settlement of the Northwest Territory—land that became the states of Ohio, Indiana, Michigan, Illinois, and Wisconsin. It served as a guide for most later westward expansion.

Two documents preceding passage of the Northwest Ordinance had an influence upon it. One, the Ordinance of 1784, embodied Thomas Jefferson's ideas for dividing the region into ten districts. Each district could become a state when its population reached 20,000. (He even chose classical names for the new states, such as Chersonessus, Assenisipia, Metropotamia, and Pelisipia.) Americans had agreed earlier that new states could be added to the Union on an equal basis with the original thirteen states. Jefferson's plan—though never officially adopted—provided a way for achieving statehood through temporary governments to be succeeded by permanent ones.

The second document was the Ordinance of 1785 "for ascertaining the mode of disposing of lands in the Western territory." Hugh Williamson of North Carolina, a friend of Jefferson's, suggested that the ancient Roman rectangular survey system be used. This was to replace the customary method of identifying property lines with trees, stones, or other natural objects.

In this scientific system, boundary lines were based on degrees of longitude and latitude; townships were divided into mile-square sections; and roads were planned to parallel boundaries at right angles. A General Land Office was set up to survey the land and sell it for no less than a dollar an acre in 640-acre sections. One square mile was set aside in each township to support public schools.

Though the Ordinance of 1785 was adopted, it did not result in a land rush. The $640 needed for a section of land was too much money for most would-be settlers. In order to stimulate development, Congress allowed large chunks of land to be purchased by stock companies. They were to encourage colonization and act as real estate agents. The Ohio Company Associates, formed in Boston in 1786, was the most important. Its members were prominent New Englanders who, in fact, drafted the Northwest Ordinance.

The ordinance specified that no fewer than three nor more than five states could be carved out of the area. A governor, a secretary, and three judges appointed by Congress were to rule each territory. When the population reached 5,000 free adult males, the citizens could elect a legislature, pass laws subject to the governor's veto, and send a nonvoting representative to Congress. When the population reached 60,000, the territory could apply for statehood.

The New England spirit showed itself clearly in the document. Important provisions included guarantees for freedom of religion, trial by jury, and freedom from arbitrary arrest. Probably most important was the stipulation prohibiting slavery.

TOWNSHIP

6	5	4	3	2	1
7	8	9	10	11	12
18	17	16	15	14	13
19	20	21	22	23	24
30	29	28	27	26	25
31	32	33	34	35	36

6 MILES

6 MILES

SECTION 25

1 MILE

1 MILE

would be chosen. There had been two constitutions. There had been times when war with either Britain, France, or Spain looked inevitable. But somehow the "vessel" had stayed afloat. And the man who had stood so near the center of the stage in the turbulent quarter-century was indeed entitled to congratulations at the end.

It had not been easy. There were times when it had seemed impossible. Every single year of the twenty-five years between Lexington and Washington's death had held out hope and fear. Washington and his fellow Americans had acquired what amounted to a habit—hoping for the best and fearing the worst at the same time.

There was plenty to fear. The Revolution might be lost, and its leaders might, as Franklin had joked, "hang separately." Or the Americans might win the Revolution only to lose their country. They might not be able to create a stable national government to hold the old colonies together. Or the new nation might be carved up by hungry European powers, just as North America had earlier been divided among several empires.

But the sense of opportunity was just as intense as the sense of danger. If Americans could bring it off—that is, if they could make the Revolution work and their government survive—then they had a chance to create the greatest nation in the world, a nation built on principles of liberty. With half a huge continent in which to expand, this nation might break down the corruptions, the inequalities, the tyrannies that had ruined people's lives in Europe. A new kind of nation, a republic, with a new kind of citizen, might grow in prosperity, power, and peace.

In the minds of most Americans, confidence and doubt lived together. They provided the backdrop against which a critical period of history was being acted out. There seemed to be only one real certainty in Washington's mind and in the minds of his countrymen: the fate of America was being decided in the years after 1775. Some even said that it was not just the fate of America but the fate of humanity that somehow hung in the balance.

Against such a backdrop every incident loomed as critical. Every issue seemed final. Every hint of success or failure was read with the anxiety of a frightened fortuneteller. In taverns and town meetings citizens debated the issues of the day. They were likely to be poorly informed by a bad press and by rumor. But of one thing they were certain: one false move and they were finished. Even this "certainty" may have been incorrect. The history of the nation might well have taken the course it did no matter what short-run decisions people made.

Still, debate was the pastime of an entire generation during and after the Revolution. Gradually, in Congress, state legislatures, and conventions at Annapolis and Philadelphia, debates grew more and more skillful. Painfully, Americans piled up a mountain of experience in political theory. Their leaders became as sophisticated and adept as any generation of politicians in any nation's history. The questions were simple and classic: What form of government best preserves the liberties of its citizens? Can a national government exist without destroying individual states? How are powers to be split among legislative bodies, executive officers, and courts? What is the relationship between a national constitution and the laws of the states?

The real problems may have been practical ones, such as Washington's problem with his western lands. But American political leaders earned a generation's experience at translating practical problems into political theory and then retranslating the theory into practice through constitutions and legislation. If Washington could relax somewhat at the end, it was because he and his generation of Americans had survived a revolutionary quarter-century with an astonishing mixture of stubbornness, skill, and plain luck.

THE CONFEDERATION PERIOD

The First and Second Continental Congresses were revolutionary governing bodies. They had no real legal standing. To the British, especially, they were little more than collections of outlaws and traitors. They were engaged in an act of frightening significance—making a government where none had existed before. They exercised powers, such as making war, that usually belong only to established governments. Even before the Declaration of Independence was drawn up, the Second Continental Congress appointed a committee to draft a new constitution in order to give the government legitimacy. Congress debated the draft constitution until November 1777, when it agreed on the new Articles of Confederation. Another year passed before a majority of the states accepted the Articles.

In the meantime, the revolutionary government, the Continental Congress, simply kept on exercising power the way it had from the beginning. The arrangement was quite undemocratic in a way. Congress had no direct "consent" from the people. But there was a war on, and politics had to be adjusted to reality. At last, in the spring of 1781, Maryland, the last state, finally ratified—five years after the original committee had been appointed. The Articles were official. They created a new national government, bearing the name "The United States of America."

Government Under the Articles In most ways the new Articles simply confirmed the practices of the old Congress. The constitution created a confederation of states, each of which was to retain its "sovereignty, freedom and independence."[1] The states were the real political entities. The Articles created a government that was somewhat like a national government but also somewhat like a treaty relationship among sovereign powers. The legislatures of the states chose delegates to the Congress. In Congress voting was by states, with each state having one vote, regardless of its population. Small states like Rhode Island and Delaware had as much legislative power as large states such as Virginia and Massachusetts. A state might choose to send as few as two delegates to Congress or as many

as seven. No matter how many delegates it had, each state had an equal vote.

Congress had some of the powers that normally belong to national governments. It could declare war and raise armies and navies. It could borrow funds. It could coin money, issue paper money, and operate a post office. It could send ambassadors to and negotiate treaties with foreign nations. In essence, the states gave Congress the power to do all the things they had willingly allowed the king and Parliament to do before the Revolution.

But the states kept for themselves powers they had refused to allow the king and Parliament: regulating commerce and raising money through taxes. Congress could not control the conditions of trade among the states or with foreign nations. And when the United States needed money, as every government does, it had to ask the states for it in a request called a "requisition." If a state did not pay its requisition, Congress was powerless to enforce the issue.

It seems obvious today that a government that has no source of revenues is no government at all. But the states had recently been in the midst of a revolution against the central authority of Parliament and the crown. They did not want to create a new central government that might subvert their liberties the way the British had tried to do. To the average American his or her "country" still meant Virginia or Pennsylvania or Massachusetts. So Americans .were ready to face the peace with the same kind of government that had conducted the war. This meant a government of states. They would work together to solve problems after they arose, but not before.

There was no federal judiciary under the Articles and no Supreme Court to make final decisions about constitutional questions. Congress had the power to settle disputes among states. This power was to work through a complicated system of arbitration, however, not through a national court. The state courts were expected to enforce federal law at the local level. There was no executive, either, although the

[1] Sovereignty is the supreme power to govern in a given region. A state, under the Articles, was sovereign; it was the highest governmental authority in its area.

Noah Webster

Noah Webster has long been identified with a single achievement—his *American Dictionary of the English Language.* This great dictionary stands as a monument to the man. But his varied accomplishments should not be lost in its shadow.

Webster's career began in 1782. While teaching in Goshen, New York, he prepared an elementary speller. It eventually became known as *The American Spelling Book,* and, more affectionately, as "the Blue-Backed Speller." It was completed with a grammar (1784) and a reader (1785).

In preparing these three books, Webster was moved by his love of country and his desire to see the United States culturally and politically independent. For Webster, education was a means of forming national character. He appealed for the adoption of an *American* system of education, stating: "Every child in America should be acquainted with his own country. He should read books that furnish him with ideas that will be useful for him in life and in practice. As soon as he opens his lips, he should lisp the praises of liberty and of those illustrious heroes and statesmen who have wrought a revolution in his favor."

Webster's combination speller-readers "taught millions to read and not one to sin." Some 20,000 copies of his speller were selling annually in 1807. After Webster compiled his "Blue-Backed Speller," he worked to promote the cause of federal copyright legislation. (Copyright guarantees authors that their works will not be reproduced without their consent.) While traveling to spread his ideas, Webster met many of the leaders of the young nation. He also became an early advocate of a strong federal government.

Webster almost single-handedly brought about uniformity of spelling throughout the United States. It was he who convinced Americans to use most of the forms that distinguish American from British spelling to this day. He chose the ending

"or" in place of "our" in words like "honor" and "color." He changed the "re" to "er" in words like "theater" and "center." He got rid of double consonants in words like "wagon." He also made spelling changes in words that are today characteristically American, such as "jail" instead of "gaol" and "plow" instead of "plough." (Some of Webster's spelling reforms did not catch on—for example, "iz" instead of "is" and "wurd" instead of "word.")

For years Webster collected notes on grammatical errors, new usages, and unfamiliar words that he noted in his wide reading. In 1828 his famous dictionary came out in two volumes. The merits of this work immediately placed it among the best of all English dictionaries. It was probably the most ambitious publication undertaken up to that time on American soil. It contained 12,000 words—many of them typically American—that had not appeared in any earlier dictionary.

All of Webster's writings appealed in some way to nationalistic sentiments. They emphasized the need for national pride and awareness. For this he deserves a place among that extraordinary group known as the founders of the American nation.

Articles did provide for a number of secretaries that might eventually develop into a cabinet system like that of the British.

Obviously, there could be no separation of powers among legislative, judicial, and executive branches under the Articles. The colonists had long been familiar with the idea of separation of powers, for they had had ample experience in the conflicts between governors and assemblies. In all the state constitutions there were elaborate schemes of checks and balances—that is, the executive, legislative, and judicial departments were separated in function but balanced in power. At this time, though, the states thought of the national government as an instrument to be used only for certain very limited purposes.

Even the limited powers of the Congress were difficult to exercise. On all important questions nine votes out of thirteen were necessary for passage of a bill. This meant that a few small states could block any piece of legislation. It was almost impossible to amend the Articles. An amendment had to have the consent of every state. It was obvious that new states would soon be admitted to the Confederation. This would make it even more difficult to ratify amendments.

During the 1780s one amendment might possibly have saved the Confederation by giving it a steady source of revenue. This was a proposal to amend the Articles to allow Congress to charge a tariff of 5 percent on all goods imported from abroad. The amendment was approved by all the states except Rhode Island. Rhode Island's refusal was enough to kill the proposal.

Answering People's Needs It is easy to dismiss the Articles as merely a weak constitution. The Confederation lasted less than a decade, and it seems obvious now that the Articles had so many flaws that a new constitution was inevitable. But the system of government contained in the Articles was really derived from the Second Continental Congress of 1775. Thus the Confederation system actually did accomplish a good deal. It fought the war. It arranged an alliance with France and wrote a peace treaty with Britain. It took control of the vast lands between the Appalachians and the Mississippi, and provided for orderly government there (see page 182). It also kept internal peace during most of the troubled years after Yorktown. These accomplishments must be counted as very real successes for any government, no matter what its constitution.

It is important to remember, too—as people like Washington sometimes forgot in their impatience—that the Articles were a product of history, not just of abstract political theory. For almost two centuries the various colonies had been proud of their independence. When they experienced trouble with the mother country, it was usually as individual colonies. And during the seedtime of the Revolution, unity was a matter of Virginia coming to the aid of Massachusetts, for example, or Pennsylvania helping New York. This kind of experience had shaped the Articles of Confederation. They were based on the theory that the real business of governing people was a matter for the states. A national government was necessary only for such purposes as waging war, conducting foreign affairs, or running a post office—functions that the states could not perform individually.

In the states themselves, political leaders were more skillful. Between 1776 and 1780 eleven of the thirteen states wrote new constitutions. (Rhode Island and Connecticut kept their old colonial charters, with a few changes.) Though the methods varied, all of these constitutions had some characteristics in common. They all divided governmental power among executive, legislative, and judicial branches. They all contained some kind of listing of the rights of citizens. And they all recognized the consent of the people as the ultimate source of political power and governmental authority.

Five Major Problems of the Confederation The Articles of Confederation created a government that was equal to its immediate tasks. But there were other problems and opportunities that the Confederation could not handle efficiently. These were the problems and opportunities that had disturbed Washington and many of his fellow participants in the Revolution—especially

An American ship, the Argo, *sails homeward after a trading voyage to France.*

younger figures like Madison and Hamilton.

The first, and in a way the most severe, problem was public finance. During the Revolution the Continental Congress had issued mountains of paper money. This paper currency was really a debt. It amounted to a vast number of promises by the government to pay off, at some future time and in "real" money, the dollar value of each bill. The states followed the same practice, so that the country was flooded with paper money of all types. The real value of this paper money depended on the hope that the national or state government would eventually be able to pay off all or part of the debt.

Congress simply could not meet its obligations. This meant that the paper money of the United States was practically worthless. In 1783 and 1784 a United States dollar could buy about fifteen cents' worth of goods. The government was nearly bankrupt. There was no effective national currency in circulation. The states paid only about a sixth of the requisitions made by Congress. They were trying to pay off their own individual debts by buying back state-issued paper money. The result was a shortage of cash. People found it difficult to conduct ordinary business.

Only a stronger government, with the power to raise money through taxes, could solve this problem. It was this realization, as much as any other, that moved political leaders in the various states to think of revising the Articles. The movement that led to the Annapolis Convention, the Philadelphia Convention, and eventually to a new government was fed by fear of financial anarchy and bankruptcy.

A second problem involved commerce. Under the Articles the states were free to make their own trade regulations, both with foreign nations and other states. Foreign trade, always extremely important in the American economy, depended, of course, on relations with foreign nations. The Revolution had not altered the basic economic relationship between America and Europe. Europe was still the principal market and manufacturing center. But the Revolution had removed

188/ the British government from the picture. Now the Americans were free from British restrictions; but they were also "free" from British protection.

Sensing American weakness at the national level, the British put restrictions on American trade that were more severe than those of the old colonial system. For example, they barred American ships from other British colonies in the New World. Old patterns of trade were completely broken. New avenues of direct trade with nations like France and Spain did not take up the slack—at least not fast enough.

To those concerned about the nation's future, it seemed clear that the national government would have to be made strong enough to write new treaties of commerce with European nations. Otherwise, Americans would be ruined. They had to depend on European markets in which to sell their tobacco and other agricultural products. And they had to be able to buy European manufactured goods on a reasonable basis in order to survive.

A third difficulty was political stability. This was what people like Washington wanted most of all. If stability could be achieved, then Americans could seize the opportunities open to a new nation. The western lands furnished an important example. A stable political situation would allow people to move west, create new states, grow more crops, and import new quantities of manufactured goods. In doing so, they would be building a great new empire for liberty. But if stability was not gained, then the British would

Independence Hall (then called the Philadelphia State House) was the meeting place of the Continental Congress and the Constitutional Convention. This view, dating from about 1778, shows a cobbled street and the water pumps that served the neighborhood.

refuse to evacuate their military posts in the Ohio Valley (which they did). The Spanish would try to break up American control of the Southwest by closing the Mississippi to American traffic (which they did). The frontier settlers would feel no loyalty to the nation, would grow lawless, and would refuse to pay debts and recognize eastern law and control (which they did).

Still another troublesome problem was the possibility of quarrels among individual states or different geographic regions of the country. Almost any law or treaty would have different effects on the North and the South, since one section depended heavily on commerce and the other was almost purely agricultural. Unless the states surrendered their sovereignty, sooner or later some issue would cause the nation to fly apart into competing regions.

Within the individual states, too, there were potential conflicts among groups that could tear state governments apart. Washington felt that Shays' Rebellion was frightening. It was even more frightening as an indication of what might happen in other states. There might be disputes between western farmers and eastern merchants or between religious groups or between political factions. If the country were to survive, it seemed essential to create a national government with enough power to settle problems among and within states.

Added to all these issues, in the minds of many political leaders, was what might be called the "problem" of democracy. The leaders of the Revolution were not democratic in ways that we would recognize. That is, they did not believe that everyone should participate directly in government. All the states had some kind of property or taxpaying qualification for voting. Only people with an economic stake in society could take part in government (and of these, only free white males). All the states had complicated barriers to popular control[2] of any branch of the government. The political theory held by almost all the Founding Fathers taught that the people

are sovereign only in an abstract sense; individuals are equal only in theory. In practice, they believed that government ought to be in the hands of men of education and property.

In almost every state, however, there was a political faction that wanted more democracy—a broader suffrage, more frequent elections, shorter terms of office for leaders. Such factions demanded laws that would protect debtors from their creditors. They tried to get the states to print more, not less, paper money. With more money the farmers could pay off their debts to bankers and merchants in cheap, almost worthless, currency. These factions demanded equal representation in the legislatures for the farming areas outside cities like New York, Boston, and Philadelphia. They talked, in other words, of what Washington would have scorned as "democratical" government. To Washington—and to most of the wealthy, educated leaders who came from the eastern seaboard—such talk could lead only to anarchy. The inherent danger in the Articles was that in any given state the "democratic" faction might get control of the government. If this happened, there would be no national power to intervene in behalf of the state's republican government. There would be no national constitution forbidding the states to abolish debts, private property, and political privilege.

During the few years between the peace of 1783 and the Philadelphia Convention, all these problems, domestic and foreign, gradually came together. The mixture might differ from person to person. John Adams might fear democracy more than Thomas Jefferson. Washington might be more concerned with western lands than Alexander Hamilton, whose principal worry was public finance. But sooner or later, in much the same way that the Revolutionary movement had built up in the colonies, the movement to revise or repudiate the Articles of Confederation grew. People in one state corresponded with their friends and relatives in another. Soon most of those who had led the Revolution were involved in a movement to make a second, peaceful revolution. They would throw off their government,

2 Used in this sense, the word "popular" refers to the people as a whole, rather than to a limited group—for example, taxpayers or the wealthy or the educated.

just as they had done in 1776, and replace it with another.

Washington's interests, plans, and fears led him to Philadelphia in exactly the same way that dozens of other people were led by their interests, plans, and fears. All the delegates went to Philadelphia sharing the conviction that something had to be done. The Articles had to be drastically altered or else thrown out. If the Articles could have been amended more easily, the Philadelphia Convention might well have simply changed them, leaving the government basically intact. As it was, there seemed to be no option but to start fresh, to draw on the experience of making state constitutions, and to build a new United States.

THE PHILADELPHIA CONVENTION

The fifty-five delegates who straggled into Philadelphia in the summer of 1787 were an extremely interesting group of politicians. As statesmen go, they were young. More were under thirty than over sixty. Together they represented an enormous amount of experience—in war, in Congress, on foreign missions, and in state governments. Thirty-one had college educations (including everyone who spoke a word in the Convention). Most of them were wealthy men who were as interested in maintaining social order as they were in experimenting with political forms.

Perhaps the most interesting fact about the Convention was that almost all its delegates had decided the main question before coming to Philadelphia. They were already committed to building a national government to replace the old Confederation. Before the first hour of debate in the hot hall where they met, most of them had agreed on another point: their essential goal was to create a government that would operate directly on *citizens of the United States*, rather than on the *states* as the old Congress had done. Since this goal was more or less taken for granted, the real questions involved methods. How would the interests of the small states and large states be reconciled? How would power be

James Madison has been called the "master builder of the Constitution." His journals are the main source for later knowledge of proceedings of the Convention.

divided among various branches of government? How would the question of slavery be handled, if at all?

For all its importance in our history, the Constitutional Convention spent much of its time in what might be called tinkering. The delegates' work was a kind of political carpentry, in which they arranged and rearranged parts to satisfy the most people. There was very little discussion of high-flown political theory. Whenever a word like "democracy" was mentioned, it was used as a scare word, to provoke fear.

All the tinkering had one objective. Delegates wanted to create a political structure that would not frighten the people, who were very much afraid of strong central government. They also wanted to avoid putting any particular state or geographic section of the country at a disadvantage. The Founding Fathers needed a consensus, a common acceptance of what they had accomplished.

The Virginia and New Jersey Plans The Convention spent much of its time discussing the

William Paterson held several important posts after the Convention—senator, governor of New Jersey, and associate justice of the Supreme Court.

and the legislature. But there was an important difference. According to the Virginia Plan, there would be both a national supreme court and other, lower federal courts. The New Jersey Plan, in contrast, provided for a supreme court only. Under this plan, therefore, the national court in most cases could only act on appeals from the state courts. Thus the Virginia Plan would have called for a judiciary whose powers might balance those of the executive and legislature. Under this plan the judiciary would be more independent of the state courts, too.

Though there were some exceptions, generally the delegates from the small states supported the New Jersey proposal, while those from large states favored the Virginia Plan. The reasons were obvious. The Virginia Plan would give the large states almost complete control of the national government. The New Jersey Plan would have made the states equal in Congress; it would have made Congress much more powerful than the other branches of government. No great principles of liberty or democracy were involved in this conflict. The issue was simple and practical. How could the new constitution be adjusted to give equal protection to the interests of both the large and the small states?

THE NEW CONSTITUTION

Out of the debate over the Virginia and New Jersey plans came a series of compromises, sometimes known as the Great Compromise. As with many compromises, the solution to the main problem was really very simple. The Convention delegates created a Congress consisting of two houses. The upper house, which they named the Senate, would have equal representation, with each state sending two senators. In the lower house, the House of Representatives, representation would be apportioned according to population.

The Senate was essentially the kind of legislature proposed in the New Jersey Plan. It protected the interests of the small states. In fact, the Convention provided that this feature of the

virtues and faults of two different plans. The first, called the Virginia Plan (which was drafted by Virginian James Madison), would have made voting in the national legislature dependent on population. Thus Virginia or Massachusetts, for example, would have had more votes than Rhode Island or Delaware. The second plan, the New Jersey Plan (proposed by delegate William Paterson of New Jersey), would have continued the system used in the Articles, giving each state the same number of votes.

There were several other important differences between the Virginia and New Jersey plans. The Virginia Plan provided for an executive with a veto power over acts of Congress. In other words, it proposed creating a strong executive, with power balancing that of the legislature. The New Jersey Plan proposed an executive, too. But it would have been composed of several people elected by the legislature, like a cabinet. And it would have had no veto power.

Both the Virginia Plan and the New Jersey Plan provided for a national judiciary, separated from and working in balance with the executive

Constitution could never be amended unless every state consented to have the number of its senators reduced. The House of Representatives, on the other hand, was a reflection of the large-state bias of the Virginia Plan.

As a concession to some of the smaller states and to states where slavery was not common, the South agreed to count a slave[3] as only three-fifths of a person. This meant that the number of representatives for a state like Virginia or South Carolina would not be so large as originally suggested by the Virginia Plan.

Powers of the Federal Government   The powers given to Congress were about the same as those exercised by the old Congress under the Articles. Congress could wage war, conduct diplomatic relations, and coin and borrow money. Two important new powers were added, powers whose absence had crippled the old Congress. The new Congress could raise revenues through taxation. Furthermore, it could regulate commerce with foreign nations and among the states.

More important in some ways was the creation of an executive branch. The Chief Executive would be called the President, and everyone knew who he would be. He would enforce the laws and serve as commander in chief of the armed forces.

The Constitution also provided for a judicial branch. There would be a Supreme Court with final power to enforce federal laws and interpret the Constitution whenever legal questions arose. In addition, Congress had the power to create other federal courts to ensure that federal law and the Constitution remained what the Constitution said they should be—the "supreme law of the land."

Checks and Balances   Among these three branches of the new government, there was to be a complicated system of relationships. Each branch was to have some independence from the others. That is, there was to be a separation of powers. The judges of the federal courts would serve for life. This would presumably make them independent. The President would owe his office to no other branch of the federal government but to the electors of the electoral college. Senators would be elected by and therefore responsible to state legislatures. Congressmen would answer to their constituents. All the officers of the new government, in other words, would have separate bases of power and support.

These separations were far from complete, however. Judges were to be nominated by the President and approved by the Senate. They could be removed from office through the process of impeachment by Congress. Nor was the presidency altogether separate. Obviously, presidential programs of almost every type would eventually require money. Funds would have to be voted by Congress. Also, presidential appointees, such as ambassadors or cabinet officers, would have to be approved by the Senate. Finally, as a last resort, a President could be removed from office through impeachment.

In certain ways, the Congress was made the most independent of the three branches of government. But its powers, too, were subject to the checks of the executive and the judiciary. The President received the power to veto acts of Congress. The federal courts were given the power to declare acts of Congress null and void (unconstitutional) if such acts were found to conflict with any provision of the Constitution.

In these and other ways, the powers of government were separate yet interdependent through a system of checks and balances. The idea behind this system was that no part of the government ought to become powerful enough to override the other branches or violate the Constitution. At any one time a strong President, a runaway Congress, or a determined Supreme Court might take the initiative on a policy question. But the other two branches would always be watching carefully—at least in theory. Each would thus protect its own powers and defend the basic structure of government as laid down in the Constitution.

---

[3] Slaves are not mentioned as such anywhere in the Constitution. Instead, they are referred to as "other persons" or "such persons."

In this cartoon of 1788, Washington and Franklin ride in a chariot, carrying the Constitution and a liberty cap (a popular symbol based on the cap a Roman slave received when he was freed). The two statesmen are drawn by thirteen men, representing the colonies.

Federalism The Constitution created a federal system of government—that is, one in which power is divided between the national government and state governments. In keeping with their general approach, Convention delegates wanted this division of powers and responsibilities to be a balanced one. The Constitution itself limited the powers that the national government could exercise. And the states were protected by retaining control over the processes of electing senators and congressmen.[4]

On the other hand, nothing was said about state sovereignty in this new Constitution. The states were forbidden to do two very important things. No state could issue paper money. Nor could any state "impair the obligation of contract." This meant that no state legislature could pass any law that significantly altered existing property relationships. The specter of Shays' Rebellion lay behind these two provisions.

Attitudes Toward Democracy The Constitution that came out of Philadelphia contained a few guarantees of individual liberties. The states and the federal government were forbidden to create titles of nobility. The federal government was forbidden to set up any religious qualifications for holding office. Except for these provisions and one or two others, the Constitution was remarkably silent about the great question of liberty, the question that had rung out so loudly in 1776.

---

[4] Senators, of course, are members of Congress also. However, the word "congressman" usually refers to a member of the House of Representatives.

As for democracy, the Constitution had nothing at all to say. Only one group of officials in the new government would be elected by the people directly—members of the House of Representatives. Even in this case the states were given complete control of property or religious qualifications for voting. Senators were to be chosen by the state legislatures. And the President would be selected by the electoral college. Justices of the Supreme Court and other federal judges would be appointed by the President (who had been chosen by the electors). Then judges would be confirmed by the Senate (chosen by the state legislatures).

Every member of the Convention would have agreed that these provisions were much better than direct popular election. The people might rule, in theory. But they would be allowed to rule only at a distance and through machinery complicated enough to slow down or stop any movement toward popular democracy at the national level. Furthermore, the federal government guaranteed each state a republican form of government. This meant that any move toward anarchy—like Shays' Rebellion—could be met by federal force. No state could fail to protect the defenders of order and property.

Was there, then, no genius to the Constitution? Was it nothing more than political tinkering resulting from a desire to protect order from the "democratical" elements in society? Many of the delegates would probably have answered no. They were practical, hard-bitten men who had been burned more than once by popular movements that threatened to get out of hand.

But for a few others, notably Madison, there was another aspect to the Constitution that not many people noticed at the time. The opening words of the document are "We the People." This Constitution, unlike the Articles and many of the state constitutions, would rest, in some sense or other, on the popular will. And it would operate directly on the people, with no intervention of state power.

The government could tax individual citizens. It could try them in its own courts under its own laws. The federal courts might even declare state or local laws unconstitutional—though this possibility was hardly discussed at all in Philadelphia. Finally (the most inspired maneuver of all), the Constitution would be ratified by specially chosen conventions in the states, not by the state legislatures. Thus the new government would not be created by the states but by "We the People." (And in this process of ratification, amendments made the Constitution more truly democratic.)

THE STRUGGLE FOR RATIFICATION

The new Constitution was drafted and approved by a majority of delegates by mid-September. (For the complete text, see the back of this volume.) Now the delegates at Philadelphia, must have felt somewhat uneasy. They had been told by their state legislatures to amend the Articles of Confederation. But they had scarcely considered this as a possibility. Instead, they had created a new government. They had held secret debates about a scheme that amounted to a coup

Alexander Hamilton wrote at least fifty-one of the eighty-five essays in The Federalist. *All were signed with the pen-name "Publius."*

d'état. They knew they had very little chance of getting all the states to accept the new government, at least not for several years. So they proposed their most radical idea of all: the new Constitution would go into effect as soon as nine state conventions had accepted it.

The Founding Fathers had some important advantages. For one thing, almost everyone agreed that something had to be done about the Articles. Another advantage was the prestige of men like Washington and Franklin. A third was the method of ratification. The state legislatures might have rejected the document in order to preserve their own powers. But a series of conventions elected for the specific purpose of judging the plan would give it a better chance of adoption. As for the document itself, delegates argued that their complicated structure of checks and balances left little to fear from the new central government. Finally, they promised to write a Bill of Rights to protect the citizens, just as soon as the new government went into effect (see page 228).

Despite all these advantages, ratification

John Jay—like Hamilton—distrusted the common people, and believed that government should be controlled by men of means and education.

was an uphill fight. A shrewd observer of American politics in 1787 would probably have predicted that the Constitution would be rejected. There was opposition in Congress. Why, some of its members argued, should that body roll over and play dead? Some members of the Constitutional Convention itself, frightened by the final result, had refused to sign the document and were ready to mount opposition. Finally, there were the old traditional state loyalties to overcome. The Constitution, much more than Patriot leaders of the Revolution, much more than the Articles, asked people to think of themselves as Americans, not solely as citizens of a state.

Generally, those who favored the Constitution were more aggressive than its opponents. They wrote more, spoke more, and lobbied more. Three young men—Madison, Hamilton, and John Jay of New York—produced a remarkable series of newspaper essays in favor of the Constitution. (The essays were later published as a book, *The Federalist*.) They have become so much a part of our history that they have even been cited as evidence in Supreme Court opinions. Madison, Hamilton, and Jay also managed to acquire the name "Federalist" for their political faction. ("Nationalist" would have been more accurate.) This seemed to leave no name for the opposition but the clumsy and empty title "Antifederalist."

The first state convention to act, that of Delaware, did so swiftly. After that the fight for ratification was close, tough, and full of bargaining. The decisions of the four largest states—Massachusetts, New York, Pennsylvania, and Virginia—were crucial. Theoretically, the Constitution could have been ratified without the participation of any of them. Actually, however, the new government would have been crippled without all of them. Pennsylvania fell into line in December 1787. But when the Massachusetts convention first met, the vote on the Constitution was 192 against, 144 in favor. The situation was as bad or worse in Virginia and New York. Eventually, in February 1788, the Federalists managed to win over Massachusetts, which voted 187 to 168 in favor of the Constitution. In Virginia the convention ended by supporting the Constitution 89 to 79 at the end of June 1788. Meanwhile, New Hampshire ratified on June 21, becoming the ninth state to do so and thus officially putting the Constitution into effect. Five other states had also ratified by the end of June. But New York still stood outside, along with North Carolina and Rhode Island.

The Antifederalists were very strong in New York. But Virginia's ratification helped turn the tide. With it, ten states had already ratified. It looked as if New York, the only large state not to do so, might stand alone. The essays of *The Federalist* also had a strong impact. New York ratified on July 26, a month after Virginia's vote. North Carolina and Rhode Island hung back until 1789 and 1790, respectively, but there was no need to wait. The old Congress simply shut up shop and ordered new elections for early in 1789.

THINGS LEFT UNSAID AND UNDONE

To Washington, Madison, Hamilton, and the other Federalists, it was clear that a crisis had been averted. They had acted with care and energy, they believed, and saved the nation from itself. The uphill struggle for ratification had been the final critical stage, but they had won. To many Antifederalists, however, a world had been lost. Now they could only engage in opposition politics in the new Congress when it finally met. Regarding the choice of President there was no question; Washington was the only conceivable man for the job. But the fight over ratification had caused men to band together into factions, with the beginnings of platforms or programs.

The Constitution said nothing at all about political parties. In fact, most of the delegates at Philadelphia said they despised the spirit of faction. But Americans had been busily organizing what amounted to political parties since at least the 1760s. (Actually, they arose even earlier, for what was the revolutionary movement but a strong expression of party spirit?) In retrospect, the rise of distinct political parties in the early years of the Republic seems logical and natural.

The Constitution said nothing about another important feature of national life. Except for the so-called three-fifths clause and provisions relating to the slave trade and fugitive slaves, it was silent on the issue of slavery. During the decades after 1787 the two most prominent features of American history were the rise of political parties and a series of crises involving slavery. The Founding Fathers were great political leaders. But they were not prophets. If they were trying to guess at the future, they badly misjudged what it held.

In the final analysis, the Constitution represented only a political structure, a kind of skeleton on which history would have to build a political and social body. The "vessel was afloat," as Washington said. But only experience would tell whether its compass, sails, and other equipment would be able to provide the order and stability that the Philadelphia Convention wanted so badly. Soon, challenges would come from directions and from people that the delegates at Philadelphia could hardly have imagined, much less prepared for.

1. Explain why both Washington and Rochambeau refused to accept the surrender of the British forces from General O'Hara.
2. Why was it necessary for Americans to fight a guerrilla war against the British? Why would one "smashing defeat" have destroyed the movement for independence?
3. Which was more of a turning point in the Revolution, Saratoga or Yorktown?
4. What was Shays' Rebellion all about? Why did it arouse such great fears? Do you think these fears were realistic?
5. How did the weaknesses of the Confederation grow out of earlier American experiences with government?
6. How would you characterize the delegates to the Constitutional Convention? On what important point did they agree? How did the new government make provision for this?
7. What were the differences between the Virginia Plan and the New Jersey Plan? How were they resolved?
8. Would it be fair to say that the Constitution was undemocratic? Why or why not?
9. Why was there opposition to the new Constitution? How did the Federalists deal with it?

Beyond the Text

1. Using the map of the Revolutionary War on page 163, locate the key military campaigns and show how each was influenced by geography.
2. The colonies won their independence in the face of some overwhelming odds. Show how each of the following contributed to the American victory: (a) British military policy; (b) French aid; (c) British problems at home and abroad; (d) American privateers.

3. The Constitution provides for the separation of powers through a system of checks and balances. What is meant by this phrase? What specific provisions were included in the Constitution to carry it out? How well do you think the separation of powers works today?

Bibliography

Nonfiction

Beard, Charles, *An Economic Interpretation of the Constitution of the United States.**
Brown, Robert E., *Charles Beard and the Constitution.**
Cunliffe, Marcus, *George Washington: Man and Monument.**
Douglass, Elisha P., *Rebels and Democrats.**
Freeman, Douglas S., *George Washington.* 7 vols.
Hamilton, Alexander, et al., *The Federalist.*
Jensen, Merrill, *A New Nation.**
———, *The Articles of Confederation.**
Main, Jackson T., *The Social Structure of Revolutionary America.**
Miller, John C., *Triumph of Freedom.**
Palmer, Robert R., *The Age of Democratic Revolution: A Political History of Europe and America, 1760–1800.* 2 vols.*
Rossiter, Clinton, *1787: The Grand Convention.**
Wood, Gordon S., *The Creation of the American Republic, 1776–1787.**

Fiction

Bellamy, Edward, *The Duke of Stockbridge.*
Melville, Herman, *Israel Potter.*
Roberts, Kenneth L., *Rabble in Arms.**

*a paperback book

UNIT THREE

FEDERAL

Americans took pride in their newly established republic. The Constitution's basic principles, accepted by most people, offered a blueprint for running a strong national government. But government is not only a matter of words. The new Constitution had to be put into practice before it would have any meaning. Could the new republic survive? During the decades after the new nation was formed—a time often known as the federal period—the United States faced so many crises that its continued existence sometimes seemed in doubt.

One of the most troubling threats was that the nation would split up, that one section or another might break away from the Union. In 1806 a former Vice President, Aaron Burr, hatched just such a conspiracy. He apparently intended to create a new republic in the Mississippi Valley.

Burr's conspiracy, which you will read about in

AMERICA

Chapter 9, failed. The United States survived this crisis, as it did many others in the years after the Revolution. Chapter 10 discusses the most important of these crises. There were the fierce political battles of the 1790s, pitting Federalists against Jeffersonian Republicans. Although Jefferson's election to the presidency cooled political tempers, he and his successors faced international problems that led to a second war with Britain in 1812. Jefferson's purchase of Louisiana created difficulties in itself; could such a dispersed nation be held together?

In the 1820s, after a so-called Era of Good Feelings, a new brand of politics emerged. It was more aggressive, more attuned to the needs and prejudices of individual voters. First in the states and then in the federal government, ''the people'' became supreme. By the time Andrew Jackson was elected President in 1828, the American political process had been revolutionized. Voting had become general among adult, white males.

Sometimes the results were unfortunate. Chapter 11 describes a New York City election that produced a good share of fraud and violence. For better or worse, however—as Chapter 12 shows—mass parties had been organized, joining together people from all parts of the country. The national capital, Washington, D.C., became the focal point for the country's political activity. The President— particularly Jackson, who dominated the 1830s—came to view himself as the direct representative of all the people.

During these decades, American politics became more democratic. And Americans showed that a republic could survive, even a democratic republic.

9

Aaron Burr, Conspirator

EARLY ON THE MORNING OF JULY 11, 1804, a pair of small barges carried two duelists across the Hudson River from New York to the New Jersey town of Weehawken. The two seconds for the duel, and the usual doctor, were also aboard. The two parties in the duel went to a level spot along the river, cleared away some of the summer brush, and carefully loaded the pistols. After the two men took up positions ten paces apart, one of the seconds called out "Present!" Each man raised his pistol in a salute similar to a fencer's "En Garde!" Without any further ceremony or signal the two men fired, one a little after the other. One of the men spun partly around and fell forward. The small, round shot had lodged in his spine, and he was bleeding internally. The other man started to rush forward as if to help or offer a gentleman's apology. But he was pulled away by his second and taken quickly back across the river to New York. The wounded man went home more slowly, lapsing in and out of consciousness. He lived with pain, doses of opium, and a grieving family, into the next afternoon. Then he died.

The dead man was Alexander Hamilton, a young hero of the Revolution. He had been first Secretary of the Treasury, and he was a leader of the Federalist party. He had achieved a remarkable career in his forty-nine years. As he lay dying, his doctor released frequent public bulletins on his condition. After his death the city of New York went

Slight but handsome, Aaron Burr was painted in Paris in 1809 by American artist John Vanderlyn. Throughout the troubles of his later life, Burr never lost his power to charm.

into official mourning. Mass meetings demanded the arrest of the "murderer," who escaped from the city after a few days. Finally, in New York and New Jersey Hamilton's opponent was indicted for murder. He fled first to Philadelphia and then south to Georgia and out of the country to Florida (still a Spanish possession). Much of the time, he traveled under an assumed name, like any ordinary fugitive from justice.

Sooner or later, however, this particular outlaw had to come out of hiding. For he was, in fact, the Vice President of the United States, Aaron Burr. He could afford to spend the late summer and early fall in the South. But Congress would soon go into session, and it was his constitutional duty to preside over the Senate. He was fairly certain that the murder charges would eventually be dropped. In the meantime, he would not be arrested if he stayed out of New York and New Jersey. Even though New York was his home, he had no reason to go there. His handsome house had been sold at auction to pay off some of his debts, and his other creditors were howling for the rest of his money. So, on November 4, the Vice President, over his head in debt and wanted for murder, took his seat as the president of the Senate. One senator, shocked at Burr's display of nerve, wrote angrily to a friend that "We are indeed fallen on evil times!"

It was not really the Senate that had fallen on evil times. The main victim (aside from the dead Hamilton, of course), was Burr himself. He was a gentleman and had fought an honorable duel—still the custom among gentlemen of the day. He had won. But he had lost, too.

Richmond Hill, Aaron Burr's New York home, stood in what is now lower Manhattan. At the time this engraving was made, in 1790, the house was occupied by John Adams. Burr moved here in 1797, but sold the house in 1803 to pay off some of his debts.

Burr had enjoyed as spectacular a career as Hamilton. Like Hamilton, he had been one of the young heroes of the Revolution. A brilliant lawyer, he was said never to have lost a case. He was also a very shrewd and successful politician. He had already been a senator from New York, and in 1800 he had narrowly missed becoming President.

Now, in the fall of 1804, Burr was in disgrace because of the duel and his debts. His term as Vice President was expiring. He had just been defeated in an attempt to become governor of New York—a defeat that Hamilton had helped bring about and that was the cause of their duel.[1] Burr was still in his forties, but it seemed that his career might be ruined.

Burr, who never allowed himself to become publicly flustered, kept up an appearance of calm. In a letter to his married daughter, Theodosia, he even made a joke of the entire affair:

> You have doubtless heard that there has subsisted for some time a contention of a very singular nature between the states of New York and New Jersey. The subject in dispute is which shall have the honor of hanging the Vice President. A paper received this morning asserts, but without authority, that he has determined in favor of New York. You shall have due notice of the time and place. Whenever it may be, you may rely on a great company, much gayety, and many rare sights, such as the lion, the elephant, etc.

To his daughter's husband, Burr hinted that the situation was more serious. The duel would not cost him his life, to be sure. But his career was a shambles, and so, he wrote, "I shall seek another country."

One thing was certain. During that winter the Vice President's mind was not on Senate business. He was busy instead with mysterious maps and a dangerous partnership. An old friend of Burr's was in Washington that winter. He was James Wilkinson, the highest ranking general in the army of the United States. The general also happened to be a spy. For years he had been Agent 13 on the Spanish espionage rolls. He was very much interested in the same sorts of maps and plans as Burr.

*T*he Vice President who was wanted for murder and the general who was a spy had known each other for many years. In fact, they had been twenty-year-old captains together during the first year of the Revolution. Under the command of Benedict Arnold, who became the most famous traitor in American history, the two men had served on an

---

[1] Hamilton had been criticizing Burr privately for many years. During the campaign for governor, letters of Hamilton were released publicly. They referred to Burr as "a dangerous man and one who ought not to be trusted with the reins of government." When Hamilton refused to apologize, Burr challenged him to a duel.

unsuccessful American invasion of Canada. Their paths had separated when Wilkinson was forced to leave the army after joining a plot against George Washington. Burr went on to become a major on Washington's staff.

Like many others in trouble, Wilkinson had gone west. He made a career in politics in western Pennsylvania and Kentucky, and he began his secret occupation as a Spanish agent. In 1791 Wilkinson was able to reenter the army and fight against the Indians in the Ohio Valley. He rose rapidly in rank, and by 1796 was the highest ranking general in the army.

From about 1794 on, Burr and Wilkinson had carried on a secret, coded correspondence. Now, together again in Washington in the winter of 1804–05, they made new plans and copied maps of Spanish possessions in the Southwest and of the western territories of the United States.

At this time Spain still ruled the American West and Southwest, as well as Mexico. (The term "Mexico" was often used to refer to all of these North American regions.) The Spanish also owned East Florida— the peninsula itself—and what was called West Florida—the area west of the peninsula, north of the Gulf of Mexico. The United States had just purchased the territory known as Louisiana, the vast region between the Mississippi River and the Rocky Mountains (see map, page 236).

In the area between the Mississippi and the Appalachians, change was the order of the day. So far, only Tennessee, Ohio, and Kentucky had been admitted to statehood. But from Michigan to Mississippi, settlers were on the move, driving out Indians and clearing land. If these western states and territories decided to secede from the Union, there was little chance that the federal government could use force to hold them.

Two very dangerous but exciting possibilities occupied the imaginations of Burr and Wilkinson. One was an invasion of Spanish territory. The other was an attempt to separate America's western lands from the rest of the Union. Involvement with Spain meant preparing for a military conquest, which was a crime under American law. Separation of the west from the rest of the country meant treason. If only one of the plans worked at first, then Burr and Wilkinson might try to combine the two. The result could be magnificent—a new nation stretching all the way from Ohio to Panama. The two plans had one very practical advantage. They required the same kind of preparation. If money could be found for it, a private army might be raised in the west. This army would travel down river by way of the Ohio, the Cumberland, the Tennessee, and the Mississippi to New Orleans. Only then would a final choice have to be made between the conquest of Spanish possessions and the separation of the west.

These schemes made a great deal of sense in 1805. After all, the United States was a small and relatively weak nation. The government exerted little control over the states and territories west of the Appalachians. It had no control at all over the new lands west of the Mississippi. It seemed only a matter of time before Mexico and the Southwest broke away from Spain in a revolution such as the Americans had recently fought against Britain. The United States and Spain had been on the verge of war for some time. If war came, the conquest of Mexico and the Southwest would become a patriotic duty. Burr and Wilkinson had influence and friends in high places. Some friends could be brought into the plan, and others could be tricked into helping. There was little need to fear the American army, even if Wilkinson had not been in command. Its strength consisted only of about 3,000 troops scattered along the Atlantic coast and through the west. Burr and Wilkinson had every reason to believe that one scheme or the other, conquest or secession, would work. It was just possible that both plans might succeed, with thorough preparation, careful timing, and a run of good luck.

The first step was to obtain money and military support from some foreign power. When Burr fled New York after the duel with Hamilton, he visited the British minister, Anthony Merry. Merry reported to his government that Burr had made an astonishing proposal.

> I have just received an offer from Mr. Burr to lend his assistance to his majesty's government in any manner in which they may think fit to employ him, particularly in endeavoring to effect a separation of the western part of the United States in its whole extent.

In late March of 1805, after a winter of planning with Wilkinson, Burr went to Merry again. The time he had a more detailed scheme. Merry reported home in a dispatch marked "Most Secret":

> Mr. Burr has mentioned to me that the inhabitants of Louisiana seem determined to render themselves independent of the United States, and that the execution of their design is only delayed by the difficulty of obtaining assurance of protection from some foreign power.

Burr wanted the British to station a squadron of ships at the mouth of the Mississippi in order to immobilize the American navy. And he wanted a "loan" of half a millon dollars. Merry was hooked. His secret dispatch ended by recommending Burr in the most favorable terms:

Wilkinson, who denounced Burr, was never fully trusted by the prosecution, either. He performed poorly in the War of 1812 and retired to write three dull and pompous volumes of memoirs.

> He certainly possesses, perhaps in a much greater degree than any other individual in this country, all the talents, energy, intrepedity, and firmness which are required for such an enterprise.

The response from England was painfully slow, so Wilkinson and Burr went ahead on their own. They managed to persuade President Jefferson to appoint Wilkinson governor of the Territory of Louisiana, which was created in 1805. Wilkinson would make his headquarters in St. Louis. Burr, meanwhile, would take a tour down the Ohio River and travel for several weeks in Kentucky and Tennessee. Then he would go down the Mississippi to New Orleans, making plans and enlisting support along the way.

Burr left Washington on horseback on April 10, 1805. Three weeks later he arrived in Pittsburgh to begin his work. He embarked on the Ohio River in style. He wrote to Theodosia on April 30:

> Arrived in good order yesterday. Find my boat and hands ready. My boat is, properly speaking, a floating house, sixty feet by fourteen, containing dining room, kitchen with fireplace, and two bedrooms; roofed from stem to stern; steps to go up, and a walk on the top of the whole length; glass windows, etc. This edifice costs one hundred and thirty-three dollars.

On this elaborate ark, as he called it, Burr went everywhere and saw everyone of any importance. He visited the senators and congressmen he knew from Washington. He stopped at plantations and country houses. Everywhere he was treated as a celebrity. At each stop, the story was the same. There might be a concert or a traveling play. There was certain to be a dinner or two with the leading citizens. Most important, there would be at least one long and guarded conversation among the men only, flavored with whiskey, secrecy, and cigars. Then Burr would hint at his plans and sound out his hosts for their possible future support.

Burr left the Ohio River at Louisville, Kentucky. Then he rode south across the state and into Tennessee. He visited Andrew Jackson at his plantation, The Hermitage. For four days he filled Jackson with the exciting prospect of a war against Spain, in which Jackson's hill-country militia could help drive the Spanish out of Florida and then off the entire continent. From Nashville Burr went down the Cumberland on one of Jackson's boats to rejoin his own great houseboat. He met Wilkinson at a small fort where the Ohio empties into the Mississippi.

Wilkinson gave Burr a military escort (even though Burr was no longer the Vice President) and an "elegant barge" for the trip down river to Natchez and New Orleans. In New Orleans Burr continued to hint at his purposes and find potential supporters. Then he headed north on horseback, through Nashville for another visit with Jackson. In St. Louis, Wilkinson's headquarters, Burr reported on his trip. Then he made the hard, slow journey back east, arriving in Washington in November. Though only a little over a year had passed since Burr's duel with Hamilton, his life had taken on a new direction, a new style, and new goals.

The next year was frustrating. Minister Merry's appeal to the British government for funds got nowhere. With a new collaborator—Jonathan Dayton, a senator from New Jersey—Burr tried to trick the Spanish themselves into financing the secession of the west. But the Spanish minister was cautious and would provide only $1,500, hardly enough to finance an army. Wilkinson was strangely silent, perhaps sensing that the time was not ripe. Burr began to suspect his colleague of being fainthearted. Worst of all, both Spain and the United States were doing everything possible to avoid a war. Against such obstacles, no amount of preparation, cunning, or timing could win out. Burr wrote Wilkinson a coded letter complaining that "Nothing has been heard from Brigadier [Wilkinson] since October." The bad news, Burr said, was that the "execution of our project is postponed till December; want of water in Ohio renders movement impracticable."

"Want of water in Ohio" was the plotters' code phrase for "lack of necessary money." Without money they had no chance unless there was a war with Spain. Unfortunately for the conspiracy, the administration of President Jefferson grounded its foreign policy on the simple principle that "Peace is our policy." Then, just at the moment when everything looked hopeless, the Spanish made a curious decision that almost led to the war Burr wanted so much.

When the United States bought Louisiana from France in 1803, its western boundary was left undefined. Technically, the United States could have claimed everything east of the Rio Grande. But the Spanish claimed the Texas region and sent in about 1,500 troops to occupy the almost empty area. Since Jefferson believed that Americans might never settle west of the Mississippi, he decided not to quarrel over Texas. Instead, he set the border with Mexico at the Sabine River. But the Spanish placed the border east of the Sabine, at a small stream named the Arroyo Hondo (see map, page 236). In the fall of 1805, after Burr had returned east from his trip to New Orleans, the Spanish moved a few troops—twenty-nine men and one officer—across the Sabine. In February 1806 an American force of sixty soldiers forced the Spanish to evacuate their post and return across the Sabine. These border incidents were small and not very dangerous, and Burr probably did not know about them. In fact, it took the government about six weeks to receive emergency messages from the border.

The country between the Sabine and the Arroyo Hondo was virtually empty, and either the United States or Spain could have given it up with no loss to national interest or security. But both sides were stubborn. Jefferson, when he finally learned of the problem, announced that he intended to hold the Sabine line. The Spanish authorities in Mexico then reinforced their garrison and once more crossed the Sabine. The American commander in the area reported to his government that the situation was desperate. He had only 200 men fit for duty, six old guns, and a shabby fort. The Spanish refused to answer his request to withdraw.

Jefferson was determined. He ordered the frontier reinforced. Early in May the President told Wilkinson himself to move his headquarters to New Orleans and take personal command of the troops in the disputed area. Now the general was in an awkward position. All along, he had been trying to juggle three roles: commanding general of the army, spy for Spain, and plotter with Burr. The problems on the border brought the three roles into painful conflict, and put him in a predicament.

In a crisis Wilkinson could choose to combine any two of his three roles, but at least one of them had to be dropped. In case of war with Spain he could be both commanding general and Burr's collaborator in the conquest of Mexico. The roles of spy for Spain and collaborator with Burr could work together if the goal were the secession of the west. Wilkinson's third option was to remain commanding general and spy for Spain. This would require him to keep peace with Spain along the Sabine but also to desert Burr and thus prevent either the conquest of Mexico or the secession of the west. The choices were extremely difficult. They depended on circumstances that Wilkinson could not completely control, such as the movements of Spanish troops and the agressiveness of Jefferson. Like many men confronting hard choices, Wilkinson moved slowly. Jefferson ordered him to leave St. Louis in May. The general hung back until August, when he finally started down river to New Orleans.

Burr's problem, as he fretted through the spring of 1806, was just the opposite of Wilkinson's. Wilkinson had too many roles to juggle; Burr had no role and was trying to find one. During the months when it seemed that there would be no war with Spain, Burr had been raising money among his friends and relatives. He had also decided to buy part of a huge land grant on the Ouachita River in what is now the state of Louisiana. If nothing else worked, he could bring in settlers and become a private prince. The preparations for the Ouachita plan—boats and armed men—were exactly the same as for the conquest of Mexico or the secession of the west.

When Burr heard the news of the border incidents on the Sabine River and that Jefferson had ordered Wilkinson to go to New Orleans, he made a fateful decision. On July 24 he sent a messenger west with a secret letter to Wilkinson written by Senator Jonathan Dayton. Dayton began by trying to convince Wilkinson that Jefferson was about to replace him as governor of Louisiana Territory. He ended by urging Wilkinson to act:

> It is now well ascertained that you are to be displaced in the next session [of Congress]. Prepare yourself, therefore, for it. You know the rest. You are not a man to despair, especially when such prospects offer in another quarter. Are you ready? Are your numerous associates ready? Wealth and glory! Louisiana and Mexico!

Jonathan Dayton (after whom Dayton, Ohio, is named) was indicted for treason in 1807, but his case was never tried.

The message was almost clear. Burr and Dayton were trying to get Wilkinson to commit himself. But to what? Dayton's words (which Burr probably dictated)—"You know the rest. . . . Louisiana and Mexico!"—left all the options open.

Burr himself wrote a letter on July 29 in the code he and Wilkinson had always used. It was much more elaborate, but it still left the choice of destinations open. Whereas Dayton's letter tried to frighten Wilkinson, Burr's tried to trick him by falsely claiming that all the pieces had fallen into place and by implying that success was certain:

> Your letter postmarked 13th May is received. I have at length obtained funds and have actually commenced. The eastern detachments from different points and under different pretences, will rendezvous on the Ohio, 1st of November.

Burr was exaggerating. The "eastern detachments" did not exist on July 29, except perhaps in his imagination. This exaggeration was small, however, compared to the lies that followed immediately:

> Every thing internal and external favors our views. Naval protection of England is secured. It [an English naval force] will meet us at the Mississippi.

The promise of English naval support was simply a lie. Minister Merry had not succeeded in getting a promise of help from London. In fact, he had been discharged by his government for his role in Burr's proposed intrigue. Burr continued trying to excite Wilkinson's imagination:

> It will be a host of choice spirits. Wilkinson shall be second to Burr only, and Wilkinson shall dictate the rank and promotion of his officers. Burr will proceed westward 1st August, never to return. Our object, my dear friend, is brought to a

Burr's famous letter of July 29 to Wilkinson was written in a combination of English words and a numbered code. (The code numbers were page-and-entry references to a dictionary that both men owned.) The opening paragraphs of the letter are quoted on the previous page. The third paragraph reads: "Burr will proceed westward 1st August, never to return. With him goes his daughter; her husband will follow in October, with a corps of worthies." (The three did meet with Blennerhassett at Lexington in October.) The next paragraph goes on to other practical details of the negotiations: "Send forthwith an intelligent and confidential friend with whom Burr may confer; he shall return immediately with further interesting details; this is essential to concert and harmony of movement. Send a list of all persons known to Wilkinson west of the mountains who could be useful, with a note delineating their characters." The letter continues on a second page and is followed by a note from Wilkinson, added when the letter was submitted as trial evidence. He denies any recollection of the May 13th letter, but supposes "it was one of Several Short notes written to him with the design to extract from him the particulars of Some grand Project."

point so long desired. Burr guarantees the result with his life and honor, with the lives, and honor, and the fortunes of hundreds of the best blood of our country.

Then Burr gave a few details of his planned movements:

Burr's plan of operation is to move down rapidly from the Falls [of the Ohio—that is, Louisville], on the 15th of November, with the first 500 or 1,000 men, in light boats now constructing for that purpose, to be at Natchez between the 5th and 15th of December, there to meet you, there to determine whether it will be expedient to seize on, or pass by, Baton Rouge [still a Spanish possession].

After setting down these details, Burr wrote a sentence that may have contained the key to the entire scheme:

The people of the country to which we are going are prepared to receive us; their agents, now with Burr, say that if we will protect their religion, and will not subject them to a foreign power, that in three weeks all will be settled.

What "country" did Burr have in mind? The Louisiana Territory or Mexico? There probably were no agents of either Louisiana or

Mexico with him at the time. Both areas were Catholic, so the protection of their religion would be a problem in one as well as the other. The most important clue may be the timetable of three weeks. Burr could hardly have hoped to put together a fleet, sail across the Gulf of Mexico to Veracruz, and conquer Mexico in such a short time. On the other hand, capturing New Orleans and proclaiming a new western nation probably could be done in three weeks, with Wilkinson's help. What Burr probably planned to do was to gather his forces, meet Wilkinson at Natchez, and then decide whether to invade Mexico, take over New Orleans, or peacefully settle the Ouachita lands. The simple fact was that his future was in Wilkinson's hands, and those hands became more unsteady every day. Burr closed his letter with a last attempt to coax Wilkinson into action: "The gods invite us to glory and fortune; it remains to be seen whether we deserve the boon." A few days after he had sent messengers west with the letter, Burr set out for the Ohio, never to return—or so he believed.

Shortly after Burr left for the west, Wilkinson started down river from St. Louis. He reached Natchez early in September and started up the Red River to the main American fort at Natchitoches. He arrived there on September 22 to find a small, unprepared garrison, with no cannon or horses ready for duty. For thirty hot, frustrating days the general bargained and hesitated and tried to reinforce his little army. At first he was tough. He wrote the Spanish military commander of Texas that his orders were "absolute." The border was the Sabine River, and the Spanish must withdraw or face the consequences. But the Spaniard was just as tough. His orders were to enforce the Spanish claim east to the Arroyo Hondo, he said, and the choice of peace or war rested with Wilkinson.

While Wilkinson carried on this correspondence with the Spanish officials, he wrote very excited letters to his American friends. For a crucial two weeks at the end of September and the beginning of October, he became convinced that war with Spain was certain. He was ready for much more than a squabble over the border between Texas and Louisiana. At last, his dream of conquering Spanish Mexico seemed about to come true. On September 26 he wrote to a friend, Senator John Smith of Ohio:

> I have made the last effort at conciliation. I shall be obliged to fight and flog them. Five thousand mounted infantry may suffice to carry us forward as far as the Grand River [the Rio Grande]. There we shall require 5,000 more to conduct us to Monterrey [Mexico], and from 20,000 to 30,000 will be necessary to carry our conquests to California and the Isthmus of Darien [Panama].

To another friend Wilkinson exclaimed, "a blow once struck, and away we go!"

It was at this critical point—with the Spanish refusing to retreat and war seemingly certain—that Wilkinson finally received Burr's coded letter of July 29. The letter had taken two months to catch up with him, and it hit him at an awkward moment. If a war did begin, Wilkinson would be pinned down in a land action in Texas. There was no way to control what Burr might do in New Orleans. If Burr were telling the truth, if he did have a thousand men and a British fleet, he could undoubtedly have his way in New Orleans. Then he could probably invade Mexico by sea before Wilkinson could get his troops assembled, much less advance to the Rio Grande. The moment had finally come when Wilkinson must choose. He received Burr's letter on October 8. He waited and thought for two agonizing weeks. He also drank more whiskey than was his usual custom, for his situation was difficult indeed.

Meanwhile, Burr was traveling in the Ohio country, having boats built and recruiting volunteers. Sometimes he said that he was going to settle the Ouachita land grant. At other times he talked of raising a force of volunteers for the war with Spain that was sure to begin soon. He visited Cincinnati, Frankfort, Lexington, Nashville, and all the settlements in-between.

Burr also established a base of operations. In the Ohio River near Cincinnati was an island owned by a wealthy Irish immigrant named Harman Blennerhassett. Blennerhassett had become involved with Burr during the winter of 1805–06. He seems to have had a vision of himself as minister to England in the new government of Mexico that Burr would establish. Whatever the vision, Blennerhassett was willing

Blennerhassett's mansion boasted paintings and furniture imported from Paris and London. He too was taken to Richmond for trial, but not prosecuted. Blennerhassett died in poverty in Europe, and his island home fell into ruins.

to put himself into debt and danger to help Burr. According to the timetable, boats would be built at Blennerhassett Island and at other points along the river. From the island, at around the beginning of December, the fleet and the volunteers would start south.

All during September and October, preparations went fairly smoothly. Many boats were completed. Dozens of volunteers were recruited, many of them the young sons of leading planters, politicians, and military men. In Kentucky, Ohio, and Tennessee, Burr's expedition—whatever its destination—was the main subject of gossip and speculation.

Some talk was good for Burr. Like any enterprise, his needed advertising. But the talk began to filter back to Washington. Jefferson's administration became first suspicious and then alarmed. Early in November a Kentucky district attorney even attempted to have Burr arrested on the grounds that he was planning an invasion of Mexico. Most Kentuckians interpreted this action as a political move. The district attorney was a member of the Federalist party, and Burr was a Republican. In addition, the district attorney had so admired Hamilton that he had taken the name as his own legal middle name. Two sympathetic juries, one in November and another in December, found Burr innocent of any crime. Still, it was clear that Burr's preparations could not go on much longer without forcing the government into some kind of response.

Burr did not know as he completed his preparations that he had already been betrayed. Wilkinson had made his decision. He would do whatever was necessary to make peace with the Spanish on the border, and then he would turn against Burr. He could then gain credit with the Spanish for protecting their interests. At home he could claim that he had saved his country from Burr's intrigues.

On October 20 Wilkinson put his plan in motion. He wrote President Jefferson two very strange letters. In the first, he enclosed an "anonymous" document—which he actually wrote himself. In it Wilkinson sounded an alarm against "a numerous and powerful association" illegally organized for the invasion of Mexico. The general had to be careful not to appear involved. He claimed:

> It is unknown under what auspices this enterprise has been projected, from whence the means of its support are derived, or what may be the intentions of its leaders.

In his second letter Wilkinson again warned the President. Again he tried to appear innocent and confused:

The magnitude of the enterprise staggers my belief. I have never in my whole life found myself in such perplexity. I am not only uninformed of the prime mover and ultimate objects of this daring enterprise, but am ignorant of the foundation on which it rests.

Wilkinson knew that when the President received these letters, he would have no choice but to move against Burr. This left only one nagging problem. If the Spanish insisted on starting a war, then Burr and his force might suddenly appear to be heroes on their way to fight the enemy. To cover this possibility, Wilkinson added an incredible postscript to his second letter to Jefferson:

Should Spain be disposed to war seriously with us, might not some plan be adopted to correct the delirium of the associates, and by a suitable appeal to their patriotism engage them in the service of their country? I do believe that I could accomplish the object.

Here was Wilkinson's escape hatch in case something went wrong. If war with Spain did come, he would simply rejoin Burr in the plan to conquer Mexico.

Now everything depended on the Spanish, and on this front Wilkinson had extraordinary luck. On October 23, three days after he wrote Jefferson, he mounted his troops to begin a slow, tense march toward the Sabine. He did not know at the time that the small Spanish force had already withdrawn west of the river. When he met no resistance, Wilkinson proposed a neutral zone between the Sabine and the Arroyo Hondo. No Spanish forces would cross the Sabine, and no American troops would cross the Arroyo Hondo. The Spanish accepted the agreement, and Wilkinson was finally free to confront Burr. He immediately headed east for Natchez and New Orleans.

Before marching east, Wilkinson sent a messenger to the Spanish authorities in Mexico asking for a payment to Agent No. 13 for keeping peace and stopping Burr's plan to conquer Mexico! The Spanish government refused to pay this particular bill. But the resourceful Wilkinson did finally manage to get Jefferson to pay the messenger $1,500 in "expenses" for the trip.

Burr was now in deep trouble, though he did not know it. There was still a slender chance that he might salvage something, but only if he moved quickly. Even by fast express Wilkinson's letter would take six weeks to get to Washington. Burr thus had until early December before the federal government could act. Wilkinson would also need several weeks to travel to New Orleans and put the city's defenses in any kind of order. If Burr could get to Natchez by his original deadline

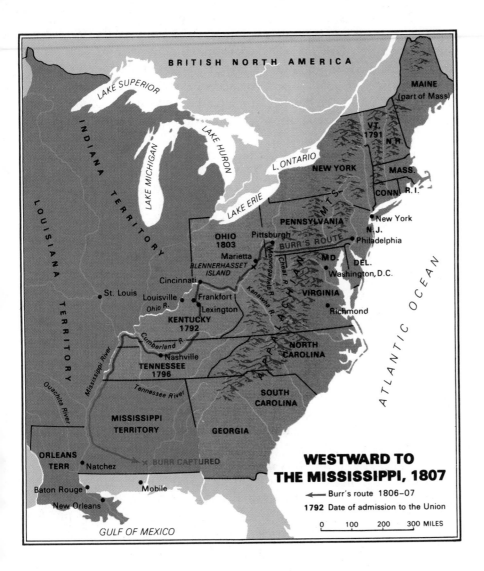

**WESTWARD TO
THE MISSISSIPPI, 1807**

⟵ Burr's route 1806–07
1792 Date of admission to the Union

0   100   200   300 MILES

of December 15, he might still have a chance to trick or surprise
Wilkinson. This meant that Burr and his collaborators had to get their
boats into the water by the middle of November. Any delay would give
the government time to act and Wilkinson time to prepare. News that
there was to be no war with Spain would soon reach Ohio and Kentucky, and this would make Burr's preparations look suspicious.

Burr's plan was certainly ambitious enough to attract intense
suspicion. He was having fifteen boats built at Marietta, Ohio, near
Blennerhassett Island. Andrew Jackson was building five more at
Nashville on the Cumberland River. At least eight others were being
bought or built in Pittsburgh and other settlements on the Ohio. These
twenty-eight boats could carry at least a thousand men and their

supplies—a force several times as large as the army Wilkinson would command in New Orleans. But the boatbuilding went more slowly than Burr had planned, and he showed no hurry to get into action.

The first four boats were launched in Pittsburgh on December 4. By this time any hope Burr might have had was gone. Ohio officials had been watching preparations at Marietta for many weeks, and they now knew of Wilkinson's treaty with the Spanish. On December 9 they seized the fifteen boats at Marietta. Harman Blennerhassett and a few other men got away down the Ohio in the four boats that had just arrived from Pittsburgh.

Burr knew nothing about these events. After his second trial in Kentucky he went to Nashville. He did not start down the Cumberland until December 22. By that time it was already much too late. Burr finally made his rendezvous with Blennerhassett and the others on December 27, at the junction of the Cumberland and Ohio rivers. There were only ten boats and less than a hundred men.

Burr would surely have quit at this point if he had known of Wilkinson's betrayal. But he still believed that a small force at New Orleans could accomplish a great deal, if Wilkinson helped. Burr already knew that Wilkinson had made peace with the Spanish. He must have thought that either the peace would be temporary or he and Wilkinson would capture New Orleans instead of Mexico. In any case, he went on down the river, completely out of communication with the rest of the world. On January 10, 1807, he pulled to shore at a small settlement just north of Natchez. A man quickly showed him a newspaper that told the story of Wilkinson's treachery. He also learned that President Jefferson had ordered his arrest. The former Vice President was once more a fugitive from justice.

General Wilkinson had already declared martial law in New Orleans and had begun to arrest Burr's friends there. Burr decided to take his chances with civilian courts in Mississippi Territory. There he hoped to be out of Wilkinson's grasp. But after a few weeks of legal maneuvering, Burr learned that Wilkinson had sent troops north to arrest him. He fled and hid with friends for about two weeks. Finally, on February 19, he was surprised and captured near Mobile. He was then taken east under military arrest for trial in Richmond, Virginia.

Burr's trial began on March 30, 1807. It lasted five months and caused more attention than any other criminal trial in America up to that time. Some of this attention was simply a result of Burr's high political position and the fact that he was charged with one of the worst

of all crimes, high treason. But his trial also had great political significance. President Jefferson committed himself actively to prosecuting
Burr, and so he became almost a party to the trial. Many Federalists,
on the other hand, became partisans of Burr in order to align themselves against the President (who was a Republican). The trial was
presided over by none other than the Chief Justice of the United States,
John Marshall. He was a Federalist and a bitter enemy of the President
(see page 223). Jefferson, Burr, and Marshall had last been together on
March 4, 1800. Then Marshall had administered the oaths of office to
President Jefferson and Vice President Burr. Now all three were locked
together in an ugly and curious political combat over whether the
President's legal staff could force the Chief Justice to convict the former
Vice President of treason.

Almost everyone believed that Burr was guilty of *something.* The
President had publicly declared that Burr was guilty before the trial
even began. The question was, however, guilty of what? Before the
Revolution, British law had made conviction in treason cases fairly
easy. The framers of the Constitution, in order to protect citizens from
the power of the federal government, had defined treason quite narrowly. Only two things, the Constitution clearly said, were treasonable.
One was giving "aid and comfort" to enemies of the United States.
The other was "levying war" against the United States. Since the
country was at peace, it technically had no enemies. So Burr had to be
convicted of "levying war." (What the term "levying" actually means
was one of the main issues of the trial.)

The Constitution contained another important provision. There
had to be two witnesses to an overt act of treason. The government
would have to prove that Burr had actually participated in an act of
war against the United States—not just that he plotted or encouraged
it. And the government would also have to have at least two eyewitnesses to the specific act.

Jefferson anxiously ordered the government's lawyers to do everything necessary to get a conviction. Still the prosecution had trouble
putting a case together. At first, Marshall refused even to begin a trial
for treason because the government could produce so few witnesses.
The strongest witness would probably be Wilkinson, but weeks passed
and he did not show up. One of Burr's lawyers pointed out that "In
Europe, a general had been known to march the same distance at the
head of his *army* in a shorter time than General Wilkinson has had to
pass from New Orleans to this place." The court recessed, one hot June
day after another, to wait for the general. Washington Irving, who was
covering the trial for a New York newspaper, commented sarcastically
on the delay. Members of the court, he wrote, used the opportunity to

go home, see their wives, have their clothes washed, and "flog their Negroes."

However the citizens of Richmond may have passed the time, they finally were treated to a sight of the general. On June 15 Wilkinson strode into court, as Irving described him, "booted to the middle, sashed to the chin, collared to the ears, and whiskered to the teeth." Wilkinson described his own courtroom appearance in a letter to Jefferson:

> I saluted the bench and my eyes darted a flash of indignation at the little traitor. This lionhearted hero, with haggard eye, made an effort to meet the indignant salutation. But it was in vain. He averted his face, grew pale, and affected passion.

Irving's newspaper story of the same meeting was a bit different:

> Wilkinson strutted into court and took his stand, swelling like a turkey-cock and bracing himself for the encounter of Burr's eye. Burr turned his head, looked him full in the face, and then cooly resumed his position. The whole look was over in an instant, but it was an admirable one.

Whoever won the exchange of looks, Wilkinson's pretrial testimony was enough—barely enough—to have Burr indicted for treason. The trial began on August 3.

The first task was the selection of a jury. Virginia was Jefferson country, and it was difficult, if not impossible, to get an unbiased jury. Even the ghost of Hamilton rose up to haunt Burr. Burr and his lawyers questioned one juror very closely, and the man turned to the courtroom and said, "I am surprised that they should be in such terror of me. Perhaps my name may be the terror, for my first name is Hamilton." (He was excused.) Finally, Burr accepted an obviously biased jury, since he hoped to win on questions of procedure and law. These would be decided by the judge, not the jury.

The government lawyers received instructions directly from the President almost every day. Determined to prove that Burr had intended to make war, they held that he had assembled an armed force at Blennerhassett Island for this purpose. According to the prosecutors, his action was what the Constitution meant by "levying war."

The strategy of Burr's defense was to make the prosecution prove its accusation. As Burr sarcastically observed, Mr. Jefferson was having a great deal of trouble even *finding* a war:

> Our President is a lawyer, and a great one, too. He certainly ought to know what it is that constitutes a war. Six months ago he proclaimed that there was a civil

war [between Burr's forces and the government]. And yet, for six months have they been hunting for it, and still cannot find one spot where it existed. There was, to be sure, a terrible war in the newspapers, but nowhere else.

Day after day, Burr and his lawyers tore holes in the government's case. The prosecution had proved only that thirty or forty men congregated at Blennerhassett Island in early December of 1806. But Burr was not even present on the island at the time.

Burr's lawyers were brilliant and cutting in their cross-examination of government witnesses. Burr, acting as his own lawyer, was even more brilliant and more cutting. One by one, the prosecution witnesses were broken. One had to admit, under Burr's questioning, that he had just been paid $10,000 by the government. Another ended by testifying *for* Burr; he admitted that, as far as he knew, Burr's force had been gathered for use only in a war against Spain. A third testified against Burr, only to have his own son follow him to the stand to swear that his father was "old and infirm, and like other old men, told long stories and was apt to forget his repetitions." Another witness, who knew Blennerhassett well, revealed that the latter was so nearsighted that it was ridiculous to imagine his participating in a military action.

Burr was sketched at the time of his trial by a French artist. Most of the audience was hostile to him. After his acquittal, a Baltimore mob hanged him in effigy, along with his chief defender, Marshall, and Blennerhassett.

The outcome depended on how Chief Justice Marshall defined treason. If he ruled that treason could mean participating in a plan that eventually led to treason, then the jury might find Burr guilty. But Burr's lawyers argued that the government would have to prove that Burr had been personally present and had participated in the act of levying war. For days lawyers for the government and for Burr argued the point. On the last day of August Marshall made his ruling. He decided in favor of Burr. To prove treason, he said, the government would have to prove by two eyewitnesses that Burr had been present and taken part in a specific act of war against the United States. Since the government had not made such a case, the jury had to deliberate only briefly. On September 1 Burr was found not guilty.

Burr had won the case, just as he had won his duel with Hamilton. But he always seemed to lose in winning. He was still in legal trouble in several states, and he was now more deeply in debt than ever. Also, much of the public was convinced that Marshall, the Federalist, had let Burr go free just to embarrass the Republican administration. Burr's career was finished. Once more, he decided to "seek another country," and he went to Europe in a self-imposed exile that lasted four years. In 1812 he came home to practice law in New York. At the age of seventy-seven he married a wealthy widow; she soon sued him for divorce (charging him with adultery!). The divorce became final on September 14, 1836. Burr died the same day, at the age of eighty.

The Republic on Trial

THE CAREER OF AARON BURR was a strange one. In many ways his life was an expression of a unique, ambitious, and unpredictable personality. But when Burr's duel with Hamilton, his western scheme, and his trial for treason are considered today, they make almost perfect sense as part of the larger history of the United States. The generation that made the Revolution and the Constitution continued to govern the United States until the 1820s. The lives of this generation were controlled by four main tendencies. Each of them was very much present in the life of Burr.

First, the development of party politics and the first two-party system occupied the minds and energies of just about every important American during the period after 1789. Burr was, first and last, a politician. He was deeply involved in almost every political battle until his duel with Hamilton. In fact, political conflict between the two men was a major factor behind the duel.

Second, the history of the United States during the decades after Washington's inauguration was tied very closely to foreign affairs. Relations with France, Spain, and Britian tended to dominate national and even local politics. Many leading politicians and military figures were involved in secret intrigues with one foreign power or another. Burr sensed this situation clearly, especially after his duel. His mind was controlled by thoughts of war with Spain and secret arrangements with Britain.

Third, the years between 1789 and the 1820s were marked by rapid expansion of territory and population. During this period the territory of the United States doubled. Thousands of pioneer settlers pushed over the Appalachian Mountains into the valleys of the Ohio, the Tennessee, and the Mississippi rivers. Burr's thoughts ran west with this expansion.

Fourth, the United States was involved in a serious test of whether the federal system would work. Each section of the country had its own special interests and institutions. It was not clear whether the nation could survive. Would the western farmers secede? Would the question of slavery divide the North from the South? Would

This anti-Republican cartoon was published in 1795. A dignified Washington leads his troops out to meet the French "cannibals." Jefferson, clutching at a chariot wheel, shouts at his followers (in a French accent), "Stop de wheels of de gouvernement."

New England leave the Union and try to go it alone? These questions were quite real and important, not just to Burr but to other leaders. leaders.

THE DEVELOPMENT
OF PARTY POLITICS

The two-party system is such a familiar feature of our national government that it is difficult for us to realize that the men who made the Constitution did not plan for it. In fact, almost all of the framers despised the idea of "factions." In the Constitution they tried to create a government that would discourage the formation of national parties.

The framers of the Constitution knew that conflict between organized groups was bound to occur. Farmers would be pitted against merchants, slaveholders against nonslaveholders, the rich against the poor. Such divisions in society were bound to lead to factions, which would struggle for domination of state governments. These struggles would bring out people's worst failings: selfishness, intrigue, ambition, and deceit. In order to gain the advantage, political parties and their leaders might stop at nothing. They might mobilize their supporters by appeals to fear and greed. And people's loyalties would not be to their country but to their party.

To combat this situation, the Founding Fathers tried to make a government that could stand above party and interest. They believed that the system of checks and balances would make it impossible for any group to gain control of the whole federal structure. The President would not be the tool of a political party, because he was elected by the electoral college, not the people. Since federal judges were to be appointed for life, they would not depend on party support for their offices. If a party formed in the popularly elected House of Representatives, then surely the Senate would counteract it. (Senators, elected for long terms of six years, would be more independent than members of the House, who had to run for election every two years.)

The Constitution forbade the states to do certain things, such as coining money and regulating interstate commerce. So the worst effects of party politics in the states could be controlled from the national capital.

The political history of the first forty years of the United States is, among other things, the story of the failure of these hopes. The national government did not prove to be above party. Political parties did emerge. The presidency did become a party office. Control of the national government became the highest prize in the conflict between one party and another. Supreme Court justices, senators, and congressmen did become party men with party loyalties. In fact, the very men who had written the Constitution to guard against parties became partisan leaders themselves. Even Washington, who had seemed in 1789 to stand loftily above all conflict and ambition, was drawn into the struggle and made a symbol of party conflict.

At first, Washington's dignity was his greatest asset. The friends of the new government knew that only he could be the first President. Only he could convince the people that the power of the central government would be fairly and evenly used. It would not operate in favor of any section or class, but in a generous and truly national way. Washington strained to create an appearance of majesty. He rode a white horse with a striking saddlecloth made from a leopard skin. He also had an elegant coach, bearing his crest and drawn by a matched team of six cream-colored horses. His house in New York was one of the grandest in the city, and it was fully staffed with servants. Almost everything Washington did was calculated to give an impression of an almost regal stateliness, far above ambition and partisanship.

Some men in Congress wanted to put an official seal upon Washington's kingly manner. Just after the first inauguration, Washington's friends in Congress drew up a message of congratulations. There was a debate over how to address the President. One of Washington's admirers went so far as to propose the title "His Highness, the President of the United States and

John Marshall

For thirty-four years, from 1801 until his death at the age of eighty in 1835, John Marshall was Chief Justice of the United States. During the formative years of the nation, he developed a large body of constitutional doctrine that still shapes laws and influences legal opinions.

Born on the Virginia frontier in 1755, the eldest of fourteen brothers and sisters, Marshall learned early to fend for himself. He had little formal education, but he read widely. In 1775 he enlisted in the army and served throughout the Revolutionary War. As a youth, Marshall distrusted the "too immediate democracy of the state legislature" and favored strong central government. His wartime experiences confirmed these views. As one biographer put it, "He became an American before he ever had time to become a Virginian."

After the war Marshall became a lawyer (after only six weeks of law school) and entered the state legislature. From then on he rose quickly. His swift, clear thinking and boldness in debate served him well. "His head was one of the best organized that I have known," said one colleague.

Marshall's experience in the legislature strengthened his Federalist opinions. He soon found himself the champion of this party in Virginia. Yet he declined to serve in the government until 1800, when he was made Secretary of State. He left this post when appointed Chief Justice. In 1803 Marshall met a critical test of the Supreme Court's power in the case of *Marbury* v. *Madison*. The Court ruled unconstitutional a 1798 federal law that would have allowed it to force President Madison to confirm the appointment of one William Marbury as a justice of the peace. This case established the principle of judicial review (not explicit in the Constitution)—that is, that the Supreme Court is the final interpreter of the constitutionality of American laws. The Constitution must be supreme, Marshall argued. Thus "a law repugnant to the Constitution is void."

Just as acts of Congress could be struck down if "repugnant," so could acts of state legislatures. *McCulloch* v. *Maryland* (1819) made this clear. A Maryland law heavily taxed the state branch of the Second Bank of the United States. When the bank refused to pay, the state sued James McCulloch, a bank officer. "The power to tax," declared Marshall, "involves the power to destroy." And the Court ruled that federal agencies, such as the bank, were beyond the reach of state laws. *Gibbons* v. *Ogden* (1824) involved two rival steamboat operators. New York State had granted Aaron Ogden a monopoly for steamboat commerce on the Hudson River. He was challenged by Thomas Gibbons. The Court's decision in favor of Gibbons established that the federal government has sole jurisidiction over interstate and foreign commerce.

To the end Marshall remained firm in his resistance to state power impinging "on the government of all." An admiring fellow judge wrote in 1833 of Marshall's contributions: "Your expositions of constitutional law are destined to enlighten, instruct, and convince future generations; they can scarcely perish but with the memory of the Constitution itself."

In 1798 Congress was the scene of a brawl between Republican Matthew Lyon, left, and Federalist Roger Griswold, right. In the Speaker's chair sits an amused Jonathan Dayton.

Protector of Their Liberties.'' After a heated debate, men of simpler taste won the day, and the letter was addressed to "George Washington, President of the United States.''

In his appointments Washington tried to fill federal offices with people from different states and with different interests. He hoped that his administration could be representative of the country at large. His Secretary of the Treasury, Alexander Hamilton, was from New York. The Secretary of State and the Attorney General, Thomas Jefferson and Edmund Randolph, were both planters from Virginia. The fourth member of what finally became known as the Cabinet was

Henry Knox of Massachusetts, Secretary of War.[1]

Hamilton's Financial Program The only man in the new government who had a clear political program was Alexander Hamilton. When he took office as Secretary of the Treasury, his job was to try to make some sense out of a confused financial situation. The United States was more than $54 million in debt. It could not operate effectively until it could pay off what it owed.

---

[1] Although Washington did consult with the heads of his executive departments, they did not hold regular meetings. The Cabinet as a formal institution did not develop until the administration of Thomas Jefferson.

Most of the debt was in the form of certificates, like the United States savings bonds we buy today. They had been printed during the 1770s and 1780s to finance the Revolution. Many of them had gone to soldiers of the Continental army as pay for their services. The certificates were promises that the government would someday, somehow, pay back in real money what it owed private citizens and foreign governments.

No one expected the federal government to be able to pay back the entire debt, so the worth of the certificates declined. Speculators bought them for a fraction of their face value. For example, a soldier who held a certificate worth ten dollars might sell it to a speculator for one dollar, on the theory that a dollar in the hand is better than ten in an uncertain future. All over the country millions of dollars in certificates had been bought up or taken in trade. The government theoretically owed the entire $54 million. But no one expected it to pay back more than a few cents on the dollar.

Individual states had also printed certificates, and they were in debt, too. Some states were paying off what they owed. Others had little money with which to do so.

Hamilton made two unexpected proposals. One, known as "funding," called for the government to pay off the entire federal debt at its full, or par, value. The other proposal was termed "assumption." The federal government would take over (assume) the states' debts and pay them off at par. The money would be paid to whoever actually held the certificates at the time. The original holders, many of them ordinary farmers who had fought in the Continental army and the state militias during the Revolution, would get nothing. The effect would be to create, by government power, a class of very rich men, men who had bought federal or state certificates for as little as a few cents on the dollar.

Hamilton did not propose to pay off federal and state debts with cash. Instead, holders of certificates would receive newly issued government bonds. Funding and assumption, plus interest on bonds, would cost a great deal of money. Hamilton called for two new taxes. One was a tax to be paid by distillers of alcoholic beverages. The other was a tariff on imports, which would not only raise money but also encourage American manufactures. The Secretary of the Treasury also proposed a national bank to help the government make all its financial transactions.

Some parts of Hamilton's program were acceptable to most people. Others aroused opposition. One group of congressmen, led by Madison, attacked the funding plan. Madison believed that speculators who had bought federal certificates should be paid half their value. He felt that the original holders should get the other half. Madison also opposed the assumption plan. Virginia had been paying off its own debt, while some other states had not. Why should Virginians be taxed to pay off the debts of other states?

Madison's congressional opposition to Hamilton's plan was powerful. He was soon joined by Jefferson, the Secretary of State. But Hamilton had strong backing, too. The disagreement over funding and assumption was settled by a classic political bargain. Madison and Jefferson promised to deliver enough votes in Congress to pass Hamilton's proposal. In return, Hamilton would deliver the votes of *his* followers for a measure providing that a new national capital would be created in the South rather than the North. The city would be called Washington, and it would be located on the Potomac River in a district that would bear the name "Columbia." The measures were passed in July 1790 and were soon signed by Washington.

Republicans Versus Federalists Within two years Hamilton had also succeeded in getting the new taxes he wanted and in establishing a national bank. But the groundwork had been laid for organized conflict between two major factions on the national level. From 1790 on, every major decision on domestic and foreign policy caused a quarrel. Jefferson and Madison, year after year, organized their forces. Slowly, almost against their wills, they formed a political party. They studied local and state elections throughout the country. They supported candidates for Congress and the Senate who they thought would be sympathetic to their views.

The followers of Jefferson and Madison were mostly small farmers and debtors. Many of them were former Antifederalists, who thought Hamilton's program was a scheme to create a powerful federal government at the expense of states' rights. Gradually, this group adopted the name Republicans (or Democratic-Republicans). This term emphasized their dedication to the interests of the people at large.

Hamilton's followers were mainly merchants, bankers, and speculators. They gradually began to call themselves Federalists. This name was derived, of course, from the term for supporters of the Constitution in 1788.

In 1792 Washington still stood "above party," and both sides joined in reelecting him. During his second term he gradually identified himself with the Federalists. He still talked of standing above party and of disliking parties more than any feature of government. But he was under constant pressure from Hamilton and his friends to support their positions. Bit by bit, Washington's second term took on the appearance of a real administration—that is, it was staffed by members of one party whose goal was achieving a specific political program.

Yet, when Washington finally gained his longed-for retirement, he wrote a Farewell Address whose main theme was a condemnation of party politics. The address was not published until September 1796. The Republicans claimed that Washington had waited until then so that they would not have time to mount a presidential campaign before the elections in November. So the address was, in its way, a political gesture, especially because of its timing. In its content, however, Washington's Farewell Address was a bitter and eloquent condemnation of political parties.

> Let me warn you in the most solemn manner against the baneful effects of the spirit of party. This spirit serves always to distract the public councils and to enfeeble the public adminis-
> tration. It agitates the community with ill-founded jealousies and false alarms; kindles the animosity [hatred] of one part against another; foments riot and insurrection. It opens the door to foreign influence and corruption.

In theory, at least, Madison and Jefferson might still have agreed. But by 1796 they had had six years of experience in opposition politics. And they had formed, like it or not, a party. The Republicans nominated Jefferson for the presidency, to run against Federalist John Adams. Despite the short time available to run a campaign, Jefferson was a close second in the electoral college. According to the awkward provisions of the Constitution, the runner-up in the electoral vote was to become Vice President. So for the next four years the United States was governed by a Federalist President and a Republican Vice President.

During Adams' term of office, party conflict reached a high pitch. Everywhere, Republicans were organizing for the election of 1800. The Federalists could sense the tide running toward Jefferson. In anger and desperation they managed to ram through Congress a series of laws designed to stifle political opposition. Three of these Alien and Sedition Acts were directed against new immigrants from Europe, most of whom became Republican voters. (One of them, for example, increased the period of residence from five to fourteen years before an alien could become a citizen.) The fourth was a law making it illegal to "oppose any measure of the government of the United States." This Sedition Act of 1798 in addition made it a crime to publish any "false, scandalous and malicious writing against the government of the United States or either house of the Congress or the President." Under the Sedition Act federal judges (appointed by a Federalist President) attempted to silence Republican criticism. One Republican candidate for Congress was even sent to prison for speeches made against Adams during the campaign of 1798.

Madison and Jefferson were able to use the Sedition Act as a means of trying to unite their

Jefferson's greatest personal attraction, according to one admirer, was "a countenance beaming with benevolence and intelligence."

party and the state governments against the Adams administration. Madison wrote a resolution for Virginia and Jefferson one for Kentucky. These so-called Virginia and Kentucky Resolutions denounced the law as unconstitutional. They held, too, that the states could resist any federal law that they judged to be a violation of the Constitution. These resolutions drew the lines very clearly for the election of 1800, and they put the Republicans firmly on the side of states' rights against federal power.

The Election of 1800 The Republicans organized an intense campaign in the summer and fall of 1800. New York was a typical and important state. The Republicans had to win it if they were to take the presidency from Adams and the Federalists. New York political affairs were in the

hands of none other than Alexander Hamilton for the Federalists and Aaron Burr for the Republicans. In the state elections of 1799 Hamilton's party had won an impressive victory. But Burr, Jefferson's candidate for the vice presidency, now went to work in the city of New York. He got Republicans to the polls by every means possible, and the result was a victory in the state legislature. Since the legislature in New York chose presidential electors, New York delivered all its electoral votes to Jefferson. Virginia, the largest state, also went to Jefferson. Although Adams held all the New England states, the Jeffersonians got more than half the votes in Pennsylvania.

The outcome was a narrow victory for Jefferson: seventy-three electoral votes to Adams' sixty-five. The presidency had changed hands, and political power had moved from one organized party to another. Burr's strategy had been crucial. New York's twelve electoral votes would have saved the presidency for Adams and the Federalists. Through hard work and careful maneuvering Burr had beaten Hamilton in New York City, and he had won the vice presidency for himself.

The result should have been clear, but it was confused by an odd provision of the Constitution. The document recognized no distinction between presidential and vice presidential candidates. It simply provided that the person having the most electoral votes would be President and the runner-up Vice President. However, all the electors who had voted for Jefferson also voted for Burr, so there was a tie vote. This meant that the election would have to be decided by the House, with each state casting only one vote.

The House of Representatives balloted for a week, with Federalists supporting Adams and the Republicans supporting Jefferson. No candidate was able to swing a majority. Thirty-five ballots were cast before Hamilton threw his support to Jefferson. Hamilton did this because, although he disliked Jefferson, he hated Burr. His action settled the election. It also made the relationship between Burr and Hamilton impos-

The Bill of Rights

The first ten amendments to the Constitution together are known as the Bill of Rights. They went into effect in December 1791, a little over three years after the adoption of the Constitution. Yet the Constitution itself came dangerously close to not being accepted because of these amendments—or lack of them.

Fifteen years earlier, in May 1776, George Mason had drafted a document that prepared the way for the Bill of Rights. This Declaration of Rights for Virginia was unanimously approved by the colony. But Mason did not fare so well at the Constitutional Convention of 1787. He was at odds with many key figures, who either opposed or ignored his basic ideas. In the end he refused to sign the Constitution and wrote a pamphlet attacking it that began: "There is no Declaration of Rights, no declaration of any kind, preserving the liberty of the press, or the trial by jury in civil causes, nor against the danger of standing armies in time of peace." The slogan "No Bill of Rights" became a powerful rallying cry for the Antifederalists.

Jefferson found the Constitution to his liking. But he too objected to the lack of a bill of rights, saying that it is "what the people are entitled to against every government on earth, and what no just government should refuse." Alexander Hamilton disagreed. He thought that

> bills of rights are not only unnecessary in the proposed Constitution but would even be dangerous. For why declare that things shall not be done which there is no power to do? Why, for instance, should it be said that the liberty of the press shall not be restrained, when no power is given by which restriction may be imposed?

Hamilton's views, as expressed in *The Federalist*, carried weight. Even so, strong sentiment for a bill of rights continued. Seven of the states had included such provisions in their own constitutions. The Antifederalists kept pressing their demands. By mid-June 1788, the necessary total of nine states had ratified the Constitution. But Virginia and New York still held back. So the Federalists wooed their opponents by promising to include the desired amendments. Finally the states ratified.

To James Madison fell the task of meeting the Federalists' promises. As head of the committee charged with drawing up the amendments, he sorted through pages of recommendations from the states. Virginia, for example, urged forty provisions. Madison and his colleagues edited this material until they had twelve amendments. These were then submitted to the states. (The original first and second amendments, dealing with apportionment of representatives and with congressional salaries, were quietly dropped as being too controversial.)

To become part of the Constitution, the amendments had to be ratified by three-fourths of the states—which at this time meant eleven, since there were now fourteen states. By an irony of history, Virginia, a leader in the movement for the Bill of Rights, became the eleventh state to ratify. By another irony, three of the original thirteen states failed to approve the amendments for years. Massachusetts, Connecticut, and Georgia finally did so in 1941, on the 150th anniversary of the Bill of Rights.

A typical town meeting

sible, and, together with events in New York, led the two men finally to the dueling ground at Weehawken.

Jefferson, a Man of New Ideas   After the election Jefferson tried to soften party divisions, as Washington had always done. He announced that "We are all Federalists; we are all Republicans." But nothing could hide the fact that a political changeover had taken place. Jefferson himself called it the revolution of 1800. He believed that the victory of his party over Hamilton, Adams, and the Federalists would cause a basic reversal in the direction of American history. His principles were different from theirs. And his party had committed itself to ideas of liberty and democracy that probably did have a profound and long-term effect on the lives of ordinary Americans.

Jefferson's conception of the good society rested on one fundamental opinion. As he put it, "Those who labor in the earth are the chosen people of God." Plain farmers, he felt, ought to be the backbone of any society. And the plain farmers of the Republic ought to have as much political power as they had virtue. They ought to control the government in a more or less direct and democratic way.

The central government ought to be devoted above all to republican simplicity. It should be small and relatively weak, so that it could not interfere with the liberties of the people. Power should be decentralized—that is, divided up among smaller authorities such as state and local governments. Then people could keep a close eye on their elected representatives.

It sometimes seemed that Jefferson's political philosophy was based on a conflict between two simple ideas: power and the people. Whatever contributed to governmental power injured people's control over their own private lives. Jefferson wanted a "government which shall restrain men from injuring one another." But government should do no more than this. It should leave men "otherwise free to regulate their own pursuits of industry and improvement."

Such a government ought to practice the strictest economy. The number of federal offices should be cut to the bare minimum. The national debt should be quickly liquidated. (It had ballooned from $54 million to about $83 million as a result of Hamilton's program of funding and assumption.) In fact, Jefferson promised to pay off the entire debt within sixteen years. To save on expenses, Jefferson reduced the army from 4,000 to 2,500 men. He cut the navy back sharply to a defensive force of coastal guns and small gunboats.

In his own life, too, the new President practiced his principles of simplicity and economy. He reduced the amount of formal entertaining at the White House. He dressed and lived quietly and simply in comparison to the aristocratic elegance of Washington. In fact, Jefferson embarrassed some Americans by receiving visitors while wearing threadbare clothes and tattered bedroom slippers.

Jefferson's was a political program that promised *not* to do things: not to maintain a powerful government with a large standing army and a powerful navy; not to allow the federal government to become powerful at the expense of the rights of the states and the people; not to pursue a financial policy that would benefit only a small class of merchants, bankers, and speculators. The heart of Jefferson's idea of government was his belief that the American people—most of whom really were plain farmers—could build a great nation if only they were let alone. Jefferson himself was a cultivated aristocrat, a highly educated man, and a wealthy slaveholding planter. But his political philosophy was one of democratic simplicity and an almost religious faith in the good sense of the people.

In the long run, Jefferson and the other Republican Presidents who followed him were the captives of history. They were forced to expand, not contract, federal power in order to meet emergencies and opportunities that came their way. But their revolution was one of ideas, not acts. Jefferson and his successors made words like "liberty" and "democracy" the most important words in the political language of Americans. And, after 1800, a democratic faith in the people became the most prominent and unique feature of American political life.

Jefferson continued to believe that political parties were evil. True, he had helped build a party that had turned the Federalists out of office. But he had done so because he believed that the Federalists were a bad party and the Republicans were a good one.

After 1800 the Republicans were committed to making their party the only party, to driving the Federalists out of existence altogether. Jefferson was elected easily for a second term in 1804. Madison won the presidency in 1808 and 1812, and he was followed into office by another Virginian, James Monroe, in 1816. By this time the Federalist party had collapsed and did not even run a candidate. Monroe won again in 1820. By 1824 the fall of the Federalists was so complete that the son of John Adams, John Quincy Adams, won the presidency as a Republican.

After 1824 a new party structure would emerge, with two new parties replacing the Republicans and the Federalists. But, for the time being, it appeared that the Republicans had actually realized the hopes of the Founding Fathers by creating a unified government.

FOREIGN AFFAIRS

During most of the twenty-five years after Washington's first inauguration, Europe was at war. Britain and France fought everywhere in Europe, around the Mediterranean, and in almost every other corner of the world. In the process other European nations and the United States were drawn into the conflict.

Events in Europe had a profound effect on the United States in two chief fields. One was the economy. Americans imported most of their manufactured goods from England, and they in turn sold many agricultural products—like tobacco and cotton—in Europe. This transatlantic trade was crucial to farmers in the southern and western states. Merchants in eastern cities also depended heavily on a brisk trade across the Atlantic. European nations at war needed the American trade, but at the same time they tried to cut their enemies off from American shipping. By turns, the English and the French attacked American ships. They even kidnapped American seamen for service in their own navies and merchant marine, a practice known as impressment.

The other field affected by European affairs was American politics. The conflict between Britain and France was an old one, going well back into the eighteenth century. Indeed, the Americans had fought their Revolution against the British with French help. But there was a new element in the conflict after 1789. In that year the French began a revolution against their monarchy. They proclaimed France a republic in 1792, and from then on they fought their wars for political as well as military reasons. In fact, the French thought of themselves as the agents of "a war of all peoples against all kings."

In the beginning many Americans favored the French Revolution. To them it meant another monarch deposed, another republic created. America's old ally, the Marquis de Lafayette, even sent Washington the key to the Bastille—a notorious Parisian prison whose capture was one of the opening events of the Revolution.

Gradually, though, the French Revolution seemed to take a dangerous turn. At the height of revolutionary fervor, in 1793 and 1794, thousands of Frenchmen, including the king and queen, were guillotined. To many Americans (especially those with Federalist sympathies) this experience was a lesson in the excesses of democracy. But others—the political disciples of Jefferson—followed their leader in stubborn sympathy with the French Revolution and its democratic changes. Thus, politics in America felt the impact of politics in Europe.

Out of this situation arose a crucial question: Could the United States remain neutral, since her trade and her politics were tied so closely to events in Paris and London? From George Washington to John Quincy Adams, American Presidents and their administrations had to devote at least as much attention to foreign as to domestic questions. In fact, much of the time, it was impossible to draw a line between the two.

This long episode in foreign policy involved almost every American political leader, from Washington, Hamilton, and Jefferson to men like Burr and Wilkinson. Burr's plans and intrigues were not the schemes of an isolated individual. Instead, he could claim the company of dozens of other public figures, all constantly involved in speculation, secret plans, and even spying. In the 1790s at least two Cabinet officers were actively working for European governments. Many senators, congressmen, and lesser politicians were so sympathetic to one European side or the other that they lost sight of American purposes and goals.

For almost twenty-five years, Americans had no real independence of Europe. They were tied to France, Spain, and Britain by every ship that left America for Europe, by developing systems of party loyalty, and by tough, troublesome issues of war and peace. Only after 1815, with peace in Europe, did Americans find release from European entanglements.

A Shaky Neutrality Several forces pushed the United States toward a new war with Britain during the 1790s. Ill feeling still lingered after the Revolutionary War. The British refused to evacuate their military posts in the Northwest Territory. They also refused to return American slaves whom they had seized during the Revolution. Many Americans sympathized with the French because of their aid during the war. In addition, there was the treaty of 1778, in which the United States pledged to come to the aid of France in case of conflict with Britain.

When France and Britain went to war in 1793, Washington's administration faced its first difficult decision in foreign policy. Partly under the influence of Hamilton, who despised the French for their democratic republicanism, Washington decided to ignore the alliance of 1778 and remain neutral. But the British made it very difficult for him. They used their position in Canada to stir up hostile Indians against American settlers. And British warships began to stop

and even seize American merchant vessels trading with French islands in the West Indies.

At the same time, the French lost a chance to cement their relations with Americans by sending over a blundering diplomat, Edmond Genêt. Genêt made the mistake of acting as though France and the United States were already allies. He did things that no representative of a foreign government can get away with for long. He set up French courts to take charge of captured English ships. He tried to talk a group of Americans into an armed attack on New Orleans (since Spain sided with Britain at the time). Worst of all, he interfered in domestic political matters. Even Jefferson, the ardent supporter of the French Revolution, could not stomach such behavior. Washington ended by demanding Genêt's recall to Paris.

In the meantime, despite Genêt's clumsiness, anti-British feeling was running high in America. There was real danger of war. Washington wanted to avoid it and settle old questions. He sent John Jay, a Federalist leader and a close friend of Hamilton, to London to negotiate a treaty.

Jay returned home in 1794 bearing a document that became known as the Jay Treaty. The British agreed to give up their Northwest posts. They made a few other concessions of a minor nature. In general, though, the treaty was unfavorable to the United States and offered no real protection to American shipping. It immediately became a political issue. Republicans opposed it, and Federalists supported it. Even Washington, who wanted desperately to avoid a war, was reluctant to sign it, but he finally did so.

Negotiations With France The Jay Treaty made American relations with France more difficult, since the French believed that anything that helped the British hurt them. Late in Washington's second administration and in the early months of Adams' presidency, the French began to intercept American shipping. Furthermore, they treated American sailors serving on British ships as pirates to be hanged. Like Washington, Adams tried to meet the crisis by insisting on neutrality and opening negotiations. He sent a team of three negotiators to Paris to try to arrange a treaty recognizing American trading rights and somehow putting an end to the embarrassing alliance of 1788.

The American mission failed. The French foreign minister, a shrewd and corrupt man named Charles Talleyrand, demanded a bribe of $250,000 for himself. He never met the Americans. Instead, he communicated with them through three anonymous go-betweens known only as X, Y, and Z. Through these agents Talleyrand also demanded that the Americans pay the government of France several million dollars as the price of peace and a treaty. Two of the three American commissioners returned angrily to America to report to a shocked President and Congress. For a time war seemed inevitable.

Adams' position was delicate. Many members of his party wanted war with France—partly to discredit the Republicans and partly to solidify their own hold on the national government. Adams moved considerably in their direction. He called for a stronger navy, better coastal defenses, and the arming of American merchant ships. He also gave in to Hamilton's demands that the army be strengthened. The retired Washington even agreed to take charge of the army in case of war, with Hamilton as his second in command. For several years American and French ships fought an undeclared war in the Atlantic.

But Adams was determined to avoid an unnecessary war, even if it hurt his position among the Federalists. In 1799 he sent another American mission to France with orders to negotiate an agreement. There the Americans found a new government in control. Its leader, Napoleon, was anxious to establish good relations with the United States. He agreed to scrap the 1778 alliance and also to end French interference with American shipping. For the time being, Adams had preserved American neutrality once more.

Trouble With Britain   After his victory in the presidential election of 1800, Jefferson began to dismantle the army and navy that Washington and Adams had expanded. Europe was temporarily at peace, and it looked as if the United States could achieve the promises of independence, freed from foreign involvements. In 1803, however, Europe again donned the familiar mask of war. The major player this time was the commanding figure of Napoleon. Over the next dozen years Napoleon's incredible ambition sent French armies all over Europe and as far from France as Egypt and Russia.

The French emperor contemplated an invasion of England, and he even thought of moving some of his armies into North America. The British were locked in what they regarded a deadly struggle for survival. For Americans the questions were the same old ones: Would they be able to carry on their vitally necessary trade with Europe? Would they be able to preserve their precious neutrality?

Beginning in 1805 British and French warships both began to intercept American merchant shipping again. The British controlled the seas, so they stopped more vessels. The British followed one practice that the French did not. They would board American vessels, pick out men whom they suspected of being British subjects, and force them into service in the royal navy. This practice of impressment, which to most Americans seemed little short of kidnapping, added to the fury that gradually built up in the United States.

Jefferson was committed to peace, to a small army and navy, and to a policy of negotiation rather than threat and bluster. But between 1805 and 1807 the British seized about a thousand American ships, and the French about five hundred. No administration, no matter how devoted to peace, could permit American ships and sailors to be treated like this.

Another crisis occurred in the summer of 1807. A British warship fired on an American vessel within view of the Virginia shore. The British ship, the *Leopard*, fired three broadsides into the American frigate, the *Chesapeake*. The *Chesapeake*'s guns were out of order, and she could return only one cannon shot. Three Americans were killed and eighteen wounded before

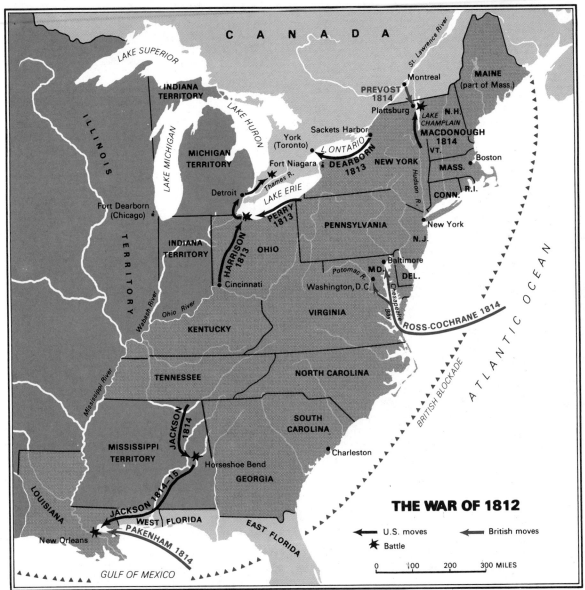

CANADA

LAKE SUPERIOR

INDIANA TERRITORY

ILLINOIS

LAKE MICHIGAN

LAKE HURON

MICHIGAN TERRITORY

Fort Dearborn (Chicago)

TERRITORY

INDIANA TERRITORY

Detroit

Thames R.

LAKE ERIE

St. Lawrence River

Montreal

MAINE (part of Mass.)

PREVOST 1814

Plattsburg

LAKE CHAMPLAIN

N.H.

MACDONOUGH 1814

VT.

Boston

MASS.

R.I.

CONN.

New York

N.J.

York (Toronto)

Sackets Harbor

L. ONTARIO

Fort Niagara

DEARBORN 1813

NEW YORK

Hudson R.

PERRY 1813

HARRISON 1813

OHIO

Cincinnati

Ohio River

Wabash River

PENNSYLVANIA

Baltimore

MD.

DEL.

Potomac R.

Washington, D.C.

Chesapeake Bay

ROSS-COCHRANE 1814

ATLANTIC OCEAN

VIRGINIA

KENTUCKY

Mississippi River

TENNESSEE

NORTH CAROLINA

BRITISH BLOCKADE

SOUTH CAROLINA

Charleston

JACKSON 1814

MISSISSIPPI TERRITORY

Horseshoe Bend

GEORGIA

JACKSON 1814-15

LOUISIANA

WEST FLORIDA

EAST FLORIDA

New Orleans

PAKENHAM 1814

GULF OF MEXICO

THE WAR OF 1812

→ U.S. moves   ← British moves

★ Battle

0   100   200   300 MILES

The American plan called for attacks against the British from Detroit, Fort Niagara, and Plattsburg, New York. In **1812** William Hull marched from Detroit into Canada. Fearing trouble from Indians on his flank, however, he retreated and surrendered Detroit without a shot. In August the American garrison at Fort Dearborn was wiped out.

In **1813** Americans were more successful. In April Henry Dearborn sailed from Sackets Harbor, New York, across Lake Ontario and burned York (now Toronto). Oliver Hazard Perry's September victory on Lake Erie forced the British to abandon Detroit. William Henry Harrison, who had moved north from Cincinnati, pursued the retreating British into Canada and defeated them at the Battle of the Thames in October.

In **1814** the Creek Indians, allied with the British, attacked Americans along the frontier. Andrew Jackson, moving south through Mississippi Territory, dealt the Creeks a heavy defeat at the Battle of Horseshoe Bend. In September British troops under Robert Ross and Alexander Cochrane sailed up Chesapeake Bay. They burned Washington, D. C., but failed to take Baltimore. That same month a British force under George Prevost moved south from Montreal. Americans led by Thomas Macdonough went north to meet them and won an important victory at the Battle of Lake Champlain. Late in the year a large British fleet commanded by Edward Pakenham moved north from Jamaica. In **1815**, in the most spectacular battle of the war, Jackson defeated them at New Orleans.

The British bombarded Fort McHenry, near Baltimore, throughout the night of September 13-14, 1814. The successful resistance of the Americans inspired a bystander, lawyer Francis Scott Key, to write the verses of "The Star-Spangled Banner."

the *Chesapeake* limped home in an odd mixture of pride and disgrace.

Facing an aroused nation, Jefferson tried to ward off a war with Britain by a device used in pre-Revolutionary days. He asked Congress for a law, the Embargo Act, which simply prohibited Americans from exporting *anything* to foreign countries. It also forbade all ships to leave American ports bound for any other nation. In short, the embargo was designed simply to halt foreign trade altogether. Jefferson hoped that the British need for American markets, plus the French desire to import American goods, would force the two nations to behave more respectfully toward American commerce.

The embargo failed. It hurt Americans more than it hurt either the British or the French, because American farmers could not export their products. The law lasted until the end of Jefferson's second administration, when he happily left Washington for his plantation, Monticello. His successor, James Madison, then had to grapple with the problem. Madison's efforts at first were only modifications of Jefferson's policy. For the embargo Madison substituted a modified policy of trade restriction with the Non-Intercourse Act of 1809. He reopened foreign trade with all nations *except* Britain and France. And he promised to resume commerce with either country if only it would respect American rights on the seas.

The War of 1812 The Madison administration experimented with one form of trade restriction or another for more than three years. Finally, Madison asked for a declaration of war, citing impressment and trade interference. Congress responded on June 18, 1812. Just two days earlier, the British had announced a favorable change in policy. But it was too late.

The Americans were involved in a war that was almost impossible for them to fight. They had little or no way of attacking the British directly. Canada was vulnerable to invasion, or so it appeared. But the United States was afraid that Britain would defeat Napoleon quickly and then turn the full power of her army and navy on North America. In such a contest the small American defense forces would have had little chance.

The first months of the war passed without much significant action. The Americans planned a three-pronged attack on Canada through Lake Champlain and the Great Lakes, but all three attempts failed. The British took Detroit, and their Indian allies massacred the Americans at Fort Dearborn (the site of Chicago).

The United States did better on water than on land, at least during the first year of the war. On the Atlantic American vessels were able to capture several British ships. Later, however, a British blockade restricted American actions. On Lake Erie Captain Oliver Hazard Perry smashed a British fleet in September 1813, restoring American control of this region.

Early in 1814 the British and their allies crushed Napoleon's armies and exiled him.[2] Britain was now free to devote more attention to the war with the United States. In August a British fleet, with troops aboard, sailed into Chesapeake Bay. Memories of the hard days of

---

[2] Napoleon escaped from exile a year later, in March 1815. After collecting another army, he was decisively defeated near Brussels at the Battle of Waterloo, in June.

The Battle of New Orleans took place on the east bank of the Mississippi about five miles south of the city. In the main skirmish, January 8, three British generals were killed.

the Revolution must have been reawakened in every American old enough to recall the loss of Philadelphia, New York, and Charleston. On August 24 British troops landed, captured Washington, and burned the Capitol and the White House.

The British planned another major invasion through New Orleans. They knew—just as Burr and Wilkinson had—the strategic value of the city and its river to the United States. Their invading force was met by Americans under the command of an old friend of Burr's, General Andrew Jackson of Tennessee. In January of 1815 Jackson met the British in a battle that soon became legendary. His riflemen and artillery, firing from carefully placed positions, tore

THE TRANS-MISSISSIPPI WEST, 1807

Lewis and Clark 1804–06
Pike 1806–07
Spanish missions

0 100 200 300 MILES

into a rigid British formation and killed or wounded over 2,000 of the enemy. Jackson's force suffered only a dozen casualties. At last, after three years of frustration, the United States had a genuine victory and a genuine military hero.

The only problem about the great victory at New Orleans was that the war was already over. For several months a group of American commissioners had been carrying on peace negotiations with the British at Ghent, Belgium. In December 1814, less than two weeks before the Battle of New Orleans, the two sides had agreed on a treaty and the war ended. The Treaty of Ghent provided only that the situation between Britain and America would remain just as it was in June of 1812. No concessions or promises were made, and no territory changed hands.

The War of 1812 made little sense at the time, and it settled no real problems. Three years after it began came Waterloo. From that time on Britain was not involved in a war with any Continental nation for a hundred years. If the Americans could have held out for three more years, British harassment of their trade would probably have stopped, and the war could have been avoided.

But at least the war was over, and the United States had not lost. In fact, many Americans, encouraged by Jackson's victory, thought of the war as a successful defense of American independence and neutral rights. They called it a Second War for Independence.

TERRITORIAL EXPANSION

One of the most obvious facts of life for the generation of Americans who lived after the making of the Constitution was growth. In 1790, at the time of the first census, there were fewer than 4 million Americans, and most of them lived on the eastern seaboard. Only about one person in every twenty-five lived over the mountains in Kentucky, Tennessee, and Ohio. But the spirit of expansion was everywhere. Every year

thousands of families set out for the Ohio Valley to make new homes. This growth and movement were very much on the minds of American political leaders. Washington felt that strenuous efforts would have to be made to tie eastern and western peoples together. Burr, on the other hand, believed that the federal government could not hold the loyalty of the western settlers.

By 1810 the population of the United States had almost doubled, to over 7 million. And by 1820 it was almost 10 million. As it grew, the population shifted steadily westward. In 1820 one of every ten citizens of the United States lived west of the Appalachian Mountains.

Everyone who looked carefully at the United States in the 1790s knew that the future lay in the west. Franklin's calculations for the future always took for granted that the Ohio and Mississippi valleys held the key to the nation's destiny. Washington thought along similar lines, and so did Jefferson. When Hamilton's death had disgraced Burr, he simply followed an American reflex: when in trouble or in doubt, look to the west for new opportunities and answers.

The Louisiana Purchase According to the peace treaty of 1783, the western boundary of the United States was to be the Mississippi River. This seemed to provide enough land to absorb the people and energies of the infant nation for decades to come. There was only one sore point. Spain still held most of the western half of the continent—and she controlled the Mississippi River and its outlet at New Orleans. The farmers west of the Appalachians depended almost entirely on the river as an outlet for their crops. (It was this traffic that Washington had wanted to divert to the east, through Virginia.)

It came as a bitter shock when the United States learned in 1801 that Spain had given Louisiana to France in a secret treaty. Now New Orleans and the vast Mississippi Valley would be in the hands not of weak Spain but of the powerful and ambitious Napoleon. In 1802 the Spanish—still theoretically in control of New Orleans—caused another shock when they de-

238/ clared that Americans would no longer have the right to use New Orleans as a port.

Jefferson summed up the horror of most Americans when he said that there was "on the globe one single spot, the possessor of which is our natural and habitual enemy. It is New Orleans." As was his custom, Jefferson turned immediately to negotiation. He made Napoleon an offer to purchase New Orleans from France for $2 million. The American negotiator, James Monroe, was greatly surprised and pleased when the French offered to sell not just New Orleans but the entire territory of Louisiana—about 800,000 square miles of lush but practically empty country.

In April 1803 the Americans closed the deal. They bought all of Louisiana for $15 million—a price that averaged out at about $2 per square mile for one of the richest unsettled areas in the world.

The purchase created some problems for Jefferson. He believed in what is called strict construction—a strict interpretation of the Constitution. Basic to his theory of government was the idea that the President and Congress could do only those things that the Constitution expressly gave them power to do. The Constitution nowhere gave the President the power to acquire new territory. In contrast to Jefferson's position was loose construction, favored by the Federalists. They felt that the government could do not only the things mentioned specifically by the Constitution but also other things that were merely implied. Thus, they would have argued, the power to make treaties implied the power to acquire territory, since acquisition was in the nature of a new treaty arrangement.[3] After some quarreling, mainly with himself, Jefferson gave up on what he called "metaphysical" questions. He asked Congress to appropriate the $15 million. The United States took formal possession of New Orleans in December of 1803, just seven

months before the duel between Hamilton and Burr.

SECTIONAL STRAINS IN A GROWING NATION

The Louisiana Purchase was approved in the Senate by a wide margin, twenty-four votes to seven. But the opposition was significant, because it pointed toward a powerful and underlying problem in American life. Most of the opponents were from New England. People there realized that the westward movement would sooner or later result in a basic shift of people, economic power, and political control away from the East to the western territories and states. The Founding Fathers had worried about whether one government could control a nation as large as the United States. The years between 1790 and 1815 were full of tests of the American motto, *e pluribus unum*—"out of many, one."

One of the fundamental purposes of the authors of the Constitution had been to control local and sectional interests and prevent uprisings like Shays' Rebellion of 1786. Between 1789 and 1815, the nation passed through several similar tests, each of which seemed to challenge national authority over the states and sections on a very fundamental level.

The Whiskey Rebellion During Washington's first administration, farmers in western Pennsylvania provoked the first major challenge to federal power. These were farmers like those who had refused to move off Washington's land and like those whom Burr would later try to recruit to his cause.

One part of Hamilton's financial program had been a tax on distilled liquor, which meant mainly whiskey. At this time the cheapest and most economical way for most western farmers to transport their grain crops to the East was to turn the grain into whiskey. So the Congress was taxing not a luxury but a basic economic product.

Many farmers resisted the tax. In the summer of 1794 they even mobbed tax collec-

[3] This difference of interpretation first came up when President Washington was deciding whether to sign Hamilton's bank bill in 1791. Jefferson, a strict constructionist, argued against it; Hamilton's loose constructionist views carried the day.

tors, much as Americans had attacked Stamp Act tax collectors a generation before. The rebellion was small, much smaller than Shays' uprising had been eight years earlier. But President Washington reacted with a series of steps that went well beyond what was needed. He called out 15,000 militiamen and marched them west toward Pittsburgh with himself at their head! This excessive display of federal military power worked immediately, of course. The rebels were totally intimidated. In his zeal Washington revealed the depth of his old concern about maintaining law and order in the west.

After the rebellion had been suppressed, Washington delivered an address to Congress in which he condemned not only the rebels but national political clubs called Democratic Societies. The societies had been formed in enthusias-

tic support of the French Revolution. Most of them were the local bases of Republican political strength. But to Washington's mind the sectional question of East versus West was closely tied to the question of Republican opposition. Anything that threatened national unity, whether it was a sectional uprising or an opposition political group, was an evil to be dealt with quickly.

The Hartford Convention During the administration of John Adams, sectional stress focused heavily on the Alien and Sedition Acts. Organized opposition came primarily from Virginia and Kentucky, in the resolutions written by Madison and Jefferson. It looked for a time as though the Republican party might become a sectional party, with strength only in the South and West, while Federalists held complete power

Even before the purchase of Louisiana, Jefferson began planning for its exploration. To lead the first expedition, he chose his private secretary, Meriwether Lewis (shown at left in Indian garb). He and William Clark— the younger brother of George Rogers Clark—spent two years gathering facts on the geography and peoples of the region. Their notebooks included the drawing of a Flathead Indian woman, right above. Another explorer sent out by Jefferson was Zebulon Pike, above left. He discovered, but failed to climb, the mountain peak in Colorado that bears his name. When he was in Mexican territory, his papers were taken from him. They remained in the Mexican archives until discovered by an American scholar a hundred years later.

in the North and East. Through the efforts of men like Burr, this split was avoided, and the Republicans built strong organizations in New York and Pennsylvania. New England continued to be the only true Federalist stronghold. It was from New England that the main opposition to the Louisiana Purchase was voiced in 1803. Whenever there was a possibility of war with Britain or France, the Republicans leaned toward war with Britain, while the Federalists leaned toward war with France.

Before the War of 1812 the New England states, which were tied closely to Britain by trade, had bitterly opposed Jefferson's embargo. New England opposed the war even more. In Congress the strongest voices for war had been those of the so-called War Hawks—Congressmen from the frontier regions who wanted to invade and annex Canada, adding even more land to the western domain at the expense of the East. Politicians and businessmen all over New England felt that the government had betrayed them and was willing to sacrifice their interests to the war fever of the rest of the country.

In opposition to the war, New England resisted militia calls and wartime taxes and continued to trade with the enemy in Canada. In 1814 the New England governors called a convention in Hartford, Connecticut, to raise the same kinds of questions that the Annapolis Convention had raised about the Articles of Confederation. In calling the convention, the governors asserted that the Constitution had failed, that the New England states were not receiving "equal rights and benefits," and that the frame of government would have to be seriously revised. A few members of the convention demanded immediate secession from the Union. The convention drafted a series of proposed amendments to the Constitution—all of which would have weakened the federal government—and sent them to Washington to the next Congress.

Time, however, cured problems that might not have been solved otherwise. When the Hartford Convention proposal reached Washington, news of Jackson's victory had just arrived, and the news of the peace treaty was not far behind. As was to happen so often in American history, sectional crisis had been resolved by events and not by statesmanship. Despite its lack of positive results, the Hartford Convention had raised what was to become the basic political question for the next generation: Would the United States be able to resolve sectional differences, or would some crisis sooner or later divide one part of the country from the other?

1. For what reasons did Burr and Hamilton become bitter enemies?
2. Why is it said of Burr's western scheme that it made "almost perfect sense as part of the larger history of the United States"?
3. Why did the framers of the Constitution oppose political parties? How did they try to prevent them? Why were they unsuccessful?
4. What were the main outlines of Hamilton's financial program? Why did Jefferson and Madison oppose it?
5. What advantages did a neutral United States hope to gain from the Napoleonic Wars? Why did both Britain and France try to prevent Americans from enjoying these advantages?
6. Why was the Jay Treaty unsatisfactory to many Americans? Why did embargoes fail to solve the trade problems of the United States?
7. Would you say that the United States won the War of 1812? Why or why not?
8. Regarding the Louisiana Purchase, Jefferson later said that he had "done an act beyond the Constitution." What did he mean? Do you agree?

Beyond the Text

1. Prepare a report on the Alien and Sedition Acts, including such points as (a) enforcement; (b) opposition; and (c) final disposition of the laws themselves.
2. Organize a panel to discuss the so-called revolution of 1800. Was Jefferson's an accurate description? If the answer is negative, discuss what you think he would have had to do to bring about a revolution.
3. Debate the topic: Americans Should Have Fulfilled the Obligations of the Treaty of 1778 and Aided France Against Britain.

4. Historians differ as to the causes of the War of 1812. Prepare individual reports for presentation to the class on the importance of each of the following: (a) neutral rights; (b) western land hunger; (c) agricultural depression; and (d) national pride.

Bibliography

Nonfiction

Bemis, Samuel F., *Jay's Treaty.**

Chambers, William N., *Political Parties in a New Nation.**

Charles, Joseph C., *Origins of the American Party System.**

Coles, Harry L., *The War of 1812.**

Cunliffe, Marcus, *The Nation Takes Shape: 1789–1837.**

Dangerfield, George, *The Era of Good Feelings.**

Fischer, David H., *The Revolution of American Conservatism.**

Hofstadter, Richard, *The Idea of a Party System.**

Levy, Leonard W., *Freedom of Speech & Press in Early American History: Legacy of Suppression.**

Miller, John C., *Crisis in Freedom.**

North, Douglass C., *The Economic Growth of the United States, 1790–1860.**

Peterson, Merrill D., *Thomas Jefferson and the New Nation.*

Schachner, Nathan, *Aaron Burr.**

Fiction

Laing, Alexander, *Jonathan Eagle.**

Roberts, Kenneth L., *Captain Caution.**

Vidal, Gore. *Burr.*

*a paperback book

11

A NEW YORK CITY MAYORAL RIOT

SHEETS OF RAIN deluged New York City on the morning of April 8, 1834. It was the first day of a three-day election. This year, for the first time, city voters were going to choose their own mayor. Excitement ran high, for this was an era of feverish political activity. To some, the chilling downpour seemed a welcome relief from the heated election campaign that had been raging for months.

It could be said, in fact, that the campaign had been going on since 1832. For it was in that year that President Andrew Jackson had declared political war on the Second Bank of the United States.[1] Chartering a bank—or refusing to do so—may not seem the stuff of which drama is made. But the so-called Bank War of the 1830s did not involve bankers alone. Because it pitted social and economic classes against each other, it aroused intense emotions among millions of Americans.

The Bank of the United States had headquarters in Philadelphia and branches in twenty-nine other cities. This bank alone could hold the government's deposits. It was a strong force also because of the credit it could extend, the bank notes it issued, and its influence on all the other banks of the country. Since the time of the First Bank, some Americans had felt that such an institution was wrong because the

---

[1] The charter of the First Bank, granted under Washington, had expired in 1811; the Second Bank was chartered in 1816.

New York's bustle is evident in this 1834 view of Broadway looking north from Canal Street. Outdoor vendors include an iceman, lower left, and a boot-seller across the street. The posts and high rails provided support for awnings stretched from shops on sunny days.

Constitution had not granted specific authority to establish it. Others opposed it because they thought that state banks should have more power.

Jackson opposed the bank, and he had been taking pot shots at it since coming into office in 1829. Its charter was not due to expire until 1836. But Nicholas Biddle, president of the bank, decided to press for early recharter in 1832. The bill passed Congress, but Jackson vetoed it in July. His veto message was a scorching attack on monopolies, foreign investors, loose interpretations of the Constitution, and aristocrats. Jackson lashed out at the rich in phrases seldom heard in American politics:

> It is to be regretted that the rich and powerful too often bend the acts of government to their selfish purposes. Distinctions in society will always exist under every just government. Equality of talents, of education, or of wealth can not be produced by human institutions. In the full enjoyment of the gifts of Heaven and the fruits of superior industry every man is equally entitled to protection by law. But when the laws undertake to add to these natural and just advantages artificial distinctions, to grant titles, gratuities, and exclusive privileges, to make the rich richer and the potent more powerful, the humbler members of society—the farmers, mechanics, and laborers—have a right to complain of the injustice of their government.

Government should give equal protection to all, special favors to none. It should, "as Heaven does its rains, shower its favors alike on the high and the low, the rich and the poor."

The bank issue dominated the presidential election of 1832. To Jackson's enemies of long standing and to those more recently acquired, his attacks seemed an invitation to class warfare. Biddle called the veto message "a manifesto of anarchy." He compared Jackson to a "chained panther biting at the bars of his cage." But 1832 was a Democratic year, and Jackson won reelection.

Now the President closed in for the kill like an *unchained* panther. The nation watched in horrified fascination as a powerful, competent financier (Biddle) and a powerful, canny politician (Jackson) went at each other without mercy. Jackson wanted to remove government deposits from the bank. When his Secretary of the Treasury refused, Jackson replaced him. Federal deposits were removed in September 1833. Biddle, meanwhile, cut down on new loans, and he demanded repayment for those already made.

The country prepared to tighten its financial belt. Jackson swore that he would never give in to the bank, no matter what happened. He assured Vice President Martin Van Buren, melodramatically yet accurately: "Were all the worshipers of the golden calf to memorialize me [send petitions] and request a restoration of the deposits, I would cut off my right hand from my body before I would do such an act. The golden calf may be worshiped by others but as for myself, I will serve the Lord." Jackson also believed that he was serving all Americans. He certainly would not confuse a small group of protesting moneymen with "the people"—*his* people.

Despite this touchy situation, some pro-bank merchants made their sentiments known to the President and Congress. A few even dared to appear in Washington to press their claims. One high-level delegation of merchants went to the White House to plead for a change in financial policy. Distress gripped the nation, they said. There was no money. The President must act. Jackson, enjoying every minute of this fight, responded with mocking advice: "What do you come to me for, then? Go to Nicholas Biddle. We have no money here, gentlemen. Biddle has all the money. He has millions in his vaults at this moment, lying idle, and yet you come to *me* to save you." So much for direct appeals.

During the winter of 1833–34 the country suffered from this Bank War. Interest rates rose, and many small businesses went bankrupt. Merchants and manufacturers, unable to borrow money cheaply, were forced to slow down business activity or even shut down. Thousands of workers in turn found themselves unemployed.

Still, something good might come out of all this—good for the bank, at least. Biddle believed that cutting down on loans might have political repercussions that would lead toward recharter. "The ties of party allegiance can only be broken by the actual conviction of existing distress in the community," observed Biddle coolly. "Nothing but the evidence of suffering will produce any effect on Congress. Our only safety is in pursuing a steady course of firm restriction—and I have no doubt that such a course will ultimately lead to the recharter of the Bank."

New York, the nation's largest city and leading money market, could not escape the impact of that "Panic Winter." The Bank War affected not only the economy but also the city's established political parties. By this time the Republicans had split into two groups. One was the Democratic-Republicans (or, more often, Democrats). It was essentially the party of Jefferson, with Jackson as its present leader. The other group was the National Republicans. It included some former Federalists, but its members were united mainly by their opposition to Jackson.

New York City political affairs were generally controlled by Democratic supporters of Andrew Jackson, campaigning under the banner

Gulian Verplanck, left, wrote poetical satires, essays on religion, and—after his defeat in the mayoral race—a life of Shakespeare. Cornelius Lawrence, right, served three successive one-year terms as mayor. During his administration occurred a disastrous fire that destroyed 600 buildings in the heart of New York's business district.

of their political club, Tammany Hall. But many Jacksonians were unhappy over the President's opposition to the bank and the apparent economic results of his policy. Some of them, especially the wealthy, felt threatened enough to leave the Democratic party entirely.

Ranged against the Jacksonians in New York City—as in the rest of the nation—were a variety of political opponents. There were disgruntled Democrats. There were National Republicans. And there were so-called Anti-Masons, who were opposed to the Masonic order because of its allegedly dangerous influence on American life. Together these groups organized the Whig party in the spring of 1834. The term "Whig" had sometimes been used by Patriots during the American Revolution. As these Americans had defended liberty against the tyranny of a hateful monarch, George III, so the Whigs of 1834 pledged themselves to overthrow, by electoral means, a ruler they considered equally hateful. (In fact, his enemies called him King Andrew I.)

Against this background New Yorkers prepared to elect a mayor. City voters had never before had a direct voice in a mayoral election. Before 1834 New York City's mayors had been chosen by the state legislators or by members of the city council. During the early 1830s such indirect election of local officials came under attack as being undemocratic, and was changed. Now New York City voters would have the right to elect their own leader.

As election day neared, Whig and Democratic appeals to the voters became more and more heated. Each side denounced the other passionately and violently, making strenuous efforts to bring out the vote. A massive election-day turnout seemed a certainty. New York's political leaders and prominent citizens wondered whether the voters would choose wisely. They also wondered whether the election itself could remain peaceful and orderly. Three days were then allotted for voting, a long time for political passions to rage. Some die-hard conservatives trembled, recalling Alexander Hamilton's remark that the people resembled "a great beast." But Democratic and Whig politicians asserted self-confidently that the voice of the people would indeed turn out to be the voice of God.

Both parties had nominated former members of Congress as their candidates for mayor. The Whig candidate was Gulian C. Verplanck, a Democrat who had split with Jackson on the bank issue. Verplanck, an honest but aloof campaigner, seemed more at home in New York's literary circles than in the rough-and-tumble of mass politics. He shied away from personal appearances. Instead Whig party organizers and newspaper editors did his electioneering and tried to build a popular image for him. One Whig editor admitted that Verplanck was a "scholar." But, he went on to argue, Verplanck was also a man

> whose name is identified with every institution for the promotion of education among the people—for the relief of those whom age or misfortune has stripped of means—a man who is identified with his native city by every tie that can bind man to his fellows.

The Democratic candidate, Cornelius W. Lawrence, although a wealthy merchant, mixed easily with the political regulars at Tammany Hall. Much of Jackson's financial policy displeased him, but Lawrence remained a loyal Democrat. He had no intention of following Verplanck's example and abandoning his party. "This will be a fair trial of the issue," predicted a Whig supporter. "Mr. Lawrence—the man who has for the sake of party proved unfaithful to the interests of the merchants, of which he is a member—on the one side, and Mr. Verplanck—who lost his seat in Congress because he would not pursue the same course—on the other."

The first day of the election was Tuesday, April 8. A ballot box had been set up in each of New York's seventeen wards (election districts). The political organizers had done their work. Not even the torrential rains could dampen the spirits of the faithful when the polls opened. Voters came out in large numbers, especially after the rain stopped at about ten in the morning. Over 20,000 voted on the first day. This was 6,500 more than had voted in New York City on the first day of the 1832 presidential election and 3,000 more than the total number of voters in a three-day election the previous fall. Signs of party organization and activity could be seen everywhere. "The parties seemed to be engaged in a death struggle," reported one impressed observer.

Certainly many businessmen in the city believed that they were engaged in a life-and-death conflict. Economic conditions had made them angry, and Democratic appeals to the masses had made them edgy. The business community opposed Jackson's unyielding position on the bank. Its fears increased when a prominent New York Democrat declared that the government should allow commerce and credit to perish rather than establish a new national bank. Most businessmen decided to close shop by late morning of the election's first day. They boarded up their stores and warehouses and marched to the Merchants Exchange on Wall Street at noon. There the troubled tradesmen listened to speakers blasting Jackson and the Democrats. Then they hoisted an American flag over the building and left to go to the polls.

What they saw at the polling places could hardly have cheered them. In the middle of the city's mercantile district was the Eleventh Ward. Here the Democrats—who controlled the city government—had appointed three election inspectors, as they did in the other sixteen wards. Not surprisingly, two of the three inspectors in the Eleventh Ward were Democrats. The polling place was a room in Hawkins' Tavern, at the corner of Allen and Houston streets. The line of voters using the main entrance to the room hardly moved because the Democratic election inspectors were allowing party loyalists to enter the polling room by two smaller side doors. "In this way," the Whigs later angrily charged, "a steady stream of Jackson voters" kept the polling rooms full, excluding "the voters at large" (who presumably included many anti-Jackson men).

The single Whig election inspector in the Eleventh Ward demanded that the two side doors be closed. His two Democratic counterparts, without blinking an eye, explained that the tavern's side rooms had been rented to private individuals and that to close the

The Democratic Chronicle.

SATURDAY EVENING, APRIL 5, 1834.

TEMPLE OF LIBERTY.

Jackson and the People
AGAINST THE
Bank and the Aristocracy.

Just before the election, a Democratic newspaper listed the candidates it backed. (Lawrence's name is followed by recommendations for offices in each ward.)

doors would interfere with their rights! Voters friendly to the Democratic cause continued to stream in from both sides.

The Whigs howled over such foul play. They hastily sent a letter by messenger to the district attorney of New York County, a Democrat, asking that voting procedures in the Eleventh Ward be declared illegal. The district attorney, Ogden Hoffman, agreed that inspectors should show no preference to any party, nor should any ballot box be the exclusive property of one party or the other. Hoffman claimed, however, that he could find nothing in the election laws that related directly to the disputed point. "Side-door balloting" continued.

The frustrations and squabbling in the Eleventh Ward were more than matched by bloody events that occurred in the Sixth Ward. This district was strongly pro-Jackson. It was nicknamed the officeholders' ward because of the many Democratic politicians and public officials who lived there. The ward also included many Irish Catholics, a good

NEW YORK CITY IN 1834

Tammany Hall in 1830 stood on Nassau Street near City Hall. Later the building was enlarged and modernized to serve as the offices of the New York Sun, *one of the city's biggest newspapers.*

portion of them recent immigrants. Politicking was serious business in the Sixth, and arguments between political partisans had broken out even before the polls opened. Fistfights between small groups of men punctuated the first morning of voting.

Early in the afternoon a crowd collected in front of Masonic Hall, the Whig party's campaign headquarters in the ward. Several members of the crowd brandished clubs, and a few carried knives. Most of them simply waved their fists in the air angrily. Suddenly, without warning, the mob surged forward into the Whig office, knocking down anyone who resisted or failed to get out of the way fast enough. Down went all the Whig banners. A bonfire of printed Whig ballots[2] soon blazed. Everything breakable in the room became a pile of debris. The attackers had felled about twenty men, and one of them lay dying.

The incidents in the Sixth and Eleventh wards, along with minor disruptions in other parts of the city, convinced Whigs that fraud and violence were destroying the democratic process. They felt too that the immigrant Irish bore the blame for much of the corruption and mayhem. Voters in 1834 did not have to register at a specified time before election day, as they do today. Under these circumstances it was much easier for a person who did not meet the residency requirements to vote fraudulently. Democratic voting inspectors were lenient. They gave ballots to many aliens who had not even filed papers indicating their intention to apply for citizenship.

The Whigs were by no means above such cheating. If it had been to their advantage, they would probably have committed similar abuses on election day. But the political loyalties of most immigrants in New York City, especially the Irish and Germans, went to the Democratic party. Whig complaints focused on

> the immense number of foreigners who are driven up every moment to the Marine Court to get out letters of naturalization. Almost every five minutes an omnibus comes up filled with them. Nine-tenths of them are Irishmen of the very lowest class, and many of them not long enough in this country to wear out the clothes they brought on their backs. They go to the court foreigners in every sense of the word, and in five minutes they come out intelligent American citizens, burning with love of country.

A few days after the election Whigs published an imaginary conversation between an Irish voter and a Democratic politician at Tammany Hall.

---

[2] At this time each political party printed its own ballots listing its candidates. A voter simply dropped the ballot of his own party into the ballot box.

A ragged, hatless, stockingless Hibernian [Irishman] presented himself, just after the election, at the bar of Tammany Hall, and after scraping and bowing three times said:

Is it Tammany Hall this is?
Yes.
Then I have come to get me pay, if you plase.
Your pay! For what?
For coming all the way from the Jarseys [New Jersey] to attend the election, to be sure, and I voted in two wards.
In *two* wards!
To be sure I did; in the 'leventh and thirteenth. And now I want me pay, if you plase.

This fabricated account was, of course, a slander on the great majority of New York Irishmen who were legal residents, American citizens, and thus legitimate voters. Their Democratic ballots did not have to be bought. Still, the newspaper article reveals some of the Whig party's attitudes toward the Jacksonian opposition—and toward non-British immigrants generally. Anti-Jackson New Yorkers felt that something drastic was needed to protect voters from the fraud and bullying they associated with the Democratic party.

Whigs had asked city officials for help earlier in the day. Mayor Gideon Lee, a Democrat, replied that all his available constables had already been assigned throughout the city. He refused to swear in more than twenty new deputies. "Twenty men against banded mobs of hundreds!" sputtered the Whig press. "We much mistake the American character if our citizens do not take the matter into their own hands."

Determined to protect themselves and the ballot boxes, 4,000 Whigs met at Masonic Hall on Tuesday night, April 8. Appropriately, they named a state militia general, Robert Bogardus, as chairman of the meeting. They resolved that:

> Whereas, the authority of the police of the city has been set at defiance by a band of hirelings, mercenaries, and bullies in the Sixth Ward, and the lives of our citizens put in jeopardy; and, whereas, it is evident we are in a state of anarchy— Resolved: That, in order to preserve the peace of the city, and especially of the Sixth Ward, the friends of the Constitution and the liberties of the citizen will meet at this place [Masonic Hall] at half-past seven o'clock A.M., and repair to the Sixth Ward poll for the purpose of keeping it open for *all* voters, until such time as the official authorities shall procure a sufficient number of special constables to keep the peace.

Masonic Hall, on Broadway between Duane and Pearl streets, looked like this in 1830. Note, on the neighboring building, an awning pulled over the sidewalk to protect pedestrians from the sun.

Some Whigs wanted even stronger action. One of them was James Watson Webb, a newspaper editor and an ex-Democrat turned rabid Jackson hater. He called for 300 well-armed men to appear at Masonic

Hall at *six* in the morning. Webb said nothing about his specific plans, but he obviously intended to bring "peace" on the "Bloody Sixth" by force if necessary.

Shortly after daybreak on Wednesday, April 9, Whigs began assembling. More men than Webb had asked for came, most of them armed. After holding a rally to instill this force with the proper spirit, Webb marched 200 of the vigilantes to City Hall. Apparently impressed by this show of force, city officials relented. The sheriff swore in the men as special constables and issued them badges. The newly appointed "peace officers" hurried immediately to the Sixth Ward.

Webb, who had served several years as an army officer, took charge. He told an unfriendly crowd that the events of the day before made the presence of the citizens' posse necessary. He announced that no man's legal rights would be interfered with. Force would be used to preserve the peace and keep the polls open. The crowd muttered, heaved a few stones, and threw some punches at the constables. By early afternoon, however, voters had free access to the polling station. Webb's men had formed double lines at both the entrance and exit of the building. Several "fierce Irishmen" were arrested, according to Whig newspaper accounts. (By this time the Whigs were assuming that all violence was the work of the Irish.)

Though relative calm reigned that day, few persons expected it to continue. Webb sent some of his constables back to Masonic Hall with instructions to remain ready for action. That night, thousands of Democrats paraded through the streets and congregated at City Hall Park. The election had one more day to run, and the crowd wanted to show the mayor and city council (then in session) how much they resented the swearing-in of the special constables. Some shouted "Down with the Courier and Enquirer building!"—a reference to the plant on Wall Street where Webb's newspaper was printed. Two members of the council rushed downtown to warn Webb of the danger, urging him to close his office in order to avoid bloodshed. Webb replied defiantly that he had not asked the city council for protection, nor did he intend to. Though he normally closed at 10 P.M., he vowed to stay open indefinitely, with lights blazing. He had with him thirty young men, all supplied with pistols, muskets, and plenty of ammunition. Five loads of paving stones lay on the roof of the building, ready to be dropped on rioters' heads.

Back at the park, meanwhile, the crowd heard more speeches and then began to move down William Street toward Wall. Webb closed his doors and waited. When the street had filled, those nearest the

NOT VERY LIKE A WHALE BUT VERY LIKE A FISH

SEVENTH WARD PROMENADES

A Whig cartoon depicts Lawrence's followers as a mob of ruffians. Their informally dressed leader is probably not Lawrence. He may be a Jacksonian Democrat named Preserved Fish, a well-known whale-oil merchant (hence the caption at top).

building began shouting threats and banging against the walls with sticks and clubs. Webb pushed his musket through a windowpane, warning that he would shoot the first man he caught in his sights. As he moved the muzzle slowly up and down the street, the crowd fled. Some of the demonstrators then appeared in front of Webb's home on Bleecker Street. They shouted insults at its owner but made no attempt to break in.

Increased violence characterized the election's final day, Thursday, April 10. In the morning fights broke out near the Sixth Ward polling place. This time, Mayor Lee stood at the head of an official party that tried to stop the fighting but only partially succeeded.

The most serious fracas occurred around noon. It began innocently enough with the supporters of both parties pushing model ships through the streets. Sailors who were aiding the Whig campaign rigged up a little frigate named the *Constitution*, put it on wheels, and draped it with Whig banners. Democrats put a similar ship model on wheels, its flag inscribed "Veto"—an approving salute to Jackson's veto of the bill to recharter the national bank. The ships had been "sailing" through the city streets for two days, often missing each other by only a block or two.

But a collision course seemed inevitable. At noon on Thursday the processions met. When the fists and missiles began flying, many Whigs came out of nearby Masonic Hall on Broadway to help the sailors. But Democratic reinforcements from the Sixth Ward soon poured in, forcing the Whigs to retreat into their headquarters.

Another call went out for Mayor Lee. He arrived, clutching his staff of office, accompanied by several city council members. But this was no moment for symbols of authority. As soon as Lee mounted the steps of the building to demand that the rioting end, a flying stick clipped him on the head and knocked him down. Though the mayor was not seriously hurt, neither he nor his police could restore order. The fighting continued, with the Democrats apparently getting the better of it. Over fifty persons were injured, many of them severely.

The outmanned Whigs knew they had to retreat, but where? "To the arsenal!" shouted some of them, and off they went to a building in which they could feel both safe and extremely well-armed. Guarded by only a few aged watchmen, the arsenal quickly fell to a group of Webb's constables. They immediately began passing out arms. Another fight, perhaps the bloodiest of all, seemed likely, since an immense crowd of Democrats had finally responded to the latest Whig move and jammed the streets surrounding the arsenal.

Once again, Mayor Lee stepped forward into an unpromising situation. He had already asked for military aid but had been refused. Both the army commander on Governor's Island and the head of the marine detachment at the Brooklyn Navy Yard replied that they lacked authority to act. The city would have to handle the explosive situation itself. The mayor then decided to use his ultimate weapon—one that he probably should have relied on after the first day's outbreak of violence—the city militia.

The crowd in front of the arsenal had grown larger and noisier. At this critical moment a militia detachment of infantry and two squadrons of cavalry marched down the street in a close column, dividing the crowd as they advanced. In the meantime, the men occupying the arsenal turned it over to Mayor Lee and his assistants. They claimed

The New York City Council still meets in this room in City Hall. After the time of this engraving—1831—the room underwent many changes, but was restored in the early 1900s.

that they had seized the building only to keep the arms out of the hands of the Democratic street fighters. With the arrival of the troops Lee in turn surrendered control of the arsenal to the commander of the militia. The infantry stayed there, while the cavalry units went to City Hall. The rioting ended, and the third day of voting came to a close.

Naturally, interest in the outcome of the election was high. After the polls had closed on the final day, city officials took the ballot boxes to City Hall under guard. The largest of these guard companies formed up in the Sixth Ward. As usual, it boasted the rowdiest crowds and the greatest threat of serious trouble. Several thousand persons trailed along after the procession bearing the disputed ballot box of the "Bloody Sixth," but there were no incidents.

Since more crowds were expected that night, newspaper editors kept their staffs on duty and well-armed. Military units patrolled the streets until dawn. They kept a special watch on banks and the Merchants Exchange—both rumored to be probable targets of mob attack.

On Friday, April 11, business ground to a halt while the election returns trickled in. Over 10,000 people jammed Wall Street, the majority of them Whigs. One of them reported:

> Such an excitement! So wonderful is the result of this election that all New York has been kept in a state of alarm. Immense crowds have been collected at Masonic and Tammany Halls, but the greatest concourse was in front of the Exchange. The street was a dense mass of people. Partial returns were coming in every few minutes. So close has been the vote that the Whigs at the Exchange and the small party for Jackson in front of the office of the *Standard* opposite shouted alternately as the news was favorable to one or the other. Up to the last moment, the result was doubtful.

As it turned out, both sides came away with something to cheer about. In a very close race Democrat Cornelius Lawrence won the mayor's office by a slim margin of only 179 votes out of the more than 35,000 cast. Lawrence's victory delighted the Democrats. They believed that it signaled the failure of Whig merchant-aristocrats to intimidate the city's "producing" classes and "create an excitement against the warm-hearted but easily aroused Irish citizens."

For their part the Whigs captured seventeen of thirty seats on the city council. Whig stalwarts praised this majority as a "triumph of good principles over violence, illegal voting, [Democratic] party discipline, and the influence of officeholders."

Leaders of each side blamed the election violence on the other, swearing that *their* people had acted only in self-defense. Whig newspapers named several persons of good standing as instigators of the Democratic mobs. These cunning but cowardly figures, they said, had egged on their gullible shock troops, the Irish, who accounted for most of those injured and arrested. Such "disgusting things cannot be permitted. Life and property in the great city of New York must not be made insecure. The mob must be taught obedience to the law."

To the editor of the principal Democratic paper, events showed clearly that the election had been a contest between rich and poor—the kind of contest President Jackson had described in his veto message. Only a blind person could miss the essential point. A would-be aristocracy had combined to oppose the just interests of laborers, farmers, and all other workers. As for the spark that touched off violence, Democrats had an easy answer. It had been unnecessarily provoked by Monday's meeting of Whigs at the Merchants Exchange.

A few days after the election Mayor Lee and the city council met to assess the damage and propose some remedies. The mayor noted that "unusual means for the preservation of the peace" had been

(continued on page 257)

AN EXPANDING FRONTIER

One of the most important features of the national experience has been the steady movement westward of the American people. They traveled through tangled forests, down rivers, and on pathways like the Allegheny road shown here, well worn by the 1830s. Americans overcame obstacles with amazing energy. In a few years they had not only tamed the wilderness, but also created whole new cities, among them Cincinnati, Louisville, Chicago, and St. Paul.

Alexis de Tocqueville praised the fearlessness of the pioneers: ''Millions of people are marching at once toward the same horizon. Their language, their religion, their manners differ; their object is the same. Fortune has been promised to them somewhere in the West, and to the West they go to find it.''

[For further information on the foreign observers quoted in this essay, see ''Notes on Sources.'']

The Squatters, by George Caleb Bingham

*A squatter is a person who, without any title to the land,
or leave asked or granted, squats himself down and declares
himself the lord and master of the soil for the time being.
There is nobody to question his right. These hardy fellows
are sometimes called the pioneers of the wilderness—and
justly so—for they go ahead of the more orderly and civilized
population and clear away the grounds in the line of march.*

[BASIL HALL, 1828]

*On our way to Pittsburgh we met with various specimens of
the backwoodsman, and I must say that, when clad in their
green hunting shirts, with deerskin caps and leggings, their
muscular attitude fully displayed in the free handling of
their long rifles, they presented the most picturesque
appearance I had ever seen. They had a way of leaning on
their guns and surveying a stranger which struck me as
singularly intelligent. It implied conviction, not inquiry. It
was a look that said, not "Who are you?" but "I know you."*

[JOHN BERNARD, 1800]

Engraving of Daniel Boone,
said to be the earliest print made
west of the Mississippi

*From camp all the trappers—
some on foot, some on horseback, according to the distance
they have to go—start every
morning in small parties in all
directions ranging the distance
of some twenty miles around.
There is much anxiety and
danger in going through the
ordinary routine of a trapper's
duty. For as the enemy is generally lurking about among the
rocks and hiding places, watching an opportunity, the hunter
has to keep a constant lookout,
and the gun is often in one hand
while the trap is in the other.*

[ALEXANDER ROSS, 1810-25]

Setting Traps for Beaver, by Alfred Jacob Miller

*The driver stopped and came to tell us ladies that he was sorry to trouble us to get out,
but that an emigrant's wagon had blocked up the ford of a creek which we had to
cross. It must not be supposed a common circumstance that an emigrant's wagon was
left in a creek. The "camping out" is usually done in a sheltered, dry spot in the
woods, not far from some little stream, where the kettle may be filled and where the
dusty children may be washed.*

[HARRIET MARTINEAU, 1835]

Emigrating westward, a family camps beside a stream

Methodist missionary on his way west

Indiana housewife outside her log cabin

A lively scene from Davy Crockett's Almanac

At one lone dwelling we found a neat, respectable-looking female, spinning under the little piazza at one side of the cabin, which shaded her from the sun. Her husband was absent on business. She had no famliy, and no companion but her husband's faithful dog, which usually attended him in his bear hunting in the winter. She was quite overcome with "lone," she said, and hoped we would tie our horses in the wood and sit awhile with her during the heat of the day. We did so, and she rewarded us with a basin of coffee. Her husband was kind and good to her, and never left her without necessity, but a true lover of bear hunting—which he pursued alone, taking only his dog with him, though it is common for hunters to go in parties to attack this dangerous animal.

[MORRIS BIRKBECK, 1818]

Pioneers cutting trees in a clearing

At intervals a log cabin, with its little space of cleared land about it, nestles under a rising ground and sends its thread of blue smoke curling up into the sky. Sometimes the ground is only just now cleared, the felled trees lying yet upon the soil and the log house only this morning begun. As we pass this clearing, the settler leans upon his axe or hammer and looks wistfully at the people from the world.

[CHARLES DICKENS, 1842]

The Mill Boy, by George Caleb Bingham

These lonely settlers are poorly off. Their corn for bread must be ground thirty miles off, requiring three days to carry to the mill and bring back the small load of three bushels. Articles of family manufacture are very scanty, and what they purchase is of the meanest quality and excessively dear. Yet the people are friendly and willing to share their simple fare.

[MORRIS BIRKBECK, 1818]

Pushed by the European population toward the northwest of North America, the Indians come, by a strange destiny, to die on the very shores where they landed in unknown centuries to take possession of America. In the Iroquois language, the Indians call themselves the "men of forever" —Ongoue-onoue. These "men of forever" have gone, and foreigners will soon leave to the heirs of a whole world only the earth of their tombs.

[FRANÇOIS-RENÉ DE CHATEAUBRIAND, 1791]

A squatter came splashing through the mud to the spot where I was and begged me to take a paddle with him in his canoe, hollowed out, as he told me, by his own hands from the trunk of a cypress. I went along with him and found his wife seated in a very nice, clean, roomy cottage made of logs, with a large fireplace lined with mud on one side, the whole whitewashed and very neat. An air of comfort pervaded the whole establishment, which I had not expected. The squatter was really quite active in his hospitality.

[BASIL HALL, 1828]

Inside a backwoodsman's home

Chippewa chieftain with a white trader

Frontier neighbors at a community scutching (beating flax to separate the fibers)

When several families settle at the same time and place, the colonists do not become brutalized as easily as the solitary settler. When he is surrounded by gloomy woods and closed horizons, cut off from association with his fellows, he soon loses those civilized habits that a community develops.

[AXEL KLINKOWSTRÖM, 1820]

Every boy, as soon as he can lift a rifle, is constantly practicing with it, and thus becomes an astonishingly expert marksman. When I was in Kentucky, a hunter offered to fire twenty times at a dollar at a distance of 100 yards, on condition that I should give him a dollar every time he struck it and that he would give me one every time he missed it. But I had seen such specimens of their rifle-shooting that I did not choose to accept his offer.

[WILLIAM BLANE, 1822-23]

Shooting for the Beef, by George Caleb Bingham. (The cow at left goes to the winner.)

It is a peculiarly happy feature of the Constitution of the United States that every state has itself an independent government. The western states of America are each a nursery of freedom. Every new settlement is already a republic in embryo. They extend political life in every direction. Every new state, therefore, is a fresh guarantee for the continuance of the American Constitution and directs the attention of the people to new sources of happiness and wealth. It increases the interest of all in upholding the general government and makes individual success dependent on national prosperity.

[FRANCIS J. GRUND, 1837]

Stump Speaking, by George Caleb Bingham

St. Paul, Minnesota, in 1856

The next moment St. Paul was before us, standing upon a high bluff on the eastern bank of the Mississippi. The town is one of the youngest infants of the Great West, scarcely eighteen months old, and yet it has in this short time increased to a population of two thousand persons. In a very few years it will certainly be possessed of twenty-two thousand, for its situation is as remarkable for beauty and healthiness as it is advantageous for trade.

[FREDRIKA BREMER, 1850]

Whatever may be the talents of the persons who meet together in society, the very shape, form, and arrangement of the meeting is sufficient to paralyze conversation. The women invariably herd together at one part of the room, and the men at the other. In justice to Cincinnati, I must acknowledge that this arrangement is by no means peculiar to that city, or to the western side of the Alleghenies. The gentlemen spit, talk of elections and the price of produce, and spit again. The ladies look at each other's dresses till they know every pin by heart, and talk of Parson Somebody's last sermon on the day of judgment or Dr. T'otherbody's new pills for dyspepsia. When the "tea" is announced, they all console themselves together for whatever they may have suffered in keeping awake.

[FRANCES TROLLOPE, 1828]

In a Cincinnati ballroom

required. Now money had to be found to pay for them. Several city watchmen had been injured, and their families needed help. Lee also thought the mayor should have the power to appoint "any number of special peace officers that may be required for any further emergency."

Lee also wanted the state legislature to approve a tough and workable voter registration law, "for ascertaining by proper proof, the citizens who shall be entitled to the right of suffrage." Twelve hundred citizens of New York City had sent in a petition urging passage of such a law. New York Governor William L. Marcy, also a Democrat, took official note of the election riots in his legislative message of January 1835. Seizure of the city arsenal, "an act tending so directly to bloodshed," called attention to the need for moving the arsenal out of the center of the city. On the question of voter registration—then a novel idea for American cities—Marcy preferred to keep the existing law of 1829 "to preserve the purity of our elections." (It would also preserve Democratic votes.) Voter registration came to New York in the late 1830s, when the Whig party gained control of the state government. Even then, the Whigs applied the "purifying" measure only to New York City.

The governor hurled some charges of his own at the "Money Power." "The moral and political condition of the electors has hitherto been sufficiently healthful to counteract the corrupting influence of money, and I hope it may long continue so."

The mayoral election of 1834 ended in stalemate and division of power, like many other episodes in Jacksonian politics. The two major parties managed to neutralize one another. Fall elections in 1834 took place without violence. This time, however, the city council acted in advance, appropriating $5,000 for "ensuring and preserving the peace at the coming election."

The election riots showed how easily Americans could move from consensus politics to political war. But, though shocked by the rioting, most American leaders rejected the notion that such violence had become the American way. They agreed with Governor Marcy, who felt "disposed to ascribe the increased efforts that appear of late to influence the elections, by the lavish use of money, to the nature of some of the questions involved in our political contests." By "some of the questions" Marcy meant the Bank War, the central issue in Jacksonian politics. It was this single question that most aroused passions and agitated the American political scene during the stormy period of Jackson's presidency.

12

The Jacksonian Era

THE THREE-DAY FRACAS in New York City in April 1834 was an unhappy example of American political violence. But it was by no means the only such event during the Jacksonian period. Riots occurred in several cities and towns, on political and other issues. Baltimore became known as the Riot City. Armed clashes there, similar to the one in New York City, continued into the 1850s. New York City itself had barely recovered from its 1834 mayoral election when another riot broke out. This one, in July, was an antiabolitionist and antiblack explosion. It, too, lasted for three days.

Political violence occurred fairly often in the young United States. Violent language had marked American politics from the earliest days. Newspaper editors and politicians wrote and spoke about their opposition party members as if they were the greatest scoundrels yet unhanged. Such violent expression often led to duels or fights and sometimes even to riots.

The Second Bank of the United States was the one issue of the Jacksonian era that, probably more than any other, led to the greatest amount

Andrew Jackson, the first President to be born in a log cabin, was actually a man of aristocratic tastes.

of violence—whether verbal or physical. This struggle, and its related problems, dominated politics throughout the 1830s. Its roots went back more than two decades. Why, after all, was there a *Second* Bank? The Jeffersonians had opposed the *First* Bank and allowed its charter to expire in 1811. Why did their Republican successors charter another one? The answer to this question lay in problems that emerged during the War of 1812 and the response to them by a Republican-controlled Congress in 1815–16.

THE ERA OF GOOD FEELINGS

The War of 1812 ended in 1815 with Andrew Jackson's spectacular victory in the Battle of New Orleans. By then American politics had been radically changed. The declining Federalists had been further weakened by charges of wartime disloyalty because of the Hartford Convention, and they had all but disappeared. For nearly ten years the so-called Era of Good Feelings characterized the political scene. Earlier, fierce battling had taken place between the two major parties. After 1815 political competition occurred among groups within the all-powerful Republican party.

This Republican party was not the same one that Jefferson had fashioned. When the war ended, Republicans adopted some of the very measures that they had condemned in the past. This proved especially true with regard to the national bank and the tariff. The federal government had gone deeply into debt during the war, and it needed more revenue. Dozens of state banks had sprung up after the expiration of the First Bank's charter. They had operated poorly during the war, and the country now clearly needed a better financial system. The government needed to pay off its debts. Moreover, there was growing pressure on it to take a more active role in promoting economic growth. Many Americans wanted federal money to be spent building a network of roads and canals, especially west of the Appalachian Mountains. They wanted a system of internal improvements, as it was then called.

Swallowing pride and party principles, the Republicans responded to these pressures by chartering a second national bank. President Madison overcame his previous objections to a national bank. A young South Carolina representative of the Southern planter interests, John C. Calhoun, introduced the bank recharter bill. It was passed in 1816, providing for a bank to run until 1836.

Next came the tariff. Like the bank issue, debate on the tariff in 1816 began with patriotic statements and a nationwide agreement, but it ended before long in fierce political squabbling. American manufacturers, located mainly in New England, were just then getting started. They wanted higher tariff duties so that Americans would buy fewer foreign goods and more of their own products. They wanted not just a revenue tariff, which would bring in funds, but a protective tariff—one set high enough to protect American producers from foreign competition.

In 1816 Calhoun and many other Southerners voted in favor of a higher, protective tariff. They did so not to enrich New England manufacturers but in order to obtain additional revenue needed by the government. National security was a primary concern. Southerners—like Americans in all sections—feared the outbreak of yet another war with Britain. They wanted the United States to be better prepared than it had been in 1812.

There was less agreement on internal improvements. The country did need a better transportation system. Here, though, Madison's constitutional conservatism stood in the way. As a Jeffersonian, he could not convince himself that the federal government had the right to spend money in this way, even though his party had shifted its attitudes on the bank and a tariff. In 1817 Congress passed a bill authorizing national funds for internal improvements, but Madison vetoed it. For the next two generations each state had to build its own roads and canals.

Madison's successor, James Monroe, continued the theme of "good feelings," the dream of national harmony and political unity. All but the most die-hard of the Federalists had made peace with the Republicans. The President issued soothing calls for an end to all party divisions. In the election of 1820 Monroe had no competition, and he won every electoral vote but one. Harmony had indeed been established in national politics—for a while.

The Panic of 1819 But trouble was already brewing. The first sign was a financial panic. Since the War of 1812, people had been speculating heavily in foreign trade and western lands. They bought on credit, hoping to reap a large profit before having to pay off their debts. Then, in 1819, the Second Bank—under new management—began calling in loans. As a result, many state banks closed, and numerous investors went bankrupt.

The Panic of 1819 affected the whole nation. But it hit western states hardest. It was the first of a series of economic downturns that would occur in the United States at approximately twenty-year intervals until 1929.

The national bank, just three years old at the time, bore the greatest blame for the hard times. Many Americans attacked the bank as a corrupting agent of aristocracy and privilege. Several state legislatures tried to tax its branches out of existence. The Supreme Court ruled such laws unconstitutional (see page 223). But the strong anti-bank feelings that had surfaced never really disappeared. Politicians would capitalize on them throughout the 1820s.

Americans had distrusted banks even during the colonial period—often with good reason, given the high rate of bank failures. In the 1820s Kentucky and Tennessee witnessed "relief wars," during which debtors organized against creditors. Everywhere, private banking interests were on the defensive. These struggles were a prelude to the Jacksonian battles of the 1830s. They also provided a training ground for several important politicians who would later join Jackson's anti-bank crusade.

The Missouri Compromise Another sign that the Era of Good Feelings was ending was the forever troublesome subject of slavery. In the

DEVELOPMENTS IN TECHNOLOGY, 1750–1860
(DATES REFER TO PATENT OR FIRST SUCCESSFUL USE)

YEAR	INVENTOR	CONTRIBUTION	IMPORTANCE/DESCRIPTION
1750	Benjamin Franklin	LIGHTNING ROD	Protected buildings against damage from electrical storms.
1775	David Bushnell	SUBMARINE	First American submarine; submerged by taking water into tanks and surfaced when water was pumped out.
1787	John Fitch	STEAMBOAT	First successful American steamboat.
1793	Eli Whitney	COTTON GIN	Simplified process of separating fiber from seeds; helped make cotton a profitable staple of Southern agriculture.
1798	Eli Whitney	JIG FOR GUIDING TOOLS	Facilitated manufacture of interchangeable parts.
1802	Oliver Evans	STEAM ENGINE	First American steam engine; led to manufacture of high-pressure engines used throughout eastern United States.
1813	Richard B. Chenaworth	CAST-IRON PLOW	First iron plow to be made in three separate pieces, thus making possible replacement of parts.
1830	Peter Cooper	RAILROAD LOCOMOTIVE	First steam locomotive built in America.
1831	Cyrus McCormick	REAPER	Mechanized harvesting; early model could cut six acres of grain a day.
1836	Samuel Colt	REVOLVER	First successful repeating pistol.
1837	John Deere	STEEL PLOW	Steel surface kept soil from sticking; farming thus made easier on rich prairies of Middle West.
1839	Charles Goodyear	VULCANIZATION OF RUBBER	Made rubber much more useful by preventing it from sticking and melting in hot weather.
1842	Crawford W. Long	FIRST ADMINISTERED ETHER IN SURGERY	Reduced pain and risk of shock during operations.
1844	Samuel F. B. Morse	TELEGRAPH	Made long-distance communication almost instantaneous.
1846	Elias Howe	SEWING MACHINE	First practical machine for automatic sewing.
1846	Norbert Rillieux	VACUUM EVAPORATOR	Improved method of removing water from sugar cane; revolutionized sugar industry and was later applied to many other products.
1847	Richard M. Hoe	ROTARY PRINTING PRESS	Printed an entire sheet in one motion, vastly speeding up printing process.
1851	William Kelly	"AIR-BOILING PROCESS"	Improved method of converting iron into steel (usually known as Bessemer process because English inventor had more advantageous patent and financial arrangements).
1853	Elisha G. Otis	PASSENGER ELEVATOR	Improved movement in buildings; when later electrified, stimulated development of skyscrapers.
1859	Edwin L. Drake	FIRST AMERICAN OIL WELL	Initiated oil industry in United States.
1859	George M. Pullman	PULLMAN CAR	First sleeping-car suitable for long-distance travel.

Voting day in Philadelphia, as elsewhere in the Jacksonian era, occasioned much rowdy excitement. During this period the number of voters increased, not only because suffrage requirements were eased but also because people took more interest in politics.

same year as the panic, the issue of statehood for Missouri came to a head. The Missouri Territory was part of the original Louisiana Purchase. Its residents had applied for admission to the Union in 1817. But then a congressman from New York demanded prohibition of slavery in the area as the price of admission. The uneasy sectional truce on the question of slavery evaporated. Congress was deadlocked on the issue for over a year. Southerners had equal voting strength in the Senate, which then had the same number of slave states and free states. Northerners controlled the House of Representatives, however, because the North had a larger population. Antislavery representatives argued that Congress could and should make abolition of slavery a condition for admitting new states. Southerners retorted that all states, old or new, were sovereign and could decide the matter of slavery for themselves.

These arguments were in progress when Maine, then a district of Massachusetts, petitioned Congress to become a separate state. Southerners would not admit Maine as a free state unless Missouri joined the Union with the right to permit slavery. Henry Clay of Kentucky, the Speaker of the House, took an active role in pushing the bargain—a free Maine, a slave Missouri. A sufficient number of Northerners in both houses agreed, and the bill passed. The Missouri Compromise of 1820 also banned slavery in the remaining areas of the Louisiana Purchase north of 36° 30′ latitude (see map, page 343).

The Missouri crisis frightened many Americans, and with good reason. They knew that truly national politics and national parties could not exist if slavery became an active issue bitterly dividing the sections of the country. Jefferson, the retired ex-President and builder of the Republican party, spoke of Missouri as a "momentous question," which, "like a fire-bell in the night, awakened and filled me with terror." The Missouri Compromise, he felt, had given the Union "a reprieve only, not a final sentence." Many other anxious politicians agreed with this analysis, though few were willing to admit it openly.

Both Northerners and Southerners preferred simply to go along with the compromise. They hoped against hope that the slavery issue could be kept quiet and localized. Yet the Missouri debates exposed the entire argument between supporters and opponents of slavery. Clearly, these sectional issues and attitudes had the power to rip the Union apart.

A RETURN TO PARTY POLITICS

By the time of the 1824 presidential election, all the major contenders for the office had problems other than Missouri on their minds. They were concerned mainly with scrambling for power at a time when the brief period of political harmony had clearly ended.

For a decade a nominating caucus (special group) of congressional Republicans had selected the party's presidential candidate. As 1824 approached, Secretary of the Treasury William H. Crawford was the main contender for the nomination. His rivals denounced the caucus, claiming that it was aristocratic and undemocratic. Others joined the attack. As the caucus became more unpopular, an alternate method of nominating candidates had to be found.

Politicians found the answer during the next few years in a new nominating device, the convention. Conventions were supposed to be more representative of a party's membership and thus more democratic than the caucus. Only members of the national or state legislature could attend a legislative party caucus. But, in theory, any party member could become a convention delegate. Grass-roots political elements could be represented at a convention. So could groups or factions that had not been able to elect people to Congress. (Behind this change was a general movement toward increasing popular participation in the governmental process. In New York City one result was the election of the mayor by the citizens themselves.)

At first, old-line politicians resisted the changeover to conventions. Yet they had little to worry about. Party bosses found that it was not difficult to manipulate convention delegates. Still, conventions did provide excellent window dressing. They gave the appearance of equality in an age when political operations were becoming more and more democratized.

The official caucus nominee was Crawford. Four presidential hopefuls—John Quincy Adams, Henry Clay, Andrew Jackson, and John C. Calhoun—refused to accept the caucus decision. When Crawford suffered a stroke that left him partly paralyzed, the caucus and its candidate seemed doomed, even though Crawford refused to leave the race. Calhoun did pull out, however, settling for the vice-presidential spot.

Jackson, a rapidly rising politician, stirred popular enthusiasm as the hero of the Battle of New Orleans. Professional politicians, who controlled the state Republican machines, did not approve of Jackson's campaign at first. But he gathered strength across the country and quickly became a serious contender.

The "Corrupt Bargain" In the election Jackson got more popular and electoral votes than his rivals, Adams, Crawford, and Clay. But he fell short of a required majority. The House of Representatives had to decide among the top three candidates, Jackson, Adams, and Crawford. Clay, though he had been eliminated, persuaded his supporters to cast their votes for John Quincy Adams. The issue was settled, and Adams was elected.

Clay's move was no more than good, hard-headed politics. Jackson and Clay (a Kentuckian) were rivals in the west. Furthermore, Clay saw eye-to-eye with Adams on many political issues, particularly the need for a national program of internal improvements.

No sooner had Clay made his decision,

The Monroe Doctrine

In President James Monroe's annual message to Congress on December 2, 1823, he included the principles of foreign policy later known as the Monroe Doctrine. Monroe and his Secretary of State, John Quincy Adams, wanted to clarify the American position in two specific problem areas. They succeeded in a wider sense, as one historian states, by planting their principles "firmly in the national consciousness."

The first problem area was the Northwest. Since 1821 Russia had been encroaching on the Oregon Country, claimed jointly by Britain and the United States. In October 1823, Adams stated bluntly that "the American continents are no longer subjects for any new European establishments." This principle was repeated in Monroe's speech.

South America was the second problem area. Eight new republics had declared their independence from Spain, but their existence was precarious. Despotic regimes in Europe were successfully crushing revolutions on the Continent, and it was no secret that Spain was eager to regain her lost colonies. In August 1823 the English foreign secretary proposed a joint British-American manifesto to warn Europe against intervention. British merchants wanted to retain their profitable new markets in South America, now open to them after the breakup of the Spanish monopoly. And Britain could back up a threat with the power of its navy.

Adams, however, did not want the United States to be "a cockboat in the wake of the British man-of-war." He suspected that the British might restrict American expansion in some way as a price for their support. Also, Britain had not officially recognized the new republics, as the United States was doing. So Adams suggested an independent course of action. Monroe agreed and decided to include a warning in his message to Congress.

Monroe declared that intervention by European monarchies in the democracies of the New World would be judged as "the manifestation of an unfriendly disposition toward the United States." He pledged the United States not to interfere with any existing European colonies in the New World and to keep out of the "internal concerns" of Europe.

The speech was acclaimed at home but viewed abroad as "arrogant." Yet the European powers took no action. Why? Two months earlier, unknown to Adams and Monroe, the English had pressured France to agree not to assist Spain in any invasion of her ex-colonies. Thus the issue had already been defused. Russia, unable to gain support for intervention, withdrew its claims to the Pacific Northwest early in 1824. The South American republics seemed indifferent to the speech. They were more impressed with "the oaken fleets of Britain" than with "the paper shield of Monroe."

So the significance of Monroe's declaration was discounted at first. In years to come, however, his principles were invoked with great reverence. The strength of the nation lent weight to his ideas.

James Monroe

however, than Adams returned the compliment by appointing Clay Secretary of State. This was the chief Cabinet spot and the post that for two decades had been a stepping stone to the White House. Adams' move was *not* good, hard-headed politics. Clay had qualifications worthy of a Cabinet post, and he served well in the State Department. But the appointment exposed both men to the charge of fraud, a "corrupt bargain," in which Clay had supposedly sold his thirty-seven electoral votes for high office and the promise of a future presidency. A popular riddle of the day among Jackson's supporters ran: "Why is Adams on shaky ground?" "Because he stands on slippery Clay!"

Jackson never took defeats calmly, and he tended to view political differences as personal quarrels. He vented his anger at Clay: "The Judas of the West has closed the contract and will receive the thirty pieces of silver." The Tennessean never doubted that Adams and Clay especially Clay, were indeed corrupt men. For three years Jackson and his followers raged at Clay and Adams in the same way that they later turned on Nicholas Biddle and the Bank of the United States.

A Second Adams Jackson, as confident as he was angry, predicted that the Adams presidency would end in failure and that the people would throw him out of office after four years. Jackson may have been too outspoken, but he was not wrong.

Like his father, John Adams—another crusty, stubborn, and inflexible man—John Quincy Adams believed in government by the most able and talented. Also like his father, John Quincy Adams learned quickly that such a belief would not make him popular with the majority of his fellow Americans. Adams had been preparing for the presidency all his life, but once he was in the White House, he found that his hands were tied. He was a minority President, lacking control of Congress. He also lacked the ability to make either himself or his programs popular with the public. Adams was bound to fail, and fail he did.

For four distressing years this very capable individual fussed and floundered. The job called for talents Adams did not possess and could not acquire. He was reserved—a "cold fish" to most people who met him. He was short-tempered with any person he considered a fool (he claimed to have met many, especially in politics). And he was completely unwilling to compromise.

President Adams' first message to Congress confirmed his lack of political skill. He urged the adoption of a wide-ranging program to improve nearly every aspect of American life—cultural and educational, as well as economic and political. His proposals would have substantially increased the powers of the federal government. Very few Americans of the time believed that this should be done. People were shocked by Adams' proposals, and Congress ignored them when it did not ridicule them.

A powerful Jacksonian opposition formed both in and out of Congress during the Adams administration. Jackson's forces made important deals in 1826 with the Republican state organizations of Virginia and New York, which had remained loyal to the bedridden Crawford two years earlier. An astute New York politician, Martin Van Buren, journeyed to Virginia to confer with leaders of the so-called Richmond Junto. Van Buren proposed an alliance to support Jackson for President in 1828. The Virginians would join his own machine, the Albany Regency, and any other groups that wanted to support Jackson.

Jackson, Van Buren argued, would be a reasonable compromise candidate. He was already very popular. He did not support the extreme states'-rights position. Nor did he favor a strong national government. Furthermore, Van Buren promised that his Northerners would see to it that slavery was kept out of national politics. The Southern states would thus be free from antislavery attacks during Jackson's presidency. In short, Van Buren wanted to revive the coalition originally formed by Burr of New York and Jefferson and Madison of Virginia. Both the original Jeffersonian group and the new Jacksonian alliance were known as Democratic–Republicans. But the Jeffersonians were more generally referred to as Republicans, while the Jacksonians called themselves Democrats. Anti-Jackson Republicans became known as National Republicans.

One political group that quickly linked up with the pro-Jackson forces was New York City's Tammany Hall. This powerful organization included in its ranks such men as Gulian Verplanck and Cornelius Lawrence. They were united as Democrats and as Jackson men—at least for the time being.

The Election of 1828   In the presidential race of 1828 the most attractive candidate was clearly Andrew Jackson. His supporters viewed him as the embodiment of all the basic American virtues, the Washington of his generation. To his critics, on the other hand, Jackson represented frontier barbarism and militarism in government.

Jackson was born in western South Carolina in 1767. He served in the Revolutionary army when he was only twelve years old. Orphaned at the age of fourteen, he migrated to Tennessee. There Jackson succeeded as a lawyer and as a businessman, especially in land sales. He soon built himself a mansion, The Hermitage, outside of Nashville, bought slaves, and planted cotton. (It was here that he received Aaron Burr in 1805.) A man of fiery temper, Jackson got into many arguments, some of which he settled in duels. His toughness earned him the nickname of "Old Hickory."

Jackson entered politics early in his career. He was in the Tennessee convention that drew up the state's first constitution. He also served briefly in both houses of Congress at the turn of the eighteenth century. Back in Tennessee he pursued business and political interests. It was as a general in the state militia that he crushed the British at New Orleans in 1815. In 1818 he fought against the Seminole Indians of Florida, a campaign that increased his great popularity.

By 1828 the Jacksonians had assembled a powerful coalition. The outcome of the contest between the frosty Adams and the fiery Jackson never seemed in doubt. The latter had the best of the political organizations behind him. He also had the services of an excellent, though unofficial, campaign manager, Martin Van Buren. Jackson also benefited from the support of a new breed of newspaper editors—brash professional politicians like Amos Kendall of Kentucky and James Watson Webb of New York City. These editors used their papers openly to build up their state political parties, as Webb did during the 1834 mayoral election in New York. At election time they tried almost any aggressive campaign technique, up to and including outright slander, to help their candidates.

The election campaign was essentially a personal, name-calling duel between Jackson and Adams and their supporters. Adams' forces accused Jackson of having lived in sin. (When he and Rachel Robards were married, years earlier, both mistakenly thought that her divorce had become final.) Jackson's forces in turn harped on the "corrupt bargain" between Adams and Clay.

The popular vote in 1828 was close, especially in the Northern states, but Jackson won— 178 electoral votes to 83. The election of 1828 not only brought Andrew Jackson to the White House, but also stimulated popular interest in national politics. In 1824 only 26 percent of those eligible to vote bothered to go to the polls. In the Jackson-Adams contest, however, 56 percent of those eligible participated. Before 1828 the biggest turnout of voters had usually occurred in state elections. After Jackson's victory national elections became more important than state contests in terms of voter participation.

JACKSON AS PRESIDENT

Like many skillfull politicians, Jackson had been deliberately vague about his policies while campaigning. He maintained this cautious course in his March 1829 inaugural address, with one exception: he called for "reform." This word was political shorthand, an indication that Jackson intended to reward his friends and punish his enemies. During the previous generation of one-party, Republican rule, turnover among public officeholders had not been great. The last large-scale shift in government employees had occurred when Jefferson became President. He removed a good many Federalists from office. Since that time a Republican elite, many of them anti-Jackson, had settled cozily into federal jobs, some for a quarter-century. Jacksonians understandably demanded that the new President replace these older officials with loyal Jackson supporters.

Jackson went further than Jefferson had. He removed about 10 percent of the federal officeholders during his first year as President and a total of about 20 percent in eight years. It was not the clean sweep hoped for by the Democratic politicos. But the Jacksonians did radically change the nature of federal patronage. Jackson

openly defended the principle of rotation in office—what came to be known as the spoils system. He agreed with William L. Marcy of New York that "to the victors belong the spoils." Jackson acted on the theory (if not always the practice) that, in a democracy, men of normal intelligence could capably fill nearly any public office. To Jackson's political opponents this view seemed dangerous. Yet rotation in office, at all levels of American government, became the standard practice after Jackson and lasted for decades.

Strengthening the Office Jackson's opponents saw him as a tyrant, an uncouth military man from the west. Needless to say, this opinion did not conform to Jackson's vision of himself as an "old Republican," a true Jeffersonian. But

A cartoon version of the Bank War portrays Jackson as a donkey trampling on branch banks. Van Buren, as a sly fox, goes after the U. S. Bank. In the background are chained dogs, representing administration newspapers, baying their approval of Jackson's antics.

Republicanism had changed significantly since Jefferson's presidency. Jackson hoped to revive what he called the "Republican principles of '98." He did not want national power to increase at the expense of the states. Yet his role as a strong President and his ability to dramatize political issues for ordinary people in every section stimulated the growth of national power.

Jackson's "old Republicanism" took several forms. In his first annual message, the President criticized the national bank. He also rejected the idea of a high, protective tariff. (Unlike some Southerners, however, he did not deny the tariff's constitutionality.)

On the issue of internal improvements Jackson held views like those of the Republican Presidents prior to John Quincy Adams. In 1830 he vetoed the Maysville Road bill, which would have involved the federal government in a road-building project in the state of Kentucky. He argued that such matters should be left in local hands. He did believe, though, that the national government could contribute to interstate projects. This is why he favored national support for the Cumberland Road, an east-west improvement that passed through several states. Jackson received firm support on this question from Martin Van Buren of New York. New York State had completed the Erie Canal in 1825 without federal money, making further major internal improvements in the state unlikely.

Jackson did much to strengthen the American presidency. He was by far the strongest Chief Executive up to his time and one of the most forceful in American history. Since Jefferson's first term, power had been steadily slipping out of presidential hands to Congress. Jackson, however, reversed the process.

During his eight years as President, Jackson restored the White House as the focal point of national politics. For one thing, he refused to agree automatically with congressional wishes. He injected himself into the legislative process with vigor, vetoing twelve bills. (This was three more vetoes than the total handed down by all the previous Presidents.) A favorite device of his was the pocket veto—delay in signing a bill until Congress adjourned. Perhaps most important, Jackson vetoed some bills simply because he thought them unwise, not necessarily because he regarded them as unconstitutional.

"Old Hickory" also became the undisputed leader of his party. He claimed to be the direct representative of the American people, since he was the only important officeholder elected by the people as a whole.

Nullification   Jackson demonstrated his forcefulness and his claim to represent all the people most strongly in the crisis over nullification. Trouble had been brewing over the federal tariff law for many years. In 1828 the South Carolina legislature published an *Exposition and Protest* (written, not too secretly, by Jackson's Vice President, John C. Calhoun). It branded protective tariffs as unjust and unconstitutional and termed the 1828 version, supported by Jackson, the Tariff of Abominations. Changes must come, the *Exposition* warned, or South Carolina would act.

By this time Calhoun had switched political positions completely. A nationalist in 1816, he had now become a leading Southern states'-rights advocate. Calhoun supported nullification—the idea that a state could nullify (refuse to enforce) a federal law. It was not just tariffs that concerned Southerners. Many feared that a more powerful federal government might be tempted to move actively against slavery. Nullification was a weapon against such tampering. Calhoun at first hid his views on nullification. By 1831, however, he had broken completely with Jackson. He now felt free to champion this position.

As Southern complaints about the tariff continued, Jackson tried to arrange for a compromise tariff bill to lower import duties. But he never lost sight of the fundamental issue, state defiance of federal law. Jackson rejected nullification totally, vowing to preserve the Union. He applied all the power of the presidency and the force of his personality to block nullification and denounce John Calhoun.

Nevertheless, South Carolina went ahead

Peter Cooper

As an old man looking backward, Peter Cooper said that his life had fallen into three parts—thirty years to get started, thirty years to gain a fortune, and thirty years to distribute it wisely. As inventor, manufacturer, and philanthropist, Cooper became a legendary figure. One historian called him ''as distinctly an American type as Benjamin Franklin, and as quickly taken to the American heart.''

Born in 1791 in New York City, the young Cooper revealed a restless nature and a talent for tinkering. As a boy, he made shoes and hats and even a simple washing machine. For his first child he devised a mechanically rocked cradle attached to a musical instrument, patented as a ''Pendulous and Musical Cradle.'' Some of his ambitious projects, such as propelling ferryboats by compressed air, were grotesque failures. Others, such as an end-less chain to haul canal boats, went unrecognized. ''I was always fussing and contriving,'' he wrote, ''and was never satisfied unless I was doing something difficult—something that had never been done before, if possible.''

He came to a turning point in 1821, when he bought a glue factory in New York. It became the foundation of his fortune. In a few years he had a monopoly in the field and was able to pursue other interests. Cooper invested in real estate and rail-roads. In 1830, for the Baltimore and Ohio Rail-road, he built and piloted the first steam locomotive in the United States, nicknamed ''Tom Thumb.'' With a good sense of the demand for iron in an increasingly industrialized economy, he bought iron mines and ironworks, producing the first structural iron for fireproof buildings. As president of the giant North American Telegraph Company, he supported Cyrus Field in his project for laying the Atlantic cable.

In 1856 Peter Cooper calculated that he was a millionaire. So he turned to the realization of his long-held dream: a workingman's institute in New York City for ''the advancement of science and art.'' He was painfully aware of his own lack of formal education, and yet he was distrustful of much ''book learning.'' Thus he wanted to develop a school ''so that the boys and girls of this city who had no better opportunity than I had to enjoy means of information would be enabled to better their condition.'' Cooper Union opened in 1859, offering free courses in science, technology, art, and design, as well as a library and a museum.

Cooper's public career included reform politics. Some of his ideas were far in advance of his time—controlled currencies, unemployment relief works programs, and government regulation of railroads. In his last years, according to one writer, he became ''an unwearied figure for social justice.''

Cooper's personal qualities explain the esteem in which the public held him. He had the self-confidence and optimism of the master craftsman. Though hard working, he was never ruthless. At his funeral in 1883, this tribute was paid: ''Here lies a man who never owned a dollar he could not take up to the Great White Throne.''

and declared the 1828 tariff "null and void" in the state. What would Jackson do? Though he might compromise on tariff rates, he would not compromise federal authority. His Nullification Proclamation of December 1832 dismissed South Carolina's nullification arguments and actions. Congress quickly passed a Force Bill reaffirming the President's right to use troops in order to put down rebellion and enforce the laws.

Jackson meant to use force if necessary. But South Carolina failed to receive moral support from other Southern states. The state's isolation left it no real hope of defending nullification. Early in 1833 Henry Clay and John Calhoun worked out a compromise bill reducing tariff rates over the next ten years to an acceptable level. The nullification issue collapsed (though to save face South Carolina declared the Force Bill unconstitutional).

An armed clash had been avoided. The Union stood firm. Jackson emerged from the struggle with more strength and greater prestige than before. The President had shown character, political skill, and moral courage—all of which he would need in his next major campaign, the war against the Bank of the United States.

The Bank War—and After Why did Jackson oppose the Second Bank of the United States and come to hate its president, Nicholas Biddle? As an investor, he had lost money in a panic in the 1790s, and he had distrusted banks ever since. As a Jeffersonian, he regarded the bank as a dangerous institution. He thought it was too large and national in scope. To him, it represented a concentration of economic power, created by the federal government, that endangered states' rights and the rights of the people. The Supreme Court declared the Bank of the United States constitutional, but Jackson felt that the President had as much right as the Court to interpret the Constitution.

The bank's president, Nicholas Biddle, was following the advice of Henry Clay when he decided in 1832 to ask Congress for a twenty-year extension of its charter. It was a presidential year. Clay, the National Republican candidate, needed an issue to defeat Jackson. Biddle's request was followed by congressional approval and presidential rejection. Jackson's stinging veto message had been drafted by Amos Kendall. He was the most influential member of the so-called Kitchen Cabinet—an informal group of Jackson's confidential advisers.

Jackson triumphed in the election of 1832, although whether the bank issue helped or hurt his campaign is difficult to judge. He was less popular with voters than when he had run as a fresh and untried candidate in 1828, and his percentage of the popular vote declined. Southerners reacted unfavorably to his antinullification stand, and the Anti-Masons siphoned off more votes. In fighting the bank Jackson had raised the threat of class war. Many of his opponents, in New York City and elsewhere, thought that he was trying to set the poor against the rich. All these disadvantages were more than offset, however, by the incredibly bungled campaign waged by Clay and the National Republicans.

When Jackson gained another four years in the White House, he was convinced that the American people wished him to crush the bank forever. He was also sure that anyone who attacked the bank was for him and anyone who supported it was against him. Those who wanted to remain Jacksonian Democrats in good standing had to join the anti-bank crusade. Those who could not support Jackson on this issue (like Verplanck in New York) switched over completely to the opposition.

In order to weaken the bank, Jackson removed federal deposits in 1833. The government would now rely on selected state banks, many of them controlled by Democrats eager to obtain interest-free government deposits. These institutions soon acquired the nickname of "pet banks." They were not all financially sound, and their collapse helped bring on the economic crisis of 1833–34—which the Jacksonians called "Biddle's Panic." Many people felt that Jackson had gone too far and that both the party and the economy had been permanently damaged. Petitions poured into Congress, asking for recharter of the bank. Among the thousands of signatures were the names of prominent Democratic merchants, including a sizable group from New York City. But the President made his stand clear. Although he had toyed previously with the idea of a different kind of national bank, he would never support recharter for "*Biddle's* Bank."

But would the issue be decided over Jackson's head? Both sides recognized that the congressional elections of 1834 would have an important influence on the outcome of the Bank War. The anti-Jackson forces gained enough recruits to form the Whig party (christened by James Watson Webb, the New York City editor). But the Democrats were too strong for them. Despite the economic hardships of the winter and spring, Jackson's candidates did well at the polls that year, not only in New York but elsewhere. They even made slight gains in the fall elections for Congress.

Jackson had won the Bank War. The Second Bank of the United States was dead. Biddle later obtained a charter for his own bank from the Pennsylvania legislature. But his institution was no longer a national bank, and thus it was no longer as powerful as it had been.

Since the mid-1820s the nation had once more prospered, and in the early 1830s the economy began to boom. The government was taking in far more money than it spent. In fact, the national debt completely disappeared during Jackson's tenure, for one of the few times in American history. Speculation in western lands had become almost a mania. American capitalists were heavily involved, and so were European investors. Since the United States was still an underdeveloped, credit-hungry nation, there was a demand for additional capital. Many new banks were chartered. Their promissory notes[1] circulated as unofficial paper money.

Jackson was worried about the speculative boom. In 1836 he issued the Specie Circular, an executive order directing government land agents to accept only gold or silver specie (hard money) as payment. The Deposit Act of that same year included the first federal regulation of the pet banks. But the Whigs added a rider providing that the federal government's surplus revenues should be distributed among the states. This money, in state hands, caused more inflation. Thus it worked against Jackson's Specie Circular.

VAN BUREN'S UNHAPPY REIGN

Jackson had been a towering figure as President in his own right. Yet his later stature rose also because of the fact that both the President who

Van Buren's shrewd manipulations gained him such nicknames as the "Flying Dutchman" and the "Red Fox of Kinderhook" (his home in New York). But his wit and cheerful disposition won him many friends.

---

[1] Promissory notes are written promises to pay a specified sum of money, either on demand or at a certain time.

A Harrison campaign poster features a trumpeting angel, and includes as well a cheering crowd and the inevitable log cabin and cider barrel.

preceded him and the one who followed him had unfortunate administrations. John Quincy Adams returned to national politics in the 1830s and 1840s as an antislavery congressman from Massachusetts. He must have felt some satisfaction over the trials of Martin Van Buren. The "Little Magician," as Van Buren was called, had squirmed his way into Jackson's confidence and had in turn been rewarded with the Democratic nomination for the presidency.

Van Buren defeated several Whig candidates to win the 1836 presidential election. Even during the campaign, though, it became clear that economic problems would soon loom large. No sooner had Van Buren been inaugurated in the spring of 1837 than he faced an economic panic, the worst the country had ever known. There were several causes. One was the Specie Circular, which had made much paper money worthless. Another was the fact that British banks raised interest rates and called in loans. In May, New York banks suspended specie payments. That is, they refused to pay out cash in exchange for paper money. Other banks soon followed.

All parts of the American business system suffered in the Panic of 1837 and the depression that followed. The price of cotton, America's chief export item, tumbled. Land sales fell from 20 million to 3-1/2 million acres in a year. Merchants found that they could not sell their goods. When sales dropped, factory owners laid off workers. Debtors could not make payments and went bankrupt.

Van Buren responded to the panic by asking Congress to create an Independent Treasury system. Like many other Democrats by then, he had come to associate the economic crisis with banking itself, whether in the form of a national bank or pet banks. Van Buren proposed that the United States should simply deposit its funds in "subtreasuries." These would be owned and managed by the government itself. Thus public funds would be separated completely from the private banking structure. The subtreasury plan was finally enacted by Congress in 1840. But it did not seriously affect the nation's economic growth, either favorably or unfavorably.

The Locofocos   Jacksonian Democrats had attacked the Second Bank of the United States as an undemocratic institution. These attacks went too far for Whig businessmen and politicians, who feared that these policies threatened their economic and political freedom. But they did not go far enough for a group of radical Democrats called Locofocos.[2] They hated the bank in particular and the wealthy in general.

Most of the Locofocos were artisans, workers, and small businessmen in the urban East. Many of them had lost their jobs in the Panic of 1837, displaced by new manufacturing techniques that were part of the factory system. Organizing local workingmen's parties, the Locofocos ardently supported political and economic equality. They hoped to turn the Democratic

---

[2] Members of the original group earned this name at a meeting in which their opponents turned off the gaslights. They promptly lit their so-called locofoco matches. These were friction matches, like those of today, and had just come into use.

party into an even more strongly anti-bank and pro-workingmen's party than it had been under Jackson and Van Buren.

Specifically, the Locofocos wanted to prevent private banks from issuing so much paper money and engaging in speculation. It was such activities, they felt, that had led to the financial panics of 1819 and 1837. Many Jacksonians—workers, farmers, and middle-class Americans—were still reeling from the effects of the past crisis. They hoped to restore a currency system based almost entirely on gold and silver. Some of them wanted to eliminate paper money altogether.

A HIGH POINT FOR WHIGS

As Van Buren's first term drew to a close, the Whigs marshaled their forces to unseat the Democrats. They had the support of most wealthy Americans. They also appealed to numerous voters among the middle class and working people. Some working people voted Whig out of fear or hatred of immigrants, who were mainly Irish and German Catholics—and Democrats. In addition, the Whig party attracted business interests concerned with economic and social expansion. Rejecting Jacksonian fears about panics and paper money, these Whigs argued that the country needed more economic development. They wanted more roads, canals, and railroads, and more credit for investors. Governments, including the federal government, should play a more active role in spurring development for the benefit of all.

The Whigs smelled victory in the presidential election of 1840. Their factions seemed united. Besides, Van Buren, as the President in office, had to shoulder the responsibility for the depression. He had warned that "all communities are apt to look to government for too much." This negative attitude toward federal power did not help his search for votes. In fact, everything that Van Buren touched (or tried to avoid) in 1840 became controversial. Many Southerners attacked him for refusing to annex Texas after

Courtesy Chicago Historical Society

Tyler, photographed some ten years after he served as President, lived the life of a Virginia country gentleman after his term of office expired.

American settlers there had set up an independent republic (see Chapter 16). Many Northerners regarded him as "soft" on slavery. Actually, Van Buren was trying to keep the slavery issue out of national politics. But ardent politicians both South and North (people like Calhoun and Adams) had other plans.

Taking advantage of the anti-Van Buren feeling, the Whigs decided to mute their own differences. Party managers ignored the Whigs' leading politicians and chose instead a candidate with a popular Jacksonian image. He was a military hero and a westerner, General William Henry Harrison.

When a Democratic editor unwisely tried to discredit Harrison as a man content to sit in front of a log cabin drinking hard cider, Whigs turned the slur into a boast. They decorated their floats with log cabins and dispensed hard cider at rallies. Campaigning for Harrison, Daniel Webster actually apologized: "Gentlemen, it did not happen to me to be born in a log cabin; but my elder brothers and sisters were born in a log cabin. Its remains still exist. I make to it an annual visit. I weep." At the same time, Whigs depicted Van Buren, the son of a small-town tavern keeper, as an overdressed, would-be aristocrat. They said he lived in luxury, perhaps on dishonestly acquired money. The charges were nonsense, for Van Buren was too smart to be dishonest. Yet the President's earlier reputation as Jackson's political wirepuller and party chieftain did him no good. Whig organization, the nation's economic troubles, and Van Buren's unpopularity combined to produce an easy victory for Harrison. Many states went Whig for the first (and last) time. A record number of Americans—almost 80 percent of those eligible to vote—participated in this national election.

The Whig party had finally arrived. But for how long would it remain? When Harrison took over in March 1841, it appeared that the Whigs would remain in power for a long time and that a real two-party system had been established. Certainly the Whig leaders by-passed as presidential candidates had cause for satisfaction. Daniel Webster became Secretary of State. Clay intended to run the administration from the Senate, since Harrison's inaugural address promised that Congress would lead the way in national affairs. Harrison regarded the veto—so often used by Jackson to browbeat Congress—as a last resort to be used sparingly, if at all.

"His Accidency" in the White House This cozy situation evaporated in less than a month, with Harrison's sudden death from pneumonia. John Tyler of Virginia became the first Vice President to succeed to the presidency. Tyler won a crucial point at the outset. He quickly rejected the suggestion that Cabinet decisions be decided by majority vote. This change—one that Harrison apparently had been considering favorably—would have permanently crippled presidential power. Though not elected to the presidency (his opponents called him "His Accidency"), Tyler made a vital contribution to maintaining the prestige and power of the office.

But Tyler scored low as party leader and direct representative of the people. A states'-rights Southerner, he infuriated Whig leaders (and damaged the Whig party permanently) by vetoing legislation that would have carried out their program. Two national bank bills met with vetoes at Tyler's hands. Most of the Cabinet resigned. The President was officially read out of the Whig party. For a while Tyler hoped he might be vindicated by winning the election of 1844. He tried to build his own organization by offering jobs to cooperative politicians. But, except for fellow Virginians and a few hungry office seekers, Tyler did not win over many regular Whig party members.

Tyler devoted much of his "accidental" presidency instead to foreign affairs. Webster negotiated a treaty with Britain over the boundary between Canada and the northeastern United States. Tyler himself became obsessed with annexing Texas. He ignored warnings that such a move would shatter the fragile sectional truce on slavery. In 1844 he appointed the Democrat John C. Calhoun Secretary of State and ordered the negotiation of a Texas annexation treaty. The Senate rejected the treaty, partly because the South Carolinian had urged it as necessary for the defense of slavery. Calhoun's undiplomatic statement underlined what everyone knew. Slavery had replaced the bank and related financial concerns as the single most important issue in American political life.

1. Why is the period after 1815 referred to as the Era of Good Feelings?
2. Why did the Republicans come to accept the need for a national bank? For a protective tariff? Why were they less willing to accept federally financed internal improvements?
3. What led to the Compromise of 1820?
4. How did the nominating convention come about? Do you think it is a more democratic method of selecting candidates than the caucus?
5. Jackson defended the spoils system as democratic. Do you agree? Why or why not?
6. Why did Southerners oppose the Tariff of 1828? Why did they accept the compromise tariff?
7. What reasons lay behind Jackson's hatred of the Second Bank of the United States? Was Clay's move to recharter the bank a politically wise one, given the facts at his disposal?
8. What factors contributed to the speculative boom of the 1830s? Why did Jackson issue the Specie Circular? Was there a connection between it and the Panic of 1837?
9. Why was Van Buren's administration a failure?
10. Why was Tyler referred to as "His Accidency"? Why was he read out of the Whig party?

Beyond the Text

1. Begin a graph charting the tariff history of the United States. Eventually it will be drawn up to the present. For the time being, it should include the tariffs from 1789 to 1846. What is the direction of the rates? Why the changes? What changes are evident in the kinds of products protected? What sections of the country benefited most? A helpful reference is Frank W. Taussig, *Tariff History of the United States.*

2. Small committees may prepare reports on various aspects of Jackson's elections and administrations. These could include: (a) Jackson's political philosophy; (b) Jackson as a politician; (c) Jackson's achievements as President. After the preparations, the heads of the committees may wish to hold a panel discussion to evaluate Jackson as a presidential leader.
3. Prepare a chart showing the stand taken by each of the three sections of the country on the following issues: the tariff; internal improvements; the sale of western lands; the Bank War.

Bibliography

Nonfiction

Dangerfield, George, *The Awakening of American Nationalism, 1815–1828.**
De Tocqueville, Alexis, *Democracy in America.**
Freehling, William W., *Prelude to Civil War: The Nullification Controversy in South Carolina, 1816–1836.**
McCormick, Richard M., *The Second American Party System.**
Meyers, Marvin, *The Jacksonian Persuasion.**
Pessen, Edward, *Jacksonian America.**
Remini, Robert V., *Andrew Jackson and the Bank War.**
Schlesinger, Arthur M., Jr., *The Age of Jackson.**
Van Deusen, Glyndon G., *The Jacksonian Era.**
Ward, John W., *Andrew Jackson: Symbol for an Age.**

Fiction

Adams, Samuel Hopkins, *Canal Town.*
Crabb, Alfred L., *Home to Hermitage.*
Gerson, Noel B., *Old Hickory.*

*a paperback book

UNIT FOUR

DIVIDED

Shortly after the Missouri Compromise of 1820, Thomas Jefferson and John Adams, aging patriots, exchanged letters on the one remaining major problem that seemed to threaten the nation's stability. "The real question, as seen in the states afflicted with this unfortunate population," wrote Jefferson in 1821, "is, Are our slaves to be presented with freedom and therefore a dagger? Are we then to see again Athenian and Spartan confederacies? To wage another Peloponnesian War to settle the ascendancy between them?" Adams was equally skeptical. "Slavery in this country," he responded, "I have seen hanging over it like a black cloud for half a century." The "black cloud" was still there when the two Founding Fathers died, in an awesome coincidence, on the same day—July 4, 1826, the fortieth anniversary of American independence.

During the 1820s and 1830s economic issues such as the Bank War and land policy deflected popular attention from the "black cloud." Only in the 1840s did the landscape once more become overcast with the problem, as

AMERICA

Americans grappled with the question of slavery's expansion. Even then, slavery did not completely preoccupy the American people. The nation doubled its population between 1830 and 1850. An industrial factory system began to develop in the North and Middle West. Millions of European immigrants landed on American shores. The country fought a war with Mexico and gained huge new territories in the West. Yet all these events occurred within a society torn by a fundamental and unresolved social problem—the place of black people in American life.

The four pairs of chapters that follow examine various phases of the American experience from the 1830s to the 1870s, with special emphasis on changing reactions to the problems of slavery and race. Chapter 13 tells the story of the most important slave revolt in United States history, led by Nat Turner. It serves as a focal point for the discussion of slavery in Chapter 14, which portrays the patterns of Southern society as they affected both slaves and their masters. Chapter 15 deals with the drama of congressional efforts to achieve a compromise over the issue of slavery in the Western territories. The resultant Compromise of 1850 and surrounding events serve as a vehicle for the exploration, in Chapter 16, of three dominant themes of the 1840s and 1850s: Northern economic growth, westward expansion, and the politics of sectional conflict.

John Brown's raid, the subject of Chapter 17, triggered extreme sectional hysteria in both South and North. It can also be seen in relation to a general climate of reform, described in Chapter 18, that characterized the ante-bellum period. Sectional differences in the United States culminated in civil war and continued in the bitter Reconstruction era that followed. The meaning of the Civil War in human terms is dramatized in Chapter 19 through an account of Sherman's devastating march through Georgia. Chapter 20 describes the major events of the Civil War and Reconstruction—the climactic struggles of a tragic and tortured period in our national past.

13

The Nat Turner Revolt

SIX POORLY CLAD BLACK MEN huddled around their campfire in the woods drinking brandy and barbecuing a pig. They had arrived at this meeting place about noon, started the fire, and waited in silence. Toward midafternoon another black man suddenly emerged from the surrounding trees. The six turned to greet him. It was this short and stocky figure for whom they had been waiting. His name was Nat Turner. A later description of him reads:

> Five feet 6 or 8 inches high, weighs between 150 and 160 pounds, rather bright complexion, but not a mulatto. Broad shoulders, large flat nose, large eyes. Broad flat feet, rather knockkneed, walks brisk and active. Hair on the top of the head very thin, no beard, except on the upper lip and the top of the chin. A scar on one of his temples, also one on the back of his neck. A large knot on one of the bones of his right arm, near his wrist, produced a blow.

Turner greeted the other blacks and joined them around the campfire. We know his companions only by their first names—Sam, Nelson, Hark, Will, Henry, and Jack.

Turner sat down, stared directly at Will, and demanded to know something he already knew quite well. Why had Will come to this rendezvous? According to Turner's later account, Will replied that "his life was worth no more than others and his liberty was as dear to him." Turner continued the questioning: "I asked him if he thought to obtain his freedom. He said he would, or lose his life."

An imaginary view of Nat Turner and four of his men conveys some of the menace evoked by his name. Illness prevented him from launching his revolt as planned, on July 4. Then, when the sun turned a "peculiar greenish blue" on August 13, he set the date at August 21.

The seven men spoke further about their plans until some time after sunset. Then, at a command from Turner, they trudged back out of the woods and through ripe tobacco fields to a clearing. Here stood a large, handsome, frame house. It belonged to a white man named Joseph Travis, who happened to own Nat Turner. An eighth black, Austin, joined them at the Travis home. Then, as Turner later recounted, "they all went to the cider press and drank, except myself."

About midnight the group gathered in front of the house. Turner climbed through a window, opened the doors to his men, and gave them guns that had been stored inside. His men now insisted that he "spill the first blood." Armed with a hatchet and accompanied by Will, Turner entered Travis' bedroom and swung wildly at the sleeping man. The blow merely grazed Travis' skull, and he jumped out of bed screaming for his wife. A second later, Will bashed his head in with an ax. Within moments, wielding his ax, Will also killed Mrs. Travis and their three oldest children, none of whom ever awoke.

The band of black men then searched the house for arms, collecting a half-dozen rifles and several pounds of gunpowder. They left soon afterward and started walking down a road that led to the town of Jerusalem (now Courtland), some fifteen miles away. They had gone only a short distance when someone remembered that the Travises had a fourth child, a baby who slept in a cradle near its parents' bed. "Henry and Will returned and killed it," Nat Turner later observed. He formed the others "in a line as soldiers" and marched his seven-man "army" down the road. With the murder of this one family began the greatest slave revolt in the history of the United States. It started on Sunday, August 21, 1831, in the sleepy Virginia county known as Southampton.

Southampton County, in southeastern Virginia, was an important agricultural area. It had several large farms that employed slave labor and might have been called plantations. Such was the Travis homestead. More common were small farms tilled by poor whites who owned no slaves. The federal census in 1830 showed that Southampton was second among Virginia counties in growing rice and potatoes. A decade later, it led the state in cotton production.

Southampton County's planters might have felt an occasional twinge of concern over their safety. Blacks in the area (most of them slaves) outnumbered whites by almost two to one. Among the 9,501 Southampton blacks counted by the 1830 census takers was a thirty-year-old, Bible-reading, visionary slave preacher named Nat Turner.

Turner was born in Southampton County on October 2, 1800. At the time, members of his family were slaves of a man named Benjamin Turner. (It was common for slaves to be given the last name of their master.) When Nat was only three or four years old, he already felt that he had been singled out by God to achieve some great work. As he said later, he thought he "surely would be a prophet." Young Nat certainly seemed a prodigy to his elders. His upbringing was unusual for a slave child, in several ways. At an early age he was taught to read and write by his parents. As a youth, he spent much time at prayer. Also, he was apparently spared much physical labor. Instead he had free time when he could study schoolbooks belonging to his master's children or simply be alone with his thoughts. He remembered other slaves turning to him for help because of his "superior judgment."

At a very early age Turner decided to pursue a lonely, almost friendless, life while awaiting the great works for which he believed God had prepared him. "Having soon discovered myself to be great, I must appear so, and therefore studiously avoided mixing in society, and wrapped myself in mystery, devoting my time to fasting and prayer."

Several times as a young man in his twenties, Turner claimed to have divine visions. His reputation as a preacher spread among whites as well as blacks in Southampton County. Yet he appeared aloof and puzzling to most of his fellow slaves. One time he escaped. But, instead of trying to reach shelter in the Great Dismal Swamp—some twenty-five miles away—he stayed in the woods for thirty days. Then he casually returned to his owner. "The Negroes found fault, and murmured against me," Nat later remarked, "saying that if they had my sense they would not serve any master in the world." By this time, however, Nat Turner believed himself destined for a greater role than that of an escaped slave, skulking in swamplands to avoid recapture. "I now withdrew myself as much as my situation would permit, from the intercourse of my fellow slaves, for the avowed purpose of serving the Spirit more fully."

Turner's vision of a divinely inspired slave revolt came to him in 1828, according to his account. "The Spirit instantly appeared to me," he said, and told him of the task ahead: "I should arise and prepare myself, and slay my enemies with their own weapons." A heavenly sign would instruct him when to begin. The signal that triggered his actual plan to revolt was an eclipse of the sun in February 1831. That month Turner outlined his general scheme to Henry, Hark, Nelson, and Sam, who later brought in Will and Jack. Turner's men began to call him the Prophet because of his mystical statements. The small band of plotters could gather easily at church meetings or barbecues to plan the rebellion, since few whites in the Jerusalem area had the slightest suspicion of an impending uprising.

Nat Turner's master in 1831, Joseph Travis, had acquired him in 1830 after marrying the widow of his former owner. Turner remembered Travis as "a kind master, who placed the greatest confidence in me; in fact, I had no cause to complain of his treatment to me." But Travis was a slaveholder. As such, he was marked by "the Prophet" for destruction.

To the very moment of revolt Nat Turner spoke more easily with the God whose commands he believed to be obeying than with his own black followers. After agreeing to meet his six companions in the woods at noon on that fateful Sunday, he joined them instead hours later, for "the same reason that had caused me not to mix with them for years before." However, once the Travis family had been chopped to pieces and the revolt was underway, Turner held back no longer. The killing began in earnest.

Some 600 yards from the Travis house lived Salathiel Francis. His home was the rebels' next stop as they obeyed Turner's command to "carry terror and devastation" along the road to Jerusalem. Their work was aided by the fact that the rebellious slaves knew most of the families in the neighborhood. When they arrived at the Francis house, Sam knocked at the door and shouted that he had a letter to deliver. It was after midnight. Yet the unsuspecting planter opened the door immediately, only to be dragged outside and beaten to death. No one else was home, so Turner and his men marched on to the home of a Mrs. Reese, whose door they found unlocked. They murdered Mrs. Reese in her bed.

By sunrise on Monday other slaves had joined the group. They now numbered fifteen, with nine mounted on horses. Monday morning they arrived at the house of Elizabeth Turner, whom Will killed, along with Sarah Newsome. No woman was raped either then or at any point during Nat Turner's march of destruction. At each stop along the way, however, the rebels also destroyed whatever valuable property they found, and they seized money, guns, and ammunition.

From the Turner residence the blacks on horseback rode on to the home of Richard Whitehead, while the others detoured to kill a slaveholding family named Bryant. As the nine armed blacks rode onto his property, Richard Whitehead stared unbelievingly from a nearby cotton patch. The blacks called to him, and, as he walked toward them, Will's ax dropped him in his tracks. Dismounting, the slaves tore through the house, putting to death the entire family. Here occurred the only murder Nat Turner acknowledged having committed personally during the entire uprising—that of Whitehead's daughter Mar-

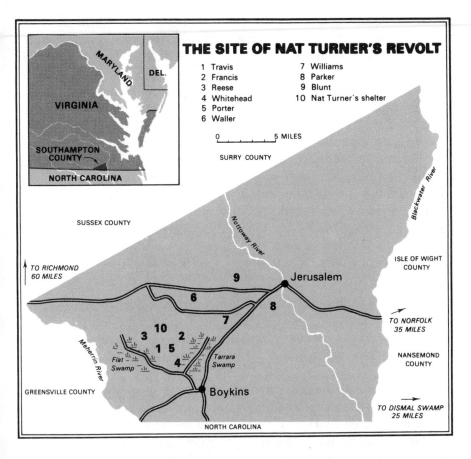

THE SITE OF NAT TURNER'S REVOLT

1 Travis
2 Francis
3 Reese
4 Whitehead
5 Porter
6 Waller
7 Williams
8 Parker
9 Blunt
10 Nat Turner's shelter

garet. Margaret "had concealed herself in the corner. On my approach she fled, but was soon overtaken, and after repeated blows with a sword, I killed her by a blow on the head, with a fence rail."

By then the six blacks who had detoured to the Bryant home returned, having "done the work of death assigned them." The entire party moved on toward Jerusalem. The mutinous slaves again broke into small bands, since several scattered slaveholding families lay in their path. The main group, led by Turner himself, rode on to Richard Porter's home, only to discover that Porter had escaped with his family. "I understood there," Nat later acknowledged, "that the alarm had already spread." He immediately returned to gather his force together.

Richard Porter's family was not alone in escaping from Nat Turner's wrath. By dawn on Monday, August 22—less than twelve hours after the revolt began—small numbers of whites began straggling into Jerusalem from the direction of the killings, rousing the town to the threatened black invasion. Within hours a rider left Jerusalem and headed north for the state capital at Richmond, about seventy miles away. He carried an urgent letter appealing for military help.

Wild rumors spread quickly across the state. In the absence of more accurate information from Southampton, the rumors threw white Virginians into a panic. Thousands of angry slaves, it was said, had banded together to take over the state. According to reports, the rebels were well-armed and commanded by soldiers from Haiti.[1] Rumor had it that Northern abolitionists (supporters of immediate freedom for the slaves) had helped incite the insurrection.

Whole companies of the state militia were hastily called up, and they headed for Jerusalem. By the time the first outside help had arrived, however, the uprising had already been crushed by Southampton County's own militia groups and armed white farmers. They had begun riding out after the small band of black rebels shortly after Richard Porter and others first sounded the alarm.

When he found Porter's family missing, Nat Turner realized the importance of marching as quickly as possible to seize Jerusalem. He knew, too, that he should keep his band together at full strength in the event of an attack. At each house along the way the rebels slaughtered the white inhabitants and urged nearby slaves to join them. By the time Turner and his men reached the home of a Captain Harris, who had also fled with his family, their ranks numbered about forty. Most seemed untroubled by Harris' absence, as they jubilantly destroyed his valuables, drank his liquor, collected his rifles, and rode on.

By this time "General Nat"—as his men reportedly started calling him—had decided on his tactics. He ordered those on horseback to ride ahead, killing whomever they met along the way. This would frighten the remaining whites in the area so that they would flee from their homes and even abandon Jerusalem to his men. Turner himself remained at the rear, directing his foot soldiers while coaxing the slaves he met to join the rebellion. When General Nat reached a house, its occupants had usually been killed, although he later commented: "I sometimes got in sight in time to see the work of death completed, viewed the mangled bodies as they lay, in silent satisfaction, and immediately started in quest of other victims." In this way Mrs. Levi Waller and her ten children were killed, then William Williams and his two small boys. Mrs. Williams was caught running away and brought back to her dead husband's side. The rebels ordered her to lie down beside him and shot her. Several other families perished as well. By

This crude drawing appeared in a tract called "Horrid Massacre in Virginia," published in 1831. A mother begs one of Turner's men to spare the lives of her children.

[1] In 1794 blacks in Haiti—led by Toussaint L'Ouverture—had overthrown French rule there. Although the French captured Toussaint, they failed to retake the colony. The success of the black revolt in Haiti frightened American slaveholders for years afterward.

Monday afternoon the rebel band numbered between fifty and sixty, "all mounted and armed with guns, axes, swords, and clubs." They were only three miles from Jerusalem. Their leader urged them to press on into the town, but several of them insisted on stopping at the plantation of James Parker, where they had relatives. Most of Turner's men rode across the fields toward Parker's house to collect their kinfolk (the Parker family had already escaped) but Turner himself remained at the roadside with seven or eight of his soldiers. This delay proved fatal for the rebels.

A local militia captain, Alexander Peete, had ridden out from Jerusalem at the head of eighteen volunteers. He was probably as startled to find Nat Turner and his small band of blacks in front of the Parker plantation as Turner was to see Peete. Turner coolly ordered his handful of followers to form ranks and prepare to fire. Shots rang out on both sides, and the white militiamen fled. The black insurgents pursued Peete's men until the retreating militiamen ran headlong into another party of armed whites who had left Jerusalem to hunt down the rebels. Turner's small band, now heavily outnumbered, scattered into the surrounding woods. Most of them were wounded. For the rest of Monday afternoon General Nat backtracked across much of the area of his earlier march. He combed the woods for his men while evading growing numbers of militiamen who searched for him. By evening he had collected almost forty men, including several new slave recruits. He placed guards around his camp and rested for the night. But the men on patrol panicked, believing the camp under attack. When order was restored, Turner's "army" had been reduced to about twenty.

"The Prophet" set out early on Tuesday morning to continue recruiting the slaves in the area. His group reached the home of Dr. Simon Blunt just before daybreak. Almost immediately, the rebels were fired on by a party of armed whites and by some of Blunt's slaves. Several of Turner's men were killed. The rest retreated to the home of Captain Harris, which had been deserted earlier. This time, another band of militia opened fire on the slaves from within the house. Most of the blacks fled into the woods, where they were quickly rounded up. Only two, Jacob and another slave named Nat, retreated to the woods with General Nat. They waited until evening, when Turner sent his last two followers in search of the rest of his original group. They never returned.

Sixty hours after the rebellion had begun, it was crushed. Nat Turner was left alone with the shattered wreckage of his mission. According to Turner's own account, God had not promised him success—only that he would perform the "great work" of "carrying terror

Also from the "Horrid Massacre" is this rendering of "Mr. Travis, cruelly murdered by his own slaves." Woodcuts like this satisfied the public taste for a visual record of sensational events, though they were usually far from accurate.

and devastation wherever we went." This he had done. In less than three days his men had killed fifty-five whites from Southampton County slaveholding families: eleven men, fourteen women, and thirty children. At least twice as many blacks were also killed during and after the revolt by white militiamen. These militiamen seldom knew whether their victims had actually taken part in the revolt.

As for Nat Turner himself, he proved more skillful in defeat than in battle. He managed to remain free, eluding thousands of whites, for almost two months. During that period, in both North and South, the black "Prophet" of Southampton County became both famous and infamous.

Just as Virginians of the seventeenth century had studied the omens that foreshadowed Bacon's Rebellion, so did most white Southerners see a train of alarming events leading up to Nat Turner's Revolt. Had not an even more widespread plot among slaves and free blacks been discovered in Charleston, South Carolina, a decade earlier? This conspiracy was led by a free black named Denmark Vesey. It was exposed in 1822, and its leaders were executed. But rumors of such plots cropped up regularly in the years before the Southampton revolt. Had not a free black in Boston, David Walker, published a widely distributed *Appeal* in 1829 calling for slave uprisings throughout the South? And, in that same city, had not a journalist and printer named William Lloyd Garrison begun publishing a notorious abolitionist newspaper called *The Liberator,* which demanded immediate and total emancipation of all slaves?

Although Boston was 500 miles from Southampton County, many Southerners blamed the abolitionist writings of Walker and Garrison for stimulating a desire for rebellion in blacks such as Nat Turner. Some even suspected antislavery Northerners of actually plotting the Southampton revolt. Almost every white Virginian, for example, would have agreed with the sentiments of the state's leading newspaper, the Richmond *Enquirer.* Only a few days after the slave rebellion had been crushed, it printed this comment:

When an appeal is actually made through the press to this unfortunate class of our community, calculated to mislead them, and while it involves us in serious trouble, leads those unhappy creatures to destruction, it is time for us to arouse from an indifference to a conduct which is daily augmenting and becoming worse and worse. To attempt to excite discontent and revolt, or publish writings having this tendency, obstinately and perversely, among us, is outrageous—it ought not to be passed over with indifference. Our own safety—the good and happiness of our slaves, requires it.

This criticism came from a newspaper whose editor, Thomas Ritchie, believed in gradual emancipation of slaves. Obviously, the reaction of proslavery Southerners was much more hysterical. Thinking about Nat Turner's Revolt, supporters of the "peculiar institution"[2] may have remembered South Carolinian Edward D. Holland's warning at the time of the Vesey conspiracy:

> Let it never be forgotten, that "our NEGROES are truly the *Jacobins*[3] of the country; that they are the *anarchists* and the *domestic enemy,*" the *common enemy of civilized society,* and the barbarians who would, IF THEY COULD, become the DESTROYERS of our race.

Southerners were fearful that Turner's insurrection would inspire other slaves to rebel. They began acting on these fears, often in an incredibly barbaric manner. An antislavery Northern observer, E. A. Andrews, wrote:

> In every town and village, an active and vigilant patrol is abroad at such hours of the night as they judge most expedient, and no Negro dares, after the prescribed hour, to be found at a distance from his quarter. Great cruelty is often practiced by the patrols toward unoffending slaves. The principal object of such visits is to terrify the slaves, and thus secure their good behavior, and especially to prevent their wandering about at night.

Andrews went south prepared to find such cruelties, and he might therefore be expected to exaggerate. But many similar accounts filled the Southern press itself.

Nowhere was the punishment of innocent slaves for Nat Turner's brief uprising more ruthless than in Southampton County itself. Nathaniel Bacon's men over a century earlier had consoled themselves for failing to find any marauding Indians by slaughtering villages of peaceful ones. In the same manner roving companies of militiamen and vigilante slave patrols—often drinking fron the same stocks that had nourished Nat Turner's band during its brief lifetime—butchered many innocent slaves unlucky enough to fall into their hands.

Throughout the South, state legislatures reacted to the acute fear of uprisings by further limiting the already restricted lives of slaves. The Virginia assembly endorsed the widely proclaimed "lesson" of Southampton County (to quote the Richmond *Enquirer*) that "no black man ought to be permitted to become a preacher" by passing a

---

[2] This term for slavery seems to have been used first by a South Carolina newspaper in the 1850s, which spoke of the dangers then threatening "the peculiar domestic institutions of the South."

[3] The Jacobins were a leftist political group of the French Revolution. Their name became synonymous with extreme and dangerous radicals.

This simple wooden building served as the Jerusalem jail when Nat Turner was confined there. In his small cell he spoke calmly to his lawyer about what Gray called the "dreadful conspiracy" and "its diabolical actors."

complete ban on "any assembly or meeting, for religious or other purposes" by either slaves or free blacks. Only whites could preach to black congregations, and slaves had to accompany their masters to church. Other new Virginia laws forbade free blacks to carry weapons, increased the penalties for blacks assaulting whites, prohibited the sale of liquor to slaves, and allowed whippings for blacks who expressed "seditious" thoughts.

In every other Southern state, within months after the Nat Turner Revolt, a flood of similar legislation tightened controls over both slaves and free blacks. These actions fulfilled the prediction made by Garrison's *Liberator* concerning the white South's reaction to the Turner uprising. "In his fury against the revolters," wrote the abolitionist editor, "who will remember their wrongs?"

While Nat Turner remained free, the object of Southern fears and fury, forty-six other blacks were brought to trial in Jerusalem for taking part in the revolt. The militiamen had obviously cast their nets too wide, for five free blacks were included among the accused. Sixteen slaves and three freemen died on the gallows for their alleged role in the revolt. Seven more were sentenced to be deported to the harsher conditions of Deep South[4] slavery. The others were acquitted, although several slaves in nearby counties were also convicted as accomplices in the uprising.

Meanwhile, Nat Turner lived a hand-to-mouth existence as a fugitive. After his last supporters had scattered on August 23, he returned to the Travis home and collected some food. In a nearby field he scratched out a shelter under a pile of fence rails. There he remained undetected for six weeks, just a short distance from his former slave cabin. Every evening the hunted rebel would leave briefly to drink water from a nearby stream. As the days wore on, he began to spend the entire night prowling through the neighborhood "gathering little or no intelligence, afraid of speaking to any human being, and returning every morning to my cave before the dawn of day."

One time when he returned, Turner saw a dog leaving his hiding place carrying a piece of meat. His days were now numbered. A few evenings later, two slaves, hunting with the same dog, passed his hideaway. The animal spotted Turner walking nearby and began barking. Turner later recalled:

> Thinking myself discovered, I spoke to the Negroes to beg concealment. On making myself known they fled from me. Knowing then they would betray me, I

---

[4] The term "Deep South" refers to the southeastern states, especially Georgia, Alabama, Mississippi, and Louisiana. The older Southern states such as Virginia and Maryland are often known as the Upper South.

immediately left my hiding place, and was pursued almost incessantly until I was taken a fortnight afterwards by Mr. Benjamin Phipps, in a little hole I had dug out with my sword, for the purpose of concealment, under the top of a fallen tree. On Mr. Phipps' discovering the place of my concealment, he cocked his gun and aimed at me. I requested him not to shoot and I would give up, upon which he demanded my sword. I delivered it to him, and he brought me to prison.

Turner was captured on October 30. Once locked in his Jerusalem cell, he was questioned by a white lawyer named Thomas R. Gray. The black insurgent apparently agreed to tell Gray his own story of the revolt. Turner's narrative, edited by Gray, appeared as a pamphlet, *The Confessions of Nat Turner,* early in 1832. At Turner's trial he pleaded not guilty, "saying to his counsel that he did not feel so." His narrative, however, was read to the court and served to convict him. After finding him guilty on November 5, Judge Jeremiah Cobb pronounced the inevitable death sentence, though with added fervor. He sentenced Turner to "be hung by the neck until you are dead! dead! dead!"

In talking to Gray, Nat Turner denied the existence of any widespread slave conspiracy. When he saw the lawyer's skeptical expression he said: "I see, sir, you doubt my word; but can you not think the same ideas might prompt others, as well as myself, to this undertaking?" The prisoner apparently impressed Gray considerably. Despite the attorney's proslavery beliefs, he defended Nat Turner against charges being made in the Southern press that he was an ignorant and cowardly black who had rebelled only to secure enough money to escape northward. "For natural intelligence and quickness of apprehension," Gray wrote, Turner "is surpassed by few men I have ever seen." Furthermore, Turner's Revolt could be understood, the lawyer argued, only as the action of "a complete fanatic warped and perverted by the influence of early impressions." Gray was probably referring to the childhood religious visions "the Prophet" claimed to have had.

The contrast between Gray's description of the actual Turner and his fearful image of the man can can be seen in this passage that Gray wrote in the *Confessions:*

> The calm, deliberate composure with which he spoke of his late deeds and intentions, the expression of his fiend-like face when excited by enthusiasm, still bearing the stains of the blood of helpless innocence about him; clothed with rags and covered with chains; yet daring to raise his manacled hands to heaven, with a spirit soaring above the attributes of man; I looked on him and my blood curdled in my veins.

Most accounts at the time agree on the dignity with which Turner spoke to questioners such as Gray and confronted his final days. "Do you not find yourself mistaken now?" Gray once asked him shortly before his death. "The Prophet" quietly responded, "Was not Christ crucified?" Calmly and without recorded last words, Nat Turner went to his death at noon on November 11, 1831.

One man who was intensely concerned with the whole episode of Nat Turner's Revolt and its aftermath was the governor of Virginia, John Floyd. His diary provides an interesting account of what the insurrection meant to a moderate white Southerner.

Floyd, born in Kentucky, had trained as a surgeon before going into Virginia politics. He had served as a Democratic congressman from 1817 to 1829. Although originally a supporter of Andrew Jackson, he felt increasingly drawn to the views of Jackson's pro-Southern Vice President, John C. Calhoun. Unlike Calhoun, however, he opposed slavery and advocated gradual emancipation.

Floyd had been governor for only a year when the Nat Turner Revolt occurred. He first heard of the rebellion on Tuesday, August 23, when the rider from Jerusalem reached Richmond. Floyd took immediate charge of preparations for quelling the uprising. Within hours he dispatched several companies of militia to Southampton County. By the end of the week the governor received definite news that the rebellion had been crushed. Yet, on August 29, his diary recorded a request from several other Virginia counties and from the town of Fredericksburg for militiamen to help quell other expected slave revolts. Virginians were obviously uneasy.

Governor Floyd insisted on being kept informed constantly about the trials of those blacks accused of taking part in the rebellion. So completely did the Nat Turner Revolt obsess him that his diary mentions little else in the following months but the Jerusalem trials, rumors of other slave conspiracies, and reflections on their meaning. By mid-September, however, Floyd became suspicious of the many reports of black unrest that flowed into Richmond. None of them seemed to materialize once state militia were sent into the area. Of one such rumor he wrote: "I do not exactly believe the report. The slaves are quiet and evince no disposition to rebel."

On several occasions Floyd expressed concern over the fate of those blacks sentenced to be sent to the Deep South. The treatment of slaves was generally much harsher there. Floyd debated whether to commute the sentences rather than "endanger the lives of these Negroes." On other occasions he reprieved some slaves who had been sentenced to death in Jerusalem. Indeed, there is evidence that the governor reviewed personally almost every convicted rebel's trial record.

Nat Turner was hanged from this tree. His death did not end white fears, though the savage reprisals against blacks—innocent as well as guilty—probably discouraged other slave uprisings.

At the same time, Floyd could not contain his fury at those Northern abolitionists who, he believed, had encouraged Nat Turner's Revolt and similar conspiracies. On September 27 he wrote:

> I have received this day another number of the *Liberator,* a newspaper printed in Boston with the express intention of inciting the slaves and free Negroes in this and the other states to rebellion and to murder the men, women, and children of those states. Yet we are gravely told there is no law to punish such an offense. The amount of it then is this, a man in our states may plot treason in one state against another without fear of punishment, whilst the suffering state has no right to resist by the provisions of the federal Constitution. If this is not checked it must lead to a separation of these states.

When not complaining about the abolitionists, the governor's diary often denounced President Andrew Jackson. Floyd considered him dangerous to Southern interests, especially on such issues as national tariff policy. After receiving South Carolinian guests returning from an antitariff meeting at Philadelphia, Floyd noted in his diary that the election of Calhoun would "turn out Jackson with all his unworthy officers, men not gentlemen, who lie and slander all men opposed to them to keep themselves in power."

The governor had little time for national politics, however. Requests for men and arms to combat expected slave revolts continued to

A page of Governor Floyd's journal from September 1831. The entry for the 27th, as well as attacking the Liberator, speaks of his willingness to recommend mercy in the case of three slaves sentenced in Southampton County, but being unable to do so because of "the forms of our infamous [state] constitution."

pour into Richmond from every section of Virginia. Floyd's diary spoke constantly about the "Northern conspirators" who he believed were planning fiendish schemes. As late as October 20, Floyd recorded hearing of a plot by "Northern fanatics" in Philadelphia to stir up a general insurrection throughout Virginia and massacre its white population. Floyd treated the rumors coming from outside his state more seriously than he did those concerning slave conspiracies within Virginia itself.

Turner's capture and execution only reinforced the determination of antislavery Virginians like John Floyd to prevent such future uprisings, not simply by supervising blacks in the state more closely but also by eliminating the source of discontent itself—that is, slavery. "There are still demands for arms in the lower counties," Floyd's diary commented on November 21. "I could not have believed there was half the fear amongst the people of the lower counties in respect to their slaves."

The problem never seemed to die down, as the governor's subsequent November entries indicate:

> Twenty-third day. I have reprieved for sale and transportation southward several slaves.
> Twenty-sixth day. I have received more applications for arms.
> Twenty-eighth day. I am preparing a message to the General Assembly. It will be ultra states' rights.

By "ultra states' rights" Floyd meant that he would demand that Northern states begin controlling the activities of abolitionists; also he would denounce the federal government for raising tariff duties, in opposition to Southern desires for lower rates.

In his "message to the General Assembly" (the state legislature) the governor also planned to deal with the question of slavery itself. His diary notes: "Before I leave this government, I will have contrived to have a law passed gradually abolishing slavery in this state, or at all events to begin the work by prohibiting slavery on the west side of the Blue Ridge Mountains."

Floyd's plan may sound surprising to us today, but it had the support of many of his fellow Virginians. In large sections of the state slavery had never assumed great economic or social importance. Men like Floyd and Thomas Ritchie of the Richmond *Enquirer* spoke for many Virginians in supporting gradual freeing of the slaves. They favored compensated emancipation—that is, slaveholders would be paid for the slaves who were freed. Most of those who favored this type of emancipation also believed in colonization—resettling former slaves elsewhere. (Africa was the location most commonly thought of.)

Opposition to slavery was particularly strong in the hilly areas and lush valleys west of the Blue Ridge Mountains. There blacks (whether slave or free) numbered less than 20 percent of the population. In the eastern sections of Virginia plantation slavery was common, and blacks numbered over 50 percent of the total population. Here supporters of abolition were less numerous.

During the early decades of the nineteenth century many anti-slavery voices such as John Floyd's were raised throughout the South. The leading organization devoted to gradual, compensated emancipation—the American Colonization Society—found many of its leaders, and followers, in the region.

Governor Floyd, though favoring gradual emancipation at the time of the 1831–32 debate in Virginia, soon afterward took a strong proslavery position.

When Floyd addressed the state legislature in December 1831, he urged its members to abolish slavery by gradual stages in Virginia. Debate began in January 1832. For three weeks Virginia's legislators wrestled with the problem of abolishing slavery. They engaged in the bluntest and most complete debate on this question ever to take place in the ante-bellum[5] South. Supporters and opponents of emancipation marshaled their arguments in long speeches detailing the benefits or dangers that would flow from such a policy. Even those who defended the institution did so mainly on the grounds that it was an unavoidable reality rather than a blessing.

A typical defense was that of a delegate named John T. Brown:

And is there, then, no apology for slavery? Is it a sin of so deep a die that none dare vindicate it? For my own part, I am not the advocate of slavery in the abstract, and if the question were upon introducing it, I should be the very last to agree to it. But I am yet to be convinced that slavery as it exists in Virginia is either criminal or immoral. It was cast upon us by the act of others. It is our lot, our destiny, and whether, in truth, it be right or wrong—whether it be a blessing or a curse—the moment has never yet been when it was possible for us to free ourselves from it. This is enough to satisfy my conscience, and I contend that the happiness of the slave does not call for his emancipation. His condition is better than that of four-fifths of the human family. He enjoys far more of the comforts of life, than the peasantry of many of the nations in Europe. The greater part of mankind must, in the nature of things, be poor and ignorant, toiling anxiously for their daily bread. All cannot be raised to the top of the scale. The Negro, of all others, is the least susceptible of elevation.

The debate ranged over many issues. What might be the economic

---

[5] "Ante-bellum" refers to the period prior to the Civil War. The term comes from Latin words meaning "before the war."

effects of emancipation? How should colonization be handled? (Both supporters and opponents of abolition agreed on this step if blacks were freed.) What was the morality of slaveholding? The specter of Nat Turner hung plainly over the entire proceedings. Few speakers, whatever their views on emancipation, bothered to disguise their anxiety over the prospect of future slave revolts. A typical antislavery speaker, for example, pleaded with his colleagues for support by reversing a standard proslavery argument. James McDowell observed:

> It is true to the letter that there is no laboring peasantry in any other part of the world who, in all external respects, are better situated than our slaves—who suffer less from want—who suffer less from hardship—who struggle less under the toils of life or who have a fuller supply of the comforts which mere physical nature demands. In all these respects the slave shares in the equalizing and benign spirit of our institutions and age.
>
> But it is in this very circumstance, in this alleviated and improved condition, that we have a principal cause of apprehension from the slave. You raise his intelligence with his condition, and as he better understands his position in the world, he were not a man if it did not the more inflame his discontent. That it has this effect we all know. The truth is proverbial: that a slave is the more unhappy as he is the more indulged. He could not be otherwise; he follows but the impulse of human nature in being so.

Petitions for and against emancipation reached the legislature from all over Virginia. Debate was halted on January 25. Finally, the legislature voted on a mild measure providing for gradual emancipation over a period of many years. It was defeated by a vote of 73 to 58. The representatives had divided along distinct regional lines. Delegates from west of the Blue Ridge Mountains (who held only 102 slaves among them) supported abolition, 49 to 6. Representatives from the eastern areas (men who together owned 1,029 slaves) opposed emancipation by a margin of 67 to 9. The eastern counties were overrepresented in the legislature, as they had been since the time of Nathaniel Bacon. Thus they carried the day for slavery.

Antislavery Virginians such as Governor Floyd felt understandably disheartened. Floyd confided to his diary the thought that Virginia itself would split into two states on the question:

> Goode, of Mecklenburgh [a slaveholder], said to me the day the debate closed upon the "slave question" that the eastern and western people were not all the same people, that they were essentially a different people, that they did not think alike, feel alike, and had no interests in common, that a separation of the state must ensue, and rather than have the subject of abolition again debated he would be glad for a separation. Both sides seem ready to separate the state if any one would propose it. I think that event from appearances highly probable.

Floyd was right, though the creation of a separate state—West Virginia— did not occur for another three decades.

s it turned out, the subject of abolition was never again debated anywhere in the ante-bellum South. Within months antislavery Southerners like Governor Floyd shifted their attention to defending what they considered Southern rights over the question of tariff nullification. Yet the rebellion did force many white Southerners to confront their own deepest convictions about the relations between master and slave. Never again would this relationship seem as clear-cut as it had before the August rebellion in Southampton County.

The most lasting result of Nat Turner's Revolt turned out to be increasingly severe Southern control of both slaves and free blacks. Many whites in the region apparently shared the fears (if not the conclusions) of the antislavery Virginia legislator who asked in January 1831:

> Was it the fear of Nat Turner and his deluded and drunken handful of followers which produced or could produce such effects? Was it this that induced distant counties, where the very name of Southampton was strange, to arm and equip for a struggle? No, it was the suspicion eternally attached to the slave himself, the suspicion that a Nat Turner might be in every family, that the same bloody deed could be acted over at any time in any place, that the materials for it were spread through the land and always ready for a like explosion.

A remarkable story was told by a black preacher who was in Virginia during the Nat Turner Revolt. Shortly after the rebellion a Southampton County slaveholder went hunting in the woods with a trusted slave, who carried his master's gun. The black had been with the slaveholder's family for many years, and he had led his master and his family to safety during the uprising. In the forest the bondsman handed the gun to his master, saying that he could no longer live as a slave. He asked his owner either to give him his freedom or to kill him. The white man hesitated for a moment, then took the gun and shot the black man through the heart.

Although this episode might never have occurred, it could be said that the choice it speaks of was given to white Virginians in the aftermath of the Nat Turner Revolt. Like the slaveholder in the story, they chose to kill the last promise of a peaceful emancipation.

Slavery in the United States

WITH THE WISDOM of hindsight, we can see that the issue of slavery was too complex to be resolved—even in one state—by a legislative debate such as that held in Virginia in 1832. The sons of these Virginians would go to war over the "peculiar institution." Their fathers and grandfathers had been wrestling with the problem unsuccessfully, after all, since the time of the Revolution.

When news of the Declaration of Independence reached England, even British supporters of the colonial cause complained about one aspect of the American Revolution. The "assigned cause and ground of the rebellion," wrote one Englishman, "is that every man hath an unalienable right to liberty. Here the words, as it happens, are not nonsense, but then they are not true. There are slaves in America, and where there are slaves, there liberty is alienated." The practice of slavery in "republican" America seemed a glaring contradiction not only to Englishmen but to the revolutionaries themselves— many of whom owned black slaves. The Declaration of Independence opened with lofty

Slave auctions were regarded as a necessary evil by many slaveowners. After turning some of his "people" over to an auctioneer, one Southerner grieved: "I did not know until the time came what pain it would give me." The auction pictured is at Richmond. The poster, from New Orleans, describes "choice Negroes" for sale.

phrases about equality. But the Second Continental Congress cautiously decided to omit a passage of the original draft that denounced human bondage. Some American leaders from Southern colonies, such as Thomas Jefferson and George Washington, expressed their concern over maintaining slavery within a democratic republic. But they did so privately.

The thirteen colonies contained about half a million slaves at the time of the Revolution. Every colony had some, but the great majority lived in the South. There were 200,000 in Virginia, 100,000 in South Carolina, and at least 70,000 each in Maryland and North Carolina. In some Southern colonies slaves composed 50 percent of the population. There were also slaves in the North. New York had 25,000 and New Jersey had about 10,000. Pennsylvania and Connecticut each had about 6,000 slaves. There were about 5,000 in Massachusetts and 4,000 in Rhode Island.

Fear of slave uprisings was common in eighteenth-century colonial America, despite the fact that only a few insurrections actually took place. Boston's Patriots were outraged by the presence of black troops among the occupying British army before the Boston Massacre. They were also angered by rumors that the redcoats were stirring up the city's small black population. Virginians were just as outraged in 1776 when the departing royal governor urged slaves to revolt against their masters and join the British in exchange for their freedom.

Along with fear of blacks' went an equal measure of contempt. Most ordinary Americans of the Revolutionary era—even those who favored abolition—believed that blacks were innately inferior to whites. "Comparing them by their faculties of memory, reason and imagination," wrote Jefferson, "it appears to me that in memory they are equal to the whites, in reason much inferior, and in imagination dull and tasteless." Few people of Jefferson's time would have quarreled with his view. (Some, though, might even have challenged the notion that a black person had a memory—or anything else—equal to a white's.)

During the Confederation period, steps

were taken to end slavery in large areas of the Republic. In the period between 1783 and 1786 Massachusetts, Connecticut, Rhode Island, New York, and New Jersey either abolished slavery outright or provided for its gradual disappearance. In Virginia the legislature passed an act in 1782 easing the process by which owners could emancipate their bondsmen. At Jefferson's direction the Northwest Ordinance of 1787 prohibited slavery in the Northwest Territory. And even though the Constitution made no provision for slavery as an institution, it did provide that the foreign slave trade be abolished after 1808.

But what would happen to slaves who were freed? Since even moderate whites feared blacks, or looked down on them, very few white Americans were prepared to accept a large free black population living among them. Most schemes for emancipation from the Revolutionary era up to the time of the Virginia legislative debate failed to resolve the problem of freed slaves. Most supporters of gradual emancipation, from Thomas Jefferson to John Floyd, believed in the need for colonization—a policy that was easier to agree on in principle than to achieve in practice.

The task of the North in emancipating its blacks after 1790 was relatively simple. The region contained only 40,000 slaves and 27,000 freed blacks; the white population totaled 1,900,000. Thus roughly 1 out of 28 people was a black. The situation was very different in the South, where there were 1,271,000 whites, 657,000 slaves, and 32,000 free blacks. In other words, over a third of the Southern population was black. By the time of the Nat Turner Revolt, through individual emancipation (a process known as manumission) and increases by birth, there were over 181,000 free blacks in the South.

Fears of an unstable free black population were obviously much greater among Southerners than among Northerners. Many white Southerners sincerely wanted to have slavery abolished. But Southern leaders from the time of the Founding Fathers until the Virginia legislative debate of 1832—and beyond—were afraid of even gradual emancipation. They thought it would pose a threat to the safety, stability, and "racial purity" of white society. Besides, slavery was profitable.

THE ECONOMICS OF SLAVERY

The ante-bellum South comprised a million square acres of territory. It stretched from Chesapeake Bay to western Texas and from the Ohio River south to the Gulf of Mexico. Although climate and terrain varied considerably in the South, most of the region had rainfall, temperature, and soil conditions adequate for producing a variety of staple cash crops.

During the colonial period Southern plantations grew tobacco, rice, indigo, and (to a much lesser extent) cotton. In some areas more than one of these crops was important. In Southampton County, for example, farmers grew both rice and cotton in bulk.

"King Cotton" Tobacco had been the South's leading export before the Revolution. But after 1800 the Southern economy came to center on cotton. The most important single factor in this change was the cotton gin. ("Gin" is short for "engine.") It was invented in 1793 by a New Englander named Eli Whitney. Before this time separating cotton fiber from the seeds was done by hand and took a long time. But with Whitney's machine one person could do the work of fifty. At the same time, improvements in technology enabled England's textile industry to process raw cotton into cloth much more efficiently than before. Thus, early in the nineteenth century, growing cotton became truly profitable in the United States.

Cotton cultivation spread throughout older states such as Georgia and South Carolina. Even more important cotton-growing areas were the as yet sparsely settled regions that eventually became the states of Alabama, Mississippi, Louisiana, Texas, and Arkansas. The United States had exported only 3,000 bales of cotton in 1790. By the time of Nat Turner's Revolt this figure had grown to 805,000 bales. By 1859, on the eve of Civil War, the figure had skyrocketed to 4 1/2 million bales. The United States—or, more particularly, the American South—had become the world's leading cotton producer. Along with this phenomenal growth went a continuing demand for more slaves to raise the crop.

Tobacco growing remained important in nineteenth-century Virginia, Kentucky, and North Carolina. Rice cultivation prospered along the South Carolina and Georgia seacoasts. Sugar-cane production dominated Louisiana agriculture. Elsewhere in the South the main crop was cotton. Cotton alone accounted for almost two-thirds of the total export trade of the United States.

Who Owned Slaves The 1850 census showed that 1,815,000 slaves were employed in cotton production. Some 350,000 worked in the tobacco fields; 125,000 raised rice; 150,000 labored on sugar plantations; and 60,000 produced hemp. Smaller numbers worked as house servants and artisans on plantations. Several thousand labored as workers in the South's few mines and factories.

Throughout the nineteenth century a constant flow of both white settlers and black slaves shifted millions of Southerners away from older seaboard regions and into the newer regions of Alabama, Mississippi, Louisiana, Arkansas, and Texas. Older states such as Virginia and Maryland declined in economic importance in the South because they produced relatively little cotton (despite the output of scattered areas such as Southampton County). Such states turned increasingly to breeding slaves as an export "crop." During the decades between Nat Turner's Revolt and the Civil War, more than 700,000 slaves were sold in the United States, mainly by owners in the Upper South to purchasers in the Deep South.

It would be incorrect to think of the Southern population as divided simply into two groups—white owners and black slaves. Many white Southerners owned no slaves at all. For example, in Southampton County at the time of Nat Turner's insurrection the majority of whites owned no slaves. Of those who did, only a tiny proportion owned enough to have been considered even small planters. Most whites who owned slaves—in that region and elsewhere in the South—worked alongside their own bondsmen in the fields.

The entire white population of the South in 1860 numbered approximately 7 million, with the total of white families estimated at 1,400,000. There were 383,635 slaveholders. This meant that almost three out of every four families held no slave property. Only 2,292 landowners owned more than 100 slaves. Some 46,000 slaveholders owned between 20 and 100 blacks. The great majority of slaveholders, owning fewer than 20 slaves, were not owners of large plantations but simply moderately successful independent farmers. Except in the richest cotton-producing areas, slaveholders generally formed a minority of local landowners.

Before the 1830s some slaveowners freed their own slaves. They expected that this policy would be generally adopted throughout the South. But new laws made the practice of manumission more difficult after the Nat Turner Revolt. In any case, most nineteenth-century slaveholders did not consider the possibility of emancipation very seriously.

A mansion in Louisiana typifies the Greek Revival style favored by wealthy Southerners. Built in 1840, it was owned by a prominent sugar planter.

Charleston Society

Charleston, South Carolina, was the cultural center of the Old South. A prosperous seaport, it was situated, as the local saying goes, "where the Ashley and Cooper rivers mingle their mighty waters to form the Atlantic Ocean." Ever since colonial times pride was no stranger to the planters of the area. Together with the town merchants, they supported concerts, lectures, plays, and libraries when such refinements were unknown elsewhere in the colonies. Charlestonians could point to the following "firsts": public library (1698), theater (1736), symphony orchestra (1762), city college (1770), and museum (1773).

The most attractive part of town was the waterfront, known as the Battery. There, fanned by sea breezes, stood the elegant mansions of the well-born and wealthy. The houses, with their sides set to the street, faced inward toward gardens lush with magnolias, wisteria, and oleander. Attached to the houses were gracious verandas decorated with delicately wrought ironwork. To Fanny Kemble, an English actress who visited the city in the late 1830s, "every house seems built to the owner's particular taste; and in one street you seem to be in an old English town, and in another in some Continental city of France or Italy. This variety is extremely pleasing to the eye."

The ebb and flow of social life was governed by the customs of the planters. From May to November, when the rice fields were under irrigation, they lived in the city to avoid the dangers of malaria. The Christmas holidays were usually spent in the countryside. By the end of January, the planters were back in town for a round of races, dinners, balls, and other entertainments. A somewhat disapproving Bostonian described the chief occupations of the upper class as "cards, dice, the bottle, and horses."

Fully half the population of the city—the slaves—did not share in these pleasures. They were subject to many restrictions because of their numbers and fears of a revolt. In colonial times, slave uprisings that had broken out in Charleston had been crushed with great severity. In 1822 came the Denmark Vesey plot. Public gatherings of blacks were forbidden. Black sailors—free elsewhere—were jailed when their ships were in port.

In 1815 Charleston was the leading port for the export of cotton and rice. But, as cotton growing spread into the Deep South, the city gradually lost its importance. Fanny Kemble found a charming aspect to the city's "air of decay, a genteel infirmity, as might be that of a distressed elderly gentlewoman." To her, Charleston in 1838 maintained "a look of state, as of former wealth and importance, a little gone down in the world yet remembering still its former dignity."

Charleston in 1831

SOUTHERN SOCIETY

The social structure of the ante-bellum South resembled a pyramid. The region's few thousand large planters stood at the top. Beneath them was the larger group of slaveholding whites, who owned enough slaves to staff a small or medium-size plantation. Further down the pyramid stood the majority of slaveholders, who owned *fewer* than ten slaves. Below them was the great mass of landowning but nonslaveholding white farmers. Toward the base of the pyramid were the lowest white Southerners, the landless and luck-less "poor whites," who generally farmed the region's less fertile hill-country areas. At the base of the pyramid were, of course, the slaves themselves, on whose labor rested the South's entire social and economic structure.

Several groups in the South stood outside the central structure of plantation power and influence. There were professionals and businessmen, people like the journalist Thomas Ritchie or the physician (and governor) Thomas Floyd. Such people were often absorbed into the plantation aristocracy by marriage, political alliance, or slave purchases. There were also free blacks—roughly 228,000 in 1860. Most of them lived in the cities of the Upper South or in New Orleans. Though better off than slaves, they were distrusted and discriminated against by Southern whites.

The plantation gentry were the elite of the South. They and their supporters dominated Southern politics up to the Civil War. Their social events, held in the larger cities and towns, set the tone for Southern society. Their impressive mansions often became centers of social life for the surrounding communities.

Though they might be compared to foreign aristocrats, Southern planters differed from them in at least two ways. (1) They were a working aristocracy. The business records of countless plantations show that the men and women who ran them were constantly concerned with the many problems of cash-crop agriculture. (2) They lived on their lands, rather than being absentee owners. This direct involvement helps account for the fact that slaveholders in the American South worked out a systematic pro-slavery argument to justify their holdings (see pages 306–08). They were the only "master class" in the Western Hemisphere to do so.

Susan Dabney Smedes, a planter's wife, once observed that "managing a plantation was something like managing a kingdom." A planter often found himself playing many roles within a brief space of time. He was an absolute ruler of his slaves. He was an aristocrat among fellow planters. He was a democratic politician among white men of all classes. He was a fellow Christian when conducting plantation religious services (often for a mixed audience of family members and slaves). The strains of moving back and forth quickly among such different roles produced anguish among some planters.

Conditions Favoring Slavery If so few Southerners actually owned slaves, why did the whole society support the slave system at times of crisis such as the Nat Turner Revolt? Probably a majority of the volunteer militiamen who had helped to quell the uprising owned no slaves, yet they seemed passionately committed to maintaining slavery. Why? At least one answer suggests itself immediately in light of the Southampton County experience. Fear of slave insurrections was intense and constant among ante-bellum white Southerners. As whites rode their nightly slave patrols in the years after the 1831 uprising, many of them must have remembered that Nat Turner's band slaughtered slaveholders and nonslaveholding whites alike. Thus concern for personal and family security helped bind together different economic classes in the South.

Southerners also favored slavery because of its psychological advantages. The existence of a slave class gave all whites—especially poor white landless farmers—some reassurance that they were superior. Black people like Nat Turner and his men had no status within Southern white society. Even the poorest, least educated white person meant more in the eyes of the law and in Southern society than a planter's brightest, most talented slave. Nat Turner acknowledged having

Slaves on sugar plantations were driven very hard. During the harvest season, many worked from sixteen to eighteen hours a day, seven days a week.

received special treatment from his original owner. But Turner had no rights that any white person was bound to respect.

Belief in the inferiority of blacks was common among almost all Southern (and Northern) whites, whatever their class. This universal sense of white supremacy blurred the sharp contrast between the South's democratic political system and its rigid economic structure, controlled by a few. Planters and poor whites, if they shared nothing else, still felt a common concern for maintaining slavery and the white racial unity it represented.

Slavery influenced status in another way. Some nonslaveholding white farmers managed to purchase blacks, and a few even broke into the planter ranks. When this happened, it bolstered the prevailing belief among white Southerners that only an economy run by slave labor could ensure a broad range of economic opportunity.

Clearly, anxiety, outright fear, and ambition helped create a feeling among almost all Southerners that their "peculiar institution" should be retained and, if necessary, defended. One other factor reinforced the consensus. Southerners were subject to fewer outside influences and new ideas than other Americans. For one thing, most white Southerners were native-born and therefore used to the customs of their region. Only 4.4

percent of the Southern population in 1860 was foreign-born, compared to 18.7 percent elsewhere in the country. Also, there were fewer big cities in the South than in other sections. Even places like Norfolk and Richmond were little more than overgrown country towns. The vibrant, unsettling qualities of urban life affected only a small minority. Most white Southerners lived on farms, plantations, or in small towns such as Jerusalem. The bulk of the South's free blacks, however, did live in towns and cities—where they were closely watched and their movements rigidly supervised. Cities thus remained the most obvious breeding ground of discontent with the slave system. And free blacks were clearly the most dangerous element within the closed world of slave society.

The Treatment of Slaves The conditions under which slaves lived varied considerably. They could be treated relatively mildly and with consideration. Nat Turner, for instance, said that he was well-treated by both his original owner and Joseph Travis. But savagely harsh practices prevailed on rice and sugar plantations in the Deep South. Slaves from other regions of the South were sent there to be punished, as was the case after Nat Turner's Revolt.

Because slaves were valuable property, an owner seldom abused them so cruelly that they died. Short of this, however, a master treated his slaves pretty much as he pleased. In times of extreme social tension, whites subjected blacks to the most degrading punishment with little fear of legal action or social criticism. Most recent scholars agree, however, that, under ordinary circumstances, slaves in the United States were generally better fed, housed, and clothed than those in Latin America during the same period. The treatment of many slaves probably did compare favorably with that of many industrial workers in the North and elsewhere—as pro-slavery people argued. (Even black rebels such as Nat Turner did not complain primarily about their *economic* conditions.) Some slaves were allowed to grow crops on private patches and to keep animals, for their own use or for sale. Almost every plantation had weekly days of rest and special holidays as well. Nat Turner's companions were probably not missed by their owners as they spent that final Sunday eating roast pig, drinking brandy, and scheming rebellion.

Yet no matter how kindly a master might treat his slaves, the slavery system was brutal, for it rested ultimately on force. "The whole commerce between master and slave," wrote Thomas Jefferson from his own experience, "is a perpetual exercise of the most boisterous passions, the most unremitting despotism on the one part, and degrading submission on the other." Slave codes, such as those strengthened throughout the South following the Nat Turner uprising, gave whites almost unrestrained physical power over their slaves. A slave master had absolute authority to decide how long his slaves should work and under what conditions. The law permitted whipping and beating of slaves. Southern newspapers and court records during ante-bellum decades were filled with accounts of how slaves had been mutilated, hanged, shot, starved to death, or even burned alive. (Indeed, the Southern press was the abolitionists' major source for reports on the mistreatment of blacks.)

The law seldom imposed more than minor penalties on whites found guilty of deliberately injuring or killing blacks. Most often, the offenders escaped punishment completely—as did the white militiamen who committed hundreds of atrocities against Southampton County blacks in 1831. Blacks, whether slaves or freemen, were not allowed to testify against whites in Southern courts of law.

It was impossible for slaves to keep their families together as units. Slave marriages had no legal status. Slave families were separated and the members were sold individually as a matter

Although some owners provided good housing for their slaves, much of it was poor, like this ramshackle cabin. Southern physicians often warned planters that they had to provide flooring, windows, and adequate space in order to prevent illness and disease.

of course. How understandably, then, did the troops of "General Nat" break ranks at the Parker plantation to collect their missing kinfolk!

ATTITUDES OF BLACKS

In spite of massive oppression, many slaves appeared to be devoted to their masters, whether from affection, loyalty, or outright fear. This attitude emerges not only from the narratives of slaveholders themselves but from other sources. The slaves who belonged to Dr. Blunt defended their master by firing upon Nat Turner's retreating band. In the Vesey plot and in an 1800 conspiracy in Virginia—led by a slave artisan named Gabriel Prosser—fellow blacks were prominent among those who betrayed the plotters. There are at least two ways of looking at this situation. On the one hand, trusted and indulged slaves such as house servants and artisans had most to lose in any slave uprising—namely, their privileged status. Therefore, they might be expected to place loyalty to their white overlords above any feeling of kinship with rebel slaves. On the other hand, an effective slave rebellion was conceivable only among well-treated bondsmen such as Prosser or Turner. Such people could move easily among other blacks in their areas without arousing the white community's suspicion.

Often in history those in an oppressed group who have privileged status, who have most to lose from rebellion, believe they have no status worth protecting and nothing to lose. So it was with the slave preachers, artisans, house servants, and freed blacks who joined the Prosser, Vesey, and Turner conspiracies. It was easy for Nat Turner's original band of supporters—Will, Hark, Henry, Sam, Nelson, and Jack—to meet with their leader. They plotted rebellion for several months at church services, weekend gatherings, and slave holidays before finally deciding to strike. Their long period of preparation shows how confident slaveholders in the region were about the loyalty of their most trusted bondsmen.

Slave revolts were relatively uncommon in the ante-bellum South. Yet blacks used a number of other ways to indicate how much they opposed the system. Driven by overwork or brutality, many slaves tried to flee from bondage. Almost every plantation owner worried about runaways. Some slaves reached freedom in the North, especially after abolitionists organized the "underground railroad" (see page 379). Other blacks simply took off and hid in the woods for a while (as Nat Turner had done), often returning voluntarily as a sign of independence. The huge number of runaways in the ante-bellum South showed that many slaves silently nursed a keen desire for freedom, despite all the efforts by slaveholders to break the will of their blacks.

Sabotage was common, too. Blacks burned crops and stole supplies. They also pretended to be sick, loafed on the job, and found other, often ingenious, ways to express their hatred for the system.

The Role of Religion   In all the efforts by blacks to undermine slavery the black church and its preachers played a significant role. Most slaves followed the religion of their masters, evangelical Protestantism.[1] It was hardly accidental that, after the Nat Turner Revolt, the Virginia legislature placed a ban on blacks such as Turner wandering freely through the countryside preaching the Gospel. Most Southern states tried to restrict the activities of black church meetings from the 1830s on—and with good reason. For one thing, slaves bent on rebellion could plot in safety at such gatherings. For another, the Bible itself—especially the Old Testament—offered to blacks prepared to interpret it that way an ideology that justified resistance. Southern whites may have regarded as strange Nat Turner's claim that a heavenly vision had instructed him to lead his people from bondage and to slaughter their oppressors. But most of his fellow

---

[1] In general, evangelical Protestants stress the teachings of the Bible rather than the authority of organized church doctrine. They also emphasize the importance of an individual's personal conversion.

John Randolph

John Randolph once said that asking one of the states to surrender part of its sovereignty was like asking a woman to surrender part of her virtue. This quip is typical of his wit. It also neatly summarizes his passionate belief in the sanctity of states' rights. To this proud, eccentric member of the Randolph family of Virginia, only Republican (Antifederalist) principles could ensure personal liberty and freedom from the ''tyranny'' of strong central government. To the end of his life he espoused these principles, sacrificing political friendships and his own promising career for the often reckless role of congressional gadfly.

In 1799, at the age of twenty-six, Randolph was elected to the House from Charlotte County. For the next thirty years, except for three two-year intervals (a single defeat, sickness, and service as a senator), he represented this district. His appearances on the floor of the House commanded attention. Usually a bit late, he would swagger in, whip in hand, booted and spurred, with one or two of his favorite hunting dogs. He would speak off the cuff in a rambling and theatrical fashion, scattering epigrams right and left. One historian described him as ''one of the most brilliant figures that ever strutted and fretted his hour upon the American public stage.''

Randolph's high point was his leadership in gaining congressional approval for the Louisiana Purchase in 1803. He did this although he felt that Jefferson was stretching his constitutional powers. Randolph himself believed in a strict interpretation of the Constitution in order to limit the scope of federal power.

His low point came in 1805, when he bungled the politically inspired impeachment trial of a Federalist judge and quarreled with Jefferson. In 1806 Randolph declared himself independent of his party, accusing Jefferson of ''pulling Federalism forward.'' His opposition to the War of 1812, which swelled the power and popularity of the federal government, cost him his congressional seat.

Randolph returned to Congress in 1815 and opposed on principle the Bank of the United States, the tariff, and other nationalistic measures. His eccentric behavior remained unchecked, but he was no longer a figure of influence. It was the Missouri Compromise of 1820 that brought him back to the limelight—as a spokesman for states' rights and for the Southern way of life. He first linked the ideas that John Calhoun later developed more fully. He also pitted himself against the architect of the compromise, Henry Clay. The two even fought a duel in 1826. According to Clay, Randolph's actions ''came near shaking this Union to the center, and desolating this fair land.''

Randolph's final position was not altogether congenial to him and to others of his generation who were uneasy about slavery. He regarded himself a friend to blacks. By the terms of his will he freed his 400 slaves. When once asked whom he considered the greatest orator he had ever known, Randolph replied, ''A slave, Sir. She was a mother, and her rostrum was the auction-block.''

slaves would have immediately understood what he meant.

The spirituals sung by slaves in their churches and elsewhere expressed a great deal. They dwelt on the belief blacks held of themselves as a "chosen" people. "We are the people of God," said one. Another proclaimed: "I'm a child of God, with my soul set free." Such images probably helped keep many slaves from adopting their masters' view of them as submissive children. The spirituals were "sorrow songs," telling of all the troubles and suffering that slaves experienced. But they rarely spoke of black inferiority, inadequacy, or unworthiness.

In their religious lives slaves found more than simply the strength to endure suffering, certain of a reward in heaven. Often, as in the case of Nat Turner, they also discovered the power to resist actively the efforts of those in authority to brutalize and degrade them. Spirituals, and the sermons of black preachers, were often prophetic. They promised a proud vision of betterment, justice, freedom, and personal worth. They taught that slaves could rise above slavery—not only in the next world, but in this one as well. Nat Turner and his fellow black ministers preached that their people could escape from bondage, through their own efforts and with the help of God. Countless deeds of slave resistance were inspired by this vision. It was embedded in the spiritual life of Southern blacks. Nat Turner's Revolt, the most extreme act of resistance by ante-bellum blacks, can be understood only as the product of such intense religious belief.

JUSTIFYING THE SYSTEM

While blacks found in the Bible a means of enduring slavery, white Southerners turned increasingly to it, and other writings, for evidence to help justify the system. Earlier proslavery advocates—such as those in the 1832 Virginia legislative debate—had apologized for slavery as a "necessary evil" inherited from the past. In the 1830s Southern political figures, led by Calhoun, began aggressively defending their peculiar institution. Southerners were disturbed for several reasons. They were shaken by such episodes as the Vesey and Turner revolts. The growth of abolitionism in the North frightened them. So did South Carolina's lonely championing of Southern interests in the nullification crises of 1832–33. In defense, they began arguing that their system of bondage was morally justified on all grounds. In 1837 Calhoun expressed this point of view: "Where two races of different origin, and distinguished by color and other physical differences, as well as intellectual, are brought together, the relation now existing in the

An antislavery cartoon, published in 1840, mocks the idea, advanced by many Southerners, that blacks had to be treated like children. Depicting black people as competent and capable was part of the strategy of those who favored colonization.

UNCLE CLEM. "Say, Massa Jim, is I wan of them onfortunate Niggers as you was reading about?"
YOUNG GENTLEMAN. "Yes, Uncle Clem, you are one of them."
UNCLE CLEM. "Well, it's a great pity about me.—I'se berry badly off, I is."

Proslavery Americans undoubtedly enjoyed this pictorial jibe at the sometimes overheated arguments of abolitionists. It appeared in Harper's Weekly *in 1861.*

slaveholding states between the two is, instead of an evil, a good—a positive good."

Slavery as a Positive Good The positive good argument dominated the thinking of white Southerners between 1832 and the Civil War. The region's leading thinkers went to enormous lengths to devise a rationale for slavery. In doing so they supported a set of beliefs that differed from the basically optimistic and democratic attitudes held by other Americans elsewhere in the country. Southerners argued that most men are naturally limited in their capacities. They said that human progress and achievement come only at the cost of enslaving peoples that are supposedly suited for such bondage. And they held that human society has always been characterized by class distinctions.

Governor James H. Hammond of South Carolina insisted that "in all social systems there must be a class to do the menial duties, to perform the drudgery of life." Without such a class, Hammond argued, "you would not have that other class which leads progress, civilization, and refinement." Slavery, then, "constitutes the very mudsill of society and of political government." George Fitzhugh, a brilliant proslavery spokesman, put it in a livelier way. He declared that "some are born with saddles on their backs, and others booted and spurred to ride them—and the riding does them good." These writers argued that whites could not be expected to perform the backbreaking tasks associated with cotton, rice, and tobacco cultivation. Slaves, therefore, became an economic necessity.

Proslavery people used a number of argu-

SLAVE STATES, 1860—PROPORTION OF WHITE AND BLACK POPULATION

(Figures rounded off to nearest whole percentage point.)

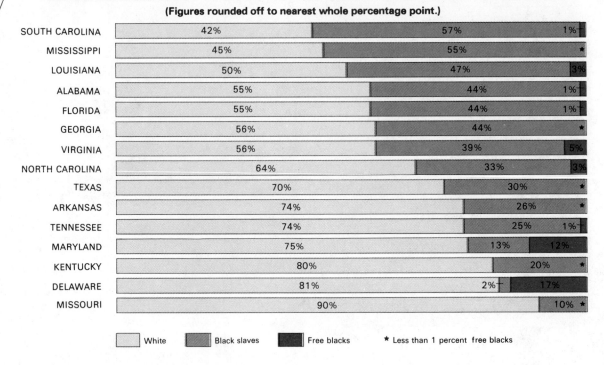

	White	Black slaves	Free blacks
SOUTH CAROLINA	42%	57%	1%
MISSISSIPPI	45%	55%	*
LOUISIANA	50%	47%	3%
ALABAMA	55%	44%	1%
FLORIDA	55%	44%	1%
GEORGIA	56%	44%	*
VIRGINIA	56%	39%	5%
NORTH CAROLINA	64%	33%	3%
TEXAS	70%	30%	*
ARKANSAS	74%	26%	*
TENNESSEE	74%	25%	1%
MARYLAND	75%	13%	12%
KENTUCKY	80%	20%	*
DELAWARE	81%	2%	17%
MISSOURI	90%	10%	*

White   Black slaves   Free blacks   * Less than 1 percent free blacks

ments in attempting to prove the virtues of slavery. They found citations in the Bible that justified enslavement, especially Saint Paul's instructions that slaves obey their masters. They pointed to the glories of Greek and Roman civilizations, both slave societies. They compared, unfavorably, the working conditions of Northern industrial laborers with those of Southern slaves. And, arguing from the false "scientific" theories of their day, they accepted the notion of the innate inferiority of black people.

Proslavery advocates also glorified planters as an aristocracy of talent and grace. Southern gentlemen were pictured as chivalrous heroes, brave and quick to defend their honor. Southern ladies were portrayed as gentle noblewomen who devoted countless leisure-filled days to such "feminine" pastimes as needlework and music. These romantic images were highly unrealistic. Yet reality and myth agreed on at least one aspect of regional life. Even hostile accounts of the slave South usually described the longstanding planter traditions of hospitality and generosity toward friends and strangers alike.

Basic to the proslavery defense was a false image of black people. Despite all the evidence to the contrary, white Southerners insisted on regarding blacks as submissive, contented, happy-go-lucky children. "A merrier being does not exist on the face of the globe," wrote one Virginian, "than the Negro slave of the United States."

This docile image fitted the hopes of Southern slaveholders better than it did the realities of their lives. But Southerners were concerned less with convincing outsiders than with persuading themselves that their proslavery arguments were true. So they convinced themselves of the happiness of their slaves despite much evidence to the contrary.

The End of Moderation A frank and hard-hitting public debate in the South over the merits of slavery, like the one held in Virginia in 1832,

This 1850 drawing manages to be inaccurate about both Southern slavery and British industrialism. Rarely did slaves have the time or energy (or heart) for carefree jollity. Nor did British workers die at forty or labor even fourteen hours a day.

would have been impossible a decade later. Even the idea of gradual emancipation, accompanied by colonization, could not be argued openly in the 1840s. By that time, no Southern state would have elected an emancipationist governor such as John Floyd. Opponents of slavery were driven from positions in Southern churches, universities, and newspapers. Freedom of thought on the slavery question no longer existed in the South during the decades before the Civil War. "Southern rights" were to be defended at all costs.

Even before this time white fears and class tensions had made the South a notoriously violent region. The vengeance taken by militiamen against Southampton County blacks after the Nat Turner uprising did not appear excessive to most white Southerners. The ante-bellum South was noted for its expert brawlers, marksmen, and duelists. Most Southerners owned guns or at least bowie knives (also known as "Arkansas toothpicks").

Once the positive good argument took hold during the 1830s, most planters and their overseers armed themselves. Slave patrols rode regularly through the hot Southern nights. Many plantations became tiny military fortresses, their owners obsessed with thoughts of runaways and rebellions. Southern whites became "militarized," not only on their plantations but also in the cities, where militia and town guards watched free blacks closely. By the late 1840s most white Southerners had accepted a view that linked the defense of slavery to every other cherished virtue. The region's leading Presbyterian minister, the Reverend J. H. Thornwell, argued in 1850 that

> the parties in this conflict are not merely abolitionists and slaveholders—they are atheists, socialists, communists, red republicans, jacobins on one side, and the friends of order and regulated freedom on the other. In a word, the world is the battleground—Christianity and atheism the combatants; and the progress of humanity the stake.

Thornwell probably spoke for the great majority of white Southerners.

The uncharitable, suspicious, and militant South of Thornwell's day seems light years away from the more leisurely, less fearful world of John Floyd and his fellow Virginians. Antislavery Southerners, of either Jefferson's generation or Floyd's, would have found little worth praising in the positive good argument. Yet leaders such as Floyd had helped prepare the way for the more aggressive Southerners who followed.

Floyd, after all, supported John C. Calhoun. Like Calhoun, he managed to combine a strong nationalist fervor with an equally passionate belief in Southern rights. He had endorsed South Carolina's attempt at nullification. He opposed slavery, but he had denounced abolitionists and roused public opinion against the "menace" of Northern "agitators." Floyd's generation found it possible to believe strongly in gradual emancipation while at the same time nursing a violent hatred for Northern advocates of immediate abolition.

The next generation had hardened its point of view. One Southerner who would have agreed with Thornwell was John Buchanan Floyd, son of the antislavery Virginia governor. John Buchanan Floyd believed wholeheartedly in slavery. Like his father, he went into politics. He served as Secretary of War from 1857 to 1860 in the Cabinet of President James Buchanan. While in this post, Floyd transferred an excessive number of arms from Northern to Southern arsenals. His aim was to stockpile military supplies for the sectional conflict everyone expected.

John Buchanan Floyd resigned from the Buchanan Cabinet in December 1860, a convinced secessionist. After Virginia joined the Confederacy in May 1861, he volunteered his services to Virginia. Exactly three decades earlier, his father had unsuccessfully urged the Virginia legislature to abolish slavery. Now John Buchanan Floyd accepted a commission from the same legislature. He would become a major general in an army dedicated to preserve the South's "peculiar institution."

1. What was unusual about Nat Turner's up-bringing?
2. Whom did Southerners blame for Nat Turner's Revolt? Do you think they were right?
3. In what ways did Governor Floyd represent moderate Southern opinion on the slavery question?
4. For what reasons were the Northern states able to abolish slavery without much trouble? Were Southerners correct in their belief that free blacks were a greater menace to slavery than the slaves themselves? Why or why not?
5. Why did cotton replace tobacco as the major staple crop of the South?
6. In what ways was slavery a unifying force in the South even for those who owned no slaves?
7. Was slavery a cruel or a benign institution? Give evidence in support of your position.
8. Why was an effective slave rebellion possible only among well-treated slaves? In what ways did most slaves show their discontent with slavery? Why are spirituals a good source for illustrating the attitudes of bondsmen about slavery?
9. On what grounds did Southerners justify slaveholding?

Beyond the Text

1. Research the Constitution to see how it legitimized slavery. Was the slave considered a person or a piece of property? Why did the Founding Fathers omit the words "slave" and "slavery"?
2. What was slavery like? To investigate this question in some depth, the class might split into three groups. One could explore slave life as ex-slaves saw it, as expressed in memoires and reminiscences. Another group might research slavery as seen by contemporary novelists, particularly Harriet Beecher Stowe and Thomas Nelson Page. The third group might look at what historians have said of slavery as an institution.
3. The question of the slave personality has been raised by historians in recent years. Was the slave a docile, faithful servant or was he a reluctant and rebellious one? Investigate this issue.
4. When the Civil War began, there were about 4 million slaves, an investment estimated at $3 billion. Research the question of the profitability of slavery from various perspectives.

Bibliography

Nonfiction

Blassingame, John W., *The Slave Community.*
Conrad, Alfred H. and John R. Meyer, *The Economics of Slavery.*
Davis, David Brion, *The Problem of Slavery in Western Culture.**
Degler, Carl W., *Neither Black nor White.**
Elkins, Stanley M., *Slavery: A Problem in American Institutional and Intellectual Life.**
Genovese, Eugene D., *The Political Economy of Slavery.**
Jordan, Winthrop D., *White Over Black.**
Lane, Anne, ed., *The Debate Over Slavery.**
Rawick, George, ed., *American Slavery,* 8 vols.
Stampp, Kenneth M., *The Peculiar Institution.**
Weinstein, Allen and Frank O. Gatell, eds., *American Negro Slavery: A Modern Reader.*

Fiction

Bontemps, Arna, *Black Thunder.**
Stowe, Harriet Beecher, *Uncle Tom's Cabin.**
Styron, William, *The Confessions of Nat Turner.**

*a paperback book

Crisis and Compromise in 1850

POTOMAC RIVER breezes chilled the air as legislators returned to Washington, D.C., in December 1849 for the opening of Congress. Senators and representatives tramped through muddy streets past the city's boarding houses, hotels, and half-finished public buildings. An incomplete stone tower jutted out like a bruised silo; when completed several decades later, it would be a monument to George Washington. The Capitol, still topped by a temporary dome, was being repaired and enlarged to make room for the growing number of congressmen who crowded into its corridors with the admission of each new state into the Union.

The mood in Washington when a new Congress convenes is normally charged with excitement. There was special reason, though, for intense feeling in December 1849. Politicians from the North and South feared that the issue of slavery would wreck the approaching Thirty-first Congress. Some brooded anxiously over the possible collapse of the Union itself.

American politicians had deliberately suppressed the slavery question in national politics since the days of the Founding Fathers. No other issue could arouse Americans to such emotion. No other issue had such power to overcome party loyalties. Southerners were particularly troubled. Fearful of abolitionist attacks since the Nat Turner uprising a generation earlier, they warned that Northern interference with slavery could lead to a breakdown of the national party system.

In his famous February 5 Senate speech, Henry Clay presents his proposals for the Compromise of 1850. Clay, a frail seventy-two, had spoken of himself as "quite weak and exhausted" that morning, but his old-time vigor returned when he spoke to his colleagues.

A struggle to elect a Speaker of the House of Representatives began almost from the moment Congress opened on December 3. The difficulty confirmed the fears about sectional political warfare. The Democratic party had dominated national politics since the days of Jackson. There were now 112 Democrats in the House and 109 Whigs. There were also 9 members of the newly formed Free Soil party.

Normally the majority party in the House agrees on its candidate for Speaker and then elects him at the opening session. But these were not normal times. The third party representatives held the balance of power, preventing either major party from having a majority.

Bitterness over slavery and sectional issues strained party lines, threatening to break them beyond repair. The Whigs nominated Robert C. Winthrop of Massachusetts, a descendant of the Puritan governor. He opposed the extension of slavery into the Western territories, but he was not an abolitionist. Still, eight Southern Whigs stormed out of the party's caucus. When the Democrats chose Howell Cobb of Georgia, a supporter of slavery, a small but significant minority of Northern Democrats balked at the choice. These defections meant that neither party could exercise control.

Vote followed vote for three weeks. After sixty-two ballots the House had still failed to select a Speaker. Even the withdrawal of Cobb's and Winthrop's names on various ballots could not break the stalement. This frustrating inaction immobilized the entire government. Congress was paralyzed. The Senate could not function without the House. President Zachary Taylor could not submit his annual message.

On December 22 both sides finally recognized the dangers, and

When this photograph of the Capitol was made in the 1840s, the building was still surmounted by a temporary iron dome. The permanent dome and the House and Senate wings, on either side of the central structure, were added between 1851 and 1865.

they changed the election system itself. House members resolved that, in order to be elected, a Speaker needed only a plurality of votes, not a majority. On the sixty-third ballot they finally chose Cobb. Several Northern Democrats who had opposed Cobb voted for him in the end. Some doubtless hoped to ease the tension. Others were simply tired. "Many members," observed Senator Daniel Webster of Massachusetts, "wished to go home for the holidays."

The new Speaker was a moderate, genial man popular with most members. He tried to heal some of the wounds by carefully allotting committee chairmanships to members from all sections of the country. But other quarrels in Congress showed that tensions remained high. Because the Speaker was a Southerner, Northerners expected that someone from their section would be chosen clerk of the House, a position of some importance and profit for the holder. Two Northern Democrats in particular wanted the job. Several Democrats from the South broke party lines, however, to help elect a fellow Southerner (though a Whig) from Tennessee. One furious Northerner felt that this action taught a simple lesson. He wrote to his brother, stating angrily that if a Northerner did not

> bow and humble and prostrate himself in the dust before their high mightinesses of the South, he must hope for nothing. My Yankee blood is fairly up in this matter, and I will see the South all d— to everlasting perdition before I will ever open my lips in its defense.

Even the President of the United States came under attack. Zachary Taylor, who owned a Mississippi plantation and dozens of slaves, should have presented no problem to the South. His career had been devoted entirely to military service. He had never held public office, nor had he even voted. Taylor had never expressed a hostile opinion on slavery—or anything else. During the campaign of 1848 the South clearly seemed more content with Taylor, a Whig, than with his two opponents. One was Lewis Cass of Michigan, a Democrat. He favored popular sovereignty—that is, allowing people in the territories to decide the slavery question for themselves. Ex-President Martin Van Buren ran on the Free Soil ticket, opposing the extension of slavery into any territory.

Taylor encouraged Southern hopes by straddling most embarrassing issues or remaining silent. Attacks on him from antislavery spokesmen in the North clinched the matter. The South supported Taylor, and he won by a narrow margin.

As President, however, Taylor seemed less acceptable to Southerners. In good Whig fashion he promised to relax the use of the presidential veto. This position caused concern among Southern Whigs, who feared that he might allow passage of the Wilmot Proviso.[1] In November 1849 a prominent Southern Whig visited the White House to learn what Taylor intended to do if Congress adopted the proviso. The President claimed to be neutral on the matter. But he added ominously that "if Congress sees fit to pass it, I will not veto it." He opposed the "coercion of the veto" as undesirable. Taylor had already stated publicly that "the people of the North need have no apprehension of the further extension of slavery." In reaction a group of Southern Whigs vowed once more to leave the Union before they would accept the Wilmot Proviso.

Two presidential statements in 1849 did little to reassure Southerners. Taylor's message to Congress in December urged all sides to avoid agitating "exciting topics of a sectional character." But Taylor did just that. He advised that, since Californians had already decided against slavery, a free California should become a state at once, bypassing entirely the territorial stage. Southerners found this idea unacceptable. They regarded as even worse Taylor's observation, in a later speech, that the New Mexico Territory (present-day New Mexico, Arizona, and part of Colorado) would probably follow California's lead in framing a state constitution prohibiting slavery. "A good Whig document," said Webster of the message, "written in a plain and simple style." But to the South it was evident that Taylor was biased against introducing slavery into newly acquired territories.

On January 21, 1850, Taylor again pleaded for action on California. His special message advised, in effect, that the people in California and New Mexico should enter the Union immediately as states. Avoid complicating the issue, Taylor seemed to say, by trying to extend the Missouri Compromise line all the way to the Pacific Ocean. Let the territorial problem solve itself.

Unfortunately for Taylor's program, the slavery problem in the territories would not go away. Slavery had already reentered national politics to stay. In the summer of 1848, during debates over the Oregon Territory, Thomas Hart Benton, a Democratic senator from Missouri, had likened the slavery issue to the biblical plague of frogs:

> You could not look upon the table but there were frogs, you could not sit down at the banquet table but there were frogs, you could not go to the bridal couch and

---

[1] The Wilmot Proviso was first proposed in 1846. It stated that slavery should be prohibited in all of the lands acquired from Mexico. Congress did not adopt the proviso in 1846, but many Northern politicians were committed to its passage.

lift the sheets but there were frogs! We can see nothing, touch nothing, have no
measures proposed, without having this pestilence thrust before us.

Ill feeling over slavery did indeed seem to crop up with every issue.
As Congress got under way in 1850, debate in the House seldom rose
above the level of name-calling. "For two years," accused Ohio Free-
Soiler Joshua Giddings, "the people of the North have been defraud-
ed, deceived, and imposed upon." Georgia's Robert Toombs warned:
"I do not hesitate to avow before this House and the country that if by
your legislation you seek to drive us from the territories of California
and New Mexico and to abolish slavery in this District of Columbia, I
am for disunion."

The problem of fugitive slaves brought further trouble. Some
Nothern states and many Northern citizens had been ignoring or
flouting the existing fugitive slave law of 1791. Early in January Senator James M. Mason of Virginia presented a bill to make the return of
captured runaway slaves easier and more certain. William H. Seward,
an antislavery Whig from New York and a man close to Taylor,
warned that he would try to nullify the effect of a new law by adding a
guarantee of trial by local jury for an alleged runaway. The Senate then
exploded into a predictable string of sectional complaints and threats.
Mississippi's Henry S. Foote branded Seward a fanatic who wished to
punish the South. Mason himself, however, defended his proposed bill
in reasonable language, and he even agreed to soften parts of it in a bid
for Northern votes.

Within a few days two important Democratic senators, Daniel
Dickinson of New York and Lewis Cass of Michigan, spoke in favor of
milder language and sectional compromise. Cass swore that he would
resign before he would vote for the Wilmot Proviso. As tempers cooled,
it became possible for someone to step forward and restore calm.

The man who took on this role was Henry Clay. He hoped to
engineer the third major compromise of his long career. In 1820, while
Speaker of the House, he had helped pass the Missouri Compromise. In
1833, together with John C. Calhoun, he had worked out a compromise
tariff bill to lower import duties and thus ease the nullification crisis.
The presidency had escaped him three times. But the seventy-three
year old senator drew consolation from his reputation as a compromiser, and he gloried in the title of "the Great Pacificator" (peacemaker). Clay knew that the issues of 1850 would be his last major
political battle.

On January 29 Clay presented his program for compromise. It
consisted of eight points, most of which would soon be joined in one
comprehensive, or omnibus, bill. (1) Congress should accept California
as a state with a free constitution. (2) In New Mexico Territory—

unfavorable ground for slavery, according to Clay and many others—there should be no congressional restriction or encouragement of slavery. (3) The slave trade should be abolished in Washington, D.C.

These were the pro-North points. Clay's additional proposals were designed to balance things sectionally. (4) The boundary between Texas and New Mexico should be established on a line favoring Texan claims. (5) The federal government should assume responsibility for the debts of Texas before it became a state. (6) Slavery itself was to be guaranteed in the District of Columbia. (7) Congress should pass a firmer fugitive slave law. (8) Congress would formally announce a policy of noninterference with the slave trade among the Southern states. (Clay's final suggestion, an attempt to sweeten the pill for the South as a whole, was later dropped.)

The North stood to gain more from Clay's proposals than the South. Admitting California as a free state would destroy the sectional balance—parity between free and slave states—that still existed in the Senate. (The House already had a Northern majority because the North had more people.) Giving the North a majority in the Senate as well as the House seemed suicidal to proslavery forces.

As for leaving the New Mexico Territory question undecided, Southern extremists feared, with good reason, that free states would eventually emerge from it. Why did this matter to a slaveholder in South Carolina? Because when such states joined the Union, they would elect antislavery congressmen who might vote to abolish slavery. The proposals regarding the Texas boundary and debt would not alter the sectional power balance. Enforcing a new fugitive slave law would depend on Northern cooperation, risky and uncertain at best.

Yet Clay made his appeal primarily to the North, asking for generosity, since the more powerful section had more to give. Northerners, he warned, must be especially understanding about slavery, although the institution did not figure in their economy or society. Slavery was woven into the fabric of Southern society, he reminded the Senate. To talk of abolition threatened the South's "habits, safety, property, life—everything."

Clay expected no help from extremists on the slavery question, and he got none. Northern antislavery advocates had never liked him much, but they bided their time and let Southern extremists voice the first criticisms of his proposals. Eight Southern senators tore into "the Great Pacificator." One angry "fire-eater" (Southern proslavery extremist) denied that Clay had proposed a compromise at all. It was, he said, "cowardly capitulation" to the North.

QUESTIONING A CANDIDATE

A cartoon of 1848 pokes fun at Taylor's unwillingness to commit himself on the issues of the day. The two disgruntled men at left have decided to turn to other candidates: John P. Hale, nominated by the Liberty party, and Van Buren ("Matty"), the Free Soil candidate.

On February 5 Clay responded with his major compromise speech. In an address lasting two and a half hours, he ignored the extremists and appealed to Northerners.

> What do you want? What do you want—you who reside in the free states? Do you want that there shall be no slavery introduced into the territories acquired by the war with Mexico? Have you not your desire in California? And in all human probability you will have it in New Mexico also. What more do you want? You have got what is worth more than a thousand Wilmot Provisos.

In the manner of a true compromiser Clay pleaded for moderation.

> Let me say to the North and to the South, what husband and wife say to each other. We have mutual faults; neither of us is perfect; nothing in the form of humanity is perfect; let us, then, be kind to each other—forbearing, forgiving each other's faults—and above all, let us live in happiness and peace together.

Calhoun in the early 1800s tried to avoid making an issue of slavery, but by 1836 he was declaring that abolition "strikes directly and fatally not only at our prosperity, but our existence as a people."

While Clay looked for votes and worked to generate "spontaneous" meetings, two leading Southerners, representing two generations of proslavery opinion, renewed the attack on his compromise proposals. Senator Jefferson Davis of Mississippi dismissed Clay's plan as misleading if not worthless. He pointed out what many congressmen perhaps chose to ignore in 1850—that no fugitive slave bill, no matter what its provisions, would work if the North chose to sabotage it. Even the Missouri Compromise line, which Davis hinted might be extended to the Pacific Ocean (thus satisfying the South), could not legally bind the states involved.

According to Davis, Northern aggression had caused the crisis. "I see nothing short of conquest on the one side, or submission on the other." He claimed that the North sought to degrade Southerners, to make them "an inferior class, a degraded caste in the Union." Unless this stopped, warned Davis, Southerners would follow the example of the thirteenth-century English barons who rose up and forced King John to sign the Magna Charta.

The other Southerner who spoke at this time was John C. Calhoun. In contrast to Davis' emotional oration Calhoun's logical address demanded specific concessions for the South. The South Carolinian had long demanded Southern unity. A year earlier Calhoun had drafted a Southern Address, a strong document of grievance and warning signed by forty-eight congressmen.

By 1850 Calhoun was old and sick. He knew that his career and life were almost over. He had already fainted in the Senate lobby several times. On one of those occasions he had been carried into the Vice-President's office to recuperate. Another South Carolinian, Robert B. Rhett, rushed over. "Ah, Mr. Rhett," Calhoun sighed, "my career is nearly done. The great battle must be fought by you younger men. . . . the South—the poor South!" On March 4 Calhoun presented his speech to the Senate. He did not actually speak, however, because of his feeble health. Senator Mason read his address for him.

Though broken in body, Calhoun remained as firm and uncompromising as ever. He argued that an exact political balance between North and South had to be maintained. No temporary, patchwork solution would do. Compromisers might chant the word "Union!" till doomsday, but it would have no more effect than intoning the word "Health!" over a dying person. What could be done? As Calhoun saw it, the North had to give slaveholders a chance to settle the West. It had to return runaway slaves, to discourage them from fleeing. It had to agree to a constitutional amendment creating a precise balance between Northern and Southern political power in the national government (despite the fact that Northern whites outnumbered Southern whites by more than 2 to 1). If the North could not accept the South on these terms, he concluded, "tell us so, and let the states we both represent agree to separate and part in peace. If you are unwilling we should part in peace, tell us so, and we shall know what to do when you reduce the question to submission or resistance."

Calhoun's defiant stand might represent the views of a minority, but still it demanded some direct response. The South Carolinian had attacked Clay's proposals and momentarily upset the majority's impulse to compromise. The man who accepted Calhoun's challenge was Daniel Webster of Massachusetts.

Webster was scheduled to speak in the Senate on March 7. In those days, a major congressional address was a great public occasion. Congressmen worked for days carefully preparing lengthy speeches. Their fellow legislators sat through the speeches and actually listened. Others, too, wanted to hear. Notice of an important speech on the congressional calendar set off a stampede for seats in the gallery. Spectators would line up for admission to the chamber, even if it meant crowding in the aisles, close-packed with other standees, for four or five hours. The Senate presented just such a picture when Webster gave his famous "Seventh of March" speech.

The portly senator rose, pulled his vest down over his paunch, raised his head, and struck a theatrical pose. "I wish to speak today," Webster began, "not as a Massachusetts man, not as a Northern man, but as an American. I speak today for the preservation of the Union. Hear me for my cause."

Webster traced the history of North-South differences. First he emphasized the contrast between the North's easy abolition of slavery after the Revolution and the South's commitment to the institution after the invention of the cotton gin and the spread of cotton culture. He did not go so far as to claim that only lack of economic dependence had made slavery seem wrong to the North. But he did argue that his listeners had to bear in mind slavery's significance to the white South. Why then had sectional conflict grown? Because, Webster said, too many radicals in the North now contended that right could be distinguished from wrong "with the precision of an algebraic equation."

Then Webster denounced both Northern abolitionists and Southern secessionists as dangerous extremists. Abolitionism was harmful, he asserted. The Wilmot Proviso was offensive and unnecessary; no one need "reaffirm an ordinance of nature nor reenact the will of God" by

Webster was a man of great eloquence in an age when long and polished speeches were more admired than they are today. For decades, American students were assigned his more famous speeches to memorize and recite.

prohibiting slavery in territories "naturally" hostile to its existence. He dismissed the idea of sectional disunion. Secession and peace were mutually exclusive. Finally, Webster argued that, although sectional tensions obviously existed, they could be eased, and major political problems could be settled. Taking Clay's cue, Webster called on the North to keep its part of the basic sectional bargain. It must not harass the South over slavery, however repugnant the slave system. It must obey the law regarding slavery and even approve a new federal law to ensure that Southerners could recapture their fugitive slaves.

When he attacked the secessionists, Webster included Calhoun, the man "who, I deeply regret, is prevented by serious illness from being in his seat today." But Calhoun was there that day, having shuffled into the Senate shortly after Webster started. Calhoun shot back: "The Senator from South Carolina is in his seat." Webster continued with hardly a pause, saying that "peaceable secession is an utter impossibility." When he had finished, the galleries broke into sustained applause. Calhoun tried for the final word: "I cannot agree that this Union cannot be dissolved. Am I to understand that no degree of oppression, no outrage, no broken faith, can produce the destruction of this Union? The Union *can* be broken." These were Calhoun's last words in the Senate.

Webster had more to worry about from Northern reaction to his speech than he did from Calhoun. Webster had opposed slavery, though he was not an abolitionist. Now his call for justice to the South, especially his support for capturing and returning fugitive slaves, infuriated Northern antislavery advocates. They responded predictably and savagely. Horace Greeley, editor of the influential New York Tribune, wrote that the speech was "unequal to the occasion and unworthy of its author." William Cullen Bryant wrote a poem about the "fallen angel," the "God-like Daniel." Theodore Parker, an abolitionist Boston preacher, claimed that he knew "of no deed in American history done by a son of New England to which I can compare this but the act of Benedict Arnold."

Other Americans, however, hailed Webster's speech for what it was—a significant and eloquent statement urging both sides to stop agitating the slavery question. Conservatives, North and South, read it with approval; 120,000 copies had been rushed into print. Even the Charleston *Mercury,* unfriendly to the North and its politics, noted that "with such a spirit as Mr. Webster has shown, it no longer seems impossible to bring this sectional contest to a close." Businessmen overwhelmingly supported the Clay-Webster position. They worried that all the squabbling about slavery would interfere with trade. William W. Corcoran, an important Washington banker, went further. He sent Webster a letter of congratulation with a check for $1,000.

With Clay and Webster clearly speaking for an older generation, it remained for a different breed of politician to be heard from. While young Southern fire-eaters continued to regard Calhoun as their mentor (even after his death on March 31), a rising group of Northern politicians looked for new leadership. William H. Seward of New York, who had just arrived in the Senate, became their spokesman.

Seward, a little man of large ambition, had played the political game astutely since the middle 1820s, mainly in his home state. First an Anti-Mason, then a Whig, Seward broke the Albany Regency's monopoly on New York state government when he became governor in 1838. He knew the value of party organization and party discipline (even at the expense of party principles) far better than most older Whig leaders. He knew also that antislavery and anti-Southern feeling was rising in the North and would soon dominate American politics.

Seward was somewhat vain and made his share of political enemies, but was well liked personally. A later historian has called him "lovable, cheerful, and generous."

Seward addressed the Senate on March 11. His speech was clearly a reaction to Webster's effort of four days earlier, although there was little similarity between the two in structure, delivery, or content. Seward read a prepared text in a monotone to a sparsely filled chamber. Still, leading senators (even Calhoun) attended because they realized the importance of Seward's views and those for whom he presumably spoke.

In essence, Seward rejected all plans for compromise. Since no real threat of disunion existed, he insisted, why compromise? Slavery, a barbarous relic of earlier and less enlightened times, would die a peaceful and natural death. Why encourage it? Congress could legislate for the territories, and it should prohibit slavery there. "I shall vote for the admission of California directly, without conditions, without qualifications, and without compromise."

Most of Seward's speech followed a Northern hard line on territorial questions, not far removed from President Taylor's stand. But the New Yorker added some statements that made his speech notorious. Did the Constitution protect slavery? "There is a higher law than the Constitution," answered Seward. Slavery must go. A moral question had been raised that transcended the "too narrow creeds" of political parties. He dismissed slavery as "temporary, accidental, partial, and incongruous." Freedom, on the other hand, was "perpetual, organic, universal, and in harmony with the Constitution."

Southerners were outraged. Even many Northerners joined in attacking Seward's "higher law" doctrine as anarchy. President Taylor

Douglas, just over five feet tall, had a massive head and shoulders, and was called the "Little Giant." Though overshadowed by his fellow-Illinoisan, Abraham Lincoln, he was one of the ablest statesmen of his era.

himself, previously close to Seward, ordered his administration newspaper to rap the New Yorker on the knuckles. These quick reactions revealed clearly that Seward, like Calhoun, spoke only for a congressional minority. But just as clearly, his stand could not be ignored.

On March 13 another Northerner, Stephen A. Douglas of Illinois, made an important speech. On the surface Douglas was critical of Clay's proposals. Actually, however, he spent more time attacking Clay's enemies and upholding popular sovereignty, his preferred solution. Douglas regarded the will of local inhabitants in the territories as all-important. He felt that the Missouri Compromise restriction of 1820, which prohibited slavery in the Louisiana Territory north of 36° 30′ latitude, was no restriction at all. Politicians in Washington, he believed, could neither establish nor forbid slavery in a territory. Local laws would prevail. They would inevitably reflect local environment and attitudes. Douglas also added his opinion that slavery could not expand west of the Mississippi beyond where it already existed—that is, Missouri, Arkansas, Louisiana, and Texas. His statement made many Southerners suspicious of Douglas and other so-called National Democrats.

At this point, a Senate fracas indicated how deep the impasse had become. It involved Thomas Hart Benton of Missouri and Henry S. Foote of Mississippi. Both were Democrats, and both wanted a compromise. Beyond this they parted ways. Benton was tall and burly, a polished and often bombastic orator. He had been in the Senate for thirty years, as long as Missouri had been a state. Although he represented a slave state, Benton did not believe in the extension of slavery. Let California join as a free state, he urged, and then solve other disputed sectional matters one by one.

Foote was short, rotund, and animated. Other senators acknowledged his considerable talents yet regarded him as a bit eccentric. Previously, Foote had been close to the Southern extremists. But he now supported Clay's proposals for compromise and strongly urged combining them into an omnibus bill.

On April 17 Benton attacked Clay's omnibus approach as pandering to Southern hysteria. Foote labeled the charge a slander. Benton then rose and headed straight toward his adversary. No match for Benton at coining phrases, Foote decided on another equalizer. He pulled a gun. Other members of the world's greatest deliberative body—as the Senate likes to call itself—quickly moved to avoid catastrophe. Stopped by a friendly senator, Benton, who rarely let a dramatic situation slip by without comment, quickly opened his shirt front and shouted, "Let the assassin fire! I am not armed. I have no pistols. I disdain to carry arms. A pistol has been brought in to shoot me with—to assassinate me!"

"I brought it here to defend myself," Foote responded lamely, at the same time handing his gun to Senator Dickinson.

"Nothing of the kind, sir," Benton retorted. "It is a false imputation. I carry nothing of the kind, and no assassin has a right to draw a pistol on me."

Foote obviously did not want to shoot Benton, yet the outrageous incident could not be ignored altogether. A special Senate committee investigated. It reported two months later but declined to recommend any disciplinary action against Foote.[2]

Benton was no stranger to violence. During the War of 1812 he brawled with Andrew Jackson; a few years later he killed a district attorney in a duel. Yet he was always ⟨ moderate on slavery.

Although congressional speechmaking played a more important role in 1850 than it does today, the real work of Congress—then as now—went on in committees. The day after the Benton-Foote confrontation, the Senate attended to more serious business. Foote moved that a select committee chaired by Clay work to resolve the sectional disputes. His resolution passed easily, 30 to 22. Thirteen senators would serve, seven Whigs and six Democrats. Seven were from slave states, and six were from free states. But only one senator from each section could be labeled an extremist.

For the next three weeks congressional activity creaked to a halt. Even the speechmakers were silent, waiting for Clay's committee to report. Its seven-point recommendation strongly resembled Clay's original plan. There was no minority report.

Few senators seemed satisfied with everything Clay's committee had proposed. When formal debate on the report began on May 13, almost every senator wanted to be heard, some several times.

T he compromise faced another challenge from outside Congress. Earlier, the Mississippi legislature had called on representatives of the slave states to meet at Nashville, Tennessee, in June 1850 to adopt methods "of resistance to [Northern] aggressions." Calhoun had supported the Mississippi move enthusiastically. His spirit would certainly be present at Nashville. Daniel Webster predicted that if the Southern extremists actually convened at Nashville, Andrew Jackson's body would turn over in its nearby grave.

Nevertheless, the Nashville Convention did take place. But—like

Foote's life seemed to embody inconsistency. A Mississippian, he opposed secession. Then he served in the Confederate congress. Still later, he quarreled with Jefferson Davis, resigned his seat, and left the South.

---

[2] As usual, Benton had the last word. Foote later tried to patch up the quarrel, announcing his intention to write a small book in which Senator Benton would figure prominently. Benton countered with an announcement that he would write a large book that would not even mention Senator Foote. Both men kept their word.

New England's Hartford Convention during the War of 1812—it proved a bit of a dud. Only nine of the slave states sent delegates, and not all of them were leaders in their own states. There was a great deal of heated talk. The meeting's final report, drafted by South Carolina fire-eater Robert B. Rhett, honored Calhoun's memory and most of his principles. Yet the convention kept cool. Delegates did not abandon their desire to defend Southern rights. But most still waited for a decision in Congress.

Most Americans observed the Nashville Convention fiasco with satisfaction, and none more so than President Taylor. The general was the nation's most important opponent of Clay's compromise, and he was angry. Clay and other Whig leaders had slighted him. Some had even made fun of him as lacking intelligence. Clay went so far as to heap praise on another general and would-be President, Winfield Scott—Taylor's rival for military glory during the war with Mexico. The President's anger boiled over whenever he heard talk of secession. Late in February a group of worried Southerners had trooped into the White House to ask Taylor if he really meant to maintain the Union at all cost. Eyes blazing (possibly thinking of Andrew Jackson's sternness at such moments), the President swore that he would blockade every Southern port if secessionists took over federal facilities. He promised to head an army of Northern and Western troops to put down any rebellion.

The situation had not yet come to a head, though. In the spring and summer of 1850 the legislative process still seemed the best solution. Yet it looked as if no compromise could jump the hurdle of a presidential veto. Taylor opposed the omnibus bill. When his own newspaper began speaking kindly of Clay, Taylor had the editor replaced by someone who would follow the administration line. Clay argued that his proposals would heal at least some, if not all, of the country's wounds on the slavery question, whereas Taylor's would heal only one, the status of California. The White House responded tartly that the original congressional resolution concerned only California and the New Mexico Territory, with no mention of such inflammatory side issues as fugitive slaves or Texan debts.

Throughout June procompromise forces made no progress. Opponents were trying to mutilate the select committee report with amendment after amendment and delay it with parliamentary obstruction. "We shall have a warm summer," Webster predicted. "The political atmosphere will be hot, however the natural may be. I am for it and shall fight it out." Arguments of "no earthly consequence start up from time to time," admitted Clay glumly, "to discourage the stoutest heart." The omnibus was stalled, perhaps permanently.

There matters stood, till Washington heat, gluttony, and divine Providence intervened. On the Fourth of July President Taylor attended ceremonies at the base of the unfinished Washington monument. Under a broiling sun he dutifully heard the ever-present Henry S. Foote (presumably unarmed this time) deliver the Independence Day oration. As the President got up to leave, aides asked him to stay and witness yet another ceremony. A handful of dust from the tomb of Thaddeus Kosciusko, the Polish hero of the American Revolution, was to be deposited in the monument. Taylor waited, standing exposed to the summer sun for an additional hour.

Back at the White House at last, Taylor refreshed himself with huge quantities of fruits, vegetables, and iced liquids. "Cucumbers and cherries with mush and milk," runs the most bizarre of the many accounts of what he consumed.

Taylor loved to eat—heartily and often. He ignored all danger warnings, verbal or internal, even one that appeared in his own official newspaper: "Do not unnecessarily heat yourselves, but, when heated, drink cold water in moderation. Ice water, in small quantities, is an excellent tonic; but some persons flood the stomach till internal chemistry can no longer overcome its effects." The President's internal chemistry broke down. He was overcome with nausea, stomach cramps, and fever. Taylor lingered on until July 9, when he died of acute gastroenteritis.

Into the White House came Vice-President Millard Fillmore. Like Seward, though always several rungs below him, Fillmore had climbed the ladder of New York Anti-Masonic and Whig politics. New Yorkers of all parties had a history of squabbling and splitting into factions. By 1850 Fillmore and Seward found themselves in warring camps. Taylor might have been on good terms with Seward, but Fillmore had no use for his fellow New Yorker. Where did Fillmore stand on the compromise? Most Southerners distrusted him, since he came from western New York, the most strongly antislavery part of the state. Fillmore's nomination and election to the vice presidency in 1848 had caused an anxious stir in the slave states. But in that election the South had placed its faith and sectional interests in Taylor's hands.

As late as April 1850, Fillmore had indicated agreement with Taylor's policies. Sometime between April and early July, however, he became a supporter of Clay's compromise. He later claimed that, just before Taylor's death, he had told the President that if the Senate tied the vote on the compromise, he, as Vice President (and president of the Senate), would break the tie with a yes vote. Daniel Webster may have had something to do with Fillmore's conversion. As Secretary of State, he emerged as the leading figure of the new administration. He exercised a strong influence over the conscientious but intellectually limited Fillmore. So did Clay, a semiofficial administration spokesman in Congress. Apparently all that remained was to push the omnibus bill through, have the new President sign it, and let peace reign. But this was not to be.

On July 31 the Senate was voting on a complicated series of amendments to the compromise. Somehow—possibly through error—the omnibus was maneuvered into a position where it could be killed. One by one, each of the bill's provisions was rejected by the Senate. The only part to be adopted was a bill granting territorial status to Utah. This passed easily, since the federal government wanted to reassert its authority over the Mormons (see page 332). Little else remained but disappointment for the procompromise forces and delight for Northern and Southern extremists. A reporter for a New York paper described the scene: "Jefferson Davis' face grinned with smiles. Old Bullion's [Thomas Hart Benton] few hairs actually bristled with delight. *He* had routed *Clay*! *He* had smashed his omnibus to atoms! Seward was dancing about like a little top." The reporter went on to describe other gleeful senators—a Northern supporter of Seward whose 'thick sides shook with sporadic spasms"; a Southerner who "looked solemn in solitary glory"; and an Ohio abolitionist shaking hands with a Louisiana fire-eater.

Clay walked out of the Senate chamber humiliated. He had fumbled his last great compromise effort. He soon left Washington for the resort town of Newport, Rhode Island—probably in a huff and surely very tired.

$\mathbf{C}$lay's failure created Douglas' opportunity. Since the omnibus package had fallen to pieces, the energetic Douglas took the logical course of action. He worked on one bill at a time. There were five altogether in addition to the Utah bill.

First was the bill settling the Texan boundary and debt. It passed on August 9. Next came the question of California. Southerners wanted to divide the region into two states—one free and the other undecided on slavery. Douglas, however, aimed to have the free-state California constitution adopted as it stood. Jeremiah Clemens of Alabama warned: "I do not know what Alabama may do, but if she determines to resist this bill by force, secession, by any means, I am at her service. If this be treason, I am a traitor—a traitor who glories in the name."

Despite talk of this kind, the Senate passed the California bill on

August 13. Next to clear the Senate was the New Mexico territorial bill.

The measure strengthening the fugitive slave laws, which would soon become the weakest link in the compromise chain, passed on August 26. In view of later reactions Northerners were surprisingly calm on the measure, perhaps because several leading antislavery figures had left Washington for cooler parts by that time. Still, twenty-one senators (fifteen of them Northerners) failed to vote on the fugitive slave bill. Had they all responded to the roll call, the bill would probably have been defeated. Douglas had applied strong and effective pressures on his Democratic colleagues in the Senate. The final bill of the compromise outlawed the slave trade in Washington, D.C. Clay himself came back to Washington in time to shepherd it through Congress on September 16.

The House of Representatives played second fiddle to the Senate throughout the dramatic 1850 session. Once the bills went through the Senate, the House passed them with little trouble early in September.

The Compromise of 1850 had initially been a Whig venture—or so Clay and Webster saw it, despite their nonpartisan appeals. But it became a reality through a series of bills shepherded through Congress by Stephen A. Douglas, a Democrat who relied largely on the votes of Democratic congressmen. Of eleven senators who supported at least five of the six compromise measures, nine were Democrats. Votes in the House of Representatives revealed the same Democratic concern for compromise. The Democrats, the party of Jefferson and Jackson, had clearly committed themselves to a new version of their old policy—keeping the slavery issue out of national politics.

In this bitter comment on the Fugitive Slave Act of 1850, Webster (center) helps a slave catcher chase a fleeing woman and child. In the accompanying caption, Webster is made to say:"Any man can perform an agreeable duty—it is not everyone that can perform a disagreeable duty."

16

A Deepening Sectional Conflict

PASSAGE OF THE COMPROMISE of 1850 and its acceptance by most Americans, North and South, seemed to close a dangerous chapter in United States history. Americans felt that they had achieved peace. Or at least they hoped so—with a fervor that showed how afraid they had been. If slavery took root as a national issue, the country itself might fall apart. The apparent escape from this danger led to a feeling of elation in 1850. Yet if the past decade was a reliable indicator of the future, the years to come would be anything but placid.

Indeed, slavery was already a national issue, even though people might have thought otherwise. It had become so through its relationship to newly acquired territories in the West—the very question that had led to the Compromise of 1850. Throughout much of American history disruptive political crises have often been involved with issues of geographic expansion. This was true in Bacon's Rebellion and in the Burr conspiracy as well. The slavery controversy was no exception.

The artist who painted this Emigrant Train Bedding Down for the Night *has somewhat ideal-ized the westward movement of the 1840s and 1850s. It was more common—though perhaps less picturesque—for a wagon train to form a circle as protection against Indian attack.*

EXPANSION INTO THE FAR WEST

Americans have generally believed that they could move freely into unsettled territories wherever available. This belief was never more stoutly held than during the first half of the nineteenth century. In this period some Americans moved into land acquired through the Louisiana Purchase. Even more attractive, however, were Far West regions that did not belong to the United States. The most important of these were the Oregon Country, claimed by Great Britain, and the Mexican-held Southwest and California.

Americans had various reasons for wanting to expand westward. Merchants were attracted to trade possibilities. Oregon, for example, offered not only furs but also a possible base for commerce with Asia. Many Americans were looking for good farming or grazing land. Even those who stayed home in the East took pride in the idea of westward expansion.

Newspapermen and politicians wrote approvingly of national growth. The phrase that best expressed the current attitude was Manifest Destiny. The term was coined by John L. O'Sullivan, a Democratic editor from New York. He wrote in 1845 that it was the "manifest destiny [of the United States] to overspread and to possess the whole of the continent which Providence has given us for the development of the great experiment of liberty and federated self-government entrusted to us."[1]

In other words, it was manifest (obvious) that fate had destined the United States for an expansionist role. Americans had a God-given mission to establish the Protestant religion, a democratic political system, and a capitalist economy in all the lands from the Atlantic to the Pacific. Many Americans shared this imperial vision in some form.

---

[1] The term "Manifest Destiny" was first used in Congress by Robert C. Winthrop, the Whig nominee for Speaker of the House in 1849.

The Mormons

To one historian, the Mormons were "the best prepared pioneers in the West." Their trek westward and their settlement in an arid desert is an American epic.

Mormons is the name commonly applied to the members of the Church of Jesus Christ of Latter-Day Saints. This sect was formed in 1830 in upstate New York by a youthful visionary, Joseph Smith, and his followers. They professed belief in much of Christian doctrine. To this they added the sacred Book of Mormon and the divine revelations made to Smith.

The Mormons won converts, but also made enemies. Their religious zeal, their closely knit farm communities, and their economic success aroused anger and envy. The practice of polygamy added to their notoriety.

Smith decided to move toward the frontier in order to find refuge. But persecution plagued the Mormons wherever they went. They were driven from Ohio and Missouri to Illinois, where Smith was murdered by a mob in 1844. The new leader, Brigham Young, believed that only in an isolated, unwanted area could his people live in peace.

Mormon pioneers in a storm

The great trek westward began in February 1846. Young led the first group of 200 wagons. Other groups followed at regular intervals. Each wagon train was divided into "hundreds" or "fifties" under the order of a captain. Each day on the trail followed a rigid schedule, from 5 A.M. to 8:30 P.M. By autumn 1846, all 15,000 Mormons were on the march, forming a broken line that stretched 300 miles. Their route took them through south-central Iowa to Nebraska, where they set up winter quarters.

In April 1847, Young and his group moved on, following the Platte River and joining the Oregon Trail. Later they branched off southward to their destination—the valley of the Great Salt Lake. In July they entered the barren plain, blistering in the midsummer sun. There were no meadows and no trees—just sagebrush. The Mormons turned this wasteland into an oasis in one of the most successful cooperative experiments in history.

Each farmer owned his own land but was assigned only the amount he could work effectively. Water rights were held in common. An irrigation system was established on a share basis. Salt Lake City was laid out in ten-acre blocks, each subdivided into eight family lots. In 1861 Mark Twain commented on the city's "general air of neatness, repair, thrift, and comfort."

In 1849 the Mormons drew up a constitution and asked Congress for statehood. Instead Congress created the Territory of Utah, naming Young as territorial governor, a post he held until 1858. Actually, effective control stayed in his hands until his death in 1877. As Twain wrote: "There is a batch of judges and other officials here, shipped from Washington, and they maintain the semblance of a republican form of government—but the petrified truth is that Utah is an absolute monarchy and Brigham Young is king!" Utah finally became a state in 1896, six years after the Mormons had abolished polygamy.

The Oregon Country   Since the late eighteenth century, many nations had shown an interest in the Oregon Country—the region between the Rockies and the Pacific coast, extending from what is now California northward to Alaska. At various times Spain, Russia, Britain, and the United States had laid claim to all or part of the area.

American merchants en route to the Far East sailed along the Oregon coast. So did traders in search of furs. In 1792 an American named Robert Gray explored and named the Columbia River. Lewis and Clark also explored the Oregon Country. In 1811 New York merchant John Jacob Astor founded a fur-trading post, Astoria, at the mouth of the Columbia River. When the War of 1812 broke out, however, he sold the post to a British company.

By 1825 both Spain and Russia had given up their claims to the Oregon Country. But British fur traders of the Hudson's Bay Company were quite active in the region. There was a spirited rivalry between them and the American traders employed by the Rocky Mountain Fur Company and Astor's American Fur Company. Great Britain and the United States agreed that the two countries would occupy Oregon jointly from 1818 to 1827. When the agreement expired, it was extended for an indefinite period.

The settlement of American families in the Oregon Country was stimulated mainly by missionaries, who went to the area in the 1830s. Methodist minister Jason Lee opened a mission in the Willamette Valley near what is now Salem, Oregon. Marcus and Narcissa Whitman, backed by the Congregationalists and Presbyterians, established a mission on the Columbia River near the present Walla Walla, Washington.

The missionaries' letters describe in glowing terms Oregon's fertile soil, magnificent rivers, and excellent climate. Small groups of settlers moved west in the early 1840s. The first major party of pioneers—a thousand strong—set out from Independence, Missouri, in 1843. The migration westward became so heavy in the late 1840s that it was known as the Oregon fever.

Pioneers made the trip to Oregon along the famous Oregon Trail. From Independence the trail led northwest and then followed the Platte River, crossing the Rockies at South Pass. Travelers to Oregon proceeded northward through the valleys of the Snake and Columbia rivers.

In 1843 Americans in Oregon organized a provisional government and petitioned Congress for annexation. Settlers from the United States now far outnumbered those from Canada and Britain. The earlier arrangements for joint occupation of the region seemed unsatisfactory—at least to Americans.

Annexation of Oregon was one of the issues in the presidential campaign of 1844. The Whigs nominated Henry Clay, who tried to avoid the question of expansion. The Democrats chose James K. Polk, governor of Tennessee and former Speaker of the House of Representatives. Polk was an ardent expansionist, and the Democratic platform stressed "All of Oregon or none." In other words, said Polk, the United States should expand northward to the 54th parallel. The British insisted on the 49th parallel as a more reasonable dividing line, since it continued westward the already existing boundary that divided the rest of the United States from Canada.

After Polk was elected, some expansionists demanded war if the British refused to yield to American demands. Their slogan was "54° 40' or Fight!" But other Americans took a calmer view. In 1846 the Polk administration negotiated a settlement with Britain that established the 49th parallel as the boundary between the western United States and Canada.

An Independent Texas   While American settlement in Oregon led to tension with Britain, expansion into Texas brought on conflict with Mexico. Spain had ceded Florida to the United States in 1819. As part of the bargain, Americans gave up their claim to Texas, which they had asserted since the purchase of Louisiana. Americans, however, were already moving into the region. In fact, traders and military adventurers from the United States helped the Mexicans win

U.S. GROWTH OF POPULATION, 1790–1860

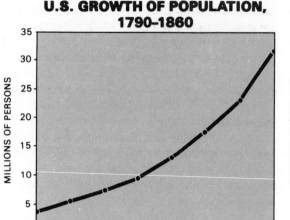

U.S. FOREIGN TRADE, 1790–1860

independence from Spain in 1821. In return the new Mexican government confirmed a large land grant previously made by the Spanish to Moses Austin.

Austin, a Missourian, had planned to colonize the Brazos River area with Americans. He died in 1821. Stephen Austin, his son, carried out the plan. In 1822 he planted a colony of 300 American families at Columbus, Texas. Most were Southerners, small slaveholders or non-slaveholding farmers. They were attracted by the possibility of practically free farmland for cotton cultivation.

During the next decade American settlers moved steadily into Texas. By 1830 there were at least 25,000 whites and 2,000 black slaves. Most of the newcomers remained Protestant despite the terms of the original Austin land grant, which committed American settlers to becoming Roman Catholics. Although Texas formed part of a state in the Mexican republic, the majority of its inhabitants were firmly committed to their American customs and beliefs.

The "invasion" of these American settlers frightened the Mexican government. Its leaders were afraid that the Texans would try to break away and join the United States. Mexico crushed one revolt in 1826. After this, Mexicans tried unsuccessfully to restrict further American im-

migration. They forbade the importation of slaves into Texas and placed heavy taxes on imported American goods. These efforts proved to be too little and too late. Americans in Texas were already encouraging their fellow countrymen to settle there. They were also agitating with the Mexicans for their own state government.

President Antonio López de Santa Anna decided to tighten Mexican control over Texas. Early in 1836 he led an army of 6,000 into the region. On March 2 the Texans met at Washington, Texas, and declared their independence from Mexico. They adopted a constitution legalizing slavery, and they set up a provisional government. As commander of the Texan army they named Samuel Houston, former governor of Tennessee and a friend of Andrew Jackson.

Meanwhile, Santa Anna had begun his siege of the Alamo, a former mission at San Antonio. For twelve days a garrison of 187 Texans led by William B. Travis withstood an attack force of 3,000. Finally, on March 6, the Alamo fell. Its defenders—including the famous frontiersman Davy Crockett—were massacred. Later in March 300 Texans were slaughtered in a similar fashion when they surrendered at Goliad. For several weeks Houston had to retreat before Santa Anna's army. Then, on April 21, he made a stand at San Jacinto. Shouting "Remember the Alamo!"

and "Remember Goliad!" Houston's men defeated Santa Anna and took the Mexican general prisoner.

Santa Anna signed a treaty (which he later repudiated) recognizing the independence of Texas. In September 1836 Texas voters ratified their new constitution and elected Sam Houston president. At the same time, they indicated their desire for annexation to the United States.

Troubles Over Annexation The annexation of Texas became a controversial issue. Northern antislavery forces did not want to add another slave state to the Union. President Jackson, who wished to avoid a sectional split, refused to endorse the proposal. So did his successor, Van Buren.

Texans then began to turn to Europe for recognition and aid, showing particular interest in Britain. Southern expansionists were alarmed by the prospect of a close alliance between cotton-hungry Britain and the cotton-producing Republic of Texas. They pressed for a treaty of annexation. So did President Tyler (who had come into office after Harrison's death in April 1841) and Secretary of State John C. Calhoun. A treaty that they negotiated in 1844, however, was rejected overwhelmingly by the Senate.

Texas, like Oregon, was an issue in the presidential campaign of 1844. One of Polk's slogans was a demand for "the reoccupation of Oregon and the reannexation of Texas." (The "re" in each case cleverly implied that the United States had always owned the disputed territories.) After Polk won, but before he took office, President Tyler exploited the popular support for expansion. He pressed for a joint congressional resolution annexing Texas. Since it was not a treaty, the resolution did not require a two-thirds Senate vote, and thus it squeaked through. Texas ratified the resolution and joined the Union in December 1845.

The Mexican War When Texas became a state, Mexico broke off diplomatic relations with the United States. This was not the only sore point between the two nations. The United States

claimed that the Texan boundary extended to the Rio Grande, whereas Mexico set it at the Nueces River. Another Mexican grievance was the growing number of Americans in California.

Early in 1846 Polk ordered General Zachary Taylor, commanding a force of 1,500, to take up a position along the Rio Grande. War fever grew among nationalists in both countries. The Mexicans refused to see John Slidell, an American diplomat sent to Mexico City to negotiate. A minor skirmish between Taylor's forces and Mexican troops along the Rio Grande gave the eager American President an excuse for war. Polk blamed Mexico for shedding American blood; Congress declared war on May 11; and the House authorized the recruitment of an army of 50,000 volunteers.

American troops, though fever in number, were better supplied and led than Mexican forces. In fact, the Mexican War served as a training ground for many young officers who later commanded armies during the Civil War. Among them were Robert E. Lee, Ulysses S. Grant, J. E. B. Stuart, George B. McClellan, and "Stonewall" Jackson.

The United States won a series of victories on Mexican soil—at Monterrey, Buena Vista, and Veracruz. In September 1847 Americans took Mexico City itself. The United States also seized New Mexico and California with small military

In difficult terrain, American forces (left), attack the Mexicans (right) at the Battle of Buena Vista.

forces supported by American settlers. Mexico had to sue for peace.

The Treaty of Guadalupe Hidalgo ended the war. Mexico gave up California, New Mexico, and the disputed area east of the Rio Grande. In return it received $15 million and the Americans' promise to assume their own citizens' outstanding claims against Mexico. The United States acquired an additional 529,000 square miles of territory at a cost of 13,000 American lives, most of them lost as a result of disease. Mexican casualties totaled approximately 14,000 killed or missing in action.

Some rabid expansionists considered even these gains minor. They wanted the United States to obey its Manifest Destiny and seize all of Mexico. The Senate prudently disregarded these suggestions, however, and ratified the treaty of peace in March 1848.

Americans in California   Many Americans who trekked west from Independence, Missouri, had destinations other than Oregon. At about the same time that Stephen Austin led his settlers into Texas, merchants were opening up the Santa Fe Trail. Year after year their trade caravans left Independence and lumbered south, loaded with goods to be sold in New Mexico. Thousands of Americans started out on the Oregon Trail but turned off before reaching the Oregon Country. One group, the Mormons, went south into Utah (see page 332). Others pushed farther west on the California Trail. Most of the pioneers went to either Sutter's Fort (Sacramento) or the Los Angeles area.

Like Texas, California originally belonged to Spain and, after 1821, to Mexico. In the early years of the nineteenth century it attracted relatively few Americans. There were only about 700 there in 1845.

Nevertheless, Polk had plans for California. Late in 1845 he wrote Thomas Larkin, the American consul at Monterey, asking him to stir up a revolt and encourage Americans in California to apply for annexation. Larkin received Polk's message in April 1846. At the same time, an explorer and military adventurer named John

In the spring of **1846**, before war was officially declared, Zachary Taylor engaged the Mexican army in two battles north of Fort Brown, Texas. After Palo Alto (May 8) and Resaca de la Palma (May 9), Taylor drove the Mexicans out of the disputed area between the Nueces River and the Rio Grande. He then crossed the lower Rio Grande and captured Matamoros (May 18) and Monterrey (Sept. 29). Before the end of the year Taylor, aided by John E. Wool, occupied Saltillo and, with General A. Quitman, went south to Victoria.

In the meantime Stephen W. Kearny led an expedition from Fort Leavenworth to Santa Fe (Aug. 15) and proclaimed New Mexico part of the United States. He left part of his army there, sent another detachment under Alexander W. Doniphan south to join Taylor, and proceeded to California. Doniphan, on his march from Santa Fe to Chihuahua, defeated the Mexicans at Valverde (Dec. 12) and El Brazito (Dec. 25). Meanwhile, Kearny had arrived in California, where John Sloat had already taken Monterey. After a temporary setback at San Pasqual (Dec. 6) Kearny joined Robert F. Stockton in San Diego.

In **1847** Kearny and Stockton were victorious at San Gabriel (Jan. 8-9). By February the Southwest was in American hands. Doniphan defeated the Mexicans at Sacramento (Feb. 28) and reached his goal, the provincial capital city of Chihuahua, on March 1. Taylor's army drove Mexican forces under Santa Anna out of a narrow mountain pass near the hacienda of Buena Vista (February 22-23).

In the winter of 1847 Winfield Scott led a force of about 10,000 with orders to take the fortified city of Veracruz. His men landed on the beaches outside the city on March 9, launching the first large-scale amphibious operation in United States military history. On March 29 he captured the city, and began an advance toward the Mexican capital. Near Jalapa, he stormed a mountain pass at Cerro Gordo (April 17-18), routing Santa Anna's army. He reached Puebla in May. Scott badly defeated Santa Anna at Contreras (Aug. 19) and Churubusco (Aug. 20), and captured the hilltop fortress of Chapultepec (Sept. 12). He smashed his way into Mexico City's last defenses on September 14, thus effectively ending the war.

C. Frémont entered the picture. Moving south from Oregon, he helped lead a revolt of settlers in the Sacramento Valley. On June 14, 1846, at Sonoma, they declared California an independent republic.[2]

Meanwhile Mexico and the United States had gone to war. American naval forces led by Commodore John Sloat took Monterey on July 7. San Francisco was captured two days later. In August Commodore Robert Stockton (who replaced the ailing Sloat) declared California an-

[2] This event is known as the Bear Flag Revolt because the homemade flag raised by the rebels was adorned with a picture of a grizzly bear. .

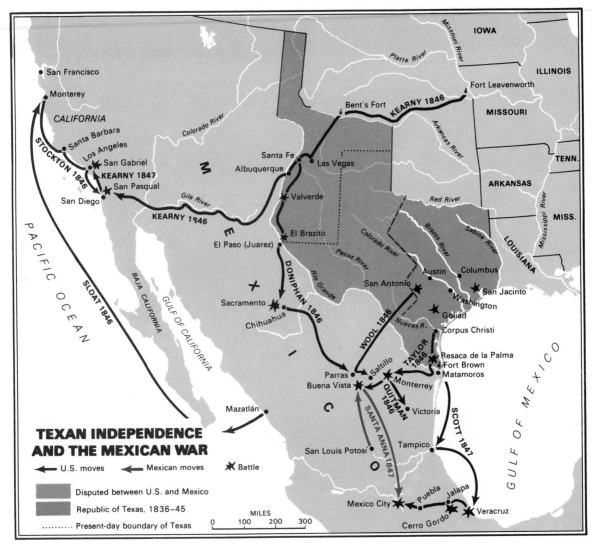

TEXAN INDEPENDENCE AND THE MEXICAN WAR

← U.S. moves ← Mexican moves ✹ Battle

Disputed between U.S. and Mexico

Republic of Texas, 1836–45

·········· Present-day boundary of Texas

MILES
0   100   200   300

nexed to the United States—with himself as governor.

The situation in California was clearly getting out of hand. Polk himself sent in Colonel Stephen Kearny, who had recently taken Santa Fe. When he arrived with a small force in November, he found Stockton and Frémont bickering over who should be in control. Early in 1847 Kearny succeeded in quelling remaining Mexican resistance in the region and in establishing his own authority as governor. California was ceded to the United States in the Treaty of Guadalupe Hidalgo, which ended the Mexican War.

Even before the treaty was ratified, an event occurred that would soon transform California. This was the discovery of gold near Sutter's Fort in January 1848. When news reached the East, the Gold Rush was on, and "forty-niners" poured into California. By 1850 there were 100,000 people there, a figure that doubled in just two years. Only a small proportion of those who joined the Gold Rush struck it rich. Most people stayed in California, though.

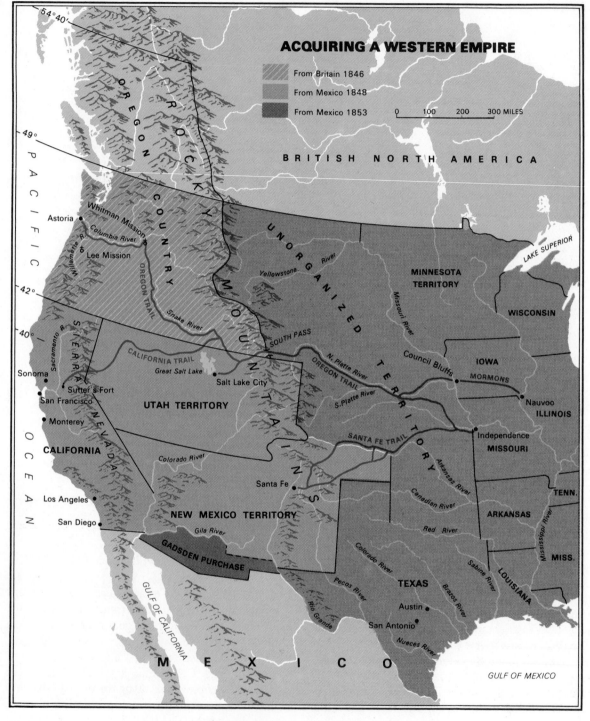

ACQUIRING A WESTERN EMPIRE

From Britain 1846
From Mexico 1848
From Mexico 1853

0   100   200   300 MILES

BRITISH NORTH AMERICA

PACIFIC

OREGON COUNTRY

ROCKY

Astoria
Whitman Mission
Columbia River
Lee Mission
Willamette R.
OREGON TRAIL
Snake River

Yellowstone River

UNORGANIZED

MINNESOTA TERRITORY

LAKE SUPERIOR

WISCONSIN

54°40'

49°

42°

40°

SIERRA

CALIFORNIA TRAIL
Sacramento R.
Sonoma
Sutter's Fort
San Francisco
Monterey

NEVADA

CALIFORNIA

Great Salt Lake
Salt Lake City

UTAH TERRITORY

Colorado River

SOUTH PASS

MOUNTAINS

OREGON TRAIL
N. Platte River
S. Platte River

SANTA FE TRAIL

Council Bluffs

MORMONS

IOWA

Nauvoo
ILLINOIS

Independence
MISSOURI

TERRITORY

Los Angeles

San Diego

NEW MEXICO TERRITORY

Gila River

GADSDEN PURCHASE

Santa Fe

Arkansas River
Canadian River

Red River

TENN.

ARKANSAS

Mississippi River

MISS.

PACIFIC OCEAN

GULF OF CALIFORNIA

Colorado River

Pecos River

Rio Grande

TEXAS

Austin

San Antonio

Brazos River

Sabine River

LOUISIANA

Nueces River

M E X I C O

GULF OF MEXICO

NATIONAL POLITICAL TENSIONS

During the 1830s and 1840s the United States had extended its boundaries to the Pacific Ocean. But these territorial gains brought major political headaches. They were the unwanted and unexpected consequences of Manifest Destiny. Were Northern or Southern patterns to dominate the new Western territories? Were the emerging new states to be slave or free? And who would decide the slavery question, Congress or the territories themselves?

National party politics in the 1840s underwent many shifts and changes, reflecting the uncertainties of a rapidly growing country. The system in existence at this time is known as the second American national party system. (The first, which took shape during the early 1800s, pitted the Federalists against the Jeffersonian Republicans.) The second system had arisen in the 1820s out of the struggle for national power between the Jacksonians and the National Republicans. It resulted in two major national parties, the Democrats and the Whigs.

The Democratic party had supporters in both the North and South, and it specifically pledged to keep slavery out of politics. The Whigs promised to do the same. In general Whigs kept this promise. Still, they usually fared better in Northern states, a fact that made them more antislavery in tone than the Democrats. Thus an antislavery politician was more likely to be a Whig than a Democrat.

Some antislavery politicians preferred to work outside the two-party system. Radical abolitionists shunned political parties altogether. Other Americans decided on organized political effort through a third party. In 1840 a small group of moderate abolitionists organized the new Liberty party. They nominated a "reformed" exslaveholder and former Alabaman, James G. Birney, for President. But they polled only 7,000 votes in the 1840 election, which helped to place Harrison in the White House. Four years later the Liberty party again ran poorly, although it took votes away from Whig candidates in several important states. Thus it

The Wilmot Proviso Until the mid-1840s party loyalties generally overcame American sectional differences. That is, a Southern Whig, for example, would consider himself a Whig first and a Southerner second, at least in matters in which party principle played a large role. But then things changed.

One man who made a difference was an obscure Pennsylvania Democratic congressman named David Wilmot. In August 1846 he introduced a proviso (amendment) to an appropriation bill requested by President Polk to buy territory from Mexico. The Wilmot Proviso stated simply that slavery would be forbidden in any states formed out of territory acquired from Mexico.

Both political parties tended to divide along

California miners pause for a photograph in 1852. In this type of sluice, water pushed gravel through, while heavier gold sank to the bottom of the trough.

sectional lines in the voting. Southerners—Whigs and Democrats alike—bitterly opposed the Wilmot Proviso. (The proslavery Whigs were sometimes known as "Cotton Whigs.") Some Northern Democrats also opposed the proviso. But many other Northerners—both Democrats and Whigs—favored it. (Northern antislavery Whigs called themselves "Conscience Whigs.")

One antislavery congressman from Illinois—a Whig named Abraham Lincoln—lost his re-election bid in 1848 partly because of his support for the Wilmot Proviso. The growing strength of antislavery feeling in the North can be seen from the fact that the proviso passed the House twice. It was defeated only in the Senate, where Southerners enjoyed equal voting strength.

Effects of the Mexican War Another factor in the growth of sectionalisn was the Mexican War. The war was understandably popular in the South, because proslavery people wanted the new territories. Northern opponents of slavery denounced the war and the prospect that the newly acquired territories might become slave states. Many Northerners saw the war as part of a conspiracy to extend the South's economic base and political power.

Even some thoughtful Southerners recognized the dangers. Calhoun supported the Mexican War, but he warned the Senate that "a deed has been done from which the country will not be able to recover for a long time, if ever. It has closed the first volume of our political history under the Constitution and opened the second."

The Election of 1848 Throughout the North many politicians seemed increasingly willing to sever old party loyalties in order to commit themselves more fully to the antislavery cause. A number of Liberty party abolitionists, anti-slavery Democrats, and Conscience Whigs banded together in 1848 to form the Free Soil party. They nominated ex-President Martin Van Buren as their candidate for the presidency.

The Free Soil platform cleverly appealed to many different segments of the population. It of course had an antislavery plank. It also included Whig economic demands, such as support for federally sponsored roads and other internal improvements. In addition it advocated Democratic social values, as in its demand for a federal homestead act that would provide free farms on public lands in the West. "Free Soil, Free Speech, Free Labor, and Free Men" ran the party's motto.

Southerners were now also banding into a party of their own, though it had no name. In Congress bloc voting on slavery issues created a Solid South that cut across earlier party lines. Thus from 1848 to 1860 Southern Whigs and Democrats usually voted as Southerners on regional interests, particularly slavery.

Despite growing sectionalism, the Whig party managed to elect its 1848 presidential candidate, Mexican war hero Zachary Taylor. Although it had been only three months in existence, the Free Soil party did well. Its presidential candidate, Van Buren, received 290,000 votes, and the party elected nine congressmen and one senator.

Aftermath of the Compromise The country soon found itself involved in the crisis over slavery in the new territories that led to the Compromise of 1850. When the sectional crisis eased momentarily, tempers cooled. Public opinion in both North and South swung heavily behind procompromise moderates such as Stephen A. Douglas and the new President, Millard Fillmore.

Antislavery Northerners, however, continued to demand exclusion of slavery from the new territories. Like Seward, they believed that "a higher law" had reserved the new lands for free labor. In 1851 Massachusetts sent Charles Sumner, a radical Conscience Whig, to the Senate. Everywhere in the North abolitionists and their sympathizers denounced the new fugitive slave measure in the Compromise of 1850.

Southern fire-eaters found themselves badly undercut by the Compromise of 1850. Yet they did not give up. After passage of the compromise, a Georgia state convention warned that any further attempt by Congress to exclude

When Sam Houston arrived in Washington, D.C., in 1846 as a senator from the new state of Texas, he was described as ''a magnificent barbarian, somewhat tempered by civilization.'' He was a stately six-foot-three and had ''a lion-like countenance capable of expressing fiercest passions.'' Flamboyant in speech and manner, he dressed in character. A favorite ensemble included a gold-headed cane, a panther-skin waistcoat, a large sombrero, and a Mexican blanket.

At age fifty-three, the freshman senator was already a legend. A runaway youth on the Tennessee frontier, he lived for years with the Cherokees, who dubbed him ''the Raven.'' He was a hero in the War of 1812. A long-time protégé of Andrew Jackson's, he became governor of Tennessee in his mid-thirties. His fame grew as the victorious commander in chief at the Battle of San Jacinto, which won independence for Texas. Twice president of the new republic, he was the prime mover in achieving annexation to the United States.

Texas was a slave state, and Sam Houston himself was a slaveholder. He was, as John F. Kennedy wrote, ''a Southerner by birth, residence, loyalty, and philosophy.'' But he was also ''one of the most independent, unique, popular, forceful, and dramatic individuals ever to enter the Senate chamber.'' He did not bind himself by sectional ties. As he said, ''I know neither North nor South; I know only the Union.'' His was the only Southern vote for all five laws that made up the Compromise of 1850. He and a Tennessean were the only Southern senators to vote against the Kansas-Nebraska Bill.

Houston's staunch defense of the Union cost him his presidential ambitions in 1852 and again in 1856. He denounced ''the mad fanaticism of the North'' and ''the mad ambition of the South,'' but he was caught between them. His vote against the Kansas-Nebraska Bill resulted in a formal censure by both the Texas legislature and the state Democrats. When he took his case to the people of Texas as an independent candidate for governor in 1857, he was defeated. But he served out his senatorial term and left the capital early in 1859. Still vigorous at age sixty-six, he was determined to make a comeback. By autumn he had done so, running again for governor and winning handily.

Houston's term of office was cut short, however. The presidential election of 1860 brought on a secessionist crisis in Texas. Pitted against a hostile legislature, Houston delayed—but could not prevent—withdrawal from the Union.

When he refused in March 1861 to take the oath of allegiance to the Confederacy, he was deposed. Gallantly, with sorrow, he bid his farewell: ''I have seen patriots and statesmen of my youth one by one gathered to their fathers, and the government which they have reared rent in twain. I stand the last almost of my race, stricken down because I will not yield those principles which I have fought for.''

slavery from the new territories or interfere with it elsewhere would lead to secession.

In 1852 the nation elected a Democratic President, Franklin Pierce of New Hampshire. Democrats also carried both houses of Congress. These victories were due partly to the fact that the Democrats, unlike the Whigs, had endorsed the Compromise of 1850. The Whig party lost in every section and never again ran a presidential candidate. Even the new Free Soil party suffered because of public support for compromise; it received only half as many votes as it had in 1848. In the South the Democrats took effective control of the region's political life. Except for the short-lived Reconstruction period, they maintained this monopoly for over a century.

DANGER SIGNALS

Obviously, the nation wanted to bury the slavery question and exclude it from political debate. But factors still at work kept the issue alive.

Attempts to enforce the Fugitive Slave Act irritated and angered Northerners. The problem was more symbolic than real, though, since fewer than 1 in 5,000 slaves escaped annually. In 1859 over 500 of the 803 runaways came from border states,[3] where owners displayed little interest in recovering their lost property. Only a handful came from the Deep South, which had demanded the tough new law, and where feelings ran highest.

Most of the runaway slaves actually recaptured were caught in the border states and received little attention. But the few slave catchers who roamed New England and the Middle West stirred up a hornets' nest. Abolitionists who stymied the efforts of "slave-nappers" became heroes to their neighbors. Few Northerners objected to the presence of runaway slaves despite their otherwise racist treatment of black people.

Moreover, Northern moderates who de-

spised abolitionists and endorsed the 1850 compromise reacted emotionally to antislavery appeals. Thousands wept over *Uncle Tom's Cabin,* Harriet Beecher Stowe's best-selling novel. Published in 1851, the book portrayed the sufferings of the fictional Uncle Tom and other slaves at the hands of their masters. Tom, the novel's black hero, was martyred at the end. He represented for Mrs. Stowe the ultimate triumph of the Christian in an evil society. *Uncle Tom's Cabin* probably won hundreds of thousands of sympathizers to the antislavery cause. Translated into twenty languages, the book sold 300,000 copies within a year. Dramatic versions appeared in Northern theatres throughout the 1850s.

President Pierce tried to keep the slavery issue out of politics by pursuing an expansionist foreign policy. During his administration American ships under Commodore Matthew C. Perry opened Japan to Western trade. The $10 million Gadsden Purchase of land from Mexico rounded out American continental borders in the Southwest. Pierce also pressured China for commercial privileges and agitated for American expansion into Cuba and Central America. Pierce, Douglas, and other Northern Democrats hoped that by stressing the national interests of Americans abroad they could destroy the virus of sectionalism at home. For a time, at least, their policies seemed effective.

The Kansas-Nebraska Act Douglas himself, however, helped to revive sectional bitterness over slavery and bring down the very compromise he had so skillfully pushed through Congress. In 1854 he introduced a Senate bill to organize the territories of Kansas and Nebraska, a sparsely settled region at that time. Douglas hoped to prevent further congressional furor over the morality of slavery expansion through popular sovereignty, allowing settlers to decide the issue for themselves. Once again, however, as in President Taylor's solution regarding California, it proved easier to devise a practical approach to the slavery issue than to enforce it.

Congress soon found itself embroiled in

[3] The border states—Delaware, Maryland, Kentucky, Tennessee, and Missouri—were slave states bordering the North that had more moderate views on controlling slaves (and, later, secession) than the rest of the South. West Virginia, which joined the Union in 1863, is usually considered a border state, too.

THE COMPROMISE OF 1850
AND THE KANSAS-NEBRASKA ACT

WASHINGTON TERRITORY 1853
OREGON TERRITORY 1848
NEBRASKA TERRITORY 1854 (Unorganized 1850)
MINNESOTA TERRITORY 1849
MAINE
VT. N.H.
MASS.
R.I.
CONN.
N.Y.
WIS.
MICH.
IOWA
PA.
N.J.
UTAH TERRITORY 1850
CALIFORNIA 1850
KANSAS TERRITORY 1854 (Unorganized 1850)
AREA OF INSET MAP
MO.
ILL.
IND.
OHIO
DEL.
MD.
VA.
KY.
NEW MEXICO TERRITORY 1850
MISSOURI COMPROMISE LINE 36°30'N
INDIAN TERR. (Unorganized 1854)
ARK.
TENN.
N.C.
S.C.
TEXAS
MISS.
ALA.
GA.
LA.
FLA.

Free states and territories

Slave states

Open to slavery by principle of popular sovereignty, Compromise of 1850

Open to slavery by principle of popular sovereignty, Kansas-Nebraska Act of 1854

Atchison
Leavenworth
KANSAS
Topeka
Lecompton
Lawrence
TERRITORY
× POTTAWATOMIE MASSACRE
MISSOURI River
MISSOURI

another quarrel between antislavery and pro-slavery members. Since Kansas and Nebraska lay within the area of the Louisiana Purchase, the status of slavery there should have been governed by the Missouri Compromise of 1820. This agreement kept slavery out of land that far north. Passage of the Kansas-Nebraska Bill would in effect repeal the Missouri Compromise. This prospect infuriated antislavery Northerners.

Douglas sponsored his bill in order to encourage settlement in the region. This would enable a transcontinental railroad to move across it to the Pacific. The bill's final version included several concessions to Southerners, whose votes Douglas needed. With the support of President Pierce the bill passed in May 1854 after months of furious debate.

Debate over the Kansas-Nebraska Act broke the uneasy truce that had more or less silenced discussions about slavery since 1850. It aroused Northern public opinion against slavery as no previous congressional measure—not even the Fugitive Slave Law of 1850—had ever done.

Two New Parties Northern outrage at passage of the Kansas-Nebraska Act took concrete form. Throughout the North in 1854 hundreds of thousands of people left the Democratic and Whig parties to join local anti-Nebraska political groups. In a few months these groups united to form the Republican party. It was a much broader coalition of Conscience Whigs, anti-Douglas Democrats, and abolitionists than the Free Soil party had been. The new party demanded complete exclusion of slavery from all remaining federal territories.

The Whig party was dying. Its members sought new political homes. While some became

344/ Republicans, others joined the recently formed American party. Members of the party were often called "Know-Nothings." Their platform was secret, and when asked about it, a party member would answer "I know nothing."

The Know-Nothings were nativists—that is, they felt that immigrants presented a threat to "native Americans." (By "native Americans" the Know-Nothings were referring, not to Indians, but to families who had been in America for two or three generations.)

Know-Nothings were particularly opposed to Roman Catholics. Hundreds of thousands of such newcomers, mainly Irish, had migrated to America in the 1840s after a potato famine in Ireland. Nativists feared the newcomers' religion, and they felt that the Catholics would not fit into American society.

Clearly, this was a time when many Americans were fearful of subversive elements in their society, elements plotting in secret to undermine democratic freedoms. Know-Nothings feared a Catholic conspiracy. Slaveholders were afraid of an abolitionist plot. And abolitionists were convinced of a slaveholders' intrigue.

"Bleeding Kansas" Many people moved to Kansas after passage of the Kansas-Nebraska Act. Most of them were farmers from both North and South. Few seemed to care whether the state became slave or free. Unfortunately, this unconcern did not last.

Antislavery Northerners formed Emigrant Aid Societies, usually under the direction of abolitionists. These societies provided money, guns, and supplies for Northern settlers in Kansas—settlers who were determined that Kansas should be a free state. At the same time, a smaller group of proslavery settlers were backed by neighboring Missourians, who often crossed the border to vote and to fight.

Armed proslavery and antislavery forces clashed fiercely in what came to be called "Bleeding Kansas." Normal political processes broke down completely. Although a large majority of Kansas settlers voted for a free-state legislature, proslavery forces and Missourians

elected their own assembly. Violence ruled the territory, and President Pierce could not maintain order.

The conflict reached Washington. In May 1856 Massachusetts Senator Charles Sumner delivered a fervent antislavery address, "the Crime Against Kansas." His speech included an attack on Senator Andrew Butler of South Carolina. Butler's nephew was a hotheaded South Carolina congressman named Preston Brooks. Two days after Sumner's speech, Brooks—determined to avenge his family's honor—marched into the Senate chamber and beat the Massachusetts senator unconscious with a cane. Sumner was injured so severely that he did not appear in Congress for three years.

ANOTHER WEAK PRESIDENT

Brooks' assault on Sumner shocked the North. Together with the Kansas-Nebraska Act and the turmoil in Kansas, it helped the Republican party in the 1856 election. The first Republican presidential candidate, General John C. Frémont, swept all but five free states. The Republicans could have won the election by taking only two more Northern states. This was a disturbing fact for those who hoped that the Compromise of 1850 had ended sectional politics. Southerners saw this very well. They provided the electoral majority for the new President, Pennsylvania Democrat James Buchanan. Former Whigs either defected to the Republicans or supported the Know-Nothings, who ran ex-President Millard Fillmore as their candidate. The Know-Nothings received only eight electoral votes. They declined after the 1856 campaign, and many of them joined the Republican party.

By the time James Buchanan took office as President in March 1857, political parties could no longer appeal to voters on a nationwide basis. The Republicans dominated the North, but they had no following in the South. The Whig party was dead. Southern Democrats generally voted as a bloc. Only Northern Democrats were still trying to bridge the widening gap between the sections. From the beginning Buchanan helped further to "sectionalize" American politics by consistently favoring the South.

The Dred Scott Decision Each year after 1854 brought events that further weakened the Compromise of 1850 and widened the rift between North and South. One such event was the Dred Scott decision.

Dred Scott, a slave, had been taken from Missouri to Illinois and later to Wisconsin. Missouri was a slave state. Illinois was a free state by virtue of the Northwest Ordinance. Wisconsin was a free territory according to the terms of the Missouri Compromise. In 1846 Scott sued for his liberty, claiming that residence in a free state and a free territory made him free. After passing through lower courts, the case reached the Supreme Court as *Dred Scott* v. *Sandford* (his owner). The Chief Justice at this time was Roger B. Taney, a Southerner and one-time leading Jacksonian Democrat.

The court handed down its decision in 1857. It ruled against Scott, saying that he had no right to sue since he was not a citizen. Furthermore, Taney ruled that blacks were inferior human beings with "no rights which any white man was bound to respect." This was bad enough from a Northern point of view. But the court went further. Taney and his colleagues in the Court majority decided that slavery could not be excluded from *any* territory. Slaves, as property, were protected wherever they were taken. (The Fifth Amendment says that no one can be deprived of property without due process of law.) In other words, the Missouri Compromise of 1820 had been unconstitutional, a position previously taken by Congress when it passed the Kansas-Nebraska Act. The Dred Scott decision shocked even moderate Northerners. When Buchanan endorsed it, they were angrier than ever.

The Emergence of Lincoln Stephen A. Douglas had helped build the Compromise of 1850—and he had helped to destroy it with the Kansas-Nebraska Act. In 1858 he ran for reelection to the Senate from Illinois. His opponent was a popular former congressman, Abraham Lincoln.

Born in Kentucky in 1809 to poor parents, Abraham Lincoln had moved with his family first to Indiana and then to Illinois. During his early years in these frontier areas the young man educated himself through extensive reading. He managed a general store at New Salem, Illinois, served as a captain of volunteers during a brief Indian war in northern Illinois, and worked as New Salem's postmaster while studying law. Lincoln was admitted to the Illinois bar in 1836. The next year he moved to Springfield and opened a law office.

Lincoln served as a state legislator from 1834 to 1842 while engaged in a private law practice. He quickly acquired a reputation for his skill as a trial lawyer and his rough frontier humor. Elected in 1846 as a Whig, the young Illinois lawyer served one term in the House. He opposed the Mexican War but remained a

Dred Scott was freed by his owner after the Supreme Court decision. He got a job as a hotel porter in St. Louis, but died of tuberculosis in 1858.

member of the Whig party. Like many Northerners, Lincoln was pried loose from former party loyalties only by passage of the Kansas-Nebraska Act in 1854. He denounced the law and, in 1856, joined the newly formed Republican party.

Lincoln's views on slavery were typical of most Northern antislavery moderates. He believed that slavery was "a moral, social, and political wrong." But he denied having any intention of interfering with the institution in the Southern states. Like most Republicans, he felt that it would die out gradually as an unprofitable labor system. He did insist, however, that slavery should be totally excluded from the Western territories.

The earliest photograph of Lincoln was taken when he was a congressman—an obscure Whig and unpopular at home because of his opposition to the Mexican War.

During a statewide series of public debates Lincoln kept Douglas on the defensive with questions about how, in view of the Dred Scott decision, settlers could legally exclude slavery from a territory under popular sovereignty. Douglas was reduced to arguing that a free-soil majority could simply refuse to enact a slave code, a weak counter to Lincoln's basic point.

In the short run the Lincoln-Douglas debates helped to reelect Douglas. But in the long run they damaged him as a national leader. His view that a territory could effectively exclude slavery in spite of the Dred Scott decision gained him votes in Illinois, but it offended Southerners.

Lincoln emerged as a major national figure in the Republican party. He had dramatized the differences between Douglas Democrats and the Buchanan-Southern Democratic coalition.

Lecompton—and After Meanwhile, the bloody border war in Kansas continued. President Buchanan insisted on submitting to Congress the Lecompton Constitution, a document drafted by a small proslavery minority in Kansas. It was supposed to serve as the basis for the territory's admission to the Union. The Lecompton Constitution legalized slavery. Congress offered a huge land grant to Kansas if the state would ratify the document, but free-state settlers voted it down in 1858 by a 9 to 1 margin. The major political effect of the Lecompton Constitution was to widen the division between Buchanan—backed by the South—and Douglas—supported by the North.

The only real achievement of the Buchanan administration lay in serving out its four years. The President was incapable of shaping the course of national events.

But Buchanan could have done little to change the hardening attitudes of both sections. Politicians had done their conventional best in 1850—as evidenced by the compromise solution they had produced then. But the time for compromise on slavery had passed. Jefferson's "fire-bell in the night" was ringing for the whole country. Its raucous sounds left poor old James Buchanan befuddled and semiparalyzed.

1. Does the settlement of 1850 deserve to be called a compromise? Why or why not? Summarize the roles played by Clay, Webster, Douglas, and Fillmore; who do you think was most important?
2. Would the slavery controversy have been less harsh if there had been no westward expansion? Explain your answer.
3. Was the American belief in Manifest Destiny the major reason for American expansion in the 1840s? Why or why not?
4. Why did Britain and the United States agree to occupy Oregon jointly? Why did Americans change their minds about joint occupation?
5. What condition did the Mexican government impose on American settlers in Texas? If Americans had complied, do you think Texas would have remained part of Mexico?
6. Why did the Senate reject the admission of Texas into the Union? What was the meaning of Polk's campaign slogan demanding "the reoccupation of Oregon and the reannexation of Texas"?
7. Explain whether you think the people of the North were justified in defying the Fugitive Slave Law.
8. What effects did the Kansas-Nebraska Act have on the two political parties? On Kansas? How was it affected by the Dred Scott decision?
9. Why did Lincoln and Douglas have a series of debates? Who got the better of the arguments?

Beyond the Text

1. Write an editorial on the Compromise of 1850 for one of the following: (a) an antislavery periodical; (b) an extreme pro-Southern newspaper; or (c) a moderate newspaper.

2. Webster and Clay both believed that slavery could not expand farther than it had by 1850. Investigate the validity of this idea for a report to the class. The question to be answered is: Had slavery reached its natural limits?
3. Report to the class on the Know-Nothing movement, focusing on its origins, its ideology, and the reasons for its eventual decline.

Bibliography

Nonfiction

Billington, Ray A., *The Far Western Frontier, 1830–1860.**

Craven, Avery O., *The Coming of the Civil War.**

———, *The Growth of Southern Nationalism, 1848–1861.*

Donald, David, *Charles Sumner and the Coming of the Civil War.*

Foner, Eric, *Free Soil, Free Labor, Free Men: The Ideology of the Republican Party Before the Civil War.**

Hamilton, Holman, *Prologue to Conflict: The Crisis and Compromise of 1850.*

Nevins, Allan, *The Emergence of Lincoln*, 2 vols.*

———, *The Ordeal of the Union*, 2 vols.*

Nichols, Roy F., *The Disruption of American Democracy.**

Singletary, Otis, *The Mexican War.**

Taylor, George Rogers, *The Transportation Revolution, 1815–1860.**

Weinberg, Albert K., *Manifest Destiny.**

Fiction

Berry, Don. *Trask.**

Nelson, Truman, *The Sin of the Prophet.*

Seifert, Shirley, *The Senator's Lady.*

*a paperback book

17

JOHN BROWN'S RAID

THE PLOT seemed so incredible that the Secretary of War refused to believe it. John B. Floyd was relaxing at a Virginia resort late in August 1859 when he received an anonymous letter. It warned of a conspiracy to incite a slave uprising throughout the South. "'Old John Brown,' late of Kansas," according to the writer, had stored a large quantity of arms in a Maryland hideaway. As the head of a "secret association," he planned to attack Virginia first, entering the state at Harpers Ferry, a northwestern border town.[1] The anonymous writer urged Floyd to send federal troops to the town.

The South had experienced no slave rebellion since the Nat Turner Revolt almost thirty years earlier. Floyd (the son of Virginia's governor at the time of the Turner uprising) was a fiery opponent of abolitionism. But he refused to believe that "a scheme of such wickedness and outrage could be entertained by any citizen of the United States." He took no action.

At this time John Brown was fifty-nine years old and a fugitive from justice. President Buchanan himself had authorized a $250 reward for his capture. Brown was wanted in connection with antislavery raids he had conducted in Kansas. It was partly because Brown's name was identified so closely with Kansas that Floyd did not take the Harpers Ferry plot seriously.

---

[1] Harpers Ferry and other West Virginia towns mentioned in this chapter were still a part of Virginia at this time; West Virginia did not become a separate state until 1863.

A sentimental version of Brown on his way to his execution was painted by Thomas Hovenden in 1884. Just before, Brown had stopped by the cell of some of his fellow-raiders and spoken to them, parting with the words: "God bless you, my men. May we all meet in heaven."

Gerrit Smith

Franklin B. Sanborn

Thomas W. Higginson

In Kansas Brown had acquired some fame but little else. In fact, his life was marked by almost total failure. He had struggled constantly to achieve financial security (an understandable goal for the father of twenty children). Brown failed first during the 1830s as an Ohio land speculator. Then, in 1842, he went bankrupt as a sheep rancher. A later career as a wool merchant also ended in failure. In 1855 Brown and his family migrated to the newly opened Kansas Territory. Here Brown soon gained a reputation as a ferocious opponent of slavery.

John Brown had always been an abolitionist. Before he moved west, his house had been a station on the underground railroad. In Kansas the situation was violent, with proslavery and antislavery forces struggling for control of the territorial government. Brown and five of his sons took an active role in what was practically a guerrilla war.

Brown was best-known for an incident that took place at Pottawatomie, Kansas, in 1856. He led a small band that murdered and mutilated five proslavery settlers. This raid was apparently in retaliation for the burning of Lawrence, Kansas (a free-state town), by slave-state advocates. None of Brown's victims owned slaves. The common thread linking them was their association with a local court that was soon to try a case in which Brown was the defendant.

In the fall of 1856 Brown went east with his sons. For the next three years he wandered across the North from Kansas to Massachusetts making speeches and holding private fund-raising meetings. Brown had long toyed with the notion of launching a direct assault on Southern slavery. He knew that this kind of action would frighten moderate abolitionists. So he usually described his aim as a simple raiding expedition southward to rescue a select handful of slaves. By early 1858, however, Brown began revealing his actual plan—"to overthrow slavery in a large part of the country."

Incredibly, Brown told about eighty Northern abolitionists of his scheme. Many had grave doubts about it. One such man was Frederick Douglass, the leading black abolitionist. Another dubious listener was an Iowa Quaker named David J. Gue. Gue had written the anonymous letter to Secretary of War Floyd. He hoped that, if Floyd ordered federal troops to Harpers Ferry, Brown would call off the raid before he and his men were all killed.

Brown could not have gotten as far as he did without the aid of six leading abolitionists, known as the Secret Six. One was Gerrit Smith, a wealthy landowner in upstate New York. The other five were all from Massachusetts. Franklin B. Sanborn was a Boston school-teacher. Thomas Wentworth Higginson and Theodore Parker were

Unitarian ministers. George Luther Stearns was a prominent merchant and manufacturer of Boston. The sixth member of the group was a physician, Samuel Gridley Howe.

Theodore Parker

At first the Secret Six, like Brown's other abolitionist supporters, believed that their leader planned some new and dramatic strike against the proslavery forces in Kansas. But then Brown began to reveal his real intentions. Neither political action nor peaceful persuasion had settled the slavery question, he said. Only a slave uprising throughout the South would make slaveholders aware of their moral guilt. God had selected him, Brown continued, to organize and lead such an insurrection. The revolt would begin in Virginia. From there it would quickly spread like a raging brushfire across the entire South. Even if the plot failed, Brown believed that the hysteria that would then sweep the South would provoke a major sectional crisis, dividing a proslavery South and an antislavery North so that civil war might result.

Brown asked the Secret Six for financial help. He refused to discuss any tactical and strategic objections they might have. He offered them, as Sanborn later remarked, "only the alternatives of betrayal, desertion, or support." Brown claimed that he now wanted "men of action." What he really wanted—and had in the Secret Six—was a group of people who would raise funds and thus fulfill their private dreams of being something more than mere talkers.

George Luther Stearns

Though some of the six wavered, in the end they all cast their doubts aside and supported Brown. Why should a slave revolt be condemned, they probably reasoned, when the "slave power" had inflicted so much violence on the free states during the previous decade? Hadn't there been undeclared warfare in Kansas? Wasn't there a massive effort by slave catchers to hunt down fugitive slaves? And what about the physical assaults on abolitionists, not to mention the savage beating of Charles Sumner on the floor of the Senate?

By the late 1850s many abolitionists—not only the Secret Six—had become convinced that there could be no peaceful solution to the slavery question. Gerrit Smith wrote the Republican governor of Vermont:

> Hitherto I have opposed the bloody abolition of slavery, but now, when it begins to march its conquering bands into the free states, I and ten thousand other peace [movement] men are not only ready to have it repulsed with violence, but pursued even unto death, with violence.

John Brown represented, for Smith and the others among the Secret Six, the obvious instrument of what they believed to be justifiable violence. At the same time, Brown's supporters preferred being

Samuel Gridley Howe

kept in the dark concerning his specific plans. They hoped to avoid being identified too closely with the scheme. "I have great faith in the wisdom, integrity, and bravery of Captain Brown," Gerrit Smith wrote Sanborn in July 1858. "Whenever he shall embark on another of his contests with the slave power, I shall again stand ready to help him." The limit on this support became clear only in the final sentences of Smith's note: "I do not wish to know Captain Brown's plans. I hope he will keep them to himself." Or, as Samuel Gridley Howe put it to Brown himself, "Don't tell me what you are about or where you are going."

Brown's ultimate destination was Harpers Ferry, Virginia. But as a base of operations he chose a farm across the Potomac River in Maryland. Brown, posing as a New York cattle buyer named Isaac Smith, had rented the farm from the Kennedy family in July 1859. He arrived with two of his sons, Owen and Oliver. A third son, Watson, joined them later.

By late August there were fifteen recruits living on the Kennedy farm. Oliver's wife, Martha, and a granddaughter of Brown's, Annie, were brought to the farm to keep house and quiet the suspicions of nosy neighbors. Most of the group were young. All but two of Brown's men were under thirty. The oldest, apart from the "Commander in Chief" himself, was a forty-eight-year-old free black named Dangerfield Newby. He had joined the company hoping to liberate his wife and seven children from a nearby Virginia plantation. As the group waited restlessly through the hot summer, hundreds of weapons reached the farm—200 revolvers, 198 rifles, and 950 iron-tipped pikes destined for use by insurgent slaves.

Several of the recruits still believed that they had come South to rescue a small group of slaves and escort them to safety in Canada. During the summer, though, Brown revealed his actual plan for a full-scale slave revolt that would spread quickly throughout the South.

Brown's men drilled, but their commander made few other preparations for the attack itself. He gathered almost no information about the slaves in the region. He did not even bother to scout the area's roads and hiding places. Nor did he develop a plan of escape in case the assault on Harpers Ferry failed.

The only preparation Brown made for possible failure was a curious effort to ensure that others besides himself would be blamed for the raid. Inside a trunk in the farmhouse, in plain view, Brown left letters that implicated his most prominent Northern supporters, among them the Secret Six.

(continued on page 353)

Travel in a Growing Nation

Almost from the beginning, Americans have been famous as travelers. (People used to say that the rocking chair was popular in the United States because, though a person might be sitting down, he could at least keep moving.) A vast continent bordered by vast oceans challenged American ingenuity. One response was the clipper ship (the one shown here was called *Lightning*)— in its time the fastest water transport known. Prince Maximilian of Wied, on his way home to Germany in 1834, wrote about the speed his ship made: "The wind was favorable and, though very strong, even our topmost sails were spread. This is an experiment which other nations do not often venture upon, but the Americans are very bold seamen." This same boldness built the roads, dug the canals, and lay the rail lines that made American transportation the best in the world.

[For further information on the foreign observers quoted in this essay, see "Notes on Sources."]

An early railroad train meeting a steamboat at the dock

The American has a perfect passion for railroads. It is not merely because his supreme happiness consists in that speed which annihilates time and space, but also because he perceives that this mode of communication is admirably adapted to the vast extent of his country, to its great maritime plain, and to the level surface of the Mississippi Valley. This is the reason why railroads are multiplied in such profusion, competing not only with each other but entering into a rivalry with the rivers and canals.

[MICHEL CHEVALIER, 1834-35]

The Erie Canal near Little Falls, New York

I like traveling by the canal boats very much. Ours was not crowded, and the country through which we passed being delightful, the placid moderate gliding through it—at about four miles and a half an hour —seemed to me infinitely preferable to the noise of wheels, the rumble of a coach, and the jerking of bad roads. The only nuisances are the bridges over the canal, which are so very low that one is obliged to prostrate oneself on the deck of the boat to avoid being scraped off it. This humiliation occurs, upon an average, once every quarter of an hour.

[FANNY KEMBLE, 1838]

At Trenton we left our boat for the most detestable stagecoach that ever a Christian built to dislocate the joints of his fellow man. The change in our movement was not more remarkable than that which took place in the tempers and countenances of our fellow travelers. Gentlemen now looked more like victims than dandies armed for conquest. The pretty ladies too, with their expensive bonnets—how sad the change! As I looked into the altered eyes of my companions, I was tempted to ask, "Look I as cross as you?" Indeed, I believe that, if possible, I looked crosser still, for the roads and the vehicle together were quite too much for my calm.

[FRANCES TROLLOPE, 1830]

Stagecoach near Trenton, New Jersey

The steamboat was fitted for the twofold purpose of carrying as many bales of cotton as could be heaped upon it without sinking, and taking in as many passengers as could enjoy the luxuries which Southern manners and a hot climate require—especially spacious cabins, abundance of fresh air, and protection from the heat of the sun.

These steamers, notwithstanding their size, draw very little water. They cannot quite realize the boast of a Western captain that "he could sail wherever it was damp," but I was assured that some of them could float in two-foot water. The high-pressure steam escapes into the air by a succession of explosions alternately from the pipes of the two engines. It is a most unearthly sound, like that of some huge monster gasping for breath.

[SIR CHARLES LYELL, 1849]

A boatman on the Missouri River

Steamboat docked at New Orleans

Interior of a steamship

On the Great Lakes there is only one means of travel, and that is the steamship. The elegance of such a ship is quite remarkable. The vessel is equipped in every possible way for the convenience of the passengers. There is, for example, a barbershop. There is also a band. Its performance on brass instruments we found none too good, but in the evenings it won general approval by presenting comical Negro songs, accompanied by the guitar, and by playing dance music, to which the youthful Yankees executed their favorite cotillion, with many dainty skips and steps.

[OLE RAEDER, 1847]

Wooding Up on the Mississippi

In the evening we embarked on board the Philadelphia *and started up the Misssissippi. As the steamboats on this river burn nothing but wood, and as their engines are mostly high-pressure, the consumption of this bulky fuel is so considerable that they are obliged to call at least twice a day at the wooding stations on the banks of the stream. The* Philadelphia *used about one cord of wood an hour. When the supply on board began to run short, the pilot cast his eye round, and upon the first convenient opportunity, he steered the boat for one of the numerous piles of firewood which occurred every few miles along the way.*

[BASIL HALL, 1828]

Yosemite Valley as seen from Glacier Point

The trail is a very remarkable piece of work. To rise 3,000 feet vertically about 4½ miles have to be traversed, and still the track is very steep. The ride up on our ponies was not absolutely free from danger, but, so long as the traveler does not lose nerve, the danger is slight. The ponies have the very sensible but slightly disquieting habit of walking to the very edge at the turns in order to make the inclined plane as easy as possible. But it was glorious! Every fresh turn, almost, introduced us to fresh views of this wonderful place. I affirm that, until I rode this trail and found myself looking down and around me from Glacier Point, I had no adequate idea of the beauty and grandeur of the Yosemite district.

[LORD RUSSELL OF KILLOWEN, 1883]

A masked holdup man in the West

I was asleep when suddenly the coach stopped, which woke me up. I heard someone outside say, "Get out one at a time & throw up your hands." Then I knew in an instant that the coach was stopped by highwaymen. The first thing I saw was a man with a double-barreled shotgun full cocked pointed at the driver and another behind the coach with 2 six-barreled pistols in his hands. When we were all out, the man with the pistols searched us. He began with me, he first took out my watch but he only looked at it & put it back & said he didn't want it. Then he searched the others. After they took our money, they handed round a bottle of whiskey for the passengers to drink. I took some just for the joke of it & because I was cold with standing out with my hands up.

[SIDFORD HAMP, 1872]

I must take this occasion to say a word of the commodiousness and other advantages of the railroads in America, which I could well observe on my trip from Chicago westward. The possibility of covering long distances by rail in the United States under unfavorable climatic conditions depends on the use of materials and devices much superior to those that serve in Italy. The front of the locomotive is furnished with an apparatus capable of removing not only the little stones, but any objects that may obstruct the roadbed, especially animals and plants torn away from the sides. At the rear of the locomotive is a little glassed-in compartment designed to protect the engineer against the elements.

[GIOVANNI CAPELLINI, 1863]

Train stopped by buffalo on the Plains

Coach car on a train

Railroad car carrying emigrants westward

Railway traveling in America is not tiring; on the contrary, it is refreshing. A train on its way to San Francisco or to Mexico is a series of moving houses. The cars are divided into rooms, and are provided with all the necessaries of life. Spacious libraries, smoking rooms, and dining rooms open out of one another, and there are bathrooms and barbershops. In the anterooms are the servants, chiefly white-coated Negroes, who are there to carry out all orders.

[COUNT VAY DE VAYA UND LUSKOD, 1908]

I suppose the reader has some notion of an American railroad car, that long, narrow wooden box like a flat-roofed Noah's ark. Those destined for emigrants on the Union Pacific are remarkable only for their extreme plainness. The benches are too short for anything but a young child. Where there is scarce elbow room for two to sit, there will not be space enough for one to lie. In all other trains, a warning cry of "All aboard!" recalls the passengers to take their seats. But all the way to San Francisco, the train stole from the station without a note of warning, and you had to keep an eye upon it even while you ate.

[ROBERT LOUIS STEVENSON, 1879]

A final handful of recruits drifted into the "Smith" farm in October. Brown decided to strike. He had already sent Martha and Annie back home and written last-minute notes to Northern relatives and friends.

There were now twenty-one "soldiers," five blacks and sixteen whites. On Sunday, October 16, Brown gathered them together for a final prayer service. He then explained his plan of attack to the newer recruits, three of whom had arrived only the previous day. First his men were to blockade the two bridges into Harpers Ferry. Then they would capture the armory buildings and a rifle factory. They would take hostages to use in the event of attack by federal troops or state militia. Once a sufficient number of blacks from the area had rallied to the invaders, the entire band would retreat toward the nearby mountains and regroup for their march southward.

At eight o'clock that moonless night Brown strode out of the farmhouse followed by eighteen of his men. He posted the remaining three as a rear guard. (One was to go to a nearby schoolhouse on Monday to await the escaping slaves who were expected to gather in the area.) Brown then climbed into a wagon filled with the weapons he had collected and rode toward a bridge that led into the silent, sleeping town across the Potomac.

Harpers Ferry was strategically located at the junction of the Potomac and Shenandoah rivers. Baltimore lay eighty miles east by rail and Washington fifty-seven miles by road. The town's main industry was arms manufacture. The federal government maintained a complex of buildings, including a fire-engine house, an armory, and an arsenal. There was also a private rifle works located on an island in the Shenandoah.

The town had a population of slightly more than 2,500. Of this total 1,251 were free blacks, and only 88 were slaves. Most of the white residents were Northerners employed as skilled craftsmen or government officials in the armory-rifle works complex.

Harpers Ferry was not a typical Southern town. There were no large plantations in the area. Neither cotton nor tobacco was grown there. The few slaveholders in the area owned small farms. Most of the local slaves were house servants. There was no large pool of plantation field hands to be rallied in the immediate area.

Several of Brown's recruits stationed themselves at the two bridges leading into Harpers Ferry. Another group overpowered the single watchman at the government-owned properties and seized control of the armory, the arsenal, and the engine house. They also took over the

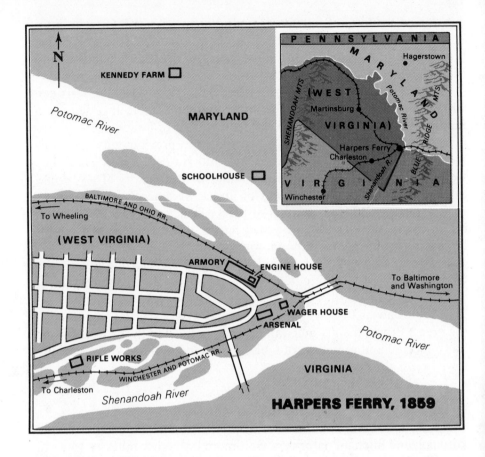

HARPERS FERRY, 1859

private rifle works. The invaders herded a small group of prisoners into the engine house as hostages. Now that he controlled millions in government munitions, Brown grew increasingly confident of success. He ordered the telegraph wires cut and dispatched a raiding party to secure more hostages from the nearby countryside. This band returned in the early morning hours of Monday, October 17, with ten freed slaves and three prisoners. Among the latter was the great-grand-nephew of George Washington, a minor slaveholder named Lewis W. Washington. Brown had particularly wanted Lewis Washington as a prisoner "for the moral effect it would give our cause having one of your name."

A train whistle signaled the beginning of danger for John Brown's plans. Shortly after midnight, an express passenger train from Wheeling reached Harpers Ferry en route to Baltimore. Trainmen found the railroad bridge barricaded and a wounded night watchman shouting warnings of armed night raiders. Brown's raiders began firing, forcing the engineer to back up the train until it was safely out of gunshot range. Just then the Harpers Ferry baggage master, a free black named

Hayward Shepherd, wandered down the track. When he tried to run in spite of a raider's command to halt, he was shot down. Shepherd died soon afterward, the first fatality in John Brown's private war against slavery.

By dawn the alarm had sounded throughout the countryside. The residents of Harpers Ferry, except for the handful Brown had taken as hostages or prisoners, armed themselves and fled in panic to a hilltop behind the town. Many of the town's blacks—both slave and free—fled with them. Church bells throughout northwestern Virginia and Maryland tolled the warning signal for slave insurrections. Militia companies began collecting their forces throughout the Blue Ridge towns that bordered on Harpers Ferry, preparing to march on the town.

Up to this point most Virginians who knew of the incident believed that *blacks* had begun a slave uprising at Harpers Ferry much like the one three decades earlier at Jerusalem. Only later in the day would the truth filter out. Brown, amazingly enough, had allowed the Baltimore express train to continue on its way. Thus he ensured that news of his invasion would pass instantly across the telegraph lines from Baltimore to Washington, Richmond, and elsewhere. It is difficult to know whether he was too dazed to act decisively or whether he deliberately wanted to publicize what he had done. In any case, by Monday noon, he and his men had clearly lost the initiative in Harpers Ferry.

Not only did Brown allow the train to proceed. He actually dawdled away Monday morning itself. Instead of collecting his hostages and making a dash for the nearby mountains, as several of his men

Harpers Ferry at the time of the 1859 raid was a small town in a dramatic setting. In this view, looking southwest, the Potomac curves down from the left and into the far distance; the Shenandoah flows past the church at right. The government buildings are near the center, not far from the bridge over the Potomac.

John Brown was fifty-six when this photograph was taken, early in 1857. (He soon grew a beard as a disguise.) One observer commented at this time that Brown had "a little touch of insanity about his glittering gray-blue eyes."

urged him to do, he squandered time with his hostages at the engine house. He even ordered breakfast for all of them from a nearby hotel, the Wager House. He divided his already outnumbered forces, sending several raiders and a few freed slaves across the Potomac to join his rear guard at the schoolhouse.

In the morning armed townspeople and men from nearby farms got the upper hand. Their rifle fire kept the raiders pinned down to their armory compound. Brown had obviously not expected his opponents to attack so quickly. Yet he remained in the town, either expecting slave reinforcements or perhaps simply making what he believed to be a divinely ordered last stand.

Brown's only means of escape, the two bridges, were retaken by militia late Monday morning. The militia dispersed the few raiders guarding the structures. One of them, the free black Dangerfield Newby, was the first of Brown's men to die in the assault. As he lay dead in the street, townspeople vented their fury at the raid on his body, beating it with sticks.

Brown finally began searching for a way to get out. Some of his men were still across the river in Maryland. Others were trapped in the rifle works. He and most of his raiders, guarding about thirty hostages by now, could not link up with either group. Brown decided to offer an exchange. He would release the hostages in return for a guarantee that he and his men could go free. Will Thompson, the first raider who carried these terms to the militia under a flag of truce, was seized by the crowd and taken away at gunpoint. Brown recognized his predicament at last. He took his remaining men, his few slave recuits, and eleven of his most prominent hostages. They barricaded themselves in the engine house. He then sent out three more people—his son Watson, another raider, and one of the prisoners. They approached the militia under another flag of truce. The two raiders were shot down, although Watson managed to crawl back to the engine house.

The streets of Harpers Ferry were filled with drunken, hysterical townspeople and militiamen by late Monday afternoon. One group caught an escaping raider near the Potomac, killed him, and then spent hours puncturing his body with bullets. Brown's remaining three men in the rifle works received similar treatment when they were forced to flee toward the river. Two of them fell dead, riddled with bullets. The third, a black named John Anthony Copeland, was rescued from lynching by a local doctor, who protected him from a mob of captors until the arrival of slightly more sober militiamen.

Among the casualties on Monday afternoon was the mayor of

Harpers Ferry, a gentle old man named Fontaine Beckham. (His will provided for the emancipation of a slave family that he owned.) He was shot by one of Brown's men. After Beckham's death the town went completely out of control. Residents and local farmers competed with frenzied militiamen in screaming at the raiders while senselessly firing their guns. A mob marched on the Wager House, where Will Thompson remained under guard. They dragged him down to the Potomac, as he shouted: "You may take my life, but eighty thousand will arise up to avenge me, and carry out my purpose of giving liberty to the slaves." The mob peppered his head with bullets before tossing the dead man into the shallow water.

The first word of the leader's identity came late Monday. He sent out yet another note from the engine house repeating his offer to exchange hostages for freedom. It was signed "John Brown." The offer was refused.

The night that followed must have been agonizing for Brown, as he struggled to retain some control over his future despite the obvious failure of his plan. Two of his sons, Oliver and Watson, lay dying. Brown and his four remaining able-bodied men took turns guarding their eleven hostages. Brown spent a good deal of time tending to his prisoners' comfort. Mainly, though, he strode quietly back and forth across the blood-spattered room, alone with his thoughts.

When Brown and his men peered out of their engine-house fortress at dawn on Tuesday, October 18, things had changed. They saw, not Monday's scruffy and jittery mob of local rabbit-shooting militia but a cool, well-dressed company of United States Marines. They were armed with rifles, bayonets, and sledge hammers for the siege that lay ahead. The marines were under the command of Colonel Robert E. Lee, accompanied by Lieutenant J. E. B. Stuart. Brown appeared neither shocked nor unhappy. One of his hostages, Lewis Washington, later observed:

> Brown was the coolest and firmest man I ever saw. With one son dead by his side, and another shot through, he felt the pulse of his dying son with one hand and held his rifle with the other, and commanded his men with the utmost composure, encouraging them to sell their lives as dearly as they could.

Lieutenant Stuart approached the engine house under a flag of truce and handed a note to Brown demanding unconditional surrender. Brown refused. He insisted that he would surrender only when he and his men were promised their freedom. Stuart repeated Lee's surrender terms and then, without warning, leaped away from the door waving

This tiny schoolhouse in Maryland was to be used as a gathering place for escaping slaves after Brown's raid. He had not intended to strike as soon as he did, but neighbors near the Kennedy farm were growing suspicious of the activity there.

In this engine house Brown and his raiders took refuge on October 17. His small band pushed the fire engines up to the doors to impede entry, but Lee's troops broke in, using a heavy ladder as a battering ram.

his cap. While thousands of excited spectators cheered wildly, a party of soldiers began battering at the oak doors of the engine house. Brown's men responded with a volley of shots. Within moments one of the doors had been broken down, and armed marines began dashing into the engine house. The first two were shot. But others swarmed in, overpowering Brown and his four remaining raiders.

Two of the four raiders were quickly bayoneted and died soon afterward. The remaining two, a Quaker youth named Edwin Coppoc and a free black named Shields Green, were captured without being seriously wounded. Brown himself knelt on the floor, his rifle cocked while awaiting the assault. Lieutenant Israel Green, the officer leading the attack on the engine house, entered the building and struck Brown with a light sword before the weary man could fire. Green then tried to run him through with his sword, practically lifting Brown off the ground. Somehow the sword struck either a bone or a belt buckle and failed to inflict a fatal wound. Nevertheless, as Brown collapsed on the ground, Lieutenant Green continued beating him over the head with his sword until his victim lost consciousness. Finally, the lieutenant regained his self-control. He ordered Brown and his men carried outside and placed on the grass, where their wounds were dressed.

Later that afternoon a detachment of militia confiscated boxes of revolvers and rifles from the Maryland schoolhouse where Brown's recruit had waited vainly for slaves to rally. Another patrol under J. E. B. Stuart occupied the Kennedy farm. By then the rest of Brown's rear guard had fled. They left behind not only hundreds of weapons but also the incriminating letters from the Secret Six and other abolitionists that Brown had abandoned so casually before the raid.

After his wounds had been dressed, Brown was taken to an office in the armory. He was guarded closely, for mobs in the streets of Harpers Ferry wanted to lynch him immediately.

On Tuesday afternoon Brown was visited by a group of politicians, military officers, and newspaper reporters who had just arrived in Harpers Ferry. Among them were Virginia Governor Henry A. Wise and Senator James M. Mason, also of Virginia. Brown did not shirk speaking to the visitors since, as he put it, he wanted "to make himself and his motives clearly understood." It was a new role for the militant man of action, who had often expressed his contempt for mere talkers. In Governor Wise's words Brown spoke "freely, fluently, and cheerfully." Whether he spoke truthfully, however, is questionable.

Senator Mason asked the old man how he had financed the raid. "I furnished most [of the money] myself," he answered. "I cannot implicate others. It is by my own folly that I have been taken." Brown insisted throughout the interview on accepting complete responsibility for the raid: "No man sent me here; it was my own prompting and that of my Maker, or that of the devil, whichever you please to ascribe it to." (If Brown had sincerely wished to avoid implicating his Northern supporters, though, he might have done so more effectively by not leaving their correspondence in plain view at the Kennedy farm.)

Brown departed most strikingly from the truth when he discussed his motives in attacking Harpers Ferry. He denied any intention of leading a violent slave revolt. He claimed that his purpose had been simply to liberate a group of slaves and lead them to freedom: "We came to free the slaves," he insisted, "and only that."

"Do you consider yourself an instrument in the hands of Providence?" one bystander asked. "I do," Brown replied. "I pity the poor in bondage that have none to help them; that is why I am here; not to gratify any personal animosity, revenge, or vindictive spirit." Brown claimed that only fear for his hostages' safety had prevented his fleeing earlier. He said too that his decision to allow the Baltimore train to proceed stemmed from his concern for the lives of its passengers.

Brown was clearly trying to suggest to his interviewers a change in his personality. His speech was free of the harsh and vindictive tone that he had used formerly in talking of Southern slaveholders. There now emerged the image of a gentle and rather sorrowful agent of Providence. Brown was directing his words more toward the Northern audience that would read newspaper accounts of the interview than toward his Southern questioners. He was trying to convey to Northern readers the belief that had led him to Harpers Ferry—that slavery could no longer be fought by peaceful means but only by such methods as he had used in his unsuccessful raid.

By late Tuesday afternoon it was possible to tally the results of John Brown's invasion scheme. The slaves he had sent to the Maryland schoolhouse had deserted the previous night and returned to their masters. One unfortunate slave captured with Brown later died in a Charleston prison. Another of his reluctant slave recruits was later found drowned near Harpers Ferry.

Seventeen people, including the two slaves, were killed during the raid or died soon afterward. Three townspeople, one slaveholder, and one marine perished. Ten of Brown's men, including two of his sons, lost their lives. Five raiders, including Brown, were captured, and the rest escaped into the Maryland mountains. Two others were caught in Pennsylvania a few days later, while five (including Brown's son Owen) fled to safety.

As a military effort, Brown's campaign failed miserably. Yet, even at its moment of failure, it began to trigger exactly the kind of sectional crisis that Brown had predicted.

Moderates in the North tried to minimize the raid's importance. They wrote John Brown off as a solitary madman whose efforts did not have support among respectable Americans of any section. "It is now well understood," editorialized *Harper's Weekly* in late October 1859, "that the insurrection was merely the work of a half-crazed white." Republican party politicians were especially eager to disassociate their peaceful antislavery views from Brown's violent tactics. "John Brown was no Republican," insisted Abraham Lincoln, and not "a single Republican [has been implicated] in his Harpers Ferry enterprise."

On the other hand, Democrats in both North and South denounced the Brown plot as an extension of Republican antislavery agitation. Senator Stephen A. Douglas, the leading Democratic spokesman of the North, called the scheme a "natural, logical, inevitable result of the doctrines and teachings of the Republican party."

More directly concerned, of course, were the Secret Six and Brown's other Northern abolitionist backers. They faced possible arrest and prison terms for their role in the episode. Newspapers throughout the country began reprinting the incriminating letters found at the

Kennedy farm. Within a week after Brown's capture Sanborn, Howe, and Stearns had fled to Canada to escape prosecution. Frederick Douglass, after writing an editorial defending the Harpers Ferry raid, sailed to England. Edwin Morton, another of Brown's abolitionist backers, also went to England. (Parker, dying of tuberculosis, had already gone to Europe.)

Gerrit Smith broke down completely. In November friends took him to an asylum for the insane, where he remained until late December, by which time he had "recovered his reason."

Higginson was the only member of the Secret Six to stand his ground. He did not try to deny involvement in the raid. But he did insist that Brown's "acquittal or rescue would do half as much good as being executed; so strong is the personal sympathy with him."

Higginson's view was shared by most abolitionists. They praised Brown for his actions—and they wanted the South to complete its work of immortalizing their hero. "Let no man pray that Brown be spared!" declared the Reverend Henry Ward Beecher. "Let Virginia make him a martyr!"

Virginia's Governor Wise seemed determined to oblige. Wise decided to charge Brown and his associates, under a Virginia statute, for treason against the state, rather than to hand over the men for trial in a federal court. The governor's position was legally questionable but politically shrewd. Brown's raid on the government arsenal and armory at Harpers Ferry had clearly broken federal laws. Nor did any of the raiders owe allegiance to Virginia. But Wise's action satisfied the general Southern clamor for swift (Southern) vengeance against the raiders. Viriginia authorities, fearful that unruly mobs in Harpers Ferry might try to lynch Brown, shifted the trial and the prisoners to Charleston. On October 26 the grand jury indicted Brown and his four accomplices—two whites and two blacks—charging them with the murder of five people, conspiracy to provoke a slave revolt, and treason against the state of Virginia. All of the raiders pleaded not guilty. The judge agreed to separate trials, Brown's being the first.

The trial of John Brown began on October 27, with the defendant reclining on a cot confronting a packed courthouse. Brown's court-appointed lawyer, Virginian Lawson Botts, startled the courtroom audience by immediately producing a telegram from a man in Akron, Ohio. He asserted that Brown and others in his family (which had lived in the Akron area for a number of years) were insane.

Botts felt that the only way to save his client's life was to have the jury commit him to an insane asylum. But Brown was not interested in saving his life. He wanted to use his trial as a national forum for preaching the antislavery gospel. He did not wish to wither away in obscurity. Finally, because of Brown's objections, his attorneys abandoned the insanity defense.

The trial came rapidly to a conclusion. On October 31, after deliberating only forty-five minutes, the jury found Brown guilty of all charges. Two days later he was carried back into court for sentencing. Before the judge could pronounce his sentence, the prisoner asked to speak. He talked for five minutes, addressing not the court so much as the country, which would read the text of his speech in newspapers the next day. He spoke slowly and eloquently, defending his actions at Harpers Ferry by distorting the facts and appealing directly and in the most emotional way for support from the antislavery North:

> In the first place, I deny everything but what I have all along admitted—the design on my part to free slaves. I intended to do as I did last winter, when I went into Missouri, and there took slaves without the snapping of a gun on either side, move them through the country, and finally left them in Canada. I designed to have done the same thing again, on a larger scale. That was all I intended. I never did intend murder or treason, or the destruction of property, or to excite or incite slaves to rebellion, or to make insurrection. . . . I see a book kissed here, which I suppose to be the Bible, or at least the New Testament. That teaches me that all things whatsoever I would that men should do to me, I should do even so to them. It teaches me further to "remember them that are in bonds, as bound with them." I endeavored to act up to that instruction.

Though Brown lied in his remarks about his plans for a slave revolt, he was truthful about his ultimate intention of liberating the slaves. This distinction was lost not only on many of Brown's Northern admirers but also on the judge, who sentenced the old man to die on the gallows on December 2. The four other captured raiders were also found guilty at their trials and, like Brown, were sentenced to hang.

In Brown's last month he continued his efforts to replace his earlier image as a vengeful border fighter with that of a forgiving yet sternly moral Christian, one who endured his final days as a prisoner with simple dignity. Brown's lawyers worked furiously to collect sworn statements from the condemned man's family and friends testifying to his insanity, in the hope of persuading Governor Wise to commit the condemned man to an asylum. They gathered a large number of such statements, many doubtless from people who were trying to save Brown's life but did not really believe him mad.

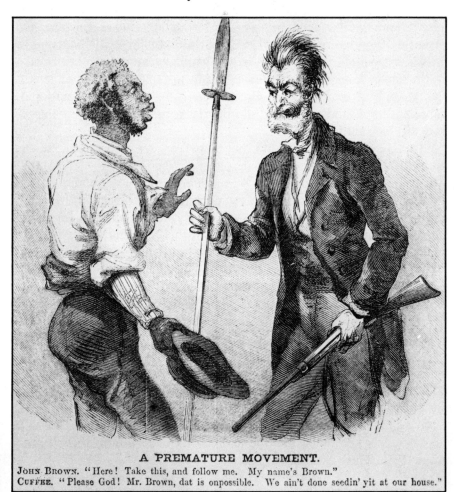

A PREMATURE MOVEMENT.

JOHN BROWN. "Here! Take this, and follow me. My name's Brown."
CUFFEE. "Please God! Mr. Brown, dat is onpossible. We ain't done seedin' yit at our house."

Trying to recruit a less than enthusiastic disciple to his cause, Brown is ridiculed in this pro-Southern view of the raid. Slaveowners liked to think that their slaves would react in this way—but most feared otherwise.

At the same time, many people wrote Wise pleading with him to spare Brown and not create an antislavery martyr, thereby increasing sectional tensions. The Governor finally rejected the many appeals for clemency, declaring Brown perfectly sane—"cool, collected, and indomitable." "He is a fanatic," Wise wrote, "but firm, truthful and intelligent." Brown could not have been more delighted at Wise's actions. He wrote: "I am worth inconceivably more to *hang* than for any other purpose."

Brown greeted a procession of visitors in his cell during his last month. Virginia officials also generously (perhaps foolishly) allowed their prisoner to receive and send a steady stream of letters to friends, family, and antislavery associates. These letters helped fix the image of Brown among Northerners as a Christian martyr for the abolitionist cause. The themes he dwelt on in his correspondence were constant: his "cheerful" resignation to death, comparisons of his own death with Christ's, his belief that his death would help achieve his aim of liberating the slaves, and his continued belief in his role as a messenger of God. In only a month's time Brown made his execution a national event. And thousands now saw him only as a brave Christian going to his death with calm nobility.

On December 1, the afternoon before his execution, Brown received a last visitor, his wife, Mary. She had traveled south, having received Governor Wise's permission to return the bodies of her husband and two sons to their New York farm for burial. Brown and his wife shared supper and discussed family matters. Before going to bed, Brown wrote a final letter to his brother Jeremiah in which he described himself as "quite cheerful and composed."

Brown rose at dawn on December 2, read his Bible briefly, and wrote a final note to Mary. He enclosed his will and gave instructions for his tombstone inscription—simply "John Brown born May 9th 1800 was executed at Charleston, Va, December 2d 1859." Soon afterward his jailers came for him and escorted him down the corridor.

Brown stepped out into a street jammed with armed men, observing wryly to his guards: "I had no idea that Governor Wise considered my execution so important." Climbing into a wagon that would take him to the gallows, Brown sat down on his own coffin. He handed one of the guards a last message (punctuated in his own unique style). It was obviously addressed to Americans in every section of the country and read as clearly as a battle order:

Brown maintained his usual calm to the very moment of his death. A few days earlier he had written to his wife: "I have been whiped, but am sure I can recover all the lost capital occasioned by that disaster; by only hanging a few moments by the neck."

Charleston, Va, 2nd, December, 1859
I John Brown am now quite *certain* that the crimes of this *guilty, land: will* never be purged *away*; but with Blood. I had *as I now think: vainly* flattered myself that without *very much* bloodshed; it might be done.

At the gallows site 1,500 federal troops and state militiamen waited, along with a huge crowd of onlookers. The day itself seemed much too pleasant for a hanging. Looking at the Blue Ridge Mountains in the distance and the cornfields that surrounded them, Brown observed: "This *is* a beautiful country. I never had the pleasure of seeing it before."

The prisoner walked quickly up the steps of the scaffold with no hesitation. For ten minutes the officials in charge stumbled about trying to take their assigned positions. Brown himself seemed the most calm and least worried person on the platform. Finally, the preparations were completed, and a hush fell over the spectators as the officials walked off the scaffold, leaving Brown alone and "as motionless as a statue." Moments later, John Brown hung dangling before the huge crowd.

Some of the Southerners present felt, like Edmund Ruffin (a proslavery Virginian), that Brown had gone to his death with "complete fearlessness." Others, like a young actor named John Wilkes Booth, remained too bitter toward the dead man to admire this courage. Several Southern military leaders were present, including "Stonewall" Jackson, later to be a Civil War hero. But it was Colonel J. T. L. Preston's voice that first broke the stillness after Brown's death. "So perish all such enemies of Virginia," Preston exclaimed. "All such enemies of the Union! All such foes of the human race!"

By the time Brown went to his death, he had become a symbol. In the North he had, of course, won the sympathies of convinced antislavery forces. But he had also captured the compassion of many who had previously been either indifferent or opposed to abolitionism. One such person was a prominent New York Democrat and conservative on the slavery issue named George Templeton Strong. A few days after the execution Strong wrote in his diary:

> Old Brown's demeanor has undoubtedly made a great impression—his simplicity and consistency, the absence of fuss, parade and bravado, the strength and clearness of his letters, all indicate a depth of conviction that one does not expect in an abolitionist (who is apt to be a mere talker). Slavery has received no such blow in my time as Brown's strangulation. The supporters of any institution are apt to be staggered and startled when they find that any one man, wise or foolish, is so convinced of its wrong and injustices as to acquiesce in being hanged by way of protest against it. One's faith in anything is terribly shaken by anybody who is ready to go to the gallows condemning and denouncing it.

When Brown died, in fact, few Republicans and Democrats in the North were willing to denounce openly the character and aims of a man whom, only a month earlier, many had attacked as an insane fanatic.

In the South the image of John Brown was naturally a different one. Here he was not the Christian martyr who was becoming increasingly popular in the North. He was, instead, a grim avenging devil figure who had tried to start a massive slave revolt. After November 1859 Northerners concentrated on the *words* that had come from John Brown's eloquent tongue and pen after his capture. But Southerners were more concerned with the *deeds* that he and his men had attempted at Harpers Ferry. After the raid several Southern towns had called militia units and vigilante companies into service, declared martial law, and began hunting down conspirators—real or imagined—in their midst. A wave of hysteria sent thousands of fearful whites, many of whom did not own slaves, patrolling their neighborhoods, searching for abolitionist invaders and unruly slaves.

The South mobilized much more quickly and effectively after John Brown's assault than it had after Nat Turner's insurrection three decades earlier. After all, Southerners had been predicting such an assault from the North for more than a generation.

Southerners regarded John Brown even more harshly after the election of Abraham Lincoln as President in November 1860. The impact of John Brown's raid was crucial in provoking what one historian has called a crisis of fear among Southerners concerning Northern-led efforts to stir up slave rebellions. It helped create the climate of intense sectional passion that led to secession and Civil War.

The impact of Brown's raid was crucial in provoking what one historian has called a crisis of fear among Southerners concerning Northern-led efforts to stir up slave rebellions. It helped create the climate of intense sectional passion that led to secession and Civil War.

Once the South had left the Union, John Brown provided a magnificent symbol for rallying a reluctant Northern public to war. "Fifty years hence," George Templeton Strong confided to his diary in February 1862, "John Brown will be recognized as the Hero or Representative Man of this struggle." He added that "a queer rude song about him seems to be growing popular." The song to which Strong refers was set to the music of another Northern tune, then also growing in popularity, "The Battle Hymn of the Republic." (Its verses were written by Samuel Gridley Howe's wife, Julia.) Brown would probably have enjoyed the "queer rude song," whose simplicity was more appealing to the ordinary soldier than Julia Ward Howe's eloquent stanzas. It ran simply:

> John Brown's body lies a-mouldering in the grave,
> John Brown's body lies a-mouldering in the grave,
> John Brown's body lies a-mouldering in the grave,
> But his soul goes marching on.

Reform in Ante-Bellum America

THE UNITED STATES had changed a great deal in the years leading up to John Brown's raid in 1859. The starkest differences were technological and economic. When the nineteenth century began, Americans lived in relatively isolated communities. Most people were concentrated along the eastern seaboard. Large cities were yet to develop west of the Appalachian Mountains. The numerous small settlements and few large towns had little direct contact with each other. Good roads were scarce. Much interstate commerce took place through waterways; Massachusetts, for example, traded with South Carolina not overland but by means of ocean-going ships.

A GROWING NATION

By the middle of the nineteenth century a so-called Transportation Revolution had taken place in the United States. Railroad trains such as the one blocked by the Harpers Ferry raiders connected major cities in the North (and some in the South) and linked regions in the interior of the country. In 1831, at the time of the Nat Turner Revolt, there had been only 73 miles of track in existence. By 1860 the United States led the world in rail transportation, with almost 30,000 miles of tracks crisscrossing the nation. When John Brown traveled east from Kansas in the late 1850s, he went much of the way by railroad.

Trade and internal migration in the eastern United States were aided by other transportation systems as well. New York State opened the Erie Canal from New York City to Lake Erie in 1825. It enabled people and goods to move easily between the coast and the interior. By 1860 there were more than 3,000 miles of canals, a network of overland turnpikes, and thousands of steamboats on the larger American rivers. Even small towns in the interior, such as Harpers Ferry, could become important transportation centers.

Another change involved communications. By 1861 the telegraph provided immediate contact among Americans in every section of the country. News of the attack on Harpers Ferry reached New York City almost as quickly as it did Richmond. For that matter, John Brown found it much easier to reach a national audience after his arrest because reporters were able to wire home their news stories. Many more Americans read about John Brown than about Nat Turner three decades earlier, especially in the North, where population tripled between 1830 and 1860.

Much of this population increase came from abroad. European immigrants averaged 250,000 a year between 1845 and 1860. They came chiefly from Ireland, Germany, and Scandinavia. Many worked as laborers in the factories and on the railroads of the Northeast. Others became farmers in the new states of the Middle West and Far West. Only a small minority went to the South, which offered fewer opportunities for small farmers and factory workers.

For the economy was also changing. Southern farmers concentrated increasingly on cotton. Northern farmers, on the other hand, produced a variety of commercial crops for both American and foreign use. Among these were corn, wheat, and fruits and vegetables grown on truck farms.

Industry too was becoming increasingly vital in the North. Manufacturing at the beginning of the nineteenth century had existed only on a small scale. Pennsylvania had a few small iron forges, for example. Massachusetts was known for handcrafted shoes. During the 1820s New England began to build a textile industry based on large-scale manufacturing, using high-speed machine tools and an expanded labor force.

Manufacturing also increased elsewhere during the ante-bellum period. At the time of John Brown's raid, over 100,000 manufacturers were producing nearly $2 billion worth of such goods as textiles, clothing, pig iron, and guns (as at Harpers Ferry). By 1860 the United States ranked fourth among the world's industrial powers.

As the country's industry grew, so did a small organized labor movement. By mid-century industrial workers had formed a few trade unions, often against strong opposition from employers. Early unions faced formidable problems. For one thing, immigrant workers provided a constant supply of nonunion labor. For another, many native-born workers were determinedly "individualistic" (a word coined by French visitor Alexis de Tocqueville). They resented the discipline imposed by union leaders striving to reform and improve working conditions.

Labor leaders were not the only Americans interested in changing society. Many wealthy businessmen also involved themselves deeply in reform activities. Throughout the ante-bellum period, in fact, the connections between economic enterprise and reform were surpisingly close. A number of prominent businessmen and landowners such as George Luther Stearns and Gerrit Smith (of the Secret Six) gave much of their wealth to movements for social change. Even John Brown himself had been as single-minded in pursuit of wealth during his earlier years as he later became in his abolitionist activities.

While those with money often took the lead,

an interest in reform was shared as well by many less wealthy Americans at this time. Reform was a distinctive characteristic of the period from the presidency of Andrew Jackson to the election of Abraham Lincoln.

BACKGROUND AND MOTIVATION OF REFORMERS

What led people to try to change so many of their customs and institutions? One factor was a belief in progress. Many Americans during the ante-bellum decades came to feel that progress was visible in all areas of national life. They thought that rapid economic growth could be matched by steady improvement in American society and values.

The belief in a divine mission for America had been understood in religious terms by seventeenth-century Puritans. Eighteenth-century Americans had thought of it in political terms. Now it was seen in social terms by ante-bellum reformers. They wanted to liberate Americans by correcting personal defects and eliminating social wrongs. They aimed to achieve worldly perfection within the nation itself—and in their own lifetimes. Most reformers believed that, in the struggle to perfect American life, they would achieve their own moral perfection as well.

Many Americans supported one or another reform activity on a part-time basis. A small number of people devoted their entire lives to the task of achieving social perfection. The reformer emerged during the 1830s and 1840s as a distinct social type in the United States. Men and women pursued reform as a vocation, especially in New England and to a lesser extent in the Middle Atlantic and Middle Western states. The novelist Nathaniel Hawthorne was once such a reformer. He wrote:

> We were of all creeds and opinions, and generally tolerant of all, on every imaginable subject. Our bond, it seems to me, was not affirmative, but negative. We had individually found one thing or another to quarrel with in our past life,

and were pretty well agreed on the futility of lumbering along with the old system any further. As for what should be substituted, there was much less agreement.

Hawthorne raised a question that many have asked about American reformers: Why did some people try to change society while most of their countrymen were content instead to tolerate existing conditions? What were the reformers' motives?

John Brown provides a good test case. Did he become an abolitionist because of frustrations, because of an inability to succeed in the economic world of his day? Was his militancy a substitute for unfulfilled personal ambitions? Or was he slightly deranged, as many of his critics (and his defense lawyers) claimed? In other words, was he attracted to reform because of psychological disturbances?

Brown's defenders would argue that no psychologically and morally sound individual who observed an evil such as human slavery could help but feel a sense of personal responsibility for its elimination. Brown's actions were extreme, but slavery was an extreme evil. His supporters would thus consider the reform impulse as normal and as a praiseworthy reaction to an obvious social problem.

Clearly the motivation of each individual reformer can only be judged on its own merits. But it is helpful to remember that the ante-bellum American reform movement occurred during an unsettled period. The economy was changing. Industry was growing and with it a new group of industrial laborers. Thousands of people were moving westward. Boatloads of immigrants arrived daily. No reformer could be unaffected by at least some of these developments, whatever the personal factors involved.

WIDE-RANGING INTERESTS

The range of reform activity can be seen by a brief listing of the major concerns of the Secret Six. Among other activities Gerrit Smith helped

Harriet Tubman

The most famous "conductor" on the Underground Railroad was a former slave, Harriet Tubman. In the years 1850 to 1861, from the passage of the Fugitive Slave Act to the outbreak of the Civil War, she made nineteen secret trips into the South, rescuing some 300 people. Rewards for her capture eventually totaled $40,000. But she eluded her enemies successfully and was never caught. In later years she claimed that "On my Underground Railroad, I never ran my train off the track, and I never lost a passenger."

Born in 1820 or 1821 on a Maryland plantation, Harriet knew only cruelty as a child. She received no schooling and thus could not read or write. Because she was thought too awkward for housework, she was made to work as a field hand. Developing great strength and endurance, she could lift huge barrels and pull a loaded wagon like an ox. A blow to the head from the plantation overseer almost killed her. It resulted in "sleepy spells" that affected her for the rest of her life. In 1844 she married a free black named John Tubman, but the marriage was unhappy.

Harriet Tubman's life as a slave did not crush her rebellious spirit. She became a determined, single-minded woman whose faith in God and hatred of the slave system sustained her. In 1849, with the aid of friendly Quakers, she escaped to Philadelphia. There she met the abolitionist William Still, who recruited her for the Underground Railroad. Still wrote in his journal at the time: "She seems wholly devoid of personal fear." And she was.

She usually gathered her "passengers" for a Saturday night departure so that a day would intervene before an ad for runaways could be posted. She carried a pistol at all times, threatening with death anyone who tried to leave the "train."

Occasionally Mrs. Tubman spoke at antislavery meetings. But she preferred to remain a woman of mystery whose whereabouts were often unknown.

Time between trips was spent with freed slaves, either in St. Catharines, Ontario, the end of her "railroad" route, or in upstate New York. Her idol was the fiery John Brown, who called her "General Tubman." Only a flareup of her head injury kept her from joining Brown in his 1859 raid on Harpers Ferry.

When the Civil War broke out, "General Tubman" volunteered her services. She worked as a spy, a nurse, and a cook for the Union forces in South Carolina. After the war, she set up a charity home for blacks in Auburn, New York, which she managed until her death in 1913.

In 1868 Frederick Douglass commended Harriet Tubman for her service. "I have wrought in the day—you in the night. I have had the applause of the crowd, while the most that you have done has been witnessed by a few trembling, scarred, and footsore bondmen and women whose heartfelt "God Bless You" has been your only reward."

Horace Mann was the first president of Antioch College, where he taught philosophy, theology, and the virtues of coeducation.

finance educational reform, temperance, dress reform, prison reform, women's rights, and vegetarianism. Franklin B. Sanborn, although interested primarily in education, was also involved in state-supported charities. George Luther Stearns financed a variety of causes, while Theodore Parker was involved in the peace movement, temperance, and prison reform. Samuel Gridley Howe worked on model educational programs for the blind, insane, and feeble-minded. He also supported his wife's work for peace and women's suffrage. Thomas Wentworth Higginson, for his part, became deeply concerned with women's suffrage and temperance. The entire group were, of course, militant abolitionists.

Education Most reformers agreed that the surest road to progress in the United States was through education. They worked to reduce illiteracy. (Probably a majority of Americans were illiterate before the Civil War.) They also tried to improve educational opportunities in a variety of ways. Outside the South, belief in state-supported primary education for every child became widespread. Public-school systems were established throughout the North. The leader of this

movement was Horace Mann of Massachusetts. During the 1830s and 1840s he reorganized his state's school system, doubled teachers' salaries, and upgraded teacher training. Formal education at the secondary-school level also grew increasingly important, especially in New England. A number of progressive primary and secondary schools opened in New England. They were financed by men like Gerrit Smith and staffed by enthusiastic young teachers like Franklin B. Sanborn.

Higher education expanded, too. State universities were established in several Southern and Middle Western states. There were also new private colleges and universities. Oberlin College in Ohio, founded in 1833, was the first coeducational college in the country. It was also one of the few schools to admit blacks, and it became a center of Middle Western antislavery agitation. Mount Holyoke in Massachussets, founded in 1837, was the first women's college.

Mass education also flourished in the antebellum period. Hundreds of mass-circulation newspapers and magazines catered to every segment of the public. The famous "penny press" dated from 1833. In that year the New York *Sun* showed other journalists the possibilities of increasing readership profitably by cutting its price to one cent.

The most influential form of adult education in this period—again outside the South—was the lyceum movement. It originated in New England in 1826. Lyceums were established by the hundreds throughout the North and Middle West. They were basically lecture halls with small libraries and facilities for discussion and study groups. Lyceums drew a steady stream of well-paid lecturers on regional and even national tours. No better device existed for mass education in a country that lacked universal literacy but valued the arts of public speaking and debating.

Any cause could gain an audience simply by sending a speaker to tour the lyceums. Hundreds of reformers made national reputations in rousing Americans to the need for hospital reform, women's rights, temperance, and abolition. Men like Theodore Parker, Samuel Gridley Howe, and William Lloyd Garrison, found the lyceum platform ideal for preaching the gospel of reform. One of the best-known was Wendell Phillips, a close associate of Garrison's.

Treatment of the Handicapped   The outstanding figure in changing public attitudes toward the treatment of the mentally ill was Dorothea Dix. A Boston schoolteacher, she spent years studying conditions in America's insane asylums. She found most inmates "confined in cages, closets, cellars, stalls, and pens, where they were chained, naked, beaten with rods, and lashed into obedience." Her detailed reports to state legislatures on the hideous conditions and her long campaign for public recognition of the problem led to many improvements in state-supported mental hospitals.

One of those who helped Dorothea Dix in her campaign to ease the sufferings of mental patients was Samuel Gridley Howe. He himself was a pioneer in the education of the deaf and blind. Before he opened his school for the blind, he spent days blindfolded so that he could better understand his pupils.

Other reformers, among them Joseph Tuckerman of Boston and Charles Loring Brace of New York, helped the "neglected poor," the unemployed, and immigrants. Their work called attention to poverty in the nation's developing cities.

Temperance   Many reformers believed that excessive drinking was the basic cause of many other evils in American society. It is probably true that nineteenth-century Americans consumed more alcoholic beverages per capita than people of today. At any rate, many Americans advocated temperance.[1] The American Society for the Promotion of Temperance, founded in 1826, led the campaign for state prohibition laws. The first of these passed Maine's legislature in 1846. A dozen other Northern and Western

Dorothea Dix, a woman of great energy, supervised the work of Union war nurses during the Civil War.

states passed similar laws during the next decade, although few remained in force for long.

Temperance advocates stumped the lyceum circuit. They preached in religious-revival fashion against the use of alcohol. They sought pledges from drunkards who promised to abandon the habit. Many children joined the cause, and so-called Cold-Water Armies staged huge temperance marches in towns and cities.

Pacifism   The peace movement gained many followers in the early nineteenth century. A Maine merchant named William Ladd founded the American Peace Society in 1828. It was weakened after a few years, when it split into two conflicting groups over the question of whether nations might use force to defend themselves. One faction condemned the use of force on any occasion. Among its leaders was abolitionist William Lloyd Garrison. He led others who believed in absolute pacifism into a new Non-Resistance Society, which condemned violence even in self-defense.

Pacifism lost followers as the slavery controversy heated up during the 1850s. Some of Garrison's followers—for example, Gerrit Smith and other associates of John Brown—not only

---

[1] When used in reference to alcoholic beverages, the word "temperance" usually means, not moderation, but rather total abstinence.

helped finance the Harpers Ferry raid but had earlier helped arm free-state settlers in Kansas. Garrison himself ended by praising John Brown's raid and supporting the Civil War.

Women's Rights   Women reformers were active in almost every progressive cause in antebellum America. In the process of trying to improve conditions for others, they came to recognize the degree to which they themselves were deprived of equal citizenship. Surely, abolitionists among them reasoned, American society should eliminate not only *black* slavery but *female* servitude as well. American women enjoyed few civil liberties, no political rights, and limited social opportunities. They could not vote. They were not allowed to attend most universities or secondary schools. A woman's property was controlled by her father or her husband. Practically all careers but marriage were considered "unfeminine," if not actually forbidden, and public activities were frowned upon.

The movement for women's rights began in earnest in 1840. In that year an antislavery meeting in London refused to admit women delegates. Two Americans—Lucretia Mott and Elizabeth Cady Stanton—met in the balcony, where they had been forced to sit as passive spectators. They began discussions that continued by letter after they had returned to the United States.

In 1848 the two women organized the first Woman's Rights Convention, at Seneca Falls, New York. The delegates issued a manifesto paraphrasing the Declaration of Independence. It stated that "all men and women are created equal" and demanded that women be given "immediate admission to all the rights and privileges which belong to them as citizens of the United States."

The women's rights movement, next to abolitionism, was the most controversial of antebellum reform crusades. Some male reformers—notably Garrison, Wendell Phillips, Gerrit Smith, Higginson, and Samuel Gridley Howe—heartily supported the feminists. Others, especially clergymen and journalists, ridiculed and attacked the movement.

Nevertheless, some progress was made during the pre-Civil War years. Women were allowed to become elementary-school teachers. Mississippi, in 1839, became one of the first states to award married women control over their own property. Girls began attending secondary schools in small numbers, and a few colleges offered higher education to women.

Probably the most important of break-

Clothing reform was advocated by some women in the ante-bellum era. Rebelling against the cumbersome dresses of the time, Elizabeth Miller designed a demure short gown with full trousers. The costume was publicized by feminist Amelia (not Lydia) Bloomer, and hence was named after her.

throughs, however, were stubbornly personal. Distinguished careers pursued by individual reformers and intellectuals dented the dominant image of woman's mental and emotional unfitness for serious vocations outside the home. Prominent women included Dorothea Dix, Lucretia Mott, and Elizabeth Cady Stanton. In 1814 Emma Willard founded a Female Seminary in which mathematics, history, and philosophy were taught. This reform came at a time when women were thought incapable of learning much besides singing and embroidery and when no college in the world admitted woman students. Susan B. Anthony, an ardent feminist (and abolitionist), worked to gain the vote for women. She once declared that she "would ignore all law to help the slave, and ignore it all to protect an enslaved woman."

Elizabeth Cady Stanton was a cousin of reformer Gerrit Smith. When she married, she insisted that the word "obey" be omitted from the ceremony.

CHANGES IN RELIGION

Underlying the many reform programs in the nineteenth century was a religious ferment that permeated American life. For many Americans the angry, wrathful God of the Puritans had been replaced by a gentler God of love. The liberal Christian reaction to Puritanism produced several new sects. One of the most important was Unitarianism. It won many followers among well-educated middle-class New Englanders early in the nineteenth century.

Unitarians believed Jesus to be a great religious teacher but not the Son of God. They denied original sin and insisted on man's innate goodness. Their most prominent leader, William Ellery Channing of Boston, was involved in many reform activities, and he steered other Unitarians into them. Of the Secret Six Parker and Higginson were Unitarian ministers; Sanborn was a close friend of Channing's.

Transcendentalism Unitarians fostered a belief in the potentially divine character of human life itself. Around this conviction a number of intellectuals in the Boston area built a philosophy called Transcendentalism.

The Transcendentalists believed in man's natural goodness, in his perfectability, and in the active presence of a divine spirit within each human being. God lived within each individual. This meant that everyone was always open to direct moral guidance. In effect, each person became his or her own church. There was no need for actual churches or ministers to mediate between God and man. According to Transcendentalist doctrines, the human soul, when correctly instructed by divine insight, often found itself right in the center of a lyceum platform preaching reform. "What is man born for but to be a Reformer, a Remaker of what man has made?" asked Emerson, the group's most influential spokesman. His disciples went about the daily work of remaking society. Some, like Franklin Sanborn, became abolitionists. Others, like Margaret Fuller, were influential journalists. Still others founded Utopian communities, which were attempts to devise model societies (see page 378).

Revivalism Much of the religious life of antebellum America was very different from Transcendentalism. Ordinary people knew little about the spiritual goals of a few New England intel-

Revival meetings were occasions for tearful outbursts, joyful shouting—and neighborly get-togethers.

during the early nineteenth century that the area became known as "the burned-over district."

Yet another nationwide period of revivalism came during the 1820s and 1830s. It was led by a great preacher, Charles G. Finney of New York. Like many other evangelical ministers of the nineteenth century, he stressed the importance of good works and constant involvement in practical morality for churches and their members.

Revivalism appealed not only to the mass of uneducated Americans but to many of the country's more successful citizens as well. And Finney helped to "harvest" a number of individuals not only for God but also for the tasks of moral reform. One of Finney's converts, Theodore Weld, became an abolitionist leader second in importance only to Garrison. Two other converts were Arthur and Lewis Tappan, wealthy New York City merchants. They became leading philanthropists and contributors to many reform causes.

lectuals. Many Protestant Americans remained firmly rooted within older churches—Congregational, Episcopal, Presbyterian, Baptist, and Methodist. Many others were caught up in revivalism—an evangelical movement that stressed emotional fervor and a very personal response to Christian teachings.

This was an age in which science had few weapons against disease. People did not live as long as they do today. Thousands of children died in infancy. The ordinary person's awareness of death was acute. Though Americans might be "officially" optimistic, there was an undercurrent of pessimism about human existence. The personal approach of the "old-time religion" offered comfort and solace.

Waves of religious fervor have periodically swept over the American people. In the mid-eighteenth century many were caught up in a movement called the Great Awakening. Another emotional outpouring, the Great Revival of the West, converted thousands on the frontier beginning about 1797. So many revivals and new religious sects passed through western New York

THE ABOLITION MOVEMENT

Of all the reforms influenced by religion, the one with the closest connections was abolitionism. Certain religious groups had been particularly active in the antislavery movement from its beginning. These included the Methodists, Episcopalians, and, particularly, the Quakers. Ethical opposition to slavery inspired many leading figures of the Revolutionary period to free their slaves. It also influenced Northern states to abolish slavery gradually by the 1820s.

A leading antislavery organization of the early nineteenth century was the American Colonization Society, founded in 1817. It worked to secure gradual, compensated emancipation of slaves. After being freed, slaves were to be transported immediately elsewhere, preferably to Africa. The society actually colonized very few blacks. But it did help found Liberia in 1822 as a refuge for ex-slaves. Many Southerners joined the American Colonization Society in an effort to resolve their moral doubts over slavery. (A leading Virginia member for a time was Governor

Henry Wise.) The society lost support in the South, however, after the Nat Turner Revolt.

Garrison and His Followers Abolitionism as an independent movement began in the 1830s. Without doubt its leading figure was William Lloyd Garrison. Born in Massachusetts, he was influenced by a fanatically religious mother. For a time he edited the first temperance paper. Then he turned to the antislavery cause and founded an abolitionist journal, the *Liberator*. It was first published in Boston in 1831. Two years later Garrison organized the American Antislavery Society.

Much of Garrison's support came from free blacks in the North. But the movement quickly grew among white sympathizers as well. By 1837 the American Antislavery Society had 145 local chapters in Massachusetts, 274 chapters in New York, and 213 in Ohio (the Middle Western center of antislavery activity). By 1843 the society had over 200,000 members.

Other abolitionist leaders included Frederick Douglass and Wendell Phillips, Garrison's Boston lieutenant. Prominent figures in New York were Gerrit Smith and the Tappan brothers. Theodore Weld dominated the Middle West. Among the best-known speakers in the Northeast were Angelina Grimké and her sister, Sarah Grimké Weld.

Garrison and his followers broke deliberately with previous antislavery groups in several ways. First, they demanded immediate rather than gradual abolition of slavery. Second, many of the abolitionists (as they came to be known) opposed the idea of colonization. They thought it was possible for black Americans to be absorbed into American society. Third, the "Garrisonians" abandoned the politeness of earlier antislavery groups. Instead they adopted a militant, aggressive style. Garrison set the tone himself in the first issue of the *Liberator:* "I *will* be as harsh as truth, and as uncompromising as justice. On this subject, I do not wish to think, or speak, or write with moderation. I am earnest—I will not equivocate—I will not excuse—I will not retreat a single inch—AND I WILL BE HEARD."

Changing Tactics The abolitionists' religious beliefs helped determine their strategy. Most were devout men and women. They believed that slavery was the country's greatest moral evil, a blot on the United States that had to be erased. Their main objection to slavery was moral. Therefore, they thought, it was essential to convince the mass of Americans, North *and* South, that slavery was immoral and unjust. Abolitionists believed that personal recognition of this fact would result in nationwide demands for an immediate end to slavery. This technique was called moral suasion.

During the 1830s Garrison and his associates made a strong effort to reach slaveholders by mailing hundreds of thousands of abolitionist newspapers and tracts to the South. After the Nat Turner Revolt the postmaster general, a Southerner, allowed Southern postmasters to refuse to deliver abolitionist propaganda. (His action clearly violated both the law and the senders' civil liberties.) Southerners held huge bonfires of antislavery material.

By the 1840s abolitionists recognized that moral suasion had failed to win over any significant number of slaveholders. They abandoned this tactic in the South, but they continued to use it in the North.

The abolitionists split into two separate wings because of opposition to Garrison. His opponents objected to him for several reasons. They resented his overbearing leadership. They also disapproved of his demand for equal status

Chicago Historical Society

Garrison was stubborn, humorless, and courageous in his crusade for abolition. In 1854 he publicly burned a copy of the Constitution, exclaiming, "So perish all compromises with tyranny!"

Utopian Communities

Utopian communities of the ante-bellum era were outgrowths of the idealism and social unrest of the time. From the 1820s through the 1840s more than a hundred colonies were set up. Most of them were inspired by religious beliefs. But some were wholly secular, established as proving grounds for new economic or social theories.

The purpose of New Harmony, Indiana, was no less than "to introduce an entire new system of society," according to its founder. He was a successful Scottish industrialist named Robert Owen. He believed that capitalism was ignorant and selfish and that socialism could bring harmony to society. In 1825 he purchased a ready-made colony of 30,000 acres from a German religious group. Within six weeks he brought together 800 colonists. But New Harmony also attracted a share of crackpots and loafers. Quarrels broke out. Owen's frequent absences left the group without strong guidance. Within two years New Harmony was disbanded.

A new recruit at Oneida

On a smaller scale was Brook Farm, a few miles from Boston. It began in 1841 as a progressive preparatory school and cooperative farm, with all pupils and group members sharing daily chores. Its leader, George Ripley, a former Unitarian minister, believed in "plain living and high thinking." He thought that people could develop fully when free from competition. Many intellectuals were associated with Brook Farm. Emerson was an occasional visitor. Nathaniel Hawthorne was a group member. (He later satirized the experiment in his novel *The Blithedale Romance*.) When a highly structured, somewhat impersonal working and living system was introduced in 1845, the farm lost its appeal for many supporters. A fire in 1846 brought the experiment to an end.

The Oneida Community in upstate New York began in 1848. Its leader, John Humphrey Noyes, believed that small industry provided a better economic base for a colony than agriculture. So members made and sold animal traps, furniture, and other consumer goods. Property was owned jointly and distributed equally. Conventional marriage was replaced by "complex marriage"; all group members were considered married to each other. Noyes and his followers believed that they were not separated by man-made laws but belonged to one another. These beliefs were criticized severely, and the group finally abolished complex marriage in 1879. Soon afterward the community was dissolved. It became a joint-stock company specializing in manufacturing silverware.

Most utopias were unable to become truly self-sufficient or maintain their isolation from the outside world. They floundered when it came to putting their high ideals into practice. Yet they did make noteworthy contributions. New Harmony sponsored a set of educational innovations: the kindergarten, the trade school, the community-supported free school. Brook Farm's combination of work and culture was highly praised. And the members of Oneida pioneered in eugenics and what we would call encounter sessions.

for women as abolitionist leaders, and for fusion of the women's rights campaign with the antislavery movement. They disliked Garrison's constant attacks on the organized churches, many of whose leaders still opposed the drive for emancipation. And they wanted to involve the movement in practical political action. (Garrison wanted instead to focus on moral agitation.)

In 1840 the anti-Garrisonians withdrew from Garrison's organization and formed the American and Foreign Anti-Slavery Society. Both groups continued their propaganda campaigns to stir up Northern public opinion until the Civil War. But their major energies shifted during the 1840s into direct political agitation at the local, state, and national levels. Abolitionism was now the central concern of all American reformers, whatever their other interests.

Reactions to the Abolitionists The abolitionists aroused intense feelings that often led to violence. It was dangerous during the 1830s to advocate immediate emancipation, even in the North. Antiabolitionist mobs, often including prominent community leaders, destroyed antislavery printing presses. Bostonians tried to lynch Garrison in 1835, dragging him through the city streets with a rope around his neck. (This incident helped convert Wendell Phillips to the movement.) In New York City a mob destroyed Lewis Tappan's home. Henry B. Stanton, another militant antislavery figure, claimed to have been attacked personally over 200 times! One abolitionist newspaper editor, Elijah Lovejoy, was lynched in Alton, Illinois, in 1837.

Those outside the South who opposed abolitionism feared the reformers almost as much as Southerners feared slave revolts. To conservative Northerners, the abolitionists seemed to threaten public order, national unity, and established institutions. In fact, race prejudice was probably more extreme in the North than in the South. Certainly free blacks in the North suffered constant abuse and discrimination.

Even white abolitionists could not wholly shed their color prejudice. Only a few treated their black associates as complete equals. Garri-

Frederick Douglass, born in Maryland, escaped from slavery in 1838. He broke with Garrison, believing in a more political approach to abolition. During the Civil War he organized two black regiments from Massachusetts. Later he served as minister to Haiti.

son at one point urged the eloquent Frederick Douglass to use more "darky" mannerisms in his speeches. Treatment like this led Douglass to break with the Boston abolitionist.

Although Northerners did not lose their racial prejudices, they gradually became more sympathetic to the abolitionists. Federal interference with antislavery mail to the South won many converts to the abolitionist cause. Even those who did not share abolitionist beliefs disliked the practice of suppressing ideas. A number of Americans who began by defending the abolitionists' civil liberties ended by joining the movement itself.

Other Northerners became aroused by the "gag rule." This resolution, passed by the House of Representatives in 1836, provided that no antislavery petitions would even be considered. Every year a small group of congressmen, led by former President John Quincy Adams, tried to repeal the gag rule. They finally succeeded in ending this crude violation of the abolitonists' right of petition in 1844.

Fugitive Slaves Probably no single aspect of the abolitionists' work did more to gain sympathy for them than their efforts to assist fugitive slaves. Black abolitionists made daring forays into the South to rescue bondsmen. Outstanding were a famous pair of women, Sojourner Truth and Harriet Tubman (see page 371). A large network of Northern sympathizers, mostly blacks but including whites, maintained the famous Underground Railroad. In its "stations"—

safe havens such as barns and cellars—escaped slaves were hidden until "conductors" could lead them onward. Along its routes ex-slaves were guided to freedom in the North and in Canada.

The 1850 Fugitive Slave Act gave almost unlimited power to private slave catchers. They roamed the Northern states during the 1850s collecting bounties from Southern planters for capturing and returning blacks who had allegedly escaped from slavery. Northern states responding to public dislike of slave catching, passed so-called personal liberty laws. They allowed local officials to withhold help in this distasteful process.

Abolitionists went a step further and actively assisted fugitive slaves. Historians estimate that Boston alone sheltered a minimum of 600 runaway blacks at any given time. Local abolitionists verged on violence to protect them.

The Fugitive's Story *engrosses three abolitionist leaders. This sculpture group is by John Rogers, one of the most popular of all nineteenth-century American artists.*

Thomas Higginson, for example, led a Boston mob that tried to prevent one fugitive from being returned to slavery. Theodore Parker, who often hid runaways in his home, wrote his sermons with a pistol within reach of his desk. When slave catchers tried to retrieve an escaped black couple who had become members of Parker's congregation, the minister managed to smuggle them out of Boston to England.

THE FAILURE OF PEACEFUL REFORM

After decades of antislavery agitation many Northerners came to believe what the abolitionists asserted—that Southern slaveholders had formed a gigantic slave-power conspiracy to control the entire nation. Several things fed their fears. Southern states drove out antislavery advocates and crushed dissent. Southerners violated federal postal statutes and the constitutional right of petition (by means of the gag rule) in order to silence abolitionists. Slave catchers roamed the North hunting blacks. And Southerners were demanding the right to transplant slavery into the new Western territories.

The reaction to John Brown's raid showed how fragile the political links between North and South had become. In the North even moderate antislavery advocates were outraged by the South's embittered defense of its "peculiar institution." They regarded President Buchanan as a turncoat. Though Brown was nominally a federal prisoner, Buchanan had simply handed him over to a Virginia court.

In the South moderates had lost control of public opinion. People there had already begun preparing for possible secession, if not war. To most Southerners Buchanan's pro-Southern attitudes no longer seemed adequate protection against "aggressions" (such as the Harpers Ferry raid) that the South believed Northern Republicans were planning. By 1860 armed defense against Northern attack seemed as reasonable to most Southerners as violent assaults against the slave system did to the antislavery North.

What was left to negotiate? How could either section compromise, when each one felt its most vital interests at stake? Brown's raid came at the end of a decade of bitter argument and violent conflict over slavery. It hastened the collapse of normal political life, since democratic politics requires moderation—which no longer had many spokesmen.

Election and Secession   The Democratic party split into sectional wings in 1860. Northern Democrats nominated Stephen A. Douglas for the presidency. The Southerners put forward their own candidate, John C. Breckinridge of Kentucky. He promised to sponsor federal laws that would protect slavery in the territories. The Republicans nominated Abraham Lincoln. A hodgepodge of former Whigs, Know-Nothings, and Democrats formed a new Constitutional Union party. They nominated a fourth candidate, John Bell, also of Kentucky. He pledged mainly to say and do nothing about the slavery question.

But a decade of agitation had worn away the basis for compromise solutions to the slavery question. It was no longer possible to wish away the issue by not talking about it. Douglas and Breckenridge split the Democratic vote. Bell carried three border states. Lincoln won the North. He became President with barely 40 percent of the popular vote, none at all from the Deep South.

Fear swept the South after Lincoln's election. "Secession fever" grew to epidemic proportions within days. South Carolina took the plunge first. Its legislature passed a secession ordinance on December 20, 1860, climaxing thirty years of leadership in defense of Southern nationalism. By February 1, 1861, six other states—Mississippi, Florida, Alabama, Georgia, Louisiana, and Texas—had adopted similar ordinances. Three days later, these seven states proclaimed the Confederate States of America in Montgomery, Alabama.

Five months separated the 1860 election and Lincoln's inauguration in March 1861. The

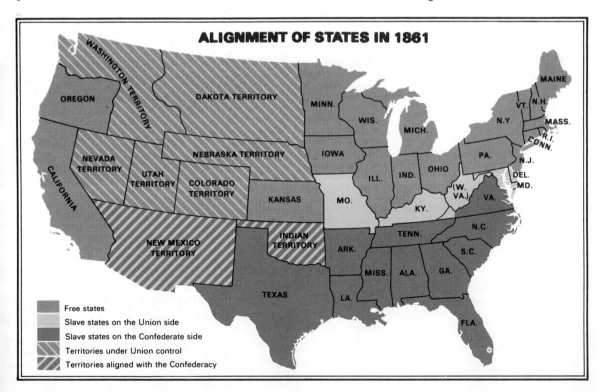

ALIGNMENT OF STATES IN 1861

Free states
Slave states on the Union side
Slave states on the Confederate side
Territories under Union control
Territories aligned with the Confederacy

"lame-duck" administration of James Buchanan did little to impede the course of secession. Buchanan condemned Southern actions and demanded obedience to federal laws. But neither he nor his government attempted to interfere as Southerners took control of federal forts, arsenals, and public property in their region.

There were various efforts to end the secession crisis by a political compromise in Congress, similar to the ones of 1820 and 1850. The most important of these was the Crittenden Compromise. It would have extended the Missouri Compromise line across the entire country, legalizing slavery south of it and prohibiting it to the north. By then, however, most Southerners were unprepared to accept any limitation, just as most Republicans opposed any extension of the system. Lincoln proposed that the North agree to enforce the Fugitive Slave Act and protect Southern slavery by constitutional amendments if necessary. But his suggestions seemed inadequate to the secessionists.

Both the Confederate states and the new Republican administration waited in March 1861 to see whether states in the Upper South would also secede. Fears about Republican intentions were widespread in states like Virginia and North Carolina, especially after John Brown's raid. But there were also more Unionists there than in the Deep South.

Lincoln's Inauguration Lincoln's inaugural address did little to calm the South. The new President promised not to invade the region or interfere with slavery where it already existed. But he made it clear that he believed the Union could not be dissolved at the whim of a state or group of states. He promised "to hold, occupy, and possess the property and places belonging to the federal government" throughout the country, including the South. And he pointed directly to the moral and political issue of slavery (and its extension) as the root of the conflict. "One section of our country," Lincoln said, "believes slavery is right, and ought to be extended, while the other believes it is wrong, and ought not to be extended. This is the only substantial dispute." Finally, he insisted that the question of war and peace was not in his hands but in those of his "dissatisfied fellow countrymen," the secessionists.

Lincoln's promise to maintain control of federal property in the South practically eliminated the possibility of a political compromise with the Confederate states. Lincoln was trapped between a desire for compromise and a need to maintain national authority, lest it collapse throughout the Upper South as well.

For weeks Lincoln and his Cabinet debated their course of action toward the Confederacy. They worried especially about whether to send relief supplies and troops to the few remaining federal posts in the region, such as Fort Sumter in Charleston harbor.

Finally, on April 4, Lincoln dispatched a relief expedition to Sumter. It carried only fresh supplies for the garrison, not reinforcements. Lincoln wanted to avoid the charge that he was making a hostile move toward the Confederacy. He even went so far as to inform the governor of South Carolina about his desire to supply Sumter peacefully. The Confederate government demanded, however, that the fort be entirely evacuated or, if necessary, destroyed. Charleston's harbor batteries opened fire at Sumter on April 12. Within two days Confederate forces had captured the fort. Virginia, Arkansas, and North Carolina all joined the Confederacy within a few weeks. So did Tennessee. Elsewhere in the border states—especially Maryland, Missouri, and Kentucky—Lincoln took firm measures to maintain Union control. "Both parties deprecated war," Lincoln later wrote, "but one of them would *make* war rather than let the nation survive; and the other would *accept* war rather than let it perish. And the war came."

1. In what ways was the United States of 1859 different from the United States in 1800?
2. What connection was there between the reform activity of the ante-bellum period and the changes taking place in American society?
3. What was the relationship between abolitionism and the women's rights movement?
4. How did Americans' attitude toward the nature of God change during the nineteenth century? Why was this new attitude favorable to reform movements? How would you characterize Unitarianism? Transcendentalism? Revivalism?
5. For what reasons did Garrison break with older antislavery groups? What was "moral suasion"? Why did abolitionists abandon this tactic in the South?
6. Did the abolitionists initiate the use of violence or did their actions provoke it? What evidence is there to indicate that not all abolitionists believed in racial equality?
7. How were moderate Northerners influenced by the "gag rule"? By the Fugitive Slave Law?
8. Did Northerners have reason to believe in a "slave power" conspiracy? Why or why not? Did Southerners have reason to believe in the possibility of a Northern attack on the slave system? Why or why not?
9. How was it possible for a "minority" President to be elected in 1860? What was Lincoln's position on the slavery issue? On the basis of the vote, what seems to have been the dominant sentiment of the country?

Beyond the Text

1. Through various committees, investigate major ante-bellum reforms (other than abolitionism) in terms of origins, personalities involved, successes, and failures.

2. The abolitionists have been called fanatics, reformers, and freedom fighters. After hearing individual reports on aspects of the abolitionist movement, hold a panel discussion to evaluate the position of the class.
3. Prepare a report on the origins, leadership, routes, and effectiveness of the Underground Railroad.

Bibliography

Nonfiction

Billington, Ray A., *The Protestant Crusade, 1800–1860.*

Filler, Louis, *The Crusade Against Slavery, 1830–1860.**

Frederickson, George, *The Black Image in the White Mind, 1817–1914.**

Griffin, Clyde S., *The Ferment of Reform, 1830–1860.**

Kraditor, Aileen S., *Means and Ends in American Abolitionism.**

Matthiessen, F. O., *American Renaissance: Art and Expression in the Age of Emerson and Whitman.**

Oates, Stephen, *To Purge This Land with Blood.**

Potter, David M., *Lincoln and His Party in the Secession Crisis, 1860–1861.**

Quarles, Benjamin, *Black Abolitionists.**

Smith, T. L., *Revivalism and Social Reform in Mid-Nineteenth Century America.*

Stampp, Kenneth M., *And the War Came: The North and the Secession Crisis.**

Tyler, Alice Felt, *Freedom's Ferment: Phases of American Social History to 1860.**

Fiction

Allis, Marguerite, *The Rising Storm.*
Fuller, Edmund, *Star Pointed North.*
Malm, Dorothea, *The Woman Question.*

*a paperback book

19

Sherman's March to the Sea

EARLY ON THE morning of November 16, 1864, the Union columns headed out of Atlanta, Georgia, bound southeast for the coastal city of Savannah. Northern troops, over 60,000 strong, with their horses, mules, and wagons, clogged the road. When they reached a hill outside Atlanta, it was natural for the soldiers to look back toward the town. Their commander, General William Tecumseh Sherman, recalled:

> Behind us lay Atlanta, smoldering and in ruins, the black smoke rising high in the air and hanging like a pall over the ruined city. Away off in the distance, on the McDonough road, was the rear of Howard's column, the gun-barrels glistening in the sun, the white-topped wagons stretching away to the south; and right before us the Fourteenth Corps, marching steadily and rapidly, with a cheery look and a swinging pace, that made light of the thousand miles that lay between us and Richmond. Some band, by accident, struck up the anthem of "John Brown's Body." The men caught up the strain, and never before have I heard the chorus of "Glory, glory, hallelujah!" done with more spirit, or in better harmony of time and place.

On that beautiful day of brilliant sunshine and clean, crisp air, the Civil War, already three-and-a-half years old, seemed exhilarating, if not remote. Sherman later recalled experiencing a "feeling of something to come, vague and undefined, still full of venture and intense interest. Even the common soldiers caught the inspiration, and many a group called out to me—Uncle Billy, I guess Grant is waiting for us at Richmond!"

Sherman's troops devastated much of central Georgia. Worse than the physical damage was the effect on Southern morale: With a Union army moving freely through their territory, few Southerners could still believe that the Confederacy might win the Civil War.

Tall, sharp-eyed, and red-haired, Sherman gained a reputation as a ruthless commander because of his march through the Confederacy. Actually, because he loved the South, he wanted to end the war quickly, and he opposed harsh reconstruction policies in the postwar era.

Although Richmond and victory for the Union were still five months away, Sherman had already made his mark in Georgia. The pall of smoke he and his troops saw above Atlanta came from the fires they had set in the town's railroad depot and machine shops. Flames soon swept into residential areas, destroying hundreds of dwellings. The general's reputation for toughness—"brutality" in the minds of most Southerners—took shape at Atlanta and on the subsequent campaign, his famous march to the sea. "We are not only fighting hostile armies," Sherman believed, "but a hostile people. We must make old and young, rich and poor, feel the hand of war."

Sherman, the tough-talking soldier, knew the South well. Born in Ohio in 1820, he attended West Point and, after graduation, spent most of his time on duty in military posts in the South. He resigned from the army in 1853. After working unsuccessfully as a bank manager in California and as a lawyer in Kansas, he tried to get back into the army. Rejected, he had to settle for the job of superintendent of a military academy in Louisiana. The school opened in 1859.

As the sectional crisis deepened, Sherman made it clear that, if Louisiana should secede from the Union, he would resign his post and do all he could to aid the national government. He kept his word when he heard of the Southern attack on Fort Sumter in April 1861. Secession, he thought, was "folly, madness, a crime against civilization." He immediately sought, and gained, reinstatement in the army. It was now more receptive to such applications, since so many regular officers had joined the Confederacy.

Sherman started as a colonel and rose rapidly in the Union high command. He served in the west as one of Grant's most trusted officers. By mid-1864, as a brigadier general, he was assigned the mission of striking from Tennessee into Georgia and seizing Atlanta. The town, though relatively small, was an important railroad center. Confederate troops under General Joseph E. Johnston and, later, General John B. Hood fought hard to hold Sherman back. They were defeated in July at two crucial battles, those of Peachtree Creek and Atlanta. After a siege of several weeks, Atlanta fell.

Sherman's troops entered the city on September 2. Although Hood at first moved south toward safety, he later wheeled northwest toward Tennessee, hoping to harass Sherman's communications so badly that his forces would have to retreat. Inadvertently, Hood's actions may have influenced Sherman in his later decision to move to the sea without regard for communications or established supply lines.

For the time being, however, Sherman wanted to rest his troops and observe Hood's movements. He decided that Hood could be kept at bay by some detachments of his own army, plus Union troops in Tennessee.

Sherman meanwhile undertook some indirect negotiations with the governor of Georgia, Joseph E. Brown. His aim was to separate the state from the Confederacy. There was reason to hope that Georgia might pull out of the war. Brown had already withdrawn his state's militia from the rebel army. And, like most Southern politicians, he detested Jefferson Davis, president of the Confederacy. Nothing came of the negotiations, though they may have impressed Sherman with the need for bringing the hardships of war home to the Southern civilian population.

When the war started, Atlanta—not then the state capital—had only 12,000 inhabitants. Many of them had fled as the Union troops approached. Others followed when Hood abandoned the town. When Sherman entered, he ordered the rest of the civilians to leave, since he did not want them clogging the town and interfering with his lines of communication. He and Hood agreed to a ten-day truce so that these civilians could move out.

By late October, Sherman had decided to march to the sea. On November 2 Grant wired: "I do not really see that you can withdraw from where you are to follow Hood without giving up all we have gained in territory. I say, then, go as you propose."

Sherman's bold plan called for his army of 62,000 men (5,000 of them cavalry) to move the 300 miles to Savannah without supply lines and without communications until they reached the Atlantic coast. There the Union navy could provide cover and supplies. Sherman's troops carried enough provisions for twenty or thirty days, but those were considered emergency rations. Food on the march would be "provided" by the local farms and plantations along the way—*not,* of course, on a voluntary basis. As a result, Georgia would be made to "howl."

Sherman's Special Field Order #120 detailed the procedure he hoped to establish. Brigade commanders were responsible for organizing foraging parties. Every morning they would move out from the four main columns under the direction of one or two "discreet officers," Foragers—or "bummers," as they soon came to be called (even by the Yankees themselves)—could seize available livestock and food supplies. They were not supposed to enter houses. Only corps commanders had the authority to order destruction of buildings, and then only in areas of resistance. Foragers for artillery units could take all the animals and wagons they needed.

If possible, foragers were to seize provisions from the rich planters rather than poor farmers. The wealthy were presumed to be more in favor of the rebellion than their humbler fellow Southerners. (This assumption fitted Northern views of secession as a conspiracy of the elite. It did not square with the facts of Southern political life.)

Sherman's field order directed his men to "forage liberally." They obeyed with a will. Men would go out in the morning on foot, seize a wagon, and then load it with everything valuable and movable they could find. One of Sherman's aides, Major Henry Hitchcock, described a foraging expedition in his diary:

> Plenty of forage along road: corn, fodder, finest sweet potatoes, pigs, chickens, etc. Passed troops all day, some on march, some destroying railroad thoroughly. Two cotton gins on roadside burned, and pile of cotton with one, also burned. Houses in Conyers look comfortable for Georgia village, and sundry good ones along road. Soldiers foraging all along, but only for *forage*—no violence so far as I saw or heard. Laughable to see pigs in feed troughs behind wagons, chickens swinging in knapsacks. Saw some few men—Whites look sullen—darkies pleased.

Stories of Union brutality, supposedly encouraged by Sherman himself, began to circulate. (They continued to circulate for generations.) But his march to the sea, devastating as it was, did not degenerate into an orgy of murder, rape, and arson. Sherman later acknowledged "acts of pillage, robbery, and violence" undoubtedly committed by some of his men. But, he argued, "these acts were exceptional and

A "bummer" goes his way, so loaded with booty that he cannot even hold the reins in his hands. For many of Sherman's men, the march through Georgia was a kind of holiday after months or years of difficult military life.

incidental. I have never heard of any cases of murder or rape; and no army could have carried along sufficient food and forage for a march of three hundred miles; so that foraging in some shape was necessary."

To Sherman, the march became just what he had ordered—harsh but, in the main, well-disciplined. The destruction of his "scorched-earth" policy centered on three main targets: railroads, the few factories on the route, and public buildings that could serve as temporary headquarters for military units.

Sherman marveled at the skill of his men in carrying out his order to "forage liberally." One fact among many proves how proficient they were: Sherman's army started the march driving 5,000 head of cattle; they ended it with over 10,000.

Where were the Confederate forces during these agonizing weeks? Some small cavalry units of the Confederate army did appear from time to time to raid foraging parties. But they had little overall effect. Hood's army had marched northwest to Tennessee and defeat. Since most Georgians of fighting age were serving with the Southern forces, the state militia had been reduced to several thousand old men and young boys. They tried to make a stand at the state capital, Milledgeville, but the Union forces swept them aside. After viewing the casualties, a northern officer wrote: "I was never so affected at the sight of dead and wounded before. I hope we will never have to shoot at such men again. They know nothing at all about fighting and I think their officers know as little."

Milledgeville fell on November 23. Georgia state officials had fled a short time before. The invading Yankee officers decided to mock the "sovereign state of Georgia." They pretended to hold a session of the state legislature, complete with resolutions and fire-eating oratory. Then they decided to repeal the ordinance of secession. When Sherman heard about these antics, he laughed. Meanwhile, his Milledgeville "legislators" ordered the burning of public buildings in the town.

Sherman's soldiers sliced a path forty to sixty miles wide through central Georgia. Every white family along the way underwent its own particular ordeal and emerged with its own sorrowful story. Tales of the devastation became commonplace: houses broken into and sacked, food and valuables hidden only to be found by the recurrent searches of intruding "bummers," treasured family possessions tossed into the flames, cotton gins and public buildings put to the torch. "Everything had been swept as with a storm of fire," wrote one Macon newspaper. "The whole country around is one wide waste of destruction."

Contrary to Sherman's conception of his foraging troops as skilled,

Mary Jones was one of the Southerners who felt the brunt of Sherman's attack. She wrote: "The foundations of society are broken up; what hereafter is to be our social and civil status we cannot see."

most Southerners in their path regarded them as greedy marauders. The experiences of two Georgia women, a mother and daughter, typified the ordeal. Mary Jones, the widow of a Presbyterian minister, owned three plantations in Liberty County, not far from Savannah. At the time of Sherman's march she and her daughter, Mary Jones Mallard, were living at the plantation known as Montevideo. Their letters and journals vividly portray the impact of war.

Mary Mallard's husband was captured on December 13 by Union cavalry near Montevideo. (Mrs. Mallard was then pregnant and expecting to give birth within days.) The first groups of "bummers" reached the Jones-Mallard household on December 15. They searched the house and made off with a number of family keepsakes. During the next two weeks, Union raiding parties—sometimes large detachments, sometimes only a few stragglers—arrived almost daily at the home. Each group searched the premises, insulted the two women, and took what food, supplies, or family items remained to be carted away.

Mary Mallard confided unhappily to her journal on December 17:

> The Yankees made the Negroes bring up the oxen and carts, and took off all the chickens and turkeys they could find. They carried off all the syrup from the smokehouse. We had one small pig, which was all the meat we had left; they took the whole of it. Mother saw everything like food stripped from her premises, without the power of uttering one word. Finally they rolled out the carriage and took that to carry off a load of chickens. They took everything they possibly could.

"Everything" included seven of the Jones family's slaves, who—like hundreds of blacks elsewhere along the army's line of march—were pressed into service as porters, laborers, or mule drivers. "So they were all carried off," Mary Mallard grieved, "carriages, wagons, carts, horses and mules and servants, with food and provisions of every kind—and, so far as they were concerned, leaving us to starvation."

Occasionally an officer would apologize for the behavior of his men. One friendly Union soldier, a Missourian, offered to show Mrs. Jones where to hide her things. Mary Mallard noted: "He said he had enlisted to fight for the *Constitution;* but since then the war had been turned into another thing, and he did not approve this abolitionism, for his wife's people all owned slaves." A few days later, a Virginian told Mrs. Jones that "there was great dissatisfaction in the army on account of the present object of the war, which now was to free the Negroes."

More often than not, however, the raiders stalked through the houses indifferent to its inhabitants. Never knowing whether soldiers coming to the door would behave politely or insolently, the two women lived in constant fear. Several times, "bummers" threatened to return and burn down their house. Yet on other occasions, Union commanders offered them protection and safe-conduct passes to Savannah, which was still in Confederate hands. The women declined to leave, partly because of Mary Mallard's pregnancy. On January 4, 1865, she gave birth to a daughter. Her mother noted in her journal:

> During these hours of agony the yard was filled with Yankees. They were all around the house; my poor child, calm and collected amid her agony of body, could hear their conversation and wild halloos and cursing beneath her windows. After a while they left, screaming and yelling in a most fiendish way as they rode from the house.

Mary Jones' journal makes it clear that Sherman had achieved his major purpose in marching through Georgia—to demoralize beyond repair what remained of the Deep South's fighting spirit. She wrote in January 1865:

> As I stand and look at the desolating changes wrought by the hand of an inhuman foe in a few days, I can enter into the feelings of Job. All our pleasant things are laid low. We are prisoners in our own home. To obtain a mouthful of food we have been obliged to cook in what was formerly our drawing room; and I have to rise every morning by candlelight, before the dawn of day, that we may have it before the enemy arrives to take it from us. . . For one month our homes and all we possess have been given up to lawless pillage. Officers and men have alike engaged in this work of degradation. I scarcely know how we have stood up under it. God alone has enabled us to "speak with the enemy in the gates," and

A Confederate soldier returns to find his home a shambles in the midst of a devastated land. The artist who drew this scene was A. J. Volck, a German-born dentist who lived in Baltimore. He was the best-known satirist to interpret the Civil War from the Southern point of view.

calmly, without a tear, to see my house broken open, entered with false keys, threatened to be burned to ashes, refused food and ordered to be starved to death, told that I had no right even to wood or water, that I should be "humbled in the very dust I walked upon," a pistol and carbine presented to my breast, cursed and reviled as a rebel, a hypocrite, a devil.

Troubling Mrs. Jones almost as much as the behavior of Sherman's soldiers was the reaction of her slaves. During the first days of Union occupation, most of them stayed on the plantation, perhaps out of fear, perhaps out of loyalty. But when it became clear that the Northern army firmly controlled the area, a number of slaves left to join the Union columns marching on Savannah. "Many servants have proven faithful," Mrs. Jones wrote in January 1865, "others false and rebellious against all authority or restraint."

Sherman himself pursued an ambiguous policy toward the ex-slaves, who were known as "contraband." He did not want them as soldiers, despite the good record of black regiments in battle when they were allowed to fight. He rejected the suggestion of General Ulysses S. Grant (by now in charge of all Union forces) that blacks be armed. He felt that his troops would object. And he had another reason. "My aim then," he later wrote, "was to whip the rebels, to humble their pride and make them fear and dread us. I did not want them to cast in our teeth that we had to call on *their* slaves to help us to subdue them."

Nevertheless, Sherman did order the formation of black "pioneer battalions"—construction units—for each army corps. "Negroes who are able-bodied and can be of service to the several columns may be taken along," Sherman instructed, "but each army commander will bear in mind that the question of supplies is a very important one, and that his first duty is to see to those who bear arms." In other words, the army was to keep blacks at a distance, using labor as needed but refraining from becoming a relief organization for ex-slaves who had left their plantations.

Sherman's prejudice against blacks was a crucial factor in his military policy. His brother John was an important antislavery Republican politican from Ohio, but William did not share his views. When still in Louisiana, he had assured Southerners that slavery was best for blacks. "All the congresses on earth," he said, "can't make the Negro anything else than what he is"—namely a slave, or a second-class noncitizen. In a letter he stated:

> I would not if I could abolish or modify slavery. I don't know that I would materially change the actual political relation of master and slave. Negroes in the great numbers that exist here must of necessity be slaves. Theoretical notions of

is the title given this draw-
ing by Northern artist Alfred
R. Waud, who reported the
war for an illustrated journal.
At the beginning of the war,
Union policy toward fugitive
blacks was so uncertain that
many runaways were re-
turned to their former masters.

Negroes leaving the plough

humanity and religion cannot shake the commercial fact that their labor is of great value and cannot be dispensed with.

Whatever Sherman's own attitudes, it was clear that, from the moment his troops left Atlanta, they sparked the imagination of Georgia's slaves. As Sherman rode through the town of Covington, a day's march from Atlanta, he found that "the Negroes were simply frantic with joy." He later recalled that "Whenever they heard my name, they clustered about my horse, shouted and prayed in their peculiar style, which had a natural eloquence that would have moved a stone."

During the following weeks, as Northern troops foraged their way across Georgia, Sherman witnessed "hundreds, if not thousands, of such scenes." He wrote later that he could still see "a poor girl, in the very ecstasy of the Methodist 'shout,' hugging the banner of one of the regiments."

Thousands of slaves did more than simply greet the liberating Northern army. They joined it, striding alongside or in back of the troop columns. Wrote Mary Jones: "Negroes in large numbers are flocking to them. Nearly all the house servants have left their homes; and from most of the plantations they have gone in a body." The ranks of contraband included strong young men and women in the prime of life, mothers carrying children, and the white-haired elderly.

More than 30,000 blacks joined Sherman's army at one time or another during its four-week march. Yet only 10,000 remained with its ranks as it entered Savannah. Many were actively discouraged from remaining with the soldiers. Neither Sherman nor most of his officers and men wished to add the task of foraging to feed a huge contraband population from the food collected each day.

Sherman later remembered personally telling an old black man at one plantation that

> we wanted the slaves to remain where they were, and not to load us down with useless mouths. We could receive a few of their young, hearty men as pioneers. But if they followed us in swarms of old and young, feeble and helpless, it would simply load us down and cripple us in our great task. I believe that old man spread this message to the slaves, which was carried from mouth to mouth, to the

Black people followed Sherman's army on foot, on horseback, and in any kind of wheeled conveyance that could be found. No one in authority was well prepared to deal with the contraband situation, and many former slaves lacked adequate shelter, food, and clothing.

very end of our journey, and that it in part saved us from the great danger we incurred of swelling our numbers so that famine would have attended our progress.

In any case, the thousands of slaves who remained with Sherman's forces did not all passively trudge along waiting to be fed and taken care of. Many played active roles. They carried supplies as porters and mule drivers. Some searched out food, animals, and equipment hidden by Confederates along the way. Others built roads or repaired bridges so that Sherman's men, equipment, and supply wagons could keep to their ten-mile-a-day pace across the swampy waterways of central Georgia. Still others helped the soldiers to destroy railroads and other strategic targets. (A favorite trick was to heat the heavy iron rails and twist them into "Sherman's neckties.")

Local blacks also served as reliable guides behind Confederate lines. One of Sherman's officers, General Oliver O. Howard, ordered one of his men to reach the Union fleet anchored off Savannah. After safely rowing a canoe past enemy posts along the Ogeechee River, the officer and his patrol

> found some Negroes, who befriended him and his men and kept pretty well under cover until evening. Then they went ashore to get a Negro guide and some provisions [after which they passed through Confederate lines]. Soon after this they came to quite a sizable Negro house, went in, and were well treated and refreshed with provisions. When they were eating they were startled by hearing a party of Confederate cavalry riding toward the house. Of course they expected to be instantly captured, but the Negroes, coming quickly to their rescue, concealed them under the floor. The coolness and smartness of the Negroes surprised even Captain Duncan, though he had believed and trusted them. The cavalry stopped but remained only a short time, and the Negroes guided our men back to their boats.

Although few blacks served the Union side so daringly during Sherman's march, the general himself acknowledged that the "large number employed as servants, teamsters and pioneers rendered admirable service."

Sherman's army marched into Savannah on December 21, along with the 10,000 black contraband. The general sent a playful telegram to "His Excellency," President Lincoln: "I beg to present you as a Christmas gift the city of Savannah, with one hundred and fifty heavy guns and plenty of ammunition, also about twenty-five thousand bales of cotton."

The message was quickly published throughout the North. Northerners had considered Sherman's army "lost" when the general had broken communication after leaving Atlanta. Sherman and his men instantly became popular heroes. "Our joy was irrepressible," said one high Washington official, "not only because of their safety, but because it was an assurance that the days of the Confederacy were numbered." Even to many Southerners, Savannah's capture seemed to foreshadow final defeat. Given the suffering Confederate soldiers and civilians had undergone by then, the prospect seemed almost welcome.

Sherman did not order the city's residents to leave, as he had done at Atlanta. With Union ships in the harbor and his troops in control of the surrounding countryside, he felt no useful military purpose would be served by evacuating or burning the city. In fact, Sherman decided to govern Savannah's 20,000 inhabitants mildly—much to their amazement and that of other Georgians. He gave people the choice of remaining or leaving for other cities still under Confederate control.

Sherman placed one of his generals in overall command of Savannah, but the Confederate mayor and city council handled most day-to-day matters. Relations between Northerners and Southerners were polite, almost cordial. Only a few hundred citizens left the city. Most people calmly went about their business. Relief ships organized by private citizens in the North arrived regularly in January 1865, bringing much-needed food and clothing. Supplies were distributed to freed blacks and needy whites. Local markets selling meat, wood, and other necessities reopened under military supervision.

*N*o city was ever occupied with less disorder or more system than Savannah," Sherman wrote on December 31. "Though an army of 60,000 men lay camped around it, women and children of an hostile people walk its streets with as much security as they do in Philadelphia." Confederate newspapers raged about the alleged "barbarities" of Sherman's forces on their march from Atlanta, exaggerating the amount of property burned, and the numbers murdered or raped. Meantime the "barbarians" occupied Savannah with little friction.

In Savannah, as on the march from Atlanta, Sherman became a hero to the liberated blacks. He wrote to his wife on Christmas Day: "They flock to me, young and old. They pray and shout and mix up my name with that of Moses and Simon and other scriptural ones as well as 'Abram Linkom.'" Hundreds of blacks hurried to see the general, wrote an aide. "There was a constant stream of them, old and young, men, women and children, black, yellow, and cream-colored, uncouth and well-bred, bashful and talkative—but always respectful and behaved—all day long."

*I*t would have come as a great shock to the blacks of Savannah to learn that their hero was at that very moment being attacked in the North for his policy toward ex-slaves. Late in December General Henry W. Halleck wrote Sherman to congratulate him on the march through Georgia and his capture of Savannah. He also warned him that powerful individuals close to the President spoke critically of him, alleging that he "manifested an almost *criminal* dislike to the Negro. "They say," added Halleck,

> that you are not willing to carry out the wishes of the government in regard to him, but repulse him with contempt! They say you might have brought with you to Savannah more than fifty thousand, thus stripping Georgia of that number of laborers, and opening a road by which as many more could have escaped from their masters; but that, instead of this, you drove them from your ranks, prevented their following you by cutting the bridges in your rear, and thus caused the massacre of large numbers by Wheeler's cavalry.

Sherman defended his decision to discourage slave runaways from joining the march on the grounds that their presence would have overburdened his army and hindered its military success. In responding to Halleck, however, he acknowledged that his sympathy for freed blacks was limited:

> Thank God I am not running for an office and am not concerned because the rising generation will believe that I burned 500 niggers[1] at one pop in Atlanta, or any such nonsense. The South deserves all she has got for her injustice to the Negro, but that is no reason why we should go to the other extreme.

It was no surprise to Sherman when Secretary of War Edwin M. Stanton arrived in Savannah on January 9, aboard the Union ship *Nevada*. Stanton was supposedly traveling on a vacation cruise and to supervise the disposition of captured Confederate cotton supplies. Actually he came to check on Sherman's handling of matters involving blacks. Stanton strongly supported Sherman's military strategy in Georgia. But he disapproved of the general's rumored hostility toward the ex-slave population, and of his refusal to use blacks as soldiers.

Sherman denied that any of his officers or troops had been hostile to slaves on their march from Atlanta. But Stanton wanted to hear about Sherman's behavior from the blacks themselves. At his request, therefore, Sherman invited "the most intelligent of the Negroes" in Savannah to come to his rooms to meet the Secretary of War. Twenty black men attended the meeting with Sherman and Stanton on January 12, 1865.

[1] This term was considered only mildly discourteous in the 1860s. It was commonly used, even by antislavery Northerners.

Never before had any major American government official met with black leaders to ask what *they* wished for their people. Each man present began by introducing himself with a brief account of his life. The average age was fifty. Fifteen of the men were ministers—mainly Baptist and Methodist—and the other five were church officials of one kind or another. Five of the leaders had been born free. Of the others, three had bought their freedom; most of the rest had been liberated by Sherman's army.

Secretary of War Stanton sat at a table facing the black visitors, making extensive notes on their remarks. Sherman, restless and uneasy over the interview, stood with two of his aides apart from the seated group. He watched the proceedings warily, pacing across the room from time to time during the exchange. The blacks had selected as their spokesman sixty-seven-year-old Garrison Frazier, a Baptist minister. He responded firmly to each of Stanton's questions.

Stanton asked first whether the men were aware of Lincoln's Emancipation Proclamation. Frazier replied that they were.

> STANTON: State what you understand by slavery, and the freedom that was to be given by the President's Proclamation.
>
> FRAZIER: Slavery is receiving by irresistible power the work of another man, and not by his consent. The freedom, as I understand it, promised by the Proclamation, is taking us from under the yoke of bondage, and placing us where we could reap the fruit of our own labor, and take care of ourselves, and assist the Government in maintaining our freedom.

Stanton then asked how black people could best maintain their new freedom. Frazier suggested that young men should be able to enlist in the army, and that other blacks ought to receive land to farm: "We want to be placed on land until we are able to buy it, and make it our own."

The Secretary of War then asked whether the men believed that freed blacks "would rather live scattered among the whites, or in colonies by yourselves?" Frazier answered: "I would prefer to live by ourselves, for there is a prejudice against us in the South that will take years to get over; but I do not know that I can answer for my brethren."

Frazier and his black associates may have considered Stanton's next question offensive. The Secretary asked whether the ex-slaves of the South were intelligent enough to sustain their freedom while maintaining good relations with Southern whites. "I think there is sufficient intelligence among us to do so," Frazier replied simply.

The black minister was then asked what he believed were the causes and object of the Civil War, and whether blacks generally supported either side. He responded shrewdly and at length. Frazier told Stanton that blacks wished only to help the Union subdue the rebellious Confederacy. He acknowledged that the North's first war aim involved bringing the South back into the Union, that Lincoln had issued the Emancipation Proclamation mainly as a means toward achieving this end. Only the South's not freeing the slaves "has now made the freedom of the slaves a part of the war." Frazier noted that the thousands of runaways who followed the Union armies, "leaving their homes and undergoing suffering," spoke clearly for the pro-Union sentiments of blacks.

Stanton then indicated that he wanted to ask a question about Sherman. The general—silently furious—left the room. In Sherman's absence, Stanton inquired about "the feeling of the colored people in regard to General Sherman" and whether Negroes regarded "his sentiments and actions as friendly to their rights and interests." Frazier's answer probably surprised Stanton, considering the rumors current in Washington:

> We looked upon General Sherman, prior to his arrival, as a man in the providence of God, specially set apart to accomplish this work, and we unanimously felt inexpressible gratitude to him. Some of us called upon him immediately upon his arrival [in Savannah], and it is probable he did not meet the Secretary with more courtesy than he met us. His conduct and deportment toward us characterized him as a friend and a gentleman. We have confidence in General Sherman, and think that what concerns us could not be under better hands.

The meeting soon ended, after Stanton thanked his black visitors for their advice.

Stanton and Sherman spent the next three days discussing the problems of policy toward the freedmen. They agreed that Sherman would issue a field order on January 16, the day after Stanton's departure from Savannah.

Special Field Order #15 set aside confiscated or abandoned land along rivers emptying into the Atlantic and on the Sea Islands—nearby islands that lay along the coast from Charleston, South Carolina, to Jacksonville, Florida. These lands were to be used exclusively for settlement by freed blacks. A freedman and his family taking up such land were to be given a "possessory title" to "not more than forty acres of tillable land" until Congress should regulate the title.

Sherman clearly viewed this scheme as a temporary one in order to provide for freedmen and their families in the area during the rest of the war, or until Congress acted. "Mr. Stanton has been here," he confidently wrote his wife on the day of Stanton's departure, "and is cured of that Negro nonsense." By now Sherman was impatient to begin his march northward. He appointed General Rufus Saxton as Inspector of Settlements and Plantations for the entire area covered by his field order. On January 21 Sherman's army left Savannah, marching into South Carolina, the symbol of Confederate resistance.

Saxton energetically arranged to transport homeless blacks in Savannah to coastal farms. He wrote urgent letters to Northern sympathizers asking for food and supplies to help sustain the new agricultural settlements. By midsummer of 1865—with the war now over—Saxton and his aides had managed to settle more than 40,000 black people on lands covered in Sherman's order.

The people faced numerous hardships—neglected soil, old equipment (and little of it), poor seed, and shortages of supplies. But the hard-working freedmen, especially those on the Sea Islands of Georgia and South Carolina, successfully grew crops of cotton and various foodstuffs. They received support not only from Saxton and the military but also from Northern white teachers and missionaries, a number of whom traveled into the area to found schools.

Most of the planning and hard work, however, came from the freedmen themselves. Many started out with little more than the clothes on their backs. One party was led by Ulysses Houston, a minister who had been present at the interview with Stanton. Before leaving for Skidaway Island, he wrote a Northern reporter: "We shall build our cabins, and organize our town government for the maintenance of order and the settlement of all difficulties." The reporter later gave this account:

> He and his fellow-colonists selected their lots, laid out a village, numbered their lots, put the numbers in a hat, and drew them out. It was Plymouth colony repeating itself. They agreed if any others came to join them, they should have equal privileges. So blooms the Mayflower on the South Atlantic coast.

The impressive success of this resettlement led many Northerners to urge that Congress enact a general land distribution policy to help all freedmen. Landless ex-slaves also came to expect that, since 40,000 Deep South blacks had quickly and effectively settled new lands, others too would receive their forty acres in the near future. Such hopes were soon dashed.

Andrew Johnson became President after Lincoln was assassinated in April 1865. Many had believed that Johnson would be sympathetic to a generous land distribution policy once in the White House, since he had been sympathetic to black rights earlier as governor of Tennessee. But a proclamation of his in May 1865 completely shattered this belief. Johnson pardoned all former Confederates except for those whose taxable property exceeded $20,000 and those who had held high military or civil positions. (Even these groups could apply for special presidential pardon.)

For the great majority of white Southerners, Johnson's proclamation not only restored civil and political rights. It also restored their property—except for slaves—even if previously confiscated as a result of

A Northern teacher reads to two of her pupils at a school on St. Helena, one of the Sea Islands off the coast of South Carolina. These former slaves were among those resettled by Sherman's Order #15.

temporary wartime orders such as Sherman's. Not only did the new President say nothing about the freedmen in his proclamation. He clearly intended them to resume their second-class economic status in the South, although no longer as slaves. Johnson made it plain that he intended landowning blacks such as those under Saxton's jurisdiction to surrender their newly acquired lands and return them to their previous owners.

Saxton now administered the freedmen's new settlements in Georgia, South Carolina, and Florida as assistant director of the Freedmen's Bureau. This agency had been recently established by Congress to coordinate federal relief assistance to ex-slaves. Heading the bureau was Sherman's former subordinate, General Oliver O. Howard. He shared President Johnson's wish to conciliate the South. Unlike the President, though, he did not want to do so at the expense of the freedmen.

Both Saxton and Howard tried to resist and delay the restoration of black-occupied lands to their former white owners. They were supported by Stanton, who attempted various maneuvers to stave off the move. But Johnson was determined. Sherman's field order was revoked in June 1865. Saxton even traveled to Washington, but without success.

In September the former landholders of Edisto Island, then under Freedmen's Bureau control, petitioned Johnson for the return of their lands. The President directed Howard to visit the island and convince the freedmen to arrange a "mutually satisfactory solution." The President left little doubt that he wanted the blacks to pack up and leave.

Howard unhappily went to Edisto in late October. Trapped between his duty and his sympathies, he met with freed blacks in a local church. They crowded in, furious at the course of events. They refused to quiet down until a woman began singing the spiritual "Nobody Knows the Trouble I Seen."

The blacks then listened to Howard as he urged them to surrender their farms and return to work for the island's former white landholders. Angry shouts of "no, no" punctuated Howard's talk. One man in the gallery cried out: "Why, General Howard, why do you take away our lands? You take them from us who have always been true, always true to the government! You give them to our all-time enemies! That is not right!"

Howard patiently explained to his audience that their "possessory titles" to the land were not "absolute" or "legal." At his insistence, a committee was formed consisting of three freedmen, three white plant-ers, and three Freedmen's Bureau representatives. It had authority to decide on the island's land ownership. (This practice was also adopted elsewhere on the Sea Islands.)

Howard still hoped to delay restoration of the property until Congress convened late in 1865. But the process of removing blacks from their assigned lands gathered momentum after he left the area to return north.

Saxton was still refusing to dispossess black landholders from the territories under his supervision, so Johnson removed him in January 1866. He was replaced by Davis Tillson, a Freedmen's Bureau official more sympathetic to presidential policy. Tillson issued an order allow-ing white owners to return to their former Sea Island farms and plantations. Tillson went so far as to charter a boat and accompany the first group, explaining personally to the blacks in residence that they would have to surrender their lands.

Blacks who were willing to sign contracts to work for white owners were allowed to remain. Others were driven from the islands either by Union troops or by white vigilante groups that began to terrorize black landholders throughout the Deep South during this period. One sym-pathetic New England schoolteacher later wrote of seeing all the freedmen on one Sea Island plantation leaving their newly acquired land with their hoes over their shoulders. "They told us that the guard had ordered them to leave the plantation if they would not work for the owners. We could only tell them to obey orders. After this many of the Sherman Negroes left the island."

For the moment, Howard's policy of delaying restoration had clearly failed. Yet shortly after Congress met in December 1865, the legislators debated the provisions of a new, postwar Freedman's Bu-reau Bill designed to protect the rights of ex-slaves in peacetime. The final version of that bill was enacted by Congress over the President's veto in July 1866. It allowed freedmen deprived of their land by Johnson's restoration policy to lease twenty acres of government-owned land on the Sea Islands with an option to buy cheaply within six years. By then, however, almost all of the "Sherman Negroes" had lost their lands.

By this time, too, Congress and Johnson were struggling bitterly over control of postwar policy toward the South. The outcome of that struggle would determine the nation's response to its millions of newly liberated blacks. Many of them probably shared the anguish of one Sea Island freedman who grieved shortly after his eviction: "They will make freedom a curse to us, for we have no home, no land, no oath, no vote, and consequently no country."

20

Civil War and Reconstruction

ON FEBRUARY 23, 1861 (at a time when Sherman had just left his post at the Louisiana military academy), Abraham Lincoln slipped secretly into Washington after an all-night train ride. His aides planned the night trip, fearing an assassination attempt at a previously scheduled stop in pro-Confederate Baltimore. On his special train the President-elect tried to sleep. But a drunken passenger kept singing the bouncy Southern melody "Dixie" over and over. Lincoln finally muttered to a companion, "No doubt there will be a great time in Dixie by and by." His concern over the impending showdown with the secessionist South was shared by most Northerners.

A thousand miles to the south the Confederacy's president-elect took a different type of journey to his own inaugural. Lincoln arrived in the nation's capital, according to one diplomat, "like a thief in the night." Jefferson Davis traveled from his Mississippi plantation to Montgomery, Alabama—first capital of the rebellious states—like a conquering hero.

Davis was a moderate Southerner. Like

Abraham Lincoln, wrote George Templeton Strong, was "a most sensible, straightforward, honest old codger; the best President we have had since Jackson's time."

Jefferson Davis suffered from poor health throughout the war. Though he was strong-willed and irritable, his devotion to the South was unquestioned.

others, he had opposed secession until after Lincoln's election. Now this group had taken charge of the South's new national government, replacing many of the zealous fire-eaters who had spread the gospel of disunion during the 1850s. Southern moderates had selected Davis as their president largely because he wanted a peaceful settlement with the North. A West Point graduate, Davis had fought ably in the Mexican War, represented Mississippi in both the House and Senate, and served as President Pierce's Secretary of War.

FIRST STEPS

While Davis pondered his cabinet, the Montgomery convention that had chosen him for president wrote a Confederate constitution. For the most part the document copied provisions of the federal Constitution. It included a bill of rights, and it even prohibited the slave trade. Slavery was pronounced legal throughout the Confederacy, of course. In a significant speech at Savannah, the vice president-elect, Alexander Stephens of Georgia, spoke candidly of the new government: "Its foundations are laid, its cornerstone rests, upon the great truth that the Negro is not equal to the white man; that slavery, subordination to the superior race, is his natural and normal condition."

The new Confederate congress began its work by legalizing for the South all Union laws that did not conflict with its new constitution. For two months after Davis' selection as president, the Confederate government waited for some sign of how Lincoln intended to deal with the secession crisis. Then came Sumter—and war.

A "Brothers' War" When the Civil War began on April 12, 1861, Americans gave it various names. For secessionists it was a "War for Southern Independence" or "the War Between the States." Northerners, on the other hand, considered it "the War of the Rebellion" or simply "the War for the Union." Both sides agreed that, whatever else, it was a "brothers' war," severing links among families, personal friends, and public figures according to their sectional loyalties.

This deeply painful division reached even into Abraham Lincoln's family. A Kentucky officer named Ben Hardin Helm was the husband of Mary Todd Lincoln's sister. He spent several days at the White House talking to old West Point friends. Some of them were already preparing to head south and join the Confederate army. As Helm—still uncertain—concluded his visit, Lincoln gave him an envelope containing a major's commission in the Union army. The two men grasped hands warmly and exchanged good-byes. A few days later came the news that Helm had chosen the Confederacy.

But another Kentuckian, Fort Sumter's Robert Anderson, accepted Lincoln's promotion to brigadier general that same month. He then left for the Middle West to help keep his native state in the Union.

A third officer, a fervent Unionist, turned down Lincoln's offer to be commander of all Northern troops. Instead, he accepted command of the Confederacy's eastern force, the Army of Northern Virginia. "If Virginia stands by the old Union, so will I," Robert E. Lee remarked. "But if she secedes (though I do not believe in secession as a constitutional right, nor that there is sufficient cause for revolution) then I will follow my native state with my sword and, if need be, with my life." When Virginia finally broke with the Union, Lee followed.

In many ways the Confederate struggle for independence resembled the American revolt against British rule two generations earlier. Some revolutionists strive for colonial independence from a ruling country. This occurred in North America in the 1770s. Other revolutions result when one section of a country tries to break away from the whole nation, leading to an internal war between the nation and the section. Such separatist revolts often occur when the people of a particular region feel that their interests and values are directly threatened by those who control the national government. This was the case in the South after Lincoln's election.[1]

Both national uprisings, such as the American Revolution, and separatist revolts, such as the Civil War, usually take place only after great soul-searching among those rebelling. The American people do not shift their loyalties easily. Washington, Franklin, and other Revolutionary leaders had served the British Empire faithfully for decades in war and peace. Lee, Davis, and other key Confederate officials had served the national government before the South seceded. They finally revolted because they believed the Southern way of life—a culture based upon slavery—was directly threatened by Republican control of the central government.

Mobilization In the early months of the Civil War most Americans seemed to expect the conflict to be bloody but brief. Few realized what lay ahead. "No casualties yet, no real mourning, nobody hurt," wrote Mary Boykin Chesnut, the wife of a high Confederate officer, in June 1861. "It is all parade, fuss, and fine feathers."

A few leaders believed the situation was more serious. Among them were Lincoln and his generals and their counterparts behind the Southern lines. Jefferson Davis, wrote Mrs. Chesnut, informed her one evening that "either way, he thinks it will be a long war, that before the end came we would have many a bitter experience. He said only fools doubted the courage of the Yankees, or their willingness to fight when they saw fit."

Nor did most Southerners underestimate the extent of Northern resources. In almost every respect—population, capital, and raw materials—the Union had the advantage over the Confederacy. Most important, the North could produce endless supplies of guns, ammunition, ships, and other war equipment. The South, on the other hand, had increasing difficulty in keeping its soldiers supplied.

---

[1] More recently, separatist revolts took place in Nigeria (where the Ibo province of Biafra revolted unsuccessfully) and in Pakistan (where the Eastern Bengali area, now known as Bangladesh, won its independence).

Neither side began with much of an army, There were only 18,000 men in the regular army in 1860, with about 1,100 officers. Only a small number of these had significant combat experience, and most of them resigned to join the Confederate Army. These officers and their Northern counterparts prepared to fight a conflict far different, in strategy and tactics, from those for which they had been trained.

Both North and South started the war using a system of volunteer enlistments. At first they recruited men for a few months, since both sides believed that the war would be short.

As the fighting dragged on, it became apparent to both sides that volunteers would not provide enough manpower. Even the cash bounties offered to those who enlisted would not bring enough volunteers. Casualties mounted in 1862. First the undermanned Confederacy and then the Union turned to drafting soldiers by lottery. Wealthy or influential young men, North and South, could, and often did, avoid going to war. They could provide a paid substitute, who might cost as much as $600. Or they could claim exemption on grounds that their civilian work was essential. (Slaveholders who grew cotton, for example, could avoid service this way.) By the end of the war the South's troop shortage had become extreme. The Confederacy then began drafting and training thousands of slaves.

Late in May 1861 the Confederate government moved its capital to Richmond. This was done partly because the large Virginia city could accommodate the growing Confederate bureaucracy more easily than Montgomery could. The move also dramatized the Confederacy's promise to defend the Upper South. Besides, Richmond was an important rail and road center. With Northern and Southern capitals and armies now only a hundred miles apart, the area of Virginia and Maryland became, for obvious reasons, the war's pivotal theater of operations.

A thick layer of gloom spread over Washington as Lincoln and his generals prepared for a Southern attack. There was talk that, for the second time in half a century, an American President might be forced to flee the White House, pursued by an invading army.

Southern Strategy Although a number of important battles were fought during the war, the Confederates generally used an overall guerrilla strategy that resembled Washington's in the American Revolution. A friend wrote Jefferson Davis complaining of the Confederacy's "purely defensive" strategy and of its reluctance to launch a full-scale attack on the North. Davis replied: "Without military stores, without the

RESOURCES OF THE UNION AND THE CONFEDERACY, 1861

	UNION	CONFEDERACY
Population	23,000,000	8,700,000*
Real and personal property	$11,000,000,000	$5,370,000,000
Banking capital	$330,000,000	$27,000,000
Capital investment	$850,000,000	$95,000,000
Manufacturing establishments	110,000	18,000
Value of production (annual)	$1,500,000,000	$155,000,000
Industrial workers	1,300,000	110,000
Locomotives	451,000	19,000
Railroad mileage	22,000	9,000

*Including 3,500,000 slaves

Lee was a vigorous fifty-five when the Civil War began. Like Washington, he fought against difficult odds and was much admired by his troops.

workshops to create them, without the power to import them, necessity, not choice, has compelled us to occupy strong positions and everywhere—selecting the time and place of attack—to confront the enemy without reserves." In other words, the South chose to conduct an "offensive defense." It tried to select the time and place for major battles carefully. At other times Southerners harassed Northern armies with cavalry raids led by such intrepid commanders

as "Stonewall" Jackson, J. E. B. Stuart, Nathan B. Forrest, and John S. Mosby.

Confederate army commanders realized that it was impossible to prevent Union invasions of the South. They knew too that they had neither the manpower nor the resources to mount a full-scale invasion of the North. So the Confederates worked instead to maintain their armies in the field while fighting back the Union troops thrown against them. They hoped that a war-weary Northern public would finally force Lincoln's government to negotiate a peaceful settlement. Lee and Davis recognized, as Washington did during the 1770s, that a revolutionary army wins by not losing—that is, by displaying the capacity to endure.

Northern Strategy   Recognizing the Southern strategy, Lincoln and his generals committed Northern armies from the beginning to a policy of total war against the South. They were dedicated to the complete destruction of Confederate military power and civil authority by every necessary means. George Templeton Strong wrote in his diary in November 1861:

> Were I dictator at this time, my military policy would be: (1) to defend and hold Washington, Western Virginia, Kentucky, Missouri; (2) to support Unionists in North Carolina and in eastern Tennessee; (3) to recover and hold (or destroy with sunken ships) every port and inlet from Hatteras to Galveston.

Strong's proposals resembled the North's actual strategy during the war, which was threefold: (1) to encircle the South in an ever-tightening military net by blockading its ports; (2) to divide the Confederacy in half by seizing control of the Mississippi and Tennessee rivers; (3) to capture Richmond and destroy the main Confederate armies in Virginia, where most Southern troops were concentrated. Strong believed, as did Lincoln and his officers, that if "the rebels of the South can be locked up and left to suffer and starve," victory would follow.

Superior to the South in its navy, the North was able to impose a blockade of Southern harbors. The Confederates counteracted with fast blockade-runners, joined by a number of private merchantmen. In the early years of the war they managed to slip past Union vessels in five out of every six attempts. But the Union blockade became increasingly effective. By 1865 it had choked off Southern cotton exports to Europe as well as imports of arms and supplies.

War in the East   The outcome of the Civil War was decided not by naval encounters but by land battles. Northern armies began poorly but improved their performance every year. Confederate forces scored impressive victories at the first and second battles of Bull Run in July 1861 and August 1862. At Fredericksburg, Maryland, in December 1862, the North suffered a crushing defeat, with over 12,000 casualties.

In May 1863, at Chancellorsville, Maryland, outnumbered Southerners won another victory, though it cost them one of their best generals, "Stonewall" Jackson. They imposed a stalemate on the Virginia front and, several times, threatened to capture Washington itself.

Lincoln searched desperately for Union commanders capable of breaking the stalemate and executing major offensive operations. In the process he appointed a succession of commanding generals—George McClellan, John Pope, McClellan again, Ambrose Burnside, Joseph Hooker, and George Meade. One time, after McClellan had failed to pursue a retreating Confederate force, he received this letter: "My dear McClellan: If you don't want to use the Army of the Potomac, I should like to borrow it for a while. Yours respectfully, A. Lincoln."

The turning point of the Civil War in the east came in July 1863. Confederate troops under Lee marched into southern Pennsylvania, where they encountered a Union force near Gettysburg. After three days of costly fighting, Lee's invasion was repulsed decisively on July 3.

Each side had over 75,000 troops involved, and the South suffered almost 25,000 casualties. "The results of this victory are priceless," rejoiced the normally pessimistic Strong. "Philadelphia, Baltimore, and Washington are safe.

Grubby-looking but brilliant, Grant was modest and reticent about his feelings. Of him Lincoln said: "I can't spare this man—he fights."

The rebels are hunted out of the North, their best army is routed, and the charm of Robert Lee's invincibility broken."

War in the West   The South's strategy of tying down and wearing out Union forces worked reasonably well in the east. Elsewhere, however, better-equipped and better-led Union troops won a series of important victories.

In February 1862 federal troops and a

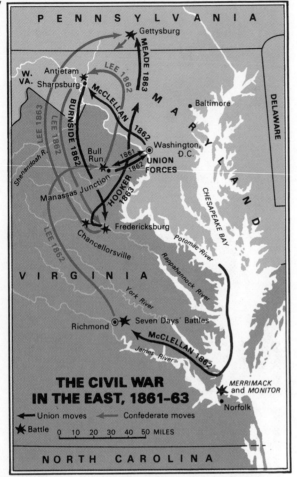

THE CIVIL WAR IN THE EAST, 1861-63

← Union moves   ← Confederate moves

★ Battle   0 10 20 30 40 50 MILES

Fighting broke out on April 12, **1861**, when Confederate batteries opened fire on Fort Sumter in Charleston harbor. The Union quickly began a naval blockade of Confederate shipping. The first major engagement occurred on July 21, at Manassas Junction, Virginia. There an advancing Union army under Irvin McDowell was defeated in the first Battle of Bull Run and driven back to Washington, D.C.

The year **1862** witnessed the first naval battle between ironclads—the Union ship *Monitor* and the Confederate ship *Virginia* (formerly the *Merrimack*)—on March 9 near Norfolk, Virginia. The Union offensives of that year began in March with McClellan's Peninsula Campaign, an attempt to take Richmond from the southeast. He advanced slowly to within a few miles of the city. Confederate forces inflicted heavy casualties on his troops at the end of May. During the subsequent Seven Days' Battles (June 26-July 2) Lee and Jackson forced McClellan to retreat and abandon the campaign. The Confederate army moved northward to win the second Battle of Bull Run (August 29-30). From there Lee and Jackson advanced into Maryland. Near Sharpsburg, McClellan engaged the Confederates in the Battle of Antietam (September 17). Although militarily the battle was a draw, Lee withdrew to Virginia. McClellan was replaced as Union commander by Burnside, whose overwhelming force was shattered at Fredericksburg (December 13).

In **1863** Hooker took command of the Union army, only to be defeated at Chancellorsville (May 2-4). However, Confederate losses there included ''Stonewall'' Jackson. Lee marched into Pennsylvania and was defeated at Gettysburg by a Union army under Meade (July 1-3). Lee retreated to Virginia, his second offensive into Union territory a failure.

gunboat flotilla led by Ulysses S. Grant captured Fort Henry, on the Tennessee River, and Fort Donelson, on the Cumberland River. These moves forced Southern General Albert S. Johnston to abandon Kentucky and parts of Tennessee to the Union.

Admiral Farragut's capture of New Orleans in April 1862 and a series of Northern victories farther up the Mississippi—capped by defeat of the Confederate fleet at Memphis in June—brought most of the river under Union control. Arkansas, Louisiana, and Texas were thus isolated from the rest of the Confederacy.

In the west the decisive point was reached the day after Lee's defeat at Gettysburg. On July 4, 1863, Vicksburg fell. This key Confederate port surrendered after a six-week siege by Union troops. A final Confederate stronghold on the Mississippi—Port Hudson, Louisiana—fell later that same month.

Grant's remarkable success in this western campaign led to his appointment as Lincoln's seventh and last commanding general. Grant appealed to Lincoln for many of the same reasons he did to most Northerners. Wrote one admirer of Grant: "He talks like an earnest businessman, prompt, clearheaded, and decisive, and utters no bosh."

Final Campaigns   Grant took command of the Union forces in the spring of 1864. In May he and Meade led a Northern force of 100,000 men against Lee's army, which had regrouped in Virginia after its Gettysburg defeat the previous year. It was in the same month that Union troops led by Sherman began their push to Atlanta.

For the remainder of the war Grant and

Meanwhile, in the west, the Union won a series of important victories in **1862.** In February Grant captured Fort Henry on the Tennessee River and Fort Donelson on the Cumberland. Moving southward in Tennessee, he was attacked at Shiloh (April 6-7), but Union reinforcements forced the Confederates to withdraw into Mississippi. Union forces also made progress in their drive to gain control of the Mississippi River. Farragut bombarded and captured New Orleans in late April and proceeded up the river to Baton Rouge. To the north, a combined naval and land expedition defeated the Confederate fleet at Memphis on June 6 and captured the city.

In **1863** the Union continued its campaign to secure mastery of the Mississippi. Grant began attacking the Confederate stronghold of Vicksburg in May, and the city surrendered on July 4. With the fall of Port Hudson on July 9, the entire Mississippi was in Union hands and the Confederacy split in two.

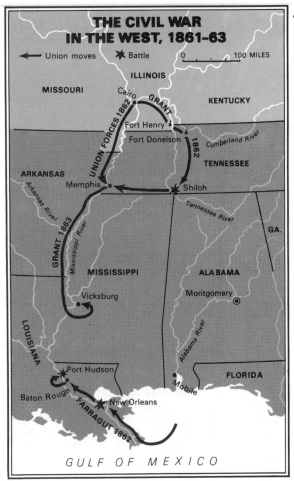

Sherman pursued the same strategy of wearing down the enemy that Davis and Lee had hoped earlier would win for the Confederacy. No longer did Union forces concentrate on capturing Richmond or other Southern territory for its own sake. Instead, Union forces struck directly at the remaining Confederate armies and resources, as Sherman did in Georgia. They aimed to inflict so heavy a price in casualties and physical devastation that a war-weary South would be forced to surrender.

Beginning in June 1864, Grant's army tied down most of Lee's forces near Petersburg, Virginia. That fall Sherman led his famous march to the sea from Atlanta to Savannah. From Savannah, Sherman's forces turned north and extended their scorched-earch tactics into South Carolina and North Carolina.

Grant's troops, meanwhile, left their Petersburg trenches for frequent assaults on Lee's thinly manned lines. By early April 1865 Grant had blocked Lee's effort to retreat southward. Lee's army had then been reduced by death and desertions from 54,000 to 30,000 men. Lee believed that further fighting was useless and that Confederate defeat was inevitable. He surrendered to Grant at Appomattox, Virginia, on April 9, 1865.

Despite pleas from Jefferson Davis for continued resistance, even if only by guerrilla bands in the Southern hills and forests, the rest of the Confederate armies still in the field surrendered

by the end of May. Union troops finally occupied Richmond after Davis and other Confederate officials had fled. For all practical purposes Southern resistance had ended by the time Jefferson Davis was captured on May 10.

LIFE ON THE HOME FRONTS

In the long run it would have been far cheaper to have purchased the abolition of slavery, although such a course was unthinkable to both sides in 1861. Estimates of the war's total cost ran as high as $3 billion for the South and $5 billion for the North. This was three to four times the total estimated value of every slave in the Con-

(continued on page 415)

Many a Civil War battle exacted enormous tolls in men. Above, Confederate dead lie in a shallow trench at Chancellorsville. Union forces, below, attack on the third day of the combat at Gettysburg. Watching a similarly dramatic panorama earlier in the war, Lee had remarked: "It is well that war is so terrible—we would grow too fond of it."

The major military actions of the fall of **1863** occurred in the west. On September 9 Union forces maneuvered the Confederates out of Chattanooga, Tennessee, without a battle. Moving south into Georgia, the Union army was stopped at Chickamauga (September 19-20) and driven back into Chattanooga. In October Grant was given command of all the Union's western armies. At the Battle of Chattanooga (November 23-25) he defeated the Confederates in engagements on Lookout Mountain and Missionary Ridge.

In **1864** Grant, now in supreme command of the Union armies, took charge of the Virginia front. He began a campaign to destroy Lee's army and take Richmond. Grant struck again and again: at the Battle of the Wilderness (May 5-6), at Spotsylvania (May 8-12), and at Cold Harbor (June 1-3). Lee parried Grant's blows, inflicting heavy casualties on his opponent. In this one-month period the Union army lost approximately 60,000 men, a number equal to Lee's total strength at the beginning of the campaign. But the North could provide reinforcements of men and supplies; the South lacked reserves of both. Grant pressed on, moving south to Petersburg. He failed to capture it in a bloody four-day battle (June 15-18). However, his subsequent nine-month seige of the town cut Richmond off from the Deep South.

In the west, Union forces under Sherman moved out of Chattanooga in May 1864 to begin their invasion of Georgia. The opposing Confederate general, Joseph E. Johnston, fought a series of defensive actions but continued falling back toward Atlanta. John B. Hood, who replaced Johnston in July, suffered heavy losses in two pitched battles near Atlanta. It was occupied by Union forces on September 2. After the fall of Atlanta, Hood moved northwest to threaten Tennessee and the Union army's long lines of communication. Sherman sent part of his army to counter Hood's forces. He led the rest of his troops in a virtually unopposed march to the sea from Atlanta to Savannah, which fell on December 22. Meanwhile, Union forces shattered Hood's army at Nashville, Tennessee (December 15–16).

In **1865** Sherman continued his scorched-earth policy as he moved north from Savannah into North Carolina, where Johnston, restored to command, slowed his advance somewhat. In Virginia the Confederates, outnumbered more than two to one by Grant's reinforced army, were unable to lift the siege of Petersburg. On April 1, Lee's last attack (at Five Forks) was repulsed, and on April 2 he evacuated Petersburg and Richmond, moving westward. A Union army under Philip H. Sheridan, which had marched south through the Shenandoah Valley, blocked his path. Virtually surrounded by an overwhelming force, Lee surrendered to Grant at Appomattox on April 9. On April 18, Johnston surrendered to Sherman at Durham Station, North Carolina. Final Confederate capitulations occurred in Alabama (May 4) and Louisiana (May 26).

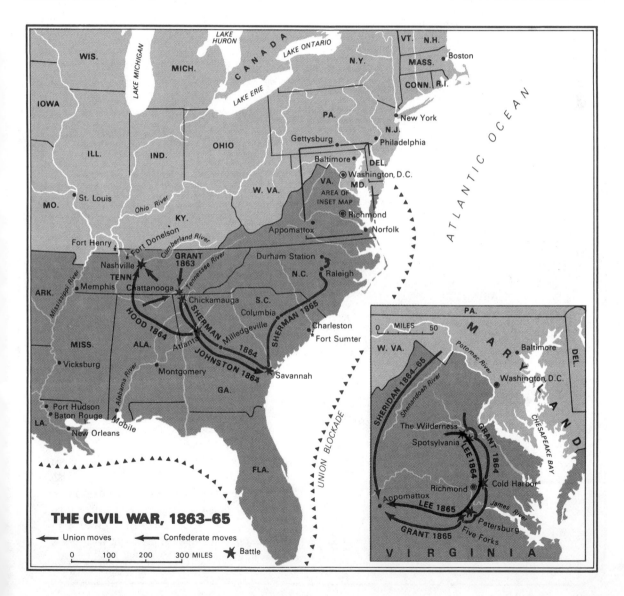

THE CIVIL WAR, 1863–65

← Union moves   ← Confederate moves

0   100   200   300 MILES   ★ Battle

The First Modern War

"The Civil War was the first of the world's really modern wars," wrote the historian Bruce Catton. The weapons of this conflict were forerunners of today's standard military equipment. And the ways in which they were used foreshadowed modern techniques of warfare.

The basic weapon for the infantry, both Union and Confederate, was the single-shot, rifled musket. Because of its rifled (grooved) barrel, it had a range and accuracy two to three times greater than earlier, smoothbore guns. Troops could now engage in deadly fire from distances of a quarter to a half mile. Trench warfare came into being as close-range or hand-to-hand combat was no longer inevitable.

What did this mean for military tactics? The old-time massive assaults, with soldiers elbow to elbow rushing forward toward the enemy, became an invitation to slaughter. (Yet generals on both sides continued to demand this classic maneuver in spite of heavy human losses.) The increased firepower of the infantry threatened both artillery and cavalry. A bank of cannon could no longer offer a solid defense when outranged by enemy riflemen. And the dash of a cavalry charge became mere vainglory when riders could easily be picked off, one by one, from afar.

Breechloading rifles, improvements on the cumbersome muzzle-loaders, and repeating rifles were introduced during the war. Other innovations included rifled cannon and a form of machine gun. The Civil War marked the beginning of a new era in naval warfare, symbolized by the first battle between ironclad ships, the *Monitor* and the *Merimack*. Other experiments in naval warfare included submarines—most were failures—and electrically controlled mines.

Transportation was modernized, with railroads used widely to move troops and supplies. The telegraph changed wartime communications. Union armies sent an estimated 6 million telegrams over 15,000 miles of wire set up by the Signal Corps. The most spectacular railroad supply system was that maintained for Sherman during his siege of Atlanta: 1,600 tons of supplies arrived daily in 16 trains from Union depots northwest of the city.

The Civil War was a modern war in the important sense that it required a break with traditional military thinking in order to achieve victory. Most Civil War generals on both sides regarded cities and territories—not enemy armies—as their objectives. They hoped to win by maneuvering rather than by fighting. By contrast, Lincoln's overall strategy was to move on all fronts simultaneously in order to crush the enemy's forces and gain control of his resources. This warfare of annihilation was a plan that tradition-bound generals scorned. Only in Grant and Sherman did Lincoln find generals who would employ his strategy successfully. They were willing to break the rules to play, and win, a new and deadly game.

Civil War mortar

federacy. Both the Union and the Confederacy had great difficulty in paying their enormous bills for war equipment, soldiers' salaries, and operating expenses. Both sides resorted to many similar financial measures: raising taxes, issuing various types of bonds, and printing vast quantities of paper money unsupported by gold or silver reserves.

Crisis in the South The overriding desire for victory led to sweeping measures in the South. Some affected the master-slave relationship. Southern slaveholders had defended their right to absolute control over their bondsmen in antebellum days. When war came, they watched helplessly as the Confederate government and Southern state governments transferred hundreds of thousands of slaves from private plantations to more urgent labor in the war effort. Slaves even became Confederate soldiers shortly before Appomattox. And throughout the war Southerners relaxed their close supervision of slave movements and activities.

Normal political life also came to a halt in the South during the war. There was no two-party system (as in the North). There was only one all-inclusive ruling, but unruly, "government party." Within the Confederacy there were people who opposed Davis' conduct of the war. They spoke their minds freely. Yet the demands of fighting a separatist revolt prevented any change in government.

The war not only changed master-slave relations and Southern politics. It also altered the Southern economy. The cherished doctrine of states' rights received rough treatment at the hands of Confederate leaders. These men were determined to assume every power they needed to wage war. Davis centralized and nationalized the economy to a remarkable degree. If occasion demanded, he interfered freely with the rights of capitalists. The Confederacy did more than seize slaves for war work. It closely regulated foreign commerce. It confiscated food and equipment from private farms for the army. It created government-run industries to produce military

CIVIL WAR MANPOWER

	UNION	CONFEDERACY
Total serving in armed forces	1,556,678	1,082,119
Killed in battle or died from wounds	110,070	94,000
Died from illness	249,458	164,000
Wounded	275,175	100,000

equipment. And it tightly controlled what was left of private enterprise.

The Confederacy even created a Cotton Bureau, which took over planters' cotton supplies. The Cotton Bureau paid a set price for the entire crop. By running the Northern blockade, the government acted as the sole Southern salesman in Europe. Government supplies of cotton were used as security for the Confederacy's foreign loans.

In spite of truly heroic effort and sacrifice the South was destitute by the end of the war. "We have no money, even for taxes, or for their confiscation," wrote Mary Chesnut in April 1865. "Our poverty is made a matter of laughing." Millions came close to starving. Confederate officials recommended the nutritional values of such fare as squirrels and rats to make up for the dire shortage of food. At the time of its surrender Lee's army had enough ammunition to provide each man seventy-five rounds—but no food.

Southern economic devastation by 1865 could be measured in many ways. Compared to 1860, there were 32 percent fewer horses, 30 percent fewer mules, 35 percent fewer cattle, and 42 percent fewer pigs. Cotton crops were destroyed or rotted unpicked in the fields. Few factories remained in operation. There was almost no trade. Only a handful of banks were left, and they were nearly empty.

Prosperity in the North "We hear they have all grown rich," Mrs. Chesnut complained about Northerners in 1865. "Genuine Yankees can

Richmond in April 1865. Only the shells of burned buildings surround the canal basin. Lee prepared to abandon the city on April 2, and mobs of its inhabitants set fire to the town on the eve of his evacuation.

make a fortune trading jackknives!'' Industrial growth in the North began before the Civil War, of course. But it was vastly accelerated by wartime demands to equip and supply the army. The number of Northern factories increased from fewer than 140,000 in 1860 to over 250,000 by 1870. Railroad mileage doubled during this decade. The growth was aided not only by government contracts for arms and military supplies. It was helped also by wartime currency inflation, huge federal subsidies to railroads, and protective tariffs for industry.

The result was enormous inflation—high prices but also tremendous profits. There was rapid expansion in industries ranging from wool production to mining, from petroleum to iron manufacturing. Farmers prospered, too, because of the increased demand for every staple crop. Most merchants and shippers shared in the boom. Banking facilities were enlarged greatly after Congress passed several new banking acts. Senator John Sherman wrote his brother General William Sherman about the impact of the war on Northern capitalists: ''They talk as confidently of millions as they formerly did of thousands.'' Aristocratic George Templeton Strong complained wistfully that the more sedate prewar culture of New York City was being ''diluted and swamped by a great flood-tide of material wealth.''

A shortage of manpower on Northern farms and in factories stimulated immigration from Europe. In 1865 alone, 180,000 new immigrants arrived on Union soil. In 1866 and 1867 the number spurted to 300,000 yearly.

Perhaps most important in the North, as in the Confederacy, was the role played by the government in stimulating economic growth. Southern Democrats had dominated Congress and the executive branch until the 1850s. They blocked measures such as the protective tariff, a national banking system, and railroad subsidies. Now the Republicans were in control. They favored industrialization and economic growth. To further their aims, they adopted the Morrill Tariff of 1861, which raised duties. They passed the National Banking Acts of 1863 and 1864; these aided national banks at the expense of state banks. In addition, Congress awarded land-grant subsidies to transcontinental railroads and stimulated western settlement with the 1862 Homestead Act, which offered land to settlers at nominal sums.

The Republicans changed not only the economic habits of the North but its political life as well. Lincoln found it no easier than Davis did to

Walt Whitman

At the outbreak of the Civil War Walt Whitman was forty-two years old. Bearded and graying, he worked off and on as a journalist in Brooklyn. Although his book of poems *Leaves of Grass* brought him little prestige and no income, he continued to revise it, writing poems whenever he could. In December 1862 he visited his wounded brother, a Union soldier in Virginia. He realized that he had to become part of the war effort. With a part-time government job in Washington, D.C., for support, he spent nearly all of the next three years serving the wounded in hospitals around the city and sometimes on the battlefields.

He described his role thus: "I have learnt a good deal of hospital wisdom. I adapt myself to each emergency, however trivial, however solemn—not only visits and cheering talk and little gifts—not only washing and dressing wounds but prayer at the bedside, etc." He entertained the veterans, both Union and Confederate, with recitations of poetry. He also led groups in "an amusing game called twenty questions."

For Whitman the essence of the war could be felt only "in the midst of its saddest results." His compassion for its victims was heightened by his own inner struggles. His optimistic views about mankind and democracy conflicted with the horror he felt toward the organized "butchery" of warfare. Not until the war ended did he resolve his own conflict. He accepted both war and peace, both evil and good, as parts of a divine plan.

In 1865 Whitman published *Drum Taps*, the poems he had written during the war. Some poems are martial outbursts—"Prelude," which describes the mobilization of the army in Manhattan, or "Beat! Beat! Drums! Blow! Bugles! Blow!" which lives up to its title. Others are quieter. They describe the cavalry crossing a ford, a bivouac, a field hospital, his own lonely vigils with the dying and the dead. In "A Sight in Camp in the Day-break Grey and Dim," the poet lifts the shrouds of an old man, a youth, and a third figure. The last has a face "calm, as of beautiful yellow-white ivory":

> Young man, I think I know you—
> I think this face of yours is the
> face of Christ himself;
> Dead and divine, and brother of all,
> and here again he lies.

Drum Taps was being printed when the news of Lincoln's assassination reached Whitman. He was inspired to write the dirge that many critics consider his masterpiece. The poem stresses that peace and beauty triumph in death, for death brings a joining of man and nature. It begins:

> When lilacs last in the door-yard bloom'd,
> And the great star early droop'd
>   in the western sky in the night,
> I mourn'd—and yet shall mourn
>   with ever-returning spring.
> O ever-returning spring!
>   trinity sure to me you bring;
> Lilac blooming perennial,
>   and drooping star in the west,
> And thought of him I love.

govern a country at war. Throughout the conflict the President was attacked from all sides of his wartime government coalition, which was known as the Union party. Abolitionist Republicans (known as Radical Republicans) denounced him for moving slowly on the question of emancipation, while War Democrats denounced him for moving at all on the problem. Moderate Republicans criticized the slow military progress of Northern armies.

Compared to the Confederacy, the North had a poor wartime record in the field of civil rights. In spite of Union victories, many Northerners opposed the war. Lincoln authorized a number of arbitrary military arrests of such civilians, especially Peace Democrats—called "Copperheads" by their enemies. He suspended the privilege of habeas corpus[2] to keep pro-Confederate Northerners in jail once arrested.

In both sections, North and South, the war interfered with civil liberties, but in different ways. Northerners were more likely to be thrown in jail for opposing the war. Southerners were more likely to be punished for resisting government confiscation of their property. These interferences involved of course the civil rights of *white* people. Neither government troubled itself much about the rights of blacks, free or slave.

FREEDOM FOR BLACK PEOPLE

As soon as the war broke out, Northern black men tried to enlist in the Union army. They were not allowed to do so, however, until the fall of 1862. Eventually, over 186,000 blacks served as Union soldiers—almost 15 percent of all Northern troops. They were usually led by white officers, and they were paid less than white troops. Union commanders were divided in their attitudes toward using black soldiers. Some welcomed them. Others, like Sherman, did not.

---

[2] This privilege, guaranteed by the Constitution, provides that an arrested person can demand that legal authorities show why he or she has been imprisoned. A writ of habeas corpus (Latin words meaning "you have the body") thus protects a person against being held in jail without cause.

The Emancipation Proclamation   Northern policy toward slavery changed during the war. Many Republicans in the government believed sincerely in emancipation. Lincoln, though, had always regarded it as secondary compared to the overriding importance of winning the war and reuniting the nation.

Like most Americans at the time, Lincoln believed that blacks were inferior. He never felt certain that 4 million ex-slaves could reach full equality with whites in the United States. Throughout the Civil War he tried unsuccessfully to link his moves toward emancipation with efforts to colonize freed blacks. None of these efforts worked out.

Lincoln had been elected on a platform that pledged to restrict slavery but not abolish it. He moved cautiously toward emancipation mainly because of his military and political problems in conducting the war. Radical Republicans in Congress kept pressuring him for swift abolition. Even many moderate Northerners became fervent converts to emancipation as war casualties mounted, if only to punish the Confederacy. Such Unionists did not change their attitudes toward *black people* (and their supposed inferiority). They only changed their minds about *slavery*.

The situation was complicated by the fact that thousands of runaway slaves took refuge with the Union army. There they were often treated—as with Sherman's army—as both a help and a hindrance. Thousands of blacks, however, did join Union army ranks. Lincoln, along with most Northerners, grew more sympathetic to emancipation.

Congress took the first step by abolishing slavery in the federal territories in June 1862. Then, in September 1862, Lincoln issued a preliminary proclamation. In it he stated that he would issue a final document on January 1, 1863, freeing the slaves in all states then in rebellion. This final document was the Emancipation Proclamation.

The Emancipation Proclamation actually freed very few people when it was issued. It did not apply to slaves in border states fighting on the Union side. Nor did it affect slaves in Southern areas already under Union control. Naturally, the states in rebellion did not act on Lincoln's order. But the proclamation did show Americans, and the rest of the world, that the Civil War was now being fought to end slavery.

For all practical purposes the 3 1/2 million black slaves in the South found themselves free within days after Lee's surrender. It was only with final ratification of the Thirteenth Amendment, however, in December 1865, that slavery was ended completely throughout the United States.

Treatment in the North   Though the Union—eventually, at least—fought to free black people, those who lived in the North faced many difficulties. In 1860 free Northern blacks numbered 225,000. Most of them were restricted to menial jobs. A rigid pattern of segregation in schools, hospitals, transportation, and other public facilities kept blacks and whites separated. Roughly 93 percent of Northern black people lived in states where they could not vote. (Only five New England states allowed blacks to cast ballots in 1865.)

Blacks were the victims of race riots throughout the North during the war. The most destructive took place in New York City in the summer of 1863. There, anger among the city's Irish working class at a new federal draft law exploded into violence during four days and nights of rioting. The new law allowed wealthy citizens to avoid the draft by buying the services of substitute soldiers—something poor laborers clearly could not afford.

Mobs of Irish workers rampaged over Manhattan Island from July 13 to July 16. They burned, looted, and killed. The rioters' main targets were free blacks and, to a lesser extent, white abolitionists and wealthy citizens. The city's outnumbered police force, also composed largely of Irishmen, fought the rioters with great bravery and discipline, finally putting down the rioting with the help of federal troops. By that time, some 1,200 persons, mostly black, had been killed. Many thousands were injured. Property

worth millions was damaged or destroyed. Other Northern cities, especially in the Middle West, experienced similar draft riots.

After the War   The Thirteenth Amendment did not settle the basic questions about the future status of black Americans, especially in the postwar South. Former slaves were now free. But free to *do* what? Free to *be* what? What did freedom mean to someone raised in slavery?

Many ex-slaves simply stayed on their plantations, working for the same masters. Their old habits altered little at first, although now the whites were often as poor as their former bondsmen. "The Negroes seem unchanged," Mrs. Chesnut wrote, referring to her one-time slaves. Other former slaves left their old homes, usually for an uncertain future.

Whatever the fate of individual freed slaves, one characteristic of Southern emancipation was its peaceful nature. Despite the fears of antebellum white Southerners, there were no blood

When the war ended, some Union commanders required surrendering forces to take an oath supporting the Constitution. These "Rebs" were sketched at Richmond.

baths, no vengeful attacks by ex-slaves on their former masters. Black people responded to their new freedom with dignity and grace.

Early in the twentieth century Benjamin Botkin and other folklorists traveled through the United States, recording the recollections of aged ex-slaves. One elderly man recalled:

> The end of the war, it come just like that—like you snap your fingers. Soldiers, all of a sudden, was everywhere—coming in bunches. Everyone was a-singing. We was all walking on golden clouds. Hallelujah! Everybody went wild! we was free. Just like that, we was free. It didn't seem to make the whites mad, either. They went right on giving us food just the same. Nobody took our homes away, but right off colored folks started on the move. They seemed to want to get closer to freedom, so they'd know what it was— like it was a place or a city.

The experience was exciting yet frightening for blacks, people like those who had joined Sherman's army on its march to Savannah. Many of them had never gone beyond the borders of their own farms. One ex-slave commented to Botkin:

> We knowed freedom was on us, but we didn't know what was to come with it. We thought we was going to be richer than the white folks, 'cause we was stronger and knowed how to work, and the whites didn't, and they didn't have us to work for them any more. But it didn't turn out that way. We soon found out that freedom could make folks proud, but it didn't make 'em rich.

As soon as the war was over, blacks began to organize and work for their own advancement. Historians sometimes overlook the fact that, even in 1860, there were 261,000 free blacks in the South. Tens of thousands of them were literate. These men and women—like the leaders who met with Stanton and Sherman—formed an important black leadership base at the end of the war. Many took part in black conventions held in a number of Southern cities in 1865 and 1866. They petitioned the federal government to assist freedmen by granting them the franchise, protecting their civil rights, and providing land and other economic help.

THE FIRST YEAR OF RECONSTRUCTION

The basic dilemma of Reconstruction for all those who lived through it, black and white, Southerner and Northerner alike, was its revolutionary nature. Like the Civil War itself, the postwar period had no examples on which to model itself, no constitutional provisions by which policy makers might be guided.

Compared with reconstruction periods that have followed more recent civil wars in Russia, Spain, and China, the American experience is notably mild. Confederate leaders were neither shot nor driven into exile. Indeed, many resumed their careers in American politics. Only a few, such as Jefferson Davis, were imprisoned, and these only for a brief period. No Confederate property was confiscated. Nor was there any forced redistribution of wealth imposed on the defeated South by the victorious North.

Lincoln's Approach   In Lincoln's Second Inaugural Address, delivered a month before his death, he called for a generous settlement with the defeated South: "With malice toward none; with charity for all . . . let us strive on to finish the work we are in, to bind up the nation's wounds."

As early as 1862 Lincoln had indicated his desire to restore a defeated Confederacy quickly and without revenge against either its leaders or people. Lincoln suggested a basis for Reconstruction in December 1863. He called for amnesty[3] (except in the case of key leaders) for Southerners who pledged loyalty to the Union. Southern states in which 10 percent of the 1860 electorate took such a loyalty oath and accepted emancipation would be restored immediately to the Union.

Governments in Arkansas, Louisiana, and

---

[3] Amnesty is a form of pardon for offenses against the government—especially to a group of persons.

Tennessee met Lincoln's provisions in 1864. But Congress refused to seat their representatives. The problem was complicated by the fact that Lincoln believed that the executive branch should control Reconstruction, whereas Congress wanted this power for itself. Congressional attitudes were partly a reaction to the vast expansion of presidential authority under Lincoln during the Civil War.

Republicans in Congress were led by Radicals Thaddeus Stevens of Pennsylvania in the House and Charles Sumner of Massachusetts in the Senate. They were afraid that the Democratic party, led by Southern ex-Confederates, would quickly return to national power. So they offered a much tougher Reconstruction plan in a measure known as the Wade-Davis Bill. It provided that a majority of voters in each Southern state take an "ironclad oath" swearing to their *past* as well as to their *future* loyalty. Obviously, if the electorate were composed only of whites, no ex-Confederate state could honestly meet this provision. The bill also required that the Southern states abolish slavery in their constitutions, repudiate the Confederate war debt, and disfranchise Confederate leaders. Congress passed the Wade-Davis Bill on July 4, 1864. Lincoln killed the measure with a pocket veto. Then Congress passed the nonbinding Wade-Davis Manifesto, reasserting the provisions of the earlier bill.

Therefore, by mid-1864, the stage was set for a postwar confrontation between the President and Congress on Reconstruction policy. Was the South to be restored quickly, its new state governments falling into the hands of ex-Confederate whites with a minimum of federal interference? (This is what Lincoln wanted, though he did urge Southern whites to allow at least educated blacks to vote.) Or should the Southern states undergo fundamental political changes before they could rejoin the Union? Should they, for instance, allow blacks to vote and hold office, while disbarring ex-Confederate leaders and perhaps confiscating their land?

Assassination   With the war almost over, Lincoln's thoughts had turned increasingly to the problem of reconstructing the South. After a trip to Richmond early in April 1865, he spent several days working out various programs.

On the night of April 14, Good Friday evening, President and Mrs. Lincoln went to Ford's Theater in Washington to see a popular play, *Our American Cousin*. Shortly after 10 P.M. a half-crazed Southern sympathizer named John Wilkes Booth shot Lincoln as he watched the play. Booth then stabbed another member of the President's party, leaped onto the stage, rushed from the theater, and rode away. (He was shot down on April 26 by Union troops that had pursued him into Virginia.)

The wounded Lincoln was taken from Ford's Theater to a nearby house. There family, friends, and government officials kept an all-night vigil. The President remained unconscious until his death at 7:22 the following morning. "Now he belongs to the ages," said Secretary of War Stanton, one of those at his bedside.

Word of Lincoln's assassination spread quickly via the telegraph. The first reaction to the event, shared by most Northerners and even many Southerners, was one of profound shock: "I am stunned," wrote George Templeton Strong, "as by a fearful personal calamity."

For Lincoln was highly popular in the North at the time of his death, a result of Union military victories beginning in 1863 and culminating in Lee's surrender. During the war itself, Southerners—as one might expect—had little affection for "Uncle Abraham." Many Northerners felt the same way, especially in the early years. One such person was Strong, an aristocrat and avowed snob. He never liked Lincoln's lack of polish and fondness for telling jokes. Yet these very qualities endeared the President to most other Americans. And even Strong, like other Unionists, responded to Lincoln's firm leadership and genuine anguish at the war's increasing toll in human suffering: "It must be referred to the Attorney General," Lincoln once told Strong about a request to pardon a criminal. "But I guess it will be all right, for me and the Attorney General's very chicken-hearted."

By the war's end, most Northerners prob-

Johnson was an honest but tactless man forced to cope with uniquely difficult circumstances. Born poor, he was a self-made man and touchy about it. Jefferson Davis said he had "the pride of having no pride."

ably agreed with Strong's high estimate of Lincoln's wartime achievement. The President's "weaknesses are on the surface," Strong wrote on April 11, 1865. "His name will be of high account fifty years hence, and for many generations thereafter."

Johnson's Plan Lincoln's death placed the burden of reconstructing the South on the shoulders of his former Vice President, Andrew Johnson. Johnson was a War Democrat from Tennessee and a one-time Radical on the Reconstruction issue. Once in the White House, however, he soon adopted Lincoln's basic proposals. Unfortunately, Johnson completely lacked Lincoln's basic sympathy for the problems of freed blacks. Also, he was a dogmatic man. He showed almost none of Lincoln's tact in dealing with political opponents.

Johnson, like Lincoln, believed that Reconstruction was a matter to be handled by the President. His position was strengthened by the fact that Congress was not in session for several months after he took office. Johnson readmitted the states of Arkansas, Louisiana, and Tennessee. In May 1865 he issued his own Reconstruction plan. It provided that whites in each Southern state who pledged their future loyalty to the Union could elect delegates to a state convention. This convention had to revoke the ordinance of secession, abolish slavery, and repudiate the Confederate war debt. Then the state would be restored to the Union. Johnson granted amnesty to almost all Confederates who took the oath of allegiance. The exceptions were wealthy people and high officials. Even they could apply for a presidential pardon. By late 1865 all the Southern states except Texas had complied with these provisions. (Texas did so early in 1866.)

Southern Regulation of Blacks Congress believed that the government had a duty to assist freedmen after the war. So in March 1865 it created the Freedmen's Bureau, a temporary federal assistance agency headed by Oliver O. Howard. The bureau distributed food and medicine to poor blacks (and whites), opened schools, supervised land distribution to freedmen, and tried to defend the civil rights of Southern blacks. (It exercised these functions in helping "Sherman's Negroes" in the resettlement program.)

The Freedmen's Bureau, however, could not protect the physical security of black Southerners without the help of Union troops. This problem was clearly a most urgent one. Brutal riots against blacks occurred in Memphis and New Orleans in 1866.

After Appomattox Union troops were mustered out of the army at a rapid rate. By the end of 1865 only 150,000 soldiers remained of the million serving six months earlier. Many of these were stationed on isolated western posts fighting Indians.

Under these conditions it was impossible for Union troops to offer the 4 million Southern blacks, most of them recently freed, any real protection. Most white Southerners had been raised to believe that blacks had no civil rights that whites were bound to respect. Killings, beatings, burnings, and other forms of physical terror directed against blacks—mostly to keep them out of politics—began soon after the war's end. Violence against blacks was often carried out by white secret societies. Several were formed after the war, primarily to keep blacks from voting. The most famous, the Ku Klux Klan, was founded in 1866. The turmoil increased during the 1870s.

Many whites in the South adopted other means to reduce black people to a state of virtual enslavement. In every Southern state new governments were elected by white voters according to the provisions of Johnson's Reconstruction plan. The Johnson state governments, as they were called, allowed no blacks to vote. They adopted so-called Black Codes to regulate the actions and bahavior of freedmen. Southern whites claimed that such codes were necessary because of the threat of social disorder as a result of emancipation. There had been no major instance, however, of blacks rioting against whites anywhere in the region.

The Black Codes had some provisions to protect blacks. They legalized marriages between blacks, for instance. They also gave blacks the

Stern, intense, and vindictive, Thaddeus Stevens attacked Lincoln throughout the war for not punishing the South harshly enough.

Charles Sumner, once admonished during an argument, "But you forget the other side," thundered in reply: "There is no other side!"

right to sue and testify in court. But the codes consisted mainly of restrictions. They supervised the movements of blacks, prevented them from carrying weapons, and forbade intermarriage between blacks and whites. Contracts, sometimes for life, forced black people to remain at their jobs. In some states blacks could not own land or work at any job other than farming without a special license. Black children were forced into certain job apprenticeships.

Reaction in the North Northern Republicans, both Radicals and moderates, attacked the Johnson state governments. They denounced the Black Codes and called for their immediate repeal. Most Radicals believed that the defeated Southern states should be treated, in Thaddeus Stevens' phrase, like "conquered provinces," until more repentant leaders emerged.

When Congress reconvened in December 1865, representatives and senators elected under the Johnson state governments applied for admission. Republicans in Congress refused to admit them. These Southerners who now claimed loyalty to the Union included fifty-eight former Confederate congressmen, six of Jefferson Davis' cabinet members, and four Southern generals. Most amazing of all was the presence of Alexander Stephens of Georgia, who eight months earlier had been vice president of the Confederacy!

The 1866 riots in Memphis and New Orleans gave Northerners additional evidence that the white South remained unrepentant. Thus it seemed inevitable that there would be a power struggle between Johnson and congressional Republicans over who would control the Reconstruction process. Who was sovereign in the federal government, the President or Congress? Who could decide?

RADICAL RECONSTRUCTION

Congress answered these questions to its own satisfaction by taking the initiative completely out of Johnson's hands. By 1867 the legislature had won control. It dominated the government for the next ten years.

The Republicans who controlled Congress developed their strategy mainly through the Joint Committee on Reconstruction, which was dominated by the Radicals. This group asserted that Southern states could be readmitted only after meeting congressional requirements. The Joint Committee moved a series of measures through Congress between 1865 and 1867. Most of the bills were vetoed by the hapless Johnson, then repassed by a two-thirds majority.

First, in February 1866, came the new Freedmen's Bureau bill. It expanded the bureau's authority to protect Southern blacks, giving it the right to try in military courts persons accused of violating the civil rights of freedmen.

A Civil Rights Act of April 1866 granted the same civil rights to blacks as those enjoyed by whites. The measure also asserted the right of the federal government to interfere in state affairs to protect a citizen's civil rights.

In order to fortify their position, congressional Republicans in June 1866 adopted and sent to the states the Fourteenth Amendment. In effect, it gave blacks full citizenship. If a state denied the vote to blacks, its representation in the House would be reduced. The amendment also forbade ex-Confederate officials from holding federal or state office again without receiving congressional pardon. The Joint Committee declared that any Southern state wishing readmission would have to ratify the Fourteenth Amendment. The Johnson state governments in the South voted against ratification. (The amendment was eventually ratified in 1868.)

President Johnson hoped his Republican opponents would be defeated in the 1866 congressional election, and he campaigned personally against them. After a wild and bitterly fought campaign, however, anti-Johnson Republicans swept the election. They carried every Union state but three.

A Harsh Program When Congress met after the election, Republicans enacted their program into law. They began with the First Reconstruc-

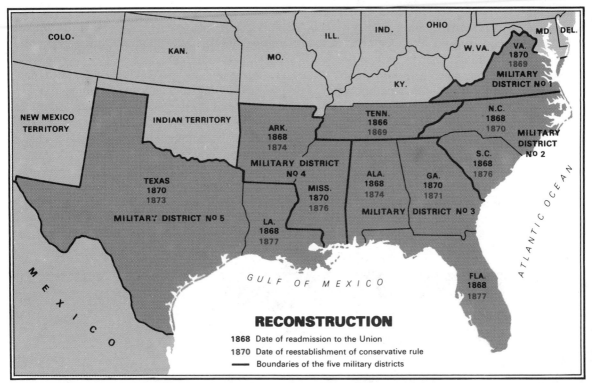

RECONSTRUCTION

1868 Date of readmission to the Union
1870 Date of reestablishment of conservative rule
——— Boundaries of the five military districts

tion Act of March 1867. Significantly, the bill's final form came from a moderate, Republican John Sherman. By this time the moderates agreed with Radicals on most key issues of Reconstruction. This law abolished the existing Johnson state governments. It provided for universal manhood suffrage—that is, for black as well as white voting.

The First Reconstruction Act also authorized temporary military rule of the South. Ten former Confederate states were still outside the Union. (Tennessee had ratified the Fourteenth Amendment and had been readmitted.) These states were divided into five military districts. To rejoin the Union, a state had to call a constitutional convention elected by universal manhood suffrage. This body, in turn, had to create a new state government that would ratify the Fourteenth Amendment and guarantee black suffrage. Three subsequent congressional acts strengthened the powers of federal army commanders in the South.

The final aspect of the Radicals' Reconstruction program involved their attempt in 1867 to remove the President through impeachment. Congress was convinced that Johnson would sabotage its Reconstruction acts, so it called itself into special session, an unprecedented step. It passed two measures on March 2, 1867. One virtually deprived Johnson of command of the American army by requiring him to issue all military orders through the General of the Army, Ulysses S. Grant. The second bill was the Tenure of Office Act. It prohibited the President from removing officials whose appointments had been made with Senate consent without again securing Senate approval. This law meant that Johnson could not fire Secretary of War Stanton. This leading Radical was the man who—along with Saxton and Howard—had tried to block presidential interference with Sherman's land distribution policy. Johnson disregarded the measure and dismissed Stanton. Then the House passed a resolution impeaching

426 / Johnson on eleven charges, including alleged violations of the two March 2 bills.

After a Senate trial the President was acquitted of the very flimsy charges. A two-thirds majority is needed to convict the President on an impeachment charge. Thirty-five senators voted for his conviction, while nineteen (including seven Republicans) voted for acquittal. Thus Johnson was saved by a one-vote margin.

The effort to unseat Johnson was the most daring episode in the Radicals' Reconstruction plans. A few Radicals such as Stevens tried to push through bills confiscating 394 million acres of land owned by the 70,000 chief leaders of the Confederacy. (Charles Sumner called the ante-bellum plantations "nurseries of the Rebellion.") But such measures found little support among the party's moderate majority, and therefore they did not pass.

Most aims of the Radicals were fairly limited. They worked chiefly for Republican political control of the national government. They also hoped that coalitions of black voters and friendly whites would dominate Southern politics, thereby preventing national revival of the Democratic party.

But Republicans did not have any direct social or economic goals. Only a small number of Radicals were committed to complete equality for black Americans. There was no large-scale

Southern blacks voted for the first time during Radical Reconstruction. Note, at right, a voter being paid off—a practice by no means limited to blacks or to Southern elections.

program to provide landless freedmen with an economic base. Many blacks had been promised "forty acres and a mule." But the thousands resettled on abandoned lands—such as "Sherman's Negroes" of the Deep South—were soon dispossessed.

After the attempt to impeach Johnson, Radicals left the problems of Reconstruction in the hands of federal commanders and new state governments in the South. The quarrel between legislative and executive branches over Southern policy ended in 1868, when Republican Ulysses S. Grant was elected President. By then the central drama of Reconstruction had shifted from Washington to the South itself.

The New Radical Governments Beginning in 1867, so-called Radical state governments were set up according to congressional regulations. New black voters made up a majority of the Radical electorate in five states—Alabama, Florida, Louisiana, Mississippi, and South Carolina. Elsewhere in the South, white Radical majorities were supported by black voters. By 1870 more than 700,000 blacks and 627,000 whites were registered as voters under the Radical state constitutions.[4]

Congress readmitted Louisiana and six other states to the Union under Radical rule in June 1868. By the end of 1870 all ten ex-Confederate states had been readmitted to the Union.

Throughout the South blacks filled public offices for the first time. These were not usually the highest offices, however. Nor did blacks hold office in proportion to their percentage of voters. Only one state legislature, that of South Carolina, ever had a black majority. No black ever became a Reconstruction Southern governor. (Some states, though, had black lieutenant governors.) There were two black United States senators and fifteen congressmen during the entire period of Radical rule.

[4] The Fifteenth Amendment, adopted in 1870, forbade any state from preventing citizens from voting because of race, color, or "previous condition of servitude." This was a clear effort to eliminate the hypocrisy of some Northern states that demanded suffrage for blacks in the South while continuing to deny it at home.

Many black political leaders were educated men. Some were among the most distinguished figures in the entire South. Francis L. Cardozo, for example, South Carolina's state treasurer, held degrees from the Universities of London and Glasgow, making him perhaps the best-educated politician in the South of either race.

Who were the Radicals in the South? They included many different groups. Some were Southerners, most of whom had been prewar Whigs or secret Union sympathizers during the war. Many Southern businessmen and even a few planters joined the Radicals. They hoped that the new governments would have enough help from Northern capitalists and Republican politicians to rebuild the South's shattered economy. Radicals also included nonslaveholding farmers, who, while they disliked blacks, hated ex-Confederates even more for having led them into what they considered "a rich man's war and a poor man's fight." These Southern-born Radicals were called scalawags (an often undeserved term) by former Confederates.

Other Radicals were Northerners. Tens of thousands of them went south after the war for a variety of reasons. Hostile whites referred to them bitterly as carpetbaggers, whose only aim was to fill their luggage with ill-gotten Southern wealth. Yet many were teachers—their carpetbags stuffed only with McGuffey's Readers. Like the people who went to the Sea Islands, their aim was to set up schools for the freedmen. Northern soldiers returned to the South seeking good land; 5,000 went to Louisiana alone. Businessmen sought opportunities to invest capital and to profit from the region's economic reconstruction. A number of politically ambitious people did arrive to take part in the Radical governments. But they were by no means all opportunists.

Charges of Corruption It has often been said that Radical state governments were corrupt. There is some truth to this charge. Legislators in South Carolina, for example, paid $200,000 for $18,000 worth of furniture for the state capitol. Louisiana's Radical governor H. C. Warmouth left the state with a personal fortune of half a million dollars, most of it acquired illegally. Similar fortunes were made throughout the South.

Several points should be noted in favor of the Radical governments, however. At this time scandals tainted the Grant administration and many Northern state and local governments. The historian John Hope Franklin has termed public dishonesty after the Civil War "bisectional, bipartisan, and biracial." (Actually, the blacks in Congress were not implicated in the Grant scandals, although many of their white colleagues were.) State governments everywhere ran up enormous debts. Postwar fortunes in the South were made by Radicals and ex-Confederates, Republicans and Democrats alike. Given the level of immorality in American politics, North and South, during Reconstruction, it seems fair to say that the Radicals were no more corrupt than other politicians at the time.

In fact, most Radical state funds were spent rebuilding a ruined economy. Somehow, the Radicals managed to begin reconstructing Southern highways, railroads, hospitals, and orphanages. They also began building schools; many Southern states had had no public-school system before the war. The rebuilding had to be done for an additional 3 1/2 million people. These were the ex-slaves, who were now citizens and entitled to the use of public facilities.

An Evaluation Historians have long debated whether Radical state governments in the South ruled poorly or well. Opinions on this question depend in part on attitudes about whether (or when) blacks should have been allowed the franchise and a role in governing. We tend to forget how short a time Radical governments actually ruled. Tennessee never underwent this type of control. Virginia, North Carolina, and Georgia returned to conservative hands by 1871. Arkansas, Alabama, and Texas did so by 1874. And it was all over by 1877.

Some provisions of the Radical state constitutions found approval even among ex-Confederates. The documents ended imprisonment for debt, for example, and did away with property qualifications for voting. Basically, ex-Confederate whites objected less to the corruption of Radical state governments than to their very existence—especially to the presence of blacks on the political slate. Radical rule did not end because of its failure to meet the economic and social problems of the South. Radicals were driven from power because of their insistence on meeting these problems through biracial political cooperation.

THE END OF RADICAL RULE

Two trends put an end to Radical Reconstruction. One was the increasing hostility of white Southerners. The other was the growing indifference of its Northern Republican sponsors.

Southern hostility not only increased, but it grew more violent. Thousands of blacks and white Radicals lost their lives to armed bands of whites such as the Ku Klux Klan and local "rifle clubs" that roamed the South during the 1870s. Federal troops and black state militia could suppress only a small number of these groups. Congress passed several Force Bills, making it a national offense to interfere with any citizen's civil rights (including his right to vote). But they had little effect, since only a few thousand federal troops remained in the South to enforce the laws against guerrilla groups like the Klan. To compound the Radicals' problem, Congress repealed its ironclad oath in 1871. No longer did Southerners have to swear that they had always been loyal to the Union. In 1872 a general amnesty restored civil rights (including the right to hold office) to all but about 600 high Confederate officials.

As white terrorists harassed the remaining Radical state governments, Northerners became indifferent. Republicans in Washington grew increasingly weary of the struggle to protect black civil rights. "The whole public," complained President Grant, "is tired of these outbreaks in the South."

The death or retirement of Radical leaders

Louisiana was one of five Southern states to have a majority of black voters. Between 1868 and 1896 the state had 133 black legislators—38 senators and 95 representatives. They were never numerous or strong enough to control political life in Louisiana, though Oscar Dunn (center) did lead a struggle against corruption and extravagance.

such as Stevens and Sumner helped restore control of Congress to more conservative, business-minded Republicans. A combination of Democrats and reform-minded "Liberal Republicans" nearly won the presidency in 1872 on a platform pledging an end to federal support for Radical regimes in the South. In 1874 the Democrats regained control of the House for the first time since before the war.

Public attention strayed even further away from the South after 1873, when a major depression swept the country. The business slump threw hundreds of thousands out of work and shifted political attention from postwar Reconstruction to the problem of economic recovery.

The Compromise of 1877 In 1876 both presidential candidates, Republican Rutherford B. Hayes and Democrat Samuel B. Tilden, promised even before the election to restore "home rule" to the South. Both pledged to remove federal support for the three remaining Radical state governments—those of Louisiana, South Carolina, and Florida. They implied that Southern whites could now handle all problems connected with blacks, including political rights.

The election ended in a unique stalemate. Two sets of returns arrived from the three states yet in Radical hands. The Radicals claimed that Hayes had won, while Democrats insisted on a Tilden majority. The nineteen doubtful electoral votes (including one disputed Oregon elector) meant the difference between a one-vote Hayes margin and a clear Tilden sweep. Congress finally accepted the recommendation of a specially appointed commission to award all the disputed votes to Hayes, thereby making him President. The South, in turn, received a pledge from Hayes that all remaining federal troops would be removed from the three Radical states, that federal subsidies would be provided for a Southern transcontinental railroad then under construction, and that a Southerner would be appointed to the Cabinet.

All these promises were met, and Radical rule promptly collapsed in the three remaining states. This so-called Compromise of 1877 marked the final surrender of the North's promise to defend black political and civil rights against the former white Confederates.

During the decades that followed, conservative governments defeated black efforts to participate in Southern politics. In every subsequent election fewer blacks voted.

Violence toward black people increased for the rest of the century. The great majority of Southern blacks farmed other people's lands as tenants or sharecroppers. They were forced into a subordinate place in Southern life, being neither slaves nor completely freedmen.

1. How did the Union and the Confederacy recruit soldiers at the beginning of the war? What changes took place in recruitment as time went on?
2. How did the basic military strategy of the Confederacy differ from that of the Union?
3. In what ways did the South change during the Civil War? Why did the absence of Southern representatives in Congress contribute to the industrial growth of the North?
4. Why was Lincoln's conduct of the war opposed by the Radical Republicans? By the War Democrats? How were people's civil rights affected in the North? In the South?
5. What were Lincoln's motives in issuing the Emancipation Proclamation? Why did it free few slaves? When did all the slaves gain their freedom?
6. Lincoln's Second Inaugural Address called for a generous settlement with the South. Did his Reconstruction plan bear this out? Why did Congress refuse to accept his program?
7. In what ways did Johnson's Reconstruction plan differ from Lincoln's?
8. What were the Black Codes and what was their purpose?
9. Why did Congress take over Reconstruction? What were the Radicals' most important moves?
10. Were the Radical Republicans truly radical in a political, economic, or social sense? Explain your answer.

Beyond the Text

1. Despite overwhelming odds, the Confederacy was able to carry on a war for four long years. Investigate the reasons for (a) its endurance, or (b) the eventual Northern victory. David Donald's collection of short essays in *Why the North Won the Civil War* can serve as a point of departure.
2. Lincoln had trouble finding good military leaders. Why was this so? Research and report to the class.
3. Blacks participated, both as voters and as legislators, in Southern politics for the first time during Reconstruction. How well did they perform?

Bibliography

Nonfiction

Catton, Bruce, *Centennial History of the Civil War,* 3 vols.

Donald, David, ed., *Why the North Won the Civil War.**

Eaton, Clement, *A History of the Southern Confederacy.**

Franklin, John Hope, *Reconstruction After the Civil War.**

McPherson, James M., *The Struggle for Equality: Abolitionists and the Negro in the Civil War and Reconstruction.**

– – – *The Negro's Civil War.*

Nevins, Allan, *The War for the Union,* 4 vols.

Patrick, Rembert W., *The Reconstruction of the Nation.**

Randall, J. G., *Lincoln the President,* 4 vols.

Randall, J. G. and David Donald, *The Civil War and Reconstruction.*

Stampp, Kenneth M., *The Era of Reconstruction, 1865–1877.**

Stampp, Kenneth M. and Leon F. Litwack, eds., *Reconstruction: An Anthology of Revisionist Writings.**

Thomas, Benjamin P., *Abraham Lincoln.*

Fiction

Basso, Hamilton, *The Light Infantry Ball.*
Campbell, Marie, *A House with Stairs.*
Crane, Stephen, *The Red Badge of Courage.**

*a paperback book

UNIT FIVE

INDUSTRIAL

Americans thought about their Civil War in many different ways. But most of them agreed, North and South, that it was somehow a conservative war. Each side thought of itself as the conserving protector of an inherited social and political order. It was difficult for Americans to understand that what lay ahead was not a restoration of stability but a surprising burst of activity and change. The United States was transformed into a modern industrial nation in the last third of the nineteenth century. That transformation is the subject of Unit Five.

In an odd way, the people who could best have understood the revolutionary transformations of American society were those who had been most completely defeated by it: the American Indians. From the time of Jamestown, they had watched white society grow in size and power. Now, the forces of expansion increased dramatically. Railroads, miners, cattle ranchers, and farmers spilled out over the Great Plains to the Pacific Coast with fresh speed and energy.

One of the tribes that felt the forces of westward expansion most directly was the Sioux. By the close of the century, this

AMERICA

determined people had been reduced from proud independence to reservation captivity. The destruction of their way of life reached a symbolic climax in 1890 in the last "battle" between Indians and United States soldiers in American history—Wounded Knee. The defeat of the Sioux is the subject of Chapter 21. The following chapter discusses the larger process of white expansion that made their final conquest inevitable.

At the same time that postwar America was expanding geographically, a new economic landscape took shape. New inventions and manufacturing processes changed the ways that Americans earned their livings and made their goods. Giant factories in enormous cities with great immigrant and working-class populations arose. With them came the inevitable conflicts between rich and poor, employers and workers, immigrants and native Americans.

One of the most important examples of conflict was a series of events in Chicago in 1885 and 1886. It began with a labor strike at the McCormick Harvester Company, led to a famous bombing incident at Haymarket Square, and ended in the trial and execution of several immigrant German Americans. Chapter 23 tells this story and Chapter 24 explores the background of industrialization that made the conflict possible.

Social and economic change created strains on political parties and governmental institutions. The examination, in Chapter 25, of the career of President James A. Garfield and of his assassination in 1881 by a crazed, disappointed office-seeker introduces the climate of political tensions. Chapter 26 then traces the conditions that made political careers such as Garfield's possible. Politicians' concern with party politics and consequent neglect of the urgent needs created by change are explored. So are the beginnings of demands for reform exemplified in the Populist movement.

What emerges, then, from the late nineteenth century is a mixed picture of incredible industrial growth and geographical expansion alongside moments of crisis and bloodshed—with political leaders looking on as almost helpless and often confused spectators.

21

"BATTLE" AT WOUNDED KNEE

THERE WAS A CONFUSION about names—there almost always was when Indians were involved. Most whites called the tribe the Sioux. But this name was just a French abbreviation of what some of the tribe's enemies had called them. They called themselves Dakota.

There was more than one Indian name for what the whites called Wounded Knee Creek, on the Pine Ridge Reservation in South Dakota. Also, whereas some people called what had happened at Wounded Knee Creek a battle, others called it a massacre. Even the man who rode out from reservation headquarters to Wounded Knee had two names. One was an Indian name, Ohiyesa. One was a white man's name, Charles Eastman. He was a Sioux, but he had been educated in white schools in New England. In fact, he was a doctor of medicine.

But there was no confusion about what Charles Eastman saw on that bright New Year's Day morning in 1891:

On the day following the Wounded Knee massacre, there was a blizzard. On the third day it cleared, and the ground was covered with fresh snow. We had feared that some of the wounded Indians had been left on the field, and a number of us volunteered to go and see.

Fully three miles from the scene of the massacre, we found the body of a woman completely covered with a blanket of snow, and from this point on we found them scattered along as they had been hunted down and slaughtered. When we reached the spot where the Indian camp had stood, among the fragments of burned tents and other belongings, we saw the frozen bodies lying

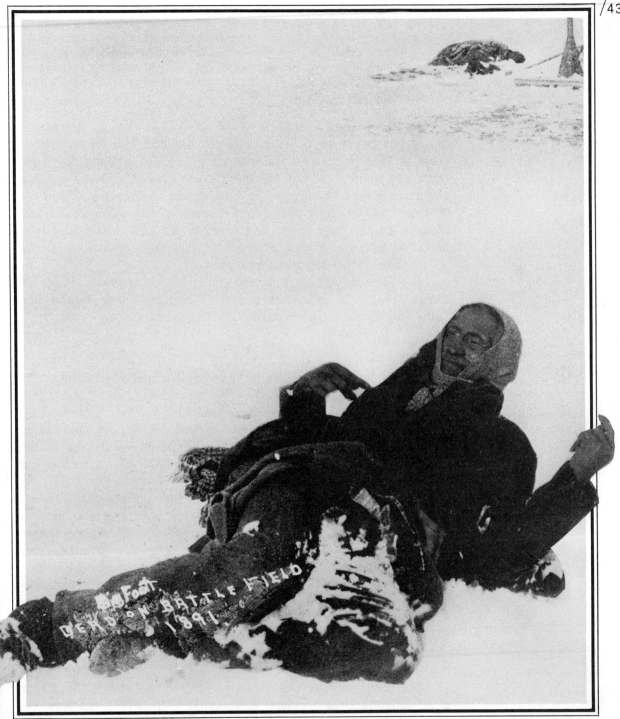

Big Foot, seventy-year-old chief of the Sioux, was one of 146 Indians killed by the U.S. Seventh Cavalry at Wounded Knee. He was found dead three days later, frozen grotesquely where he had fallen.

close together or piled one upon another. I counted eighty bodies of men, who were almost as helpless as the women and babes when the deadly [gun] fire began, for nearly all their guns had been taken from them.

Although they had been lying in the snow and cold for two days and nights, a number had survived. Among them I found a baby of about a year old, warmly wrapped and entirely unhurt. Under a wagon, I discovered an old woman, totally blind and helpless.

Eastman began to load the few survivors into wagons to return to the agency (reservation headquarters), where he had set up a small hospital. Two groups of white men stayed behind at Wounded Knee. One was a troop of the U.S. Seventh Cavalry. The other was a group of about thirty white civilians who had agreed to bury the dead, at a charge of two dollars a body. They found the body of the chief of the Indians, an old man named Big Foot, frozen half sitting, half lying down. Ill with pneumonia, he had been lying on a blanket on the winter ground when the shooting started.

It took until the next day to dig a big open grave. Then 146 Indians—128 men and women and 18 children—were buried. The battle and massacre (it was partly both) was over.

Wounded Knee was the last and most tragic moment in a long, difficult, and often ugly process: the conquest of the Sioux Indians. The conquerors were the white citizens and blue-coated soldiers of the United States. The process began before the Civil War. At that time the Sioux were a powerful tribe, probably numbering well over 20,000. They hunted on millions of square miles of the plains west of the Missouri River.

The Sioux resisted the invasion of white miners, farmers, and ranchers. They fought often, and they usually won. In the summer of 1876 they won two astonishing victories over the bluecoats, as they called the cavalry. On Rosebud Creek, in what is now Montana, they attacked a large column of cavalry and infantry and forced the soldiers into a retreat. Then, just a few days later, the Seventh Cavalry, with General George A. Custer commanding, attacked a large Sioux camp on the Little Bighorn River, just a few miles from Rosebud Creek. Custer divided his force, and the Indians killed Custer as well as most of the Seventh, one of the most experienced cavalry units operating in the West.

But there were too many other soldiers. Though the Sioux were never defeated, their surrender was inevitable. In 1877, just a year after "Custer's last stand," the great war chief Crazy Horse led many of his followers onto a reservation that had been recently set aside for the

The Sioux moved onto reservations such as this one at Pine Ridge, South Dakota, in 1877. They raised horses for hunting buffalo, which provided them with food, clothing, and skins for their portable tepees.

Sioux. Crazy Horse was murdered a short time later. Some of his people fled to Canada to join the other outstanding Sioux leader, Sitting Bull. About 2,500 Sioux then tried to survive in Canada. But hunger and cold—and the fact that white people had slain most of the buffalo—finally drove them back to the reservation. In 1881 Sitting Bull surrendered—"came in," as it was said. This was the end of a golden age for the Sioux, one that had lasted more than a century.

Originally, the Sioux inhabited the forest and lake country between Minnesota and the Great Lakes. They built permanent bark houses and lived by farming and hunting small game. About the middle of the eighteenth century the Sioux were driven westward from their forest homes onto the Great Plains by another tribe, the Chippewas. The Chippewas had come into contact with the French and had traded their furs for guns. The guns gave the Chippewas an overwhelming advantage. The Sioux had to retreat.

There were seven main divisions of the Sioux. The division that moved farthest west and became most prosperous was the Tetons. The Tetons in turn consisted of seven bands, among them the Oglalas, the Brules, and the Hunkpapas.

Plains life for the Sioux centered on the buffalo, the horse, and the rifle. These Indians became nomadic. They gave up their permanent homes for portable tepees made of buffalo hides. The tepees, and the poles over which they were stretched, could be dragged from place to place by horses. Buffalo provided meat and skins for clothing and shelter. Hunting and warfare were the primary occupations of the Sioux. A man gained prestige depending on his skill and courage at hunting and in battle.

The whites, with their cannon, railroads, and reservations, destroyed the Sioux way of life. The whites slaughtered the buffalo until there were practically none left. The whites insisted that the Sioux live in permanent log homes on the reservation. Government rations of beef, flour, and beans were substituted for the hunt. The whites disapproved of the Sioux religion and forbade the sacred Sun Dance, the Indians' most holy annual ritual. White Indian agents (those in charge of the reservations) insisted that a Sioux man have only one wife. Reservation life undercut the old Sioux society completely. The authority of warriors and chiefs collapsed with the end of a hunting economy and tribal warfare.

What was happening to the Sioux was simple and tragic. They had been defeated by a much more powerful and complex society. Some of them—the "nonprogressives"—might resist in certain ways. They might refuse to plant crops, for example, or continue to wear Indian clothing. But their defeat was still almost complete. They had long ago gladly accepted some of the white man's ways and tools: the horse, the rifle, the metal kettle that was so much better than their old buffalo-skin buckets. Such things had been useful in the old life. But the United States government had plans and hopes for the Sioux that were utterly at odds with the old Indian ways.

American policy was aimed at one long-range goal—to make the Indians into self-supporting farmers. Each family would receive its own land. Indians would cook on a stove instead of over a fire, wear white people's clothes, and, if possible, worship the white man's God instead of the old God of the Sioux, Wakan Tanka. To well-intentioned reformers in the East this meant "raising the Indian to civilization." To whites in the West it meant a final end to the Indian as a barrier to westward expansion.

For the Indians these changes meant a divided world. Even those who wanted to cooperate most—the so-called progressive Indians— lived something of a double life. An Indian man might wear a white man's clothes, plow and harvest crops, marry only one woman, send his children to white schools or even become a member of the Indian Police.[1] But the memory of the old life—a life now dead in fact—was still alive.

The deep conflict between Indian and white ways came to the surface in 1883, when a Senate investigating committee visited the

[1] The Indian police, recruited from young reservation Indians, helped the Indian agents keep order.

Sioux. Sitting Bull, who had been one of the Sioux leaders at the Battle of the Little Bighorn, came to testify. But the chairman would not recognize Sitting Bull as chief. Sitting Bull got up and left. All the Indians followed him. But several of the progressive Indians returned to plead with the committee to use its influence with the Great Father[2] to get better treatment for the Indians. Soon even Sitting Bull swallowed his hurt pride and returned to apologize.

Then Sitting Bull gave a remarkable account of what defeat had meant to the Sioux. They had been wealthy in their own terms, with land, ponies, and buffalo aplenty. In one lifetime the white man had reduced them to poverty.

> Whatever you wanted of me I have obeyed. The Great Father sent me word that whatever he had against me in the past had been forgiven and thrown aside, and I accepted his promises and came in. And he told me not to step aside from the white man's path, and I am doing my best to travel in that path. I sit here and look around me now, and I see my people starving. We want cattle to butcher. That is the way you live, and we want to live the same way. When the Great Father told me to live like his people, I told him to send me six teams of mules, because that is the way the white people make a living. I asked for a horse and buggy for my children; I was advised to follow the ways of the white man, and that is why I asked for those things.

Sitting Bull's ideas were a little confused, at least by white standards. But he summed up neatly the dilemma of the Sioux. He was still proud of himself and his tribal ways. He resented the whites' failure to understand this pride. But another side of him recognized defeat and was prepared to plead with the whites not for less civilization but for more. In Sitting Bull, and in almost all the other reservation Indians, pride, resentment, hunger, and begging were so intermixed that a meaningful pattern of life was almost impossible.

The situation was the same among all the Sioux. During the 1880s the Indians were gradually becoming "civilized." But the hunger and anger were just below the surface. Some crucial event or idea was all that was needed to bring the conflict with the whites back into the open, tip the scales one way or another, and offer the Indians a clear choice between the old life and the new.

A new idea did come, and from an unpredictable direction. In the summer of 1889—about a dozen years after Crazy Horse had surrendered his band of hostiles—the Sioux began to hear rumors of an Indian messiah (or savior) who had come to earth in the west. They

---

[2] Great Father, or White Father, was the title used by the Indians for the President of the United States.

had learned enough of Christianity on the reservation to understand the alien notion of a messiah. If it were true that a messiah had come to save the Indians from the whites, surely it was worth investigating they thought.

The Messiah was said to be at the Paiute reservation at Walker Lake, Nevada. Three of the six Sioux reservations[3] selected important men to make the trip west. It was about a thousand miles away— farther than almost any of the Sioux had ever traveled. Pine Ridge Reservation sent eight men, including Kicking Bear, who was to become the most effective disciple of the new Messiah. From Rosebud went Short Bull. The Cheyenne River Reservation, smaller than either Pine Ridge or Rosebud, sent one man.

The eleven Sioux started west by train. Railroads had by then penetrated all the major Western areas, and Indians hopped freight cars with little or no opposition from the white railroad men. When the Sioux reached Wyoming, they found that other tribes—Cheyennes, Arapahoes, Bannocks, and Shoshonis—had also sent wise men to seek the Messiah. The whole group then traveled south to Walker Lake. There the Paiutes gave them wagons to complete the pilgrimage. Soon they were in the presence of the Messiah.

His Indian name was Wovoka, his white name Jackson Wilson. He was about thirty-five years old. He was a Paiute, but he had grown up close to a white ranching family named Wilson. (They gave him his English name.) The Wilsons were a religious family. From them Wovoka had learned in some detail how Jesus had controlled the wind and the seas, how he had promised eternal life to his followers, and how other whites had crucified him. Wovoka was apparently the son of a Paiute shaman, or medicine man.[4] One day in 1889, when he was ill (and perhaps delirious) with a high fever, there was an eclipse of the sun. This led him to believe that he had been taken up to heaven. After talking with God, he had been returned to earth to bring salvation to the Indians.

Wovoka's doctrines were a fairly straightforward Indian version of some of the basic teachings of the New Testament. In a sermon to some visiting Cheyennes he summarized his new faith:

> You must not hurt anybody, or do harm to anyone. You must not fight. Do right always.

Wovoka, the Messiah, claimed to be sent by God to save his people. He preached non-violence and brotherly love. He demanded of his followers only that they dance the Ghost Dance and await the resurrection of their dead.

[3] One so-called Great Sioux Reservation had been created in 1868. It consisted of about 43,000 square miles in what is now South Dakota, and it was administered from several agencies on or near the land. In 1889 the Sioux territory, much reduced in size, was broken up into six separate reservations— Pine Ridge, Rosebud, Lower Brule, Crow Creek, Cheyenne River, and Standing Rock.

[4] Almost all American Indians relied on shamans, men or women who were thought to have supernatural powers such as foretelling the future or curing the sick.

Do not tell the white people about this. Jesus is now upon the earth. The dead are all alive again. I do not know when they will be here; maybe this fall or in the spring. When the time comes there will be no more sickness and everyone will be young again.

Ghost shirts, emblazoned with bright-colored thunderbirds and buffaloes, were supposed to protect Indians from the white man's weapons in battle.

In a simplified way Wovoka was telling his disciples that the dead would be resurrected soon. The earth would tremble; he often said that a new earth would cover the old. But true believers need not be afraid, because they would soon enjoy perfect life, youth, and health. In the meantime, the Indians should live in peace with the whites.

Wovoka gave the visiting Cheyennes some clay for making the sacred red paint of the Paiutes. Symbols drawn with it were signs of their salvation. Then he advised them: "When you get home, you must make a dance to continue five days. You must all do it in the same way."

This was the famous Ghost Dance from which Wovoka's new religion soon took its name. During the five days it lasted, men and women sang certain songs and went into hypnotic trances. It was during the dance that Indians were supposed to be able to visit their departed relatives in heaven.

After Short Bull returned to South Dakota, he gave his version of the Ghost Dance religion to his excited Sioux audience. The tone was much more militant than Wovoka's. Short Bull promised punishment for those who refused to be converted—just as the Christian missionaries promised damnation for those who rejected their Messiah. And Short Bull emphasized that the Ghost Dance would enable the Sioux to see their dead relatives. He also promised victory over the hated and feared soldiers for those who wore holy shirts into battle. The shirts were supposed to protect wearers from whites' bullets.

It was not only Short Bull who brought this interpretation back from the trip to Wovoka. A similar version of the Ghost Dance faith emerged on all the Sioux reservations during the summer of 1890. The Sioux were offered a new ritual, the Ghost Dance, and a new faith, which held that the whites would soon be buried in the earth and the Indians would once again own the plains. Nevertheless, most of the Sioux probably rejected the Ghost Dance and decided to continue along the white man's path. For many, though, the religion of Wovoka offered great hope for the return of the old life and the end of their humiliating captivity.

There is no way of knowing how sincere Short Bull was. Nor is there any way of knowing whether Sitting Bull—who soon became a disciple of the Ghost Dance—really believed in the coming resurrection. But there can be no doubt that large groups of Sioux did accept the Ghost Dance.

gents on all the reservations tried to stop the dances, using Indian police. But, time and again, the dancing Sioux refused to be cowed. They threatened their own police with rifles, insulted the agents, and began to behave like the Sioux of the 1870s. The agents reacted in various ways. When the police failed to make the Sioux obey, some of the agents refused to issue rations to those Indians who were active Ghost Dancers. At least two of the agents asked for federal troops. One, a new agent at Pine Ridge, was so incompetent that the Indians named him Young-Man Afraid-of-Indians. White newspapermen, always hungry for a sensational news story, began to write about "hostile" Sioux. And white settlers in the Dakotas began to demand protection from the government.

Finally, after a tug of war between the Department of the Interior and the Department of War in Washington, the government authorized the army to send infantry and cavalry onto the reservations. This move brought about the first real confrontation since 1876 between the Sioux and the dreaded bluecoats. On November 20, 1890, cavalry and infantry units occupied Pine Ridge and Rosebud. A few days later the entire Seventh Cavalry arrived at Pine Ridge. This was Custer's unit, and it included many veterans of the Little Bighorn.

The effect on the Sioux of the appearance of the troops was overpowering. Instead of retreating to the outer edges of the reservations, most of the Indians at Pine Ridge and Rosebud immediately left their cabins and camps and gathered around the agency buildings. They pitched their tepees in rambling confusion and hoped that they would not be suspected of any wrongdoing. It was as though the only

During the Ghost Dance, which went on for five days, the Sioux worked themselves into a trance. Believers thought they could visit their dead while in this state.

way to be safe from the rifles and cannon of the army was to be right under the noses of the officers and agents.

Thus the arrival of the army segregated the Indians. Those who wanted peace with the whites—those who had the good sense to be afraid—had gathered at the agencies. Only the most militant of the Ghost Dancers, led by Kicking Bear and Short Bull, decided to hold out. They were gathered along the creeks not far from the Pine Ridge Agency—at Medicine Root, Porcupine, and Wounded Knee.

About a week after the cavalry's arrival, several hundred of the militant Indians broke for open country. They plundered the farms of the peaceful Indians who had fled to the agencies, and they raided the agencies' cattle herd for beef. Then about 600 warriors and their families struck out for a low plateau at the northwest corner of Pine Ridge. This area was known as the Stronghold. Here the Indians had grass, water, cattle, ponies in large numbers, and plenty of guns and ammunition. They announced that they intended to stay all winter, dancing, and then see what the spring brought.

Kicking Bear spread the doctrines of the Messiah to Sitting Bull and the Standing Rock Reservation. But he gave the new faith a militant interpretation that caused a white reaction.

Fortunately, the officer in command at Pine Ridge decided to be cautious. He sent one messenger after another to the Stronghold, promising that there would be no punishment if the Indians surrendered and returned to the agency. In turn the Indians had to agree to give up the Ghost Dance and return the cattle and other things they had taken. The messengers were badly treated, but some of the men at the Stronghold wanted to surrender. It seemed clear that sooner or later the Indians would disagree among themselves and the threat of uprising would be broken. The situation at Pine Ridge settled into a stalemate, with neither side ready to force a confrontation.

Now the scene of the action shifted north to Standing Rock, where Sitting Bull kept his camp. The nonprogressive Indians regarded Sitting Bull almost reverently. He was probably not as great a war chief as Crazy Horse had been. But Sitting Bull had held out against the whites longer than any other Sioux leader. And his people believed that he had extraordinary powers as a medicine man.

The agent at Standing Rock was James McLaughlin, a tough, fair, and experienced agent. For years he had struggled to gain moral leadership of the Indians, and for years Sitting Bull had stood in his way. McLaughlin had been looking for a way to break Sitting Bull's strong hold over the nonprogressive Indians at Standing Rock. When Sitting Bull took up the forbidden Ghost Dance, McLaughlin decided that arresting him would be the best course. McLaughlin wanted to delay the arrest until winter, when the Indians stayed indoors to avoid the bitter cold and to rest. The agent also believed that the arrest should be made by the Sioux Indian police, not by the cavalry units stationed near the agency at Fort Yates.

In November 1890 McLaughlin began to enlarge his Indian police force. He ordered them to keep a close watch on Sitting Bull's camp and make certain that the old chief did not leave.

In mid-December McLaughlin learned that Sitting Bull had been invited to the Stronghold, where he would join the Pine Ridge and Rosebud Sioux under Short Bull and Kicking Bear. The agent was determined to stop Sitting Bull from taking his group to Pine Ridge. He knew what kind of stalemate had developed there, and he felt that Sitting Bull's presence might be enough to tip the scales toward open warfare between the Sioux and the cavalry. So McLaughlin ordered Sitting Bull's arrest. He commanded the Indian police, who were led by an experienced lieutenant, Bull Head, to sneak into Sitting Bull's camp at dawn on December 15. They were to arrest the chief and bring him into the agency.

Bull Head and the police met the command with mixed feelings. Most of them were progressives. They prayed to the white man's God before starting their mission. But the thought of Sitting Bull still brought back memories of the great days of the Sioux. One of the police, He Alone, whose white name was John Lone Man, later remembered the way he felt when the orders were read and translated to the police. (The English here is the work of an educated relative of his.)

> I'm simply expressing my viewpoint as one who had reformed from all the heathenish ways, formerly one of the loyal followers of Chief Sitting Bull. But ever since I was about ten years of age, I had participated in a good many buffalo hunts and fought under Sitting Bull. But the most important fight I took part in was the Custer fight. After this fight I still went with Sitting Bull's band to Canada. Even after Sitting Bull was returned to Standing Rock Reservation, I remained in his camp, where I tamed down somewhat. We all felt sad.

The police gathered in the early evening of December 14 and passed the night telling war stories. Then, just before dawn, Bull Head ordered He Alone and the thirty or so other police to get ready.

Sitting Bull's camp stood on the north bank of the Grand River. The police, circling from the east, crossed the river to cut off any possible escape southward toward Pine Ridge. Soon they could see Sitting Bull's log cabin. In front of it stood the very tall tepee that was the headquarters for the Ghost Dance. Sitting Bull's two wives, his son Crow Foot, and several other children and relatives lived in the cabin. Other tepees were scattered around it. The police paused for a moment, then crossed the river again. He Alone recalled:

Sitting Bull and his family accepted reservation life in 1881, five years after defeating Custer at Little Bighorn. The unsettling mixture of pride, resentment, and recognition of defeat is visible on his face. This potentially explosive mixture stirred white fears.

We rode up as if we attacked the camp. We quickly dismounted, and while our officers went inside we all scattered around the cabin. It was still dark, and everybody was asleep, and only dogs greeted us.

Bull Head knocked at the door, and the Chief answered, "*How, timahel hiyu you.*" [All right, come in.]

Bull Head said, "I come to arrest you. You are under arrest."

Sitting Bull said, "How. Let me put on my clothes and go with you."

When Sitting Bull started to go with the police, one of Sitting Bull's wives burst into a loud cry which drew attention. No sooner had this started, when several leaders were rapidly making their way toward Sitting Bull's cabin. Bear That Catches, particularly, came up close saying, "Now, here are the metal breasts [5] just as we had expected. You think you are going to take him. You shall not do it."

By now the entire camp was up and angry. The police might still have been able to arrest the sleepy Sitting Bull if Crow Foot, his seventeen-year-old son, had not intervened. Sitting Bull had been grooming Crow Foot to be a chief, filling his youthful head with tales of courage in battle. As He Alone described it, Crow Foot upset the delicate balance of fear and anger:

> Just about this time, Crow Foot got up, moved by the wailing of his mother and the remarks of Bear That Catches, and said to Sitting Bull, "Well, you always called yourself a brave chief. Now you are allowing yourself to be taken by the metal breasts."

[5] "Metal breasts" was a reference to the policemen's badges.

Sitting Bull then changed his mind, and said, "*Ho ca mni kte sni yelo.*"
[Then I will not go.]

Lieutenant Bull Head said to the chief, "Come now, do not listen to any
one."

I said to Sitting Bull, "Uncle,[6] nobody is going to harm you. Please do not let
others lead you into any trouble."

But the chief's mind was made up not to go, so the three head officers laid
their hands on him, pulling him outside. By this time, the whole camp was in
commotion. Bear That Catches pulled out a gun from under his blanket and fired
into Lieutenant Bull Head, wounding him. I ran up toward where they were
holding the chief, when Bear That Catches raised his gun. He pointed and fired at
me, but it snapped [misfired]. I jerked the gun away from his hands and laid him
out. It was about this moment that Lieutenant Bull Head fired into Sitting Bull
while still holding him, and Red Tomahawk followed with another shot which
finished the chief.

There was more shooting, and soon the Ghost Dancers ran for a
line of trees. After a time the police took shelter in Sitting Bull's cabin.
The inner walls of the cabin were unfinished but hung with strips of
brightly colored sheeting, sewn together and tacked to the walls.
Suddenly, one of the policemen noticed a movement in a corner,
behind the sheeting. He Alone raised the curtain:

There stood Crow Foot, and as soon as he was exposed to view, he cried out,
"My uncles, do not kill me. I do not wish to die." Lieutenant Bull Head said, "Do
what you like with him. He is the one that has caused this trouble." I do not
remember who fired the shot that killed Crow Foot—several fired at once.

Just after Crow Foot was killed, the cavalry units from Fort Yates
arrived. The remaining members of Sitting Bull's band scattered
toward the south.

Four Indian policemen had died at Sitting Bull's camp. Two more,
including Lieutenant Bull Head, died later from their wounds. At least
eight of Sitting Bull's people had died. Their bodies were left where
they fell. Only Sitting Bull was buried. A few moments after the
ceremonies for the dead police, his body was put in a plain grave at the
Fort Yates cemetery. The only people there were three officers as
witnesses, along with the four guardhouse gravediggers who shoveled
the dirt over the simple wooden coffin.

None of Sitting Bull's followers was present at his burial. Most of
them—about 400—had fled south and west from the Grand River
camp. The authorities at Standing Rock had a number of nightmarish

---

[6] Indians often used words like "Uncle" and "Father" as terms of respect.

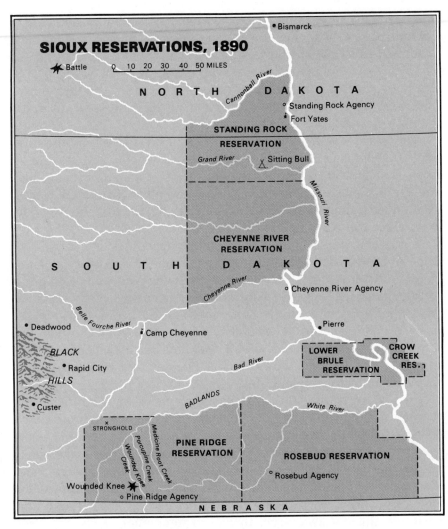

SIOUX RESERVATIONS, 1890

★ Battle   0 10 20 30 40 50 MILES

• Bismarck

N O R T H   D A K O T A

Cannonball River

○ Standing Rock Agency

✦ Fort Yates

STANDING ROCK RESERVATION

Grand River   ⋋ Sitting Bull

Missouri River

CHEYENNE RIVER RESERVATION

Cheyenne River

○ Cheyenne River Agency

S O U T H   D A K O T A

Belle Fourche River

• Deadwood

✦ Camp Cheyenne

• Pierre

BLACK

• Rapid City

HILLS

Bad River

LOWER BRULE RESERVATION

CROW CREEK RES.

• Custer

BADLANDS

White River

× STRONGHOLD

Medicine Root Creek

Porcupine Creek

Wounded Knee Creek

PINE RIDGE RESERVATION

ROSEBUD RESERVATION

○ Rosebud Agency

Wounded Knee ★

○ Pine Ridge Agency

N E B R A S K A

ideas about what might happen next. Most likely, the Standing Rock Ghost Dancers might join Chief Big Foot on the Cheyenne River, where the dance had been in full swing for weeks. Then, too, the frightened Sitting Bull group might strike out for the Stronghold, where Short Bull and Kicking Bear still held out. Or they might set Big Foot in motion toward the Stronghold too, with terrible results. A potential "domino" effect could ignite the entire Sioux reservation system, once the news of Sitting Bull's death spread.

Agent McLaughlin immediately sent friendly scouts to find Sitting Bull's band. Upon finding them, the scouts were able to persuade over half to return to the Standing Rock Reservation. Some of the others simply scattered and sooner or later went back to their homes around Grand River. The rest—fewer than a hundred—headed south to join Big Foot.

They reached a camp that was already nervous and confused. Big Foot had been a great chief. But he was old now, in his seventies, and his control over his band was slipping. The band's medicine man, Yellow Bird, was a fanatical Ghost Dancer. Many of the young braves were ready to bring about their hoped-for victory over the whites. There were about 200 in the band, and all of them were aware of mounting pressure from the white soldiers.

The War Department had ordered Big Foot's arrest, on the false theory that he was almost as large a source of potential trouble as Sitting Bull had been. An observation camp, Camp Cheyenne, had been established by the cavalry just a few miles up the Cheyenne River. Infantry units from the east were trying to cross the Missouri River, which was partially ice-covered.

For several days Big Foot wavered among various alternatives. At one point he was convinced by messengers from the cavalry to go to the Cheyenne River Agency. But many of his young men wanted to go to the Stronghold instead. Big Foot had also been invited by the Pine Ridge chiefs to go there to settle the troubles. He had a great reputation as a diplomat, and he was offered a hundred ponies to heal the split between the "friendly" Sioux and the Ghost Dancers at Pine Ridge. Most of the time, however, Big Foot seemed to want only to stay put at his own camp and wait.

Finally, for reasons that are difficult to guess, Big Foot made his decision. He would go to Pine Ridge, make peace, and accept the gift of ponies. What he did not realize was that leaving his reservation when the whites were so frightened of a Sioux "uprising" would make him a fugitive "hostile" in the eyes of the military. Almost immediately, new orders went out for Big Foot's arrest. His band was to be disarmed and their horses taken. Then they would be marched to the railroad and sent to Omaha—far away from their own reservation lands. Big Foot never understood that this was the army's plan. He assumed that he was going to Pine Ridge on a mission of peace.

Big Foot's band left camp on December 23, under the cover of night. As soon as the officers at Camp Cheyenne realized that the old chief had gone, a desperate series of cavalry units started patrolling the line between Big Foot's camp and the Stronghold. But the chief passed east of the patrols. The band moved very slowly, for Big Foot had caught pneumonia. He rode in a wagon without springs. Soon Big Foot was bleeding through his nose. And it was bitterly cold for the old man. At one point, in a pass through a steep wall along the Bad River, Big Foot's men had to dig out a road for the wagon. Big Foot managed to reach Porcupine Creek, only about thirty miles from the Pine Ridge Agency, without being sighted by the army. He sent men ahead to tell the Sioux he was coming.

On December 28, five days after starting south, Big Foot's band was finally "captured" by the Seventh Cavalry. When the Indians and cavalry met, there was a tense moment. The cavalry formed a skirmish line and brought up cannon. Big Foot's braves formed a battle line in front of his wagon. But then the cavalry commander came forward. He and Big Foot shook hands, and the chief accepted an "escort"—going, he thought, to Pine Ridge. Together, the cavalry and the Indians made their way to a trading post at Wounded Knee Creek.

The officer in charge had wisely not tried to disarm the Sioux, and he let them keep their horses for the trip. He even transferred Big Foot into an ambulance wagon. When the two groups reached Wounded Knee, the Indians were issued rations. The rest of the Seventh Cavalry came from Pine Ridge to join the patrol. The Indians pitched their tepees in a low hollow near a ravine that led into the creek. There were 102 men, and 230 women and children. The soldiers—a total of about 500—camped on a rise just to the north. Armed sentries surrounded the Indians, but on the whole everything seemed peaceful enough.

Soon the Indians settled down and the cavalry—except for the ring of sentries around the Indian camp—went to sleep. Only a few officers, veterans of the Little Bighorn disaster, stayed up late. They celebrated over a keg of whiskey someone had brought from the agency.

The next morning Colonel James Forsyth, commander of the Seventh Cavalry, asked all the men of Big Foot's group to gather in a council between the tepees and the cavalry encampment. The sentries remained in place. The rest of the cavalry units drew up, mounted, around the Sioux men and their camp. Forsyth asked the Indians for their weapons.

Big Foot tried diplomacy. From his ambulance bed he quietly advised his men to give up the bad guns but hide the good ones. Soon Forsyth sent twenty of the Indians to the tepees to bring the guns. Meanwhile, however, the Sioux women (who understood the value of a weapon) had hidden the rifles that the Sioux had bought, stolen, or taken in battle. The Indians returned to the council with only two old, broken cavalry carbines.

Forsyth heightened his search. He placed a line of troops between the Sioux braves and their camp and sent his own men into the tepees. But this search uncovered only thirty rifles, most of them old and useless. This left one other real possibility: the Sioux were hiding their rifles under the blankets they kept draped over their shoulders against the cold.

By now the situation was very delicate. Forsyth ordered Big Foot brought out on his blanket. The medicine man, Yellow Bird, was dancing around, chanting Ghost Dance songs, urging the young braves to be firm. In the tepees women were hastily packing, ready to run.

Suddenly, one Indian, Black Coyote, pulled a rifle from his blanket and began to shout, holding the weapon over his head. He was probably deaf and, by the Indians' own testimony, a little insane. Two soldiers grabbed him and struggled for the rifle. It went off, firing overhead. In what may have been a signal, Yellow Bird threw a handful of dust into the air. Several braves pulled rifles from their blankets and aimed at the cavalry. "By God, they have broken," an officer shouted. The Indians fired, and at about the same moment came the command "Fire! Fire on them!"

No one could stop what happened next. Big Foot was quickly killed. Cavalry carbines ripped into the group of Sioux men. The bullets that did not find a Sioux body passed on across the ravine into the tepees. Women ran this way and that, followed by children. Some of the Indians broke toward the creek, where they were cut down by waiting cavalrymen. Others ran into the ravine.

Some officers did what they could to prevent women and children from being shot down. But the Indians (at least those who still had weapons) were fast and accurate with their repeating rifles, and the soldiers sometimes fired at anything that moved. When the artillery on the hill opened up on the Indians in the ravine, the shells exploded on all without regard to age or sex. Apparently, too, some of the soldiers broke ranks and chased down fleeing Indians. These were the bodies Charles Eastman found miles away from Wounded Knee.

The actual battle lasted only a few minutes and the cavalry's mopping-up only a short time longer. About 150 braves rode out from Pine Ridge, too late and too few to help their comrades. The cavalry gathered their own dead (25) and wounded (39) and returned to the Pine Ridge Agency. They took some of the wounded Sioux with them and left the rest on the field. There were at least 146 Indian dead— about half of them men. Some bodies were probably taken away during the next two days, before Eastman's party arrived to rescue the living and bury the rest. All in all, probably 200 Sioux and whites had died.

Wounded Knee was followed by a few small skirmishes. But soon Pine Ridge was pacified. The Stronghold Indians had given up while Big Foot's band was on the march. The Ghost Dance was over. Spring came and went, but the earth did not cover the white man, as the Messiah had promised. Paul Weinert, the cannoneer at Wounded Knee, received a Congressional Medal of Honor for his action at the edge of the ravine.

The Sioux who died at Wounded Knee were buried in a mass grave. With them died the last remnants of Indian resistance on the Western plains.

A small white church was later built at the Sioux mass grave, on what came to be called Cemetery Hill. In 1903, with the help of missionaries, the Indians put up their own small monument, burying Wounded Knee in the past.

This monument is erected by surviving relatives and other Ogalalla [Oglala] and Cheyenne River Sioux Indians in memory of the Chief Big Foot Massacre, Dec. 29, 1890. Col. Forsyth in command of U.S. troops. Big Foot was a great chief of the Sioux Indians. He often said, "I will stand in peace till my last day comes." He did many good and brave deeds for the white man and the red man. Many innocent women and children who knew no wrong died here.

Settling the Last Frontier

THERE IS NOTHING unique about the history of the Sioux. It is true they resisted the whites longer and more ferociously than most other Indians, east or west. And they were the only tribe that, inspired by the Messiah's new religion, developed a militant resistance to reservation life. But, despite these differences, they were finally defeated in a manner typical of the way in which white Americans subdued all the Indians.

The defeat of the Sioux and the other Plains Indians was just one part of continental expansion. White Americans had begun moving west in the 1830s. In the decades after the Civil War this movement increased in speed and recklessness.

THE LAST WEST

Until the 1840s America had a clearly drawn frontier. It was possible at each census before

MOVEMENT OF THE FRONTIER, 1790–1890

Frontier in
— 1790
— — 1810
······ 1830
— 1850
— — 1870
······ 1890

then to draw a zigzag line, north to south across the country, showing how far settlement had advanced in each decade. But after the Mexican War this was no longer true. The drift of pioneers into Oregon, the settlement of Texas and Utah, and the discovery of gold in California created isolated pockets of white settlement thousands of miles beyond the old frontier line near the Mississippi. By the early 1850s it was evident that the Pacific Coast would be settled fairly quickly, organized into territories, and carved into states. California had already been admitted to statehood as part of the Compromise of 1850. Oregon entered the Union nine years later.

Between the Pacific Coast and the old frontier in eastern Kansas and Nebraska lay a vast stretch of plains and mountains. It formed an area larger than the whole nation when Washington was President. This region was the last frontier, the last region to be settled by white Americans.

The Great Plains begin in the first tier of states west of the Mississippi River, and extend west to the Rockies. In 1836 the Senate Committee for Indian Affairs declared that the Great Plains were an "uninhabitable region." The Indians there "are on the outside of us, and in a place which will forever remain on the outside." In fact the plains were given an official name, "The Great American Desert." The weather there is dry. There is no water in many of the rivers during most of the year. The land is not covered with trees but with stubborn grass. Only the Indian and the buffalo seemed able to thrive. The Rocky Mountain region also seemed to offer little to encourage settlement. For many years its great peaks and high valleys were the home only of small Indian bands and a few American fur traders.

There were many reasons why this myth that the West could not be settled came to an end. Three of the earliest and most important factors were gold, railroads, and cattle. As min-

*Virginia City, Nevada, sprang up after the discovery of silver nearby in 1859. Mark Twain
described it as "the liveliest town that America ever produced" in its early years.
Schools, churches, and "respectable" businesses replaced saloons and gambling halls after
the initial excitement of silver fever had died down.*

ers, railroad men, and ranchers moved into the region, they systematically seized Indian lands. Then came the final pioneers of the last West, the farmers. In 1890 the Census Bureau announced that the frontier no longer existed.[1]

THE MINING FRONTIER

The discovery of gold and silver had been responsible for the rapid development of California. Miners who reached the Pacific Coast too late to find gold easily soon began to drift east over the mountains, looking for new bonanzas. In 1858 prospectors found gold near Pike's Peak in Colorado. Soon people were pouring into new, ramshackle towns like Denver, Pueblo, and

Boulder. Their covered wagons proclaimed "Pike's Peak or Bust!" A year after the first strike about 100,000 people—mostly men without their families—had moved into the area. Like most other Western gold and silver strikes, the Pike's Peak boom did not last. The earliest prospectors soon raked off the surface gold. The remaining precious metal was buried deep in the mountains, where it could be mined only with expensive machinery that individual miners could not afford. Within three months in 1859 the population of the Colorado gold fields dwindled to about 50,000. But enough men stayed to create a pocket of white settlement in the mountains.

A similar process was under way farther west, in what is now Nevada. Miners from California found gold near the western border of the region in the late 1850s. In 1859 they discovered the famous Comstock Lode. One of the richest

[1] The Census Bureau, of course, was referring only to the territory beyond the Mississippi River to the west coast. Alaska, which was purchased from Russia in 1867 by Andrew Johnson's Secretary of State William Seward, was still largely unsettled in 1890. That territory was really America's last frontier.

single mines in America, it produced over $200 million worth of gold and silver in the thirty years after its discovery. Thousands of men rushed over the mountains from Sacramento to build nearby Virginia City. Soon the town had five newspapers, a miniature stock exchange, and a horde of prospectors, saloonkeepers, prostitutes, and gamblers. A few men became enormously wealthy. Most of the prospectors, however, went away disappointed.

Some miners who stayed found small pockets of loose gold that could be mined with a pan or a sluice, a simple trough that runs water downhill over dirt and loose rocks, washing out the heavy gold dust. This kind of mining, called placer mining, soon washed off the free metal near the surface. The only way to make the gold fields pay off on a large scale over a long period was to invest money in machinery that could dig out hard rock below the surface. This meant that the miner's frontier quickly became a corporate frontier, exploited by mining companies owned by Eastern investors. Within a few years any

successful field soon became an industrial development. And the prospectors scattered again in search of a new discovery and easy pickings elsewhere.

The California Gold Rush that had excited so many thousands of Americans in 1849 was repeated over and over again throughout the West. In the late 1850s a small strike was made in eastern Washington, but it soon petered out. Restless miners headed farther east, up the Snake and Salmon rivers into Idaho. There they built Boise, Silver City, and other new mining towns. By 1861, the start of the Civil War, there were probably 30,000 white men in Idaho.

During the Civil War—while their countrymen were battling at Bull Run and Chickamauga—white miners moved from Idaho into Montana. There they struck gold and silver at Last Chance Gulch (which later became the city of Helena) and Alder Gulch (Virginia City). By 1863 Idaho had enough citizens to organize as a territory, and Montana followed only a year later.

Open-pit mining, utilizing expensive heavy machinery to dig through the surface of hard rock to the ores below, helped turn the miner's frontier into a corporate frontier.

The Telegraph

Modern telegraphy and the name of Samuel F. B. Morse are forever linked. Morse was the inventor of the first usable telegraph in the United States. Yet the telegraph key and the code for transmitting messages that bears Morse's name were devised by others. But it was Morse's gift to see the possible use of electricity in communications. He persisted in the face of great odds to prove his ideas.

The inventor's fascination with electricity won him a university teaching post. He could then pursue his special interest. In 1836 he completed a crude apparatus consisting of a transmitter of electrical impulses and a receiver that made marks on a moving strip of paper in response. But the impulses could travel only a few feet by wire. His real breakthrough—and the basis for his status as an inventor—came from his addition of a relay device for reinforcing the electric current. This made long-distance telegraphy feasible.

In 1838 he applied for aid from Congress to continue his research but was refused. Although years

of poverty and frustration followed, he did not give up. Finally, in 1843, he was granted $30,000 to build an experimental telegraph line from Washington, D.C., to Baltimore. On May 24, 1844, at the Capitol building, Morse transmitted the first formal message: "What hath God wrought?" The quotation was from the Old Testament, and the event became legendary.

At first the government decided to operate the telegraph service as a government agency, like the post office. But private companies were formed in the East, with Morse holding patent privileges. Early in 1847 Congress mistakenly concluded that the telegraph business would be unprofitable. It turned over the Washington-Baltimore line to Morse's partners. The rush to build telegraph lines began.

Lines from New York to other major cities were set up first. By 1848 Florida was the only state east of the Mississippi without telegraph service. Poor message service was common, often because of bad weather. But the popularity of the telegraph increased. Newspapers and stockbrokers were the most eager customers.

The 1850s saw the birth of many rival companies, for equipment was cheap and financing became easy. Gradually, a few giants emerged. Western Union, formed in 1856, was the leader. Its fabulous growth is shown by the increase in capital stock from $385,000 in 1858 to $41,000,000 in 1867. A few years later the company held 66,000 of the 73,000 miles of national lines.

Other landmarks in the growth of the telegraph were the spanning of the continent (1861), the invention of the stock ticker (1866), and the beginning of successful transatlantic cable service (1866). Probably more than any other invention, the telegraph knit together the nation. For his part, Samuel Morse acquired wealth and fame—and a series of costly law suits with rival inventors and telegraph companies.

This 1859 sketch shows a stage near Tucson, Arizona, on the Butterfield Overland Express route. Passengers had to endure the rough ride through desert lands on springless seats.

The last Western gold rush occurred in 1874. In the Black Hills of South Dakota, in the heart of the Great Sioux reservation, an army expedition commanded by General Custer found traces of gold. According to a treaty between the United States and the Indians, the hills belonged to the Sioux "forever." For a short time the government tried to prevent white men from entering the Black Hills. But the pressure to find gold was too great. Within two years about 7,000 whites had built Deadwood and Custer City. The Sioux lands had been decisively invaded.

TRANSPORTATION WEST

The influx of miners, together with the settlement of Oregon and California, led to demands for quick, safe, and economical land transportation between the settled East and the Far West. Every new mining town wanted to be linked to the rest of the country. People who lived on the west coast wanted an overland route as an alternate to the long sea voyage from the east coast around South America.

Trail, Stage, and Pony The Oregon Trail, Santa Fe Trail, and other routes followed by pioneers in the 1840s and early 1850s were more or less protected by army posts along the way. But they were far from being real roads. Something else seemed necessary.

In 1858 the first stage road was finally cut through the countryside for the Butterfield Overland Express. Its route ran 2,000 miles from St. Louis south through Indian Territory,[2] then across Texas, New Mexico, and Arizona. The ride was rough and usually very hot, and the trip took twenty-four days. But the road was faster than the sea voyage. Soon other stage and freighting companies were opening additional roads across Colorado and Utah to California.

In 1860 businessmen set up a mail service known as the pony express. Small, lightweight boys, like jockeys, rode big horses (not ponies) in relays between St. Joseph, Missouri, and Sacramento, California. The young riders were able to carry a message across the country in ten days. The pony express prospered for only about a year, however. In 1861 the first telegraph line was put through to the west coast. The time for sending and receiving cross-country messages was then cut to a split second.

---

[2] This region—corresponding roughly to the present state of Oklahoma—was set aside in 1834 for Indians removed from east of the Mississippi. Later, parts of it were reserved for Western Indians, too.

A Transcontinental Railroad All these ways of getting people, goods, and information across the country were only preludes to the most dramatic and successful method of all, the railroad. A transcontinental railroad had been a dream since the 1840s—to move people through the West to California. The North and South, however, had not been able to agree on the western part of the route. The North wanted a line to run from Chicago to San Francisco. The South insisted on a route through Texas to southern California.

The Civil War ended this competition. By seceding, the South lost its right to participate in the decision making. In 1862 Congress settled on a route between San Francisco and Council Bluffs, Iowa. The same law provided for enormous financial support from the federal government. There would be two companies. The Central Pacific would build east from San Fran-

cisco. The Union Pacific (a patriotic name for wartime) would go west across Nebraska and Colorado. They were to meet somewhere in the middle. Each railroad would be given a right of way 400 feet wide. In addition, the government would lend the railroads up to $48,000 for each mile of track laid—less for flat country, more for mountain track. Most important, the railroads would be given 6,400 acres for every mile of track completed. In 1864 this land allowance was doubled.

The Central Pacific started building toward the east slowly. The company lacked funds, and labor was scarce. But gradually these problems were resolved. The Lincoln administration cooperated by including mountains in the flat-country category, thereby entitling the railroad to the largest possible loans. The labor problem was soon solved by importing thousands of Chinese. In all of 1864 the railroad laid only

A railroad line spanning the continent would not have been possible without the help of thousands of Chinese laborers, who did much of the work on the Central Pacific.

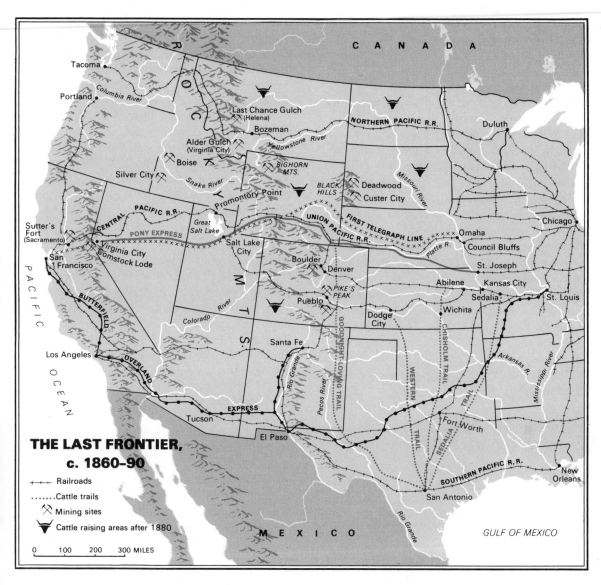

THE LAST FRONTIER,
c. 1860–90

+–+–+ Railroads
· · · · · Cattle trails
⚒ Mining sites
🐃 Cattle raising areas after 1880

0   100   200   300 MILES

about 20 miles of track, but by 1867 the pace was up to 20 miles a month.

At the other end of the proposed route the Union Pacific also built slowly. It picked up speed by bringing in thousands of Irish immigrants to lay rails. In 1868 alone the Union Pacific laid 425 miles of track.

In May 1869, after only five years of construction, the two work gangs met at Promontory Point, Utah, just east of the Great Salt Lake. The last tie put down was coated with silver, the last spike was gold. A telegraph operator cabled east and west: "Hats off—prayer is being offered." Then there was a wait of almost fifteen minutes. Again the telegraph clicked: "We have got done praying. The spike is about to be presented." Railroad officials took turns with the hammer—the first blow was a bad miss—but the work was done. The two locomotives eased forward until they touched. The nation celebrated almost as wildly as it had at the end of the Civil War. Chicago's parade was seven miles long. The nation was joined, east to west, across a desert that an earlier generation had believed would never be settled.

During the next fifteen years three more routes were opened across the Rockies. Iowa, Missouri, Kansas, and Nebraska were crisscrossed by rails. In the process the government gave the railroad companies almost 180 million acres of public land, and it lent them over $100 million. Because of complicated regulations that allowed railroads to delay choosing the land they wanted to keep along their rights of way, they could keep great stretches of land for years. At one point the railroads controlled—at least on paper—almost all of Iowa and Wisconsin. The Northern Pacific, whose route crossed the northern tier of states between Lake Superior and the Pacific, had a strip of land larger than many European nations. The same kind of situation developed in Arizona and New Mexico. By 1885 the railroads held land totaling almost a sixth of the entire country.

FROM BUFFALO TO CATTLE

What mattered in the long run was not the paper land grants. The railroads did make millions of dollars in profits from land sales. But the real effect of the railroads was to open new avenues of profit in the plains environment. Obviously railroads benefited the corporations that were taking gold, silver, and lead from the Rockies. They also helped to create an entirely new industry— ranching. Building the railroads hastened the destruction of the plains buffalo herds. But it also made possible the exploitation of another animal, the cow.

Early in the sixteenth century the Spanish had begun importing European cattle into America. Over the years the cattle had multiplied. Some had escaped and become wild, especially in southern Texas around the Nueces River. These were the famous Texas longhorns—lanky, tough, long-horned, and too dangerous to be captured or herded on foot. They roamed at will over the open range, a huge expanse of grass that was part of the public domain. By 1860, there were probably 5 million head of longhorns in Texas.

The Mexicans had learned to rope, brand, and even herd longhorns. In fact, it was Mexicans and not Americans who were the first cowboys. They originated almost all of the tools of the cowboy's trade, from his big hat and kerchief to his tooled leather saddle and boots. Mexico, however, had no real market for beef. The situation was different in the United States.

The Civil War sent beef prices soaring in both North and South. The beef herd in the Northern states was smaller at the end of the war than at the beginning. At the same time, the population had grown by more than 20 percent. Thus the demand for beef increased, and so did the price. A man could buy a longhorn steer in Texas for as little as three dollars. The same steer in Chicago would be worth ten times as much.

The Long Drive   By 1866 the Missouri Pacific Railroad had pushed its line west to Sedalia, Missouri, just east of Kansas City. That same year the first large group of Texans drove enormous herds north across Indian Territory to reach the rail line. The men ran into many difficulties. Part of the route passed through dense forests. The longhorns, unaccustomed to woods, panicked and refused to be driven through the trees. The Indians (whose treaty gave them control of any white travel across their land) harassed the cowboys. This early attempt showed, however, that it was possible to herd cattle safely over hundreds of miles to the railroad—and thus to Eastern markets.

Thus began the twenty-year era of the "long drive." As the years passed, the railroads extended farther west. New cattle towns replaced Sedalia. Among them were Abilene (probably the most successful), Wichita, and Dodge City. Between 1866 and 1888 Texans drove as many as 6 million head of cattle over the grasslands to Kansas.

For those who succeeded, the profits of the long drive were enormous. Cattlemen claimed that as much as 40 percent profit per year was not unusual. Like the miner's frontier, the cattleman's bonanza soon attracted thousands of eager Easterners. Each usually had a few hundred dollars and a dream of running a vast ranch. Like the prospectors, most of the would-be ranchers were disappointed. Many of them returned home or switched to another line of work such as running a store or saloon.

The long drive, despite the romantic myth of the cowboy it fostered, was a business. It required capital if it was to succeed on a big scale. In the end only the lucky few who had been there first (like the prospectors in California or Nevada) became "cattle barons." In the long run, it was Eastern and European investors, with enough capital to buy and move large herds, who controlled most of the industry.

The End of the Open Range The long drive had a brief existence. Gradually, people north of Texas realized that as the railroads came closer, it made sense to breed and feed cattle nearby instead of bringing them up from Texas. During the 1880s the long drive from Texas was replaced by an even wilder cattle bonanza in other plains territories to the north. In 1860 there were no cattle at all in the northwestern plains, and there were only a few in Kansas and Nebraska. By 1880 Montana, the Dakota Territory, Wyoming, and Colorado had great herds, totaling almost 4 million head.

But the days of the open range, when cattle wandered on public land from one spring to the next, could not last long. The cattle industry soon found itself in a situation faced earlier by tobacco and cotton growers—overproduction. Rapid expansion led to an overstocked range. The grass could not support so many cattle. The increased

The long drives of cattle from the rich grasslands of the Southwest to Northern markets lasted through the 1880s. They created vast fortunes for a few fortunate cattle barons and gave the country the legend of the cowboy.

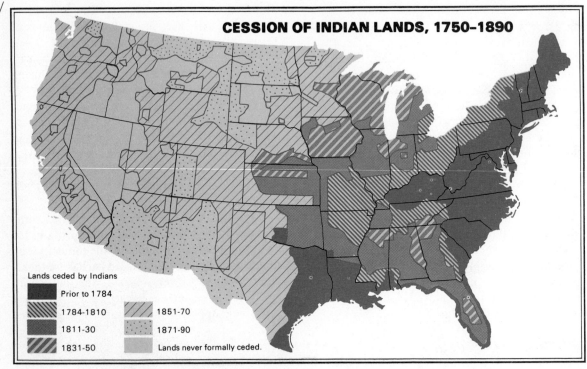

CESSION OF INDIAN LANDS, 1750–1890

Lands ceded by Indians
- Prior to 1784
- 1784–1810
- 1811–30
- 1831–50
- 1851–70
- 1871–90
- Lands never formally ceded.

supply also caused prices to fall. Between 1885 and 1886 the price of a steer dropped from thirty dollars to ten dollars. The following winter on the plains was the bitterest in memory. Thousands of cattle starved and froze to death. The cattle bonanza was over.

THE DEFEAT OF THE WESTERN INDIANS

The miners, railroads, and cattlemen brought about the final chapter in the conflict between whites and Indians. It was a conflict older than Jamestown and as dark as any aspect of American history. The whites cloaked their actions with high-sounding expressions like "civilization against savagery" or "Manifest Destiny." But the facts were very simple: the white men came and took the Indians' lands.

White people in the New World had always regarded the Indians as a problem. For most whites—whether they were French, Spanish, or English— the Indians were seen either as a people to be exploited through trade or slavery or as a barrier to westward expansion. A few whites sympathized with the Indians and did what they could to protect them from the worst aspects of white civilization. But even to those who were sympathetic, help meant teaching the Indian to "adjust to civilization."

The Indians might be a problem for the whites but the whites meant disaster for the Indians. At stake for the whites was only the delay of continental expansion for a generation or so. The stakes were much higher for the Indians. They were in danger of losing their culture, their freedom, their identity as human beings and, in many cases, their lives. This was true from the time Cortes invaded Mexico, through Bacon's Rebellion and the removal of the Cherokee and other tribes westward,[3] down to the final conquest of the tribes of the West.

Advantages of the Whites White people's ways were overpowering to the Indians. In the first place, the whites' methods of dealing with the environment were totally unlike those of the Indians. Some Indians farmed a little. But the whites were able to cultivate vast stretches of land, first with teams of mules or oxen, then with machinery. Some Indians, like the Navajos, made ornaments out of silver or gold. But the whites came for gold and silver in droves. Big new towns and frightening machines and explosives changed the face of the mountains and valleys of the Rockies. The Indians hunted wild animals, which seemed numerous enough to last forever. But the whites killed off wild animals, fenced in the range, and raised great herds of cattle instead.

These were the main white weapons—farming, mining, and ranching. Along with these the whites brought strange powers and "medicine" that made the Indians' situation hopeless indeed—the railroad, soldiers' machine guns and cannons, and the telegraph.

Another weapon of the whites against the Indians was something they did not use on purpose—indeed, the whites feared it themselves. This was disease. Smallpox, measles, and other sicknesses may have wiped out as many as half the Western Indians before any significant number of whites even arrived in their territory. The germs traveled with traders and so preceded actual white migrations by decades. The Indians had no inherited resistance or immunity to many diseases of the whites, since the germs had been "imported" from Europe. Indians died by the band and even by the tribe from sicknesses that only made most whites uncomfortable.

Finally, the whites had an advantage that probably counted more than anything else—

These Mandan Indians survived a smallpox epidemic in 1872. Indians had no immunity to white men's diseases like smallpox and therefore died by the thousands when exposed to them.

people. They poured west by the thousands. In one change of seasons, between one Sun Dance and another, the whites seemed to be able to throw up towns like San Francisco, Denver, or Deadwood—towns larger than the whole Sioux nation.

One by one, the tribes of the Great Plains, the California-Intermountain area, and the Northwest Coast were made to realize that the whites were a force they could neither understand nor control. Some groups, like the Sioux, the Kiowas, and the Apaches, fought back. They were sustained by their myths, their magic, and their hatred of the cavalry that invaded their villages, shooting men, women, and children. But, in the end, all the tribes were defeated. Only something as unusual as the Messiah's Ghost Dance could convince the Indians—and only a few at that—that there was any way to combat the enveloping white civilization.

---

[3] In the 1830s the federal government forced the so-called Five Civilized Tribes—the Cherokees, Chickasaws, Choctaws, Creeks, and Seminoles—to move from the Southeast to Indian Territory. The Indians suffered so much on the trip west that the journey became known as the trail of tears.

Dealing with the Tribes From the beginning, United States policy toward the Indians had been contradictory. On the one hand, the government treated tribes as independent nations with whom it could make treaties. On the other hand, Indians were not citizens but wards of the government, subject to federal control. In addition, the nation was growing with incredible speed. Again and again, government aims that seemed practical in one decade were obsolete ten years later.

In California and Oregon, and in the frontier regions of the Rockies, relations between whites and Indians were poorly controlled by the government. Groups of whites simply drove the Indians out, murdering many of them in the process. The Indians of California suffered especially. They had settled around Spanish missions and learned farming and various crafts. After the Spanish missions were closed down in the 1830s, the Indians were defenseless against the greedy whites. In the ten years after the Gold Rush of 1849, some 70,000 of these mission Indians died from starvation, whites' diseases, and outright murder.

On the Great Plains whites might band together to attack Indians. But the government and its army played a much larger role there than it did farther west. After 1850 the history of Indian-white relations settled down to a fairly steady rhythm of treaties, uprisings, war, and new treaties. The Indians were always the losers. Even when they won the battles, they lost in making the treaties.

This process began in 1851 at Fort Laramie on the Oregon Trail. To protect the trail, the government called hundreds of Indian leaders together and persuaded them to agree not to bother the wagon trains passing across their territory. Each tribe accepted boundaries to its hunting grounds. In return the government promised to leave them in peace.

These agreements left the Indians in possession of almost all the Great Plains. But accepting boundaries laid out by Washington opened the door to a new government tactic—getting each tribe to give up part of its lands in separate treaties. By 1865 the Indians had given up all of Kansas, most of Nebraska, the central half of Utah, and almost all of Texas.

The Sand Creek Massacre Much Indian land was surrendered peacefully, in return for promises of peace and annual shipments of government supplies, called annuities. But in 1861 in Colorado, a government attempt to move Cheyennes and Arapahoes onto a small reservation at Sand Creek resulted in a three-year guerrilla war by the Indians. In 1864 the leader of the warring Indians, Black Kettle, tried to make peace with the whites. The army and the territoral government refused. The unyielding commander of the Colorado militia, Colonel John Chivington, told Black Kettle: "My rule for fighting white men or Indians is to fight them until they lay down their arms and surrender."

Black Kettle led his people to a camp at Sand Creek, where he hoped to be left in peace. But the Indians woke on November 29, 1864, to find 1,000 of Chivington's militia surrounding them. The militia rushed the camp, shooting at everything that moved. When the "fight" was over, 450 Indians were dead. Only about 50 had escaped the massacre. The next year the Cheyennes and Arapahoes had to sign a new treaty. It forced them to leave their Colorado plains for a barren corner of Indian Territory.

Negotiations with the Sioux The Sioux fared better, at least for a time. Their agreement at Fort Laramie in 1851 gave them one of the largest hunting areas in the West—most of the Dakota Territory and the region around the Powder River in eastern Wyoming and southern Montana. But by 1865 miners had crowded into Montana at Bozeman, Virginia City, and Helena. These towns soon demanded a road connecting them with the Oregon Trail. This road would cross the Yellowstone River, skirt the Sioux hunting areas around the Big Horn Mountains, and cross directly over the valley of the Powder River.

In the summer of 1865 the cavalry moved into the area to construct forts and begin work

I am tired of fighting. The old men are all dead. [My brother] who led the young men is dead. It is cold, and we have no blankets. The little children are freezing to death. My people, some of them, have run away to the hills. No one knows where they are. I want to have time to look for my children and see how many I can find. Maybe I shall find them among the dead. Hear me, my chiefs. From where the sun now stands, I will fight no more forever.

With these words Chief Joseph of the Nez Percé surrendered to American troops on October 5, 1877, in the Bearpaw mountains of Montana. The "rebellion" of the Nez Percé, started four months earlier, ended. It began when the Indians were forced to leave their homeland in the Wallowa Valley of Oregon. They had eluded their pursuers by a roundabout route through the rugged mountains of Idaho, Montana, and Wyoming. Hopeful of refuge in Canada, they were only thirty miles from the border when they were attacked. The Indians held out four days. Finally, after being told that his people would be sent to a reservation in Idaho, Joseph surrendered. He handed his rifle to his captors and made his solemn promise of peace. He never broke that promise.

He came from a proud and peaceful people. (The Nez Percé, French for "pierced nose," were named for their habit of wearing ornamental pieces of shell.) They were buffalo hunters, cattle breeders, and superb horsemen. In 1855 they had agreed to reservation status in order to keep their land. But, in 1863, when gold was discovered there, the reserve was drastically reduced. Joseph's father refused to sign away his ancestral lands. He and some other chiefs separated from the "treaty Indians." This bold move went unchallenged for years.

In 1871, at age 30, Joseph became chief When settlers began moving into the Wallowa Valley, Joseph protested. President Grant responded by declaring the area a reservation "for the roaming Nez Percé." But in 1875 this policy was reversed.

Joseph's people were ordered to leave their homeland for a reservation in Idaho.

The young braves resisted at first, but Joseph convinced them that war was futile. In great sorrow the exodus began: about 250 warriors, 450 women, children, and old people, and 2,000 horses. Whites harassed the group and stole some horses. The braves retaliated, killing some whites. Although a man of peace, Joseph would not abandon his people. So, with federal troops closing in, he planned an escape to Canada. Outnumbered, he played a grim game of hide-and-seek, counterattacking only when provoked.

But Joseph was unable to help his people. They were not sent to the Idaho reservation as promised. Instead, they were placed on the plains of Oklahoma. Many died there. Joseph made several trips to Washington, to plead for relocation, but his eloquence failed. Forbidden to return to his homeland, he died in 1904. The official cause of death was described as a broken heart.

A wagon train expedition, protected by Colonel George Custer's cavalry, entered the Black Hills of South Dakota in search of gold in 1874. Within three years the Sioux were forced off their lands and onto reservations.

on the road. A Sioux chief, Red Cloud, led his people in a two-year attack on the road and the forts. And in 1868 the government made a new treaty that seemed to give the victory to Red Cloud. The road was abandoned. But the Sioux, in return, had to agree to a reservation that included only the Dakotas west of the Missouri—the so-called Great Sioux Reservation. Accord-

ing to the treaty, they could still hunt in the Powder River country. For the first time, however, they had accepted a reservation to replace the large domain that their 1851 treaty had recognized.

The same commission that made the 1868 agreement with the Sioux dealt with other Plains tribes in the same way. Reservations were created in Indian Territory for the southern groups—the Kiowa, Comanche, Arapaho, Cheyenne, Osage, and Pawnee tribes. Between 1868 and 1874 the northern tribes—Crow and Blackfoot, Shoshoni and Mandan—also accepted new, restricted reservations. By 1876 the Plains Indians had given up over three-fourths of the land they had held under the Fort Laramie Treaty.

The Battle of the Little Bighorn The policy of concentrating Indians on reservations was applied once again in the Black Hills area of South Dakota. The treaty of 1868 guaranteed the Tetons complete possession of the Black Hills. But in 1874 rumors of gold led to a reconnaissance of the area by a military column of the Seventh Cavalry under Colonel George Custer. Custer's men found gold, and the resulting rush into Deadwood and other mining towns made conflict between the Sioux and the whites inevitable.

The Grant administration tried for a time to hold the prospectors back. The army even removed some of them. But finally the government gave in and allowed the prospectors to enter the Black Hills "at their own risk." The next step was as cruel and illegal as any the government ever took against the Sioux. To prevent clashes between the miners and the Indians, Washington ordered all the Sioux to report to reservation agencies. Any who remained outside would be considered automatically "hostile" and liable to attack. Many of the Sioux obeyed the order. But about 8,000 of them defied the government and gathered in the area of the Big Horn Mountains for their annual summer encampment and Sun Dance.

In June 1876 the army launched powerful forces of infantry, cavalry, and artillery against these Indians. One column, marching north from the Platte River, met Crazy Horse at Rosebud Creek on June 17. The army was beaten back in fierce fighting. Crazy Horse returned to the Sioux camp at the Little Bighorn River, where 8,000 Teton Sioux had gathered—the most powerful single force of Indians the army would ever face. Another army column advanced from the east. On June 25 the Seventh Cavalry, again under Custer's command, rode foolishly to the attack. The Sioux killed almost all of Custer's force in the most famous (and, from the white point of view, perhaps the most stupid) Indian battle in American history.

Another cycle of treaty, war, and new treaty was about to be completed. Within a year the Sioux were forced to give up their important Black Hills area. They were now forced onto a reservation covering only the central part of South Dakota, between the Missouri River and the Black Hills. But their troubles were not over. A railroad was pushing toward the reservation, and the remaining Sioux stood in its path. Farmers and ranchers were also beginning to look longingly at the land that the Sioux still held.

A Changing Indian Policy At this time a new government policy toward Indians was beginning to take shape. Reformers—many of them missionaries and people who had never spent a day with an Indian—were promoting the change. It was not enough, they argued, to concentrate the Indians on reservations. They had to be "civilized"—converted to Christianity and white people's way of life. The best way to do this, the reformers felt, was to make the Indians into landholding farmers. Each one would receive land and be taught how to plow and plant.

When the Indians had agreed to give up land, they did so as tribes, not as individuals surrendering private property. The reformers believed that this attitude toward land ownership was harmful. To counteract it, they proposed that the Indians be given land as separate individuals. For once, Eastern reformers and Western exploiters agreed. The latter, who were anxious to break up the reservations, could do simple arithmetic. In almost every case, after individual allocations were made, there would still be reservation land left over. It, too, would become available to whites.

The new policy became law in the Dawes Act of 1887. Each Indian family head received 160 acres, each single adult 80 acres, and each dependent child 40 acres. The whites began to apply the policy immediately. In 1888, after a great deal of argument and some trickery, the Sioux were persuaded to accept the new policy.

The same policy was applied to the other Plains Indians. The resulting demoralization provided a fertile ground for the new Ghost Dance religion. No matter what the intentions of the people who wrote and supported the Dawes Act, it was a disaster for the Indians. In 1887 the Indians held about 130 million acres of land. By 1930 total Indian landholdings had been reduced to less than 50 million acres.

With the new policy came even stronger efforts to convert the Indians to white civilization—to make them "walk the white man's road," as Sitting Bull put it. These efforts hardened the conflicting attitudes of the progressive Indians, who accepted the new ways, and the nonprogressives, who clung to the old ones. The division was dramatized when Sitting Bull was arrested by Indian police from his own tribe. Even after the "reforms" of the 1880s American policy toward the Indians was a calamity. They were reduced to a condition in some ways worse than that of the freed slaves in the South.

FARMING ON THE PLAINS

Mining, railroads, and cattle ranching had created a scattered pattern of settlement on the Great Plains and in the Rockies. Miners gathered in towns that were separated by hundreds of miles. Railroads created towns but only along their rights of way. And ranchers needed only a few cowhands to handle even very large herds. The actual white settlement of the plains had to await the slower migrations of farmers away from the Mississippi and onto the dry grasslands.

The Homestead Act The pace and pattern of settlement depended very much on government encouragement. In its youth the Republican party had been the party of "free soil," which meant both agriculture without slavery and free land for any American. One of the first measures promoted by the Lincoln administration was the Homestead Act of 1862. According to this law, any citizen (or any immigrant who had taken the first step toward becoming a citizen) could claim 160 acres of public land, just by paying a fee of $10. If he "lived upon or cultivated" the land for five years, the land became his, free and forever. If the homesteader did not want to wait five years, he could pay for the land at $1.25 an acre and own it immediately.

The Homestead Act resulted in over half a million claims, totaling 80 million acres. But if its purpose was to give away most of the public lands of the West to simple farmers, it was a failure. Much more land was given to railroads and states or sold directly to speculators than was ever acquired by small farmers.

Moreover, many of the homestead claims were phony. By law it was possible to transfer ownership at any time to any other person or corporation. So for example, a rancher could have each of his hands claim a homestead and then (for a small bribe) transfer ownership to the ranch. Any land speculator could do the same, just by paying a bribe to a stranger passing through.

Other Land Acts Congress made the situation worse by passing several more laws that promoted corruption and the robbery of public land. First, in 1873, came the Timber Culture Act, which allowed a homesteader (or a rancher or speculator) to claim an additional 160 acres if he would plant trees on 40 of the acres. In 1877 Congress passed the Desert Land Act, which allowed an individual to claim 640 acres of land if he would begin irrigation. Under the law ranchers took up section after section of land, especially in the Southwest, since they needed it for grazing cattle. They had their friends swear that it was irrigated (even if they had only poured a bucket of water on it in the presence of their "witnesses").

Even more corruption resulted from the Timber and Stone Act of 1878. This law applied to forest land that could not be farmed but that was highly profitable for timber. Under this law any citizen or immigrant could purchase up to 160 acres of Western forest for $2.50 an acre. Lumbermen used the same tricks that ranchers and other speculators used. They imported sailors, prospectors, and others to buy land and then sign it over to a company for a small fee. And since one good log sold for about $2.50, every tree but the first from any acre of land was pure profit. Under these laws over 20 million more acres of potentially valuable public land fell into the hands of corporations and speculators.

Hardships and Solutions Despite the fact that many of the profits went to land speculators and big corporations, Western lands were opened to the American people. Though they might have to pay ten dollars an acre to a speculator instead of getting free homestead land from the government, farmers moved out onto the plains anyway. The majority came from the states bordering the Mississippi. Most of the rest were immigrants. Almost no workers from Eastern cities made the trip west. But the men and women who did go to the plains performed a monumental task. In the thirty years after 1870 they brought more land under cultivation than had been cleared and plowed by all the generations of farmers from the settlement of Jamestown to the Civil War.

These farmers confronted problems that they had not met farther east. They found that their old ways of plowing and planting would not work. For one thing, rainfall was scarce, rivers often ran dry, and the water table[4] was low. Farmers had to haul water from long distances or collect it in holes when it did rain. New well-digging machinery invented in the 1880s and 1890s, however, enabled people to dig

---

[4] The water table of an area is the supply of water within the ground.

From the 1860s through the 1880s settlers rolled across the plains in prairie schooners like these, conquering one frontier after another. Hardships endured along the way paled in comparison with those met in taming the land.

deeper wells. And steel windmills made it easier to pump the water up. Plains dwellers also developed dry farming. This technique—by which a farmer covers a plowed field with a blanket of dust—conserves the moisture in the soil.

Another problem on the plains was lack of wood. Farmers living there often made their first homes from cakes of sod. For fuel they burned old hay or dried cow dung. Fencing was a special problem until the invention of barbed wire in the 1870s.

A farm family soon learned that, while sixty acres of land could support them farther east, five times as much was needed on the plains. Plowing, planting, and harvesting extensive acreage were greatly aided, nevertheless, by the invention of mechanized farm equipment (see Chapter 24).

Nature seemed to do things on a grand scale on the plains. In the summer the wind blew hot and twice as hard as in the East. In winter blizzards howled down out of the mountains, burying homes and killing livestock. Tornadoes, dust storms, and plagues of locusts and grasshoppers were frequent.

Dry years drove thousands of farmers back east. Many of those who stayed barely survived. In the end, though, farmers turned the plains into the world's most efficient area for producing wheat, corn, and other grains. By 1880 American

Homesteaders like this Montana farmer took advantage of the government offer of cheap land in the West. Many failed, but those who mastered the harsh climate turned the Great Plains into the bread basket of America.

flour—like American beef and pork from the same area—was being exported in great quantities all over the world.

In all this the Indian was, of course, the great loser. The whites' successes on the plains did seem to prove what white Americans had always believed—that the Indians could not make "proper" use of their environment because they lived too much with it and not enough from it. White men were able to exploit even the tough plains environment, to draw from it enough food to feed not only most of the United States but part of the rest of the world, too. The Indian, in contrast, had been willing to settle for the little he needed to maintain his way of life. A full century was to pass before white Americans began to ask themselves seriously whether the Indian's way was not somehow at least as good as theirs. Only one thing was certain: in his "primitive" way the Indian had respected nature more. He had never viewed his world as an object to be owned, changed, and exploited. This, at least in part, was what the battle at Wounded Knee was all about.

1. What present-day states make up what used to be called "The Great American Desert"? Why was the area called that?
2. Why did the mining frontier become a "corporate frontier"?
3. Why was no transcontinental railroad built before the Civil War? How did the government aid the building of a transcontinental line? Was this government policy of aid worth the cost?
4. What was the purpose of the long drive? Why did it end? To what does the phrase "open range" refer? Why did it lead to the overproduction of cattle?
5. What was the attitude of most Americans, including sympathizers, toward the Indians?
6. Describe the major weapons used by whites in overpowering Indians.
7. Cite examples to show that no matter what policy they followed—warfare or treaty-making—the Indians were always the losers.
8. Were those who were attempting to promote individual land ownership and farming among the Indians mistaken? Why or why not? Cite the Dawes Act in your answer.
9. What was the purpose of the Homestead Act? Show how it and other land acts failed to achieve this purpose.

Beyond the Text

1. Look into Frederick Jackson Turner's thesis on the meaning of the closing of the frontier and prepare a discussion defending or opposing it.
2. Discuss the cowboy in fact and in fiction. Include in the discussion the significance of the black cowboy in the development of the frontier.
3. Debate the proposition: The Culture of the Indians Was As "Good" As That of the Whites Who Tried to Eliminate It.
4. In 1972–73 Indian activities at Wounded Knee again became prominent. Check newspapers and magazines to determine what were the issues between the Indians and the government, what tactics were used, and what success these tactics had.
5. What problems did the Great Plains area present to settlers, and how did they solve these problems? Specifically investigate how the pioneers provided fencing and building materials in an area where there was no lumber, and how they acquired water in an area of low annual rainfall.

Bibliography

Nonfiction

Adams, Andy, *Trail Drive.*
Atherton, Lewis, *The Cattle Kings.**
Billington, Ray A., *Westward Expansion.*
Billington, Ray A., ed., *The Frontier Thesis.*
Brown, Dee, *Bury My Heart at Wounded Knee.**
Fee, Chester A., *Chief Joseph.*
Josephy, Alvin, Jr., *The Indian Heritage of America.**
Monaghan, Jay, *Custer.**
Robbins, Roy M., *Our Landed Heritage.**
Shannon, Fred A., *The Farmer's Last Frontier.*
Utley, Robert M., *The Last Days of the Sioux Nation.**
Webb, Walter P., *The Great Plains.**

Fiction

Allen, Henry, *No Survivors.*
Blackburn, Thomas W., *A Good Day to Die.**
Cather, Willa A., *My Antonia.**
Grey, Zane, *The U.P. Trail.**

* a paperback book

CHAPTER

23

STRIKE AND VIOLENCE IN CHICAGO

April 15, 1885

My Dear Virginia,

We have had a week of trial and anxiety on the great subject of disturbances in our main factory—the serious labor troubles we have encountered—a great "strike," and all the resulting derangement of our relations—old and pleasant as they were—with our workmen.

Trouble has come to hundreds of families in consequence; hatred and fierce passions have been aroused; and an injury has resulted to our good name.

It began with a few molders[1] and went on, one force operating on another, until 1,200 men went out, part of them by intimidation and part of them led by ignorant and blind passion. It ended by our conceding the terms demanded.

What a sore heart I have carried these days!

Your Devoted Mother

THIS LETTER was written by a bewildered woman in her early seventies to her daughter. The writer, Nettie Fowler McCormick, was the widow of Cyrus Hall McCormick. An ambitious and ingenious Virginia farm boy, McCormick had made millions of dollars from the invention and

---

[1] Molders are factory workers who pour molten iron into molds to make metal parts for various machines.

Workers gathered in Haymarket Square to protest police treatment of striking workers. The speakers' oratory was fiery and the police ordered the crowd's dispersal, leading to violence that was to set back the labor cause for some time.

Cyrus Hall McCormick invented the first successful reaping machine in 1834. He turned his invention into a booming business, employing new sales methods such as installment buying.

manufacture of the reaper, a machine that harvested crops mechanically. He opened his Chicago factory, the McCormick Harvester Works, in the 1840s. It was the largest producer of harvesting machines in the world.

Nettie McCormick had always paid close attention to the family business. Now, just a year after her husband's death, a stable and profitable enterprise seemed to be falling to pieces before her eyes. At first, she remembered, her husband had known all the original twenty-three workmen by name. He had worked alongside them in the little Chicago factory. Even after a few years, when there were about 200 workers making over 1,000 reapers a year, he could still name those who had been with the company for any length of time.

As the business grew, relations with the workers had become more difficult. During the Civil War, when labor had been scarce and prices jumped every week, there had been many strikes or threats of strikes. McCormick had been forced to agree to one wage increase after another. But the company had survived and continued to grow.

In 1884, the year Cyrus Hall McCormick died, it had shown a profit of 71 percent! The plant covered dozens of acres. Its modern machinery, including two huge steam engines that supplied the power, filled twelve full acres of factory floor space. About 1,300 men (depending on the season of the year) put in six ten-hour days a week at the plant. They turned 10 million feet of lumber and thousands of tons of iron into about 50,000 reapers a year. And these machines that poured out of the factory were making possible an agricultural revolution in the United States.

Most of the McCormick workers had seemed contented enough. Nine out of ten were Germans, Norwegians, or Swedes. Most lived just west of the plant in neighborhoods that Cyrus McCormick had built, little industrial suburbs with Swedish and German street names. All the McCormicks agreed that the trouble had to lie with one small group, the molders, who worked in the huge foundry. The molders were largely Irish—"fighting Irish," as one plant official called them. And they had a union, Molders Local No. 233. This union had been making trouble for the McCormicks since the Civil War, twenty years earlier.

There were only about ninety molders and about an equal number of semiskilled helpers in the foundry. But their work was crucial to the production of reapers. And the molders had always been well-organized. Whenever prices rose, they were the first to demand a wage increase and threaten a strike. Whenever Cyrus McCormick cut wages, the molders were always the first, and usually the only, group of workmen to fight back.

Nettie Fowler McCormick, wife of the founder of the McCormick Works, understood little of the underlying causes of worker discontent at the plant in 1885.

As Nettie McCormick had said, the molders were in the forefront of the recent strike. In December 1884 the company's new young president, Cyrus McCormick II, announced a 15-percent cut in pay for the molders and at least a 10-percent pay reduction throughout the factory. At first even the molders seemed to accept the cut. Actually, they were only biding their time until production reached its annual spring peak. Then, in March 1885, they demanded a restoration of wages. When McCormick refused, the molders went on strike.

McCormick was anxious to prove himself. He sent telegrams to company agents all over the Middle West asking them to send strike-breaking molders to Chicago. He hired the strikebreakers and housed them inside the plant grounds. They were actually listed on the McCormick payroll as "scabs," the union's insulting name for men who replaced striking workers. Company records referred to their barracks as "scab house."

Then came that awful day, April 14. Police were scattered throughout the city to patrol a local election. Striking union men attacked McCormick workers all around the plant. A horse-drawn bus carrying Pinkerton guards into the plant with a case of Winchester repeating rifles was set upon and burned. The rifles disappeared into the crowd, and the police captain—an Irishman named O'Donnell who was probably sympathetic to the strikers—did nothing!

Naturally enough, Cyrus McCormick went to the mayor of Chicago to demand better police protection for his plant and his scabs. But the Mayor, Carter Harrison, knew that the McCormicks were his political enemies. All he did was recommend that young Cyrus reach an agreement with the molders. The last straw came when old Philip Armour, head of a large meat-packing company in Chicago and a veteran of many labor troubles, told McCormick that he was already beaten and had no choice but to give in to the molders.

Everything seemed to run counter to young McCormick's wishes—Mayor Harrison's unwillingness to help, the obvious sympathy between the police and the strikers, and Armour's negative advice. So he gave in. He tried to hold the wage increase to 10 percent, but the molders refused to accept it. He ended by restoring the original 15 percent.

The strike confirmed the McCormicks' view of the Irish molders as troublemakers. Their attitude was shared by the Pinkerton Detective Agency, hired by McCormick as a private police force during the strike. A Pinkerton man submitted this report on the "fighting Irish":

> The assault on the Pinkerton police during the strike of last week was urged by Irishmen, who are employed at McCormick's as molders and helpers. These

Irishmen are nearly all members of the Ancient Order of Hibernians, who have a most bitter enmity against the Agency.

To the Pinkerton Agency there seemed to be only one possible conclusion:

The Germans who participated in McCormick's strike were merely tools, and the Irish were the real instigators both in inaugurating the strike and in the outrages which followed—and in forcing Mr. McCormick to come to terms at a 15 percent increase.

In April 1885, when Mrs. McCormick wrote to her daughter, Cyrus McCormick II was busy trying to analyze the strike. He wrote to his mother:

The whole question of these labor troubles is vast and important and throws more new light on a department of our manufacturing interests which we have not hitherto studied with sufficient depth and understanding.

McCormick was only twenty-five at this time. Three years earlier his father had taken him out of Princeton to help run the factory. When his father died two years later, young McCormick had become president of the company. In handling the strike perhaps he had made mistakes, he thought, the mistakes of inexperience. As he mulled over the preceding weeks, McCormick came to two firm conclusions. First, he agreed with his mother and the Pinkerton report that the molders had been the chief villains. Second, he grew more and more determined to defeat their union. He felt that he and his company could not afford to be dictated to by any union, especially one composed of only a few highly skilled workers who could, at will, stop production entirely.

McCormick went to work at once to "weed out" the offending Irish molders. He focused his efforts on a daring technological gamble. During the summer of 1885, the summer following the strike, the McCormick Company bought a dozen new pneumatic molding machines. They were supposed to perform mechanically most of the foundry tasks that the skilled molders had always done by hand. The machines were expensive, and they were experimental. No one knew whether they would work. McCormick hoped that they would enable the company to rid itself once and for all of the troublesome molders.

In August the McCormick foundry was closed for two months so that the machines could be installed. The closing was not unusual, since reapers were manufactured seasonally—much like automobiles are today, with new model seasons every fall. August and September were always light months at the Harvester works. But when the foundry reopened for full production, not one molder who had participated in the spring strike was back on the payroll.

McCormick seemed to have won a complete victory. All he had done was spend a vast sum of money on the new machinery. A few months after the machines went into operation, he wrote his mother triumphantly that the machines

> are working even beyond our expectations and everybody is very much pleased with the result. Two men with one of these machines can do an average of about three days work in one. Add to this fact that we have only nine molders in the whole foundry (the rest are all laborers), and you can see what a great gain this will be to us.

McCormick was being more optimistic than he should have been— probably to reassure his anxious mother. Actually, there were troubles with the machines. In October the McCormick Company complained to the manufacturer that the castings turned out by the pneumatic molding device were too brittle to use. And in November Cyrus McCormick was called home from a trip to New York because of a crisis in the foundry. He wrote in his diary for Wednesday, November 11: "Telegram from mother urging come home at once about molding machines—probably failure. Critical situation."

The machines were fixed, but even when they worked they seemed to require an endless amount of labor to keep them functioning. Before the machines were installed, the total wage bill in the foundry was about $3,000 a week. After the machines had been in operation for about six months, the wages at the foundry totaled $8,000 a week,

Prior to the mechanization of the molding floor at the McCormick Works, much of the labor was done by unskilled and semiskilled workers. Pouring the molten metal into molds was the job of the common laborer, but working the metal into shape required more skill and was more highly paid.

more than double the old labor cost. Most of the labor was common, unskilled work. But gradually the company had to hire additional new molders to supervise the work. Economically, the machines were a complete failure.

Still, the new technology had broken the molders union at McCormick. And the union was unhappy. The leader of the molders was a veteran union man named Myles McPadden. He devised a new scheme. It was much more dangerous to the McCormicks than the old union, with only ninety members. If there was to be no molders union, then McPadden would simply organize all the other workers in the plant into one union or another. The workers were discontented, so the time was ripe. By February of 1886 he had succeeded in organizing every major group of workers in the plant. The skilled workers—blacksmiths, machinists, and so on—joined the Metalworkers Union. McPadden encouraged the others to join the Knights of Labor, a general nationwide union. Only 300 of the 1,400 McCormick workers remained nonunion. The lines of a new strike battle were shaping up clearly.

During this time McCormick was busy, too. After his frustrated attempt to get Mayor Harrison to help, McCormick had gone to some lengths to make peace with the powerful political leader of the city. In every election before 1885 the McCormicks had opposed Harrison. After that year they supported him. As a result, Captain O'Donnell, the Irish police official who had been sympathetic to the workers in the spring of 1885, was replaced. The new man in charge of the area where the works were located was Police Inspector John Bonfield.

Bonfield had a reputation as a tough antilabor cop. He had once literally beaten his way through a crowd of strikers, shouting a slogan for which he became famous: "Clubs today spare bullets tomorrow." If there was going to be trouble in 1886, McCormick could count on the police in a way impossible a year before.

In mid-February 1886 a union committee representing all three unions—the Knights of Labor, the Metalworkers, and the Molders—presented McCormick with a series of demands:

> First, that all wages of laboring men be advanced from $1.25 to $1.50 a day. Second, that all vise hands[2] be advanced to $2.00 a day, and that blacksmith helpers be advanced to $1.75. Third, that time the men spend in the water closet [the toilet] not be limited as heretofore. Fourth, that, inasmuch as the molding

---

[2] "Vise hands" refers to workers who used a vise, a tool for holding metal being worked. They had a skill and were, therefore, to receive higher wages than the "laboring men," who were unskilled workers.

machines are a failure, the preference should be given the old hands. The scabs in the foundry must be discharged, and a pledge given that no man would be discharged for taking part in a strike.

The company offered to meet some of the demands, but not the fourth, which must have made Cyrus McCormick furious. The unions rejected the counteroffer and called a strike.

Before the strike was scheduled to begin, however, the company announced a complete shutdown of the plant for an indefinite period of time. Union pickets started marching near the plant, but they were kept away by 400 city policemen, now under Bonfield's command. To show its gratitude, the company served free hot meals to the police, with Cyrus McCormick sometimes personally pouring the coffee.

After two weeks the works were reopened, but only to nonunion employees. There was a loyal force of only 82 men. The company furnished them with pistols. McCormick hoped they would lead an enthusiastic rush for jobs. But only 161 men showed up the first day. The second day was not much better. Once again the company's agents scoured the region for workers. Gradually, the company's situation improved a little. McCormick was actually willing to sacrifice almost half a year's production in order to settle the union question once and for all.

For the men on strike the situation was just as important. If they lost, their future at McCormick (or any other manufacturing plant in the city) was dim. As March turned into April, stomachs grew tighter and tempers hotter. The explosion McCormick had avoided the year before by giving in to union demands now looked inevitable.

The situation at McCormick was complicated by the fact that during the spring of 1886 there were strikes all over Chicago. On May 1 all the unions in Chicago began a general stike for the eight-hour day. This was one of the largest and most heated labor actions in American history. The strike at McCormick merged with the more general agitation, involving thousands of skilled and unskilled workers from plants all over the city.

Then on May 3, two days into the strike for an eight-hour day, a lumber workers union held a mass meeting to hear an address by August Spies, a radical labor agitator. The meeting took place on Black Road, just a short distance from the McCormick factory. Some McCormick men were at the meeting, even though none was a lumber worker.

The McCormicks had been so desperate for workers that they had already granted the eight-hour day (with ten hours' pay) to their scab workers. So, at 3:30, two hours before the former 5:30 closing, the bell at the plant rang, and the strikebreaking workers left the plant. The striking union men at the meeting watched the strikebreaking workers leave the plant on their new short schedule.

The sight proved too much. Several hundred men, some of them McCormick strikers and some of them lumber workers, mobbed the scabs leaving the plant, driving them back inside the gate. The strikers began to smash windows, unleashing anger that had been building for months. About 200 policemen, under Inspector Bonfield, were there. Suddenly, they began firing their revolvers into the crowd, forgetting Bonfield's slogan about using clubs to spare bullets. When the noise died away, two workers were dead and several others were wounded.

August Spies, who had been addressing the meeting of lumber workers near the McCormick Works, followed the crowd and witnessed the violence that occurred. The next day, in the newspaper office where he worked, he heard that a mass meeting was scheduled at Haymarket Square to protest the shootings at McCormick. A circular announcing the meeting was being printed in both German and English when Spies arrived at the paper:

Attention Workingmen!

GREAT

MASS-MEETING

TO-NIGHT, at 7.30 o'clock,

AT THE

HAYMARKET, Randolph St., Bet. Desplaines and Halsted.

Good Speakers will be present to denounce the latest atrocious act of the police, the shooting of our fellow-workmen yesterday afternoon.

Workingmen Arm Yourselves and Appear in Full Force!

THE EXECUTIVE COMMITTEE.

Spies agreed to address the meeting, but he insisted that the final line in the circular be omitted. About 200 of the circulars had already been printed, but the line was removed from the rest. Few of the

20,000 circulars that were finally distributed on the streets of Chicago contained the threatening reference to arms.

August Spies was not, strictly speaking, a workingman. He might best be described as a radical journalist. At the time of the Chicago troubles he was thirty years old and the editor of the *Arbeiter-Zeitung*, a German-language newspaper with a radical viewpoint. He was also the business manager of an organization called the Socialistic Publishing Society, a propaganda organization of a small political party known as the Socialist Labor Party. (This party still exists and runs candidates for national office in several states.)

From time to time Spies had been in trouble with the police. Only a year before, during the McCormick strike of 1885, he had angered the police by intervening in the case of a poor German servant girl. She had been arrested by the police and held in jail for several days. When Spies and the girl's mother went to the jail, they discovered that the girl had been molested repeatedly. Rather than keep quiet, Spies swore out a warrant for the police sergeant in charge of the jail. He lost the case for lack of evidence, but he became well-known to the Chicago police.

Spies was, in short, a politically active radical who did not hesitate to condemn people in positions of authority. He was also a committed socialist politician. Furthermore, he hoped that the rally at Haymarket would attract enough people to fill the square, which could hold about 20,000.

Spies reached Haymarket Square late, at about 8:30 on the night of May 4. He must have felt disappointed. No meeting was in progress, and there were only about a thousand people scattered around the square. The other main speaker, a socialist named Albert R. Parsons, was nowhere in sight. Spies climbed on a wagon, sent someone to look for Parsons, and began his talk. He was a good speaker, and soon the small crowd became enthusiastic:

> The fight is going on. Now is the chance to strike for the oppressed classes. The oppressors want us to be content. They will kill us. The day is not far distant when we will resort to hanging these men. [Applause, and shouts of "Hang them now" came from the crowd.] McCormick is the man who created the row on Monday, and he must be held responsible for the murder of our brothers! [More shouts of "Hang him!"]

Spies went on in the same vein for about an hour, trying to rouse his working-class audience to anger and a sense of solidarity against their "oppressors." Then someone announced that Albert R. Parsons had been found. Spies turned over his wagon rostrum to the second speaker.

The crowd had been waiting for Parsons, for he had a reputation as a spellbinder. Unlike Spies and many other Chicago socialists, he was a native American. Parsons, born in Alabama in 1848, came from a family whose ancestry went back to 1632 in New England. He was a self-trained printer in Texas before the Civil War. During the war he fought for the Confederacy in a Texas artillery company. After the war Parsons became converted to socialism. He moved to Chicago, the center of working-class politics in the United States.

Like Spies, Parsons was not a worker at all but a political journalist. He edited a radical workingmen's paper called *The Alarm*. The Haymarket rally was just one more in a long series of political speeches for him. His speech was much like Spies', with a slightly stronger tone:

> I am not here for the purpose of inciting anybody, but to speak out, to tell the facts as they exist, even though it shall cost me my life before morning. It behooves you, as you love your wife and children—if you don't want to see them perish with hunger, killed or cut down like dogs in the street—Americans, in the interest of your liberty and independence, to *arm*, to *arm* yourselves!

Here again there was applause from the crowd and shouts of "We'll do it! We're ready!"

What Parsons and Spies did not know was that the crowd was full of police detectives. Every few minutes one or another ran back to a nearby station house to report what the speakers were saying. Waiting in the station were almost 200 policemen, fully armed, and under the command of none other than John Bonfield.

Parsons and Spies probably did not notice Mayor Carter Harrison in the crowd, either. Only the mayor's presence had kept Bonfield from breaking up the meeting. As Parsons finished, the mayor left; it was obvious to him that everything was peaceful. It was almost ten o'clock and rain was in the air. Most of the crowd, too, began to drift off as the third speaker, Samuel Fielden, began to talk.

Suddenly, 180 policemen (a group almost as large as the crowd itself) marched into the square and up to the wagon where Fielden was speaking. One of the captains turned to the crowd and said: "In the name of the people of the State of Illinois, I command this meeting immediately and peaceably to disperse." After a moment the police captain repeated his order. The crowd was already starting to melt away (it was almost 10:30 by now). Fielden had stopped speaking and was climbing down from the wagon platform. "We are peaceable," Fielden said to Bonfield.

At that moment, without any warning, a dynamite bomb was thrown (it is not known from where or by whom) at the police. The fuse burned for a second or two after the bomb struck the ground. Then it went off with a deafening roar. Screams split the air as people ran in all directions. A number of policemen lay on the ground, one dead and the others wounded. Quickly, the police re-formed their ranks, and some of them began to fire into the crowd. Other policemen waded into the confusion swinging their clubs. The uproar lasted only a minute or two. Then suddenly the square was empty.

In addition to the one dead policeman there were seventy-three wounded, six of whom died later. Four civilians were killed, and the official reports listed twelve as wounded. The twelve were those who had been too badly hurt to leave the square. Probably several times as many limped or struggled home and never became official statistics.

Like most riots, the Haymarket affair had been short. And, considering what could have happened, very few people were hurt. But the incident occurred on the heels of trouble at the McCormick plant, in the midst of the eight-hour strike, with 80,000 Chicago workingmen off the job. Thus the Haymarket bomb touched off a near panic in the city and much of the rest of the nation. Thousands of respectable citizens convinced themselves that a dangerous conspiracy of anarchists, socialists, and communists was at work to overthrow the government and carry out a bloody revolution. One of the leading business magazines of the day, *Bradstreets'*, spoke for thousands of Americans when it said of the Haymarket incident:

> This week's happenings at Chicago go to show that the threats of the anarchists against the existing order are not idle. In a time of disturbance, desperate men have a power for evil out of proportion to their numbers. They are desperate fanatics who are opposed to all laws. There is no room for anarchy in the political system of the United States.

Also important was the fact that many people had been frightened and angered by a recent flood of immigration from Europe to Ameri-

A contemporary sketch of what happened after a bomb exploded in Haymarket Square shows workers as well armed as police in battlelike poses. Pictures such as this fed the popular notion of union men as anarchists.

ca—and many of the "anarchists" were also foreigners. Not only in Chicago, but all over the nation, newspaper editorialists and public speakers demanded the immediate arrest and conviction of the alien radicals who had conspired to murder honest policemen and subvert law and order. The result was a swift and efficient series of illegal raids by the Chicago police. They arrested people and searched property without warrants. They imprisoned people without charging them and threatened potential witnesses. All in all, the authorities arrested and questioned about 200 "suspects"—probably none of whom had anything at all to do with the bombing.

In this heated atmosphere, fueled by journalists who whipped up unreasonable fears of an anarchist conspiracy, a jury met to determine if indictments could be brought against anyone for the violence. It decided that, although the specific person who threw the bomb could not be determined, anyone who urged violence was a "conspirator" and as guilty of murder as the bomb thrower. On the basis of this decision another jury met and indicted thirty-one persons on counts of murder. Of the thirty-one, eight were eventually tried, all of them political radicals. Most had not even been present at the Haymarket bombing.

The effect of the Haymarket Affair had now become clear. What had begun weeks before as an ordinary strike at the McCormick Works had been transformed into a crusade against political radicalism, most of which was said to be foreign in origin. Only Parsons and Samuel Fielden were not German or of German descent. The names of the other six would have been as natural in Berlin or Hamburg as in Chicago: August Spies, Michael Schwab, Adolph Fischer, George Engel, Louis Lingg, and Oscar Neebe.

In one way or another, all the defendants had some connection with the labor movement and with political agitation for revolution. Several of them were anarchists, though their ideas about anarchism as a philosophy were vague. They might as well have called themselves socialists, as several of them did at one time or another. In general, they were intellectuals. Their jobs were connected with radical journalism in either the English- or German-language press. They did not all know each other, but by the time their trial was over, most of them were probably "comrades," a word they used more and more in the months ahead.

On the other side of the battle were all the forces of law, order, and authority. True, some agreed with Mayor Harrison that the Haymarket meeting had been peaceful, that the whole idea of a conspiracy was a false and legally incorrect notion. But most of Chicago society (including even many elements of the labor movement) favored a quick conviction and the hanging of all eight defendants. The judge who tried the case, the prosecuting attorney, most business leaders, almost all the local clergymen—almost everyone who had anything to say in Chicago—were convinced before the trial that the defendants were guilty. Moreover, most of Chicago's leading citizens, and their counterparts in the rest of the country, agreed that the trial was a struggle to the death between American republicanism and foreign anarchism. The entire established order of American society, with very few exceptions, was determined to make an example of the "conspirators."

The Haymarket trial began on June 21, 1886. The first three weeks of the seven-week trial were spent selecting a jury. Under Illinois law the defense had the right to reject a total of 160 jurors on peremptory challenges—that is, without having to discuss a juror's qualifications and abide by the judge's decision. As one prospective juror after another was called, it became clear that most of them were extremely prejudiced against the defendants. The defense attorneys quickly used up their 160 challenges. They then had to show cause for turning down a juror and depend on the judge, Joseph Gary, to rule fairly. Again and again, plainly biased jurors were accepted by the judge—whose own prejudice against the defendants became apparent as the process went on. The result was a jury composed of twelve citizens who obviously wished to hang the defendants.

In his opening statement prosecuting attorney Julius Grinnell set the tone of the entire trial:

> Gentlemen, for the first time in the history of our country people are on trial for endeavoring to make anarchy the rule. I hope that while the youngest of us lives this will be the last and only time when such a trial shall take place. In the light of the 4th of May, we now know that the preachings of anarchy by these defendants, hourly and daily for years, have been sapping our institutions. Where they have cried murder, bloodshed, anarchy, and dynamite, they have meant what they said. The firing on Fort Sumter was a terrible thing to our country, but it was open warfare. I think it was nothing compared with this insidious, infamous plot to ruin our laws and our country.

It was obvious that this would not be an ordinary murder trial. The defendants would be judged by their words and beliefs. A ninth "conspirator," Rudolph Schnaubelt, had fled. The prosecution would try to prove that he had thrown the bomb. The next step would be to convict the other eight of conspiracy, which would carry the same penalty as murder itself. And they would be convicted by the fact that they had made speeches and written newspaper articles urging violent revolution. Day after day the prosecution offered evidence about the defendants' beliefs, their writings, and even pamphlets they had supposedly helped to sell.

The prosecution had weak cases against the individual defendants. They were able to prove that one of the defendants, Lingg, had actually made bombs. But Lingg was a stranger to most of the others, and he had not even been at Haymarket Square. Parsons, Spies, Fischer, and Schwab had left the square before the bomb was thrown. George Engel proved that he had been home drinking a glass of beer with his wife. In the end the prosecution's case rested on a theory of "general conspiracy to promote violence." No evidence of a single violent act was brought into court that could withstand even the mildest cross-examination by the frustrated defense attorneys.

After four weeks of testimony the jury retired. The jury members had been instructed by Judge Gary in such a way as to make conviction almost inevitable, and they needed only three hours to discuss the matter. After this short deliberation the jury filed solemnly back into the courtroom. It was ten o'clock, August 19, 1886, when the foreman read the verdict:

> We the jury find the defendants Spies, Schwab, Fielden, Parsons, Fischer, Engel, and Lingg guilty of murder in the manner and form as charged, and fix the penalty at death. We find Oscar Neebe[3] guilty of murder in the manner and form as charged, and fix the penalty at imprisonment in the penitentiary for fifteen years.

Years later Judge Gary recalled that "the verdict was received by the friends of social order with a roar of almost universal approval."

Before they were sentenced, each of the defendants made a speech to the court. Spies spoke for all of them when he said, in a German accent that he never lost:

> There was not a syllable said about anarchism at the Haymarket meeting. But "anarchism is on trial," foams Mr. Grinnell. If that is the case, your honor, very well; you may sentence me, for I am an anarchist. I believe that the state of classes—the state where one class dominates and lives upon the labor of another class—is doomed to die, to make room for a free society, voluntary association, or universal brotherhood, if you like. You may pronounce the sentence upon me, honorable judge, but let the world know that in A.D. 1886, in the state of Illinois, eight men were sentenced to death because they believed in a better future.

There were appeals, of course, first to state courts and then to the Supreme Court of the United States. One by one the appeals failed. Then there were pleas to the governor of Illinois for mercy, and the sentences of Fielden and Schwab were commuted to life. Lingg, the

---

[3] Oscar Neebe was the youngest defendant; almost no evidence had been presented against him. Most of the jury's three-hour deliberation was devoted to his case.

Courtesy Chicago Historical Society

Albert Parsons, August Spies, /487
George Engel, and Adolph
Fischer were hanged on
November 11, 1886, after one
of the most unfair trials in
American history.

bomb maker, who was probably half-mad, committed suicide in jail—using dynamite set off by a fuse that he lit with his jail-cell candle. The other four condemned men—Engel, Spies, Parsons, and Fischer—were hanged on November 11.

As the four stood on the scaffold, ropes around their necks and hoods over their heads, Spies broke the deep silence of the prison yard by shouting: "There will come a time when our silence will be more powerful than the voices you strangle today!"

At the McCormick Works the situation had returned to normal months earlier. On May 7, 1886, three days after the Haymarket bombing, Cyrus McCormick was able to write in his diary: "A good force of men at the works today, and things are resuming their former appearance." Three days later, taking full advantage of the public outrage over the "devilish plot," as McCormick called it, at Haymarket Square, the McCormick Works quietly resumed the ten-hour day. On Monday, May 10, McCormick wrote: "Things going smoothly. We returned to 5:30 closing hour today, instead of 3:30."

CHAPTER

24

Factories, Cities, and Immigrants

THERE IS a popular type of nursery rhyme that tells a story by linking together a strange sequence of events—a chain of odd happenings somehow related to one another. These events build upon each other. The final result is totally unrelated to each event but quite impossible without any one of them. One of the most popular concerns "the house that Jack built." A rat (soon to suffer an unkind fate) begins the sequence: "This is the rat that ate the malt that lay in the house that Jack built." Each line of the rhyme adds something new to the series. Before long a curious group of characters enters the system, each doing his odd bit to tickle the fancy of a child:

This is the farmer, sowing the corn,
That kept the cock that crowed in the
    morn,
That waked the priest all shaven and
    shorn,
That married the man all tattered and
    torn,
That kissed the maiden all forlorn,

That milked the cow with the crumpled
　　horn,
That tossed the dog,
That worried the cat,
That killed the rat,
That ate the malt,
That lay in the house that Jack built.

Such nursery rhymes have a simple appeal apart from their quaint images and galloping rhythms: they put isolated people, animals, and things together into a system. In most cases the system only works once: the cock crows one time, and the poor rat can only die once in the house that Jack built. But still the result is a system—a whole with parts that work together to achieve some purpose.

THE INDUSTRIAL SYSTEM

This chapter examines the creation of a new system in the United States: the industrial order. Like the house that Jack built, this system involved a large number of parts that had to fit more or less together if the system was to work at all.

In some sense industry is as old as human society. People have always made things—tools, weapons, clothing, and so on. But, beginning in the eighteenth century, their ability to make goods began to increase rapidly. The so-called industrial revolution that resulted originated in England and spread quickly to the rest of Western Europe and the United States. By the time of the Civil War this revolution was well under way in North America, fed by inventions like the steam engine, the cotton gin, and the reaper. After the war, industrialization drastically altered the basic patterns of life in the United States.

Everything had to be changed, since every element in this new house that people built had to hang together. Raw materials, like coal and iron for making steel, had to be found and developed. Cheap transportation, like railroads, had to be available to bring these materials to

factories and to take finished products from them. Workers had to be hired to operate the factories. And agriculture had to be improved so that fewer and fewer farmers would be needed to grow more and more food. More and more machines had to be used to feed more and more factory workers, who would in turn make still more machines. Nothing could happen at all unless everything else happened—and in the proper order, too. Just as the farmer had to sow the corn to feed the cock and so on until the rat was dead, every factory functioned as part of a chain of invention, materials, transportation, and workers.

The McCormick Harvester Company, for example, was only one part of a complicated series of events and machines. The reapers made at the McCormick Works enabled farmers on the Great Plains to produce unheard-of quantities of grain. Some of this grain was milled into flour, for bread eaten by people like McCormick's molders. Other farm products fed cattle, which were slaughtered in big cities at other factories owned by men like Philip Armour.

The new transcontinental railroads were necessary to take the reapers west and bring the flour and beef east. Since there were not enough workers to lay the new rails, Irish and Chinese were encouraged to immigrate. The McCormick plant, too, was tended by immigrants, and it was German immigrants who were the main victims of the Haymarket Riot. The city of Chicago itself was a new kind of city, built around railroads and factories, in a way that no other American city had ever been built—a great barracks for the workmen at dozens of factories like the McCormick Works.

In achieving its own industrial system, the United States was transformed. It had once been a nation in which nine out of every ten people lived on farms or in rural communities. By the end of the nineteenth century it was the world's most productive industrial nation. The landscape had been remade. (Many Americans would later decide it had been ruined by careless exploitation.) The people had been changed, too. There had always been immigrants to the United

States. But new industries attracted different types of immigrants in great numbers. In the end the daily lives and even the language of Americans were changed. New words like "telephone," "subway," "scab," and "millionaire" became common speech. They signaled just how deep and complete the change had been and how different this new house was from the old.

TECHNOLOGICAL CHANGE

Few of the men and women who made or watched the industrial revolution understood its complexity. Most of them probably regarded it as a product of technological change—the invention of new types of machines or the improvement of existing ones. Though this was important, it was not the whole story. Certainly one of the most obvious changes of the nineteenth century was that many things that had once been done slowly by hand were now being done rapidly by machine.

An Agricultural Revolution Agriculture was a prime example of the replacement of hand labor by machine power. The most rapid and striking introduction of new agricultural technology took place on the Great Plains. On these flat and treeless expanses, plowing, planting, and harvesting could be done on a scale that would have stunned colonial settlers and even most plantation owners of the Old South. But what happened on the plains was just an exaggerated version of what went on in all phases of American agriculture: the industrialization of the farm.

At first, the new machinery was fairly simple. McCormick's earliest reapers, built before the Civil War, were small. They were drawn by one horse and worked by one or two men. Another invention—a steel plow that could cut deeper and faster than the old iron plow—was a small step. But gradually the new technology gained force and speed. Reapers were soon equipped with automatic binders that could fasten grain into bunches mechanically. The single steel plow was soon modified into a multiple, or gang, plow that could cut three or four furrows at one time.

Soon other new machines appeared. One could plow and plant at the same time. Another, the combine, added to the reaper a mechanical thresher, which could separate grain from stalks automatically. A combine could move quickly through a wheatfield, gathering wheat and leaving behind only waste to be plowed under in the spring. The machine worked without a single person's hand touching either the earth or the wheat plants.

During most of the nineteenth century new machinery was still driven primarily by animals. Some steam engines were used, but the final mechanization of farms had to await the gasoline-driven tractor in the twentieth century. Still, even before the tractor, the life of the American farmer had been fundamentally altered by technology. Farming gradually came to resemble the running of factories, in which a product for sale was processed and made ready by machinery. Nor was it just grain farmers in the West who experienced this revolution. Dairy farmers acquired milking machines and automatic separators, which could divide cream from milk in a matter of seconds. Sooner or later, almost every step in all but a few kinds of agriculture was mechanized.

The result of the mechanical changes in agriculture was to double and redouble the volume and pace of food production. In 1840 it took more than three hours of human work time to produce a bushel of wheat. In the 1890s the time had been cut to ten minutes. In 1840 a bushel of corn required almost five hours of labor, from planting to final processing. In the 1890s the time had been cut to forty minutes.

Hand in hand with the reduction of hours was a marked decrease in the number of farmers needed to produce food. Mechanization made it possible for a tiny minority of Americans to feed the large majority. Those who left farms were then free to work for the railroads and in oil fields, iron mines, factories and offices—thereby aiding the process of rapid industrialization.

The amount of land under cultivation dou-

The introduction of machines such as the combine greatly increased farm efficiency. The combine was so called because it brought together a reaper and a thresher in one machine.

bled between the Civil War and 1900. The net result of the agricultural revolution was an enormous abundance of food.

Improving Rail Transport The agricultural revolution depended not only on new technology on the farms but also on new machinery to take food from farms and bring it to cities—that is, railroads. It was railroads that brought Wyoming beef, Kansas wheat, and Louisiana rice to the table of a McCormick molder. Without the new railroad network built after the Civil War, the mechanization of agriculture would have had small effect.

Railroads, just like farms, benefited from new technological developments. The principle of the steam engine remained the same. But almost every other mechanical aspect of railroading changed drastically during the generation after Appomattox.

The old railroads had used iron rails, small and dangerous wood-burning engines, and tiny, rickety coaches and freight cars. The new lines used steel rails that would last for many years without cracking or rusting. Because they could support almost twenty times as much weight as iron rails, larger engines and cars could be built. The typical pre-Civil War engine had weighed about 20 tons. By 1900 some engines weighed as much as 300 tons. The coal-burning locomotive became a giant source of power that could pull huge freights over the most difficult grades efficiently and safely. Freight cars increased in weight from 10 tons to over 100 tons. At the same time, the length of trains grew from 20 cars to as many as 100. The new trains were also faster; by 1900 many locomotives could travel over a hundred miles an hour.

Railroad mileage increased, too. In 1870—even after the completion of the first transcontinental line—there were only about 60,000 miles of track in the United States. By 1900 there were over 250,000 miles. This total was greater than the entire railroad mileage of Europe, including Russia. Other inventions like the telegraph and the electric signal made it possible to control complicated traffic patterns and freight yards. The trains and tracks of 1900 were as dramati-

Alabama, rich in iron ore and coal, became a center of the steel industry. Steel was produced in giant blast furnaces, like these of the Tennessee Coal, Iron, and Railroad Company of Ensley, Alabama, and transported by rail to other centers.

cally different from those of 1850 as the jet airplane is from the first wobbly passenger craft of the 1920s. These new giants of the landscape transformed the nature of moving food, objects, and people from one place to another.

MANUFACTURING

Taken by themselves, the technological changes in agriculture and the railroads would have meant little. They were important only in their relation to other parts of the new industrial order. In this system it was manufacturing that was crucial.

By 1900—a little more than a century after Washington had taken the oath of office—the United States was the leading manufacturing nation in the world. Many factors made this growth possible. Americans found new beds of coal. They discovered iron ore in Michigan and Minnesota. They opened oil fields in Pennsylvania, the Ohio Valley, and the southern Great Plains. These raw materials and energy sources

fed in turn the new factories of Pittsburgh, Chicago, and dozens of other cities. Mechanized agriculture made it possible for millions of people to move to cities to work in industrial plants. A high tariff kept down competition from foreign manufactured goods. Most important of all were the new machines and processes that enabled Americans to produce so much so quickly.

The Steel Industry   Steel was (and still is) very close to the heart of the new economy. It is stronger than iron, more resistant to rust, and easier to shape or mold. People had been making small quantities of steel for centuries, but the process was slow and difficult, since it depended on hand labor. In the 1850s an Englishman named Henry Bessemer invented a converter that could turn iron into steel by blowing a blast of hot air through the molten iron. The process was spectacular to watch, sending a brilliant shaft of sparks and smoke toward the sky. The economic results were just as startling. For the first time it was possible to produce steel in massive quantities.

The combination of the Bessemer converter,

the demand for steel from the railroads and other industries, and the discovery of additional sources of iron ore and coal created a new industry. In 1870 the United States produced only about 77,000 tons of steel. By 1900, however, steel production had increased to over 11 million tons a year—an increase of almost 2,000 percent. Pittsburgh became the first (and is still the largest) of the steel towns. But eventually cities like Birmingham, Alabama, and Gary, Indiana—built almost entirely around the steel industry—sprang up in what had recently been open countryside.

Other Industries   What happened in steel was repeated in dozens of other industries. The sewing machine and other inventions made it possible to manufacture shoes and clothing on a mass scale. Steam-powered mills using steel equipment could cut lumber or grind wheat or print newspapers with a speed and efficiency no one had dreamed of earlier (see chart, page 639).

Another new industry grew up based on electricity. The foremost American in this field was the versatile Thomas A. Edison. Throughout the late nineteenth century a stream of inventions poured from his laboratories. These included the phonograph, the first practical electric light bulb, the storage battery, the dynamo, the electric voting machine, and the motion picture.

An industry also developed rapidly around the discovery of oil and new ways of refining it. It yielded kerosene to light lamps and fuel stoves. Heavier oils lubricated the motors of the new technology. Beginning around 1900, it became important as a source of gasoline for the internal combustion engine (see Chapter 32). This vast industry had simply not existed in 1800.

A revolution in communications began in 1876, on the hundredth anniversary of the Declaration of Independence. In that year a young inventor named Alexander Graham Bell exhibited the first working model of the telephone. At first the telephone was purchased only by individuals who wanted to communicate between two specific locations, like a house and a factory or office. But soon there were enough

phones in use to create the first telephone exchange. It was opened at New Haven, Connecticut, in 1878. Other cities and towns followed suit.

Soon cities began to link up with each other. The first connection linked New York and Boston in 1884. New York and Chicago were joined in 1892. By 1915, when lines connected New York and San Francisco, it was possible to place calls between any two cities in the nation.

The only way to measure the magnitude of what was happening to the United States is to use statistics. In 1869 the value of American manufactured goods was about $1 1/2 billion. By the end of the century the figure was more than $4 1/2 billion. In 1869 about 2 million workers ran American shops, mills, and facto-

In 1877 the telephone was the subject of a humorous song. By the turn of the century it had revolutionized communications in every major city in the United States. Just fifty years after its invention almost every middle-class American home had its own telephone.

ries. Simple arithmetic shows that the market value of the average person's yearly work was only about $940. By 1900, when almost 5 million men and women worked in industry, the average market value of their yearly efforts was almost doubled, to nearly $1,800.

Comparatively, by the 1890s the United States had more steel, more rails, more electric trolleys, more telephones, and more electric lights than any other nation in the world. To accomplish all this, Americans mined more metal, cut more lumber, dug more iron ore, and pumped more oil than any other country.

THE GROWTH OF BIG BUSINESS

Technology and manufacturing were crucial in making the United States an industrial nation. Equally vital were new methods of organizing industry and business.

The Factory System At the beginning of the Civil War the majority of Americans who worked in industry were employed in small shops and mills—a tailor shop, for example, or a blacksmith's, or harnessmaker's. In 1870, when the revolution in industry was already well under way, the average industrial plant had only 8 employees. A median plant (one halfway between the largest and the smallest) had 30 workers. By 1914 the average plant had 28 workers, and the median 270. In 1870 no factory in America employed over 1,000 workers. By 1914 several had over 10,000 workers.

What was occurring, in other words, was a change that went beyond the technology of production and the rate of manufacturing. It was nothing less than a parallel revolution. The factory was replacing the traditional small shop.

In a traditional shop (or in home manufacture of items like cloth or soap) work centers on the person. Power is supplied mainly through human toil. The same worker is involved in all stages of production, from spinning thread, for example, to weaving the final cloth.

The idea behind a factory (first introduced into England in the late eighteenth century) is very different. Work in a factory centers on a machine. Power is mechanical, not human. Parts are nearly identical, and so they are interchangeable.[1] Most important is the division of labor. Each worker specializes, performing only one step in a chain. He may never touch or see the raw material. Or he may never look at or handle the final product. The result is mass production—manufacturing large numbers of articles in standard shapes and sizes.

Changes in Organization Factories were inevitably larger than shops. They cost more money to build and equip with machinery. People needed more and more capital in order to enter and compete in almost any line of business. As the factory system grew, so did the size of companies.

Growth in turn demanded changes in the organization of business. Mass production required a sizable investment. This made it difficult for family firms and partnerships to be truly competitive. So large corporations gradually replaced companies owned by one family or a few partners.

The corporation is an old idea. The Virginia Company and the Massachusetts Bay Company were both corporations. The idea is as simple as it is old. If many people invest in an enterprise by buying stock in it, the company can grow much larger than if it is funded by only a few individuals. If the company fails, each investor has lost only the value of his stock. He cannot be held responsible for any of the corporation's debts.

Just as there had been American factories before the Civil War, so had there been corporations. But their number increased greatly after the war. The corporation became the standard way of organizing business, just as the factory became the characteristic method of organizing production.

---

[1] A pioneer in this field was Eli Whitney, the inventor of the cotton gin. In 1799 he developed the principle of interchangeable, machine-tooled parts for muskets he was making for the army.

"Welcome Carnegie, generous son" was the message of the banners on the streets of Dunfermline, Scotland. A festive crowd gathered to welcome back Andrew Carnegie and his mother to his birthplace. It was 1877. Thirty-three years before, when Andrew was twelve, the Carnegies had fled a life of grinding poverty for a promising New World. Now they returned to receive the honorary citizenship of the city and to dedicate the first Carnegie library outside the United States. Carnegie considered it a high moment of his life.

Carnegie never lost his relish for the good life of a multimillionaire. But more important to him was the "business" of being a philanthropist—the planning and supervision of his give-away. In a famous magazine essay in 1889 entitled "The Gospel of Wealth," he declared that it was a "disgrace" for a rich man to die rich. His wealth was merely held in trust for the benefit of society. The rich man should spend his fortune wisely in his own lifetime. He should act as a "trustee and agent for his poorer brethren, bringing to their service his superior wisdom, experience, and ability to administer, doing for them better than they would or could do for themselves."

Carnegie believed in "scientific philanthropy." By this he meant that wealth should not be used for charity but "to stimulate the best and most aspiring poor of the community to further efforts for their own improvement." Since he was self-educated, he wished to encourage the reading habit. To Carnegie libraries were a prime field for "investment," for there were few at that time. Consistent with his self-help policy, he granted support for the buildings only, very rarely for books. He expected the communities to maintain the libraries properly. At a cost of over $50 million nearly 2,800 libraries were built. A third were located outside the United States. This allowed Carnegie to boast that the sun never set on Carnegie libraries.

Carnegie's sentimental journey to Dunfermline began his career as a philanthropist. To him it was

an enjoyable hobby. He built libraries and spread his gospel of wealth. He "collected" honorary citizenships from fifty-four cities. To "Dear Smoky Pittsburgh," as he put it, he gave a cultural center. It later became the Carnegie Institute of Technology. Only after he had sold Carnegie Steel in 1901 did he devote full time to the distribution of his fortune.

From then until his death in 1919, philanthropy was his primary concern. He worked at it with characteristic zest, scanning the growing list of his contributions as eagerly as he used to eye stock reports. Although he hobnobbed with philosophers, he appointed businessmen as executives of his funds. Most important, he broadened his base for gift giving into other areas—scientific research, colleges and universities, peacemaking. He managed to give away $350 million, 90 percent of his fortune. Almost $125 million was used to set up the Carnegie Corporation. This philanthropic trust was the largest the world had ever known. It remains a living legacy, fulfilling Carnegie's hopes "to continue to benefit humanity for generations untold."

Mass production required not only corporate investment. It also demanded that each firm market its product efficiently on a broad national scale, instead of selling just locally. To remain in business, a corporation had to create effective distributing and selling divisions. It had to buy raw materials on a large scale. Ideally, in fact, it would purchase its own supply of raw materials—for example, a forest for a paper company or cotton plantations for a textile mill.

In other words, mass production made it profitable for a company to invest money in all the stages of its industry, from original materials to final sales. Economists call this phenomenon vertical integration. It involves a business firm not only in manufacturing but in all the other stages and phases relating to the business. An oil company that owned wells, pipelines, and refineries and had its own sales force would be almost perfectly integrated. It would be freed from dependence on any other economic unit—except, of course, customers.

Competition and Consolidation The new industrial order brought a new kind of competition into the American economy. Before mass production small shops and mills had catered to limited territories. They competed only where one territory bordered another. But large corporations needed large markets to absorb their massive outputs. Thus a number of companies might find themselves competing for the same customers.

To win a big market, a corporation might advertise heavily. It might hire high-pressure salesmen and reward them with big commissions. But the most obvious way to win a market was to cut prices. A large company with efficient factories and lower production costs could force its competitors into bankruptcy simply by lowering prices beyond the point where the smaller firms could stay in business.

In one industry after another a few corporations gradually emerged as the leading firms. Each was too large and powerful to be driven out of business by the others. Each was too small to be able to control the whole market. Whenever this happened—and it happened sooner or later in most industries—the firms entered a period of cutthroat competition.

Most American businesses did not welcome such competition. In the 1880s and 1890s they tried to find ways to avoid it. The railroads led the way. Railroad owners had witnessed the havoc and ruin that could be created when one railroad waged a price war with another. By a process of trial and error the railroads worked out private agreements among themselves to control freight rates. Railroads also developed a system of grouping their customers in "pools"; each line was entitled to a certain share of the market. Gradually, too, the railroads had become consolidated into a few major lines, each one absorbing dozens of smaller companies. The Pennsylvania and New York Central railroads dominated the Northeast. The Southern Railway controlled much of the South. The Louisville and Nashville line was supreme in the Ohio Valley.

By agreements and consolidations the railroads had become the models for big business. Other industries soon copied what railroad leaders had learned and used the economic devices they had developed. Consolidation became the order of the day.

No matter what industry was involved, the process was the same. First, a few large competing firms would emerge. A period of intense and costly competition would follow. Then firms would consolidate as a way of avoiding competition. During its period of rapid growth the McCormick Harvester Company was competing with a handful of other large manufacturers of agricultural machinery. In the years after the Haymarket Affair, however, the McCormicks began to realize that competition was wasteful and unnecessary. Early in the twentieth century McCormick merged with its competition to form the huge International Harvester Company. Since then, it has produced practically all the harvesting machinery manufactured in the United States.

A similar development occurred in the steel industry, which was dominated for almost half a century by a Scotch immigrant, Andrew Carne-

(continued on page 497)

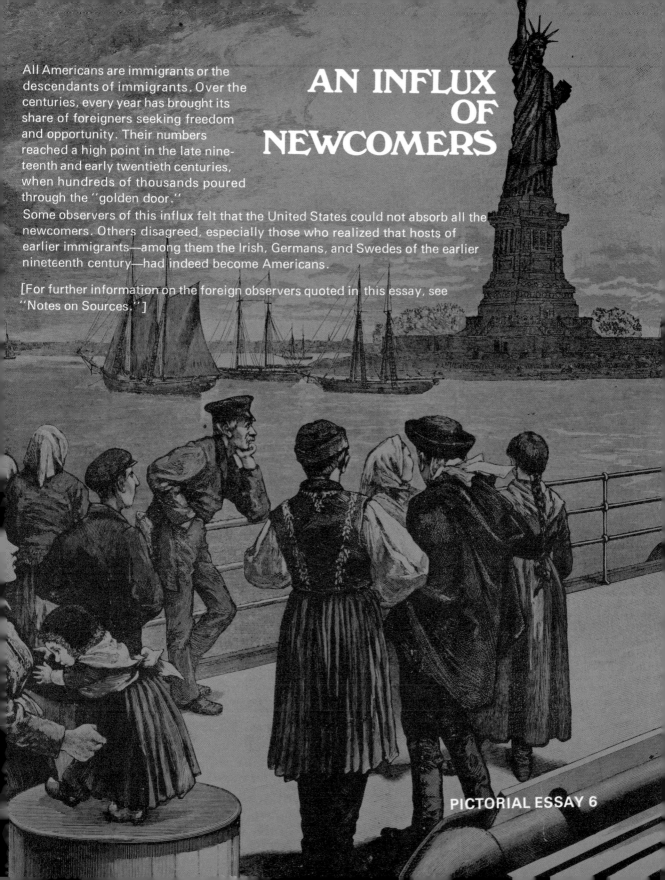

AN INFLUX OF NEWCOMERS

All Americans are immigrants or the descendants of immigrants. Over the centuries, every year has brought its share of foreigners seeking freedom and opportunity. Their numbers reached a high point in the late nineteenth and early twentieth centuries, when hundreds of thousands poured through the "golden door."

Some observers of this influx felt that the United States could not absorb all the newcomers. Others disagreed, especially those who realized that hosts of earlier immigrants—among them the Irish, Germans, and Swedes of the earlier nineteenth century—had indeed become Americans.

[For further information on the foreign observers quoted in this essay, see "Notes on Sources."]

PICTORIAL ESSAY 6

My uncle Olaf, a seaman, used to come to us between voyages, and he was all the time talking about America; what a fine place it was to make money in. The schoolmaster told us one day about the great things that poor Swedes had done in America. A man who had lived in America once came to visit near our cottage. He said that food was cheap in America and that a man could earn nearly ten times there as in Sweden. So at last it was decided that my brother was to go to America.

[AXEL JARLSON, 1903]

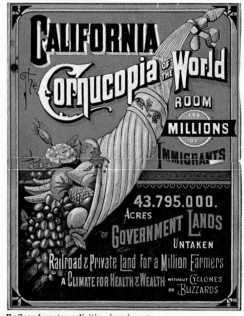

Railroad poster soliciting immigrants

The emigrants flocked into the mess-room from the four doors to twenty immense tables spread with knives and forks and toppling platters of bread. Nearly all the men came in in their hats—in black glistening ringlety sheepskin hats, in fur caps, in bowlers, in sombreros, in felt hats with high crowns, in Austrian cloth hats, in caps so green that the wearer could only be Irish. A strange gathering of seekers, despairers, wanderers, pioneers, criminals, scapegoats.

[STEPHEN GRAHAM, 1913]

Between Decks in an Emigrant Ship

We carried our luggage out at eight, and in a pushing crowd prepared to disembark. At 8:30 we were quick-marched out of the ship to the Customs Wharf and there ranged in six or seven long lines. All the officials were running and hustling, shouting out "Come on!" "Hurry!" "Move along!" and clapping their hands. Our trunks were examined and chalk-marked on the run—no delving for diamonds—and then we were quick-marched further to a waiting ferry-boat [for Ellis Island].

[STEPHEN GRAHAM, 1913]

Immigrants disembarking in New York City

A doctor examining boys at Ellis Island

I visited Ellis Island yesterday. The central hall is the key. All day long, through an intricate series of metal pens, the long procession files, step by step, bearing bundles and trunks and boxes, past this examiner and that, past the quick, alert medical officers, the tallymen and the clerks. On they go, from this pen to that, pen by pen, toward a desk at a little metal wicket— the gate of America. Ellis Island is quietly immense. It gives one a visible image of one aspect at least of this world-large process of filling and growing and synthesis which is America.

[H. G. WELLS, 1906]

Waiting for processing at Ellis Island

We were carefully examined, and when my turn came the examining officials shook their heads and seemed to find me wanting. I confessed that I had only five cents in my pocket and had no relatives here, and that I knew of nobody in this country except Franklin, Lincoln, and Harriet Beecher Stowe, whose Uncle Tom's Cabin *I had read in a translation. One of the officials, who had one leg only and walked with a crutch, with a merry twinkle in his eye said in German: "You showed good taste when you picked your American acquaintances." I learned later that he was a Swiss who had served in the Union army during the Civil War.*

[MICHAEL PUPIN, 1874]

George Bellows, *Cliff Dwellers*

Italian saw sharpener at work on the sidewalk

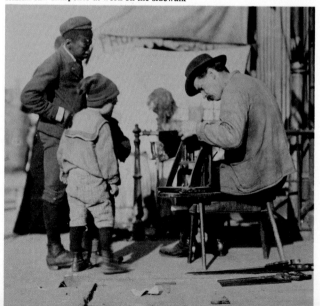

There was a bootblack named Michael on the corner. When I had time I helped him and learned the business. Francisco, too, worked for the bootblack, and we were soon able to make the best polishes. Then we thought we would go into business.

We had said that when we saved $1000 each we would go back to Italy and buy a farm, but now that the time is coming we are so busy and making so much money that we think we will stay. We meet many people and are learning new things all the time. We were very ignorant when we came here, but now we have learned much.

[ROCCO CORRESCA, 1902]

Immigrant iron workers in Pennsylvania

The work given to the new arrivals is generally of a rudimentary nature, but it teaches them to work, and the wages, although low, at least enable them to live, besides giving them the chance of joining the great labor unions of the country and taking if ever so small a part in the industrial pursuits of the people among whom they have come to live.

[COUNT VAY DE VAYA UND LUSKOD, 1908]

←*The inhabitants seem to have come from all quarters of the globe and to represent every known type. The streets, wide as they are, are yet too narrow to hold the masses of people who surge to and fro in them. Everyone is busy; everyone carries a parcel containing articles of clothing or food. Bargaining goes on in all the languages imaginable, and one hears an Italian praising his oranges as in the piazza of St. Lucia; a German discussing sausages of doubtful origin with a French urchin, who plays the part of a chef at the corner of the street; and Russian emigrants share their vodka, as a token of friendship, with Polish Jews.*

[COUNT VAY DE VAYA UND LUSKOD, 1908]

Jewish hot potato vendor, New York City

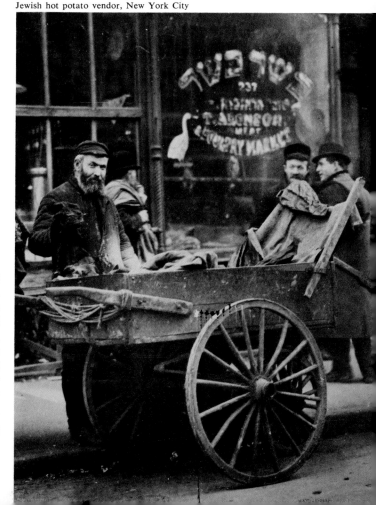

In the evening my sister and I took a walk; she went shopping and asked me to go with her. I saw a Jewish sign (in Hebrew letters) in a window reading "Kosher Butcher." I stopped and admired it very much and said to my sister, "This is the first time I see Hebrew letters in a window." In Rumania it is not allowed. Then I started to realize what anti-Semitism really meant and what an anti-Semitic country Rumania was.

[ROBERT MYERS, 1913]

Program for festivities at a Milwaukee *Turnverein* (German social and athletic club)

German band, Cincinnati

The German in America is badly off. Where in the world can he find a wife? He has little opportunity for family life. So the young people get acquainted only in public places, in restaurants, concerts, the theater, balls. But what can they learn of each other there? Everything, except that which relates to a wife and her duties.

[KARL GRIESINGER, 1858]

Polish store, Chicago

Those who are Americanized are American, and very patriotically American. Those who are not thus nationalized are not in the least internationalized. They simply continue to be themselves; the Irish are Irish; the Jews are Jewish; and all sorts of other tribes carry on the traditions of remote European valleys almost untouched. Very often these exiles bring with them not only rooted traditions, but rooted truths.

[G. K. CHESTERTON, 1921]

Returning to the log house, we spent the evening—twenty-one Swedes altogether—in games, songs, and dancing, exactly as if in Sweden. I felt myself happy in being with my countrymen, happy to find them so agreeable and so Swedish still in the midst of a foreign land.

[FREDRIKA BREMER, 1850]

Harvesting, by the Swedish American painter Olaf Krans

Irish politicians, Chicago

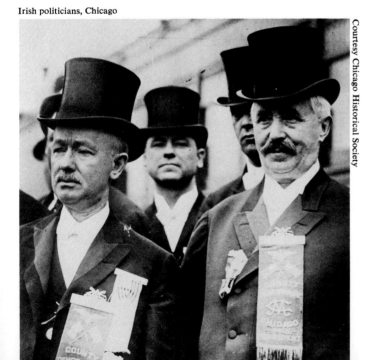

Courtesy Chicago Historical Society

I made the acquaintance of two local celebrities (Irish), namely Paddy Ryan and Michael McDonald. Paddy is a fighting man lately defeated in the twenty-four-foot ring by a compatriot, Sullivan. Michael McDonald runs a granite quarry. But his principal importance arises from his political position. He is supposed to direct and control what is called the rowdy element in Chicago—largely made up of our countrymen—and this gives him very great local influence. He is a rough diamond, with a decisive, masterful way about him, which clearly marks him out as a leader of men. His friends claim for him that he returned the present mayor of Chicago—the first Democratic mayor returned for Chicago for thirty years.

[LORD RUSSELL OF KILLOWEN, 1883]

The Chinese have built a great part of the Northern Pacific from the Continental Divide to the Pacific. As we sped along, we came upon their encampments again and again in forest glades, by the shores of the rivers and lakes, on the outskirts of the cities—always a community apart. It is said to their credit that they insist, when they can, on being located near water for purposes of personal cleanliness.

[LORD RUSSELL OF KILLOWEN, 1883]

Chinese workmen on a Western railroad

In a place so exclusively Mexican as Monterey, you saw not only Mexican saddles but true vaquero riding—men always at the gallop up hill and down dale, and round the sharpest corner, urging their horses with cries and gesticulations and cruel spurs, checking them dead with a touch, or wheeling them right-about-face in a square yard. In dress they ran to color and bright sashes. Not even the most Americanized could always resist the temptation to stick a red rose into his hatband.

[ROBERT LOUIS STEVENSON, 1879]

Mexican horseman in California

gie. Carnegie was a classic example of the "rags-to-riches" success story.[2] At thirteen he came to America with his family and immediately went to work. At eighteen he was a telegraph clerk for the Pennsylvania Railroad. During the quick railroad expansion of the Civil War years, Carnegie realized that iron and steel for rails and bridges were the keys to the railroads' future, and that railroads, in turn, were the key to an expanding economy. He saved every cent and invested daringly but successfully. By 1872 he was able to build his own steel plant near Pittsburgh.

Carnegie's company grew with the industry. By 1890 he was producing almost a third of a million tons of steel. By 1900 this amount had nearly tripled. At the same time, Carnegie worked to achieve vertical integration. He bought iron ore deposits, steamers to transport ore on the Great Lakes, railroad cars, and all the other facilities he needed for making steel.

In the meantime the process of competition had eliminated all but a few other steel companies. In 1892 the Carnegie Company was reorganized to combine seven other corporations in which Carnegie had acquired a controlling interest. In 1901 the largest steel concerns in the nation were all merged into one great new corporation, the United States Steel Corporation. The power behind this consolidation was another dominant figure of the period, J. Pierpont Morgan, a New York banker and financier. Morgan spent nearly a half-billion dollars to buy out Carnegie and set up this supercorporation. Like International Harvester, the giant company dominated its industry. It produced almost all of some forms of steel and three-fifths of the total steel made in the United States.

The Trust   An even more stunning example of consolidation brought John D. Rockefeller into control of the oil industry. Rockefeller started out as a poor boy, like Carnegie. He too saved every cent (except for the 10 percent tithe he regularly

gave to the Baptist Church). Starting with one /497 refinery in Cleveland, Rockefeller created the Standard Oil Company in 1872. Using every means of competition, Rockefeller was able to absorb seventy-four competing firms in six years!

Rockefeller also created a new device that made it even easier to consolidate an industry—the trust. A trust in industry is an arrangement in which several companies sell themselves to a group of trustees. The companies are paid for with shares in the new trust itself. Only paper changes hands, but the result is a group of directors who control the operations of several companies.

Through the Standard Oil Trust the Rockefeller interests acquired almost total control of the oil industry. The trust could phase out unnecessary plants. It could take full advantage of mass production and distribution techniques to sell kerosene for Americans' lamps or oil to lubricate their machines. Rockefeller himself summed up adequately the reasons for the trust:

> It has revolutionized the way of doing business all over the world. The time was ripe for it. It had to come, though all we saw at the moment was the need to save ourselves from wasteful conditions [of competition]. The day of combination is here to stay. Individualism has gone, never to return.

One by one the main American industries passed from competition to consolidation. It might occur through giant corporations created by mergers, like International Harvester or United States Steel. Or it might result from the formation of trusts—which involved everything from cottonseed oil to sugar to whiskey. By 1900 a few large concerns controlled almost all the major facilities of production and distribution in the United States.

THE NEW AMERICANS

The house that Jack built needed people—a farmer, a priest, a maiden—to make the system

---

[2] Actually, many successful businessmen of this period came from comfortable middle-class homes. But enough had emerged from poverty to keep the success myth alive.

U.S. GROWTH OF POPULATION, 1870-1910

go. The new industrial order needed people to make it work, too. The growth in agriculture, railroads, and industry demanded millions of people, both as workers and consumers.

The American population kept pace with the growing industrial order. For every 100 persons living in the United States in 1870, there were 126 in 1880. In 1890 there were 158, in 1900 there were 190, and in 1910 a surprising 230! In one generation the population more than doubled, from about 40 million in 1870 to over 90 million forty years later.

These were the millions who moved into the Great Plains and the Rockies, bringing about the final collapse of the Western Indians. These were the millions that bought McCormick's harvesters, worked in his factory, and built the railroads that carried his reapers into every flat corner of the country where grain could be planted and harvested by machine.

These millions, however, were not just more of the same kinds of Americans who had lived here in Jacksonian times. They were a new people, with different languages, different religions, and different ways of life. Andrew Jackson's common man was almost certain to be a "native" American—white, and Protestant and a farmer. His parents or grandparents might have immigrated to the United States, but they would probably have come from England or Scotland.

When they arrived here, they would have found the language, the way of worshiping God, and the customs familiar and comfortable.

The common man in New York in 1900 was more likely to be a Jew from Poland or a Roman Catholic from Italy. He probably lived in a city and had a job in a factory. His English might be poor, his memories of the "old country" at least as important to him as his hopes for the new. He represented a social revolution that had accompanied the revolutions in technology, industry, and business—the creation of an urban immigrant working class.

Shifting Trends in Immigration There had always been immigrants in America, at least from the time when the Indians began to cross over from Asia into Alaska. Over the years since the American Revolution the actual proportion of immigrants to the total population did not change much. Two other things happened instead: (1) the nature of the immigrant population changed; and (2) the immigrants (along with other Americans) began to congregate in urban centers. These two changes made factory cities like Chicago the gathering places for a new kind of American: the poor immigrant from a country where English was not spoken and where an Anglo-Saxon Protestant was rare.

In 1790 the United States took its first census under the new Constitution. Nine out of ten Americans (except for the black slaves in the South) had English or Scotch ancestors. This pattern changed somewhat with the "old immigration" of the 1840s and 1850s, when large numbers of Germans, Scandinavians, and Irish began to immigrate. Most of the Germans and Scandinavians, however, were Protestants, though their languages were strange to American ears. And though many "native" Americans resented the Irish because of Catholicism, these immigrants at least spoke English. In 1865 the United States had only about 200,000 inhabitants who had been born in Southern or Eastern Europe. They were easily absorbed by a total population of about 40 million.

By 1914 this picture changed dramatically.

IMMIGRATION BY REGION, 1860–1920

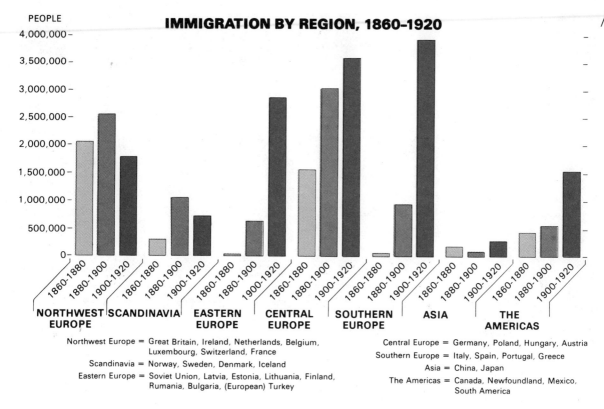

PEOPLE

4,000,000 –
3,500,000 –
3,000,000 –
2,500,000 –
2,000,000 –
1,500,000 –
1,000,000 –
500,000 –
0 –

NORTHWEST EUROPE | SCANDINAVIA | EASTERN EUROPE | CENTRAL EUROPE | SOUTHERN EUROPE | ASIA | THE AMERICAS

(1860–1880, 1880–1900, 1900–1920 for each region)

Northwest Europe = Great Britain, Ireland, Netherlands, Belgium, Luxembourg, Switzerland, France
Scandinavia = Norway, Sweden, Denmark, Iceland
Eastern Europe = Soviet Union, Latvia, Estonia, Lithuania, Finland, Rumania, Bulgaria, (European) Turkey

Central Europe = Germany, Poland, Hungary, Austria
Southern Europe = Italy, Spain, Portugal, Greece
Asia = China, Japan
The Americas = Canada, Newfoundland, Mexico, South America

A "new immigration"—mainly from Italy, Russia, and Austria-Hungary—flooded into the United States. Poverty drove many of these people from their home countries. Some men left to avoid the military draft, which discriminated against the poor. Jews wanted to escape the official anti-Semitism of Russia and Poland. Armenians fled from persecutions carried out by the Turkish government. The new immigrants were drawn to the United States by advertisements of cheap steamship transportation, by rumors of free land and golden opportunity, and by a massive propaganda campaign conducted by railroads anxious for workers and customers to buy up their lands.

Immigration from Southern and Eastern Europe amounted to only a trickle in the 1860s and 1870s. But by the 1890s over half the immigrants to America were from Southern and Eastern Europe. In the next decade—the peak decade for all forms of immigration in the history of the United States—the proportion of new immigrants had risen to over 75 percent. In simple terms this means that over 6 million Italians, Russian Jews, Hungarians, and other immigrants from Southern and Eastern Europe came here between 1901 and 1910.

Reactions to the Newcomers The strike at McCormick and the Haymarket Affair occurred just before the peak of the new immigration burst over the United States. But prejudice had already been aroused by the Irish and Germans and by the beginnings of the influx from Eastern and Southern Europe. Both the McCormick strike and the trial of the so-called Haymarket radicals occurred in an atmosphere of fear and bigotry. The Pinkerton report on the "fighting Irish" molders and the newspaper comments on foreign "anarchists" make it clear that events would have been different in Chicago had the bewildering fact of immigration not existed.

The new immigrants were not only different in culture, language, and religion. They also be-

The new immigrants from Southern and Eastern Europe fueled the industrial machine by their labor. Forced to live in cities where the jobs were, they clustered in crowded and unsanitary ghetto areas like New York's Lower East Side.

haved in different ways. They moved into a society that was no longer predominantly agricultural and rural but urban. So they did not fan out onto farms as most of the old immigrants had done. Instead, they followed the lead of millions of other Americans and settled in cities. Two-thirds of foreign-born residents in the United States lived in towns or cities by 1900.

Bewildered and ofter victimized in America, new immigrants clustered together in their own city neighborhoods, or ghettos.[3] People from a particular province or even a particular village would move into buildings on the same block, re-creating much of the culture of their Old World homes. As the new immigration increased, so did nativist, antiforeign sentiment. Ghetto dwellers earned a reputation among "native" Americans

for being clannish, dirty, superstitious, and generally undesirable. They were considered strange, chattering in their odd languages, and somehow suited only for city life. Actually, of course, they were no more "natural" city dwellers than the English who came to Virginia and Massachusetts in the seventeenth century. They were simply caught in a phase of the industrial revolution—the creation of an urban society.

Becoming "American" In the era of the new immigration the goal was assimilation—taking on the traits of the new society so as to blend with it. But becoming an "American" was not an easy process for most Europeans who migrated to this country in the late nineteenth century. Foremost was the problem of language. Real assimilation meant being able to take advantage of American economic and political opportunities. And this in turn depended upon learning the language.

---

[3] The word "ghetto" dates back to the Middle Ages. It is Italian and may come from *borghetto,* meaning a small settlement outside the town. The term originally applied to the Jewish quarter of a city.

Since a knowledge of English brought with it an almost immediate economic advantage over those who could not speak or write the language, most immigrant groups sacrificed the income they would have received from their children's labor to send their children to the free public schools. Workers often attended special night school classes after their exhausting days in the factories. A Jewish immigrant, Mary Antin, wrote:

> Education was free. It was the one thing that my father was able to promise us when he sent for us; surer, safer than bread or shelter. On our second day in the country a little girl from across the alley came and offered to conduct us to school. We five children between us had a few words of English by this time. We knew the word "school." We understood. This child, who had never seen us till yesterday, who could not pronounce our names, who was not much better dressed than we were, still was able to offer us the freedom of the schools of Boston!

Countless immigrants must have felt similar emotions at the discovery that schooling—so restricted in Europe—was so readily available in the United States. As Mary Antin said: "No application made; no questions asked; no examinations, rulings, exclusions; no fees."

Learning English was the first step in assimilation. After that many immigrants joined some form of voluntary association that put them in contact with native-born Americans. The most available of such groups for city dwellers were the political parties. They provided favors, food, and jobs for poor and needy immigrants (see page 530). They also helped "Americanize" them.

"Boss" Richard Croker of Tammany Hall in New York described the function of his political machine as taking the city's newcomers, who "do not speak our language and do not know our laws, yet are the raw material with which we have to build up the state," and turning them into Americans. He asserted that a

Children old enough to work in factories did so by day and attended school at night. The goal was assimilation: shedding enough of the old folkways to enter "native" American society.

World's Columbian Exposition

Chicago was the proud host for the World's Columbian Exposition of 1893. To commemorate Columbus' discovery of America (and to boost Chicago), the city invested $15 million. In two years almost 700 acres of sandy wasteland on the shore of Lake Michigan were transformed into a magnificient setting known as the White City. There, reflected in an artful landscape of canals and lagoons, stood massive exhibit buildings of gleaming white plaster. These structures, with their domes, arches, columns, and heroic statues, were, according to one commentator, "as white and as richly ornamented as a congregation of royal brides." At night the buildings shone brightly, illuminated by thousands of electric bulbs. The Age of Electricity was at hand, and White City was its symbol.

The fair lasted six months, from May through October. Attendance totaled an almost incredible 27,500,000 visitors. Though the year brought hard times to many financially, this did not deter the crowds. Some people even used their life savings for a trip to Chicago. Twenty-seven nations took part in the exposition. Spain sent a full-size model of Columbus' flagship, *Santa Maria*. France built a replica of the Great Hall of Versailles. The most advanced products and processes in manufacturing, agriculture, mining, and transportation were displayed. All forty-four of the states had exhibits. Montana contributed a solid silver statue of a woman. California sent a knight in a suit of armor made entirely of prunes. The ferris wheel was invented for use at the fair. This giant device, over 250 feet high, could carry 2,160 persons. Also noteworthy was Little Egypt, the hootchy-kootchy dancer. Attempts to close her show failed.

The exposition can be credited with three major achievements. First, it brought together major talents in architecture, engineering, and the fine arts. Second, the harmonious beauty of White City that resulted from its creators' innovative teamwork was itself an accomplishment. Third, the fair provided a forum for the discussion of many serious subjects—economics, labor, education, women's rights, and religion.

The architecture of White City had a widespread, long-lasting influence. Its neoclassic style was copied by banks, courthouses, and railroad stations throughout the land. To Chicago architect Louis Sullivan, designer of a modernistic exhibit building at the fair, Neoclassicism represented a step backward in the development of a truly American style. But his was a minority opinion. Most people agreed with city planner Daniel Burnham, who said: "The American people have seen the classics on a grand scale for the first time. I can see all America constructed along the lines of the fair, in noble, dignified classic style."

In the long run White City had even greater impact upon the American landscape. It opened peoples' eyes to the values of civic planning. A flowery tribute was paid by the Chicago *Tribune*, which saluted the fair with the words: "This splendid fantasy of the artist and architect seemed to foreshadow some faraway time when all the earth should be as pure, as beautiful, and as joyous as the White City itself."

Chicago Historical Society.

political machine like Tammany "looks after them for the sake of their vote, grafts them upon the Republic, makes citizens of them, in short; and although you may not like our motives or our methods, what other agency is there by which so long a row could have been hoed so quickly or so well?"

Another strong influence on the new immigrants was a small number of immigrants who had arrived before the great influx. They had learned English and then helped recruit workers from Europe for factory labor in the United States. They often paid the newcomers' transportation and helped them settle in the ghettos of American cities.

Such men were sometimes called *padrones* (an Italian word meaning "patrons"). They might be paid by three different groups: (1) employers, for supplying cheap labor; (2) political machines, for delivering the votes of immigrants once they became citizens; and (3) the immigrants themselves, for favors received. Often the *padrones*—who existed among Jewish, Greek, Armenian, Polish, and other immigrant groups as well as among the Italians—were ward leaders in political organizations. They provided a link between the concerns of the ghetto newcomers and those of the citywide machine.

URBANIZATION

In the ancient world only two great cities—Rome and Alexandria—had populations of over half a million people. By the time George Washington was born, Rome and Alexandria had long ago declined. The only cities to have reached a comparable size since were London and Paris. At the time of the Haymarket Affair, however, Chicago had become a great city. In fact, by 1900 the United States had six cities with more than half a million inhabitants—more than had existed anywhere before 1800.

The process of urbanization was not confined to the United States. All the industrializing nations of Western Europe experienced it, too.

The factory system demanded high concentrations of workers, and the agricultural revolution made it possible for millions of people to leave their farms—whether in Germany or in Maine—and move to towns.

The United States experienced three great migrations in the generation after the Civil War. One was from the East to the Great Plains and the Far West. Another was from Europe to America. The third was from the country to the city. Of the three the movement from farm to city was easily the most extensive.

In 1790 only about three Americans out of every hundred lived in towns larger than 8,000. By the end of the century this proportion had grown 1,000 percent; almost a third of the nation lived in cities of over 8,000. In 1800 there had been only six cities larger than 8,000; in 1900 there were over 400.

This increase was not gradual and smooth. Most of it came in the half century after the end of the Civil War. During this period at least 15 million "native" Americans moved out of farming areas and into cities, and their number was swelled by an almost equal number of new immigrants who settled in cities instead of on farms. Statistics tell the story. Between 1870 and 1900 the population of the United States increased by about 35 million people. During the same period the urban population increased by about 24 million. The cities, which cover such a small proportion of the land, had absorbed more than two thirds of the total increase!

Technological Factors A city is not just a collection of people in a small area. Like industry, modern cities were made possible by technological change. In the centuries before the industrial revolution the size of a city had been determined mainly by the transportation available. It could not be too big, because a person had to be able to walk or travel by wagon or carriage to a marketplace or job and back home again. After about 1880, however, cities began to experience a transportation revolution. The introduction of electricity made it possible to replace slow and

504/ awkward horse-drawn transport with fast, clean trolleys, elevated trains, and subways. These improvements meant that people could live many miles from their place of work and still be part of a vast city.

Electricity also made it possible to light city streets. Cleveland, in 1879, became the first city to have electric street lighting. Similarly, the introduction of the telephone in the 1880s meant that homes, offices, and factories could be tied together in an almost instantaneous communications network.

At first city buildings themselves were a limiting factor. Even with the thickest walls, a stone or brick building could not extend higher than fifteen stories. To build a structure even this high, builders had to make windows smaller and smaller because glass could not support the weight. A second problem was that human legs could tolerate only so many stairs. The first problem was solved by the invention of the skyscraper. This development was pioneered by a Chicago architect, Louis Sullivan. Skyscraper construction—in which walls were hung on steel frames—made possible structures as tall as a hundred stories. Thus even more people could be concentrated, level upon level, on smaller parcels of land. The second problem was solved in the 1880s by the invention of the electric elevator.

Technological change turned American cities (and European ones, too) into points at which power, innovation, and wealth came to-

A turn of the century view of a typical Midwestern city, Kansas City, Missouri, shows that the pulse of American life had quickened and taken on an increasingly urban character. The city itself was being transformed—trolleys transported people as once horses had done.

The growth of New York City depended upon improved transportation facilities like the Brooklyn Bridge. The bridge's completion in 1883 made it possible to live outside Manhattan and commute to work by steam car, carriage, or on foot.

gether with poverty, ignorance, and disease. Cities like New York and Chicago contained the factories, offices, and homes of families like the McCormicks or the Rockefellers. They were also magnets that drew people from the farms of America and Europe, people who came in search of work and success.

Problems and Contradictions In all the major American cities a new phenomenon, the tenement slum, began to appear. The new cities might tower with skyscrapers and glisten with electric lights. But they were also centers of grinding poverty and disease, especially the

immigrant ghettos. In New York City certain parts of the Lower East Side became crowded with Jewish and Italian immigrants. According to statistics, more than 30,000 people were squeezed into half a dozen city blocks. The density was 986 people per acre, making this the most populous area in the entire world!

Middle-class Americans became aware of the poverty and suffering of the slum population largely through the writings of a New York police reporter named Jacob Riis. Riis, himself an immigrant, had come to America from Denmark in 1870. For years he collected information and photos of the people in New York City's various ethnic ghettos. He published his findings in 1890, in a book called *How The Other Half Lives: Studies Among the Tenements of New York*. The scenes Riis described were familiar to most city workers, wherever they lived.

> Cherry Street. Be a little careful, please! The hall is dark and you might stumble over the children pitching pennies back there. Not that it would hurt them; kicks and cuffs are their daily diet. They have little else. Here where the hall turns and dives into utter darkness is a step, and another, another. A flight of stairs. You can feel your way, if you cannot see it. Close? Yes! What would you have? All the fresh air that ever enters these stairs comes from the hall-door that is forever slamming, and from the windows of dark bedrooms that in turn receive from the stairs their sole supply of the elements God meant to be free, but man deals out with such niggardly hand.

The city, with its extremes of wealth and poverty, skyscrapers and slums, mansions and tenements, was a focus for many of the problems and contradictions of the new industrial order. The main foundations of the industrial house-that-Jack-built had been laid—in agriculture, railroads, factories, corporations, the labor force, and cities. There was much that people might proudly call progress. Indeed, Americans of the nineteenth century liked nothing better than to boast about the country's fantastic rates of growth.

But the new industrial order meant more than growth. It created new problems that Americans were slow to recognize and even slower to solve. The workers at McCormick, the McCormick family, the Chicago police, and the other actors in the Haymarket Affair—all were caught in a web of difficulties that would almost certainly lead to violence and persecution. Haymarket was not an event that can be understood simply as a local occurrence or in terms of the personalities of a McCormick or an Irish molder. The strike at McCormick and the Haymarket Affair have to be seen as the outcomes of a host of dislocations and contradictions resulting from fundamental changes in the entire social and economic system.

1. What changes occurred during the agricultural revolution? Why could there have been no agricultural revolution without a parallel revolution in transportation?
2. What factors account for the industrial supremacy of the United States at the turn of the century?
3. In what ways is the factory system different from the small shop? What factors are necessary to bring about mass production?
4. Why was cutthroat competition necessary to the new industrial order? How did pools eliminate competition? What advantages did trusts have over pools as a form of business consolidation?
5. Who were the new immigrants? Compare the reasons for their coming with those of the old immigrants. Why was resentment greater toward the former?
6. What is the meaning of assimilation? Was it preferable to letting the immigrants keep their own ways? Why or why not?
7. What groups contributed to the tremendous growth of cities? What technological developments aided that growth?

Beyond the Text

1. Were the big businessmen of this era "robber barons" or "industrial statesmen"?
2. Horatio Alger propularized the "rags to riches" myth. Report on the myth and its validity for the post–Civil War years.
3. Men like McCormick, Carnegie, and Rockefeller accumulated millions of dollars at a time when most factory workers barely made ends meet. At the same time these men spent millions on various philanthropies. How did they justify the accumulation and the distribution of their money? Do you agree with their philosophy?
4. Bigotry appears to occur in cycles in American history. Investigate the reasons for its reappearance in the 1880s and determine from which segments of the population it came at that time and why. Compare this cycle of bigotry with the Know-Nothing movement of the 1850s.

Bibliography

Nonfiction

Barnard, Harry, *Eagle Forgotten: The Life of John Peter Altgeld.*
Bremner, Robert H., *From the Depths: The Discovery of Poverty in America.**
Carnegie, Andrew, *Autobiography of Andrew Carnegie.*
Cawelti, John G., *Apostles of the Self-Made Man.**
David, Henry, *History of the Haymarket Affair.**
Ginger, Ray, *Eugene V. Debs: A Biography.**
Hays, Samuel P., *The Response to Industrialism.**
Higham, John, *Strangers in the Land.*
Hofstadter, Richard, *Social Darwinism and American Thought.**
Miller, William, ed., *Men in Business.**
Nevins, Allan, *John D. Rockefeller*, 2 vols.
Rayback, Joseph G., *A History of American Labor.**
Schlesinger, Arthur M., *The Rise of the City: 1878–1898.**
Wiebe, Robert H., *The Search for Order: 1877–1920.**
Wyllie, Irvin G., *The Myth of the Self-Made Man in America.**

Fiction

Barber, Elsie O., *Hunt for Heaven.*
Dreiser, Theodore, *Jennie Gerhardt.*
Gerdell, Alexander, *The Race and the Tiger.*

* a paperback book

25

THE ASSASSINATION OF GARFIELD

ON THE MORNING OF July 2, 1881, the President of the United States, James Abram Garfield, was strolling toward a waiting train in a railroad depot in Washington. The train, scheduled to depart at 9:30 A.M., was to take him on the first leg of a trip to Williams College, his alma mater. There he was to address a class reunion and enroll his two sons. Walking alongside the President and chatting with him was the Secretary of State, James G. Blaine, a close political associate and friend. Already inside the train were Garfield's two sons and other members of his Cabinet.

The President and the Secretary of State walked toward the train platform. Neither noticed a thin, bearded figure, dressed in shabby and unpressed clothing, staring at them from a few feet away. The two men broke off their conversation for a moment and prepared to step aboard the train.

Suddenly the man who had been watching them drew a pistol from his pocket. He pointed it at the President and fired twice. Garfield fell to the ground. The President managed to cry "My God!" before he fainted. Blood spurted onto his gray traveling suit. He lay wounded and unconscious where he fell.

At the sound of the shots, Blaine had lunged toward the assassin. But when he saw the President lying on the floor, he quickly returned to his side. Along with others who had reached the scene, Blaine raised

SHOT DOWN.

President Garfield Dangerously Wounded.

AN ASSASSIN'S WORK.

Fired at Entering the Railroad Depot at Washington.

THE SERIOUS HIP WOUND.

Carried in an Ambulance to the White House.

CHEERFUL IN THE FACE OF DEATH.

Grave Symptoms Succeeded by a More Hopeful Condition.

A STRONG MAN'S STRUGGLE

Arrest and Imprisonment of the Criminal.

CHARLES JULES GUITEAU.

An Erratic Creature of Low Antecedents—His Strange History.

MRS. GARFIELD'S SORROW

She Reaches Washington and Meets Her Husband.

INTENSE EXCITEMENT—WORLDWIDE SYMPATHY

SCENE OF THE ASSASSINATION.

Map of Washington Showing Location of the Baltimore and Potomac Railroad Depot.

After less than six months in office President Garfield was shot by a disgruntled office seeker, Charles Guiteau, as Secretary of State James G. Blaine looked on. Though the President was in a public place, he had no Secret Service protection.

the wounded man's head from the floor. Garfield regained consciousness almost immediately.

Garfield's two sons and the Cabinet members rushed from the train to join the crowd of onlookers. Some railroad workers gently lifted the heavy-set man and placed him on a ragged mattress, brought hastily from a nearby room. The first physician to arrive was Dr. Smith Townsend, the District of Columbia health officer. The doctor assumed from Garfield's appearance that the chief executive was dying. Townsend gave the injured man aromatic spirits of ammonia and some brandy to ease his pain. Then he inspected the more serious of the two wounds Garfield had received—the one on the lower right side of his back. Garfield winced. The doctor's touch had reopened the wound. Townsend's face and manner remained grim but, somewhat mechanically, he assured Garfield that his back wound was not serious. "I thank you, doctor," replied Garfield in evident pain, "but I am a dead man."

After firing the shots, the assassin calmly returned his pistol to his pocket. Then, as anxious and curious spectators surrounded the bleeding President, he rushed toward a railway station exit. Just as he reached it, the exit's massive door burst open. The man who had shot the President found himself face to face with Patrick Kearney, a District of Columbia patrolman. Kearney had been running toward the sound of the shots. In an attempt to flee past the policeman, the slender, dark-complexioned figure mumbled in an excited voice, "I have a letter to send to General Sherman."[1]

Kearney, sensing that the agitated man was somehow connected with the earlier pistol cracks, held him for a moment. Several railroad employees raced to the exit and reported that the President had been shot. The policeman verified this by peering at Garfield's body, which still lay on the station floor. Then he rushed his prisoner away from the scene. As they left the station, the man finally spoke, saying: "I did it. I will go to jail for it; [Vice President] Arthur is President."

When Kearney reached the police station, his fellow officers would not believe that Garfield had been shot. It took a few minutes before they accepted the patrolman's story. Kearney himself, still excited over having captured the man who had tried to kill the President, did not even bother to seize the prisoner's gun until they had reached the stationhouse. For that matter, only then did the patrolman think of asking the assassin his name. The prisoner reached into his pocket,

---

[1] William Tecumseh Sherman was then commanding general of the American army.

withdrew a small printed calling card, and handed it to Kearney, who stared at the name and address: Charles Guiteau, Chicago, Ill.

There had been some change back at the railroad depot. Several people had carried the President onto a police ambulance, which rushed him back to the White House. There he was placed in a second-floor bedroom. Dozens of physicians, family members, government officials and well-wishers scurried about the sickroom for the remainder of the day. A horde of newspapermen also managed to reach the sickroom door. They pestered each visitor to the President's bedside for fresh news of his condition.

The physicians all agreed that Garfield's back wound was too serious to allow immediate removal of the bullet. They felt they could do nothing but give the President large, continual doses of morphine to dull his pain. Their frequent bulletins to the waiting reporters seldom varied in content: "The President's wounds were grave. He remains pale, weak, and cold. Although he is not bleeding profusely *externally,* there was every chance of massive *internal* hemorrhaging."

To doctors and reporters alike, this meant only one thing: the President was dying. Several members of Garfield's Cabinet joined his family and physicians in the sickroom. Together they waited for further developments throughout the long night. At one point the Secretary of War walked out into the corridor for a breath of air. He turned to a reporter and said: "How many hours of sorrow I have passed in this town." With this remark, Robert Todd Lincoln, Abraham Lincoln's son, reentered the sickroom.

Garfield's spirits, and his condition, improved greatly once his wife reached his bedside. She had left her New Jersey resting place hurriedly after receiving word of her husband's shooting. A special train brought her to Washington. Arriving at the White House in early evening, she spent a few minutes alone with Garfield. Then she stationed herself outside his sickroom, praying and waiting for news. The President, after being told that she had gone to bed, fell asleep himself.

An hour later Garfield awoke. He turned to the attending physician, D. W. Bliss, who had taken charge of his treatment, and asked about his chances for recovery. He told the physician, as Dr. Bliss later remembered, "that he desired a frank and full statement, that he was prepared to die and feared not to learn the worst." Dr. Bliss, somewhat less than frank, replied: "Mr. President, your injury is formidable [but] in my judgment you have a chance for recovery." Garfield smiled and, placing his hand upon the doctor's arm, answered simply: "Well, doctor, we will take that chance." The warmth, good humor, and

The public's view of Garfield as a homespun, simple man was reinforced by the fact that he was "the last of the log cabin Presidents." This painting of his birthplace in Orange, Ohio, gives us a nostalgic view of the pure and pastoral life of Garfield's youth.

optimism that had characterized James Abram Garfield throughout his rise to the presidency did not desert him during this final struggle for life.

Garfield's rise to the presidency parallels the success story of several other nineteenth-century American Presidents. He was a man of humble origins. Like Presidents William Henry Harrison and Abraham Lincoln before him, he had the good sense to be born in a log cabin. The log cabin had become the American symbol of homespun integrity and was therefore very useful to budding politicians.

Garfield, who was born in Ohio in 1831, was a seventh-generation American. His ancestors came to Massachusetts Bay with John Winthrop. His father was a pioneer Ohio farmer, who died when Garfield was two. His mother, Eliza, raised the future President and three other children in bitter rural poverty.

As a boy, Garfield worked at a variety of jobs, helping to support his mother while striving to earn an education. After graduating from a neighboring school called Western Reserve Eclectic Institute (later changed to Hiram College), Garfield worked his way through Williams

College in Massachusetts. He graduated from there in 1856. Returning to Ohio, Garfield served first as a teacher and then—though still in his twenties—as principal of Hiram Institute. In 1858 he married Lucretia Rudolph, his childhood sweetheart.

Throughout the 1850s Garfield exhibited the talents that were later to win him high political office. In 1859 he ran for, and won, the Republican seat in the Ohio senate. He made friends easily, worked furiously, displayed great tact and an ability to compromise, took few extreme positions, and—above all—sought to please. When the Civil War began, the young state legislator organized a volunteer infantry regiment composed largely of his former students. Although he had no previous military experience, he mastered the appropriate army training manuals quickly and well.

Colonel Garfield's regiment was assigned to the Union army command in Kentucky. There it defeated a much larger force of Confederate soldiers at the Battle of Middle Creek in January 1862. This victory earned Garfield the rank of brigadier general. After fighting at the Battle of Shiloh, he had to leave the field because of poor health. When he returned to active duty in 1863, he served with distinction during the important Battle of Chickamauga. Garfield left the army in December 1863 with the rank of major general. He had been elected to the House of Representatives that fall.

Garfield was then thirty-two and extremely popular in Ohio's Western Reserve district. This area returned him to Congress seven more times. His skill as a legislative leader and orator quickly made him a leading Republican in the House. So great was his personal popularity that Ohio voters reelected him despite the fact that they did not agree with him on many issues.

Garfield, like all successful officeholders, quickly learned the skill of political survival: when to speak out on an important question, when to blur an issue, and when to remain silent. During Hayes' administration Garfield's talent for bringing together different viewpoints within the Republican party led to his selection as House minority leader. Early in 1880 he was elected by the Ohio legislature to a six-year Senate term. But he never filled this seat.

It was in that year that the Republicans held their convention to nominate a presidential candidate. They were bitterly divided among three leading contenders—former President Ulysses S. Grant, Senator John Sherman of Ohio, and Senator James G. Blaine of Maine. There was a three-way deadlock on thirty-four ballots. On the thirty-fifth a break occurred. On the thirty-sixth Garfield, who had gone to the convention as Sherman's campaign manager, emerged with his party's nomination for President.

Blaine quickly became a close political ally. Sherman remained

Garfield was the ideal compromise candidate. A tireless worker and an able speaker, he rarely took a strong independent stance. Not an extremely ambitious man, he seems to have had responsibility thrust upon him rather than to have actively sought it.

cordial, if suspicious. Grant's managers (particularly the influential New York senator Roscoe Conkling) never forgave Garfield, despite the fact that Chester A. Arthur, Conkling's colleague from New York, was chosen Garfield's running mate. Garfield and Conkling did eventually smooth their differences, and the Republicans carried a close election with a popular plurality of only 10,000 votes. James Garfield, a mild-mannered and unforceful politician, became President of the United States.

During his years in Congress Garfield and his family had lived modestly. When Congress was in session, they stayed in Washington. At other times they made their home in Mentor, Ohio, a small agricultural town on Lake Erie, twenty-five miles from Cleveland. They had a farm there, which they called Lawnfield. Garfield enjoyed the farm work and rural way of life. He left Mentor for the last time in 1881, for Washington and his inauguration. The letters he wrote during his few months as Chief Executive show that he often yearned to return to the peaceful isolation of Lawnfield.

Although Garfield had been a professional politician for more than twenty years by the time he entered the White House, he retained an avid interest in cultural matters. This interest, no doubt, was a carry over from his days as a student, teacher, and college principal. Throughout his adult life he corresponded with some of the country's leading men of letters and reformers.

But Garfield himself was not a reformer. Throughout his legislative career he allied himself with railroad, industrial, and other established interests. He expressed skepticism about reforms dealing with women's suffrage, contempt for proposals to assist the Indians, and indifference toward efforts to aid blacks. Above all, Garfield was a party "regular"—a politician whose primary concern was advancing his own fortunes and those of his party.

Garfield did not know that one of the proposals he ignored would eventually mark him for an assassin's bullet. The issue was civil-service reform, which advocated filling government posts by qualifying tests rather than by political appointment. Some minor steps toward such reform were taken by Garfield's predecessor in the White House, Rutherford B. Hayes. But Garfield let the matter drop when he became the President.

Instead, he put up with the hundreds who came weekly to the Executive Mansion in search of government jobs. True, they annoyed him. Daily, as he walked through his own offices and living quarters, he was besieged by a "band of disciplined office hunters who drew papers on me as highwaymen draw pistols."[2] One of these constant job-seeking visitors to the White House who "drew papers on the President was a forty-year-old Chicago lawyer, bill collector, and itinerant preacher named Charles Julius Guiteau.

Charles Julius Guiteau's life was an interesting contrast to that of James Abram Garfield. Garfield had married happily and raised a family. His efforts as student, educator, soldier, and politician were all rewarded. The President remained secure in his early religious beliefs. He numbered among his friends and admirers not only the most powerful people in America but also many of its intellectuals. The road from log cabin to White House had been, by and large, a smooth one that he traveled with outer serenity and inner contentment. Garfield represented, for many of his generation, living proof of the continued American formula for achievement: personal integrity plus hard work plus trained intelligence yields success and happiness.

Both the personal life and public career of Charles Guiteau had been marked by frustration and failure. He was born the fourth of six children on September 8, 1841, in Freeport, Illinois. Jane Howe Guiteau, his mother, died when he was seven. The boy was raised by his father, Luther Wilson Guiteau, a Freeport bank official and religious disciple of John Humphrey Noyes.[3] Charles was usually cared for by his older sister, Frances, who maintained an interest in the boy's welfare even after her marriage to George Scoville, a Chicago lawyer.

Guiteau, like Garfield, worked extremely hard as a young man, helping his father at the bank and tending to family chores. Both young men were enthusiastic Republicans; both were physical- and mental-fitness buffs; and both dreamed of eventual success. Guiteau had fought many stormy quarrels with his domineering father. In 1859, the same year that Garfield became principal of Hiram Institute, Guiteau decided to leave Freeport to seek his fortune.

The first goal he set for himself was obtaining a college education. Guiteau went to the university college at Ann Arbor, Michigan, where he attempted to register. But the teachers there asked that he first train for university work by enrolling at a Michigan preparatory school. Lonely, lacking funds, and keenly feeling his lack of academic preparation, Guiteau turned to religion for solace. Not surprisingly, he became interested in his zealous father's faith, the teachings of John

---

[2] White House security measures were not as strict then as they are now. Visitors were free to come and go, so that they might well run into the President as he was walking elsewhere in the Executive Mansion.

[3] John Humphrey Noyes was the founder of the Oneida Community, an experimental communal colony in upstate New York.

Humphrey Noyes. In June of 1860 Guiteau left Ann Arbor to join the Oneida Community.

The Oneida Community, like other utopian settlements in mid-nineteenth-century America, was based upon religious fellowship and the principle that both work and worldly goods would be shared. Guiteau was no happier at Oneida than he had been in Ann Arbor. He was unpopular among other members of the community. Neither then, nor at any other point in Charles Guiteau's life, did he manage to keep a single close friend. A bad-tempered, solitary, and nervous figure, he often came under attack for selfishness and conceit at the community's important mutual-criticism sessions. In 1865 Guiteau left the community.

For the next fifteen years Guiteau's life consisted mainly of a series of career failures. He constantly borrowed from family members. He was always in debt and often ran away to escape arrest. He flitted between periods spent in New York City and in Chicago (where his sister lived). Hoping and expecting some great new career—which would be achieved instantly—Guiteau generally found himself teetering on the edge of despair.

Guiteau ran through a succession of jobs with alarming ease. After leaving the Oneida Community, he tried to found a religious newspaper. But he failed. He spent a short time in 1867 as a subscription and ad salesman for the Reverend Henry Ward Beecher's influential weekly paper, the *Independent*. He soon gave up the post. Then he spent a year threatening a lawsuit against Noyes and his other former brethren at the Oneida Community. He tried to blackmail them into paying him $9,000. Otherwise, he threatened to publicize the colony's controversial sexual practices.[4] Guiteau's own father denounced his son publicly for this betrayal of Oneida. Guiteau finally stopped his abusive letters to Noyes after the latter threatened to prosecute him.

Guiteau next moved to Chicago, where he apprenticed in a law office. He was admitted to the Illinois bar in 1868. He made only one appearance as a trial lawyer. Inevitably, he lost the case. After this his legal practice consisted almost entirely of bill collecting, a trade he followed with little success until 1875.

In 1869 Guiteau had married an eighteen-year-old girl, Anne Bunn. The union lasted five turbulent years, during which he often beat his wife severely and sometimes even locked her in a closet overnight. In 1874 his wife divorced him.

By then, Guiteau had acquired a reputation as a sleazy and dishonest bill collector. He served a brief jail sentence in 1875 for petty

---

[4] The community held that traditional marriage and family patterns bred selfishness and, thereby, many evils in society. Therefore, monogamy was banned, and children were cared for by the entire community.

fraud and abruptly that same year, shifted his career plans once more. The penniless lawyer now announced plans to raise $200,000 in order to purchase a Chicago newspaper. Attempts to borrow the money quickly failed. Guiteau retreated to his family again. During a visit to his sister Frances, he threatened her with an ax. A physician who examined Guiteau after this incident recommended that he be placed in an insane asylum. Guiteau fled.

Now Guiteau adopted yet another vocation. He became an itinerant preacher and wandered across the country, selling religious pamphlets and preaching a version of John Humphrey Noyes' theology. Apparently Guiteau earned almost no money between 1875 and 1881. Yet somehow he managed to survive on the misplaced trust of creditors.

Charles Guiteau truly believed that Garfield's death was a necessity that would unite the Republican party and save the Republic. He claimed that the idea had come to him under "divine pressure."

In 1880 a new vision of success appeared to Guiteau. This time it was a political one. He wrote an incoherent pro-Garfield essay and had it privately printed. Then he attached himself to the Republicans' New York City campaign headquarters. There he became one of the many unwanted and unused hangers-on. Though he did nothing to bring it about, Guiteau viewed Garfield's election as a personal triumph. He immediately began making plans to apply for a high post in the diplomatic corps.

Guiteau wrote several letters to Garfield and other important Republican leaders to carry out his plan. In them he asserted his importance in the party's New York victory and requested assignment to various foreign ministries. Eventually, he decided on the Paris consulship. He moved to Washington—one jump ahead of his creditors—to press this claim.

During the early months of Garfield's presidency, from March to June 1881, Guiteau became a familiar face at the White House and in the State Department corridors. He pestered Garfield and Blaine about the Paris post at every chance, by letter and even in person (when he managed to push his way through). "Never bother me again about the Paris consulship so long as you live," Blaine shouted at the pesky figure after one such May encounter. By then, Guiteau had decided that Blaine was a "wicked man," He demanded Blaine's dismissal in notes to Garfield that became increasingly intimate in tone. A new scheme for glory now began to hatch in Guiteau's crazed mind: a plan to murder the President.

Guiteau was not familar with firearms. As his obsession grew more vivid, he purchased a revolver and practiced target shooting on the banks of the Potomac. He took to following the President and observ-

Roscoe Conkling, head of the Stalwarts, was a political boss who believed that "parties were not built by deportment or gush." He ruined his political career in an attempt to thwart Garfield's policies.

ing his daily routine. On several occasions prior to the fateful day he came close to executing his scheme, only to back down at the last minute. By shooting Garfield, his odd reasoning ran, not only would his political friends be raised to power but he too would share in it.

Finally, on July 2, 1881, Charles Julius Guiteau, a failure's failure, managed to carry out the last of his innumerable schemes. He shot the President. Guiteau later acknowledged:

> I have had an idea [since my youth] that I should be President, and it has never left me. When I left Boston for New York, in June 1880 [to campaign for Garfield], I felt that I was on my way to the White House. My idea is that I shall be nominated and elected as Lincoln and Garfield were—that is, by the act of God.

Many blamed Garfield's opponents among the Republican party's Stalwart wing[5] (somewhat unfairly) for having allowed the assassin even a minor place within their ranks in New York during the 1880 campaign. Some even blamed Vice President Arthur. Until Garfield selected him as a running mate, Arthur had been a loyal associate of the country's leading Stalwart, Senator Roscoe Conkling of New York. Arthur remained loyal to Conkling despite his new responsibilities as Vice President.

In May 1881 Garfield insisted on appointing an anti-Conkling Republican to an important patronage post—Customs Collector for the Port of New York. Conkling and his New York Stalwart colleague, Thomas C. Platt, both resigned from the Senate. Arthur supported their decision. Conkling and Platt hoped, by resigning, to put pressure on their Senate colleagues to reject the President's nominee on the grounds of "senatorial courtesy." They planned to win Senate reelection from the New York state legislature and then to return to Washington with added power. This was the dispute between Garfield and the Stalwarts that Guiteau claimed had triggered his decision to kill the President.

In the end Conkling and Platt lost the struggle—and their power. The two were brought down in July 1881 by Conkling's personal arrogance and an ill-timed peek over an Albany hotel transom by a political opponent. Platt withdrew from the contest the same day that Garfield was shot in order not to hurt Conkling's chances. It was no use. Neither man gained reelection. Thus, ironically, Garfield had begun to win his struggle against Conkling for control of the Republi-

Senator Thomas C. Platt, a faithful political crony of Roscoe Conkling, followed his lead in resigning from the New York State legislature. Promptly dubbed "Me Too" Platt, his loyalty cost him his Senate seat.

[5] The Stalwart wing was centered in New York. It actively opposed civil-service reform. Guiteau claimed to be a Stalwart, acting for the good of that faction in shooting Garfield.

can party at the very moment he was cut down by a maddened office seeker claiming to be a Stalwart.

Garfield himself never blamed his political opponents for the shooting. Garfield also forgave the political treachery of his Vice President, who had supported Conkling's reelection bid. During Garfield's struggle to recover from the shooting, Arthur remained at his New York City home, grief-stricken and withdrawn from public notice. Garfield turned the daily management of government over to his Cabinet. The rumors of a Stalwart conspiracy guiding Guiteau's hand quickly died away.

The wounded President lingered between life and death for seventy-nine days. He remained in his second-floor sickroom, only rarely writing official dispatches or dealing with government business. Doctors, medical consultants and free advice poured into the White House to assist in the President's treatment. But the bullet remained lodged in his back while physicians continued their painful probing. Nothing seemed to help.

A reproduction of a contemporary sketch shows two doctors attempting to discover the location of the bullet in Garfield's body through the use of a strange telegraph-like apparatus. They never succeeded in removing the bullet.

At first the President's condition improved. But a mid-July rally turned into a late-July decline. In Washington's sweltering summer heat, Garfield ran a fever that only occasionally broke. His normally robust 200-pound frame shrank to 120 pounds by late August. When early September brought a record heat wave, the doctors decided to move Garfield to the cooler temperatures of his oceanside summer house at Elberon, New Jersey. He was carried there by special train on September 6, but his condition continued to deteriorate. Persistent job seekers continued to plague him. Still, almost to the end, his spirits remained good. He even tried to cheer those around him.

On the night of September 19, with only an old friend, Captain D. G. Swain, and one servant attending him, Garfield's final agony began. He awoke suddenly, clutched his heart, and cried out, "How it hurts here!" Swain handed the President a glass of water, but it failed to help. The President cried: "Swain, can't you stop this?" Then Garfield fell into a coma. Within moments Dr. Bliss and Mrs. Garfield entered the room. Mrs. Garfield sat down calmly and held her husband's hand. But the strain was too much, and she had to leave the room. Dr. Bliss remained with his patient for a few minutes, then walked quietly to a nearby study and wrote in his medical log: "Applying my ear over the heart, I detected an indistinct fluttering that continued until 10:35 when he expired. The brave and heroic sufferer, the nation's patient, has passed away."

The waiting had ended; the grieving began. Garfield's seventy-nine days of suffering before death, borne with stoic dignity, made the slain President a hero in the eyes of his countrymen. His body was brought back to Washington on September 21 to lie in state in the Capitol rotunda. Thousands—Southerners and Northerners, Democrats and Republicans alike—filed past to pay their last respects. The world's rulers also mourned. The President's widow received condolence messages from Queen Victoria of England; the emperors of China, Russia, and Japan; the kings of Belgium, Italy, and Spain; the Pope; and the sultan of Turkey.

American advocates of civil-service reform found an obvious moral in Garfield's assassination by a disappointed office seeker. Throughout his long death agony reformers organized countless meetings protesting the spoils system and demanding government appointments based on merit alone. "Garfield dead," one historian later wrote, "proved more valuable to reformers than Garfield alive."

The great majority of Americans, however, mourned Garfield's passing more sincerely. On September 23 a special train carried the

President's casket from Washington to Cleveland for burial. Crowds lined the entire route to honor the dead President, just as sixteen years earlier throngs had wept as Lincoln's funeral train followed a similar route from the East back to Illinois. Some 250,000 people from throughout the Middle West jammed Cleveland's streets for Garfield's funeral ceremony. Thousands of tributes—sermons, memorial leaflets, and letters—reached his widow at their Mentor home. The nation's grief seemed remarkably intense, considering the fact that Garfield, unlike Lincoln, had not been a war leader. Moreover he had held the highest office in the nation only a few months.

In New York Walt Whitman heard of the President's death. In his journal he wrote some lines that expressed the genuine sorrow of most of his less eloquent countrymen:

> The sobbing of the bells, the sudden death-news everywhere,
> The slumberers rouse, the rapport of the People,
> (Full well they know that message in the darkness,
> Full well return, respond within their breasts, their brains, the sad
>   reverberations,)
> The passionate toll and clang—city to city, joining, sounding, passing,
> Those heart-beats of a Nation in the night.

Another New Yorker also recoiled at the awful news that evening. At Chester Alan Arthur's house the bell rang at midnight. A reporter informed the servant who answered the door that Garfield had died. "Oh, no, it cannot be true," cried Arthur, who overheard the news. "It cannot be. I have heard nothing." His face was pale, and he was crying. When the reporter persisted, Arthur could say only "I hope—My God, I do hope it is a mistake."

The man who had just become President turned and walked back to his study, where a small group of silent friends now waited. The bell rang again, and a messenger handed Arthur a telegram sent by a number of Garfield's Cabinet members. It confirmed the President's death and advised Arthur to take the oath of office immediately. Arthur's friends rushed out to find a judge who could administer the oath. Someone checked it for the exact wording. Within minutes a state supreme court justice, roused from his bed, administered the oath of office to the Vice President. The next morning President Chester A. Arthur left for Washington.

On September 20, two days after Garfield's death, his assassin sent a letter to Chester Arthur. He wrote, "My inspiration is a godsend to you, and I presume you appreciate it. It raises you from $8,000 to $50,000 a year. It raises you from a political cipher to President of the

This caricature of Garfield's assassin shows some of his crazed intensity of purpose. We can easily believe that he wrote: "I presume the President was a Christian, and that he will be happier in Paradise than here."

United States with all its power and honors. For the Cabinet I would suggest as follows . . . ." President Arthur never answered the letter. Instead, he ordered Guiteau tried promptly. He personally helped select the prosecuting attorneys.

Guiteau, however, still seemed convinced that the Stalwarts would somehow rescue and reward him. His confidence waned, though, as the trial date neared. He continued to deny responsibility for the killing. He insisted that divine inspiration made him pull the trigger. "I am here as God's man, and don't you forget it." No independent lawyer would touch the case, despite a newspaper appeal for such assistance. When the trial began on November 14, 1881, Guiteau's brother-in-law, George Scoville, served as defense counsel.

Lines between the defense and prosecution arguments were drawn clearly from the start. Scoville argued that his client was an insane religious fanatic and therefore could not be held legally responsible for his actions. Furthermore, the defense insisted that Garfield's wounds were not necessarily mortal. The President had died, Scoville claimed, only because of incompetent medical treatment after the shooting.

Both defense arguments had merit, although the prosecution, of course, denied them. It insisted that Guiteau, although morally evil, had killed the President while in complete possession of his faculties. He had done so for calculated political motives—namely, as a malicious and disappointed job seeker.

The case against Guiteau, then, centered on the question of his sanity. Both prosecution and defense attorneys presented "expert" medical testimony to prove their respective contentions. A majority of the doctors who had examined Guiteau found the prisoner sane within the prevailing legal definitions of sanity, which were far broader than those today. Guiteau demonstrated his unbalanced mental state by frequently interrupting the trial to shout abusive statements at everyone, including his own lawyer. He continued to claim divine inspiration.

The prosecution argued that such outbursts were merely a cynical act by Guiteau, who was trying to portray himself as mad. Apparently the jury also believed this. It took only a half-hour on January 25, 1882, to find Guiteau guilty of murder. The prisoner vented his anger by shrieking: "My blood will be upon the heads of [this] jury. God will avenge this outrage." One doctor who had observed the trial daily, George M. Beard, a noted psychologist, disagreed strongly with the jury's decision. Beard later wrote:

> The physicians called in to make a diagnosis mistook the symptoms of insanity for the symptoms of wickedness. [This] error is quite as natural for nonexperts in insanity in our time as that of the village physician of Salem, Dr. Griggs, in witchcraft times, in attributing insanity to possession by the devil.

Nevertheless, on February 3, Judge Walter Cox sentenced Guiteau to hang.

Before sentencing, Guiteau addressed the court a final time. He insisted again that Garfield's killing had been "God's act, not mine." He compared his fate to Christ's and threatened bloody divine vengeance on the United States if he hung. In the months before his execution the condemned man continued to believe that President Arthur would issue a last-minute reprieve or pardon.

Finally, Guiteau recognized the reality ahead of him. Four days before his death, while in his cell, he scrawled a "Scene between the Almighty and my murderers." In this imaginary scene God confronts Guiteau's persecutors, including President Arthur, and condemns them along with the entire American nation. A few days later, on June 30, 1882, Charles Guiteau was hung. He went to the scaffold, fighting back tears and singing a childlike hymn he had written especially for the occasion. Then he gave a final shout: "Glory hallelujah! I am with the Lord. Glory, ready, go!"

26

Politics in Transition

THE ECONOMIC and social landscape of the United States in the nineteenth century underwent dramatic change. The period might best be termed a transitional one. It was characterized by the emergence of a new, industrial society. In the decades after the Civil War the preindustrial issues that dominated the ante-bellum era were overridden in importance by the realities of a rapidly maturing industrial society. New economic and social factors, some of them grim, were changing life. They included: transcontinental railroads, a truly national market for goods, a growing monopoly in oil, the factory system, and new technology in steel and other industries. In addition, there were deplorable urban living conditions, millions of new, non-English-speaking immigrants, rising labor violence, growing discontent among farmers, and brutal poverty among workers and farmers.

These factors were clearly visible. But both Republican and Democratic politicians managed to avoid confronting them. Not until a paralyzing business depression in the 1890s and the rise of a new third party, committed to reform, did politicians finally start to deal with the problems brought about by industrial development. Before then, in the 1870s and 1880s, political leaders were more concerned with traditional issues, particularly the currency and tariffs. They argued, for example, over whether the amount of currency in circulation should be expanded or reduced. And they debated whether the United States would benefit more from raised or from lowered tariffs.

Why did politicians avoid considering the problems of the new industrial society? Basically, they (and voters too) were still intensely involved with the emotional questions arising out of the Civil War and Reconstruction. But with the ending of war and the termination of Radical rule in the South, old issues had disappeared. This transitional generation of politicians was simply unprepared to face the new problems of an industrial nation.

A GENERATION OF ORDINARY MEN

Through the 1870s and 1880s politics continued along at an unhurried pace. Leaders tried to avoid difficult issues. In large part the people who entered politics during this period were ordinary men, like Garfield. They displayed little achievement beyond their ability to win votes.

In *The American Commonwealth* (1888) James Bryce, an English historian, noted that in a country where all careers are open to those having talent and where "political life is unusually keen and political ambition widely diffused," the highest positions in the land are seldom "won by men of brilliant gifts."

Why did eminent figures usually not choose to run for political office in this period? First, for talented people American politics did not seem interesting and important. This situation contrasted with that in European countries, where officeholders in national governments generally held much more power over people's lives. Thus, first-rate men were attracted to vocations in which they felt they could make a significant impact. Politics was not one such vocation.

A second reason for the lack of brilliant people in politics was that success generally required a slow rise through the party ranks. The long apprenticeship in party loyalty necessary to achieve office discouraged ambitious people who wished to move quickly into positions of prominence. Also American voters, then as today, were distrustful of anyone who seemed overly eager for political power, although he or she might have been very capable.

Finally, persons of outstanding ability may not have entered politics simply because the era seemed a quiet one, at least compared with the age preceding it. Profound ideological questions no longer separated the parties. The problems of slavery, sectional divisions, and civil war were settled. Few issues were significant enough to attract talented people into politics.

Small-Town Background Given the lure of other fields, the slowness of the process of reaching the top, and the relative quietness of the times, the quality of those who held high public

President Garfield's home in Mentor, Ohio was the kind of country setting most national politicians of this era preferred. Their living patterns represented a nostalgia for an older, simpler way of life in an increasingly complex industrial society.

office is hardly surprising. Nor is it surprising to find that those who did make politics their career shared very similar patterns of life. It was far more likely for someone like Garfield to become President than for a man like his assassin Guiteau.

In fact, most successful figures in late nineteenth-century national politics, including the great majority of congressmen and senators, had backgrounds similar to that of Garfield. They came from small towns and cities like Garfield's Mentor, Ohio, rather than from large cities or predominantly rural areas. Furthermore, most began their careers in such professions as law, business, the ministry, or teaching.

During the 1860s and 1870s the number of politicians having business interests increased. But despite this fact most politicians were nonetheless provincial in their values and outlook on life. They tended to be more comfortable with their preindustrial way of thinking. They remained aloof and sheltered from the habits and problems of urban-industrial society. They brought to national affairs a viewpoint similar to that of their pre–Civil War counterparts. Most national elected officials, in fact, had little direct personal contact with the major new realities of a changed America—cities, industries, and immigrants.

As with most of the national politicians of this period, the presidential candidates—especially the Republicans—were men with roots in small cities and towns. And all the Republican candidates but James G. Blaine in 1884 came from the Middle West. Thus, even if a man like Charles Guiteau had managed to build a successful career for himself in a city like Chicago or New York, his urban ties would probably have blocked his road to the White House.

Guiteau may have been more successful as a Democrat, however. The Democrats generally nominated presidential candidates from big cities during these years: Horatio Seymour (1868), Horace Greeley (1872), Samuel Tilden (1876), and Grover Cleveland (1884, 1888, 1892). But of this group only Cleveland succeeded in becoming President. Thus, while they controlled the big cities and even had respectable showings in congressional elections, the Democrats largely failed to take the biggest prize of all—the presidency.

Civil War Experience As important as a small-town background seemed to be in achieving political success, there was another factor at least as important in advancing a politician's career—his Civil War record. This was true at all levels in American politics but particularly in regard to seeking the presidency. Indeed, another reason why Guiteau could never have become President was that he had not served in the Union Army.

For many Northern voters Republicanism was practically a family religion, sanctified by wartime sacrifices. (Most Northerners had lost at least one family member in the fighting.) The "martyrdom" of Lincoln and Garfield practically guaranteed the presidency for the Republican party.

The Republican presidential candidates were usually Civil War generals. General Hayes succeeded General Grant in the presidency. He, in turn, was succeeded by General Garfield. As death and old age thinned out the number of high-ranking officers, Colonel Benjamin Harrison, and, finally, Major William McKinley entered the White House.

The Democrats, for their part, failed to choose nominees having a military background, at least on the national level. The single Democratic candidate who was a Union military man was General Winfield Scott Hancock. He lost to Garfield in 1880. It is understandable that Union officers were not nominated. The Democrats depended, for the most part, on Southern support for victory. In local and regional elections, of course, where Southern support was irrelevant, Democrats could play on old Civil War loyalties to win elections. But, again, the presidential prize eluded them.

Codes of Personal Conduct The victorious politicians of this period, besides sharing a small-town background and Civil War experience, were also strong believers in the strictest of

John Peter Altgeld

"He was a lover of his fellow man." With these words in 1902 the famous lawyer Clarence Darrow eulogized his friend the former governor of Illinois. "When John P. Altgeld died," he continued, "the poor and weak and defenseless lost their truest friend."

Indeed, John Peter Altgeld had been a friend of the unfortunate. He himself had been poor, and he never forgot how it felt. He was born in 1847 in Germany. When he was three months old, his parents brought him to Ohio. There his father, an illiterate, narrow man who scorned "book learning," struggled with little success to earn a living at farming.

Young John shared his father's long hours of grinding labor on the farm. He did not share his scorn for books, however. He attended school when he could, which was rarely. At sixteen he went to fight in the Civil War. Then he drifted for a while, doing whatever work he could find. Finally he began to study law on his own and in 1875 moved to Chicago.

By 1886 he was a successful lawyer, made prosperous by investments in real estate. He entered public life, first as a judge and then, in 1893, as the first Democratic governor of Illinois in thirty-six years.

It was a time when government did not know how to meet the pressing problems created by the country's rapid shift from agriculture to industry. Altgeld's inauguration speech showed that he had some ideas on how to deal with this new situation. He outlined his plans for reforms in health and labor conditions, the prison system, civil service, education, personal liberty, and taxation.

Altgeld was beset by crisis from the start. Long before he became governor, he had been troubled by the Haymarket Affair. The three convicted men who had not been executed were still in prison in Illinois. Many people demanded their release. Altgeld agonized for six months. He wanted to see

Chicago Historical Society

justice done, but he knew the consequences. As he said to his friend Darrow, "If I pardon those men, it will not meet with the approval that you expect; from that day I will be a dead man politically."

Nevertheless, he pardoned the prisoners and published a detailed message stating his reasons. He used the trial records to document his conclusions that the judge and jury were prejudiced and that the evidence was insufficient to prove guilt.

Altgeld's dire prediction of political death proved correct. He was not elected to a second term. But another, happier prediction also proved true. Shortly after he became governor, he told a friend that he would soon present a broad program of reforms. All of them, he said, would one day be enacted into law. It probably took longer than he hoped, but by the 1920s virtually every one of his reforms was either the law of the state or the law of the land.

Grover Cleveland was elected President despite his failure to meet Victorian moral standards. His political incorruptibility and reform-mindedness were assets in office.

moral codes. They usually presented themselves to the public as family men, who lived their private lives according to the rigid ethical precepts of American middle-class culture. We do not know, of course, whether this was fact or sheer image building. The author of Garfield's semiofficial campaign biography wrote, for example: "No profane word, no unseemly jest is ever heard at Lawnfield [his home]. No wines sparkle on its table. The moral atmosphere is sweet, pure, and healthgiving to heart and soul. It is a Christian family—a Christian home."

Prior to the Civil War a politician's personal habits and morality had rarely influenced the success of his political career. Neither Andrew Jackson's background of frequent duels nor Henry Clay's frequent gambling prevented these men from seeking the highest prizes in American politics. During the middle of the nineteenth century, however, the American family adopted a stern moral code on such questions as sexual behavior, drinking, and gambling. Voters began to apply these standards to vote seekers as well. Thus, had Guiteau chosen to run for office, his stormy relationship with Anne Bunn would probably have been used against him.

Perhaps the only national politician of the era to successfully overcome hostility toward "loose" morality was Grover Cleveland. He won the presidency in 1884 despite the fact—brought out in the campaign—that in his youth he had fathered an illegitimate child. Ironically, voters that year were offered a choice between repudiating either Cleveland's single offense against private morality or James G. Blaine's questionable public morality. While a senator during the 1870s, Blaine had allegedly accepted money and stocks from railroad companies in return for political favors. When the returns were in, the electorate had registered its preference for a candidate with a single confessed private lapse to one probably tainted with several instances of political corruption.

ELECTING A PRESIDENT

National politics during the 1870s and 1880s was not oriented toward issues, although some of the older issues did play a part in the elections. Basically, politicians were concerned with party affiliation and moral, ethnic, and religious differences among the electorate. Three basic factors shaped presidential elections of the late nineteenth century: a close balance in voting strength between the two major parties, high voter turnout, and a stress on party regularity.

The Closeness of Contests The statistics for every presidential election of the era show clearly that the parties were evenly matched. In the disputed 1876 election Republican Rutherford B. Hayes was elected by one electoral vote, although he had received almost 250,000 fewer votes than his Democratic opponent, Samuel J. Tilden. In 1880 Garfield defeated the Democratic candidate, Winfield Scott Hancock, by a comfortable electoral majority. But his nationwide popular margin was a mere 7,368 votes. Actually, Garfield received only a plurality of the votes—48 percent; a third-party candidate, James B. Weaver of the Greenback-Labor party, cut into the major parties' totals.

Democrat Grover Cleveland's presidential election history is an interesting one, for he crossed and recrossed the narrow line between victory and defeat. In 1884 Cleveland won with less than 49 percent of the popular vote. His margin in the popular vote was only 63,000. When he was defeated by Republican Benjamin Harrison in the 1888 election, Harrison received the majority of electoral votes despite receiving 96,000 fewer popular votes. Cleveland again became President in 1892 when he received 360,000 more votes than Harrison. In this race a new third party, the Populists, received over 1 million votes. Thus a President-elect once more won with only a plurality, not a majority, of the popular vote.

The closeness of these presidential contests helps to explain the efforts usually made by both Republicans and Democrats to blur their basic differences over issues at the national level. Although the Republicans supported high protec-tive tariffs, for example, there were many in the party, including Garfield, who favored much lower rates. Similarly, the Democrats were a low-tariff party. But Cleveland's decision to press the tariff-reduction issue during his first term cost the party support from many high-tariff Democrats and independents who might other-wise have voted for him when he ran again. In order to make its position seem close to that of the other party, and thus hopefully to gain votes, each party had to suppress its conflicting factions on issues such as the tariff.

Because of the narrow margins of victory in each presidential election, both Republicans and Democrats were essentially in competition for the support of a small group of swing voters in a few doubtful states. These voters shifted from party to party throughout this period. Business help was often invaluable in swinging the key votes and deciding the outcome of the election. Thus Garfield's election in 1880 owed much to

Election night, 1892, in New York City is typical of voter enthusiasm in this era. Despite political corruption and the lack of great issues, excitement over politics ran high.

The Tweed Ring

New York City in the mid-1800s was growing rapidly. European immigrants, as well as native-born Americans, poured into the city in search of work in the booming urban-industrial society. In 1840 the city population numbered 300,000. By 1870 it had reached 950,000 inhabitants, about 400,000 of them foreign-born.

The effects on the city were staggering. Housing, public transportation, sanitation, and health facilities became dangerously inadequate. So did the existing methods for governing the city. The old residents—the "best people"—had governed a city where their way of life was the norm. Now they found themselves surrounded by what they considered strange and threatening intruders. And they quickly made their hostility known.

Not everyone shared their view of the newcomers, however. A political club with headquarters at Tammany Hall saw them in a different light—as potential voters. As quickly as the older residents alienated the new arrivals, Tammany welcomed them with open arms.

Tammany's leader was William Marcy Tweed. He

saw the immigrant as the basis for a strong constituency that would secure political power for him and his associates. So "Boss" Tweed courted the immigrant. He sent his people to meet ships bringing immigrants in. The confused and uprooted strangers soon learned who would help them get jobs, find places to stay, and become citizens.

Once they were settled in wards, or political districts, the immigrants learned that the ward leader knew of their existence. When they had a death in the family, he sent flowers. When they had trouble with the law, he used his influence. In return for these blessings new citizens were generally glad to give their votes.

Thus in 1866 the Tweed Ring, the country's first big city political organization, or "machine," was born. Ward leaders could deliver the vote to maintain the Tweed Ring in political office. Tweed's people could then levy taxes and decide on the allocation of money for projects. Tweed could in turn offer the ward leaders jobs on these projects for their voters—as well as other profitable favors.

With their power base secure, the Tweed Ring plundered New York City. Of every tax dollar, only fifteen cents went for legitimate uses. The rest went into the pockets of the ring, the overpaid builders, or bribe-welcoming officials.

Soon though, New Yorkers learned the price they were paying. Thomas Nast, a brilliant political cartoonist, began exposing Boss Tweed and his ring. The Tweed operation could not withstand the light of publicity. By the mid-1870s it was destroyed. Many of its members were imprisoned; its leader became a fugitive hiding out in Spain.

Although the Tweed Ring robbed New York City of anywhere from $30,000,000 to $200,000,000, it did leave a legacy. The way it built and maintained its support on the ward level was to remain standard practice in many American cities for nearly a hundred years.

the fact that John D. Rockefeller instructed his thousands of salesmen in various states in the Middle West to work actively for the Republican ticket. Similarly, in 1888, Harrison's victory was due in part to corporate donations that helped finance intensive drives for votes in a few key swing states.

Turnout of Voters Another basic factor in presidential elections in the late nineteenth century was a surprisingly high voter turnout. This phenomenon is somewhat more difficult to explain. There were no dramatic public issues bitterly dividing the two parties as there had been earlier—and would be in the near future. Part of the explanation, however, can be found in the popular view of elections as spectacles.

Both parties waged furious campaigns. Republicans "waved the bloody shirt"—that is, they reminded the voters of Southern Democratic disloyalty during the Civil War. Democrats, in turn, pointed to the corrupting influence of business on the Republican party.

Political campaigns were often the greatest shows in town. Huge numbers of voters marched in torchlight parades. They listened for hours to familiar but rousing partisan oratory. As participants in and spectators of such grand displays, voters reaffirmed their strong faith in their party identifications.

Importance of Party Loyalty Political loyalties among politicians and voters were clear and strong during this period. However blurred the political issues might be, this kind of loyalty strengthened the parties as institutions in American life.

Among politicians party loyalty or regularity was extremely important at the national level. Presidential power, which had reached a high point with Lincoln's wartime authority, declined after the crisis of civil war ended. Presidents were largely at the mercy of Congress in achieving their programs. The President's political task was twofold: (1) to "carry" enough congressmen of his own party into office when he was elected; and (2) to hold their loyalty once he won.

Concerning the former, Presidents were not too successful. No President during this entire era governed for his entire term with a majority of his own party in control of Congress. The Democrats, for example, won control of the House in 1874, lost it in 1880, regained it in 1882, lost it in 1888, and won it back in 1890. Although Republicans controlled the Senate throughout this period, except for the 1879–81 session, for all but two years they held no more than a slim three-vote Senate majority. There was considerable turnover in congressional membership during the 1870s and 1880s, particularly in the House.

It was even more difficult for a President to hold the party loyalty of congressmen after election. There were numerous factions in both parties. Various means of keeping the party together seemed to work, however. By the end of the era, congressional caucuses were a device used in both parties. They generally decided the legislative policies that all members were expected to, and usually did, abide by. A congressman who did not support the party could be disciplined in a number of ways. Leaders might deny him important committee assignments. They might refuse to help him in the passage of the numerous private bills that every congressman introduces yearly on behalf of his constituents. If necessary they would oppose his renomination. In these circumstances, most congressmen, of course, obeyed the dictates of their party's leaders.

Party loyalty among American voters was more easily assured. American voters adhered as firmly to their party allegiances as they did to their religious faiths. If one was raised as a Democrat or as a Republican, one usually remained a Democrat or a Republican for life.

Recent studies point to the importance of ethnic and religious backgrounds as factors in the political behavior of most Americans in the period following the Civil War. A voter's ethnic, cultural, and religious ties shaped his party loyalty as much as it did his attitudes on specific economic or political issues. For example, in order to help capture the votes of the immigrants, who badly needed employment, civil-service reformers in each party complained about the use of the spoils system by urban political machines in the other party. Although jobs were dispensed through political patronage under the spoils system, and thus recent immigrants were unlikely to get them, few of these immigrants favored introducing a merit system. This, they felt, might result in jobs being awarded mainly to native-born Americans who had had greater opportunity to receive education and training.

Religious beliefs were also a factor in determining political affiliation. Recent voting studies have shown that during this period the more an individual's religion stressed correct behavior rather than strict adherence to doctrine alone, the more likely he was to vote Republican. Some Protestant religious denominations viewed politics as a moral battleground in which state power should be used to regulate ethical behavior. For example, they supported laws prohibiting the sale of alcohol. Members of these denominations tended to support Republicans for office, whether in the 1850s or the 1890s. Certainly Republican opposition at the state level to using public funds for parochial schools (schools particularly important for many new immigrant families) and the party's support for prohibition (viewed as an assault on Democratic-voting Catholic immigrant "drinkers") attracted large numbers of native-born Episcopalian, Congregationalist, Presbyterian, and other similar voters.

This does not mean that immigrant groups and church members voted in blocs for a single party. Nonetheless, ethnic and cultural ties did indeed influence political loyalties in the period of the 1870s and 1880s.

THE REPUBLICANS IN POWER

For three decades, from 1861 to 1892, the Republicans (except for Democrat Cleveland's 1885–89 term) governed nationally, despite the close political balance between the parties. During this period, as already stated, the President was extremely dependent on Congress. In fact, more often than not, Congress—not the President—determined party policies and the legislation that emerged from Washington.

Americans did not seem to want strong Presidents during this period. Certainly they did not appear to need them because of the relative quietness of the times. So, none of the Republican Presidents—Grant, Hayes, Garfield, Arthur, or Harrison—managed to wrest control of Republican policies from the Senate and House leaders.

Men like Blaine and Conkling remained the party's most influential national spokesmen throughout the period. They largely shaped national legislation during the era. Since they were Republicans, they believed in an effective and energetic national economic policy. In general, the purpose of this policy was to encourage industrial expansion. For this they were often criticized by Democratic politicians who retained their party's traditional faith. This Democratic faith rested on the belief that government should not meddle actively in the economic lives of Americans.

But the Republican party, founded in an era when the national government had to expand its powers to preserve the Union, saw nothing wrong with continuing this trend at the war's end. To encourage economic development, party leaders aided business in every possible way. In accomplishing this purpose, they forged an informal alliance between the national government and the great majority of businessmen—bankers, industrialists, and merchants in foreign trade. While this alliance did further economic growth, it had other less fortunate consequences as well. It gave the era a reputation for corruption unparalleled in American history until then.

Corruption Under Grant It is ironic that people who lived by strict small-town moral codes in their private lives found it difficult to maintain the same kind of integrity in public affairs. Political corruption was widespread in this period. The Grant years in particular saw some of the worst offenses against honest government in the nation's history.

A series of Cabinet scandals during Grant's administration involved many people close to the President himself. His Secretary of the Navy sold work to contractors rather than take honest bids. His Secretary of War sold extremely profitable tradeships on Indian reservations. Department of Interior officials worked hand in hand with dishonest land speculators.

Some of the worst scandals involved the Department of the Treasury. Grant's Secretary of the Treasury farmed out the collection of unpaid taxes to a private contractor who kept half the collections. The President's own private secretary protected a Whiskey Ring of corrupt Treasury inspectors. These officials received millions of dollars in bribes from liquor distillers to avoid payment of government revenue taxes. Through Grant's personal bungling the Department of the Treasury cooperated with two New York stock speculators, James Fisk and Jay Gould, to manipulate government selling of bullion. The two men cornered the gold market briefly in September 1869, forcing anyone else who needed gold to pay an exorbitant price to get it. Although they caused a panic in the money market, Fisk and Gould made a fortune on the deal. Once they were exposed, Grant did little to punish the guilty parties in his administration.

The opportunities for politicians to profit through corrupt practices increased vastly as a result of the economic boom of the 1860s and 1870s. Many national leaders like Garfield had carefully watched their money while young to further their educations and careers. Suddenly they were responsible for handling billions of dollars in government funds. Politicians found themselves able to reap tidy sums (and benefit the country) simply by helping businessmen with government funds or favorable legislation.

The railroads were notorious seekers after these government favors. Railroad owners paid millions in bribes to public officials each year to secure cash subsidies, gifts of government land, and favorable legislation. Both Garfield and

Elected for being a great military man, Ulysses S. Grant was not a great President. His appointees, chosen more for personal loyalty than administrative competence, blackened his administration's record with scandals.

Blaine were linked to such transactions, although no specific criminal charges were ever made against either of them.

During Grant's administration, Garfield apparently profited, along with numerous other public officials, from a shady company known as the Crédit Mobilier. This was a purchasing and construction corporation organized by a few stockholders of the Union Pacific Railroad in the late 1860s. The Union Pacific stockholders retained control of the Crédit Mobilier, to which they awarded huge and fraudulent contracts connected with building the railroad. Congressmen of both parties, including Garfield, were bribed with money and stocks in the Crédit Mobilier to avoid congressional inquiry into these transactions. Before the affair was exposed in 1873, the Crédit Mobilier (despite the Union Pacific's virtual bankruptcy) had paid yearly dividends to stockholders that often exceeded

300 percent of the original investment. Moreover, sometimes these excessive profits went to Congressmen who paid nothing for the stock in the first place!

Although the Grant administration provides the most famous instances of scandal, governmental corruption was not limited to the national level or to Republicans alone. In fact, some of the worst instances of corruption took place at the city level, where Democrats were more likely to be in control. New York City, for instance, was run by a Democratic political organization, or "machine," known as the Tweed Ring (see p. 30). Its political leader, "Boss" William Marcy Tweed, and members of his machine stole over $100 million in public revenues ($14 million in one profitable day).

Civil-Service Reform An important source of Tweed's money was from kickbacks forced from people who wanted city jobs. Once in office, the machine politicians had the power to distribute jobs. Many reformers of the era thought that this spoils system for filling political posts should be eliminated and replaced with a merit system. This system, they thought, would do away with much of the corruption in high places that had plagued the country at all levels.

Grant's successor, Rutherford B. Hayes, ordered that officeholders not be asked to make political contributions or be required to do political campaigning. But these orders were largely ignored. Garfield, as noted in the previous chapter, backed away from Hayes' civil-service commitment. With Garfield's assassination public attention focused on Guiteau not merely as an actual assassin but as a symbol of the various evils that Americans identified with the spoils system of selecting officeholders.

Although the most blatant instances of national corruption had taken place a decade or more earlier, in 1883 Congress responded to the public outcry by passing the Pendleton Act. President Arthur, himself a one-time spoilsman, had lobbied hard for the bill. The act established a bipartisan Civil Service Commission, appointed by the President. Its purpose was to conduct competitive examinations to choose officeholders on the basis of merit. Arthur appointed three solid reformers as civil-service commissioners.

The original measure did not solve the entire problem, however, for the merit system affected only about one of every ten federal jobs. The others were to be filled as political appointments. Nonetheless, the Pendleton Act gave the President the authority to expand the number of positions classified as merit jobs. By 1900 over 40 percent of federal posts had been brought under the civil-service heading. This percentage has expanded in every decade since.

CONTINUING BUSINESS INFLUENCE

The assault on the spoils system did not have much effect on business influence within the national government. Businessmen tried less often to buy favors from individual politicians. Instead, increasing numbers of them began either running for office themselves or supporting politicians committed to business policies through legal campaign contributions. Industrialists and bankers poured millions into Republican campaign treasuries.

Even more important than business involvement in presidential contests, however, was the growing importance of senators who represented large corporate interests. By 1900 such businessmen, most of them Republicans, comprised a third of the Senate. Fifteen senators were involved in railroads; fifteen in extractive industries—minerals, oil, and lumber; nine in banking and finance; six in commerce; and three in manufacturing. Wealthy members of both the House and Senate were not captives or "puppets" of the business interests with which they held close ties. But on issues affecting the national economic life their policies tended to favor businessmen and monied interests rather than farmers, laborers, and the poor. And they made only token efforts to regulate American industry or finance.

This pro-Greenback cartoon portrays a gold-nosed government octopus linking itself to big business with its tentacles while strangling labor, farmers, and small business.

Currency Expansion   Favoritism toward business interests is shown clearly in the monetary programs enacted by Congress in the era. The debate involved the amount of currency in circulation. Farmers and most other debtors favored an increase in the amount of money issued by the government. Businesses, on the other hand, especially banking interests, wanted the opposite.

To understand the farmers' demands, it is important to keep in mind that this group was experiencing especially hard times during this period. The mechanization of agriculture was a mixed blessing to farmers. It greatly added to their efficiency; but it helped create vast surpluses and consequent falling prices. Wheat, for example, which sold for $2.50 a bushel in 1868 dropped to an average of 78 cents a bushel in the late 1880s.

While prices continued dropping, the cost of running farms remained high. Many farmers, for instance, were at the mercy of railroads that held a monopoly on transportation in their areas. These railroads often charged excessively high rates for carrying agricultural products to markets. Besides the cost of transportation, the cost of land, machinery, and tools was quite high.

Faced with high costs and declining prices for their own products, farmers usually went into debt by mortgaging their land and goods. In the 1880s the number of mortgages soared. Of the total number of farms in the country, over 40 percent were mortgaged. In some areas, like Kansas, the figure was closer to 60 percent. Interest rates on these mortgages were high—6 to 15 percent on land and 10 to 18 percent on goods.

Farmers felt that government could relieve their distress by pumping more money into the economy. The government had increased the amount of paper money—greenbacks—in circulation during the Civil War in order to finance the war effort. After the war the government began to withdraw these greenbacks from circulation. This cutback in currency was hitting the indebted farmer particularly hard because he had borrowed when money was "cheap" or plentiful. Now he had to pay his debts in currency worth much more than its original value.

From the bankers' point of view, of course,

the situation was ideal. They had a stake in seeing that money became scarcer. They would profit more on the repayment of loans, since the value of a dollar increases as its supply decreases. The government agreed with this viewpoint. During the Hayes administration, the Specie Resumption Act of 1875 reduced the number of greenbacks in circulation. This was a direct slap at debtor interests, particularly farmers. The act gave an even more direct favor to the financial community. It provided that bonds issued during the Civil War should be paid off in gold. The banking community, of course, held most of these bonds. The provision meant that war bonds

An antitariff cartoon of the 1880s shows the spiraling bad effects of a high tariff. The tariff wall results in a glut of products on the home market, consequent cuts in production, and then widespread unemployment.

that had been bought with greenbacks worth less than 40 cents to the dollar could now be turned in for currency worth 100 cents to the dollar.

This resumption of specie payments, as it was called, so enraged some farmers that they banded together to form a third party. They were joined by many recruits from labor and became the Greenback-Labor party in 1878. In the short run the movement was unsuccessful, since it failed to win many votes or to change the government's policy in currency. In the long run, however, it was significant in laying the basis for an agrarian movement far more powerful during the 1890s.

Agitation for expanding the currency did not stop after the initial failure of the greenback movement. In fact, a new strategy was tried—a demand that silver be used to back the dollar. In 1873 the government had stopped coining silver and put the country back on the gold standard— that is, backed money with gold alone. But in the 1870s the supply of silver increased tremendously because of the discovery of new silver deposits in the West. Many charged that silver had been demonetized illegally. By the 1880s farmers and other debtor groups saw in the "remonetizing" of silver a way of getting cheaper money. This in turn would raise crop prices and secure them relief from their debts.

Those who agitated for silver were partially successful during the 1870s. The Bland-Allison Act of 1878 required the Department of the Treasury to buy not less than $2 million and not more than $4 million worth of silver each month to back the dollar. Unfortunately, the government continuously bought the lesser amount. Though the silver interests were placated, farmers did not get much relief.

The Tariff Issue   Another government policy that tended to favor business interests at the expense of other segments of society involved the tariff. The tariff debate, as old as the country itself, took on new importance with the coming of the industrial age. The original justification for a tax on imports was to protect infant industries from the competition of foreign manufacturers. But long after competition from abroad ceased to be a threat, the tariff still remained high on most goods. And it was going higher.

Again those particularly hurt by the tariff were the farmers. They complained that they had to sell their goods competitively on an open world market. But they had to purchase tariff-protected manufactured and processed goods such as farm machinery and oil. In fact, consumers in general suffered from the imposition of high tariffs. Without the competition of cheaper imported goods, they paid whatever prices domestic manufacturers set. These were often determined by monopolistic practices.

Republicans were by no means the only supporters of high protective tariffs. Factions in both parties backed business interests (or farmer interests) on this matter. But it was not until a Democrat, Grover Cleveland, took office that there was a serious challenge to high tariffs. Cleveland's advocacy of a lowered tariff provided the leading issue in his reelection bid in 1888. He was defeated, as was noted earlier, partly because he had alienated the protariff faction in his own party. But his downfall came mostly because businessmen poured millions of dollars into the campaign of the Republican candidate, Benjamin Harrison.

Harrison repaid his business backers by supporting the highest tariff in the nation's history. The McKinley Tariff of 1890—named after its sponsor, William McKinley (who, with business backing, would himself become President a few years later)—aimed not just at discouraging competition but at eliminating it altogether. It raised rates from an average of 38 percent to an average of almost 50 percent. It clearly marked a triumph for American industrialists.

Token Reform Although business influence was at its height, the government could not afford to ignore the public altogether. Some steps were taken in this period to deal with elements in the changed economy. But these proved to be less than effective. Congressmen from both parties joined in passing two basically mild bills to regulate the new giant industries.

The Interstate Commerce Act in 1887 set up a federal commission (the ICC) to oversee "reasonable and just" rates on the nation's railroads. Congress did not provide the commission with any strong enforcement powers, however. Its only avenue was the courts, and these generally consisted of probusiness conservatives. Moreover, the persons who were appointed as commissioners during the 1890s were sympathetic to the railroads. This, of course, further prevented the ICC from making any serious efforts to regulate the lines in order to ensure fair and equal treatment for all shippers.

A second law, the Sherman Antitrust Act of 1890, was also supposed to curb big business. Anticipating public reaction to the high McKinley Tariff congressmen hoped that the Sherman Act would quiet agitation. Unfortunately, it provided only mild and ineffective penalties against companies that formed combinations in restraint of trade. Furthermore, it was rarely applied during the 1890s. Only five years after the law was passed, the Supreme Court handed down a decision in *U.S. v. Knight* that exempted most industries from its provision. A monopoly, according to the Court, was not itself illegal. It became so only when it served to restrain interstate trade.

The immediate effect of such token efforts was to prevent a massive public outcry. In the long run, though, they only added further grievances to the growing list of problems confronting the country. The nation had lived through more than two decades of conservative rule resulting from the informal alliance of business and government. The public was ready for reform, and pressure was mounting in various parts of society to bring that about.

THE POPULIST CRUSADE

The first sector of the population to voice the need for change and take steps in this direction were the farmers. Their lot had been difficult throughout this period. It worsened in the late 1880s with the onset of a severe farm depression

Populist conventions mixed the gaiety of a county fair with the fervor of a revivalist meeting. This one in New York in 1896 decided against running an independent slate and endorsed Democrat William Jennings Bryan, marking the end of the party.

affecting especially the South and the West. The price of farm products continued to decline while production costs skyrocketed. Angry at their political powerlessness within the existing party system, farmers decided to strike out on their own in a new third party.

They called themselves the Populist party. Although they managed to attract some support from working-class and middle-class reformers, most Populist leaders and party members came from the ranks of previous farmer protest organizations. They met in Omaha in 1892 to assemble a reform program. Ignatius Donnelly, foremost Populist writer and orator, wrote their platform. In its preamble he charged:

The controlling influences dominating both

these parties have permitted the existing dreadful conditions to develop without serious effort to prevent or restrain them. Neither do they now promise us any substantial reform. Instead, they have agreed together to drown the outcries of the people [in the campaign ahead] with the uproar of a sham battle over the tariff, so that capitalists, corporations, national banks, rings, trusts, the demonetization of silver may all be lost sight of.

The Party's Program   At the convention a program was adopted that was followed in most essentials by Populist candidates throughout the 1890s. The program reflected the party's largely rural and agrarian base. Therefore, although there were planks that defended the right of unions to organize and denounced the oppression of factory workers, these were not central Populist concerns. And, although the platform also demanded a graduated federal income tax, direct election of senators, and other constitutional or political reforms, these were not central Populist concerns either.

What the new party wished, above all, was a series of reforms designed to help American farmers overcome what they felt were the unfair handicaps imposed upon agriculture in the United States by industrial growth. The most important of these demands was strict regulation or government ownership of the nation's railroads, which farmers believed discriminated against them. They also wanted an increase in the supply of money through remonetizing silver, since the Bland-Allison Act had been largely ineffective. Finally they proposed establishing a government subtreasury warehouse system, at which farmers could deposit their crops and receive loans up to 80 percent of the current market value of these crops. They would redeem the crops and sell them when open market prices had risen to acceptable levels.

The impact of the Populist crusade was felt by the two major parties as soon as the 1892 election results were in. After only six months of life the new third party had carried four states with twenty-two electoral votes. It had received over a million popular votes and elected a number of congressmen and senators.

Failure of the Movement   Despite this dramatic success, just four years later the Populists aligned with the Democrats to support William Jennings Bryan for President, only to lose badly at the hands of Republican William McKinley. By 1900, although they ran a presidential candidate, they were no longer a major political force. A key factor affecting the Populist decline was the spread of the economic depression. This depression that had first hit farmers in the late 1880s soon affected other groups in the economy. Business entered a slump, and millions of workers were laid off. By 1894, at the height of the depression, probably one out of every five workers

was unemployed. Four out of five were living at a subsistence level.

Strangely, the decline that had earlier spurred the nation's farmers to take active steps for their own relief had no such effect on the rest of the country's workers. They failed to join the Populist movement. Several factors help to explain this. For one, the Populists never succeeded in breaking down the traditional political loyalties of most Americans since party loyalty was extremely important to voters at this time. Even under the impact of economic depression, people remained with their parties.

It was also true that the depression occurred during a Democratic administration—Cleveland's second term. This resulted in political gains for the major opposition party even more impressive than those made by the Populists. In fact, Republicans almost doubled their number of House members in 1894—moving from 127 to 244—while the Democrats lost 113 seats. This was the most rapid major reversal of national political strength in American history, marking the first step in ending the close balance between the parties that had existed during the 1870s and 1880s.

Besides the depression working against them, there were other problems that the Populists could not overcome. The South presented the Populists with a unique set of problems that impeded their growth. There the new party attempted, for the first time since Reconstruction days, to create a biracial political coalition of black and white farmers against the business interests that still dominated most Southern state governments. For a time they made striking gains. Georgia Populist leader Tom Watson told farm audiences from both races: "You are made to hate each other, because upon that hatred is rested the keystone of the arch of financial despotism which enslaves you both." But the political opponents of Southern Populism played upon such deeply felt racial fears and hostilities so effectively that, by the end of the decade, the new party had lost almost all its influence in the South. In that region, in fact, Populism had the ironic effect by 1900 of raising the race issue to an intensity and importance that it has maintained throughout most of the twentieth century.

Populist strength was sapped, especially in the industrial states, by internal tensions among its diverse sources of support. Such tensions between utopians and pragmatists often characterize reform movements. The Populists' agrarian leaders tended to be the movement's practical figures. Their overriding concern was for specific, immediate, and achievable goals such as free coinage of silver, the subtreasury plan, and other measures that would improve the economic bargaining position of most American farmers. On the other hand, many middle-class and working-class reformers joined the Populist party in order to use it as a vehicle to overhaul American economic institutions. It was not surprising, therefore, that the latter groups, along with some of the more radical farm leaders, opposed the party's decision to support Bryan against Republican William McKinley in 1896 rather than run its own uncompromising candidate.

Bryan's Defeat All of these factors and others contributed to William McKinley's smashing defeat of Bryan in 1896. McKinley had the almost united financial support of the business community in the election. It was driven into McKinley's camp by its unbounded fears of Bryan's and Populist reform. The careful organization of McKinley's campaign by his astute manager Mark Hanna also contributed to the Republican victory.

Perhaps the most striking feature of the 1896 election, however, was the Republicans' ability to put together a national majority that cut across class lines. McKinley won the votes not only of industrialists and the middle class but also of a majority of urban workers. Bryan failed to capture the cities and the votes of most industrial laborers, despite prolabor planks in the Democratic platform. Many urban workers clearly felt that their economic interests were better protected by a probusiness Republican President than by a Democratic candidate who spoke (in the rich twang of Midwestern rural America no less) mainly about the problems of farmers.

But if Bryan failed in 1896 to create that farmer–laborer–small-businessman coalition that he believed could win national power and make needed political and economic reforms, he did lay the groundwork for such reformers, not only within the Democratic party but among Republicans as well. In the process of laying the groundwork for reform, Bryan set a precedent for active presidential campaigning that almost all subsequent major party candidates followed in the twentieth century. Within a decade Theodore Roosevelt, McKinley's Republican successor as President, would use a similar energetic personal style of campaigning to drum up public support for reform measures. In the end, therefore, the struggle for change in American society gathered momentum during the late 1890s despite Bryan's defeat, despite the disappearance of Populism, and even despite the country's return to economic prosperity.

This 1896 caricature of William Jennings Bryan denounces him for having deserted the Democratic party in 1892 to support the Populist candidate, James B. Weaver, and then returning four years later in search of the Democratic presidential nomination.

1. Was it accurate to say that "Garfield dead proved more valuable to reformers than Garfield alive"? Why or why not?

2. Why do historians refer to politicians of this era as preindustrial? Why were successful Democrats likely to come from big cities? Why was Union Army experience not an asset for a Democrat seeking national office?

3. How might the importance of swing voters in this era be explained? Why was voter turnout so high at this time?

4. Is it accurate to say that the Republican party had become the party of big business by this time?

5. For what reason were recent immigrants more likely to oppose civil-service reform than were native-born Americans? Why were Catholics more likely to be Democrats than Republicans?

6. What did reformers hope would result from civil-service reform? What steps did the Pendleton Act take to bring it about? Why was it inadequate?

7. For what reasons did farmers favor and bankers oppose an increase in the amount of money in circulation? What evidence is there to show that the government carried out the bankers' wishes?

8. What steps did the government take to regulate industry? Why are these measures regarded as "token" reform?

9. Why was the Populist party founded? How did internal dissension work against its success? Why didn't urban workers support William Jennings Bryan for President?

Beyond the Text

1. Because Garfield lingered for seventy-nine days, questions arose as to his ability to perform his duties of office. Who determines if the President is unable to perform his duty? If the Vice President takes over how can a President, once recovered, regain his powers?

2. Historians have rated American Presidents according to these categories: Great, Near Great, Average, Below Average, and Failure. Evaluate the Presidents elected between 1876 and 1900. Consult *Life Magazine* (November 1, 1948) and Thomas A. Bailey's *Presidential Greatness* in preparing an answer.

3. Ethnic and religious affiliations determined voting behavior in the 1870s and 1880s. Are they still important in present-day presidential elections?

Bibliography

Nonfiction

Faulkner, Harold U., *Politics, Reform & Expansion, 1890–1900.**

Garraty, John A., *The New Commonwealth: 1877–1890.*

Hicks, John D., *The Populist Revolt.**

Kirkland, Edward C., *Industry Comes of Age.**

Kleppner, P., *The Cross of Culture.*

Marcus, Robert D., *Grand Old Party: Political Structure in the Gilded Age.**

Morgan, H. Wayne, *From Hayes to McKinley.*
———, ed., *The Gilded Age.**

Rothman, David J., *Politics of Power: The United States Senate, 1869–1901.**

Sproat, John G., *"The Best Men": Liberal Reformers in the Gilded Age.**

Wiebe, Robert H., *The Search for Order: 1877–1920.**

Woodward, C. Vann, *The Origins of the New South: 1877–1913.**

Fiction

Adams, Henry, *Democracy.**
Dowdey, Clifford, *Sing for a Penny.*
Ford, Paul L., *The Honorable Peter Stirling.*

*a paperback book

UNIT SIX

PROGRESSIVE

The new century brought to Americans confidence in their own ability to control the nation's destiny. It also brought concern for the unresolved problems of industrial growth, urban squalor, and immigrant poverty. The business depression of the 1890s had ended by 1898, returning the country's middle and upper classes to full prosperity. A global empire had been won almost without cost or exertion. Reformers across the land increased their efforts in the early 1900s while, in the White House itself, a young new President, Theodore Roosevelt, pushed political, economic, and social reforms. Truly there seemed cause for such confidence.

The chapters that follow describe the three decades of confidence, concern, and change within American society from 1900 to the New Era of the twenties. The first of these chapters on the Triangle Fire dramatizes the lives of southern and eastern European immigrant workers in New York City garment factories. Underpaid and impoverished, they struggled to unionize the clothing industry. Only when a flash fire killed scores of young female workers

AMERICA

at the Triangle Company did their appeal for better working conditions receive a hearing.

Chapter 28 then opens with a discussion of the urban world within which most of these recent immigrants lived. The chapter explores the varieties of industrial reform efforts. Since the political life of progressive America (1900–17) often concerned the struggle for change, Chapter 28 also examines the connections between reform activities and partisan politics.

Popular confidence rose during these decades partly because of the ease with which the United States assumed a leading role in world affairs. Chapter 29 portrays one of the unhappier consequences of that new role—the unsuccessful revolt by Filipino nationalists against American takeover of their islands. The Philippine Revolt serves as the context for a general discussion in Chapter 30 of American foreign policy. The chapter traces developments from the country's brief involvement in the Spanish-American War to its costlier participation in the First World War. The connections between domestic concerns in progressive America and the nation's actions as a major global power emerge clearly.

Rounding out the unit are two chapters on the evolution of the United States as a technological society during the first third of the twentieth century. One of the most widely publicized instances of American technological superiority was Charles Lindbergh's pioneering flight across the Atlantic in 1927. His feat captured the imagination of a machine-oriented world. Lindbergh's story unfolds in Chapter 31.

In the accompanying chapter the achievements, attitudes, and patterns of the optimistic, mechanically advanced America that produced Lindbergh's flight are examined. From the vantage point of the 1970s, the United States of the progressive era may seem, whatever its problems, a less complicated and perhaps even happier society. Certainly this country's leaders—even most of its critics—looked to the future with a measure of confidence that withstood involvement in a world war and collapsed only during the 1930s under the onslaught of the Great Depression.

THE TRIANGLE FIRE

IN SEPTEMBER 1909, 200 Jewish and Italian immigrant workers at New York City's Triangle Shirtwaist Company walked off their jobs. The previous year, Triangle's owners had organized an Employees Benevolent Association, a so-called company union, designed to head off unions organized by the workers themselves. But the tactic had not worked. Protesting miserable working conditions and poor pay, the workers at Triangle—most of them young women—sought to gain recognition of their union by their employers. They were led by officials from the recently organized International Ladies' Garment Workers' Union (ILGWU). They had also received the support of the Women's Trade Union League (WTUL).

The Triangle strikers and workers in other shirtwaist shops in the city had a number of complaints. They were forced to work in crowded, unclean factories. Fire hazards and unsanitary conditions presented a serious threat to their health. Windows and doors in the shops were often nailed shut. Rarely did the sun penetrate the factory lofts, which workers referred to as sweatshops.

Long hours and low wages added to the workers' discontent. Most employees in New York's garment factories worked a fifty-six-hour, six-day week. When a factory owner had a rush order, he could force employees to work overtime at night or on Sunday without pay. Wages in the shirtwaist industry were as low as $6 a week. Employers often

The Triangle Shirtwaist Company occupied the top three floors of the ten-story Asch Building in Lower Manhattan. A fire raged on those floors on March 11, 1925 that was ultimately to affect the working conditions of a large segment of American laborers.

deducted penalties from the workers' pay for mistakes made in sewing clothes. They charged the workers fees for "renting" the machines and using electricity. In addition, employees were subjected to a series of petty fines for talking, smoking, and singing on the job.

It was against such conditions, in the face of active opposition by the police who were openly sympathetic to the factory owners, that workers finally took a stand.

The strike dragged on into winter. Workers at nonstriking shirt-waist companies grew angrier as they watched police and hired thugs abuse the striking employees. On the evening of November 22 the city's shirtwaist workers held a mass meeting at Cooper Union to discuss the situation. Among the reformers and union leaders asked to speak were Samuel Gompers, president of the American Federation of Labor (AFL); Abraham Cahan, editor of the *Jewish Daily Forward;* and Mary Dreier, president of the Women's Trade Union League. Gompers, a moderate in labor disputes, surprised the audience by stating that "there comes a time when not to strike is but to rivet the chains of slavery upon our wrists."

Within a few days between 10,000 and 20,000 workers, mainly young women, had walked off their jobs. The strike affected over 500 shirtwaist and dressmaking companies, including all the smaller shops and most of the big companies in the city. "The Uprising of the Twenty Thousand," as the ILGWU called the walkout, was the first industry-wide strike of immigrant workers in New York City. It was also the largest strike by women ever held in the United States to that time.

The shirtwaist[1] industry was a relatively recent one. The 1900 federal census described it as a "branch of the garment industry that has developed during the last decade." Before 1900 many of the garments produced in New York City and elsewhere came from work-shops in ghetto slum apartments. Families were paid according to the number of garments produced. This piecework system proved ineffi-cient. Clothing production gradually shifted to new loft buildings constructed especially for the trade.

By 1910 New York had become the national center for the gar-ment industry. The city's 600 shirtwaist and dress factories employed over 30,000 workers. They sold more than $50 million worth of cloth-ing annually. In the new shops skilled machine operators, usually men, supervised crews of young women who performed simple, unskilled tasks in preparing shirtwaists and dresses. At large factories such as

---

[1] The shirtwaist was a tailored blouse for women that was styled somewhat like a man's shirt. It was usually made of sheer cotton to give it a "feminine" look.

Triangle the machine operators, called contractors, were paid by the owners not only for their own work but for the labor of their crews as well. The contractors, in turn, paid weekly salaries to their female assistants. This system was often abused by dishonest contractors, who cheated young women workers out of their proper wages.

Four out of every five workers in the garment trades were women. In the Uprising of the Twenty Thousand 75 percent of the strikers were young women between the ages of sixteen and twenty-five. Almost all had been born abroad or to recently arrived immigrant families. Most of the workers were either Jewish or Italian. Most of the factory owners were Jews.

The 1909 garment trade's strike marked the first time that many of these immigrant workers managed to set aside their mutual fears and suspicions to work for common economic interests. The strike brought Jewish and Italian women together on the picket line and in the union. Thus it set a pattern for future cooperation in the labor movement among the city's ethnic communities. Jewish union organ-

Sweatshops like the one shown were common in the garment industry. Unskilled women laborers usually worked under skilled male machine operators in crowded, poorly ventilated, and unsafe shops.

izers learned a smattering of Italian, while Italian leaders acquired enough Yiddish to make themselves understood. Political and community leaders from each ethnic group also worked together on behalf of the strikers. Meyer London, a socialist lawyer who later became the country's first Jewish congressman, cooperated with Fiorello LaGuardia, a young state legislator who later became the country's first Italian congressman. LaGuardia, the son of a Jewish mother and an Italian father, symbolized the alliance then being forged by the two groups.

Several hundred black workers who were frequently hired as scabs in the garment factories joined the Uprising of the Twenty Thousand. One black shirtwaist striker—a "real born American," as she described herself—kept a diary of the events. In it she recorded her shop's reaction to the November 22 call for a general strike:

> It's a good thing, this strike is. It makes you feel like a real grown-up person. I simply can't get over the way little Ray Goldousky jumped on a chair and suddenly, without a minute's notice, stopped the electricity [in the shop]. Why, we were simply stunned. Before you could say Jack Robinson, we all rose, slipped on our duds, and marched down the stairs, shouting, yelling, and giggling about our walkout, as they called it.

Similar incidents in New York's garment factories shocked the industry's manufacturers into taking action against the strikers. Several weeks before the general walkout, the Triangle Company's owners, Blanck and Harris, proposed to other employers that an employers' mutual protective association be founded to counter efforts by workers to organize unions. Not until their own shops began striking, however, did other manufacturers agree to the idea. Then they joined together to form the Associated Waist and Dress Manufacturers. It directed antistrike activities. These activities ranged from encouraging police brutality against strikers to organizing company unions among the minority of workers who did not support the strike.

Employers also tried using "carrot-and-stick" tactics. They offered incentives to those who remained on the job and hired hoodlums to beat up workers on the picket line. The anonymous shirtwaist striker noted in her diary that the Triangle Company promised nonstrikers "from fifteen to twenty dollars weekly, free lunch, and dancing during the noon hour."

These tactics, however, failed to break the morale and unity of the shirtwaist strikers. The Uprising of the Twenty Thousand continued throughout the bitterly cold winter of 1909–10. Reformers, labor unions, and other sympathizers contributed over $60,000 to aid the striking workers. But the strike fund supplied only a fraction of the money that the workers and their families needed for food, clothing, rent, medical care, and other expenses. "As the days go by," one striker wrote in her diary on December 1, "the girls suffer more and more. During the tedious picket duty they get frozen, catch colds, go without food until they're nothing but shadows of their former selves—it's real disheartening." On December 27, she noted proudly that "girls with sore throats and girls with broken noses, girls with wet, torn shoes and girls without hats or coats, shivering from cold and faint with hunger [all voted] to stay on strike."

The Triangle strike was an important event not only for women garment workers but also for women's suffrage reformers, ghetto community leaders, labor officials, and socialist politicians. All these groups donated time and money to make the strike a success.

Members of New York's economic and social elite posted bail bonds for arrested strikers. Wealthy New York socialites such as Mrs. Henry Morgenthau, Mrs. O. H. P. Belmont, Anne Morgan, and Mrs. J. B. Harriman raised funds for strike benefits and worked to secure the release of jailed employees. Mrs. Belmont even offered her Madison Avenue mansion as security for an $800 bail bond. When a judge asked sarcastically whether the mansion was adequate security, Mrs.

Strikers in the shirtwaist strike of 1909–10 sold copies of the Call, *a New York socialist daily, in order to publicize their demands and raise money for their living expenses while on strike.*

Belmont replied: "I think it is. It is valued at $400,000. There is a mortgage of $100,000 on it, which I raised to help the cause of the shirtwaist makers and the women's suffrage movement."

These "uptown" supporters were joined by several of the city's most active reform groups: The Women's Trade Union League, the National Women's Suffrage Association, the Political Equality Association, and the National Civic Federation. The WTUL raised 20 percent of the strike benefit fund and joined the picketers in support of the walkout. Early in December the WTUL, which led a march on City Hall to plead the strikers' cause, had organized many marches on behalf of women's suffrage legislation.

A host of muckraking reporters,[2] academics, social workers, and other professionals also worked on behalf of the strikers. Many of these middle- and upper-class reformers were German Jews whose ancestors had come to the United States during the mid-nineteenth century. The strike gave them an opportunity to display their solidarity with poorer Jews from the Lower East Side, most of whom had recently left Eastern Europe for the United States.

Everywhere on the Lower East Side community leaders and organizations worked in support of the strike. They included union officials from the United Hebrew Trades, Socialist party orators from both the Jewish and Italian communities, sympathetic rabbis and priests, and editors of Jewish newspapers. A number of other New York newspapers supported the striking workers, as did many of the city's residents. An open meeting held on December 5 drew over 8,000 pro-strike demonstrators. Pressure mounted on the garment trade employers to resolve the dispute.

A settlement was finally reached in February 1910. The agreement came in two stages. It represented a victory for the union, though not a total triumph. At first the shirtwaist workers rejected several compromise offers arranged by arbitrators who brought the two sides together. Then a number of smaller manufacturers began settling privately with the ILGWU. They agreed to hire only union members and not to deal with contractors who employed nonunion help. But larger manufacturers such as Triangle continued to insist on the right to maintain an open (or nonunion) shop, as opposed to a closed (or union) shop. Eventually, some of the larger firms agreed to a settlement, promising workers higher wages and better working conditions. In the agreements, however, neither the union nor the union shop was recognized.

By February 15, 1910, only 1,100 workers, from 13 shops, were

---

[2] Muckraking reporters were writers of the late nineteenth and early twentieth centuries who exposed corrupt conditions in business and government.

still away from their jobs. The ILGWU officially declared the strike over. Over 300 firms had accepted the union's terms completely, and 19 shops (including Triangle and other large firms) had agreed to open-shop compromises. The garment workers made several important gains in the settlements: reduction of the workweek to 52 hours, a two-hour limit on night work, wage increases of 12 to 15 percent, and a promise by employers to end the contractor system of payment.

Later that year, prominent Jewish citizens of New York City helped to arrange a second agreement between employers and workers. Louis Brandeis, a Boston lawyer, served as chief arbitrator between union and management. Brandeis skillfully played on the common Jewish background of garment employees and garment employers. Many of the employers themselves had begun as poor workers.

On Labor Day evening both sides agreed to a "Protocol of Peace," which became a milestone in American industrial relations. Its provisions included the end of the contractor system and the charges levied against workers for materials and electricity. There was also an agreement by employers to give preference to union workers in hiring. Garment employees were guaranteed a six-day, 54-hour week in all shops, an end to night work after 8:30 P.M., and limits on the amount of overtime an employer could require. The agreement also called for the creation of a board of arbitration to settle major disputes between workers and bosses. A Joint Board of Sanitary Control—representing union, management, and the public—was set up to oversee health and safety conditions in garment factories. Although the agreement eventually broke down, the Protocol represented a significant victory for the ILGWU. Its membership skyrocketed from 400 to 60,000 workers in the months following the "Uprising."

At the Triangle Company, however, the union remained unrecognized. Many strikers were not rehired, and most of the strikebreakers who had worked during the walkout were kept on the payroll. Some workers complained that the major effect of the settlement was to end the phonograph music and dancing contests that had been provided for nonstriking employees. Otherwise work returned to normal at the country's largest shirtwaist shop, at least until the afternoon of March 25, 1911.

The Triangle Shirtwaist Company occupied the top three floors of a new loft structure, the Asch Building, in lower Manhattan. The ten-story building, constructed in 1901, was located on the northwest corner of Green Street and Washington Place. It stood next to New

York University and a block east of Washington Square. Since the turn of the century, over $150 million had been spent on the construction of loft factories in lower Manhattan. The new buildings, made of brick or stone, were supposed to be fireproof, but they had wooden frame interiors that could easily catch fire. Few of the buildings had adequate fire escapes or staircases.

Using such buildings, manufacturers took advantage of cheap insurance rates, low operating costs, and a concentrated labor supply. State law required employers to allow 250 cubic feet of air per worker. But the law did not specify where the air space should be. Loft buildings, with their ten-foot-high ceilings, enabled owners to crowd hundreds of employees onto a floor and still meet the space requirements. (The extra space was above the worker's heads; it was not distributed among employees.) At Triangle about 500 people jammed the Asch Building's top three floors.

The Triangle employees never had a fire drill. Even though several small fires had occurred on the premises in 1909, no improved safety measures had been taken. There were only two narrow staircases leading down from the Triangle's three floors. All but one of the doors leading to the stairways were kept closed (often bolted) to prevent employees from loitering or stealing fabric. The single fire escape in the building went down only to the second floor, so that it was difficult to reach the street in case of emergencies. The only other means of descent were two small freight elevators, each about five feet square. Huge piles of cloth, tissue paper, rags, and cuttings covered the company's tables, shelves, and floors. The floors and machines were soaked with oil, and barrels of machine oil lined the walls. All these factors made the Triangle factory highly flammable.

As the day's work drew to a close on Saturday, March 25, 500 Triangle workers finished their chores and prepared to leave the building by the one open door on the eighth floor. A company guard stationed at the exit checked the women's handbags for cloth fragments. The time was 4:30 P.M. Saturday's weather was brisk and sunny—a perfect early spring afternoon.

Hardly had the guard rung the closing bell when a young woman employee on the eighth floor ran up to Samuel Bernstein, the company's production manager, and cried: "There is a fire, Mr. Bernstein." The manager and several other men, who had battled a small fire on the floor two weeks earlier, tried to put out the blaze with pails of water. But the flames shot up even higher. One of the men later remembered: "It was like there was kerosene in the water; it just seemed to spread it." Bernstein quickly realized that it would be impossible to stop the fast-spreading flames. He shouted to an assistant: "You can't do anything here. Try to get the girls out!" Bernstein and a few others tried to lead the stunned workers out in orderly fashion. But screams of "Fire!" soon filled the eighth floor.

Panic and confusion spread with the inferno. The 225 eighth-floor workers scurried across the smoke-filled room toward the various exits. As they ran, many called out the names of relatives—sisters and brothers, fathers and mothers—who also worked for Triangle. A young bookkeeper on the floor, Diana Lipschitz, sent an urgent message by interoffice teletype to the tenth floor: "The place is on fire. Run for your lives." The bookkeeper who received the message at first thought that Diana was joking. But the flames soon spurted through the tenth-floor windows, igniting bundles of cloth. Employees on that floor spread the alarm and hurried toward the exits. Because the Asch Building was supposedly fireproof, the blaze could not damage the walls or floors. But the flames curved in a swirling mass through the eighth-floor windows and engulfed the ninth and tenth floors within minutes.

On every floor workers pressed against one another in a desperate effort to reach the exits. The intense heat from the surrounding flames seared their bodies. Those on the eighth floor who had pushed their way down the congested stairway collapsed on lower floors, where firemen later found them.

Employees on the ninth floor, meanwhile, had not received even a teletype warning of the blaze. They learned of the danger only when the fire darted through the windows, bursting into pockets of flame. Most of the women dashed frantically toward exits. Others froze in fear and remained at their machines. When they discovered that the door next to the freight elevators was locked, the women rushed toward the other stairway. Over 150 workers fought for access to the twenty-inch passageway that led to the open stairway.

On the tenth floor those who did not escape via the roof crowded into the two freight elevators. Jammed with fleeing workers, the cars began their descent to the ground floor. Then, some workers still trapped on the top floors started jumping into the elevator shafts to land on top of the descending elevators. One elevator operator, Joseph Zito, recalled that so many girls hit the top of his car that it would not work: "It was jammed by the bodies." Nineteen bodies were later found wedged into one of the elevator shafts. The other elevator broke down when its power circuit became waterlogged by the spray of the fire hoses.

By 4:45 P.M. the top three floors of the Asch Building were engulfed in flames. Escape was no longer possible.

A fireman looks on helplessly as the fire in the Asch Building rages out of control just fifteen minutes after its start. Rescue efforts had to be abandoned.

By this time, the fire on the top floors of the Asch Building was visible in the street below. Within minutes a crowd gathered around the building to watch the blaze. One policeman watching the scene observed: "It's mighty hard work burning one of those fireproof buildings, but I guess it's lucky it's Saturday afternoon. It looks as if everyone is out of the place." Suddenly, an object that looked like a bale of dress material dropped from an eighth-floor window. A reporter from the *New York World,* who had joined the bystanders, described what followed:

"Somebody's in there all right," exclaimed a spectator. "He's trying to save the best cloth."

Another seeming bundle of cloth came hurtling through the same window, but this time a breeze tossed open the cloth, and from the crowd of 500 persons there came a cry of horror.

The breeze had disclosed the form of a girl shooting down to instant death on the stone pavement beneath.

Before the crowd could realize the full meaning of the horror, another girl sprang upon another window ledge. It seemed that she had broken open the window with her fists. Her hair, streaming down her back, was all ablaze, and her clothing was on fire.

She stood poised for a moment with her arms extended, and then down she came. Three other girls at the same moment threw themselves from various windows, and other girls could be seen clinging to the window frames, struggling for breath and trying to decide between the death within the factory room and the death on the stone pavement and sidewalk below.

The firemen's nets caught only a few of those who jumped. More often, as Fire Captain Howard C. Ruch recalled, the bodies—which struck the ground with a force almost a thousand times their actual

The sidewalk in front of the Triangle Company was strewn with the bodies of those who had jumped to their death at the height of the blaze. The fire department's safety nets were too weak to break the victims' fall.

weight—"didn't break through the nets; they just carried them to the sidewalk. The force was so great it took the men off their feet; they turned somersaults over onto the bodies." Sometimes, a group of girls would join hands before jumping from the ledge, soothing their fears in a joint death fall.

Fifteen minutes after the firemen arrived the fire was brought under control. In those few minutes 46 people jumped to their deaths. The charred remains of 100 workers were later recovered from inside the building. Most of those who perished were Jewish. All but 21 of the victims were women, and a dozen were so badly burned or disfigured that they were almost unrecognizable. In fact, 7 were never identified.

Hundreds of workers had managed to escape the flames. Those injured, stunned, and weeping survivors soon filled the hospitals and ghetto apartments of the Lower East Side. Police officials hurriedly tried to find coffins for the dead. On East 26th Street a huge, enclosed pier was converted into a temporary morgue. The Triangle dead were piled up on sidewalks near the Asch Building while firemen watered down the smoldering building.

Police Department "death wagons" rode throughout the evening, bringing the dead to the temporary morgue. Policemen searched through personal belongings in an effort to identify victims. Fourteen engagement rings were later found on one floor of the Triangle factory alone. These and other rings collected at the morgue testified to one particularly bitter aspect of the tragedy. Some of the victims had stuffed their skimpy pay envelopes inside their clothing. Others still had their wages clutched in their hands.

Many of the Jewish families on the Lower East Side had relatives or friends working at Triangle, and the community's grief was almost unbearable. Tens of thousands rushed to the East 26th Street pier searching for missing friends or relatives. They were joined by numerous Italian and other immigrant familes. The police finally let the frantic throng file through the pier a few dozen at a time. Inside the temporary morgue the bodies of the Triangle victims had been laid out in coffins in neat rows.

Heartbreaking scenes of recognition filled the night. A mother, discovering her daughter's body, would break down into uncontrollable wailing and have to be escorted out. A young woman, finding her sister's charred body, would simply faint. Some women completely lost control and tried to kill themselves, either by swallowing poison or by jumping off the pier. Police and onlookers stopped at least a dozen such attempts.

Thousands of mourning relatives and friends filed through the temporary morgue on the East 26th Street pier to identify the victims. Some were never identified.

In the days following the fire the Triangle victims were buried quietly by their families. Friends and relatives from the Lower East Side attended the funerals. They poured out their grief and sorrow. Reformers and community leaders arranged a series of memorial meetings to honor the victims. A fund-raising appeal conducted by the Red Cross, Jewish community groups, and the WTUL collected over $120,000 to assist needy families. Several of the victims had been the sole support of their families, in either New York or "the old country." Half a dozen families had lost two sisters (one a widow with five children); another had lost two brothers. In one Italian family a mother and two daughters were killed in the fire.

On April 5 a symbolic mass funeral was held in lower Manhattan. Over 100,000 people—mainly women who lived and worked on the Lower East Side—marched silently in the rain for five hours to honor the Triangle dead. The memorial service was the climax of a week of mourning and protest. The march had been organized by the garment unions to demonstrate labor solidarity. "Come and pay your respects to our dead," intoned the *Forward,* "every union man with his trade, with his union." Most of the marchers wore armbands that read simply: "We mourn our loss." One group of women garment workers carried a banner that said: "We demand fire protection."

In the streets of Manhattan over 400,000 spectators watched as the mourners marched toward Washington Square to the beat of muffled drums. Almost all the Triangle survivors marched. The procession was led by an empty hearse draped in black and drawn by six white horses. "The skies wept," began the *World's* story on the event.

Later that afternoon the seven unidentified victims—coffin numbers 46, 50, 61, 95, 103, 115, and 127 in the police records—were buried. Catholic, Protestant, and Jewish clerics read brief prayers before the coffins were lowered. The mourners, meanwhile, continued their march to Washington Square Park, where they were to proceed up Fifth Avenue to 34th Street. As they approached the Asch Building, the women who marched gave way completely to their emotions. As one paper reported, they uttered "one long-drawn-out, heart-piercing cry, the mingling of thousands of voices, a cry that was perhaps the most impressive expression of human grief ever heard in this city."

Who was to blame for the tragedy? This question haunted New Yorkers in the weeks that followed the Triangle disaster. "That a terrible mistake was made by somebody," *The New York Times* observed, "is easier to say now than to point out just where the blame for this destruction of human life may be placed."

The city's fire department bore a share of the responsibility, despite the bravery of those who fought the blaze. The department had failed to enforce even those few mild safety laws that were on the books. Moreover, its equipment was inadequate for fighting fires in the city's new loft buildings. The tallest fire ladders reached only the sixth floor, although half the city's factory workers worked in lofts above this floor. Some of the department's safety nets were so weak that they broke under the force of falling bodies.

The City Buildings Department too had to accept a measure of the blame. The Asch Building, like most of New York City's garment shops, lacked adequate safety features. Several months earlier, a factory inspector had warned the owners of the Asch Building of such violations as insufficient exits and locked stairway doors. But the department made no effort to ensure that these conditions were corrected. There were only 47 inspectors in Manhattan to check over 50,000 buildings. Of these buildings 13,600 had been listed as dangerous by the fire department the previous month. Inspectors managed to visit 2,000 buildings in March, but the Asch Building was not among them.

Nor were the fire insurance companies innocent of blame. Insurance brokers in New York suffered heavy losses from the numerous fires that occurred in the city's loft buildings. Yet the insurance industry failed to insist on safety standards that might have reduced fire hazards. Rather, they preferred to pay off after a fire and then raise a company's premium costs. Higher policy rates also meant higher commissions for insurance brokers. During the 1890s a group of insurance companies attempted to offer cheaper rates to manufacturers who installed sprinkler systems in their factories. These companies were soon driven out of business by the city's powerful insurance industry. It was simply easier and more profitable to leave the "fireproof" firetraps alone and to settle afterward.

At the time of the fire the Triangle Shirtwaist Company carried insurance policies totaling $199,750. The Triangle owners eventually collected full repayment for their losses in equipment and property damage. They were also given an extra indemnity of $64,925, or $445 for each worker killed. The company's owners defended themselves against charges of responsibility for the fire by pointing out that building inspectors had never entered a complaint against the firm and that an employee carelessly dropping a cigarette might well have started the fire.

On April 11, a week after the public funeral for the Triangle victims, Isaac Harris and Max Blanck were indicted by a grand jury and charged with manslaughter. Their trial began in New York eight months later on December 4. Crowds of women gathered outside the courtroom each day screaming "Murderers! Murderers!" A heavy police guard was called in to protect the defendants. Harris and Blanck—"the shirtwaist kings"—engaged as their defense counsel a well-known Jewish layer, Max D. Steuer.

In order to simplify the case, the state decided to try the pair only for responsibility in the death of a single worker, Margaret Schwartz, who died in the fire because of the locked ninth-floor door. Most testimony centered on three questions. (1) Was the ninth-floor door kept locked regularly? (2) Was it locked at the time of the fire? (3) Most importantly, did Blanck and Harris know it was locked?

The prosecutor called a number of Triangle employees. They testified that the ninth-floor door had been locked regularly and was locked when the fire began. Defense attorney Steuer then called other Triangle workers and supervisors. They testified not only that a key was always kept in the door but that the door was always left open. Steuer tried to persuade the jurors that prosecution witnesses had been coached before coming to the witness stand. But the state offered convincing rebuttal evidence that defense witnesses had lied, that they actually knew the door was kept locked.

In instructing the jury members, the judge pointed out that unless they believed Blanck and Harris were aware of the locked doors "beyond a reasonable doubt," they would have to acquit the defendants. The jury took less than two hours to find the shirtwaist kings not

Not much remained of the "fireproof" Asch Building after the fire had run its course. The Triangle owners collected insurance money for losses in equipment and property damages though their company had inadequate safety features.

guilty. As one jury member later told a newsman: "I believed that the [door] was locked at the time of the fire. But I could not make myself feel certain that Harris and Blanck knew that it was locked."

One interesting sidelight to the tragedy emerged during the trial. The Triangle owners kept their exit doors locked for fear that employees would steal garments or pieces of fabric. At one point the prosecutor asked Isaac Harris: "How much in all the instances would you say was the value of all the goods that you found had been taken by these employees? You would say it was not over $25, wouldn't you?" Harris turned pale before responding: "No, it would not exceed that much."

If Harris and Blanck had been convicted, the Triangle fire might have been forgotten more easily. The public might have been satisfied that justice had been done. As it turned out, the acquittal of Blanck and Harris sparked a new effort to improve the conditions under which New York City's laborers worked. Responding to public pressure, the state legislature created the New York Factory Investigating Commission in June 1911 to study working conditions in the state.

Among the commission's most active members were two politically powerful New York City Democrats, State Assembly Majority Leader Alfred E. Smith and State Senate Majority Leader Robert F. Wagner, Sr. They helped throw the Tammany machine's full support behind the commission's many proposals for reform. Other members included Samuel Gompers of the AFL and Mary Dreier of the WTUL. Many experts on factory safety and working conditions assisted the commission. Among them were progressive reformers such as Belle and Henry Moskowitz, and young social workers such as Frances Perkins, who later became the nation's first woman Cabinet member as Secretary of Labor.

The Triangle Commission went far beyond an investigation of fire hazards alone. It studied almost every type of labor problem in New York. In 1911 the group held public hearings in the state's major manufacturing cities and heard 222 witnesses. Staff field inspectors visited 1,836 factories in 20 industries. Smith, Wagner, and their associates talked with factory workers who had lost limbs because of unsafe machinery. They examined the "doctored" records kept by many companies on employees' wages and hours. Commission inves-

By 1900 at least 1,700,000 children under sixteen were in the labor market. One result of the Triangle fire was the passage of laws limiting child labor and improving working conditions for women and children.

tigators watched hundreds of women leaving ten-hour shifts at 5 A.M. They studied the horrible conditions in the disease-ridden tenements where workers lived.

On farms in upstate New York, commission members observed migrant women working alongside their children for eighteen hours a day or more. In canneries across the state they saw children of five working full time. The conditions wore no party label; the worst offenders among New York's manufacturers included both Republicans and Democrats. In the factory of a leading upstate Democratic progressive, for example, Smith and Wagner found "the vilest and most uncivilized conditions of labor in the state."

During the four years that commission members and staff toured the state, they gathered material for thirteen volumes of reports. These were submitted to the state legislature. The reports did not gather dust. Between 1911 and 1915, Smith and Wagner introduced over sixty bills based on their investigations. Despite much conservative opposition in the legislature, the two Tammany Democrats managed to pass fifty-six of their proposals by fusing the votes of Democratic regulars and antimachine reformers. The bills they passed called for the creation of a Bureau of Fire Prevention and the enforcement of strict fire safety codes (including compulsory fire drills and the installation of sprinklers in factories). Two other major bills provided for an increase in the number of factory inspectors and a strengthening of the supervisory authority of the state's Department of Labor.

One of the most hard-fought proposals in the legislature was a bill calling for a 54-hour workweek for women and minors. When cannery owners objected to the measure, Smith replied sarcastically that they wished to revise the Bible to read "Remember the Sabbath to keep it holy—except in canneries." The bill passed. Other laws forbade night factory work for women, prohibited smoking in factories, and called for better ventilation and sanitary facilities. Child labor was outlawed in tenement manufacturing and canneries. Sunday work was forbidden ("one day's rest in seven"), and insurance (workmen's compensation) was provided for employees injured in accidents. Other laws forbade employment of children under fourteen and required improved working facilities, rest periods, and minimum wages for women and children.

In the Triangle Commission's four years of existence Smith and Wagner helped to pass the most enlightened code of industrial reform in the country. Their work served as a model for legislators in other states and foreshadowed many of the federal laws enacted under the New Deal. Out of the ashes of tragedy had come new hope for workingmen.

New Waves of Reform

THE MISERABLE working conditions that provoked the great shirtwaist industry strike of 1909 were typical of American manufacturing in the half-century of industrial growth that followed the Civil War. Workers in manufacturing plants toiled an average of 59 hours each week. They earned less than $10 per week for their back-breaking labor.

By contrast their employers—the manufacturers, bankers, and merchants who directed the course of economic development in the United States—profited handsomely from the workers' long hours and low wage rates. Between 1860 and 1900 the country rose from fourth to first place among the world's industrial nations, producing more in 1900 than Britain, France, and Germany combined.

The rewards for business success during this period were high indeed. In 1890 an estimated 200,000 people owned 70 percent of the country's wealth. A survey taken in 1892 showed that close to 4,000 people had become millionaires since the Civil War. Almost all these individuals made their fortunes in manufacturing, railroads, trade, or finance. This great concentration of wealth in America's upper classes only added to the discontent of the nation's industrial laborers.

Union organization seemed to hold the only promise of changing the working conditions of American workers. But despite the efforts of union leaders and rank-and-file organizers throughout the period, no strong, united workingman's association emerged among the industrial labor force of the United States. Instead, in this era of economic growth industry-wide unions like the ILGWU came and went. Several unions also attempted, with varying degrees of success, to organize American workers. The ILGWU, for example, was only the latest in a line of unions attempting to organize the garment industry, the earlier ones having failed at the task.

At the turn of the century 10 million men and women, over a third of the entire labor force, worked in factories. Yet the union movement had succeeded in organizing less than 4 percent of America's industrial workers. What was this union tradition? Why had it failed to mobilize the country's underpaid, overworked, and poorly treated laboring masses?

THE RISE OF ORGANIZED LABOR

Those who led and took part in the Uprising of the Twenty Thousand inherited a tradition of industrial union activity more than a half-century old. In Jacksonian America factory workers and craftsmen attempted to form their own unions. Few of these trade organizations lasted beyond the Civil War. In the half-century after the war a number of major unions were formed. Almost all these unions employed the strike weapon, though rarely with complete success. During the 1880s, for example, over 24,000 strikes occurred in the United States, involving over 6 1/2 million workers.

During the turbulent depression years of the 1890s, 3 million people were thrown out of work, perhaps 15 to 20 percent of the country's work force. Over 7,000 strikes were called during this period. Between 1894 and 1896 numerous small armies of the unemployed marched on Washington demanding federal relief assistance.

By the early twentieth century the infant ILGWU, which was to lead the great shirtwaist strike of 1909, had counterparts in every other industry in the country. Like the garment union, most of these organizations were small and had to struggle for existence. The experience of the 1909 garment workers' strike demonstrates many of the difficulties unions encountered in organizing.

Difficulties in Union Organization For one thing, few unions were as successful as the ILGWU in persuading workers from different ethnic backgrounds to put aside their fierce hatreds and work for common goals. Indeed, the 1909–10 strike was the first time that most of New York City's Jewish and Italian workers had joined together in one union. More often, tensions among nationality groups, differences in language, and racial hostilities within the working class hampered union organization.

Employers skillfully exploited these ethnic and national hostilities to divide workers. When Jews went on strike, Italians would work, and vice versa. When both groups went on strike, blacks were called in to scab. Furthermore, the influx of southern and eastern European immigrants in the late nineteenth and early twentieth centuries kept wage rates down in most industries. More often than not, the labor supply greatly exceeded demand. Employers had little difficulty filling the unskilled and semiskilled positions at their plants.

Employers resorted to a variety of tactics to defeat the efforts of union organizers. These included the use of strikebreakers (such as the hoodlums who attacked ILGWU picketers), and the hiring of scabs (another tactic employed by Harris and Blanck). Employers also used blacklisting—the denial of work to union officials by all the firms in an industry—and lockouts of striking workers. Firms like the Triangle Company sometimes enlisted the aid of sympathetic policemen and judges who harassed strikers with arrests and court action. Another important weapon of management was the yellow-dog contract, in which new workers agreed not to join a union as a condition of their employment.

Attempts at Union Organization   At the national level the union movement faced a number of difficulties in the half-century after the Civil War. Several national unions rose and fell because of unsuccessful strikes, the opposition of the middle class, and the inability of unions to hold the loyalty of most workers. The National Labor Union played a prominent role briefly during the depression of the 1870s. The Knights of Labor, under the leadership of Terence V. Powderly, became a major force in the labor movement in the following decade. These unions favored improvement of the American worker's economic state and a broad program of reform within American society.

The Knights had many self-employed or salaried middle-class Americans in its membership. During the 1880s it tried unsuccessfully to organize a series of strikes and to set up cooperative factories and stores—owned by the workers themselves—as an alternative to the privately run corporations. Leaders of the Knights were blamed for the Haymarket Affair of 1886 and were attacked as "anarchists," Actually, they had played no part in the bombing. Membership in the Knights of Labor nevertheless declined from 700,000 in 1886 to 74,000 by 1893. The union played an insignificant role in the labor movement during the 1890s, joining finally with the agrarian-led Populist party. By 1900 it had lapsed into obscurity.

The leading force within American unionization during this period was the American Federation of Labor (AFL). It was a loose confederation of independent craft unions and semi-industrial affiliates such as the ILGWU. The AFL was formed in 1881 under the leadership of Samuel Gompers. A one-time socialist, Gompers criticized earlier union organizations such as the Knights for stressing general reforms in American society.

The labor movement, Gompers believed, should concentrate exclusively on winning economic gains for the working class. It should leave the tasks of reform to others. Union leaders should devote all their time and energy to raising workers' wages, reducing hours, and improving

Samuel Gompers, shown here at a meeting to organize the 1909 garment workers' strike, founded the American Federation of Labor around such craft unions. Using both the strike and collective bargaining, he forged a powerful national labor organization.

working conditions. Gompers also believed that unions should avoid independent political action, such as the affiliation of the Knights with the Populist party in the 1890s. Instead, labor should support its political friends and oppose its enemies, regardless of party. When asked at a congressional hearing what the unions wanted, Gompers replied simply: "More!"

By the time of the New York garment industry strike the AFL, under Gompers' leadership, had become the country's dominant national labor organization. It was also the most powerful union politically and economically up to that time.

REFORMERS IN THE LATE NINETEENTH CENTURY

Union leaders were not the only people concerned about the conditions of American workers. Socialists, middle- and upper-class reformers, and city politicians all worked to improve conditions for American laborers. Their suggested solutions to the problems posed by industrial society, though, were as different as the backgrounds out of which these reformers emerged.

The Socialist Vision In the late nineteenth century a group of socialist writers became the first generation of critics to tackle the dilemmas of urban-industrial America. They were grouped as socialists because they held in common the belief that ownership and control of industry, land, and so forth should be shared by the community as a whole. These writers put forth a series of proposals for a complete overhaul of American institutions. In *Progress and Poverty* (1877–79) Henry George attacked the inequities of the American economic system. Edward Bellamy's *Looking Backward* (1888) presents a vision of a socialist Utopia. His book became a best-seller in the 1880s and 1890s. Henry Demarest Lloyd's *Wealth Against Commonwealth* (1894) attacked the corrupt business practices of the Standard Oil Company. Other influential

critics of American industrial life included economist Richard Ely, "social gospel" minister Washington Gladden, and utopian writers Ignatius Donnelly and William Dean Howells.

Uppermost in the minds of these late nineteenth-century reformers was the notion that, if conditions in the nation's slums, factories, and farms were not improved quickly and drastically, the United States would explode into class warfare. Surely, they reasoned, abused workers would not tolerate such conditions indefinitely. They believed that a social catastrophe was close at hand. It could be prevented only by an immediate and total alteration in the nation's social and economic structure.

They offered no single remedy. Some, like Lloyd, Bellamy, and Howells, believed in a socialist commonwealth. They argued, though, over the details of Utopia and how to achieve it. Others, like George and Ely, felt that a single tax on unearned income from land would somehow provide enough money to solve the nation's problems. All these reformers were united in their belief that a single problem underlay all the social ills of the United States. Find and correct this overriding problem—"the root of our social difficulty" as George put it—and Americans could begin moving toward an era of moral and social perfection.

In this utopian vision of the United States these late nineteenth-century reformers resembled their pre-Civil War, preindustrial counterparts. Garrison, Emerson, and Fuller had also walked a thin line between social criticism and religious prophecy. However "practical" their remedies, therefore, people like George and Bellamy were basically seers. They preached a gospel of total reform, without which total catastrophe would result.

The Settlement House Movement The struggle to improve the lives of the immigrant poor, both in the factories and in the ghettos, was aided by a number of middle-class reformers and socially conscious members of the American upper class. Women like Mrs. Belmont and other affluent leaders of the Women's Trade Union League who were active in the shirtwaist strike are representative of this trend.

During the 1880s and 1890s many college-educated women became concerned especially with the slum conditions under which immigrant workers lived. They helped to organize settlement houses in the ghettos of east coast and Middle Western cities. There, foreign-born workers received food and shelter, and learned how to speak English. They were given help in understanding and exercising their rights as Americans. In 1889 Lillian Wald founded the Henry Street Settlement in New York City. Jane Addams and Ellen Gates Starr founded Chicago's Hull-House that same year.

By 1910 over 400 settlement houses had been established in the country's slum districts. On New York's Lower East Side settlement workers assisted the victims of the Triangle fire and their families. In the previous year they had provided money and support for the striking garment workers. As valuable instruments for Americanizing immigrant communities, the settlement houses helped immigrants to improve their working and living conditions at a time when most middle-class Americans remained indifferent or even hostile toward the foreign-born poor.

Municipal Reorganization For some reformers, the settlement house movement seemed an inadequate response to the many problems of America's enlarged industrial cities. It was somewhat like putting bandages over a festering infection without treating the infection itself first. For such reformers the roots of the infection seemed clear: the inefficiency and corruption of urban political machines in alliance with equally corrupt business interests. Democratic politicians such as Al Smith and Robert Wagner, Sr., viewed New York's Tammany machine as the logical friend of the immigrants. But reformers such as Henry George and, later, Fiorello La-Guardia believed that the machines merely exploited the immigrants, using their trust and votes to line the pockets of ward heelers, city officials, and local businessmen.

Reform groups such as the National Civic Association (which later helped to organize the Triangle Fire Commission investigation) sparked a concern among voters for driving the political machines from office. These groups sought to run urban government more efficiently and less corruptly than the machines.

Municipal reformers then, as today, came largely from middle-class or upper-class backgrounds. They included businessmen, lawyers, ministers, and journalists—professionals concerned with the concentration of power in the hands of working-class-supported political machines and giant corporations. Many were native-born Protestants. Most had little direct contact with foreign-born, largely Catholic and Jewish immigrants until they began a career of reform.

Quite often, these basic cultural differences among immigrants and reformers made it difficult, it not impossible, for the two groups to join successfully. Their interests were also often in direct conflict. New immigrants depended on the very political favors—jobs and other assistance from local political bosses—that the reformers wanted to eliminate. Moreover, the immigrant culture was more tolerant of gambling and drinking than the reformer's tradition of stern Protestant moralism. These differences over values certainly diluted the effect of municipal reformers in curing urban ills.

A NEW GENERATION OF REFORMERS

Many of those who had opposed unions and other reform movements prior to the 1890s gradually became convinced of the need for basic reforms in American society. They had been deeply affected by the tumultuous events of the '90s: the depression, the social unrest on farms and in factories, the deepening class conflict.

By the turn of the century many middle-class Americans saw the dangers. Conservative journalists such as William Allen White, "big business" lawyers such as Clarence Darrow and

"Even as a little child, she seemed inclined toward special work of some sort. In fact, she was anxious for a career." This is how, with some dismay, Mrs. John H. Addams described her stepdaughter Jane. After all, a girl born to a prosperous family in Cedarville, Illinois, in 1860 was not supposed to have such ambitions. She was expected to attend a ladies' seminary, travel in Europe in search of culture, and then return home to marry.

Jane fulfilled the first two expectations. But instead of marrying, she worried over what that "special work" could be. She knew that it was not missionary work or teaching. For eight years she traveled, read, and attended the social functions that suited Mrs. Addams' plans for her. It was a period of frustration, nervousness, and unhappiness. "I am filled with shame that with all my apparent leisure, I do nothing at all," she wrote.

At long last, during a European trip, an idea began to take shape in her mind. She told her friend and traveling companion, Ellen Gates Starr, about it. Jane wanted to move into a large house in a poor neighborhood. There she and other educated young people who wanted to do something important could live among the poor. They could share the problems of poverty and help to improve the neighborhood. In no way would this be an attempt to "uplift the masses." Instead it would be a learning experience for all concerned.

Jane Addams and Ellen Starr soon returned to the United States to put the plan into effect. They located a house, formerly owned by a man named Hull, in a poor area in Chicago. They unpacked their things, invited the neighbors to stop in, and waited.

Before long two things happened. First, neighbors, most of them immigrants, started coming—to attend lectures and form clubs. Second, a number of talented and energetic men and women moved into Hull-House. They saw the social settlement as a place where they could enjoy stimulating intel-

Chicago Historical Society

lectual company and at the same time do something about growing urban problems.

Soon Hull-House was truly the neighborhood center. Here working mothers brought their children for day care. Here newly formed labor unions met. People of all ages came to attend classes in music, art, homemaking, and handicrafts. Residents and neighbors joined in community betterment projects.

Under Jane Addams' leadership Hull-House took on another, more far-reaching task. It became a clearing house for several reform movements. The residents researched urban problems and then tried to convince those in power to do something about them. They pressured legislators to act on such matters as child labor, factory inspection, recognition of labor unions, protection of immigrants, and industrial safety.

By the time of Jane Addams' death in 1935, Hull-House stood as a monument to her philosophy: "Without the advance and improvement of the whole, no man can hope for any lasting improvement in his own moral or material condition."

George Norris, and middle-of-the-road Republicans such as Theodore Roosevelt had all concluded that the future political and social health of the American republic depended on a variety of reforms. They sought improvements in the conditions under which the urban poor lived. They also wanted to bring giant trusts under governmental supervision in the public interest. These various reform interests came together in a movement that historians have labeled "progressivism."

The Progressive Movement However different progressive reformers were in their social and economic concerns, most shared certain fundamental beliefs. For one thing, unlike the Bellamys and Georges of the previous generation, they did not believe in imminent social catastrophe. Rather, they were highly nationalistic and optimistic about the future of the United States. Herbert Croly, one of their most influential writers, argued that this "promise of American life" consisted of "an improving popular economic condition, guaranteed by democratic political institutions, and resulting in moral and social [improvement]."

Nationalism and reform, then, went hand in hand. Both impulses were based on an idealistic faith in American potential. Most progressives believed that a decent society for all Americans could be created through gradual reform, rather than through revolutionary changes. The reformers of the previous generation had not been so confident.

Progressive reformers harnessed their optimism about domestic affairs to a firm belief in the value of Christian morality. It was within this "ethical climate" that much reform legislation of the era took shape. To Frances Perkins the new climate was dominated by "the idea that poverty is preventable, that poverty is destructive, wasteful, demoralizing, and that poverty in the midst of potential plenty is morally unacceptable in a Christian and democratic society." An end to poverty, injustice, and unregulated economic power, the preservation of the nation's natural resources, a return to honest government—all this, the progressives believed, would follow from applying Christian ethics to reshaping the social environment.

Another belief shared by progressive thinkers was a confidence in the use of "experts" to manage public affairs. Professional advisers such as those who had assisted the Triangle Commission would provide rational, "scientific" measurement of the country's problems; they would also suggest efficient means for tackling social ills.

Progressive reformers called for the establishment of legislative investigating bodies at all levels of government, and the use of expert advisers—brain trusts—to help city and state governments develop programs of reform. They wanted to create regulatory agencies to supervise business practices. Progressives also favored the establishment of nonpartisan commissions or councils to eliminate machine corruption in city government. The independent commission form of city government originated in Galveston, Texas, in 1900. By 1914 it had spread to over 400 American cities, although not to most larger ones.

Finally, most reformers of the era believed strongly in the value of publicizing social problems as a first step toward solving them. As early as 1898 Congress had established a commission to study the giant business trusts. The commission eventually published nineteen volumes on American social and economic problems. In addition, many states set up investigatory groups to study business corruption. This technique of exposure was carried out most systematically under the reform governorship of Robert M. LaFollette in Wisconsin from 1901 to 1906. LaFollette's efforts to uncover business abuses and press for needed social legislation set a pattern for reform administrations in other states.

Newspapers and magazines provided a forum for investigations of social problems by muckraking journalists. Ida Tarbell wrote an explosive expose of the Standard Oil Company. Lincoln Steffens studied corrupt city political machines. David Graham Phillips examined Senate corruption. Magazines such as *McClure's* and *Harper's Weekly* increased their circulation to the hundreds of thousands by becoming champions of reform.

New Politics for the Cities Nowhere was the belief in rational government stronger than at the local level. Here progressives were as appalled by corrupt city politics as they were by dirty tenements and unsafe factories. All three conditions came under the attack of municipal reformers. Beginning in the 1890s, reform groups won control of a number of cities and began dealing with slum and factory conditions. In New York City, for example, after driving Tammany Hall from power in 1901, Mayor Seth Low worked closely with reformers to improve parks and playgrounds, tighten housing laws, and strengthen the city's health services to the poor. But, despite his efforts, much remained to be done, as conditions in the city at the time of the Triangle fire demonstrated.

In other cities too the concern for social reform proved strong. During the 1890s and 1900s three remarkable Middle Western businessmen—all self-made millionaires—became pioneers in urban reform. Their cities served as models for social reformers throughout the country.

Hazen Pingree, mayor of Detroit, Michigan, from 1889 to 1896 and then governor of the state, fought corruption by politicians and local industrial groups, especially street railways and gas companies. Pingree authorized the construction of a city-owned electric lighting plant and urged public ownership of other such utilities. In Toledo, Ohio, Samuel M. "Golden Rule" Jones, mayor of the city from 1897 to 1904, established free kindergarten day-care facilities for working mothers, pressed for a minimum hourly wage and other social legislation, and supported public ownership of utilities.

Thomas Johnson, Cleveland's mayor from 1901 to 1909, became a social reformer after reading Henry George's *Progress and Poverty*. He too fought the private utility interests and urged public ownership. Johnson sponsored a number of social welfare projects, including the

Ida M. Tarbell's stunning exposés revealed the way giant corporations gained advantage over competitors by securing special rates—rebates —from railroads. Her landmark study of the oil industry appeared in McClure's magazine, which established it as the leading muckraking periodical.

Lincoln Steffens, one of the leading reformer journalists, wrote numerous articles exposing political corruption in city government. His autobiography gives an accurate account of the development of the muckraking movement.

Upton Sinclair is best remembered for his novel, The Jungle, *that told of the brutal and unsanitary conditions in Chicago's stockyards. The public revulsion it aroused resulted in the passage of the Meat Inspection Act of 1906.*

Tom Johnson, Cleveland's reform mayor, instituted reforms, including city planning, that made that city one of America's best-governed. He had his own political machine, observing, "It all depends on whether a boss is a good one or a bad one."

construction of municipal bathhouses (a crucial urban health measure, since many tenement houses did not have adequate bathroom facilities) and careful inspection of consumer meat and dairy products.

All three Middle Western mayors ran nonpartisan governments, dominated by professional administrators and reformers who took over the jobs that had formerly been filled by appointees. Unfortunately, driving political machines from office did not always produce improvements in ghetto or factory conditions. Many municipal reformers were less interested in improving slum conditions than in eliminating the power and corruption of immigrant-supported political machines. In Pittsburgh, for example, two-thirds of those involved in trying to revise the city's charter came from upper-class backgrounds and were closely tied to the city's leading banks and industries.

Changes at the State Level Many of the major reforms of this period were achieved at the state level. In a number of states progressive reformers were elected governors. Among them were Rob-

ert LaFollette in Wisconsin, Charles Evans Hughes in New York, Hoke Smith in Georgia, Hiram Johnson in California, and the transplanted Southern-born president of Princeton University, Woodrow Wilson, in New Jersey. Each state had its special problems, each its particular group of "entrenched interests." In Massachusetts, the railroads and insurance companies dominated; in California it was the powerful and corrupt labor unions.

Almost all reform governors fought for stricter regulation of railroads, public utilities, and industries within their states. They tried to force corporations to pay a fair share of taxes and conserve natural resources like forests and mines, which provided raw materials for industry. Finally, they fought to make state government more democratic through such reforms as the initiative, the referendum, and the recall.[1]

During the first two decades of the century many states enacted broad programs of social legislation dealing with the wages and hours of factory workers, the employment of women and children, and safety conditions in tenements and factories. Maryland adopted the first state workmen's compensation law in 1902. A year later Oregon passed a law restricting women's industrial work to ten hours per day. Illinois adopted the first measure providing public assistance to mothers with dependent children in 1911. And Massachusetts passed the first minimum wage law (applying to women and children) in 1912. All these measures were landmarks in the struggle of progressive reformers to achieve economic and social justice for all Americans.

Amending the Constitution Suffrage—the right to vote—had been a central concern of the women's rights movement for several decades. In

---

[1] The initiative is a device by which a small number of citizens, sometimes as little as 5 percent, can bypass the legislature and vote upon measures at general elections. The referendum forces legislatures to return proposed laws to the electorate, who then approve or reject the proposals. The recall, perhaps the most controversial device, allows the electorate to remove an elected official from office. It requires a special election, called after a certain number of voters have signed a petition asking for the official's removal.

1910 the American labor force employed over 8 million women, including a number of college-educated women who had entered the professions. During this period 36 percent of all professional jobs were held by women. Yet, prior to World War I only eleven states had granted women the right to vote.

Between 1914 and 1919 women's rights advocates gave the suffrage issue national importance by conducting a massive campaign of petitions, lobbying, picketing, and nonviolent demonstrations. The campaign was sponsored by two national associations of women's suffrage advocates, led by Carrie Chapman Catt and Anna Howard Shaw. The picketing and demonstrations that had brought public sympathy for the demands of shirtwaist employees during the Triangle strike worked with similar effect for the suffragettes. The involvement of women in war work during World War I brought the movement increased public support. In June 1919

Congress responded by passing the Nineteenth Amendment, giving women the right to vote. The amendment received final state ratification in August 1920. Later that year, for the first time, American women in every state voted in a presidential election.

Another progressive interest, the temperance movement, had been a concern of reformers since before the Civil War. Municipal reformers joined the anti-alcohol drive for two major reasons. First, there was much political corruption associated with urban liquor dealers. Secondly, reformers felt that alcoholism was destroying the moral fiber and social well-being of many Americans.

The prohibitionists made their first gains at the local and state levels. A number of Southern and Western states voted themselves "dry." During World War I many of the same groups that later pushed the women's rights amendment through Congress secured passage of the Eight-

Women concentrated on making political gains in the early twentieth century. An intense campaign, and their increasing importance in the labor market, finally gained them full suffrage on a nationwide basis by constitutional amendment—the Nineteenth.

eenth Amendment, which forbade the sale and distribution of alcoholic beverages. Ratified by the states in January 1919, the amendment took effect the next year. It was considered the most impressive yet the most debatable triumph of progressive moralism.

In 1913 progressive reformers won two other important victories. The Sixteenth Amendment instituted a federal income tax. And the Seventeenth Amendment provided for direct election of senators. An amendment prohibiting child labor passed Congress under intense reform pressure. It met strong opposition from the business community, however, and failed to win ratification by the states.

PROGRESSIVISM IN THE WHITE HOUSE

With the death of William McKinley on September 14, 1901, Theodore Roosevelt became the third man in less than forty years to succeed to the presidency because of an assassin's bullet. At forty-three he was the nation's youngest President. Roosevelt came to the White House with a distinguished career in public service. He had served as state legislator, federal official, city police chief, army colonel, governor of New York, and Vice President. An energetic and impulsive man, Roosevelt responded candidly to McKinley's death: "It is a dreadful thing to come into the presidency this way; but it would be a far worse thing to be morbid about it."

Roosevelt's Square Deal for America Roosevelt moved cautiously during the next few years to take control of the Republican national machinery from McKinley's close friend Senator Mark Hanna of Ohio. In his first term he made few reform proposals. He did, however, publicize reform more and more, especially as his second term drew to a close. During this period no other American did as much as Theodore Roosevelt to educate his fellow citizens to the need for political and social change. He called the presidency "a bully pulpit." He often mounted its steps to criticize "malefactors of great wealth" and others—trusts, political bosses, destroyers of natural resources—who endangered his vision of a "square deal" for all Americans.

But Roosevelt did far more than simply publicize reform. Despite his strong party loyalties and keen appreciation of political patronage, he brought into government service a remarkable number of reformers. Roosevelt appointed William Howard Taft as Secretary of War, conservationist Gifford Pinchot as chief of the Forest Service, James R. Garfield (the son of the former President and a dedicated conservationist) as Secretary of the Interior, and the great jurist Oliver Wendell Holmes, Jr., as Supreme Court justice. Unlike his Republican predecessors in the White House, Roosevelt worked for the support of the black community. He consulted Booker T. Washington, president of the Tuskegee Institute in Alabama, as his chief adviser on Southern Republican appointments.

Underlying Roosevelt's actions and policies during his administration were certain firm beliefs shared by other progressives as well. Among them was the belief that government must begin intervening in the economy to bring unregulated businesses under control. It was argued that such a move would reduce class tensions in American society as well. Toward this end Roosevelt lobbied actively to push several important reform measures through Congress. The Elkins Act of 1903 forbade railroads to give rebates[2] to large industrial companies. The Hepburn Act of 1906 strengthened the powers of the Interstate Commerce Commission (ICC) to regulate the nation's railroads.

In these and other regulatory measures Roosevelt received the support of several members of the business community. For many business leaders, federal action seemed the most rational response to the country's growing industrial problems. Thus the railroads favored tighter federal regulation to eliminate the rebate system

---

[2] Rebates were special rates, lower than the published ones, granted secretly to users who accounted for a large share of freight traffic. Farmers felt especially cheated by these special rates, usually granted to industries.

Theodore Roosevelt surrounded himself with conservationists like John Muir who believed that the natural environment must be protected. Through Roosevelt's influence 148,000,000 acres of forests were set aside for national parks like Yosemite, seen in the background.

and avoid even more rigid state regulation. Similarly, giant lumber corporations endorsed federal intervention to enforce a rational set of guidelines for the industry.

An energetic outdoorsman, Roosevelt did much to educate the American public to the need for environmental protection. The Newlands Act, passed in 1902, authorized federal funds for the construction of dams and reclamation projects in the West. In 1907 he signed an executive order converting over 17 million acres of forest land in Western states to national reserves. Roosevelt also withdrew from private sale many

valuable natural resources, including coal and mineral lands, oil reserves, and water-power sites. In 1908 he summoned the nation's conservation experts to a White House National Conservation Congress. Its purpose was to plan future policies for the protection of natural resources.

Busting the Trusts In 1902 Roosevelt began a policy of "trust busting." He moved to break up many of the giant corporations that had been organized by industry mergers during the previous decade. At first Roosevelt sought only to

The Bull Moose Convention

"We stand at Armageddon, and we battle for the Lord!"

Theodore Roosevelt shouted this rallying cry to Progressives at the Republican convention in June 1912. He was a man with a mission. He wanted to regain the presidency because he had a Progressive program, his "New Nationalism," that he wanted to see enacted into law. In his characteristic way he was ready to do battle. "I feel as fit as a bull moose," he told reporters.

When he lost the nomination, the Progressives would not accept the end of their dream. On August 5, 1912, they met as the newly formed Progressive, or "Bull Moose," party. Here in Chicago they would nominate Roosevelt as their presidential candidate.

The religious note that Roosevelt had sounded at the Republican convention seemed to find its real audience here. One historian has described the delegates as "a group of well-dressed, serious citizens with the respectability of Sunday School superintendents." The gathering seemed more like a religious revival meeting than a political convention. Speaker after speaker took the podium to deliver rousing, emotion-packed sermons on social justice. An already converted audience listened intently and often tearfully. Occasionally they would be moved to respond with hymns, feet stomping, and quotes from the Bible.

These were the men and women who for years had sought reforms in their own communities. They were frequently isolated from the rest of society because of their beliefs. One writer described them as "men of character who had fought against local grafting politicians. College professors, social workers, businessmen of vision and independence, farmers tired of seeing agriculture on the cross—[all] were enlisting in a cause they loved for unselfish service."

On the second day of the convention Roosevelt rose to present his "Confession of Faith" in political and economic reform. Before he could speak, 15,000 people came to their feet to welcome him. They poured out all of the emotions that had been building in them since he was denied the Republican nomination.

Roosevelt did not disappoint them. His mood matched theirs. When it came time for him to accept their nomination, he launched the crusade in fervent, enthusiastic terms:

> Six weeks ago here in Chicago, I spoke to the honest representatives of a convention which was not dominated by honest men; a convention wherein sat, alas! a majority of men who, with sneering indifference to every principle of right, acted so as to bring to a shameful end a party which had been founded over half a century ago by men in whose souls burned the fire of lofty endeavor. Now to you men who, in your turn, have come together to spend and be spent in the endless crusade against wrong, to you who face the future resolute and confident, to you who strive in a spirit of brotherhood for the betterment of our nation, to you who gird yourselves for this great new fight in the never-ending warfare for the good of mankind, I say in closing what I said in that speech in closing: We stand at Armageddon, and we battle for the Lord.

regulate the trusts through appropriate legislative channels. He asked Congress to pass legislation authorizing the federal licensing of corporations, full disclosure of company earnings and profits, and other supervisory measures. But the conservative majority in Congress rejected these proposals. So Roosevelt took on the trusts himself, using the powers given to the President by the 1890 Sherman Antitrust Act.

The President's first target was the National Securities Company. This was a consolidation of three major railroad systems: the Northern Pacific, the Great Northern, and the Chicago, Burlington, and Quincy. New York banking houses, led by Rockefeller and J. P. Morgan, had organized the merger to put an end to damaging competition among the three lines. Roosevelt ordered his Attorney General, Philander C. Knox, to file suit against the Northern Securities Company for violating the Sherman Act. In 1903 the Supreme Court declared the merger illegal and ordered the Northern Securities Company dissolved.

Roosevelt brought similar antitrust actions against several other giant corporations. These included Standard Oil, the American Tobacco Company, and DuPont. In this policy, which proved highly popular politically, Roosevelt asserted the supremacy of federal authority over private economic interests.

In his antitrust compaign Roosevelt insisted that he opposed not large corporations as such but corporate action against the public interest. The exact nature of that interest, Roosevelt felt, was something the President must judge. He wrote: "Our objection to a given corporation must be not that it is big, but that it behaves badly." In 1902 Roosevelt used his authority to force the settlement of a coal strike that threatened to deprive residents of the east coast of fuel during the winter months. With the aid of Wall Street banker J. P. Morgan he forced coal company executives to accept a settlement favorable to the United Mine Workers. It was the first time that an American President had intervened in a labor dispute on behalf of the striking workers.

Roosevelt's actions toward big business

were not always consistent, however. He came to private arrangements with U. S. Steel and other giant corporations to avoid invoking antitrust action. In some labor disputes though, he called in federal troops as strikebreakers. Perhaps he believed that the federal government had to play the role of a neutral third party in resolving major disputes on industrial relations.

When Roosevelt left the White House in 1909, he bequeathed to his hand-picked successor, William Howard Taft, a well-formulated set of reform proposals for congressional action. These proposals included thorough governmental regulation of business, federal supervision of the stock market, a federal workmen's compensation law, and compulsory arbitration of labor disputes.

Taft and the Old Guard The new President showed little interest in carrying out Roosevelt's proposals. Not that Taft opposed reform completely. During his four years as President he supported constitutional amendments providing for an income tax and for direct election of senators. In addition, Taft initiated twice as many antitrust actions as Roosevelt. But unlike his predecessor, he never acquired an image as a trust buster. Under Taft's administration Congress established the eight-hour day for government workers, widened the ICC's authority to include interstate communications systems, and extended a tax on corporate profits. Taft also gave genuine and vigorous support to the conservation movement.

In other areas, however, Taft remained a conservative, politically allied to the Republican Old Guard. In 1910 Taft's Interior Secretary Richard Ballinger made an agreement with private firms allowing them to develop valuable coal and water-power sites in Alaska. Chief Forester Gifford Pinchot objected to this decision, but Taft supported Ballinger and fired Pinchot. This move infuriated Roosevelt and marked the beginning of a political break between the two men.

Taft also supported Republican conservatives in their battle for control of Congress against a coalition of reform Democrats and Republicans. He worked actively for the defeat of leading Republican insurgents in the 1910 congressional election. Again Taft's actions angered Republican reformers, among them Senator Robert LaFollette, the party's most prominent progressive. Later that year Taft cooperated with the Republican Old Guard in helping to pass the Payne-Aldrich Tariff, a high-tariff measure beneficial to big business. The battle over the Payne bill split congressional Republicans into conservative and progressive wings. Long before the close of his term in office, Taft had lost the support of most Republican reformers. They turned again to Teddy Roosevelt for leadership.

The Election of 1912   Roosevelt did not disappoint them. Beginning in 1910, he toured the country, supporting party insurgents against Taft, and denouncing the Ballinger-Pinchot affair. He made it evident that he wished the Republican party's nomination for an unprecedented third term in the White House. Roosevelt's active campaigning helped him to capture the presidential primaries in six states. But in most states presidential nominations were made by party conventions rather than by primary elections. Taft had gained control of the party machinery during his four years in office. Thus in June 1912 the Republican national convention nominated Taft for a second term.

Republican progressives led by Roosevelt and LaFollette then split from party ranks. In August 1912 they organized the Progressive (or Bull Moose) party, which nominated Roosevelt for the presidency. The new party-attracted the attention of the country's leading reformers. Its 1912 convention, held in Chicago, was attended by such figures as Jane Addams, William Allen White, and George W. Perkins—all activists in the era's various reform movements (see page 574).

The Progressive party platform reflected a broad concern for major reforms in American life. It called for tighter governmental regulation of giant industries and financial companies, national presidential primaries, women's suffrage, and the initiative, referendum, and recall. Progressives also favored the prohibition of child labor, minimum wage standards for women, workmen's compensation, and a variety of banking and currency reforms.

On July 2, the Democrats nominated for the presidency a moderate reform candidate, Governor Woodrow Wilson of New Jersey. The Democratic platform favored collective bargaining for unions and revisions in the country's banking system. Unlike the Progressives, the Democrats sought the abolition of giant corporations rather than their regulation. Wilson called his program the New Freedom.

The Republicans, too, ran on a platform of moderate reform. They favored, among other legislation, tighter regulation of trusts and banking and currency changes. Thus, although Taft was more conservative than either Roosevelt or Wilson, he could hardly be considered an opponent of reform. A fourth candidate, Socialist Eugene V. Debs, ran on the most radical platform of all. In this curious election of 1912 all four candidates were committed in varying degrees to reform.

In the end the Republican split sent Wilson to the White House. Roosevelt received 4,126,000 votes and Taft 3,483,000. Had these votes been combined, the Republicans could have retained control of the presidency. Wilson received 6,286,000 popular votes, less than 45 percent of the total. But he won enough state pluralities to capture a majority of electoral votes. For the first time since the depression of the 1890s, the presidency returned to Democratic hands. In the election the Democrats gained control of both houses of Congress. Thus the new President had a working majority to pass his legislative program.

Wilson and the New Freedom   During his first term in office Wilson proceeded to enact his programs. Though he applied stern moral standards to the conduct of foreign relations, Wilson was a skillful realist about domestic affairs. He quickly tossed the notion of breaking up the trusts into the political ashcan. Instead, adopting Roosevelt's more moderate idea of regulating giant corporations, he helped push several bills through Congress to achieve this purpose.

The Federal Trade Commission Act of 1914 established a bipartisan body to supervise industry and prevent unfair methods of competition in interstate commerce. The Clayton Antitrust Act, passed that same year, strengthened the 1890 Sherman Act by spelling out specific business practices that violated the antitrust laws. The Clayton Act also restrained the government from using court injunctions against striking unions.[3] Though on paper the new law seemed a powerful weapon, it actually did little to regulate the behavior of giant corporations or aid organized labor. In 1913 Wilson helped to steer through Congress the Underwood Tariff, the first downward revision in tariff rates since before the Civil War.

In December 1913 Congress passed the Federal Reserve Act, which created the present American banking system. The new law established twelve regional Federal Reserve banks, which were to serve member banks in their various geographic districts across the country. The Federal Reserve banks issued paper currency, supervised bank credit, and controlled other banking practices. The act also required existing national banks to become members of the Federal Reserve.

Wilson was supported in all these measures by his close associations with Southern Democrats. Some historians have called his election "the revolution of 1912" because, for the first time since the Civil War, Southerners regained a large measure of national influence. Born and raised in the South, Wilson felt most comfortable with those from his native region, many of whom became his closest advisers. He appointed a number of Southerners ambassadors and awarded some with other high-level government jobs. Several of his Cabinet members came from the South; others, like Wilson himself, were of

Southern background ("the South in exile," as some called it).

The Senate Majority Leader, Thomas Martin of Virginia, and the House Majority Leader, Oscar Underwood of Alabama, worked closely with the new President. During Wilson's administration fifteen out of seventeen Senate committees were led by Southern chairmen. These senators helped to formulate Wilson's domestic program and steer it through Congress. The Federal Reserve Act was largely the work of three Southerners, including Wilson's Secretary of the Treasury, Carter Glass of Virginia. The Clayton Antitrust Act was sponsored by Henry Clayton of Alabama and House Majority Leader Underwood led the fight for the tariff-revision bill.

Protest and Progress Wilson's Southern background had less fortunate consequences, however. Segregation officially came to Washington under Wilson's regime. Governmental offices and other public facilities in the city were ordered segregated by race. In doing this, Wilson was only following a practice that had become common after Reconstruction. In the late nineteenth century "Jim Crow" laws[4]—that is, laws keeping blacks and whites apart in all public places—were enacted throughout the South (with little protest from the North). In 1896, in the case of *Plessy* v. *Ferguson,* the Supreme Court ruled that "separate but equal" facilities were constitutional. The decision was based to some extent on pseudoscientific assumptions of the day shared by many middle-class progressives in both the North and South. They believed that blacks (as well as southern and eastern Europeans) were essentially inferior. With the approval of the court, white supremacy asserted itself in segregated railroad cars, restaurants, schools, and other public facilities and institutions.

In the early twentieth century the problems of black Americans were brought to the nation's attention by a group of young black businessmen and professionals under the leadership of the

---

[3] An injunction is a court order requiring or forbidding certain activities. Business and government have sometimes used the injunction as an antiunion weapon to prevent strikes.

[4] The laws got their name from a song sung by Thomas Rice in a Negro minstrel show.

W. E. B. DuBois, the first black to receive a Ph.D. from Harvard, founded the NAACP to agitate for black political rights. When he died in 1963, his goals were beginning to be realized, though he himself, disheartened, had moved to Africa.

great scholar W. E. B. DuBois. In 1905 they founded the militant Niagara Movement to press for an end to Booker T. Washington's policy of "accommodation" with whites.[5] The leaders of the Niagara group sought a return to active agitation for complete political and civil equality of blacks with whites—the earlier goals of Radical Reconstruction.

Four years later, members of the Niagara Movement and white supporters of black civil rights formed the National Association for the Advancement of Colored People (NAACP). DuBois was appointed editor of the NAACP's journal, *The Crisis.* Active in the new organization were several reformers who would support the garment workers' strike that same year: Lillian Wald, Jane Addams, and publisher Oswald Garrison Willard (William Lloyd Garrison's grandson). The NAACP grew rapidly in the next

---

[5] Washington believed that it was more important for blacks to achieve economic gains than political ones. He preached patience, conservatism, and the primacy of education in achieving material prosperity to his black followers.

decade. It quickly took the lead in opposing the segregationist policies of the Wilson administration.

Wilson found himself under growing pressure from other groups of reformers as his first term drew to a close. There seemed little chance that he could again slip into the White House through a split in Republican ranks. Roosevelt had rejoined his party, and most Progressives were unhappy with Wilson's refusal to support social welfare legislation. Concerned over the political situation, Wilson began a determined campaign to win over reform-minded voters by pushing several progressive measures through Congress.

The Federal Farm Loan Act, passed in May 1916, aided domestic agriculture by expanding the credit resources of American farmers. The Adamson Act, passed the same year, provided an eight-hour day for workers in interstate commerce. The Kern-McGillicudy Act created a model workmen's compensation program for federal employees. In August of 1916 Congress attempted to deal with the problems of child labor by passing the Keating-Owen Act, which outlawed the interstate shipment of products manufactured by children under fourteen. (Two years later the law was declared unconstitutional.) Wilson nominated progressive lawyer Louis Brandeis to the Supreme Court and fought for his confirmation in Congress against conservative opposition. Brandeis became the first Jewish Supreme Court justice.

During the election of 1916 Democrats stressed Wilson's skill at maintaining American neutrality in the growing war in Europe (see Chapter 30). But it was the President's energetic sponsorship of reform measures that won him the support of the labor movement and most middle-class reformers. In a hard-fought campaign against Republican Charles Evans Hughes, Wilson won reelection by narrow popular and electoral margins. In his second term he devoted most of his attention to the problems of fighting a war and winning the peace. Domestic reform took a back seat to world affairs during Woodrow Wilson's last four years in office.

1. Why has the "Protocol of Peace" come to be regarded as a milestone in American industrial relations?
2. Why were unions largely unsuccessful in organizing workers in the early years of the twentieth century?
3. Was the membership of large numbers of self-employed workingmen in the Knights of Labor a hindrance to its effectiveness? Why or why not? Why did Samuel Gompers believe that reform activity and independent political action by unions hindered their effectiveness?
4. Why did many reformers of the late nineteenth century believe that a social catastrophe was imminent? How did men like Edward Bellamy and William Dean Howells propose to avoid it?
5. Why did some reformers believe that settlement houses were inadequate responses to urban problems? What was their solution?
6. Who were the progressives and what beliefs did they share? What were some of their accomplishments at the city and state levels?
7. Did Theodore Roosevelt want to break up all trusts? Why did he believe it necessary to move against the Northern Securities Company?
8. Was President Taft a progressive? For what reasons did he and Roosevelt have a falling-out? How did that falling-out affect the election in 1912?
9. Why did Wilson begin to press for social welfare legislation at the end of his first term? Cite some examples of this legislation.

Beyond the Text

1. Compare and contrast the Knights of Labor and the AFL with regard to (1) structure, (2) membership, and (3) attitudes toward the strike.
2. Compare Theodore Roosevelt and Woodrow Wilson in terms of their aims, their accomplishments, and their influence on history.
3. Booker T. Washington and W. E. B. DuBois represented two different approaches to black advancement in American society. Describe their differences and indicate which you think more correct.

Bibliography

Nonfiction

Aaron, Daniel, *Men of Good Hope: A Story of American Progressives.**

Davis, Allen F., *Spearheads for Reform: The Social Settlements & the Progressive Movement, 1890–1914.**

Flexner, Eleanor, *Century of Struggle: The Women's Rights Movement in the United States.**

Grob, Gerald N., *Workers and Utopia.**

Hays, Samuel P., *Conservatism and the Gospel of Efficiency.**

Hofstadter, Richard, *The Age of Reform.**

Kolko, Gabriel, *The Triumph of Conservatism.**

Lasch, Christopher, *The New Radicalism in America, 1889–1963.**

Link, Arthur S., *Woodrow Wilson and the Progessive Era, 1910–1917.**

McKelvey, Blake, *The Urbanization of America, 1860–1915.*

Mowry, George E., *The Era of Theodore Roosevelt, 1900–1912.**

———, *Theodore Roosevelt & the Progressive Movement.**

Taft, Philip, *The A. F. of L. in the Time of Gompers.*

Fiction

Sinclair, Upton, *The Jungle.**
Smith, Chard P., *Ladies Day.*
Stone, Irving, *Adversary in the House.**

*a paperback book

The Philippines Revolt

AT AGE THIRTY, Emiliano Aguinaldo was a seasoned revolutionary. The son of a prosperous farmer from the island of Luzon, he was a member of the Katipunan, the Filipino movement for independence. In August 1896 Aguinaldo joined a revolt against Spain, which had held the Philippines as a colony since the sixteenth century. Two months later the rebels proclaimed the existence of the Tagal Republic. When the first president of the republic died, Aguinaldo became president and commander in chief of the insurgent forces.

But revolutionary organization and high-sounding titles alone could not defeat the Spanish in the field. Nor could Spain's colonial power crush the rebels. In December 1897, after more than a year of seesaw guerrilla warfare, both sides recognized the stalemate and signed a treaty.

Spain, apprehensive over the threats posed to its Caribbean empire by rebellion in Cuba and political unrest in Puerto Rico, agreed to consider reforms in the Philippines. In turn, Aguinaldo and other leaders of the rebellion agreed to leave their country for three years. They went to Hong Kong, a British colony on the southern coast of China. Meanwhile, the Spanish deposited 400,000 pesetas in a Hong Kong bank in the rebels' name. If Spain enacted the promised reforms, this trust fund would be used to educate Filipinos abroad. If Spain failed, the insurgents could use the money to buy arms and resume the war.

The American fleet's destruction of the Spanish fleet in Manila Bay on May 1, 1898 brought the United States into an era of overseas expansion. Gaining the Philippines from Spain proved easier than winning the loyalties of the Filipino people, as events of the next four years would show.

The Filipinos soon became convinced that they had been tricked. Spanish Governor-General Miguel Primo de Rivera did not declare a general amnesty, as expected. Reforms acceptable to the rebels did not come to pass. The trust fund that rested in Hong Kong now seemed to the rebels to be no more than hush money, a bribe to silence Filipino leaders. From their headquarters in the British colony, the insurgents began planning for future campaigns.

During this period rebellion in Cuba brought on a crisis in Spanish-American relations. (Americans and their government were sympathetic to freedom movements in Latin America.) As Spain and the United States moved closer to war, the Filipino rebels thought about an alliance with the United States. Then, in April 1898, Aguinaldo was told that the American consul in Singapore, W. Spencer Pratt, wanted to discuss important matters of interest to both countries. The Filipino agreed to meet with Pratt in Singapore.

The Aguinaldo-Pratt talks took place in the Raffles Hotel, legendary center of "East Asian intrigue" and British colonial power at the turn of the century. Pratt claimed that Spain had broken the terms of the truce. He urged Aguinaldo to resume the rebellion. The consul added some important news: "As of the other day, Spain and America have been at war. Now is the time for you to strike. Ally yourselves with America, and you will surely defeat the Spaniards!"

Aguinaldo was clearly interested in this proposal, but he remained cautious: "What can we expect to gain from helping America?" Pratt assured him: "America will give you much greater liberty and many more material benefits than the Spanish ever promised you."

When Aguinaldo asked whether such an arrangement could be put in writing, Pratt sidestepped. He obviously had no authority to speak for Washington. Yet he continued to offer verbal assurances: "The American Congress and President have just made a solemn declaration disclaiming any desire to possess Cuba and promising to leave the country to the Cubans after having driven away the Spanish and pacified the country. Cuba is at our door while the Philippines are 10,000 miles away." In short, Pratt suggested, there was no chance that the United States would occupy the Philippines.

Consul Pratt also told Aguinaldo that he would try to arrange for the rebels to be transported to Manila on American ships. Pratt contacted Commodore George Dewey, commander of the United States Pacific fleet in Hong Kong. The cable to Dewey read: "Aguinaldo, insurgent leader, here. Will come Hong Kong. Arrange with Commodore for general cooperation insurgents Manila if desired." The Yankee sailor answered quickly and tersely: "Tell Aguinaldo come as soon as possible." When informed of Dewey's okay, Aguinaldo promised that if his forces obtained sufficient arms the rest of the Filipino people would rise against the Spanish. Pratt, seldom at a loss for reassuring words, added that Dewey felt that "the United States would at least recognize the independence of the Philippines under the protection of the United States Navy."

But Commodore Dewey never met with Aguinaldo before the United States Pacific squadron sailed for Manila. A few years later he denied all knowledge of a political deal. By then Commodore Dewey had been promoted to admiral, a rank created especially for him by Congress: he had become a national hero. Dewey dismissed Consul Pratt as a "busybody interfering with other people's business," a man whose letters he simply filed and ignored. Toward the Filipinos Dewey adopted a paternal and disapproving stance. "They seemed to be all very young, earnest boys," he recalled. "I did not attach much importance to what they said or to themselves."

Certainly Dewey did not believe the rebels' boasts that they already had 30,000 armed men in the Philippines, with many more available. Why then did Dewey agree to take Aguinaldo and other Filipino leaders to Manila? By his own account, to get rid of them. "They were bothering me. I was very busy getting my squadron ready for battle, and these little men were coming aboard my ship at Hong Kong and taking a good deal of my time." So he consented to transport the rebels, though in the end only one Filipino went along.

Despite his denials, Dewey did want something from the Filipinos. He needed troops to occupy Manila and other parts of the Philippines if and when he defeated the Spanish navy. Aguinaldo and his followers might help Dewey accomplish the job.

Commodore George Dewey created the conditions for United States involvement in protracted guerrilla warfare in the Philippines. He needed Filipino help to defeat Spain but did not reckon with Filipino nationalist feelings after the conflict.

On May 1, 1898, American forces defeated the Spanish navy in Manila Bay. The spectacular victory reaffirmed the rise of American military power on the world scene. The United States squadron blew the remnants of the decaying Spanish navy out of the water. (Some of Spain's ships were hulks, rotting at dockside, with guns that would not function.) Within a few hours it was over. Spain no longer ruled the Philippines. Yet Manila remained to be captured and occupied. The Spanish army had not been routed, nor had its commander indicated a willingness to surrender.

The victory at Manila Bay reopened the question of Dewey's need for Filipino support. From his ships Dewey could do nothing. Spanish artillerymen had allowed Dewey to anchor close to Manila's shore, but the commodore knew that opening fire would expose the city to prolonged bombardment. Moreover, his small Marine battalion was an

Emilio Aguinaldo was evaluated differently by his enemies and his own people. To Dewey he was at first a nuisance and later an "Oriental despot." To the Filipinos, however, he symbolized their hope for independence.

insufficient landing force. The commodore felt that with 5,000 troops he could end the war in one day. But he did not have 5,000 troops. Insurgent Filipinos comprised the only immediately available source of military manpower.

Early in May Dewey sent for the rebel leader. Aguinaldo and a dozen of his associates in Hong Kong arrived in Manila on a United States Navy auxiliary vessel. Within a few days Dewey and Aguinaldo met for the first time. Their versions of the encounter are as different as the men themselves.

According to Aguinaldo, the American commander repeated the familiar promises about American disdain for acquiring colonies and its support of Filipino independence. Dewey also requested that the insurgents resume fighting. He supplied them with sixty-two rifles and some abandoned Spanish naval guns. The United States commander stressed that all promises were guaranteed "by the word of honor of Americans." Finally, Aguinaldo claimed that Dewey instructed him to have a Filipino national flag prepared. It would be hoisted as soon as Spain surrendered.

Dewey presented an equally questionable account of the events. Shortly after meeting with Aguinaldo, Dewey claimed, the Secretary of the Navy instructed him to avoid entangling the United States in alliances with the Filipino insurgents. Dewey complied because he was bound by obedience and because he did not like the insurgents. He had little faith in their cause. He considered the soft-spoken Aguinaldo an "unimpressive little man," though he recognized the Filipino's enormous prestige among his people.

Dewey admitted that the insurgents might be of service in clearing the shoreline from the naval base of Cavite to Manila City. Thus he allowed the rebels to enter the Cavite arsenal. But he warned that the Filipinos and the Americans should keep their distance. The United States commander continued to maintain that Aguinaldo had been forced on him by the barrage of pleas from the American consuls in Hong Kong and Singapore. Dewey also insisted that he never believed the Filipinos wanted independence. How could they? Aguinaldo "considered me as his liberator, as his friend."

Friend would soon become foe, and Aguinaldo himself bore some of the blame for his later disillusionment with the United States. During his months of exile in Hong Kong and his first few weeks back in the Philippines, Aguinaldo seemed to accept everything the Americans promised. His proclamations and public letters of the time praised the United States in lavish terms.

The distance that Dewey sought to create between himself and Aguinaldo was quickly established. American officers began complaining about the many Filipinos inside the Cavite naval base. These "natives," they argued, might be friends or foes. So Dewey told Aguinaldo that he and his men must leave the arsenal but could remain in the town of Cavite. From this headquarters the Aguinaldo movement grew. Enlistees poured in, many of them armed with captured Spanish rifles.

On May 21 Aguinaldo felt militarily strong enough to issue a proclamation outlining his ultimate aims: "Everything appears favorable for attaining independence. The hour has arrived for the Philippines to belong to her sons." Aguinaldo advised his men to fight a "civilized" war, warning that "if we do not conduct ourselves thus, the Americans will decide to sell us or else divide up our territory, as they will hold us incapable of governing our land." Like it or not, Aguinaldo knew, the Filipinos would have to deal with the United States. Neither Japan nor the European powers had demonstrated a willingness to confront America over the fate of the Philippines.

Throughout May Manila remained in Spanish hands. The Americans had made no commitments to the rebels, but United States troops were on the way. In June the Filipino insurgents announced the establishment of a provisional government and issued a declaration of independence.

The declaration also recognized the dictatorship of Emilio Aguinaldo. On June 23 Aguinaldo dissolved the dictatorship and declared himself president of the revolutionary government. In an effort to win support from the United States and other nations, the Filipinos promised to work for two primary goals: independence and the establishment of a representative, republican government.

By the time Aguinaldo formally declared independence, he and his forces controlled most of Cavite province and almost surrounded Manila. From the panic-stricken city, Dewey received requests from Spanish officials to help evacuate foreign and Spanish civilians, as well as wounded soldiers. Some were placed aboard foreign ships in the harbor. Aguinaldo, mindful of the need to wage war in a manner approved by Europeans, allowed civilians and wounded soldiers to pass through his lines. His cooperative spirit reached its height in mid-July when he helped pick the spot for a landing of United States soldiers. Thanks to the insurgents' advice, admitted Dewey, "we were able to land our troops within easy striking distance of their objective," a position more than halfway between Cavite and Manila.

But American gratitude did not mean acceptance of the Filipino forces as a political entity. According to Dewey, in fighting their way up the coast and surrounding Manila, the insurgents had merely prepared "a foothold for our troops when they should arrive." American Army units, under General Wesley Merritt, entered Manila on June 30. From then on, the war against Spain became an exclusively American affair.

American soldiers quickly moved to replace the Filipinos in the trenches dug near the Manila fortifications. One of General Merritt's officers tried to convince the insurgents to pull out of the line and turn their trenches over to the Americans. In return he offered to supply the rebels with cannon and other artillery. The local Filipino commander consulted Aguinaldo. Aguinaldo would comply, but only if the request and the offer were put in writing. This concession demonstrated the Filipino leader's desperate desire for legal recognition of his government's standing. Pull out first—then we will furnish the paper, answered the Americans. Aguinaldo ordered his troops out of the trenches. But they never saw the cannon, nor did their commander receive written confirmation. Once again, as in Cavite, Aguinaldo yielded to an American request under American pressure. This decision proved extremely costly to the rebel cause.

With insurgent forces neutralized and Aguinaldo's political status in doubt, the American capture of Manila proceeded swiftly and with little bloodshed. On August 13 the city capitulated. The United States now ruled the Philippines. A War Department dispatch dated August 17 declared that Filipino insurgents would not form part of the occupation forces:

> The United States, in possession of Manila City, Manila Bay and harbor, must preserve the peace and protect persons and property within the territory occupied by the military and naval forces. The insurgents and all others must recognize the military occupation and authority of the United States.

What was in store for the Philippines beyond the period of military occupation? In Washington President McKinley began the process of reconciling the facts of conquest with the arguments of territorial expansionists. At first McKinley opposed taking all the Philippines, though he held open the possibility that conditions might change. The President favored keeping Luzon, the large island in the northern part of the archipelago, and establishing a United States naval base at Manila. McKinley wished to show Europe that "a lofty spirit" guided American actions. But he also supported the "general principle of holding on to what we get."

These statements reflect McKinley's personality and his tactical approach to political decision making. The President worked hard to create the impression that he was forced to act. He wanted to make it appear that public opinion and the pressure of events directed the outcome of the Philippine conflict. In reality, as McKinley surely realized, the decision to take Manila made full-scale American involvement in the Philippines unavoidable.

In October 1898 Spanish and American negotiators met at the bargaining table in Paris, to write a peace treaty. When the American delegates left for France, McKinley still appeared to be uncertain about how to deal with the Philippines. But he later wrote the head of the delegation: "There is a very general feeling that, whatever it might prefer as to the Philippines, the United States is in a situation where it cannot let go." McKinley argued that the islands were too interconnected by history and commercial ties, too dependent on Luzon, for a selective policy of partition to work. The United States could not ignore the moral obligations imposed by its victory. But neither could it overlook Spain's inability to rule the islands. Finally, the United States would not allow their transfer to another foreign power. It became the responsibility of Secretary of State John Hay to work out the details of an arrangement.

The Treaty of Paris, which ended the Spanish-American War, was signed on December 10. Spain agreed to grant Cuba independence and to cede to the United States Puerto Rico and the tiny Pacific island of Guam. The United States also received the Philippine Islands, for which it paid Spain $20 million. "A goodly estate indeed!" crowed the head of the American delegation. He wrote President McKinley: "Perhaps the treaty may be an acceptable Christmas offering to you from the American commission."

During the negotiations between the United States and Spain, Aguinaldo tried desperately to gain legal standing for his revolutionary government. On August 6, shortly before Manila capitulated, he issued a memorandum to all foreign powers. It asked recognition of the belligerent status of the insurgents, a first step toward full diplomatic recognition. It also asked support for their ultimate aim of independence. But other countries refused to recognize the rebels. Nor did the United States indicate a willingness to consider Philippine independence seriously. Filipino insurgents were not America's allies, stated a directive from Washington. They had merely cooperated with Americans "against a common enemy."

Under these circumstances tension between Americans and Filipinos mounted. In December 1898 President McKinley sent a message to the new military commander in the Philippines, General Elwell S. Otis. The President assured Otis that the United States wished to pursue a policy of "benevolent assimilation" in the islands and bestow the "blessings of good and stable government." But he warned Otis that all obstacles to achieving these ends were to be removed. Before publishing McKinley's message, General Otis cut out several sections critical of the Filipino rebels. When a junior United States officer in the city of Iloilo mistakenly printed the entire text, Filipino resentment grew.

The insurgents' reactions in January 1899 were firm but still friendly. Aguinaldo rejected the American claim to rule his country and accused the United States of betraying a loyal ally. In the United States another Filipino leader, Felipe Agconcillo, tried to reason with the new colonial power in terms of its own declared ideals: "I cannot believe that in any possible action on the part of the American republic toward my country there is an intention to ignore, as to the ten millions of human beings I represent, the right of free government." He concluded his memo with the warning that the accidental or impetuous act of one Filipino or American soldier might trigger a full-scale war.

On February 4, 1899, the situation changed radically. An American soldier on guard duty near Manila challenged a Filipino to halt. When the Filipino disobeyed, the sentry shot and killed him. Fighting between Americans and Filipinos, confined during the previous six months to isolated incidents, broke out all along the outskirts of Manila. The war was on. And as even Dewey had to admit: "Perhaps the insurrection was bound to break out."

Inevitably, each side circulated conflicting reports about the incident. The Filipinos accused the Americans of deliberate provocation, adding that they were unprepared to launch attacks and that several of their leaders were on leave. They also asserted that Aguinaldo had believed the initial exchange of shots to be accidental. The day after the incident, the rebels claimed, one of their generals proposed an immediate cease-fire to General Otis. But Otis rejected the offer, and ordered the fighting to continue "to the grim end."

McKinley responded with an equally one-sided account. First, he brushed off the cease-fire claim: "There appears to have been no such application." Second, McKinley claimed, no American officer had promised the rebels independence. The most that Aguinaldo could have hoped for when he returned to Manila was the ouster of Spain. Their ambitions had led the Filipinos to launch an "unprovoked attack" on American troops.

Throughout the war American military leaders tried to downgrade the enemy. American officials viewed Aguinaldo as a bandit, who robbed his own people and lived in luxury on the proceeds of his looting. Whatever Aguinaldo's shortcomings, he remained the leading

Filipino insurgent for two years, the chief symbol of resistance to colonial power and of hope for independence.

General Otis, who predicted a quick and easy suppression of the rebellion, failed at the job. Otis boasted that his 21,000 troops would crush the insurgents in a few weeks. He repeated this promise with depressing regularity for the next twelve months. The gap between Otis' fantasies and the realities of the Philippine war can be measured by the increased number of troops the General soon demanded. Shortly after the outbreak he asked for 35,000. A year later he had 70,000 and wanted 30,000 more.

In the spring of 1899 the United States Army drove northward from Manila to occupy—or pacify, as the government called it—the island of Luzon, center of Tagal resistance. In April American forces captured the insurgent capital of Malolos. Aguinaldo and his followers fled farther north. But in mid-May they had to give up their provisional capital at San Isidro. Then, instead of mounting an all-out American attack, General Otis halted the advance. The rainy season had just begun, and many of the troops were scheduled for immediate return

THE PHILIPPINES REVOLT, 1896–1902

home. So Otis, a cautious field commander, suspended military operations.

Back in the White House McKinley remained optimistic. He assured Theodore Roosevelt that "Otis had things entirely in hand and that the insurrection would be speedily put down certainly after the opening of the dry season."

In the meantime, the Schurman Commission, a mixed civilian-military commission headed by the president of Cornell University, Jacob Schurman, was formed to investigate conditions in the Philippine Islands. A preliminary report, issued in the fall of 1899, found much to praise in the Filipinos. It expressed great interest in the islands' natural resources and potential for economic growth. But the report stressed that immediate self-government was out of the question and that the American presence must continue to assure peace and order. The commissioners concluded: "Whatever the future of the Philippines may be, there is no course open to us now except the prosecution of the war

Combat in the Philippines was perhaps the most grueling experienced to that time. Fought in jungle terrain against twin unseen enemies—the guerrilla insurgents and disease—the war produced over 7,000 American casualties.

until the insurgents are reduced to submission." The report delighted McKinley.

Most Americans agreed that Filipinos were unprepared for self-government. Some, like Republican Senator George F. Hoar of Massachusetts, protested that Filipinos should be left to govern themselves, whatever the results. But the majority felt otherwise. They predicted that an American pullout would quickly produce internal wars and anarchy. This they were sure would be followed just as quickly by the intervention of other foreign powers. Theodore Roosevelt hoped that Filipinos might be able to govern themselves at some future, undetermined date. But he warned that the "consent-of-the-governed doctrine must not be pushed to an extent that would restore savagery."

William Howard Taft, at the time a federal judge, went to the Philippines as the first American governor. He expounded on the theory of Filipino inferiority. In 1902 the Senate committee investigating the war asked Taft whether Filipinos were in fact so ignorant that a few leaders could easily misguide them. Taft replied: "That is quite possible, and that is one of the chief reasons why the Filipino people are utterly unfit for self-government." Americans had to lead the way, Taft asserted, for the Filipinos lacked any knowledge of how to carry on a government. The United States could not remain "blind to their serious defects, many of which are due to the environment, social and political, which has been presented by their history of three hundred years."

General Robert P. Hughes spoke more bluntly. In referring to one of the Filipino ethnic groups, he testified: "These people do not know what independence means. They probably think it is something to eat. They have no more idea what it means than a shepherd dog."

The suspension of American offensive operations in the spring of 1899 gave Aguinaldo and his followers time to regroup—and make a key decision. The insurgents knew they could not defeat the rapidly growing United States forces in conventional warfare. From then on, Aguinaldo and his staff decided, Filipino rebels would engage in guerrilla tactics. In order to succeed, they would have to depend on their own countrymen's support, voluntary or forced, and on their ability to blend in with the civilian population.

Aguinaldo's tactical switch posed new and serious problems for the United States Army. When General MacArthur resumed his northward advance in Luzon in October 1899, his men had trouble distinguishing friend from foe among the Filipinos. The guerrillas tried to wear down the enemy by ambushing American patrols and firing at

War atrocities committed by Americans, such as the burning of the native district of Manila in 1899, caused divisions of popular sentiment at home. Mark Twain suggested bitterly that the field of stars on the flag be "replaced by a skull and crossbones."

night into towns occupied by United States troops. Along the trails between villages Filipino rebels set up booby traps—pits lined with sharpened bamboo spears and covered with foliage. General Hughes complained: "As to actual engagements, there were very few. It was very hard to get an engagement of any kind. You could get what we would call a little skirmish, and probably there would be ten or twelve killed."

Though Americans denied that the Filipino army had any legal standing, guerrilla prisoners were not automatically executed as rebels. Instead, a generous American amnesty policy for the insurgents allowed for a decent gap between the official United States position and the actual treatment of those Filipinos who wished to surrender.

Many insurgents did surrender and swear allegiance to the United States. Some even joined American troops to crush the rebels. Combat reports often mentioned the Macabebe soldiers. They were Filipinos who fought with and supported the United States throughout the war. But American officials in the Philippines rejected the idea of forming an all-Filipino regiment. "To put in command of a Filipino a thousand men with a thousand rifles would not be wise," warned Taft. Still, many Filipinos cooperated with the Americans, and, as in most wars, the majority of the population remained uninvolved. These facts bolstered the American argument that Aguinaldo and his forces actually hurt the Filipinos more than anyone else.

Filipinos who continued to resist and rejected the American offer of amnesty received rough treatment. Captured insurgent leaders were shipped to Guam, and "enlisted men" were imprisoned. For a short while Americans even set up security camps for Filipino civilians. This same tactic, when employed by Spain in Cuba, had enraged the American public. In the insurrectionary province of Batangas American officials ordered a ban on all trade, hoping that wealthy Filipinos who supported the insurgents would yield to the pressure.

In the field, United States soldiers routinely burned Filipino villages. Sergeant Leroy Hallock testified that he had participated in the burning of a village of over 3,000 people. He claimed that he had heard of other burnings, including a town of 10,000 inhabitants. Another enlisted man recalled: "If a column was marching along and was fired upon, it was the practice to burn the buildings in that neighborhood. That impressed the natives with the fact that they could not fire upon us with impunity, although they did not often do very great damage."

No specific orders had been issued authorizing such indiscriminate reprisals, but they continued. Colonel Arthur L. Wagner defended the policy on practical and religious grounds:

> It is not always possible to discriminate between those who are active enemies and those who are not. We know that a certain community has been conducting itself badly. In such a case it would be justifiable to destroy the town, although we might burn the property of inoffensive people, if the town were notoriously a nest of *ladrones*—that is, [thieves, insurgents]. The Almighty destroyed Sodom, notwithstanding the fact that there were a few just people in that community—less than ten.

Early in 1900 the superior military strength of the United States forces began to make itself felt. In May General Otis resigned rather than work under the all-civilian Taft Commission, which had been sent to Manila to set up a civil government. Otis' replacement, General Arthur MacArthur, harried the Filipino guerrillas whenever and wherever he could find them.

The biggest setback for the insurgents' cause came with the capture of Aguinaldo himself. During late 1900 and early 1901 Aguinaldo's whereabouts remained a mystery. Some American military men and journalists began circulating rumors of his death. MacArthur knew better. In February 1901 United States troops captured an insurgent soldier carrying dispatches from Aguinaldo to rebel officers in the field. The messages did not pinpoint the location of rebel headquarters, but they indicated that the captive knew where to find Aguinaldo. Interrogation began, and before long the courier talked: Aguinaldo could be found in the village of Palanan, in the mountains of Luzon near the northeast coast.

But how could the Americans get to Aguinaldo? Thirty-six-year-old Brigadier General Frederick Funston, head of a volunteer regiment from Kansas, had a plan. The intercepted messages called for the movement of small groups of rebel reinforcements toward Aguinaldo's headquarters. Funston decided to use eighty Macabebe scouts pretending to be rebel reinforcements. He and four other American officers would go along, supposedly as prisoners. One additional and crucial element remained: several Tagals loyal to the United States would be needed to pose as leaders of the expedition. Funston found three such men, plus the messenger who had been captured. General MacArthur gave his approval but with misgivings. Instead of wishing Funston well, he remarked: "I fear I shall never see you again."

The march to Palanan proved more difficult than the capture itself. The expeditionary force landed by gunboat on the east coast of Luzon, about a hundred miles from its objective. The men had to struggle for several days through rough terrain near the shoreline, heavy rains, and dense jungle. It had been decided, for reasons Funston never made clear, that the Tagal officers and the Macabebes would enter the village about an hour before the Americans.

On March 23, 1901, the Macabebes arrived in the rebel camp.

Filipino guerrillas were not highly regarded as soldiers by the American military. General Arthur MacArthur claimed that they "could not hit a stack of barns" with their guns. But it took 70,000 American troops three years to defeat them.

They were relieved to find only a handful of insurgent soldiers to greet them. The Tagal officers entered rebel headquarters to confer with Aguinaldo and his staff. As the conversation wore on, all but two of the insurgent officers drifted out of the room. An expedition officer leaned out the window to give the Macabebes the signal to open fire. Aguinaldo, thinking that his own men were firing in the air to welcome the fresh troops, rushed to the window to tell them to stop wasting ammunition. At that point one of the Tagal officers seized Aguinaldo. The others opened fire on the insurgent guards.

It was all over before Funston and his American companions arrived. Funston rushed to the headquarters, and Aguinaldo asked if the "capture" was some kind of joke. When Funston identified himself, Aguinaldo let his shoulders drop in resignation and defeat. On March 28 the group returned to Manila. Aguinaldo was imprisoned in the governor's mansion. When General MacArthur arrived, ever skeptical, he asked Funston: "Where is Aguinaldo?" Funston had the triumphant pleasure of replying: "Right in this house."

Frederick Funston reaped most of the acclaim for the capture of Aguinaldo, including a Medal of Honor. But it was the Tagals and the Macabebes who actually captured the Filipino rebel leader.

Aguinaldo had sworn many times that he would never be taken alive. For several weeks American officers pressured him to swear an oath of allegiance to the United States. On April 19 he agreed to take the oath. He promised to issue a proclamation calling on Filipinos to lay down their arms in order to avoid further bloodshed. Aguinaldo's declaration suddenly made him a hero in American eyes. *The New York Times,* which had once described Aguinaldo as an "enslaver" and a "criminal aggressor," now found him to be "honest and sincere," a "natural leader of men with considerable shrewdness and ability."

On July 4, 1901, Taft took over as the civil governor of the Philippines. He left a revealing account of his reception in Manila: "The populace that we expected to welcome us was not there, and I cannot describe the coldness of the army officers and the army men who received us any better than by saying that it somewhat exceeded the coldness of the populace." By the end of the year President Roosevelt reported to Congress with a mixture of satisfaction and exasperation: "The insurrection has become an affair of local banditti and marauders. Encouragement, direct or indirect, to these insurrectos stands on the same footing as encouragement to hostile Indians in the days when we still had Indian wars."

Still, the rebellion—the ill-fated and barely understood war of national liberation—continued. Its center shifted southward to the island of Mindanao. The inhabitants of the island were Moros. They

More than 20,000 Filipino insurgents died in the three-year conflict—and independence was not achieved.

were Moslems who opposed the American presence but who had never accepted the authority of the Tagals in Manila. Fire fights and armed conflict broke out. One fire fight in northern Mindanao left ten Americans dead and forty wounded. Fighting between American troops and Moro rebels continued off and on for another twelve years.

In the meantime, the "unfriendly" island of Samar exploded. Company C of the regular Ninth United States Infantry was stationed on the island in the fishing village of Balangiga. Hundreds of Filipino workmen, supposedly loyal to the United States, fell on the Americans with knives, bolos (machetes), and bare hands. A few soldiers escaped in a boat to another island. They were the only survivors. The massacre at Balangiga would not be forgotten. For the next six months American troops called for revenge, in the same way that a previous generation of American soldiers had sought to avenge Custer's defeat at the Little Bighorn.

Major Littleton Waller of the Marines received the punitive assignment. The area commander, General Jacob ("Hell Roaring Jake") Smith, told Waller that he wanted the Samar rebellion ended quickly. Smith ordered Waller to remove all Filipino civilians from the island's interior and place them in stockades. Those who resisted, especially those capable of bearing arms, were to be considered enemies and shot. Waller asked what the cutoff point was. Anyone more than ten years old, replied Smith. Waller and his men did as they were told.

The pacification of Batangas province followed the same script. Miguel Malavar, head of the revolutionary government there, had

5,000 men and was better organized than the rebels on Samar. The American general, J. Franklin Bell, an ambitious young man who only three years before had been a lieutenant, saw his chance and took it. He waged an intense campaign, herding thousands of civilians into security camps. In April 1902, after several months of dodging and fighting on the run, Malvar surrendered. The last sustained pocket of armed Filipino resistance had been eliminated.

The war between American troops and Filipino rebels had lasted more than three years. Countless Filipinos lost their homes in the burning of towns and villages. Thousands of rebel soldiers were killed or wounded in the fighting. The United States had not gained an easy victory. Almost as many Americans died in the Filipino conflict as in the war with Spain. And the rebellion had cost the United States $160 million, or eight times the "indemnity" paid to Spain for the islands.

On July 4, 1902, the United States government declared the Philippine insurrection officially over. President Roosevelt, who had become President after McKinley's assassination, sent a special message to the Army. The President praised American soldiers for the rapid accomplishment of their mission, despite great hardships in more than 2,000 skirmishes and battles. Teddy Roosevelt was still mentally fighting Indians, for he went on to say: "Utilizing the lessons of the Indian wars [the army] relentlessly followed the guerrilla bands to their footholds in mountains and jungle and crushed them." With surprisingly few exceptions, the President maintained, American troops had been humane and kind to both prisoners and civilians. They had fought bravely against "a general system of guerrilla warfare conducted among a people speaking unknown tongues, from whom it was almost impossible to obtain the information necessary for successful pursuit or to guard against surprise and ambush." The Army, declared Roosevelt, had added honor to the flag.

30

Becoming a World Power

By 1900 Many Americans came to question the presence of American soldiers in the Philippines. Wasn't the war with Spain fought to liberate Cuba, an island ninety miles off the coast of Florida? Then why was the United States involved in places halfway round the globe? Whose interests were served by such overseas commitments? Answers to these questions lay tangled in the history of late nineteenth-century America and in the international power struggles of an imperialist age.

For most of the nineteenth century Americans had been more than content to search for and use the wealth of their own country. America was their Garden of Eden. And although many of its products were sold overseas (much cotton went to Britain, for example), the United States had avoided foreign political ties. America had allied itself with a foreign power only once in its history—during the Revolutionary War, when it signed an alliance with France. Concerned with domestic problems and opportunities, Americans had concentrated on developing their own continent.

GAINING AN OVERSEAS EMPIRE

Two major factors helped to change this attitude and promote American interests overseas. First, domestic industry grew at an astounding rate during the second half of the nineteenth century. A massive and efficient transportation network was constructed across the American continent. Much of the country's agriculture was mechanized, and heavy industries were established. By 1900 the United States was the world's leading economic power, one that could play an influential role beyond its own territorial borders.

Second, the major nations of Europe had been scrambling for empire in Asia and Africa. They were carving up these two continents into colonial dependencies, much as Spain had done three centuries earlier in the New World. As the nineteenth century ended Americans entered into the same race. American power was to expand not only into the Caribbean and the rest of Latin America but into the Far East as well.

Arguments for Empire   Basically, the United States shunned overseas political involvement. But many Americans argued for commercial

In this illustration Uncle Sam looks longingly over the sea and says, "The world is my market; my customers are all mankind." Industrial and agricultural growth encouraged the late nineteenth-century belief in the necessity of overseas outlets to absorb American surpluses.

U.S. FOREIGN TRADE, 1870-1910

expansion during the late nineteenth century. Why shouldn't the United States seek additional markets for its agricultural products and manufactured goods? The periodic recessions and depressions in the decades following the Civil War reinforced the argument for commercial expansion. Many business leaders had begun to feel that domestic markets were saturated. The new industrial complex seemed to be producing more goods than Americans could buy. Substantial cuts in production were out of the question. They would only put large numbers of American workers and farmers out of work. In turn, unemployment might cause political unrest and social instability. Perhaps the surplus from American factories and farms could be channeled into enlarged and more profitable markets overseas.

Other expansionists argued for American imperialism on strategic grounds. The chief spokesman for this point of view was Alfred T. Mahan, a naval officer and instructor at the Naval War College. In 1890 Mahan advanced his theory in a series of lectures, which he later published as *The Influence of Sea Power on World History*. Mahan asserted that through the ages naval power had been primarily responsible for national or imperial power. He also held that no country could maintain commercial expansion without a strong navy and overseas ports

(bases, for example, such as the Philippines and other Pacific islands).

Mahan's ideas quickly gained favor with imperialists in every major European country. More important, they also influenced several American foreign policy makers at the turn of the century. Chief among the American advocates of a strong navy were Roosevelt, McKinley's Assistant Secretary of the Navy, and John Hay, who served as Secretary of State under McKinley and later under Roosevelt himself.

Expansionism also had its defenders outside the business and military communities. Many Americans prided themselves on the myth of Anglo-Saxon racial superiority and the dominance of Western culture. For both selfish and humanitarian reasons they argued that the United States had a moral duty to uplift and enlighten its less civilized neighbors. The culture and religion of the Anglo-Saxons should be exported to "heathen" lands for everyone's good. This spirit was captured in 1899 by the British poet of imperialism, Rudyard Kipling. His "White Man's Burden" was written and first published in the United States. It reflected the mood of many Americans who were then debating the virtues of keeping the Philippines.

Current theories of evolution seemed to support the claims of Anglo-Saxonists. In his book *Origin of Species* (1859) Charles Darwin argued that through the process of natural selection only the "fittest" would survive. Individual animal species might adapt and prosper while others declined and perhaps disappeared. So-called social Darwinists extended these generalizations to the domains of the social scientist, businessman, and politician. That is, individual nations and empires might attain greatness at the expense of their less fit neighbors. These ideas were powerfully "scientific" supports for the missionary zeal of the expansionists.

Extending the Monroe Doctrine Although the United States moved cautiously and with uncertainty at first, it soon began to behave like a world power. Its debut on the world scene as a leading economic power provoked a great deal of controversy. But as the nineteenth century drew to a close, the prospect of increasing commercial activity abroad became highly attractive to American businessmen and politicians alike.

Even Grover Cleveland, who opposed acquiring new territories, supported commercial expansion. The severe depression that began during his second administration (1893–97) gave the President added reason to seek foreign markets. Commercial expansion might cure some of America's economic ills. It might help the nation start its slow climb back to prosperity. But a drastic change would be needed in the pattern of America's overseas trading. Historically, farm products—not manufactured goods—had been the country's main export and source of foreign exchange. American business leaders began arguing for expanding the sale of industrial goods to nonindustrialized countries such as China, the Philippines, and Latin American nations.

As early as 1889 Benjamin Harrison's Secretary of State, James G. Blaine, had organized the first Pan American Congress to promote American commerce in the Western Hemisphere and increase United States influence in Latin American affairs. During the 1890s a significant number of American businessmen responded to this opportunity by investing in Latin America. The United States thus began the process of replacing Britain as Latin America's major foreign investor. Both Harrison and Cleveland supported these efforts.

Cleveland's Latin American policy received a major test in 1895 when a crisis arose between Britain and Venezuela. The two nations disagreed over the boundary line between Venezuela and British Guiana. When the British threatened to use force against Venezuela, some Americans demanded that President Cleveland step in and apply the Monroe Doctrine to curb the European power. Stung by accusations of cowardice and beset by domestic problems, Cleveland decided to force a confrontation. He insisted that Britain submit to arbitration of the boundary dispute. Sensing that Cleveland was not bluffing, the British agreed.

The President's actions led to an important extension of the Monroe Doctrine: European powers could no longer resolve conflicts in the Western Hemisphere by military means. In a note to the British government Secretary of State Richard Olney declared that the United States considered itself "practically sovereign" in this hemisphere. The will of the United States, Olney boasted, "is law." American industrial power and growing military and naval power made these phrases more than empty words.

The Problem of Cuba Another incidence of American expansionism concerned Cuba, the island ninety miles south of Florida. Americans have always been interested in Cuba. From the early decades of the republic American politicians eyed the island with interest and greed. By the beginning of the nineteenth century Spain had lost most of its overseas empire. The remnants of that empire—Cuba, Puerto Rico, and the Philippines—became all the more valuable to the Spanish as their power waned. During the second half of the nineteenth century substantial American trade developed with the Spanish islands of the Caribbean. The situation appeared stable. But periodically groups of Americans called for absorbing Cuba, either by purchase or force.

Cubans resented Spanish rule, which was repressive and corrupt. They had revolted unsuccessfully in the 1860s. By the 1890s they had had enough. At that time, the economic crisis in the United States had reduced the American sugar trade with Cuba. The Spanish island colony suffered sharply from the effects of the American depression. In 1895 a Cuban revolutionary movement called Cuba Libre ("Free Cuba") moved for independence. The Cuban rebels embarked on a new war of national liberation, a war similar to the revolution then under way against Spanish rule in the Philippines.

Neither Cuba Libre nor the Katipunan in the Philippines had sufficient strength to push out the Spanish without outside help. Cuban rebels engaged in guerrilla warfare to wear down Spanish soldiers. The Cubans also burned sugar plantations and anything else of value, hoping to drive out Spanish landowners. In response, Spanish officials set up *reconcentrados*, or "detention camps," for civilians suspected of helping the rebels. Thousands of Cubans died in the camps because of poor food, inadequate sanitation, and lack of medical attention.

The United States had been sympathetic but strictly neutral during the earlier Cuban revolution. But in the 1890s Americans gave increasing support to the Cuban rebels. A variety of factors led Americans toward direct intervention in Cuba. First, Americans had little sympathy for Spain and its culture. Many still believed in the "Black Legend."[1] Second, Spanish troops were committing atrocities. Little did most Americans think that their own soldiers would shortly be acting in a similar manner to suppress the Filipino revolt. Third, many American businessmen had investments in Cuba, though these investments were small. Finally, Americans' new determination to become the dominant Caribbean power made events in Cuba of vital concern to Washington.

The Cuban question soon became a leading issue in United States politics. During the 1896 presidential election year Congress passed a resolution calling for recognition of the belligerent status of the Cuban rebels. President Cleveland, a Democrat who opposed territorial expansion, rejected the resolution. Cleveland's successor in the White House, Republican William McKinley, also opposed intervention in Cuba. McKinley was apparently less eager for expansion than most other members of his party. The Republican platform of 1896 was openly proexpansionist and favored involvement in the Caribbean. McKinley remained firm.

But events in Cuba and America's desire to impose its will in the Caribbean won over McKinley's promises. "Jingoism"—boastful patriotism—soon took hold of the nation. Two sensationalist New York City papers, William Randolph Hearst's *Journal* and Joseph Pulitzer's *World*, helped to stir up the interventionist frenzy. Both Hearst and Pulitzer ran stories, some of them deliberate lies, attacking Spanish cruelty in Cuba and praising the rebels. The stories spread to other newspapers across the country. By early 1898 it had become clear that Spain could not put down the Cuban rebellion. Nor would the United States allow the stalemate to continue much longer.

On the night of February 15, 1898 an explosion aboard the U.S.S. *Maine* in Havana harbor settled the issue of United States intervention. The battleship had been sent to Cuba to demonstrate American concern for the Cuban situation. The explosion killed 260 American sailors. Spain, which had the most to lose from American intervention in Cuba, hastily sent notes of regret to Washington. The cause of the explosion was never determined. But public opinion in the United States placed the blame squarely on the Spanish. "Remember the Maine!" became the slogan of American interventionists. The United States government began to pressure Spain to grant Cuba independence. But Madrid would not accept the loss of its Cuban colony.

On April 11, 1898, McKinley sent a message to Congress, asking for authority to use armed forces in Cuba. The President described Americans as "a Christian, peace-loving people" who still hoped to achieve a just solution through diplomacy rather than war. But Spain would not modify its position, even with the certainty of American armed intervention. By late April both nations were at war.

War with Spain The Spanish-American War of 1898 was over within a few months. American forces dominated Spanish military and naval power. Spanish soldiers and sailors fought bravely, but they were hopelessly ill-equipped for war. Spain won no battles and suffered heavy losses. American casualities were light. Many more soldiers died from disease than from combat.

[1] This was the English notion—dating back to the days of Queen Elizabeth and the defeat of the Spanish Armada—that the Spanish were a particularly cruel and treacherous people.

The year 1900 had been called the yellow-fever year in Cuba. The Spanish-American War had brought thousands of American troops there. Hundreds of them lay near death from the disease in Columbia Barracks in Havana. Doctors and nurses worked untiringly to try to save them, too often with no effect.

Early that year a tall slender officer, very military in appearance, with a serious but kind face strode into the office of the Surgeon General of the Army in Washington, D.C. He was Major Walter Reed, an army doctor who had just arrived from Cuba. He had come to ask that he be sent back there with equipment and personnel. With these he would study the permanently damaging and often fatal yellow fever.

As a practicing doctor and a scientist, Reed was well suited to the job he sought. In 1869 he had earned a medical degree from the University of Virginia in his home state. He was eighteen at the time. From there he went to New York City, where he earned a second medical degree. As an army doctor he specialized in the new science of bacteriology, studying the causes and transmission of diphtheria and typhoid fever.

Now he urgently wanted to discover how yellow fever was transmitted. The theory then accepted was that a person caught it upon coming into contact with the clothing or bedding of an infected person. Reed did not agree. He thought that a certain kind of mosquito carried the disease and infected people with its bite. He was determined to discover which theory was correct.

Soon his orders came through. He was to return to Cuba to organize and direct the work of three doctors "for the purpose of pursuing scientific investigation of yellow fever." The dry wording of his orders did not hint at the danger involved. Only humans contracted yellow fever Therefore humans, not animals, would be subjected to experiments.

Reed and his group set up the experimental situation. In one building volunteers slept on bedding used by yellow-fever victims. In another volunteers lived in uncontaminated surroundings but were exposed to the suspected mosquitoes.

It was not long before the results were clear. None of the persons who slept on soiled bedding was infected. But those bitten by the mosquitoes did contract yellow fever; in fact one of them died as a result, as did one of the three doctors. The discovery was credited with being "worth more than the cost of the Spanish-American War, including lives lost and money expended."

Armed with the knowledge that the mosquito was indeed the culprit, United States sanitary engineers went out to clean up the filth in which the mosquitoes bred. They were so successful that by 1902 there was not one case of yellow fever in Cuba. It was also eradicated from the United States, where epidemics had periodically struck cities on the eastern seaboard. And when work began on the Panama Canal, mosquito-control measures were taken. These removed the workers from the peril of yellow fever. Walter Reed's persistence had paid off.

When the fighting ended in the summer of 1898, United States forces had won Cuba and occupied Puerto Rico. In the Philippines Dewey's squadron held Manila Bay while awaiting the arrival of American troops. Spanish officials reluctantly agreed to meet with American negotiators to hammer out a treaty that would end Spain's status as an imperial power.

During the short struggle American expansionists achieved their longstanding wish of an-

---

Military action in the Spanish–American War of 1898 occurred on two fronts: the Philippines and Cuba. Hostilities commenced in the Pacific. The United States Asiatic Squadron under Commodore George Dewey sailed from Hong Kong in late April to attack the Spanish Philippines. On May 1 Dewey destroyed the Spanish naval force in Manila Bay with no loss of American lives.

In the Caribbean theater the Spanish fleet under Admiral Pascual Cervera arrived in Santiago harbor in May and was blockaded there by an American naval squadron. The blockade was reinforced June 1 under the command of Rear Admiral William T. Sampson. In late June United States troops under General William R. Shafter landed in Cuba at Daiquiri and Siboney and marched on Santiago. This force included the Rough Riders, a volunteer cavalry regiment under Colonel Leonard Wood and Lieutenant Colonel Theodore Roosevelt. On July 1 the troops captured the heights north and east of Santiago in the battles of El Caney and San Juan Hill. They then began an artillery bombardment of Santiago.

On July 3 Admiral Cervera attempted to run the United States blockade and escape from Santiago harbor. But Sampson's force destroyed the entire Spanish fleet in a four-hour battle along the coast. The Spanish garrison of Santiago soon surrendered (July 17). Hostilities were ended in the Caribbean by July 25.

In the Pacific Dewey's naval squadron was reinforced in July by the arrival of American troops under General Wesley Merritt. On August 13 United States troops and Filipino guerrillas occupied the city of Manila.

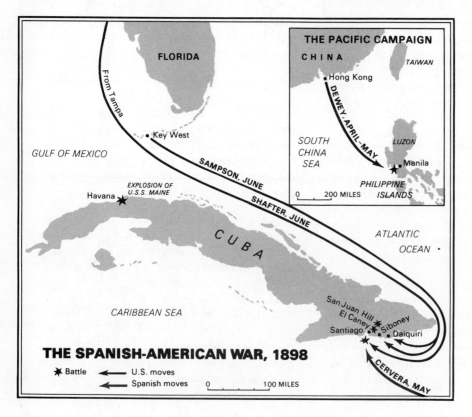

THE SPANISH-AMERICAN WAR, 1898

★ Battle ⟵ U.S. moves
⟵ Spanish moves   0 ⊢⊢⊢⊢⊢⊢⊢ 100 MILES

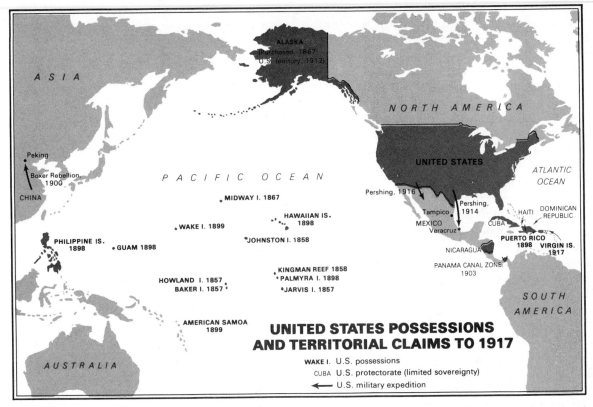

UNITED STATES POSSESSIONS AND TERRITORIAL CLAIMS TO 1917

WAKE I. U.S. possessions
CUBA U.S. protectorate (limited sovereignty)
← U.S. military expedition

nexing Hawaii. In 1893 a revolutionary movement backed by American businessmen successfully overthrew the Hawaiian monarchy and sought annexation to the United States. But like Texas between 1836 and 1845, Hawaii had to sit out a period of uneasy independence—five years—until United States politics entered into an expansionist phase. By mid-1898 annexationist forces had gained a majority in the House and the Senate. Congress passed a joint resolution declaring Hawaii a territory of the United States.

When Spanish and American negotiators met in Paris to work out the terms of a peace, the fate of the Philippines had not yet been established. But all signs pointed to a continued American presence on the islands. President McKinley's stance of indecision fooled few people—least of all Emilio Aguinaldo and other Fil-

ipino leaders. The President had clearly been drawn into the expansionist camp. For several months McKinley played a waiting game while expansionist forces in the Senate gathered support for a Spanish-American treaty.

In the end, McKinley demanded what he perhaps had in mind all along. Determined to "educate the Filipinos, and uplift and civilize and Christianize them," McKinley asked Spain to give up all the Philippines. The Spanish had to agree. The Treaty of Paris was signed in December 1898. The United States gained control of Cuba, the Philippine Islands, and Guam.

Most Americans had supported the war with Spain. But the Treaty of Paris, which proposed immediate acquisition of an American overseas empire, ran into stiff opposition. Many Americans feared that imperialism would endanger American democracy. Others objected to imperialism on moral grounds. Nations or cultures, they argued, should not be taken over by larger nations merely because they were too weak to resist. An anti-imperialist movement organized to fight the peace treaty. In the Senate many Democrats and a minority of Republicans opposed imperialism. William Jennings Bryan, the Democratic presidential candidate of 1896, led the antitreaty forces.

But at the last minute Bryan changed his course. The day before the vote on the treaty, fighting broke out between American troops and Filipino rebels. Americans regarded the uprising as a show of ingratitude on the part of the Filipinos. Bryan announced that the challenge had to be met firmly. He threw his support to the treaty, though he declared that he would continue to oppose imperialism. The Senate ratified the Treaty of Paris in February 1899. Bryan, who again opposed McKinley in the election of 1900, attempted to make imperialism the central issue of the campaign. Bryan and the Democrats were defeated overwhelmingly. The American people had voted for empire.

The Search for Asian Markets   Early in the nineteenth century a few American businessmen had entered into a prosperous trade with China. But even with the "opening" of Japan in the 1850s, the volume of United States trade in Asia never reached the proportions anticipated by American business leaders. By the end of the century overproduction in America's factories generated new and powerful pressures for foreign trade. The lure of the China market made itself felt again.

But participation in the China market could not be accomplished without political involvement in Asia. The European powers had already carved up China into "economic spheres of influence."[2] American businessmen believed they could compete successfully in China if they were given a fair opportunity. In September 1899

---

[2] A nation often established with other nations a world area where it would hold a dominant economic position. Once other countries agreed to accept this arrangement, the area in question would be free from the competition of other nations.

Secretary of State John Hay sent a series of diplomatic notes to Japan and the major European powers. In the notes he asked them to support a new trade policy in China. This policy became known as the Open Door. Hay recognized the existence of foreign spheres of influence in China, but he asked the European nations to grant other countries free-trade privileges within these spheres—thus keeping the Chinese door open to all who wanted to trade there. Hay also called on the European powers to guarantee Chinese "territorial integrity"—that is, to avoid outright political partition of the country. The European nations did not formally reject Hay's proposals, though some grumbled about American interference. Hay announced boldly that the Open Door was accepted by all.

While America was seeking support for its Open Door policies, a group of Chinese nationalists, called Boxers, organized to drive foreigners from their country. In 1900 they began killing foreign missionaries and diplomats. Survivors fled to Peking and the temporary safety of the British legation. There, they withstood a two-month siege until troops from their own countries relieved them. The United States participated by rushing in troops from bases in the Philippine Islands. The Boxer Rebellion was ended. Within a few months peace—and imperialism—were reestablished. In July Hay issued a second series of diplomatic notes. In them he asked the victorious European powers to preserve Chinese territorial integrity. Hay reaffirmed America's desire to "safeguard for the world the principle of equal and impartial trade with all parts of the Chinese Empire." Not wishing to risk a major war, the imperialist powers agreed not to divide up China. They accepted instead a sum of money from the Chinese in payment for their losses.

In comparison with other powers, the United States had acted as a friend and protector of China. But did the Open Door represent an American willingness to guarantee Chinese territorial integrity? The United States had not signed a formal agreement with China, or with any other foreign nation, to enact its Open Door policy. Hay quickly admitted that his country would not go to war to enforce the Open Door—not in 1900 at any rate. European imperialistic powers had battled to a draw in China with the creation of economic spheres of influence. Hay's Open Door declarations filled the partial vacuum created by this stalemate. The Open Door would work to America's advantage only as long as no other major power embarked on an all-out push to dominate China.

INTERVENTION IN LATIN AMERICA

The growth of United States industrial and military power, combined with America's interest in the Caribbean, meant that Britain's position as the leading Caribbean power would not last long. In 1895, during the first Venezuelan crisis, the Cleveland administration had asserted America's new role in the Western Hemisphere. The events of the next decade confirmed this role.

Building a Canal to the Pacific   Britain proved very cooperative in the building of a canal across Central America. A fifty-year-old treaty between Britain and the United States became an early casualty of America's new attitude of expansion. The 1850 treaty called for participation by both nations in the construction of any transoceanic canal. In February 1900 Secretary Hay negotiated another accord with the British ambassador, Lord Pauncefote. Under the Hay-Pauncefote Treaty Britain granted the United States exclusive rights to build a canal. But the American government was prohibited from fortifying it. This compromise did not satisfy the United States Senate. The treaty was quickly rejected. Hay returned to the negotiating table, pulled a few teeth from the reluctant British lion, and produced a second agreement. The revised treaty placed no limitations on military fortification of the canal. The United States had only to promise that during peacetime all nations could use the canal on equal terms.

Americans next turned their attention to the

This Chinese Boxer, a member of the society whose official title was the Fist of Righteous Harmony, believed that his country's survival depended upon expulsion of foreign powers threatening to divide China for economic profit. The Boxer Rebellion nearly led to the extinction of China as a national entity.

question of where the Central American canal should be built. The shortest route was across the Isthmus of Panama, a province owned by Colombia. The Colombian government had sold the rights to the Panama site to a French company, headed by Ferdinand DeLesseps (builder of Egypt's Suez Canal). After several unsuccessful attempts to build a canal, the French offered to sell their rights for $109 million. Another proposed site, in Nicaragua, was a much longer route. But it was less expensive and free of foreign entanglements.

President Roosevelt and Congress argued the relative merits of both routes and initially favored the Nicaraguan site. Then, early in 1902, the French company lowered the price for sale of its rights to $40 million. Roosevelt quickly changed his mind in favor of the Panama site. Permission also had to be gotten from Colombia. In January 1903 Secretary Hay signed a treaty with Colombia agreeing to pay $10 million and an annual rent of $250,000 for a hundred-year-lease on a canal zone in Panama.

But the Colombian senate, in a burst of patriotic pride and financial self-interest, rejected the canal treaty. President Roosevelt complained about the "bandits" of Colombia and their insistence on national honor. Roosevelt considered intervening in Panama under the terms of an 1846 treaty with Colombia. This granted the United States the right to maintain "free transit" across the isthmus. But United States troops were then busy fighting in the Philippines. Besides, the 1846 treaty required the agreement of Colombian authorities for the use of force in Panama.

In November 1903 a revolt in Panama settled the canal question. The revolt was organized by Phillipe Bunau-Varilla, an agent of the French canal company. The Panamanian rebels received immediate United States aid. American ships were sent in to prevent Colombian forces

Roosevelt's famous boast that "I took the canal zone and let Congress debate" is caricatured here. Roosevelt is seen heaving his shovelful of Panamanian soil on Bogota, capital of Colombia, the country from which Panama was detached.

from landing on the isthmus. Within a few days the new Panamanian government declared independence. Bunau-Varilla was appointed its chief representative to the United States. Bunau-Varilla and Secretary Hay quickly came to an agreement on an American-operated canal. Under the treaty the United States granted diplomatic recognition to Panama and obtained a perpetual lease on a canal zone.

Roosevelt's "big stick" diplomacy in Panama received sharp criticism from some Democrats in Congress. But the majority of Americans approved of the deeds and the bluster of their President. Some years later Roosevelt acknowledged with few apologies: "I took the canal zone and let Congress debate, and while the debate goes on, the canal does also."

In 1914 the Panama Canal opened to merchant shipping. The canal was acclaimed as a marvel of American engineering. It also put the finishing touch on a program for United States domination of the Caribbean and economic penetration of Latin America.

Policing the Caribbean While negotiations were being carried on in Panama, a second international crisis erupted in Venezuela. The dispute involved an attempt by European powers to collect debts owed their citizens by Venezuela. In December 1902 Britain, Germany, and Italy sent warships to blockade the Venezuelan port of LaGuaira. An international court decided that the three nations that had blockaded Venezuela should be given priority in collecting their debts.

Roosevelt contested this decision. America could not permit European powers to use force to settle disputes in the Western Hemisphere. When a similar financial crisis arose in 1905 in the Dominican Republic, another Caribbean country, Roosevelt moved quickly to avoid European intervention. American officials took over the government and the financial affairs of the Dominicans.

In 1904 Roosevelt announced to Congress that the United States would not tolerate "chronic wrongdoing" by any Latin American country. If political or economic developments in

Latin America invited the danger of European intervention, the United States would intervene first. The President's message, which became known as the Roosevelt Corollary to the Monroe Doctrine, asserted the role of the United States as an "international police power" in the Caribbean. The statement was actually a broad departure from the earlier doctrine.

Dollar Diplomacy   Theodore Roosevelt's successor, William Howard Taft, pursued Roosevelt's policies in Latin America. He favored economic penetration of foreign nations, a policy that became known as dollar diplomacy. Taft urged American capitalists to invest millions of dollars in overseas ventures, especially in the Caribbean. Such investments, he said, would bring Wall Street handsome profits. More important, they would serve the interests of American security. Also, American guardianship of the Western Hemisphere would benefit the people of Latin America. It would ensure them political stability and economic growth.

Nicaragua mounted the most serious challenge to the new American policy. Nicaraguan president José Zelaya, a strong opponent of the United States, tried to avoid the snares of dollar diplomacy. In 1909 he canceled special economic privileges granted to an American mining company. Zelaya's downfall came quickly. A revolutionary movement, supported by American businessmen, overthrew the Nicaraguan president. The United States granted diplomatic recognition to the new regime, took over the government's finances, and sent in the marines to protect American interests. The pattern for implementing dollar diplomacy had been clearly established.

Idealism Versus Intervention in Mexico   In 1913 Woodrow Wilson, a Democrat, moved into the White House. In his campaign Wilson promised a more liberal internationalism. He wanted a new foreign policy to curb the growing imperialist impulse. Wilson's choice for Secretary of State, the anti-imperialist William Jennings Bryan, gave some indication that Repub-

lican policies would be modified or abandoned. Wilson stated that his aim in Latin America was to support "the orderly processes of just government based upon law, and not upon arbitrary or irregular force, and to cultivate the friendship of our sister republics of Central and South America."

But idealistic aims proved no match for big-power politics. As President, Wilson used military force in Latin America even more than his Republican predecessors. Seeking to bring peace and "constitutional liberty" to the unstable governments of Latin America, he sent troops into the Caribbean to put down a rebellion in Haiti. A year later, in 1916, the President ordered United States Marines into the Dominican Republic. There a military government was established under the Department of the Navy. Troops remained in both countries throughout Wilson's administration.

Wilson played his strongest and most controversial role as a moralist when he intervened in the Mexican revolution that had begun in 1910. The President at first refused to recognize the government of General Victoriano Huerta, who had risen to power in 1913. An unsavory politician, Huerta had ordered the murder of his predecessor, Francisco Madero, Mexico's first freely elected president in decades. Wilson wanted Huerta to resign and permit free elections in Mexico. Though such goals might have been welcomed by the Mexican people, they could hardly be imposed from outside by persuasion alone.

Huerta refused to budge from the presidential palace in Mexico City. But Wilson remained determined to "teach the South American republics to elect good men." Early in 1914 the President allowed ships to supply arms to Huerta's foes. In April Huerta's forces arrested a group of American sailors who had landed at the port of Tampico. Washington demanded formal apologies. Huerta agreed but only on the condition that the United States support his government. Wilson and Bryan refused. When the President learned that an arms shipment from Germany—intended for Huerta's forces—was

General John J. Pershing and his hastily mobilized American troops invaded Mexico in 1916 in pursuit of "Pancho" Villa. The mission was a failure and may even have convinced Germany of America's military unpreparedness.

nearing the Mexican port of Veracruz, he decided to act.

In the meantime, Congress had granted Wilson permission to use armed forces against Huerta. A message went out to the United States naval commander in the Caribbean: "Take Veracruz at once." American forces quickly seized Veracruz. Mexican opposition rose within a few days. Fighting broke out, and both sides suffered heavy casualties. Wilson, who had not anticipated bloodshed, found himself in an embarrassing position. Americans protested the involvement—and the death of United States soldiers. Withdrawal of troops had to be arranged by a mediating commission of three South American countries.

Wilson's problems regarding Mexico were not over, however. Huerta was overthrown in July 1914 by the Constitutionalist forces of Venustiano Carranza. As the new president tried to consolidate power, civil war again broke out in Mexico. In November 1915 Wilson gave

unofficial support to Carranza's government. This move angered other pretenders to the Mexican presidency, particularly "Pancho" Villa. Operating in northern Mexico, Villa decided to teach the "gringos" a lesson. Early in 1916 Villa's forces stopped a train and killed sixteen American engineering students. Villa then crossed the border to raid the New Mexico town of Columbus, an act of revenge that cost seventeen American lives. The calculating and cold-blooded Villa hoped to lead America into military intervention in Mexico. Then, as the leading opponent of the United States, he would gain support from those people who supported Carranza.

Villa guessed correctly about United States intervention. But he misjudged its political consequences. Americans were enraged by Villa's actions. General John J. Pershing—soon to gain fame and glory as commander of the United States Army in France—led a "punitive" expedition deep into Mexico. Villa could not be found. Instead, American troops fought a bloody skirmish with Carranza forces. The battle was unwanted by both sides. The incident threatened another Veracruz. But anti-interventionists in Congress won out over those who wanted war. Early in 1917 Pershing's forces were withdrawn from Mexico. For most Americans it had become clear that Wilson's Mexican policy meant continuous trouble. By this time, too, the American people had become far more concerned with developments in Europe, where a destructive war had been raging since 1914.

THE UNITED STATES AND WORLD WAR I

Europe had enjoyed a period of relative peace during the century after Napoleon's defeat in 1815. International rivalries did not die down, and many short but limited wars broke out. Yet Europeans had managed to avoid a general war. European leaders relied on the balance of power to maintain peace and political stability. Two powerful blocs kept each other in check: the Central powers (Germany, Austria-Hungary, and Turkey) and the Allies (Britain, France, and Russia). But a buildup of arms on both sides foreshadowed trouble. In 1914 the assassination of Archduke Franz Ferdinand, heir to the Austro-Hungarian throne, set off a chain reaction that resulted in World War I.

The United States tried to stay out of the war. Whatever their personal opinions or sympathies, most Americans preferred neutrality. In 1914 Wilson issued a proclamation calling on all Americans to remain impartial "in thought as well as in action." But over the next three years a combination of factors edged the United States closer and closer to the side of the Allies and involvement in the European war.

The Road to War European powers violated America's rights as a neutral nation. American shippers tried to continue, and even expand, commerce with both sides. As in the case of the Napoleonic Wars a century before, American interests quickly clashed with those of Britain, the world's leading sea power. The British declared the North Sea a military zone. Before a neutral ship could pass through British waters, it had to enter a British port. There the ship's cargo was examined for contraband (war materials). British escorts would then lead the neutral ship through minefields to safety. Many Americans protested, and Wilson publicly condemned the British practice. But the United States clearly was not going to make the issue a cause for war. No American lives were lost as a result of the British

EUROPE AT THE START OF WORLD WAR I

regulations. No American seamen were impressed into the British navy, as in the War of 1812.

The Germans knew that their navy was no match for British sea power. For the most part German battleships and cruisers remained at anchor in home ports. Instead, the Germans turned to the submarine as a means of crippling their enemies. The British blockade of Continental Europe, launched soon after the war, threatened the German people with starvation. Germany fought back by declaring all-out submarine warfare. The Germans announced that any ships found in the waters surrounding the British Isles would be torpedoed without warning. Loss of life in such cases usually ran high.

Wilson denounced the German declaration as a violation of American neutral rights. Many Americans condemned submarine warfare as immoral. In the spring of 1915 the British passenger liner *Lusitania* was torpedoed by a German submarine off the Irish coast. Over 1,000 people died, including 128 Americans. Germany refused to accept responsibility for the incident or pay indemnities for American losses. The Germans pointed out that Americans had been publicly warned not to sail on British ships. Besides, the *Lusitania* carried arms as well as passengers. But Wilson drafted a strongly worded note to the Germans insisting that they end their surprise attacks.

Economic factors also contributed to American intervention on the side of the Allies. The United States had always traded more with Britain than with Continental Europe. The onset of world war, combined with British domination of the seas, ensured an expanded trade with Britain and its allies. Americans might have to endure annoying British regulations, but at least most American ships could get through to Britain. Between 1914 and 1916 Allied purchases in America quadrupled. It soon became apparent that Britain and France would need loans in order to continue trading. Wall Street stood ready. Anti-interventionists, led by Secretary of State Bryan, argued that such loans were contraband and would inevitably drag the United States into the war. Again Wilson proclaimed strict neutrality. He did not move to prohibit credit to the Allies, however. The loans were, after all, big business, and the United States economy was booming.

Another important factor influencing American involvement in the war was close cultural and political ties with Britain. Since the end of the nineteenth century relations between Britain and America had improved dramatically, though the two nations had not entered into a formal alliance. Most Americans sympathized with Britain and its allies. German Americans, as well as Irish Americans who opposed Britain's policies in Ireland, were notable exceptions. Perhaps the strongest supporter of Britain was Wilson himself. The President admired British culture and the parliamentary form of government. In contrast, Germany's image in America had suffered a complete change during the nineteenth century. Americans once viewed Germany as a country of poets and philosophers but came to see it as a stark and frightening nation of militarists.

Within the context of these three factors—neutral rights, economic interdependence, and cultural ties—Wilson tried to maintain a course of neutrality. By 1916 the war had become a stalemate. Neither side seemed capable of gathering enough strength to defeat the other. Hundreds of thousands of soldiers died in a series of brutal, inconclusive battles. Wilson attempted to use American prestige and the threat of use of power to negotiate a European peace. His trusted adviser, Colonel Edward M. House, crossed the Atlantic several times to confer with foreign ministers and heads of state. European statesmen listened to House—America was too powerful to ignore—but they did not heed his message. They had fought too long and suffered too many losses to accept Wilson's "peace without victory." The British and French skillfully played along with Wilson and House, banking ultimately on American intervention to bring an Allied victory.

The war dragged on indecisively for three years. Early in 1917 Germany renewed unrestricted submarine warfare, cutting off food and supplies to the French and British. Germans also launched a massive land offensive that threatened to destroy the Allies. Germany knew that this action would bring the United States into the war. But Berlin hoped to smash the Allies before a large American force could be mobilized and sent to Europe.

Wilson acted. Early in 1917 Washington received news of a revolution in Russia and the establishment of a constitutional government. The overthrow of the Russian czar removed many of the moral problems that Wilson faced in seeking support for American involvement on the side of the Allies. In April the President asked Congress to declare war on Germany. Wilson called upon Americans to embark on a great crusade, a "war to end all wars" and to make the world safe for democracy. In his message to Congress Wilson noted: "It is a fearful thing to lead this great peaceful people into war. But right is more precious than peace."

The Great Crusade When the United States entered World War I, the major European powers were nearly exhausted. On both sides men previously considered too old or too young for combat were pressed into military service. But after April 1917 the Allies suddenly had a great new reservoir of manpower to draw upon—the young manhood of the United States. The regular American army was small. Close to a million soldiers had to be recruited. But America prepared willingly to meet the demands of Wilson's crusade. Military conscription was accepted by most Americans with far fewer objections than during the Civil War or during the war in Vietnam.

The German submarine campaign achieved startling success during the first six months of 1917. The Allied navies soon devised an effective countermeasure: the convoy system. A single ship crossing the Atlantic had little chance against the German submarine fleet. But a large group of troop ships and freighters traveling together could reach Europe in relative security. The rate of sinkings by German submarines fell

THE WESTERN FRONT, 1918

← Allied moves ← German moves
★ Battle
······· Farthest German advance
- - Armistice line   0   50 Miles

War broke out in July 1914, one month after Serbian nationalists had assassinated Archduke Franz Ferdinand of Austria. Although the United States was a neutral for the first three years of the conflict, its ships were at times seized by the British and some were sunk by the Germans. In early 1917, after the Germans renewed unrestricted submarine warfare against all shipping, the United States broke off diplomatic relations with Germany. Provoked by continued German submarine attacks, the United States declared war on Germany in April of that year. The United States entered the war on the side of the Allies as an associated power. In June an American Expeditionary Force under General John J. Pershing arrived in France.

In March 1918, after years of trench warfare, the Germans began an offensive with the Second Battle of the Somme, intending to reach the English Channel. The Allies (including the United States) later set up a unified command for the Western Front under French General Ferdinand Foch. In May the German armies approached to within fifty miles of Paris. The turning point of the war came in July–August, when the German advance was stopped at the Second Battle of the Marne. Allied advances in the second half of 1918 were marked by major offensives at Belleau Wood in June–July, Ypres in August, St. Mihiel in September, and the Meuse-Argonne Forest drive of September–November.

The military position of the Central Powers deteriorated rapidly during the summer of 1918. On November 11, an armistice was signed, putting an end to the war.

The Fight Over the League of Nations

On July 19, 1919, Woodrow Wilson submitted the Treaty of Versailles with its League of Nations covenant to the United States Senate. A poll taken earlier in the year showed that sixty-four senators—the necessary two-thirds majority—favored ratification. But time and events had reduced that figure. Everyone knew that trouble lay ahead.

One source of the trouble was Wilson himself. He had created hostility by neglecting to ask any leading Republican to accompany him on the peacemaking mission. Then, too, he was a stubborn man. Once he made a decision, he was certain that it was right. He refused to compromise.

Another source of trouble lay in the diverse reactions of the senators to the treaty and the League. Some thought the treaty dealt unfairly with various nations, but they favored the League of Nations. Others had no trouble with the treaty itself but feared that the League would take away American independence and possibly lead the United States into war again. And there were those who thought the treaty provisions were unjust and that the League would only uphold these injustices. Several Republicans objected to the League simply because they thought that members of both parties should have had a stake in its creation.

Battle lines were being drawn. There were forty-seven Democrats and forty-nine Republicans in the Senate, divided into three discernible groups. First there were those who were willing to ratify the treaty immediately—forty-three Democrats. Then there were the "reservationists"—about thirty-five Republicans and one Democrat—who wanted some of the provisions changed before they would agree to vote for ratification. Finally there were the "irreconcilables"—the remaining Republicans, including three Democrats. This last group vowed never to sign the treaty under any circumstance.

At the center of this controversy was Senator Henry Cabot Lodge of Massachusetts, the new chairman of the Foreign Relations Committee. Lodge disliked Wilson and objected to the treaty, which he thought was too easy on Germany. He was therefore, at heart, an irreconcilable. But he thought he knew a better way of defeating the treaty. As he said to one senatorial colleague, "I do not propose to beat it by direct frontal attack, but by the indirect method of reservations."

Before the treaty went to the Senate for a vote, it was stalled for two months in the unfriendly Foreign Relations Committee. When it emerged, forty-nine revisions and amendments were attached to it. The disheartened Wilson was adamant. Democratic senators were not to vote for it with these "Lodge reservations." "Never! Never!" said Wilson. "I'll never consent to accept any policy with which that impossible name is so prominently identified."

He kept his word, and enough Senate Democrats stayed loyal to him to defeat the treaty with reservations. On November 19 it was all over. The Senate adjourned and the treaty that Wilson thought would be his crowning achievement would not be considered again. The United States would never join the League of Nations.

Isolationist Senators Borah, Lodge, and Johnson refuse to give a lady—Peace—a seat.

The Meuse-Argonne offensive in World War I was noted for its vastness—1,200,000 American troops—and its human costliness—over 120,000 casualties. Sergeant Alvin York, the prewar conscientious objector, became famous here for his single-handed capture of 132 Germans.

rapidly. Most important, nearly all American soldiers completed the passage to France safely.

The large but still untested American army—General John J. Pershing's American Expeditionary Force—went into action late in 1917. French generals, hungry for more manpower, had originally called for small-sized American units, which they wished to integrate into their own commands. Pershing worked cooperatively with the French commanders and with the Allied commander in chief, Marshal Ferdinand Foch. But he and other senior American officers insisted that the Americans operate as an independent army.

American soldiers soon received their own piece of the Western front to defend. American troops helped the Allies hold their positions. Then they joined the Allied counteroffensive in the summer and fall of 1918. By November Germany was beaten. The Kaiser fled into exile in Holland. Worn out by four years of brutal warfare and beset by unrest at home, Germany asked for peace.

At home America organized its wartime economy as quickly and effectively as it had mobilized its soldiers. The United States had begun to prepare for war as early as 1916. In that year Congress created the Council of National Defense, a mixed governmental and business

commission. During the war the council supervised a network of agencies that controlled every aspect of the American economy. Under Bernard Baruch the War Industries Board supervised the allocation of raw materials and set production goals. The Food Administration controlled prices, and a War Trade Board regulated imports and exports. Congress established at least half a dozen other agencies, all of which reported to the President.

Wilson used his presidential war powers to the limit in waging a battle against dissent. Most Americans supported the war. But sizable minorities did not. German Americans opposed United States support of the Allies for ethnic reasons. Socialists and radicals condemned the war as a "capitalist" venture for profit. During the first months of American participation German Americans suffered the abuse (and sometimes the assaults) of their fellow citizens. But when it became certain that Germany would have to yield to the Allies, radicalism came to be regarded as the prime threat to Wilsonian peace. In November 1917 communist forces in Russia overthrew the new constitutional government and withdrew their nation from the war. With the new "red scare" radical dissenters replaced German Americans as the nation's principal outcasts.

A government propaganda machine, the Committee on Public Information, was set up to publicize war efforts and to censor information or newspaper opinions unfavorable to the Allied cause. Congress enlarged the war against dissent by passing strict laws against treason. By the time the war ended, almost all Americans had been enlisted in the crusade.

Wilson the Peacemaker   At the war's end Wilson turned his energies and ideals to the formidable task of obtaining a fair and lasting peace. The President had outlined his proposals for peace—the Fourteen Points—even before the armistice. The Germans surrendered in November 1918, hoping that Wilson's peace program would guide Allied policy.

The American President called for a new world order. It would help to eliminate worldwide political and economic rivalries. He sought to substitute international cooperation for the unstable and dangerous balance-of-power politics that had led the world to war. Wilson also proposed national self-determination for ethnic groups in the decaying European empires. Finally, Wilson called for a "general association of nations," a league of all the countries in the world. The league's members would cooperate actively to avoid future international conflicts.

In January 1919 Allied negotiators met at Versailles, a city outside of Paris. The peace conference was attended by Wilson and other Allied heads of state: Premier Georges Clemenceau of France, Prime Minister David Lloyd George of Britain, and Premier Vittorio Orlando of Italy. Clemenceau's overconcern with French security, though understandable, gave Wilson the most trouble. Lloyd George sought a middle ground, though he always kept the interests of the British Empire in mind. Orlando, junior partner of the Allies, did not participate in most of the "summit" deliberations.

The treaty that emerged from Versailles was a compromise. But it was surprisingly in tune with Wilsonian goals. The President was defeated overwhelmingly on several issues. Despite Wilson's call for "open convenants of peace, openly arrived at," most of the treaty negotiations took shape in secret conferences among the Allied "Big Three"—Wilson, Lloyd George, and Clemenceau. Wilson compromised on national self-determination, allowing European leaders to redraw the political map of Europe. He agreed that Germany and its allies should pay staggering amounts in war damages. Allied powers greedily divided up Germany's colonies, ignoring the wishes of the inhabitants of those areas. Nonetheless, most of the Fourteen Points were incorporated into the treaty. Perhaps most important for Wilson, the Treaty of Versailles called for the establishment of an international peacekeeping body, the League of Nations.

But dedication to ideals does not ensure success in politics, as Wilson quickly found out. Wilson brought the treaty and the League home to debate and disaster (see page 614). A small group of isolationists in the Senate were opposed to any American participation in an international league. They feared that a headlong rush into internationalism would curb essential American rights and hurt American interests. Other American senators wanted to be convinced. If Wilson had confided in these senators and attempted to work out a compromise with them, the treaty and the League of Nations might have been saved.

Wilson, however, saw all opposition as betrayal of the highest trust, the cause of world peace. He cracked the whip of party discipline over Democratic senators and went on the campaign trail seeking public support for his treaty. The trip ended tragically when Wilson suffered a stroke, which left him partially paralyzed. During 1919 the Senate rejected several versions of the treaty.

Wilson began looking ahead to the presidential election of 1920, which he hoped to turn into a "solemn referendum" on the League. The election became instead a referendum on Wilsonian politics. Republican Warren G. Harding, who promised Americans a retreat from internationalism and a return to "normalcy," won a landslide victory. All hope for American participation in the League of Nations vanished.

1. Why did Aguinaldo and the Filipino insurgents go to war against the American occupation troops?
2. Why didn't the insurrection come to an end when Aguinaldo swore an oath of allegiance to the United States? When did it end?
3. Explain the connection between mounting interest in overseas expansion and industrial growth in the United States.
4. How did Captain Mahan, Kipling, and the Social Darwinists justify the need for expansion?
5. Why did the United States support Cuban independence? What events led to the Spanish-American War.
6. Why did American businessmen expect to benefit from the Open Door Policy? Was the policy harmful or beneficial to the Chinese?
7. Describe some of the efforts of the United States to police the Caribbean during Roosevelt's administration. How did the Roosevelt Corollary to the Monroe Doctrine justify such intervention?
8. In what way did Woodrow Wilson claim he was going to change American foreign policy? Was the Mexican intervention consistent with this claim? Explain.
9. Could the United States have avoided intervening in World War I? In what ways was the American contribution to the Allied victory a major one?
10. What was the purpose of Wilson's Fourteen Points? Was the Treaty of Versailles in line with them? Why or why not? Why did the United States reject the treaty?

Beyond the Text

1. Since newspapers played such a significant role in bringing on the Spanish-American War, discuss the questions: Is public opinion too easily swayed to serve as a guide for setting national policy? Should newspapers be limited in the kinds of news they report?
2. Compare Roosevelt's actions in taking the Canal Zone with those of President Nixon in sending troops into Cambodia without congressional consent. Should presidential power in foreign affairs be curbed?
3. Who was responsible for the defeat of the League of Nations—Wilson or the Senate?

Bibliography

Nonfiction

Bailey, Thomas A., *Woodrow Wilson and the Great Betrayal.**

———, Woodrow Wilson and the Lost Peace.*

Beale, Howard K., *Theodore Roosevelt and the Rise of America to World Power.**

Beisner, Robert L., *Twelve Against Empire: The Anti-Imperialists, 1898–1900.**

Friedel, Frank, *The Splendid Little War.*

LaFeber, Walter, *The New Empire: An Interpretation of American Expansion, 1860–1898.**

Levin, N. Gordon, Jr., *Woodrow Wilson and World Politics.**

Link, Arthur S., *Wilson the Diplomatist.**

May, Ernest R., *Imperial Democracy.**

———, *The World War & American Isolation, 1914–1917.**

Mayer, Arno J., *Politics & Diplomacy of Peacemaking.**

Morgan, Howard W., *America's Road to Empire.**

Murray, Robert K., *The Red Scare.**

Williams, William A., *The Tragedy of American Diplomacy.**

Wolff, Leon, *Little Brown Brother.*

Fiction

Castor, Henry, *The Year of the Spaniard.*

Cummings, E. E., *The Enormous Room.**

Dos Passos, John, *Three Soldiers.**

*a paperback book

31

LINDBERGH'S FLIGHT

THE CAPTAIN was a little man, dapper and very French. But he sought a big prize: $25,000 for the first man to fly an airplane from New York to Paris. His name might sound somewhat strange—even funny—to American ears: René Fonck. But his reputation was incredible. He had been the youngest French air ace in the Great War of 1914 (as World War I was known until World War II). Without being seriously injured himself, he had shot down at least seventy-five German planes. In a war that had turned the new aviators into overnight heroes, Fonck's reputation for skill, courage, and "dash" was probably greater than that of any other pilot. Now, in the summer of 1926, he was preparing for a flight that could make him an even greater hero, both in France and in the United States.

Compared with any of the planes Fonck had flown during the war, his new silver-colored craft was huge. Like most of the other large aircraft of the day, it had three engines and two wings—a biplane, it was called. Its large cabin was equipped for a crew of four: a pilot, a copilot, a mechanic, and a radio operator. The problem that Fonck faced was simply getting the plane off the ground with enough fuel to fly the 3,600 miles to Paris. All summer he tested the plane in New York, gradually increasing the gasoline load for each test.

At daybreak on September 21 Fonck's plane was pulled onto the east-west runway at Roosevelt Field, a small airport on Long Island. The wind was blowing from the west, as it almost always does after

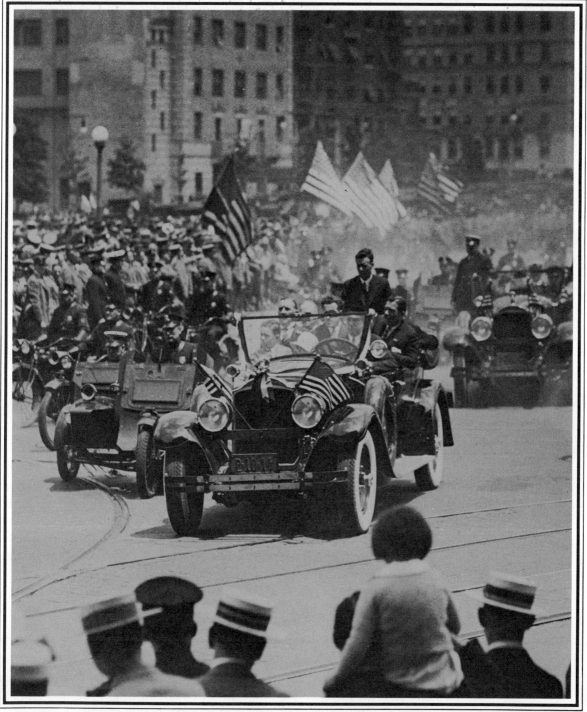

The American public was intoxicated by Lindbergh's adventure, a solo flight across the Atlantic. He was honored as a national hero in cities throughout the country—here in a parade in New York City.

dawn on Long Island. So Fonck would take off from east to west. To get the plane off the ground he and his crew would have to attain a speed of eighty miles an hour. One by one, the engines were turned up to their maximum power. After blocks were pulled away from the wheels, the plane began to move. It lurched slightly, having over 2,000 gallons of gasoline aboard, and chased its own awkward shadow down the dirt runway.

When the plane passed the halfway point on the small airstrip, it did not have the speed needed for takeoff. The small crowd of onlookers waited for Fonck to cut power. But something had gone wrong, either with the pilot or with his controls. The plane simply roared on. The runway ended. The plane took a sharp, short drop into a gully, then exploded and burst into flames. Somehow Fonck got out, and so did his navigator. But the copilot and the radio operator burned to death.

Despite the crash, the man who had offered the $25,000 prize—Raymond Orteig, a Frenchman who managed two hotels in New York—announced that his offer still stood. For a while Fonck's crash made headlines and kept alive the idea of a New York–Paris flight. Late in February 1927 others began to announce that they would make the flight. It was soon obvious that a real contest was developing. It would not be merely a battle between one airplane and the ocean but a race among several aviators and their planes. The stage was set for what the public began to sense would be the greatest thrill of the decade.

By the end of March 1927 there were four serious contenders. One was the *America*, a plane piloted by Admiral Richard E. Byrd, who had gained fame as the first man to fly to the North Pole. Byrd was backed with over $100,000 from a wealthy New York merchant. His three-engined plane, with a wingspread of over seventy feet, was huge by the standards of the day. It seemed to have the best chance.

A second entry was another trimotored craft, the *American Legion,* named after and supported by the veterans' organization. It too was backed with $100,000. Unlike Fonck's plane and Byrd's *America* the *American Legion* carried only two men. A third entry was a plane known as the *Columbia,* a single-winged, single-engined craft. The *Columbia* would soon set the world endurance record by flying for over fifty hours. Finally, there was a French entry, a single-engined biplane called the *White Bird.* Its pilot and copilot, a pair of French aces from the Great War, planned to make the flight in reverse—from Paris to

New York. The *White Bird* was said to have the most powerful gasoline engine ever put into an airplane.

By mid-April the weather had warmed up enough to make flight over the North Atlantic seem possible. On April 16 Commander Byrd took his *America* up from a New Jersey airport for its first test flight. Byrd and three crewmen tested the plane for a few hours and then brought it down for its first landing. The heavy landing gear touched ground smoothly. But almost at once there was a sound of splintering wood and wrenched metal. The *America* flipped over and skidded to a halt on its back. All four men managed to escape. Byrd had a broken wrist, and two of the other crewmen were badly hurt. They would not be able to fly again for weeks.

Ten days later the *American Legion* was in Langley Field, Virginia, undergoing its last test flight. The plane had flown well in earlier attempts. But both its designers and pilot knew it was too heavy. To find out whether the plane could make the Paris flight, the pilot and copilot decided to fly it from Virginia to New York with a full load of gasoline. The takeoff was slower than usual. For a moment it seemed as if the plane would not clear a line of trees at the end of the runway. To avoid them, the pilot banked to the right a few degrees. The slight turn was too much. It upset the delicate balance of the plane. The *American Legion* slid downward into a wet marsh and turned over. The pilot and copilot were trapped inside the cabin that filled first with gasoline fumes and then with water. By the time rescuers came wading through the marsh, the two men were dead.

Four men had been killed and three others hurt, and the race over the Atlantic had not yet begun. On both sides of the ocean, in America and in France, newspapers brought public excitement to a high pitch. Surely one of the planes would make it, sooner or later. But no one knew what might happen next or who might be injured or killed. The race to Paris had the competitive excitement of a World Series or a heavyweight championship fight. And it had the danger and drama of war. In the United States the race was almost as important as the war of 1898, the sinking of the *Lusitania,* or the declaration of war in 1917. And in France the excitement was heightened by the memory of Fonck's crash. Moreover, two other young ace pilots from the Great War, Charles Nungesser and Francis Coli, held great promise. Both had been wounded a total of twenty-six times in air combat. Between them they had won almost every medal that their government could award.

At dawn on May 8 Nungesser and Coli took off for New York from Le Bourget airport near Paris. A great crowd gathered to watch the two heroes and their *White Bird*. Nungesser got the wheels off but too soon. The *White Bird* dropped back down on the runway with a thud. Finally, it gathered speed and left the ground almost two-thirds of a mile down the long strip.

The next morning American newspapers reported that the plane had been sighted over Newfoundland. Paris celebrated with an excitement that almost matched that on the day of the armistice. Nungesser and Coli had dropped their landing gear over the ocean to save weight and lessen wind resistance. New Yorkers watched the harbor where the Frenchmen hoped to land and float until they could be reached by waiting boats. But the *White Bird* was never seen again. In France the celebrations quickly came to a shocked end.

The death toll of the New York–Paris race had reached six in less than a year. The world's most experienced pilots—backed by large sums of money, flying the best airplanes that modern technology could provide, with the most powerful motors ever developed—had all failed.

The man who was finally going to win the race to Paris had been reading every newspaper report he could find on all the airplane tests, takeoffs, and crashes. When Fonck's plane burned, Charles Lindbergh was flying air mail between Chicago and St. Louis. When Byrd and the others announced that they would enter the competition, Lindbergh was in San Diego supervising the construction of a new plane for himself. When Nungesser and Coli took off from Paris, he was waiting in San Diego for the weather to clear over the Rocky Mountains and the Great Plains, so he could fly east to St. Louis. From there he would go on to New York to make his attempt.

Lindbergh had only $2,000 of his own money, carefully kept for him by his mother in Detroit. He was only twenty-five years old. He looked even younger, so that almost everyone called him a boy. Worst of all, he decided on what struck everyone as a suicidal idea: to make the flight in a single-engine plane with only himself in the cockpit. He had been able to persuade some St. Louis businessmen to back him to the extent of $15,000. But this was a small sum compared to the support that Byrd's group and the *American Legion* had. Still, late in the summer of 1926, just before Fonck's crash, Lindbergh had come to an almost religious conviction that he could make the Paris flight.

At first Lindbergh tried to negotiate with several large aircraft companies. He was turned down. No one wanted to risk a company's reputation on an insane stunt like flying from New York to Paris alone. Then Lindbergh sent a plain but daring telegram to Ryan Airlines, a small, little known factory in California:

RYAN   AIRLINES,   INC.   FEB.   3,   1927

SAN   DIEGO,   CALIFORNIA

CAN   YOU   CONSTRUCT   WHIRLWIND   ENGINE   PLANE

CAPABLE   FLYING   NONSTOP   BETWEEN   NEW   YORK   AND

PARIS.   IF   SO   PLEASE   STATE   COST   AND   DELIVERY   DATE.

Surprisingly, the answer came quickly. The small company could build the plane, and it could do so for the amount of money Lindbergh had at his disposal. But it would take three months, the telegram said. Lindbergh answered:

RYAN   AIRLINES   FEB.   5,   1927

SAN   DIEGO,   CALIFORNIA

COMPETITION   MAKES   TIME   ESSENTIAL.   CAN   YOU

CONSTRUCT   PLANE   IN   LESS   THAN   THREE   MONTHS.

PLEASE   WIRE   GENERAL   SPECIFICATIONS.

This drawing shows the plane Ryan airlines built for Lindbergh. Although the goal of the design was simplicity, sacrificing safety to the need for carrying as much gasoline as possible, the plane was quite a sophisticated piece of machinery.

Again the company answered quickly, making as much of a guess as a calculation. It could build a plane capable of carrying 380 gallons of gasoline at a cruising speed of 100 miles per hour, with an engine rated at only 200 horsepower. (This was less than half the power of the big engine that had taken the *White Bird* out over the Atlantic. It was much less than the power supplied by the three engines of Byrd's great *America* as well.) Most important, the company promised to have the plane ready in time.

By the last week in February Lindbergh was in San Diego working out the details on his plane. Neither Lindbergh nor the engineer who designed the plane knew how far it was to Paris. They drove to the San Diego public library to measure off the distance on a globe with a piece of string. Lindbergh remembered it this way:

> "It's 3,600 miles." The bit of white grocery string under my fingers stretches taut along the coast of North America, bends down over a faded blue ocean, and strikes the land mass of Europe. It isn't a very scientific way of finding the exact distance between two points on the earth's surface, but the answer is accurate enough for our first calculations. The designer was making quick calculations in pencil on the back of an envelope. "Maybe we'd better put in 400 gallons of gasoline instead of 380," he concludes.

Lindbergh's project was simple, almost amateurish: quick telegrams, bits of string stretched across a public-library globe, figures on the back of an envelope, and "maybe" calculations. But with no more detailed or expert plans, he decided to go ahead.

The mechanics and carpenters at Ryan started work at once on the plane that Lindbergh would call the *Spirit of St. Louis*. They built it almost literally around the pilot. The narrow, simple cockpit was just large enough to hold Lindbergh's tall, skinny body (and then only if the overhead ribs were hollowed out a little to make room for his head). In the end the plane would be only about three feet taller than Lindbergh himself. Moreover, it would have a smaller engine that any of the other planes in the race. But this was the secret of Lindbergh's plane—simplicity. He would build the smallest, simplest plane possible, a machine designed with only one purpose: to carry enough gasoline for the trip. Everything else—comfort, safety, complicated navigating equipment—would be sacrificed to save weight, weight that could be turned into gallons of gasoline.

On April 26, the day the two pilots of the *American Legion* were killed in Virginia, the *Spirit of St. Louis* was finished. Two days later Lindbergh was ready for his first test flight. He shoved himself into his

(continued on page 625)

The Maturing of American Culture

Generations of foreigners, while admiring American
achievements in other fields, criticized the nation's artistic
backwardness. Even Americans who patronized the arts—
like this eager visitor in Frank Waller's 1881 painting of
the Metropolitan Museum—were said to appreciate money
more than merit. Such views were exaggerated, yet held some
truth. Until the late nineteenth century, a distinctive American
culture was slow to emerge. But the situation changed in the
next few decades. By the 1920s foreigners were admiring
American literature, painting, architecture, and music.
The United States had found a cultural voice of its own.

[For further information on the foreign observers
quoted in this essay, see ''Notes on Sources.'']

PICTORIAL ESSAY 7

PE 7–2 / American art is still in a stage of evolution; the painters of today are the precursors of those who shall adorn the Golden Age which is to come. Though there have been, and are, individual artists of distinguished merit and ability, art itself is not yet fully developed nor understood. The nation has had hitherto neither time, opportunity, nor inclination to interest itself intelligently in the fine arts.

[COUNT VAY DE VAYA UND LUSKOD, 1908]

Behold! Mark Twain had curled himself up in the big armchair, and I was smoking reverently, as befits one in the presence of his superior. The thing that struck me first was that he was an elderly man; yet, after a minute's thought, I perceived that it was otherwise, and in five minutes, the eyes looking at me, I saw that the gray hair was an accident of the most trivial. He was quite young. I was shaking his hand, I was smoking his cigar, and I was hearing him talk—this man I had learned to love and admire fourteen thousand miles away.

[RUDYARD KIPLING, 1889]

Mark Twain in 1907. By this time the writer had gained world-wide acclaim for such books as *The Adventures of Tom Sawyer* (1876), *Life on the Mississippi* (1883), and *The Adventures of Huckleberry Finn* (1885).

American paintings are no longer strange to Europe. In the art division of the last Paris Exposition, Americans took their share of the honors, and they are highly appreciated at most of the Berlin and Munich picture shows. Sargent and Whistler are the best known. Sargent, as the painter of elegant ladies, prosperous men, and interesting children, has undoubtedly the surest and most refined gift with his brush of any son of the New World. Whistler is doubtless the greater, the real sovereign. He fathoms each human riddle, and expresses it intangibly, mysteriously. Everything is mood and suggestion, the dull and heavy is lightened, the whole is rendered in rich twilight zones.

[HUGO MUNSTERBERG, 1904]

The Last of Old Westminster, painted by James Abbott McNeill Whistler in 1862. The scene is London, where Whistler lived for much of his life. This work was followed by a number of outstanding portraits, including the famous one of his mother (which he actually titled *An Arrangement in Grey and Black*).

Miss Cassatt is a true phenomenon. In more than one of her canvases she is on the verge of becoming a notable artist with unparalleled natural feeling, penetrating observation, and a welcome subjection before the model which is the accomplishment of peerless artists.

[ALBERT WOLFF, 1881]

The Bath, by Mary Cassatt, dates from about 1891. The artist—who lived most of her adult life in Paris—liked to paint mothers and children. She communicated feelings of warmth and tenderness without sentimentality.

The taste for plastic art [in the United States] has slowly worked upward. Recent movements have left many beautiful examples of sculpture. Cities are jealously watchful now that only real works of art shall be erected, and that monuments which are to be seen by millions of people shall be really characteristic examples of good art. More than anything else, sculpture has at length come into a closer sympathy with architecture than perhaps it has in any other country. Such a work as Saint-Gaudens' Shaw Memorial in Boston is among the most beautiful examples of modern sculpture. Vigorous and mature is the American, in plastic art as well as in poetry.

[HUGO MUNSTERBERG, 1904]

This work, showing Augustus Saint-Gaudens in his studio, was painted by Kenyon Cox in 1908. The sculptor was known for his public statuary, including Lincoln, in Lincoln Park, Chicago; General Sherman, near Central Park in New York City; and the Shaw Memorial on Boston Common.

Mr. and Mrs. Isaac Newton Phelps Stokes, portrayed by John Singer Sargent in 1897. These prominent New Yorkers, though pictured in informal dress, epitomize the wealth and refinement typical of Sargent's subjects.

PE 7–4 / People are inclined to smile at me when I suggest
that you in America are at the commencement of a
period of fine and vigorous art. The signs, they say, are
all the other way. Of course you ought to know best.
All the same, I stick to my opinion with British
obstinacy, and believe I shall see it justified.

[JOHN GALSWORTHY, 1919]

*Willa Cather builds her imagined world almost as
solidly as our five senses build the universe around
us. She has within herself a sensitivity that constantly presents her with a body of material which
would overwhelm most of us. She has also a quality
of mountain-pony sturdiness that makes her push on
unfatigued under her load and give an accurate account
of every part of it.*

[REBECCA WEST, 1927]

On the threshold of her career, in 1902, Willa
Cather had yet to gain a name for herself.
She became noted for such novels as *O
Pioneers!* (1913) and *My Antonia* (1918).

*Sloan's canvas of girls
under the elevated has
more of New York in
it than anything else
I know.*

[DIEGO RIVERA, 1942]

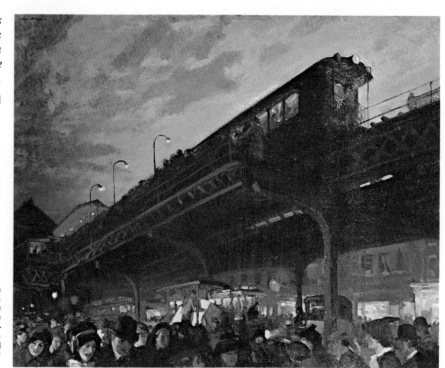

Six O'Clock was painted by John
Sloan in 1912. He was one of a
group called The Eight. They were
known more familiarly as the
Ashcan School because they depicted scenes of everyday city life
rather than the more formal and
traditional subjects favored by
academic artists.

Characteristic of Frank Lloyd Wright's so-called "prairie houses" is this home in River Forest, Illinois. It was built in 1908. Wright's later works, noted for their daring innovation, included the Imperial Hotel in Tokyo, the Johnson administration building in Racine, Wisconsin, and the Guggenheim Museum in New York City.

Most of Wright's country houses, fitted into the oceanlike endlessness of the prairie, are very low, joined with, indeed pressed down toward, the earth. As a consequence the interior rooms spread out horizontally from one another. Therefore these houses do not seem like some grotesque thing which has grown out of the earth; they appear native to the soil and fitted to it, like the farmhouse.

[LUDWIG HILBERSHEIMER AND UDO RUKSER, 1920]

The chances are that Robert Frost will become a national figure, a sage, a Yankee sage. He has personal thought; he has wisdom; he has a basic conception from which he can speak. He likes the nation, every nation, and he dislikes the state, every state. He is a puritan, but he goes by the dictates of the heart.

[PADRAIC COLUM, 1936]

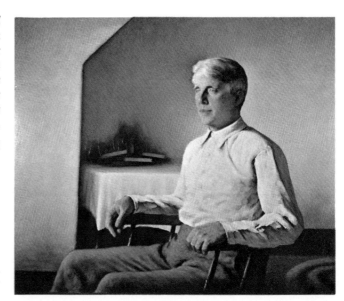

Robert Frost, as seen by artist James Chapin in 1929. The New England writer had by this time published some of his best-known poems, among them "Mending Wall," "Birches," and "Stopping by Woods on a Snowy Evening."

The mission which this land has, like all others, is to discover it's own being, to fulfill it's task of representing itself. And if one puts his ear to the ground, then one hears millions of forces at work to forge and shape this individual being.

[ANTON ERKELENZ, 1927]

Eugene O'Neill is one of the really great figures in modern drama. O'Neill is an example of what I mean when I say America is producing, and will produce in ever greater quantities, an art I feel is indigenous; it belongs to the American soil. No European dramatist could possibly have written those plays. The drama, under him, has found a new type of artistic expression.

[GERHART HAUPTMANN, 1932]

Eugene O'Neill in 1921, at the start of his career. His greatest plays came later: *Desire Under the Elms* (1924), *Mourning Becomes Electra* (1931), and *The Iceman Cometh* (1946). In 1936 he became the first American playwright to win the Nobel prize.

A scene from *Beyond the Horizon*, by O'Neill. Produced in 1920, it was the first full-length play by the dramatist to be acted.

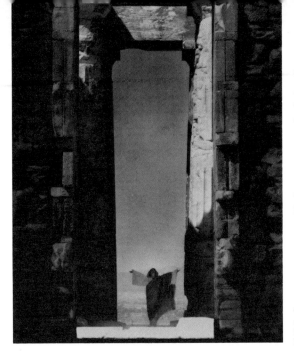

What she gives us is a sort of sculpture in transition. Imagine a dozen statues expressive, say, of the cardinal phases of despair—the poses and gestures and facial expressions of the moment in which each of these phases reaches its maximum of intensity. Then imagine some hundreds of statues that represent, in faultless beauty, every one of the moments of slow transition between these cardinal phases, and you get the art of Isadora Duncan.

[ERNEST NEWMAN, 1921]

The great American photographer Edward Steichen captured some of the magic of dancer Isadora Duncan in this 1921 photo, taken at the Parthenon. Her flowing Grecian costumes and striking interpretive power transformed modern dance.

Gershwin's Rhapsody [in Blue] is by far the most interesting thing of its kind I have yet met with. It really has ideas and they work themselves out in a way that interests the musical hearer. Perhaps it is better not to prophesy. What is at present certain is that Gershwin has written something for a jazz orchestra that is really music, not a mechanical box of tricks.

[ERNEST NEWMAN, 1924]

Mexican artist David Siqueiros painted this *Portrait in a Concert Hall* (George Gershwin) in 1936. The composer, who died the following year, had followed his *Rhapsody in Blue* (1923) with *An American in Paris* (1928) and *Porgy and Bess* (1935).

The young Ernest Hemingway was painted by Henry Strater in 1922. His best work, yet to come, included *The Sun Also Rises* (1926), *A Farewell to Arms* (1929), and *For Whom the Bell Tolls* (1940).

The outstanding achievement of American literature is the swiftness with which it strode from provincialism to half-acknowledged universality. Before 1800 there is nothing, save in the field of politics, which could command, or even deserve to command, a European audience; by 1900 it is true to say that there were few forms of creative effort in which Americans had not done work of the highest quality. America had moved to the very front of the cosmic stage. Henceforth it might be disliked; it could not be neglected.

[HAROLD LASKI, 1948]

It is hardly an exaggeration to say that Ernest Hemingway, more than any of his American colleagues, makes us feel we are confronted by a still young nation which seeks and finds its exact form of expression.

[NOBEL PRIZE CITATION, 1954]

Lunched with Sinclair Lewis. He is full of imagination. He tells me he wrote four or five novels before he wrote Main Street, *but they were not successes. I asked him why that had not discouraged him. He laughed, he said it was no use being discouraged, that writing novels was all he could do, he might starve at it, but he was incapable of any other form of work. (Truly an artist!)*

[CLARE SHERIDAN, 1921]

Sinclair Lewis, photographed with his wife in 1916. A year after his meeting with Clare Sheridan, he published one of his best-known novels, *Babbitt*. In 1930 he became the first American to win the Nobel prize for literature.

The cockpit of the Spirit of St. Louis *was a model of stripped-down efficiency. The wicker seat was probably uncomfortable but lightweight. Only side windows were thought necessary since there was not much to see in flight. Leg room was limited by the controls.*

seat in the cockpit. He could touch both sides of the fuselage with his elbows. To the front the cockpit was blind. Shiny metal sloped all the way up from the engine to the top of the wing. There were only two side windows and a glassed-in skylight overhead. For takeoffs and landings he had to lean out one of the side windows. But the plane was designed for only one important takeoff and landing. The rest of the time, over the Atlantic, there would be nothing to see but ocean, clouds, sun, and stars.

Directly in front of Lindbergh's face was a small cluster of instruments—an air-speed indicator, a turn-and-bank indicator, a fuel-flow meter, a compass, and one or two others. The plane carried a pitifully small survival kit containing a rubber raft, a flashlight, a canteen of water, some matches, and string. Surrounding the cockpit were nothing but gasoline tanks. One tank rested in the nose between the pilot and the engine. Another lay behind the cockpit in the fuselage. And there were more tanks in the wings overhead. There was no radio, no heater to provide warmth at freezing altitudes, no sextant for navigational sightings, not even a parachute. The *Spirit of St. Louis* was built to carry only gasoline—over a ton of it, as it turned out, weighing more than the plane and the pilot put together.

To Lindbergh, as he walked onto the sunny runway in San Diego, the *Spirit of St. Louis* was a thing of beauty and awe:

> What a beautiful machine it is, resting there on the field in front of the hangar, trim and slender, gleaming in its silver coat! All our ideas, all our calculations, all our hopes, lie there before me, waiting to undergo the acid test of flight. For me, it seems to contain the whole future of aviation.
> "Off! Throttle closed."
> I'm in the cockpit. The chief mechanic turns the propeller over several times. "Contact!"
> He swings his body away from the blade as he pulls it through. The engine catches, every cylinder hitting. This is different from any other cockpit I've been in before. The big fuel tank in front of me seems doubly large, now that I'm actually to fly behind it.
> I signal the chocks [blocks in front of the wheels of the plane] away. The *Spirit of St. Louis* rolls lightly over the baked-mud surface of the field.

The *Spirit of St. Louis* moved very quickly. Its tanks were almost empty for this first test flight.

> The tires are off the ground before they roll a hundred yards. The plane climbs quickly, even though I hold its nose down. There's a huge reserve of power. I spiral cautiously upward. I straighten out and check my instruments. I circle over the factory, watching little figures run outdoors to see the machine built actually flying overhead. I rock my wings and head across the bay.

During the next week Lindbergh tested the *Spirit of St. Louis* for speed, control, and, most important, takeoff under load. More and more gasoline was filtered by hand into the tanks for each run. With a load of slightly over 300 gallons the plane took off easily. But continued landings with large loads were dangerous. Lindbergh decided to stop the tests.

The *Spirit of St. Louis* had needed a little more than 1,000 feet of runway to take off with 300 gallons. From this and other data, the Ryan designers made a theoretical calculation that, fully loaded with 400 gallons, the plane would need 2,500 feet of hard runway. Rather than tempt fate, as the crew of the *American Legion* had done by testing with a full load, Lindbergh decided to trust the plane and the designer's arithmetic. He was ready. And he knew Byrd's *America* had been repaired and was undergoing final tests. The *Columbia* too was ready. Both planes were poised on Long Island. Time counted more than tests.

But time seemed to work against Lindbergh. A big storm blanketed the western United States, moving with painful slowness eastward. Lindbergh had to wait several days until the rain and clouds had moved east. On the evening of May 10 he began the first leg of his trip, from San Diego to St. Louis. He flew the 1,500 miles in record time. It was the longest nonstop solo flight ever made. Then, after a night's sleep, he headed for New York.

Lindbergh arrived on Long Island on May 12. He had set another record for the fastest transcontinental flight in history. The crews of Byrd's *America* and the *Columbia* came over to shake his hand and wish him luck. There was a crowd. Newspaper photographers and reporters pushed and shoved their way to Lindbergh, shouting for pictures and answers to their questions. A crowd of people climbed to the roof of a small building next to the hangar where Lindbergh parked the plane. Their weight caused a wall to collapse. Something new and strange was happening to Lindbergh. The newspapers and the public were making him into a hero, almost a myth.

Even without Lindbergh, the New York–Paris contest had all the elements of an exciting publicity event: death, drama, and competition. But Lindbergh added new elements. He was going alone, so he could become an object of hero worship in ways that the crews of the other planes could not. Moreover, he was young, and along with his youth went other personality traits that soon endeared him to the newspapers. He was tall, thin, blue-eyed, handsome in a boyish way. Above all, he was modest, shy, and simple.

All these traits combined presented a picture of an innocent young man ready to dare the impossible, alone. Lindbergh was the honest, plain-spoken, cowboy-like young man from the West. He was a modern David challenging the Eastern Goliaths, with their money, their experience, their financial backers, and their head start. In short, he was an underdog. The *Spirit of St. Louis,* too, was simple and seemingly innocent compared with the other planes in the race. It was a sentimental favorite as well.

Lindbergh could not leave his hotel room without being mobbed by people anxious to touch him "just for luck." And the newspapers played his story for all it was worth. They nicknamed him "Lucky," "The Flyin' Fool," or just "Lindy." (He had always been "Slim" to his friends.) All the hero worship that the Americans of the 1920s usually reserved for baseball players like Babe Ruth or movie stars like Rudolf Valentino was now showered on the twenty-five-year-old air-mail pilot. The worship was made more serious by the fact that "The

What attracted the public to Lindbergh, besides his boyish good looks, was the power he had of symbolizing what was best about the country: not just daring, but moral courage and independence of spirit.

Flyin' Fool" was doing something real and dangerous, not merely hitting baseballs or posing for motion picture cameras.

In most ways this public personality created for the new celebrity was only a myth. Lindbergh may not have had Byrd's $100,000, but he had finally obtained solid backing from St. Louis businessmen. And even if the *Spirit of St. Louis* was smaller than the other planes, it was still a sophisticated piece of machinery, created by advanced technology. It was a little silly for newspapers to write of Lindbergh and his plane as though they were a cowboy hero and his beloved horse.

Nor was Lindbergh's background as simple as the newspapers tried to make it appear. He came from a well-to-do and educated family. His father had been a congressman. Lindbergh had been to college for a time and held a commission as captain in the Army Air Service Reserve and the Missouri National Guard. He had been chief pilot for the air-mail company in St. Louis. He was, despite his youth, an experienced professional pilot, flying an advanced aircraft.

But there was just enough truth to the mythical picture to make it stick. It probably infected Lindbergh somewhat, too. He had always been a bit wild, even though he was shy. Cars, motorcycles, ice boats— anything that involved speed—had always fascinated him. When he was just twenty he dropped out of college to learn to fly. This had started him on a short and dangerous career. He bought his first craft, a war-surplus plane, even before he had made a solo flight, and he almost crashed it on his first takeoff.

Lindbergh had barnstormed all over the West, crashing regularly and surviving only with luck. He had walked on airplane wings while in flight and done dangerous parachute jumps for one aerial circus after another. Four times he had been forced to parachute for his life from planes that had collided, run out of gas, or gotten lost at night.

All this—combined with Lindbergh's shyness and boyishness, his faith in himself and his plane—did smack of something religious and mythical. So the hero worship that began almost as soon as he reached Long Island was probably inevitable. At times the publicity and the public attention irritated Lindbergh. Reporters went so far as to burst into his hotel room without knocking to discover what kind of pajamas, if any, he wore to bed. But the irritation could not overcome the excitement. Lindbergh was becoming, even before takeoff, a national hero.

The *Columbia* was scheduled to take off on May 13, the day after Lindbergh reached Long Island. But the weather was closed in over New York and the North Atlantic. The same storm that had delayed

Lindbergh in San Diego was making its slow progress north and east. So the *Columbia* had to wait. Lindbergh was able to test and tune his engine, to check and recheck every instrument. A noisy crowd that sometimes numbered over a thousand gathered around the hangar to watch him. By May 16 he was ready. As far as he could tell, Byrd was ready too. The weather was suitable for all three planes to take off. In the *Columbia* organization there was a legal quarrel over who would be the pilot. One of the men who had trained for the flight had secured a court order preventing the plane from taking off without him. But the court order could be lifted at any minute. So there seemed to be a real chance that two or possibly even three planes would take off from Roosevelt Field on the same morning.

The storm persisted for three more days. Then, on the evening of May 19, the forecast called for clearing skies. Though it was not clearing rapidly, Lindbergh made his decision. He would fly the next morning. This would mean taking off into a rainy sky from a muddy field. He bought five sandwiches "to go." A few hours later the *Spirit of St. Louis* was towed to the west end of the Roosevelt Field runway. Lindbergh had decided to take off at night instead, when the wind was east to west. This was the opposite direction from the one Fonck had taken the preceding autumn. Not far behind the *Spirit of St. Louis* was the scorched area, marked by a bent propeller stuck into the ground as a tribute, where Fonck's plane had burned.

Slowly, carefully, mechanics strained five-gallon cans of gasoline into Lindbergh's plane. The tanks were oversized. They had a capacity of 450 gallons instead of the 400 that the designers had planned earlier. Lindbergh decided to fill them to the brim, even though it meant a dangerous overload for the takeoff. In the hangers of the *America* and the *Columbia,* there was only darkness and silence. No one else was going to fly.

As he looked over the situation, Lindbergh wondered whether he should go. He was overloaded with gasoline. The field was muddy. The wheels of the *Spirit of St. Louis* sank into the earth as though warning him that flight was out of the question. The wet weather affected the engine, which turned about thirty revolutions per minute slower than it should have at full power. Worst of all, the process of getting ready took so long that Lindbergh lost the night wind. By the time he was ready to fly, the breeze had shifted to his back, creating a tailwind of five or six miles per hour. This meant he would need even more speed on takeoff.

Lindbergh's only guidelines were the San Diego tests. They had demonstrated theoretically that he should be able to take off in 2,500 feet on a hard runway with no wind and with full engine power. At the

Moments before the takeoff, Lindbergh readied himself for the flight, while policemen guarded and his backers inspected the plane that would carry him to Paris.

end of the Roosevelt Field runway were a ditch, a tractor, some telephone wires and then a hill with a line of trees. He had to clear them all. He considered towing the *Spirit of St. Louis* through the misty rain and mud to the other end of the runway to get the help of the wind. He thought about postponing the flight altogether. But he decided to go.

Lindbergh looked around at the crowd that had gathered to watch. Nearby there were the mechanics, the engineers, several policemen, all looking into the dark cockpit at his pale face.

Their eyes are intently on mine. They've seen the planes crash before. I lean against the side of the cockpit and look ^head, through the idling blades of the propeller, over the runway's glistening surface. I study the telephone wires and the shallow pools of water through which my wheels must pass. A curtain of mist shuts off all trace of the horizon. Sitting in the cockpit, in seconds, minutes long, the conviction surges through me that the wheels *will* leave the ground, that the wings *will* rise above the wires, that it *is* time to start the flight.

I buckle my safety belt, pull goggles down over my eyes, turn to the men at the blocks, and nod. Frozen figures leap to action. I brace myself against the left side of the cockpit and ease the throttle wide open.

The *Spirit of St. Louis* feels more like an overloaded truck than an airplane. The tires rut through mud as though they really were on truck wheels. Even the breath of wind is pressing me down. The engine's snarl sounds inadequate and weak.

A hundred yards of runway passes. How long can the landing gear stand such strain? I keep my eyes fixed on the runway's edge. I *must* hold the plane straight. Pace quickens—the tail skid lifts off ground—I feel the load shifting from wheels to wings. The halfway mark is just ahead, and I have nothing like flying speed.

The halfway mark streaks past. Seconds now to decide. I pull the stick back firmly, and—*the wheels leave the ground!* The wheels touch again. I ease the stick forward. Almost flying speed and nearly 2,000 feet ahead. The entire plane trembles. Off again—right wing low—pull it up—ease back onto the runway. Another pool, water drumming on the fabric [covering the fuselage]. The next hop's longer. I could probably stay in the air, but I let the wheels touch once more.

The *Spirit of St. Louis* takes herself off next time. Full flying speed. The controls taut, alive, straining—and still a thousand feet to the telephone wires. If the engine can hold out one more minute. Five feet, twenty, forty. Wires flash by underneath. Twenty feet to spare!

Green grass below—a golf links. People looking up. A low, tree-covered hill ahead. The *Spirit of St. Louis* seems balanced on a pinpoint, as though the slightest movement of controls would cause it to topple over and fall. Five thousand pounds suspended from those little wings. Five thousand pounds on a blast of air.

Now I'm high enough to steal glances at the instrument board. The earth inductor compass needle leans steeply to the right. I bank cautiously northward until it rises to the center line—65 degrees—the compass heading for the first 100-mile segment of my great-circle route to France and Paris. It's 7:54 A.M. Eastern daylight time.

Back in San Diego, when Lindbergh and the designer of the *Spirit of St. Louis* had measured the distance of the flight across a library globe, the string had made a straight line between New York and Paris. But on a flat map, where the lines of latitude are straightened out into parallels, the route had to bend into an arc known as a great circle. The route Lindbergh would take curved north and east from New York, up the east coast over Cape Cod, then out over the ocean to Nova Scotia. Lindbergh planned to change his course every hundred miles (about one hour's flying time in the *Spirit of St. Louis*). He would head a few degrees farther south and east across the southern coast of Newfoundland and out over the North Atlantic.

As Lindbergh flew up the coast on this route, people waited on streets and housetops to watch him pass. Despite the fact that his navigating equipment was primitive, he managed to reach the Nova Scotia coast only a few miles off course. Every hour excited messages were telephoned to New York giving details of his progress. In the twelfth hour of his flight, Lindbergh passed over St. John's, New-foundland, then out over the ocean:

> I come upon it suddenly—the little city of St. John's, after skimming over the top of a granite summit. Farther ahead, the entrance to the harbor is a narrow gap with sides running up to the crest of a low coastal range. Twilight deepens as I plunge down into the valley. It takes only a moment, stick forward, engine throttled, to dive down over the wharves (men stop their after-supper chores to look upward) and out through the gap. North America and its islands are behind. Ireland is 2,000 miles ahead.

Throughout the flight Lindbergh faced the ever-present dangers of engine failure, storms, and the possibility of a structural weakness in the *Spirit of St. Louis* itself. But between Newfoundland and Ireland there were two additional dangers. The first was sleep. Lindbergh had not slept at all the night before his takeoff. During the next night and the day after, as he flew over the ocean, he fought back the terrible temptation to close his eyes for just a few seconds of rest. Despite its virtues, the *Spirit of St. Louis* was not a very stable plane. Lindbergh knew that if he relaxed his hold on it for more than a moment, he might crash. He had to hold his eyes open with his hands. Once he even had to hit himself full force in the face to keep awake.

The second danger was ice. This hazard hit Lindbergh suddenly after he had climbed over 10,000 feet, trying to clear a bank of clouds about 200 miles east of Newfoundland. He was suddenly aware of being cold himself. (He had left the glass out of the side windows of the *Spirit of St. Louis*, hoping that the fresh air and engine noise would keep him alert.) Cold? He jerked himself wide awake. If *he* was cold, what about his plane?

> Good Lord! There are things to be considered outside the cockpit! How could I forget! I jerk off a leather mitten and thrust my arm out the window. My palm is covered with stinging pinpricks. I pull the flashlight from my pocket and throw its beam on a strut. The entering edge is irregular and shiny! *Ice*!
> I've got to turn around, get back to clear air—quickly!

Lindbergh fought the urge to turn quickly. He knew that if he did, the ice on the wings might cause the plane to go out of control. Instead, he eased the *Spirit of St. Louis* around in a long, slow curve back toward Newfoundland.

> I throw my flashlight [beam] onto the wing strut. Ice is thicker! Steady the plane. Everything depends on the turn indicator working till I get outside the cloud. Just two or three more minutes.
> My eyes sense a change in the blackness of my cockpit. I look out through the window. How bright! What safety have I reached! I was in the thunderhead for ten minutes at most, but it's one of those incidents that can't be measured by minutes. Such periods stand out like islands in a sea of time.

After this brief but dangerous encounter with the night sky, Lindbergh picked his way cautiously toward Ireland and dawn. (Since he was flying west to east, into the sunrise, he was experiencing the shortest night of any man before him in history.) He sipped cautiously at the quart canteen of water. For the rest of the time he just flew his plane, waiting for moonrise, then sunrise, then land fall. He later recalled the twenty-eighth hour of his flight.

> I keep scanning the horizon through breaks between squalls. Is that a cloud on the northeastern horizon, or a strip of low fog—or—*can it possibly be land*? It looks like land, but I don't intend to be tricked by another mirage. I'm only sixteen hours out of Newfoundland. I allowed eighteen and one-half hours to strike the Irish coast.
>
> But my mind is clear. I'm no longer half asleep. The temptation is too great. I can't hold my course any longer. The *Spirit of St. Louis* banks over toward the nearest point of land.
>
> I stare at it intently, not daring to believe my eyes, watching the shades and contours unfold into a coastline. Now I'm flying above the foam-lined coast, searching for prominent features to fit the chart on my knee. I've climbed to 2,000 feet so I can see the contours of the country better. Yes, there's a place on the chart where it all fits—Valentia and Dingle Bay, *on the southwestern coast of Ireland*! I can hardly believe it's true. I'm almost exactly on my route, closer than I hoped to come in my wildest dreams back in San Diego. What happened to all those detours of the night around the thunderheads? Where has the swinging compass error gone?
>
> Intuition must have been more accurate than reasoned navigation.
>
> The southern tip of Ireland! Of course, over two hours ahead of schedule; the sun still well up in the sky, the weather clearing!

Now it was easy. So easy that Lindbergh himself fell into the temptation of making a myth out of his own achievement:

> I'm angling slowly back onto my great-circle route. I must have been within three miles of it when I sighted Ireland. An error of fifty miles would have been good dead reckoning under the most perfect conditions. Three miles was—well, what was it? Before I made this flight, I would have said carelessly that it was luck. Now, luck seems far too trivial a word, a term to be used only by those who've never seen the curtain drawn or looked on life from far away.

After Ireland the landmarks appeared rapidly—a lighthouse, the coast of England and the coast of France, "like an outstretched hand to meet me." For the first time Lindbergh felt hungry. He ate one of the sandwiches, stale and dry now, that he had bought in New York. He picked up a series of beacon lights marking the route between London and Paris. Then the city arose before him. He circled the brightly lit Eiffel Tower and then turned northeast to look at Le Bourget. "You can't miss it," he had been told. He was like a tourist.

It was almost ten o'clock at night in Paris. Lindbergh was confused by an incredible number of lights around the dark spot where the airport ought to be. A factory, he thought. He did not know that he had suddenly become the most famous man in the world. Thousands of Parisians had rushed out to the airport to greet the American flyer. The little roads toward Le Bourget were jammed with cars with headlights blazing.

Finally, Lindbergh was able to pick out floodlights showing the edge of a runway. He dragged the field once, flying low over it to check for obstructions—a tractor or maybe some sheep let out to crop the

As the clock struck 10 P.M. the Spirit of St. Louis *came to rest on the runway at Le Bourget airport. To the French, who had gathered by the thousands to celebrate the "Flying Fool's" success, Lindbergh was the epitome of "a real American."*

grass, he thought. He brought the plane in as carefully as possible, as though he were teaching a student to fly. The plane felt sluggish. By his own guess he still carried a lot of gasoline. His own reflexes seemed slow. Lindbergh had never landed the *Spirit of St. Louis* at night. He glided in at an angle so he could peer out his side window.

> It's only a hundred yards to the hangars now. I'm too high, too fast. Drop wing. Left rudder. Careful. Still too high. I push the stick over. Below the hangar roofs now. Straighten out. A short burst of the engine. Over the lighted areas. Sod coming up to meet me. Careful. Easy to bounce when you're tired. Still too fast. Tail too high. Hold off. Hold off. But the lights are far behind. Ahead, there's nothing but night. Give her the gun and climb for another try?
>
> The wheels touch gently. Off again. No, I'll keep contact. Ease the stick forward. Back on the ground. Off. Back, the tail skid too. Not a bad landing, but I'm beyond the light. Can't see anything ahead. The field *must* be clear. Uncomfortable, though, jolting into blackness. Wish I had a wing light, but too heavy on the takeoff. Slower now, slow enough to ground-loop safely. Left rudder. Reverse it. The *Spirit of St. Louis* swings around and stops rolling, resting on the solidness of earth, in the center of Le Bourget.
>
> I start to taxi back to the floodlights and hangars. But the entire field ahead is covered with running figures!

About 100,000 Frenchmen had broken through police lines to rush onto the field. They were almost hysterical over the new American hero. All day—and all the previous day—the transatlantic cables, the radios, and the newspapers had been full of news about the flight. As soon as Lindbergh taxied back to the hanger, the crowd rushed his plane. He was afraid (as he would be for months whenever he landed at a crowded airport) that people would run into his spinning propeller. And when he tried to climb out of the *Spirit of St. Louis*, the crowd grabbed him. For a long time he could not touch French soil but was passed from shoulder to shoulder. He shouted for a mechanic to take care of his plane. No one could hear or understand him.

In the log he kept of the flights of the *Spirit of St. Louis* Lindbergh made this brief, slightly bitter entry: "May 20. Roosevelt Field, Long Island, New York, to Le Bourget Aerodrome, Paris, France. 33 hours. 20 min. Fuselage fabric badly torn by souvenir hunters."

The first part of the log entry, the flight, was what seemed significant to Lindbergh. But the second part—the half-crazy hero worship of the "souvenir hunters"—is just as important in understanding Lindbergh's achievement. Not just in Paris but even more in dozens of American cities, Lindbergh was adored. People crowded around wherever he went. They grabbed his hats in restaurants. Even his shirts and underwear were stolen by laundry employees for souvenirs. From the time Lindbergh landed at Le Bourget, his life was not his own. He had become a public hero.

A "New Era"

Occasionally, some particular event or act (like John Brown's raid or, more recently, the assassination of President Kennedy in 1963) causes masses of people to undergo a great excitement. At such times most people are not really interested in facts about the event. Instead, they project significance into the event. They see historical actors as demons or heroes, usually in unrealistic ways. By doing so, they make some new sense out of their own lives.

So it was that Charles Lindbergh became a hero and a symbol to the American people. More than any other individual of his generation, Lindbergh captured the imagination, the admiration, and the hopes of his contemporaries.

On the surface, there was no solid reason to make Lindbergh into a hero. His flight had proven nothing except that a superb pilot with an airplane built especially for the purpose could fly 3,600 miles. The *Spirit of St. Louis* could not carry any cargo or passengers. (In fact, Lindbergh refused to carry even one pound of mail for an offer of $1,000.) Even more important, Lindbergh had not even been the first man to fly the Atlantic.[1] But, in 1927, when Lindbergh made his famous trip, almost no one could remember these earlier pilots, while Lindbergh's name became a household word.

A number of extraordinary changes in American society had prepared the way for Lindbergh's fantastic reputation. And the ways Americans chose to celebrate Lindbergh as their hero suggests a great deal about the nature of the new society that was beginning to emerge in the period after World War I.

REACHING A MASS AUDIENCE

One of the reasons for Lindbergh's rapid rise to fame was the publicity he received from the press and the radio. Since the 1890s the newspapers of the United States had been increasing in number and circulation. They competed fiercely for the attention of the public. This expansion of newspapers was only part of an important revolution in communications that began in the nineteenth century and still continues today.

One by one, new inventions brought people's lives closer together. These included the telegraph, the telephone, the phonograph, the camera, the radio, and the motion picture. They created a world in which whole nations and continents could share almost simultaneously in distant events. Lindbergh's flight was "covered" intensely by the press, which transmitted its stories over telegraph and telephone lines. Lindbergh was also photographed mercilessly. His activities were recorded both in newspaper photographs and in the newsreels that accompanied the early silent motion pictures. Hour-by-hour reports of his famous flight were transmitted on the radio—an invention that had come into use only a few years before. As soon as Lindbergh landed in Paris, the news was flashed back to the United States by transatlantic telegraph cable.

[1] Before 1919, a British dirigible (a balloon powered by propeller engines) had crossed from New York to England twice. An American seaplane had made the flight, landing several times on the ocean, in 1919. That same year, two pilots had made it *nonstop* from Newfoundland to Ireland, to win a prize of $50,000, more than twice the prize Lindbergh won.

In many ways Lindbergh the hero was the creation of mass communications. He was the first celebrity to have the full advantage of every modern form of communication except television. (Television did not come into wide use until after World War II.)

The Communications Revolution The revolution in communications began with the telegraph, which linked California and New York more than half a century before Lindbergh's flight. During the same period newspapers began to attract a mass audience. The telephone, too, contributed to the rapid and widespread circulation of information. In the first part of the twentieth century the number of telephones in use skyrocketed, from a little over 1 million in 1900 to more than 10 million in 1915. By the time Lindbergh took off for Paris, practically every middle-class American home had its own telephone.

But the communications revolution did not gather full speed until the invention of the radio. The principle of wireless transmission of sound was almost as old as the telephone. In 1887 a German scientist proved the existence of electrical waves in space. He speculated that they might be turned into signals. An Italian inventor, Guglielmo Marconi, applied the theory to wireless transmission of telegraph signals in 1896. From then on it was only a matter of assembling the appropriate tubes, transmitters, and receivers.

In 1920 Americans heard their first commercial radio broadcast. The station was KDKA in Pittsburgh, and the program was a news report on the 1920 presidential election. Soon after that the winner of the election, Warren G. Harding, installed a radio set in the White House. Gradually Marconi's invention was transformed from a toy into a commercial reality. By the time Lindbergh made his flight to Paris, an estimated 10 million sets were in use in the United States, almost one for every telephone.

Two other inventions, the phonograph and the camera, furthered the revolution in mass communications. Thomas A. Edison found a way

With the broadcast of the Harding-Cox election returns in November 1920, KDKA in Pittsburgh gave birth to commercial radio. The broadcast opened a new era in communications.

of capturing and recreating sound that was to make music available to millions at an instant. George Eastman's perfection of the camera made it possible for newspapers to include pictures on their pages.

All these changes allowed millions of people to participate indirectly in events that they were not present to witness. In other words, these developing communications facilities had created a potential public that could take part in any happening, frown at any villain, worship any hero.

A Middle-Class Public The new public to which Lindbergh was such a hero was overwhelmingly white and well-to-do. Despite a growing literacy in America, newspapers still appealed primarily to a middle-class audience. Radios and telephones too were almost exclusively middle-class conveniences. In 1927 millions of Americans still regarded the phonograph and the camera as strange novelties. Blacks, poor farmers, and poor immigrants in the cities were largely excluded from the new prosperity.

Thus, if Lindbergh represented values, they were not necessarily the values of all Americans. Rather they were primarily the beliefs and hopes

of white middle-class citizens. It was easy to confuse these citizens with the whole nation. The American ambassador to France proclaimed at the time that Lindbergh was the best possible representative "of the spirit of our people." The *New Republic* magazine said that "he is US personified." But the "people" and "US" were primarily the middle-class public defined by the communications network.

THE MACHINE AND THE MAVERICK IN A TECHNOLOGICAL SOCIETY

Americans were fond of calling the period after World War I the New Era. Much of what they meant by the phrase was summed up symbolically in Lindbergh's airplane. The New Era was above all a machine age, a triumph of advanced technology. Compared with a modern jet or a moon rocket, the *Spirit of St. Louis* was a very primitive machine. But to millions of Americans of the 1920s it was the final and glistening outcome of the industrial and technological revolution that had begun in the preceding century. It symbolized what they believed was happening in the United States: the creation of a new kind of

DEVELOPMENTS IN TECHNOLOGY, 1865–1930
(DATES REFER TO PATENT OR FIRST SUCCESSFUL USE)

YEAR	INVENTOR	CONTRIBUTION	IMPORTANCE/DESCRIPTION
1869	George Westinghouse	AIR BRAKE	Provided smoother and quicker braking action for railroad cars.
1874	Joseph Glidden	BARBED WIRE MANUFACTURE	Speeded the end of open grazing of cattle.
1876	Alexander Graham Bell	TELEPHONE	Made out of a cigar box, wire, and two toy magnets; revolutionized communication.
1877	Thomas Alva Edison	PHONOGRAPH	Extended availability of music to millions.
1879	Thomas Alva Edison	INCANDESCENT BULB	Made possible electric lighting.
1880	W. E. Sawyer	PRINCIPLE OF SCANNING	Established the possibility of using only a single wire or channel for transmission of a picture, thereby making television possible.
1888	George Eastman	HAND CAMERA	Revolutionized newspaper journalism.
1888	Nikola Tesla	FIRST MOTOR TO BE RUN BY ALTERNATING CURRENT	Made the transmission of electrical power over long distances possible.
1892	John Froelich	MOTORIZED TRACTOR	Powered by a 20-hp., single-cylinder gasoline engine; greatly increased agricultural efficiency.
1895	George B. Selden	INTERNAL COMBUSTION AUTOMOBILE ENGINE	Initiated a new mode of transportation.
1896	Guglielmo Marconi	WIRELESS TELEGRAPH	Formed the basis for radio transmissions.
1903	Orville & Wilbur Wright	FIRST FLIGHT OF A HEAVIER-THAN-AIR CRAFT	Marked the beginning of the air age.
1904	Thomas Alva Edison	SOUND MOTION PICTURE	Inaugurated a new entertainment/information medium.
1913	William M. Burton	CRACKING OIL-REFINING PROCESS	Made possible production of gasoline from kerosene.
1917	Ernst F. W. Alexanderson	HIGH-FREQUENCY ALTERNATOR	Made worldwide wireless transmission possible.
1918	Peter C. Hewitt F. B. Crocker	HELICOPTER	First helicopter to rise successfully from the ground.
1922	Herbert T. Kalmus	TECHNICOLOR PROCESS	Made possible color film.
1926	Robert Hutchings Goddard	ROCKET	First liquid-propellant rocket.

civilization, a miracle of progress in which every barrier to human comfort and achievement would be broken by industry and invention.

The United States of the mid-1920s was much more thoroughly industrialized than it had been at the turn of the century. Total steel production, for example, quadrupled during the period between the death of McKinley and Lindbergh's flight to Paris. The total value of all manufactured goods increased almost eight times in the same period. The number of people engaged in agriculture declined to about one-fourth of the total population. American cities grew at an astounding pace. By 1930, three years after Lindbergh's flight, 40 percent of the total population of the United States lived in twenty-five large metropolitan centers. In short, Lindbergh appealed to a society that was overwhelmingly industrial and urban and fundamentally dependent on machines and factories.

Electric Power and Assembly Lines In some ways the New Era was an extension of the revolution in industry that had occurred after the Civil War (see Chapter 24). The factory system had continued to expand. New and more complex forms of machinery were developed to produce more and more goods. But if the basic trends were the same, there were some new elements too. The New Era, much more than the old, was driven by electricity and organized around assembly lines.

In 1870, when the industrial revolution was making its first powerful impact, steam power and water wheels were used equally to drive industry. Steam continued to be the main form of motor energy in industry until about 1917. But steam had its drawbacks, and the introduction of electricity made possible extraordinary advances in industry.

Again, the basic inventions belonged to the nineteenth century. Within the ten-year period from 1877 to 1887 the dynamo for generating electricity and the motor for converting it into motion were both perfected. This was largely the work of Thomas Edison. During these same years Edison introduced his incandescent light into homes and streets. In 1882 the first commercial electric-power station, the Edison Illuminating Company, was built in New York.

While electric lighting brightened life in offices, houses, and streets, the electric motor helped transform industrial production. In 1900 electric motors provided only one-twentieth of the power used in American industrial plants. By World War I this figure had increased to about one-third. When Lindbergh flew to France, just ten years later, electricity provided almost two-thirds of the total industrial power in American factories and mills. Between 1870 and 1920 the amount of raw energy used by American industry, measured in horsepower, increased by well over 1,000 percent!

The development of the moving-belt assembly line also had far-reaching effects on industrial production. Assembly lines were first introduced on a large scale by Henry Ford at his automobile plant in Michigan in 1913. The principle was a simple one. Workers were placed in a row in the order of their jobs. The product

This photograph of a day's production of car chassis at a Detroit Ford plant vividly illustrates the increase in output possible by the use of the assembly line. Mass-production methods cut assembly time from 12½ to 1½ hours.

As much as any other single factor, automobiles caused the dramatic change in American life in the twentieth century. Yet the man who did the most to put the nation on wheels, Henry Ford, disliked the change. The older he grew, the more fondly he looked back on the America of his youth. He valued its rural base, Puritan work ethic, and simple pleasures.

Life began for Henry Ford on a farm near Dearborn, Michigan, on July 30, 1863. Early in his life two traits became apparent: he loved machinery, and he hated farming. He was a born tinkerer. By the time he was thirteen, he could disassemble and reconstruct a watch. He was forever fixing his father's farm machinery and his mother's household appliances. When he ran out of repairs at home, he repaired neighbors' watches, clocks, and machinery.

As soon as he could, he left the farm for Detroit to become a machinist. He quickly learned his trade and was soon a well-paid, highly skilled workman. In his spare time he worked on a gasoline buggy in an old brick shed behind his home. By 1896 he was able to drive it through a hole knocked out of the shed wall. Mounted on four bicycle wheels was a two-cylinder, four-horsepower engine. Mounted on that was a buggy seat. To steer it he used a curved stick like the tiller on a boat.

From this awkward beginning he built a billion-dollar industry over the next fifty years. But as he grew from home-shop tinkerer to industrial tycoon, he never really changed his boyhood attitudes. They remained those of an agrarian Populist of the 1880s and 1890s.

As a result, Henry Ford was a mass of contradictions. While he professed a firm belief in the value of the individual workman and of hard and useful work, he developed an assembly-line process that was truly dehumanizing. He broke down each of the jobs involved in making a car into its tiniest steps. Consequently, a workman did only one thing—like tightening a single bolt—all day long. Ford was even proud of the fact that 43 percent of the jobs in his factories could be mastered in no more than one day.

While he was an expert businessman, as shown by his development of an enormous personal fortune and a vastly profitable corporation, Ford disliked many aspects of capitalism. He had an abiding mistrust of bankers and moneymen.

And while he continued to turn out millions of cars, making Americans a highly mobile and rootless society, he romanticized the stable, well-rooted small-town life. He so loved nineteenth-century rural America that he spent twenty years constructing a reproduction of the community he grew up in—Greenfield Village. There skilled artisans worked at jobs that had long since been taken over by assembly lines.

Henry Ford died an old man of eighty-four, puzzled and unhappy with the people and the world he had done so much to transform.

(in this case the automobile) was then moved past them while each man performed an assigned task. The idea might be simple, but the savings in time and motion were dramatic. Each worker, using a specialized tool to perform a small task, could now produce much more in a given day. Ford's assembly line was copied by dozens of other industries. By the middle of the 1920s it was a standard technique.

Effects of Mechanization The industrial revolution continued. The changes brought about by the electric motor and the assembly line made the lives of most Americans in 1927 very different from their lives a generation or two earlier. More and more, the ways people lived and worked were determined by machines and technological innovations. More and more, mechanical devices replaced human energy and skill.

This process of mechanization had two deep effects on American society. First, it made modern Americans more conscious of the efficient use of time and effort than any other people in the history of the world. Second, it threatened to standardize life by reducing the area of imagination and individuality in peoples' daily working environment. The celebration of Lindbergh was connected to both these consequences.

In planning his flight, Lindbergh was almost ruthlessly efficient. The *Spirit of St. Louis* was a nearly perfect machine. It was designed to perform one simple task in the most effective way, with a minimum of wasted energy. Like a machine in a modern factory, the plane represented the harnessing of energy to a carefully designed instrument for the performance of a rigidly defined task. Much of what Americans admired in Lindbergh was precisely what they admired in their own society—his technological achievement.

But there was another side to Lindbergh. He was a maverick. Some of the pet names the newspapers gave him, like "The Flyin' Fool" and "Lucky," made his daring seem more important than his technical skill. Lindbergh seemed to go against the trend toward standardization of life in the New Era. He represented individual imagination, as well as engineering and piloting skill. A large part of Lindbergh's fame probably rested on this contradiction. His flight was both a triumph of technology and a victory for individual daring.

WHEELS AND WINGS: THE MOTOR AGE

The development of electricity had a powerful effect not only on industry but also on American home life. New inventions like the electric washing machine and refrigerator (which utilized small, inexpensive motors) changed the working and eating habits of American families. And a dozen other smaller electric appliances—from toasters to thermostats for home furnaces—helped usher in American consumers' vision of a New Era.

Perfecting the Automobile The largest change in American social life was brought about by the gasoline engine. The basic principle of the internal combustion engine was understood by the middle of the nineteenth century. The principle was simple. Instead of burning fuel externally to convert water into steam, the internal combustion engine burned fuel in an explosive way inside a chamber. The force of the explosion was then used to drive a piston or a rotor. The first internal combustion engine was built and operated in the 1860s in France. Power for the new engine was available in the form of gasoline, a "waste" product in the making of kerosene, the basic fuel oil of the nineteenth century.

It was only a matter of time, then, until someone perfected the engine, mounted it on a "horseless carriage," and so created the automobile. No one, however, could have begun to guess at the end of the nineteenth century just how rapid the development of the automobile would be. Nor could they foresee the surprising range of consequences it would have on the ways Americans lived.

The first man in the United States to build a workable automobile powered by a gasoline en-

The automobile early became a symbol of the "good life." Here a family picnics on the grass with their Model T Ford parked behind them.

gine was probably Ransom E. Olds. (His rickety machine was the forerunner of the present-day Oldsmobile.) Five years later, in 1895, Henry Ford put together his first car. The new machine was noisy, unreliable, and expensive. Still, a few Americans were willing to pay the price and stop their ears against the noise. By 1900 there was about 8,000 of the curious new machines operating in the country.

But Ford was not so much an inventor of the automobile as the inventor of a style and a method of production. In the early years of the century Ford began simplifying the automobile. He cut away every fancy decoration and convenience that had been adapted from the luxurious carriages of the day. Moreover, he reduced costs by turning out standardized, mass-produced machines. The results were astonishing. In 1907 the average price of an automobile was over

$2,000. The next year Ford introduced a model selling at only $850. By 1914 he was able to cut the price to a little over $500. By the mid-1920s Ford was selling his assembly-line Model T for less than $300. The car was similar in many ways to the *Spirit of St. Louis.* It was the simplest machine possible, designed to do a plain task in the most efficient way.

Other automobile makers began to imitate and compete with Ford. The result was an exploding new industry. By the 1920s the manufacture of automobiles was by far the largest consumer products industry in the United States. It employed tens of thousands of workers at large and growing factories centered in Detroit. The automobile had a remarkable impact on other industries, especially steel and rubber, which provided the raw products for the assembly lines. The oil industry also underwent a major expan-

The prosperity in the 1920s that enabled millions of Americans to purchase automobiles gave rise to that most modern phenomenon—the traffic jam.

sion. The automobile turned gasoline into the main stock-in-trade of the petroleum companies.

Life in the Motor Age The most obvious impact of the automobile was not on industry but on American social life. By 1927 Ford had made 15 million cars. About 20 million American families owned an automobile. The immediate result was that horses and other draft animals disappeared from the landscape and the streets.

But the automobile had less obvious and predictable effects. First, the automobile encouraged Americans to move farther and farther away from cities, out into the suburbs. From about the time of Lindbergh's trip to Paris, the "lure of the suburbs" attracted more and more middle-class Americans. Second, cars and buses transformed American education, especially in small towns and farm areas. The school bus made it possible to consolidate school districts into larger units. Gradually the simple one-room schoolhouse, with one or two teachers for all the grades, disappeared.

Finally, the automobile, the truck, and the bus almost destroyed the principal industry of the late nineteenth century, the railroad. By the early 1930s the railroads had lost most of their passenger traffic to the car and the bus. The trucking industry took away most of the railroads' valuable freight traffic. The train, with its mighty steam engine, had been the great symbol of the early industrial revolution. By the middle of the twentieth century much of the railroad industry was sick and unprofitable.

In the long run the automobile proved to have unwanted as well as unpredicted consequences. Among these the modern decay of central cities was the most serious. Gradually large sections of cities like New York, Boston, and Chicago became the slums of the poor, who could not afford suburban homes. Also, although no one in Lindbergh's day could have predicted it, the automobile caused a major problem of air pollution. Smog resulted from the exhausts of millions of cars and trucks burning hundreds of millions of gallons of gasoline every year.

To most Americans, though, the automobile was an unquestioned miracle. To those who could afford it, it meant freedom to move at will through the city or the countryside. It also gave status, as manufacturers introduced more elaborate models, some costing ten times as much as

Ford's Model T. And the automobile meant adventure. Middle-class Americans could get behind the wheel of a powerful, complicated piece of machinery—just as Lindbergh climbed into the cockpit of his machine—and be off on an exciting journey of motion and speed every day. Like Lindbergh, too, Americans went beyond a concern with efficiency and practicality to a romantic affection for their machines. They polished them, paraded them, and gave them pet names like the "old bus," the "flivver," the "tin Lizzie," and the "merry Oldsmobile." Despite its defects, Americans loved the car.

Development of Air Transportation For the first quarter of the twentieth century the automobile had the greatest social and economic impact on America. The development of the aircraft industry and airline passenger service did not become truly important until years after Lindbergh's flight. But the airplane was in many ways more thrilling than the automobile. (This was why Lindbergh and other pilots could make a living in the 1920s barnstorming across America in their aerial circuses.) Like the automobile, the airplane depended on the small, powerful, and efficient gasoline engine.

The first men in history to fly a heavier-than-air craft were Orville and Wilbur Wright. Their primitive biplane had no engine and no cockpit: the pilot simply lay down on the lower wing. They managed to get the flimsy craft into the air for a few seconds at Kitty Hawk, North Carolina, in 1903. The development of airplanes was slow after that. The advent of World War I brought about a quick jump in design, engine power, and reliability. The war also romanticized flight by creating a new kind of celebrity, the flying ace.

The main civilian use of the airplane was shipping mail. The government began service in 1918. Later private companies (like the one Lindbergh worked for in St. Louis) took over the service. The operation was dangerous. A majority of the pilots were killed in crashes during the early years. But by the mid-1920s there was

regular, all-weather air-mail service between most major cities in America.

Lindbergh's flight, combined with the introduction of larger airplanes like Byrd's *America,* did more than any other single event to encourage the growth of air transportation. Lindbergh had faith in the future of aviation. Soon after his return to America in 1927, he began a flying tour of the country to promote air mail and air transportation. By 1930, just three years after his solo transatlantic flight, there were 43 domestic airline companies, operating over 30,000 miles of flying routes.

NEW MANNERS AND MORALS

All these changes—the development of mass communications, the expansion of industry, the introduction of a new technology—brought about another revolution. This revolution marked a dramatic difference in the manners and morals of the American people. Americans of the 1920s knew they were living in a time when the world was undergoing rapid change. They coined new words and phrases—like the "roaring twenties," the "lost generation," and "flaming youth,"—to describe what was happening to them. Americans were adopting habits and moral standards that their parents found shocking and offensive.

A Revolution for Women At the center of the revolution in manners were women. The revolution that would change women's lives did not begin in the 1920s. During the first two decades of the twentieth century, many middle- and upper-class women had adopted new patterns of behavior (including divorce) that broke with the traditions of nineteenth-century Victorian America. But because of the impact of World War I and the influence of books, radio, and advertising, the trend started at the turn of the century began to affect ever-widening circles of women. By the 1920s the revolution was in full bloom.

Politically, women were new creatures. After

decades of agitation, they finally won the right to vote with the passage of the Nineteenth Amendment in 1920. But this new political role was only a small part of the emancipation of women. The new woman of the 1920s wanted to do everything. "Everything" included more opportunities than her mother had had.

She was much more likely than her mother to attend college. She might go to work, too. By 1930, 10 million women were employed in the American labor force. This new experience of education and work made women more likely to remain single, or, if they did marry, to get di-

vorces. The divorce rate in 1930 was twice what it had been before the war. This did not mean that marriages were more unhappy. It meant, instead, that women were less likely to put up with a bad marital situation. They would demand their freedom instead.

The new woman dressed differently, too. The fashionable woman that gradually emerged in the decade of Lindbergh's flight was the flapper. She wore her hemlines shorter—above the knee rather than at the ankle. And her dresses were made of thin material, designed to move with her body as she walked or danced.

The flapper symbolized the new woman's daring—her flouting of traditional social and moral restraints. Short, bobbed hairdos, knee-length skirts, and sheer silk stockings identify these four women as flappers, as does their surroundings—a nightclub.

The flapper took off the corsets that had constrained women of an earlier generation. She put on more make-up and perfume and jangled with more jewelry on her wrists and around her neck. In advertisements or movies (and more and more in real life) she was likely to have a cocktail in one hand and a cigarette holder in the other—the ultimate in the new sophistication of the 1920s.

The Jazz Age The new woman was part of a changing culture. A freedom of action and belief unheard of before seemed to go hand in hand with the triumph of industrial technology, with its prosperity and sense of unlimited possibilities for life. Both men and women listened to new music—jazz—and danced new steps. Instead of formal waltzes and other Victorian dances, they moved to the fast Charleston and the Black Bottom. They also danced close together in the slow fox trot. Many older Americans were shocked by these changes. But these dances became part of the new culture, sweeping their way through high-school gymnasiums and college campuses across the country.

The sexual ideas of Americans were changing, too. The ideas of the Austrian psychologist Sigmund Freud on sex began to be discussed at the dinner table and in the polite magazines of the middle class. Words like "bitch" appeared in novels published by respectable publishers and read by respectable people. "Petting" and "necking" became part of the everyday vocabulary of magazine readers and even ministers. In the movies sex became a major box-office attraction. Stars like Theda Bara and Clara Bow appeared on the screen in thin clothing, locked in long, passionate embraces with their leading men. When Clara Bow was advertised as the "It" girl, hardly anyone needed to ask what "It" meant.

Americans drank more too. Despite prohibition (see page 651) liquor was easy to obtain. And since liquor was illegal, millions of Americans became technically criminals on an almost daily basis. Probably half the respectable, middle-class families in the nation had their regular

The "Jazz Age" gave birth to the blues, an especially plaintive, bittersweet music of black American origin. Bessie Smith, one of the best American jazz artists, made the singing of the blues uniquely her own.

Movie Stars as Public Idols

In its earliest years the American film industry had no movie stars. Instead, each studio had a number of anonymous "players" who were used over and over again in "the pictures." As time went on, moviegoers began to single out certain favorite players. They gave them names so that they could discuss them. There was the "Biograph girl," so named because she worked for Biograph Studios. There were "the little girl with the golden curls" and "the little fellow." All were anonymous, and all were loved by their fans.

Before long the public was clamoring to know who these players were. Letters poured into the studios demanding their real names. The studios did not want to comply. Once their players became famous, it was feared they would want higher salaries. For a time the public was infuriated. But the studios held firm.

Then an industry maverick, Carl Laemmle, recognized that there was money to be made in revealing players' names. If the public knew the names of their favorites, they would know in what films they were appearing. This, in turn, would ensure these films success at the box office. Laemmle began by luring the popular "Biograph girl" to his studio. He told the world she was Florence Lawrence and featured her in movies under her own name.

The "star system" was born. The public created it, and the studios exploited it. And Hollywood did not always wait for movie fans to find their own favorites. Through clever and imaginative press agentry, the studios could create, package, and distribute stars.

One such press-agent creation was the "vamp," Theda Bara. Born to an Egyptian mother and a French father, she grew up learning the secrets of the Orient. She possessed an evil power over men, and she had a name that could be respelled "Arab Death." At least that was what the fans were told about her. She thrilled them when she looked up from her tiger-skin rug, turned her hypnotic eyes on her leading man, and said, "Kiss me, my fool." Actually, she was Theodosia Goodman, a tailor's daughter who grew up in Cincinnati. But that was not the kind of background that sold tickets.

Stardom was not a job—it was a way of life. As one student of the film culture has put it:

> Stars lived like stars, larger than life. Clara Bow, the original 'It' girl, queen of the 'Jazz Babies,' received 100,000 fan letters a year, gave parties for whole football squads, owned a Kissel roadster (colored red to match her hair) with two red Irish setters trained to ride on the running boards, earned $4,000 a week and spent it all.

Hollywood gave people what they wanted—idols whose tastes, fashions, and manners they could imitate, whose luxurious lives seemed so much more adventurous and exciting than their own. Above all, Hollywood epitomized America's rags-to-riches dream: a tailor's daughter could indeed become a highly paid, glamorous, and adored celebrity.

bootlegger. Terms like "bathtub gin" and "speakeasy" became part of the national language. Especially in colleges, drinking became a regular pastime of the "flaming youth" of the decade.

The Search for Innocence   As their own lives became more and more confused, Americans began to celebrate innocence. In their movies and sports they created simple, naïve heroes who were guided by straightforward codes of justice and virtue. The most popular type of movie hero of the decade was the cowboy, a symbol of innocent, preindustrial man. And the most popular movie star of the period, Rudolf Valentino, played roles that put him on horseback in a country far removed from Fords and factories and modernity. It was no accident too that the greatest sports hero of the decade, George Herman Ruth, was innocently nicknamed "Babe."

Lindbergh stirred the deep urge of people to believe in innocence. His youth, honesty, and simple determination made him seem much purer than the public that worshiped him. Lindbergh did not smoke or drink. He displayed no interest in women, at least at the time of his flight. And his boyish face looked out at the world through clear blue eyes. They seemed to say that everything was still the same, that the world had not lost its innocence after all.

A CONSERVATIVE TIDE

For millions of Americans the continuing atmosphere of change that dominated the period after World War I seemed threatening. In national politics, the 1920s was a decade of sharp reaction against all the reforms of the progressive period. But the reaction went much deeper than politics. Not every American participated, but a large and active segment of society believed that dramatic action was necessary to save their country from the dangers of "foreign" political ideas, from alcohol, from new ideas like evolution, and from the influence of Catholic and Jewish immigration.

into a hero in 1927 did so because he seemed so clean, so morally upright, so much a product of middle-class standards and morals. As much as anything else, this conservative reaction, with its simple values and direct methods, gave the period its peculiar tone and color.

The Red Scare   The conservative reaction focused sharply on radicalism. The Russian Revolution, which had brought the communist government of the Bolsheviks to power, was followed by communist uprisings in Germany and Hungary. These developments created an atmosphere of fear in the United States. Many people, including a number of powerful leaders in federal and state governments, believed that a communist conspiracy was at work among them, ready to "radicalize" the country.

In 1919 a series of spectacular strikes and the outbreak of political sabotage fed the fear. In the spring of that year two small groups of anarchists attempted to bomb the homes and offices of a number of government officials and businessmen. The bombs, sent through the mails, were probably the work of mentally unstable persons. Certainly they had nothing to do with the tiny organized Socialist and Communist parties of the country.

In fact, the bombers were incompetent. One large package of bombs was never delivered because it did not have enough postage. Another bomb only damaged the house of its intended victim, but it blew the bomber himself—an Italian anarchist—to bits. A third, addressed to a Georgia politician, was opened by his maid (a black worker, not a capitalist). She lost her hands as a result. But the bombings did convince many people that revolution was at hand.

One of the people who was most convinced was Woodrow Wilson's Attorney General, A. Mitchell Palmer. Like Wilson, Palmer was a liberal and a strong antiradical. The Attorney General also had his eye on the Democratic nomination of 1920. So he used the "red scare" to make his department the center of the action. He obtained an extra appropriation for hunting

Nicola Sacco and Bartolomeo Vanzetti entered a courthouse to make their final appeal in 1927. They were convicted essentially because they were Italians at a time when hatred of aliens ran high, and anarchists in a politically conservative era.

down radicals. With the money he formed a new antisubversive division of the Justice Department, headed by J. Edgar Hoover.

Beginning in November of 1919 the Justice Department conducted a series of raids against radical groups, seeking out suspected communists at union meetings, at Communist party headquarters, and in their homes. The most spectacular of the raids, which came on New Year's Day 1920, resulted in the arrest of 6,000 people. In the end the Palmer raids led to the conviction of only a handful of citizens, most of them for minor crimes. Immigrant aliens, who were Palmer's main targets, suffered more. About 600 were eventually deported, mostly to the Soviet Union.

Palmer's campaign created an atmosphere of near hysteria among many Americans. It led to one tragedy that did more than any other

single event of the 1920s to divide Americans of different political beliefs. In 1920 two Italian anarchists were arrested in Boston on a charge of robbing a shoe company and murdering two of its employees. Their trial soon became a political event, a test of the established authority against political radicalism. The trial was unfair. Even the judge privately referred to the defendants, Nicola Sacco and Bartolomeo Vanzetti, as anarchists.

But in the political air of the red scare Sacco and Vanzetti were convicted and sentenced to death. The process of appeals was long and unsuccessful. Finally, in 1927, the year of Lindbergh's flight, both men were executed in the electric chair. To the small number of American liberals and radicals of the 1920s, Sacco and Vanzetti were the century's greatest martyrs. They were modern counterparts of the victims of the Salem witch trials and the Haymarket Affair. But to most Americans, they were just Italian radicals who had been properly punished.

The red scare also made it possible for those Americans who feared immigrants and their ethnic and religious differences to restrict immigration. In February 1921 (over the veto of President Wilson) Congress passed a law that limited immigration, especially from countries in southern and eastern Europe. According to the law, the number of immigrants from a country in any given year could not exceed 3 percent of the number of people of that nationality who were already in the United States in 1910. In 1924 the law was made even more restrictive. Quotas would now be based on resident population in 1890, immigration limited to 150,000 a year after 1927, and Asians totally excluded. The effect of the laws was to end, almost at once, the flow of immigration.

Prohibition and Reaction   Like the red scare and the movement for immigration restriction, the prohibition of alcohol in the 1920s had roots in the progressive period. In 1919 the states had passed the Eighteenth Amendment, which empowered Congress to prohibit the sale of alcoholic beverages. The amendment marked the victory of a long campaign of temperance. It provided another rallying point for conservative, small-town Americans. They divided society into the "drys" and the "wets" and opposed any politician who did not favor prohibition.

The prohibition movement failed to stop Americans from drinking. In most cities people continued to drink whiskey in speakeasies. The sale of bootleg whiskey was controlled largely by organized gangs of criminals. Gangs like the one led by Al Capone in Chicago bribed public officials and policemen to cover up their operations. But for most conservative Americans prohibition was above all a moral crusade. It was an issue they could use to split their countrymen into two camps: one composed of decent people, the other of riffraff.

Another conservative campaign of the 1920s was the attempt of many Protestant Americans—again, especially in the South and the Middle West—to prevent schools from teaching dangerous or un-American ideas. In several Southern states this crusade aimed mainly at the idea of evolution. The notion of biological evolution was an old one. It became scientifically respected in the nineteenth century through the work of Charles Darwin. By the 1920s practically every scientist in the world believed that animals, including man, had evolved over a long period of time. But this seemed to many people to go against the fundamentals of their religion. They saw it as a challenge to the biblical story of creation.

Several state legislatures forbade their schools to teach the doctrine of evolution. In 1925 John Scopes, a schoolteacher in Dayton, Tennessee, decided to challenge the law. He was arrested, and his trial became almost as much a spectacle as the trial of Sacco and Vanzetti.

Scopes was defended by the most famous criminal lawyer in the United States, Clarence Darrow of Chicago. William Jennings Bryan led the prosecution. Bryan, an aging but still powerful leader of millions of fundamentalists, stood ready to smite the forces of modernism. He was humiliated on the witness stand by Darrow. Reporters from every major American newspaper—and several European papers—covered the events.

Scopes lost the trial and was fined $100. The Tennessee law stayed on the books. But after the Scopes trial the direction of education in the South and elsewhere shifted away from Bryan's intellectual conservatism toward the acceptance of modern science. Bryan's crusade, like many other conservative movements of the 1920s, was only a temporary victory over twentieth-century ideas and social habits.

Extremism: The Klan   The most spectacular popular conservative movement of the period was the revitalization of the Ku Klux Klan. The Klan, which had died after Reconstruction, was reorganized in Georgia in 1916. Its membership grew slowly until the early 1920s. Then, like other conservative movements, the Klan gained

652/ a large following. By the middle of the decade it had about 5 million members, most of them from the South and Southwest. But the Klan also had supporters in the Middle West. It was strongest of all in Indiana, where for a few years it controlled the state government.

The Ku Klux Klan was an extremist organization. It usually attracted only the most violently conservative Americans. With its white hoods, burning crosses, the use of violence, and intense prejudices, the Klan represented the worst aspects of American life. Secrecy, rituals, and bizarre offices ("Dragons," "Kleegals," and so on) characterized the Klan. It provided many Americans with a way of expressing anger at the way "their" country had been "taken over" by foreigners, Jews, Catholics, liberal intellectuals, blacks, and gangsters.

The Klan was not so much typical of American conservatism in the 1920s as it was a symbol. Millions of conservative Americans were deeply troubled by the direction their country had taken during the preceding generation—and by worries about the future. Like the prohibition movement and Protestant fundamentalism, the Klan, even at the height of its power, seemed destined to lose in the long run.

The country was running headlong and at breakneck speed into the future. Technology had brought prosperity, and prosperity had fostered change. Nothing but a catastrophe was likely to slow the pace. Americans in the 1920s could foresee no such event. But by 1929 the event was upon them. The stock market crash of that year signaled the end of the New Era and the beginning of much bleaker times.

The lunatic fringe of the 1920s had considerable strength, as this parade of Klansmen in the nation's capital in 1925 indicates. Terror was the Klan's chief method of warding off members' own fears of a rapidly changing America.

1. Why might it be said that Lindbergh was a hero created by the mass media? Why was his public essentially a white and well-to-do one? Explain whether this makes any difference in the significance of his feat.
2. Which technological developments do you think were most basic in bringing about the New Era? Defend your selections.
3. In what ways was it possible for Lindbergh to be both an embodiment of the New Era and a maverick?
4. How was Henry Ford able to lower the cost of his cars so sharply between 1900 and the mid-1920s?
5. What were the effects of the invention of the automobile on the city, education, and the transportation industry? Were these effects advantageous?
6. In what ways may it be said that there was a "new woman" emerging in the 1920s? Could she have appeared without other changes occurring in the New Era? Why or why not?
7. Why was there a conservative reaction in the United States during the 1920s? To what evidence would the conservatives have pointed to prove the existence of a "radical" plot? Would the evidence have convinced you?
8. How did the immigration law of 1921 practically end the flow of "new" immigration?
9. Who were the religious fundamentalists? Why did they believe that the theory of evolution conflicted with the Bible?

Beyond the Text

1. Discuss the effects of mass-production techniques on individuality in America, considering the following questions: (1) How does the assembly line affect a worker's pride? (2) What is the effect of mass-produced products on consumers?
2. Compare the Sacco-Vanzetti case with the trial of those involved in the Haymarket Affair as to the attitudes of the judges, the bias of the jurors, the nature of the evidence, and the general intolerance of the times.
3. By the 1920s America had definitely become an urban nation. Investigate and report on the conflict between urban and rural values as shown in: (1) prohibition, (2) fundamentalism, and (3) the revival of the Ku Klux Klan. Davis' *The Social and Cultural Life of the 1920s* is a useful reference.

Bibliography

Nonfiction

Allen, Frederick L., *Only Yesterday.**
Chalmers, David, *Hooded Americanism.**
Cohen, Stanley, *A. Mitchell Palmer.*
Furniss, Norman F., *The Fundamentalist Controversy, 1918–1931.*
Jacobs, Lewis, *The Rise of the American Film.**
Kazin, Alfred, *On Native Grounds.**
Leighton, Isabel, ed., *The Aspirin Age: 1919–1941.**
Leuchtenburg, William E., *The Perils of Prosperity, 1914–1932.**
Morris, Lloyd, *Not So Long Ago.*
Murray, Robert K., *Red Scare: A Study in National Hysteria, 1919–1920.**
Nevins, Allan and Frank Hill, *Ford.*
Porthro, James W., *Dollar Decade: Business Ideas in the 1920s.*
Ross, Walter S., *The Last Hero: Charles A. Lindbergh.*
Sinclair, Andrew, *The Age of Excess.*

Fiction

Anderson, Sherwood, *Kit Brandon.*
Dos Passos, John, *U.S.A.**
Fitzgerald, F. Scott, *The Great Gatsby.**

*a paperback book

UNIT SEVEN

MODERN

Fifteen million Americans were unemployed on March 4, 1933, when the new President, Franklin Delano Roosevelt, was inaugurated. Roosevelt stirred his audience when he told his stricken countrymen: "Let me assert my firm belief that the only thing we have to fear is fear itself." A despairing nation responded eagerly to Roosevelt's determination to act quickly and boldly in confronting the emergency.

Twenty-eight years later another new President, John Fitzgerald Kennedy, also used his inaugural speech to proclaim new energy in national affairs. "Let the word go out," Kennedy intoned, "that the torch has been passed to a new generation of Americans [willing] to pay any price, bear any burden, to assure the survival and the success of liberty."

Roosevelt's address rallied Americans to begin the process of economic recovery. Kennedy's speech summoned Americans to leadership of the Western world. The three decades between these two orations saw the United States emerge from economic catastrophe to become the strongest and most prosperous country in

AMERICA

world history. The following chapters trace the steps in this evolution.

The defeat of the Bonus Marchers in 1932, narrated in Chapter 33, symbolized the old order's inability to respond effectively to the vast human suffering of the times. Most of the marchers were unemployed World War I veterans who had come to Washington seeking aid. It took the New Deal to provide such assistance. The accompanying chapter discusses both the discredited political assumptions of the 1920s and the experimental world of Roosevelt's New Deal. It also portrays the Great Depression's impact upon American social practices.

The attack on Pearl Harbor, dramatized in Chapter 35, highlights the beginning of a shift in national attention from domestic to foreign concerns. Roosevelt and his successors, determined to avoid future "Pearl Harbors," led the country in a search for collective security through treaty alliances. The wartime "Grand Alliance" of the United States, Great Britain, and the Soviet Union rapidly deteriorated after

World War II. A new era of Cold War between the Western allies and the Soviet communist camp began. Pearl Harbor thus vaulted the United States into a position of world leadership. Chapter 36 traces the development of that role from the 1930s to the Kennedy administration.

Running parallel to Cold War developments in foreign affairs were anticommunist rumblings at home. The Alger Hiss case figured prominently in this. Hiss was a former high government official who was convicted in 1950 of having lied about involvement with Russian agents. His case came to symbolize for many the threat of communism to American society. The Red Scare that the incident touched off was central to many of the political, social, and economic developments that the next chapter discusses. Among those developments the nation's return to affluence, the rise of a "military-industrial complex," and the beginnings of certain social problems that would haunt the next decade are discussed. The dramatic flare-up of some of those problems during the Kennedy-Johnson-Nixon years is the subject of the Epilogue.

Defeat of the Bonus Marchers

THE WITNESS shifted nervously but stood his ground. Having waited a long time to testify, he was not going to be put off. Without formally addressing the committee or saying so much as a polite "Gentlemen," he began: "My comrade and I hiked here from nine o'clock Sunday morning, when we left Camden. I done it all by my feet—shoe leather. I come to show you people that we need our bonus. We wouldn't want it if we didn't need it."

The witness was Joseph T. Angelo, veteran of World War I. He was addressing a committee of the House of Representatives of the United States Congress in 1931. The committee was hearing witnesses testify about a controversial matter: the immediate payment of a "bonus" to all the veterans of the war. The country was in the third year of a depression, and the bonus would pay about $1,000 each to over 3 million veterans and their families.[1] It would, in fact, be the greatest program of direct relief for the poor ever undertaken by the federal government.

For six days officials of the Republican administration testified. President Herbert Hoover was opposed to the bonus. The testimony of government officials reflected this opposition. A few congressmen, and one or two officials of veterans' organizations, spoke out for the bonus. But they were outnumbered by a long string of bank vice presidents, insurance executives, and other businessmen. The testimony was dull.

---

[1] Congress had set up the bonus (a combination of life insurance and a pension) in 1924. It was not due to be paid until 1945, except to heirs of veterans who died earlier.

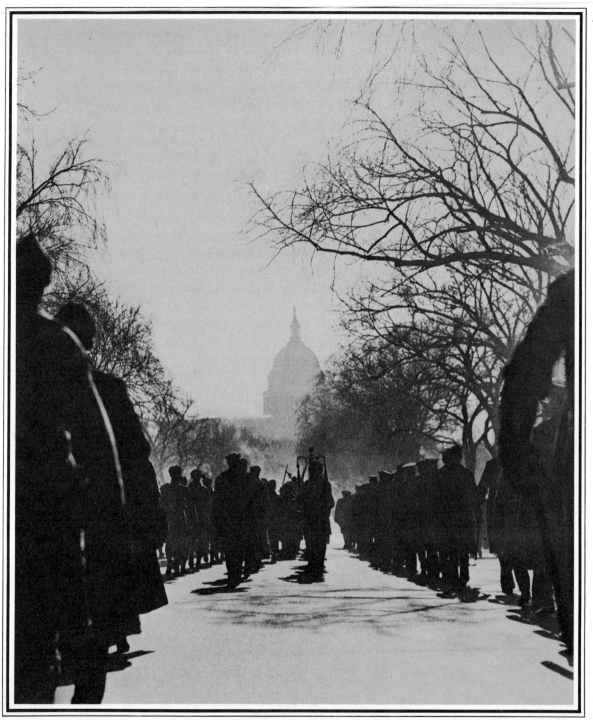

Disciplined regiments of World War I veterans marched silently and gravely to the Capitol in June 1932. This was a veterans' parade with a difference—the men did not want the people's gratitude now, but a bonus that would help them through hard times.

It was full of statistics designed to prove that the bonus would bankrupt the federal treasury and bring about a dangerous inflation.

But now for the first time an ordinary veteran, with no job, a hungry family, and a plain man's English, was testifying. Before Angelo finished, the committee and the audience were stirred into a mixture of laughter, admiration, and stunned confusion.

> I have got a little home back there [in Camden, New Jersey] that I built with my own hands after I came home from France. Now, I expect to lose that little place. Last week I went to our town committee and they gave me $4 for rations. That is to keep my wife and child and myself and clothe us; and also I cannot put no coal in my cellar.

Here, in the poor grammar and tired face of the witness, was the whole meaning of the depression that had begun in 1929. Angelo said he spoke for hundreds like himself in New Jersey. But he spoke, too, for millions all over the country who had not worked for a long time, who stood in bread lines, and who built the shacks in the shabby little towns they wryly called Hoovervilles.

But Angelo was also a veteran. So he spoke from his experience of the two most important events in his time—the war that people still called the Great War and the depression they were beginning to call the Great Depression. There was no economic theory or political philosophy in his testimony. He was just a hungry man who had fought in France.

> All I ask of you, brothers, is to help us. We helped you, now you help us. My partner here has a wife and five children, and he is just the same as I am. He hiked down here at the same time with me, and our feet are blistered. That is all I have to say. And I hope you folks can help us and that we can go through with the bonus. We don't want charity; we don't need it. All we ask for is what belongs to us, and that is all we want.

Some of the congressmen were confused. Others were curious. Following the custom of congressional committees, they began to question the witness:

MR. FREAR: What is your business?

MR. ANGELO: Nothing. I am nothing but a bum.

MR. FREAR: You say you have not worked for two years?

MR. ANGELO: I have not worked for a year and a half. But there is no work in my home town.

MR. RAINEY: You are wearing some medal. What is it?

MR. ANGELO: I carry the highest medal in America for enlisted men, the Distinguished Service Cross.

MR. RAINEY: You have a Distinguished Service Cross? What is that for?

MR. ANGELO: That is for saving Colonel Patton.

George S. Patton was already a well-known army officer. (In World War II he would become one of the most famous and controversial of America's generals.) Congressman Rainey continued the questioning and pressed Angelo for details. Angelo responded with a startling tale. He had been part of a 305-man unit attacked by German machine guns in the Argonne Forest in 1918. When the battle was over, he said, most of the men were dead. Colonel Patton was wounded, and only he—Angelo—was left standing. Then Angelo showed the committee a tie-pin made from a bullet he said was taken from Patton's leg in France. Neither the watch nor the medal had ever gone to "Uncle," Angelo's pet name for the pawnshop that had swallowed up his other possessions.

The afternoon was wearing on, but Angelo had roused the attention of the committee members and the audience as none of the other witnesses had. So the congressmen began to ask about his life. As Angelo answered, the audience sometimes laughed, sometimes applauded. He told them of working in a DuPont plant, making munitions for the British before the United States entered the war. When Congress declared war in 1917, he enlisted at once. But he was almost rejected because he weighed a mere 107 pounds. Only after ten doctors had poked at him and a general had watched him do a handspring and jump a table was he accepted.

Then, obviously agitated, Angelo wound up with another statement:

> I can make money. I can make lots of money. Now, I could go bootlegging. It is just the same way I could have went to France and I could have run out on my outfit. Which is the best, to be a live coward or a dead hero?
>
> When this was put on me, brothers, I wasn't worried when I went through. I don't have nothing to worry about. I wasn't married, and I got a wonderful send-off when I went to France. My father throwed me out. [Laughter.] And when I came back, I went home to my father. I saw a big, fat woman sitting in the seat. I knowed her from next door. I said, "She is the last woman you want on earth. Pop, what is she doing here?" He says, "That is my wife." I says, "Oh, My God!" She says, "Get out of here," and that was my welcome home, and I got out. [Laughter.]
>
> So, folks, I tell you all I will say to you is, help us through with the bonus. That is the best answer for you folks to give to the fellow at home. Don't forget me for a job. [Applause.]

Joe Angelo was three things: a veteran, a bum, and a victim of the most serious economic depression in American history. In each of these roles he was not just an individual grappling with purely personal problems. He represented over 4 1/2 million soldiers (about half of whom had actually been sent to Europe) suddenly discharged into civilian life in 1918 and 1919. These veterans organized—like other veterans in America's previous wars. More than a million joined the new American Legion and the Veterans of Foreign Wars. They thought of themselves as a special type of citizen, with a special claim on their country's gratitude.

As a bum, Angelo also spoke for countless people, many of them veterans, who had worked unsuccessfully at one job or another but mostly drifted through the 1920s. Naturally, the depression added millions of new "bums." Angelo, who had not been able to find work for a year and a half, was only one of a great, restless mass of unemployed. When he appeared before the congressional committee, at least 5 million men and women were classed as unemployed. Probably another 5 million were able to find only part-time work. Almost every other worker in America had his wages cut after the stock market crash of 1929. Few people could doubt in 1931 that unemployment was one of the most serious problems the United States had ever faced.

Joe Angelo's instinct was to turn to Washington for help. On his walk from Camden he had met other small groups of veterans with the same idea. The unemployed, the veterans, and the bums (often one man was all three) were looking more and more to the federal gov-

A group of New York veterans gathered in the yards of the Baltimore and Ohio Railroad at Jersey City, New Jersey, on June 4, 1932. These angry, frustrated men were hoping to seize a train for Washington where they could demand payment of their bonus.

ernment for relief. They had one fairly good chance of getting help from a reluctant Congress and a stubborn President—payment of the bonus. This, in Angelo's words, was "the best answer for you folks to give."

Angelo wanted $1,000 immediately, instead of waiting until 1945 to collect a larger amount. This was the heart of an issue that was about to create the most dramatic crisis of the depression—the massing in Washington of a "Bonus Army." Behind the crisis lay the old task of writing a final chapter to the World War and the new, complicated task of dealing with the depression. But for the marchers in the Bonus Army, the problem was quite simple: When and how would they be able to collect their bonus in full?

Veterans could already borrow money against the promise of the government to pay. Over 2 million had taken out loans that averaged $100 each—just enough to pay a back grocery bill, buy some coal for winter, or meet a medical emergency. But veterans everywhere were beginning to ask for ten times more, the payment of the entire bonus. And they found some sympathetic ears in Congress. Representative Wright Patman of Texas introduced a bill to authorize printing almost $2 1/2 billion in new paper money to pay the bonus. As time passed there was more and more talk of the bonus, not only in Washington but wherever knots of hungry veterans gathered.

In November 1931 a group of veterans left Seattle to ride freights to the capital. All over the country others were doing likewise. A movement began that would shake the Hoover administration.

For two years the President had been telling the nation that the depression was not so serious and would soon end. Administration officials had always played down unemployment statistics. They portrayed the crisis as a temporary economic slump that would cure itself. Meanwhile, Hoover kept to his principle that the federal government should not provide direct relief to poor individuals. The veterans who were hitchhiking and jumping freight trains headed toward the capital were not so sure of their principles. Certainly they lacked the President's political experience and skills. But they knew that they needed the bonus.

By May 1932, 300 more men from Portland, Oregon, left for Washington in a group. They called themselves the Bonus Expeditionary Force—a play on the name of the American army in France, the American Expeditionary Force. They elected a leader, Walter F. Waters, once an army sergeant, now an unemployed foreman in a fruit cannery. They rode freight cars east and, by late May, reached East St.

Louis, Illinois. There they tried to hop new trains going farther east. When railroad police told them to leave, they began to break up trains by uncoupling cars. They also soaped the rails in some places, making it impossible for engines to move.

The state called for its national guard to drive the veterans away. A scuffle occurred, but no one was hurt badly. The marchers were soon on their way again—in national guard trucks Illinois provided them in return for their promise to leave the state peacefully. But, most important, for the first time, the newspapers and the public heard in a notable way about the Bonus Army. Other veterans soon followed suit.

The scene was repeated everywhere. Merchants and mayors, railroad officials and governors, found that it was easier to supply trucks or boxcars than to stop the veterans. Thus a steady stream of bonus marchers was emptying into Washington. Each group had a leader or two, and their purpose was the same. They were in Washington to demand their bonus, even if they had to wait there until 1945 to get it.

One man deeply interested in the veterans' cause was Pelham D. Glassford, a West Point graduate and the youngest American in the World War to become a brigadier general. In 1931 Hoover appointed Glassford superintendent of Washington's police force. So he would have to deal with the Bonus Expeditionary Force in the capital.

Glassford hoped that the Bonus Army either would not come or would go home quickly. But as the marchers arrived, he became sympathetic and helpful. He regarded them as "his boys." He assigned them quarters in abandoned buildings on Pennsylvania Avenue. The location was at the heart of official Washington, between the White House and the Capitol.

At Glassford's suggestion, also, the marchers made a "muster," or list of their groups, to make it easier to track down criminals and keep out the "Reds" and radicals. Gradually the marchers formed companies and then regiments. They elected Walter Waters, leader of the Portland group, commander of the Bonus Expeditionary Force. He appointed junior officers and divided the men into companies named after states. Soon, the Bonus Army had a structure of command like the regular army.

Glassford's original decision to let the marchers camp along Pennsylvania Avenue was based on his hope that few would come. Soon it was obvious that the Bonus Army was much too large and dangerous (and embarrassing to the administration) to be in the center of things. Glassford sent most of the marchers to a new campsite a few miles southeast of Capitol Hill. The place was Anacostia Flats, a muddy land-fill near the forks of the Potomac and Anacostia rivers. There, about 6,000 veterans built a shabby but orderly camp, with shacks and tents arranged in winding rows.

At Anacostia Flats the veterans tried to re-create their old army life. They woke to bugles, conducted roll calls, and had inspections. A company of men was assigned every day to "KP." Waters exercised strict discipline.

Other aspects of camp life were more relaxed. Some men had brought their wives and children. The Salvation Army set up a post office, a library, and a recreation room. Glassford managed to borrow some field kitchens and other equipment. He supervised the distribution of food donated by Washington citizens, American Legion posts, and others. At one point Glassford gave several hundred dollars of his own money to buy food. There was even a newspaper to keep the veterans informed about the progress of bonus legislation in Congress.

By June 6, 1932, the veterans were ready for their first direct action. About 7,000 left their separate camps around the city and lined up neatly in six "regiments" to parade through Washington. The men felt fairly hopeful as they moved along. The Patman bill, which was in the House, seemed as if it would pass soon. The rumors that they were controlled by communists, spread by some politicians to smear the Bonus Army, were not given much credit. Best of all, their parade had drawn a crowd of about 100,000, mostly Washington clerical workers. Every time another company with its American flag passed, the crowd applauded.

Shortly after dark the long line of march reached a monument circle near the Capitol. (They were forbidden to pass the White House or go to the Capitol itself.) Orders were given to fall out, and the marchers broke ranks to walk quietly back to Anacostia. They had heard that in less than a week the House would vote on the bonus bill. If it passed both the House and the Senate and was signed by Hoover, most of the veterans could collect the thousand dollars needed to get their hungry families through another depression year.

The parade was simply a beginning. Veterans kept coming to Washington—the police estimated a hundred every hour. On June 15, when the House passed the bill, there were probably 15,000 veterans, plus some of their wives and children, scattered around Washington. Anacostia Flats was crowded, but new shacks kept going up. By now the ex-soldiers had stripped half the city of every stray board or door, every spare piece of tin or canvas. One man moved a burial vault onto the flats and took up residence in it. The camp was about level with the river, and had to be protected by a levee. When it rained, mud was a foot deep. But the Bonus Army kept building.

General Pelham D. Glassford here watches some men at Anacostia Flats prepare a stew for their dinner. Although as chief of police he was responsible for dealing with the alarming number of veterans arriving in the capital, Glassford was not unsympathetic to the Bonus Marchers' cause.

Obviously some kind of crisis might soon develop. Health officials predicted a typhoid epidemic. Waters predicted victory when 100,000 more veterans arrived. Hoover's advisers predicted that communists would take over the Bonus Force.

The Bonus Army and the administration were both waiting for the Senate to vote on the Patman bill. Hoover was sure he would win. The House elected in 1930 was Democratic. Since it was the first body of politicians to graduate from the depression, it was full of representatives who had recently promised their constituents direct action. But only a third of the Senate had been elected in 1930. The majority were still firmly Republican and loyal to the President. Both houses were striving for a July adjournment. (It was an election year, and everyone wanted to get home to campaign.) The administration hoped that the Bonus Army would simply disappear after the Senate voted and Congress adjourned.

On June 17 the Senate would debate and vote on the bonus. Waters commanded his marchers to go to the Capitol and fill the galleries, steps, and grounds. By noon, there were 10,000 marchers in and around the Capitol.

Inside, the Senate debated. Men would leave the galleries every few minutes to report to the marchers out on the steps. The opponents of the bill argued Hoover's position on what should be done about the depression: the government ought to cut spending, not spend more. Direct relief to individuals was not a federal responsibility. Recovery would come as large banks, businesses, and railroads regained their health. Then jobs would become available, and the economy would escape from radical tinkering.

Many senators supporting the bill argued that since the veterans were hungry and would be able to collect the bonus in thirteen years anyway, they should have it now. But one or two senators gave a more complicated justification for the bonus. In a depression, they insisted, the government should spend money, not save it. If the government printed 2 1/2 billion new dollars for the bonus, the money would swiftly circulate. The veterans would be only the first to gain. Then the stores where they spent their payments would get the money. These stores, in turn, would order more goods from wholesalers and manufacturers. So every bonus dollar would become a dollar in motion, moving through the economy and stimulating all business. Naturally, when the depression was cured, the government would stop deficit spending—that is, spending more than it raised in taxes. The economy would return to normal. The government would only "prime the

Thousands of veterans waited tensely on the steps of the Capitol, as the Senate debated the fate of their bonus. The eventual defeat of the Patman bill that would have made their dream a reality nearly triggered a violent confrontation between them and the marines.

pump" with its paper dollars. The happy results would then be automatic.

Though the argument went on, it soon became clear that only a political miracle could save the bonus. The Senate was much too conservative to experiment with such legislation. Even some of the liberal senators who usually opposed Hoover questioned the bill. What was needed, they said, was a general bill for relief of all the unemployed. Veterans should receive no special favors.

Finally, after eight o'clock, someone came from the galleries and whispered to Waters. The bill had lost decisively, 62 to 18. Waters climbed the steps and turned to face the largest body ever gathered in Washington to demonstrate for a cause. The marchers had been waiting for hours, and for a moment it seemed as if they might riot. Marines were stationed nearby, just in case. Members of the administration wanted to ready machine guns, but Glassford persuaded them not to. Waters shouted: "Comrades![2] I have bad news. Let us show them we can take it on the chin. Let us show them we are patriotic Americans." There was a muttering from the crowd. Then a gigantic roar came from 10,000 throats. Waters pleaded for calm:

> We are not telling you to go home. Go back to your camps. We are going to stay in Washington until we get the bonus, no matter how long it takes. And we are one hundred times as good Americans as those men in there who voted against it. But there is nothing more to be done tonight.

[2] This was an old term from the war, not a communist greeting.

The situation was tenser than any in the capital since the Civil War. Ten thousand disappointed people, who had kept good discipline for weeks, were ready to break and mob the Senate. Waters played a final card to keep order: "I call on you to sing 'America,' he shouted. After a few false starts, the men obeyed. Gradually, the song gathered strength.

The emergency was over, at least for the moment. The singing died out, and bugles sounded assembly. The men milled about, looking for their outfits for the march back to camp. It was dark now, and the nervous men waiting in the White House and the Capitol could take a deep breath. The bonus was dead, at least until Congress reconvened in December, after the presidential elections.

But the Bonus Army did not disappear. The government issued reports that the men were leaving. The Bonus Force and the police reported, however, that new recruits were arriving about as fast as old ones left. Estimates of the size of the force issued by the government, police, newspapers, and the Bonus Army itself varied widely. At its largest the Bonus Army probably numbered just under 20,000 men. Membership shifted constantly; perhaps as many as 50,000 veterans

Veterans inhabited eye-sores such as these, located on government property close to the Capitol. In an election year the government felt especially threatened by their well-publicized presence.

were in Washington at one time or another during June and July of 1932.

The government offered to lend the marchers train fare or gas money to leave town, plus seventy-five cents a day for other expenses. Many veterans simply took the money and stayed in town. Others used it to recruit new members. Thus, a month after the Senate defeated the Patman bill, there were about as many marchers as ever. The police estimated 15,000 people, two-thirds of them now crowded into Anacostia Flats.

By July, with no hope of a bonus from Congress, the veterans' mood soured. Their newspaper published more militant calls for action. Waters began to allow the small group of about 150 communists to eat occasionally at the Anacostia mess. (He had always thrown them out before.) He even began to talk about a permanent organization of veterans in politics, which he would call "Khaki Shirts," in imitation of the "Brown Shirts" that Adolf Hitler had organized.

In the White House, too, opinions were getting stronger. After the Senate defeated the bonus, the President decided the marchers had no business squatting on government land. He also decided they were not truly patriotic veterans asking for relief. Instead he believed they had been

organized and promoted by the communists, and included a large number of hoodlums and ex-convicts determined to raise a public disturbance. They were frequently addressed by Democratic congressmen, seeking to inflame them against me.

The differences grew sharper, the summer hotter, and tempers shorter. On July 16 the most serious incident so far broke out at the Capitol. Congress was about to adjourn. Waters order his men to make one last symbolic demonstration. By midday nearly 7,000 Bonus Marchers were at the Capitol. Their mood was much uglier than a month before. Senators and congressmen crowded near every window to watch. Even Glassford lost his nerve.

Glassford ordered Waters taken into custody and moved to the basement of the Capitol. When the veterans saw what was happening, they stopped cheering Glassford and began to boo and jeer. "Waters! Waters!" they shouted. Glassford was forced to bring the Bonus Army's commander onto the platform. After a short, harsh exchange with Glassford, Waters tried to calm his people. Then he ordered them to move to the middle: "Use the center steps. But I want you to keep a lane open for the white-collared birds, so they won't rub into us lousy rats. We're going to stay here until I see Hoover!"

The demonstration was clearly dangerous. Several congressmen came out of the Capitol to speak to the demonstrators, trying to cool them off. Finally the Speaker of the House, John Nance Garner, agreed to meet with Waters and a committee of his aides inside the building. Garner handled the situation well. He made a few empty promises of help and was photographed with Waters. When the conference was over, Waters went back outside and ordered his followers to their camps. For a second time an extremely touchy and potentially violent situation had been controlled.

In the White House, however, tempers were also growing shorter. Hoover had just been renominated by the Republicans to run for a second term. The Democrats would meet soon to nominate Franklin D. Roosevelt, then governor of New York. Hoover knew the campaign would be rough. But he knew he would win if he overcame the widespread idea that he was responsible for the depression. A favorite tactic of Hoover's closest associates was to picture him as the firm opponent of all kinds of radicalism.

Unfortunately, the Bonus Army was the most visible kind of radicalism. Hoover had always opposed the bonus. Now he and his advisers decided to move firmly against the veterans. Some even hoped for an incident. Then it would appear that the government had to defend its very life against a radical insurrection.

A few days after Congress adjourned, the administration decided to move. The tensest point in Washington was the two square blocks on the south side of Pennsylvania Avenue, just a block from the Capitol and a mile from the White House. The buildings here were part of a triangle of structures that had been condemned to make way for a government building program. All over the triangle veterans camped in and around vacant and half-demolished structures, eye-sores that embarrassed the administration. On July 21, on instructions from the Treasury Department, the commissioners who governed the District of Columbia (and were directly responsible to the administration) ordered the veterans to evacuate the two blocks. For various reasons the order was not carried out at once. But Waters told his people to be ready to leave. Glassford was locating another site farther away, where they could take their few possessions and settle again.

Finally, at about 10 A.M. on July 28, Treasury officials accompanied by Glassford and his police entered the area. The veterans began to evacuate the buildings and vacant lots, leaving behind everything that they could not carry or push along in small carts or baby carriages. Everything went peacefully, though a few veterans had to be taken out under arrest. Before noon the first building was empty. In the mean-

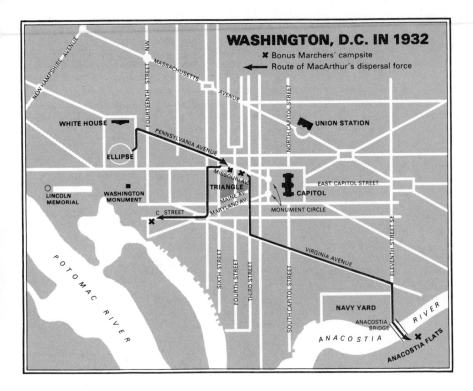

WASHINGTON, D.C. IN 1932

✖ Bonus Marchers' campsite
← Route of MacArthur's dispersal force

time, a large crowd of Washington citizens gathered to watch. Their sympathies were divided between the police and the veterans.

Then, a little past noon veterans from other camps filtered into the area, mixing with the crowd. One group came to stage a formal demonstration. Paul Anderson, a journalist, watched what happened next:

> At noon, three bonus men, one carrying a large American flag, started across the block, followed by several hundred. When the leaders encountered a policeman, he grabbed the flag. There was a scuffle, and one of the marchers was hit on the head with a night stick. He wrested it from the officer and struck the cop, and there was a shower of bricks from the buddies in the rear. It looked like an ugly mess, but the cops kept their heads, and no shots were fired.
>
> Glassford dashed into the heart of the melee, smiled when a brickbat hit him on the chest, and stopped the fighting. Within two minutes, the veterans were cheering Glassford.

For another half-hour the police continued their work. The veterans were leaving the buildings, but they stood around outside, many on big piles of bricks. No one is certain what happened next. Some witnesses said a policeman tried to clear veterans out of a building that had not even been ordered vacated. They resisted. Another observer said that a policeman started climbing some makeshift stairs, lost his balance, and fell. In a panic he pulled his revolver and began to fire wildly into a crowd near him. General Glassford gave what may be the most accurate account:

> I was about twenty yards away from the building when I heard a commotion. I went to the second floor. One officer had started up the steps, and near the rear, I heard some say, "Let's get him!"
>
> As he started up the steps, bricks started falling on him [Glassford was not certain whether the bricks were being thrown or were just falling], and as I leaned over the railing above, I saw him fall and draw his gun, firing two shots.

Other policemen also started shooting. Then veterans began to throw bricks at every policeman in sight. Again Glassford acted quickly to prevent a vicious riot. He ran outside, shouting, "Stop that shooting!" The firing ended, and the bricks stopped flying. Ambulances rushed to take away the injured. One policeman was hurt seriously by a brick. One Bonus Marcher was dead; another died later of gunshot wounds.

The battle of the Bonus Army might have ended here. Glassford had the situation in hand. The veterans were moving out of the buildings as they had been ordered. On the whole they were reluctant but still willing to cooperate. Waters had supported Glassford every step of the way. Within another hour or two the evacuation of the two blocks

When the Bonus Marchers were ordered to clear the federal property on which they had been squatting, fights broke out between them and the police that led to a larger battle.

would have been complete. But the administration also had decided to act. Hoover ordered the Chief of Staff of the Army, General MacArthur, to bring troops into the city to restore civil peace.

The troops—about 500 at first, then later over 1,000—formed up behind the White House. They came armed with bayoneted rifles and heavy blue canisters of tear gas. There were cavalry with sabers, a machine-gun squadron, several infantry companies, and even a half-dozen tanks. MacArthur put the troops under the command of General Perry L. Miles. But he later wrote, "In accordance with the President's request, I accompanied General Miles." With MacArthur was his aide, Major Dwight David Eisenhower. And in the cavalry was George S. Patton (who had no way of knowing that Joe Angelo had come back to Washington and was out in the troubled city with about 12,000 of his buddies, waiting).

At about four o'clock the cavalry led the way, the iron shoes of their horses clattering on the asphalt of Pennsylvania Avenue. Then came tanks, more cavalry, the infantry, and the mounted machine gunners. They rode, walked, and rumbled up to the triangle, pushing the crowds back and surrounding the buildings. Without any conference or hesitation the troops (who wore gas masks and carried fixed bayonets) began to throw tear-gas bombs into the buildings. They were going to clear the entire area.

The veterans did not resist. A few hung back, and had to be jabbed at with bayonets. Mostly they stumbled out of the area and toward Anacostia. MacArthur, who also had tears streaming down his face from the tear gas, ordered most of his men to herd the veterans south. Another detachment moved west, to attack the small, separate camp of the communist group.[3] Suddenly, it became clear that the general intended to clear the entire District. In the triangle, smoke began to rise. There, the troops had set fire to the shacks, tents, and scattered belongings of the Bonus Army.

MacArthur's forces kept pushing the straggling veterans before them with bayonets and sabers. The sun was going down behind them. Ahead lay the drawbridge to Anacostia. The Bonus Army's rear guard hurried across the bridge at about sunset. Waters had already given the order to evacuate Anacostia and had sent word to MacArthur asking for time to move women and children out of the camp. On the flats about 7,000 men were scurrying around, trying to keep order in a forced retreat.

From the time the troops first appeared, the bonus marchers gave

General Douglas MacArthur with his aide, Dwight David Eisenhower, led the forces that finally cleared Washington of Bonus Marchers. MacArthur later claimed that if the situation had continued the institutions of government would have been threatened.

---

[3] Communists in this camp included James Ford, their candidate for Vice President. On July 31 the New York *Times* ran a front-page article quoting the communists. "We agitated for the bonus and led the demonstration of the veterans in Washington." However, the communists were never the Bonus Force's prime movers.

Troopers used tear gas in a final effort to clear the Bonus Marchers out of Washington.
The veterans were forced to retreat and in the main did not resist.

no resistance. They hung back, they booed, they swore—but they moved. MacArthur left his tanks north of the river and paused before Anacostia Flats for an hour before sending the infantry. But when they went onto the flats, the soldiers threw tear gas everywhere. Stragglers were treated very roughly. The soldiers then set fire to the camp. (Many of the veterans has already put matches to their borrowed army tents.) Next they moved out of the camp to the nearby area where many of the veterans still stood watching their shacks burn. As the troops rushed up the hill which was not federal property, they continued to throw tear gas. One woman, whose baby had actually been born since the Bonus Army's arrival, told this story:

> The troops came up the hill, driving the people ahead of them. As they passed by the house [where the woman was staying], one of them threw a tear-gas bomb over the fence into the front yard. The house was filled with gas, and we all began to cry. We got wet towels and put them over the faces of the children. About a half an hour later, my baby began to vomit. I took her outside in the air and she vomited again. Next day, she began to turn black and blue.

A few days later the baby died—the third and last fatality of the battle of the Bonus Army.

The day after the action was a time for summing-up. The White House and other administration officials issued statements. MacArthur gave his version in a press conference:

That mob was a bad-looking mob. It was animated by the essence of revolution. They had come to the conclusion, beyond the shadow of a doubt, that they were about to take over either the direct control of the government, or else to control it by indirect methods. It is my belief that had the President not acted today, he would have been faced with a grave situation. Had he let it go on another week, I believe that the institutions of our government would have been severely threatened.

To this version of the threat posed by the Bonus Force, MacArthur added a simple lie—that it was the veterans who had burned their shacks in the triangle.

Another kind of summing-up came from Joe Angelo, who told a newspaper reporter his story. He was at Anacostia Flats, watching a group of infantrymen in gas masks overrun the shack he had been living in. They were urged on by a tough, confident cavalry officer. Angelo blinked the burning tear gas out of his eyes and recognized George S. Patton. Then like the rest of the Bonus Army, he ran. Soon he was back home in Camden, from where he had started his long hike to Washington a year and a half before.

On July 29, 1932, in a blazing finale that brought the battle of the Bonus Army to an end, the camps at Anacostia Flats went up in flames.

34

Prosperity and Depression

Most Of The Bonus March veterans who went to Washington were as politically innocent as Joe Angelo. Some of their leaders had a little political knowledge—and the tiny fraction who were communists thought they understood the basic problems of American society and sought a revolutionary solution. But the great rank and file of the marchers were simply caught in a web of circumstances they did not understand or want.

These people had been affected deeply by all the technological and social changes of the 1920s. But when they came to Washington in 1932 to demand their bonus, the veterans faced a much more frightening challenge. The 1920s had been difficult times in many ways; life grew more and more unsettled and confused. But in 1929 every problem of living in a modern society came to a head in an economic depression. Millions of Americans—not just Bonus Marchers—came to realize that their government had grown too rigid to deal effectively with the realities of unemployment, hunger, and economic collapse.

The Bonus Marchers asked the federal government to take an unusual step to meet an unusual difficulty. The Hoover administration's refusal to pay the bonus was part of the political reality of inflexibility and conservatism that had developed in the 1920s. But, soon after the marchers were driven out, an election swept Hoover out, too. Franklin Delano Roosevelt became President, promising a New Deal that would end the depression and cure some of the economic ailments of the preceding decade. A generation that had already lived through sweeping technological and social changes now was to experience equally vast changes in the American economy and government—changes that the Bonus Army experienced and, in a small way at least, helped to bring about.

HARDING'S CONSERVATIVE REVIVAL

With the end of World War I the Republicans sensed a mood in the country of relaxation from the demands of reform and war on which the Wilson administration had built its policies. They met full of hope at their national convention in Chicago in 1920. They were still the majority party. President Wilson's illness had disorganized the Democrats.

Still, the party was split into two factions. The convention deadlocked for six ballots because no candidate could get a majority. Then a few party leaders huddled in the most famous "smoke-filled room" in American history and chose a presidential candidate—Warren Gamaliel Harding.

Harding was a small-town newspaper publisher and politician. He had risen through the ranks of Ohio Republicans to become a senator. A handsome but simple man, he was puzzled by complicated issues like taxation, the tariff, and foreign affairs. He was "one of the boys," who enjoyed a night of whiskey and poker with his cronies. He had never proposed an important law or policy, nor made an important speech, in his whole career. But he had a face that voters wanted to trust. And the people who ran the party knew they could trust him, too. He was a

party regular. He would not have any strange ideas about regulating business or supporting labor unions or propose any odd reforms. He was, in a word, conservative.

For Vice President, the Republicans nominated Calvin Coolidge, another small-town politician who had become governor of Massachusetts. Coolidge was less a party regular than Harding, but he was just as conservative. And no one imagined, anyway, that he would every be anything but Vice President.

The Democrats nominated a lackluster candidate, James M. Cox. They did try to spice up the ticket with a dashing young New Yorker, Franklin D. Roosevelt. Roosevelt had served as assistant secretary of the navy under Wilson. The

Warren Harding, who won the presidency by being one of the boys, was aware of his limitations. About his search for a capable economic advisor he said: "I don't know where to find him and haven't the sense to trust him when I find him." His candor was winning but, unfortunately, prophetic.

convention hoped the Roosevelt name would attract voters who remembered his cousin Theodore. But probably no Democratic ticket could have won in 1920. The voters wanted a change. Sixty percent of them voted for Harding. They also sent large Republican majorities to both the House and Senate, making it one of the most complete victories in the history of American national politics. Harding carried every state outside the Democrats' solid South and cracked even that by winning Tennessee. The repudiation of Wilson's New Freedom seemed complete.

Return to Normalcy Harding took office with a slogan that coined a new word. He said the country needed a "return to normalcy." No dictionary defined "normalcy," but almost every American probably knew what the President meant. Harding believed that there had been too much experimentation, too many attempts to regulate the economy and the working lives of Americans, too much speculation about new diplomatic arrangements such as the League of Nations. Normalcy meant letting things take their natural course—not interfering in the decisions of businessmen or in the complex affairs of other nations. Normalcy meant, in short, a return to simpler times and uncomplicated politics.

Harding's relaxed conservatism was not actually a well-defined policy. Rather it was a wish for fewer policies and less activity by the government. For his Cabinet the President chose people sympathetic to the practices of industrial and business leaders. His most important appointment, in fact, was Secretary of the Treasury Andrew Mellon, a Pennsylvania industrialist who owned the only important company then making aluminum in the United States.

Mellon helped to shape the small amount of legislation that the Harding administration presented to Congress. His pet bill was one cutting the income tax on the wealthy from a maximum of 65 percent to 25 percent. (Congress at first reduced the limit to only 50 percent, but Mellon later got most of what he wanted.) He also proposed, and got from Congress, much higher tariffs on imports, a policy that benefited American business and industry by limiting foreign competition.

The Ohio Gang Specific legislation was less important in Harding's conservative administration than its general relaxation of federal controls over business. Harding did not try to tear down the established regulatory agencies, like the Interstate Commerce Commission or Federal Reserve Board. Instead, he merely appointed persons to these agencies who were so friendly toward corporations that they administered the law gently or not at all. And Harding named as his Secretary of Commerce Herbert Hoover, who had made a fortune as a mining engineer and investor. Hoover used the Commerce Department to help, not hinder, the activities of American businessmen. His approach typified the triumphant conservatism of Harding's administration.

Unfortunately, Harding also brought to Washington a group of friends who soon became known as the Ohio Gang. Some held seemingly harmless positions, like Old Doc Sawyer, a doctor in less than good standing with the medical profession. Old Doc became the White House physician, with the rank of army brigadier general. Other Ohio Gang members took more important positions such as Attorney General and Secretary of the Interior.

After two years in office, Harding, who was personally honest about money, began to realize that his appointees were stealing and peddling influence. In the spring and summer of 1923 two administration officials committed suicide while being investigated. In June Harding began a long vacation in the West. As he left, he complained to a journalist, "My God, this is a hell of a job. I have no trouble with my enemies. But my friends! They're the ones that keep me walking the floor nights!"

Two months later, in California after a trip to Alaska, Harding suffered from what Old Doc Sawyer called food poisoning. Harding now had to pay in person for this political appointment, for Sawyer was wrong. The President had suffered a heart attack instead; on August 2 he died.

In a way, Harding was lucky. He was mourned by his countrymen almost as much as Lincoln had been. He was spared the knowledge of a new scandal that would later become almost synonymous with his name.

Albert Fall, Harding's Secretary of the Interior, had finagled Interior Department control of oil reserves set aside for the navy. There were two large reserves, at Elk Hill in California and at Teapot Dome in Wyoming. Private oil interests were willing to pay almost any price to drill the land. They did.

Two oil company executives, Edward L. Doheny and Harry F. Sinclair, gave and "lent" Fall almost a half million dollars in return for secret leases allowing them to drill on the reserves. The secret leaked out faster than the oil. The Government managed to cancel the leases, but Fall went to prison for a year. He was the first Cabinet officer in American history to be put behind bars.

When the Teapot Dome scandal, involving the bribing of Republican officials, broke, a Memphis newspaper published this cartoon entitled, "Assuming Definite Shape."

COOLIDGE AND BUSINESS

When Harding died, Vice President Calvin Coolidge became President. Though privately a talkative man, "Silent Cal," as Coolidge was called, spoke very little in public. He kept most of Harding's appointees, and basically followed his predecessor's policies for the rest of the term. As the 1924 election approached, there was little doubt about what the Republicans would do. Their convention enthusiastically nominated Coolidge.

The Democrats experienced a struggle between two wings of their party. One represented the rural South and West, the old Bryan supporters. They were at least as conservative as the Republicans. The other wing was newer and based in the Northern cities. It was made up mostly of "wets" (opponents of prohibition) and depended heavily on the support of immigrants (many of them Catholics or Jews). After 103 ballots the convention settled on a compromise candidate, John W. Davis.

Coolidge was conservative. But so was Da-vis, who was associated with the firm of J. P. Morgan. Once more the time seemed right, as in 1912, to try a third party. The Progressive candidate was Robert La Follette, now nearly seventy but still a fiery opponent of business interests. He did well. Coolidge won the election easily, though, with 15 million votes. But La Follette managed to get almost 5 million votes, and to carry Wisconsin's electoral vote. Davis and his badly split party could muster only 8 1/2 million votes, less than a third of the total.

Coolidge's second term in office was a continuation of the conservative policies of the earlier years, but without the scandals of 1921–23. Mellon and Hoover still exercised great influence. The new administration went on supporting high tariffs, low taxes on corporations and the wealthy, and a hands-off policy on trusts. It had an essentially do-nothing approach to farm problems and a negative attitude toward labor as well. The entire conservative politics of the 1920s was summed up in Coolidge's most famous sentence: "The business of America is business."

Still, the President was popular, and doubtless he could have been nominated for a second full term and won. But his second most famous sentence was: "I do not choose to run." Coolidge may have meant simply that he would accept a draft. Still, for once, "Silent Cal" had spoken too soon and said too much. The Republicans took him literally and turned to Herbert Hoover, the most prestigious official in the administration.

The Democratic Challenge of 1928 The Democrats partially healed their old split, hoping for victory. Governor Alfred E. Smith of New York won the nomination easily. Smith and Hoover were almost perfect contrasts. Hoover was conservative, even gloomy. He dressed in neat blue suits and was the perfect representative of stability and efficiency. Above all he opposed any extension of federal power over private enterprise (unless, as with tariffs, federal power could be used to help business).

Smith, on the other hand, was a happy, talkative, cigar-chomping Irish American politician. He wore a brown derby and checked suits and talked with an urban twang. His Catholicism and the fact that he was a "wet" disturbed rural voters, especially in the South. During the campaign Hoover accused Smith of socialism because the New Yorker favored federal ownership of electric power generating facilities.

But Smith did not really differ much from Hoover on economic policies. The contest was actually between two political styles. And Hoover won. He came close to Harding's record with 58 percent of the vote. In doing so, he cut deeply into the South, where he carried Virginia, Tennessee, North Carolina, Florida, Arkansas, and Texas. Hoover amassed 21 million popular votes, more than Coolidge and La Follette combined in 1924.

Plainly, the Republican regime was still in full swing. Hoover could look to the future with even more confidence than Harding or Coolidge. Surely a strong industrial system—watched over at a distance by a friendly government—would now move the nation into unheard-of prosperity.

BOOM AND BUST

On the surface, at least, the 1920s was a decade of great prosperity. Progress seemed inevitable as more and more cars, radios, washing machines, and other goods poured off assembly

One of every four farms was sold for debt or taxes from 1920 to 1932. Farm machinery proved costly not only in purchase price but in the overproduction and falling prices it caused. Dust storms on the plains in the thirties proved the final blow to many more farms like the one pictured.

lines. More workers were producing more goods than ever before. The United States seemed to have created an economic miracle.

American buyers and investors were confident. The New York Stock Exchange, where the economy's pulse seemed most vital, enjoyed an amazing boom period after 1923. Sales on the Exchange quadrupled between 1923 and 1930. As sales increased, so did the prices of stocks. Americans were on an investment binge. The total amount of money they kept in stocks and bonds increased faster than any other economic factor during the period (much faster, for example, than actual production or sales of goods).

Much of the new investment was made on credit. According to the rules of the New York Stock Exchange, investors could buy stock by putting some money down and owing the rest to their brokers. These "brokers' loans" showed how little of the investment rush was real money and how much was pure speculation. By 1927 almost $4 billion was still owed on such loans. The whole structure of the stock market was rickety.

Such investment was really a form of gambling. If a stock cost $10 a share and an investor expected it to go up, he could buy a share and wait for the price to rise. But he could also buy ten shares, one for cash and the other nine on loan. When the stock went up, he could then sell his shares at the new price, pay off his broker, and pocket the difference in cash. There would be a problem though if the stock went down. Then, when the broker's loan was due, the investor might have to sell not only his ten shares of stock but other assets as well. If the stock market fell too low, he could be ruined.

Year after year, the gambles paid off. More and more ordinary people with only small amounts of money began to play the market. The prospering economy appeared to justify their confidence.

A Warped Economy But this prosperity was very unevenly distributed through the population. There were many large pockets of people throughout the country who did not share it at

all. Blacks in both the South and the North did not benefit much. Nor did most farmers, whose lives had long been difficult.

The problem of farmers was an especially hard one to solve. During the war they had been relatively prosperous, producing both for the home front and the battle front overseas. But after the war, the demand in both markets decreased. Complicating the picture, farmers greedily bought up new farm machinery, such as new gasoline-powered tractors. Mechanization increased production. But since the market was smaller than it had been, the effect was overproduction and a sharp drop in prices.

The position of laborers was better. Except for "sick" industries such as coal mining and textiles, conditions of labor had improved and living standards had risen. The progress occurred despite the fact that the union movement was not growing. The lack of growth resulted from the cautious and conservative policies of the leading union movement, the AFL, and a campaign by manufacturers to win acceptance of the open (that is, nonunion) shop. Perhaps because wages seemed to be rising, labor was not militant in organizing. But, a dangerous trend was developing in the economy: the power of people to buy goods was not keeping pace with the volume of goods being produced.

This problem did not result from conscious decisions by any group. The new technology let factories turn out more and more goods. So the total output of products for sale increased much faster than the population. This increase should have meant that almost everyone could have more of life's comforts and conveniences. For this to happen, manufacturers would have to raise wages or lower prices, or both, as production became cheaper. Then the people who actually made the goods could afford to buy them.

But businessmen generally raised wages less than they should have. They also kept prices high. In the short run, their measures meant higher profits—and higher profits for corporations meant the price of their stock rose. They could either invest the profits in still larger factories to produce still more goods. Or they could invest them in stock, to heat up the stock market even more. Many corporations did both.

The result was a warped economy. The amount of goods that could be produced ran far ahead of the people's power to purchase them. Sooner or later, an adjustment had to be made. Otherwise factories would have to close until the surplus cars, clothes, tools, and other items could be bought. For a time the problem could be avoided in two ways. The surplus products could be sold, on credit, to people who could not really afford them. A family could pay for a car, for example, over two or three years. Or, the surplus could be exported to foreign countries. But both credit and exporting could help a warped economic system only briefly.

The Stock Market Crash These facts were difficult to see. On the surface, the economy had never looked better, and Americans continued to bet on the future by speculating in stocks. In 1928 the average price of industrial stocks increased by about 25 percent. An investor who bought, say, $1,000 worth of stock in January could sell it in December for $1,250. Or he could take the extra $250 and invest it in some new gamble. Most speculators did the latter.

Then, after a few rumblings and warnings, the bubble burst. The stock market was not a sure indicator of economic health or disease. In 1929 reality finally caught up with it.

In September the most popular index of stock prices stood at 452. Two months later it was 234. What this meant, in plain terms, was that the market value of stocks on the Exchange had been halved. Most of the holders of the $4 billion in brokers' loans were ruined. So were many of the brokers. On the worst day of all, "Black Tuesday," October 29, the market index fell 43 points. Other days were almost as bleak and ruinous. Stock prices continued to slide. They reached bottom in 1932. Then most stocks were worth little more than a tenth of their cost in September 1929. The Great Depression had begun.

It was difficult then, and still is, for people to understand why the panic on Wall Street should have had any effect on the real economy. The factories were still there, ready to roll out goods. The farms were still there, ready to produce food. All the hands willing to work before Black Tuesday were still there, still willing to work.

But, month by month, the entire economic machine ground down. The stock market crash was the crucial link in the chain of events leading to this breakdown. It caused people to make some grim decisions: not to buy or invest. Many foreclosed on loans made to others because they needed money to pay off their own loans. So storekeepers sold less. And factories made less or closed down altogether.

Farmers behind on their payments lost their farms as banks desperately tried to collect hard cash. The banks needed cash because millions of people with savings accounts, frightened now, lined up at tellers' windows to withdraw their money. The banks often could not produce the cash because they had invested or lent it. So even the banks began to fail.

Builders of houses or offices stopped construction because they could not borrow money to continue. Down at the bottom of this tangle were plain workers who, by the millions, received notices that they need not come to work anymore. Their jobs disappeared. Since they could not work, they could not buy; since they could not buy, others could not sell or make goods.

The jobless were not just the old-line poor. Many had been solid, middle-class citizens, bank tellers or factory foremen. Others were farmers, who had barely managed to survive throughout the decade. Now they had lost their farms forever. They came to cities, looking for food and work, or they began to drift, looking for migrant workers' jobs. People combed garbage heaps for food for their families. They made soup from dandelions. Mostly, however, they waited in a cold, gloomy fog of despair for something to happen.

Hoover's Optimism The question posed by the depression and symbolized by the Bonus March was simple. Could the federal government be

Amid the bright lights of Times Square hundreds of New York's hungry formed bread lines in 1932. Ironically, scarcity was not the problem. As Socialist Norman Thomas remarked: "It remained for us to invent bread lines knee-deep in wheat."

used as a tool for dealing with economic disaster? In the past the answer had been no. Other depressions had been allowed to run their course without any federal attempt to bring early recovery or relieve human suffering. But the Great Depression was by far the worst ever. Now the industrial economy was so large and complicated that its collapse affected people far more. Countless millions were jobless, banks were failing by the thousands, and tens of thousands needed food. Something had to be done.

At first the Hoover administration was optimistic. The stock market crash was called a needed adjustment. The economy, Hoover announced, was fundamentally sound. Recovery would be natural and would come soon. Meanwhile, no federal action of any kind was needed.

Surprisingly, most Democrats agreed. In the congressional elections of 1930, the Democrats made prohibition as big an issue as the depression. Nor did the voters heavily punish the administration for its failure to bring about recovery. The Democrats won the House but the Senate stayed Republican. Hoover was still predicting that a return to prosperity was just around the corner.

But things kept getting worse. In 1929, over 600 banks shut down; in 1930, over 1,000; in 1931, 2,000. For farmers there seemed to be no bottom. Wheat in 1931 sold for $.36 a bushel compared to $1.03 in 1929. No one even knew how many people were unemployed by 1932, but guesses ran as high as 15 million. For those who still had jobs, pay envelopes grew smaller. By 1932 wages in industry were less than half what they had been in 1928.

As he faced all these facts—or, sometimes, tried not to face them—the President grew gloomy and confused. He tried to stay optimistic in public, believing business confidence was crucial to recovery. In private, however, he was trapped between two different beliefs. A humane man, he did not like to see people suffer. But he still thought that government should not interfere in the economy. Free enterprise would bring the nation back to its feet.

Most important, Hoover believed that the federal government must never give direct relief to the poor, unemployed, and hungry. Direct federal welfare, he thought, would destroy people's moral character. It would make them dependent instead of healthy, strong personalities. This set of attitudes, which he referred to as individualism made Hoover seem insensitive and cruel. He became the target of bitter jokes. People named their shantytowns Hoovervilles and called an empty pocket, turned inside out, a Hoover flag. Reluctantly, Hoover decided that the government must act.

New Federal Powers   Early in 1932 Hoover signed a law creating a new federal agency, the Reconstruction Finance Corporation (RFC). It could lend up to $2 billion to banks, insurance companies, and railroads. These loans, the administration believed, would be used especially by the banks to make other loans to businesses. Businesses would in turn use the money for new construction or to reopen factories. Their moves would create new jobs and save old ones. Thus, eventually RFC loans would end up in the pockets of workers, who would then spend the money and create new demand, resulting in more new production, and so on, in a circle of recovery.

The President also went against his own beliefs by signing another law empowering the RFC to lend relief money to state governments. But the amount of the loans was too small to help much. Pennsylvania, for example, could borrow only enough to provide three cents a day to its unemployed workers. Also, the RFC loans to business were far too small to aid the economy effectively. Compared to previous government activity, Hoover's actions were bold experiments in the use of federal power. But, measured against what was actually needed, they were too little too late as the Bonus Marchers recognized.

The Election of 1932   This state of affairs led to the dramatic election of 1932. When the Democrats met, they could smell victory. The Republicans had renominated Hoover, and, against him, almost any Democrat seemed sure to win. The tide was running toward Franklin Roosevelt, who had been working diligently for the nomination for months.

In contrast to Hoover, the nominee was a cheerful, brash man who was an experienced politician. In 1921 Roosevelt was crippled by polio. But he fought back with energy and could stand with the help of braces and canes. He brought a spirit of energy and experimentation lacking in the Hoover administration. He even broke a long tradition by going to the convention to accept the nomination in person (flying there, to symbolize his modernity). Standing before the cheering delegates, he announced that he would be different:

> Let it be symbolic that I broke tradition [by coming to the convention].
> Republican leaders not only have failed in material things, they have failed in national vision, because in disaster, they have held out no hope. I pledge you, I pledge myself to a new deal for the American people.

In the campaign no one quite knew what this "new deal" would be. Roosevelt was vague, but promised that the government would relieve suffering, provide jobs, and stabilize the economy. This promise, plus the fact the country blamed Hoover for causing the depression, was enough to give FDR, as he was often called, a smashing victory.

Roosevelt received almost 23 million votes to Hoover's 15 million. Just as important, the Democrats, for the first time in modern history, won large majorities in both the House and Senate. On inauguration day, March 4, 1933, Roosevelt expressed his optimistic belief that the government could and should act to heal the

After the stock market crash people lost confidence and began to withdraw their money from banks. As a result banks, like this one in New York City, failed or were closed by state order.

nation: "Let me assert my firm belief that the only thing we have to fear is fear itself. This nation asks for action, and action *now*."

ROOSEVELT'S NEW DEAL

The words were brave. They had to be, for the crisis had reached panic proportions. A growing sense of despair had spread throughout the country. Millions roamed the country in search of food, shelter, and employment. Some even returned to Europe in search of work. As radios blared popular songs such as "Brother, Can You Spare a Dime?" bread lines and Hoovervilles were set up in every major city. Private, local, and state relief funds were proving insufficient for the emergency. Never had the majority of Americans been so pessimistic about the country's future.

Of immediate concern to Roosevelt was keeping the entire banking system from collapsing. Many banks were failing. A bank "holiday" closing all banks to protect them from bankruptcy, was declared in Michigan. Hoover, the night before he left office, said, "We are at the end of our rope." Roosevelt simply stretched his constitutional powers and declared a national bank holiday until further notice. Then, only five days after the inauguration, he sent to Congress an Emergency Banking Relief Act, which allowed the RFC to buy stock in banks. The law would allow the government to save a failing bank by providing cash to pay its depositors. Amazingly, the act passed both houses of Congress in eight hours! The New Deal was under way.

The Debate Over Meaning Ever since the 1930s Americans have debated almost endlessly

MAJOR NEW DEAL DOMESTIC LEGISLATION

YEAR	ACT/ADMINISTRATION	PURPOSE
BANKING, CURRENCY, SECURITIES		
1933	EMERGENCY BANKING RELIEF ACT	To save failing banks by providing them with cash to pay their depositors.
	GLASS-STEAGALL ACT	To curb speculation by banks; set up the Federal Deposit Insurance Corporation to "insure" savings deposits up to $10,000.
	"TRUTH IN SECURITIES" ACT	To require corporations floating new securities to register them with the Federal Trade Commission.
1934	GOLD RESERVE ACT	To enable the President to fix the gold content of the dollar.
	SECURITIES EXCHANGE ACT	Set up the Securities and Exchange Commission to regulate the Stock Market.
1935	BANKING ACT	To reform and strengthen the Federal Reserve System by directing interest rates.
DIRECT RELIEF		
1933	FARM CREDIT ADMINISTRATION	To provide emergency relief to farmers in the form of mortgages.
	FEDERAL EMERGENCY RELIEF ACT	Set up the Federal Emergency Relief Administration to provide grants in aid to the states; also set up the Civil Works Administration to relieve unemployment by a temporary work relief program.
	FRAZIER-LEMKE FARM BANKRUPTCY ACT	To enable some farmers to regain their farms even after the foreclosure of mortgages.
	HOME OWNERS REFINANCING ACT	Set up the Home Owners' Loan Corporation to provide emergency relief to home owners in the form of government financed mortgage loans.
	NATIONAL INDUSTRIAL RECOVERY ACT	Set up the Public Works Administration to contract for heavy construction projects in order to increase emloyment.
	UNEMPLOYMENT RELIEF ACT	Set up the Civilian Conservation Corps to provide jobs for the unemployed on conservation projects.
1934	NATIONAL HOUSING ACT	Set up the Federal Housing Administration to insure mortgages for new construction and home repairs.
1935	WORKS PROGRESS ADMINISTRATION	To relieve unemployment by light public works projects.
1937	FARM SECURITY ADMINISTRATION	To make short-term loans for rehabilitation of farms, and long-term loans for purchase of farms.

YEAR	ACT / ADMINISTRATION	PURPOSE

REGULATION OF INDUSTRY AND AGRICULTURE

YEAR	ACT / ADMINISTRATION	PURPOSE
1933	AGRICULTURAL ADJUSTMENT ACT	Set up the Agricultural Adjustment Administration to encourage stability in agriculture by attempting to control agricultural production.
	NATIONAL INDUSTRIAL RECOVERY ACT	Set up the National Recovery Administration to encourage corporations to create associations for planning production and controlling prices; created a blanket code of minimum wages and maximum hours.
1935	CONNALLY ACT	To prevent overproduction of oil.
	GUFFEY ACT	To control the coal industry.
	NATIONAL LABOR RELATIONS ACT (WAGNER ACT)	To give federal protection to the labor movement by making it illegal for an employer to refuse to recognize a labor union.
	PUBLIC UTILITIES HOLDING COMPANY ACT	To limit the development of holding companies and discourage financial concentration in public utilities.
1936	ROBINSON-PATMAN ACT	To prohibit wholesalers or manufacturers from giving preferential discounts or rebates to large buyers.
	WALSH-HEALY ACT	To set minimum wages and maximum hours for work done on federal contracts (enacted after NRA declared unconstitutional).
1938	AGRICULTURAL ADJUSTMENT ACT	To cut back farm production through marketing quotas, soil conservation payments, export subsidies, and crop loans. It began storage of surpluses.
	FAIR LABOR STANDARDS ACT	To establish minimum wages and maximum hours; forbade child labor.

REFORM

YEAR	ACT / ADMINISTRATION	PURPOSE
1933	TENNESSEE VALLEY AUTHORITY	Set up the Tennessee Valley Authority to develop the nation's water resources and, therefore, provide cheap electric power.
1935	SOCIAL SECURITY ACT	To create a system of old-age insurance for Americans.
	WEALTH TAX ACT	To make the federal income tax more equitable.

MISCELLANEOUS

YEAR	ACT / ADMINISTRATION	PURPOSE
1934	RECIPROCAL TRADE AGREEMENTS ACT	To lower tariff barriers in order to improve foreign trade.
1939	HATCH ACT	To remedy corrupt campaign practices by prohibiting active political campaigning and soliciting by federal officials.
	REORGANIZATION ACT	To reorganize the executive branch for greater efficiency.

To inspire the American people with a new sense of confidence, Franklin Roosevelt initiated a series of radio broadcasts when he took office. During these "fireside chats" he explained his proposals simply and reassuringly. They won him needed support.

and sometimes angrily about the basic nature and meaning of the New Deal. For some the New Deal was a revolution. They argue that it departed from the normal patterns of American politics to institute new and radical habits of federal regulation of economic and social life. But many other Americans believe that the New Deal produced few really fundamental changes. Roosevelt's programs, according to this view, left both the Constitution and the capitalist economy more or less intact. In fact, Roosevelt's only real purpose was to preserve the American social, economic, and political system from the kinds of revolution that were occurring in some European nations.

There is truth on both sides, depending on what comparisons are made. Compared with previous peacetime Presidents, Roosevelt looks quite revolutionary. The New Deal did take some drastic steps toward federal regulation, control, and planning of the economy. But when compared to the wartime presidencies of Lincoln

or Wilson, Roosevelt's response to the depression appears to be less unusual. Also, when the New Deal is seen as part of the progressive tradition that spans the twentieth century, Roosevelt's "revolution" looks tame indeed.

Those who argue the question often assume that the New Deal was a systematic program based on a coherent political theory. It was not. The New Deal was, instead, a series of laws and executive orders that were designed to meet the problems at hand. There was only one basic idea behind these acts: federal power should be used to cure the depression and, if possible, prevent future collapses of the economy. What held the New Deal together was not ideas, really, but the personality of Roosevelt himself. And that personality was itself confused and contradictory.

The Man Behind the Program   Roosevelt was forty-seven when the stock market collapsed, fifty-one when he became President. His ideas about the world were already formed. There is no evidence that the depression changed them significantly.

He was in many ways a tradition-minded man. He was a wealthy aristocrat, educated in the country's most exclusive private schools, and a graduate of Harvard. He owned a great estate, where he liked to play at being a gentleman farmer. An Episcopalian in religion, he was a commonplace capitalist in private life. He came naturally to his career in regular Democratic party politics because of his family background. Unlike other great American Presidents, he was not a scholar or writer. All in all, Roosevelt was a suave, smiling, confident man who seemed to take the institutions and beliefs of his nation very much for granted. A more unlikely candidate for leader of a revolution is hard to imagine.

On the other hand, Roosevelt's confidence opened his mind to experiments. Because he had no serious doubts about American values and institutions, he could accept almost any concrete suggestion for reform. Above all, he often said, the country demanded action. As long as the action was limited in its scope and possible consequences, he was willing to try almost any-

"About the only value the story of my life may have is to show that one can, without any particular gifts, overcome obstacles that seem insurmountable; that, in spite of timidity and fear, in spite of a lack of special talents, one can find a way to live widely and fully." With these words Eleanor Roosevelt modestly introduced her autobiography in 1960.

Indeed, timidity and fear seemed to be the dominant personality traits of the first half of Eleanor's life. She was born in 1884 to a beautiful mother, a society belle, and a handsome and charming father, the brother of Theodore Roosevelt. But it soon became obvious that she had inherited neither her mother's looks nor her father's ease with people. "I was a shy, solemn child even at the age of two, and I am sure that even when I danced I never smiled." Her mother, somewhat ashamed of her plain daughter, told a visitor in Eleanor's presence, "She is such a funny child, so old-fashioned that we always call her 'Granny.'"

It was an agonizing childhood. "Looking back I see that I was always afraid of something: of the dark, of displeasing people, of failure. Anything I accomplished had to be done across a barrier of fear." By the time she was eight, her mother was dead. Just before her tenth birthday she lost her father too.

Such unhappiness could have resulted in great bitterness. In Eleanor Roosevelt, however, it developed instead into a deep compassion for all human beings and their sufferings. At first it showed itself in the charity work she did. This was in keeping with the young society matron she became after her marriage to her distant cousin Franklin Delano Roosevelt in 1903. But as her horizons expanded, she channeled her compassion into a lifelong crusade for human rights.

In the 1920s she allied herself with the causes of better working conditions and greater political participation for women. With the coming of the

depression she concerned herself with helping hungry, jobless workers.

When her husband became President at the height of the depression, she became his eyes and ears in the field of social conditions. She crossed the country visiting farms, factories, even coal mines. Then she reported her findings to him—what people were thinking, what they needed, how they were bearing up. She became his unofficial ambassador to blacks, and she worked tirelessly to have equal rights extended to them.

In the 1940s Mrs. Roosevelt moved her crusade onto the world scene. She became a delegate to the United Nations and served as chairman of the commission to draft the Universal Declaration of Human Rights. Through her work for that body's Educational, Scientific, and Cultural Organization (UNESCO), she became an international symbol of the eternal struggle for the rights of man.

After her death in 1962, a saddened United Nations listened to United States Ambassador Adlai E. Stevenson eulogize her: "Yesterday I said I lost more than a friend; I lost an inspiration. She would rather light candles than curse the darkness, and her glow has warmed the world."

thing. If his first try did not work, he could easily try something different because he believed the nation was healthy and would survive.

Roosevelt knew that the depression was serious and that the stakes were high. But he was sure, too, that sooner or later limited reforms would revive the economy. Then all that would be needed was a gentle system of laws and regulations to prevent the worst mistakes of the 1920s and to protect against future disasters.

No wonder, then, that Roosevelt was secretive, even coy, whenever anyone asked him during the 1932 campaign just what he had in mind. The New Deal was never a systematic plan but a loosely connected series of "programs." Each was designed to attack what FDR or his advisers thought was an unfortunate problem.

These advisers—most of them academic economists or social scientists or old law school friends—became known as the "Brain Trust." Some members of the Brain Trust did have well-thought-out schemes of social reform in mind. Also, dozens of minor officials who came to Washington to work in the administration had much more radical ideas than Roosevelt.

But the President himself thought in very specific terms. As a result he sent to Congress a confused stream of proposals for new governmental agencies. Many of them were known by their initials, so that the government soon resembled what one jokester called an "alphabet soup." FDR's first few months in office, called the "hundred days," saw intense but helter-skelter activity and experiment that resulted in many new laws.

Relief and Stabilization Measures   Part of the New Deal was aimed at one simple goal: to relieve the hunger and disaster brought to millions by the depression. At first, direct relief was felt needed. The Federal Emergency Relief Act of 1933 answered that need by distributing billions of dollars to the states, which then doled out the money to millions of needy families.

But charity in the form of direct relief was thought to be degrading by many unemployed.

The WPA's immediate goal was to provide relief for the unemployed. But in its six-year life span it compiled a remarkable record of public construction, including more than 600,000 miles of road, like this one in Tennessee. Moreover, it introduced the notion of government aid to the arts. This mural in a Madison, Wisconsin, auditorium is a product of that aid.

Thus a Public Works Administration (PWA) was established in 1933. It eventually spent over $4 billion, placing people in government jobs constructing roads, public buildings, and other such projects. In 1935 a similar program, the Works Progress Administration (WPA), was set up that extended the definition of public works to include everything from light construction projects to the production of plays, concerts, and other works of art. Between 1935 and 1941 more than 8 million Americans were employed by the WPA, which spent over $11 billion on 250,000 such projects. Both the PWA and the WPA were created to give only temporary work relief until the private economy could provide jobs. They represented the kind of direct federal intervention in the economic lives of citizens that Hoover most feared. But Roosevelt, seeing the need, plunged ahead.

Other important New Deal laws were designed to give immediate emergency relief to farmers and ordinary homeowners. Under this legislation, the federal government began to make mortgage loans to families in danger of losing their homes to banks. These laws saved thousands of farms and homes. But they also helped the banks, which were paid in full instead of being saddled with practically worthless property.

This direct relief—while it might mean most to those who benefited from it—was not the most important part of the New Deal. The cornerstone of Roosevelt's program, from the hundred days to the end of the New Deal, were laws aimed at stabilization rather than recovery. Roosevelt believed that the basic economic institutions were sound. But he thought that the economy was subject to unpredictable ups and downs. These wild motions of the economy were what caused businessmen, bankers, farmers, and consumers to lose confidence. Depressions and delayed recoveries resulted. By planning and controls the important parts of the economy could be stabilized. Federal power would be used wherever needed to prevent businesses and farms from failing.

Banks, for example, had proved to be one of the most fragile economic institutions. Roosevelt

had already used the powers of the federal government to rescue them. Later, he persuaded a willing Congress to go further.

A new Federal Deposit Insurance Corporation (FDIC) was given the power to insure savings deposits up to $10,000. This plan would make it almost impossible for a bank to fail, thereby wiping out a family's savings. The effect was to create enough confidence in the banks that people were willing to deposit money in them once more. Banks not only survived but began to make the loans necessary to recovery.

A smiliar logic guided the two programs that were closest to the heart of the New Deal: the National Industrial Recovery Act and the Agricultural Adjustment Act, both passed in 1933. The two laws sought to regulate the basic units of the economy—privately owned farms and business corporations—without altering their private, capitalistic character.

The National Industrial Recovery Act was, in essence, a repeal of parts of the old Sherman Antitrust Act (see page 537). Under a federal agency known as the National Recovery Administration (NRA), corporations were encouraged to create associations for planning production and controlling prices. Such a step was in many ways an abandonment of competition, but the administration was prepared during the depression to sacrifice competition to stability.

For workers, the act also proposed that employers agree on uniform standards for labor practices, wages, and hours. When some companies were slow to cooperate, the NRA created a blanket code of minimum wages and maximum hours. Companies that cooperated were awarded a flag with the NRA symbol, a blue eagle, to fly as evidence of their public spirit. Up to a point it worked. Some workers—those who had jobs to begin with—began to work shorter days and take home larger salaries.

The Agricultural Adjustment Act was a similar but more radical attempt to alter the economics of agriculture. It recognized that the farmer had a peculiar problem. When prices fell, manufacturers could cut back production. This reduction in supply would, sooner or later, raise prices. But farmers had always met falling prices by trying to grow more, not less.

The Agricultural Adjustment Act created an Agricultural Adjustment Administration (AAA) with the power to pay farmers not to plant and harvest crops. It could also buy up agricultural products such as cotton or wheat and store them. This scheme would reduce supply and raise prices. In other words, a government agency, with the voluntary cooperation of farmers, would try to control agricultural production. The goal was to enable farmers to earn as much as they had during the prosperous years 1909-14, a standard known as parity.

The AAA worked better than the NRA. Using its new powers, the government plowed under about 10 million acres of cotton. It also killed about 5 million pigs—a controversial act, when many people did not have enough to eat. But these drastic measures worked—helped along by a drought in 1933 and 1934 that destroyed much of the wheat and corn crops. In 1933 farm prices reached 55 percent of parity; by 1936, 90 percent.

Attempts at Reform The relief and stabilization programs made up the bulk of New Deal legislation. But Roosevelt also attempted a more fundamental (occasionally, even revolutionary) remodeling of American society. These measures appear quite small when compared to more recent exercises of federal power. But at the time they seemed to many people to hint at radical and permanent changes in the ways Americans lived and worked.

The Tennessee Valley Authority (TVA) was an attempt to change the basic social and economic structure of an entire region (see page 691). The Civilian Conservation Corps (CCC) hired thousands of young men to plant trees, improve parks, and clean up streams. Roosevelt even tried (without success) to revive the old practice of homesteading, to lure people from the city into agriculture.

More important to most citizens, however, were two laws of 1935 that lasted well beyond the depression. Both were designed to give pro-tection to groups of people that Roosevelt felt were always at an economic disadvantage: workers and the elderly. The first, the National Labor Relations Act (popularly known as the Wagner Act), made it illegal for an employer to refuse to recognize a labor union. The law also contained a list of "unfair labor practices" forbidden employers. It was clearly the most powerful piece of prolabor legislation ever signed into law by an American President.

As a result of the act labor unionism tripled in membership, from a low of 3 million members in the early 1930s to about 9 1/2 million by 1941. This rapid growth in unionism was not gained without strife though. The AFL, a crafts union movement, was challenged by the Congress of Industrial Organizations (CIO), which stressed organization of workers by industry. In general most businessmen opposed all unions, but many opted for negotiation with one group rather than the numerous craft unions. Sit-down strikes at General Motors plants in 1936 and near warfare a year later in the steel industry forced industrialists to accept the CIO formula for organizing labor.

Older people had suffered more in the depression than any other group of people, except perhaps for farmers in the South and Southwest. The Social Security Act of 1935 was an attempt to create a system of insurance for Americans. (The system was modeled on programs already common in many European countries and even some American states.) The law provided that workers and their employers would each contribute a small part of each year's earnings to a common fund. When a person reached retirement age (or could no longer work because of illness), he or she would receive a small pension from the fund. If a worker died, the survivors would receive benefits. The law, though modest, was the biggest step the federal government had ever taken toward becoming what Roosevelt's critics called a "welfare state."

Taken together, TVA, Social Security, the Wagner Act, and others were a definite though incomplete move in the direction of federal planning, welfare, and control of the economy

The Tennessee Valley Authority

Though the Great Depression was severe throughout America, it was nowhere felt more keenly than in the Tennessee River Valley. This 40,000 square miles of territory spanned seven states. Loggers had long since come, chopped down its forest, and left. Each year fifty-two inches of rain fell, swelling its rivers to flood stage and washing out the meager crops. There was little industry and less hope for more. Income was not even half the national average. The extreme poverty resulted in poor schools, government, and health conditions.

Shortly after becoming President, Franklin D. Roosevelt announced a far-reaching plan for the area. It was by far the most creative experiment to date in American history. He wanted Congress to set up the Tennessee Valley Authority, a regional planning agency that would revive the area by taking full advantage of its natural resources. The TVA would direct the building of a series of dams for flood control and thus make successful farming possible. It would construct hydroelectric plants along the rivers and make these rivers navigable. The cheap power and easy water transport would make the area appealing to industry.

The TVA would also be charged with reforesting the area, making proper use of marginal lands, and in general planning for the economic and social well-being of the people in the region. Adult education, improved health conditions, and greater recreational opportunities were included in the planning.

Objections to the plan came from owners of the power plants already in the area. They objected to competing with the government in producing and selling electric power. Also, there were those who objected to the idea of "social planning." Somehow it seemed communistic to them; according to Representative Joe Martin of Massachusetts, the TVA was "patterned closely after one of the Soviet dreams. I think I can accurately predict than no one in this generation will see materialize the industrial-empire dream of the Tennessee Valley."

Martin could not have been less accurate. Congress authorized the TVA and work began. Soon the valley began to develop as agricultural methods improved, industry moved in, education renewed itself, and new recreational areas emerged. Historian Arthur M. Schlesinger, Jr., has outlined the physical successes of the TVA experiment and then concluded that

> there was something less tangible yet even more penetrating: the release of moral and human energy as the people of the Valley saw new vistas open up for themselves and for their children. The jagged river, flowing uselessly past worn-out fields, overcut forests, ramshackle huts, its muddy waters reflecting the dull poverty of the life around—all this was giving way to a shimmering network of green meadows, blue lakes, and white dams.

The Tennessee river, which was once the destroyer, was becoming man's servant. There was new hope stirring in the land. The project was an apt symbol of the time. It represented man's capacity through the use of political and technical intelligence to change the conditions of life and transform defeat into victory.

THE TENNESSEE VALLEY AUTHORITY, 1933

and the environment. They did *not* attempt any change in the political system as previous American reform movements had done. There was no important civil rights legislation and no use of taxation to cause a significant change in class structure. If attempting to stabilize the inherited system was revolutionary, then Roosevelt was a radical. But if failing to demand deep changes in politics, race relations, and class structure was conservative, then he was a conservative. In his own curious way, he was both.

THE END OF THE NEW DEAL

Roosevelt did everything possible to make the 1936 election a test of the voters' response to the New Deal. The result was the greatest victory in the history of American elections until then. Roosevelt surpassed even Harding's triumph of 1920, winning 61 percent of the popular vote. His Republican opponent, Alfred Landon of Kansas, carried only Maine and Vermont. A third-party candidate, Congressman William Lemke, polled less than 1 million votes. Lemke's Union party attracted the followers of three leading extreme opponents of the New Deal: Senator Huey Long of Louisiana, Dr. Francis Townsend, and Father Charles Coughlin.

Long's populistic "Share Our Wealth" program had urged, among other things, increased federal taxation of wealthy individuals and corporations. Some of Long's ideas on taxation were included in the 1935 Wealth Tax Act— though the act did practically nothing to redistribute wealth. Dr. Townsend's income-grant plan for the elderly, supported by millions of senior citizens organized into Townsend clubs, was undercut by passage of the 1935 Social Security Act. And Father Coughlin, a Catholic priest who drew an audience of millions with his radio programs, lost much of this following by attacking the New Deal in increasingly intemperate and anti-Semitic terms. By the election of 1936 none of these extremist elements threatened Roosevelt's hold on the American voter.

With his New Deal programs as tools, Roosevelt succeeded in forging from the depression a new political coalition of farmers and urban working people. The Democratic party, for the first time in a century, became the majority party in the nation, a position it still holds.

Despite this political success the economic and social problems of the depression had not been solved. In 1936 the gross national product (the total volume of all money transactions in any given year) had reached only the level of 1931. Unemployment remained high since many factories were still closed. There was measurable improvement in the lives of American farmers, but they were a distinct minority of the population. For everyone else, the depression remained a stubborn fact.

Offsetting this inability to achieve economic recovery was the New Deal's undeniable success in restoring political and social stability to American life. The relatively small vote for extremist candidates in 1936 reflected a general faith among most Americans that, whatever their failings, the two major parties would somehow guide the country through the economic crisis. The millions of poor citizens who worked on federal projects such as the WPA and the additional millions who received direct relief assistance now had more reason for hope than during the dark winter of 1932–33. Similarly, the large number of citizens whose houses had been saved by federally guaranteed mortgages and who now left their money safely in federally guaranteed bank accounts had greater cause for optimism than earlier.

Catholics, Jews, and blacks owed the New Deal a particular debt. For the first time in American history these groups were heavily represented in top-level government positions. Of the 214 federal judges appointed by the 3 preceding Presidents, for example, only 8 were Catholics. Roosevelt, on the other hand, named 51 Catholics among the 196 federal judges appointed during the New Deal era. The roll call of New Deal officials and advisors—including names such as Corcoran and Cohen, Frankfurter

Father Charles Coughlin, whose national radio broadcasts mixed calls for the nationalization of banks, utilities, and natural resources with a persistent antisemitism, drew his support from the right.

The most prominent of FDR's critics on the left was Huey Long. To secure the presidency by stirring up resentment over the maldistribution of wealth, he proposed heavy taxation of the rich and large handouts for the poor.

and Farley, Kennedy and Bunche—symbolized this change for ethnic Americans. To these men, and to lesser-known Americans from immigrant backgrounds, Roosevelt offered opportunities for public service and influence on a scale undreamed of during previous periods.

For all this, the New Deal never managed to achieve economic recovery from the depression itself. Even the limited recovery that was achieved before 1936 was soon wiped out. After the election, instead of pushing ahead Roosevelt announced that he would begin phasing out parts of the New Deal because the country was on the way back to prosperity. Partially as a result of this move, a depression within a depression began in 1937. The resulting new decline in business was even steeper that in 1929-30. Millions of people began to lose faith in the government's power to bring about full recovery. In fact, only the transition to a wartime economy after 1939 finally ended the depression for good.

Post-Election Reaction   Adding to Roosevelt's problems of dealing with the new decline were the political problems he encountered. In the early days, he had depended on strong support from Democratic congressmen and senators from the South. After 1936 this support began to weaken. A new coalition in Congress of conservative Southerners and Northern Republicans made it almost impossible to enact significant new legislation, even if Roosevelt had wanted it. FDR's appeal to blacks in the South, plus his pro-labor policies, had turned many Southern white supporters against him. Roosevelt was soon deprived of his working majorities in both the House and the Senate.

A second difficulty that affected Roosevelt's popularity was the Supreme Court's rulings on several important New Deal laws. The NRA, parts of the AAA, and several other Roosevelt programs were declared unconstitutional in 1935 and 1936. The President believed that, unless something were done the Court would soon strike down other laws, like the Social Security Act or the Wagner Act.

Roosevelt grew increasingly restless. He publicly complained that the Court was behind the times. He grumbled that "nine old men" were defying the people's will as it had been expressed in the election victory of 1936. Then, in the first year of his second term, Roosevelt proposed a scheme to "pack" the Court. For every justice over seventy, he argued, the President should be empowered to appoint one additional justice to the Court. This, he said with obvious insincerity, would ease the heavy work load of the judiciary.

The battle that followed in Congress and in the press had two curious effects. First, it seems to have frightened some of the justices into a friendlier attitude toward New Deal legislation. Within weeks of the court-packing announcement, the Court ruled favorably on two such laws. One wit remarked that "a switch in time saved nine."

Second, and more important, public opinion shifted against Roosevelt. The public disliked his tampering with the Constitution and pressured Congress to reject the plan. Afterward, the administration proposed little new legislation on social and economic questions. The New Deal was over. Soon the attention of both the President and the people would turn more urgently to events in Europe and Asia.

1. Why did President Hoover refuse to support the Bonus bill for veterans? Why was the bill able to pass the House but not the Senate?
2. What did Harding mean when he urged a return to "normalcy"?
3. What did Coolidge mean by his famous statement, "The business of America is business"?
4. Would it be fair to call Al Smith a conservative Democrat? Why or why not?
5. What danger was there in having so many Americans buying stock and using credit at this time?
6. Why did the stock market crash help bring on the Great Depression?
7. Why did Hoover believe that the government should do nothing directly to bring the nation out of a depression? In what way did the government provide some indirect relief?
8. What steps did the New Deal take to provide direct relief to the needy?
9. How did the National Industrial Recovery Act and the Agricultural Adjustment Act attempt to protect the economy from unpredictable ups and downs? Why did the AAA prove to be more successful than the NIRA?
10. Why is the Wagner Act regarded as the most significant labor law in American history? Was the Social Security Act a radical governmental measure?
11. Why can it be said that the New Deal ended in 1937?

Beyond the Text

1. Using the Statistical Abstract of the United States, compare the economic status of the American farmer of the 1920s and 1930s with farmers today as to the (1) number engaged in farming, (2) percentage of the population this represents, (3) average income, and (4) relations with the government. On the basis of this information, are farmers better or worse off today?
2. "Hoover's limitations lay in the inadequacy of his philosophy; Roosevelt's strength lay in his lack of philosophy." Investigate the validity of this assertion. You may want to consult the essays on the two men in Hofstadter's *The American Political Tradition*.
3. Have a panel discussion to look into the reasons why the New Deal was unable to end the depression.
4. Prepare a report on Father Coughlin, Huey Long, and Dr. Francis Townshend. Focus on the kinds of programs they offered, the credibility of the programs, and the sources of their support.

Bibliography

Nonfiction

Galbraith, John K., *The Great Crash, 1929.**
Handlin, Oscar, *Al Smith and His America.**
Hicks, John D., *Republican Ascendancy, 1921–1933.**
Leuchtenburg, William E., *Franklin D. Roosevelt and the New Deal.**
MacArthur, Douglas, *Reminiscences.*
Mitchell, Broadus, *Depression Decade.*
Romasco, Albert U., *The Poverty of Abundance: Hoover, the Nation, the Depression.**
Schlesinger, Arthur M., Jr., *The Age of Roosevelt, 3 vols.**
Soule, George, *Prosperity Decade.**
White, William Allen, *A Puritan in Babylon.*
Williams, T. Harry, *Huey Long.**

Fiction

Steinbeck, John, *The Grapes of Wrath.**
Warren, Robert Penn, *All the King's Men.**
Wright, Richard, *Native Son.**

*a paperback book

35

"Remember Pearl Harbor"

ON DECEMBER 7, 1941, while negotiations to avoid war between the United States and Japan were proceeding in Washington, 353 Japanese planes attacked Pearl Harbor. This massive, audacious, and extremely successful attack on the Americans' principal—and supposedly impregnable—naval base in Hawaii came before Japan had even declared war. Grim-faced and resolved, President Roosevelt went before Congress to call it "unprovoked and dastardly" and "a day which will live in infamy."

Until this assault Congress, like the country as a whole, had been sharply split between interventionists and isolationists. Now Congress and most Americans were furious at this shrewdly planned, superbly executed, and deadly raid. It dealt a staggering blow to American power in the Pacific. Congress swiftly and overwhelmingly voted to enter World War II. During the rest of the long, terrible conflict the single slogan that most readily aroused Americans to action was: "Remember Pearl Harbor!"

The attack on Pearl, referred to as Operation Z by the Japanese, had a history. A key figure in planning the attack was Admiral Isoruko Yamamoto, head of the Japanese Imperial Navy. If Japan's national

Battleship Row, Pearl Harbor, is seen here from a Japanese bomber during the surprise attack. The Japanese commander of the air strike said of the sight: "Below me lay the U.S. Pacific Fleet in a formation which I would never have dared to imagine. A fleet should always be on alert since surprise attacks can never be discounted."

Isoroku Yamamoto, commander-in-chief of the Japanese Imperial Fleet, was a strong advocate of the navy's use of air power. Responsible for planning naval operations, he was the mastermind of the audacious attack on Pearl Harbor.

interest called for war with the United States, the admiral reasoned, why not strike directly at the enemy fleet's Pacific home base? No mere "battleship admiral," the air-minded Yamamoto knew the possibilities of carrier-based warfare.

When the admiral took command in 1939, war plans still called for letting the American fleet plow west to meet the Japanese fleet near Iwo Jima or Saipan, fairly close to Japanese bases. Yamamoto extended the battle line far to the east shortly after reviewing some impressive results achieved by carrier-based planes in maneuvers. He also never forgot the example of his own personal hero, Admiral Heihachiro Togo, who in 1904 had battered the Russian fleet in Port Arthur in a surprise attack. Yamamoto had served under Togo and been wounded in the stunning Japanese victory over the Russian navy a year later.

Yamamoto was neither a visionary nor overly optimistic. He was quite dubious about defeating the United States in war. He knew the country, having studied at Harvard and worked at the Japanese embassy in Washington during the 1920s. He returned to Japan sobered by American industrial might. He harbored no illusions about conquering the United States. An invasion of continental United States never figured seriously in Japanese war plans. "If I am told to fight regardless of the consequences," Yamamoto told the Japanese premier in 1940, "I shall run wild for the first six months, but I have utterly no confidence for the second or third years."

Others in the Japanese military shared Yamamoto's fears over the probable consequences of war with the United States. Then why venture such a dangerous policy, such a desperate gamble? By 1940 Japan was an authoritarian society ruled by a civilian-military government. Its leaders agreed that the country needed to gain most of its basic objectives. Most important was access to the raw materials vital for a modern industrial nation. Without them heavily populated Japan would become a third- or fourth-rate power. Without expansion the Japanese would be forced to tighten their belts even to stay alive.

So Japan decided to expand. In 1931 it took Manchuria from a helpless China. America and Western Europe objected strongly but ineffectively. In 1937 Japan launched a full-scale invasion of the rest of China. Despite Western protests the Japanese captured the coastal portions and overran much of the Chinese interior. By mid-1940 Japan's ally Hitler had conquered the French, the Dutch, and much of Europe, isolating Great Britain. Therefore, Tokyo figured it could now expand Japanese control into Southeast Asia. It planned to establish a massive sphere of influence, "the Greater East Asia Co-Prosperity Sphere."

The Japanese asked: Why should Britain reap the benefits of

Malaya's tin reserves? Why should the Dutch exploit and profit from the oil of the East Indies? Why should France have the rubber and other raw materials of Indochina? And why should America, thousands of miles from Asia, take such a high-and-mighty tone about China? "Asia for the Asians!" proclaimed the Japanese. They did not add that Japan would simply take over the role of the exploiter. If Tokyo could win this huge area without force, so much the better. But if not, it was prepared to wage war.

Thus, by early 1941, Admiral Yamamoto was contemplating his strategy. Success hinged on two factors: the attackers must achieve total surprise; and, the bulk of the American fleet, especially the capital ships (battleships and carriers), would have to be at their moorings the day of attack.

While Japanese and American diplomats in Washington continued their negotiations, naval aviators began months of intensive practice. When Yamamoto caught wind of grumbling and possible foot-dragging, he threatened to resign if the plan was scrapped. Objections ceased. Yamamoto became for the moment the symbol of the Japanese navy. Under no condition would his fellow officers accept his resignation. Operation Z (named for the signal flag that Admiral Togo hoisted before trouncing the Russians) became a reality. If diplomacy failed, only the date of the attack on America remained to be fixed.

Meanwhile, political developments ominously paralleled the course of these military preparations. After France had fallen to Germany, Japan grabbed the northern half of French Indochina. It held back from the southern half—as well as from British Malaya and the Dutch East Indies (present-day Indonesia)—after the United States warned that action in these areas would have grave consequences. Roosevelt banned shipments of aviation gasoline and scrap metal to Japan, and increased American support to China. The American ambassador to Japan, Joseph C. Grew, noted: "We are getting ready, steadily, for the ultimate showdown."

By summer 1941 matters were even more tense. Hitler invaded Russia; Japan could now pursue its Asian policy without fear of Stalin. Japan advanced, occupying southern Indochina in late July. The Americans, British, and Dutch responded by seizing all Japanese financial assets in their jurisdiction. They also ended Japan's access to their raw materials. The United States also gave an official warning that, if Japan took any further steps "by force or threat of force," the Americans would defend their "legitimate rights and interests."

In diplomacy's stilted language, these were strong words. The Japanese premier suggested that he and President Roosevelt hold a summit meeting, possibly in Hawaii. This could not be arranged. On October 16 a new premier, General Hideki Tojo, came to power. He was an all-out militarist.

Yet the national interests of both countries favored more negotiations. Further talks would hide Japanese war preparations—especially Operation Z, now in high gear. Washington would also benefit. It could use the extra time to reinforce its Pacific bases, particularly in the Philippines. In November 1941 Japan sent a veteran diplomat, Saburo Kurusu, to Washington to head a negotiating team. Diplomatic exchanges would obviously continue for at least a few more weeks.

At the same time, table-top maneuvers at the Japanese Naval War College demonstrated the most effective route for the Pearl attack force. The fleet would sail in a wide arc across the nearly deserted waters of the North Central Pacific. Then it would turn sharply south on reaching a point 500 miles north of Hawaii. Yamamoto thought that this route would give the best chance for surprise.

On November 5, while the Japanese and Americans negotiated in Washington, Yamamoto issued a secret order outlining the first phase of the Japanese offensive against Hawaii. The twenty-three attack ships included six carriers and two battleships under Admiral Chuichi Nagumo. He disliked the plan and still hoped the madcap attack would somehow be canceled.

The Japanese strike force sailed on November 26. The attack date had been set for December 7 (Sunday morning) in Hawaii. The American navy—even though on military alert because of the dangerous diplomatic situation—had weekends off. So its ships usually anchored in the harbor on Friday and stayed there until Monday. Nagumo's orders did contain one escape clause. If the Washington negotiations succeeded, the attack was off. The fleet would then wait in the North Pacific for new orders.

Yet any chance that diplomacy could ease the crisis was now vanishing. On November 20 the negotiator Kurusu made Tokyo's final offer: Japan would leave southern Indochina but remain in the northern part, as well as in China. The United States must not only lift its ban on oil but also cut off aid to China. Secretary of State Cordell Hull immediately rejected these terms. Fearful of being called appeasers, Roosevelt and Hull would make no concessions. The American note of November 26—the very day the strike force set sail—stated that America's embargo would continue until Japan abandoned both Indochina and China.

Roosevelt and Hull, along with their top civilian and military colleagues, had good reason to distrust the sincerity of Japanese negotiations. Operation Magic of American naval intelligence had cracked Japan's diplomatic codes. On November 22—two days after Kurusu's final offer and four days before the formal American reply to it—a cable intercepted from Tokyo read: "THIS TIME WE MEAN IT, THAT THE DEADLINE [November 29] CANNOT BE CHANGED! AFTER THAT THINGS ARE AUTOMATICALLY GOING TO HAPPEN."

If Admiral Kimmel had initiated air reconnaissance of the seas around Pearl Harbor, Operation Z might have been discovered and foiled. But neither he nor anyone else in authority expected Japanese hostilities to begin there.

What things? Most likely, reasoned the leaders in Washington, the Japanese planned to attack the Philippines and British and Dutch holdings in Asia. But Hawaii seemed beyond the range of effective Japanese assault. So American short-sightedness was beginning to aid the future success of Operation Z. Knowledge of Magic was restricted to Washington's inner circle. This kept Tokyo from realizing its code had been broken. Thus American brass in Hawaii had no notion of Magic.

Hawaiian military commanders received some warning on November 27 to expect a hostile move by Japan. But Washington took no action during the next ten days. Only four Magic decoding machines existed then: two in Washington, one in the Philippines, and another in London. There were none in Hawaii. The commanders there, Admiral Husband E. Kimmel and General Walter C. Short, were not even told about Magic.

Admiral Kimmel had seriously considered, but then rejected, the idea of taking his fleet out of Pearl Harbor. In open water, he felt, the ships would be too vulnerable. His four carriers were not then available to provide air cover. (Three were bringing warplanes to American-held Pacific islands; the fourth was in San Diego for repairs.) Besides, moored safely in Pearl, his ships could be protected by the several hundred army planes stationed at Hawaiian bases. Still, Kimmel might well have sent most of the battleships out with the carriers to the other Pacific islands.

General Short reacted to the war warning by increasing the army's antisabotage defenses. Sabotage, he apparently thought, might come from Hawaii's large Japanese-American community. Instead of widely spacing his aircraft or protecting them in concrete shelters already constructed on the major fields, Short ordered the planes bunched together, wing tip to wing tip. True, fewer soldiers could then protect them against saboteurs. But Japanese Americans in Hawaii never aided Japan, although some Japanese diplomats were spies.

Premier Tojo is shown in a respectful posture before Emperor Hirohito at a ceremony celebrating the Japanese Empire's 2,600th anniversary. Tojo's rise to power helped determine Japan's course toward war. Hirohito's role was largely symbolic, but he supported Tojo's militarism and anti-Americanism.

In short, Magic had been botched. Hawaiian commanders never received copies of important decoded messages. These messages piled up at the few overworked decoding centers. As far back as September, and with increasing frequency thereafter, Tokyo asked the Japanese consulate in Honolulu for details on the location of American warships in the harbor. By November such naval maps were being transmitted to Tokyo twice a week. Some of these Magic intercepts were not deciphered and translated for many days after reception. Especially revealing Japanese messages of November 29, for example, waited until December 5 to be deciphered. Even then, they received little attention.

Even key Washington officials, including Roosevelt and Hull, apparently did not take the Magic decodings very seriously.[1] For in Tokyo the die had been cast. Hull's note of November 26 refusing to lift the American embargo infuriated Premier Tojo. He thought it proved beyond all doubt American insincerity in the negotiations. Tojo persuaded Emperor Hirohito to let Operation Z proceed. A palace meeting ratified the decision for war. Hirohito did not attempt to intervene. He believed, as he later told an aide, that the United States was looking for nothing less than Japan's humiliation.

---

[1] On November 25 Roosevelt told Secretary of War Henry L. Stimson of his fears that Japan would strike on December 1 without declaring war, "for the Japanese are notorious for making an attack without warning." Stimson wanted to bomb Japanese convoys if they moved farther south. Roosevelt rejected the notion because "we are a democracy."

One point remained unsettled. Japan had signed the Hague Convention. It required a formal declaration of war before a nation could start hostilities. But could this "paper" commitment override the need for surprise in attacking Hawaii? Absolutely not, insisted Yamamoto. Any kind of advance warning would endanger the Japanese fleet. Yet several ministers, including Tojo, argued initially for avoiding the dishonor of a sneak attack by some advance warning.

But the argument was useless: the nature of Operation Z made all such talk pointless. In the end Tokyo instructed Kurusu to present the final note—not a declaration of war—at 1 P.M. on Sunday, December 7. The first wave of Japanese planes would start bombing at the same time. Should Kurusu continue negotiating or at least pretend to? Of course he should, Tojo decided; it would facilitate operations. In Washington Kurusu asked a Japanese newspaperman rhetorically, "Am I being used as a smoke screen?" Indeed he was.

Kurusu had to help screen the task force then steaming across the North Pacific. After leaving on November 26, the fleet enjoyed seven days of uneventful sailing. The weather cooperated. Light winds made refueling at sea relatively easy. Cloudiness and generally poor visibility decreased chances of detection. Security precautions were rigidly enforced. No radio contact was made except within the fleet. At night a blackout was enforced. Most ships communicated by signal flags and blinkers. They did not even discard garbage, to avoid leaving a trail.

The fleet's passage north of the American base at Midway provided cause for some real concern. No American planes or ships spotted them, however. On December 6 there was the final fueling. Japanese intelligence from Hawaii reported the presence of many American warships but no carriers or heavy cruisers. It was decided that the force would strike and destroy whatever was at hand.

A little past noon on December 6 all hands were summoned on deck. Their officers read them the emperor's war message. Yamamoto had also sent a statement: "The moment has arrived. The rise or fall of our empire is at stake." Then Admiral Togo's flag, the signal flag that gave its name to Operation Z, went up above the attack fleet's flagship. The crews shouted *"Banzai!"*—their battle cry— and turned the ships south toward Hawaii. All was ready for the great moment.

The launch itself was almost perfect. Pilots and flight crewmen were aroused at 3:30 A.M. The news that the Americans apparently had not adequately protected their ships encouraged the Japanese airmen. At zero hour (6 A.M.) the carriers were 200 miles from Oahu. As the ships rolled and pitched, the lead pilots waited eagerly for the order to take off. When it came, the first wave of 183 planes left the 6 carriers in 15 minutes, bettering their fastest practice runs. With Commander Mitsuo Fuchida in command, flying one of the high-level bombers, the air fleet headed for its target.

Fuchida led the attack planes in. He listened meanwhile to Honolulu radio which obligingly gave a fine weather report for the assault. The forecast was for cloudiness over the mountains. This cloud cover would hide the planes until just before they attacked.

The first wave passed over the northern coast of Oahu at 7:40 A.M. It was almost exactly the time Kurusu was scheduled to give Secretary Hull the note breaking off negotiations. The sight of all their unsuspecting targets delighted and amazed the Japanese pilots. Fuchida later recalled his own surprise at seeing ships of the American fleet anchored less than a thousand yards apart from one another. They would be an easy target for a surprise attack.

Overconfidence and negligence had made Americans complacent. Many viewed the Japanese as a society adept in imitating Western ways but with little creativity. Informed Americans knew that the Japanese had a history of attacking first and declaring war later. But most thought they would not dare attack the United States. In 1932 the American navy itself had successfully "attacked" the harbor during a mock raid. The event was quickly forgotten. The Navy Department filed the report in its archives as just another war-games exploit.

There were certainly some warnings during 1941. In January a Peruvian diplomat in Tokyo reported that a drunken Japanese official had boasted about Japan's plan to sink the American fleet and knock out Pearl Harbor. Ambassador Grew passed the "fantastic" rumor along to Washington. A few months later Grew noted that Japan was "capable of sudden and surprise action" with "a determination to risk all."

The shortcomings of American defensive reactions were considerable, in view of what was known about Japanese intentions and how much could have been learned if the data from Magic had been properly exploited. One man who worried a great deal was Admiral Kimmel. After November 27—the day Kimmel received the war warning from Washington—naval intelligence lost track of the Japanese fleet. Kimmel asked the head of his intelligence section at Pearl where the fleet was. The officer admitted he did not know. Not entirely in jest, Kimmel asked: "You mean to say that it could appear rounding

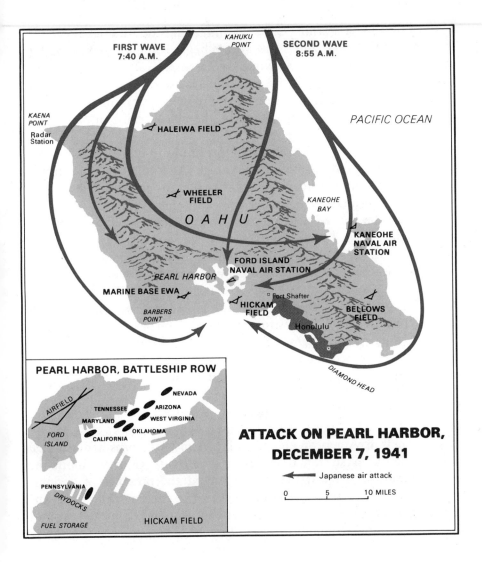

ATTACK ON PEARL HARBOR, DECEMBER 7, 1941

Diamond Head [a famous high point close to Pearl Harbor] without our knowing it?" The intelligence officer answered: "I hope that it would be spotted before that."

Yamamoto had no intention of parading his ships past Diamond Head, impressive though the sight would have been. Instead, his planes crossed over Oahu's northern coast. At 7:49 A.M. Fuchida broke radio silence to signal Nagumo (and Yamamoto also, since Japan picked up the message). Attack by the first wave had begun, blessed with the key element of surprise. Fuchida's first signal was "*To-To-To,*" repeating the opening syllable of the Japanese word for "charge." Soon he sent an even more welcome message: "*Tora* [Tiger], *Tora, Tora,*" which meant that the Americans were almost completely unprepared.

A special Japanese invention, the midget submarine operated by a crew of two, was used in the advance attack upon American battleships. The submarines failed in their mission that day and were not widely used in the war.

Yet that same morning came warnings that the Americans did not heed. Five full hours before the attack began, Magic in Washington had decoded the final Japanese message breaking off negotiations. The officer in charge took the intercept straight to Admiral Harold R. Stark, chief of naval operations. Though impressed, Stark did not phone Admiral Kimmel, who simply stood by the war warning of November 27.

In Hawaii itself two excellent opportunities to rouse the American garrison were missed just before the attack. At 6:30 A.M. the antitorpedo net at the entrance to Pearl was opened to let a ship enter. The captain of an American destroyer was watching. When he saw what looked like the top of a submarine coming in behind the ship, he sounded the alarm. The unidentified craft was one of several "midget" Japanese subs. (A large Japanese submarine fleet preceded the Operation Z task force, but it did not accomplish much on December 7.)

American submarine captains had been prohibited from entering Pearl Harbor underwater. Thus any submerged craft would be considered an enemy ship. The destroyer fired and hit the small sub. As it began to sink, depth charges finished it off. The destroyer's captain immediately radioed navy headquarters about the incident. But the message did not reach Kimmel's chief of staff until 7:12, and he discounted its importance.

Yet another chance to prepare for the attack slipped away. This occurred on Oahu's north coast, precisely where Fuchida's squadrons would penetrate American air space. The Army Air Corps had installed a movable radar station there. At 6:45 Private George Elliott, the enlisted man on duty at the station, noted the presence of a single plane on the radar screen. The plane was approaching Oahu from the north. It may have been the observation seaplane launched from a Japanese cruiser. He paid little attention to it.

But at 7:06 Elliott noted much larger blips on the screen, again moving toward Oahu from the north, and rapidly growing larger. He asked the advice of another soldier. They decided to call signal headquarters at Fort Shafter. But the only officer on duty there, a pilot, told them to forget about it. He knew that a dozen American planes were scheduled to arrive from California that morning. A group of B-17s—called Flying Fortresses—was indeed in the air, very close to Hawaii. Again the Japanese had benefited from a stroke of luck. Fuchida's first wave was confused with reinforcements from the States.

After sending the signal "*Tora, Tora, Tora*," Fuchida fired a blue flare from his bomber. It informed pilots in planes without radios that surprise had been achieved. It would produce a prearranged pattern of attack, with the slow-flying but deadly torpedo bombers going in first.

But apparently one group of pilots, their vision obscured by the cloud cover, had not seen the luminous signal. At least they did not wiggle their planes' wings in response. Fuchida then committed one of the few Japanese mistakes of the day. He fired a second flare.

This changed the flight plan. Two flares meant that dive bombers would attack first. Fighters and some dive bombers were to concentrate on American airfields and antiaircraft installations rather than on the fleet. Happily for the Japanese, the commander of the torpedo bomber wing ignored the second flare. His forty heavy but superbly piloted aircraft peeled off and glided down to the prescribed low altitudes, heading straight for their principal targets, the battleships.

Meanwhile, in answer to the second signal, the faster planes went hunting for American aircraft at Wheeler, Hickam, Haleiwa, Bellows, and other fields. Wheeler housed most of the American fighter planes. These planes, already tested in combat, could hold their own against the more maneuverable Japanese fighters. But, owing to General Short's fear of ground sabotage, Wheeler's planes had been crowded together like sheep in a pen. The attackers quickly destroyed a third of the planes and damaged many more. Fires broke out in the hangars and storage buildings. One of them contained ammunition that exploded, causing additional losses.

American military aviation tried to respond but it was useless. At Wheeler, for instance, most of the pilots were still sleeping. But Lieutenants George Welch and Ken Taylor, who were breakfasting at the officers' club, saw the dive bombers swoop. They rushed for a car and speeded at a hundred miles an hour to an auxiliary airstrip unknown to the Japanese. There they took off, headed for a Japanese squadron, and shot down three planes before landing to refuel. During the dogfight

The devastation on the ground after the attack was extensive. By 10 A.M. Hickam Naval Air Station was in chaos and a smoking ruin.

one of the three machine guns in Welch's plane jammed. Taylor was wounded twice.

At Kaneohe Naval Air Station the commanding officer was drinking his morning coffee. When he heard planes, he glanced up. To his anger several V formations of planes—all flying lower than regulations allowed—were turning toward the right into the bay where most of his thirty-three new flying boats were at anchor. He leapt to his feet shouting, "Those fools know there is a strict rule against making a right turn!" His young son who was with him answered, "Look, red circles on the wings!" Realizing it was the Japanese rising-sun symbol, the commander rushed to his headquarters and set up a fierce antiaircraft fire against the invaders.

At the moment of attack only a fourth of the antiaircraft guns on the ships moored in the harbor were manned. Land-based antiaircraft guns could not respond immediately because ammunition had been stored to prevent deterioration. Their effectiveness increased as the morning wore on, however. Unluckily, the B-17s arrived from California about then. Weary after fourteen hours in the air, the American bomber pilots and crews thought they had flown into a nightmare. Columns of smoke rose from the ground. Airfields were ablaze, including the one the B-17s were supposed to use on Ford Island. Incredibly, not one Flying Fortress was shot out of the air. All landed at various fields, though some were shot at and destroyed after landing.

Ironically, Admiral Kimmel and General Short had scheduled a golf match with each other that morning. Kimmel rose early. At about 7:30 he received a phone call from a staff officer. The destroyer *Ward* had sighted a submerged submarine and dropped depth charges. Kimmel headed for his office. Just as he was leaving, he received another call adding some details about the *Ward* incident. Suddenly, the officer at the other end shouted that Japanese planes were attacking. Kimmel ran out to his garden, which overlooked the harbor. What he saw astonished him. The carnage was under way. The sky over the bay seemed alive with attack planes. Kimmel knew that his ships were doomed.

Kimmel got to his headquarters at 8:10, during the height of the first-wave attack. There was nothing he could do but stand at the window and watch his fleet and men under attack. A spent Japanese bullet crashed through the window and bounced off Kimmel's chest. He felt that "it would have been merciful had it killed me."

Fuchida's pilots were not concerned with Kimmel. They wanted to destroy the American fleet. Disappointed over not finding carriers in port, they concentrated on the battleships. Seven of the eight were lined up on Battleship Row in the harbor. Five were moored to the docks, and two were on an "outside" parallel column. Thus two of the inside battleships could not be attacked by torpedoes. The dive bombers went after them. Soon every battleship had been hit.

On the *Nevada,* at one end of the row, Bandmaster Oden McMillan stood with his musicians, ready to play morning colors at 8 A.M. As they began "The Star-Spangled Banner," a Japanese plane dropped its deadly burden on the nearby *Arizona,* then peeled off just feet above the band. The *Nevada's* deck officer, Ensign Joe Taussig, shouted over the public-address system: "All hands, general quarters. Air raid!" The *Nevada,* though damaged, tried to steam out to sea. The Japanese bore in, hoping to sink her at Pearl Harbor's mouth and thus close the port indefinitely. The *Nevada* took six bomb hits but made it to the other side of the bay, keeping the channel clear.

The *Oklahoma* took four torpedoes within one minute and began to capsize. The *California* sustained hits that caused her to settle slowly and finally sink. And so on down the row: *Tennessee, West Virginia, Maryland, Pennsylvania.* Fuchida, who was supervising the attack in his bomber overhead, frowned in slight puzzlement as his pilots raced in. They were bunched up in their assault, instead of diving in stages as first arranged. But their formation no longer really mattered—every enemy ship was a sitting duck.

The worst blow for the Americans came when the *Arizona* blew apart and sank, trapping more than a thousand men inside. Later, it was claimed that a bomb had gone straight down her stack. But the probable cause of the disaster was the detonation of the ship's ammunition store. Whatever the cause, a gigantic pillar of fire and smoke rose 500 feet. The shock was so tremendous that, far above, Fuchida could feel his bomber tremble. Miraculously, many survived this searing blast. Some of these survivors tried to swim to shore and safety, but burning oil engulfed most of them.

The second wave, 170 additional planes, came in at 8:55. Fuchida and his pilots had taken more time than planned because of additional bomb runs. The fresh attackers went to work shortly after the first wave pulled out. They encountered considerably more opposition from heavy antiaircraft fire and lost twenty-one planes. Towering columns of smoke cut visibility. Still, the second wave of bombers did considerable damage in its one-hour attack, knocking out some ships not previously hit. They withdrew at 9:45 to return to their carriers.

On Battleship Row the rescue effort began at once. Most of the giant ships were ablaze. One had overturned, while another had settled

The Japanese victory would have been more complete and would have had more serious consequences for the United States if American aircraft carriers had been in port. As it was, the Japanese had to be satisfied with destroying American battleships.

straight down into the mud. In the plotting room of the heavily damaged *West Virginia* Ensign Victor Delano watched smoke and oily water seep in. He and several others headed forward to another compartment. Just before closing a watertight door, they heard frantic calls from six seamen, blown from the deck above them by the explosions, but had to go on. Delano then returned to the plotting room, risking his life to help a wounded sailor. Neither he nor his companions could get their footing on the oil-slick deck. The ship's angle compounded the problem.

Luckily, one compartment wall was a switchboard. By grabbing its knobs, they were at last able to reach the door. As the men moved forward, they could hear the shouts and pleas of others, sealed off by the watertight doors in flooding compartments. The damage-control officer had ordered the doors closed. He knew that this order condemned many men to death. But opening the doors would merely cause the ship to sink quickly and doubtless drown even more men. Many, however, did make their way to the upper decks or swam to the surface by escaping through portholes. The harbor was filled with boats and launches busily rescuing survivors.

The overturned *Oklahoma* posed special problems. Dozens of men, perhaps hundreds, were still alive in a crazy house where floors had become ceilings. Partial flooding meant that air pockets existed in most compartments. There, survivors could exist for awhile, if they treaded water or grasped whatever protruded from walls. About thirty men trapped in the dispensary waited an hour. Noting with alarm the decreasing amount of oxygen in the air, they decided to move. But where?

Diving into the water that covered most of the dispensary, they found a porthole. Though no one knew where it led, staying in the dispensary meant sure death. Those who were thin enough to squeeze through the porthole swam clear of the ship and were rescued. Others tried but could not squeeze through the porthole. They died in the dispensary.

Another group of sailors trapped near the *Oklahoma's* center seemed doomed beyond any hope. Amazingly, one of them dove downward through a funnel. He emerged directly under the capsized ship, reached topside, then swam clear of the wreckage and reached the surface. He led rescuers to his mates.

The rescue crews relied on this kind of information. Without it, they had no way of locating the living. Rescuers banged on ship hulls, and survivors lost no time in signaling back. Yet the sounds seemed to come from everywhere and nowhere. Several times crews laboriously cut holes in hulls, then found nobody.

When they did, they had sometimes unwittingly added to the tragedy. Acetylene torches consumed the oxygen in the air pockets once the hull had been punctured. Slower working pneumatic drills allowed the precious air to escape as the water rose in the compartments. Despite these dangers inaction would surely spell doom for the trapped. So people worked through the night. They had surprisingly good results in the number of men saved.

Japanese airmen fashioned a striking yet limited victory at Pearl Harbor. The casualty figures were all in their favor.[2] But, in the long run, Operation Z failed to cripple American power. First, no American carrier was in port; the war that followed conclusively showed that

---

[2] All 8 battleships in Pearl on December 7 were either sunk, capsized, or were badly damaged. Ten other ships, including 3 cruisers and 3 destroyers, were also casualties. In military aviation 188 American planes were destroyed, and nearly all the others were damaged. About 100 civilians and 2,403 men in uniform died. Japan lost only 29 planes, 5 two-man submarines, and a total of 54 lives.

carriers were more vital than battleships. Second, American plane losses would soon be dwarfed by the huge air armadas that were already beginning to roll out of American factories. Third, the naval base itself had not suffered severe damage. Fourth, and probably most significant of all, the Japanese—concentrating on ships and planes—ignored the oil storage tanks. If Hawaii's fuel supply had been destroyed (as it easily could have been), Japan might have: (1) driven the carriers and other ships still functioning back to California for oil; (2) made Pearl useless as a base for several months and perhaps a year; and (3) thus given Japan freedom to expand in the Pacific without worrying about counterattacks. Instead, Pearl began to function right after December 7 as the staging area for a massive American build-up of military power.

By bombing the harbor, Japan gained some time—but little more. Even some of the sunken battleships came back to haunt their attackers. All but two were put back in service. But these consequences lay in the future. December 7 was Japan's day. The assault on Hawaii was only part of a mighty Japanese drive. Simultaneous attacks took place on the Philippines and on British and Dutch colonies.

Some diplomatic strings remained to be tied. The final Japanese note to Secretary Hull was supposed to be delivered at 1 P.M. But delay in decoding and typing the long document kept the Japanese diplomats from arriving at Hull's office until 2 P.M. In the meantime, Hull had read the Magic intercept of the note. Roosevelt got the news of the attack at 1:47 from Secretary of the Navy Knox.

Roosevelt called Hull at 2:05. The Japanese diplomats had just arrived and were in the waiting room. Roosevelt instructed Hull to receive them but say nothing about the attack. The Japanese ambassador, by way of apology, said he had been told by his government to hand over the note at 1 P.M. Hull pretended to read it (he knew its contents already) and handed it back saying it was "crowded with infamous falsehoods and distortions." With a disgusted shrug Hull dismissed the envoys.

In Tokyo Ambassador Grew still hoped to achieve something positive. The day before the attack, Roosevelt had sent a personal appeal for peace to Emperor Hirohito. Grew asked for an audience with the emperor. At 7 A.M. Grew was awakened and told that the foreign minister wished to see him. Hoping to see Hirohito, Grew rushed to the ministry, only to be handed the note breaking off negotiations. Two hours later he heard that Japan had declared war on the United States and its European allies.

Japan greeted the news of war and the victory at Pearl Harbor jubilantly. Newspaper extras appeared on the streets, and the radio

Secretary of State Cordell Hull and Japanese negotiators met several times to prevent a
direct confrontation. But both sides took hard-line stands, so that the course of events
was determined weeks before the final meeting at 2:00 P.M. on December 7.

alternated between martial music and patriotic slogans. At the end of
December the fleet returned to Japan, and the government and people
welcomed the heroes of Operation Z with celebrations and medals.
Hirohito granted an audience to Nagumo, Fuchida, and several other
task force leaders. The rising sun reached its zenith. But as usual the
clearheaded Yamamoto warned that "this war will give us many
headaches in the future."

Roosevelt and most Americans never doubted this. On December
8, when the President asked Congress to declare war on Japan, he
assured his listeners that, whatever the cost, Japan would be van-
quished. He was right.

36

The United States as a Superpower

AFTER PEARL HARBOR anything seemed possible for the Japanese. Their plan for domination of Asia (the Greater East Asia Co-Prosperity Sphere) became a reality, at least temporarily. Japan had signed a mutual security treaty with Nazi Germany, and Hitler hastily declared war on the United States just after Pearl Harbor.

Only twenty-three years had elapsed since the end of World War I. Now another generation of American youth would have to fight overseas. Ironically, America's entry into the war came after a decade of intense isolationist feeling.

In the late 1920s and the 1930s isolationism gathered strength in America while dictatorships flourished overseas. In Japan the emperor continued to reign, but the role of the military greatly increased. In Europe new regimes emerged. A fascist dictator, Benito Mussolini, seized power in Italy in 1922. In Germany Nazi party chief Adolf Hitler became chancellor in 1933. When he started to rearm Germany, the peace settlement of 1919 began to collapse in Europe.

Most Americans heartily disliked the new

fascist regimes, which denied liberty and worshipped dictators. Worse still was the deadly anti-Semitism of the Nazis. But Americans also disliked the idea of war with the dictatorships (including Soviet Russia, where Joseph Stalin had made himself a communist dictator).

A profound disillusionment with World War I had spread throughout the United States. It no longer seemed a clean-cut crusade to "make the world safe for democracy." Instead, some regarded it as a capitalist war that the United States supposedly fought to protect loans made to European Allies by American bankers. This in turn had benefited the arms manufacturers, the "merchants of death." Republican Senator Gerald P. Nye of North Dakota developed these themes in sensational congressional hearings during the early 1930s. Nye's claims helped pressure Americans into favoring isolationism as a foreign policy.

THE NEUTRALITY ACTS

President Roosevelt quickly recognized the fascist threat to American interests and security. But he could do little. In domestic matters Congress followed his lead. In foreign affairs, however, things were different. Congress concentrated specifically on the causes of American involvement in World War I. Billions of dollars in war loans remained unpaid. So in 1934 Congress banned further loans to countries that had not paid their debts. Then the Neutrality Act of 1935 limited Roosevelt's ability to respond effectively to overseas aggression, even if American interests were endangered.

This law attempted to close the gap between a President's control of foreign relations and Congress' right to declare war. Henceforth, if war broke out anywhere, the President had to issue a proclamation of neutrality. More important, the law forbade shipping arms to any nation at war, whether victim or aggressor. Roosevelt sought power to ban or "embargo" shipments to unfriendly or aggressor nations while permitting arms to go to the victims of

Charles A. Lindbergh and Senator Gerald P. Nye stirred popular sentiment for isolationism. Nye's munitions industry investigations uncovered less noble reasons for this country's entrance into World War I, which led Lindbergh to campaign for nonintervention in future world power struggles.

aggression. Congress refused this request. It also rejected Wilson's internationalism by ordering Roosevelt to warn Americans that in wartime they traveled on belligerent ships at their own risk. Congress wished no repetition of the "mistakes" of 1917.

Yet isolationist hopes proved no match for events in the later 1930s. Italy invaded Ethiopia in October 1935. Roosevelt invoked the Neutrality Act, this time willingly, since an arms embargo would hinder Italy more than Ethiopia. He also asked American oil producers for a "moral embargo" on shipments to Italy, limiting amounts to prewar levels. Ethiopia fell to the Italian invaders. Italy then quit the League, following the example of Japan and Germany. The foundations for the Axis alliance had been laid.

Further Triumphs for the Dictators The menace to the Western democracies increased in 1936. Hitler armed the Rhineland, which had been demilitarized after World War I. General

Francisco Franco, leader of Spain's fascists, led a revolt—which was ultimately successful—against the Spanish government. France and Britain declared a noninterventionist policy toward Spain. This clearly favored the fascists, for Italy and Germany had intervened by sending planes and some troops to help Franco. Congress reacted by passing a second Neutrality Act, tightening the isolationist provisions of the first law.

So the first series of fascist moves, instead of weakening isolationism, strengthened it. Believing the Atlantic and Pacific oceans gave the United States ample security, isolationists argued that America should be a fortress prepared for any outside attack. But the United States should not meddle in foreign politics or wars.

Isolationists were not pacifists. They favored American rearmament, particularly a larger, two-ocean navy. As for Britain and France, most isolationists wished both countries well. Still, they did not think that the United States should or could guarantee the security of other Western powers. Europeans would have to fight their own wars.

Rise of the Interventionists In October 1937 Roosevelt sent up an anti-isolationist trial balloon, only to see it shot down quickly. In his "Quarantine Speech" he noted that an "epidemic of world lawlessness is spreading." Thus it was foolish to assume "that America will escape, that America may expect mercy, that this Western Hemisphere will not be attacked." To counter the threat, Roosevelt called for a quarantine of aggressor nations. Though some Americans agreed, the massive and negative outcry afterward caused Roosevelt to abandon his proposal.

A small but growing number of interventionists insisted, however, that the fascist Axis powers—if left unchecked—would eventually attack America. They saw Hitler as a madman whose ravings against "decadent" Western civilization showed what policies he would pursue. Isolationism was unworkable because not even wide oceans or great industrial power could make the United States secure if it stood alone.

Thus whatever aid America gave fascism's opponents would help the nation itself. Like the isolationists, interventionists saw a world moving toward war. But they also foresaw United States involvement—sooner or later. Better sooner, they thought, while Americans still had some overseas friends.

Events in 1938 and 1939 emphasized the failure of appeasement—the policy of buying off dictators with compromises. Compromises only brought new demands. France and Britain sold out part of Czechoslovakia to Germany at Munich in September 1938. Not satisfied yet, Hitler merely kept on expanding. He absorbed Austria as part of the German Third Reich. In March 1939 he occupied all of Czechoslovakia. Then he threatened Poland.

Roosevelt had approved of appeasement at Munich, but by 1939 he realized his mistake. He began a long campaign to repeal, or at least soften, the neutrality laws. He spoke of "many methods short of war" that might discourage aggression. But Congress would have to allow some presidential flexibility. Congress did not budge. No one can say to what extent American inertia and isolationism helped Hitler decide on war. Nevertheless, the American attitude surely encouraged him. On September 1, 1939, Germany invaded Poland. Britain and France declared war on Germany two days later, and World War II was underway.

GLOBAL CONFLICT

The start of World War II put American views on neutrality to a real test. Hitler quickly conquered Poland and divided it with Russia. Roosevelt was legally bound to issue a proclamation of neutrality. He was far from neutral, however. Nor did he try to hide his pro-Allied sentiments.

Defeat of the Axis was basic in Roosevelt's mind. If American isolation meant defeat for Britain and France, American security would be disastrously, perhaps fatally, damaged. Thus, Roosevelt would go to war before letting the other Western democracies perish.

Since 1900 American foreign policy had

increasingly involved British-American cooperation. Roosevelt developed a close friendship with Winston Churchill, Britain's prime minister.[1] Still, neither sentiment nor deep concern for the fate of democracy elsewhere in the world provided Roosevelt's chief motivation. He saw the savagery of dictators, especially Hitler. He concluded that, once Europe and Asia had been overrun by these "New Barbarians," America's turn would come.

Although Roosevelt accepted the risk of war, Congress would probably never have declared war prior to Pearl Harbor. Thus, Roosevelt's carefully worded pro-Allied efforts had to be made bit by bit. First, he asked Congress to repeal the arms embargo so that the United States might sell war goods to other Western powers. This passed with surprising ease. Now Britain and France might buy American arms but only on a "cash-and-carry" basis. Many Americans still hoped Hitler would be defeated without the necessity of making war loans to the Allies or placing American ships in Atlantic war zones.

These unreal hopes evaporated in the spring of 1940. Hitler launched a series of spectacular and successful campaigns that conquered much of Continental Europe. By May five countries had been overrun—Denmark, Norway, Luxembourg, the Netherlands, and Belgium. In June the "impossible" happened: France collapsed before the Nazi onslaught and agreed to German occupation of half its territory, including Paris. This left Britain the only effective Axis opponent.

Steps Toward Intervention These events profoundly disturbed Americans and shifted the isolationist-interventionist balance. Americans were shocked by the well-publicized sight of Hitler inspecting his new toy—the city of Paris—and dancing a little victory jig. What would come next? Americans might accept Allied defeats in limited wars, but this war seemed to have no limit.

[1] The Roosevelt-Churchill correspondence consisted chiefly of long, candid cables between the two men. Roosevelt ended one such message: "It is fun to be in the same decade as you."

Interventionists, who wanted massive aid for the battered Allies, grew bolder and better organized. Heroic British resistance to a German air assault on their homeland armed these interventionists with plenty of effective propaganda. The Committee to Defend America First, however, fought against any American involvement in the war. The America Firsters, like Charles Lindbergh, hero of the 1920s, argued that the war was simply none of our business. Many felt that a seemingly invincible Germany should not be stirred up unnecessarily.

Roosevelt moved shrewdly (1) to rearm America and (2) to aid Britain to the extent

This photo of Hitler, now known to have been doctored to make a little leap into a grotesque victory "jig," proved effective in turning American sentiment toward war.

legally permissible and politically possible. Since 1940 was also a presidential election year, he had to be cautious. Meanwhile, Roosevelt broke the traditional ban on third-term Presidents by running again. Significantly, Republican isolationists could not nominate their man, Senator Robert A. Taft of Ohio. An internationalist named Wendell Willkie, a utilities executive with little political experience, won the nomination.

In the midst of the campaign Roosevelt made a daringly unneutral move. He transferred fifty World War I destroyers to the British navy. In exchange the United States received a dozen British air and naval bases in the Western Hemisphere. Churchill said of this: "It marked the passage of the United States from being neutral to being nonbelligerent [but involved]." Roosevelt won the election by a narrower margin than in 1936. Republican gains meant that Roosevelt had to take the views of the opposition party into greater account in facing the world crisis.

Every President who wins reelection usually regards it as a mandate for his policies. Now Roosevelt went even further than the destroyers-for-bases swap. He asked Congress for a Lend-Lease program. Under this law, passed in March 1941, the President could "lend" war material to countries whose security was deemed vital to American interests. The United States would become the "arsenal of democracy." By the end of World War II over $50 billion in Lend-Lease equipment and supplies had been distributed to America's allies.

Undeclared Naval Hostilities Further support for Britain soon materialized. The American navy patrolled the western half of the North Atlantic, freeing British ships for duty nearer Europe. American ships and planes fed data on Nazi submarines to the Royal Navy. British ships used American ports freely, while this country kept sixty-five Axis ships tied in its harbors. Some Americans joined the British or Canadian air forces, and British pilots trained at American airfields. The situation, as Germany knew, was not at all neutral. But Hitler was not yet ready to declare war on America; in the summer of 1941 he had attacked his Russian "ally."

But American "nonbelligerence" soon provoked German countermeasures. When American warships began escorting Allied shipping halfway across the Atlantic, German submarines (or U-boats) responded. Several American destroyers were fired on; several merchant ships went down. In October a German submarine sank an American destroyer near Iceland. Congress then removed the last restriction of the neutrality laws: armed American ships could take war supplies directly to Britain. An undeclared naval war raged in the Atlantic.

Some members of the Roosevelt Cabinet wanted an immediate declaration of war against Germany. But Roosevelt preferred to continue active nonbelligerence. He would arm those fighting the Axis (including Soviet Russia). He would cement relations with Britain, as in the meeting with Churchill that produced the Atlantic Charter.[2] He would also let the Axis powers decide when to declare war.

THE UNITED STATES AT WAR

Japan, not Germany, made the decisive move. The assault on Pearl Harbor and other bases in the Pacific on December 7, 1941, ended the isolationist-interventionist debate. It also united the nation. Roosevelt's critics, including Lindbergh of America First, now pledged their hearty support for the war. One major isolationist, Michigan's Republican Senator Arthur H. Vandenberg, conceded that Pearl Harbor opened his eyes: "That day ended isolationism for any realist."

Could the war with Japan have been avoided? Not unless one of the two nations, Japan or the United States, had changed its basic policy. Japan intended to expand in China and South-

[2] The Atlantic Charter stated common British and American beliefs: The right of people to choose their own form of government and the need for world-wide economic cooperation and an international security system to prevent future wars.

east Asia. The United States would never recognize Japan's partial conquest of China. It would equally oppose any Japanese moves against Allied colonies, such as British Malaya or the Dutch East Indies. Neither side would budge. Japan's decision to expand by force made conflict with America almost inevitable. An attack on only British, French, and Dutch holdings would have been wiser for Tokyo, nevertheless. Had American territory remained untouched, Congress might well have refused to declare war.

Americans had a long job ahead. It was made even longer just after Pearl Harbor when Germany and Italy honored their Axis commitments by declaring war on the United States. In one way, however, this step simplified matters. American leaders believed that Hitler, the greatest threat to democracy, should be defeated first. Japan could not be ignored—Americans would indeed "Remember Pearl Harbor"—but the war in Europe against Germany, Italy, and their Axis allies received top priority. Hitler, then at the height of his power, relished the idea of smashing Franklin "Rosenfeld." (Hitler had the strange notion that Roosevelt, an Episcopalian since birth, was Jewish.)

Whatever his motives, Hitler's actions caused the creation of the Grand Alliance, a coalition of all nations fighting the Axis. America, Britain, and Russia were senior partners. Starting with a declaration by "United Nations," signed in January 1942 by twenty-six countries, the alliance grew to forty-seven members by 1945. This provided the basis for the United Nations (UN). Technically, all were equal. But in reality the great powers ran the war largely to suit themselves.

Joining the Allies was a new step for the United States. Even in World War I, America was only an "associated power" rather than an "ally." The difference went beyond hairsplitting over the meaning of words. World War II was unique; Americans felt their own security threatened. The world had indeed changed.

Big Three Relations Within the Grand Alliance, or United Nations, the closest cooperation

existed between Britain and the United States. Churchill and Roosevelt met almost a dozen times to develop the partnership and sometimes to prepare a united front against Russia, the other major ally. It was not that the Soviet Union was an uncooperative ally. After withstanding the first German offensive of 1941 (a surprise attack by a former ally), the Russians fought the Germans tenaciously. The Nazi army was spending itself in Russia, winning many battles but nothing decisive. Churchill and Roosevelt hastened to assure Stalin, the Soviet dictator, of their esteem. They promised military aid as soon as possible.

But Stalin wanted immediate action by his allies in the West. Specifically, he called for an Anglo-American invasion of Western Europe launched across the English Channel in 1942. But instead of a dangerous, and probably disastrous, cross-channel invasion of occupied France that year, Western leaders settled for landings in North Africa. This move took little pressure off Russia. Stalin angrily rejected suggestions that this weak move represented a so-called second front against Germany.

Further friction developed during preliminary discussions of the postwar political settlements. Stalin, like Roosevelt and Churchill, never doubted his side would win. He wanted a hand in carving national boundaries after the war. Roosevelt conceded on this point, but Churchill usually tried to pacify but contain Stalin. Roosevelt often urged the postponement of political decisions until later in the war.

Events in Asia and the Pacific The war was fought on many fronts. After the Japanese struck Pearl Harbor, they took over most of Southeast Asia. First they conquered the rest of French Indochina (Vietnam, Laos, and Cambodia). Then Malaya, Singapore, and Burma—all British colonies—fell. The Dutch East Indies came next. Australia was so sure its turn had come that it almost withdrew its troops from North Africa for a last-ditch homeland defense.

Meanwhile, the Japanese occupied most of America's colony, the Philippines. General

WORLD WAR II IN THE PACIFIC

← Japanese advances
← Allied advances
⋯⋯ Extent of Japanese conquest
◄-- Allied air operations
✦ Battle or campaign

0   1000 MILES

The day after the Japanese surprise attack on Pearl Harbor on December 7, 1941, the United States declared war on Japan. On that same day, the Japanese invaded Thailand and Malaya. By late December they had captured Guam, Hong Kong, and Wake Island. The Japanese invasion of the Philippines began December 10; they took Manila on January 2, 1942. General Douglas MacArthur retreated to Australia.

In February 1942 the Japanese took Singapore and by early March, most of the Dutch East Indies. In June they seized two of the Aleutian Islands. The Battle of the Coral Sea was fought between Japanese and Allied forces on May 7–8, which stopped Japan's advance on Australia. The air and naval battle of Midway (June 3–6) was a turning point in the Pacific war, and within two months the United States was for the first time on the offensive.

The first major Allied offensive, beginning in August 1942, was fought at Guadalcanal. The Japanese were driven from it in February 1943. During March–August the Japanese were driven from the Aleutians. In the second half of 1943 the South Pacific offensive took place. It gave the Allies control of the waters adjacent to the Solomon Islands. A Central Pacific offensive was launched in November under Admiral Chester

Nimitz, during which the Allies took the Solomons, Gilberts, Marshalls, and Marianas. In December General Joseph W. Stilwell began a campaign in Burma; Burma was not completely retaken, however, until May 1945.

In June 1944 air attacks were opened against cities on the Japanese home islands. The Philippines campaign of June–December saw General MacArthur's return there. The naval Battle of Leyte Gulf (October 23–25) was a decisive defeat for Japan. It destroyed most of its remaining sea power. The Philippines campaign ended after the taking of Manila.

After heavy fighting, United States Marines took Iwo Jima in March 1945 and conquered Okinawa by late June. In May–August the greatest air offensive in the Pacific was launched against the Japanese home islands, culminating in the dropping of atomic bombs on Hiroshima (August 6) and Nagasaki (August 9). On August 8, the Soviet Union declared war on Japan and invaded Manchuria.

Japan surrendered and sued for peace on August 10. President Harry Truman announced August 14 as V-J Day. Japan's formal surrender took place September 2 in Tokyo Bay aboard the United States battleship *Missouri*.

(continued on page 721)

Pleasures and Pastimes in a Mass Society

"The Americans are a queer people: they can't play. Americans rush to work as soon as they get up. They can't play. They try to, but they can't." Canadian humorist Stephen Leacock indulged in some poetic license when he described his neighbors to the south. Americans do play, of course. They enjoy light entertainment. They love competitive sports. And they find pleasure in the simple satisfactions of everyday life. (A happy man indeed is greeting *The New Television Set* in Norman Rockwell's 1949 painting.)

Foreign observers sometimes complain about the "canned" amusements of a mass society, but even French critic André Maurois commented favorably on them. He wrote, "Americans who never meet each other and who live under different skies come to have innumerable common memories and brotherly thoughts."

For further information on the foreign observers quoted in this essay, see "Notes on Sources."

PICTORIAL ESSAY 8

Stronger than in various other countries, and perhaps also than in Turkey, seems to be the predilection in America for the lighter types of musical and theatrical entertainment—for jazz and operettas, or for comedies and thrillers rather than plays that have a pessimistic note or are centered around philosophical and social themes.

[ÖMER CELÂL SARC, 1959]

Broadcasting a radio drama, 1934

Scene from *Oklahoma!* (original production, 1943)

I could not agree that the creation of films is not an art at all, only an industry. It is actually a curiously mixed activity, coming into a new category, needing all the resources and organization of a large industry, but by no means devoid of genuine artistic impulses. The public looked to films for general entertainment, on a scale hitherto unknown, and accepted the moving pictures as a substitute for theaters, books, gossip, and dreams.

[J. B. PRIESTLEY, 1935-36]

A scene from *Gold Diggers of 1933*

Let's listen to Louis Armstrong on Broadway, the black Titan of the cry, of the apostrophe, of the burst of laughter, of thunder. An imperial figure, Armstrong makes his entrance. His voice is as deep as an abyss, it is a black cave. He bursts out laughing, he roars and puts the trumpet to his mouth. With it he is in turn demoniac, playful, and massive, from one second to another, in accordance with an astounding fantasy. The man is extravagantly skillful; he is a king.

[LE CORBUSIER, 1947]

Louis Armstrong

Elvis Presley and fans

Female teenagers are in the habit of greeting their heroes, the young crooners —the one best known being Elvis Presley, of the writhing hips and thighs—with a shrill yell that seems to issue from a single throat. The picture of young and well-dressed girls comporting themselves in this fashion is enough to send cold shivers down an adult's spine. Significantly, however, it has been observed that only the girls in the rows lit up by the stage lights break out in this yell; that is, only those who can be seen by the others. Moreover, they are looking not so much at the singer as at the other members of their own group.

[HERBERT VON BORCH, 1962]

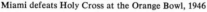
Miami defeats Holy Cross at the Orange Bowl, 1946   Willie Mays at second base, 1957

I do not pretend to understand even the coarser of the finer points of American college football, which must have been originally devised during an early revolutionary phase of American life, for like a revolution it is an odd mixture of secret plotting, with so many heads motionless and close together, and sudden violent action. When either side pressed towards goal, we all stood up. The danger over or the prize lost, we sat down again. The enormous clock ran off the seconds when the ball was actually in play. It stopped when the game stopped. And the game was always stopping.

[J. B. PRIESTLEY AND JACQUETTA HAWKES, 1954]

I have studied hundreds of photos of Louis in his big fights, of Louis preparing for his big fights, of Louis just after his big fights. His face almost never changes. The man is dignified, in the toughest sport in the world, whether he's giving a licking or taking one. You cannot get away from this impression of the man being so superbly equipped to fight that he didn't need the window-dressing of a big grin of confidence, or glib phrases by the publicity boys. Louis wasn't just a great fighter. He was an admirable man.

[HARRY CARPENTER, 1964]

The Brown Bomber, Louis and Schmeling Fight, by Robert Riggs

Robinson's character was the key. A fierce competitor, Jackie had in the early days to curb his angry pride. He ignored insults, and won recognition as a baseball player, on equal terms with others, whether white or black. Today ability is the key, not pigmentation. Some day Jackie's greatest honor will come when he is simply a name in a record book, when, because there was a Jackie Robinson and others like him, future generations have forgotten there was ever a need for a Jackie Robinson.

[CANADIAN SPORTSWRITER]

Cheerleaders at a high-school basketball game

To observe the North American in a large crowd within the United States—at a World Series game or a popular football game—is one of the most cheering spectacles in the world. Here we have an enormous mass of people, well balanced, attractive, determined to enjoy to the utmost an afternoon of relaxation, applauding their favorite team but wihout ill will or malevolence toward the adversary, on the contrary always disposed to recognize and applaud the courage and skill of the opposition.

[DANIEL COSÍO VILLEGAS, 1959]

We went into a bowling alley. It is the old game of skittles which the dwarfs of Rip Van Winkle played, but it has been brought up to date. Instead of a wild gully, I found a bar with tables and chairs: the bowling alleys, set side by side, are of varnished wood, and when the bowling ball has knocked over the ninepins, it falls through a trap door and is returned by an automatic device to the player. The game is so popular that the alleys are booked for days in advance. It is monotonous to watch.

[SIMONE DE BEAUVOIR, 1947]

Bowling at a fifty-six-lane alley, California

Woman playing bingo in Muncie, Indiana

Father and son tossing a football, Newton, Iowa

America is a modern land where technical ingenuity is apparent at every point, in the equipment of a kitchen as well as of a car, but at the same time a land of gardens, of flowers, of home activities, where a man, away from his office or his work-place, enjoys tinkering at his bench, making a piece of furniture, repainting his house, repairing a fence, or mowing his lawn. A land of luxury but also of simple pleasures. There is an America that strolls in the parks in its suburban Sunday clothes, or cavorts on the beaches, and plays base-ball everywhere.

[JACQUES FREYMOND, 1959]

Teenagers at a "sock hop," Carlsbad, New Mexico

Wisconsin Farm Auction, by Joan Arend Kickbush

Girls jumping rope, Cleveland

The American smile, which has been so ridiculed by those who believe the intelligent thing is to know everything already—without, of course, knowing much of anything at all—seems to me to be the expression of love for one's fellow man, of the basic fact that in the United States it is firmly believed that living together is a blessing. This is derived, in my opinion, from the historical makeup of the United States and from the American spirit, from its loneliness and the fact that for so long the presence of other men was an occasion for joy.

[JULIAN MARIAS, 1959]

Children playing at an open water hydrant, New York City

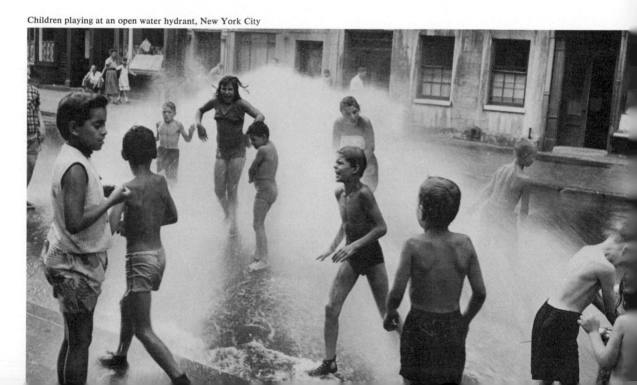

Douglas MacArthur, the commander there when the Philippines were attacked (on the same day as Pearl Harbor), was ordered to Australia. What remained of the American army—including Filipino units—held out bravely for several months on the Bataan peninsula near Manila until overwhelmed by superior force. Most Filipinos opposed the Japanese invasion. The islands had been promised independence; the war upset this time table, forcing a postponement until 1946.

The Japanese drive of 1941–42 was soon halted. Though a naval battle in the Coral Sea in May 1942 brought neither side victory, it removed the threat of a Japanese invasion of Australia. In June a key naval battle took place near Midway. Japanese strategy called for capture of Midway, then a move against Hawaii. Japan probably should have made these two attacks right after Pearl Harbor. By mid-1942, however, things had changed. American aircraft carrier strength, though limited, was undamaged. Also, because Magic had broken the Japanese code, the American navy knew where to concentrate.

Midway signaled the end of traditional naval warfare. Planes replaced guns and torpedoes as the most important offensive weapons. Enemy aircraft carriers were therefore the main target. Four Japanese carriers were sunk but only one American flat-top.[3] More important, the troop transports turned back toward Japan. The Japanese never again made a serious thrust in the mid-Pacific.

Coral Sea and Midway set the stage for Allied offensive operations. In August 1942 Americans landed on Guadalcanal in the Solomon Islands. The battle there was long and fierce—a warning of what lay ahead. This "island hopping" followed a bloody course from Guadalcanal in 1942 to Okinawa in 1945. In a series of landings on the various islands in between

---

[3] All four carriers Japan lost at Midway had been used to attack Pearl Harbor. Likewise lost at Midway—or during the harsh fighting that followed in the Solomon Islands—were nearly all the daring Japanese pilots of December 7. Neither the flat-tops nor the aviators were ever properly replaced. Admiral Nagumo, who led the victory at Pearl and the defeat at Midway, survived until 1944. Then he died, evidently by suicide, during the American capture of Saipan.

The war in the Pacific was fought by island-hopping— retaking island by island territory captured by the Japanese. This Marine landing in the Solomons in 1943 helped save Australia from conquest.

United States troops fought for every bit of territory, notably the first few yards of each beachhead. Japanese resistance never let up. Even losing battle after battle did not diminish the enemy's will to fight.

After Midway Americans had sea and air superiority. The American fleet, especially the number of carriers, grew enormously. Even when the Japanese navy or air force came out in full force (as when the United States recaptured the Philippines in 1944), Japan suffered staggering losses. On one day American pilots shot down nearly 500 Japanese planes. At Leyte Gulf Japan's navy was almost destroyed.

American submarines (though less publicized than German U-boats) sank hundreds of Japanese ships. Many of them were carrying raw materials from Southeast Asia to Japan's factories. By early 1945 Japan had no hope for victory. The war in China ground on inconclusively. The Pacific, which three years before had seemed to be Japan's, was now an American lake. The only way left to preserve Japanese martial honor or punish the American invaders was suicide assaults by *Kamikaze* pilots.[4]

Events in Europe and the Mediterranean The Allies mounted an equally relentless (and equally successful) effort in Europe and the Meditteranean. American and British forces overran North Africa and routed German General Erwin Rommel's *Afrika Korps*. In 1943 the Allies invaded Sicily and then mainland Italy. Meanwhile, massive preparations for invading France went on, with Britain as the staging area.

On another front the Russians took terrible losses. Yet they stopped the farthest German penetration at the Volga River in the Battle of Stalingrad. For the next two years the "Eastern Front" repeatedly saw Russian advances and German retreats.

The invasion of France on June 6, 1944, put Hitler's neck in the noose. Despite strong resistance Allied invaders stormed Normandy beaches. Happily, Hitler insisted that the Normandy invasion was unimportant. He refused to concentrate his available forces there. After several nerve-racking weeks American tank columns led by General George S. Patton pushed beyond Normandy and raced across France.

But the Nazi army could not be crushed in 1944. It withdrew toward the Rhine. Germany, as helpless now as Japan, was the target of massive air attacks. (Over 1,000 Allied planes participated in a single raid on Berlin.) Hitler still dreamed of victory, though he mistakenly believed his own people were betraying him. He forbade his generals to retreat. He hastened the murder of millions in concentration camps. Yet neither ravings nor cruelty produced military victories. Early in 1945 the Allies pushed ahead on all fronts.

The Big Three leaders—Roosevelt, Stalin, and Churchill—had long been preparing for victory. Stalin and Churchill met in Moscow in October 1944. There they began carving out spheres of influence. Roosevelt wanted to end the war first and then make such decisions. The Axis must accept defeat and unconditional surrender; the Allies should not squabble until they had won. Thus the 1943 Big Three meeting at Teheran, Iran, dealt mainly with wartime strategy.

By early 1945 territorial questions could not be postponed. Germany would surely surrender that year; Japan was next in line. Russian participation in the invasion of Japan could mean a shorter campaign, with fewer Western casualties. What price would Stalin demand, though, to bring Russia into the Pacific war? The answer emerged at the Yalta Conference of February 1945, a Big Three meeting at a Russian resort in the Crimea.

Stalin set a high though not outlandish price. He wanted Russian power in the Far East to equal its extent in 1904, before his country lost the Russo-Japanese War. Russia was to receive the northernmost islands of the Japanese chain, plus territorial and commercial rights in Manchuria and northern China. In return, Stalin would declare war against Japan within three months of the end of the war in Europe.

Roosevelt's military advisers warned that

---

[4] *Kamikaze* pilots crashed their planes, loaded with bombs, into ships.

WORLD WAR II IN EUROPE

Extent of Axis control

Neutral nations

Allies

Allied offensives

Battle

When Germany was at the height of its power, its armies had overrun much of European Russia, defeated France, occupied Norway and Denmark, and held much of North Africa. In December 1941 England and the Soviet Union were the only Allies in Europe still undefeated by Germany.

The first United States troops for the European theater of the war arrived in northern Ireland in January 1942. Six months later in North Africa, the British checked the Axis advance at El Alamein. In November General Eisenhower's Allied forces landed in North Africa. By May 1943 the Germans had been defeated there. In Europe the Russians defeated the German armies, attacking Stalingrad in December 1942 after a four-month siege—a major turning point. Thereafter the Russians began to take the offensive.

The Allied invasion of Italy began in July 1943. Italy's unconditional surrender to the Allies in September was followed by stiff German resistance in northern Italy. The Germans were not finally defeated there until 1945.

The air offensive against Germany began in January 1944 in preparation for an Allied invasion. On June 6, D-Day, Allied armies invaded Normandy in northern France in a surprise attack. By August 10 this offensive was concluded and a second front in southern France was opened that began a drive up the Rhone Valley. All of France, Belgium, and Luxembourg was liberated by September. By this time the Russians had driven the Germans out of the Soviet Union and into Eastern Europe.

The battle for Germany began in September 1944. The first large German city to fall, Aachen, was taken in October. Within five months Belgrade, Budapest, and Warsaw had fallen.

A German counteroffensive in the west was launched in December 1944. The Germans almost succeeded in breaking through the American line in the Battle of the Bulge, but they were repulsed. Then a British offensive was launched in the Netherlands. By March United States troops had penetrated the Ruhr Valley and crossed the Rhine; a month later, they reached the Elbe. The Russians entered Berlin late in April. Berlin fell on May 2. The formal end of the war in Europe occurred on May 8. Germany surrendered unconditionally to the Allies.

The strain of war was visible on FDR's face as he met with his allies, Churchill and Stalin, for the last time at Yalta. The concessions made to Stalin there to secure Russia's entrance into the Pacific war were denounced by some postwar critics as "appeasement."

invading Japan without Russia might cost the United States a half-million casualties. The President had no wish for this. Nor could he count on the still untested atom bomb to end the war. Stalin's offer seemed the only choice.

Yalta also planned for the dismemberment of Germany. The Allied powers (the Big Three and France) would each occupy a section. Germany must also pay reparations for the wartime destruction it had caused. Stalin wanted to weaken Germany so that the Germans might never attack Russia again. Reparations would keep Germany feeble. Moreover, splitting Germany into occupation zones assured Stalin that the eastern zone would remain firmly in Soviet control.

A HOT WAR TURNED COLD

Within a half year of Yalta, the Axis was subdued. In April 1945 Hitler committed suicide in Berlin as the Allies overran Germany. Four months later the Pacific war ended spectacularly and ominously. On August 6 an American atom bomb largely obliterated the Japanese city of Hiroshima, killing over 70,000 (see page 726). Three days later Nagasaki suffered a similar fate. Japan surrendered, though many Japanese wished to fight to the death.

History's greatest war ended with unconditional surrender by the Axis. Yet victory found the Grand Alliance anything but united. Differences over postwar policy produced visible strains, with the possibility of a new and dangerous confrontation. The United States and Russia were now superpowers. Their growing disagreements would soon be called a Cold War.

Soviet-American cooperation broke down completely after World War II. Eastern and central Europe came under Russian domination. The Baltic countries of Latvia, Lithuania, and Estonia ceased being independent nations. Finland avoided the same fate by curbing its foreign policy in a treaty with Russia. The countries between Western-occupied Germany and Russia, plus the Balkan nations, became Soviet satellites. (Yugoslavia would later break away.) A Russian Soviet empire emerged. Countries on its borders (Greece, Turkey, and Iran, for example) all felt the pressure of the new superpower.

The United States had hoped for cooperation, not conflict, among the major powers after the war. The status quo and isolationism of earlier periods were dead. Americans could not pull back as in 1919 and expect to maintain their interests in a vacuum. World War II had exhausted Britain and France. If North Atlantic leadership of the world were to continue, the United States had to step in. Thus Washington pushed for a new world organization, despite the League of Nations' failure and America's own sorry role in that failure.

Roosevelt wanted a league. Unlike Wilson, though, he made sure that Republicans participated in sessions that preceded the founding of the United Nations in 1945 (soon after Roosevelt's death). The UN differed from the League in various ways. It was located in New York, not Geneva. More important, the great powers established a Security Council whose permanent members (the United States, Britain, France, Russia, and China) could defeat any proposal with a single negative vote. This big-power veto, a recognition of both national sovereignty and great-power interests, gravely limited UN effectiveness in crisis situations. Yet the veto was desired by all the large powers.

Containment in the Mediterranean American hopes for postwar stability suffered as a result of Roosevelt's death. The late President did not possess a precise blueprint for peacetime policy. He had become increasingly disillusioned over Russian behavior. But he did possess enormous prestige. This was not true of Vice President Harry S Truman, a man without experience in either high-level administration or foreign policy. President Truman's baptism of fire in summit diplomacy—direct meetings by heads of gov-

ernment—came in July 1945. He, Stalin, and Britain's new prime minister, Clement Attlee, met at Potsdam, Germany. Full agreement proved impossible. With Japan still undefeated, Truman accepted postponement of various pending issues.

Russia's expansionism and the weakness of America's allies soon ruled out further delay. By 1947 Western Europe seemed ready to collapse. Britain, France, Italy, and West Germany (not yet a separate country) were sliding downward, perhaps toward a chaos that could only benefit Russia. Britain had to give up its empire. The British move that most affected the United States was its decision to end aid to Greece and Turkey, Britain's anticommunist Mediterranean allies. The Russians and Turks had been at odds for centuries. The post–World War II period proved no exception. The Soviets tried to gain parts of eastern Turkey and establish bases at the Dardanelles, Turkey's (and Russia's) gateway to the Mediterranean.

The Greeks (unfriendly toward the Turks but now allied with them as another target of Russian expansionism) also needed help. A communist guerrilla movement was fighting the Greek government. Only active American intervention could keep Greece and Turkey out of the Soviet sphere. In March 1947 the President enunciated the Truman Doctrine "to help free peoples to maintain their free institutions" against the threat of "subjugation by armed minorities or by outside pressures." Congress appropriated $400 million to aid Greece and Turkey.

The congressional action and Truman's strong words were highly significant. They proved the Cold War had truly begun. The United States would, by threat of a third world war, contain Russia within the areas the Soviets had occupied or dominated by 1947. The support Truman received from Republicans in Congress signaled that the policy of containment had bipartisan support as well.

Containment in Western Europe After containing the Russian advance in the eastern Med-

Hiroshima

The silence in the skies above Hiroshima was broken only by the sound of two approaching B-29s. There had already been one alert on that warm morning of August 6, 1945. But now the all clear had sounded. The people of Hiroshima were used to a weather plane flying overhead at this hour—around 8:00 A.M.—so they did not pay much attention to the sky.

But these were not weather planes. One of them was the *Enola Gay*. Its mission was to drop the first atomic bomb on enemy territory. At about 31,000 feet the bomb-bay doors opened. The bombardier released "Little Boy," a weapon that had twenty times the power of a ton of TNT. At 2,000 feet the bomb detonated.

A young Hiroshima girl who was riding a trolley gave this account:

> At that moment my eyes were suddenly blinded by a flash of piercing light and the neighborhood was enveloped in dense smoke of a yellow color like poison gas. Instantly everything became pitch dark, and you couldn't see an inch ahead. Then a heavy and tremendously loud roar. The inside of my mouth was gritty as though I had eaten sand,

and my throat hurt. I looked toward the east, and I saw an enormous black pillar of cloud billowing upward. 'It's all over now,' I thought.

As the plane made a sharp turn to avoid the blast, the tail gunner looked down at the falling bomb. Within seconds he was looking directly into the center of the atomic detonation. He watched the shock wave approach the plane like a shimmering heat wave. The mushroom cloud started forming immediately. He described it as "a bubbling mass of purple-gray smoke, and you could see it had a red core to it and everything was burning inside."

Within an instant 70,000 people died. Another 30,000 would later die of radiation burns and a strange new disease, radiation sickness. Approximately 75 percent of the buildings in Hiroshima were destroyed. As another eyewitness said of those first few seconds, "Everything had crumbled away in that one moment and changed into streets of rubble, street after street of ruins."

What caused the decision to use this devastating weapon? President Truman had been told that if the Japanese fought to the end of their own islands, as they vowed to do, the war would last more than another year, and a half million American lives would be lost. He thought a quick one-two punch—one atomic bomb dropped, followed swiftly by a second on another target—would force Japan to surrender.

Historians have conjectured that there may also have been other reasons. Soviet-American relations were strained. Truman may have wanted to show the Russians that American strength was superior. Or he may have wanted to end the war before the Soviet Union could occupy Asia as it had Europe.

The atomic bomb did end the war. Three days after Hiroshima was bombed, Nagasaki suffered the same fate. The next day the Japanese asked for peace terms.

iterranean, the United States turned to Western Europe. Secretary of State George C. Marshall (see page 731) announced in mid-1947 American willingness to contribute huge sums toward European reconstruction. All Europe was included; even Russia sent envoys to a preliminary conference. But the Russians quickly withdrew and kept their satellites from joining the European Recovery Program (ERP), better known as the Marshall plan.

Congress moved more cautiously than on Greece and Turkey. But a communist takeover of Czechoslovakia in 1948 spurred it on. Billions of dollars flooded into Western Europe, stimulating the area's economic recovery. This also ended any early possibility that European communist parties would reach power through elections.

The Western allies took an added step in containing communist advances in Europe by creating a formal military alliance in 1949. The North Atlantic Treaty Organization (NATO) included a dozen North Atlantic nations (see page 729). They pledged to take any action necessary "including the use of armed force, to restore and maintain the security of the North Atlantic area." To implement the promise to defend any NATO country attacked by an outside power, large numbers of United States troops went to Germany. The American navy took over from Britain in the Mediterranean.

Through NATO the United States in effect became the policeman for the Western world, a break with American tradition. Not since the French alliance of 1778 had the United States allied itself formally with another power. NATO made the containment policy a firm one. Though the Soviets exploded their first nuclear weapon in 1949, they knew further expansion to the west was unthinkable. NATO was soon functioning effectively, with General Dwight D. Eisenhower (Supreme Allied Commander in Europe during World War II) heading NATO's forces. Obviously Washington would not allow a Russian "iron curtain" to fall over Western Europe.

The Struggle for Mainland China Unsettling events in Asia contrasted sharply with the suc-

cess of containment in Europe. Postwar China /727 was particularly disappointing for Americans. Civil war broke out there between the communists under Mao Tse-tung and the Nationalists under Chiang Kai-shek. Mao had fought for control of China long before the Japanese invasion. War with Japan temporarily united the two sides, but afterward, they returned to civil war.

By 1948 it became clear the Nationalists would lose. The next year Chiang fled to the island of Taiwan, while on the mainland Mao proclaimed his communist government, the People's Republic of China (often referred to as Red China). Massive American military intervention might have prevented the communist takeover. A few American leaders thought so, though even fewer recommended it. But later large-scale American involvement in Vietnam casts grave doubt on that course. In any case, two certainties remain: by 1949 Red China possessed considerable power, and this power would increase.

The Korean Conflict The United States refused diplomatic recognition to Red China. Yet soon after the Chinese civil war ended, Americans were forced to recognize the Red Chinese army in combat. The scene was Korea, which had regained independence from Japan in 1945. But now Korea had been divided into communist-occupied North Korea and American-occupied South Korea. The communist North invaded the South in June 1950, perhaps because Washington had declared Korea outside the zone of American vital interest.

When South Korea asked for American help, Truman quickly provided it. Available combat forces (two American divisions stationed in Japan) went at once to Korea. Also, a Soviet mistake let Truman make the American response a United Nations venture. In June 1950 Russia was boycotting all UN meetings. The Security Council promptly branded North Korea an aggressor and authorized a UN military force to repel the attack. General Douglas MacArthur, occupation leader of Japan, also headed the UN army (mostly American soldiers) in Korea.

The Korean conflict was a success and a failure for the United States. Two Koreas still exist. Thus the 1950–53 military effort there did prevent a communist takeover. But this venture became a political liability for Democrats and a lasting frustration for all Americans. After a year of seesaw campaigns up and down the Korean peninsula, fighting settled close to the original dividing line.

Total victory became unattainable because the war had limited aims. Washington too permitted only limited means to achieve them. MacArthur, a great soldier and a great egotist, was especially frustrated. He had sent his troops to within sight of China's border in 1950, provoking full-scale Chinese intervention in Korea and an American retreat. Despite this—and the risk of bringing Russia into combat also—MacArthur wanted to bomb China and fight the war more vigorously. Truman refused. When MacArthur aired his contrary views in public, Truman fired him.

Warfare in Korea was conventional in employing large numbers of men with standard weaponry in set battles. But since it was fought for limited aims—containing rather than destroying the enemy—it foreshadowed recent combat in Vietnam.

U.S. POSTWAR ALLIANCES

YEAR ESTABLISHED	ALLIANCE	MEMBERS	PURPOSE
1948	ORGANIZATION OF AMERICAN STATES (OAS)	Argentina, Barbados, Bolivia, Brazil, Chile, Colombia, Costa Rica, Cuba, Dominican Republic, Ecuador, El Salvador, Guatemala, Haiti, Honduras, Jamaica, Mexico, Nicaragua, Panama, Paraguay, Peru, Trinidad-Tobago, United States, Uruguay, Venezuela	To provide for the common defense of the Western Hemisphere and settle economic and political hemispheric problems.
1949	NORTH ATLANTIC TREATY ORGANIZATION (NATO)	Belgium, Canada, Denmark, France, Great Britain, Iceland, Italy, Luxembourg, the Netherlands, Norway, Portugal, United States Greece, Turkey (1952) West Germany (1955)	To coordinate military defense (under a central military command) against external communist aggression. An armed attack on one member is an attack on all.
1951	ANZUS PACT	Australia, New Zealand, United States	To provide security against external attack in the southern Pacific region.
1951–60 1951 1954 1954 1960	BILATERAL MUTUAL-DEFENSE TREATIES	Philippines, United States Taiwan, United States South Korea, United States Japan, United States	To provide specific commitments to the military defense of the Far East.
1954	SOUTHEAST ASIA TREATY ORGANIZATION (SEATO)	Australia, France, Great Britain, New Zealand, Pakistan, Philippines, Thailand, United States	To build up Southeast Asia economically and militarily against possible communist aggression. Joint resistance to external attack is not required.
1955	BAGHDAD PACT; Reorganized in 1959 as CENTRAL TREATY ORGANIZATION (CENTO)	Iran, Pakistan, Turkey, United Kingdom Iraq (1955–59)	To provide economic and military assistance to the Middle East. The United States is a nonmember but gives extensive aid, primarily military, and is represented on some of the organization's councils.

REPUBLICANS BACK IN POWER

Truman fought the war his way; he and his party then paid the political price. Though Korea did not decide the election of 1952, it figured prominently. In promising to go to Korea if elected, the Republican candidate, Eisenhower ("Ike"), implied that he could end the conflict. This he did. Yet the truce signed in 1953 resulted less from Ike's tour of Korea than from exhaustion on both sides. Americans were happy to see the war end, though quite unhappy about the war itself. In this sense Korea was a prelude to the Vietnam nightmare.

When Republicans regained the presidency in 1952, after twenty years, they promised changes in foreign policy. Something beyond containment, something active, seemed possible to President Eisenhower and John Foster Dulles, his Secretary of State. Dulles quickly established himself as second in command in Eisenhower's administration. In foreign affairs he was first. Dulles talked tough about communism. He called Russian satellites captive nations, hinting that

John Foster Dulles is the protective nurse guarding the "children" of Asia from the lure of the "Red Piper of Peking" by herding them around the SEATO carriage.

their liberation was near. He warned that major communist wrongdoing could bring "massive retaliation" from the United States. Finally, Dulles stated he would go to "the brink of war" (including nuclear war) in pursuing his policies.

To back up his words, Dulles lined up more allies. In the Far East, the Southeast Asia Treaty Organization (SEATO) was organized in 1954. Although similar in many ways to NATO, the new alliance had some vital differences. Dulles limited his country's commitment by promising an American response to communist aggression only. Nor did the treaty set up a joint military command among the signers. Several important Asian nations (India and Indonesia, among others) would not join SEATO.

In the Middle East Dulles' initiative produced yet another anticommunist alliance, the Baghdad Pact of 1955. It included Pakistan, Iraq, Turkey, and Iran. Britain obligingly helped organize this group for Dulles, while the United States poured military and economic aid into its member nations.

Problems from Vietnam to Suez Almost at once these Dulles moves began to go awry. In French Indochina communism could not be contained. After World War II France hoped to carry on the business of her empire as usual there. But a nationalist guerrilla movement erupted under Ho Chi Minh. By 1954 the com-

munists had all but driven the French army from North Vietnam. The United States had been supplying the French with arms. When France, its NATO ally, started losing, Washington considered intervening directly. Instead, Dulles tried to salvage half a country.

The Geneva accords of 1954 (not signed by the United States, though Dulles was present as an observer) temporarily divided Vietnam into northern and southern sectors. The communists expected to win a promised nationwide election that was never held. Instead, Dulles helped install a pro-American Catholic, Ngo Diem, as head of South Vietnam. The United States thus acquired problems and responsibilities that would later haunt Americans.

War there would not come until the Democrats took office. But the Eisenhower-Dulles foreign policy quickly suffered other setbacks. In the fall of 1956 the ideas of "liberating" Eastern Europe and "containing" Russia's growing influence in the Arab world went up in the smoke of two crises: Hungary and Suez. The Soviets ruthlessly crushed Hungary's attempt to establish a government more responsive to its own needs. Washington deplored the events in Hungary but took no action.

Suez proved equally embarrassing for the United States. In Egypt a nationalist government under Gamal Abdel Nasser took over the Suez Canal. When Israel, Britain, and France invaded Egypt simultaneously, Nasser sought help from Russia. The threat of Russian intervention convinced the United States that the invaders should withdraw. Foreign troops did leave Egypt, though this humiliation of its NATO allies embarrassed the United States.

Further embarrassment came when Russia sent up the world's first space satellite in 1957. This Soviet scientific achievement shocked Americans. In response, Washington accelerated its space program and began pumping money into scientific education.

America "Moving Again" The Eisenhower foreign policy was less activist after Dulles, dying of cancer, retired in 1959. Eisenhower made

George C. Marshall

One of George C. Marshall's biographers has described him as "the least typical of generals." He notes that what is remarkable in him is a "beautifully balanced mind thinking in terms of the dignity and integrity of the country which gave him birth."

Marshall was a soldier-statesman in the tradition of George Washington and Andrew Jackson. He was a military genius who turned diplomat, Secretary of State, and Secretary of Defense after the close of his career as a professional soldier. His actions in war caused President Harry Truman to state in 1945: "In a war unparalleled in magnitude and horror, millions of American gave their country outstanding service. General of the Army George C. Marshall gave it victory." His actions in peace won him the Nobel Peace Prize in 1953. He was the first soldier ever to receive it.

Marshall was an absolute master of organization and military strategy. But he sometimes considered this talent a liability, for although his army career involved two world wars, he was never to lead troops in battle. He was considered too valuable a planner to be risked in field command.

In the 1930s Marshall had a tedious job as an instructor in the Illinois National Guard. But by 1936 his star began to rise. He was promoted to Chief of Staff of the Army on September 1, 1939, the opening day of World War II in Europe. Between that day and the end of the war Marshall built up the army and air corps from fewer than 200,000 men to over 8 million. Without his planning it has been estimated that the invasion of Europe would have come a full year later than it did in 1944.

At war's end Marshall wished to retire. But President Truman asked him to undertake a diplomatic mission to China to try to bring the warring Nationalist and communist forces together in a coalition government. The soldier hero's second career as a controversial statesman began.

After China Marshall was named Secretary of State. He found himself in a new war—the Cold War with the Soviet Union. He helped to hammer out the Truman Doctrine and, of course, the Marshall Plan. Then he tried to retire again. This time, however, Truman wanted him to become Secretary of Defense.

In 1951 Senator Joseph McCarthy, whose crusade against communism became a witch hunt, lashed out at Marshall. He published a speech attacking Marshall's wartime strategy, his mission to China, and his actions as Secretary of State. McCarthy accused this public servant of being "a man steeped in falsehood," who was guilty of "invariably serving the world policy of the Kremlin."

Marshall resigned soon after this vicious attack, because his effectiveness in office had been greatly reduced. It was a melancholy ending to a frequently brilliant and selfless career in the service of the nation. He was remembered by one of his colleagues in the State Department as "the image of the American gentleman at his best—honorable, courteous, devoid of arrogance, exacting of others but even more of himself, intolerant only of cowardice, deviousness, and cynicism."

The Khrushchev-Eisenhower meeting at Camp David, Maryland, in 1959 produced a temporary thaw in the Cold War. Khrushchev's new policy of peaceful coexistence with the West provided economic competition as an alternative to direct military confrontation in the world.

some personally satisfying overseas tours. He even hosted Russia's new dictator, Nikita Khrushchev, on an American visit. But attempts at more summit diplomacy failed miserably. A summit conference, slated for Paris in 1960, collapsed largely because an American spy plane, piloted by an agent of the Central Intelligence Agency, was shot down over Russia just before the conference.

Eisenhower was not active in the presidential campaign of 1960, even though his foreign policy came under attack. Eisenhower and Dulles, despite some reforms, had maintained the basic postwar policy of containment. But in the President's final term the United States frequently seemed not to be acting but reacting, often too late, to Soviet initiatives. Democratic candidate John F. Kennedy made shrewd use of this issue in his campaign against Republican Vice President Richard M. Nixon. During the famous Nixon-Kennedy television debates, Kennedy stated:

> I want people in Latin America and Africa and Asia to start to look to America, not [to] Khrushchev or the Chinese Communists. Can freedom be maintained under the most severe attack it has ever known? I think it can be, and I think in the final analysis it depends upon what we do here. I think it's time America started moving again.

Kennedy's promise to get the country "moving again" won him a narrow election victory. Americans looked forward to the 1960s, keenly anticipating his fulfillment of that pledge. But when the turbulent sixties had become history, many looked back with nostalgia to the eight quiet years of the Eisenhower era.

1. Why is the attack on Pearl Harbor now regarded as "a striking yet limited victory" for the Japanese?

2. What factors contributed to American disillusionment with world politics after World War I?

3. How did Congress try to avoid what it believed had been the "mistakes" of 1917? How did Roosevelt get around these laws in his cash-and-carry, destroyers-for-bases, and lend-lease programs?

4. Could the war with Japan have been avoided? Why or why not?

5. What was the significance of the Battle of Stalingrad? Of the battles of the Coral Sea and Midway?

6. What was the "high but not outlandish" price Stalin demanded for Russian participation in the war against Japan? Why was the United States willing to pay the price?

7. What was the meaning of the "containment" policy? Why was it adopted? What steps were taken in Europe to implement it?

8. Why was Russia unable to prevent the UN from acting in South Korea? Why is the Korean conflict considered both a success and a failure for the United States?

9. Was Eisenhower's foreign policy more active against communism than Truman's had been? Why or why not?

Beyond the Text

1. Roosevelt's policy of unconditional surrender, adopted at the Casablanca Conference in 1943, has been attacked by many who believe it prolonged the war. Why has this charge been made?

2. The decision to drop the atomic bomb has been much debated. What alternate strategies were proposed and rejected? Was there any possibility that the bomb need not have been dropped?

3. Debate the proposition: The United States, More Than Russia, Bears the Responsibility for Bringing on the Cold War.

Bibliography

Nonfiction

Alperovitz, Gar, *Atomic Diplomacy: Hiroshima & Potsdam.**

Barnet, Richard J., *Roots of War.**

Buchanan, A. Russell, ed., *The United States & World War Two,* 2 vols.*

Burns, James M., *Roosevelt: The Soldier of Freedom.**

Divine, Robert A., *Roosevelt & World War Two.**

Feist, Herbert, *From Trust to Terror: The Onset of the Cold War, 1945–1950.**

FitzGerald, Frances, *Fire in the Lake.**

Gaddis, John L., *The United States & the Origins of the Cold War.**

Kolko, Joyce and Gabriel, *The Limits of Power.**

LaFeber, Walter, *America, Russia and the Cold War, 1945–1971.**

Maddox, Robert J., *The New Left & the Origins of the Cold War.*

Smith, Gaddis, *American Diplomacy During the Second World War.**

Ulam, Adam B., *The Rivals: America & Russia Since World War Two.**

Walton, Richard J., *Cold War & Counterrevolution.**

Wiltz, John E., *From Isolation to War, 1931–1941.**

Fiction

Buck, Pearl S., *Command the Morning.**
Heller, Joseph, *Catch 22.**
Hersey, John, *Hiroshima.**

*a paperback book

THE ALGER HISS CASE

WHITTAKER CHAMBERS, star witness in the Hiss case, reflected on the importance of the case some years later and wrote to his children:

Beloved Children,

I am sitting in the kitchen of [our Maryland farm] writing a book. In it I am speaking to you. But I am also speaking to the world. To both I owe an accounting.

It is a terrible book—terrible in what it tells about men, more terrible in what it tells about the world in which you live. It is about what the world calls the Hiss-Chambers case, or even more simply, the Hiss case. It is about a spy case. All the props of an espionage case are there—foreign agents, household traitors, stolen documents, microfilm, furtive meetings, secret hideaways, phony names, an informer, investigations, trials, official justice.

But if the Hiss case were only this, it would not be worth my writing about or your reading about. It would not be what, at the very beginning, I was moved to call it: "a tragedy of history."

For it was more than human tragedy. Much more than Alger Hiss or Whittaker Chambers was on trial in the trials of Alger Hiss. Two faiths were on trial. Human societies, like human beings, live by faith and die when faith dies. At heart, the Great Case was this critical conflict of faiths; that is why it was a great case. On a scale personal enough to be felt by all, but big enough to be symbolic, the two irreconcilable faiths of our time—communism and freedom—came to grips in the persons of two conscious and resolute men. Both had been schooled in the same view of history (the Marxist view). Both were trained by the same party in the same selfless, semisoldierly discipline. Neither would nor could yield without betraying, not himself, but his faith [and] both knew, almost from the beginning, that the Great Case could end only in the destruction of one or both of the contending figures.

Alger Hiss and Whittaker Chambers silently confront each other before the House Un-American Activities Committee in August 1948. The hearings touched off a Red scare that was to have widespread effects in the fifties.

My children, as long as you live, the shadow of the Hiss case will brush you. In time you will ask yourselves the question: What was my father?

I will give you an answer: I was a witness. A witness, in the sense that I am using the word, is a man whose life and faith are so completely one that when the challenge comes to step out and testify for his faith, he does so, disregarding all risks, accepting all consequences.

Alger Hiss, chief among those high government officials accused of communist connections, related the circumstances surrounding his involvement in the investigation:

In August 1948 I was living in New York City. For the preceding year and a half I had been president of the Carnegie Endowment for International Peace. To accept that position I had resigned from the State Department, where I was director of the office responsible for proposing and carrying out our policies in the United Nations.

My new work was closely related to what I had been doing in Washington, for the Endowment had decided to concentrate its activities on support of the United Nations as the appropriate means of furthering Andrew Carnegie's aim "to hasten the abolition of international war, the foulest blot upon our civilization."

On Monday, August 2, 1948 a reporter reached me by telephone at my apartment. He told me that, according to information coming from the Committee on Un-American Activities of the House of Representatives, a man named Chambers was going to appear before the committee the next morning and call me a communist. The reporter asked whether I had any comment.

I did not. The untruthful charge of communism had been the lot of many who had been New Deal officials in the Washington of the 1930s and the early 1940s. I had not taken such charges seriously when made against others, and I saw no reason why I or anyone else should pay much attention to a similar fanciful charge that might now be made against me.

The next morning a witness named Whittaker Chambers appeared before the committee and said that years before he had been "attached" to "an underground organization of the United States Communist party" in Washington. He said that I had been a member of that group.

As I knew no one named Whittaker Chambers I chose to make my denials not only to the newspapers but in the same setting where the charges had been made. Therefore, I sent a telegram to the committee that same afternoon saying that I wanted to appear to deny Chambers's charges under oath.

Richard Nixon, then an obscure congressman from California, considered the case the first major crisis he would face while in public life:

My name, my reputation, and my career were ever to be linked with the decisions I made and the actions I took in that case, as a thirty-five-year-old freshman congressman in 1948. Yet, when I was telling my fifteen-year-old daughter, Tricia, one day about the [subject], she interrupted me to ask, "What was the Hiss case?"

I realized for the first time that a whole new generation of Americans was now growing up who had not even heard of the Hiss case. And now, in retrospect, I wonder how many of my own generation really knew the facts and implications of that emotional controversy that rocked the nation. I experienced [the case] not only as an acute personal crisis but as a vivid case study of the continuing crisis of our times, a crisis with which we shall be confronted as long as aggressive international communism is on the loose in the world.

The Hiss case began for me personally when David Whittaker Chambers appeared before the House Committee on Un-American Activities to testify on communist infiltration into the federal government. Never in the stormy history of the committee was a more sensational investigation started by a less impressive witness.

Chambers did not ask to come before the committee so that he could single out and attack Alger Hiss. The committee had subpoenaed him. Both in appearance and in what he had to say, he made very little impression on me or the other committee members. None of us thought his testimony was going to be especially important.

AUGUST 3, 1948. Six congressmen took their seats in a near empty House committee hearing room: Karl E. Mundt (South Dakota), John McDowell (New Jersey), John E. Rankin (Mississippi), J. Hardin Peterson (Florida), F. Edward Hebert (Lousiana), and Richard M. Nixon (California). Robert E. Stripling, chief investigator of the House Un-American Activities committee (HUAC), called the sole witness waiting to testify—David Whittaker Chambers. Chambers, not an impressive-looking witness, still had quite good credentials. He had combined two public careers over the previous twenty years as a journalist and a gifted translator. Educated at Columbia College, he was fluent in several languages and had translated into English such popular works as the children's book *Bambi*.

Chambers had been subpoenaed the previous day. In answer to Stripling's questions Chambers said that in the 1920s and 1930s he had been a Communist party member "and a paid functionary of the party." He added:

> In 1937 I repudiated Marx's doctrines and Lenin's tactics. For a number of years I had served in the underground, chiefly in Washington, D.C. The underground group [included] Alger Hiss. The purpose of this group at that time was not primarily espionage. Its original purpose was the communist infiltration of the American government. But espionage was one of its eventual objectives.

The committee members questioned Chambers at length about his charges. He pointed out that on several previous occasions in the past decade, he had given similar testimony to high State Department

On his role as star witness in the case against Alger Hiss, Chambers said, "I have testified against him with remorse and pity, but in the moment of history in which this nation now stands, so help me God, I could not do otherwise."

officials and to the FBI. No action, however, had ever been taken against any officials he had named as communists. The witness went on to suggest that he and Hiss had been particularly close:

> MR. STRIPLING: When you left the Communist party in 1937, did you approach any of these seven [alleged underground members] to break with you?
>
> MR. CHAMBERS: No. The only one of those people whom I approached was Alger Hiss. I went to the Hiss home one evening at what I considered considerable risk to myself and found Mrs. Hiss at home. Mrs. Hiss is also a member of the Communist party. Mr. Hiss came in shortly afterward, and we talked and I tried to break him away from the party. As a matter of fact, he cried when we separated; but when I left him, he absolutely refused to break. I was very fond of Mr. Hiss.

Despite repeated questions by committee members, Chambers stood by his charges and pointedly denied that the alleged communist underground group within the New Deal had ever committed espionage:

> These people were specifically not wanted to act as sources of information. These people were an elite group, which it was believed would rise to positions—as, indeed, some of them did—notably Mr. Hiss—in the government. Their position in the government would be of much more service to the Communist party.

Newsmen present promptly reported the hottest news item in the morning's testimony: a senior editor of *Time* magazine had accused the president of the Carnegie Endowment of being a secret Soviet agent!

August 5, 1948. It was now Alger Hiss' turn to appear before the committee. He offered a striking contrast to his stout and untidy accuser. His handsome face seemed cool and relaxed. His tall, lean body was fitted with elegant, carefully pressed clothes. Furthermore, he displayed none of Chambers' evident nervousness under questioning. Hiss began his testimony with a prepared statement.

> I am not and never have been a member of the Communist party. I do not and never have adhered to the tenets of the Communist party. I am not and never have been a member of any communist-front organization. I have never followed the Communist party line, directly or indirectly. To the best of my knowledge, none of my friends is a communist. To the best of my knowledge I never heard of Whittaker Chambers until 1947, when two representatives of the Federal Bureau of Investigation asked me if I knew him and various other people. I said I did not know Chambers. So far as I know, I have never laid eyes on him, and the statements made about me by Mr. Chambers are complete fabrications. I think my record in the government service speaks for itself.

Committee members questioned Hiss at length about his impressive government career. It included being secretary to the great Chief

Justice Oliver Wendell Holmes and assistant counsel to the Senate's
Nye Committee (see Chapter 36). He also served with the Solicitor
General of the United States and then held high posts in the State
Department until he left in 1947 to head the Carnegie Endowment.

Then HUAC members and Stripling questioned Hiss about
Chambers' accusations:

> MR. MUNDT: I wonder what possible motive a man who edits *Time* magazine
> would have for mentioning Alger Hiss in connection with [communist involve-
> ment].
>
> MR. HISS: So do I, Mr. Chairman. I have no possible understanding of what
> could have motivated him.

The committee members recognized by this time that, in Stripling's words, there was "very sharp contradiction" between Hiss and
Chambers. One of the two men was a monumental liar. Yet according
to Mundt, both men were "witnesses whom normally one would
assume to be perfectly reliable. They have high positions in American
business or organizational work. They both appear to be honest. They
both testify under oath [yet their] stories fail to jibe."

At this point Congressman Nixon suggested that Hiss and Chambers "be allowed to confront each other so that any possibility of a
mistake in identity may be cleared up." The other HUAC members
ignored Nixon's suggestion, and the questioning continued. After Hiss
concluded his testimony, a large crowd of spectators and reporters
rushed up to congratulate him. Nixon later expressed the feelings of
most of them—and of most members of HUAC—when he said that a
terrible mistake had been made. The committee, he thought, owed an
apology to Hiss. It should not have allowed Chambers to testify without first checking into the possibility of such a mistake.

A journalist confirmed this reaction when he asked Hiss: "How is
the committee going to dig itself out of this hole?" HUAC was already
being criticized widely for its careless handling of hearings. There was
even a strong possibility that President Truman, if he won the upcom-
ing 1948 election, would ask Congress to disband the committee. That
same morning, while Hiss was denying Chambers' charges before the
committee, Truman denounced HUAC's current spy investigation. He
called it a red herring organized by the Republican-dominated committee to distract the public from the party's failure to pass an effective
domestic economic program.

Thus, from the beginning, the Hiss-Chambers testimony was an
issue in national politics, threatening Republican chances in the fall
elections. "This case is going to kill the committee," one reporter told
Nixon after the morning session had ended, "unless you can prove

Chambers' story." The reporter did not know that this was exactly what Nixon intended to do.

Richard Milhous Nixon was then a freshman representative from Southern California. His family, like millions of others, had suffered during the depression. He had worked hard from his earliest years. After largely supporting himself through college and law school, Nixon worked briefly in Washington and then served as a naval officer during World War II. Returning to California, he ran for Congress. In his campaign he charged his Democratic opponent with being a radical and procommunist. The tactic was successful, and he won the election. During his first year and a half in Congress, he had not acquired any wide reputation beyond his home district. Soon this would change.

Nixon later wrote that when HUAC met privately after Hiss testified, "it was in a virtual state of shock." For his part Nixon argued:

> While it would be virtually impossible to prove that Hiss was or was not a communist—for that would simply be his word against Chambers'—we should be able to establish whether or not the two men knew each other. If Hiss were lying about not knowing Chambers, then he might also be lying about whether or not he was a communist.

Nixon managed to persuade the acting committee chairman, Karl Mundt, to appoint him head of a subcommittee to question Chambers again. This time the session was to be private, with no spectators or press present.

August 7, 1948. The HUAC subcommittee headed by Nixon questioned Chambers secretly in New York City. Nixon asked in what period Chambers had known Hiss as a communist. The witness answered "roughly, between the years 1935 and 1937." Chambers said Hiss knew him not by his real name but "by the party name of Carl." He also asserted that he collected Communist party membership dues from Mr. and Mrs. Hiss. According to Chambers, therefore, Hiss was a member of the communist underground infiltrating the government. Moreover, he was also a dues-paying member of the party itself. At this point Nixon plunged into a detailed, rapid-fire series of questions testing whether Hiss had known Chambers. Specifically, Nixon noted, he wanted to know "What should one man know about another if he knew him as well as Chambers claimed to know Hiss?"

Chambers apparently remembered a great deal about the Hisses, although as Nixon later admitted: "All of this information might have been obtained by studying Hiss' life without actually knowing him. But some of the answers had a personal ring of truth about them beyond

Alger and Priscilla Hiss at first denied any knowledge of Chambers, then conceded that they knew him under another name when he exposed numerous details of their personal lives to the committee.

the bare facts themselves." Chambers claimed he had seen the Hisses on numerous occasions. He had been a guest at their home several times. He also seemed to recall a great many details about the Hisses' private lives: nicknames for one another, eating and drinking habits, pets, personal mannerisms, relatives, the exteriors and furniture of their various homes.

Perhaps the most damaging details that Chambers provided about Hiss during the questioning concerned two episodes. One was the transfer of a car Hiss owned to another communist. The other impressed Nixon because it had a "personal ring of truth." It concerned a hobby the Hisses had in common. Both were amateur ornithologists, bird watchers. Chambers testified, "I recall once they saw, to their great excitement, a prothonotary warbler." At this point Congressman McDowell, also a bird lover, interrupted to ask, "A very rare specimen?" Chambers replied, "I never saw one. I am also fond of birds."

The mass of detail concerning the Hisses' lives—birds, cars, homes, nicknames, and the like—restored a faith in Chambers' honesty among committee members.

August 16, 1948. At this closed session of HUAC Hiss seemed under severe strain. The cool composure of his earlier appearance before the committee had given way to a mixture of nervousness and anger. Nixon showed Hiss two pictures of Chambers and asked again whether he knew the man "either as Whittaker Chambers or as Carl or as any other individual." Hiss began to waver admitting that "the face has a certain familiarity." Chief counsel Stripling and the committee members confronted Hiss with Chambers' detailed claims concerning their friendship. They probed for evidence confirming the *Time* editor's account.

Hiss repeatedly protested the committee's refusal to provide him with a transcript of Chambers' earlier testimony. He became increasingly hostile. He was angry that the committee found it difficult to decide whether truth was on the side of Chambers—"a confessed former communist" and "self-confessed traitor"—or himself, a highly respected man. Stripling, in turn, snapped back sharply that Chambers had "sat there and testified for hours. He said he spent a week in your house, and he just rattled off details like that. He has either made a study of your life in great detail or he knows you."

Moments after this exchange Hiss announced: "I have written a name on this pad in front of me of a person whom I knew in 1933 and 1934 who not only spent some time in my house but sublet my apartment." Hiss was not sure this person—a free-lance writer named

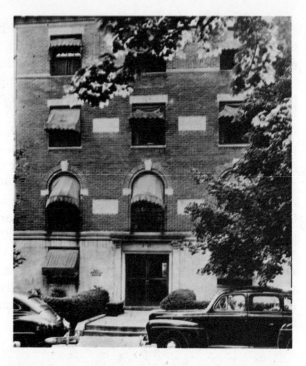

Alger Hiss lived in this apartment house in Washington, D.C., from 1934-35. He admitted that he let Chambers sublet his apartment for a time in 1935.

George Crosley—was Chambers. He insisted that he had not seen Crosley since 1934. Hiss gave a detailed account of this relationship, claiming to have met Crosley while he was legal counsel to the Nye Committee in 1933.

Crosley, he said, wished to write several magazine articles about the Nye Committee's munitions-industry investigation. Hiss added that he took a liking to the young journalist. When moving his family to a new apartment, Hiss briefly sublet his old apartment to Crosley and his family. At the same time he gave the journalist "an old Ford we had kept for sentimental reasons." Crosley never paid the rent money, according to Hiss. As for the car, "I threw it in along with the rent" because of a desire to "get rid of it." Deciding that he "had been a sucker and [Crosley] was a sort of deadbeat using me for a soft touch," Hiss said he never saw the man again after 1935. (He later changed the date to mid-1936.)

Hiss also remembered taking several drives with Crosley and giving him "loans [he] never paid back." Once Crosley gave him "a rug he said some wealthy patron gave him. I have still got the damned thing." At one point Nixon asked Hiss about his hobbies. When the witness mentioned bird watching, Congressman McDowell asked: "Did you ever see a prothonotary warbler?" "I have right here on the Potomac," Hiss replied, unaware of Chambers' earlier testimony.

Several members of HUAC remarked during Hiss' testimony that either he or Chambers was obviously committing perjury. "Whichever one of you is lying is the greatest actor that America has ever produced," exclaimed Congressman Hebert. Before adjourning the bitterly tense executive session, the committee decided to have Chambers and Hiss testify publicly, together, nine days later on August 25. Actually, the pair confronted one another the following day at a hurriedly arranged HUAC meeting in New York City.

August 17, 1948. The session was moved up, according to Nixon, to prevent Hiss from gaining "nine more days to make his story fit the facts." In fact there may have been another motive. The committee was uneasy over the death of Harry Dexter White, a former high Treasury Department official. He had died of a heart attack. White had appeared before a HUAC public hearing a few days earlier to deny charges leveled by Chambers that he had been either a party member or procommunist. He had asked for a postponement because of his bad heart but was refused. White had proved a good witness in his own defense despite the committee's attempt to browbeat him. Nixon and the other HUAC subcommittee members obviously hoped to divert public outrage over White's untimely death following this grueling interrogation. They would shift attention to the still active Hiss-Chambers investigation.

Throughout the session, Hiss was extremely irritable, angry, and defensive. He observed that Harry Dexter White's death had upset him greatly, so that testifying would be difficult. He also protested that the committee (despite promises to the contrary) had leaked portions of his previous day's testimony to the press. (Both Nixon and Stripling denied this charge.) Finally Chambers, who had been waiting in an adjoining room, was brought in.

MR. NIXON: Sit over here, Mr. Chambers. Mr. Chambers, will you please stand? And will you please stand, Mr. Hiss? Mr. Hiss, the man standing here is Mr. Whittaker Chambers. I ask you now if you have ever known that man before.
MR. HISS: May I ask him to speak? Will you ask him to say something?
MR. NIXON: Yes. Mr. Chambers, will you tell us your name and your business?
MR. CHAMBERS: My name is Whittaker Chambers. [At this point, Hiss walked toward Chambers.] I am senior editor of *Time* magazine.
MR. HISS: Are you George Crosley?
MR. CHAMBERS: Not to my knowledge. You are Alger Hiss, I believe.
MR. HISS: I certainly am.
MR. CHAMBERS: That was my recollection. [Chambers read from a magazine so that Hiss could test his voice pattern.]

Hiss then announced that Chambers was probably the man he knew as Crosley. Nixon and Stripling began a lengthy series of questions comparing Hiss' version of the relationship with Crosley—apartment rental, car transfer, gift of a rug, and other details—with the facts previously supplied by Chambers. Hiss of course denied that Crosley had been more than a casual acquaintance, saying, "He meant nothing to me." Chambers again stressed their common bond, stating, "I was a communist, and you were a communist." At last Hiss acknowledged, "I am perfectly prepared to identify this man as George Crosley." But he denied knowing whether "Crosley" had ever been a communist and pointed out that "it was a quite different atmosphere in Washington then than today." He insisted he had known Crosley only as a journalist.

August 25, 1948. The hearing room was clogged with reporters and spectators. The hearing lasted nine hours. (Hiss testified for six, Chambers for three.) Not only Hiss but all seven other alleged members of the communist cell whom Chambers had named had meanwhile testified before HUAC. Except for Hiss' brother, Donald, who joined Alger in specifically denying any communist associations, the others refused to say whether they had been communists. In their refusals all cited the Fifth Amendment, which provides protection from possible self-incrimination.

From the start Hiss, accompanied by his lawyer, treated the occasion as a kind to trial. He was convinced that HUAC believed Chambers and wished mainly to prepare evidence for a perjury charge against him. Therefore, Hiss was extremely guarded in responding. He qualified his answers with phrases such as "to the best of my recollection" more than 200 times. On several occasions he accused HUAC of believing Chambers largely for political reasons. The Republican-controlled committee, he claimed, wanted to expose a top civil servant closely identified with Democratic-sponsored programs like the New Deal, the Yalta agreements, and the United Nations.

The day went badly for Hiss. At the start both Hiss and Chambers were directed to stand. Hiss again identified the *Time* editor as Crosley. Chambers again claimed to have known Hiss in the communist underground. Some of the most damaging passages for Hiss involved the Ford car. He had previously testified turning it over to Crosley along with his apartment.

MR. NIXON: Did you give Crosley a car?

MR. HISS: I gave Crosley, according to my best recollection . . .

MR. NIXON: You certainly can testify yes or no as to whether you gave Crosley a car. How many cars have you given away in your life, Mr. Hiss?

MR. HISS: I have had only one old car of a financial value of $25 in my life. That is the car I let Crosley use.

A smiling Alger Hiss shakes hands with President Truman at a conference to establish the United Nations. Because Hiss was a New Deal liberal, his fall from grace carried the implication that the government was permeated with communists.

MR. NIXON: My point now is, is your present testimony that you did or did not give Crosley a car?

MR. HISS: Whether I transferred title to him in a legal, formal sense; whether I gave him the car outright; whether the car came back—I don't know.

Unfortunately for Hiss, a title search by HUAC agents produced evidence that Hiss had transferred the car on July 23, 1936, to William Rosen, the alleged communist about whom Chambers had testified earlier. The Hiss signature on the document had been notarized by W. Marvin Smith. He was a lawyer with the Justice Department. Smith told HUAC that he knew Hiss and that Hiss had personally signed the transfer in his presence. (Strangely, Smith fell, jumped, or was pushed to his death soon after he testified.)

Hiss now counterattacked. He denounced HUAC's investigation as a political attack on liberal Democrats. He reviewed his fifteen years of impressive public service and named as references for his achievements, personal character, and loyalty thirty-four prominent public figures. Nixon termed this an effort by Hiss to prove his "innocence by association," an ironic reference considering HUAC's past reputation for trying to show a witness' guilt by association.

During this day's testimony the two major witnesses reversed their previous roles completely. Chambers was now a cool, placid witness, calmly answering every question put to him. Hiss testified nervously and emotionally. But Hiss emphasized that a number of Chambers' most obvious statements about him were incorrect. Thus Hiss was not deaf in one ear, the Hisses were not teetotalers, their stepson was not a "puny little boy," and Hiss did attend church. Despite these and other important errors about the Hisses, Chambers still displayed remarkable familiarity with their private life.

Hiss offered some explanation for this apparent familiarity. He claimed that Chambers, with access to *Time*'s excellent research records, could have discovered most of the personal material on Hiss in such publications as *Who's Who*. Congressman Hebert retorted: "Nobody could have read in *Who's Who* that you found a rare bird [the prothonotary warbler]." Hiss responded that he had "told many, many people." But this did not persuade the committee.

For his part, Chambers denied that he harbored any secret reason for wishing to ruin Hiss, as the latter charged. He went so far as to call Alger Hiss "the closest friend I ever had in the Communist party." Fighting back tears, he said softly:

> I am [not] working out some old grudge, or motives of revenge or hatred. I do not hate Mr. Hiss. We were close friends, but we are caught in a tragedy of history. Mr. Hiss represents the concealed enemy against which we are all fighting, and I am fighting.

By the time HUAC finally adjourned its August 25th session at 8 P.M., Alger Hiss had been placed on the defensive. Three days later HUAC issued an interim report. It called Hiss' testimony "vague and evasive," Chambers' "forthright and emphatic." In the committee's opinion "the verifiable portions of Chambers' testimony have stood up strongly; the verifiable portions of Hiss' testimony have been badly shaken."

The next act in this "tragedy of history" took place on a national radio show, *Meet the Press*. There, Chambers charged that "Alger Hiss was a communist and may be now." Several weeks passed without Hiss responding. His supporters grew impatient. "Mr. Hiss has created a situation," complained the liberal Washington *Post*, "in which he is obliged to put up or shut up." Finally, on September 27, Hiss brought suit against Chambers for libel. By then the election campaign was in full swing. HUAC members (including Nixon) had returned to their various states. An exciting four-way battle for the presidency crowded "the Hiss-Chambers case" off the front pages.

Nixon himself faced no reelection problem. He had won his district's Democratic *and* Republican nominations, then possible under California's cross-filing system that allowed candidates to enter both primaries. He did campaign for other Republicans, however, regaling crowds with a dramatic account of the Hiss investigation.

In the presidential election Truman ran against Governor Thomas E. Dewey of New York, who avoided the anticommunist issue because he believed no case could be made against Truman as "soft" on communism. After a hard-fought campaign Truman won a startling reelection victory. The Democrats, moreover, regained control of Congress.

Prospects for continuing the Hiss-Chambers inquiry looked bleak, since Truman still considered it a political red herring directed against his administration. After the election many in Washington thought the President would try to abolish HUAC. The Hiss case itself dropped from public attention and went into its legal phase—a libel suit.

Deeply depressed by Truman's victory, Chambers even contemplated suicide (an action he considered at other critical points in the case). He also fretted at the possibility that a Justice Department controlled by Democrats might indict him, not Hiss, for perjury. Pressed for written proof of his charges and under severe emotional strain, Chambers (according to his own account) took a mid-November trip to Brooklyn. There he visited a nephew with whom, he claimed, he had left a package ten years earlier. The nephew drew from a disused dumbwaiter shaft the "proof" Chambers needed—a dusty envelope containing papers that (Chambers later insisted) he had forgotten about until the libel suit jogged his memory.

The papers were dated from early 1937 through April 1938. If genuine, they indicated that Hiss had lied in claiming not to have seen "Crosley" or Chambers after mid-1936. Furthermore, the papers had apparently been typed on an old Woodstock typewriter that belonged to the Hisses until 1937 or 1938. (The exact date that the Hisses got rid of the machine would later become a major point at issue.) Chambers hurried back to his farm with this evidence and hid the microfilms. On November 17, he submitted some of the material to Hiss' attorneys at a pretrial hearing—sixty-five pages of copied State Department documents, four memos in Alger Hiss' handwriting, and the envelope in which they had been hidden for a decade.

Chambers now claimed that he had tried until then to "shield" Alger and Priscilla Hiss from exposure as Soviet spies. But because of the pressures imposed by Hiss' libel suit, he had to reveal "that Alger Hiss had also committed espionage." Chambers then testified to Hiss' attorneys about a new claim. He allegedly was a courier for Hiss while the latter stole secret State Department documents. Some of these Mrs. Hiss had retyped while others Chambers had microfilmed. The *Time* editor now asserted that he had actually left the party in April 1938 rather than in 1937, since some of the stolen documents dated from the later period. Hiss vigorously denied this new charge. His lawyers grilled both Chambers and his wife sharply about the numerous contradictions between his previous and his new testimony.

The typed documents were explosive evidence. The Hiss and Chambers lawyers immediately turned them over to Alex Campbell, the head of the Justice Department's Criminal Division. Campbell warned both parties to the libel suit not to discuss the envelope's

Under pressure to provide HUAC with all the evidence against Hiss in his possession, Chambers led two HUAC investigators to the pumpkin patch on his farm (an arrow identifies the patch) and retrieved the microfilms from a hollowed-out pumpkin.

contents (neither Campbell nor Hiss then knew of the microfilms) until the material had been investigated. But then a story in the pro-Hiss Washington *Post* indicating that the Justice Department might drop its investigation of Hiss spurred Nixon into action. Before leaving for a Caribbean vacation, Nixon signed a subpoena ordering Chambers to provide HUAC with any further evidence he had relating to his charges against Hiss.

On the night of December 4 HUAC staff members served the subpoena. A few hours earlier, because of rumors that Hiss investigators were prowling around his farm, Chambers had taken the microfilms from his bedroom and hidden them in his pumpkin patch. Now he went to the hollowed-out pumpkin, removed the microfilms inside, and handed them to the HUAC representatives. "I think this is what you are looking for," he said. Within hours the press began headlining Chambers' mysterious "pumpkin papers" (actually not papers but microfilms). That same day Hiss confirmed the existence of the typed stolen documents produced on November 17.

The Justice Department finally swung into action. Both Chambers and Hiss were called several times, beginning on December 6, to testify before a New York federal grand jury. After a hurried and well-publicized return from his Caribbean vacation, Nixon led HUAC in a new series of hearings. At one of these new sessions Assistant Secretary of State John Peurifoy (in charge of security matters) testified. He declared that the Soviet Union or any other foreign country possessing these microfilmed documents would have been able to break all the secret State Department codes then in use.

Clearly, the Republican-controlled HUAC, which had no legal authority to put Hiss on trial, was competing with the Democratic-controlled Justice Department for jurisdiction in what was now a criminal case. Nixon frankly stated that his committee "did not trust the Justice Department to prosecute the case with the vigor it deserved." On December 9 Truman again labeled the case a red herring. On December 10 Chambers resigned from *Time*.

On December 13 the FBI produced for the grand jury several old letters typed by Priscilla Hiss on the same machine that had typed the State Department documents. That day, Alger Hiss left the Carnegie Endowment on a three-month paid leave of absence. He never returned. The New York grand jury indicted Hiss on two counts of perjury on December 15. The first was for claiming he had not stolen State Department records and given them to Chambers. The second was for swearing he had not seen Chambers after January 1, 1937.

Only the statute of limitations and the absence of witnesses who could back up the charge kept the grand jury from charging Hiss with espionage.

The former State Department official underwent two trials. The first ended on July 8, 1949, with a deadlocked jury that had voted 8 to 4 to convict Hiss. The prosecutor at both trials, Thomas Murphy, presented several types of evidence to prove the government's perjury charges. These included evidence that the two men knew one another more intimately (after 1936) than Hiss admitted, that Hiss had been a communist, and that Hiss had stolen the State Department documents. The weakest link in the government's case concerned Hiss' alleged communism. Only one witness, a professional ex-communist named Hede Massing, confirmed Chambers' claim that Hiss had been a party member. Her testimony was effectively challenged, however, by a reputable defense witness who swore that Mrs. Massing had told him an entirely different (and more innocent) story about Hiss.

At both trials Chambers repeated the story he first told to Hiss' attorneys in November 1948 during pretrial hearings involving the libel suit. According to this story, Hiss had been recruited for espionage by Chambers' communist superior during the fall of 1937. Chambers changed the date to January 1937 at the first trial, which made it possible for Hiss to have stolen all of the documents in question. Chambers said he served as Hiss' courier until April 1938. Then he broke from the party. (He previously testified to leaving the party months earlier.) At this point he turned the final batch of stolen documents over to his nephew in Brooklyn for safekeeping.

The microfilms and retyped State Department messages were at the heart of the case against Hiss. Prosecutor Murphy called them "immutable" witnesses, therefore presumably reliable ones. At neither trial did Hiss' attorneys challenge an FBI expert. He testified that a comparison of typing on the documents with other letters written by Mrs. Hiss on the same machine established her as the typist. Nor did they challenge the argument that the documents had been typed on a Woodstock machine belonging to Hiss. Hiss did claim he had given the machine away sometime before the material was typed. But this claim was never proved conclusively in court, one way or the other.

The jury at the second trial convicted Hiss of perjury on both counts. After that Hiss' lawyers began arguing that the typewriter itself was a false piece of evidence constructed by either Chambers or the FBI. They also argued that the typed documents had been prepared only to implicate Hiss. (This argument, of course, did not affect the microfilmed documents or the handwritten Hiss memos.) Since the defense had actually located the typewriter in question prior to the first

A withdrawn and beaten Alger Hiss sits on a New York subway trying to ignore headlines telling of his indictment the day before on perjury charges. He was eventually convicted but on highly disputed evidence.

trial, Hiss' supporters began arguing that the FBI somehow gained possession of the machine earlier, then "planted" it on the defense. This remains unproven even today, though those who argue that Alger Hiss was innocent tend to assume some degree of FBI involvement.

Another troubling point about Chambers' story concerns his claim to have broken with the Communist party as late as April 1938, in time to have received from Hiss the last of the secret documents. A mass of documentary evidence—too extensive to reprint here—indicates that Chambers actually broke with the party earlier that year, probably in February, when he began working as a free-lance translator. If this was true, or course, Chambers could not possibly have collected the last few months' worth of stolen government papers from Hiss. This would cast grave doubt on the authenticity of *all* the secret documents.

Thus two sets of "immutable witnesses" exist in this confusing case. The first involves Chambers' break with communism sometime

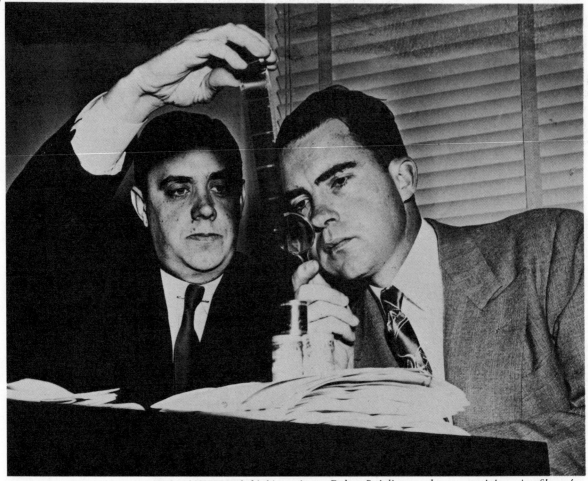

Richard Nixon and chief investigator Robert Stripling are shown examining microfilms of secret State Department documents, the most damaging evidence against Hiss, though their authenticity has been challenged.

before March 1938. The second concerns a collection of State Department documents allegedly stolen by Hiss but dating through April 1, 1938. The essential mystery of this episode centers on the difficulty in resolving these two facts.

Unfortunately for Hiss, the defense did not stress this point at either of his trials. Instead, they paraded a distinguished group of Americans before the jury to testify to Hiss' excellent career and good character. At the same time, they tried to throw doubt on Chambers' reliability. They placed a psychiatrist on the stand who labeled Chambers "a psychopathic personality" with irrational hostilities.

Prosecutor Murphy ridiculed these defense efforts at both trials. He pointed repeatedly to the evidence that Hiss' lawyers could never adequately explain—the stolen government documents. The twelve jurors at the second trial, overlooking Chambers' inconsistencies, all believed Murphy. On January 21, 1950, they found Hiss guilty. Later appeals to overturn the verdict were rejected, and Hiss served forty-four months in prison. He emerged in November 1954, still proclaiming his innocence.

Hiss, now a convicted perjurer, did not return to the Carnegie Endowment, of course. He has had a series of obscure and ill-paying business jobs. He has written his version of the episode and worked continuously to revive public interest in the case. Chambers returned to his Maryland farm, did special assignments as a journalist, and wrote his memoirs. In 1961, he died from a heart attack.

Nixon won a Senate seat in 1950, largely because of his efforts in the Hiss case. He went on to become Vice President in 1953. The House Committee on Un-American Activities temporarily regained its public prestige as a result of Hiss' conviction. Truman abandoned his effort to abolish it.

Less than three weeks after Hiss' conviction, a then obscure Wisconsin senator announced: "I have here in my hand a list of 205 known to be members of the Communist party and who, nevertheless are still working and shaping the policy of the State Department." With Joseph R. McCarthy's speech a new era of anticommunist politics in the United States acquired its leader—and its name.

38

Affluence and Anticommunism

THE DEPRESSION ENDED—with a bang, not a whimper—when Japan attacked Pearl Harbor. The war years changed the lives of the two key figures in the Hiss case very little. Alger Hiss remained a top official of the State Department, while Whittaker Chambers rose in importance on *Time* magazine. But Richard Nixon saw his life altered dramatically. Although reared as a Quaker, Nixon yearned for some role in the war effort. He first joined a new government agency, the Office of Price Administration (OPA), created to regulate wartime price levels. Then the young lawyer joined the Navy and served on various Pacific islands, handling duties as a supply officer.

Nixon returned to a restless year of private practice in California before winning his first race for Congress in 1946. The war had clearly opened up significant career possibilities for Nixon, as it did for millions of his contemporaries. A nation still climbing uncertainly out of the depression in 1941 had regained, by war's end, most of its pre-1930 affluence and self-confidence.

THE WORLD WAR II HOME FRONT

Almost 4 million Americans were still unemployed on the eve of Pearl Harbor. They were receiving relief assistance from New Deal welfare and Social Security programs. Other millions still labored at government-sponsored jobs for agencies such as the WPA. Some 40 percent of America's families lived below the $1,500 annual minimum income needed for a family of four. (This amounted to only $30 a week to cover food, housing, clothing, and everything else!) Over 7 1/2 million workers earned salaries below the legal minimum wage of 40 cents an hour.

Still, there were many signs of change in 1941. The economy, thanks largely to $8 billion spent on defense production, was now strong, almost booming. Of the country's 134 million people, 56 million held civilian jobs. A tenth of them worked on defense contracts at top wages. Farm prices reached a new high in 1940, as did average hourly wages in the two dozen major defense-oriented industries.

Moreover, on the eve of war, most Americans supported the pro-Allied policies of the Roosevelt administration. A 1941 Gallup poll revealed that 85 percent believed that the United States would eventually enter the war against Hitler. Still, Americans did not expect a war to improve their condition much. Twelve years of depression had left the country somewhat doubtful of future prospects and skeptical of idealistic visions. Another poll released the week Pearl Harbor was attacked showed that many thought they would have to "work harder after the war." Only a small number felt that the chances for success after a war would be better than before it.

Bolstering Morale The government went to great lengths to counteract pessimism and ensure the cooperative involvement of most Americans in the war effort. The Office of Civilian Defense (OCD) sponsored various programs to stimulate patriotism. These included "town meetings" throughout the country. Their basic objective was "that of awakening all the elements of the community to their responsibilities for total participation for victory." Patriotic sentiments were also aroused by stage, screen, and radio productions. They tried to bolster national morale, particularly in the first year, when news from the fronts was often grim.

Usually such entertainment aimed at stirring up hatred toward the enemy, Germans and Japanese. Seldom did it assert any positive American war goals. Movie heroes such as John Wayne and radio idols like Jack Armstrong ("the all-American boy") battled tirelessly against Japan's fanatical "yellow hordes" or Nazi saboteurs. American advertising encouraged sales of government war bonds or warned defense workers and soldiers to beware of possible spies in their midst. ("Loose lips sink ships!") Such efforts were remarkably successful in achieving greater homefront efforts.

Mobilizing the Economy Conversion to military preparedness had preceded Pearl Harbor. Total mobilization of both the American people and their economy, however, advanced swiftly after December 1941. An army of 1,600,000 existed then. By war's end the number of troops who had served or were serving in the army, navy, marines, air corps (then still part of the army) and coast guard exceeded 15 million—including 200,000 women.

The home front resembled a big factory. A few statistics tell much of the story. Many Americans felt that Roosevelt was being unrealistic when in 1942 he called for an output of 60,000 planes, 45,000 tanks, and 8 million tons of shipping. Yet in 1944 the nation's factory workers—keeping plants open 24 hours daily on continuous shifts—produced over 96,000 planes. By 1945 the country's naval yards had turned out over 55 million tons of merchant shipping and 71,000 warships. Federal purchases grew from $6 billion in 1940 to $89 billion by 1944.

Total federal spending during the three and a half years of war amounted to over $320 billion, an amount twice as large as the total of all previous spending from 1789 to 1941! The government financed this vast increase through higher taxes on both corporations and individuals. Even after taxes, though, corporate profits doubled from 1939 to 1944 (reaching $10 billion that year). Much of the government's revenues came from taxes or public borrowing through war bonds. A still higher percentage came from running huge budget deficits throughout the war. The American national debt grew to $247 billion by 1945, nearly six times that of 1941.

Meanwhile, prosperity returned to the United States, and unemployment vanished. Many women took full-time factory jobs to meet the shortage of labor created by the armed forces' need for men. Public confidence in the business community increased after the widespread hostility apparent during the depression decade.

Rationing and Inflation Full employment during the war gave millions of Americans bigger bank accounts. It put more money in their pockets, though they had less to spend it on. "Disposable income" (income after taxes) increased from $67 billion in 1939 to $140 billion by 1945. Consumer spending alone rose from $62 billion in 1939 to $106 billion by 1945. Wartime rationing and shortages of consumer goods led to an increase in prices for available products or services. Higher wages and profits led, in turn, to higher inflationary prices for most consumer goods when they were available.

When gas and tires were rationed during the war, Whittaker Chambers remembered walking long distances to catch public transportation. Most Americans used gas sparingly and only on special occasions. The great majority, despite the inevitable complaining, accepted the need for such rationing with good humor. But many less honest individuals profited from selling goods at inflated prices illegally on the "black market."

Significant numbers of women belonged to the labor force that produced the winning margin in World War II, a continuous flow of planes from American factories.

The government tried to control inflation and regulate prices—which rose an average of 2 percent monthly during the war—by establishing official wage and price levels. It set ceilings on legal prices through OPA. Richard Nixon remembered his experiences in this agency as a time when he "became more conservative [and] greatly disillusioned about bureaucracy." Yet OPA did succeed in holding down runaway inflation throughout the war years, despite an enormous increase in the disposable income of most Americans.

On the farms conditions improved at this time, too. Farm income doubled during the war because of the insatiable demand for agricultural products by the armed forces and civilians alike. Despite a decline in the number of farm laborers, increased mechanization helped double farm output from 1941 to 1945. During the war legislation by powerful farm bloc Democrats brought farmers' incomes to an all-time high.

Average weekly earnings among industrial workers also increased by 100 percent during the war years. Both the AFL and CIO made "no-strike" pledges. But the number of strikes increased as prices and profits continued rising at a level greater than wage increases. Union membership increased from 10 to 15 million. The demand for factory workers led to a reduction of total unemployment from 5.6 percent of the work force in 1941 to 1 percent by war's end. More important, the war guaranteed the future of industrial unionism, which had grown with New Deal encouragement during the depression.

The Atomic Bomb The period's single most significant scientific and military achievement, which would notably affect postwar American policy, was the development of the atomic bomb. Wartime scientific research was placed in the hands of an Office of Scientific Research and Development (OSRD), headed by Vannevar Bush and James Conant. The United States benefited greatly from the work of refugee scientists, many of them Jews who had fled Nazi Germany or fascist Italy. Albert Einstein, Leo Szilard, and Enrico Fermi led this intellectual

Because of fears for his Jewish wife, Enrico Fermi fled Fascist Italy in 1938 for the United States. He and his refugee colleagues created the weapon that could have given the Axis powers victory—the atomic bomb.

migration. It affected not only science but many other aspects of American life and culture.

At a cost of billions a massively organized project was undertaken to develop an atomic bomb before the Germans, who were working on a similar project. The secret program, known as the Manhattan Project, involved scientists, technicians, and industrial workers. It included design laboratories at Columbia University, the University of Chicago, the University of California at Berkeley, and—most important—at a central headquarters near Los Alamos, New Mexico. There, under the leadership of physicist J. Robert Oppenheimer, the first device was assembled. It was detonated on July 16, 1945, at Alamorgordo, New Mexico.

The bombs dropped subsequently at Hiroshima and Nagasaki led directly to Japan's defeat in August 1945. By then the United States had spent over $350 billion to achieve victory in World War II at a tremendous cost in American casualties.

The Relocation Policy The country paid not only a high cost in human life but also a certain

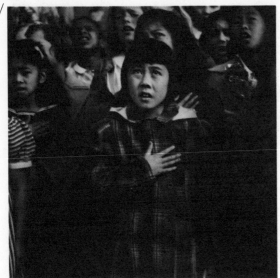

Japanese American children are shown saluting the flag in their San Francisco elementary school two days before their relocation to internment camps.

moral cost for its victory. For the Japanese attack on Pearl Harbor led to what the American Civil Liberties Union called "the worst single invasion of citizens' liberties" during the war. This was the confining in relocation centers of 112,000 Japanese Americans (more than half of them born in the United States). After Pearl Harbor white residents of west coast states feared an internal threat from the Japanese Americans. They appealed to President Roosevelt to remove the entire community from the west coast.

Actually, there was no evidence whatsoever of sabotage. But officials such as California's attorney general Earl Warren (later a great civil libertarian as the Chief Justice of the United States) urged their evacuation to protect the region's civil defense. Bowing to these pressures, President Roosevelt signed an executive order in February 1942 authorizing the relocation of Japanese Americans to nine inland centers. Driven from their homes into these American versions of concentration camps, these loyal Japanese Americans needlessly suffered loss of their freedom, homes, land, and dignity. This unfair treatment did not deter over 33,000 Japanese Americans from enlisting and fighting bravely

for the United States. Although the Supreme Court upheld the relocation policy, the government later paid compensation to the displaced for their property losses.

THE TRUMAN YEARS

Franklin D. Roosevelt, reelected for an unprecedented fourth term in 1944, died in April 1945. He left to Vice President Truman the responsibility for governing the world's most militarily powerful and economically properous nation. On learning of Roosevelt's death, Truman quite understandably felt "as though the moon and all the stars and all the planets have fallen on me." Confronted with the galaxy of postwar domestic and foreign problems that existed, Truman had excellent reasons for such feelings.

Harry Truman was an accidental President. Roosevelt had chosen him for the vice-presidential nomination in 1944 almost as an afterthought. Truman had little formal preparation for holding the office. While Vice President, for example, he was not even told about the atomic bomb. Less than four months after taking office, he had to make the fateful decision to drop it on Japan.

A Missouri farm boy who served in World War I, Truman entered politics as a member of the notorious Pendergast machine that ran Kansas City politics. Although personally honest, he served this corrupt political machine loyally. Truman rose through its ranks and was first elected to the Senate in 1934.

Several facts helped Truman secure the vice presidency in 1944. Hard-working and extremely liberal (by Missouri's border-state standards), he had fought the Ku Klux Klan in his home state, battled loyally for New Deal programs, and served with distinction as chairman of a Senate committee that investigated national defense spending. He first seemed understandably insecure as President. ("Boys, if you ever pray," he said to newsmen, "pray for me now.") But he quickly caught on.

Many of Truman's most pressing concerns

during his first months in office were vitally important decisions on war policy and postwar settlements (see Chapter 36). Of immediate concern to the new President, once Japan surrendered, was the fact that the men overseas wanted to come home quickly. ("No Boats, No Votes," was the gist of GI mail.) Congress and President Truman responded by rapidly demobilizing (releasing from duty) the great bulk of American armed forces. By mid-1946 an army and air force of over 8 million troops the previous year was reduced to less than 2 million. A navy of almost 4 million was cut back to less than 1 million. Total military strength fell to 1 1/2 million by mid-1947, and Congress had ordered even this number reduced to under 1 million by January 1948.

Postwar Economic Policy Congress allowed the 1940 draft to expire in mid-1947. Cold War military planning focused more and more on the defense shield provided by America's monopoly of nuclear weapons. Furthermore, the discharged servicemen found that Congress had provided more generously for them than for the Bonus Marchers. Under the Servicemen's Readjustment Act (which most people called the GI Bill of Rights) more than $13.5 billion was spent on veterans in the next decade. This money went not only for college educations and vocational training, but also for special unemployment insurance (for a year) to smooth the return to civilian life. Funds were spent as well on medical help at veterans' hospitals and rehabilitation programs for the wounded. Finally, low-interest loans were available to veterans to start businesses and buy or build homes. This was particularly helpful because of the dire housing shortage at war's end.

The 1944 Democratic platform also promised to guarantee full postwar employment. There was widespread fear among the public, and many economists too, that without war spending the country would suffer a major postwar recession. A Council of Economic Advisers, created by Truman's Maximum Employment Act, committed Washington for the

first time to using the nation's resources to ensure "maximum employment, production, and purchasing power." By mid-1946 Congress had also ended most wartime price and wage controls, cut taxes over $6 billion, and begun to tackle the massive problems of reconversion to a peacetime economy. These efforts were hindered by a wave of strikes and runaway inflation.

Auto workers struck for 113 days beginning in November 1945, and miners for a shorter period in mid-1946. Truman's decision to have the soft coal mines run by the government (control that continued until June 1947) lost him much support from businessmen. A railroad strike was settled the same month the mines were seized (May 1946) only when Truman threatened to take over the railroads, too. More strikes occurred in 1946 than in any other single year in American history. Over 4,750,000 workers were involved.

Truman also faced a hostile congressional coalition of Republicans and antiadministration Southern Democrats in every area of his domestic program. This coalition responded to the strikes and general unrest among American unions with a tough law (passed over Truman's veto) regulating the labor movement. The Taft-Hartley Act of 1947 limited the President to seeking an eighty-day injunction to stop any strike that endangered "national health or safety" (rather than taking an extreme step like running an industry under government supervision). The new law also (1) required unions to accept a sixty-day "cooling-off" period before striking, (2) outlawed the closed shop, (3) restricted union involvement in political campaigns, and (4) required that union officials (but not company officers) take an oath that they were not communists.

The Taft-Hartley Act did not succeed in limiting the gains of already existing unions. However, it did impede union activity in industries, such as Southern textiles, that were not yet fully organized. Congress also passed the Twenty-second Amendment to the Constitution limiting future Presidents (although not Truman) to two full terms. This was a direct slap at FDR's four-term success. In various ways the Eightieth Congress prevented Truman from getting his own legislative program.

The Fair Deal The President called his program the Fair Deal. He viewed it essentially as an effort to continue the social welfare policies of Roosevelt's New Deal. Thus, soon after he took office, Truman had proposed to Congress legislation that would guarantee full employment, vastly expanded public housing, and raise farm price supports. Other proposals were to continue a permanent Fair Employment Practices Committee to block discrimination against blacks and other minorities, nationalize atomic energy, and increase the minimum wage. A few parts of the program passed quickly. Congress approved a civilian Atomic Energy Commission in mid-1946 that took control of peaceful uses of atomic energy. Most of the program, however, was blocked by the same Republican–Southern Democratic coalition that opposed Truman on so many issues.

Truman went on the offensive in 1948. He proposed not only the enactment of his entire Fair Deal program but also a set of civil rights proposals to guarantee first-class citizenship for black Americans. These proposals included a permanent FEPC, measures against lynching and the poll tax, plus other laws that would ensure blacks full federal protection of their civil and political rights. After his renomination by a divided Democratic convention in 1948, Truman called Congress into special session to dramatize its opposition to his programs. He requested repeal of the Taft-Hartley Act and passage of civil rights, housing, health, and Social Security programs. Congress rejected it all.

This rejection allowed Truman to conduct his successful "whistle-stop" campaign (see Chapter 37) against what he called the "do-nothing Eightieth Congress." The public liked Truman's new stance as an aggressive, "give-em-hell" fighter. The Man from Independence scored the most smashing upset in American presidential history. The Democrats also recaptured both houses of Congress.

Still dominated in large measure by the

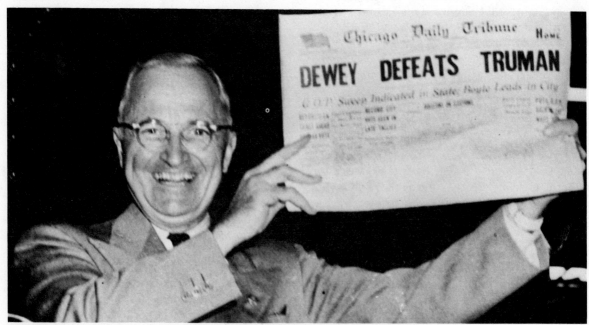

The culmination of Harry Truman's 1948 whistle-stop campaign was this triumphant pose before a crowd at St. Louis' Union Station. He called the headline "one for the books."

Republican–Southern Democratic coalition, the new Eighty-first Congress blocked Truman's farm program and his request for a permanent FEPC. But it did pass a major low-income housing and urban-renewal program, raised the minimum wage, abolished segregation in the armed forces, and enlarged existing conservation programs. All in all, it enacted more liberal legislation than any Congress since that of 1937–38.

The onset of the Korean War in June 1950, however, diverted the primary attention of Congress and the Administration from home-front reforms to foreign policy. Little important domestic legislation passed in Truman's final two years in office. His energy between 1950 and 1952 was spent primarily fighting the Korean War and improving American security against communism abroad. Ironically, he also had to defend his administration against its alleged "softness" towards communism at home.

McCARTHYISM: "THE SECOND RED SCARE"

Truman reacted angrily whenever Republicans charged that his and Roosevelt's administration had "sold out" Eastern Europe and China to communist control. To Republican cries of "Twenty Years of Treason," Truman replied that he had welded the free nations of Western Europe into military and political alliances against the Soviet Union's expansionism. The Truman Doctrine, the Marshall Plan, and NATO had largely restored European stability. China had been lost—not for lack of American help—but through Chiang Kai-shek's political and military weakness.

Elsewhere, American troops (along with UN forces) defended South Korea against communist attack. Further, the Seventh Fleet prevented communist invasion of the Chinese Nationalists' last stronghold, the island of Taiwan. To achieve this global strategy of containment, the Truman administration had increased defense expenditures from $13 billion in 1949 to $22.5 billion the next year and $44 billion by

1951. Military expenses absorbed two-thirds of the federal budget in 1952, up from only one-third in 1950. In the process of increasing defense spending so swiftly and enormously, the country's gross national product rose from $264 billion in 1950 to $339 billion by 1952. A continued high level of economic prosperity was almost assured.

None of these facts, however, silenced Republican critics. They continued to attack Truman and Secretary of State Dean Acheson. Nor were Republican anticommunist investigators like those on HUAC happy with Truman's efforts to rid the federal government of suspected subversives. The President, despite assurances from the FBI that the problem was under adequate control, had issued an executive order in May 1947, setting up a Loyalty Review Board. Its purpose was to check every federal employee and dismiss any found questionable "on reasonable grounds for belief in disloyalty." Over the next five years, such loyalty boards checked out over 6 1/2 million government employees and their families. Of this number only 490 were dismissed on loyalty grounds. The boards uncovered no cases of espionage, but the investigations wrecked the careers of many loyal government officials accused without proof.

Prosecution of Leading Communists Under mounting pressure from Congress after Alger Hiss' indictment, Truman prosecuted the eleven leaders of the American Communist party under the 1940 Smith Act. They were prosecuted for organizing a group advocating the overthrow of the American government by force. The Communist party leaders were convicted in 1949, and other prosecutions of communists began. The Supreme Court upheld the convictions in 1951. Through such actions Truman contributed to a growing climate of American fear over communism.

No single episode did more to spread this Red scare than the indictment and eventual conviction of Alger Hiss. The fact that Dean Acheson and other high administration officials testified on behalf of Hiss lent a touch of credibility to charges that the Democrats, under Roosevelt and Truman, were soft on left-wingers.

At this point Senator Joseph McCarthy began a series of speeches. It mattered little that McCarthy's figures for "known communists" in the State Department varied from speech to speech. Britain had just arrested communist Klaus Fuchs for atomic espionage; the new communist government had full control of the Chinese mainland; and Americans were jittery over possible new Russian moves against Berlin. Accordingly, many people were prepared to believe that something dire was about to befall the United States.

McCarthy's charges offended several Republicans in Congress, including Senators Margaret Chase Smith of Maine and Ralph Flanders of Vermont, who both denounced him publicly. Yet he was extremely useful to his party, despite his wild charges of disloyalty and communist activity in government. A significant number of Americans approved of McCarthy's relentless attacks. McCarthy's method, like that of most successful demagogues, was simple. He used "the multiple untruth," a statement so complex and many-sided that it was extremely difficult to deny intelligently.

A Flow of Political Melodrama Among those McCarthy tried to smear were George Marshall (author of the Marshall Plan), Philip Jessup (later chief UN delegate under President Nixon), Secretary of State Dean Acheson, and even President Truman himself. Truman had helped establish the credibility of politicians like McCarthy with his loyalty program. Other Truman administration activities did lend some support to the widespread popular belief that (in the words of Truman's own Attorney General) "many communists in America [were] everywhere—in factories, offices, butcher stores, on street corners." McCarthy turned this tactic of "Red-baiting" against the Democrats themselves. For a time, he had remarkable success. Little about his methods was new. He used the tactics of HUAC and even borrowed Nixon's files on the subject. From these he wrung a con-

stant flow of political melodrama out of the noisy pursuit of "secret conspirators" and (occasionally) admitted communists. There were, after all, some American communists, even a few who had reached middle-level posts in the Roosevelt years.

The onset of the Korean War in June 1950 gave McCarthy and other Republican opponents of Truman additional ammunition. If communists were killing our soldiers in Korea, many Americans reasoned, why give possible Reds the benefit of any doubt in this country? Loyalty oaths and security investigations soon involved millions of people in industries and labor unions, public schools and universities, as well as in government jobs at every level.

There is much irony in the fact that Truman spent his last two years in office using American and UN forces against communist aggression in Korea while trying to prove that he was not a dupe or agent of communism at home. Truman's attorney general carried on a vigorous prosecution of alleged communist agents. In April 1951 Julius and Ethel Rosenberg were convicted of having directed a spy ring that transmitted to the Russians diagrams and other data on the firing mechanism and internal structure of the atomic bomb. According to the Rosenbergs' accusers, this information speeded up by years completion of the Soviet atomic bomb, first exploded in 1949. The Rosenbergs received the death sentence, while their accomplices were sentenced to long prison terms.

Such episodes persuaded Congress that tighter laws were needed to protect the country against domestic communists. So it passed the McCarran Internal Security Act in 1950. This law established a Subversive Activities Control Board to keep track of communist activities in America. The act made membership in the Communist party illegal and also ordered communist organizations to register with the Attorney General. Other provisions barred former members of totalitarian groups from the United States and forbade communists to hold federal office or receive passports. Many of these provisions have since been declared unconstitu-

To Senator Joseph McCarthy communism was a nationwide threat. He accused the Democrats of communist sympathies and also charged that the Protestant clergy had been infiltrated.

tional by the Supreme Court. But the act passed by a two-thirds majority over Truman's veto, which showed how politically potent the anticommunist issue had become.

"Korea, Communism, and Corruption" The Democratic administration was very unpopular by 1952. Many voters accepted McCarthy's reckless charges against Truman and his associates, despite the Democrats' strong commitment to Cold War foreign policies. Truman's decision to seize the steel industry to prevent a nationwide strike in April 1952 (declared unconstitutional by the courts two months later) reminded Americans of his earlier troubles with labor and management. Several scandals involving big businessmen and Truman's associates had also come to light. So Republicans raised the issue of widespread government corruption. The Korean War dragged on, with American casualties mounting in the most unpopular war fought by the nation until the Vietnamese conflict.

The issues of "Korea, communism, and corruption" that Republicans stressed in 1952 would probably have brought about the election of any candidate after twenty years of Democratic rule. Still, the out-of-power party took no chances. At their 1952 convention the Republicans rejected the candidacy of the able conservative Senator Robert A. Taft of Ohio because they were not sure he could win. They nominated General Dwight David Eisenhower—World War II hero, university president, commander of American NATO forces, and easily the most popular public figure in the country. The party then reaffirmed its concern for the anticommunist issue by nominating Richard Nixon as Vice President.

The Democrats drafted Governor Adlai Stevenson of Illinois, a man who, though able, was assailed by Republicans as an "egghead" because of the intellectual quality of his campaigning. Stevenson's efforts to defend Democratic achievements and promise a continuation of Fair Deal reform fell flat. Many voters were tired after two decades of depression, reform, world war, and Cold War. The public voted to make its grandfatherly first citizen, Dwight Eisenhower, President by an overwhelming 33 to 27 million popular margin and a 442 to 89 electoral majority. After two decades in the political wilderness the Republican party returned to full national power, winning not only the White House but also Congress.

THE EISENHOWER YEARS

With Eisenhower's inauguration in 1953, control of the federal government returned essentially—for the first time since Herbert Hoover—to businessmen. The new President's Cabinet officers were either corporation executives or closely allied to the business community. Eisenhower was determined to run a less activist presidency than either Truman or Roosevelt and was suspicious of the federal bureaucracy and New Deal–Fair Deal social welfare programs. He set himself the task of keeping the nation calm. Wall Street lawyers such as Herbert Brownell (Attorney General) and John Foster Dulles (Secretary of State), corporation presidents George M. Humphrey (Secretary of the Treasury) and Charles E. Wilson (Secretary of Defense) typified Eisenhower's advisers.

Eisenhower interfered less often than Roosevelt or Truman with his various department heads. Instead, he allowed each to make his own decisions with minimal overall supervision. Frequently, for example, Dulles and not Eisenhower made essential foreign policy decisions. Similarly George Humphrey slashed departmental budgets throughout the government—except for the military. Here the Joint Chiefs of Staff generally got programs they wanted. The chain of command under Eisenhower thus resembled that of a loosely organized corporation. Each department head exercised considerable independence under a President who acted like a genial chairman of the board.

The Republican party's right-wingers became a real problem for Eisenhower. McCarthy, by his actions as head of the Senate's Government Operations Committee, posed a serious threat to Eisenhower's ability to rule. He publicly led the successful opposition to Eisenhower's nomination of career diplomat Charles E. Bohlen as ambassador to Russia because Bohlen had been Roosevelt's interpreter at Yalta! McCarthy also sent his committee's chief counsel, Roy M. Cohn, to tour Europe. Cohn proceeded to berate American diplomats for being "soft" on communism and to demand that allegedly "radical" books, including those of Mark Twain, be taken from the shelves of United States Information Agency libraries.

McCarthy's Fall Until 1954 the administration had tried to compromise with the senator. In that year, however, McCarthy opened an investigation of subversion in an army base at Fort Monmouth, New Jersey. This attack on the military and Eisenhower's army secretary, Robert Stevens, for "coddling" communists proved to be the last straw. It forced a reluctant Eisenhower to take a public stand against McCarthy and his tactics.

Senate hearings considered McCarthy's charges against the army. They reviewed the army's countercharges that the senator had sought special favors for an aide, David Schine, drafted into the service. The hearings were watched on television by over 20 million Americans. McCarthy proved an adept television performer. But even more adept was the army counsel, Joseph N. Welch. He baited McCarthy into losing his temper, thus widely exposing the browbeating tactics that McCarthy had used so effectively against unfriendly witnesses before his committee in the past. McCarthy's influence began to decline.

In December 1954 the Senate (supported by the Eisenhower administration) "condemned" Senator McCarthy for "conduct unbecoming a member." After this censure he lost his remaining political influence. He died in May 1957. But "McCarthyism" lingered on.

The reckless hunt for possible communist

Polio is a disease of civilization that strikes hardest where sanitation is highest. It is also a disease that most frequently strikes children. It can keep a victim bedridden for weeks, but much worse it can cause severe paralysis or even death. Since 1894 when the first cases of polio appeared in the Green Mountains of Vermont, epidemics of the disease had been a common and dreaded occurrence. And nothing could be done to prevent them until in 1953 a young researcher, Dr. Jonas Salk, announced the development of a polio vaccine.

Jonas Salk's discovery was not one of medicine's happy accidents but rather the result of years of intensive research. Salk himself is said to have worked sixteen hours a day, six days a week over a long period of time before succeeding. His background had prepared him for such a test of endurance. The son of an immigrant garment worker, he largely put himself through school by part-time jobs and scholarships. The promise he had shown while earning his medical degree led to the offer of a research post that would start him on his career in immunology.

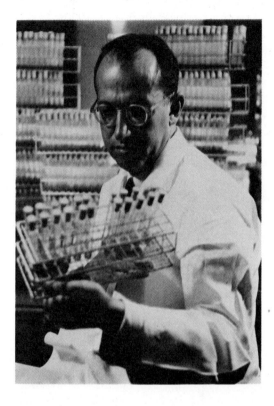

The polio vaccine that Salk finally developed was made by growing a representative strain of each of three types of polio virus in a broth made with monkey kidney. The viruses were then killed with formaldehyde, which rendered them incapable of causing the disease. However, they did not lose the power to stimulate the human body to produce antibodies. These antibodies would give a person at least limited immunity to polio.

Salk, his wife, and their three sons were among the first to receive his vaccine. Then in the Fall of 1954 a massive twelve-state test, sponsored by the National Foundation for Infantile Paralysis, was held. Almost 2 million schoolchildren in the primary grades participated. Half the children received the vaccine; the other half did not. The results were conclusive: in April 1955 the vaccine was pronounced safe and effective in preventing polio.

Salk's discovery catapulted him to instant, and largely unwanted, fame. He became a public figure deluged with offers to lecture and even to make his life into a movie. Finally, in 1955 he was awarded a congressional gold medal for ''great achievement in the field of medicine.'' Salk, however, was more concerned with the common good and science than with public praise. He refused to accept any cash awards and eagerly returned to his laboratory at the University of Pittsburgh to continue his research.

Thanks to the dedication and perseverance of Dr. Salk, the scourge of polio is today largely a thing of the past. In 1952, before the vaccine was available, nearly 58,000 cases of polio were reported in the United States. By 1960, after the vaccine was used, that number was reduced to 3,000.

subversives in American society, without proof of guilt or adequate safeguards for defense, continued to be a problem during the 1950s. Many thousands of Americans lost their jobs, suffered ruined careers because of blacklisting in their professions, and went to jail or even into exile because of it. The list of victims is long. It includes industrial workers, labor union officials, as well as prominent editors, broadcasters, and others in the arts. Screenwriter Dalton Trumbo went to jail for refusing to admit having once been a communist. He said of the era in 1970:

> It will do no good to search for villains or heroes or saints or devils because there were none; there were only victims. In the final tally, we were *all* victims because almost without exception each of us felt compelled to say things he did not want to say, to do things he did not want to do, to deliver and receive wounds he truly did not want to exchange. That is why none of us— right, left, or center—emerged from that long nightmare without sin.

"Peace, Progress, and Prosperity" The Eisenhower years signified far more than simply the tail end of McCarthyism. Eisenhower avoided tampering with New Deal–Fair Deal programs, even presiding over some extensions for them. He created the Department of Health, Education, and Welfare, approved a measure that added 7 million people to the Social Security rolls, signed another that raised the minimum wage, and supported a housing act that greatly increased urban-renewal projects. The country prospered. Few Americans worried much until the 1960s about the decline of public facilities such as schools, hospitals, and public transport systems. These received little federal attention in the 1950s.

Furthermore, Eisenhower avoided the type of scandal that had rocked Truman's second administration. His relations with the Democratic leaders who ran Congress were generally amicable, unlike Truman's with congressional Republicans. Eisenhower regularly consulted House Majority Leader Sam Rayburn and Senate Majority Leader Lyndon Johnson, the two Texans who dominated Congress during the 1950s.

When the President decided to run for reelection in 1956, despite a serious heart attack in 1955, there were no issues that the Democrats could exploit. Eisenhower had negotiated peace in Korea, run a basically budget-conscious and honest administration, and toned down McCarthyism. Also, he had flown to Geneva in 1955 for a summit meeting on peaceful coexistence with Russia's post-Stalin leaders (the first such meeting since Potsdam). He kept the country out of major foreign involvements in the Indochina crisis of 1953 and the Hungarian and Suez crises of 1956. Not surprisingly, Eisenhower again whipped Adlai E. Stevenson, winning a landslide 58 percent of the popular vote.

There seemed little public interest during the 1950s in rocking a very prosperous national boat. Eisenhower provided an image of safe, solid leadership that appealed even to many Democrats. Some American's, though—particularly writers and intellectuals—worried out loud about the cheapening of America. They saw supermarkets, suburbs, and superhighways as the products of a spiritually bankrupt society. They feared that their countrymen had betrayed American ideals in the name of material prosperity. For most Americans, however, the facts spoke in more positive and glowing terms.

Farm income had almost doubled by 1960, netting more for farmers than even the thriving war years. Moreover, the much larger pie had to be divided among a smaller farm population. Median family income rose from $4,293 in 1950 to $5,904 in 1960. By 1956 white-collar workers outnumbered those in blue-collar jobs. Even for those in the latter group (particularly those unionized) real spendable income increased by 60 percent between 1940 and 1960. Much of this prosperity came in new industries—dealing with military weapons systems and space technology. These greatly expanded after the Russians sent the world's first missile, Sputnik I, into space in 1957. Suddenly, Americans found they had a lot of catching up to do if they were to equal the Russians in scientific pursuits. Many people re-

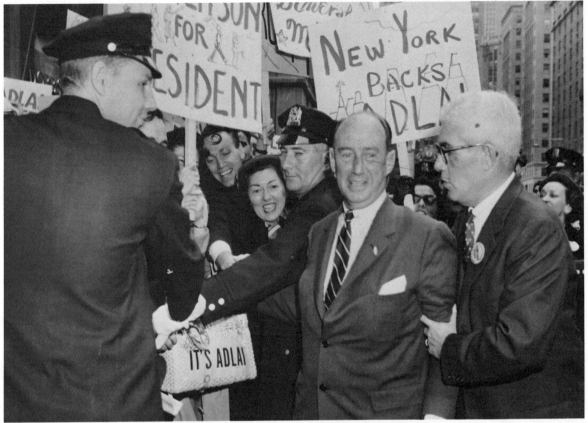

Adlai Stevenson, twice the Democratic nominee for President, was an eloquent and witty campaigner. But Eisenhower's image as a war hero and elder statesman proved unbeatable.

alized that education had been lacking and government funds were quickly demanded to inject the schools and universities with new monies for expansion and updating of their facilities.

UNSETTLED PROBLEMS

Yet various social and economic problems of enormous scope remained during the Eisenhower era. These would haunt Americans in the 1960s. For one thing, the affluent society remained a myth in 1960 for the 42 million people (almost a third of America's families) with annual family income levels of less than $4,000. The "invisible poor," as Michael Harrington described them, were not "invisible" by their own choice. They were not so much unseen as

ignored by those who had made dramatic economic gains.

"Making it" often involved drawing firm barriers between oneself and those left behind. Groups heavily represented among the poor were the elderly, unskilled or nonunion workers, migrant farm laborers, blacks and Spanish Americans. The average black family income in 1960, for example, was $3,838 compared with $6,508 for white families.

The wartime FEPC had opened thousands of jobs in Northern industries to blacks. President Truman's 1950 executive order desegregated the armed forces and barred discrimination in federal employment. The next great civil rights advance for blacks came in 1954. The Supreme Court, in the famous case of *Brown v. Board of Education of Topeka, Kansas,*

Brown v. Board of Education of Topeka

Linda Brown held her father's hand tightly as they walked along one spring morning in Topeka, Kansas. He was taking her to school. But she was not going where she usually went, to Monroe Elementary, twenty blocks from her home. Instead she was going to enroll at Sumner Elementary, four blocks away. Nine-year-old Linda was mystified by the change in routine.

Reverend Oliver Brown was not mystified. He knew exactly what he was doing. He wanted to enroll his daughter in the elementary school nearest their home. His request for a transfer had been denied. Sumner was a school for white children, he was told, and Linda was black.

The school officials were well within the law in denying Linda entrance. It was 1951. If a community chose, it could segregate the races in any public facilities—schools, buses, restrooms, and so on. These segregation policies had been judged constitutional by the Supreme Court in the *Plessy v. Ferguson* decision in 1896. At that time the Court found that separate facilities did not deny anyone "the equal protection of the laws" promised by the Fourteenth Amendment, as long as these facilities were "equal."

But Reverend Brown did not believe that his daughter was receiving equal school facilities. So he brought suit against the Topeka Board of Education. The three-man federal court that heard the case found Topeka's schools to be equal and so decided against him. He then appealed. The Supreme Court agreed to hear his case, along with several others also based on school segregation and the Fourteenth Amendment.

The case came before the Court on December 9, 1953. It continued for over a year. The decision the Court handed down on May 17, 1954, presents the question the justices faced: "Does segregation of children in public schools solely on the basis of race, even though the physical facilities and other 'tangible' factors may be equal, deprive children of the minority group of equal educational opportunities?"

They answered this question with a firm, "We believe that it does." Among the reasons they gave was the effect of such segregation on black students: "To separate them from others of similar age and qualifications solely because of race generates a feeling of inferiority as to their status in the community that may affect their hearts and minds in a way unlikely ever to be undone."

Then they stated their final decision: "We conclude that in the field of public education the doctrine of 'separate but equal' has no place. Separate educational facilities are inherently unequal." These words, in effect, gave legal backing to Oliver Brown's belief. His daughter, and millions of blacks like her, had been deprived of their Fourteenth Amendment right to equal protection under the law.

Later, the Supreme Court instructed schools to move "with all deliberate speed" to desegregate their facilities. In the years since the decision segregated schools have not disappeared from the American scene. But the decision signified that segregation can no longer be considered the law of the land.

ruled unanimously that segregation in public-school education was illegal.

Although 792 of 2,985 biracial school districts had been integrated by 1959, none were in the Deep South or Virginia. There massive resistance from leading politicians and local White Citizens Councils raised the level of racial tension to dangerous heights. In 1956 a hundred Southern congressmen promised to overturn the *Brown* decisions by "all lawful means." Then in 1957 at Little Rock, Arkansas—with white parents threatening violence against court-ordered desegregation—Governor Orval Faubus called out the National Guard to bar nine black students from a high school. After a court order removed the guard, a riot broke out. Eisenhower, himself a moderate on the segregation issue, sent federal paratroopers to help escort the nine children into the school.

Elsewhere, one Virginia county even closed its public schools to avoid integration. The University of Alabama, after a riot on the campus, expelled a black student admitted under Supreme Court order. Meanwhile, blacks in Montgomery, Alabama, led by an eloquent young minister, the Reverend Martin Luther King, Jr., organized a boycott against segregation on local buses in December 1956. Segregation on interstate buses had been banned the previous month. King's "direct action" tactics spread to other Southern cities. Soon he and other Southern black ministers formed the Southern Christian Leadership Conference (SCLC) to fight discrimination and all forms of bigotry.

In February 1960 a student wing of the SCLC held the first sit-in at a Greensboro, North Carolina, lunch counter to protest segregation in public eating places. Two mild civil rights acts in 1957 and 1960 somewhat strengthened federal authority against efforts to keep blacks from voting or exercising other rights. But as the sixties began, Americans knew the major battles to secure full equality for blacks were still ahead.

Other critical problems faced the nation as Eisenhower's second term ended. He himself

emphasized a major one in a January 17, 1961, farewell speech.

> The conjunction of an immense military establishment and a permanent armaments industry of vast proportions is new in the American experience. The total influence—economic, political, even spiritual—is felt in every city, every state house, every office of the federal government. We must guard against the acquisition of unwarranted influence, whether sought or unsought, by the military-industrial complex. We must never let the weight of this combination endanger our liberties or democratic processes.

A fair warning, but Eisenhower himself had speeded the growth of the "military-industrial complex." Militarists and industrialists became more powerful during the ten years following. Still, the checks of the American system have kept them from getting complete control of the nation's political or economic structure.

Return of the Democrats America faced still other unsolved problems, but it entered the 1960s in a confident mood, sure of its purposes and powers. This confidence would not long remain. Still both 1960 presidential candidates reflected this basic assurance about the American future.

Richard Nixon, while defending the Eisenhower record, promised progressive and dynamic new policies. John Kennedy urged Democrats to rally behind him for similarly vigorous leadership. Little separated the two candidates in terms of issues, domestic or foreign. Kennedy did attack a presumed decline of American prestige abroad under Eisenhower and an alleged missile gap that threatened to make the Soviet Union dominant.

Kennedy benefited from a united party. His Texas Protestant running mate, Lyndon Johnson, helped keep much of the South Democratic for the Catholic Kennedy. He also profited from television debates with Nixon, which helped undercut the Republican charge of inexperience and youth. (Kennedy was forty-three, the youngest man ever elected President.) Most of

In his inaugural address John Kennedy challenged a complacent citizenry with the words:
"Ask not what your country can do for you; ask what you can do for your country."

all, his election resulted from the strong support he received among Catholics and blacks—over 70 percent. Nixon received only mild backing from Eisenhower. Nixon's earlier career as a "Red hunter" haunted him and hurt him severely among Democratic and independent voters in 1960. Still Kennedy won by a tiny popular margin of only 113,000 votes out of 68,800,000 cast.

In his inaugural address Kennedy promised to lead the United States toward a New Frontier headed by young people: "The torch has been passed to a new generation of Americans, born in this century, tempered by war, [and] disciplined by a hard and bitter peace." The sense of promise and hope was strong among Americans that day, as the youthful new chief executive issued "a call to bear the burden of a long twilight struggle, year in and year out against the common enemies of man: tyranny, poverty, disease, and war itself." Few Americans doubted in 1961 that the country felt itself adequate to these great tasks.

1. In what way did the Hiss case help Nixon become President?
2. How did the war in Europe help bring the United States out of the depression? Why did higher wages and profits lead to inflationary prices? How was the government able to keep this inflation under control?
3. Which character traits did Truman bring to the Presidency that would make his terms of office successful? Which hindered him?
4. In what ways was the Fair Deal a continuation of the New Deal? Why was labor unhappy with the Taft-Hartley Act?
5. Why was Truman himself in part responsible for McCarthy's credibility?
6. In what ways did the Eisenhower administration extend some New Deal–Fair Deal legislation?
7. Why did many artists and writers believe that America in the 1950s had become spiritually bankrupt? Do you agree with them?
8. What is the significance of the *Brown* decision? To what does the phrase "massive resistance" refer? How did blacks like Martin Luther King deal with this resistance.

Beyond the Text

1. Discuss the reasons for the decision to evacuate the Japanese Americans from the West Coast of the United States. Consider in your discussion the following questions: How did the government justify the move? Why was similar action not taken against the Japanese in Hawaii or against the German Americans and Italian Americans? On what grounds did the Supreme Court uphold the action? Do you consider the relocation justified?
2. Truman's election victory confounded the experts. Why were all the pollsters wrong? Why did a three-way split in the Democratic party aid rather than jeopardize his victory?
3. Using Michael Harrington's *The Other America,* investigate and then hold a panel discussion on poverty in America in the 1950s and beyond. Consider such questions as why it was (or is) so widespread, why most Americans in the 1950s were not aware of its extent, and what approaches might be considered in the elimination of poverty.

Bibliography

Nonfiction

Brooks, John, *The Great Leap: The Past Twenty-Five Years in America.**
Commoner, Barry, *The Closing Circle.**
Galbraith, John K., *The Affluent Society.**
———, *The New Industrial State.**
Goldman, Eric F., *The Crucial Decade & After: America, 1945–1960.**
Latham, Earl, *The Communist Controversy in Washington: From the New Deal to McCarthy.**
Lubell, Samuel, *The Hidden Crisis in American Politics.**
Murphy, Paul L., *The Constitution in Crisis Times, 1918–1969.**
Parnet, Herbert S., *Eisenhower & the American Crusades.*
Polenberg, Richard, *War & Society: The United States, 1941–1945.**
Revel, Jean Francois, *Without Marx or Jesus.**
Silberman, Charles E., *Crisis in Black & White.**
White, Theodore H., *The Making of the President, 1960.**
Yarmolinsky, Adam, *The Military Establishment.**

Fiction

Frankel, Ernest, *Tongue of Fire.**
Graham, Lorenz B., *North Town.*
King, Larry L., *The One-Eyed Man.*

*a paperback book

EPILOGUE

Recent American History

The Cuban Missile Crisis

When the Soviet Union began supplying Cuba with missiles, the Cold War reached crisis proportions. As the nation watched, President Kennedy announced a counteraction that brought the world perilously close to nuclear confrontation.

ON OCTOBER 22, 1962, President John F. Kennedy appeared on television to deliver a speech his press secretary had described earlier as one of extreme urgency. The President was grave. His voice was tense, his face drawn. The Soviet Union, he announced, was placing offensive nuclear missiles on the island of Cuba. The United States would not tolerate this threat to its security. Therefore, he said, he had ordered a "difficult and dangerous effort." Beginning the next morning, the United States would place a "quarantine" on all offensive weapons being shipped to Cuba. (The President called it a quarantine instead of a blockade because a blockade would be an act of war.)

Kennedy also announced that other steps would be taken. But the quarantine was the most important and dangerous. Intelligence reports indicated that about twenty Russian ships were in the Atlantic, headed for Cuba. A dozen of them probably contained missiles or missile components. Thus what Kennedy had announced was a very dangerous confrontation between the two great nuclear powers. It was one

that he and some of his advisers believed might lead to the terrible war that had been a nightmare for the world since 1945.

The President's speech was part of a crisis that had long been building. In 1958 a Cuban revolutionary, Fidel Castro, had overthrown the dictator Fulgencio Batista. Castro then began to take over American property in Cuba, establish a communist government, and build close diplomatic and military connections with the Soviet Union.

In response the Eisenhower administration attempted to isolate Cuba economically and diplomatically. But, very early in his presidency, Kennedy approved a more direct and, as it turned out, much less sensible tactic. He financed and supported an attempted invasion of Cuba at the Bay of Pigs. The invasion, mounted in 1961 by 1,200 anti-Castro Cuban exiles, was based on completely false intelligence reports that the Cuban people would rise up to welcome their "liberators" once a foothold on Cuba was established. There was no uprising. The invaders were beaten quickly and with almost ridiculous ease by the Cuban defenders, the second largest armed force in the hemisphere.

Then, the next year brought the Soviet military build-up. At first it seemed to involve only antiaircraft missiles and bombers, with Russian crews and advisers. But by September, the Soviet Union began to send offensive missiles as well. American planes with sophisticated photographic equipment kept surveying Cuba. On October 15 one plane brought home the first photographs of missile bases being constructed just ninety miles from Florida.

For the next three days Kennedy presided over long, tense meetings with advisers. Some, mostly military people, urged an immediate air attack on the missile bases and other targets. Perhaps, they argued, this might even result in the overthrow of Castro's government. Others

An American reconnaissance plane photographed Soviet freighters, loaded with intermediate-range ballistic missile parts, in a Cuban port.

wanted more cautious steps, such as the quarantine (dangerous though it was). After all, they pointed out, air attacks could kill hundreds of Russians in Cuba and thus provoke immediate retaliation on the United States. Finally Attorney General Robert F. Kennedy, the President's brother, pointed out that an air attack would kill many thousands of Cubans and look suspiciously like the Japanese attack on Pearl Harbor.

The President finally decided on the quarantine and made his television announcement. The next morning he sat with his brother and waited while Russian ships approached the 500-mile quarantine limit. American ships and planes were ready to stop them and turn them back—with force, if necessary. Robert Kennedy later wrote this description of the agonizing wait:

> This was the moment we had prepared for, which we hoped would never come. I think these few minutes were the time of gravest concern for the President. Was the world on the brink of a holocaust? Was it our error? A mistake? Was there something further that should have been done? Or not done? His hand went up to his face and covered his mouth. He opened and closed his fist. His face seemed drawn, his eyes pained, almost gray. We stared at each other across the table.

Just before 10:30 a messenger came in. He reported that two of the Russian ships seemed to have stopped abruptly in the water. Soon, all the Soviet ships near the quarantine line either stopped or turned back. The immediate crisis was over. The Russians had decided to play a careful game.

There was an enormous sigh of relief in the White House. But the relief was short-lived. Some Russian vessels resumed their course toward Cuba. Possibly these vessels were oil tankers containing no weapons. But, to make the quarantine effective, sooner or later a ship must be stopped, boarded, and searched. The President waited two days for the right moment. Then he carefully chose a ship that he felt carried only oil. The ship flew a Panamanian flag and was working on contract for the Soviet Union. It had no Russian crewmen. Two American destroyers pulled alongside, ordered it to stop engines, and sent armed search parties aboard. There was no resistance.

Soviet restraint and the President's cautious procedures had avoided a direct military confrontation. But, all week Russians in Cuba had continued work on the existing missile sites. In fact, they had speeded up their work. So the fundamental issue still remained. Would the United States tolerate missiles already there, or would the Russians remove them?

The first Soviet response to quarantine had been warlike language but restrained actions. Then, on the afternoon of Friday, October 26, the President received a personal letter from the Soviet premier, Nikita Khrushchev, which changed the tone of the confrontation and also contained a formula for ending it:

> You can be calm. We are of sound mind, and understand perfectly that if we attack you, you will respond the same way. I think that you also understand this. If you have not lost your self-control, Mr. President, we and you ought not to pull on the ends of the rope in which you have tied the knot of war, because the more the two of us pull, the tighter the knot will be tied. And a moment may come when that knot will be tied so tight that even he who tied it will not have the strength to untie it. Then let us not only relax the forces pulling on the ends of the rope, let us take measures to untie that knot. We are ready for this.

In this remarkable letter, which marked a definite turning point in the Cold War, Khrushchev suggested a way to resolve the specific issue of the missiles in Cuba. If the United States would end the quarantine and publicly proclaim it would never again support any kind of invasion of Cuba, then the Soviet Union would remove the missiles already in place and send no more.

The very next day Kennedy accepted the proposal. Khrushchev replied with more warmth than had been shown since the start of the Cold War: "I express my satisfaction and thank you for the sense of proportion you have displayed."

Superpower Politics

THE CUBAN missile crisis contained two separate elements. One was obvious, the other ignored by most people at the time. Both were at the core of the history of American relations with the rest of the world in the years after Kennedy's inauguration. The first and obvious element was the confrontation and then relaxation between the two nuclear superpowers. The missile crisis was not merely the closest approach to nuclear war since World War II. It was also the beginning of a process of easing tensions (or "detente," as it is often called), which eventually ended the Cold War. The second, less obvious element in the missile crisis, however, was that it represented a definite American intervention in Cuban affairs. The United States, in effect, modified the old Monroe Doctrine once more, asserting again its right to control the foreign affairs of smaller nations in the Western Hemisphere.

Both of these elements—more peaceful relations with the world's other great powers and continued intervention in the affairs of smaller nations—ran clearly through the policies of Presidents Kennedy, Johnson, and Nixon. The combination was a bit baffling. While the United States moved toward peaceful relations with the Soviet Union and China, it frequently took more forceful action in smaller countries. It was almost as though Theodore Roosevelt's foreign policy slogan—"speak softly and carry a big stick"— had been split up. The soft words would be reserved for the world's other great powers, the big sticks for smaller nations.

The trend toward soft words and relaxed tensions with the Soviet Union (and, under Nixon, with China) began to be implemented the very next year after the missile crisis. At that time the United States and the Soviet Union came to their most significant agreement since World War II—a treaty banning any further testing of nuclear weapons in the atmosphere. Eventually almost every nation (except France, Cuba, and China) also signed this agreement. But the Kennedy administration thought of the test-ban treaty as only a first step in a long process of negotiated disarmament that might take decades to complete.

"CLIENT" NATIONS

The happy ending of the missile crisis and the signing of the test-ban treaty appeared, in 1962 and 1963, very small steps toward ending the Cold War. There were still many powerful obstacles to the relaxation of conflicts between what American politicians liked to call the free West and the communist East. NATO continued to be a cornerstone of United States policy. The Warsaw Pact represented the Russian counterpart to NATO in Eastern Europe. Germany remained a divided nation. The British, French, and American occupation zones were united into "Free" West Germany facing the communist East Germany. The city of Berlin was still split politically and physically, with the western part of the city completely dependent on outside help.

Beyond Europe both the United States and the Soviet Union cultivated close relationships with "client" nations and political movements. Each gave massive military and economic support to friendly governments. Each helped finance and provide weapons for revolutionary movements in unfriendly countries throughout Asia, Latin America, and Africa. In fact, this "Third World,"—the underdeveloped nations outside Europe and North America—was the main East-West battleground of the 1960s. As a result, the United States and the Soviet Union seemed to be creating dozens of potential areas of confrontation in nations where neither country's deepest interests were at stake.

In the Middle East, for example, the Soviet Union grew closer and closer to Egypt and some other Arab nations. The United States (which also supported some pro-Western Arab governments) provided economic and military aid for Israel. Thus when war broke out in 1967 between Israel and the Arabs, Americans and Russians found themselves involved in a potential conflict over which they had no real control. The 1967 war was short (and a smashing victory for Israel). So the two nuclear superpowers avoided a crisis. But the threat continued into the 1970s.

In October 1973 fighting broke out once more in the Middle East. Egypt and Syria—aided by other Arab nations—attacked Israel, attempting to recover territory lost in 1967. This time, Israel was not able to win such a quick military victory. It did turn back the Egyptian and Syrian attacks and did capture new territory in both Arab countries. But once more the United States and the Soviet Union found themselves rushing huge shipments of planes, tanks, and other equipment to the opposing sides, trying to maintain the balance of power there.

On the Chinese-American front of the Cold War, an even more obvious source of danger was American support for the Taiwan regime of Chiang Kai-shek, one of the most powerful American client states. The survival of this Nationalist Chinese republic remained the greatest barrier to American recognition of the mainland government of Communist China. The United States Seventh Fleet still patrolled the narrow straits between China and Taiwan. Both President Kennedy and his successor, Lyndon Johnson, reaffirmed the old American pledge to protect Chiang Kai-shek's government. By the mid-1960s almost no spot on the globe seemed free from the potential for setting off nuclear war.

CHANGING WORLD CONDITIONS

Certain conditions taken together, however, made it possible for the Cold War opponents to begin settling differences. First, the cost of building advanced weapon systems and maintaining huge armies and navies was more difficult to bear each year. Obviously, the economies of both nations could not continue to support vast military budgets and at the same time produce the consumer goods their civilian populations demanded.

Second, and more important in the long

run, the world of the 1960s was different from that of the 1950s. Since World War II the United States and the Soviet Union had been the unchallenged superpowers. But by the late 1950s, and even more rapidly in the 1960s, other power centers emerged to compete with the two nuclear giants. Greatly helped by the Marshall Plan, the Western European nations recovered from the war completely. Then they developed their industrial systems to capacities undreamed of before World War II. France and Great Britain both developed modest nuclear arms of their own.

At the same time the cornerstone of American defense policy in the 1950s, NATO, grew steadily weaker. One of the most important members, France, dropped out of the organization altogether and also ordered all NATO troops out of France. The nations that did remain as members were much less dependent on NATO in the 1960s than they had been during the more critical years of the Cold War.

As economic competitors, too, the countries of Western Europe became a third great power by uniting in the European Common Market. West Germany and Japan, after being overpowered and occupied in 1945, recovered with almost miraculous speed. Neither was permitted to rearm (and neither seemed to want to become a military force). Yet in every other way the two former enemies of the United States assumed the role of great powers.

Third, and most important of all, both the United States and the Soviet Union experienced difficulties with their allies that compelled them to approach the Cold War in new ways. Nations like France, Great Britain, and Germany were no longer unquestioning friends in the conflict with the Soviet Union. For Moscow relations were even more strained. Under the leadership of Mao Tse-tung and Chou En-lai, China developed rapidly both economically and militarily. With this came a serious split between the two great communist powers.

The conflict began in propaganda, with Mao and Khrushchev firing words back and forth across their border. Soon both countries heavily fortified this border. In 1969 a dangerous but brief shooting skirmish occurred between Russian and Chinese soldiers. At the same time, the Russians were having great difficulty controlling their client states in Eastern Europe. Gradually, American political leaders realized that "international communism" was not a united movement but was instead badly divided.

To a limited extent under Lyndon Johnson—and far more rapidly under his successor, Richard Nixon—the United States actively pursued a detente with both China and the Soviet Union. By the early 1970s it was possible for Americans

The foreign and economic ministers of Western Europe are shown conferring at a Common Market meeting in 1961. Since then, with its growing economic power, that bloc of nations has become an influential third force in world politics.

During President Nixon's visit to China in February 1972, he and Premier Chou En-lai reviewed the Chinese Red Guard. Televised scenes like this startled the American public, long accustomed to thinking in Cold War terms.

to speak of the end of the Cold War. In 1972 Nixon visited China, and the United States finally accepted Chinese membership in the United Nations. Many hours of the President's trip to Peking were telecast back to the United States. Americans watched with some amazement as Nixon and the Chinese leaders exchanged hearty toasts and warm words. In 1972–73 Nixon and Soviet leader Leonid Brezhnev exchanged cordial visits to each other's capitals.

In October 1973, at a critical point in the new war between Israel and its Arab neighbors, the detente was put to an important practical test. Brezhnev flew to Cairo to talk to Arab leaders; Henry Kissinger, who had become Secretary of State, then flew to Moscow to see Brezhnev and went from there to Israel. Quickly the United States and the Soviet Union called a meeting of the UN Security Council to vote a cease-fire proposal. China, now a full member of

the council, went along and did not exercise its veto power.

After a shaky beginning the cease-fire was effective. Apparently, the superpowers had been able to work together to stop the war, though it remained to be seen whether they could impose real peace in the Middle East—or anywhere else. Still, there could be little doubt that detente was becoming one of the basic goals of foreign policy for all three major parties to the Cold War.

GLOBAL INTERVENTION

The habit of aggressive intervention was harder to break than the habit of Cold War, however. The 1960s had begun with American sponsorship of the Bay of Pigs invasion—a direct military attempt to overthrow a foreign government. At the same time, the Kennedy administration was pouring millions of dollars into the small new nation of Laos (part of the old French colony of Indochina) to support a pro-West government against forces that the United States claimed were communist.

The oldest theater for American intervention is Latin America. For decades the United States had had a contradictory policy of combining military intervention and economic assistance. Early in his administration President Kennedy announced an impressive sounding Alliance for Progress for Latin America. The alliance was a program of loans, grants in aid, and technical assistance. It was designed to attack the problem of poverty that made life in most of Latin America miserable for the poor and uncertain for the well-to-do.

Confidently, Kennedy said that the alliance would not be used to support military governments just because they happened to be anticommunist. But in the ten years after the alliance was formed, military leaders overthrew republics in several important Latin American nations. The United States recognized these new military governments—and in some cases probably helped them seize power. And so, whether American leaders planned it that way or not the

With the defeat of the French at Dienbienphu in 1954, Vietnam was, in effect, divided into two countries: North Vietnam with its capital at Hanoi, and South Vietnam with its capital at Saigon. Soon Communists and nationalists began guerrilla and terrorist activity against the Saigon government, which received support and increasing amounts of military aid from the United States. These guerrilla forces, formally titled the National Liberation Army, came to be known as the Viet Cong.

In August 1964 North Vietnamese torpedo boats reportedly fired on United States ships in the Gulf of Tonkin. President Johnson ordered the bombing of North Vietnamese naval bases in retaliation. The United States was soon bombing North Vietnam regularly and also areas in South Vietnam held by the Viet Cong. In turn, United States naval bases, such as the one at Danang, were attacked. American bombers then attacked eastern Laos in an attempt to stop the flow of men and supplies from North Vietnam over the Ho Chi Minh trails. United States military involvement increased until nearly 540,000 American troops were in Vietnam.

In early 1968 the Vietcong launched their Tet Offensive—simultaneous attacks on the major cities of South Vietnam. During an American counterattack, a massacre of Vietnamese civilians by American soldiers occurred at My Lai. In the same year President Johnson called a limited halt to the bombing of North Vietnam on March 31 and a full bombing halt on November 1. In 1970 occasional air attacks were resumed.

United States and South Vietnamese forces drove deep into Cambodia in April 1970 in an effort to locate and destroy Vietcong bases there. In February 1971 South Vietnamese troops, with United States air support, crossed the border into Laos in an unsuccessful attempt to cut the Ho Chi Minh trails.

In March of 1972 the Vietcong and North Vietnam launched a massive offensive, capturing the provincial capital of Quang Tri and scoring other successes; in May the United States began systematic bombing of all North Vietnam and mined North Vietnamese rivers, canals, and ports—including Haiphong Harbor.

Under President Nixon the number of American troops in Vietnam was drastically reduced—down to 65,000 in May 1972—and combat duties were transferred to South Vietnamese forces under a policy of "Vietnamization." In 1973 a cease-fire was concluded in Vietnam.

THE WAR IN SOUTHEAST ASIA

← United States and South Vietnamese troop moves
← National Liberation Army moves
◉ Capital cities   0 _____ 100 MILES

alliance helped to stabilize governments that were neither democratic nor economically progressive. In 1964 Lyndon Johnson followed a more traditional path of intervention when he sent 20,000 American soldiers and marines into the Dominican Republic to prevent establishment of a new government believed to be friendly to Castro's Cuba.

These interventions paled in size and importance beside the American involvement in a confused guerrilla war in two artificial nations in Indochina, North and South Vietnam. The country had been divided when the French withdrew from the region in 1954 (see Chapter 36). A northern capital was set up in Hanoi and a southern one in Saigon. When elections to unite the country were not held, a National Liberation Front, composed of local communists and supported by the North, tried to bring down the Saigon government.

The Eisenhower administration had supported the South Vietnamese government with money, military equipment, and a few military advisers. Kennedy deepened this commitment by sending more American advisers and more weapons. But apparently no amount of money, arms, or advice would enable Saigon to hold out against the National Liberation Front (or "Vietcong," as they were also called). In 1965, after an alleged incident with North Vietnam involving American ships in the Tonkin Gulf, President Johnson committed American forces to battle. With congressional approval—but without a declaration of war—Johnson bombed North Vietnam with more force than had been used against Germany during World War II. He eventually sent more than 500,000 American troops to Indochina.

American involvement in Vietnam began with a limited commitment of military advisers, like this Green Beret soldier. American advisers remained in 1973, though combat troops had been withdrawn.

The war went badly for the Americans. The Vietcong and their strong supporters from the North matched the huge military concentration of American troops, machines, and weapons. If anything, the military position in the South kept growing worse. At home the war became the most divisive and heated political issue in decades. It led to a powerful peace movement that first centered on college campuses, but then spread with astonishing strength.

Under domestic political pressure Johnson announced in the spring of 1968 that he was seeking negotiations with the National Liberation Front and North Vietnam. In the election that followed, Hubert Humphrey and Richard Nixon both campaigned for the presidency on a promise to end the war. Still, somehow, the conflict lasted four more long years. Finally, just before election day in 1972, Nixon's foreign-policy expert Henry Kissinger announced that "peace is at hand." But at Christmas the United States resumed the bombing of North Vietnam while battles continued in the South. Finally, a peace agreement was signed early in 1973, involving all four parties to the struggle—the United States, North Vietnam, South Vietnam, and the National Liberation Front.

Even with international supervision, this peace settlement seemed almost impossible to enforce. True, the United States withdrew all its combat forces from South Vietnam and stopped bombing the North. But, as the year wore on, American planes were still bombing Cambodia heavily to try to prevent the collapse of the pro-West government there.

Finally, on August 15, 1973, under severe pressure from a Democratic Congress determined to end American military involvement in Indochina, Nixon stopped bombing Cambodia. The United States had spent billions of dollars on the longest air war in history. But, when the warplanes were all finally grounded, there was little assurance that any part of Indochina would soon see true peace.

As though in preparation for a siege, workmen erected this cyclone fence topped with barbed wire around the Democratic convention hall in Chicago.

"The Battle of Chicago," 1968

IN THE SUMMER of 1968, the city of Chicago prepared to serve as host for the Democratic convention. The preparations included an unusual preoccupation with security. The area around the International Amphitheater, where the convention would meet, began to resemble a fortress under siege. Around the amphitheater workers erected a cyclone fence topped with barbed wire. They also set up rolls of barbed wire at crucial points outside the fence. For blocks around they sealed manhole covers to prevent any underground attack on the amphitheater. The Democratic mayor of Chicago, Richard J. Daley, often met with his own police officials and representatives of the state government. They laid plans to summon the National Guard, and even federal troops if necessary.

The barbed wire, the sealed manholes, and the other preparations took place in a dense atmosphere of rumor. The Chicago police heard, and sometimes believed, that black militants were planning to assassinate white leaders. Groups of "hippies"—a term then used for young persons with long hair or unusual cloth-ing—were supposedly going to add LSD to the Chicago water supply. Other "radicals"—a term even more vague than "hippie"—were supposedly planning to mix ground glass into the food served in downtown Chicago restaurants.

Meanwhile, thousands of people, most of them young, were coming into Chicago. They came not to attend the convention as such but to protest the Johnson administration's domestic and foreign policy. By the time the convention opened, perhaps as many as 10,000 young men and women were camping in Chicago's parks, making and hearing speeches, trying to organize a coherent movement. Some practiced judo and karate. Some listened to music or read poetry. Some smoked marijuana or used other drugs. Some were earnest, even prayerful. But for the most part the young people just lounged or drifted in small groups.

Chicago city officials, some newsmen, and many other Americans simply grouped the young people under the fuzzy label "demonstrators." Actually, it is difficult to generalize about them. Most were under thirty. Many were college students and members of solidly middle-class families. Most were white. They were not, in other words, part of a revolutionary movement of the poor and downtrodden. Politically, they ranged from moderate critics of American military involvement in Indochina to revolutionaries determined to "bring down the system."

Their mood was a curious mixture of picnic gaiety and deep anger at what they regarded as the American government's betrayal of freedom and democracy. They wanted the convention to do two things (neither of them likely). First, they wanted the Democrats to condemn the long war in Indochina. Second, they wanted the party to nominate someone other than the man they considered the "regular" candidate, Vice President Hubert Humphrey. But these two wishes were drowned in a more general conviction: the party would fail them; the entire political system was hopelessly unresponsive; and all they could do was to make their presence felt by going outside politics, into the streets.

Out of this frustration a tactic developed. One group of demonstrators, calling themselves Yippies (for Youth International party), ceremoniously named a pig Pigasus and nominated him for President. The Yippies, in particular, became steadily more strident. They searched for profanities to shout at the police and other officials, profanities harsh enough to convey their anger. Soon, too, the demonstrators decided that if they could provoke the police or National Guard into violence, the whole world would see just how brutal, just how "fascist," the system had become.

For their part, Mayor Daley and other officials also developed a tactic. Again and again, they expressed their fear that the demonstrators had come to Chicago to create violence. The city, the mayor announced, would stand firm. There would be no permits for parades. The demonstrators would not be allowed to approach the amphitheater. Nor could they use the city's parks as campgrounds at night. The police would be in the streets, fully armed and ready.

Thus, on both sides, the stage was set for a violent, dramatic encounter—the "battle of Chi-cago." The trouble began the night before the convention was to open. All that day demonstrators had crowded into Lincoln Park, which lies along the shore of Lake Michigan, about two miles north of the amphitheater. By 11 P.M., according to a curfew announced by the city, the park was supposed to be cleared. But about a thousand young people remained, apparently determined to resist the curfew. Their spirits were fed by mimeographed sheets circulated by the Yippie organization. One of these read:

> Laugh at professors; disobey your parents; burn your money; you know life is a dream and all of our institutions are man-made illusions. Break down the family, church, nation, city, economy. What's needed is a generation of people who are freaky, crazy, irrational, sexy, angry, irreligious, childish, and mad; people who burn draft cards, burn high-school and college degrees; people who lure the youth with music, pot, and acid. The white youth of America have more in common with Indians plundered than they do with their own parents. Burn their houses down, and you will be free.

At 10:30 the police ordered Lincoln Park cleared. The immediate result was confusion. Many in the crowd simply melted away. Others stayed and shouted slogans like "The streets belong to the people." After a long pause the police began to "sweep" the park. Most Chicago police simply tried to keep order on this first night's encounter with the demonstrators. But an official report later described the ways some police behaved:

> Police followed another group of persons who had sought [refuge in an apartment building nearby] and hit one member of the group on the head with a baton [a night stick]. As the student raised his hand to feel his head, he was hit again, and two fingers were broken. Other officers ran up the exterior staircase of an apartment building and used their shotguns to force downstairs six or seven persons who had sought refuge there.

The crowd surged up and down Clark Street. More tear gas canisters exploded, sending people on the run, grabbing handkerchiefs, and

(continued on page 785)

The Land Americans Have Shaped

How to describe the United States of today? Travelers use words like "size," "diversity," "achievement," "efficiency," "wealth." All are valid. But all seem somewhat abstract without a sense of the people who have worked to make America what it is. Their monuments may be as modest as a tiny New England village—this one in Vermont—or as vast as Boulder Dam. Clearly, they have transformed the land first explored by Europeans over 450 years ago. Wrote Mohamed Mehdevi of Iran: "My imagination could not keep pace with the trials and labors that must have gone into this spanning and building of a continent, an achievement of man. And it had been done not by heroes and great warriors, but everyone."

[For further information on the foreign observers quoted in this essay, see "Notes on Sources."]

PICTORIAL ESSAY 9

Skyscrapers, New York City

New York is a vertical city. It is a catastrophe with which a too hasty destiny has overwhelmed courageous and confident people, though a beautiful and worthy catastrophe. Nothing is lost. Faced with difficulties, New York falters. Still streaming with sweat from its exertions, wiping off its forehead, it sees what it has done and suddenly realizes: "Well, we didn't get it done properly. Let's start over again!" New York has such courage and enthusiasm that everything can be begun again, sent back to the building yard and made into something still greater, something mastered!

[LE CORBUSIER, 1947]

Levittown, Pennsylvania

Already, three out of every five American families own homes. The horizontal trend which has replaced the vertical trend of the skyscrapers is covering the great green spaces around the cities with the individual houses of suburbia. Suburbia is a way of life. In the family-centered society which America has become in recent years, suburbia is regarded as the ideal place to rear children. In this world of carefully mowed lawns there already lives one-third of the nation.

[HERBERT VON BORCH, 1962]

South Carolina plantation

On the banks of the Mississippi stands a stately home with pillared porch, dappled oak alley and a spacious lawn, on which magnolias shed their heavy-lidded blossoms. The home is open to visitors on Sundays, though a family is in residence. There is a guide in the shape of an overpowering lady who waits until the number of visitors meets her approval. The lady praises the past in a voice that echoes in the marble halls.

[JAN DE HARTOG, 1961]

The Americans are proud of their Lincoln and Jefferson Memorials, and they enjoy showing visitors their National Art Gallery, a splendid white Tennessee marble building which looks pink after a rain. Next we visited the Library of Congress. As we walked around the city this evening in the warm moist air filled with swirling leaves, we saw the dome of the Capitol illuminated against the dark sky. Washington is not a provincial city but a melting pot for people from every state who come to do business, petition, or simply visit.

[NIKOLAI MIKHAILOV AND ZINAIDA KOSSENKO, 1960]

Joint session of Congress

The Capitol, Washington, D.C.

Assembly line workers, Detroit

I became aware of the pace of work in North America, a pace that was not the international one but that of Uncle Sam. During the eight-hour day people really attended to their job, and it was taken for granted that the chiefs would set an example of punctuality and dedication. Among us Chileans, and I believe also in all the Latin countries, the boss enjoys the privilege of arriving late at the office and staying away whenever he feels like it, and the employees, by the same token, can refrain from showing too much devotion to their work. Compared with us, the North Americans strike me as a much more powerful and better run machine.

[AMANDA LABARCA H., 1959]

Steel works, Gary, Indiana

University of Chicago Law Library, designed by Eero Saarinen

American architecture has beauty, audacity, and a superb sense of scale, absorbing what is best in modern architecture in Western Europe, adapting itself to American needs, scenery, and wide horizons, and yet presenting what is exciting, new, and vital. The architect works in freedom and according to the needs he must satisfy and the function his building must perform.

[MORRIS BROUGHTON, 1959]

Then there are the cities, and especially those small towns that hold the secret of the United States—with their frame houses, their adjoining gardens always open to the view, their grass of a succulent and hospitable green, their tall, powerful trees, their modest and silent intimacy, softened in the whiteness of the snow or expressed passionately in the floral effusion of the springtime; their hospitable and secluded churches, their bustling schools, their solitary streets along which there shine at night, among the trees, the lights of so many open windows; and the business streets with the bank, the gasoline station, the tempting and ingeniously arranged shop windows.

[JULIAN MARIAS, 1959]

Parade at Taylor, Wisconsin

Wheat farm on the Great Plains

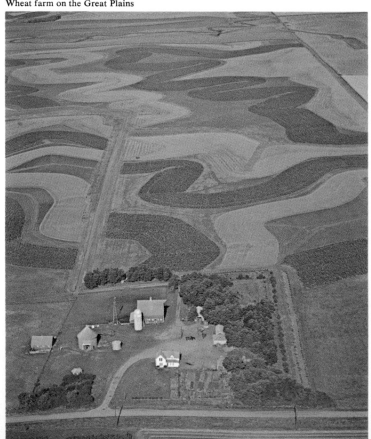

If you come from the Eastern states, or farther east still, from Europe, going west is a continuous journey of suspense, from the moment you are over the Appalachians and know that the Atlantic has gone for good. In the Midwest, the sky is a little wider, and the prairie is a kind of sea all its own; so much so that in the wheatlands of Kansas you get the illusion of great heaving yellow swells, and the silos float by like battleships on the horizon.

[ALISTAIR COOKE, 1968]

Taos Pueblo, New Mexico

Taos is the most characteristic of all the reservations. We were struck at once by its beauty. On two sides of an open space, traversed by a stream, are enormous blocks of buildings, as high as they are long, in which adobe houses are encrusted and super-imposed one above the other. The dominant color is a dull yellow, but red and violet cloths, hung up to dry on the flat roofs and fluttering in the breeze, light up the sombre background.

[SIMONE DE BEAUVOIR, 1947]

Hoover Dam (Boulder Dam), on the Arizona-Nevada border

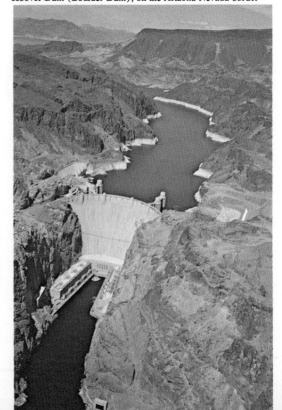

Boulder Dam is something more than a vast utilitarian device, a super-gadget. Enchanted by its clean functional lines and at the same time awed by its colossal size, you might be tempted to call it a work of art; as if something that began with utility and civil engineering ended somewhere in the neighborhood of Beethoven's Ninth Symphony.

[J. B. PRIESTLEY, 1935-36]

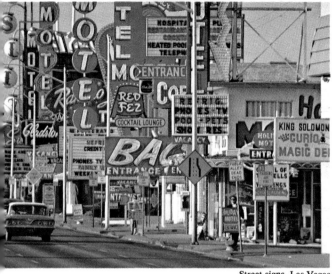

Street signs, Las Vegas

A feature of Las Vegas hotels is that there are no windows or clocks. Gamblers must not be reminded to go to bed. The less expensive gambling avenue caters for a poorer class of tourist and is known as Glitter Gulch. Its electric signs made it as bright as day. It is ridiculous to sneer at the lighted advertisements of the U.S. Romantic historians are always saying how wonderful Elizabethan London must have been "with all those painted inn signs swinging in the wind." Well, here you have it still alive. Why sneer? It is living, it is folk art, it is exquisite from an aircraft, and I personally like to be saluted by an electric cowboy a hundred feet high who waves his arm in a gesture of Hi!

[T. H. WHITE, 1964]

Harbor Freeway, Los Angeles

Just leaving my hotel [in Los Angeles] I feel lost —the distance to the nearest drugstore is the same as between two villages in France. One's helplessness in such vastness is paralyzing. In a car with a girl I said: "Let's go somewhere out of town...." "But where?" she asked. "Oh, no matter where ...," I smiled, "... where the city ends." "Los Angeles never ends," she said firmly.

[LEOPOLD TYRMAND, 1966]

San Francisco at night

We sped toward the Mark Hopkins [and went to] the top floor. The walls were of glass, and we walked slowly around the room, looking at the myriad lights below; it was far more beautiful than Los Angeles at night, than even New York itself, because of the bay traced out in shining lines against a background of dark water and also those fiery ladders rising from the sea. We looked for a long time. There are, in such travels, moments which are promises and others which are only memories: this one was complete in itself.

[SIMONE DE BEAUVOIR, 1947]

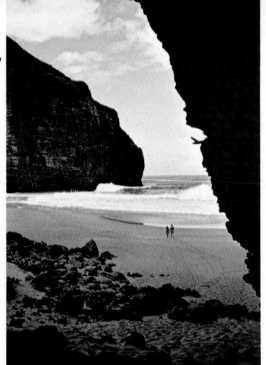

Beach and cliffs, Kauai Island, Hawaii

There is enough wilderness in the world to increase very greatly the number of national parks and to see to it that some of them are preserved in their original condition with access kept so strenuous that the solitary walker is most unlikely to be crowded out.

And this perhaps is the ultimate meaning of the wilderness and its preservation—to remind an increasingly urbanized humanity of the delicacy and vulnerability of all the living species—of tree and plant, of animal and insect —with which man has to share his shrinking planet. As he learns to observe their interdependence and their fragility, their variety and their complexity, he may remember that he, too, is a part of this single web and that if he breaks down too thoroughly the biological rhythms and needs of the natural universe, he may find he has destroyed the ultimate source of his own being. If somewhere in his community he leaves a place for silence, he may find the wilderness a great teacher of the kind of planetary modesty man most needs if his human order is to survive.

[BARBARA WARD AND RENÉ DUBOS, 1972]

Glacier Peak Wilderness, Washington

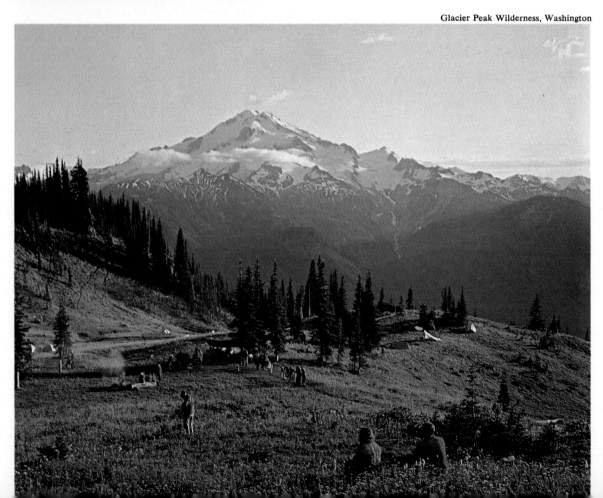

choking for air. Police jabbed a young, blond-haired girl in the stomach. Despite her screams, police continued to hit her until she fell to the pavement. Gradually, the crowd dispersed, and the violence ended.

The next evening—the first day of the convention—police and demonstrators enacted an almost identical script. The demonstrators were more obscene and sullen than before, while the police were more violent. To millions watching both the convention and the disorders on television, it was becoming obvious that the important action was not only in the amphitheater but also in the streets and parks.

The next day battle lines were drawn even more severely. Early in the evening a leader of a radical black political group, Bobby Seale of the Black Panthers, told a crowd in Lincoln Park: "There are pigs—Lyndon Johnson, Hubert Humphrey, and Nixon—in this society." He was followed by Jerry Rubin, a young white radical, who attempted to tie black and white radicalism together: "We whites have been suppressed as blacks have for the past hundred years. We're going with the blacks. If they try to keep us out of the park, then we'll go to the streets. They bring out the pigs to protect the pigs they nominate."

Later, the police cleared Lincoln Park in what had by now become the customary manner. But much of the action had shifted to Grant Park, just across from the huge Conrad Hilton Hotel, the convention's official headquarters. The police declared the hotel off limits. The demonstrators rallied, heard speeches, and shouted insults. One or two even undressed and paraded naked to try to provoke the police. Finally the tired police were relieved by troops of the Illinois National Guard, who did not attempt to enforce the city's curfew. The crowd remained in Grant Park, undisturbed all through the night.

The next day, about 10,000 people gathered in Grant Park. The National Guard went off duty for a while, replaced by policemen. When the crowd declared its intention of marching to the amphitheater, police officials quickly forbade this.

By nightfall several thousand unorganized people were packed at one corner of the block-long Hilton. Nervous police lined up to protect the hotel. Other police tried to clear the streets. The crowd had no place to go—and no plan, either. The lights of television crews added to the unreality of the scene. On an upper floor in the hotel Hubert Humphrey waited for the vote that would nominate him. He could smell and taste faint tear-gas fumes floating up from below.

Just before 8 P.M. the "battle of Chicago" reached its climax. On millions of television sets around the country Americans watched in fascination as two events occurred together: The convention went on with the cumbersome and traditional speeches, demonstrations, and roll calls. Outside the police once more broke discipline and began to attack the demonstrators. A reporter for a Saint Louis newspaper described his experience this way:

> The crowd tried to reverse gears. People began falling over each other. I was in the first rank between police and the crowd and was caught in the first surge. You could hear shouting and screaming. I saw a youth running by me also trying to flee. A policeman clubbed him as he passed, but he kept running.

Another newspaper reporter experienced the battle this way:

> To my left, the police caught a man, beat him to the ground, and smashed their clubs on the back of his unprotected head. He was elderly, somewhere in his mid-fifties. As I stopped to help him, the police turned on me. It was the most slow and confused and the least experienced people who got caught and beaten.

Not all the violence was done by the police. Some demonstrators fought back with rocks, glass bottles, and kicks. Some policemen were hurt by bottles, ash trays, even pieces of furniture hurled from the hotel. About a hundred policemen claimed injuries (most of them delivered by thrown objects) at or near the Hilton. Nobody knows how many demonstrators were hurt. But,

With the Democrats about to nominate Hubert Humphrey inside, the passions of demonstrators outside intensified—but so did the reaction of the police. Here police are shown dispersing demonstrators outside convention headquarters.

on televison, what showed was the almost unbelievable picture of hundreds of nightsticks being raised and brutally lowered.

The main battle was over quickly. By 8:15 the police were in control. The crowd scattered to other parts of the city, where several small skirmishes occurred. Around midnight the police at the Hilton were again relieved by guardsmen. By 1 A.M. the remaining crowd in Grant Park was officially described as orderly. At the amphitheater the party had nominated Humphrey.

Oddly, there were almost no pieces to pick up. The federal government eventually indicted eight leaders on various charges. But a spectacular trial produced no convictions. Little or no disciplinary action was taken against the Chicago police.

What remained, for many people, besides confused memories of the battle, was one small but dramatic incident at the convention itself.

Abraham Ribicoff, a liberal senator from Connecticut, was making a nominating speech for George McGovern of South Dakota, another liberal senator. In the middle of the speech Ribicoff stared down at Richard Daley, who had become a symbol of the kind of traditional party leadership that the protest centered on. If George McGovern were President, Ribicoff said coldly, there would be no "Gestapo tactics in the streets of Chicago." As the television camera zoomed in for a close-up of Daley's angry face, the mayor shouted back something unintelligible.

All too intelligible, however, was the open anger between Ribicoff and Daley. This was the real significance of the "battle of Chicago." It clearly demonstrated the bitter split in the Democratic coalition that had held power for so long. In that sense the battle almost assured Hubert Humphrey's defeat and Richard Nixon's election as President.

Politics at Home

DURING THE SAME summer of 1968 Russian tanks and troops stormed into Prague, Czechoslovakia, to stamp out a movement to liberalize that nation's communist government. The Americans demonstrating in Chicago drew parallels between themselves and the people of Prague. Both, they claimed, were victims of cruel and repressive regimes based only on military power. The parallel was false in several ways, however.

In 1968, the United States was ending almost four decades of national politics dominated by a Democratic party dedicated more or less to reform, not repression. In a dozen important areas of life—such as social welfare, education, or civil rights—defenders of the political system could point to many important successes. One of the strangest facts about the critical summer of 1968, then, was that hundreds of thousands— perhaps millions—of middle-class young people rebelled against a style of politics that had been, at least on the surface, devoted to improving the lot of the poor, the elderly, and several exploited minorities.

KENNEDY'S "THOUSAND DAYS"

The decade of the 1960s began on a note of hope and experimentation. John Fitzgerald Kennedy brought to the White House in 1961 a public personality full of energy, wit, and enthusiasm. But, basically, the political mind of the new President, like many members of his administration, was the product of Roosevelt's New Deal and Truman's Fair Deal. Most of the legislation Kennedy succeeded in getting from Congress during the thousand days he was President reflected this traditional reforming trend. Social Security was extended to cover more self-employed people. The minimum wage went up to $1.25 an hour. New money for public housing was appropriated. There was an increase in federal aid to education and in funding for urban renewal and redevelopment.

Still, compared to the promising rhetoric and style of the President and many of his key colleagues, the actual legislative achievement was embarrassingly small. Most of the Kennedy program was enacted in the first year of his presidency. After this his domestic record in Congress was even more skimpy.

Much of what President Kennedy wanted to accomplish was simply bottled up or defeated in Congress. He attempted to create a new Department of Urban Affairs, but Congress refused to approve the legislation. A bill providing federally assisted medical care for the elderly (Medicare) failed to pass the Senate. A new, strong civil rights act could not get off the ground in either house of Congress. Without much help from the President, Congress did approve the Twenty-fourth Amendment. It prohibits any state from requiring payment of a poll tax as a qualification for voting. The old opposition group of conservative Southern Democrats and Republicans that had formed in the 1930s remained very powerful.

TRAGEDY IN TEXAS

In the 1962 election a number of congressmen friendly to the administration lost their seats. It was clear, too, that the President had become increasingly unpopular among some Southerners because of his liberal position on civil rights. To smooth over some of these difficulties, Kennedy decided to visit Dallas, Texas, in November 1963 to make a speech. Before the scheduled speech there was a motorcade through downtown Dallas. The route was well publicized to attract a large crowd. As the car carrying the President passed the Texas School Book Depository, a rifle fired several times. The President jerked forward and fell to the floor of the car, bleeding. He was rushed to a hospital but died very quickly.

In the days that followed Americans watched in sorrow, confusion, and astonishment. Vice President Lyndon Johnson, also in Texas at the time, flew back at once to Washington in the presidential plane with Mrs. Kennedy. He took the oath of office on the aircraft, still uncertain whether the assassination was part of a larger plot. The mystery was soon cleared up. The disgruntled young assassin, Lee Harvey Oswald, was captured. But, as he was being moved from one jail to another, in full view of television cameras beaming their picture to another nationwide audience, Oswald was shot to death by a Dallas night-club owner named Jack Ruby.

Most of the young people who, six years later, were the radicals, hippies, and demonstrators in Chicago were high-school students at the time of the assassination. With their parents they watched the murder, the funeral, and then Oswald's murder.

Other generations of Americans had entered adult life against a background of depression or war. To this new generation—at least to its white, middle-class majority—the violence at Dallas was probably the single most memorable introduction to the realities of modern life. The lessons drawn from it were confirmed again and again as the decade passed.

JOHNSON'S GREAT SOCIETY

Lyndon Johnson set to work promptly to become, as he put it, "President of all the people." Taking full advantage of the wave of emotion following Kennedy's assassination, he made his motto, "Let us continue." He also used all the knowledge and skill he had accumulated during a long career in Congress. Within twelve months of Kennedy's death Johnson managed to move some of the most cherished and difficult liberal proposals through Congress. He called his program the Great Society.

First, and perhaps most significant, the new President made a passionate plea for a new civil rights law. The first Southerner in the White House since Woodrow Wilson, he demanded full equality for blacks and other racial minorities. He even quoted the most stirring song of the civil rights movement: "We shall overcome." The effect was electric. For the first time in its history the Senate voted to end a filibuster against civil rights legislation. It passed the Civil Rights Act of 1964.

The law required that every state apply exactly the same standards to blacks and whites for voting or face suits in special courts. More important, at least in the short run, the act forbade any kind of discrimination in such public accommodations as trains, hotels, swimming pools, and restaurants. (Amazingly, throughout the South, there was rapid and widespread acceptance of this revolutionary aspect of the new law.) But the Civil Rights Act went even further. It authorized the federal government to cut off aid to any school district that did not move toward racial integration. It also forbade discrimination on the basis of either race or sex in employment.

Aside from civil rights Johnson devoted major efforts to his "war on poverty." To create the Great Society, the President asked Congress to set up a new government agency, the Office of Economic Opportunity (OEO). Under the legislation that Johnson wrung from a suddenly cooperative Congress, the OEO would provide education and vocational training to unemployed young people, make grants to cities for their own antipoverty programs, and finance part-time jobs for students and others who needed support. The dollar amounts appropriated were not large at first. But the legislation moved the federal government into more direct assistance for the poor than at any time since the depression.

Obviously, Johnson would be the unanimous choice of the Democrats in 1964. The Republicans nominated Senator Barry Goldwater of Arizona. Goldwater was an outspoken conservative, more so than any Republican candidate since Herbert Hoover. His book, *Conscience of a Conservative,* set forth a political philosophy opposed to most of the reform legislation passed during the New Deal, the Fair Deal, Kennedy's New Frontier, and Johnson's Great Society. Goldwater even hinted that he might seek an end to the Social Security system. For the first time in at least a generation the voters had an apparently clear-cut choice between a frank conservative and a liberal who stood squarely in the Roosevelt-Truman-Kennedy tradition of reform.

Lyndon Johnson's legislative experience helped him get an impressive domestic program through Congress during his presidency. This same activism in foreign affairs, however, proved his downfall.

The outcome was spectacular. Johnson and his vice-presidential candidate, Hubert Humphrey, won 61 percent of the vote, the largest popular margin of victory in modern history. Goldwater carried only his own Arizona, plus five states in the Deep South. Johnson also swept large numbers of Democratic governors, congressmen, and senators into office. Jubilantly, he interpreted the election as a national referendum on public policy. He set to work with more energy than ever to perfect the Great Society.

IMPROVING THE GREAT SOCIETY

The next two years, 1965 and 1966, were unquestionably Johnson's most impressive. He won a doubled appropriation for OEO from Congress. A law providing $3 billion in federal aid to education at all levels was a victory long overdue. An old sore spot was at least partially cured when Congress agreed to eliminate the national-origins quota restrictions on immigration. The new system replaced the former quotas, so heavily weighted in favor of northern Europe. Two general limits, one for the Western Hemisphere, the other for the rest of the world were substituted.

Most significant of all for many Americans was the passage of the Medicare bill. Since the Truman administration Democrats had tried without success to provide some form of federal medical assistance for the elderly and the poor. The Medicare law, administered through the Social Security system, provided such medical insurance for the elderly.

As though the Civil Rights Act of 1964 had not been spectacular enough, Johnson asked for and won a new law, the Voting Rights Act of 1965. It aimed primarily at guaranteeing voting rights to blacks. For the first time since the Civil War and Reconstruction the national government stepped directly into the process of registering voters. The law provided that in any district where fewer than half the eligible voters had participated in the 1964 election, federal registrars could be sent to enroll new voters under carefully controlled conditions.

But landslide victories in American politics often turn sour. Lyndon Johnson's victory was to be no exception. Two years after his landslide the President was in deep political trouble. By the 1966 congressional elections a reaction was clearly building in the country against some elements of his Great Society program. Accordingly, the Republicans in 1966 took forty-seven seats from the Democrats in the House of Representatives, plus three in the Senate. From this point on Johnson found it difficult indeed to deal with Congress. His administration was nearly stagnant in the area of domestic legislation and reform. It also became badly divided and embattled over the issue of the war in Indochina.

Part of the obvious political reaction of 1966 was not due to Lyndon Johnson and his policies but to the Supreme Court. Under the vigorous leadership of Chief Justice Earl Warren, the Court continued to make determined rulings on minority rights and integration. It also threatened many established patterns in American politics by a revolutionary decision, neatly summed up as "one man, one vote." This ruling declared that electoral districts for Congress and the state legislatures had to be drawn so that they contained almost equal numbers of people. This seemingly innocent idea meant that longstanding imbalances between urban and rural areas would soon end. For generations cities had been underrepresented in both state and national legislatures. In contrast rural areas had enjoyed disproportionate political representation. The Court ruling threatened this practice and shifted the balance of political power toward the cities.

Also, in a dramatic series of decisions, the Court enlarged the rights of defendants in criminal cases. Critics said these rulings made it nearly impossible for state and local authorities to enforce criminal law properly. The Court also angered many conservatives when it forbade prayers of any kind in public schools. Billboards went up carrying the demand "Impeach Earl Warren." Because he publicly agreed with many of its rulings and because many Court members were clearly identified with the Democratic Presidents who had appointed them, President Johnson shared much of the criticism leveled at the Court.

THE FALL OF LYNDON JOHNSON

The Johnson administration could easily have survived criticism from those conservatives who opposed the war on poverty, the civil rights legislation, and the Supreme Court decisions. But the President was also coming under still wider and sharper attack because of the deepening American involvement in the Indochina War. As the presidential primaries of 1968 approached, the attack gained force. Senator Eugene McCarthy, a Democrat from Minnesota, announced that he would run in Democratic primaries against the President—a most unusual step for a politician. Waiting in the wings—hesitating about whether to become a candidate himself—was Robert F. Kennedy, now a senator from New York.

To the astonishment of a great many professional politicians, Senator McCarthy effectively utilized thousands of young volunteers in the New Hampshire primary in March. He did not actually defeat the President but came close enough to embarrass him. And it appeared likely that McCarthy might actually win the next important primary election in Wisconsin, just weeks away.

In this tense political atmosphere the President went on national television on the last day of March. He announced that he would cut American military activity in Indochina and would try to start negotiations to end the war there. Then, after a slight pause, he announced that he would not seek reelection. He spoke

Antiwar activists united around Senator Eugene McCarthy to give him a significant showing against President Johnson in New Hampshire's primary. Though McCarthy ultimately lost the nomination, the response he evoked probably led Johnson not to seek reelection.

quietly, with the emotion that marked most of his public speeches. But he had done an astonishing thing.

Johnson's announcement meant that the Democratic nomination was open. Robert Kennedy quickly entered the race. Vice President Hubert Humphrey was on a few primary ballots as a kind of administration stand-in. But the primaries boiled themselves down to a contest between two liberals, McCarthy and Kennedy. Both shared much the same support and had very similar ideas. McCarthy won some primaries, Kennedy others. Gradually, attention focused on the last primary, in California. There, Kennedy won by a narrow margin. There, too, leaving a victory celebration in a Los Angeles hotel, he was murdered by a young Syrian immigrant, Sirhan Sirhan.

This assassination turned the Democratic convention into an unequal struggle between a liberal wing, led but not controlled by Eugene McCarthy, and the party regulars, who rallied behind Hubert Humphrey. The latter group had enough support to nominate Humphrey.

THE REPUBLICAN RETURN

Some of the young people who went to Chicago rejected normal politics and demanded "revolution." But many, probably a majority, had actually worked for the nomination of McCarthy or Robert Kennedy. For them Kennedy's assassination and McCarthy's impending defeat were just the events that made Chicago's violence seem the inevitable outcome of their political experience. They had come close to compelling a major party to take a fundamentally new political turn. But they had failed—or, as they saw it, the Democrats had failed them. It is this fact that explains why the Democratic party—not the Republican party—was the target of their opposition.

For their part the Republicans simply reached back into history to nominate Richard Nixon. They adopted a generally conservative

Governor George Wallace's third-party candidacy in 1968 siphoned off nearly 10 million votes, making that election one of the closest in recent history.

platform, including a virtual endorsement of the war in Indochina. To the Chicago "radicals"—and their supporters around the nation—the Democratic party was the more evil precisely because it had made the closer approach to virtue.

The election was complicated still further by the third-party candidacy of Governor George C. Wallace of Alabama. Wallace, a Democrat and conservative, was a blunt-spoken opponent of racial integration and federal power. He appealed to his supporters' distrust of big, impersonal government bureaucracy. He also tried to persuade working-class Americans that they had been taxed unfairly to support welfare programs and other federally financed social experiments. With these ideas Wallace attracted a large and mixed body of support.

Wallace's candidacy, the Republicans' continuing position as a minority party, and a late surge of loyalty by Democrats made the election fairly close. Richard Nixon won by a smaller percentage of the vote than he had received in losing in 1960. The percentage of people voting for President was also the lowest in years.

NIXON'S DOMESTIC POLICIES

The narrowness of the election and continued Democratic control of Congress weakened the Nixon administration. Clearly Nixon would not be able—even if willing—to reverse the long tendency toward increased federal power. The President did attempt to reduce the size of the Great Society's social welfare budget. Also, he appointed new members to the Supreme Court, including Chief Justice Warren Burger. They would, he believed, change the direction the Court had taken under Earl Warren.

In many ways, however, Nixon's hands were tied. The Senate rejected some of his appointees to the Supreme Court, questioning their qualifications and conservative political views. Congress also refused to act on one of Nixon's major domestic programs, a proposal to replace what he had called the welfare mess with a system of guaranteed incomes at $1,600 a year. The figure was below what was then the official definition of the poverty line. In addition, it was coupled with a demand that the unemployed either accept work or enroll in vocational-training programs. In short, the welfare reform proposal was simply too conservative for the Democratic Congress to accept.

Probably Nixon's most serious domestic concern during his first term of office was the economy. Despite continued growth it seemed unhealthy and unstable. The most important evidence of this—aside from serious and rising unemployment figures—was a decided rise in prices. Finally, under severe pressure the President acted in August 1971. He announced a "New Economic Policy," with several "phases" designed to impose federal controls on wages and prices. In the first phase all prices and wages were frozen. This assertion of government power was quite out of character with Nixon's long previous opposition to federal economic controls.

Aside from the New Economic Policy little that emerged on the home front during the President's first term was surprising. There was no major change in social welfare legislation and no new civil rights laws of any kind. There was a new amendment to the Constitution (the Twenty-sixth), allowing all citizens over eighteen years of age to vote. But this law was a result of congressional, not presidential, efforts.

CONFLICT IN 1972

Because of Nixon's domestic performance and the troubled state of the economy, the Democrats appeared to have a good chance to regain the presidency in 1972. Several candidates emerged as leaders in primaries and state conventions: George Wallace, Hubert Humphrey, Edmund Muskie of Maine (vice-presidential candidate with Humphrey in 1968), and George McGovern (the man who had tried to reorganize Robert Kennedy's support in the 1968 convention).

By careful organization and by taking skillful advantage of party reforms made in 1968 and afterward, McGovern won delegates faster than any other candidate. Finally, he defeated Humphrey and Wallace in a close California primary. McGovern was too liberal for most of the professionals in the party. Consequently, party regulars made determined efforts at the convention to block his nomination. But he had enough delegates (though barely enough) to win nomination and to name Senator Thomas Eagleton of Missouri as his running mate.

In many ways McGovern's success resulted from the Chicago convention of 1968. His support included many who had supported Robert Kennedy or Eugene McCarthy in 1968. He also had the help of thousands of people who had either been in the streets at Chicago or been appalled by the police violence there. But McGovern's nomination did not heal the party division that had caused Humphrey's defeat four years before.

On the contrary, McGovern's victory deepened the division. Many old-line Democratic politicians refused to rally behind him. He represented, at least to many of his followers, something new on the American political scene.

The new politics, as it was called, centered on youth, the rights of ethnic minorities, and the liberation of women.

During the primary campaigns McGovern had proposed several controversial schemes. He suggested, for example, that every family whose income was below $10,000 should receive a yearly cash grant of $1,000. This was to be paid for, according to McGovern, by higher taxes in the high-income brackets. Many middle-class voters were unconvinced that it would not raise their taxes as well. After his nomination McGovern attempted to back away from such proposals, seeking the moderate support he would need to win. But the memory of some of his primary proposals lingered on. McGovern's program seriously alienated many customary sources of Democratic political power in labor unions, among farmers, and among middle- and lower-middle-class voters.

Still, McGovern's showings in various public-opinion polls were better than Humphrey's had been at convention time in 1968.

George McGovern, in attempting to open the Democratic party to groups shut out of the 1968 convention, alienated the traditional base of Democratic support—blue-collar workers. Richard Nixon capitalized on this to win in a landslide.

But his candidacy was badly hurt when newspapers began to report that Eagleton had been treated for psychiatric disorders. McGovern at first announced his support for Eagleton. But soon he asked for the vice-presidential candidate's resignation, an act the voters interpreted as indecisiveness. Sargent Shriver, a brother-in-law of John and Robert Kennedy, became Eagleton's replacement. But the damage had been done. In November Nixon won almost 61 percent of the popular vote and all electoral votes except those of Massachusetts and the District of Columbia. The President entered his second term with a landslide reminiscent of Johnson's in 1964.

CONSTITUTIONAL CRISES

During the campaign the President had promised that if he won the victory he hoped for, then the first six months of his new term would be just as exciting as Franklin Roosevelt's "hundred days." In ways that he would not have predicted the President was correct. Not just the first six months of the new term but its first year was marked by more political surprises and turmoil than any period since the secession winter of 1860-61. By the first anniversary of his reelection the President's victory had turned to ashes. The Nixon administration entered a series of crises that finally rendered him almost powerless, brought his standing in public opinion polls to its lowest ever, and created a very real possibility of presidential impeachment.

The crisis began in an odd way. Early on the morning of June 17, 1972, policemen surprised five men in the headquarters of the Democratic party in a Washington building known as the Watergate. The men carried walkie-talkies, cameras, burglars' tools, and electronic "bugging" equipment. In the days that followed, embarrassing connections between the Watergate burglars and the Nixon administration began to emerge. One of the burglars was employed by the President's own reelection committee. Another carried the phone number of a White House consultant. Investigators soon discovered that the apparent leader of the burglary had received over $100,000 that could be traced to the Nixon campaign organization.

At first the White House dismissed the incident as a "third-rate burglary attempt." John Mitchell, who had resigned as attorney general to direct the Nixon campaign, brushed it aside as a "bizarre incident." When investigations led to the indictment of two middle-level employees of the White House and the Nixon campaign, McGovern tried to make "Watergate" an election issue. But the seven men accused in the crime pleaded guilty without involving the President or his administration, and the incident did not affect the outcome of the election. On inauguration day the President could still hope that the crime would not affect his second term either.

Then in the spring of 1973, from many different sources, new accusations and confessions began to spill. By the beginning of summer two former Cabinet members—Mitchell and Secretary of Commerce Maurice Stans—had been indicted in a related case. The current attorney general and two of the President's top assistants had been forced to resign because of their possible involvement in an attempt to "cover up" the Watergate crime. A number of powerful and less powerful men began publicly to confess to perjury and obstruction of justice.

The President was forced to appoint a Special Prosecutor with full power to investigate not only Watergate but other related accusations. In the meantime the Senate had created a special committee, headed by Democratic Senator Sam Ervin of North Carolina, to investigate the entire campaign of 1972. The committee held public hearings that attracted an even larger audience than the McCarthy hearings of 1954. Stunned and confused, Americans saw the President's own counsel, John Dean, accuse him of participating in an attempt to buy the silence of the Watergate burglars. They also saw the acting head of the FBI admit that he had burned evidence. For weeks a train of witnesses, including several Cabinet members and men with offices

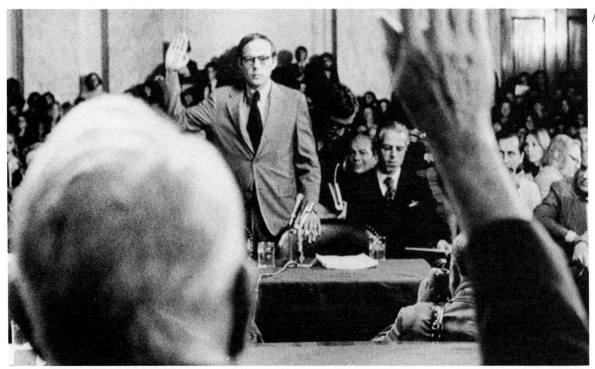

The Watergate hearings reached a dramatic climax with the testimony of John Dean, here being sworn in before the Senate investigating committee by its chairman, Sam Ervin. To test the truthfulness of Dean's testimony, Senate investigators subpoenaed presidential tapes, and a confrontation with the executive branch resulted.

only a few feet from the President's, painted a picture of intrigue and irregularity that threw serious doubt on the meaning of the 1972 election. Even more shockingly, the testimony sometimes appeared to implicate the President himself.

In the midst of these dramatic hearings a minor White House technician revealed that the President had systematically recorded his conversations. Immediately the Ervin committee and Special Prosecutor Archibald Cox subpoenaed the tapes. The President vigorously refused to surrender them, claiming that it was essential that any President be able to conduct conversations in private. The legal status of the tapes formed the basis for a constitutional encounter between the President on one side and the judiciary and Congress on the other—an encounter that everyone expected to be resolved only by a "definitive decision" of the Supreme Court.

While the President and the nation waited for such a decision, the administration suffered another serious blow. Vice President Spiro Agnew was under investigation for accepting bribes. According to the charges, both during his Maryland career and as Vice President, Agnew had taken large sums of money from construction executives who were anxious to secure government contracts. Agnew repeatedly and indignantly denied the charges until, early in October, he pleaded *nolo contendere* (no contest) to a charge of tax evasion—in an attempt to avoid further prosecution and a possible prison sentence. Simultaneously he resigned as Vice President. Making the first use of the Twenty-fifth Amendment, the President nominated Republican Congressman Gerald Ford of Michigan as his choice to replace Agnew. The nomination required congressional approval.

While the administration was digesting the

After pleading no contest to a tax evasion charge at a Baltimore federal court, Vice President Spiro Agnew resigned his office. He claimed that he acted to avoid a divisive struggle in the courts.

shock of the Vice President's resignation, a federal appeals court ruled that Nixon must turn over the presidential tapes and other documents to a federal judge. After a tense delay the President announced that he would neither obey the appeals court nor appeal the case to the Supreme Court. He was willing, however, to produce written versions of the tapes. At the same time he ordered Archibald Cox to take no further legal action to obtain the tapes. The Special Prosecutor refused, and the President ordered the attorney general to fire him. In his turn the attorney general refused and resigned. The assistant attorney general followed suit. Finally the solicitor general, third man in the Justice Department, agreed to carry out the President's order. Overnight the President had gotten rid of Cox but had also lost the first two men in the department that was investigating possible White House involvement in crimes.

The result was an outcry of public indignation that one of the President's own aids described as a "fire storm." Washington was suddenly flooded with letters and telegrams demanding the impeachment of the President. Then, just as suddenly, Nixon announced that he would obey the court's order and surrender the tapes. This gesture helped to cool the demands for impeachment. But several congressmen had already introduced impeachment resolutions, and a House committee announced that it was going to proceed at "full speed" with hearings on possible impeachment.

The President had steadily narrowed the circle of denials and refusals with which he had originally tried to surround himself. He was now laid open to the ultimate constitutional action that might be taken against him. He had seen his administration severely wounded by resignations and indictments. He had heard himself publicly accused of criminal behavior by other political leaders. After his promise to surrender the tapes—a promise he had refused to make until his impeachment seemed likely—the President appeared to have no remaining cards to play. The initiative had shifted almost completely to the courts and to Congress. Richard Nixon, a President who was extremely fond of making spectacular moves and decisions, could only wait while the other branches of government came to their decisions.

Neil Armstrong took this photograph of Edwin Aldrin preparing a scientific experiment on the surface of the moon. Their successful lunar landing fulfilled John Kennedy's promise of 1961 to put Americans on the moon before 1970.

THE MOONSHOT

IT WAS NOT so much the height of the rocket as its weight that was remarkable. True, it was as tall as sixty of any of the men aboard it. But it weighed a fantastic 6 1/2 million pounds. It stood on a launch pad at Cape Kennedy, Florida, waiting to be shot into space toward the moon. Almost at its peak three astronauts waited. Two of them were destined to be the first human beings ever to step onto the moon. All over the United States people watched on television, just as they had watched the Democratic convention in Chicago a year before. This time, however, it was not violence they awaited but a spectacular triumph of human skill and technology.

The name of the rocket, "Saturn," was taken from antiquity. The moonshot was the eleventh in a series with another classical name, "Apollo." But the astronauts' capsule had a patriotic name, "Columbia." And the small "Lunar Excursion Module" in which two of them would drop onto the surface of the moon also bore a name Americans treasure as a national symbol, "Eagle."

When the Saturn roared to life on July 15,

the three astronauts experienced only mild excitement. Their hearts speeded up a bit, but they were experienced, well-trained men for whom the moment of lift-off was almost routine. Slowly at first and then with almost unbelievable speed the rocket roared upward. Within minutes, the astronauts were orbiting the earth weightlessly. Then they were launched on a course aimed at the moon almost a quarter of a million miles away.

For the next two days the men moved farther and farther from the earth's field of gravity. Late on July 17 they passed that invisible point in space where the moon's gravity becomes stronger than the earth's. After this, they literally fell toward the moon, reaching a silent speed of over 5,000 miles per hour. Saturday night, July 18, they disappeared behind the moon, in the first of several orbits they would make while preparing to separate the Columbia from the Eagle. After separation the Eagle would aim for a target on the moon named the Sea of Tranquillity.

The separation was completed early Sunday. Several hours later the two astronauts in the Eagle fired the rockets that would slow their craft down. It began its final controlled fall toward the moon's surface. At the last moment two astronauts, Neil Armstrong and Edwin Aldrin, could see they were headed for a rough, rocky crater. Quickly, they took control of the awkward-looking little Eagle away from the computers. Firing rockets to slow their fall, they dropped farther. Armstrong's heartbeat increased to 156 per minute, more than twice the normal pulse.

Suddenly, the rockets stopped firing as the ship came to rest on the surface. Armstrong reported to the space headquarters in Houston, Texas: "Houston: Tranquillity Base here. The Eagle has landed." It was 4:17 P.M., Eastern Daylight Time, July 20, 1969.

Hours later, just before 11 o'clock that night, Armstrong opened the hatch of the Eagle and climbed carefully down a short ladder toward the surface. He moved uncertainly, clumsy in his pressurized white spacesuit. With him he carried a heavy back-pack to provide him with air and cool his suit against the 250-degree temperature of the moon's morning. Finally, he planted a heavy boot on the powdery moon and said, through the static of his radio, "That's one small step for man, one giant leap for mankind."

Aldrin followed Armstrong down the ladder. The astronauts planted an American flag, stiffened with wires to make it "fly" on the airless moon. Awkwardly, the astronauts stepped back and saluted the bit of red, white, and blue cloth that stood out oddly against the bleak, gray moonscape. Then they placed a plaque on the surface to mark their achievement. Unlike the flag, the plaque credited the event to the entire human race:

> Here men from the planet earth first set foot upon the moon, July, 1969, A.D. We came in peace for all mankind.

With these ceremonies completed, the two set out to explore the area around their spacecraft. They moved around in odd hops, six or eight feet long, in the moon's weak gravity. They took samples of lunar "soil" and collected forty-five pounds of moon rocks. These would be their only "payload" on the trip home. Finally, they crawled back up the ladder to the Eagle.

On Monday afternoon, after about one earth day on the moon, the Eagle's rockets were fired. Leaving its heavy base behind, the craft lifted precariously off the moon. There followed an orbital chase of the mother ship, Columbia, in which the third astronaut had been orbiting and waiting. The link-up was successful. Aldrin and Armstrong reentered the Columbia for the trip home. They pointed their craft across the darkness and cold of space to a spot in the Pacific where they would splash down. The trip home began. As though to remind himself and all people of the humility they ought to feel in the face of their own accomplishment, Aldrin read a verse from the Bible over the Columbia's radio: "When I consider the heavens, the work of Thy fingers, the moon and the stars which Thou has ordained, what is man that Thou art mindful of him?"

New Directions in the Economy

ALDRIN'S SCRIPTURAL passage, the use of patriotic names and the flag, the plaque declaring peace— all these aspects of the moon landing marked it as an achievement of the human spirit. But, at bottom, it was more significant as the most striking single symbol of America's rapid technological change and economic growth during the 1960s.

The rocket and the electronic and computer technology that made the moon flight possible exemplified a marked change in the nature of American economic life. The space program as a whole showed just how productive the economy had become. All during the post–World War II period productivity had steadily increased. Then in the 1960s the economy rose to a rate of production few economists could have predicted. The billions of dollars spent to send Armstrong and Aldrin after their forty-five pounds of rocks were billions that came out of what the government considered surpluses.

PATTERNS OF CHANGE

In several important ways the economy of the 1960s and 1970s differed noticeably from American economies of the past. First, it was oriented much more to consumer goods than to heavy industrial goods. The mainstay of the modern economy had clearly become, by 1960, the cars, clothing, household appliances, and other items that ordinary families bought from year to year.

Second, though continuing a long-term trend, the new economy was built more and more on credit. Home mortgages, bank loans, and installment purchases enabled Americans to buy more goods than most other people in the world could even dream of getting. From 1945 to 1970, in fact, the volume of consumer credit increased ten times. It was this, and not industrial technology, that some economists said was the most important American "invention."

Third, the new economy was characterized by an increasing reliance on computer technology. Computers ran banks, oil refineries, even some libraries. By the 1970s many ordinary supermarket cash registers were linked to large computers that regulated the flow of stock to the market shelves. Computers were changing the practice of medicine, too. Even professional football teams used computers to help determine strategies and player trades. Thus by 1969 the "on-board computer" that helped fly the astronauts to the moon and back was no longer a strange science-fiction fantasy. It was as common a feature of American society as the Ford automobile had been in the 1920s.

Fourth, and perhaps most important, the American economy was changing rapidly from a system that rested on a solid basis of production to one that centered on service. Economists divide economic activity into three principal types. The first (characteristic of the American economy in the colonial period) is called primary, or extractive. It involves taking goods directly from nature, as a tobacco planter, a fur trader, or a goldminer does. The second type (basic to the industrial revolution of the nineteenth and twentieth centuries) involves the production of artificial goods like automobiles, steam engines, and airplanes.

The third type of economic activity involves services. The money people spend on policemen's salaries or advertising or going to movies is spent not for a touchable, physical "good" (as economists call it). Rather, it goes for a service that cannot be resold or stored away for later use. In the simplest terms the United States had, by the beginning of the 1960s, developed a service economy. By 1960 more workers were employed to perform services than to produce goods, a trend that seems likely to continue into the future.

SIGNS OF GROWTH AND WEAKNESS

All these changes occurred in an atmosphere of growth and prosperity. Between 1961 and 1968 the United States experienced the longest and most spectacular period of peacetime economic expansion in its history. Inflation in the prices of goods and services was held down to a low of about 1 percent per year. Economic growth, on the other hand, occurred at a rate of about 5 percent. This meant that the total value of all goods and services Americans bought and sold and paid for in taxes doubled between 1956 and

U.S. FOREIGN TRADE, 1920-70

Exports   Imports

Figures indicate surplus (+) or deficit (−) in millions of dollars

1971, from less than $500 billion to more than $1 trillion.

Americans took this kind of growth more or less for granted. About 1968, however, problems began to develop that cast doubt on both the stability and wisdom of these growth patterns. For one thing the rate of growth itself slowed down rather drastically. Also, between 1968 and 1973, inflation rose at a rate that frightened many economists, businessmen, and politicians. In fact, prices soared at a rate of about 6 percent a year, despite efforts by the Nixon administration to control them.

At the same time, the rate of increase in Gross National Product, the most convenient measurement of economic growth, slowed to less than half that of the period 1961–68. Unemployment then became a critical problem. Nationally, the unemployment figure hovered around 5 percent of the work force, or about one worker out of every twenty. But in some industrial states unemployment neared 10 percent in the early 1970s. All three factors—the slowing growth rate, inflation, and unemployment—became major political issues for the second Nixon administration and major daily worries for Americans.

The domestic economy's lack of strength also weakened the dollar abroad. Since World

War II the dollar had been the world's strongest currency. But America's leveling growth rate and rising inflation caused the dollar's value to decrease in relation to other currencies like the German mark and Japanese yen. President Nixon had to keep devaluing the dollar—that is, to accept official reductions in the amount of money it took to exchange an American dollar for another nation's currency.

PROBLEMS IN AN AFFLUENT SOCIETY

These weaknesses in the American economy were worrisome enough. But they were further complicated by other noneconomic problems.

For one thing, it became more apparent than ever that affluence was not shared equally. In general, the history of the American economy has seen the spreading of wealth to middle- and lower-income groups. Thus in 1929 the richest 20 percent of Americans received almost 60 percent of the money every year. But by 1960 the same group received only about 45 percent. After 1960 this kind of democratic change slowed almost to a stop. Almost no shift occurred in the distribution of income over the next dozen years. Clearly, the problem of poverty was not being solved by economic growth and change.

A second nagging issue that became increasingly important after the mid-1960s was the mounting problem of urban decay. The failure of Americans to keep their great cities clean, safe,

When the dollar was devalued in February 1973, brokers in international currency were deluged with calls. The dollar's weakness was a sign of the economy's illness.

U.S. GROWTH OF POPULATION, 1920-70

Finally, a new interest in the natural environment began to cast doubt on the wisdom of economic growth itself. This new concern for "ecology" (the delicate relationship between man and his natural surroundings) questioned the very concept of productivity. The criticism of growth by those interested in the environment took many forms. For one thing, ecologists insisted on the necessity of slowing down the rate of population increase, both in the United States and the whole world. Overpopulation threatened massive famines. For another, they warned that the world could support only so much economic activity before it began to collapse. In so doing they awakened a new consciousness of the fragility of the earth's resources and wildlife.

For the first time in their history large numbers of Americans began to worry about such matters as the "death" of Lake Erie, the disappearance of whole species of wildlife, and, by the 1970s, an "energy crisis" that actually threatened shortages of gasoline and electricity. Against such a background President Nixon announced the indefinite postponement of any more manned space explorations. Astronaut Aldrin's biblical question, "What is man?" seemed more urgent—and profound—than ever before.

and livable (despite general prosperity) suggested to some observers that mere growth was not the solution. Partly because of the movement by blacks for civil rights and the rioting that often broke out in large cities, many Americans began to ask for a reexamination of national priorities. They challenged the use of valuable resources for superhighways or moon landings instead of for the more obvious and pressing problems of urban poverty and decay.

Suds from phosphate detergents dumped into Lake Erie created a serious hazard to life along the lakefront. Pollution of the natural environment is one of the ongoing problems of industrial civilization.

A Man and His Dream

MARTIN LUTHER KING, JR., stepped to the microphone and looked out on some 200,000 people still massed patiently on the mall before the Washington Monument. They had been coming to Washington for days. There a great march and demonstration for civil rights and racial equality was to be held. And now, on August 28, 1963, they had listened to speeches and sung hymns and freedom songs almost all day. Many of them were veterans of the 1955–56 bus boycott in Montgomery, Alabama, or of countless other sit-ins and demonstrations that had followed.

Huge as it was, the crowd was only a small part of what many participants called simply the movement. It represented hundreds of local groups that had organized and marched and sat-in and struggled for the integration of schools, lunch counters, hotels, and swimming pools. They worked for better jobs and equal pay for blacks, for the right to vote, for equal housing—for all those concrete goals summed up in the word "freedom." Now, in Martin Luther King, they were about to hear the man who, more than

Two hundred thousand people, black and white, filled the Washington Memorial mall in August 1968 to give a visible form to Martin Luther King's dream of racial harmony.

any other American, was the movement's voice.

His voice could captivate listeners. A well-trained voice of a professional minister, it was deep and strong—with a well-timed tremble on the important words that he wished to emphasize. He had all the skills of the country preacher, black or white: simplicity, repetition, and homely images.

It was the voice of an experienced political leader too. From the beginnings in Montgomery King had become not just a spokesman for the movement but also one of its strategists. He had already organized and led massive protests against segregation. He had learned how to provoke white leaders to serve his cause. Some of his younger followers already complained that he was too conservative, too committed to winning cooperation from white liberals. They would complain more and more as the years passed.

Some complained, too, that King's passionate devotion to nonviolence made the movement weak. In the end, they argued, the only thing white racists could understand was force and power. But King had so far managed to thread his way skillfully through such criticisms and the need to inspire passion in the blacks, who were the only real base of the movement.

King's voice was also that of a man whose courage few people doubted. He had lined up with his followers (many of them children) against policemen's clubs, firehoses, and dogs. Earlier in the year he had gathered thousands of blacks in Birmingham, Alabama, against what was probably the most vicious police repression of a protest demonstration in modern American history. And he had seen the insides of several jails and state prisons as a result of his work. Whenever blacks had become violent, he had gone into saloons and pool halls to plead with them to be gentle and forgive the violence they experienced.

In any other man such passion and such well-publicized courage might have looked a little foolish. It would have been easy for King to seem ridiculous or pretentious. But he always managed, somehow, to stop short of the point where he might become a holier-than-thou joke to less visionary people, white or black.

Today, before the immense crowd, with television cameras focused relentlessly on him, he would prove again that he could put meaning into words like "hope" and "freedom" and "faith." At first he read from the speech he had carefully prepared, hammering away at one point. It had been a hundred years since the Civil War, and still the promises of equality had not been redeemed. One hundred years and black Americans were still crippled, lonely, and poor.

Then King stopped reading and began to improvise, drawing on all his training and experience in the pulpit. He drew, too, on the encouraging shouts and cheers that began to roll up from the crowd. Soon something like an overpowering conversation began to take place. The crowd urged him on, and King repaid their cheering with one ringing phrase after another. "I have a dream today," he began. The noise of the crowd came back to him. It pushed him into a shouted, trembling meditation that soon brought the audience to its feet:

> I have a dream that my four little children will one day live in a nation where they will not be judged by the color of their skin but by the content of their character.

And then, again, the electrifying assertion:

> I have a dream today.

And again, the roar.

> I have a dream that one day the state of Alabama, whose governor's lips are presently dripping with the words of interposition and nullification,[1] will be transformed into a situation where little black boys and black girls will be able to join hands with little white boys and white girls and walk together as sisters and brothers.
> I have a dream today.

Then King passed swiftly into the comforting language of biblical faith:

> I have a dream that one day every valley shall be exalted, every hill and mountain shall be made low, the rough places will be made plain,

[1]Interposition is the idea that a state may oppose a federal policy, such as desegregation, with which it disagrees. Nullification means that a state fails to enforce a particular federal law within its territory.

and the crooked places will be made straight, and the glory of the Lord shall be revealed, and all flesh shall see it together.

The speech already had tremendous emotional impact. But King had still more to say. He chose an American patriotic song for his final theme:

This will be the day when all of God's children will be able to sing with new meaning, "My country, 'tis of thee, sweet land of liberty, of thee I sing. Land where my fathers died, land of the pilgrim's pride, from every mountainside, let freedom ring."

Probably no other man in America could have used such words so movingly. But King had an astonishing talent for giving new toughness to familiar language. So the massive crowd only cheered harder as he went on:

And if America is to be a great nation, this must become true. So let freedom ring from the prodigious hilltops of New Hampshire. Let freedom ring from the mighty mountains of New York. Let freedom ring from the heightening Alleghenies of Pennsylvania!

Let freedom ring from the snowcapped Rockies of Colorado!

Let freedom ring from the curvaceous peaks of California!

But not only that; let freedom ring from Stone Mountain of Georgia!

Let freedom ring from Lookout Mountain of Tennessee!

Martin Luther King, Jr., was the most eloquent spokesman for racial justice in the 1960s. For many, his passionate plea for nonviolence was undercut by his own violent death at the hands of an assassin.

Let freedom ring from every hill and molehill of Mississippi! From every mountainside, let freedom ring!

When we let freedom ring, when we let it ring from every village and every hamlet, from every state and every city, we will be able to speed up that day when all of God's children, black men and white men, Jews and Gentiles, Protestants and Catholics, will be able to join hands and sing in the words of the old Negro spiritual, "Free at last! Free at last! Thank God almighty, we are free at last!"

Judged by his own professional standards, the speech was probably not Martin Luther King's best. But it was really not so much a speech as an event. What he and the crowd had managed to create together was one of those very rare moments when people give expression to their highest ideals and best hopes. Jefferson did it in the opening sentences of the Declaration of Independence. Lincoln did it at Gettysburg. In the last few minutes of his speech King somehow became the conscience of the America of the 1960s.

But against his dream some unhappy realities had to be placed. These realities called him and his movement quickly and regularly back to frustration and failure. Less than three weeks after King put his dream into words, he hurried back to Birmingham. There he had been leading a long protest against segregation. Someone had tossed a bomb into a black church, killing four young girls. In the same day, Birmingham police killed two blacks. At the funeral King spoke bitterly of the "stale bread of hatred and the spoiled meat of racism."

There were some victories for the dream, too. The Civil Rights Act of 1964 was at least as much the creation of King as of Lyndon Johnson. The Nobel Prize for peace he won the same year was one of the highest recognitions the world could give his talents and contributions. Yet there was always the hard and ever-present reality of poverty and racism. The movement stumbled on, often splintered by criticism within. King turned north, taking the movement to Chicago to demand attention for black poverty and deprivation in Northern cities. There he encountered resistance as stiff as any he had met in the South. He became increasingly concerned with the war in Indochina, which he considered an immediate evil almost as important as the old problem of race. The reality of Indochina, too, often seemed incurable.

Five years after his great speech, a frustrated King was trying to plan another march on Washington. This one, he said, would be a "last desperate demand" for an end to "the worst chaos, hatred, and violence any nation has ever encountered." In early April 1968, however, he interrupted the planning to go to Memphis, Tennessee, to help in a strike of black sanitation men against the city. On April 4 he walked onto a balcony outside his motel room and leaned over the rail to talk to a friend in the parking lot two stories below. In a nearby building a rifle fired. The bullet passed through King's jaw and neck; in a short time he was dead.

Social Dreams and Realities

OF ALL THE urges that move Americans probably none is more pronounced than the need to feel that their experience is somehow new and different from other peoples' in other times. Americans keep finding ways to assert they have been singled out for a unique destiny that will separate them from history and move them into a special future. This need is as old as the first English settlements of North America. John Winthrop was fond of reminding his fellow Puritans that they had embarked on an experiment that would set them apart from the rest of mankind.

The leaders of the American Revolution, too, had a deep sense of uniqueness and experimentation. In his turn, Lincoln asked for a "new birth of freedom." Similarly, in the twentieth century, one President after another has tried to identify himself with newness. So we have seen Theodore Roosevelt's New Nationalism, Woodrow Wilson's New Freedom, and Franklin Roosevelt's New Deal. Even conservatives have insisted on the newness of their ideas. Herbert Hoover bravely announced that the United States had entered a "New Era." And Dwight Eisenhower often spoke of a "new prosperity."

But perhaps no generation of Americans has been as touched by the rage for newness as that of the 1960s. John F. Kennedy enjoyed pointing out that the "torch" of leadership had at last been passed to men and women "born in this century." He even called his program the New Frontier.

But if there was any reason to think of the 1960s as truly new or different, the reason did not lie in politics at all. All the political campaigns and crises of the Kennedy, Johnson, and Nixon years were acted out against a background of deep social change and conflict that made presidential politics seem almost irrelevant. Part of the underlying meaning of the "battle of Chicago" was that national politics had continued in a more or less traditional pattern while society at large had undergone fundamental changes.

The enormous public pressure that finally forced Johnson and Nixon to try to end the war in Indochina was also a signal that traditional habits of foreign policy were being rejected by

Among those influenced by King's advocacy of nonviolent tactics was Cesar Chavez, leader of the Mexican American farm workers. Here he ends a twenty-three day fast in support of striking grape growers by breaking bread with Robert Kennedy.

growing numbers of Americans. The moon landing, too, suggested that if the 1960s and 1970s had any unique significance, it was not to be found primarily in politics but rather in deep changes in America's economics and technology.

MOVEMENTS FOR CHANGE

In such an atmosphere, it seemed possible to believe a new era had in fact arrived. In 1963 Martin Luther King's proclamation, "I have a dream," made as much sense as any dream in American history. Not just for the 200,000 or more whites and blacks who assembled to hear King but for millions of others it seemed reasonable to hope that a new era had at last arrived. Old promises of freedom and equality, long-denied and half-forgotten, surfaced again. They found expression in dozens of organized movements demanding peace, equality, or freedom.

The 1960s saw many such movements. As the symbolic leader of the most powerful movement of all, King stood nearer the center of his generation's struggles than any other American. Like the "radicals" at Chicago a few months after his murder, King demanded changes of a political nature—new civil rights laws, for example. But, again like the young demonstrators in Chicago, King expressed a dream that went well beyond politics. In his lifetime dozens of groups of Americans, many of them overlapping, joined militant movements that aimed at change. Women, blacks, Mexican Americans, Indians, homosexuals, college students—one group after another began to complain bitterly about their exploitation by the Establishment and to demand "liberation."

The civil rights movement, for which King spoke so effectively, was the largest and in some ways the most successful. But it was only one movement among many. Growing from it (and adopting many of its tactics) was the whole range of protests and organized demands that gave the period from 1960 onward so much of its unique flavor and tone.

College students on campuses from California to New York organized little "revolutions." They took over buildings, marched, sang, and issued manifestoes demanding an end to the Indochina war. Other Americans engaged in campaigns to legalize abortion, homosexuality, and the use of marijuana. Toward the end of the decade millions of women began crusading for women's liberation, an end to what they regarded as the injustices of a society dominated by men.

All these drives existed on the edges of politics, though they affected politics deeply. Certainly King's speech affected the passage of the Civil Rights Act of 1964, and the peace movement probably forced Lyndon Johnson's decision not to run for reelection in 1968. But they were far more than political phenomena. The movements of the 1960s went deeper into society than politics normally does. They also reflected, more accurately than surface political events, some of the profound changes in the nature of American society.

Moreover, the movements of the period seemed to thrive most on direct action outside the ordinary channels of politics. In the process they created a new vocabulary and a new style of behavior. The new vocabulary was full of words like "protest," "demand," "demonstration," and "confrontation." The new style was one of action, often illegal and sometimes violent and deadly.

RESISTANCE AND POLARIZATION

To most Americans—especially to those who were not black or Puerto-Rican, young, or students in college—all these movements and their loud demands were frightening. Public opinion polls showed very clearly that a majority of Americans actually approved the way the Chicago police had handled the demonstrations.

The movement for black civil rights inspired other movements like Women's Liberation. These demonstrators use the foremost symbol of freedom as the backdrop for their demands for political and economic equality.

And, for all the vocal opposition to the Indochina war that students and others created, this war was supported most of the time by an equal number of citizens.

Such ordinary Americans—the people Richard Nixon called the silent majority, or middle America—were shocked by the "radicalism" of many of the groups of the 1960s. To them, and to most of their professional political leaders, it was painfully obvious that black "militants," "hippies," and student "revolutionaries" represented a critical danger to the country. It was among this decided majority of Americans that Republicans like Richard Nixon and conservative Democrats like George Wallace and Richard Daley found their base of support.

This conflict between a confused, sometimes frightened, and often angry middle America on one side and those demanding social change on the other gave the years after 1960 much of their air of crisis. The lines seemed clearly drawn. At one pole stood millions of people demanding changes in society, in laws, in politics, even in what many people regarded as simple good manners. At the other pole was the desire by this not-always-silent majority for "law and order." The slogan, a rather vague phrase, stood for the preservation of traditional patterns of family life, race relations, and attitudes toward drugs, pornography, abortion, plus many other social details.

Part of the genius of Martin Luther King's 1963 speech was the skill with which he attempted to cut through the atmosphere of polarization. His Washington audience was at least one-fourth white. The television audience was many times as large and doubtless had even more whites. For this audience King was able to link civil rights closely to the most cherished rhetoric of patriotic Americans—even to the music they had all learned in schools: "From every mountainside, let freedom ring."

BLACK MILITANCY

But King's experience after 1963 also mirrored the increasing tensions and frustrations of a divided society. In all the movements of protest and reform there were growing demands for more immediate change, more direct action, more violence. Long before King's assassination, a struggle had developed among young black leaders. It would eventually challenge the essentially nonviolent definition that King wanted his own group to have. The challenge focused on

Within a decade the tone of the civil rights movement changed dramatically. Quiet picketing gave way to strident mass protest. Rising expectations and growing frustrations offer some explanation.

what quickly became known as militancy. Some black leaders thought King's tactics were too slow, too peaceful, and too dependent on white cooperation. So they demanded a more aggressive strategy.

In 1966, two years before King's death, two of the most important black organizations underwent fierce struggles for control between militants and moderates. In the Student Nonviolent Coordinating Committee (the group that had begun the sit-ins of the early 1960s) a young man named Stokely Carmichael, whose slogan would soon become "Black Power," won control. The Congress of Racial Equality elected a young, aggressive leader named Floyd McKissick.

Even before this, another black, much more radical than King, Malcolm Little (or Malcolm X as he was known after he joined the religious and militant Black Muslims) had already presented a serious challenge to King's moderate leadership in New York and other Northern cities. Malcolm X himself was killed at a New York rally in 1965. His death—combined with King's and with the killing of several Black Panther party leaders in Chicago in 1970—opened the way for a more and more splintered contest for public leadership of black Americans.

UNANSWERED QUESTIONS

No one—not even King—really knew the answers to two critical questions: Who really spoke for black America? Even more fundamentally, did "the black community" really exist as a unified social and political whole? As far as voting statistics and other figures indicated, militant leaders had only a small following. Millions of blacks seemed to be going quietly about their daily lives. In the process they appeared to be changing an impressive range of statistics about the place of black people in American society.

In the 1960s, for example, the proportion of blacks whose jobs could be labeled skilled, clerical, or professional increased from about one out of every five to one out of every three. At the same time the proportion of blacks finishing

high school jumped from a little over one-third to almost two-thirds. In the South the number of blacks attending integrated schools rose from only 6 percent in 1965 to 38 percent in 1969. In Northern cities family income among blacks rose from about 75 percent of the figure for whites in 1960 to practical equality in 1970.

But despite such encouraging statistics, a turn for the worse appeared about 1970. Over the next three years black family income actually declined in proportion to that of whites. And unemployment statistics (which had improved during the 1960s) once again became even worse for blacks than for whites. Educational statistics continued to improve. But in the tough reality of jobs and income the situation of blacks seemed to be starting a slide downward from some of the gains of the preceding decade.

At the same time it was also obvious that the poorest group of Americans by far was still the lower-income fifth of the black population. In Northern cities great black ghettos had been created in the years since World War II. Nothing could hide the fact that the millions who lived in them did not participate at all in whatever overall improvement took place in the general condition of blacks.

It was undeniably true that blacks who happened to be well off were making progress in political terms. Thurgood Marshall became the first black justice on the Supreme Court; Edward Brooke of Massachusetts was elected as the first black senator since Reconstruction; Robert Weaver was the first black man ever appointed to the Cabinet. The election of black mayors in Cleveland, Newark, and Los Angeles also appeared to be a sign of very real gains. Yet such facts as these could not hide the equally obvious truth that those blacks who were poor and obscure lived lives that were wracked with hunger, disease, drugs, crime, and early death.

Black poverty continued to provide the widespread potential constituency for such organizations as the Black Panther party and the Black Muslims. There was no lack of evidence of violent unrest among urban black populations in the cities outside the South. In 1964, just one

Slums such as this one in the Brownsville section of New York are a continuing reminder that King's dream of equality is still a task for the nation into its third century of existence.

year after King announced his hopeful dream, New York's Harlem exploded into rioting and burning that shocked and surprised the entire nation.

Similar outbreaks of violence followed during the next four years in the Watts area of Los Angeles, as well as in Chicago, Detroit, Newark, New Haven, Washington, Cleveland, and a dozen other important cities. The "disturbances" were not planned. They were not the result of any kind of "conspiracy" among black radicals. They even had some beneficial results. It was partially in response to urban violence that new antidiscrimination laws and programs for the relief of poverty were passed.

Still, the powerful fact that millions of poor black people packed into urban ghettos were deeply hostile to the system of law and stability was a source of anxiety to millions of Americans, both black and white. For reasons that were almost impossible to grasp, the intensity of urban violence, of confrontation of all kinds, in almost all the movements of the 1960s began to slacken off after 1970. Whatever the reason for the relative peace of these years, it was most certainly not that the problems of the 1960s had been solved. True, the war in Indochina appeared to be over. However, every other complaint of the troubled Kennedy and Johnson years still remained.

Above all, it remained an open question whether Americans could—or would—ever deal successfully with the problems of racism and black poverty that Martin Luther King had dreamed of solving. His dream was one kind of answer. His assassination was another. Both were answers rooted in the American past. But no one could tell which answer would be final—whether the riots and assassinations would continue a long history of blunders and failures or whether the dream of 1963 would ever be realized.

1. Was the agreement that led to the removal of Russian missiles from Cuba of greater advantage to the United States or to Russia?
2. How does the existence of "client" nations prevent the full relaxation of Soviet-American tensions? Which of these client relationships do you think is potentially the most dangerous?
3. In what way did the increasing cost of arms help bring on the detente? How did the increasing number of power centers in the world help?
4. Is the Alliance for Progress a continuation of dollar diplomacy? Is the military intervention in Indochina a justifiable extension of the containment policy?
5. Why did demonstrators gather in Chicago for the Democratic National Convention in 1968? Why were they so pessimistic about their chances of success?
6. Show how Kennedy's philosophy is basically New Deal–Fair Deal.
7. What programs made up Johnson's "Great Society"? Given his domestic record do you think he could have run successfully in 1968?
8. In what ways did Nixon try to change the political direction of the country?
9. Why is the American economy today referred to as a consumer economy? a service economy? What is the connection between this country's affluence and its ecological problems?
10. What was the significance of Martin Luther King's "I Have a Dream" speech? Why was King's leadership rejected by the militants?

Beyond the Text

1. American interventions in Laos, the Dominican Republic, and Vietnam seem to have been initiated on behalf of unpopular but anticommunist governments. Should the United States support such governments?
2. Debate the proposition: The Expenditure of Vast Sums of Money to Reach the Moon Is Money Unwisely Spent.
3. It is claimed that black liberation movements often set the style and tone of other movements in the 1960s. Compare the goals and tactics of women, Mexican Americans, Indians, and other minority groups to test this statement's validity.

Bibliography

Nonfiction

Ashby, Darell, ed., *The Discontented Society.**
Berman, Ronald, *America in the Sixties.**
Burner, David, Robert Marcus, and Thomas West, *A Giant's Strength: America in the 1960s.**
Cleaver, Eldridge, *Soul on Ice.**
Draper, Theodore, *Abuse of Power.**
Fall, Bernard B., *Viet-Nam Witness: 1953–1966.*
Friedan, Betty, *The Feminine Mystique.**
Goldman, Eric F., *Tragedy of Lyndon Johnson.**
King, Martin Luther, *Why We Can't Wait.**
Muse, Benjamin, *The American Negro Revolution.**
Phillips, Kevin, *The Emerging Republican Majority.**
Schlesinger, Arthur M., Jr., *Thousand Days.**
Shaplen, Robert, *Time Out of Hand: Revolution & Reaction in Southeast Asia.**
Sullivan, Walter, ed., *America's Race for the Moon.*
White, Theodore H., *The Making of the President, 1964,* 1968,* 1972.*

Fiction

Brown, Claude, *Manchild in the Promised Land.**
Kesey, Ken, *One Flew Over the Cuckoo's Nest.**
Wolfe, Tom, *Electric Kool-Aid Acid Test.**

*a paperback book

THE DECLARATION OF INDEPENDENCE

In Congress, July 4, 1776. *The unanimous Declaration of the thirteen united States of America,*

When in the Course of human events, it becomes necessary for one people to dissolve the political bands which have connected them with another, and to assume among the powers of the earth, the separate and equal station to which the Laws of Nature and of Nature's God entitle them, a decent respect to the opinions of mankind requires that they should declare the causes which impel them to the separation.—

We hold these truths to be self-evident, that all men are created equal, that they are endowed by their Creator with certain unalienable Rights, that among these are Life, Liberty and the pursuit of Happiness.—

That to secure these rights, Governments are instituted among Men, deriving their just powers from the consent of the governed,—

That whenever any Form of Government becomes destructive of these ends, it is the Right of the People to alter or to abolish it, and to institute new Government, laying its foundation on such principles and organizing its powers in such form, as to them shall seem most likely to effect their Safety and Happiness. Prudence, indeed, will dictate that Governments long established should not be changed for light and transient causes; and accordingly all experience hath shown, that mankind are more disposed to suffer, while evils are sufferable, than to right themselves by abolishing the forms to which they are accustomed. But when a long train of abuses and usurpations, pursuing invariably the same Object evinces a design to reduce them under absolute Despotism, it is their right, it is their duty, to throw off such Government, and to provide new Guards for their future security.—

Such has been the patient sufferance of these Colonies; and such is now the necessity which constrains them to alter their former Systems of Government. The history of the present King of Great Britain is a history of repeated injuries and usurpations, all having in direct object the establishment of an absolute Tyranny over these States. To prove this, let Facts be submitted to a candid world.—

He has refused his Assent to Laws, the most wholesome and necessary for the public good.—

He has forbidden his Governors to pass Laws of immediate and pressing importance, unless suspended in their operation till his Assent should be obtained; and when so suspended, he has utterly neglected to attend to them.—

He has refused to pass other Laws for the accommodation of large districts of people, unless those people would relinquish the right of Representation in the Legislature, a right inestimable to them and formidable to tyrants only.—

He has called together legislative bodies at places unusual, uncomfortable, and distant from the depository of their public Records, for the sole purpose of fatiguing them into compliance with his measures.—

He has dissolved Representative Houses repeatedly, for opposing with manly firmness his invasions on the rights of the people.—

He has refused for a long time, after such dissolutions, to cause others to be elected; whereby the Legislative powers, incapable of Annihilation, have returned to the People at large for their exercise; the State remaining in the mean time exposed to all the dangers of invasion from without, and convulsions within.—

He has endeavoured to prevent the population of these States; for that purpose obstructing the Laws for Naturalization of Foreigners; refusing to pass others to encourage their migrations hither, and raising the conditions of new Appropriations of Lands.—

He has obstructed the Administration of Justice, by refusing his Assent to Laws for establishing Judiciary powers.—

He has made Judges dependent on his Will alone, for the tenure of their offices, and the amount and payment of their salaries.—

He has erected a multitude of New Offices, and sent hither swarms of Officers to harrass our people, and eat out their substance.—

He has kept among us in times of peace, Standing Armies without the Consent of our legislatures.—

He has affected to render the Military independent of and superior to the Civil power.—

He has combined with others to subject us to a jurisdiction foreign to our constitution, and unacknowledged by our laws; giving his Assent to their Acts of pretended Legislation:—

For quartering large bodies of armed troops among us:—

For protecting them, by a mock Trial, from punishment for any Murders which they should commit on the Inhabitants of these States:—

For cutting off our Trade with all parts of the world:—

For imposing Taxes on us without our Consent:—

For depriving us in many cases, of the benefits of Trial by Jury:—

For transporting us beyond Seas to be tried for pretended offences:—

For abolishing the free System of English Laws in a neighbouring Province, establishing therein an Arbitrary government, and enlarging its Boundaries so as to render it at once an example and fit instrument for introducing the same absolute rule in these Colonies:—

For taking away our Charters, abolishing our most valuable Laws, and altering fundamentally the Forms of our Governments:—

For suspending our own Legislatures, and declaring themselves invested with power to legislate for us in all cases whatsoever.—

He has abdicated Government here, by declaring us out of his Protection and waging War against us.—

He has plundered our seas, ravaged our Coasts, burnt our towns, and destroyed the lives of our people.—

He is at this time transporting large Armies of foreign Mercenaries to compleat the works of death, desolation and tyranny, already begun with circumstances of Cruelty & perfidy scarcely paralleled in the most barbarous ages, and totally unworthy the Head of a civilized nation.—

He has constrained our fellow Citizens taken Captive on the high Seas to bear Arms against their Country, to become the executioners of their friends and Brethren, or to fall themselves by their Hands.—

He has excited domestic insurrections amongst us, and has endeavoured to bring on the inhabitants of our frontiers, the merciless Indian Savages, whose known rule of warfare, is an undistinguished destruction of all ages, sexes and conditions.

In every stage of these Oppressions We have Petitioned for Redress in the most humble terms: Our repeated Petitions have been answered only by repeated injury. A Prince, whose character is thus marked by every act which may define a Tyrant, is unfit to be the ruler of a free people.

Nor have We been wanting in attentions to our British brethren. We have warned them from time to time of attempts by their legislature to extend an unwarrantable jurisdiction over us. We have reminded them of the circumstances of our emigration and settlement here. We have appealed to their native justice and magnanimity, and we have conjured them by the ties of our common kindred to disavow these usurpations, which, would inevitably interrupt our connections and correspondence. They too have been deaf to the voice of justice and of consanguinity. We must, therefore, acquiesce in the necessity, which denounces our Separation, and hold them, as we hold the rest of mankind, Enemies in War, in Peace Friends.—

We, therefore, the Representatives of the united States of America, in General Congress, Assembled, appealing to the Supreme Judge of the world for the rectitude of our intentions, do, in the Name, and by Authority of the good People of these Colonies, solemnly publish and declare, That these United Colonies are, and of Right ought to be, Free and Independent States; that they are absolved from all Allegiance to the British Crown, and that all political connection between them and the State of Great Britain, is and ought to be totally dissolved; and that as Free and Independent States they have full Power to levy War, conclude Peace, contract Alliances, establish Commerce, and to do all other Acts and Things which Independent States may of right do.—

And for the support of this Declaration, with a firm reliance on the protection of divine Providence, we mutually pledge to each other our Lives, our Fortunes and our sacred Honor.

John Hancock
(MASSACHUSETTS)

NEW HAMPSHIRE
Josiah Bartlett
William Whipple
Matthew Thornton

MASSACHUSETTS
Samuel Adams
John Adams
Robert Treat Paine
Elbridge Gerry

DELAWARE
Caesar Rodney
George Read
Thomas McKean

NEW YORK
William Floyd
Philip Livingston
Francis Lewis
Lewis Morris

NEW JERSEY
Richard Stockton
John Witherspoon
Francis Hopkinson
John Hart
Abraham Clark

NORTH CAROLINA
William Hooper
Joseph Hewes
John Penn

MARYLAND
Samuel Chase
William Paca
Thomas Stone
Charles Carroll
    of Carrollton

SOUTH CAROLINA
Edward Rutledge
Thomas Heywood, Jr.
Thomas Lynch, Jr.
Arthur Middleton

RHODE ISLAND
Stephen Hopkins
William Ellery

CONNECTICUT
Roger Sherman
Samuel Huntington
William Williams
Oliver Wolcott

PENNSYLVANIA
Robert Morris
Benjamin Rush
Benjamin Franklin
John Morton
George Clymer
James Smith
George Taylor
James Wilson
George Ross

VIRGINIA
George Wythe
Richard Henry Lee
Thomas Jefferson
Benjamin Harrison
Thomas Nelson, Jr.
Francis Lightfoot Lee
Carter Braxton

GEORGIA
Button Gwinnett
Lyman Hall
George Walton

THE CONSTITUTION OF THE
UNITED STATES OF AMERICA

We the People of the United States, in Order to form a more perfect Union, establish Justice, insure domestic Tranquility, provide for the common defence, promote the general Welfare, and secure the Blessings of Liberty to ourselves and our Posterity, do ordain and establish this Constitution for the United States of America.

> The preamble establishes the principle of government by the people, and lists the six basic purposes of the Constitution.

ARTICLE I • LEGISLATIVE DEPARTMENT

Section 1. All legislative Powers herein granted shall be vested in a Congress of the United States, which shall consist of a Senate and House of Representatives.

Section 2. The House of Representatives shall be composed of Members chosen every second Year by the People of the several States, and the Electors in each State shall have the Qualifications requisite for Electors of the most numerous Branch of the State Legislature.

> Representatives serve two-year terms. They are chosen in each state by those electors (that is, voters) who are qualified to vote for members of the lower house of their own state legislature.

No Person shall be a Representative who shall not have attained to the Age of twenty-five Years, and been seven Years a Citizen of the United States, and who shall not, when elected, be an Inhabitant of that State in which he shall be chosen.

Representatives and direct Taxes shall be apportioned among the several States which may be included within this Union, according to their respective Numbers, which shall be determined by adding to the whole Number of free Persons, including those bound to Service for a Term of Years, and excluding Indians not taxed, three-fifths of all other Persons. The actual Enumeration shall be made within three Years after the first Meeting of the Congress of the United States, and within every subsequent Term of ten

> The number of representatives allotted to a state is determined by the size of its population. The 14th Amendment has made obsolete the reference to "all other persons"—that is, slaves.
>
> A census must be taken every ten years to determine the number of representatives to which each state is entitled. There is now one representative for about every 470,000 persons.

Source: House Document #529. U.S. Government Printing Office, 1967.
[NOTE: *The Constitution and the amendments are reprinted here in their original form. Portions that have been amended or superseded are in brown type.] The words printed in the margins explain some of the more difficult passages.*

Years, in such Manner as they shall by Law direct. The Number of Representatives shall not exceed one for every thirty Thousand, but each State shall have at Least one Representative; and until such enumeration shall be made, the State of New Hampshire shall be entitled to chuse three, Massachusetts eight, Rhode Island and Providence Plantations one, Connecticut five, New York six, New Jersey four, Pennsylvania eight, Delaware one, Maryland six, Virginia ten, North Carolina five, South Carolina five, and Georgia three.

"Executive authority" refers to the governor of a state.

When vacancies happen in the Representation from any State, the Executive Authority thereof shall issue Writs of Election to fill such Vacancies.

The Speaker, chosen by and from the majority party, presides over the House. Impeachment is the act of bringing formal charges against an official. (See also Section 3.)

The House of Representatives shall chuse their Speaker and other Officers; and shall have the sole Power of Impeachment.

Section 3. The Senate of the United States shall be composed of two Senators from each State, chosen by the Legislature thereof, for six Years; and each Senator shall have one Vote.

The 17th Amendment changed this method to direct election.

Immediately after they shall be assembled in Consequence of the first Election, they shall be divided as equally as may be into three Classes. The Seats of the Senators of the first Class shall be vacated at the Expiration of the second Year, of the second Class at the Expiration of the fourth Year, and of the third Class at the Expiration of the sixth Year, so that one third may be chosen every second Year; and if Vacancies happen by Resignation, or otherwise, during the Recess of the Legislature of any State, the Executive thereof may make temporary Appointments until the next Meeting of the Legislature, which shall then fill such Vacancies.

The 17th Amendment also provides that a state governor shall appoint a successor to fill a vacant Senate seat until a direct election is held.

No Person shall be a Senator who shall not have attained to the Age of thirty Years, and been nine Years a Citizen of the United States, and who shall not, when elected, be an Inhabitant of that State for which he shall be chosen.

The Vice President may cast a vote in the Senate only in order to break a tie.

The Vice President of the United States shall be President of the Senate, but shall have no Vote, unless they be equally divided.

The president *pro tempore* of the Senate is a temporary officer; the Latin words mean "for the time being."

The Senate shall chuse their other Officers, and also a President pro tempore, in the absence of the Vice President, or when he shall exercise the Office of President of the United States.

No President has ever been successfully impeached. In 1868 the Senate fell one vote short of the two-thirds majority needed to convict Andrew Johnson. Twelve other officials —ten federal judges, one senator, and one Secretary of War—have been impeached; four of the judges were convicted.

The Senate shall have the sole Power to try all Impeachments. When sitting for that Purpose, they shall be on Oath or Affirmation. When the President of the United States is tried, the Chief Justice shall preside: And no Person shall be convicted without the Concurrence of two thirds of the Members present.

Judgment in Cases of Impeachment shall not extend further than to removal from Office, and disqualification to hold and enjoy any Office of Honor, Trust or Profit under the United States: but the Party convicted shall nevertheless be liable and subject to Indictment, Trial, Judgment and Punishment, according to Law.

Elections for Congress are held on the first Tuesday after the first Monday in November in even-numbered years.

Section 4. The Times, Places and Manner of holding Elections for Senators and Representatives, shall be prescribed in each State by the Legislature thereof; but the Congress may at any time by Law make or alter such Regulations, except as to the Place of chusing Senators.

The 20th Amendment designates January 3 as the opening of the congressional session.

The Congress shall assemble at least once in every Year, and such Meeting shall be on the first Monday in December, unless they shall by Law appoint a different Day.

Section 5. Each House shall be the Judge of the Elections, Returns and Qualifications of its own Members, and a Majority of each shall constitute a Quorum to do Business; but a smaller number may adjourn from day to day, and may be authorized to compel the Attendance of absent Members, in such Manner, and under such Penalties as each House may provide.

Each House may determine the Rules of its Proceedings, punish its Members for disorderly Behavior, and, with the Concurrence of two thirds, expel a Member.

Each House shall keep a Journal of its Proceedings, and from time to time publish the same, excepting such Parts as may in their Judgment require Secrecy; and the Yeas and Nays of the Members of either House on any question shall, at the Desire of one fifth of those Present, be entered on the Journal.

Neither House, during the Session of Congress, shall, without the Consent of the other, adjourn for more than three days, nor to any other Place than that in which the two Houses shall be sitting.

Each house of Congress decides whether a member has been elected properly and is qualified to be seated. (A quorum is the minimum number of persons required to be present in order to conduct business.) The House once refused admittance to an elected representative who had been guilty of a crime. The Senate did likewise in the case of a candidate whose election campaign lent itself to "fraud and corruption."

Section 6. The Senators and Representatives shall receive a Compensation for their Services, to be ascertained by Law, and paid out of the Treasury of the United States. They shall in all Cases, except Treason, Felony and Breach of the Peace, be privileged from Arrest during their Attendance at the Session of their respective Houses, and in going to and returning from the same; and for any Speech or Debate in either House, they shall not be questioned in any other Place.

No Senator or Representative shall, during the Time for which he was elected, be appointed to any civil Office under the Authority of the United States, which shall have been created, or the Emoluments whereof shall have been encreased during such time; and no Person holding any Office under the United States, shall be a Member of either House during his Continuance in Office.

Congressmen have the power to fix their own salaries. Under the principle of congressional immunity, they cannot be sued or arrested for anything they say in a congressional debate. This provision enables them to speak freely.

This clause reinforces the principle of separation of powers by stating that, during his term of office, a member of Congress may not be appointed to a position in another branch of government. Nor may he resign and accept a position created during his term.

Section 7. All Bills for raising Revenue shall originate in the House of Representatives; but the Senate may propose or concur with Amendments as on other Bills.

Every Bill which shall have passed the House of Representatives and the Senate, shall, before it become a Law, be presented to the President of the United States; If he approve he shall sign it, but if not he shall return it, with his Objections to that House in which it shall have originated, who shall enter the Objections at large on their Journal, and proceed to reconsider it. If after such Reconsideration two thirds of that House shall agree to pass the Bill, it shall be sent, together with the Objections, to the other House, by which it shall likewise be reconsidered, and if approved by two thirds of that House, it shall become a Law. But in all such Cases the Votes of both Houses shall be determined by Yeas and Nays, and the Names of the Persons voting for and against the Bill shall be entered on the Journal of each House respectively. If any Bill shall not be returned by the President within ten Days (Sundays excepted) after it shall have been presented to him, the Same shall be a Law, in like Manner as if he had signed it, unless the Congress by their Adjournment prevent its Return, in which Case it shall not be a Law.

Every Order, Resolution, or Vote to which the Concurrence of the Senate and House of Representatives may be necessary (except on a question of Adjournment) shall be presented to the President of the United States; and before the Same shall take Effect, shall be approved by him, or being disapproved by him, shall be repassed by two thirds of the Senate and House of Representatives, according to the Rules and Limitations prescribed in the Case of a Bill.

The House initiates tax bills but the Senate may propose changes in them.

By returning a bill unsigned to the house in which it originated, the President exercises a veto. A two-thirds majority in both houses can override the veto. If the President receives a bill within the last ten days of a session and does not sign it, the measure dies by pocket veto. Merely by keeping the bill in his pocket, so to speak, the president effects a veto.

The same process of approval or disapproval by the President is applied to resolutions and other matters passed by both houses (except adjournment).

These are the *delegated,* or *enumerated,* powers of Congress.

Duties are taxes on imported goods; *excises* are taxes on goods manufactured, sold, or consumed within the country. *Imposts* is a general term including both duties and excise taxes.

Naturalization is the process by which an alien becomes a citizen.

Government *securities* include savings bonds and other notes.

Authors' and inventors' rights are protected by copyright and patent laws.

Congress may establish lower federal courts.

Only Congress may declare war. *Letters of marque and reprisal* grant merchant ships permission to attack enemy vessels.

Militia refers to national guard units, which may become part of the United States Army during an emergency. Congress aids the states in maintaining their national guard units.

This clause gives Congress the power to govern what became the District of Columbia, as well as other federal sites.

Known as the *elastic clause,* this provision enables Congress to exercise many powers not specifically granted to it by the Constitution.

Section 8. The Congress shall have Power to lay and collect Taxes, Duties, Imposts and Excises, to pay the Debts and provide for the common Defence and general Welfare of the United States; but all Duties, Imposts and Excises shall be uniform throughout the United States;

To borrow money on the credit of the United States;

To regulate Commerce with foreign Nations, and among the several States, and with the Indian Tribes;

To establish an uniform Rule of Naturalization, and uniform Laws on the subject of Bankruptcies throughout the United States;

To coin Money, regulate the Value thereof, and of foreign Coin, and fix the Standard of Weights and Measures;

To provide for the Punishment of counterfeiting the Securities and current Coin of the United States;

To establish Post Offices and post Roads;

To promote the Progress of Science and useful Arts, by securing for limited Times to Authors and Inventors the exclusive Right to their respective Writings and Discoveries;

To constitute Tribunals inferior to the supreme Court;

To define and punish Piracies and Felonies committed on the high Seas, and Offenses against the Law of Nations;

To declare War, grant Letters of Marque and Reprisal, and make Rules concerning Captures on Land and Water;

To raise and support Armies, but no Appropriation of Money to that Use shall be for a longer Term than two Years;

To provide and maintain a Navy;

To make Rules for the Government and Regulation of the land and naval Forces;

To provide for calling forth the Militia to execute the Laws of the Union, suppress Insurrections and repel Invasions;

To provide for organizing, arming, and disciplining the Militia, and for governing such Part of them as may be employed in the Service of the United States, reserving to the States respectively, the Appointment of the Officers, and the Authority of training the Militia according to the discipline prescribed by Congress;

To exercise exclusive Legislation in all Cases whatsoever, over such District (not exceeding ten Miles square) as may, by Cession of particular States, and the acceptance of Congress, become the Seat of the Government of the United States, and to exercise like Authority over all Places purchased by the Consent of the Legislature of the State in which the Same shall be, for the Erection of Forts, Magazines, Arsenals, dock-Yards, and other needful Buildings;—And

To make all Laws which shall be necessary and proper for carrying into Execution the foregoing Powers, and all other Powers vested by this Constitution in the Government of the United States, or in any Department or Officer thereof.

This clause concerns the slave trade, which Congress did ban in 1808.

The *writ of habeas corpus* permits a prisoner to appear before a judge to inquire into the legality of his or her detention.

Section 9. The Migration or Importation of such Persons as any of the States now existing shall think proper to admit, shall not be prohibited by the Congress prior to the Year one thousand eight hundred and eight, but a tax or duty may be imposed on such Importation, not exceeding ten dollars for each Person.

The privilege of the Writ of Habeas Corpus shall not be suspended unless when in Cases of Rebellion or Invasion the public Safety may require it.

No Bill of Attainder or ex post facto Law shall be passed.

No capitation, or other direct, Tax shall be laid, unless in Proportion to the Census or Enumeration herein before directed to be taken.

No Tax or Duty shall be laid on Articles exported from any State.

No Preference shall be given by any Regulation of Commerce or Revenue to the Ports of one State over those of another; nor shall Vessels bound to, or from, one State, be obliged to enter, clear, or pay Duties in another.

No Money shall be drawn from the Treasury, but in Consequence of Appropriations made by Law; and a regular Statement and Account of the Receipts and Expenditures of all public Money shall be published from time to time.

No Title of Nobility shall be granted by the United States: And no Person holding any Office of Profit or Trust under them, shall, without the Consent of the Congress, accept of any present, Emolument, Office, or Title, of any kind whatever, from any King, Prince, or foreign State.

Section 10. No State shall enter into any Treaty, Alliance, or Confederation; grant Letters of Marque and Reprisal; coin Money; emit Bills of Credit; make any Thing but gold and silver Coin a Tender in Payment of Debts; pass any Bill of Attainder, ex post facto Law, or Law impairing the Obligation of Contracts, or grant any Title of Nobility.

No State shall, without the Consent of the Congress, lay any Imposts or Duties on Imports or Exports, except what may be absolutely necessary for executing its inspection Laws: and the net Produce of all Duties and Imposts, laid by any State on Imports or Exports, shall be for the Use of the Treasury of the United States; and all such Laws shall be subject to the Revision and Controul of the Congress.

No State shall, without the Consent of Congress, lay any duty of Tonnage, keep Troops, or Ships of War in time of Peace, enter into any Agreement or Compact with another State, or with a foreign Power, or engage in War, unless actually invaded, or in such imminent Danger as will not admit of delay.

ARTICLE II • EXECUTIVE DEPARTMENT

Section 1. The executive Power shall be vested in a President of the United States of America. He shall hold his Office during the Term of four Years, and, together with the Vice President, chosen for the same Term, be elected, as follows.

Each State shall appoint, in such Manner as the Legislature thereof may direct, a Number of Electors, equal to the whole Number of Senators and Representatives to which the State may be entitled in the Congress: but no Senator or Representative, or Person holding an Office of Trust or Profit under the United States, shall be appointed an Elector.

The Electors shall meet in their respective States, and vote by Ballot for two persons, of whom one at least shall not be an Inhabitant of the same State with themselves. And they shall make a List of all the Persons voted for, and of the Number of Votes for each; which List they shall sign and certify, and transmit sealed to the Seat of the Government of the United States, directed to the President of the Senate. The President of the Senate shall, in the Presence of the Senate and House of Representatives, open all the Certificates, and the Votes shall then be counted. The Person having the greatest Number of Votes shall be the President, if such Number be a Majority of the whole Number of Electors appointed; and if there be more than one who have such Majority, and have an equal

---

Marginal notes:

A *bill of attainder* is an act of legislation that declares a person guilty of a crime and punishes him or her without a trial. An *ex post facto* law punishes a person for an act that was legal when performed but later declared illegal.

The object of Clause 4 was to bar direct (per person) taxation of slaves for the purpose of abolishing slavery. The 16th Amendment modified this provision by giving Congress the power to tax personal income.

States are hereby forbidden to exercise certain powers. Some of these powers belong to Congress alone; others are considered undemocratic.

States cannot, without congressional authority, tax goods that enter or leave, except for a small inspection fee.

Federal officials are ineligible to serve as presidential electors.

The 12th Amendment superseded this clause. The weakness of the original constitutional provision became apparent in the election of 1800, when Thomas Jefferson and Aaron Burr received the same number of electoral votes. The 12th Amendment avoids this possibility by requiring electors to cast separate ballots for President and Vice President.

Number of Votes, then the House of Representatives shall immediately chuse by Ballot one of them for President; and if no Person have a Majority, then from the five highest on the List the said House shall in like Manner chuse the President. But in chusing the President, the Votes shall be taken by States, the Representation from each State having one Vote; a quorum for this Purpose shall consist of a Member or Members from two thirds of the States, and a Majority of all the States shall be necessary to a Choice. In every Case, after the Choice of the President, the Person having the greatest Number of Votes of the Electors shall be the Vice President. But if there should remain two or more who have equal Votes, the Senate shall chuse from them by Ballot the Vice President.

The Congress may determine the Time of chusing the Electors, and the Day on which they shall give their Votes; which Day shall be the same throughout the United States.

A naturalized citizen may not become President.

No person except a natural born Citizen, or a Citizen of the United States, at the time of the Adoption of this Constitution, shall be eligible to the Office of President; neither shall any Person be eligible to that Office who shall not have attained to the Age of Thirty-five Years, and been fourteen Years a Resident within the United States.

The Vice President is next in line for the presidency. A federal law passed in 1947 determined the order of presidential succession as follows: (1) Speaker of the House; (2) president *pro tempore* of the Senate; and (3) Cabinet officers in the order in which their departments were created. (So far, death has been the only circumstance under which a presidential term has been cut short.) This clause has been amplified by the 25th Amendment.

In Case of the Removal of the President from Office, or of his Death, Resignation, or Inability to discharge the Powers and Duties of the said Office, the same shall devolve on the Vice-President, and the Congress may by Law provide for the Case of Removal, Death, Resignation or Inabiltiy, both of the President and the Vice President, declaring what Officer shall then act as President, and such Officer shall act accordingly, until the Disability be removed, or a President shall be elected.

The President shall, at stated Times, receive for his Services, a Compensation, which shall neither be encreased nor diminished during the Period for which he shall have been elected, and he shall not receive within that Period any other Emolument from the United States, or any of them.

Before he enter on the Execution of his Office, he shall take the following Oath or Affirmation:—"I do solemnly swear (or affirm) that I will faithfully execute the Office of the President of the United States, and will to the best of my Ability, preserve, protect and defend the Constitution of the United States."

This clause suggests written communication between the President and "the principal officer in each of the executive departments." As it developed, these officials comprise the Cabinet—whose members are chosen, and may be replaced, by the President.

Section 2. The President shall be Commander in Chief of the Army and Navy of the United States, and of the Militia of the several States, when called into the actual Service of the United States; he may require the Opinion in writing, of the principal Officer in each of the executive Departments, upon any subject relating to the Duties of their respective Offices, and he shall have Power to Grant Reprieves and Pardons for Offenses against the United States, except in Cases of Impeachment.

Senate approval is required for treaties and presidential appointments.

He shall have Power, by and with the Advice and Consent of the Senate, to make by and with the Advice and Consent of the Senate, shall appoint Ambassadors, other Treaties, provided two thirds of the Senators present concur; and he shall nominate, and public Ministers and Consuls, Judges of the supreme Court, and all other Officers of the United States, whose Appointments are not herein otherwise provided for, and which shall be established by Law: but the Congress may by Law vest the Appointment of such inferior Officers, as they think proper, in the President alone, in the Courts of Law, or in the Heads of Departments.

Without the consent of the Senate, the President may appoint officials only on a temporary basis.

The President shall have Power to fill up all Vacancies that may happen during the Recess of the Senate, by granting Commissions which shall expire at the End of their next Session.

Section 3. He shall from time to time give to the Congress Information of the State of the Union, and recommend to their Consideration such Measures as he shall judge necessary and expedient; he may, on extraordinary Occasions, convene both Houses, or either of them, and in Case of Disagreement between them, with Respect to the Time of Adjournment, he may adjourn them to such Time as he shall think proper; he shall receive Ambassadors and other public Ministers; he shall take Care that the Laws be faithfully executed, and shall Commission all the Officers of the United States.

The President delivers a "State of the Union" message at the opening of each session of Congress. Woodrow Wilson was the first President since John Adams to read his messages in person. Franklin D. Roosevelt and his successors followed Wilson's example.

Section 4. The President, Vice President and all civil Officers of the United States, shall be removed from Office on Impeachment for, and Conviction of, Treason, Bribery, or other high Crimes and Misdemeanors.

ARTICLE III • JUDICIAL DEPARTMENT

Section 1. The judicial Power of the United States, shall be vested in one supreme Court, and in such inferior Courts as the Congress may from time to time ordain and establish. The Judges, both of the supreme and inferior Courts, shall hold their Offices during good Behaviour, and shall, at stated Times, receive for their Services, a Compensation, which shall not be diminished during their Continuance in Office.

Federal judges hold office for life and may not have their salaries lowered while in office. These provisions are intended to keep the federal bench independent of political pressure.

Section 2. The judicial Power shall extend to all Cases, in Law and Equity, arising under this Constitution, the Laws of the United States, and Treaties made, or which shall be made, under their Authority;—to all Cases affecting Ambassadors, other public Ministers and Consuls;—to all Cases of admiralty and maritime Jurisdiction;—to Controversies to which the United States shall be a Party;—to Controversies between two or more States;—between a State and Citizens of another State;—between Citizens of different States;—between Citizens of the same State claiming Lands under Grants of different States, and between a State, or the Citizens thereof, and foreign States, Citizens or Subjects.

This clause describes the types of cases that may be heard in federal courts.

The 11th Amendment prevents a citizen from suing a state in a federal court.

In all Cases affecting Ambassadors, other public Ministers and Consuls, and those in which a State shall be Party, the supreme Court shall have original Jurisdiction. In all the other Cases before mentioned, the supreme Court shall have appellate Jurisdiction, both as to Law and Fact, with such Exceptions, and under such Regulations as the Congress shall make.

The Supreme Court handles certain cases directly. It may also review cases handled by lower courts, but Congress in some cases may withhold the right to appeal to the highest court, or limit appeal by setting various conditions.

The trial of all Crimes, except in Cases of Impeachment, shall be by Jury; and such Trial shall be held in the State where the said Crimes shall have been committed; but when not committed within any State, the Trial shall be at such Place or Places as the Congress may by Law have directed.

The 6th Amendment strengthens this clause on trial procedure.

Section 3. Treason against the United States, shall consist only in levying War against them, or in adhering to their Enemies, giving them Aid and Comfort. No Person shall be convicted of Treason unless on the Testimony of two Witnesses to the same overt Act, or on Confession in open Court.

Treason is rigorously defined. A person can be convicted only if two witnesses testify to the same obvious act, or if he confesses in court.

The Congress shall have Power to declare the Punishment of Treason, but no Attainder of Treason shall work Corruption of Blood, or Forfeiture except during the Life of the Person attainted.

Punishment for treason extends only to the person convicted, not to his or her descendants. ("Corruption of blood" means that the heirs of a convicted person are deprived of certain rights.)

ARTICLE IV • RELATIONS AMONG THE STATES

States must honor each other's laws, court decisions, and records (for example, birth, marriage, and death certificates).

Section 1. Full Faith and Credit shall be given in each State to the public Acts, Records, and judicial Proceedings of every other State. And the Congress may by general Laws prescribe the Manner in which such Acts, Records and Proceedings shall be proved, and the Effect thereof.

Each state must respect the rights of citizens of other states.

The process of returning a person accused of a crime to the governmental authority (in this case a state) from which he or she has fled is called *extradition*.

The 13th Amendment, which abolished slavery, makes this clause obsolete.

Section 2. The Citizens of each State shall be entitled to all Privileges and Immunities of Citizens in the several States.

A Person charged in any State with Treason, Felony, or other Crime, who shall flee from Justice, and be found in another State, shall on demand of the executive Authority of the State from which he fled, be delivered up, to be removed to the State having Jurisdiction of the Crime.

No Person held in Service or Labour in one State, under the Laws thereof, escaping into another, shall, in Consequence of any Law or Regulation therein, be discharged from such Service or Labour, but shall be delivered up on Claim of the Party to whom such Service or Labour may be due.

A new state may not be created by dividing or joining existing states unless approved by the legislatures of the states affected and by Congress. An exception to the provision forbidding the division of a state occurred during the Civil War. In 1863 West Virginia was formed out of the western region of Virginia.

Section 3. New States may be admitted by the Congress into this Union; but no new State shall be formed or erected within the Jurisdiction of any other State; nor any State be formed by the Junction of two or more States, or parts of States, without the Consent of the Legislatures of the States concerned as well as of the Congress.

The Congress shall have Power to dispose of and make all needful Rules and Regulations respecting the Territory or other Property belonging to the United States; and nothing in this Constitution shall be so construed as to Prejudice any Claims of the United States, or of any particular State.

A *republican* form of government is one in which citizens choose representatives to govern them. The federal government must protect a state against invasion and, if state authorities request it, against violence within a state.

Section 4. The United States shall guarantee to every State in this Union a Republican Form of Government, and shall protect each of them against Invasion; and on Application of the Legislature, or of the Executive (when the Legislature cannot be convened) against domestic Violence.

ARTICLE V • AMENDING THE CONSTITUTION

An amendment to the Constitution can be proposed (a) by Congress, with a two-thirds vote of both houses, or (b) by a convention called by Congress when two-thirds of the state legislatures request it. An amendment is ratified (a) by three-fourths of the state legislatures, or (b) by conventions in three-fourths of the states. The twofold procedure of proposal and ratification reflects the seriousness with which the framers of the Constitution regarded amendments. Over 6,900 amendments have been proposed; only 26 have been ratified.

The Congress, whenever two thirds of both Houses shall deem it necessary, shall propose Amendments to this Constitution, or, on the Application of the Legislatures of two thirds of the several States, shall call a Convention for proposing Amendments, which, in either Case, shall be valid to all Intents and Purposes, as part of this Constitution, when ratified by the Legislatures of three fourths of the several States, or by Conventions in three fourths thereof, as the one or the other Mode of Ratification may be proposed by the Congress: Provided that no Amendment which may be made prior to the Year One thousand eight hundred and eight shall in any Manner affect the first and fourth Clauses in the Ninth Section of the first Article; and that no State, without its Consent, shall be deprived of its equal Suffrage in the Senate.

ARTICLE VI • GENERAL PROVISIONS

All Debts contracted and Engagements entered into, before the Adoption of this Constitution, shall be as valid against the United States under this Constitution, as under the Confederation.

This Constitution, and the Laws of the United States which shall be made in Pursuance thereof; and all Treaties made, or which shall be made, under the Authority of the United States, shall be the supreme Law of the Land; and the Judges in every State shall be bound thereby, any Thing in the Constitution or Laws of any State to the Contrary notwithstanding.

The supremacy clause *means that if a federal and a state law conflict, the federal law prevails.*

The Senators and Representatives before mentioned, and the Members of the several State Legislatures, and all executive and judicial Officers, both of the United States and of the several States, shall be bound by Oath or Affirmation, to support this Constitution; but no religious Test shall ever be required as a Qualification to any Office or public Trust under the United States.

Religion may not be a condition for holding public office.

ARTICLE VII • RATIFICATION

The Ratification of the Conventions of nine States shall be sufficient for the Establishment of this Constitution between the States so ratifying the Same.

DONE in Convention by the Unanimous Consent of the States present the Seventeenth Day of September in the Year of our Lord one thousand seven hundred and eighty-seven and of the Independence of the United States of America the Twelfth. In Witness whereof We have hereunto subscribed our Names.

The Constitution would become the law of the land upon the approval of nine states.

G° WASHINGTON
Presid* and deputy from
VIRGINIA

Attest: *William Jackson,* Secretary

DELAWARE
Geo: Read
Gunning Bedford, jun
John Dickinson
Richard Bassett
Jaco: Broom

MARYLAND
James McHenry
Dan: of St Thos Jenifer
Danl Carroll

VIRGINIA
John Blair
James Madison Jr.

NORTH CAROLINA
Wm Blount
Richd Dobbs Spaight
Hu Williamson

SOUTH CAROLINA
J. Rutledge
Charles Cotesworth
*   Pinckney*
Charles Pinckney
Pierce Butler

GEORGIA
William Few
Abr Baldwin

NEW HAMPSHIRE
John Langdon
Nicholas Gilman

MASSACHUSETTS
Nathaniel Gorham
Rufus King

CONNECTICUT
Wm Saml Johnson
Roger Sherman

NEW YORK
Alexander Hamilton

NEW JERSEY
Wil: Livingston
David Brearley
Wm Paterson
Jona: Dayton

PENNSYLVANIA
B Franklin
Thomas Mifflin
Robt. Morris
Geo. Clymer
Thos. FitzSimons
Jared Ingersoll
James Wilson
Gouv Morris

AMENDMENTS

AMENDMENT I • (1791)

Establishes fredom of
religion, speech, and the
press; gives citizens the
rights of assembly and
petition.

Congress shall make no law respecting an establishment of religion, or prohibiting the free exercise thereof: or abridging the freedom of speech, or of the press; or the right of the people peaceably to assemble, and to petition the Government for a redress of grievances.

AMENDMENT II • (1791)

States have the right to
maintain a militia.

A well regulated Militia, being necessary to the security of a free State, the right of the people to keep and bear Arms, shall not be infringed.

AMENDMENT III • (1791)

Limits the army's right to
quarter soldiers in private
homes.

No Soldier shall, in time of peace, be quartered in any house, without the consent of the Owner, nor in time of war, but in a manner to be prescribed by law.

AMENDMENT IV • (1791)

Search warrants are required
as a guarantee of a citizen's
right to privacy.

The right of the people to be secure in their persons, houses, papers, and effects, against unreasonable searches and seizures, shall not be violated, and no Warrants shall issue, but upon probable cause, supported by Oath or affirmation, and particularly describing the place to be searched, and the persons or things to be seized.

AMENDMENT V • (1791)

To be prosecuted for a serious
crime, a person must first
be accused *(indicted)* by a
grand jury. No one can be
tried twice for the same
crime *(double jeopardy)*.
Nor can a person be forced
into self-incrimination by
testifying against himself
or herself.

No person shall be held to answer for a capital, or otherwise infamous crime, unless on a presentment or indictment of a Grand Jury, except in cases arising in the land or naval forces, or in the Militia, when in actual service in time of War or public danger; nor shall any person be subject for the same offence to be twice put in jeopardy of life or limb; nor shall be compelled in any criminal case to be a witness against himself, nor be deprived of life, liberty, or property, without due process of law; nor shall private property be taken for public use, without just compensation.

AMENDMENT VI • (1791)

Guarantees a defendant's
right to be tried without
delay and to face witnesses
testifying for the other side.

In all criminal prosecutions, the accused shall enjoy the right to a speedy and public trial, by an impartial jury of the State and district wherein the crime shall have been committed, which district shall have been previously ascertained by law, and to be informed of the nature and cause of the accusation; to be confronted with the witnesses against him; to have compulsory process for obtaining witnesses in his favor, and to have the Assistance of Counsel for his defence.

[The date following each amendment number is the year of ratification.]

AMENDMENT VII • (1791)

In suits at common law, where the value in controversy shall exceed twenty dollars, the right of trial by jury shall be preserved, and no fact tried by a jury, shall be otherwise reexamined in any Court of the United States, than according to the rules of the common law.

A jury trial is guaranteed in federal civil suits involving more than twenty dollars.

AMENDMENT VIII • (1791)

Excessive bail shall not be required, nor excessive fines imposed, nor cruel and unusual punishments inflicted.

AMENDMENT IX • (1791)

The enumeration in the Constitution, of certain rights, shall not be construed to deny or disparage others retained by the people.

The listing of specific rights in the Constitution does not mean that others are not protected.

AMENDMENT X • (1791)

The powers not delegated to the United States by the Constitution, nor prohibited by it to the States, are reserved to the States respectively, or to the people.

Limits the federal government to its specific powers. Powers not prohibited the states by the Constitution may be exercised by them.

AMENDMENT XI • (1798)

The Judicial power of the United States shall not be construed to extend to any suit in law or equity, commenced or prosecuted against one of the United States by Citizens of another State, or by Citizens or Subjects of any Foreign State.

A state cannot be sued by a citizen of another state in a federal court. Such a case can be tried only in the courts of the state being sued.

AMENDMENT XII • (1804)

The Electors shall meet in their respective states and vote by ballot for President and Vice-President, one of whom, at least, shall not be an inhabitant of the same state with themselves; they shall name in their ballots the person voted for as President, and in distinct ballots the person voted for as Vice-President, and they shall make distinct lists of all persons voted for as President, and of all persons voted for as Vice-President, and of the number of votes for each, which lists they shall sign and certify, and transmit sealed to the seat of the government of the United States, directed to the President of the Senate; —The President of the Senate shall, in presence of the Senate and House of Representatives, open all the certificates and the votes shall then be counted;—The person having the greatest number of votes for President, shall be the President, if such number be a majority of the whole number of Electors appointed; and if no person have such majority, then from the persons having the highest numbers not exceeding three on the list of those voted for as President, the House of Representatives shall choose immediately, by ballot, the President. But in choosing the President, the votes shall be taken by states, the representation from each state having one vote; a quorum for this purpose shall consist of a member or members from two-thirds of the states, and a majority of all the states shall be necessary to a choice. And if the House of Representatives shall not choose a President whenever the right of choice shall devolve upon them, before the fourth day of March next following, then the Vice-President shall act as President, as in the case of

Revises the process by which the President and Vice President were elected (see Article II, Section 1, Clause 3). The major change requires electors to cast separate ballots for President and Vice President. If none of the presidential candidates obtains a majority vote, the House of Representatives— with each state having one vote—chooses a President from the three candidates having the highest number of votes. If no vice presidential candidate wins a majority, the Senate chooses from the two candidates having the highest number of votes. The portion printed in color was superseded by Section 3 of the 20th Amendment.

the death or other constitutional disability of the President.—The person having the greatest number of votes as Vice-President, shall be the Vice-President, if such number be a majority of the whole number of Electors appointed, and if no person have a majority, then from the two highest numbers on the list, the Senate shall choose the Vice-President; a quorum for the purpose shall consist of two-thirds of the whole number of Senators, and a majority of the whole number shall be necessary to a choice. But no person constitutionally ineligible to the office of President shall be eligible to that of Vice-President of the United States.

AMENDMENT XIII • (1865)

Abolishes slavery.

Section 1. Neither slavery nor involuntary servitude, except as a punishment for crime whereof the party shall have been duly convicted, shall exist within the United States, or any place subject to their jurisdiction.

Section 2. Congress shall have power to enforce this article by appropriate legislation.

AMENDMENT XIV • (1868)

This section confers full civil rights on former slaves. Supreme Court decisions have interpreted the language of Section 1 to mean that the states, as well as the federal government, are bound by the Bill of Rights.

Section 1. All persons born or naturalized in the United States, and subject to the jurisdiction thereof, are citizens of the United States and of the State wherein they reside. No State shall make or enforce any law which shall abridge the privileges or immunities of citizens of the United States; nor shall any State deprive any person of life, liberty, or property, without due process of law; nor deny any person within its jurisdiction the equal protection of the laws.

A penalty of a reduction in congressional representation shall be applied to any state that refuses to give all adult male citizens the right to vote in federal elections. This section has never been applied. The portion printed in color was superseded by Section 1 of the 26th Amendment. (This section has also been amplified by the 19th Amendment.)

Section 2. Representatives shall be apportioned among the several States according to their respective numbers, counting the whole number of persons in each State, excluding Indians not taxed. But when the right to vote at any election for the choice of electors for President and Vice-President of the United States, Representatives in Congress, the Executive and Judicial officers of a State, or the members of the Legislature thereof, is denied to any of the male inhabitants of such State, being twenty-one years of age, and citizens of the United States, or in any way abridged, except for participation in rebellion, or other crime, the basis of representation therein shall be reduced in the proportion which the number of such male citizens shall bear to the whole number of male citizens twenty-one years of age in such State.

Any former federal or state official who served the Confederacy during the Civil War could not become a federal official again unless Congress voted otherwise.

Section 3. No person shall be a Senator or Representative in Congress, or elector of President and Vice-President, or hold any office, civil or military, under the United States, or under any State, who, having previously taken an oath, as a member of Congress, or as an officer of the United States, or as a member of any State legislature, or as an executive or judicial officer of any State, to support the Constitution of the United States, shall have engaged in insurrection or rebellion against the same, or given aid or comfort to the enemies thereof. But Congress may by a vote of two-thirds of each House, remove such disability.

Section 4. The validity of the public debt of the United States, authorized by law, including debts incurred for payment of pensions and bounties for services in suppressing insurrection or rebellion, shall not be questioned. But neither the United States nor any State shall assume or pay any debt or obligation incurred in aid of insurrection or rebellion against the United States, or any claim for the loss or emancipation of any slave; but all such debts, obligations and claims shall be held illegal and void.

Makes legal the federal Civil War debt, but at the same time voids all Confederate debts incurred in the war.

Section 5. The Congress shall have power to enforce, by appropriate legislation, the provisions of this article.

AMENDMENT XV • (1870)

Section 1. The right of citizens of the United States to vote shall not be denied or abridged by the United States or by any State on account of race, color, or previous condition of servitude.

Gives blacks the right to vote.

Section 2. The Congress shall have power to enforce this article by appropriate legislation.

AMENDMENT XVI • (1913)

The Congress shall have power to lay and collect taxes on incomes, from whatever source derived, without apportionment among the several States, and without regard to any census or enumeration.

Allows Congress to levy taxes on incomes.

AMENDMENT XVII • (1913)

The Senate of the United States shall be composed of two Senators from each State, elected by the people thereof, for six years; and each Senator shall have one vote. The electors in each State shall have the qualifications requisite for electors of the most numerous branch of the State legislature.

Provides for election of senators by the people of a state, rather than the state legislature.

When vacancies happen in the representation of any State in the Senate, the executive authority of such State shall issue writs of election to fill such vacancies: *Provided,* That the legislature of any State may empower the executive thereof to make temporary appointments until the people fill the vacancies by election as the legislature may direct.

This amendment shall not be so construed as to affect the election or term of any Senator chosen before it becomes valid as part of the Constitution.

AMENDMENT XVIII • (1919)

Section 1. After one year from the ratification of this article, the manufacture, sale, or transportation of intoxicating liquors within, the importation thereof into, or the exportation thereof from the United States and all territory subject to the jurisdiction thereof for beverage purposes is hereby prohibited.

Legalizes prohibition—that is, forbidding the making, selling, or transporting of intoxicating beverages. Superseded by the 21st Amendment.

Section 2. The Congress and the several States shall have concurrent power to enforce this article by appropriate legislation.

Section 3. This article shall be inoperative unless it shall have been ratified as an amendment to the Constitution by the legislatures of the several States, as provided in the Constitution, within seven years from the date of the submission hereof to the States by the Congress.

AMENDMENT XIX • (1920)

Gives women the right to vote.

The right of citizens of the United States to vote shall not be denied or abridged by the United States or by any State on account of sex.

Congress shall have power to enforce this article by appropriate legislation.

AMENDMENT XX • (1933)

The "lame duck" amendment allows the President to take office on January 20, and members of Congress on January 3. The purpose of the amendment is to reduce the term in office of defeated incumbents—known as "lame ducks."

Section 1. The terms of the President and Vice-President shall end at noon on the 20th day of January, and the terms of Senators and Representatives at noon on the 3d day of January, of the years in which such terms would have ended if this article had not been ratified; and the terms of their successors shall then begin.

Section 2. The Congress shall assemble at least once in every year, and such meeting shall begin at noon on the 3d day of January, unless they shall by law appoint a different day.

Section 3. If, at the time fixed for the beginning of the term of the President, the President elect shall have died, the Vice-President elect shall become President. If a President shall not have been chosen before the time fixed for the beginning of his term, or if the President elect shall have failed to qualify, then the Vice-President elect shall act as President until a President shall have qualified; and the Congress may by law provide for the case wherein neither a President elect nor a Vice-President elect shall have qualified, declaring who shall then act as President, or the manner in which one who is to act shall be selected, and such person shall act accordingly until a President or Vice-President shall have qualified.

Section 4. The Congress may by law provide for the case of the death of any of the persons from whom the House of Representatives may choose a President whenever the right of choice shall have devolved upon them, and for the case of the death of any of the persons from whom the Senate may choose a Vice-President whenever the right of choice shall have devolved upon them.

Section 5. Sections 1 and 2 shall take effect on the 15th day of October following the ratification of this article.

Section 6. This article shall be inoperative unless it shall have been ratified as an amendment to the Constitution by the legislatures of three-fourths of the several States within seven years from the date of its submission.

AMENDMENT XXI • (1933)

Section 1. The eighteenth article of amendment to the Constitution of the United States is hereby repealed.

Repeals the 18th Amendment.

Section 2. The transportation or importation into any State, Territory, or possession of the United States for delivery or use therein of intoxicating liquors, in violation of the laws thereof, is hereby prohibited.

States may pass prohibition laws.

Section 3. This article shall be inoperative unless it shall have been ratified as an amendment to the Constitution by conventions in the several States, as provided in the Constitution, within seven years from the date of the submission hereof to the States by the Congress.

AMENDMENT XXII • (1951)

Section 1. No person shall be elected to the office of the President more than twice, and no person who has held the office of President, or acted as President, for more than two years of a term to which some other person was elected President shall be elected to the office of the President more than once. But this Article shall not apply to any person holding the office of President when this Article was proposed by the Congress, and shall not prevent any person who may be holding the office of President, or acting as President, during the term within which this Article becomes operative from holding the office of President or acting as President during the remainder of such term.

Limits a President to only two full terms plus two years of a previous President's term.

Section 2. This article shall be inoperative unless it shall have been ratified as an amendment to the Constitution by the legislatures of three-fourths of the several States within seven years from the date of its submission to the States by the Congress.

AMENDMENT XXIII • (1961)

Section 1. The District constituting the seat of Government of the United States shall appoint in such manner as the Congress may direct:

A number of electors of President and Vice-President equal to the whole number of Senators and Representatives in Congress to which the District would be entitled if it were a State, but in no event more than the least populous State; they shall be in addition to those appointed by the States, but they shall be considered, for the purposes of the election of President and Vice-President, to be electors appointed by a State; and they shall meet in the District and perform such duties as provided by the twelfth article of amendment.

By giving the District of Columbia three electoral votes, Congress enabled its residents to vote for President and Vice President.

Section 2. The Congress shall have power to enforce this article by appropriate legislation.

AMENDMENT XXIV • (1964)

Section 1. The right of citizens of the United States to vote in any primary or other election for President or Vice-President, for electors for President or Vice-President, or for Senator or Representative in Congress, shall not be denied or abridged by the United States or any State by reason of failure to pay any poll tax or other tax.

Forbids the use of a poll tax as a requirement for voting in federal elections.

Section 2. The Congress shall have power to enforce this article by appropriate legislation.

AMENDMENT XXV • (1967)

Outlines the procedure to be followed in case of presidential disability.

Section 1. In case of the removal of the President from office or of his death or resignation, the Vice-President shall become President.

Section 2. Whenever there is a vacancy in the office of the Vice-President, the President shall nominate a Vice-President who shall take office upon confirmation by a majority vote of both Houses of Congress.

Section 3. Whenever the President transmits to the President pro tempore of the Senate and the Speaker of the House of Representatives his written declaration that he is unable to discharge the powers and duties of his office, and until he transmits to them a written declaration to the contrary, such powers and duties shall be discharged by the Vice-President as Acting President.

Section 4. Whenever the Vice-President and a majority of either the principal officers of the executive departments or of such other body as Congress may by law provide, transmit to the President pro tempore of the Senate and the Speaker of the House of Representatives their written declaration that the President is unable to discharge the powers and duties of his office, the Vice-President shall immediately assume the powers and duties of the office as Acting President.

Thereafter, when the President transmits to the President pro tempore of the Senate and the Speaker of the House of Representatives his written declaration that no inability exists, he shall resume the powers and duties of his office unless the Vice-President and a majority of either the principal officers of the executive department or of such other body as Congress may by law provide, transmit within four days to the President pro tempore of the Senate and the Speaker of the House of Representatives their written declaration that the President is unable to discharge the powers and duties of his office. Thereupon Congress shall decide the issue, assembling within forty-eight hours for that purpose if not in session. If the Congress, within twenty-one days after receipt of the latter written declaration, or, if Congress is not in session, within twenty-one days after Congress is required to assemble, determines by two-thirds vote of both Houses that the President is unable to discharge the powers and duties of his office, the Vice-President shall continue to discharge the same as Acting President; otherwise, the President shall resume the powers and duties of his office.

AMENDMENT XXVI • (1971)

Lowers the voting age to eighteen.

Section 1. The right of citizens of the United States, who are eighteen years of age or older, to vote shall not be denied or abridged by the United States or any state on account of age.

Section 2. The Congress shall have the power to enforce this article by appropriate legislation.

Quotations by these foreign observers appear in the nine Pictorial Essays. Minor adaptations have been made in some quoted material, chiefly to modernize spelling and grammar. In the essays, the writer's name is followed by a date or dates. These represent the years in which the observations were made, if known. If the exact period is not known, the date represents the year in which the account was first published in the original language.

Anburey, Thomas *(Essay 2)* An officer in the British army during the Revolution, he journeyed through Canada and several of the colonies between 1776 and 1781. His *Travels Through the Interior Parts of America* was published in 1789.

Beaujour, Felix de *(Essay 2)* French consul-general in the United States from 1804 to 1816. His *Sketch of the United States at the Commencement of the Nineteenth Century* (1814) was highly critical of Americans as crude and money-grubbing.

Beauvoir, Simone de *(Essays 8, 9)* The noted French writer and philosopher made a nationwide tour of the United States between January and May 1947. *America Day by Day* (1953), based on her travels, shows her as an intelligent and sensitive reporter of the American scene.

Bernard, John *(Essays 3, 4)* This English actor made several professional tours in the United States between 1797 and 1811. Selections from his witty and gossipy *Retrospections of America* appeared at intervals later in the nineteenth century.

Birkbeck, Morris *(Essay 4)* An Englishman who relocated in southern Illinois in 1818. His writings greatly influenced other would-be settlers. The two quotations given here are from his *Letters From Illinois* (1818).

Blane, William *(Essay 4)* Little is known of this young Englishman other than that he lived from 1800 to 1825. His *Excursion Through the United States and Canada During the Years 1822-23* was published anonymously three years after his death.

Bremer, Fredrika *(Essays 4, 6)* A Swedish novelist well known in her day, who traveled in America from 1849 to 1851. Her impressions, in the form of letters to her sister, appeared in *Homes of the New World* (1853).

Broughton, Morris *(Essay 9)* A South African journalist and editor of *The Cape Argus,* he came to the United States in 1956 as a guest of the State Department. By his estimation, he traveled over 10,000 miles and visited over thirty states during his three-month stay here.

Burnaby, Andrew *(Essay 2)* A clergyman of the Church of England, Burnaby traveled in the colonies in 1759-60. His firm loyalty to the British crown is evident in his *Travels Through North America,* first published in 1775.

Cabeza de Vaca, Álvar Núñez *(Essay 1)* After his stay among the Indians in North America, the Spanish explorer led an expedition in South America and served as governor of Paraguay. He returned to Spain in 1544. His account of his years in North America, *Los Naufragios* ("The Shipwrecked") was published in 1542.

Capellini, Giovanni *(Essay 5)* An Italian professor of geology, Capellini toured the western United States in 1863. He recorded his scientific observations in a journal published in 1867.

Carpenter, Harry *(Essay 8)* An English sports expert, Carpenter was boxing and general sports columnist for *The London Daily Mail* from 1954 to 1962, as well as a full-time correspondent for the BBC. In his *Masters of Boxing* (1964) he spoke of Joe Louis as the "headmaster" of boxing.

Castañeda, Pedro de *(Essay 1)* This Spaniard—one of the 300 men who accompanied Coronado on his expedition in the 1540s—was the most famous chronicler of the jounrney. Little is known of him except his birthplace, Najera, Spain.

Champlain, Samuel de *(Essay 1)* The renowned French explorer was the chief founder of New France. He made a number of voyages to Canada in the early seventeenth century, and published several different accounts of them.

Chastellux, Marquis de (Francois-Jean de Beauvoir) *(Essay 3)* A French army officer, he served as aide to Rochambeau during the American Revolution. His *Travels in North America in the Years 1780, 1781, and 1782* (1786) is a vivid and generally accurate account.

Chateaubriand, François-René de *(Essay 4)* This French novelist visited the United States for four months in 1791, but did not publish his *Travels in America* until 1827. It is a romantic work devoted mainly to the Indian as a "noble savage" rather than to the author's own experiences.

Chesterton, G. K. *(Essay 6)* The English poet and novelist visited the United States on a lecture tour in 1921. His book, *What I Saw in America,* was published in London in 1922.

Chevalier, Michel *(Essay 5)* As a young French engineer, he was sent by his government in 1834-35 to study transportation and public works in the United States. He praised the country in *Letters on North America* (1836).

Cobbett, William *(Essay 3)* Opinionated and outspoken, this English journalist was twice forced to flee to the United States, where he lived from 1792 to 1800 and again from 1817 to 1819. The selection quoted is from *A Year's Residence in the United States of America* (1818).

Colum, Padraic *(Essay 7)* This Irish man of letters made his home in the United States after 1914. He was a friend of many writers, including Robert Frost.

Columbus, Christopher *(Essay 1)* The great explorer kept a journal account of his first voyage, which he presented to the Spanish monarchs. It has since been lost, but an abstract of it was made earlier by the Spanish missionary Bartolomé de Las Casas.

Cooke, Alistair *(Essay 9)* Of Anglo-Irish birth, this popular journalist and broadcaster has lived primarily in the United States since the 1930s, and became an American citizen in 1941. He is the author of many books on American culture. This selection comes from *Talk About America* (1968).

Corresca, Rocco *(Essay 6)* An Italian immigrant, he typified the penniless hopefuls who flocked to America to make their fortune. His "Biography of a Bootblack" appeared in a magazine, *The Independent,* in December 1902.

Dal Verme, Francesco *(Essay 2)* Member of a noble Milanese family. The journal and letters concerning his travels in 1783-84 were meant only for his relatives, but were published in 1969 as *Seeing America and its Great Men.*

Danckaerts, Jasper *(Essay 2)* A Dutchman, he belonged to a small Calvinist sect, the Labadists. He and Peter Sluyter spent thirteen months in America in 1679-80 looking for a place for the Labadists to settle (they chose Maryland). Danckaerts' journal was discovered in the nineteenth century by an American, and published in 1867.

Dickens, Charles *(Essay 4)* The famous English writer first toured the United States in 1842. His *American Notes,* published that same year, was highly critical of Americans. Out of this experience came his novel *Martin Chuzzlewit.*

Dubos, René—See Ward, Barbara

Erkelenz, Anton *(Essay 7)* A member of the German parliament, he wrote a book called *America Today* (1927), in which he expressed an optimistic belief that the United States would some day create a culture uniquely its own.

"A Fidalgo of Elvas" *(Essay 1)* Nothing is known of this chronicler of De Soto's expedition other than his nationality, Portuguese, the language of his narrative. He was clearly a modest man, since he mentioned himself only once in the entire account (first published in 1557).

Freymond, Jacques *(Essay 8)* On his first trip to the United States (1949-1950), Fremond, a Swiss historian, studied at Yale University and made an extended auto tour of the country. He returned for a two-month trip in 1955.

Galsworthy, John *(Essay 7)* The noted English writer gave a series of speeches in the United States that were published in a volume called *Addresses in America* (1919).

Gilbert, Bartholomew See Gosnold, Bartholomew

Gosnold, Bartholomew *(Essay 1)* An Englishman, he led an expedition—including Bartholomew Gilbert as navigator—of the first Europeans to explore Cape Cod. They also visited Martha's Vineyard, which Gosnold named after his daughter and because of its lush growth of strawberries, grapes, and other fruit.

Graham, Stephen *(Essay 6)* A British traveler and journalist who visited the United States in 1913. These quotations are from his work *With Poor Immigrants to America* (1914).

Grassi, Giovanni *(Essay 3)* This Italian Jesuit priest spent the years 1810-17 in the United States. His report, emphasizing general characteristics rather than specific people or places, appeared in 1819.

Griesinger, Karl Theodor *(Essay 6)* This German historian spent five years in the United States, although he did not find the American form of democracy to his liking. His *Living Pictures from America,* published in 1858, is characterized by a cutting and ironical humor.

Grund, Francis J. *(Essay 4)* A Bohemian journalist who spent several years in the United States during the 1830s. His book of observations—*The Americans in Their Moral, Social, and Political Relations*—was published in 1837.

Hall, Basil *(Essays 4, 5)* A retired English naval officer, he visited the United States in 1820 and in 1827-28. His *Travels in North America* (1829) is a valuable description.

Hamp, Sidford *(Essay 5)* This English youth was only seventeen when his uncle—who had helped found Colorado Springs—arranged for him to travel to the United States on a scientific expedition. His diary reflects his youthful enthusiasm.

Hartog, Jan de *(Essay 9)* A Dutch author and playwright who made a leisurely voyage in 1958-61 from Houston to Nantucket, largely by inland waterways. He gives a charming account of his adventures in *Waters of the Western World,* published in 1961.

Hauptmann, Gerhart *(Essay 7)* In 1932 this German playwright, a Nobel prize winner, visited the United States. He remarked on leaving that the high points of his trip had been meeting O'Neill and attending *Mourning Becomes Electra.* The critique quoted here is from an interview the same year with an American correspondent.

Hawkes, Jacquetta—See Priestley, J. B.

Hawkins, John *(Essay 1)* The famous English naval commander visited America on many of his voyages. The excerpt quoted is from Richard Hakluyt's great compendium of travel accounts, *Principall Navigations, Voiages, and Discoveries of the English Nation.*

Heriot (or Harriot), Thomas *(Essay 1)* An English mathematician and astronomer, he traveled to Roanoke as a surveyor on Sir Richard Grenville's 1585 expedition (financed by Raleigh). His *Brief and True Report of the new-found Land of Virginia* appeared in 1588.

Hilbersheimer, Ludwig and Udo Rukser *(Essay 7)* These German architects praised the innovations of American architecture and especially the work of Frank Lloyd Wright. Their article appeared in a 1920 issue of the German journal, *Art and Artist*.

Jarlson, Axel *(Essay 6)* The story of this Swedish farmer's immigration to America illustrates how the members of a single family helped each other to settle in the United States. Jarlson's narrative was published in the January 8, 1903, issue of *The Independent*.

Josselyn, John *(Essay 2)* An English traveler who visited the American colonies in 1638-39 and again in 1663-71. This quotation is taken from the second of two books he wrote, *An Account of Two Voyages to New-England* (1674).

Kalm, Peter *(Essay 2)* A Swede who traveled in America from 1748 to 1751. As a botanist, he was interested mainly in plants and farming. (Mountain laurel is named after him— *Kalmia latifolia*.) His *Travels* appeared at intervals between 1753 and 1761.

Kemble, Fanny *(Essay 5)* A leading English actress, she first toured the United States in 1833-34, when she met and married a Philadelphian who owned cotton and rice plantations in Georgia. Her *Journal of a Residence on a Georgian Plantation in 1838-39* (1863) is an animated account.

Kipling, Rudyard *(Essay 7)* Between March and September 1889, the famous English writer (then only twenty-four) sent thirty-seven letters back to an Indian newspaper, as he traveled from India to England via the Far East and the United States. The last of his letters is titled "An Interview with Mark Twain." All this correspondence was published in *From Sea to Sea* (1890).

Klinkowström, Axel *(Essays 3, 4)* A member of an old Swedish family, Baron Klinkowström served as a naval officer, and visited the United States in 1818-20 primarily to investigate the practical workings of the steamboat. His *Letters on the United States* appeared in 1824.

Kossenko, Zinaida—See Mikhailov, Nikolai

Labarca H., Amanda *(Essay 9)* A distinguished Chilean educator, feminist, and public servant, she visited the United States ten times between 1911 and 1952. She represented Chile in the first General Assembly of the United Nations in 1946.

Lambert, John *(Essay 3)* Little is known of this Englishman's life except his trip to North America in 1806-09 to investigate the possibilities of hemp cultivation in Canada. The chief result was his *Travels Through Lower Canada and the United States of North America* (1810).

Lane, Ralph *(Essay 1)* This Englishman sailed on Grenville's 1585 expedition, and remained to become the first governor of Virginia. He and the rest of the colony, however, returned to England with Drake in 1586. The quotation is from Hakluyt's *Voyages*.

Laski, Harold *(Essay 7)* A noted British socialist, he taught history at Harvard University from 1916 to 1920. After returning to England, he devoted himself to teaching, writing, and journalism. His *American Democracy* was published in 1948.

Leacock, Stephen *(Essay 8)* The Canadian humorist and man of letters was also a distinguished political scientist and professor at McGill University. This quotation is from *Stephen Leacock's Laugh Parade*, published in 1940.

Le Corbusier (Charles Edouard Jeanneret) *(Essays 8, 9)* This Swiss-born French architect has been called "the voice and conscience of modern architecture." He visited the United States several times during his lifetime. His book *When the Cathedrals Were White* (1947) was devoted mostly to his impressions of America.

Lederer, John *(Essay 2)* This scholar and student of medicine explored the Piedmont and the Blue Ridge Mountains in 1669-70, the first European to do so. He then moved to New England, returning to his native Germany in 1675. His *Discoveries*, written in Latin, was translated and published in London in 1672.

Leigh, Charles *(Essay 1)* A merchant, he sailed from his native England in 1597 to trade and to plunder Spanish ships. His description of Newfoundland, from Hakluyt's *Voyages*, is one of the few accounts of his many travels to survive.

Lyell, Sir Charles *(Essay 5)* The leading English geologist of the nineteenth century, he made four trips to the United States. His steamboat description is from *A Second Visit to the United States of North America* (1849).

Marias, Julian *(Essays 8, 9)* A Spanish philosopher, he helped found Madrid's Institute of Humanities. In 1951–52 Marias was a visiting professor at Wellesley College.

Martineau, Harriet *(Essay 4)* A writer, she spent the years 1834-36 in the United States, returning to her native England an ardent abolitionist. Her *Society in America* was published in 1837.

Maurois, André *(Essay 8)* The noted French critic and novelist was a frequent visitor to the United States, where he was a popular lecturer. In 1939 he published *Thirty-Nine States, Journal of a Voyage to America*, from which this quote is taken.

Maximilian of Wied, Prince *(Essay 5)* This Prussian aristocrat traveled in the western United States in 1832-34. He was accompanied by a young Swiss artist, Charles Bodmer; the result of their stay was *Travels in the Interior of North America* (1839-41), with maps and illustrations by Bodmer.

Mehdevi, Mohamed *(Essay 9)* An Iranian journalist and diplomat, he first became acquainted with the United States as a foreign student in Florida. *Something Human* (1962) was the result of his adventures hitchhiking from Florida to the West Coast.

Mikhailov, Nikolai and Zinaida Kossenko *(Essay 9)* This Russian geographer and his wife, a psychiatrist, made a tour of America in 1960. Their account first appeared in a Moscow publication the same year and was later published in the United States as *Those Americans, a Travelogue* (1962).

Moreau de Saint-Méry, M. L. E. *(Essay 3)* A French judge, he fled to the United States in 1794 to escape the Revolution. He remained until 1798, an embittered critic of the American scene. His *Voyage to the United States* remained in manuscript form until it was published in 1913.

Münsterberg, Hugo *(Essay 7)* This German philosopher and professor at Harvard University wrote *The Americans* (1904) in order to dispel German prejudice against Americans.

Myers, Robert *(Essay 6)* A Jewish immigrant from Rumania, Myers came to the United States in 1913 and later became active in the labor movement. His recollections, *Stimmer* ["stutterer"]: *The Boy Who Couldn't Talk*, were published in 1959.

Newman, Ernest *(Essay 7)* From 1910 to 1940 he was the major British music critic. His review of Isadora Duncan quoted here was written in April 1921. Several years later, he moved to New York City, where he wrote music reviews for the *New York Evening Post*. The November 17, 1924, edition carried his appreciation of Gershwin's *Rhapsody in Blue*.

Oñate, Juan de *(Essay 1)* Born in the New World, he founded the province of New Mexico in 1598 and was its governor until 1609. Though convicted of misconduct in office, he was later pardoned.

Priestley, J. B. *(Essays 8, 9)* The English novelist and critic lived in the United States in 1935–36; *Midnight on the Desert* (1937) grew out of this experience. In 1954 he and his wife Jacquetta Hawkes (an author and anthropologist) traveled in the American Southwest. Their wry and amusing collaboration, *Journey Down a Rainbow,* for which each wrote alternating chapters, was published in 1955.

Pupin, Michael Idvorsky *(Essay 6)* Born in Yugoslavia, the brilliant physicist sold all his belongings in order to come to America. In 1924 he won a Pulitzer Prize for *From Immigrant to Inventor* (1923), the story of his life.

Raeder, Ole *(Essay 5)* A leading Norwegian lawyer and judge, he was sent to the United States in 1847 to study the jury system. He regularly sent home newspaper dispatches, which were eventually published in 1929 as *America in the Forties*.

Rivera, Diego *(Essay 7)* In 1942 the celebrated Mexican artist spoke of his contemporary, John Sloan, to American art critic Walter Pach. Rivera himself had visited the United States in the 1930s, where he painted frescoes in Detroit, San Francisco, and New York. He was much impressed with American technology.

Ross, Alexander *(Essay 4)* A Scot, he worked for John Jacob Astor's Pacific Fur Company from 1810 to 1813, then for the Canadian North West Company until 1825. His *Fur-Hunters of the Far West* appeared in 1855.

Rukser, Udo—See Hilbersheimer, Ludwig

Russell of Killowen, Lord *(Essays 5, 6)* Born in Ireland, this lawyer first visited America in 1883 and wrote a *Diary of a Visit to the United States of America* (published in 1910). He served as lord chief justice of England from 1894 until his death in 1900.

Sarc, Omer Celâl *(Essay 8)* This Turkish economist has spent much time in the United States. In 1950 he visited universities across the country as a guest of the State Department. He also taught at Columbia University and worked for the United Nations.

Schoepf, Johann David *(Essay 3)* A German scientist, he came to America as a physician for Hessian troops in 1777, and remained in this country until 1784. His *Travels in the Confederation* appeared in 1788.

Settle, Dionise *(Essay 1)* A mariner who sailed on the second of Frobisher's three expeditions to North America. This account is from Hakluyt's *Voyages*.

Sheridan, Claire *(Essay 7)* A celebrated British sculptress, known for her busts of Lenin, Trotsky, and Gandhi. She met Sinclair Lewis in Washington, D.C., in April 1921. A vivid account of their meeting appeared in her book *My American Diary,* published the following year.

Stevenson, Robert Louis *(Essays 5, 6)* The Scottish writer crossed the United States in 1879 to visit an American woman he had met in Europe (and whom he eventually married). *Across the Plains* was published in 1892.

Tocqueville, Alexis de *(Essays 3, 4)* This French statesman and writer was sent to the United States in 1831 by his government in order to study American penitentiaries. He is best known, however, for his two-volume *Democracy in America* (1835, 1840), widely regarded as one of the most insightful commentaries ever written on the United States.

Trollope, Frances *(Essays 4, 5)* An English novelist (and the mother of novelist Anthony Trollope), she visited the United States in 1827-30, trying unsuccessfully to set up a store in Cincinnati. Her *Domestic Manners of the Americans* (1832) is a humorous critique that much offended Americans of the time.

Tyrmand, Leopold *(Essay 9)* A journalist born in Warsaw, Poland, he moved to the United States in the 1960s. Portions of his writings, dealing with his experiences as a European in America, appeared in *The New Yorker*. They were collected in *Notebooks of a Dilettante* (1967).

Vay de Vaya und Luskod, Count *(Essays 5, 6, 7)* A Hungarian nobleman, he traveled widely as a diplomat for the Roman Catholic Church. Visiting the United States several times between 1903 and 1906, he described his travels in *The Inner Life of the United States* (1908).

Verrazano, Giovanni da *(Essay 1)* The Italian navigator commissioned by France is believed to have been the first European to enter New York Harbor and sail up the Hudson River. Gilbert and Gosnold had his account with them when they explored Cape Cod.

Vizcaíno, Sebastián *(Essay 1)* A Spanish trader, he was commissioned by the viceroy to explore California, which he did in 1596 and again in 1602-03.

Von Borch, Herbert *(Essays 8, 9)* This German writer's book *The Unfinished Society* (1960) was based on notes he made while working in the United States as a newspaper correspondent.

Wansey, Henry *(Essay 2)* An English clothier who retired to take up scholarship, he visited the United States in 1794. His observations were published in 1796 under the title of *An Excursion to the United States of North America*.

Ward, Barbara and René Dubos *(Essay 9)* Barbara Ward, an English social scientist, lectured frequently in the United States in the period after World War II. *Only One Earth* (1972) was written with the Pulitzer-prize winning microbiologist, René Dubos, who was born in France but moved to the United States in 1924.

Wells, H. G. *(Essay 6)* The famous English novelist visited Ellis Island during his first trip to the United States in 1905. He wrote of his impressions in *The Future of America* (1906).

West, Rebecca *(Essay 7)* Born in Ireland, she became known for her writings on history and politics. Her essay on Willa Cather was originally published by the *New York Herald Tribune* in September 1927, and was reprinted in *The Strange Necessity* (1928).

White, T. H. *(Essay 9)* Best known for his books on King Arthur, this English author kept a journal while on a lecture tour in the United States. It was later published as *America at Last, the American Journal of T. H. White* (1965).

Wolff, Albert *(Essay 7)* A French art critic, he wrote for the noted Franch newspaper, *Le Figaro*. This selection is quoted from his 1881 review of the Impressionists' sixth group exhibition.

144, Colonial Williamsburg; 146, Metropolitan Museum of Art–Bequest of Charles Allen Munn, 1924; 148, Shelburne Museum, Inc.; 151, John Carter Brown Library; 152, I. N. Phelps Stokes Collection–N.Y.P.L. Prints Division; 154, John Carter Brown Library; 156, Henry Francis duPont Winterthur Museum; 159, House of Delegates–Annapolis, Md.; 160, Pierpont Morgan Library; PE 3-1, N.Y. Historical Society; PE 3-2(top), Daughters of the American Revolution Museum–Washington, D.C.; (bottom), Moravian Historical Society–Nazareth, Pa.; PE 3-3(top), Connecticut Historical Society; (bottom), Newport Historical Society; PE 3-4(top), N.Y.P.L. Rare Book Collection; (bottom), N.Y. Historical Society; PE 3-5 (top left), Detail of "The Shop and Warehouse of Duncan Phyfe 168-172 Fulton Street, N.Y.C."–Metropolitan Museum of Art Rogers Fund, 1922; (top right), (N. Heideloff) Gallery of Fashion (London, 1794)–N.Y.P.L.; (bottom), "The Dinner Party" by Henry Sargent–Boston Museum of Fine Arts–Gift of Mrs. Horation A. Lamb in Memory of Mr. and Mrs. Winthrop Sargent; PE 3-6(top), Abby Aldrich Rockefeller Folk Art Collection; (bottom), Metropolitan Museum of Art Rogers Fund, 1942; PE 3-7, National Gallery of Art–Gift of Edgar William and Bernice Chrysler Garbisch; PE 3-8 (top), Ann Parker; (bottom), Firestone Library–Princeton University; 167, National Gallery of Art–Gift of Edgar William and Bernice Chrysler Garbisch; 170, N.Y.P.L. Manuscript Division; 171, Virginia State Library; 179, (B. Bowen) History of the Centennial Celebration of Washington's Inauguration; 181 & 185, N.Y.P.L. Picture Collection; 187, Peabody Museum of Salem; 188, Historical Society of Pennsylvania; 190, Thomas Gilcrease Institute; 191, Culver Pictures, Inc.; 193, Am. Antiquarian Society; 194, N.Y. Historical Society.

UNIT THREE

Page 198, Culver Pictures, Inc.; 201, N.Y. Historical Society; 202, Museum of the City of New York; 205, Independence National Historical Park Collection; 209, Corcoran Gallery of Art; 210, Newberry Library; 212, Cincinnati Historical Society; 219 & 221, N.Y. Historical Society; 223, N.Y.P.L. Picture Collection; 224, Library of Congress; 227, White House Collection; 228, Culver Pictures, Inc.; 234, N.Y. Historical Society; 235, New Orleans Museum of Art; 239(left), Granger Collection; (center), Independence National Historical Park Collection; (right), Missouri Historical Society; 243, 246(left), N.Y. Historical Society; (right), Museum of the City of New York; 248, 250, 251, 253, 255, N.Y. Historical Society; PE 4-1, (Maximilian, Prince of Wied) Travels in the Interior of North America (1833)–N.Y.P.L. Rare Book Collection; PE 4-2(top), Museum of Fine Arts of Boston–Bequest of Henry L. Shattuck in Memory of the Late Ralph W. Gray; (bottom), Missouri Historical Society; PE 4-3(top), Northern Natural Gas Company Collection of the Joslyn Art Museum–Omaha, Neb.; (bottom left), Granger Collection; (bottom right), Culver Pictures, Inc.; PE 4-4(top left), Northern Natural Gas Company Collection of the Joslyn Art Museum–Omaha, Neb.; (top right), (F. J. Meine) The Crockett Almanacks (Chicago, 1955)–N.Y.P.L. Rare Book Collection; (bot-

tom), detail of "Spring Burning Up Fallen Leaves" by George Harvey–Brooklyn Museum; PE 4-5(top), Collection of Mr. and Mrs. Leslie Cowan–Columbia, Mo.; (center), N.Y. Historical Society; (bottom) Glenbow-Alberta Institute–Courtesy American Heritage Publishing Co.; PE 4-6(top), "Flax Scutching Bee" by Linton Park–National Gallery of Art–Gift of Edgar William and Bernice Chrysler Garbisch (Courtesy Time/Life Books, © Time, Inc.); (bottom), detail of "Shooting for the Beef" by George Caleb Bingham; PE 4-7, Boatmen's National Bank of St. Louis; PE 4-8(top), Minnesota Historical Society; (bottom), (Mrs. Frances Trollope) Domestic Manners of the Americans (Kiel, Germany, 1835); 259, Corcoran Gallery of Art; 262, Historical Society of Pennsylvania; 264, James Monroe Memorial House and Library; 267, Library of Congress; 269, The Cooper Union; 272, Benjamin Harrison Home.

UNIT FOUR

Pages 276 & 279, Culver Pictures, Inc.; 284 & 285, Virginia State Library; 288, Virginia State Library; 290, N.Y.P.L. General Research and Humanities Division/Astor, Lenox, and Tilden Foundation; 291 & 293, Virginia State Library; 297, N.Y. Historical Society; 299, Louisiana Tourist Development Commission; 300, Yale University Art Gallery; 302, Glenbow-Alberta Institute; 303, Duke University Library; 305, Virginia State Library; 306, N.Y. Historical Society; 307 & 309, Library of Congress; 313, N.Y. Historical Society; 314, 319, 320, 321, 323, 324, 325, Library of Congress; 329, Worchester Art Museum; 331, Corcoran Gallery of Art–Gift of Mr. and Mrs. Lansdell K. Christie; 332, N.Y. Historical Society; 335, Library of Congress; 339, California State Library Picture Collection; 341, Intern'l Museum of Photography at George Eastman House; 345, Missouri Historical Society; 346, Culver Pictures, Inc.; 349, Metropolitan Museum of Art–Gift of Mr. and Mrs. Carl Stoeckel, 1897; 350(top), Library of Congress; (center), N.Y.P.L. Picture Collection; (bottom), Boston Athenaeum; 351(top), N.Y.P.L. Picture Collection; (center & bottom), Library of Congress; PE 5-1, Permission of Frost and Reed, London–Courtesy Mariners Museum, Newport News, Va.; PE 5-2(top), Kennedy Galleries, Inc.; (bottom), N.Y. Historical Society; PE 5-3, "Travel by Stagecoach Near Trenton, New Jersey" by Paul Svenin–Metropolitan Museum of Art Rogers Fund, 1942; PE 5-4(top), Thomas Gilcrease Institute–Tulsa, Okla.; (bottom), Tulane University; PE 5-5(top), Mariners Museum–Newport News, Va.; (bottom), Boatmen's National Bank of St. Louis; PE 5-6(top), California Historical Society–San Francisco/San Marino; (bottom), Thomas Gilcrease Institute–Tulsa, Okla.; PE 5-7, Smithsonian Institution; PE 5-8(top), Library of Congress–Courtesy American Heritage Publishing Co.; (bottom), Granger Collection; 355, Baltimore and Ohio Railroad; 357, Virginia State Library; 358, Baltimore and Ohio Railroad; 362, N.Y. Historical Society; 363, Library of Congress; 365, Virginia State Library; 371, Library of Congress; 372, Metropolitan Museum of Art–Gift of I. N. Phelps; 373, 374, 375, Library of Congress; 376, N.Y. Historical Society; 378, Library of Congress; 379, Kansas State

Historical Society–Topeka, Kan.; 380, Mabel Brady Garvan Collection–Yale University Art Gallery; 385, Library of Congress; 386, Brady Collection–U.S. Signal Corps/National Archives; 388, N.Y.P.L. Prints Division; 390, Charles Colcock Jones Papers/Manuscript Dept. Special Collections Division–Tulane University Library; 391, N.Y.P.L. Prints Division; 393, Library of Congress; 394, Library of Congress; 401, Penn Community Services Cultural Program; 405 (right) Brady Collection–U.S. Signal Corps/National Archives; 408, Valentine Museum–Richmond, Va.; 409, Brady Collection–U.S. Signal Corps/National Archives; 412, Library of Congress; 414, National Archives; 416, 417, 419, 422, 423, Library of Congress; 426, Virginia State Library; 429, Louisiana State Museum.

UNIT FIVE

Page 432, Culver Pictures, Inc.; 435, Smithsonian Institution/National Anthropological Archives; 437, U.S. Signal Corps/National Archives; 440, 441, 442, Smithsonian Institution/National Anthropological Archives; 443 & 445, U.S. Signal Corps/National Archives; 451, Nebraska State Historical Society; 454, Library of Congress; 455, Minnesota Historical Society; 456, N.Y.P.L.; 457, Permission of Huntington Library–San Marino, Cal.; 458, Southern Pacific Railroad; 461, Library of Congress; 463, Manitoba Archives; 465, Smithsonian Institution/National Anthropological Archives; 466, Naval Observatory/National Archives; 469, Western History Department–Denver Public Library; 470, Bureau of Reclamation/National Archives; 473, Library of Congress; 474 & 477, International Harvester Company Historical Archives; 491 & 492, Library of Congress; 493, A.T.&T.; 495, Library of Congress; PE 6-1, Culver Pictures, Inc.; PE 6-2(top), N.Y. Historical Society; (bottom), Metropolitan Museum of Art; PE 6-3(top & center), Bettmann Archive; (bottom), N.Y.P.L. Picture Collection; PE 6-4(top), Los Angeles County Museum of Art; (bottom), Museum of the City of New York; PE 6-5(top), Bettmann Archive; (bottom), N.Y.P.L. Picture Collection; PE 6-6(top left), Wisconsin State Historical Society; (top right), Missouri Historical Society; (bottom), Chicago Historical Society; PE 6-7(top), Illinois Department of Conservation; (bottom), Chicago Historical Society; PE 6-8(top), Thomas Gilcrease Institute–Tulsa, Okla.; (bottom), Franklin D. Roosevelt Library–Hyde Park, N.Y.; 500, Intern'l. Museum of Photography at George Eastman House; 501, Photo by Jacob A. Riis–Jacob A. Riis Collection, Museum of the City of New York; 504, Kansas State Historical Society–Topeka, Kan.; 505, Museum of the City of New York; 509(newspaper), Library of Congress; (photo), Culver Pictures, Inc.; 512, Library of Congress; 514, Photo by Elroy Sanford–Lake County Historical Society/President James A. Garfield Museum; 517 & 518, Library of Congress; 519 & 522, Culver Pictures, Inc.; 525, Library of Congress; 528, N.Y.P.L. Picture Collection; 529, Culver Pictures, Inc.; 533, N.Y.P.L. Picture Collection; 535 & 536, Culver Pictures, Inc.; 538, Bettmann Archive; 540, Culver Pictures, Inc.

UNIT SIX

Page 542, Culver Pictures, Inc.; 545 & 547,

Brown Brothers; **549,** N.Y. Historical Society; **553, 554, 556, 559,** Brown Brothers; **560,** Library of Congress; **564,** Brown Brothers; **569(top & center),** Library of Congress; **(bottom),** Culver Pictures, Inc.; **570,** Cleveland Public Library Picture Collection; **571, 573, 574, 578,** Library of Congress; **581,** Bettmann Archive; **583,** Naval Photographic Center; **584,** U.S. Signal Corps/National Archives; **590 & 592,** Library of Congress; **594 & 595,** U.S. Signal Corps/National Archives; **596,** Library of Congress; **599,** N.Y. Historical Society; **603,** Library of Congress; **607,** U.S. Signal Corps/ National Archives; **608,** Library of Congress; **610,** U.S. War Dept. General Staff/ National Archives; **614,** Library of Congress; **615,** U.S. Signal Corps/National Archives; **619,** Culver Pictures, Inc.; **623,** National Air and Space Museum/Smithsonian Institution; **PE 7-1,** Painting of the Museum's Interior in 1881 by Frank Waller, Photo by Francis G. Mayer–Metropolitan Museum of Art; **PE 7-2(top),** Culver Pictures, Inc.; **(bottom),** Museum of Fine Arts of Boston; **PE 7-3(top),** Art Institute of Chicago; **(bottom left),** Metropolitan Museum of Art; **(bottom right),** Museum of Modern Art–Gift of Friends of the Sculptor in 1908; **PE 7-4(top),** N.Y.P.L. Picture Collection; **(bottom),** Phillips Gallery; **PE 7-5 (top),** Hedrich Blessing; **(bottom),** Amherst College Collection; **PE 7-6(top),** Culver Pictures, Inc.; **(bottom),** Museum of the City of New York; **PE 7-7(top),** Edward Steichen; **(bottom),** Courtesy Mr. Ira Gershwin and The Humanities Research Center–University of Texas at Austin; **PE 7-8(top),** Museum of Art of Ogunquit; **(bottom),** Brown Brothers; **625,** National Air and Space Museum/Smithsonian Institution; **627 & 630,** Brown Brothers; **634,** National Air and Space Museum/Smithsonian Institution; **638,** Westinghouse Broadcasting Company, Inc.; **640 & 641,** Ford Archives; **643,** Brown Brothers; **644,** Michigan History Division;

646 & 647, Bettmann Archive; **648,** Culver Pictures, Inc.; **650,** United Press International; **652,** Wide World Photos.

UNIT SEVEN
Page 654, Art by Ed Malsberg; **657,** United Press International; **660,** Wide World Photos; **663,** United Press International; **665,** Wide World Photos; **666,** Acme News-Pictures, Inc.; **670,** Wide World Photos; **671,** United Press International; **672,** Underwood and Underwood; **673 & 675,** Wide World Photos; **677,** Cartoon by Alley–*Memphis Commercial Appeal;* **678, 681, 683, 686,** Wide World Photos; **687,** United Press International; **688(top),** Wide World Photos; **(bottom),** United Press International; **693,** Culver Picures, Inc.; **697,** Navy Dept./National Archives; **698,** Naval Photographic Center; **701,** United Press International; **702,** U.S. Office of War Information/National Archives; **706, 707, 710,** Navy Dept./ National Archives; **713,** United Press International; **715,** Acme Newspapers, Inc.; **717,** United Press International; **PE 8-1,** Detail of "The New Television Set" by Norman Rockwell–Permission Los Angeles County Museum of Art; **PE 8-2(top left),** Culver Pictures, Inc.; **(top right),** Eileen Darby/ Graphic House; **(bottom),** Brown Brothers; **PE 8-3(top),** Globe Photos; **(bottom),** Time-Life Picture Agency; **PE 8-4(top left),** Acme Newspictures, Inc.; **(top right),** Hy Peskin/ Time-Life Picture Agency; **(bottom),** Capricorn Art Gallery; **PE 8-5(top),** Francis Miller/Time-Life Picture Agency; **(bottom),** Ralph Crane/Time-Life Picture Agency; **PE 8-6(top),** Margaret Bourke-White/Time-Life Picture Agency; **(bottom),** Leonard McCombe/ Time-Life Picture Agency; **PE 8-7(top)** Nina Leen/Time-Life Picture Agency; **(bottom),** University of Wisconsin Dept. of Photocinema; **PE 8-8(top),** Frank Scherschel/ Time-Life Picture Agency; **(bottom),** Peter Stackpole/Life Magazine © Time Inc.; **721,**

U.S. Information Agency/National Archives; **724,** Acme Newspictures, Inc.; **726,** U.S. Office of War Information/National Archives; **728,** U.S. Information Agency/National Archives; **730,** Estate of David Low; **731, 732, 735, 738,** Wide World Photos; **740,** United Press International; **742, 745, 748, 751, 752,** Wide World Photos; **756 & 757,** Wide World Photos; **758,** Dorothea Lange Collection–Oakland Museum; **760,** United Press International; **763, 765, 767, 768, 770,** Wide World Photos.

EPILOGUE
Page 773, Art by Ed Malsberg; **774 & 775,** United Press International; **779,** Wide World Photos; **780 & 782,** United Press International; **783,** Wide World Photos; **PE 9-1,** Esther Henderson/Rapho Guillumette; **PE 9-2(top),** Charles Moore/Black Star; **(bottom),** V. Bucher/Photo Researchers; **PE 9-3(top),** Bruce Roberts/Rapho Guillumette; **(bottom left),** Fred J. Maroon/Photo Researchers; **(bottom right),** Porterfield Chickering/Photo Researchers; **PE 9-4(top),** Ford Motor Company; **(bottom),** Hedrich-Blessing; **PE 9-5(top),** Lucio Woods/ Photo Researchers; **(bottom),** F. Hulnegle/ Monkmeyer; **PE 9-6(top),** Myron Wood/ Photo Researchers; **(bottom left),** Georg Gerster/Rapho Guillumette; **(bottom right),** Ray Manley/Shostal Photos; **PE 9-7(top),** Russ Kinne/Photo Researchers; **(center),** Tom McHugh/Photo Researchers; **(bottom),** Joe Munroe/Photo Researchers; **PE 9-8(top),** Jack Fields/Photo Researchers; **(bottom),** Ray Ateson; **786, 789, 791,** Wide World Photos; **792,** United Press International; **793,** Wide World Photos; **795 & 796,** United Press International; **803 & 805,** Wide World Photos; **808 & 809,** United Press International; **810(left),** Wide World Photos; **(right)** United Press International; **812,** Wide World Photos.